Psychology
From Inquiry to Understanding

FOURTH EDITION

Scott O. Lilienfeld
Emory University

Steven Jay Lynn
Binghamton University

Laura L. Namy
Emory University

 Pearson

330 Hudson Street, NY, NY 10013

Portfolio Manager: Erin Mitchell
Content Producer: Pamela Weldin
Content Developer: Julie Kelly
Portfolio Manager Assistant: Stephany Harrington
Director of Field Marketing: Jonathan Cottrell
Senior Field Marketing Manager: Debi Doyle
Executive Product Marketing Manager: Chris Brown
Content Producer Manager: Amber Mackey
Content Development Manager: Sharon Geary
Associate Director of Design: Blair Brown
Design Lead: Kathryn Foot
Technical Manager: Caroline Fenton
Digital Producer: Lindsay Verge
Full-Service Project Manager: Ron Watson, Integra
Compositor: Integra
Printer/Binder: LSC Communications
Cover Printer: Lehigh Phoenix Color/Hagerstown
Cover Design: Lumina Datamatics, Inc.
Cover Credit: Getty Images

Acknowledgments of third-party content appear on page 791 which constitutes an extension of this copyright page.

Library of Congress Cataloging-in-Publication Data
Names: Lilienfeld, Scott O., 1960- author. | Lynn, Steven Jay, author. |
  Namy, Laura L., author.
Title: Psychology : from inquiry to understanding / Scott O. Lilienfeld,
  Steven Jay Lynn, Laura L. Namy.
Description: 4 Edition. | Hoboken, NJ : Pearson, [2017] | Revised edition of
  the authors' Psychology, [2014]
Identifiers: LCCN 2016057913 | ISBN 9780134552514 | ISBN 0134552512
Subjects: LCSH: Psychology.
Classification: LCC BF121 .P824 2017 | DDC 150—dc23 LC record
available at https://lccn.loc.gov/2016057913

2 17

Student Edition:
ISBN 10:   0-134-55251-2
ISBN 13: 978-0-134-55251-4

A La Carte Edition:
ISBN 10:   0-134-58820-7
ISBN 13: 978-0-134-58820-9

Brief Contents

Contents

My deepest gratitude to David Lykken,
Paul Meehl, Tom Bouchard, Auke Tellegen,
and my other graduate mentors
for an invaluable gift that I will always cherish:
scientific thinking.

—Scott Lilienfeld

To Fern Pritikin Lynn, my wife, my heart and
my soul. And to my daughter, Jessica Barbara Lynn,
the light of my life.

—Steven Jay Lynn

With profound appreciation for my NSF colleagues
who expanded my horizons further than
I ever could have imagined.

—Laura L. Namy

About Revel and the New Edition

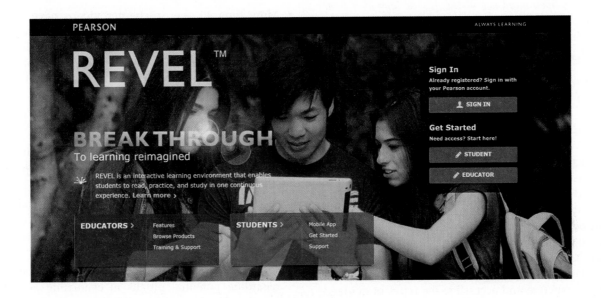

"Why don't we remember what happened to us as babies?" **"Is human intelligence purely genetic?"** "Can people actually become addicted to gambling or sex?" **"Does everyone see colors the exact same way?"** **"Is the polygraph test really a 'lie detector'?"** "Should we trust most self-help books?"

Every day, our students are barraged with information—and misinformation—that shapes how they understand the world and their place in it. Whether it's from social media, movies, self-help books, or advice from friends, our students encounter information and explanations—often many of which are inaccurate—about sex and romance, drug abuse, intelligence testing, parenting, mental illness, psychotherapy, and scores of other topics. Much of the time, the questions about these issues that most fascinate students are precisely those that psychologists routinely confront in their research, teaching, and practice. This is both a blessing and a curse—on the one hand, we as instructors have a natural "hook" because students find the topic inherently interesting. On the other hand we also face the challenge of coaxing students away from their intuitions, so that they can begin to think scientifically about evidence regarding mind, brain, and behavior.

As consumers of information, we all need help evaluating the bewildering variety of claims stemming from the vast world of popular psychology. This goal is especially critical in a world in which fake news is becoming increasingly challenging to

distinguish from real news. Without a framework for evaluating evidence, making sense of these often contradictory assertions can be a bewildering task for anyone. It's no surprise that the untrained student can find claims regarding topics such as memory and mood-enhancing drugs, the overprescription of stimulants, the effectiveness of antidepressants, and the genetic bases of psychiatric disorders difficult to evaluate. Moreover, it is challenging for those who haven't been taught to think scientifically to resist the allure of extraordinary psychological claims that lie on the fringes of scientific knowledge, such as extrasensory perception, subliminal persuasion, astrology, alien abductions, lie-detector testing, handwriting analysis, and ink-blot tests, among many others. Without a guide for distinguishing adequate from inadequate evidence, our students are left to their own devices when it comes to weighing the merits of these claims.

Our goal in this text, therefore, is to empower students to apply scientific thinking to the psychology of their everyday lives. By applying scientific thinking—thinking that helps protect us against our tendencies to make mistakes—we can better evaluate claims about both laboratory research and daily life. In the end, we hope that students who have read our text will emerge with the critical thinking skills and open-minded skepticism needed to distinguish psychological misinformation from psychological information. The text is designed to encourage students to keep an open mind to new claims but to insist on and evaluate evidence informing these claims. Indeed, our overarching motto is that of space scientist James Oberg (sometimes referred to as "Oberg's dictum"): *Keeping an open mind is a virtue, just so long as it is not so open that our brains fall out.*

What's New in This Edition?

Psychology: From Inquiry to Understanding continues to emphasize the importance of scientific-thinking skills. We are especially excited, in the fourth edition, to leverage Revel™, a multimedia instructional platform, to provide more interactive demonstrations, video examples, and self-tests. These activities engage student interest and provide regular opportunities for them to apply their knowledge to both real-world and research examples. We take seriously the compelling evidence that testing is an effective learning tool and have introduced interactive exercises that are low-stakes (i.e., ungraded) tests of their comprehension, with immediate feedback. Our intention in using this new interactive multimedia platform is to bring psychological phenomena to life and render concrete and accessible the types of evidence available to psychological scientists. We believe that Revel will create a sense of excitement and empowerment about the use of inquiry to foster understanding. To this end, we have updated the fourth edition to include not only new evidence and topic areas, but also new techniques for engaging student attention and facilitating learning.

From presenting chapter-opening videos produced by award-winning documentarians, to creating interactive demonstrations, to asking students to test their ability to distinguish supported from unsupported claims, this edition maintains the vision and tone students enjoyed in the previous editions. In addition, it introduces exciting interactive opportunities to apply their knowledge as they learn. We have also significantly updated the content by integrating new findings, highlighting fresh debates and challenges to psychology (e.g., the replicability crisis), and introducing new sections on emerging areas of research.

GENERAL CHANGES

- New documentary-style, chapter-opening videos—in which subjects share their insights, daily experiences, or personal stories—will engage students and awaken an interest in them to learn more about the topics covered in each chapter.
- New "Challenge Your Assumptions Polls" allow students to compare their intuitions about psychological topics with those of their peers across institutions.

- Fully revised "Evaluating Claims" scenarios prompt students to use scientific-thinking skills to evaluate claims they are likely to encounter in various forms of media. This feature makes use of a fully interactive branching narrative in which readers navigate the scenario by making individual choices.
- New Fact vs. Fiction feature tests students' ability to distinguish supported from unsupported claims in a low-stakes interactive assessment.
- More than 40 new in-chapter videos have been filmed or specially selected for this edition. These videos cover a variety of key topics in introductory psychology, from animating complex psychological concepts to demonstrating experiments to diagnosing and classifying disorders.

NEW CONTENT AND UPDATED RESEARCH

- **Chapter 1 (Psychology and Scientific Thinking)** features new timely coverage of the replicability crisis as well as enhanced discussion of confirmation bias.
- **Chapter 2 (Research Methods)** provides broader discussion of the role of response styles in psychological assessment and enhanced guidance on evaluating claims on the Internet.
- **Chapter 3 (Biological Psychology)** includes new content regarding potential pitfalls in evaluating evidence from functional brain-imaging studies, as well as an introduction to epigenetics.
- **Chapter 4 (Sensation and Perception)** provides expanded coverage of inattentional blindness, the neuroscience of magic, and extrasensory perception. This chapter also provides greater coverage of multiple illusions, including afterimages, the moving spiral, and color constancy and "the dress."
- **Chapter 5 (Consciousness)** features enhanced discussion of a variety of topics including synesthesia, the brain just prior to death, effects of LSD on the brain, and Hobson's dream theory of protoconsciousness. The coverage of sleep has been significantly augmented to include expanded coverage of sleep disorders, sleep in nonhuman species, and the amount of sleep needed on a daily basis. Discussion of hallucinations, mystical experiences, and the effects of hallucinogenic drugs has also been expanded.
- **Chapter 6 (Learning)** includes new coverage of Little Albert, greater discussion of the role of classical conditioning in disgust reactions, and greater coverage of learning in unsupervised environments and of the role of mirror neurons in learning.
- **Chapter 7 (Memory)** includes new research on individual differences and context effects in false memories, memory and politics, overcoming memory biases, and the neural basis of spatial memory in Clark's nutcracker. The chapter

offers enhanced coverage of interventions to potentially decrease the risk of dementia and memory loss that accompanies aging, as well as cross-cultural differences in early memories.

- **Chapter 8 (Thinking, Reasoning, and Language)** features enhanced coverage of behavioral economics and neuro-economics, a description of distributed cognition, a new *Psychomythology* box on myths about sign language, and expanded coverage on learning to read.

- **Chapter 9 (Intelligence and IQ Testing)** provides new coverage of molecular genetic research on intelligence, the effects (or lack thereof) of brain-training programs on intelligence and working memory, the predictive validity of IQ tests, the effects of early intervention programs on IQ, sex differences in mental abilities, stereotype threat and IQ, emotional intelligence, and grit.

- **Chapter 10 (Human Development)** includes a discussion of epigenetics, new sections differentiating premature birth from low birth weight (including their causes and consequences), discussion of the research on early menarche, an updated *Psychomythology* box on apps designed to increase infant intelligence, expanded coverage of temperament and attachment, a new section on transgender development, and updated citations of current evidence on the developing brain.

- **Chapter 11 (Emotion and Motivation)** features new coverage of research on primary and secondary emotions, the facial feedback hypothesis, nonverbal behaviors and lie-detection methods, positive psychology, and self-esteem. The chapter also includes new discussion of bariatric surgery, binge eating and purging disorders, as well as enhanced coverage of intrinsic/extrinsic motivation, Maslow's hierarchy of needs, the glucostatic theory of hunger, sexual desire, and similarity and attraction.

- **Chapter 12 (Stress, Coping, and Health)** includes new coverage of posttraumatic growth, yoga, stress and social media, hookah smoking and electronic cigarettes, and apps for meditation. The chapter also features expanded coverage of PTSD, the tend-and-befriend response and oxytocin, optimism, coronary heart disease, controversies related to moderate drinking, and complementary and alternative medicine.

- **Chapter 13 (Social Psychology)** offers new coverage of the replicability crisis and its implications for social psychology, cultural differences in the fundamental attribution error, scientific controversies concerning the Milgram obedience and Zimbardo prison studies, viewpoint diversity, political polarization, "brainwashing," potential media influences on aggression, cyberaggression, psychological research on correcting misconceptions, stereotyping and outgroup-homogeneity, and implicit prejudice, and prejudice-reduction interventions.

- **Chapter 14 (Personality)** includes new coverage of molecular genetic research on personality, neuroscience research purportedly offering support for psychodynamic assertions, controversy regarding the efficacy of psychodynamic therapy, the ability to infer personality from social media, and cross-cultural research on the five-factor model of personality.

- **Chapter 15 (Psychological Disorders)** offers new coverage of the recent developments in diagnosis of mental disorders, including the development of the Research Domain Criteria (RDoC); discussion of inflammation as a potential trigger of depression and schizophrenia; genetics, the immune system and "overpruning" of synapses in schizophrenia; and the role of sleep disturbances in dissociation. Coverage has also been expanded on suicide, borderline personality disorder, and psychopathic personality.

- **Chapter 16 (Psychological and Biological Treatments)** includes new coverage related to meeting needs for psychological services, existential therapy, ecological momentary assessment, unified integrative psychotherapy protocols, and customized psychotherapeutic interventions. The chapter also features expanded coverage of Alcoholics Anonymous, nonspecific factors in psychotherapy, combining medication with psychotherapy, and transcranial stimulation.

Content Highlights

From Inquiry to Understanding: The Framework in Action

As instructors, we find that students new to psychology tend to learn best when information is presented within a clear, effective, and meaningful framework—one that encourages inquiry along the path to understanding. As part of our text's distinctive inquiry-to-understanding framework, our pedagogical features and assessment tools work to empower students to develop a more critical eye in understanding the psychological world and their place in it.

THINKING SCIENTIFICALLY In Chapter 1, we introduce readers to the **Six Principles of Scientific Thinking**, which comprise an integrated framework for the lifelong learning of psychology. Colored arrows indicate whenever the principles are referenced to reinforce these scientific thinking principles in readers' minds. In this way, readers come to understand these principles as key skills for evaluating claims in scientific research and in everyday life. These six principles, which we employ (a) throughout every chapter and (b) within our new Evaluating Claims feature to drive home their relevance and importance to the learning material, are:

Ruling Out Rival Hypotheses

Have important alternative explanations for the findings been excluded?

Replicability

Can the results be duplicated in other studies?

Correlation vs. Causation

Can we be sure that A causes B?

Extraordinary Claims

Is the evidence as strong as the claim?

Falsifiability

Can the claim be disproved?

Occam's Razor

Does a simpler explanation fit the data just as well?

APPLICATIONS OF SCIENTIFIC THINKING In keeping with the text's theme, the fully reconcieved **Evaluating Claims** feature prompts students to use scientific thinking skills to evaluate claims they are likely to encounter in various forms of media. This interactive feature uses a unique branching narrative where user input dictates the flow of content.

A new feature for the fourth edition, **Fact vs. Fiction** invites students to test their ability to distinguish empirically supported versus unsupported claims. These self-tests are peppered throughout each chapter.

Throughout the text, **Psychomythology** boxes focus in depth on a widespread psychological misconception. In this way, students will come to recognize that their commonsense intuitions about the psychological world are not always correct and that scientific methods are needed to separate accurate from inaccurate claims. **Mysteries of Psychological Science** boxes tell the story of how psychological science has helped to shed light on a longstanding psychological mystery.

ACTIVE LEARNING Students learn best by doing, by applying their knowledge, and by engaging in interactive opportunities to test their understanding. We have developed a comprehensive array of active learning tools designed to test not only students' basic mastery but also their scientific reasoning skills. The Revel format provides a platform for active learning to occur outside (as well as inside) the classroom. We capitalize on these new avenues of instructional technology to deliver pedagogical tools and learning applications directly to the student.

INTEGRATED CULTURAL CONTENT Wherever relevant, we infuse the text with discussion of cultural factors that shape behavior, cultural variability in practice, and replications across cultural and ethnic groups. It is increasingly important in today's global society to highlight both generalizability of psychological phenomena and cases that are culturally unique, and to adopt a broader perspective on how cultural context influences behavior and thought. A cultural perspective also allows students to better understand the potential boundary conditions on psychological findings.

A Focus on Meaningful Pedagogy: Helping Students Succeed in Psychology

Our goal of applying scientific thinking to the psychology of everyday life is reflected in the text's pedagogical plan. The features in the text, the built-in quizzing, and the print and media supplements were designed to help students achieve a mastery of the subject and succeed in the course.

Challenge Your Assumptions polls, located at the start of every chapter, ask students what they believe they know about psychology, and instantaneously compare their responses with those of other students taking the course. These questions also serve to preview the key topics that will be discussed in each chapter. New documentary-style **Chapter-Opening Videos** help students connect emotionally to the material.

Each chapter is organized around **Numbered Learning Objectives,** which are listed at the start of each major section. (All instructor supplements are also keyed to these learning objectives.) The in-chapter assessment material is also organized around these objectives. Students' understanding of important terminology is enhanced with our on-page **Glossary.**

Color-coded biological art and animations orient students at both the micro and macro levels as they move throughout the text and forge connections among concepts. **Interactive photo captions** test students on their scientific-thinking skills and invite them to evaluate whether the photo is an accurate depiction of psychological phenomena.

Each chapter contains relevant and interesting **Fact vs. Fiction** self-tests designed to challenge students' ability to distinguish supported from unsupported claims. **Journal Writing Prompts** invite students to write short critical thinking–based responses to questions about the chapter content.

An **Experiment Simulations appendix** in Revel, correlated to each chapter, allows students to participate in online simulations of virtual, classic psychology experiments and research-based inventories, helping to reinforce what they are learning in class and in their book.

Putting Scientific Thinking to the Test: Innovative and Integrated Supplements

Psychology: From Inquiry to Understanding is accompanied by a collection of teaching and learning supplements designed to reinforce the scientific thinking skills from the text. These supplements "put scientific thinking to the test" by reinforcing our framework for evaluating claims and assessing students' ability to think scientifically in a variety of psychological and real-world situations.

NEW! Learning Games Fun Activities to Help Students Master Concepts Learning Games, powered by mLevel, take studying to the next level with a series of fun, interactive games that drive learning. Enabling students to master Introductory Psychology concepts, Learning Games' powerful analytics allow you to track student performance and engagement in real time by course, activity, topic, and learning objective. Learning Games are available for study (and play!) via students' computer or mobile device. To purchase mLevel for Lilienfeld, Lynn & Namy's Psychology: From Inquiry to Understanding 4e, please visit pearson0006.mlevel.com

MyPsychlab MyPsychLab is an online homework, tutorial, and assessment program that truly engages students in learning. It helps students better prepare for class, quizzes, and exams—resulting in better performance in the course—and provides educators with a dynamic set of tools for gauging individual and class progress. MyPsychLab comes from Pearson, your partner in providing the best digital learning experience.

Learning Catalytics Learning Catalytics is a "bring your own device" student engagement, assessment, and classroom intelligence system. It allows instructors to engage students in class with real-time diagnostics. Students can use any modern, web-enabled device (smartphone, tablet, or laptop) to access it.

PRESENTATION AND TEACHING RESOURCES The Instructor's Resource Center (www.pearsonhighered.com/irc) provides information and the following downloadable supplements.

Test Bank (ISBN 0134637593) This test bank contains more than 3,000 multiple-choice, true/false, short-answer, and essay questions, each referenced to the relevant page in the textbook. All test items are mapped to the chapter learning objectives. An additional feature for the test bank is the

inclusion of rationales for the *conceptual and applied* multiple-choice questions. The rationales help instructors to evaluate the questions they are choosing for their tests and give instructors the option to use the rationales as an answer key for their students.

A Total Assessment Guide chapter overview makes creating tests easier by listing all of the test items in an easy-to-reference grid. All multiple-choice questions are categorized as factual, conceptual, or applied, and are correlated to each of the chapter's learning objectives.

MyTest (ISBN 0134627628) The fourth edition test bank is also available through Pearson MyTest (www.pearson-mytest.com), a powerful assessment-generation program that helps instructors easily create and print quizzes and exams. Instructors can write questions and tests online, allowing them flexibility and the ability to efficiently manage assessments at any time, anywhere.

Instructor's Resource Manual (ISBN 0134637658) The Instructor's Resource Manual is a comprehensive tool for class preparation and management, each chapter includes learning objectives, a chapter outline, lecture and discussion suggestions, "think about it" discussion questions, activities and demonstrations, and suggested video resources.

Interactive Powerpoint Slides (ISBN 0134637690) These slides draw students into the lecture and provide wonderful interactive activities, visuals, and videos. The slides are built around the text's learning objectives. Icons integrated throughout the slides indicate interactive exercises, simulations, videos, and activities that can be accessed directly from the slides if instructors want to use these resources in the classroom. Many of the textbook figures are presented in layers (like a set of transparency overlays) within the slides to allow instructors to step through more complex diagrams or processes.

Standard Lecture Powerpoint Slides (ISBN 0134637674) These ADA compliant PowerPoint slides provide an active format for presenting concepts from each chapter and feature relevant figures and tables from the text, and are designed to be compatible with assistive technology requirements.

Art Powerpoint Slides (ISBN 0134637623) These slides contain only the photos, figures, and line art from the textbook.

Pearson Assessment Bank for the APA Guidelines for the Undergraduate Psychology Major 2.0 A unique bank of assessment items allows instructors to assess student progress against the American Psychological Association's (APA) Guidelines for the Undergraduate Psychology Major 2.0 (2013).

APA Correlation Guide This detailed correlation guide, which appears in the Instructor's Manual, shows how the learning outcomes in the text and the test bank questions correspond to the APA Learning Goals and Outcomes.

Test Item File for Your Learning Management System For instructors who only need the test item file, we offer the complete test item file in Blackboard, WebCT, and other LMS formats at www.pearsonhighered.com/irc.

Final Word and Thanks

The author team has been passionate about our vision for the book and our commitment to helping engage students in the process of evaluating evidence. We have been honored and thrilled by the enthusiasm and support the book has received. Over the years since our first conception of this text, we have benefited from the input of literally hundreds of colleagues and students who have contributed in various ways to bringing it to fruition and continuing to improve its impact. We stand in awe of our fellow-instructors' love of the discipline and the enthusiasm and imagination they bring to the psychology classroom every day. We are incredibly grateful to them for joining us on this journey. We especially want to acknowledge Nancy Woolf's and Barry Beyerstein's contributions to earlier editions of the text.

In addition, the authors would like to extend our heartfelt gratitude and sincere thanks to a host of people who worked on or with the Pearson team. We consider ourselves remarkably fortunate to have had so much support for implementing our vision and priorities. To a person, they have been truly delightful, helpful, creative, energetic, wonderful collaborators and team members. Needless to say, this project was a monumental team effort, and every member of the team played an invaluable role in its inception. We owe special thanks to Erin Mitchell, Executive Editor, for her remarkable wisdom and insight, not to mention her supportive and encouraging approach and reassurance during this process; as well as Julie Kelly, our developmental editor, for her thoughtfulness, organizational acumen, limitless patience, and relentlessly positive attitude. We also thank Pam Weldin, Caroline Fenton, Kim Norbuta, Brooke Wilson, Ron Watson, Lindsay Verge, Ben Ferini, Mike Lackey, and Renae Horstman for their extensive efforts on behalf of our book. We are grateful to James Evans for his invaluable help with tracking down references. We also wish to extend our particular appreciation to Megumi Nishikura, Greg Moyer, and the entire Blue Chalk team for their visionary, effective, and elegant work on our chapter opening videos.

Over the course of the first three editions, feedback from users of the text has been extraordinarily helpful in refining the content, and we welcome additional feedback on this edition. We invite you to share your experiences using the fourth edition by writing to Scott Lilienfeld at slilien@emory.edu.

OUR REVIEW PANEL We are indebted to the members of our review panel from the third and previous editions who evaluated chapters and provided expert analysis on critical topic areas. Others served on an advisory council, participated in focus groups, conducted usability studies, ran class testing of chapters, and attended our faculty forums for the text. Their input proved invaluable to us, and we thank them for it.

Bethany Fleck Dillen, *Metropolitan State University of Denver*

Johnathan Forbey, *Ball State University*

Chelsea Hansen, *Upper Iowa University*

Alicia MacKay, *Tulsa Community College*

Wanda Moore, *Eastfield College and University of Phoenix*

Kaneez Naseem, *Monroe College*

Danielle Richards, *College of Southern Nevada*

Wayne Robinson, *Monroe Community College*

Amy Skinner, *Troy State University*

O'Ann Steere, *College of DuPage*

Anton Villado, *Rice University*

Karen Yanowitz, *Arkansas State University*

Eynav Accortt, *Miami University*

Marlene Adelman, *Norwalk Community College*

Luis Aguerrevere, *Stephen F. Austin State University*

Mark Akiyama, *Diablo Valley College*

David Alfano, *Community College of Rhode Island*

Cathy Alsman, *IvyTech Community College of Indiana*

Nicole D. Anderson, *Grant MacEwan College*

Gina Andrews, *Volunteer State Community College*

Wendy Ann Olson, *Texas A&M University*

Mary Ann Schmitt, *North Virginia Community College–Manassas*

Pamela Ansburg, *Metropolitan State College of Denver*

Clarissa Arms-Chavez, *Auburn University–Montgomery*

Renee Babcock, *Central Michigan University*

Louis E. Banderet, *Northeastern University*

Ted Barker, *Northwest Florida State College*

Jason Barker, *University of Illinois at Springfield*

Jack Barnhardt, *Wesley College*

Robert Barry Stennett, *Gainesville State College*

Tammy D. Barry, *University of Southern Mississippi*

Mark Basham, *Regis University*

David Baskind, *Delta College*

Scott C. Bates, *Utah State University*

James Becker, *Pulaski Technical College*

Matt Bell, *Santa Clara University*

Stefanie M. Bell, *Pikes Peak Community College*

Jennifer Bellingtier, *University of Northern Iowa*

Michael Benhar, *Suffolk County Community College*

Dr. Martin van den Berg, *California State University, Chico*

Joy Berrenberg, *University of Colorado Denver*

Sylvia Beyer, *University of Wisconsin–Parkside*

John Bickford, *University of Massachusetts–Amherst*

John Billimek, *California State University–Long Beach*

Joseph Bilotta, *Western Kentucky University*

Belinda Blevins-Knabe, *University of Arkansas–Little Rock*

Christopher Bloom, *Providence College*

Tracie Blumentritt, *University of Wisconsin–La Crosse*

Fred Bonato, *St. Peter's College*

Ronald Boothe, *University of Washington–Tacoma*

Michael C. Boyle, *Sam Houston State University*

Conna Bral, *Kirkwood Community College*

Michele Y. Breault, *Truman State University*

Eric Bressler, *Westfield State University*

Robert Brill, *Moravian College*

Nathan Brody, *Wesleyan University*

Gayle L. Brosnan Watters, *Slippery Rock University*

Thomas Brothen, *University of Minnesota*

Charles Brown, *University of South Alabama*

Jay Brown, *Southwest Missouri State University*

Veda Brown, *Prairie View A&M University*

Brad Brubaker, *Indiana State University*

Eric L. Bruns, *Campbellsville University*

Susan Buckelew, *University of Tennessee at Martin*

Amy Buddie, *Kennesaw State University*

Susan R. Burns, *Morningside College*

Alyson Burns-Glover, *Pacific University*

Glenn Callaghan, *San Jose State University*

Catherine Camilletti, *University of Texas at El Paso*

David E. Campbell, *Humboldt State University*

Thomas Capo, *University of Maryland*

Etzel Cardena, *University of Lund*

Cheryl Carmichael, *Brooklyn College*

Jessica Carpenter, *Elgin Community College*

Lorelei A. Carvajal, *Triton Community College*

Francis Catano, *Southern New Hampshire University*

Richard Catrambone, *Georgia Institute of Technology*

Robin Cautin, *Manhattanville College*

Christopher Chabris, *Union College*

Shawn Charlton, *University of Central Arkansas*

Monali Chowdhury, *Ohio State University*

Jennifer Cina, *Barnard College*

Rachel Clark, *University of Minnesota–Twin Cities*

Job Clement, *Daytona Beach Community College*

Andrea Clements, *Eastern Tennessee State University*

Mark Cloud, *Lock Haven University*

Lorry Cology, *Owens Community College*

Mary Coplen, *Hutchinson Community College*

Luis A. Cordon, *Eastern Connecticut State University*

Katherine Corker, *Michigan State University*

Keith P. Corodimas, *Lynchburg College*

Gregory M. Corso, *Georgia Institute of Technology*

Helene Deacon, *Dalhousie University*

Dawn Delaney, *Madison Area Technical College*

Kathryn Demitrakis, *Central New Mexico Community College*

Ben Denkinger, *Hamline University/Augsburg University*

Bruce J. Diamond, *William Paterson University*

Anastasia Dimitropoulos White, *Case Western Reserve University*

G. William Domhoff, *University of California–Santa Cruz*

Dale Doty, *Monroe Community College*

Vicki Dretchen, *Volunteer State Community College*

Michael Dreznick, *Our Lake of the Lake College*

Perri B. Druen, *York College of Pennsylvania*

Michael G. Dudley, *Southern Illinois University–Edwardsville*

Kimberley Duff, *Cerritos College*

Robert Dushay, *Morrisville State College*

Jane Dwyer, *Rivier College*

David Echevarria, *University of Southern Mississippi*

Carla Edwards, *Northwest Missouri State University*

Naomi V. Ekas, *Texas Christian University*

David R. Entwistle, *Malone College*

Audrey M. Ervin, *Delaware County Community College*

Yousef Fahoum, *University of Arkansas–Little Rock*

Matthew Fanetti, *Missouri State University*

Allison Farrell, *University of Minnesota*

Celeste Favela, *El Paso Community College*

Linda Fayard, *Mississippi Gulf Coast Community College*

Joseph R. Ferrari, *DePaul University*

Donald Fischer, *Missouri State University*

Joseph M. Fitzgerald, *Wayne State University*

Bethany Fleck, *University of Tampa*

Christine Floether, *Centenary College*

Stephen Flora, *Youngstown State University*

Roy Fontaine, *Pennsylvania College of Technology*

Johnathan Forbey, *Ball State University*

William F. Ford, *Bucks County Community College*

Daniel J. Fox, *Sam Houston State University*

Janet Frick, *University of Georgia*

Dr. Michael B. Frisch, *Baylor University*

Chelsea Fry, *Midlands Technical College*

Lana Fry, *West Texas A&M University*

Ellen Furlong, *Ohio State University*

Deborah Garfin, *Georgia State University*

Doug Gentile, *Iowa State University*

Marjorie A. Getz, *Bradley University*

Bryan Gibson, *Central Michigan University*

Vicki Gier, *University of South Florida*

Debra L. Golden, *Grossmont College*

Adam Goodie, *University of Georgia*

Randy Gordon, *University of Minnesota–Duluth*

Richard M. Gorman, *Central New Mexico Community College*

C. Allen Gorman, *Angelo State University*

Gladys Green, *State College of Florida*

Joseph P. Green, *Ohio State University–Lima*

Jeff D. Green, *Virginia Commonwealth University*

Gary J. Greguras, *Louisiana State University*

Mark Griffin, *Georgia Perimeter College–Dunwoody*

R. J. Grisham, *Indian River Community College*

Jennifer Grossheim, *University of Northern Iowa*

Laura Gruntmeir, *Redlands Community College*

Amy Hackney-Hansen, *Georgia Southern University*

Kelly Hagan, *Bluegrass Community and Technical College*

Erin Hardin, *Texas Tech University*

Richard Hass, *Rowan University*

Robert Hayes, *Westfield State University*

Traci Haynes, *Columbus State Community College*

Bert Hayslip, Jr., *University of North Texas*

Rebecca Hendrix, *Northwest Missouri State University*

Jeffrey B. Henriques, *University of Wisconsin–Madison*

Robert Hensley, *Mansfield University*

Rebecca Hester, *Western Carolina University*

Michael Hillard, *Albuquerque Tech Vocational Institute*

Robert Hines, *University of Arkansas–Little Rock*

Matthew Holahan, *Carleton University*

Mark Holder, *UBC, Okanagan*

Shareen Holly, *Providence College*

Lynne Honey, *Grant MacEwan College*

Joseph Horvat, *Weber State University*

Dr. Tharon Howard, *Clemson University*

Joanne Hsu, *Houston Community College–Town and Country*

Christopher R. Huber, *University of Minnesota*

Allen Huffcutt, *Bradley University*

Tammy Hutcheson, *Garden City Community College*

Matthew I. Isaak, *University of Louisiana–Lafayette*

Linda Jackson, *Michigan State University*

James Jakubow, *Florida Atlantic University*

Cameron John, *Utah Valley University*

Kenneth W. Johns, *University of Winnipeg*

James Johnson, *Illinois State University*

James R. Johnson, *Central New Mexico Community College*

Brian Johnson, *University of Tennessee at Martin*

Kevin W. Jolly, *University of Texas at El Paso*

Samuel Jones, *Jefferson State Community College*

Lance Jones, *Bowling Green State University*

Kerry Jordan, *Utah State University*

Laura M. Juliano, *American University*

Deana Julka, *University of Portland*

Michael J. Kane, *University of North Carolina–Greensboro*

Paul M. Kasenow, *Henderson Community College*

Melissa Kelly, *Millsaps College*

Colin Key, *University of Tennessee at Martin*

Girwan Khadka, *Washington State University*

Shirin Khosropour, *Austin Community College*

Melvyn King, *SUNY Cortland*

Kevin King, *University of Washington*

Katherine Kipp, *Gainesville State College*

Cynthia Koenig, *St. Mary's College of Maryland*

Brenda E. Koneczny, *Lake Superior College*

Elissa Koplik, *Bloomfield College*

Shannon Kundey, *Hood College*

Caleb W. Lack, *University of Central Oklahoma*

Travis Langley, *Henderson State University*

G. Daniel Lassiter, *Ohio University*

Natalie Lawrence, *James Madison University*

Timothy J. Lawson, *College of Mount St. Joseph*

Lindette Lent Baas, *Arizona Western College*

Tera Letzring, *Idaho State University*

Mary B. Lewis, *Oakland University*

Robin Lightner, *University of Cincinnati*

Linda Lockwood, *Metropolitan State College of Denver*

Susan D. Lonborg, *Central Washington University*

Christopher R. Long, *Ouachita Baptist University*

Christopher Lowry, *BYU Idaho*

Don Lucas, *Northwest Vista College*

Margaret Lynch, *San Francisco State University*

Amy Lyndon, *East Carolina University*

Angelina MacKewn, *University of Tennessee at Martin*

Na'im Madyun, *University of Minnesota–Twin Cities*

Sonya Major, *Acadia University*

Mike Majors, *Delgado Community College*

Joanne Malkani, *SUNY Adirondack*

Jean Mandernach, *University of Nebraska at Kearney*

Mike Mangan, *University of New Hampshire*

Julia Manor, *University of Minnesota*

David Marcus, *University of Southern Mississippi*

Anne Marie Perry, *Massasoit Community College*

Howard Markowitz, *Hawaii Pacific University*

Nicole Martin, *Kennesaw State University*

Robert Martinez, *University of the Incarnate Word*

Cindy Matyi, *Ohio University–Chillicothe*

Dawn McBride, *Illinois State University*

Wanda McCarthy, *University of Cincinnati–Clermont College*

Tammy McClain, *West Liberty State College*

William McIntosh, *Georgia Southern University*

Michael McIntyre, *University of Winnipeg*

Ann McKim, *Goucher College*

Jessica McManus, *Kansas State University*

Barbara McMasters, *University of Cincinnati–Raymond Walters College*

Steven E. Meier, *University of Idaho*

Joe Melcher, *St. Cloud State University*

Richard Miller, *Western Kentucky University*

Robin Morgan, *Indiana University Southeast*

Jason Moses, *El Paso Community College*

Thomas J. Mount, *Yakima Valley Community College*

Morrie Mullins, *Xavier University*

Glenn Musgrove, *Broward Community College–Central*

Janie Nath, *Cerritos College*

Margaret Nauta, *Illinois State University*

Cindy Nordstrom, *Southern Illinois University–Edwardsville*

Larry Normansell, *Muskingum University*

Peggy Norwood, *Red Rocks Community College*

Mark O'DeKirk, *Meredith College*

Cynthia O'Dell, *Indiana University Northwest*

Kim O'Neil, *Carleton University*

Tony Obradovich, *Portland Community College*

Carlotta Ocampo, *Trinity College*

Michie Odle, *SUNY Cortland*

Elaine Olaoye, *Brookdale Community College*

David Osburn, *Arkansas Tech University*

Luz Ospina, *Brooklyn College*

Barbara Oswald, *Miami University*

Larry Pace, *Anderson University*

Tibor Palfai, *Syracuse University*

Jack Palmer, *University of Louisiana at Monroe*

Dominic Parrott, *Georgia State University*

David Payne, *Wallace Community College*

Terry F. Pettijohn, *Coastal Carolina University*

Brady J. Phelps, *South Dakota State University*

Jacqueline Pickrell, *University of Washington*

Julie Piercy, *Central Virginia Community College*

Lloyd R. Pilkington, *Midlands Technical College*

Alan Pope, *University of West Georgia*

Frank Provenzano, *Greenville Technical College*

Barbara Radigan, *Community College of Allegheny County*

Reece Rahman, *University of Pittsburgh at Johnstown*

Christopher K. Randall, *Kennesaw State University*

Meera Rastogi, *University of Cincinnati– Clermont College*

Celia Reaves, *Monroe Community College*

Dennis T. Regan, *Cornell University*

Ann Renken, *University of Southern California*

Tanya Renner, *Kapi'olani Community College*

Amira Rezec, *Saddleback College*

Kymberly Richard, *Northern Virginia Community College*

Harvey Richman, *Columbus State University*

Sheldon Rifkin, *Kennesaw State University*

Michelle Rivera, *University of Maine*

Jermaine Robertson, *Florida A&M University*

Christopher Robinson, *University of Alabama–Birmingham*

Wayne Robinson, *Monroe Community College*

James Rodgers, *Hawkeye Community College*

Scott Roesch, *San Diego State University*

Wade C. Rowatt, *Baylor University*

Claire Rubman, *Suffolk County Community College*

Linda Ruehlman, *Arizona State University*

John Ruscio, *The College of New Jersey*

Melinda Russell-Stamp, *Northwest Missouri State University*

Ron Salazar, *San Juan College*

Catherine Sandhofer, *University of California–Los Angeles*

Sherry Schnake, *Saint Mary-of-the-Woods College*

David A. Schroeder, *University of Arkansas*

Caitlin Schultz, *University of North Dakota*

Nicholas Schwab, *University of Northern Iowa*

Joseph Sclafani, *University of Tampa*

Eric Seemann, *University of Alabama–Huntsville*

Layton Seth Curl, *Metropolitan State College of Denver*

Amy Shapiro, *University of Massachusetts, Dartmouth*

Heidi Shaw, *Yakima Valley Community College*

Wayne Shebilske, *Wright State University*

Laura Sherrick, *Front Range Community College–Westminster*

Elisabeth Sherwin, *University of Arkansas–Little Rock*

Mark Sibicky, *Marietta College*

Lawrence Siegel, *Palm Beach State College*

Randy Simonson, *College of Southern Idaho*

Royce Simpson, *Spring Hill College*

Lisa Sinclair, *University of Winnipeg*

Amy Skinner, *Gordon College*

John Skowronski, *Northern Illinois University*

Dale Smith, *Olivet Nazarene University*

Vivian Smith, *Lakeland Community College*

Valerie T. Smith, *Collin County Community College*

Patrice Smith, *Carleton University*

Todd Smitherman, *University of Mississippi*

Jeanne Spaulding, *Houston Community College–Town and Country*

Susan Spooner, *McLennan Community College*

Jennifer Steeves, *York University*

Jakob Steinberg, *Fairleigh Dickinson University*

James Stringham, *University of Georgia*

Alexandra Terrill, *Washington State University–Vancouver*

James Todd, *Eastern Michigan University*

Richard Topolski, *Augusta State University*

Richard W. Townsend, *Miami-Dade College–Kendall*

Casey Trainor, *Augustana College*

Lisa L. Travis, *University of Illinois– Urbana Champaign*

Chantal Tusher, *Georgia State University*

Amy Van Buren, *Sacred Heart University*

Cynthia Vance, *Piedmont College*

Barbara VanHorn, *Indian River Community College*

Jennifer Vencill, *Texas Tech University*

Anré Venter, *University of Notre Dame*

Carrie Veronica Smith, *University of Delaware*

Janice Vidic, *University of Rio Grande*

Anton Villado, *Rice University*

Paul Vonnahme, *New Mexico State University*

Jeffrey Wagman, *Illinois State University*

Mark Walter, *Salisbury University*

Jason Warnick, *Arkansas Tech University*

Gillian Watson, *University of British Columbia*

Kathy Weatherford, *Trident Technical College*

Jeff Weatherly, *University of North Dakota*

Nambrath Rajkumari Wesley, *Brookdale Community College*

Mark West, *Rutgers University*

Virginia Wickline, *Miami University*

David R. Widman, *Juniata College*

Sharon Wiederstein, *Blinn College– Bryan*

Colin William, *Columbus State Community College*

Thomas W. Williams, *Western Kentucky University*

Keith Williams, *Richard Stockton College of New Jersey*

Kevin M.P. Woller, *Rogers State University*

Marc Wolpoff, *Riverside City College*

Tara Woolfolk, *Rutgers University– Camden*

John W. Wright, *Washington State University*

Thresa Yancey, *Georgia Southern University*

Karen Yanowitz, *Arkansas State University*

Jennifer Yanowitz, *Utica College*

Dean Yoshizumi, *Sierra College*

Michael Zinser, *University of Colorado–Denver*

Michael Zvolensky, *University of Vermont*

Meet the Authors

SCOTT O. LILIENFELD received his BA in psychology from Cornell University in 1982 and his PhD in clinical psychology from the University of Minnesota in 1990. He completed his clinical internship at Western Psychiatric Institute and Clinic in Pittsburgh, Pennsylvania, from 1986 to 1987. He was Assistant Professor in the Department of Psychology at SUNY Albany from 1990 to 1994 and is now Samuel Candler Dobbs Professor of Psychology at Emory University and a Visiting Professor at the University of Melbourne in Australia. He is a Fellow of the Association of Psychological Science and was the recipient of the 1998 David Shakow Award from Division 12 (Clinical Psychology) of the American Psychological Association (APA) for Early Career Contributions to Clinical Psychology. More recently, he received the James McKeen Cattell Award from the Association for Psychological Science for outstanding career contributions to applied psychology and the Ernest Hilgard Award from APA Division 1 (General Psychology) for the integration of psychology across disciplines. Dr. Lilienfeld is president of the Society for a Science of Clinical Psychology within Division 12 and past president of the Society for the Scientific Study of Psychopathy. He is editor of *Clinical Psychological Science* and until recently was a regular columnist for *Scientific American Mind* magazine. He has authored or coauthored fourteen books and more than 350 journal articles and chapters. Dr. Lilienfeld has also been a participant in Emory University's "Great Teachers" lecturer series, a Distinguished Speaker for the Psi Chi Honor Society at the annual APA convention, and a keynote speaker at numerous national and international conventions.

STEVEN JAY LYNN received his BA in psychology from the University of Michigan and his PhD in clinical psychology from Indiana University. He completed an NIMH Postdoctoral Fellowship at Lafayette Clinic, Detroit, Michigan, in 1976 and is now Distinguished Professor of Psychology at Binghamton University (SUNY), where he was the director of the Psychological Clinic and is currently the directory of the Laboratory of Consciousness and Cognition. (2007–2016). Dr. Lynn is a fellow of numerous professional organizations, including the American Psychological Association and the Association for Psychological Science, he is a diplomate in clinical and forensic psychology (ABPP), and he was the recipient of the Chancellor's Award of the State University of New York for Scholarship and Creative Activities. Dr. Lynn has authored or edited 22 books and more than 350 other publications and was named on a list of "Top Producers of Scholarly Publications in Clinical Psychology Ph.D. Programs" (2000–2004/Stewart, Wu, & Roberts, 2007, *Journal of Clinical Psychology*). Dr. Lynn is the founder and editor of *Psychology of Consciousness: Theory, Research, and Practice* (APA), and he has served on 11 other editorial boards, including the *Journal of Abnormal Psychology*. Dr. Lynn's research has been supported by the National Institute of Mental Health and the Ohio Department of Mental Health. His research has been featured in numerous media outlets, including the *New York Times, New Scientist Magazine, Discover Magazine, CBS Morning Show,* ABC's 20/20, Discovery Channel, and the Academy Award-winning documentary, *Capturing the Friedmans.*

LAURA L. NAMY received her BA in philosophy and psychology from Indiana University in 1993 and her PhD in cognitive psychology at Northwestern University in 1998. She is now Director of the Center for Mind, Brain, and Culture at Emory University where she is also Professor of Psychology and Core Faculty in Linguistics. She recently completed a three-year term at the National Science Foundation as a Program Director in the Behavioral and Cognitive Sciences Division. She is past editor-in-chief of the *Journal of Cognition and Development* and a Fellow of the American Psychological Association. Her research focuses on the origins and development of verbal and nonverbal symbol use in young children, sound symbolism in natural language, and the role of comparison in conceptual development.

APA Correlation for Lilienfeld 4e

The APA Guidelines for the Undergraduate Psychology Major, Version 2.0

APA Learning Outcomes and Objectives	Text Learning Objectives and Features
Goal 1: Knowledge Base in Psychology	
Demonstrate fundamental knowledge and comprehension of major concepts, theoretical perspectives, historical trends, and empirical findings to discuss how psychological principles apply to behavioral problems.	
1.1 Describe key concepts, principles, and overarching themes in psychology.	
1.1a Use basic psychological terminology, concepts, and theories in psychology to explain behavior and mental processes	*Learning Objectives:* 1.4a, 3.1a, 3.1b, 3.1c, 3.2a, 3.5a, 4.1a, 5.1b, 6.1a, 6.1b, 6.2b, 6.2c, 6.2d, 6.3a, 6.3b, 7.1b, 7.1c, 7.2b, 7.3a, 8.2a, 8.2b, 8.2c, 8.3d, 9.1a, 9.2a, 9.2b, 10.1a, 10.3a, 11.1a, 11.1b, 11.2a, 12.2a, 13.1a, 13.3a, 13.4a, 14.2a, 14.3a, 14.4a, 14.5a, 15.1a
1.1b Explain why psychology is a science with the primary objectives of describing, understanding, predicting, and controlling behavior and mental processes	*Learning Objectives:* 1.1b, 7.1a, 7.2a, 7.2c Chapter 13: Mysteries of Psychological Science: Why Are Yawns Contagious?
1.1c Interpret behavior and mental processes at an appropriate level of complexity	*Learning Objectives:* 3.4a, 3.4b, 4.6a, 8.3a, 9.3a, 9.3b, 14.2b
1.1d Recognize the power of the context in shaping conclusions about individual behavior	*Learning Objectives:* 4.6b
1.1e Identify fields other than psychology that address behavioral concerns	*Learning Objectives:* 6.1c, 6.2e, 8.3b, 8.4a, 8.4b, 9.2c, 9.2d, 10.1b, 12.4b, 12.5c

APA Learning Outcomes and Objectives	Text Learning Objectives and Features
1.2 Develop a working knowledge of the content domains of psychology	
1.2a Identify key characteristics of major content domains in psychology (e.g., cognition and learning, developmental, biological, and sociocultural)	*Learning Objectives: 5.2a, 6.1a, 6.1b, 6.2a, 6.2c, 6.2d, 7.1b, 8.1a, 8.1b, 10.2c, 10.4d*
1.2b Identify principle research methods and types of questions that emerge in specific content domains	*Learning Objectives: 4.1b*
1.2c Recognize major historical events, theoretical perspectives, and figures in psychology and their link to trends in contemporary research	*Learning Objectives: 1.4a, 1.4c, 5.2a, 5.3b, 9.2b, 11.3b, 11.4a, 12.2a, 14.2a, 14.2b, 14.3a, 14.3b, 14.4a, 14.4b, 14.5a, 14.5b, 14.6a, 14.6b,14.6c, 16.2a, 16.2b, 16.4a*
1.2d Provide examples of unique contributions of content domain to the understanding of complex behavioral issues	*Learning Objectives: 1.4b, 1.4d, 3.3a, 3.5b*
1.2e Recognize content domains as having distinctive sociocultural origins and development	*Learning Objectives: 7.4a, 10.4e* Chapter 7: Mysteries of Psychological Science: Why Can't We Remember the First Few Years of Our Lives?
1.3 Describe applications that employ discipline-based problem solving	
1.3a Describe examples of relevant and practical applications of psychological principles to everyday life	*Learning Objectives: 1.4d, 3.1d, 4.5c, 4.6c, 5.1c, 6.1c, 6.2e, 7.2d, 7.3c, 7.5b, 8.3c, 9.2c, 10.2a, 10.2b, 12.1a, 12.3a, 12.4a, 12.5a, 12.5b, 16.3a, 16.3b, 16.3c* Chapter 3: Mysteries of Psychological Science: How Do We Recognize Faces? Chapter 12: Psychomythology: Are Almost All People Traumatized by Highly Adverse Events?
1.3b Summarize psychological factors that can influence the pursuit of a healthy lifestyle	*Learning Objectives: 4.5b, 5.1a, 5.4a, 7.3b, 10.2d, 11.4b, 12.5a, 12.5b* Chapter 16: Psychomythology: Are Self-Help Books Always Helpful?
1.3c Correctly identify antecedents and consequences of behavior and mental processes	*Learning Objectives: 5.3a, 6.2a, 11.5b, 12.2b*
1.3d Predict how individual differences influence beliefs, values, and interactions with others, including the potential for prejudicial and discriminatory behavior in oneself and others	*Learning Objectives: 9.4a, 9.4b, 10.4a, 10.4b, 10.4c, 13.5a, 13.5b* Chapter 9: Psychomythology: Do College Admissions Tests Predict Grades?
Major concepts are reinforced with learning tools: Writing Space, Experimental Simulations, MyPsychLab Video Series, Visual Brain, and instructor's teaching and assessment package. Text features such as Evaluating Claims and Fact Versus Fiction also reinforce learning objectives.	
Goal 2: Scientific Inquiry and Critical Thinking	
Understand scientific reasoning and problem solving, including effective research methods.	
2.1 Use scientific reasoning to interpret behavior	
2.1a Identify basic biological, psychological, and social components of behavioral explanations (e.g., inferences, observations, operational definitions, interpretations)	*Learning Objectives: 1.1a, 3.1a, 3.2b, 6.4a*
2.1b Use psychology concepts to explain personal experiences and recognize the potential for flaws in behavioral explanations based on simplistic, personal theories	*Learning Objectives: 1.3a, 16.5a, 16.5b* Chapter 3: Psychomythology: Are Some People Left-Brained and Others Right-Brained?
2.1c Use an appropriate level of complexity to interpret behavior and mental processes	*Learning Objectives: 1.2a, 3.2a, 4.6d, 9.1b, 10.1b, 11.1a, 11.3a, 11.4a, 12.1b, 12.3b, 12.4c, 13.4b, 14.1a* Chapter 4: Psychomythology: Psychic Healing of Chronic Pain
2.1d Ask relevant questions to gather more information about behavioral claims	*Learning Objectives: 1.3b, 4.6d, 5.2b, 5.3a, 11.2b, 13.1b, 13.4c, 16.5a, 16.5b* Chapter 4: Mysteries of Psychological Science: How Does Magic Work? Chapter 6: Mysteries of Psychological Science: Why Are We Superstitious? Chapter 10: Psychomythology: Creating "Superbabies" One App at a Time Chapter 16: Mysteries of Psychological Science: Why Can Ineffective Therapies Appear to be Helpful?
2.1e Describe common fallacies in thinking (e.g., confirmation bias, post hoc explanations, implying causation from correlation) that impair accurate conclusions and predictions	*Learning Objectives: 1.1a, 1.2a, 1.3a, 1.3b, 9.5b*
2.2 Demonstrate psychology information literacy	
2.2a Read and summarize general ideas and conclusions from psychological sources accurately	*Learning Objectives: 2.5a, 2.5b, 6.5a*
2.2b Describe what kinds of additional information beyond personal experience are acceptable in developing behavioral explanations (i.e., popular press reports vs. scientific findings)	*Learning Objectives: 1.1a, 2.5b, 9.5a*
2.2c Identify and navigate psychology databases and other legitimate sources of psychology information	*Learning Objectives: 1.2a* Chapter 7: Psychomythology: Smart Pills
2.2d Articulate criteria for identifying objective sources of psychology information	*Learning Objectives: 1.2b, 2.5b* Chapter 1: Mysteries of Psychological Science: Why Do We Perceive Patterns Even When They Don't Exist? Chapter 8: Psychomythology: Common Misconceptions About Sign Language

(continued)

APA Learning Outcomes and Objectives	Text Learning Objectives and Features
2.2e Interpret simple graphs and statistical findings	*Learning Objectives: 2.4a, 2.4b, 2.4c*
2.3 Engage in innovative and integrative thinking and problem-solving	
2.3a Recognize and describe well-defined problems	*Learning Objectives: 4.2a, 4.3a, 4.4a, 4.5a, 5.4b*
2.3b Apply simple problem-solving strategies to improve efficiency and effectiveness	
2.3c Describe the consequences of problem-solving attempts	
2.4 Interpret, design, and conduct basic psychological research	
2.4a Describe research methods used by psychologists, including their respective advantages and disadvantages	*Learning Objectives: 2.2a, 2.2b, 3.4a, 9.2a, 14.1a*
2.4b Discuss the value of experimental design (i.e., controlled comparisons) in justifying cause-effect relationships	*Learning Objectives: 2.2c*
2.4c Define and explain the purpose of key research concepts that characterize psychological research (e.g., hypothesis, operational definition)	*Learning Objectives: 1.3b* Chapter 2: Mysteries of Psychological Science: How Do Placebos Work?
2.4d Replicate or design and conduct simple scientific studies (e.g., correlational or two-factor) to confirm a hypothesis based on operational definitions	*Learning Objectives: 2.5a*
2.4e Explain why conclusions in psychological projects must be both reliable and valid	*Learning Objectives: 2.4b, 14.6b, 14.6c* Chapter 14: Psychomythology: How Accurate Is Criminal Profiling?
2.4f Explain why quantitative analysis is relevant for scientific problem solving	*Learning Objectives: 2.4b*
2.4g Describe the fundamental principles of research design	*Learning Objectives: 2.5a, 9.3a, 9.3b*
2.5 Incorporate sociocultural factors in scientific inquiry	
2.5a Relate examples of how a researcher's value system, sociocultural characteristics, and historical context influence the development of scientific inquiry on psychological questions	*Learning Objectives: 2.1a, 5.2a, 9.2b, 16.2a* Chapter 5: Psychomythology: Age Regression and Past Lives Chapter 6: Psychomythology: Are We What We Eat?
2.5b Analyze potential challenges related to sociocultural factors in a given research study	*Learning Objectives: 8.3b, 8.3c*
2.5c Describe how individual and sociocultural differences can influence the applicability/generalizability of research findings	*Learning Objectives: 7.4a, 7.5a, 7.5b,*
2.5d Identify under what conditions research findings can be appropriately generalized	*Learning Objectives: 2.5a*
Scientific inquiry is reinforced with learning tools: Writing Space, Experimental Simulations, MyPsychLab Video Series, Visual Brain, and instructor's teaching and assessment package. Text features such as Evaluating Claims and Fact Versus Fiction also reinforce learning objectives.	
Goal 3: Ethical and Social Responsibility	
Develop ethically and socially responsible behaviors for professional and personal settings.	
3.1 Apply ethical standards to psychological science and practice	
3.1a Describe key regulations in the APA Ethics Code for protection of human or nonhuman research participants	*Learning Objectives: 2.3a, 2.3b*
3.1b Identify obvious violations of ethical standards in psychological contexts	
3.1c Discuss relevant ethical issues that reflect principles in the APA Code of Ethics	*Learning Objectives: 2.3b, 7.5b*
3.1d Define the role of the institutional review board	*Learning Objectives: 2.3a*
3.2 Promote values that build trust and enhance interpersonal relationships	
3.2a Describe the need for positive personal values (e.g., integrity, benevolence, honesty, respect for human dignity) in building strong relationships with others	*Learning Objectives: 11.3a, 11.3b*
3.2b Treat others with civility	*Learning Objectives: 11.3b*
3.2c Explain how individual differences, social identity, and world view may influence beliefs, values, and interaction with others and vice versa	*Learning Objectives: 13.1a, 13.2a, 13.3b, 13.5a, 13.5b* Chapter 15: Psychomythology: The Insanity Defense: Controversies and Misconceptions
3.2d Maintain high standards for academic integrity, including honor code requirements	
3.3 Adopt values that build community at local, national, and global levels	
3.3a Identify human diversity in its many forms and the interpersonal challenges that often result from the diversity	*Learning Objectives: 8.3c, 9.2d, 13.5a, 13.5b* Chapter 15: Mysteries of Psychological Science: More Than a Pack Rat: Why Do People Hoard?
3.3b Recognize potential for prejudice and discrimination in oneself and others	*Learning Objectives: 9.2d, 15.1a, 15.1b, 15.1c*
3.3c Explain how psychology can promote civic, social, and global outcomes that benefit others	*Learning Objectives: 8.4a, 8.4b, 12.5a, 13.5b, 16.1a*

APA Learning Outcomes and Objectives	Text Learning Objectives and Features
3.3d Describe psychology-related issues of global concern (e.g., poverty, health, migration, human rights, international conflict, sustainability)	*Learning Objectives: 9.2d, 9.4b, 10.3b, 10.3c, 11.4b, 11.4c, 11.4e, 12.4c, 12.5a, 12.5b, 15.3c, 15.4b* Chapter 14: Mysteries of Psychological Science: Where Is the Environmental Influence on Personality?
3.3e Articulate psychology's role in developing, designing, and disseminating public policy	*Learning Objectives: 8.3c, 9.2d, 13.3a, 13.3b, 13.5b*
3.3f Accept the opportunity to serve others through civic engagement, including volunteer service	*Learning Objectives: 9.2d, 15.1a, 15.1b, 15.1c*
Ethics and social responsibility are reinforced with learning tools: Writing Space, Experimental Simulations, MyPsychLab Video Series, Visual Brain, and instructor's teaching and assessment package. Text features such as Evaluating Claims and Fact Versus Fiction also reinforce learning objectives.	

Goal 4: Communication

Demonstrate competence in written, oral, and interpersonal communication skills and be able to develop and present a scientific argument.

4.1 Demonstrate effective writing in multiple formats

4.1a Express ideas in written formats that reflect basic psychological concepts and principles	
4.1b Recognize writing content and format differ based on purpose (e.g., blogs, memos, journal articles) and audience	*Learning Objectives: 2.5b*
4.1c Use generally accepted grammar	
4.1d Describe how writing using APA writing style is different from regular writing or writing in other conventions	*Learning Objectives: 2.5b*
4.1e Recognize and develop overall organization (e.g., beginning, development, ending) that fits the purpose	
4.1f Interpret quantitative data displayed in statistics, graphs, and tables, including statistical symbols in research reports	*Learning Objectives: 2.4a, 2.4b, 16.5a*
4.1g Use expert feedback to revise writing of a single draft	*Learning Objectives: 2.5a*

4.2 Exhibit effective presentation skills in multiple formats

4.2a Construct plausible oral argument based on a psychological study	
4.2b Deliver brief presentations within appropriate constraints (e.g., time limit, appropriate to audience)	
4.2c Describe effective delivery characteristics of professional oral performance	
4.2d Incorporate appropriate visual support	
4.2e Pose questions about psychological content	*Learning Objectives: 2.4c* Chapter 4: Mysteries of Psychological Science: How Does Magic Work? Chapter 5: Mysteries of Psychological Science: Why Do We Experience Déjà Vu? Chapter 11: Mysteries of Psychological Science: Why Do We Cry?

4.3 Interact Effectively with Others

4.3a Identify key message elements in communication through careful listening	*Learning Objectives: 2.4c*
4.3b Recognize that culture, values, and biases may produce misunderstandings in communication	
4.3c Attend to language and nonverbal cues to interpret meaning	
4.3d Ask questions to capture additional detail	Chapter 9: Mysteries of Psychological Science: Why Smart People Believe Strange Things
4.3e Respond appropriately to electronic communications	
Communication goals are reinforced with learning tools: Writing Space, Experimental Simulations, MyPsychLab Video Series, Visual Brain, and instructor's teaching and assessment package. Text features such as Evaluating Claims and Fact Versus Fiction also reinforce learning objectives.	

Goal 5: Professional Development

Apply psychology-specific content and skills, effective self-reflection, project management skills, teamwork skills and career preparation to support occupational planning and pursuit.

5.1 Apply psychological content and skills to professional work

5.1a Recognize the value and application of research and problem-solving skills in providing evidence beyond personal opinion to support proposed solutions	
5.1b Identify a range of possible factors that influence beliefs and conclusions	*Learning Objectives: 4.6c, 4.6d, 10.3c*
5.1c Expect to deal with differing opinions and personalities in the college environment	*Learning Objectives: 11.4e, 11.5a*
5.1d Describe how psychology's content applies to business, healthcare, educational, and other workplace settings	*Learning Objectives: 4.5c, 6.1c, 6.2e, 7.3c* Chapter 7: Psychomythology: Smart Pills
5.1e Recognize and describe broad applications of information literacy skills obtained in the psychology major	

(continued)

APA Learning Outcomes and Objectives	Text Learning Objectives and Features
5.1f Describe how ethical principles of psychology have relevance to non-psychology settings	
5.2 Exhibit self-efficacy and self-regulation	
5.2a Recognize the link between effort and achievement	
5.2b Accurately self-assess performance quality by adhering to external standards (e.g., rubric criteria, teacher expectations)	
5.2c Incorporate feedback from educators and mentors to change performance	
5.2d Describe self-regulation strategies (e.g., reflection, time management)	
5.3 Refine project management skills	
5.3a Follow instructions, including timely delivery, in response to project criteria	
5.3b Identify appropriate resources and constraints that may influence project completion	
5.3c Anticipate where potential problems can hinder successful project completion	*Learning Objectives: 12.1a, 12.2b*
5.3d Describe the processes and strategies necessary to develop a project to fulfill its intended purpose	
5.4 Enhance teamwork capacity	
5.4a Collaborate successfully on small group classroom assignments	
5.4b Recognize the potential for developing stronger solutions through shared problem-solving	Chapter 13: Psychomythology: Is Brainstorming in Groups a Good Way to Generate Ideas?
5.4c Articulate problems that develop when working with teams	*Learning Objectives: 13.2a, 13.2b*
5.4d Assess one's strengths and weaknesses in performance as a project team member	*Learning Objectives: 13.2b*
5.4e Describe strategies used by effective group leaders	
5.4f Describe the importance of working effectively in diverse environments	
5.5 Develop meaningful professional direction for life after graduation	
5.5a Describe the types of academic experiences and advanced course choices that will best shape career readiness	*Learning Objectives: 11.4a, 16.1b*
5.5b Articulate the skills sets desired by employers who hire people with psychology backgrounds	
5.5c Recognize the importance of having a mentor	
5.5d Describe how a curriculum vitae or resume is used to document the skills expected by employers	
5.5e Recognize how rapid social change influences behavior and affects one's value in the workplace	
Professional development goals are reinforced with learning tools: Writing Space, Experimental Simulations, MyPsychLab Video Series, Visual Brain, and instructor's teaching and assessment package. Text features such as Evaluating Claims and Fact Versus Fiction also reinforce learning objectives.	

The Story of Revel—Why Revel?

Watch WHY REVEL?

Revel is an immersive learning experience designed for the way today's students read, think, and learn. Revel uses interactives and assessments integrated within the narrative that enhance content as well as students' overall learning experiences.

The story of Revel is simple: When students are engaged in the course content, they learn more effectively and perform better.

When creating your course, you have many choices as to how to supplement your lectures and curriculum. So ask yourself these questions: How do I know if my students are reading their assigned materials? Do I want my students to have a better understanding of the concepts presented in this class through course materials and lectures? Do I want to see my students perform better throughout the course? If you answered "yes" to these questions, choose Revel.

Narrative Tells the Story

With Revel, students are introduced to a new learning experience, one in which content, reading, and interactive learning become one.

We've talked to hundreds of instructors about their biggest challenges in teaching the Introduction to Psychology course. We've heard some consistent answers: students are not engaged; students come to class unprepared; students are unable to think critically. However, the most common answer is that students do not read, which leads directly to, and in fact magnifies, the other challenges that instructors identified—lack of student engagement, lack of student preparedness, and an inability to think critically. Our goal in developing Revel was to research why students aren't reading and to solve that problem first and foremost as a gateway to deeper learning.

Research and Data

Research shows that for students, reducing the extraneous cognitive load – that is, the mental effort being used in the working memory – is key to learning and retention. When students read or study in order to process and retain information, the information must move from the working memory to the

long-term memory. Put simply, reducing extraneous cognitive load increases long-term memory.

Our research also tells us that students do not see the benefits of reading their textbooks. Students perceive their instructor's dynamic lectures and class notes as their main source for learning and view their assigned text as simply a repetition of that classroom experience. In a student's mind, why would they read? What are the benefits?

We share the same goals: to give your students the motivation to read by adding value to their interaction with the course materials, and to make it easier for you to assign reading.

If that's important to you, choose Revel.

The Story of Revel— The Solution

Watch THE REVEL SOLUTION

Revel is learning reimagined.

Revel benefits your students. Revel's dynamic content matches the way students learn today. Narrative is supported and enhanced by interactive content and as a result, reading becomes a pleasure rather than a chore. Revel also enables students to read and interact with course material on the devices they use, anywhere and any time. Responsive design allows students to access Revel on their tablets, desktop computers, or mobile devices with content displayed clearly in both portrait and landscape view.

Revel benefits you. Revel allows you to check your students' progress and understanding of core concepts through regular and consistent assessment. End-of-module and end-of-chapter quizzes in Revel allow students opportunities to check their understanding at regular intervals before moving on; their grades are reported to the instructor dashboard.

Revel also offers no-, low-, and high-stakes writing activities for students through the journal, shared-writing, and essay activities.

Revel lets you monitor class assignment completion as well as individual student achievement. Do you want to see points earned on quizzes, time on task, and whether a particular student's grade is improving? If so, choose Revel.

Support and Implementation—Getting Started with Revel

More than 5,000 Revel instructors are connecting and sharing ideas. They're energizing their classrooms and brainstorming teaching challenges via Pearson's growing network of faculty communities. The Revel community is an open, online space where members come together to collaborate and learn from each other. If you're currently teaching with Revel or considering Revel for use in your class, we invite you to join the Revel community.

Getting started with Revel is easy:

- **Identify the Problems You Want to Solve**
  Do you want students to come to class more prepared, having read their assigned reading? Are your goals focused on improving student success in your course? Are you looking to increase student engagement? Are you interested in 'flipping your classroom' so that students learn basic course content outside of class, allowing for more active and applied in-class learning?

- **Keep it Simple**
  The process of accessing and navigating these learning solutions needs to be simple and intuitive. Revel has built-in, frequent, low-stakes assessments for students to easily assess their understanding of the material, without getting sidetracked from their required reading assignment.

- **Track Learning Gains**
  Educators who track and measure learning gains are able to make informed decisions about product implementations, course transformations, and redesigns. In addition, they can increase their ability to prove institutional effectiveness, meet accreditation standards, track quality-enhancement plans, and fulfill grant requirements.

Course Creation, Set-Up, and Assignments

If you have used a Pearson digital product in the past like a MyLab, you can use your same Pearson account info to sign in to Revel.

If you do not have a Pearson account already, click **Educator** in the **Get Started** box, and click **I would like to request access**.

After sign in, you will arrive at Revel's course homepage. Select **Search for Materials** in the upper right- hand corner and enter the title, author, ISBN or keyword of the text you'll be using. When you find your text, click **Create Course**. Fill in your course information, and click **Save**.

The first time you log in to Revel as an instructor you will be prompted to "start creating assignments." Click **Get Started**.

You are now ready to:

- select content to choose textbook content, interactive media, and graded assignments;

- set due dates to make sure students know what Revel reading and assessments are due and when;

- publish assignments to push content and assignments to students.

BUILDING AN ASSESSMENT PLAN Revel includes various quiz types to use for both formative and summative assessments. To get started, simply assign each Revel module that you intend to cover in your course. Be sure to consider your assignment due dates. If your goal is for students to come to class more prepared, then be sure to make assignments due before those topics are covered in class.

Additionally, think about how you will measure success in this Revel course. What are the quantifiable goals you want to achieve? Pertinent metrics might include one or both of the following:

- an analysis of student engagement using Revel's built-in reporting features

- a comparison of in-class exam scores, final course grades, or retention rates with those of previous semesters.

Dashboard and Analytics

Because students tend to skip optional assignments, it is critical that Revel contributes to the overall course grade. The recommendation of experienced educators is that Revel should represent at least 10-20% of the total course grade.

Remember that when you assign a chapter or section in Revel, you are assigning reading, interactives, videos, and assessments. All you need to do is pick the chapters and topics you want to cover, and then assign them to your students on the Revel assignment calendar. The Performance Dashboard allows you to export the student grades and provides total points earned for easy manual adjustments to external gradebooks.

Instructional design research suggests that certain habits of mind and dispositions are associated with critical thinking skills. Writing can be used as a tool to foster critical thinking. To get students to move toward adopting these habits and dispositions, *instruction and assessment should be appropriately complex, and focused on supporting, eliciting, and assessing skills such as evaluation, analysis, synthesis, collaboration, and critical reflection.* (Cope, Kalantzis, McCarthey, Vojak & Kline, 2011; Liu, Frankel, & Roohr, 2014).

As a reminder, all Revel product information can be found on the Pearson Revel site.
https://www.pearsonhighered.com/Revel/

Chapter 1
Psychology and Scientific Thinking

A Framework for Everyday Life

1.1a Explain why psychology is more than just common sense.

1.1b Explain the importance of science as a set of safeguards against biases.

1.2a Describe psychological pseudoscience and distinguish it from psychological science.

1.2b Identify reasons we are drawn to pseudoscience.

1.3a Identify the key features of scientific skepticism.

1.3b Identify and explain the text's six principles of scientific thinking.

1.4a Identify the major theoretical frameworks of psychology.

1.4b Describe different types of psychologists and identify what each of them does.

1.4c Describe two great debates that have shaped the field of psychology.

1.4d Describe how psychological research affects our daily lives.

Challenge Your Assumptions

Is psychology different from common sense?

Should we trust most self-help books?

Is psychology a science?

Are claims that can't be proven wrong scientific?

Are all clinical psychologists psychotherapists?

For many of you reading this text, this is your first psychology course. If you're like most people, much of what you've learned about psychology comes from watching television programs and movies, reading self-help books and popular magazines, surfing the Internet, using Facebook, Twitter, and other forms of social media, and talking to friends. In short, most of your psychology knowledge probably derives from the popular psychology industry: a sprawling network of everyday sources of information about human behavior.

Before reading on, try your hand at this little test of popular psychology knowledge.

Test of Popular Psychology Knowledge

1) Most people use only about 10 percent of their brain capacity.	True / False
2) Newborn babies are virtually blind and deaf.	True / False
3) Hypnosis enhances the accuracy of our memories.	True / False
4) All people with dyslexia see words backward (like *tac* instead of *cat*).	True / False
5) In general, it's better to express anger than to hold it in.	True / False
6) The lie-detector (polygraph) test is 90–95 percent accurate at detecting falsehoods.	True / False
7) People tend to be romantically attracted to individuals who are opposite from them in personality and attitudes.	True / False
8) The more people present at an emergency, the more likely it is that at least one of them will help.	True / False
9) People with schizophrenia have more than one personality.	True / False
10) All effective psychotherapies require clients to get to the root of their problems in childhood.	True / False

(left margin: Interactive)

Beginning psychology students typically assume that they know the answers to most of the preceding 10 questions. That's hardly surprising because these assertions have become part of popular psychology lore. Yet most students are surprised to learn that *all* 10 of these statements are false! This exercise illustrates a take-home message we'll emphasize throughout this text: *Although common sense can be enormously useful for some purposes, it's sometimes completely wrong* (Chabris & Simons, 2010; Watts, 2014). This can be especially true for psychology, a field that strikes many of us as self-evident, or even obvious. In a sense, we're *all* psychologists because we deal with psychological phenomena like love, friendship, anger, stress, happiness, sleep, memory, and language in our daily lives (Lilienfeld et al., 2009). As we'll discover, everyday experiences can often be helpful in allowing us to navigate the psychological world, but they don't necessarily make us experts (Kahneman & Klein, 2009). Put a bit differently, familiarity with human nature doesn't equal understanding of human nature (Lilienfeld, 2012).

Journal Prompt

Were you surprised by the results of this quiz? Where do you recall learning about the myths that you thought were true? Why do you think many of these myths persist despite scientific evidence to the contrary?

1.1: What Is Psychology? Science Versus Intuition

1.1a **Explain why psychology is more than just common sense.**
1.1b **Explain the importance of science as a set of safeguards against biases.**

William James (1842–1910), the Harvard psychologist often regarded as the founder of American psychology, once described psychology as a "nasty little subject." As James noted, psychology is exceedingly difficult to study, and simple explanations of behavior are few and far between. If you enrolled in this course expecting cut-and-dried answers to psychological questions, such as why you become angry or fall in love, you're likely to come away disappointed. But if you enrolled in the hopes of acquiring more insight

psychology

the scientific study of the mind, brain, and behavior

levels of analysis

rungs on a ladder of analysis, with lower levels tied most closely to biological influences and higher levels tied most closely to social influences

---

Figure 1.1 Levels of Analysis in Depression.

We can view psychological phenomena, in this case the disorder of depression, at multiple levels of analysis, with lower levels being more biological and higher levels being more social. Each level provides unique information and offers a distinctive view of the phenomenon at hand.

SOURCE: Based on a figure from Ilardi, Rand, & Karwoski, 2007.

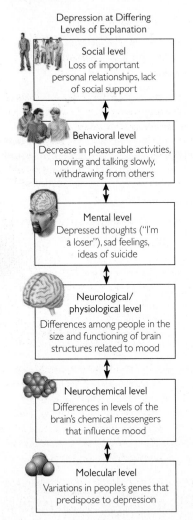

Depression at Differing Levels of Explanation

Social level
Loss of important personal relationships, lack of social support

Behavioral level
Decrease in pleasurable activities, moving and talking slowly, withdrawing from others

Mental level
Depressed thoughts ("I'm a loser"), sad feelings, ideas of suicide

Neurological/physiological level
Differences among people in the size and functioning of brain structures related to mood

Neurochemical level
Differences in levels of the brain's chemical messengers that influence mood

Molecular level
Variations in people's genes that predispose to depression

---

into the hows and whys of human behavior, stay tuned, because a host of delightful surprises are in store. While reading this text, prepare to find many of your preconceptions about psychology challenged. Also be prepared to encounter new ways of thinking about the causes of your everyday thoughts, feelings, and actions, and to apply your newfound skills to evaluating psychological claims in daily life. If we've done our job as authors, you'll emerge from this text equipped with tools to more thoughtfully evaluate assertions from the Internet, movies, television shows, news sources, and social media. In short, you'll become a better consumer of psychological knowledge.

Psychology and Levels of Analysis

The first question often posed in introductory psychology texts could hardly seem more straightforward: "What is psychology?" Although psychologists disagree about many things, they agree on one thing: Psychology is remarkably challenging to define (Henriques, 2004; Lilienfeld, 2004). In part, that's because psychology is a vast discipline, encompassing the study of perceptions, emotions, thoughts, and observable behaviors from an enormous array of perspectives. For the purposes of this text, we'll simply refer to **psychology** as the scientific study of the mind, brain, and behavior.

Psychology is a discipline that spans multiple **levels of analysis**. We can think of levels of analysis as rungs on a ladder, with the lower rungs tied most closely to biological influences and the higher rungs tied most closely to social and cultural influences (Ilardi & Feldman, 2001; Kendler, 2005; Schwartz et al., 2016). The levels of analysis examined in psychology stretch all the way from what psychologists call "neurons to neighborhoods." That is, they span molecules to brain structures on the lower rungs to thoughts, feelings, and emotions and to social and cultural influences on the higher rungs, with many levels in between (Cacioppo et al., 2000; Satel & Lilienfeld, 2013) (see Figure 1.1). The lower rungs are more closely tied to what we traditionally call "the brain"; the higher rungs to what we traditionally call "the mind." But as we'll see, "brain" and "mind" are just different ways of describing the same material "stuff" at different levels of analysis: What we call the "mind" is really just the brain in action. Although research psychologists often differ in which rungs they choose to investigate, they're united by a commitment to understanding the causes of human and animal behavior using the best available tools of science.

We'll cover all of these levels of analysis in the coming chapters. When doing so, we'll keep one crucial guideline in mind: *To fully understand psychology, we must consider multiple levels of analysis.* That's because each level tells us something different, and we gain new knowledge from each perspective. Think of viewing a major city from the vantage point of a tall hotel's glass elevator (Watson, Clark, & Harkness, 1994). As you ascend, you'll obtain different glimpses of the city. At the lower elevations, you'll acquire a better grasp of the details of the city's roads, bridges, and buildings, whereas at the higher elevations, you'll acquire a deeper perspective of how the roads, bridges, and buildings fit together and interact. Each elevation tells you something new and interesting. The same is true when ascending the ladder of levels of analysis in psychology.

It's easy to fall into the trap of assuming that only one level of analysis is the "right" or "best" one. Some psychologists believe that biological factors—like the actions of the brain and its billions of neurons (nerve cells)—are sufficient for understanding the major causes of behavior. Others believe that social factors—like parenting practices, peer influences, and culture—are sufficient for understanding the major causes of behavior (Meehl, 1972). In this text, we'll steer clear of these two extremes, because both biological and social factors are essential for a complete understanding of psychology (Kendler, 2005; Schwartz et al., 2016).

What Makes Psychology Distinctive—and Fascinating

Another key theme of this text is that we can approach psychological questions scientifically, and in much the same way as we can approach questions in biology, chemistry, and physics. Yet in some ways, psychology is distinctive from other sciences, if not unique. A host of challenges make the study of mind, brain, and behavior especially complex; yet it's precisely these challenges that also make psychology fascinating because they contribute to scientific mysteries that psychologists have yet to solve. Here, we'll touch briefly on five especially intriguing challenges that we'll be revisiting throughout the text.

First, human behavior is exceedingly difficult to predict, in part because almost all actions are **multiply determined**, that is, produced by many factors. That's why we need to be skeptical of *single-variable explanations* of behavior, which are widespread in popular psychology. Although it's tempting to explain complex human behaviors, such as violence, in terms of a single causal factor like poverty, personality traits, bad upbringing, or genes, such behaviors are almost surely the result of the interplay of an enormous array of factors (Stern, 2002).

Second, psychological influences are rarely independent of each other, making it difficult to pin down which cause or causes are operating. Imagine yourself as a scientist attempting to explain why some women develop **anorexia nervosa**, a severe eating disorder. You could start by identifying several factors that might contribute to anorexia nervosa, such as anxiety-proneness, compulsive exercise, perfectionism, excessive concern with body image, and exposure to television programs that feature thin models. Let's say that you want to focus on just one of these potential influences, such as perfectionism. Here's the catch: Women who are perfectionists also tend to be anxious, to exercise a lot, to be overly concerned with their body image, to watch television programs that feature thin models, and so on (Egan et al., 2013). The fact that all of these factors tend to be interrelated makes it tricky to pinpoint which one actually contributes to anorexia nervosa. The odds are high that they each play at least some role.

Third, people differ from each other in thinking, emotion, personality, and behavior. These **individual differences** help to explain why we each person responds in different ways to the same objective situation, such as an insulting comment from a boss (Harkness & Lilienfeld, 1997). In this respect, psychology is far more complicated than chemistry, because people—unlike most carbon atoms—aren't identical. Entire fields of psychology, such as the study of intelligence, interests, personality, and mental illness, focus on individual differences (Cooper, 2015; Lubinski, 2000). Individual differences make psychology challenging because they make it difficult to come up with explanations of behavior that apply to everyone. At the same time, they make psychology endlessly fascinating, because people we might assume we understand well often surprise, or even shock, us in their reactions to life events.

Fourth, people often influence each other, making it difficult to pin down precisely what causes what (Wachtel, 1973). For example, if you're an extraverted person, you're likely to make the people around you more outgoing. In turn, their outgoing behavior may "feed back" to make you even more extraverted, and so on. This is an example of what Stanford researcher Albert Bandura (1973), who is the most-cited living psychologist, called *reciprocal determinism*—the fact that we mutually influence each other's behavior. Reciprocal determinism can make it enormously challenging to isolate the causes of human behavior (Wardell & Read, 2013).

Fifth, people's behavior is often shaped in powerful ways by culture. Cultural differences, like individual differences, place limits on the generalizations that psychologists can draw about human nature (Henrich, Heine, & Norenzayan, 2010; Morris, Chiu, & Lui, 2015). To take one example, Richard Nisbett and his colleagues found that European-American and Chinese participants often attend to strikingly different things in pictures (Chua, Boland, & Nisbett, 2005). In one case, the researchers showed people a photograph of a tiger walking on rocks next to a river. Using eye-tracking technology, which allows researchers to determine where people are moving their eyes, they found that European Americans tend to look mostly at the tiger, whereas Chinese tend to look mostly at the plants and rocks surrounding it. This finding dovetails with evidence that European Americans tend to focus on central details, whereas Asian Americans tend to focus on peripheral or incidental details (Nisbett, 2003; Nisbett et al., 2001).

All five of these challenges are worth bearing in mind as we move onto later chapters. The good news is that psychologists have made substantial progress toward addressing all of them. As we'll discover, a deeper and richer appreciation of these challenges helps us to better predict—and in some cases understand—behavior.

Psychology may not be one of the traditional hard sciences like chemistry, but many of its fundamental questions are even more difficult to answer.

multiply determined

caused by many factors

anorexia nervosa

psychiatric condition marked by extreme weight loss and the perception that one is overweight even when one is massively underweight

individual differences

variations among people in their thinking, emotion, personality, and behavior

In the museum of everyday life, causation isn't a one-way street. In conversations, one person influences a second person, who in turn influences the first person, who in turn influences the second person, and so on. This principle, called *reciprocal determinism*, makes it challenging to pinpoint the causes of behavior.

In a study by Chua, Boland, and Nisbett (2005), European Americans tend to focus more on the central details of photographs, like the tiger itself (*left*), whereas Asian Americans tend to focus more on the peripheral details, like the rocks and leaves surrounding the tiger (*right*).

Do Opposites Attract?

Marriages like that of Mary Matalin, a prominent conservative political strategist, and James Carville, a prominent liberal political strategist, are rare. Despite the commonsense belief that opposites attract, psychological research shows that people are generally drawn to others who are similar to them in beliefs and values.

naive realism

belief that we see the world precisely as it is

Figure 1.2 Naive Realism Can Fool Us.

Even though our perceptions are often accurate, we can't always trust them to provide us with an error-free picture of the world. In this case, take a look at *Shepard's tables,* courtesy of psychologist Roger Shepard (1990). Believe it or not, the tops of these tables are identical in size: One can be directly superimposed on top of the other (get out a ruler if you don't believe us!).

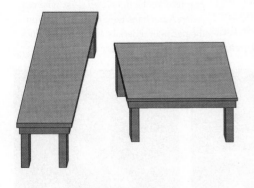

Why We Can't Always Trust Our Common Sense

To understand the causes of our behavior and that of others, most of us rely on our common sense—that is, our gut intuitions about how the social world works. Many popular books, such as Malcolm Gladwell's blockbuster bestseller *Blink* (2005), reinforce this view, implying that we should often, if not usually, trust our common sense. Yet, as we've already discovered, our intuitive understanding of ourselves and the world is frequently mistaken (Cacioppo, 2004; Chabris & Simons, 2010; Van Hecke, 2007).

As the quiz at the start of this chapter showed us, our commonsensical understanding of psychology is sometimes not merely incorrect but entirely backward. For example, although many people believe the old adage "There's safety in numbers," psychological research actually shows that the more people present at an emergency, the *less* likely at least one of them will help (Darley & Latané, 1968a; Fischer et al., 2011; Latané & Nida, 1981).

Let's consider another illustration of why we can't always trust our common sense. Read the following well-known proverbs, most of which deal with human behavior, and ask yourself whether you agree with them:

1. Birds of a feather flock together.
2. Absence makes the heart grow fonder.
3. Better safe than sorry.
4. Two heads are better than one.
5. Actions speak louder than words.
6. Opposites attract.
7. Out of sight, out of mind.
8. Nothing ventured, nothing gained.
9. Too many cooks spoil the broth.
10. The pen is mightier than the sword.

To most of us, these proverbs all ring true. Yet in fact, each proverb contradicts the proverb across from it. So our common sense can lead us to believe two things that can't both be true simultaneously—or at least that are largely at odds with each other. Strangely enough, in most cases, we never notice the contradictions until other people, like the authors of an introductory psychology textbook, point them out to us. This example reminds us of why scientific psychology doesn't rely exclusively on intuition, speculation, or common sense.

NAIVE REALISM: IS SEEING BELIEVING? We trust our common sense in part because we're prone to **naive realism** (Lilienfeld, Lohr, & Olatanji, 2008; Ross & Ward, 1996). We assume that "seeing is believing" and trust our intuitive perceptions of the world and ourselves. In daily life, naive realism generally serves us well. If we're driving down a one-lane road and see a tractor trailer barreling toward us at 85 miles per hour, it's a good idea to get out of the way. Much of the time, we *should* trust our perceptions, or at least pay pretty close attention to them.

Yet appearances can sometimes be deceiving. The earth *seems* flat. The sun *seems* to revolve around the earth (see Figure 1.2 for another example of deceptive appearances). Yet in both cases, our intuitions are wrong.

Similarly, naive realism can trip us up when it comes to evaluating ourselves and others. Our common sense assures us that people who don't share our political views are biased but that we're objective. Yet psychological research demonstrates that just about all of us tend to evaluate political issues in a biased fashion (Pronin, Gilovich, & Ross, 2004). So our tendencies toward naive realism can lead us to draw incorrect conclusions about human nature. In many cases, "believing is seeing" rather than the reverse: Our beliefs shape our perceptions of the world, often in ways we don't realize (Gilovich, 1991; Gilovich & Ross, 2016).

WHEN OUR COMMON SENSE IS RIGHT. That's not to say that our common sense is always wrong. Our intuition comes in handy in many situations and sometimes guides us to the truth (Gigerenzer, 2007; Gladwell, 2005; Myers, 2002). For example, our snap (five-second) judgments about whether someone we've just watched on video is trustworthy or untrustworthy tend to be right more often than we'd expect by chance (Fowler, Lilienfeld, & Patrick, 2009). Common sense can also be a helpful guide for generating hypotheses that scientists can later test in rigorous investigations (Redding, 1998). Moreover, some everyday psychological notions are indeed correct. For example, most people believe that happy employees tend to be more productive on the job compared with unhappy employees, and research shows that they're right (Kluger & Tikochinsky, 2001).

But to think scientifically, we must learn when—and when not—to accept our common-sense conclusions. Doing so will help us to become more informed consumers of popular psychology and ideally, to make better real-world decisions. One major goal of this text is to provide you with a framework of scientific thinking tools for doing so. This thinking framework can help you to better evaluate psychological claims, not just in your courses, but in everyday life.

Psychology as a Science

A few years ago, one of our academic colleagues was advising a psychology major about his career plans. Out of curiosity, he asked the student, "So why did you decide to go into psychology?" The student responded, "Well, I took a lot of science courses and realized I didn't like science, so I picked psychology instead."

We're going to try to persuade you that the student was mistaken—not about selecting a psychology major, that is, but about psychology not being a science. A central theme of this text is that modern psychology, or at least a hefty chunk of it, is scientific. But what does the word *science* really mean, anyway?

We might assume that *science* is just a word for all of that complicated stuff people learn in their biology, chemistry, and physics classes. But in reality, science isn't a body of knowledge. It's a systematic *approach* to evidence (Bunge, 1998; Chalmers, 2013). Specifically, science consists of a set of attitudes and skills designed to prevent us from fooling ourselves and fooling others. Science begins with *empiricism*, the premise that knowledge should initially be acquired through observation. Yet such observation is only a rough starting point for obtaining psychological knowledge. As the phenomenon of naive realism reminds us, observation isn't sufficient by itself, because our senses can fool us. Science refines our initial observations, subjecting them to stringent tests to determine whether they are accurate. The observations that stand up to rigorous scrutiny are retained; those that don't are revised or discarded.

Survey data show that a large percentage, and perhaps even a majority, of the general public doubts that psychology is scientific (Janda et al., 1998; Ferguson, 2015; Lilienfeld, 2012). Some of this skepticism probably reflects the fact that few psychologists who appear on the news or other popular media outlets are scientists. So it's not entirely surprising that in a poll of the American public, only 30 percent agreed that "psychology attempts to understand the way people behave through scientific research"; in contrast, 52 percent believed that "psychology attempts to understand the way people behave by talking to them and asking them why they do what they do" (Penn & Schoen and Berland

Naïve Realism

Interactive

Here's another case in which our naive realism can trick us. Take a look at these two upside-down photos. They look quite similar, if not identical. See next page for "flipped" versions.

Naïve Realism

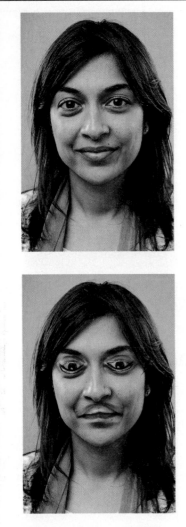

Interactive

Now you can see a noticeable difference between these two images.

scientific theory

explanation for a large number of findings in the natural world

hypothesis

testable prediction derived from a scientific theory

Some creationists have argued that evolution is "just a theory." Cobb County, Georgia, briefly required high school biology textbooks to carry this sticker (Pinker, 2002).

> This textbook contains material on evolution. Evolution is a theory, not a fact, regarding the origin of living things. This material should be approached with an open mind, studied carefully, and critically considered.
>
> *Approved by*
> *Cobb County Board of Education*
> *Thursday, March 28, 2002*

Associates, 2008, p. 29). In fact, scientific psychologists almost always rely on systematic research methods, of which talking to people is only one component, and often not the most important. Another reason why many people question psychology's scientific status is that psychology is intimately familiar to all of us; memory, learning, love, sleep and dreams, personality, and the like are part and parcel of everyday lives. Because these psychological phenomena are so recognizable to us, we may assume that we understand them (Lilienfeld, 2012). Indeed, children and adults alike tend to regard psychology as simpler and more self-evident than physics, chemistry, and biology (Keil, Lockhart, & Schlegel, 2010), which probably helps to explain why these other fields are often called the "hard" sciences. Yet as we'll see in later chapters, there are many ways in which psychology is even "harder" than physics, because behavior— especially human behavior—is often far more challenging to predict (Cesario, 2014; Meehl, 1978).

WHAT IS A SCIENTIFIC THEORY? Few terms in science have generated more confusion than the deceptively simple word *theory.* Some of this confusion has contributed to serious misunderstandings about how science, including psychological science, works. We'll first examine what a scientific theory is and then address two misconceptions about what a scientific theory *isn't.*

A **scientific theory** is an explanation for a large number of findings in the natural world, including the psychological world. A scientific theory offers an account that ties multiple observations together into one pretty package.

Still, good scientific theories should do more than account for existing data. They should generate predictions regarding new data we haven't yet observed. For a theory to be scientific, it must lead to novel predictions that researchers can test. Scientists call a testable prediction a **hypothesis**. In other words, theories are general explanations, whereas hypotheses are specific predictions derived from those explanations (Bolles, 1962; Meehl, 1967). Based on their tests of hypotheses, scientists can provisionally accept the theory that generated these hypotheses, reject this theory outright, or revise it (Proctor & Capaldi, 2006). Now, let's consider two common misconceptions about what a theory is.

Misconception 1: *A theory explains one specific event.* The first misunderstanding is that a theory is a specific explanation for an event. The popular media get this distinction wrong much of the time. We often hear television reporters say something like, "The most likely theory for the robbery at the downtown bank is that it was committed by two former bank employees who dressed up as armed guards." But this isn't a "theory" of the robbery. For one thing, it attempts to explain only one event rather than a variety of diverse observations. It also doesn't generate testable predictions.

Misconception 2: *A theory is just an educated guess.* A second myth is that a scientific theory is merely a guess about how the world works. People often dismiss a theoretical explanation on these grounds, arguing that it's "just a theory." (McComas, 1996).

In fact, *all* general scientific explanations about how the world works are theories. A few theories are extremely well supported by multiple lines of evidence. For example, the Big Bang theory, which proposes that the universe began in a gigantic explosion about 14 billion years ago, helps scientists to explain a diverse array of observations. They include the findings that (1) galaxies are rushing away from each other at remarkable speeds; (2) the universe exhibits a uniform background radiation strongly suggestive of the remnants of a tremendous explosion; and (3) powerful telescopes reveal that the oldest galaxies originated about 14 billion years ago, right around the time predicted by the Big Bang theory. Like all scientific theories, the Big Bang theory can never be "proven" because it's remotely conceivable that an even better explanation might come along one day. Nevertheless, because this theory is consistent with many differing lines of evidence, the overwhelming majority of scientists accept it as a good explanation.

Identify Theories and Hypotheses

1) Sarah's motivation for cheating was fear of failure.
   a. Theory
   b. Hypothesis

2) Darwin's evolutionary model explains the changes in species over time.
   a. Theory
   b. Hypothesis

3) The universe began in a gigantic explosion about 14 billion years ago.
   a. Theory
   b. Hypothesis

4) Our motivation to help a stranger in need is influenced by the number of people present.
   a. Theory
   b. Hypothesis

5) Crime rates in Nashville increase as the temperature rises.
   a. Theory
   b. Hypothesis

1) b, 2) a, 3) a, 4) b, 5) b.

Fact vs. Fiction

Academic psychologists are more skeptical of many weakly supported claims, such as extrasensory perception, than are their colleagues in more traditional sciences, such as physics and chemistry. (See bottom of page for answer.)

○ Fact

○ Fiction

Darwinian evolution, the Big Bang, and other well-established theories aren't merely guesses about how the world works, because they've been substantiated over and over again by independent investigators. In contrast, many other scientific theories are only moderately well supported, and still others are questionable or entirely discredited. Not all theories are created equal.

So when we hear that a scientific explanation is "just a theory," we should remember that theories aren't merely guesses. Some theories have survived repeated efforts to refute them and are well-established models of how the world works (Kitcher, 2009).

SCIENCE AS A SAFEGUARD AGAINST BIAS: PROTECTING US FROM OURSELVES. Some people assume that scientists are objective and free of biases. Yet all scientists, including psychological scientists, are human and have their biases, too (Greenwald, 2012; Mahoney & DeMonbreun, 1977). The best scientists, though, strive to become aware of their biases and to find ways to compensate for them. In particular, the best scientists realize that they *want* their pet theories to turn out to be correct. After all, they've typically

Answer: Fact. Compared with physicists, chemists, and biologists, psychologists are considerably less likely to believe that extrasensory perception is an established scientific phenomenon (Wagner & Monnet, 1979). That may be because psychologists are more aware than most other scientists of how biases can affect the interpretation of ambiguous data.

Figure 1.3 Diagram of Wason Selection Task.

In the Wason selection task, you must pick two cards to test the hypothesis that all cards that have a vowel on one side have an odd number on the other. Which two will you select?

Here are four cards. Each of them has a letter on one side and a number on the other side. Two of these cards are shown with the letter side up, and two with the number side up.

Indicate which of these cards you have to turn over in order to determine whether the following claim is true:

If a card has a vowel on one side, then it has an odd number on the other side.

confirmation bias

tendency to seek out evidence that supports our beliefs and deny, dismiss, or distort evidence that contradicts them

Top, Astronomer Percival Lowell sits next to his telescope. *Bottom,* one of Lowell's sketches of his Martian "canals", which he erroneously believed to provide evidence of extraterrestrial intelligence. Lowell's observations almost surely stemmed in part from confirmation bias.

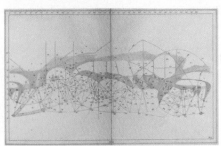

invested months or even years in designing and running a study to test a theory; sometimes it's even a theory they've developed. If the results of the study are negative, they'll often be bitterly disappointed. They also know that because of this deep personal investment, they may bias the results unintentionally to make them turn out the way they want (Greenwald et al., 1986).

Scientists are prone to self-deception, just like the rest of us. As a consequence, there are several traps into which scientists can fall unless they're careful. We'll discuss two of the most crucial next; we should bear in mind that we're all vulnerable to these biases in our everyday lives.

Confirmation Bias. To protect themselves against bias, good scientists adopt procedural safeguards against errors, especially errors that could work in their favor. In other words, scientific methods are tools for overcoming **confirmation bias**, the tendency to seek out evidence that supports our beliefs and deny, dismiss, or distort evidence that contradicts them (Nickerson, 1998; Risen & Gilovich, 2007). There's an old saying that "once you have a hammer, everything starts looking like a nail." This expression is nice illustration of confirmation bias because it highlights the point that once we have a belief in mind, we tend to look for and find evidence that supports it.

Because of confirmation bias, our preconceptions often lead us to focus on evidence that bolsters our beliefs, resulting in psychological tunnel vision (Wagenmakers et al., 2012). One of the simplest demonstrations of confirmation bias comes from research on the *Wason selection task*, one example of which is displayed in Figure 1.3 (Wason, 1966). There, you'll see four cards, each of which has a number on one side and a letter on the other side. Your task is to determine whether the following hypothesis is correct: *All cards that have a vowel on one side have an odd number on the other side.* To test this hypothesis, you need to select *two* cards to turn over. Which two will you pick? Decide on the answer before reading on.

Most people select the *E* and *5* cards. If you selected *E*, you were right, so give yourself one point there. But if you selected *5*, you've fallen prey to confirmation bias, although you'd be in good company because the substantial majority of people make this mistake. Although *5 seems* to be a correct choice, it can only confirm the hypothesis, not disconfirm it. Think of it this way: If there's a vowel on the other side of the *5* card, that doesn't rule out the possibility that the *4* card also has a vowel on the other side, which would disconfirm the hypothesis. So the *4* card is actually the other card to turn over because it's the only other card that could demonstrate that the hypothesis is wrong.

Confirmation bias wouldn't be especially interesting if it were limited to cards. What makes this bias so important is that it extends to many domains of daily life, including friendship, romance, politics, and sports (Nickerson, 1998; Rassin, Eerland, & Kuijpers, 2010). For example, research shows that confirmation bias affects how we evaluate candidates for political office—including those on both the left and right sides of the political spectrum. If we agree with a candidate's political views, we quickly forgive the candidate for contradicting himself or herself, but if we disagree with a candidate's views, we criticize him or her as a "flip-flopper" (Tavris & Aronson, 2007; Westen et al., 2006). Similarly, in a classic study of a hotly contested football game, Dartmouth fans were more likely than Princeton fans to see Princeton players as "dirty" and as committing many penalties, whereas Princeton fans were more likely than Dartmouth fans to view Dartmouth players in the same way (Hastorf & Cantril, 1954). When it comes to judging right and wrong, our side almost always seems to be in the right; the other side always seems to be in the wrong.

Confirmation bias also helps to account for how scientists, even brilliant ones, can be led astray. Percival Lowell (1855–1916) was an influential American astronomer who was renowned for his keen powers of observation. Today, though, he is perhaps best known for falling prey to what may have been the most prolonged visual illusion in scientific history. Around the turn of the 20th century, Lowell became convinced that he had discovered dozens of canals on Mars, which he believed provided definitive evidence of intelligent life on the Red Planet.

Using his powerful telescope, he "observed" these canals for decades, and "discovered" more and more of them over time (Sagan & Fox, 1975).

What had happened? Several decades before, an Italian astronomer had detected similar features on the Martian surface, and referred to them as "canali." The astronomer actually wasn't sure what to make of them, but because *canali* became translated into English as canals," Lowell and others assumed that they were likely the products of an extraterrestrial civilization. Interestingly, not long before Lowell starting "seeing" his canals, the Suez Canal had been built in Egypt, so the ideas of canals was very much a topic of discussion in popular culture. So, almost certainly, Lowell was psychologically predisposed to perceive canals on Mars, and sure enough he did. He was a victim of confirmation bias. Remarkably, it was not until the 1960s, when the United States finally sent unmanned missions to photograph the Martian surface, that the idea of Martian canals was disconfirmed.

As it turns out, there's a curious postscript to this story. Although it's less well known, Lowell also claimed to observe "spokes" on the surface of Venus; we now know that these features were a product of his imagination because the surface of Venus isn't visible from earth. In 2003, a research team may have figured out the mystery. They noticed that Lowell's spokes on Venus bore a striking similarity to the blood vessels in the human eye (Sheehan & Dobbins, 2003). Moreover, because of the peculiar construction of his telescope, Lowell was probably seeing his eye faintly reflected in his line of vision. So Lowell was probably mistaking planetary canals and spokes for the blood vessels in the back of his own eye!

Although we'll be encountering a variety of biases in this text, confirmation bias is the "mother of all biases." That's because it's the bias that can most easily fool all of us into seeing what we expect to see and often what we want to see (Gilovich, & Ross, 2016). For that reason, it's probably the most crucial bias that psychologists need to counteract. What distinguishes psychological scientists from nonscientists is that the former adopt systematic safeguards to protect against confirmation bias, whereas the latter don't (Lilienfeld, Ammirati, & Landfield, 2009; MacCoun & Perlmutter, 2016).

Belief Perseverance. Confirmation bias predisposes us to another shortcoming to which we're all prone: **belief perseverance** (Lewandowsky et al., 2012; Nestler, 2010). In everyday language, belief perseverance is the "don't confuse me with the facts" effect. Because none of us wants to think we're wrong, we're usually reluctant to give up our cherished notions. For example, even though numerous widely publicized studies have shown that vaccines don't cause autism (technically called *autism spectrum disorder*), one in three parents continues to believe that they do (Nyhan & Reifler, 2015). In a striking laboratory demonstration of belief perseverance, Lee Ross and his colleagues asked students to inspect 50 suicide notes and determine which were real and which were fake (in reality, half were real and half were fake). They then gave students feedback on how well they did. They told some students that they were usually right; others, that they were usually wrong. Unbeknownst to the students, this feedback was unrelated to their actual performance. Yet, even after the researchers informed the students that the feedback was bogus, students based their estimates of ability on the feedback they'd received. Students told they were good at detecting real suicide notes were convinced that they were better at it than students told they were bad at it (Ross, Lepper, & Hubbard, 1975).

Beliefs endure. Even when informed that we're wrong, we don't completely wipe our mental slates clean and start from scratch.

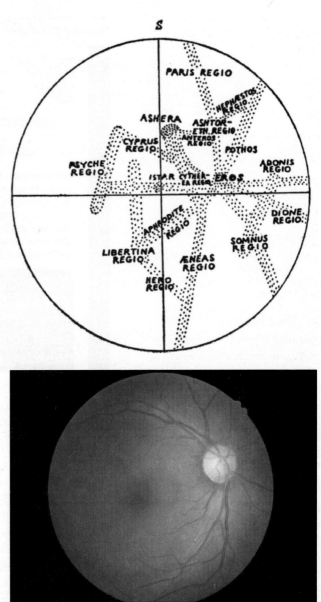

Top, The "spokes" on Venus observed by Percival Lowell. *Bottom*, Blood vessels in the human eye. Do you notice a similarity? One author team did (Sheehan & Dobbins, 2013).

belief perseverance

tendency to stick to our initial beliefs even when evidence contradicts them

Metaphysical Claims

The image on the left is probably pseudoscientific because it makes extreme claims that aren't supported by evidence. The image on right is metaphysical because it makes a claim that science cannot test

Metaphysical Claims: The Boundaries of Science

metaphysical claim

assertion about the world that's not testable

It's essential to distinguish scientific claims from **metaphysical claims** (Popper, 1965). Metaphysical claims include assertions about the existence of God, the soul, and the afterlife. These claims differ from scientific claims in that we could never test them using scientific methods. (How could we design a scientific test to conclusively disprove the existence of God?)

This point doesn't mean that metaphysical claims are wrong, let alone unimportant. To the contrary, some scholars contend that questions concerning the existence of God are even more significant and profound than are scientific questions. Moreover, regardless of our beliefs about religion, we should treat these questions with respect. But it's crucial to recognize that there are certain questions about the world that science can—and can't—answer (Gould, 1997; Novella, 2013). Science is a wonderful tool for investigating claims about the natural world, but it can't answer questions that lie outside of this world. So, it needs to respect the boundaries of religion and other metaphysical domains. Testable claims fall within the province of science; untestable claims don't (see Figure 1.4). Moreover, according to many (although admittedly not all) scholars, there's no inherent conflict between science and the vast majority of religious claims (Dean, 2005). One can quite comfortably adhere to one's religious views while embracing psychology's scientific tools and findings.

Figure 1.4 Nonoverlapping Realms of Knowledge.

Scientist Stephen Jay Gould (1997) argued that science and religion are entirely different and nonoverlapping realms of understanding the world. Science deals with testable claims about the natural world that can be answered with data, whereas religion deals with untestable claims about moral values that can't be answered with data. Although not all scientists and theologicians accept Gould's model, we adopt it for the purposes of this text.

SOURCE: Gould, 1997.

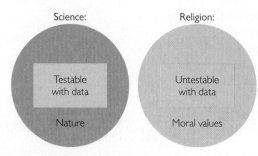

Recognizing That We Might Be Wrong

Good scientists are keenly aware that they might be mistaken (Tavris & Aronson, 2007; Sagan, 1995). That's a crucial insight because initial scientific conclusions are often wrong or at least partly off base. Medical findings are prime examples (Prasad & Cifu, 2015). Eating a lot of chocolate reduces your risk for heart disease; oops, no, it doesn't. (We'll bet you were disappointed to learn that.) Drinking a little red wine now and then is good for you; no, actually, it's bad for you. And on and on it goes. It's scarcely any wonder that many people just throw up their hands and give up reading medical reports altogether. One researcher (Ioannidis, 2005) found that about a third of findings from published medical studies don't hold up in later studies. (Of course, we have to wonder: Do we know that the results of *this* analysis will hold up?) But the beauty of this admittedly messy process is that scientific knowledge is almost always tentative and potentially open to revision. The fact that science is a process of continually revising and updating findings isn't a source of weakness. Instead, science's capacity for self-correction actually lends it strength as a method of inquiry. It does mean, though, that we usually acquire knowledge about the world slowly and in small bits and pieces.

One way of characterizing this process is to describe science, including psychological science, as a *prescription for humility* (Firestein, 2015; McFall, 1997). Good scientists don't claim to "prove" their theories and try to avoid committing to definitive conclusions unless the evidence for them is overwhelming. Such terms and phrases as *suggests*, *appears*, and *raises the possibility that* are widespread in scientific writing and allow scientists to remain tentative in their interpretations of findings. Many beginning students understandably find all of this hemming and hawing a bit frustrating; They may wonder: "But what I am supposed to believe?"

Yet, as Carl Sagan (1995) observed, the best scientists hear a little voice in their heads that keeps repeating the same words: "I might be wrong." Science forces us to question our findings and conclusions and encourages us to ferret out mistakes in our belief systems (O'Donohue, Lilienfeld, & Fowler, 2007). Science also forces us to attend to data that aren't to our liking, whether or not we want to. As social psychologists Carol Tavris and Elliott Aronson (2007) have widely observed, science is a method of "arrogance control." It helps to keep us honest.

1.2: Psychological Pseudoscience: Imposters of Science

1.2a Describe psychological pseudoscience and distinguish it from psychological science.

1.2b Identify reasons we are drawn to pseudoscience.

You might have enrolled in this course to better understand yourself, your friends, or a boyfriend or girlfriend. If so, you might well be thinking, "But I don't want to become a scientist. In fact, I'm not even interested in research. I just want to understand people."

Not to worry. We're not trying to persuade you to become a scientist. Instead, our goal is to persuade you to *think scientifically*: To become more aware of your biases and to take advantage of the tools of science to try to compensate for them. By acquiring these skills, you'll be equipped to make better educated choices in your everyday life, such as what weight loss plan to choose, what type of psychotherapy to recommend to a friend, and maybe even what potential romantic partner to pursue. You'll also learn how to avoid being duped by bogus claims. Not everyone needs to become a scientist, but the good news is that just about everyone can learn to think like one.

Subliminal self-help tapes supposedly influence behavior by means of messages delivered to the unconscious. But do they really work?

The Amazing Growth of Popular Psychology

Distinguishing real from bogus claims is crucial because the popular psychology industry is huge and continually expanding. On the positive side, this fact means that the American public has unprecedented access to psychological knowledge. On the negative side, the remarkable growth of popular psychology has led not only to an information explosion but also to a *misinformation explosion*, because there's scant quality control over what this industry produces (Lilienfeld, 2012).

For example, about 3,500 self-help books are published every year (Arkowitz & Lilienfeld, 2006). Some of these books are effective for treating depression, anxiety disorders, and other psychological problems, but about 95 percent of all self-help books have never been examined in research studies (Gould & Clum, 1993; Gregory et al., 2004; Rosen, 1993) and evidence suggests that a few of them may even worsen people's psychological problems (Haeffel, 2010; Rosen, 1993; Salerno, 2005).

Coinciding with the ongoing expansion of the popular psychology industry is the enormous growth of treatments and products that claim to cure almost every imaginable psychological ailment. There are more than 600 "brands" of psychotherapy (Eisner, 2000), with new ones emerging every year. Fortunately, research shows that some of these treatments are helpful for numerous psychological problems. Yet the substantial majority of psychotherapies remain untested, so we don't know whether they help (Baker, McFall, & Shoham, 2009). Some may even be harmful (Lilienfeld, 2007, 2016).

Fortunately, not all psychology information in popular culture is inaccurate. For example, some self-help books base their recommendations on solid research about psychological problems and their treatment. In addition, we can often find excellent articles in the *New York Times, Scientific American,* and *Discover* magazines, as well as other media outlets that present high-quality information regarding scientific psychology. In addition, hundreds of Web sites provide helpful information and advice concerning such psychological topics as memory, personality testing, and psychological disorders. The Web sites of such organizations as the Association for Psychological Science (www.psychologicalscience.org), American Psychological Association (www.apa.org), Canadian Psychological Association (www.cpa.ca), and National Institute of Mental Health (www.nimh.nih.gov/index.shtml) are good starting points for obtaining accurate information regarding human behavior. In contrast, many other psychology Web sites contain misleading or erroneous information, so we need to be armed with accurate knowledge to evaluate them.

What Is Pseudoscience?

pseudoscience

set of claims that seems scientific but isn't

Everything we've discussed thus far highlights a crucial point: We need to distinguish claims that are genuinely scientific from those that are merely imposters of science. The name for an imposter of science is **pseudoscience**. In particular, *pseudoscience lacks the safeguards against confirmation bias and belief perseverance that characterize science.* We must be careful to distinguish pseudoscientific claims from metaphysical claims, which, as we've seen, are untestable and therefore lie outside the realm of science. In principle, at least, we can subject pseudoscientific claims to research tests.

Pseudoscientific and other questionable beliefs are widespread. A 2009 survey of the U.S. public shows that 25 percent believe in astrology, 26 percent believe that trees and other objects possess magical energies, 18 percent believe that they've had encounters with ghosts, and 15 percent have consulted psychics (Pew Research Center, 2009). The fact that many Americans *entertain* the possibility of such phenomena isn't by itself worrisome because a certain amount of open-mindedness is essential for scientific thinking, given that all scientific knowledge is provisional. Instead, what's troubling is that many Americans appear convinced that such phenomena exist even though the scientific evidence for them is weak, as in the case of psychics, or essentially nonexistent, as in the case of astrology. Moreover, it's troubling that many poorly supported beliefs are more popular, or at least more widespread, than well-supported beliefs. To take merely one example, there are about 20 times as many astrologers as astronomers in the United States (Gilovich, 1991); as a consequence, the general public may often have a difficult time distinguishing accurate from inaccurate claims regarding astronomy. The same principle holds for psychology.

WARNING SIGNS OF PSEUDOSCIENCE. Several warning signs can help us distinguish science from pseudoscience; we've listed some of the most useful ones in Table 1.1. They're extremely helpful rules of thumb, so useful in fact that we'll draw on many of them in later chapters to help us become more informed consumers of psychological claims. We can—and should—also draw on them in everyday life. None of these signs is by itself proof positive that a set of claims is pseudoscientific. Nevertheless, the more of these signs we see in the case of a given claim, the more skeptical of this claim we should typically become.

Pseudoscientific and otherwise questionable claims have increasingly altered the landscape of modern life.

Table 1.1 Some Warning Signs That Can Help Us Recognize Pseudoscience.

Sign of Pseudoscience	Example
Overuse of ad hoc immunizing hypotheses	The psychic who claimed to predict the future failed all controlled tests in the lab, but that's because the experimenters inhibited his extrasensory powers.
Exaggerated claims	Three simple steps will change your love life forever!
Overreliance on anecdotes	This woman practiced yoga daily for three weeks and hasn't had a day of depression since.
Absence of connectivity to other research	Amazing new innovations in research have shown that eye massage results in reading speeds 10 times faster than average!
Lack of review by other scholars (called *peer review*) or replication by independent labs	Fifty studies conducted by the company all show overwhelming success!
Lack of self-correction when contrary evidence is published	Although most scientists say that we use almost all our brains, we've found a way to harness additional brain power previously undiscovered.
Meaningless "psychobabble" that uses fancy scientific-sounding terms that don't make sense	Sine-wave filtered auditory stimulation is carefully designed to encourage maximal orbitofrontal dendritic development.
Talk of "proof" instead of "evidence"	Our new program is proven to reduce social anxiety by at least 50 percent!

Here, we'll discuss three of the most crucial of these warning signs.

Overuse of ad hoc immunizing hypotheses. Yes, we know this one is a mouthful. But it's actually not as complicated as it appears because an **ad hoc immunizing hypothesis** is just an escape hatch that defenders of a theory use to protect this theory from being disproven. For example, some psychics have claimed to perform remarkable feats of extrasensory perception (ESP) in the real world, like reading others' minds or forecasting the future. But when brought into the laboratory and tested under tightly controlled conditions, most have bombed, performing no better than chance. Some of these psychics and their proponents have invoked an ad hoc immunizing hypothesis to explain away these failures: The skeptical "vibes" of the experimenters are somehow interfering with psychic powers (Carroll, 2003; Lilienfeld, 1999c). Although this hypothesis isn't necessarily wrong, it makes the psychics' claims essentially impossible to test.

Lack of self-correction. As we've learned, many scientific claims turn out to be wrong. Fortunately, in science, incorrect claims tend to be weeded out eventually, even though it often takes longer than we might like. In contrast, in most pseudosciences, mistaken assertions never seem to go away because their proponents fall prey to belief perseverance, clinging to them stubbornly despite contrary evidence. Moreover, pseudoscientific claims are rarely updated in light of new data. Most forms of astrology have remained almost identical for about 4,000 years (Hines, 2003) despite the discovery of outer planets in the solar system (Uranus and Neptune) that were unknown in ancient times.

Overreliance on anecdotes. There's an old saying that "the plural of anecdote isn't fact" (Park, 2003). A mountain of numerous anecdotes may seem impressive, but it shouldn't persuade us to put much stock in others' claims. Most anecdotes are *I know a person who* assertions (Nisbett & Ross, 1980; Stanovich, 2012). This kind of secondhand evidence—"I know a person who says his self-esteem skyrocketed after receiving hypnosis"—is commonplace in everyday life. So is firsthand evidence—"I felt less depressed after taking this herbal remedy"—that's based on subjective impressions.

Pseudosciences tend to rely heavily on "anecdata," scientists' informal term for anecdotal evidence. In many cases, pseudoscientists base claims on the dramatic reports of one or two individuals: "I lost 85 pounds in three weeks on the Matzo Ball Soup Weight-Loss Program." Compelling as this anecdote may appear, it doesn't constitute good scientific evidence (Davison & Lazarus, 2007; Loftus & Guyer, 2002). For one thing, anecdotes rarely tell us anything about cause and effect. Maybe the Matzo Ball Soup Weight-Loss Program caused the person to lose 85 pounds, but maybe other factors were responsible. Perhaps he went on an additional diet or started to exercise frantically during that time. Or perhaps

ad hoc immunizing hypothesis

escape hatch or loophole that defenders of a theory use to protect their theory from falsification

he underwent drastic weight-loss surgery during this time but didn't bother to mention it. Anecdotes also don't tell us anything about how representative the cases are. Perhaps most people who went on the Matzo Ball Soup Weight-Loss Program gained weight, but we never heard from them. Finally, anecdotes are often difficult to verify. Do we really know for sure that he lost 85 pounds? We're taking his word for it, which is a risky idea in science; it's also a risky idea in everyday life.

Simply put, most anecdotes are extremely difficult to interpret as evidence. As clinical psychologist Paul Meehl (1995) put it, "The clear message of history is that the anecdotal method delivers both wheat and chaff, but it does not enable us to tell which is which" (p. 1019).

WHY ARE WE DRAWN TO PSEUDOSCIENCE?   There are a host of reasons why so many of us are drawn to pseudoscientific beliefs.

Perhaps the central reason stems from the way our brains work. *Our brains are predisposed to make order out of disorder and find sense in nonsense.* This tendency is generally adaptive because it helps us to simplify the often bewildering world in which we live (Alcock, 1995; Pinker, 1997; Shermer, 2011). Without it, we'd be constantly overwhelmed by endless streams of information that we don't have the time or ability to process. Yet this adaptive tendency can sometimes lead us astray because it can cause us to perceive meaningful patterns even when they're not there (Carroll, 2003; Davis, 2009).

Here's a striking example. The Nobel Prize–winning physicist Luis Alvarez once had an eerie experience: Upon reading the newspaper, he read a phrase that reminded him of an old childhood friend he hadn't thought about for decades. A few pages later, he came upon that person's obituary! Initially stunned, Alvarez (1965) performed some calculations and determined that given the number of people on earth and the number of people who die every day, this kind of strange coincidence probably occurs about 3,000 times across the world each year.

patternicity

the tendency to perceive meaningful patterns in their absence

Mysteries of Psychological Science
Why Do We Perceive Patterns Even When They don't Exist?

Our tendency to see patterns in meaningless data is so profound that science writer Michael Shermer (2008) gave it a name: **patternicity**. Although patternicity can lead to errors, it probably stems from an evolutionarily adaptive tendency (Reich, 2010). If we eat a specific food, say a bacon cheeseburger, for lunch tomorrow and become violently ill soon afterward, we'll tend to avoid bacon cheeseburgers for a while. We'll do so even though it's likely that the link between the cheeseburger and our becoming ill was purely coincidental. No matter—our brains tend to seek out patterns and connections among events, because of a basic evolutionary principle: "Better safe than sorry." All things being equal, it's usually better to assume that a connection between two events exists than to assume that it doesn't, especially when one of the events is physically dangerous.

We all fall prey to patternicity from time to time (Hood, 2014). If we think of a friend with whom we haven't spoken in a few months and immediately afterward receive a phone call from him or her, we may jump to the conclusion that this striking co-occurrence stems from ESP. Well, it *might*.

But it's also entirely possible, if not likely, that these two events happened at about the same time by chance alone. For a moment, think of the number of times one of your old friends comes to mind and then think of the total number of phone calls you receive each month.

You'll realize that the laws of probability make it likely that at least once over the next few years, you'll be thinking of an old friend at about the same time he or she calls.

Our tendency to underestimate coincidences almost surely fuels patternicity. "Streaks" of several consecutive heads (H) or tails (T) in a row when flipping a coin, like HTTHTTTTTHHHTHHTTHH, are far more common than we believe. They're even inevitable in long random sequences. Indeed, the sequence above is almost perfectly random (Gilovich, 1991). Because we tend to underestimate the probability of consecutive sequences, we're prone to attributing more significance to these sequences than they deserve ("Wow ... I'm on a winning streak!").

Another manifestation of patternicity is our tendency to detect eerie coincidences among persons or events. To take one example, read through each of the uncanny similarities between Abraham Lincoln and John F. Kennedy, two great American presidents who were the victims of assassination, listed in Table 1.2.

Pretty amazing stuff, isn't it? So extraordinary, in fact, that some writers have argued that Lincoln and Kennedy are somehow linked by supernatural forces (Leavy, 1992). In actuality, though, coincidences are everywhere. They're surprisingly easy to detect if we make the effort to look for them. Because of patternicity, we may attribute paranormal significance to coincidences that are a result of chance.

Table 1.2 Some Eerie Commonalities Between Abraham Lincoln and John F. Kennedy.

Abraham Lincoln	John F. Kennedy
Was elected to Congress in 1846	Was elected to Congress in 1946
Was elected President in 1860	Was elected President in 1960
The name "Lincoln" contains seven letters	The name "Kennedy" contains seven letters
Was assassinated on a Friday	Was assassinated on a Friday
Lincoln's secretary, named Kennedy, warned him not to go to the theater, where he was shot	Kennedy's secretary, named Lincoln, warned him not to go to Dallas, where he was shot
Lincoln's wife was sitting beside him when he was shot	Kennedy's wife was sitting beside him when he was shot
John Wilkes Booth (Lincoln's assassin) was born in 1839	Lee Harvey Oswald (Kennedy's assassin) was born in 1939
Was succeeded by a president named Johnson	Was succeeded by a president named Johnson
Andrew Johnson, who succeeded Lincoln, was born in 1808	Lyndon Johnson, who succeeded Kennedy, was born in 1908
Booth fled from a theater to a warehouse	Oswald fled from a warehouse to a theater
Booth was killed before his trial	Oswald was killed before his trial

(The term *paranormal* describes phenomena, such as ESP, that fall outside the boundaries of traditional science.) Moreover, we often fall victim to confirmation bias and neglect to consider evidence that *doesn't* support our hypothesis. Because we typically find coincidences to be far more interesting than noncoincidences, we tend to forget that Lincoln was a Republican whereas Kennedy was a Democrat; that Lincoln was shot in Washington, D.C. whereas Kennedy was shot in Dallas; that Lincoln had a beard, but Kennedy didn't; and on and on. Recall that scientific thinking is designed to counteract confirmation bias. To do so, we must seek out evidence that contradicts our ideas. In extreme forms, patternicity leads us to embrace conspiracy theories, in which individuals detect supposedly hidden connections among numerous largely or entirely unrelated events (Douglas & Sutton, 2011).

Journal Prompt

Do you know someone who believes in a conspiracy theory? What is it and what evidence is consistent with this theory? What evidence is inconsistent with it?

A final reflection of patternicity is our tendency to see meaningful images in meaningless visual stimuli. Any of us who's looked at a cloud and perceived the vague shape of an animal has experienced this version of patternicity, as has any of us who's seen the oddly misshapen face of a "man" in the moon. Another entertaining example comes from the photograph in Figure 1.5a. In 1976, the *Mars Viking Orbiter* snapped an image of a set of features on the Martian surface. As we can see, these features bear an eerie resemblance to a human face. It was so eerie, in fact, that some individuals maintained that the "Face on Mars" offered conclusive proof of intelligent life on the Red Planet (Hoagland, 1987). In 2001, during a mission of a different spacecraft, the *Mars Global Surveyor,* the National Aeronautics and Space Administration (NASA) decided to adopt a scientific approach to the face on Mars. NASA was open-minded but demanded evidence. It swooped down much closer to the face and pointed the *Surveyor's* cameras directly at it. If we look at Figure 1.5b, we'll see

Patternicity can lead us to perceive meaningful people or objects in largely random stimuli. The "nun bun," a cinnamon roll resembling the face of nun Mother Teresa, was discovered in 1996 in a coffee shop in Nashville, Tennessee.

Figure 1.5 Face on Mars.

At the top (*a*) is the remarkable "Face on Mars" photo taken by the *Mars Viking Orbiter* in 1976. Some argued that this face provided proof of intelligent life on other planets. Below (*b*) is a more detailed photograph of the Face on Mars taken in 2001 that revealed that this "face" was just an illusion.

(a)

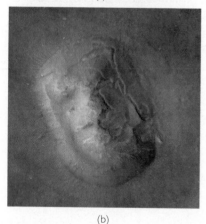

(b)

terror management theory

theory proposing that our awareness of our death leaves us with an underlying sense of terror with which we cope by adopting reassuring cultural worldviews

Fact vs. Fiction

Interactive

Conspiracy theories can lead us to believe two logically inconsistent things at the same time (such as the idea that a person is simultaneously alive and dead). (See bottom of page for answer.)

○ Fact

○ Fiction

what NASA found: absolutely nothing. The patternicity in this instance was a consequence of a peculiar configuration of rocks and shadows present at the angle at which the photographs were taken in 1976, a camera artifact in the original photograph that just happened to place a black dot where a nostril should be, and perhaps most important, our innate tendency to perceive meaningful faces in what are basically random visual stimuli.

Finding Comfort in Our Beliefs. Another reason for the popularity of pseudoscience is motivational: We believe in large part because we want to believe. As the old saying goes, "hope springs eternal": Many pseudoscientific claims, such as astrology, may give us comfort because they seem to offer us a sense of control over an often unpredictable world (Shermer, 2002). Research suggests that we're especially prone to patternicity when we experience a sense of a loss of control over our surroundings. Jennifer Whitson and Adam Galinsky (2008) deprived some participants of a sense of control—for example, by having them try to solve an unsolvable puzzle or recall a real-life experience in which they felt helpless—and found that they were more likely than other participants to perceive conspiracies, embrace superstitious beliefs, and detect patterns in meaningless visual stimuli (see Figure 1.6). These results may help to explain why so many of us believe in astrology, ESP, and other belief systems that claim to foretell the future; they lend us a sense of control over the uncontrollable (Wang, Whitson, & Menon, 2012).

According to **terror management theory**, our awareness of our own inevitable death leaves many of us with an underlying sense of fear, even dread (Solomon, Greenberg, & Pyszczynski, 2000; Vail, 2012). We cope with these feelings of terror, advocates of this theory propose, by adopting cultural worldviews that reassure us that our lives possess a broader meaning and purpose—one that extends well beyond our vanishingly brief existence on this planet.

Answer: Fact. Research shows that many of the same people who are convinced that Princess Diana (who died in a car accident in Paris in 1997) was the victim of an intentional murder plot are also certain that she faked her own death and is still alive (Wood, Douglas, & Sutton, 2012).

Can terror management theory help to explain the popularity of certain paranormal beliefs, such as astrology, ESP, and communication with the dead? Perhaps (Whitson, Galinsky, & Kay, 2015). Our society's widespread beliefs in life after death and reincarnation may stem in part from the terror that stems from knowing we'll eventually die (Lindeman, 1998; Norenzayan & Hansen, 2006). Two researchers (Morier & Podlipentseva, 1997) found that compared with other participants, participants who were asked to contemplate death reported higher levels of beliefs in the paranormal, such as ESP, ghosts, reincarnation, and astrology, than did other participants. It's likely that such beliefs are comforting to many of us, especially when confronted with reminders of our demise, because they imply the existence of a dimension beyond our own.

Terror management theory doesn't demonstrate that paranormal claims are false; we still need to evaluate these claims on their own merits. Nonetheless, this theory suggests that we're likely to hold many paranormal beliefs regardless of whether they're correct.

THINKING CLEARLY: AN ANTIDOTE AGAINST PSEUDOSCIENCE. To avoid being seduced by the tempting charms of pseudoscience, we must learn to avoid commonplace pitfalls in reasoning to which we're all prone. Students new to psychology commonly fall prey to *logical fallacies*: traps in thinking that can lead to mistaken conclusions. It's easy for us to commit these errors because they seem to make intuitive sense. We should remember that scientific thinking often requires us to cast aside our beloved intuitions, although doing so can be extremely difficult for all of us.

Here we'll examine three especially important logical fallacies that are essential to bear in mind when evaluating psychological claims; we can find other fallacies in Table 1.3. All of them can help us to separate science from pseudoscience, and more generally, avoid falling prey to dubious assertions in everyday life.

Figure 1.6 Regaining Control.

Do you see an image in either of these pictures? Participants in Whitson and Galinsky's (2008) study who were deprived of a sense of control were more likely than other participants to see images in both pictures, even though only the picture on the bottom contains an image (a faint drawing of the planet Saturn).

Table 1.3 Logical Fallacies to Avoid When Evaluating Psychological Claims.

Logical Fallacy	Example of The Fallacy
Error of using our emotions as guides for evaluating the validity of a claim (*emotional reasoning fallacy*)	"The idea that day care might have negative emotional effects on children gets me really upset, so I refuse to believe it."
Error of assuming that a claim is correct just because many people believe it (*bandwagon fallacy*)	"A lot of people I know believe in astrology, so there's got to be something to it."
Error of framing a question as though we can only answer it in one of two extreme ways (*either-or fallacy*)	"I just read in my psychology textbook that some people with schizophrenia were treated extremely well by their parents when they were growing up. This means that schizophrenia can't be the result of environmental factors and therefore must be completely genetic."
Error of believing we're immune from errors in thinking that afflict other people (*not me fallacy*)	"My psychology professor keeps talking about how the scientific method is important for overcoming biases. But these biases don't apply to me because *I'm* objective."
Error of accepting a claim merely because an authority figure endorses it (*appeal to authority fallacy*)	"My professor says that psychotherapy is worthless; because I trust my professor, she must be right."
Error of confusing the correctness of a belief with its origins or genesis (*genetic fallacy*)	"Freud's views about personality development can't be right because Freud's thinking was shaped by sexist views popular at the time."
Error of assuming that a belief must be valid just because it's been around for a long time (*argument from antiquity fallacy*)	"There must be something to the Rorschach Inkblot Test because psychologists have been using it for decades."
Error of confusing the validity of an idea with its potential real-world consequences (*argument from adverse consequences fallacy*)	"IQ can't be influenced by genetic factors because if that were true, it would give the government an excuse to prevent low-IQ individuals from reproducing."
Error of assuming that a claim must be true because no one has shown it to be false (*appeal to ignorance fallacy*)	"No scientist has been able to explain away every reported case of ESP, so ESP probably exists."
Error of inferring a moral judgment from a scientific fact (*naturalistic fallacy*)	"Evolutionary psychologists say that sexual infidelity is a product of natural selection. Therefore, sexual infidelity is ethically justifiable."
Error of drawing a conclusion on the basis of insufficient evidence (*hasty generalization fallacy*)	"All three people I know who are severely depressed had strict fathers, so severe depression is clearly associated with having a strict father."
Error of basing a claim on the same claim reworded in slightly different terms (*circular reasoning fallacy*)	"Dr. Smith's theory of personality is the best because it seems to have the most evidence supporting it."

Candace Newmaker was a tragic victim of a pseudoscientific treatment called *rebirthing therapy*. She died of suffocation at age 10 after her therapists wrapped her in a flannel blanket and squeezed her to simulate birth contractions.

Stem-cell research is controversial on both scientific and ethical grounds. To evaluate this and other controversies properly, we need to be able to think critically about the potential costs and benefits of such research.

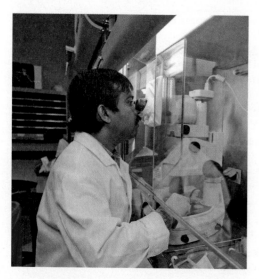

Emotional Reasoning Fallacy. "The idea that day care might have negative emotional effects on children gets me really upset, so I refuse to believe it."

The *emotional reasoning fallacy* is the error of using our emotions as guides for evaluating the validity of a claim (some psychologists also refer to this error as the *affect heuristic*) (Kahneman, 2011; Slovic & Peters, 2006). If we're honest with ourselves, we'll realize that findings that challenge our preexisting beliefs often make us uncomfortable or angry, whereas findings that confirm these beliefs often make us happy or at least relieved. We shouldn't make the mistake of assuming that because a scientific claim makes us feel upset or indignant, it must be wrong. In the case of scientific questions concerning the psychological effects of day care, which are scientifically controversial (Belsky, 1988; Hunt, 1999), we need to keep an open mind to the data, regardless of whether they confirm or disconfirm our preconceptions.

Bandwagon Fallacy. "A lot of people I know believe in astrology, so there's got to be something to it."

The *bandwagon fallacy* is the error of assuming that a claim is correct just because many people believe it. It's an error because popular opinion isn't a dependable guide to the accuracy of an assertion. Before 1500, almost everyone believed the sun revolved around the earth, rather than vice versa, but they were woefully mistaken.

Not Me Fallacy. "My psychology professor keeps talking about how scientific methods are important for overcoming biases. But these biases don't apply to me, because *I'm* objective."

The *not me fallacy* is the error of believing that we're immune from errors in thinking that afflict other people. This fallacy can get us into deep trouble because it can lead us to conclude mistakenly that we don't require the safeguards of science. Many pseudoscientists fall into this trap: They're so certain their claims are right—and uncontaminated by mistakes in their thinking—that they don't bother to conduct scientific studies to test these claims. Yet even scientists can fall prey to this error if they're not careful.

Social psychologists have uncovered a fascinating phenomenon called *bias blind spot*, which means that most people are unaware of their biases but keenly aware of them in others (Pronin, Gilovich, & Ross, 2004; Ross, Ehrlinger, & Gilovich, 2015). None of us believes that we have an accent because we live with our accents all of the time. Similarly, few of us believe that we have biases because we've grown accustomed to seeing the world through our own psychological lenses. To see the not me fallacy at work, watch a debate between two intelligent people who hold extremely polarized views on a political issue. More likely than not, you'll see that the debate participants are quite adept at pointing out biases in their opponents, but are oblivious of their own equally glaring biases. People who are highly intelligent are just as prone to bias blind spot as are other people (West, Meserve, & Stanovich, 2012), so we shouldn't assume that more knowledge, education, or sophistication make us immune to this error. Bias blind spot reminds us yet again that we all need to be humble and that science can assist us in this regard.

The Dangers of Pseudoscience: Why Should We Care?

Up to this point, we've been talking a lot about pseudoscience. Why? Pseudoscience can be dangerous, even deadly. This point applies to a variety of questionable claims that we encounter in everyday life. There are three major reasons why we should be concerned about pseudoscience.

1. **Opportunity Costs: What We Give Up.** Pseudoscientific treatments for mental disorders can lead people to forgo opportunities to seek effective treatments (Lazar, 2010; Lilienfeld, Lynn, & Lohr, 2014), a phenomenon known as *opportunity costs*. As a consequence of opportunity costs, even treatments that are themselves harmless can cause harm indirectly by causing people to forfeit the chance to obtain a treatment that works. For example, data suggest that in the United States at most a third of people with major depression, a severe disorder associated with a dramatically heightened risk for suicide, receive any treatment at all (Layard & Clark, 2014). Moreover, among those who do receive treatment, most people with major depression receive treatments that aren't especially effective for their condition,

such as herbal remedies, long-term psychoanalysis (Freudian therapy), and energy therapies, the last of which we'll discuss in the chapter. Only a minority receive scientifically supported interventions, such as *cognitive-behavioral therapy*, which focuses on changing clients' maladaptive behaviors, as well as their unhealthy views of themselves, others, and the world.

2. **Direct Harm.** Pseudoscientific treatments sometimes do dreadful harm to those who receive them, causing psychological or physical damage, or on rare occasions, even death (Barlow, 2010; Lilienfeld, 2007, 2016). The tragic case of Candace Newmaker, a 10-year-old child who received treatment for her behavioral problems in Evergreen, Colorado, in 2000, illustrates this point (Mercer, Sarner, & Rosa, 2003). Candace received a treatment called *rebirthing therapy*, which is premised on the scientifically doubtful notion that children's behavioral problems are attributable to difficulties in forming attachments to their parents that stem from birth—in some cases, even before birth. During rebirthing, children or adolescents reenact the trauma of birth with the "assistance" of one or more therapists (Mercer, 2002). During Candace's rebirthing session, two therapists wrapped her in a flannel blanket, sat on her, and squeezed her repeatedly in an effort to simulate birth contractions. During the 40-minute session, Candace vomited several times and begged the therapists for air, complaining desperately that she couldn't breathe and felt as though she was going to die. When Candace was unwrapped from her symbolic "birth canal," she was dead (Mercer, Sarner, & Rosa, 2003).

3. **An Inability to Think Scientifically as Citizens.** Scientific thinking skills aren't just important for evaluating psychological claims; we can apply them to all aspects of our lives. In our increasingly complex scientific and technological society, we need scientific thinking skills to reach educated decisions about climate change, genetically modified foods, stem-cell research, vaccine safety, novel medical treatments, and parenting and teaching practices, among dozens of other claims (Mooney & Kirshenbaum, 2010).

The take-home message is that pseudoscience matters. That's what makes scientific thinking essential; although far from foolproof, it's our best safeguard against errors to which we're all prone.

This welcome sign for the state of Missouri captures the central motto of scientific skepticism.

1.3: Scientific Thinking: Distinguishing Fact From Fiction

1.3a   **Identify the key features of scientific skepticism.**
1.3b   **Identify and explain the text's six principles of scientific thinking.**

Given that the world of popular psychology is chock-full of remarkable claims, how can we distinguish psychological fact—that is, the body of psychological findings that are so dependable we can safely regard them as true—from psychological fiction?

Scientific Skepticism

The approach we'll emphasize throughout this text is **scientific skepticism**. To many people, *skepticism* implies closed-mindedness, but nothing could be further from the truth. The term *skepticism* derives from the Greek word *skeptikos*, meaning "to consider carefully" (Shermer, 2002). The scientific skeptic evaluates all claims with an open mind but insists on persuasive evidence before accepting them. So we should be certain to distinguish skepticism from cynicism, which implies a dismissal of claims before we've had the opportunity to adequately evaluate them.

As Carl Sagan (1995) noted, to be a scientific skeptic, we must adopt two attitudes that may seem contradictory but aren't: (1) a willingness to keep an open mind to all claims and (2) a willingness to accept claims only after researchers have subjected them to careful scientific tests. Scientific skeptics are willing to change their minds when confronted with evidence that challenges their preconceptions. At the same time, they change

" …and, as you go out into the world, I predict that you will, gradually and imperceptibly, forget all you ever learned at this university."

You'll probably forget many of the things you learn in college. But you'll be able to use the approach of scientific skepticism throughout your life to evaluate claims.

SOURCE: © Science CartoonsPlus.com.

scientific skepticism

approach of evaluating all claims with an open mind but insisting on persuasive evidence before accepting them

their minds only when this evidence is persuasive. The motto of the scientific skeptic is the Missouri principle, which we'll find on many Missouri license plates: "Show me" (Dawes, 1994).

Another feature of scientific skepticism is an unwillingness to accept claims on the basis of authority alone. Scientific skeptics evaluate claims on their own merits and are reluctant to accept them until they've met a high standard of evidence. Of course, in everyday life we're often forced to accept the word of authorities simply because we don't possess the expertise, time, or resources to evaluate every claim on our own. Most of us are willing to accept the claim that our local government keeps our drinking water safe without conducting our own chemical tests. While reading this chapter, you're also placing trust in us—the authors, that is—to provide you with accurate information about psychology. Still, this doesn't mean you should blindly accept everything we've written hook, line, and sinker. Consider what we've written with an open mind, but evaluate it skeptically. If you disagree with something we've written, get a second opinion by asking your instructor or by sending us an e-mail.

critical thinking

set of skills for evaluating all claims in an open-minded and careful fashion

A Basic Framework for Scientific Thinking

The hallmark of scientific skepticism is **critical thinking**. Many students misunderstand the word *critical* in *critical thinking*, assuming incorrectly that it implies a tendency to attack all claims. In fact, critical thinking is a set of skills for evaluating all claims in an open-minded and careful fashion. We can also think of critical thinking in psychology as *scientific thinking* because it's the form of thinking that allows us to evaluate scientific claims not only in the laboratory, but also in everyday life (Lilienfeld, Ammirati, & David, 2012; Willingham, 2007).

Just as important, scientific thinking is a set of skills for overcoming our biases, especially confirmation bias, which, as we've learned, can blind us to evidence we'd prefer to ignore (Alcock, 1995; Begley & Ioannidis, 2015). In particular, in this text, we'll be emphasizing *six* principles of scientific thinking (Bartz, 2002; Lett, 1990). We should bear this framework of principles in mind when evaluating all psychological claims, including claims in the media, in self-help books, on the Internet, in your introductory psychology course, and, yes, even in this text. Table 1.4 offers a number of user-friendly tips for critically evaluating information on the Internet; most of these tips should also be of help with evaluating information in other popular sources. Such tips are increasingly crucial in an age in which fake and real online news stories are becoming more challenging to distinguish. Indeed, recent evidence suggests that college students often can't differentiate fake from real news stories (Stanford History Education Group, 2016).

Table 1.4 Five Questions to Ask Yourself When Evaluating Psychological Web Sites.

1. Does the site refer to peer-reviewed psychological literature, that is, articles in reputable journals?	If yes, that's a good sign. You can check the website of each journal to find out whether it's peer-reviewed.
2. Does the site contain multiple references to articles published in questionable journals?	If so, be skeptical. See the following list for a guide to such journals: https://scholarlyoa.com/publishers/
3. Does the site consist primarily of references to anecdotes or personal testimonials rather than to controlled scientific studies?	If so, be skeptical.
4. Does the site make extreme claims (such as "This treatment has been proven to work" or "This diagnostic technique is virtually 100 percent accurate"), or does it instead make more qualified claims (such as "This treatment has been supported by most of the research evidence" or "This diagnostic technique has been found to be reasonably valid in several controlled studies").	Beware of websites touting unqualified claims.
5. Has the website been recently updated?	If not, you may want to think twice before accepting its claims.

Figure 1.7 The Six Principles of Scientific Thinking That Are Used Throughout This Text.

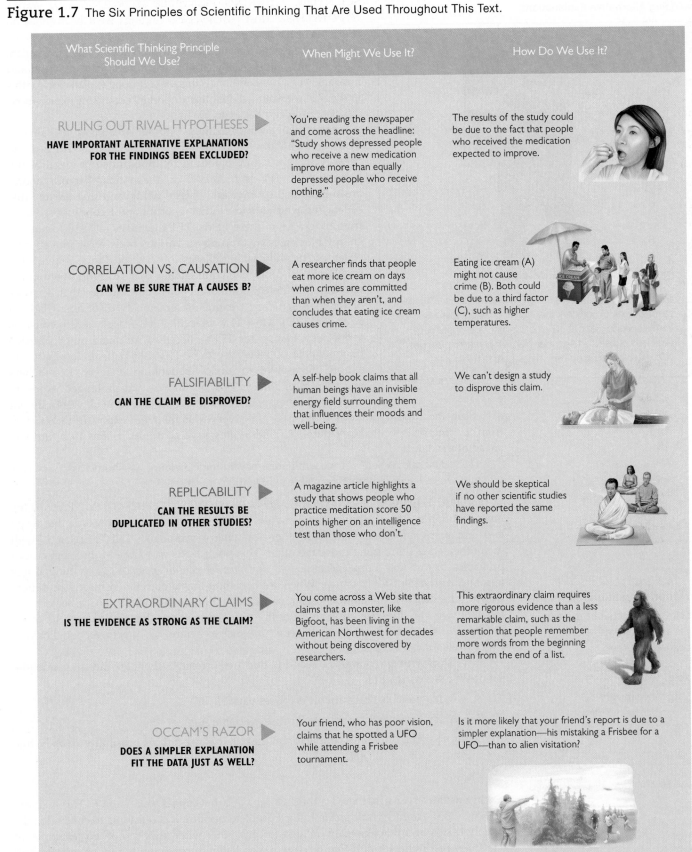

What Scientific Thinking Principle Should We Use?	When Might We Use It?	How Do We Use It?
RULING OUT RIVAL HYPOTHESES ▶ **HAVE IMPORTANT ALTERNATIVE EXPLANATIONS FOR THE FINDINGS BEEN EXCLUDED?**	You're reading the newspaper and come across the headline: "Study shows depressed people who receive a new medication improve more than equally depressed people who receive nothing."	The results of the study could be due to the fact that people who received the medication expected to improve.
CORRELATION VS. CAUSATION ▶ **CAN WE BE SURE THAT A CAUSES B?**	A researcher finds that people eat more ice cream on days when crimes are committed than when they aren't, and concludes that eating ice cream causes crime.	Eating ice cream (A) might not cause crime (B). Both could be due to a third factor (C), such as higher temperatures.
FALSIFIABILITY ▶ **CAN THE CLAIM BE DISPROVED?**	A self-help book claims that all human beings have an invisible energy field surrounding them that influences their moods and well-being.	We can't design a study to disprove this claim.
REPLICABILITY ▶ **CAN THE RESULTS BE DUPLICATED IN OTHER STUDIES?**	A magazine article highlights a study that shows people who practice meditation score 50 points higher on an intelligence test than those who don't.	We should be skeptical if no other scientific studies have reported the same findings.
EXTRAORDINARY CLAIMS ▶ **IS THE EVIDENCE AS STRONG AS THE CLAIM?**	You come across a Web site that claims that a monster, like Bigfoot, has been living in the American Northwest for decades without being discovered by researchers.	This extraordinary claim requires more rigorous evidence than a less remarkable claim, such as the assertion that people remember more words from the beginning than from the end of a list.
OCCAM'S RAZOR ▶ **DOES A SIMPLER EXPLANATION FIT THE DATA JUST AS WELL?**	Your friend, who has poor vision, claims that he spotted a UFO while attending a Frisbee tournament.	Is it more likely that your friend's report is due to a simpler explanation—his mistaking a Frisbee for a UFO—than to alien visitation?

Developing Alternative Explanations

Scientific thinking involves ruling out rival hypotheses. In this case, we don't know that this woman's weight loss resulted from a specific diet plan. During this time, she might have exercised or used another diet plan. Or perhaps the larger pants she's holding up were never hers to begin with.

SCIENTIFIC THINKING PRINCIPLE #1: *RULING OUT RIVAL HYPOTHESES.* Most psychological findings we'll hear about on television or read about online lend themselves to multiple explanations. Yet more often than not, the media report only one explanation. We shouldn't automatically assume it's correct. Instead, we should ask ourselves a key question: Is this the *only* good explanation for this finding? Have we ruled out other important competing explanations (Huck & Sandler, 1979; Platt, 1964)?

Let's take an increasingly popular treatment for anxiety disorders, Thought Field Therapy (TFT; Feinstein, 2012), is an "energy therapy" now practiced by thousands of mental health professionals. TFT is premised on the notion that our bodies are surrounded by invisible energy fields, and that anxiety disorders (as well as some other psychological conditions) result from blockages in these fields. TFT therapists attempt to remove energy blockages by tapping on various body areas in a specific order, often while asking clients to hum song tunes. Here's the problem: Well-controlled studies show that TFT works better than nothing, but there's not a shred of good evidence that it works better than standard treatments for anxiety disorders. (Pignotti & Thyer, 2009). Most TFT advocates have neglected to consider a rival explanation for TFT's success: Like many other effective treatments for anxiety disorders, TFT asks patients to repeatedly expose themselves to anxiety-provoking imagery. Researchers and therapists alike have long known that prolonged exposure itself can be therapeutic (Bisson, 2007; Craske et al., 2014). By not excluding the rival hypothesis that TFT's effectiveness stems from exposure rather than from tapping on specific body parts, TFT advocates have advanced claims that run well ahead of the data.

The bottom line: Whenever we evaluate a psychological claim, we should ask ourselves whether we've excluded other plausible explanations for it.

SCIENTIFIC THINKING PRINCIPLE #2: *CORRELATION ISN'T CAUSATION.* Perhaps the most common mistake laypersons make when interpreting studies is to conclude that when two things are associated with each other—or what psychologists call "correlated" with each other—one thing must cause the other. This point leads us to one of the most crucial principles in this text: *Correlational designs don't permit causal inferences*, or, putting it less formally, *correlation isn't causation.* When we conclude that a correlation means causation, we've committed the **correlation–causation fallacy**. This conclusion is a fallacy because the fact that two variables are correlated doesn't necessarily mean that one causes the other. Incidentally, a **variable** is anything that can *vary*, such as height, IQ, or extraversion. Let's see why correlation isn't causation.

If we start with two variables, A and B, that are correlated, there are three major explanations for this correlation.

1. A → B. It's possible that variable A causes variable B.
2. B → A. It's possible that variable B causes variable A.

So far, so good. But many people forget that there's also a third possibility, namely, that

3.

In this third scenario, there's a third variable, C, that causes *both* A and B. This scenario is known as the *third variable problem*. It's a problem because it can lead us to conclude mistakenly that A and B are causally related to each other when they're not. For example, in one study researchers found that teenagers who listen to music with a lot of sexual lyrics have sexual intercourse more often than teenagers who listen to music with tamer lyrics (Martino et al., 2006). So listening to sexual lyrics is *correlated* with sexual behavior. One newspaper summarized the findings of this study with an attention-grabbing headline: "Sexual lyrics prompt teens to have sex" (Tanner, 2006). Like many headlines, this one went

correlation–causation fallacy

error of assuming that because one thing is associated with another, it must cause the other

variable

anything that can vary

well beyond the data. It's possible that music with sexual lyrics (A) causes sexual behavior (B). But it's also possible that sexual behavior (B) causes teens to listen to music with sexual lyrics (A) or that a third variable, like impulsivity (C), causes teens to listen to music with sexual lyrics *and* to engage in sexual behavior. Given the data reported by the authors, there's no way to know. *Correlation isn't causation.*

The bottom line: We should remember that a correlation between two things doesn't demonstrate a causal connection between them.

SCIENTIFIC THINKING PRINCIPLE #3: *FALSIFIABILITY.* The Austrian philosopher of science Sir Karl Popper (1965) observed that for a claim to be meaningful, it must be **falsifiable**, that is, capable of being disproved. If a theory isn't falsifiable, we can't test it. Some students misunderstand this point, confusing the question of whether a theory is *falsifiable* with whether it's *false*. The principle of falsifiability doesn't mean that a theory must be false to be meaningful. Instead, it means that for a theory to be meaningful, it *could* be proven wrong if there were compelling evidence against it. For a claim to be falsifiable, its proponent must state clearly *in advance,* not after the fact, which findings would count as evidence for and against the claim (Dienes, 2008; Proctor & Capaldi, 2006).

A key implication of the falsifiability principle is that a theory that explains everything—a theory that can account for every conceivable outcome—in effect explains nothing. That's because a good scientific theory must predict only certain outcomes but not others. If a friend told you he was a master "psychic sports forecaster" and predicted with great confidence that "Tomorrow, all of the major league baseball teams that are playing a game will either win or lose," you'd probably start giggling. By predicting every potential outcome, your friend hasn't really predicted anything.

If your friend instead forecasted "The New York Yankees and New York Mets will both win tomorrow by three runs, but the Boston Red Sox and Los Angeles Dodgers will lose by one run," this prediction could be either correct or incorrect. There's a possibility he'll be wrong—the prediction is falsifiable (Meehl, 1978). If he's right, it wouldn't prove he's psychic, of course, but it might at least make you wonder whether he possesses some special predictive abilities.

The bottom line: Whenever we evaluate a psychological claim, we should ask ourselves whether one could, in principle, disprove it or whether it's consistent with any conceivable body of evidence.

SCIENTIFIC THINKING PRINCIPLE #4: *REPLICABILITY.* Barely a week goes by that we don't hear about another stunning psychological finding on the evening news: "Researchers at Cupcake State University detect a new gene linked to excessive shopping"; "Investigators at the University of Antarctica at Igloo report that alcoholism is associated with a heightened risk of murdering one's spouse"; "Nobel Prize–winning professor at Cucumber State College isolates brain area responsible for the enjoyment of popcorn." One problem with these conclusions, in addition to the fact that the news media often tell us nothing about the design of the studies on which they're based, is that the findings often haven't been replicated. **Replicability** means that a study's findings can be duplicated consistently. Replication is the cornerstone of a dependable science. If researchers' findings can't be duplicated, it increases the odds that the original findings were the result of chance. *We shouldn't place too much stock in a psychological finding until it's been replicated.*

Indeed, over the past decade, psychological scientists have become increasingly aware of the importance of replication (Asendorpf et al., 2013; Lilienfeld & Waldman, 2016; Nosek, Spies, & Moytl, 2012). Some of this heightened awareness stems from difficulties in replicating certain findings in psychology that had been previously assumed to be well-established (Lindsay, 2015; Pashler & Wagenmakers, 2012). Some of it also stems from the **decline effect** (Schooler, 2011). For example, early studies of the effectiveness of newly developed medications for schizophrenia showed larger effects than did more recent studies (Leucht et al., 2009). The same decline in effectiveness over time may hold for parenting interventions for autism spectrum disorder (Ozonoff, 2011) and the effectiveness of cognitive-behavioral therapy for depression (Johnsen & Friborg, 2015). Although psychologists aren't sure how widespread a problem the decline effect is, virtually all agree that it sometimes exists.

THE FAMILY CIRCUS.   By Bil Keane

"I wish they didn't turn on that seatbelt sign so much! Every time they do, it gets bumpy."

Correlation isn't always causation.

SOURCE: Family Circus © Bil Keane, Inc. King Features Syndicate.

falsifiable

capable of being disproved

replicability

when a study's findings are able to be duplicated, ideally by independent investigators

decline effect

fact that the size of certain psychological findings appears to be shrinking over time

Psychologist Brian Nosek at the newly launched Center for Open Science (COS) at the University of Virginia. Nosek has been a pioneer in the effort to determine the extent to which psychological findings are replicable.

According to a few researchers, tens of thousands of Americans have been abducted by aliens and brought aboard spaceships to be experimented on. Could it really be happening, and how would we know?

In 2012, University of Virginia social psychologist Brian Nosek and his collaborators launched the *Open Science Collaboration*, a coordinated effort by a team of dozens of psychologists around the globe to try to replicate widely cited studies in psychology, some about which we'll be reading in later chapters (Carpenter, 2012). In 2015, they published a "bombshell" article that attempted to replicate 100 published findings in social and cognitive psychology; social psychology examines the effects of other people on our behaviors and attitudes, whereas cognitive psychology examines thinking processes. To the surprise of many, they found that only about 40 percent of the original findings could be replicated (Open Science Collaboration, 2015). This sobering result doesn't mean that the original positive findings were wrong; it's instead possible that the later findings were wrong, or that the original findings hold up only in certain settings or among certain groups of individuals, such as Americans as opposed to non-Americans (Gilbert et al., 2016). In any case, the pioneering results of the Open Science Collaboration tell us that we can't take the replicability of psychological results for granted.

Most replications aren't exact duplications of the original researchers' methods. Most involve introducing minor variations in the original design or extending this design to different participants, including those in various cultures, races, and geographical locations. In general, the more we can replicate our findings using different participants in different settings, the more confidence we can place in those findings (Schmidt, 2009; Shadish, Cook, & Campbell, 2002).

We should bear in mind that the media are far more likely to report initial positive findings than failures to replicate. The initial findings may be especially fascinating or sensational, whereas replication failures are often disappointing—they don't make for juicy news stories. It's especially crucial that investigators other than the original researchers replicate the results because this increases our confidence in them. If I tell you that I've created a recipe for the world's most delicious veal parmigiana, but it turns out that every other chef who follows my recipe ends up with a meal that tastes like an old piece of cardboard smothered in rotten cheese and six-month-old tomato sauce, you'd be justifiably skeptical. Maybe I flat-out lied about my recipe. Or perhaps I wasn't following the recipe closely and was instead tossing in ingredients that weren't even in the recipe. Or perhaps I'm such an extraordinary chef that nobody else can come close to replicating my miraculous culinary feats. In any case, you'd have every right to doubt my recipe until someone else replicated it. The same principle goes for psychological research.

The literature on ESP offers an excellent example of why replicability is so essential. Every once in a blue moon, a researcher reports a striking new finding that seemingly confirms the existence of ESP (Bem, 2011). Yet time and again, independent researchers haven't been able to replicate these tantalizing results (Galak et al., 2012; Ritchie, Wiseman, & French, 2012; Hyman, 1989; Lilienfeld, 1999c), which might lead a skeptical observer to wonder whether many of the initial positive findings were merely a result of chance.

The bottom line: Whenever we evaluate a psychological claim, we should ask ourselves whether independent investigators have replicated the findings that support this claim; otherwise, the findings might be a one-time-only fluke.

SCIENTIFIC THINKING PRINCIPLE #5: *EXTRAORDINARY CLAIMS REQUIRE EXTRAORDINARY EVIDENCE.* Throughout the text, we'll be abbreviating this principle as "Extraordinary Claims." This principle was proposed in slightly different terms by 18th-century Scottish philosopher David Hume (Sagan, 1995; Truzzi, 1978). According to Hume, the more a claim contradicts what we already know, the more persuasive the evidence for this claim must be before we accept it.

A handful of researchers believe that every night, hundreds and even thousands of Americans are being lifted magically out of their beds, taken aboard flying saucers, and experimented on by aliens, only to be returned safely to their beds hours later (Clancy, 2005; McNally, 2012). According to some alien abduction advocates, aliens are extracting semen from human males to impregnate female aliens in an effort to create a race of alien–human hybrids.

Of course, alien abduction proponents *might* be right, and we shouldn't dismiss their assertions out of hand. But their claims are pretty darned extraordinary, especially because they imply that tens of thousands of invading flying saucers from other solar systems have inexplicably managed to escape detection by hundreds of astronomers, not to mention air traffic controllers and radar operators. Alien abduction proponents have been unable to provide even a shred of concrete evidence that supposed abductees have actually encountered extraterrestrials—say, a convincing photograph of an alien, a tiny piece of a metal probe inserted by an alien, or even a strand of hair or shred of skin from an alien. Thus far, all that alien abduction proponents have to show for their claims are the self-reports of supposed abductees. Extraordinary claims, but decidedly ordinary evidence.

The bottom line: Whenever we evaluate a psychological claim, we should ask ourselves whether this claim runs counter to many things we know already and, if it does, whether the evidence is as extraordinary as the claim.

Evaluating Claims REMARKABLE DIETARY CLAIMS

Interactive

You're a busy, overworked college student (well, we suppose you knew that already). You like to drink coffee to wake you up in the morning and stay alert in the afternoon, and you especially love those delicious, but fattening, specialty coffee drinks. As much as you enjoy coffee and want to drink it to decrease your fatigue, you also don't want to put on weight.

A new coffee shop, *Moonbeams*, has just opened up a few blocks from campus. *Moonbeams* is advertising a yummy, "grande" size Caramel Frappuccino. They call it the "Weight Buster," with the claim that "Incredible as it sounds, you can actually lose weight by drinking our Weight Buster!" When you ask the store manager how that's possible, she says "Our company recently conducted a rigorous study of six people who drank at least one Weight Buster every day for 2 weeks. All of them lost weight, ranging from 2 pounds to 9 pounds. Science doesn't lie!"

Scientific skepticism requires us to evaluate all claims with an open mind but to insist on compelling evidence before accepting them. How do the principles of scientific thinking help us to evaluate *Moonbeams'* claim that you can lose weight by drinking the "Weight Buster"?

Consider how the six principles of scientific thinking are relevant as you evaluate this claim.

1. **Ruling Out Rival Hypotheses**
   Have important alternative explanations for the findings been excluded?
   The results of the study are open to many alternative interpretations, so they don't necessarily demonstrate that drinking the Weight Buster leads to weight loss. For example, perhaps people who drank the calorie-laden drink also consumed less food because they knew that the drink was fattening. Or maybe the six people who drank the coffee knew they were being studied, so they worked especially hard to lose weight.

2. **Correlation versus Causation**
   Can we be sure that A causes B?
   This critical thinking principle isn't especially relevant to this scenario (because the study doesn't describe a correlation), so try another one.

3. **Falsifiability**
   Can the claim be disproved?
   The claim that the Weight Buster helps people to lose weight could in principle be falsified, but it would require an experimental design with random assignment to conditions. Note that *Moonbeams* didn't conduct that study, or if they did, they're not telling you what they found.

4. **Replicability**
   Can the results be duplicated in other studies?
   According to the store manager, the evidence that the Weight Buster leads to weight loss was based on only a single study. We should be skeptical of findings based on only one study, especially when these results are extremely surprising.

5. **Extraordinary Claims**
   Is the evidence as strong as the claim?
   The assertion that a large, creamy, and sugary drink causes weight loss is pretty darn extraordinary. Yet the evidence

Wilhelm Wundt (*right*) in the world's first psychology laboratory. Wundt is generally credited with launching psychology as a laboratory science in 1879.

introspection

method by which trained observers carefully reflect and report on their mental experiences

One of William James's doctoral students was Mary Whiton Calkins (1863–1930), who became the first female president of the American Psychological Association in 1905. Despite being an outstanding student at Harvard University, the faculty denied her tenure because of her gender—and despite James's recommendation of her. Calkins made significant contributions to the study of memory, sensation, and self-concept.

about 140 years, and much of this time was spent refining techniques to develop and modify research methods that were free from bias (Coon, 1992). Throughout its history, psychology has struggled with many of the same challenges that we confront today when reasoning about psychological research. So it's important to understand how psychology evolved as a scientific discipline, one that relies on systematic research methods to avoid being fooled.

Psychology's Early History

We'll start our journey with a capsule summary of psychology's bumpy road from non-science to science (a timeline of significant events in the evolution of scientific psychology can be seen in Figure 1.8).

For many centuries, the field of psychology was difficult to distinguish from philosophy. Most academic psychologists held positions in departments of philosophy—psychology departments didn't even exist back then—and didn't conduct experimental research. Instead, they mostly sat and contemplated the human mind from the armchair. In essence, they relied on common sense.

But beginning in the late 1800s, the landscape of psychology changed dramatically. In 1879, Wilhelm Wundt (1832–1920) developed the first full-fledged psychological laboratory in Leipzig, Germany. Indeed, 1879 is commonly regarded as the birth year of scientific psychology. Most of Wundt's investigations and those of his students focused on basic questions concerning our mental experiences: How different must two colors be for us to tell them apart? How long does it take us to react to a sound? What thoughts come to mind when we solve a math problem? Wundt used a combination of experimental methods, including reaction time procedures, and a technique called **introspection**, which required trained observers to carefully reflect and report on their mental experiences. Introspectionists might ask participants to look at an object, say an apple, and carefully report everything they saw. Soon, psychologists elsewhere around the world followed Wundt's bold lead and opened laboratories in departments of psychology, launching psychology as a full-fledged scientific discipline.

Before becoming a science, though, psychology also needed to break free from another influence: spiritualism. The term *psychology* literally means the study of the "psyche," that is, spirit or soul. In the mid- and late 1800s, Americans became fascinated with spirit mediums, people who claimed to contact the dead, often during séances (Blum, 2006). These were group sessions that took place in darkened rooms, in which mediums attempted to "channel" the spirits of deceased individuals. Americans were equally enchanted with psychics, individuals who claimed to possess powers of mind reading and other extrasensory abilities. Many famous psychologists of the day, including William James, invested a great deal of time and effort in the search for these paranormal capacities (Benjamin & Baker, 2004; Blum, 2006).

They ultimately failed, and psychology eventually developed a respectful distance from spiritualism. It did so largely by creating a new field: the psychology of human error and self-deception. Rather than asking whether extrasensory powers exist, a growing number of psychologists in the late 1800s began to ask the equally fascinating question of how people can fool themselves into believing things that aren't supported by evidence (Coon, 1992)—a central theme of this book.

The Great Theoretical Frameworks of Psychology

Almost since its inception, psychological science has confronted a thorny question: What unifying theoretical perspective, if any, best explains behavior?

Five major theoretical perspectives—structuralism, functionalism, behaviorism, cognitivism, and psychoanalysis—have played pivotal roles in shaping contemporary psychological thought. Many beginning psychology students understandably ask, "Which of these perspectives is the right one?" As it turns out, the answer isn't entirely clear. Each theoretical viewpoint has something valuable to contribute to scientific psychology, but each has its limitations (see Table 1.5). In some cases, these different viewpoints aren't

Table 1.5 The Theoretical Perspectives That Shaped Psychology.

Perspective		Leading Figures	Scientific Goal	Lasting Scientific Influence
Structuralism ◄ E. B. Titchener		E. B. Titchener	Uses introspection to identify basic elements or "structures" of experience	Emphasis on the importance of systematic observation to the study of conscious experience
Functionalism ◄ William James		William James; influenced by Charles Darwin; James Angell	To understand the functions or adaptive purposes of our thoughts, feelings, and behaviors	Has been absorbed into psychology and continues to influence it indirectly in many ways
Behaviorism ◄ B. F. Skinner		Ivan Pavlov; John B. Watson; Edward Thorndike; B. F. Skinner	To uncover the general principles of learning that explain all behaviors; focus is largely on observable behavior	Influential in models of human and animal learning and among the first to focus on the need for objective research
Cognitivism ◄ Jean Piaget		Jean Piaget; Ulric Neisser; George Miller	To examine the role of mental processes on behavior	Influential in many areas, such as language, problem solving, concept formation, intelligence, memory, and psychotherapy
Psychoanalysis ◄ Sigmund Freud		Sigmund Freud; Carl Jung; Alfred Adler	To uncover the role of unconscious psychological processes and early life experiences in behavior	Understanding that much of our mental processing goes on outside of conscious awareness

contradictory because they're explaining behavior at different levels of analysis. As we wend our way through these five frameworks, we'll discover that psychology's view of what constitutes a scientific approach to behavior has changed over time and continues to evolve today.

STRUCTURALISM: THE ELEMENTS OF THE MIND. Edward Bradford Titchener (1867–1927), a British student of Wundt who emmigrated to the United States, founded the field of structuralism. **Structuralism** aimed to identify the basic elements, or "structures," of psychological experience. Adopting Wundt's method of introspection but going much further, structuralists dreamt of creating a comprehensive "map" of the elements of consciousness—which they believed consisted of sensations, images, and feelings—much like the periodic table of the elements we can find in every chemistry classroom (Evans, 1972).

Nevertheless, structuralism eventually ran out of steam. At least two major problems did it in. First, even highly trained introspectionists often disagreed on their subjective reports, suggesting that they weren't arriving at a truly objective set of basic elements of consciousness. Second, German psychologist Oswald Kulpe (1862–1915) showed that participants asked to solve certain mental problems engaged in *imageless thought:* thinking unaccompanied by conscious experience. If we ask an introspecting participant to add 10 and 5, he or she will quickly respond "15," but he or she will usually be unable to report what came to mind when performing this calculation (Hergenhahn, 2000). The phenomenon of imageless thought dealt a serious body blow to structuralism because it demonstrated that some important aspects of human psychology lie outside conscious awareness.

Structuralism correctly emphasized the importance of *systematic observation* to the study of conscious experience. Nevertheless, structuralists went astray by assuming that a single, imperfect method—introspection—could provide all of the information needed

Figure 1.10 The Face of Psychology Has Changed Dramatically over the Past Three Decades.

Interactive

Percent of female PhD recipients (y-axis: 0% to 100%)

Categories: Clinical, Developmental, Industrial/organizational, Experimental, Cognitive, Counseling

Legend: 1974 | 1990 | 2005

Across most areas, the percentage of women earning doctoral degrees has increased. In clinical and developmental psychology, women comprise three-fourths to four-fifths of those attaining PhD

SOURCE: Based on data from American Psychological Association [APA], 2007.

"The title of my science project is 'My Little Brother: Nature or Nurture.'"

SOURCE: © The New Yorker Collection 2003 Michael Shaw from cartoonbank.com. All Rights Reserved.

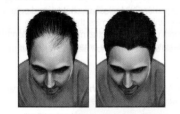

The fact that American men spend billions of dollars per year on hair replacement treatments is difficult to square with evolutionary hypotheses suggesting that women prefer bald men. The bottom line: Beware of unfalsifiable evolutionary stories.

evolutionary psychology

discipline that applies Charles Darwin's theory of natural selection to human and animal behavior

The Great Debates of Psychology

Now that we've learned a bit about the past and present of psychology, we need to set the stage for things to come. Two great debates have shaped the field of psychology since its inception and are likely to continue to shape it in the future. Because these debates are alive and well, we'll find traces of them in virtually all of the chapters of this text.

THE NATURE–NURTURE DEBATE. The nature–nurture debate poses the following age-old question: *Are our behaviors attributable mostly to our genes (nature) or to our rearing environments (nurture)?*

As we'll discover in this text, the nature–nurture debate has proven especially controversial in the domains of intelligence, personality, and psychopathology (mental illness). Many early thinkers, such as British philosopher John Locke (1632–1704), likened the human mind at birth to white paper that hadn't been written on. Others following his lead referred to the mind as a *tabula rasa* ("blank slate"). For Locke and his followers, we enter the world with no genetic preconceptions or preconceived ideas: We're shaped exclusively by our environments (Pinker, 2002). For much of the 20th century, most psychologists assumed that virtually all human behavior was exclusively the product of learning. But research conducted by *behavior geneticists*, who use sophisticated designs such as twin and adoption studies, shows that most important psychological traits, including intelligence, interests, personality, and many mental illnesses, are influenced substantially by genes (Plomin et al., 2016). Increasingly, modern psychologists have come to recognize that human behavior is attributable not only to our environments, but also to our genes (Bouchard, 2004; Harris, 2002).

Because just about everyone now agrees that both genes and environment play crucial roles in most human behaviors, some people have declared the nature–nurture debate dead (Ferris, 1996). Yet we still have a great deal to learn about how much nature or nurture contributes to different behaviors and how nature and nurture work together. Indeed, we'll discover in later chapters that the old dichotomy between nature and nurture is far less clear-cut—and far more interesting—than once believed. Nature and nurture intersect in complex and surprising ways.

One domain of psychology that's shed light on the nature–nurture debate is **evolutionary psychology**, which applies Darwin's theory of natural selection to human and animal behavior (Barkow, Cosmides, & Tooby, 1992; Dennett, 1995; Tooby & Cosmides, 1989). It begins with the assumption, shared by William James and other functionalists, that many human psychological systems, like memory, emotion, and personality serve key adaptive functions: They help organisms survive and reproduce. Darwin and his followers suggested that natural selection favored certain kinds of mental traits, just as it did physical ones, like our hands, livers, and hearts.

Biologists refer to *fitness* as the extent to which a trait increases the chances that organisms that possess this trait will survive and reproduce at a higher rate than competitors who lack it. Fitness has nothing to do, by the way, with how strong or powerful an organism is. By surviving and reproducing at higher rates than other organisms, more fit organisms pass on their genes more successfully to later generations. For example, humans who have at least some degree of anxiety probably survived at higher rates than humans who lacked it, because anxiety serves an essential function: It warns us of impending danger (Barlow, 2000; Damasio & Carvalho, 2013).

The Great Debates Assessment

Interactive	Below is a series of short scenarios describing different positions on the Nature-Nurture and the Free Will-Determinism debates. Read each item carefully and determine which side of the specified debate is illustrated.	
	1) Behavioral theory suggests that animals and people are driven primarily by their past reinforcement history when engaging in behavior. Which side of the Free Will-Determinism debate does this theory adopt?	a. Free Will b. Determinism
	2) Humanistic theory and therapies often refer to people's abilities to control their own destiny regardless of their past difficulties. Which side of the Free Will-Determinism debate does this theory adopt?	a. Free Will b. Determinism
	3) Sigmund Freud believed that humans are born with an innate sense of aggression that must be later reined in by the ego and superego. In short, all humans are born with these negative characteristics. In making the claim that we're born with a propensity toward aggression, which side of the Nature-Nurture debate did Freud adopt?	a. Nature b. Nurture
	4) Social psychologists believe that humans learn their behavioral customs (such as how to interact with authority figures and even how and when to express emotion) through their socialization and from parents and important adult figures. Which side of the Nature-Nurture debate does this reflect?	a. Nature b. Nurture

1) b, 2) a, 3) a, 4) b.

Still, evolutionary psychology has received more than its share of criticism (Kitcher, 1985; Panksepp & Panksepp, 2000; Rose & Rose, 2010). Many of its predictions are extremely difficult to falsify. In part, that's because behavior, unlike the bones of dinosaurs, early humans, and other animals, doesn't leave fossils. As a consequence, it's far more challenging to determine the evolutionary functions of anxiety or depression than the functions of birds' wings. For example, two researchers speculated that male baldness serves an evolutionary function, because women supposedly perceive a receding hairline as a sign of maturity (Muscarella & Cunningham, 1996). But if it turned out that women preferred men with a lot of hair to bald men, it would be easy to cook up an explanation for that finding. ("Women perceive men with a full head of hair as stronger and more athletic.") Evolutionary explanations could account for either outcome. Evolutionary psychology has the potential to be an important unifying framework for psychology (Buss, 1995; Confer et al., 2010), but we should beware of evolutionary explanations that can fit almost any piece of evidence after the fact (de Waal, 2002).

THE FREE WILL–DETERMINISM DEBATE. The free will–determinism debate poses the following question: *To what extent are our behaviors freely selected rather than caused by factors outside our control?*

Most of us like to believe that we're free to do what we want whenever we want. You may believe that at this very moment, you can decide to continue reading to the end of the chapter or take a well-deserved break to watch TV. Indeed, much of our legal system is premised on the concept of free will. We punish criminals because they're supposedly free to abide by the law but choose otherwise. One major exception is the insanity defense, in which the legal system assumes that severe mental illness can interfere with people's free will (Hoffman & Morse, 2006; Stone, 1982). Some prominent psychologists argue that we all possess free will (Baumeister, 2008).

Yet many others maintain that free will is actually an illusion (Bargh, 2008; Sappington, 1990; Wegner, 2002). Arch-behaviorist Skinner (1971) argued that our sense of free will stems from the fact that we aren't consciously aware of the thousands of subtle environmental influences impinging on our behavior at any given moment. Much like puppets in a play who don't realize that actors are pulling their strings, we conclude mistakenly that we're free simply because we don't realize all of the influences acting on our behavior. For Skinner and others, our behaviors are completely determined.

Some psychologists argue that most or even all of our behaviors are generated *automatically*—that is, without conscious awareness (Gazzaniga, 2012; Kirsch & Lynn, 1999; Libet, 1985). We may even come to believe that something or someone else is producing

Increasingly, today's fire trucks are lime-yellow rather than red. That's because psychological research has demonstrated that lime-yellow objects are easier to spot in the dark than are red objects.

Thanks to psychological research, advertisers know that placing a model's face on the left and written text on the right of an advertisement best captures readers' attention.

basic research

research examining how the mind works

applied research

research examining how we can use basic research to solve real-world problems

A classic simultaneous eyewitness lineup. Although police commonly use such lineups, most research suggests that they're more prone to error than are sequential lineups.

behaviors we ourselves are generating. For example, people who engage in *automatic writing*—writing sentences while seemingly in a trance—typically insist they're being compelled to do so by some outside force. But there's strong evidence that they're generating this behavior themselves, although unconsciously (Wegner, 2002). According to many determinists, our everyday behaviors are produced in the same way—triggered automatically by influences of which we're unaware (Bargh & Chartrand, 1999). Still other psychologists aren't convinced; they believe that we maintain a great deal of conscious control over our behavior (Newell & Shanks, 2013).

How Psychology Affects Our Lives

As we'll discover throughout this text, psychological science and scientific thinking offer a host of important applications for numerous aspects of everyday life. Psychological scientists often distinguish basic from applied research. **Basic research** examines how the mind works, whereas **applied research** examines how we can use basic research to solve real-world problems (Nickerson, 1999). Within most large psychology departments, we find a healthy mix of people conducting basic research, such as investigators who study the laws of learning, and applied research, such as investigators who study how to help people cope with the psychological burden of cancer.

APPLICATIONS OF PSYCHOLOGICAL RESEARCH. Surveys show that few people are aware of the substantial impact of psychology on their everyday lives (Lilienfeld, 2012; Wood, Jones, & Benjamin, 1986). Indeed, psychological science has found its way into far more aspects of contemporary society than most of us realize (Salzinger, 2002; Zimbardo, 2004a). Let's look at a sampling of these applications from a pamphlet produced by the American Psychological Association:

- If you live in or near a big city, you may have noticed a gradual change in the color of fire engines. Although old fire engines were bright red, most new ones are lime-yellow. That's because psychological researchers who study perception found that lime-yellow objects are easier to detect in the dark. Indeed, lime-yellow fire trucks are only about half as likely to be involved in traffic accidents as are red fire trucks (American Psychological Association, 2003; Solomon & King, 1995).

- As a car driver, have you ever had to slam on your brakes to avoid hitting a driver directly in front of you who stopped short suddenly? If so, and if you managed to avoid a bad accident, you may have psychologist John Voevodsky to thank. For decades, cars had only two brake lights. In the early 1970s, Voevodsky hit on the bright (pun intended) idea of placing a third brake light at the base of cars' back windshields. He reasoned that this additional visual information would decrease the risk of rear-end collisions. He conducted a 10-month study of taxis with and without the new brake lights and found a 61 percent lower rate of rear-end accidents in the first group (Voevodsky, 1974). As a result of his research, all new American cars have three brake lights.

- If you're anything like the average American, you see more than 100 commercial messages every day. The chances are that psychologists had a hand in crafting many of them. The founder of behaviorism, John B. Watson, pioneered the application of psychology to advertising in the 1920s and 1930s. Today, psychological researchers still contribute to the marketing success of companies. For instance, psychologists who study magazine advertisements have discovered that human faces better capture readers' attention on the left side rather than the right side of pages. Written text, in contrast, better captures readers' attention on the right side rather than the left side of pages (Clay, 2002).

- To get into college, you probably had to take one or more tests, like the SAT or ACT. If so, you can thank—or blame—psychologists with expertise in measuring academic achievement and knowledge, who were primarily responsible for developing these measures (Zimbardo, 2004a). Although these tests are far from perfect predictors of academic performance, they do significantly better than chance in forecasting how students perform in college (Geiser & Studley, 2002; Sackett, Borneman, & Connelly, 2008; Sackett et al., 2009).

- Police officers often ask victims of violent crimes to select a suspect from a lineup. When doing so, they've traditionally used *simultaneous lineups,* in which one or more suspects and several decoys (people who aren't really suspects) are lined up in a row, often of five to eight individuals. These are the kinds of lineups we've most often seen on television crime shows. Yet psychological research shows that *sequential lineups—* those in which victims view each person individually and then decide whether he or she was the perpetrator of the crime—are often more accurate than simultaneous lineups (Cutler & Wells, 2009; Steblay et al., 2003; Wells, Memon, & Penrod, 2006), although these more accurate line-ups may come at the cost of allowing a certain number of guilty people go free (Clark, 2012). As a result, police departments around the United States are increasingly using sequential rather than simultaneous lineups (Lilienfeld & Byron, 2013).

- For many years, many American public schools were legally required to be racially segregated. Before 1954, the law of the land in the United States was that "separate but equal" facilities were sufficient to guarantee racial equality. But based in part on the pioneering research of psychologists Kenneth and Mamie Clark (1950), who demonstrated that African American children preferred white to African American dolls, the U.S. Supreme Court decided—in the landmark 1954 case of *Brown v. Board of Education of Topeka, Kansas*—that school segregation exerted a negative impact on the self-esteem of African American children.

The classic doll studies of Kenneth and Mamie Clark paved the way for the 1954 Supreme Court decision of *Brown v. Board of Education,* which mandated racial integration of public schools.

So, far more than most of us realize, the fruits of psychological research are all around us. Psychology has dramatically altered the landscape of everyday life, in most cases for the better.

Journal Prompt

Can you think of other ways that psychological research can be applied to our everyday lives?

When it comes to evaluating psychological claims in the news or entertainment media, there's a simple bottom-line message: We should always insist on rigorous research evidence.

THINKING SCIENTIFICALLY: IT'S A WAY OF LIFE. As you embark on your journey to the rest of the field of psychology, we leave you with one crucial take-home point: Learning to think scientifically should help you make better decisions not only in this course and other psychology courses, but also in everyday life (Gawande, 2016). Each day, the news and entertainment media bombard us with confusing and even contradictory claims about a host of topics: herbal remedies, weight-loss plans, parenting methods, insomnia treatments, speed-reading courses, urban legends, political conspiracy theories, unidentified flying objects, and "overnight cures" for mental disorders, to name only a few. Some of these claims are partly true, whereas others are entirely bogus. Yet the media typically offer little guidance for sorting out which claims are scientific, pseudoscientific, or a bit of both. Moreover, online "news" sources are increasingly a bewildering blend of genuine and fake stories.

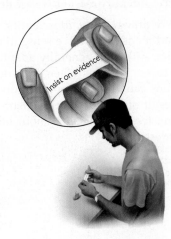

Fortunately, the scientific thinking skills you've encountered in this chapter—and that you'll come to know and (we hope!) love in later chapters—can assist you in successfully navigating the bewildering world of popular psychology and popular culture. The trick is to bear three words in mind throughout this text and in daily life: *Insist on evidence*. By recognizing that common sense can take us only so far in evaluating claims, we can come to appreciate the need for scientific evidence to avoid being fooled—and to avoid fooling ourselves. But how do we collect this scientific evidence, and how do we evaluate it? Stay tuned: We'll find out in the next chapter.

Summary: Psychology and Scientific Thinking

1.1: What Is Psychology? Science Versus Intuition

1.1a **Explain why psychology is more than just common sense.**

Psychology is the scientific study of the mind, brain, and behavior. Although we often rely on our common sense to understand the psychological world, our intuitive understanding of ourselves and others is frequently mistaken. Naive realism is the error of believing that we see the world precisely as it is. It can lead us to frequently embrace false beliefs about ourselves and our world, such as believing that our perceptions and memories are always accurate.

1.1b **Explain the importance of science as a set of safeguards against biases.**

Confirmation bias is the tendency to seek out evidence that supports our hypotheses and deny, dismiss, or distort evidence that doesn't. Belief perseverance is the tendency to cling to our beliefs despite contrary evidence. Scientific methodology consists of a set of safeguards against these two errors.

1.2: Psychological Pseudoscience: Imposters of Science

1.2a **Describe psychological pseudoscience and distinguish it from psychological science.**

Pseudoscientific claims appear scientific but don't play by the rules of science. In particular, pseudoscience lacks the safeguards against confirmation bias and belief perseverance that characterize science.

1.2b **Identify reasons we are drawn to pseudoscience.**

We're drawn to pseudoscientific beliefs because the human mind tends to perceive sense in nonsense and order in disorder. Although generally adaptive, this tendency can lead us to see patterns when they don't exist. Pseudoscientific claims can result in opportunity costs and direct harm as a result of dangerous treatments. They can also lead us to think less scientifically about other important domains of modern life.

1.3: Scientific Thinking: Distinguishing Fact From Fiction

1.3a **Identify the key features of scientific skepticism.**

Scientific skepticism requires us to evaluate all claims with an open mind but to insist on compelling evidence before accepting them. Scientific skeptics evaluate claims on their own merits and are unwilling to accept them on the basis of authority alone.

1.3b **Identify and explain the text's six principles of scientific thinking.**

Six key scientific thinking principles are ruling out rival hypotheses, correlation versus causation, falsifiability, replicability, extraordinary claims, and Occam's Razor. Replicability has assumed particular importance over the past decade in light of the realization that certain psychological findings are challenging for independent investigators to reproduce.

1.4: Psychology's Past and Present: What a Long, Strange Trip It's Been

1.4a **Identify the major theoretical frameworks of psychology.**

Five major theoretical orientations have played key roles in shaping the field. Structuralism aimed to identify the basic elements of experience through the method of introspection. Functionalism hoped to understand the adaptive purposes of behavior. Behaviorism grew out of the belief that psychological science must be completely objective and derived from laws of learning. The cognitive view emphasized the importance of mental processes in understanding behavior. Psychoanalysis focused on unconscious processes and urges as causes of behavior.

1.4b **Describe different types of psychologists and identify what each of them does.**

There are many types of psychologists. Clinical and counseling psychologists often conduct therapy. School psychologists develop intervention programs for children in school settings. Industrial/organizational psychologists often work in companies and business and are involved in maximizing

If the
that r
forde
lives.
highli

employee performance. Many forensic psychologists work in prisons or court settings. Many other psychologists conduct research. For example, developmental psychologists study systematic change in individuals over time. Experimental psychologists study learning and thinking, and biological psychologists study the biological bases of behavior.

1.4c   Describe two great debates that have shaped the field of psychology.

Two great debates are the nature–nurture debate, which asks whether our behaviors are attributable mostly to our genes (nature) or our rearing environments (nurture), and the free will–determinism debate, which asks to what extent our behaviors are freely selected rather than caused by factors outside our control. Both debates continue to shape the field of psychology.

1.4d   Describe how psychological research affects our daily lives.

Psychological research has shown how psychology can be applied to such diverse fields as advertising, public safety, the criminal justice system, and education.

S
to the
dure
the fa
them,
keybo
T
of wh
by the
photo
child
the ch
T
In vir
flashe
Roma
tion
Unbel
dren t
the ch
our n
disco
ting a
"See
tainir
tated
versio

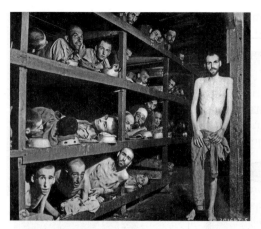

A widely publicized 1992 poll by the Roper organization asked Americans the following confusing question, which contained two negatives: "Does it seem possible or does it seem impossible to you that the Nazi extermination of the Jews never happened?" A shocking 22 percent of respondents replied that the Holocaust may not have happened. Yet when a later poll asked the question more clearly, this number dropped to only 1 percent. Survey wording counts.

The term *narcissism* derives from the Greek mythological character Narcissus, a handsome hunter who fell in love with his own reflection in a pond and died while staring at it. According to some psychologists, narcissism and similar personality traits can sometimes weaken the validity of self-reports because individuals with high levels of such features often view themselves far more positively than is deserved.

Reliability is necessary for validity because we need to measure something consistently before we can measure it well. Imagine trying to measure the floors and walls of an apartment using a ruler made of Silly Putty, that is, a ruler whose length changes each time we pick it up. Our efforts at accurate measurement would be doomed. Nevertheless, reliability doesn't guarantee validity. Although a test must be reliable to be valid, a reliable test can be completely invalid. Imagine we've developed a new measure of intelligence, the "Distance Index-Middle Width Intelligence Test" (DIMWIT), which subtracts the width of our index finger from that of our middle finger. The DIMWIT would be a highly reliable measure of intelligence, because the widths of our fingers are unlikely to change much over time (high test-retest reliability) and are likely to be measured similarly by different raters (high interrater reliability). But the DIMWIT would be a completely invalid measure of intelligence because finger width has nothing to do with intelligence.

When interpreting the results of self-report measures and surveys, we should bear in mind that we can obtain quite different answers depending on how we phrase the questions (Schwarz, 1999; Smith, Schwarz, & Roberts, 2006). One researcher administered surveys to 300 female homemakers. In some surveys, women answered the question "Would you like to have a job, if this were possible?," whereas others answered the question "Would you prefer to have a job, or do you prefer to do just your housework?" These two questions seem remarkably similar. Yet although 81 percent of those who were asked the first question said they'd like to have a job, only 32 percent who were asked the second question said they'd like to have a job (Noelle-Neumann, 1970; Walonick, 1994). Moreover, we shouldn't assume that people who respond to survey questions even understand the answers they're giving. In a survey conducted in late 2015, 30 percent of U.S Republicans and 19 percent of U.S. Democrats said that they supported bombing Agrabah (Berenson, 2015). There's only one problem: Agrabah doesn't exist. It's the fictional country in Disney's film *Aladdin*.

ADVANTAGES AND DISADVANTAGES OF SELF-REPORT MEASURES. Self-report measures have a key advantage: They're easy and cheap to administer. All we need are a pencil, paper, and a willing participant, and we're off and running. Moreover, if we have a question about someone, it's often a good idea to first ask that person directly (Samuel, in press). Most of us possess access to subtle information regarding our emotional states, such as anxiety or guilt, about which outside observers aren't aware (Grove & Tellegen, 1991; Sellbom et al., in press).

Self-report measures of personality traits and behaviors often work reasonably well. For example, people's reports of how outgoing or shy they are tend to be moderately associated with the reports of people who've spent a lot of time with them. These associations are somewhat higher for more observable traits, like extraversion, than for less observable traits, like anxiety (Gosling, Rentfrow, & Swann, 2003; Kenrick & Funder, 1988; Vazire, 2010).

Still, self-report measures have their disadvantages, too. First, they typically assume that respondents possess enough insight into their personality characteristics to report on them accurately (de Waal, 2016; Nisbett & Wilson, 1977; Oltmanns & Turkheimer, 2009). This assumption is questionable for certain groups of people. For example, people with high levels of narcissistic personality traits, like self-centeredness and excessive self-confidence, view themselves more positively than others do (Campbell & Miller, 2011; John & Robins, 1994). (The word *narcissistic* derives from the Greek mythological character Narcissus, who fell in love with his reflection in the water.) Narcissistic people tend to perceive themselves through rose-colored glasses.

Second, self-report questionnaires typically assume that participants are honest in their responses. Imagine that a company required you to take a personality test for a job you really wanted. Would you be completely frank in your evaluation of yourself, or would you minimize your personality quirks? Not surprisingly, some respondents engage in **response sets**—tendencies to distort their answers to questions, often in a way that paints them in a positive light (Edens, Buffington, & Tomicic, 2001; McGrath et al., 2010; Paulhus, 1991).

One response set is the tendency to answer questions in a socially desirable direction, that is, to make ourselves look better than we are (Paunonen & LeBel, 2012; Ray et al., 2012). We're especially likely to engage in this response set when applying for an important job. This response set can make it difficult to trust people's reports of their abilities and achievements. For example, college students overstate their SAT scores by an average of 17 points (Hagen, 2001). Other research shows that when hooked up to a fake lie-detector machine, female undergraduates report more lifetime sex partners than they ordinarily report, suggesting that they typically understate the true numbers (de Waal, 2016). Fortunately, psychologists have devised clever ways to measure this response set and thereby compensate for it in clinical practice and research (van de Mortel, 2008). For example, within their measures they might embed several questions that measure respondents' tendency to make themselves seem perfect (like "I never get upset at other people."). Positive responses to several of these items alert researchers to the possibility that people are responding to questionnaires in a socially desirable fashion.

A nearly opposite response set is *malingering,* the tendency to make ourselves appear psychologically disturbed with the aim of achieving a clear-cut personal goal (Ebrahim et al., 2015; Rogers, 2008). We're especially likely to observe this response set among people who are trying to obtain financial compensation for an injury or mistreatment on the job, or among people trying to escape military duty—in the last case, perhaps by faking insanity. Just as with socially desirable responding, psychologists have developed methods to detect malingering on self-report measures, often by inserting items that assess nonexistent or extremely implausible symptoms of mental illness (like "I often hear barking sounds coming from the upper left corner of my computer screen.").

People accused of crimes sometimes engage in malingering to keep out of trouble. Vincent Gigante, who earned the nickname of the "Oddfather," was a Mafia crime boss who was repeatedly charged with murder and extorting money from others. For a full three decades beginning in the late 1960s, he dressed peculiarly and muttered to himself, at times walking around New York City in a robe and slippers, accompanied by a bodyguard. Hospitalized 22 times for psychiatric reasons, he was diagnosed with schizophrenia and other severe mental disorders (Resnick & Knoll, 2005). Gigante finally admitted to making all of this up to escape prosecution (he was eventually convicted and died in prison).

response set

tendency of research participants to distort their responses to questionnaire items

RATING DATA: HOW DO THEY RATE?   An alternative to asking people about themselves is asking others who know them well to provide ratings on them. In many job settings, employers rate their employees' work productivity and cooperativeness in routine evaluations. Rating data can circumvent some of the problems with self-report data, because observers may not have the same "blind spots" as the people they're rating (who are often called the *targets* of the rating). Imagine asking your introductory psychology instructor, "How good a job do you think you did in teaching this course?" It's unlikely she'd say "Just awful." In fact, there's growing evidence that observers' ratings of personality traits, such as conscientiousness, are often more valid than are self-reports of these traits for predicting students' academic achievement and employees' work performance (Connelly & Ones, 2010; Samuel, in press).

Like self-report measures, rating data have their drawbacks too; one such shortcoming is the *halo effect*. This is the tendency of ratings of one positive characteristic to "spill over" to influence the ratings of other positive characteristics (Guilford, 1954; Moore, Filippou, & Perrett, 2011). Raters who fall victim to the halo effect seem almost to regard the targets as "angels"—hence the halo—who can do no wrong. If we find an employee physically attractive, we may unknowingly allow this perception to influence our ratings of his or her other features, such as conscientiousness and productivity (Rosenzweig, 2014). Indeed, people perceive physically attractive people as more successful, confident, assertive, and intelligent than other people even though these differences often don't reflect objective reality (Dion, Berscheid, & Walster, 1972; Eagly et al., 1991).

Student course evaluations of teaching are especially vulnerable to halo effects because if you like a teacher personally you're more likely to give him or her "a break" on the quality of teaching. Conversely, if you detest a teacher, you're more likely to punish him or her by providing poor ratings on teaching quality (this reverse halo effect is sometimes called the *horns effect*—picture a devil's horns—or pitchfork effect.) (Corsini, 1999).

In one study, Richard Nisbett and Timothy Wilson (1977) randomly placed participants into one of two conditions. Some participants watched a videotape of a college professor with a foreign accent who acted friendly to his students; others watched a videotape of the same professor (speaking with the same accent) who acted unfriendly to his students. Participants watching the videotapes not only liked the friendly professor better, but rated his physical appearance, mannerisms, and accent more positively. Students who like their professors also tend to give them high ratings on characteristics that are largely irrelevant to teaching effectiveness, including the quality of the classroom audiovisual equipment and the readability of their handwriting (Greenwald & Gillmore, 1997; Williams & Ceci, 1997).

Correlational Designs

correlational design

research design that examines the extent to which two variables are associated

Does being an outgoing person go along with being less honest? Are people with higher IQs snobbier than other people? Are more narcissistic presidents more successful than other presidents (apparently yes; see Watts et al., 2013)? These are the kinds of questions addressed by another essential research method in the psychologist's toolbox, the correlational design. When using a **correlational design**, researchers examine the extent to which two variables are associated. Recall that a *variable* is anything that can vary across individuals, like impulsivity, creativity, or religiosity. When we think of the word *correlate*, we should decompose it into its two parts: *co-* and *relate*. If two things are correlated, they relate to each other—not interpersonally, that is, but statistically.

Whereas naturalistic observation and case studies allow us to describe the state of the psychological world, correlational designs can often allow us to generate predictions about the future. If SAT scores are correlated with college grades, then knowing people's SAT scores allows us to forecast—although by no means perfectly—what their grades will be. Conclusions from correlational research are limited, however, because we can't be sure *why* these predicted relationships exist.

IDENTIFYING WHEN A DESIGN IS CORRELATIONAL.   Identifying a correlational design can be trickier than it seems, because investigators who use this design—and news reporters who describe it—don't always use the word *correlated* in their description of findings. Instead, they'll often use terms like *associated, related, linked,* or *went together.* Whenever researchers conduct a study of the extent to which two variables "travel together," their design is correlational even if they don't describe it that way. So, if you read a study that says "Researchers find that people's weight is positively associated with their liking of classical music" (we're just making that up), that's a correlational study even though the word *correlation* doesn't appear in it.

CORRELATIONS: A BEGINNER'S GUIDE.   Before we get too much further, let's lay some groundwork by considering two basic facts about correlations:

1. Correlations can be *positive, zero,* or *negative.* A *positive* correlation means that as the value of one variable changes, the other goes in the same direction: If one goes up, the other goes up, and if one goes down, the other goes down. If the number of college students' Facebook friends is positively correlated with how outgoing these students are; this means that more outgoing students have more Facebook friends and less outgoing students have fewer Facebook friends. A *zero* correlation means that the variables don't go together at all. If math ability has a zero correlation with singing ability and vice versa, then knowing that someone is good at math tells us nothing about his singing ability. Finally, a *negative* correlation means that as the value of one variable changes, the other goes in the opposite direction: If one goes up, the other goes down, and vice versa. If social anxiety is negatively correlated with perceived physical attractiveness, then more socially anxious people would be rated as less attractive, and less socially anxious people as more attractive.

2. *Correlation coefficients* (the statistics that psychologists use to measure correlations), at least the ones we'll be discussing in this text, range in value from -1.0 to 1.0. A correlation coefficient of -1.0 is a perfect negative correlation, whereas a correlation coefficient of $+1.0$ is a perfect positive correlation. We won't talk about how to calculate correlation coefficients, because the mathematics of doing so gets a bit technical (those of you who are really ambitious can check out www.easycalculation.com/statistics/correlation.php to learn how to calculate a correlation coefficient). Values lower than 1.0 (either positive

or negative values), such as 0.23 or 0.69, indicate a less-than-perfect correlation coefficient. To find how strong a correlation coefficient is, we should look at its *absolute value*, that is, the size of the coefficient without the plus or minus sign in front of it. The absolute value of a correlation coefficient of $+0.27$ is 0.27, and the absolute value of a correlation coefficient of -0.27 is also 0.27. Both correlation coefficients are equally large in size—and equally informative—but they're going in opposite directions.

So, here's a quick quiz question: Which correlation is larger, 0.79 or -0.79? If you guessed that this is a trick question, give yourself a point. The right answer is, "They're equally large."

Identify the Type of Correleation

Indentify the type of correlation being used.

1) The more days participants reported exercising per week, the lower their weight tended to be.	a. Positive Correlation b. Negative Correlation c. Zero Correlation
2) Participants reaction times tended to increase when their blood alcohol level (BAC) increased.	a. Positive Correlation b. Negative Correlation c. Zero Correlation
3) People who missed more days of class tended to have lower GPAs.	a. Positive Correlation b. Negative Correlation c. Zero Correlation
4) There is no systematic relationship between IQ and head size.	a. Positive Correlation b. Negative Correlation c. Zero Correlation
5) The more negative life events people experience, the more likely that they are diagnosed with depression.	a. Positive Correlation b. Negative Correlation c. Zero Correlation
6) There is no relationship between a student's height and her exam scores in a class.	a. Positive Correlation b. Negative Correlation c. Zero Correlation

1) b, 2) a, 3) a, 4) c, 5) a, 6) c.

Interactive

THE SCATTERPLOT. Figure 2.4 shows three panels depicting three types of correlations. Each panel shows a **scatterplot**, which is a grouping of points on a two-dimensional graph (it's called a *scatterplot* because the dots are scattered around the line). Each dot on the scatterplot depicts one person. As we can see, each person differs from others in his or her scores on one or both variables.

The panel on the left displays a fictional scatterplot of a moderate ($r = -0.5$) negative correlation, in this case, the association between the average number of beers that students drink the night before their first psychology exam and their scores on that exam. We can tell that this correlation coefficient is negative because the clump of dots goes from higher on the left of the graph to lower on the right of the graph. Because this correlation is negative, it means that the more beers students drink, the worse they tend to do on their first psychology exam. Note that this negative correlation isn't perfect (it's not $r = -1.0$). That means that some students drink a lot of beer and still do well on their first psychology exam (yes, we know that's not fair) and that some students drink almost no beer and do poorly on their first psychology exam.

Next, the middle panel shows a fictional scatterplot of a zero ($r = 0$) correlation coefficient, in this case the association between the students' shoe sizes and scores on their first psychology exam. The easiest way to identify a zero correlation is that the scatterplot looks like a blob of dots that's pointing neither upward nor downward. This zero correlation

scatterplot

grouping of points on a two-dimensional graph in which each dot represents a single person's data

Figure 2.4 Diagram of Three Scatterplots.

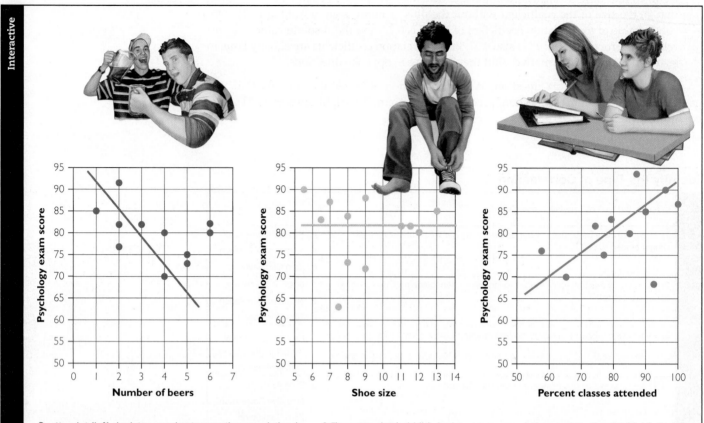

Scatterplot (*left*) depicts a moderate negative correlation (*r* = − 0.5); scatterplot (*middle*) depicts a zero correlation; and scatterplot (*right*) depicts a moderate positive correlation (*r* = 0.5)

Just because we know one person who was a lifelong smoker and lived to a ripe old age doesn't mean there's no correlation between smoking and serious illnesses, like lung cancer and heart disease. Exceptions don't invalidate the existence of correlations.

means there's no association whatsoever between students' shoe sizes and how well they do on their first psychology exam. If we tried to guess people's exam grades from their shoe sizes, we'd do no better in our predictions than flipping pennies.

Finally, the panel on the right shows a fictional scatterplot of a moderate (*r* = 0.5) positive correlation, in this case, the association between students' attendance in their psychology course and their scores on their first psychology exam. Here, the clump of dots goes from lower on the left of the graph to higher on the right of the graph. This positive correlation means that the more psychology classes students attend, the better they tend to do on their first psychology exam. Because the correlation isn't perfect (it's not *r* = 1.0), there will always be the inevitable annoying students who don't attend any classes yet do well on their exams, and the incredibly frustrated souls who attend all of their classes and still do poorly.

Unless a correlation coefficient is perfect, that is, 1.0 or −1.0, there will always be exceptions to the general trend. Because virtually all correlations in psychology have an absolute value of less than one, *psychology is a science of exceptions*. To argue against the existence of a correlation, it's tempting to resort to "I know a person who …" reasoning (see LO 1.2a). So if we're trying to refute the overwhelming scientific evidence that cigarette smoking is correlated with lung cancer, we might insist, "I know a person who smoked 5 packs of cigarettes a day for 40 years and never got lung cancer." But this anecdote doesn't refute the existence of the correlation because the correlation between cigarette smoking and lung cancer isn't perfect. Because the correlation is less than 1.0, such exceptions are to be completely expected—in fact, they're required mathematically.

ILLUSORY CORRELATION. Why do we even need to calculate correlations in the first place? Can't we just use our eyeballs to estimate how well two variables go together?

No, because psychological research demonstrates that we're all poor at estimating the sizes of correlations. In fact, we're often prone to an extraordinary phenomenon termed

Fact vs. Fiction

Two variables can be perfectly correlated ($r = 1.0$) and still be different. (See bottom of page for answer.)

○ Fact

○ Fiction

illusory correlation, which is the perception of a statistical association between two variables where none exists (Chapman & Chapman, 1967, 1969; Dawes, 2006). An illusory correlation is a statistical mirage. Here are three striking examples:

1. Many people are convinced of a strong statistical association between the full moon and a variety of strange occurrences, like violent crimes, suicides, psychiatric hospital admissions, dog bites, hockey fights, and births—the so-called lunar lunacy effect (the word *lunatic* derives from *Luna,* the Roman goddess of the moon). Some police departments even put more cops on the beat on nights when there's a full moon, and many emergency department nurses insist that more babies are born during full moons (Hines, 2003). Yet a mountain of data shows that the full moon isn't correlated with any of these events: That is, the true correlation is almost exactly $r = 0$ (Margot, 2015; Plait, 2002; Rotton & Kelly, 1985).

2. Many individuals with arthritis are convinced their joint pain increases during rainy weather, yet carefully conducted studies show no association between joint pain and rainy weather (Quick, 1999).

3. Have you ever repeatedly pressed the "walk" button at a pedestrian crosswalk and had the distinct sense that you were influencing traffic? If so, you may well have experienced an illusory correlation. In many major U.S. cities, such as New York City, the vast majority of crosswalk buttons are "placebo buttons" that do nothing (Mele, 2015). The same goes, incidentally, for many or most elevator "close door" buttons and switches on office thermostats.

Illusory Correlation and Superstition.   Illusory correlations form the basis of many superstitions (Vyse, 2000). Take the case of Wade Boggs, Hall of Fame baseball player and one of the game's greatest hitters. For 20 years, Boggs ate chicken before every game, believing this peculiar habit was correlated with successful performance in the batter's box. Boggs eventually became so skilled at cooking chicken that he even wrote a cookbook called *Fowl Tips.* It's unlikely that eating chicken and belting 95-mile-an-hour fastballs into the outfield have much to do with each other, but Boggs perceived such an association. Countless other superstitions, like keeping a rabbit's foot for good luck and not walking under ladders to avoid bad luck, probably also stem in part from illusory correlation.

Why We Fall Prey to Illusory Correlation.   So you may be wondering: How on earth could so many people be so wrong? In fact, we're all susceptible to illusory correlation, so this phenomenon is an inescapable fact of daily life. To understand why, we can think of much of everyday life in terms of a table of four probabilities, like that shown in Table 2.2. As you can see, we call this table "The Great Fourfold Table of Life."

illusory correlation

perception of a statistical association between two variables where none exists

Although legend has it that animals and humans behave strangely during full moons, research evidence demonstrates that this supposed correlation is an illusion.

Table 2.2   The Great Fourfold Table of Life.

		Did a Crime Occur?	
		Yes	**No**
Did a Full Moon Occur?	**Yes**	(A) Full moon + crime	(B) Full moon + no crime
	No	(C) No full moon + crime	(D) No full moon + no crime

Answer: Fact. For example, the harder we push down on our car accelerator, the faster our car will move. But the force applied to the accelerator and the movement of the car itself are two different things.

Many superstitions, such as avoiding walking under ladders, probably stem in part from illusory correlation.

Let's return to the lunar lunacy effect. As we can see from the Great Fourfold Table of Life, there are four possible relations between the phase of the moon and whether a crime is committed. The upper left-hand (A) cell of the table consists of cases in which there was a full moon and a crime occurred. The upper right-hand (B) cell consists of cases in which there was a full moon and no crime occurred. The bottom left-hand (C) cell consists of cases in which there was no full moon and a crime occurred. Finally, the bottom right-hand (D) cell consists of cases in which there was no full moon and no crime.

Decades of psychological research lead to one inescapable conclusion: We tend to pay too much attention to the *upper left-hand (A) cell* of the fourfold table (Eder, Fielder, & Hamm-Eder, 2011; Lilienfeld et al., 2010). This cell is especially interesting to us, because it typically fits what we expect to see, causing our confirmation bias to kick in. In the case of the lunar lunacy effect, instances in which there was both a full moon and a crime are especially memorable ("See, just like I've always said, weird things happen during full moons."). Moreover, when we think about what occurs during full moons, we tend to remember instances that are the most dramatic, and that therefore come most easily to mind. In this case, these instances are usually those that grab our attention, namely, those that fall into the (A) cell (Gilovich, 1991).

Unfortunately, our minds aren't good at detecting and remembering *nonevents*, that is, things that don't happen. It's unlikely we're going to rush home excitedly to tell our friend, "Wow, you're not going to believe this. There was a full moon tonight, and nothing happened!" Our uneven attention to the different cells in the table leads us to perceive illusory correlations.

How can we minimize our tendencies toward illusory correlation? One way is to force ourselves to keep track of disconfirming instances—to give the other three cells of the fourfold table a little more of our time and attention. When James Alcock and his students asked a group of participants who claimed they could predict the future from their dreams—so-called prophetic dreamers—to keep careful track of their dreams by using a diary, their beliefs that they were prophetic dreamers vanished (Hines, 2003). By encouraging participants to record all of their dreams, Alcock forced them to attend to the (B) cell, the cell consisting of cases that disconfirm prophetic dreams.

The phenomenon of illusory correlation explains in part why we can't rely on our subjective impressions to tell us whether two variables are associated—and why we need correlational designs. Our intuitions often mislead us, especially when we've learned to expect two things to go together (Majima, 2015; Myers, 2002). Indeed, adults may be more prone to illusory correlation than are children, because they've had years to build up expectations about whether certain events—such as full moons and odd behavior—go together (Kuhn, 2007). Fortunately, correlational designs help us to control for the problem of illusory correlation, because they force us to weigh all cells in the table equally.

CORRELATION VERSUS CAUSATION: JUMPING THE GUN. As we've seen, correlational designs can be extremely useful for determining whether two (or more) variables are related. As a result, they can allow us to predict behavior. For example, they can help us discover which variables—such as personality traits or history of crimes—predict which inmates will reoffend after being released from prison, or what life habits—such as heavy drinking or cigarette smoking—predict heart disease.

Still, there are notable limitations to the conclusions we can draw from correlational designs. As we learned previously (LO 1.2a), the most common mistake we can make when interpreting these designs is to jump the gun and draw *causal* conclusions from them: Correlation doesn't necessarily mean causation. Although a correlation *sometimes* reflects a causal relationship, we can't tell from a correlational study alone whether it does.

Incidentally, we shouldn't confuse the correlation versus causation fallacy—the error of equating correlation with causation—with illusory correlation. Illusory correlation refers to perceiving a correlation where none exists. In the case of the correlation versus causation fallacy, a correlation exists, but we mistakenly interpret it as implying a causal association. Let's look at two examples of the correlation versus causation fallacy (see Figure 2.6 for some other examples).

Correlation vs. Causation ▶

Can we be sure that A causes B?

1. A statistician with too much time on his hands once uncovered a substantial negative correlation between the number of PhD degrees awarded in a state within the United States and the number of mules in that state (Lilienfeld, 1995). Yes, *mules*. Does this negative correlation imply that the number of PhD degrees (*A*) influences the number of mules (*B*)? It's possible—perhaps people with PhDs have something against mules and campaign vigorously to have them relocated to neighboring states. But this scenario seems rather unlikely. Or does this negative correlation instead imply that mules (*B*) cause people with PhD degrees (*A*) to flee the state? Maybe, but don't bet on it. Before reading the next paragraph, ask yourself whether there's a third explanation.

   Indeed there is. Although we don't know for sure, the most likely explanation is that a *third variable, C,* is correlated with both *A* and *B*. In this case, the most probable candidate for this third variable is *rural versus urban status*. States with large rural areas, like Wyoming, contain many mules and few universities. In contrast, states with many urban (big city) areas, like New York, contain few mules and many universities. So in this case, the correlation between variables *A* and *B* is almost certainly the result of a third variable, *C*.

2. One team of researchers found a positive correlation over time between the number of babies born in Berlin, Germany (A), and the number of storks in nearby areas (B) (Hofer, Przyrembel, & Verleger, 2004). Specifically, over a 30-year period, more births were consistently accompanied by more storks. As the authors themselves noted, this correlation doesn't demonstrate that storks deliver babies. Instead, a more likely explanation is again a third variable, population size (C): Highly populated city areas are characterized both by large numbers of births, because big cities have lots of hospitals, and storks, which tend to be attracted to inner-city areas.

We shouldn't rely on the news media to help us distinguish correlation from causation because they frequently fall prey to the correlation versus causation fallacy. For example, consider the headline example in Figure 2.5 "Facebook Addiction Affects Brain Like Cocaine, Gambling." (Navarro, 2016). The article's title—note the word *affects*—clearly implies a *causal* link between Facebook addiction and brain functioning. Yet, the study described in the article demonstrates nothing of the sort because it's correlational. The researchers found that undergraduates who reported being "addicted" to Facebook and other social media sites displayed some of the same brain-imaging

Figure 2.5 Confusing Correlation with Causation.

SOURCE: Jon Mueller, Newspaper Headlines That Confuse Correlation With Causation.

Facebook Addiction Affects Brain Like Cocaine, Gambling: Study

Low Self-Esteem "Shrinks Brain"

A Surprising Secret to a Long Life: Stay in School

Housework Cuts Breast Cancer Risk

Fear of hell makes us richer, Fed says

Wearing a helmet puts cyclists at risk, suggests research

Winning World Cup lowers heart attack deaths

Eating fish prevents crime

Third Variables in Correlation

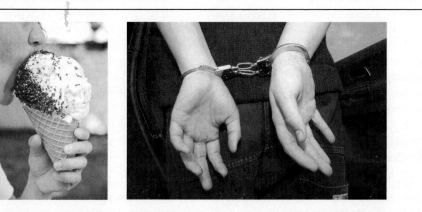

There's a positive correlation between the amount of ice cream consumed and the number of violent crimes committed on that day, but that doesn't mean that eating ice cream causes crime, nor that committing a crime leads to eating more ice cream. A third variable that might explain this correlation is that on hotter days, people both commit more crimes (in part because they go outside more often, and in part because they're more irritable) and eat more ice cream.

Two examples of confusing correlation with causation:

(*Top*) An analysis (Vigen, 2015) showed that between the years 2002 and 2010, shark attacks were highly correlated ($r = 0.77$) with tornadoes. That is, across these years, more shark attacks were associated with larger numbers of tornadoes. (*Bottom*) Another analysis (Vigen, 2015) showed that between 1999 and 2010, the number of film appearances featuring actor Bruce Willis was highly correlated ($r = 0.81$) with the number of people killed by exploding boilers. Needless to say, these correlations are extremely unlikely to directly reflect causal relationships. That's good news for you Bruce Willis fans out there (and for any of you who might happen to be shark fans).

abnormalities as did people with more traditional addictions, such as those to drugs or gambling. The findings are interesting, but they don't demonstrate that Facebook addiction affects the brain. It's entirely possible, for example, that certain brain characteristics predispose people to become addicted to Facebook, or that a third variable, such as impulsivity, gives rise to both.

The bottom line: We should be on the lookout for headlines and news stories that proclaim a causal association between two variables. If the study is based on correlational data alone, they're almost always taking their conclusions too far.

Experimental Designs

If observational designs, case studies, and correlational designs don't allow us to draw cause-and-effect conclusions, what kinds of designs do? The answer: experimental designs, often known simply as "experiments." These designs differ from other designs in one crucial way: When performed correctly, *they permit cause-and-effect inferences*. To see why, we need to understand that in correlational designs, researchers are measuring *preexisting* differences in participants, like age, gender, IQ, and extraversion. These are differences over which investigators have no control; researchers can't make a participant younger or older, for example. In contrast, in experimental designs, researchers *manipulate* variables to see whether these manipulations produce differences in participants' behavior. Putting it another way, in correlational designs, the differences among participants are *measured*, but in experimental designs they're *created* (Cronbach, 1975).

WHAT MAKES A STUDY AN EXPERIMENT: TWO COMPONENTS. Although news reporters frequently use the term *experiment* rather loosely to refer to any kind of research study, this term actually carries a specific meaning in psychology. To be precise, an **experiment** consists of *two* ingredients:

experiment

research design characterized by random assignment of participants to conditions and manipulation of an independent variable

1. Random assignment of participants to conditions
2. Manipulation of an independent variable

Both of these ingredients are necessary for the recipe; if a study doesn't contain both of them, it's *not* an experiment. Let's look at each one in turn.

Random Assignment.   By **random assignment**, we mean that the experimenter randomly sorts participants into one of two groups. By using this procedure, we tend to cancel out preexisting differences between the two groups, such as differences in their gender, race, or personality traits. One of these two groups is the **experimental group**; this group receives the manipulation. The other is the **control group**; this group doesn't receive the manipulation. Scientific thinking doesn't come naturally to the human species.

When viewed through this lens, it's perhaps not surprising that the concept of the control group didn't clearly emerge in psychology until the turn of the 20th century (Coover & Angell, 1907; Dehue, 2005). Before then, many psychologists thought that they could figure out whether a treatment worked without using control groups. Yet as the prefrontal lobotomy example painfully taught us, they were wrong.

To consider an example of how random assignment plays out in the case of an actual experiment, let's imagine we wanted to find out whether a new drug, Miraculin, is effective for treating depression. We'd start with a large sample of individuals with depression. We'd then randomly assign (say, by flipping a coin) half of the participants to an experimental group, which receives Miraculin, and the other half to a control group, which doesn't receive Miraculin.

Incidentally, we shouldn't confuse random assignment with *random selection*, which, as we discussed, is a procedure that allows every person an equal chance to participate. Random selection deals with how we initially choose our participants, whereas random assignment deals with how we assign our participants *after we've already chosen them*.

Manipulation of an Independent Variable.   The second ingredient of an experiment is manipulation of an independent variable. An **independent variable** is the variable the experimenter manipulates. The **dependent variable** is the variable that the experimenter measures to see whether this manipulation has produced an effect. To understand this distinction, remember that the dependent variable is "dependent on" the level of the independent variable. In the experiment using Miraculin as a treatment for depression, the independent variable is the presence versus absence of Miraculin. In contrast, the dependent variable is the level of participants' depression following the experimental manipulation.

When we define our independent and dependent variables for the purposes of a study, we're providing what some psychologists term an **operational definition**—a working definition of what they're measuring. For example, an investigator who wants to measure the effects of a novel psychotherapy on chronic worrying could operationally define his or her dependent measure as "Worrying more than two hours per day for four consecutive weeks." It's important to specify how we're measuring our variables because different researchers may define the same variables in different ways and end up with different conclusions as a result. Imagine that two researchers used two different doses of Miraculin and measured depression using two different scales, one that operationally defines depression as an extremely sad mood lasting two weeks or more and another that operationally defines depression as moderately or extremely sad mood lasting five days or more. The investigators might well end up drawing drastically different conclusions about Miraculin's effectiveness because their measures told different stories. Still, operational definitions aren't like "dictionary" definitions of a word, in which just about all dictionaries agree on the "right" definition (Green, 1992; Lilienfeld et al., 2015). Different researchers can adopt different operational definitions for their own purposes.

CONFOUNDS: SOURCES OF FALSE CONCLUSIONS.   For an experiment to possess adequate internal validity—the ability to draw cause-and-effect conclusions—the level of the independent variable must be the *only* difference between the experimental and control groups. If there's some other difference between these groups, there's no way of knowing whether the independent variable itself exerted an effect on the dependent variable. Psychologists use the term *confounding variable*, or confound, to refer to any variable that differs between the experimental and control groups other than the independent variable (Brewer, 2000). In our depression treatment example, let's imagine that the patients who received Miraculin, but not those in the control group, also received a few sessions of psychotherapy. This extra treatment would be a confounding variable because it's a variable other

random assignment

randomly sorting participants into two groups

experimental group

in an experiment, the group of participants that receives the manipulation

control group

in an experiment, the group of participants that does not receive the manipulation

independent variable

variable that an experimenter manipulates

dependent variable

variable that an experimenter measures to see whether the manipulation produces an effect

operational definition

a working definition of what a researcher is measuring

The control group is an essential part of the "recipe" for a psychological experiment.

Does yoga help people to lower their blood pressure and relieve stress? Only an experiment, with random assignment to conditions and manipulation of an independent variable, gives us permission to infer a cause-and-effect relationship.

"FIND OUT WHO SET UP THIS EXPERIMENT. IT SEEMS THAT HALF OF THE PATIENTS WERE GIVEN A PLACEBO, AND THE OTHER HALF WERE GIVEN A DIFFERENT PLACEBO."

SOURCE: © ScienceCartoonsPlus.com.

than the independent variable that differed between the experimental and control groups. Because of this confound, there's no way to know whether the differences between groups on the dependent variable (level of depression) resulted from Miraculin, psychotherapy, or both.

CAUSE AND EFFECT: PERMISSION TO INFER.   The two major features of an experiment—random assignment to conditions and manipulation of an independent variable—permit us to infer cause-and-effect relations, if we've done the study right, that is. To decide whether to infer cause-and-effect relations from a study, here's a tip that will work 100 percent of the time. *First*, using the criteria we've outlined, ask yourself whether a study is an experiment. *Second*, if it isn't an experiment, don't draw causal conclusions from it, no matter how tempting it might be.

Unfortunately, when reporting studies about physical or psychological health, the news media rarely tell us whether the data came from an experimental or a correlational design. For instance, they might report that "Large new study finds that drinking chocolate milk is linked to lower rates of liver cancer." But they typically don't tell us whether the data came from an experiment, in which participants were randomly assigned to drink lots of chocolate milk or not, or from a correlational study, in which the researchers merely examined how much chocolate milk people typically drink and examined whether that variable is associated with liver cancer risk. If, but only if, the study is an experiment can we draw reasonably confident causal inferences from it.

Before going further, let's make sure the major points concerning experimental designs are clear. Read the description of the acupuncture study, and answer the four questions.

PITFALLS IN EXPERIMENTAL DESIGN.   Like correlational designs, experimental designs can be tricky to interpret because there are numerous pitfalls to beware of when evaluating them. We'll focus on the most important traps here, and explain how psychological scientists have learned to control for them.

The Placebo Effect.   To understand the first major pitfall in experiments, imagine we've developed what we believe to be a new "wonder drug" that supposedly treats attention-deficit/hyperactivity disorder (ADHD) in children. We randomly assign half of our participants with this condition to receive the drug and the other half to receive no treatment. At the conclusion of our study, we find that children who received the drug are much less inattentive and hyperactive than are children who received nothing. That's good news, to be sure, but does it mean we can now break out the champagne and celebrate the news that the drug is effective? Before reading the next paragraph, try to answer this question yourself.

If you answered no, you were right. The reason we can't celebrate just yet is that we haven't controlled for the placebo effect. The term *placebo* derives from the

---

Acupuncture Study: Assess Your Knowledge.

Interactive

Introduction

A researcher hypothesizes that acupuncture, an ancient Chinese medical practice that involves inserting thin needles into specific places on the body, can allow stressed-out psychology students to reduce their anxiety. She randomly assigns half of her participants to undergo acupuncture and half to receive no treatment. Two months later, she measures their anxiety levels and finds that people who received acupuncture are less stressed out than participants who received no treatment.

1. Is this a correlational or an experimental design?

2. What are the independent and dependent variables?

3. Is there a confound in this design? If so, what is it?

4. Can we infer cause and effect from this study? Why or why not?

Feedback

1. This study is experimental because there's random assignment to groups and the experimenter manipulated whether or not participants received treatment.

2. The independent variable is the presence versus absence of acupuncture treatment. The dependent variable is the anxiety level of participants.

3. There's a potential confound in that those who received acupuncture knew they were receiving treatment. Their lower anxiety may have been the result of expectations that they'd be feeling better following treatment.

4. Yes. But because of the confound, we don't know why the experimental group was less anxious. But we can conclude that *something* about the treatment reduced anxiety.

Latin for "I shall please." The **placebo effect** is improvement resulting from the mere expectation of improvement (Kaptchuk, 2002; Kirsch, 2010). Participants who received the drug may have improved merely because they knew they were receiving treatment; this knowledge could have instilled confidence and hope. The placebo effect is a powerful reminder that expectations can create reality.

In medication research, researchers typically control for the placebo effect by administering a sugar pill (sometimes referred to as a "dummy pill," although this term isn't meant as an insult to either the researchers or patients), which is itself often called a *placebo*, to members of the control group. In this way, patients in both the experimental and control groups don't know whether they're taking the actual medication or a placebo, so they're roughly equated in their expectations of improvement. In the Miraculin study, a placebo effect might have been operating, because participants in the control group didn't receive a placebo; they received nothing. So participants in the experimental group might have improved more than those in the control group because they were aware they were getting treatment.

To avoid placebo effects, it's critical that patients not know whether they're receiving the real medication or a placebo. That is, patients must remain **blind** to the condition to which they've been assigned, namely, experimental or control. If patients aren't blind to their condition, then the experiment is essentially ruined because the patients may differ in their expectations of improvement. These differences thereby generate a confound.

Two different things can happen if the "blind is broken," which is psychological lingo for what happens if patients happen to find out which group (experimental or control) they're in. First, patients in the experimental group (the ones receiving the drug) might improve more than do patients in the control group (the ones receiving the placebo) because they're becoming aware that their treatment is real rather than fake. Second, patients in the control group might become resentful that they're receiving a placebo, and therefore try to "beat out" the patients in the experimental group ("Hey, we're going to show those experimenters what we're really made of."). As a consequence, the participants in the control group may, surprisingly, outperform those in the experimental group. Psychologists sometimes refer to this phenomenon as the *John Henry effect*, after an African American folk hero and steel worker from the 1870s who tried to outperform an automated steel drill, only to die in the process (Adair, 1984).

Writers sometimes describe the placebo effect as being entirely in people's heads. Yet the placebo effect is every bit as real as that of actual drugs (Kaptchuk & Miller, 2015; Mayberg et al., 2002). Placebos show many of the same characteristics as do genuine drugs, such as having a more powerful effect at higher doses (Rickels et al., 1970). Placebos injected through a needle (researchers usually use a salt and water solution for this purpose) tend to show more rapid and powerful effects than placebos that are swallowed (Buckalew & Ross, 1981), probably because people assume that injectable placebos enter the bloodstream more quickly than pill placebos. Some patients even become addicted to placebo pills (Mintz, 1977). And placebos we believe to be more expensive tend to work better than placebos we believe to be cheaper (Ariely, 2008), probably because we assume that if something costs more, it's probably more effective. As the old saying goes, "You get what you pay for."

This joke advertisement reminds us that the effects of placebos can sometimes be just as powerful as those of real medications.

Unless we're careful, placebo effects can trick us into concluding that an intervention works even when it doesn't. For example, scores of companies market fast-paced video games that claim to boost memory, attention, and other thinking-related skills. Nevertheless, because participants expect to improve in their memory and attention after playing these games, the positive results advertised by these companies are probably attributable to placebo effects (Boot et al., 2013). As another example, some researchers maintain that up to 80 percent of the effectiveness of antidepressants, such as Prozac or Zoloft, is attributable to placebo effects (Kirsch, 2010; Kirsch & Saperstein, 1998), although others suspect the true percentage is somewhat lower (Dawes, 1998; Klein, 1998; Kramer, 2016). There's growing evidence that placebos are roughly equivalent to antidepressant medication in cases of mild or moderate depression, but not in severe depression, in which antidepressants display a clear edge over placebos (Fournier et al., 2010; Kirsch, Deacon, & Huedo-Medina, 2008).

Placebo effects aren't equally powerful for all conditions. They seem to exert their strongest effects on subjective reports of depression and pain, but their effects on objective measures of physical illnesses, such as cancer and heart disease, are weaker (Hröbjartsson & Götzsche, 2001). Also, the effects of placebos may be more short-lived than those of actual medications (Rothschild & Quitkin, 1992).

Mysteries of Psychological Science
How Do Placebos Work?

As we've seen, our expectations can sometimes exert a powerful influence over our health. There've been cases in which a patient's health improves based on the mere expectation of a treatment or cure. But how do placebos work?

In our attempt to answer this question, we'll travel back in time to the mid-18th century, when physician Frans Anton Mesmer was all the rage in Paris. Mesmer, who lent his name to the term *mesmerism* (a synonym for hypnosis), claimed to cure people of all manners of physical and psychological ailments. Mesmer believed that an invisible magnetic fluid filled the universe and triggered emotional illnesses when it became imbalanced in people's bodies. Dressed in a flowing cape, the flamboyant Mesmer merely needed to touch his patients with a magnetic wand to cause them to shriek, laugh, and enter a stupor, followed by the abrupt disappearance of their symptoms. Mesmer became so much in demand that he took to magnetizing trees for the masses, which supposedly afforded the same cures but in far less time.

But the French government was skeptical of Mesmer's extraordinary claims, wondering whether they were supported by evidence. So they appointed a commission, headed up by none other than Benjamin Franklin, who was U.S. Ambassador to France at the time, to investigate Mesmer's assertions. Franklin set up a series of clever tests to find out whether Mesmer's techniques were as magical as they seemed (Kihlstrom, 2002; Lynn & Lilienfeld, 2002). For example, in some cases, the members of Franklin's commission magnetized a tree but told people that it wasn't magnetized; in other cases, they didn't magnetize a tree but told people it was. People experienced fainting spells only when they *believed* the trees had been magnetized, even if they hadn't been.

Franklin had pulled off two impressive scientific feats. First, he was among the first people to stumble on what eventually came to be known as the placebo effect. Second, and just as important, he had found an ingenious way to isolate this effect. Here's the formula: Present participants with a manipulation in which only some are exposed to the supposed treatment (in this case, a magnetized tree), but others to a control treatment (a nonmagnetized tree), while ensuring that all participants are "blind" to the treatment they're receiving. This is the essence of the same research approach that psychological scientists use in controlled studies today.

Inspired by Franklin's insights, scientists today are homing in on an understanding of how placebo effects work. One promising clue comes from research on the effects of surgery on patients with Parkinson's disease, a condition marked by severe movement problems, including tremors. Parkinson's disease is caused by a deterioration in brain areas rich in the chemical messenger dopamine, which plays a vital role in both movement and the anticipation of reward. In a study that would have made Franklin proud, researchers attempted to treat

Although Mesmer believed he was curing people using his remarkable magnetic powers, he probably was just harnessing the power of the placebo effect.

patients with Parkinson's disease by implanting fetal cells containing dopamine into their brains. To control for the placebo effect, the investigators randomly assigned other patients with Parkinson's to a condition in which they received surgery but no injection of fetal cells (patients were blind to which condition they were in). As expected, patients who received the fetal cell implants improved in their movement and quality of life (McRae et al., 2004). Yet remarkably, patients assigned to the placebo control condition did too. Later research showed that this effect was generated by a burst of dopamine in control participants' brains (Benedetti, 2013). The prospect of improvement had boosted their brain's reward systems, as well as eased their movement abnormalities, both of which are controlled partly by dopamine.

These findings suggest that at least some placebos work in part by jacking up the activity of dopamine, although other chemical messengers are probably involved too (Hall, Losalzo, & Kaptchuk, 2015; Lidstone et al., 2010). By enhancing hope, the placebo effect may often capitalize on our brain's natural reward system. Were he alive today, Franklin might not have been surprised, because he understood that expectations of hope can themselves be therapeutic.

The Nocebo Effect. The placebo effect has an "evil twin" of sorts: the nocebo effect (Benedetti, Lanotte, & Lopiano, 2007; Freeman et al., 2015; Häuser, Hansen, & Enck, 2012). The *nocebo effect* is harm resulting from the mere expectation of harm (*nocebo* comes from the Latin phrase meaning "to harm"). The ancient African, and later Caribbean, practice of voodoo presumably capitalizes on the nocebo effect: People who believe that others are sticking them with pins sometimes experience pain themselves. In one study, individuals who were allergic to roses sneezed when presented with fake roses (Reid, 2002). In another case, researchers deceived a group of college students into believing that an electric current being passed into their heads could produce a headache. More than two-thirds of the students reported headaches, even though the current was imaginary (Morse, 1999). One patient even experienced serious physical symptoms, such as extremely low blood pressure, after overdosing on fake pills that he thought were antidepressants (Enck & Hauser, 2012).

People who believe in the power of voodoo, a supernatural practice popular in Haiti, West Africa, and some regions of the U.S. state of Louisiana, may experience pain when one of their enemies inserts a pin into a doll intended to symbolize them. This is an example of the *nocebo effect*, a psychological phenomenon that demonstrates that the expectation of pain can itself create pain.

Journal Prompt

People who believe in the power of voodoo may experience pain when one of their enemies inserts a pin into a doll intended to simulate them. As your text notes, this phenomenon illustrates the nocebo effect. What other examples from the realm of superstition might be nocebo effects?

The Experimenter Expectancy Effect. Including a control condition that provides a placebo treatment is extremely important, as is keeping participants blind to their condition assignment. Still, there's one more potential concern with experimental designs. In some cases, the participant doesn't know the condition assignment, but the experimenter does.

When this happens, a knotty problem can arise: the **experimenter expectancy effect** or *Rosenthal effect* (Rosenthal & Rubie-Davies, 2015). It occurs when researchers' hypotheses lead them to unintentionally bias a study's outcome. It may be worth underlining the word *unintentionally* in the previous sentence, because this effect doesn't refer to deliberate "fudging" or making up of data, which fortunately occurs relatively rarely in science (John, Loewenstein, & Prelec, 2012). Instead, in the experimenter expectancy effect, researchers' biases affect the results in subtle ways, almost always outside of their knowledge. In some cases, these researchers may end up falling prey to confirmation bias, seeming to find evidence for their hypotheses even when these hypotheses are wrong.

Because of this effect, psychological investigators now always try to conduct their experiments in a **double-blind** fashion. By double-blind, we mean that neither researchers nor participants know who's in the experimental or control group. By voluntarily shielding themselves from the knowledge of which subjects are in which group, researchers are guarding themselves against confirmation bias. Double-blind designs represent science at its best because they show how good scientists take special precautions to avoid fooling themselves and others.

One of the oldest and best-known examples of the experimenter expectancy effect is the infamous tale of German teacher Wilhelm von Osten and his horse (Fernald, 1984; Heinzen et al., 2015). In 1900, von Osten had purchased a handsome Arabian stallion, known in the psychological literature as Clever Hans, who seemingly displayed astonishing mathematical abilities. By tapping with his hooves, Clever Hans responded correctly to mathematical questions from von Osten (such as, "How much is 8 plus 3?"). He calculated square roots, added and subtracted fractions, and could tell the time of day. He could even give accurate answers to more specific questions, like the number of men in front of him who were wearing black hats. Understandably, von Osten was so proud of Clever Hans that he began showing him off in public for large throngs of amazed spectators.

You might be wondering whether Clever Hans's feats were the result of trickery. A panel of 13 psychologists who investigated Clever Hans witnessed no evidence of fraud on von Osten's part, and concluded that Clever Hans possessed the arithmetic abilities of a 14-year-old human. Moreover, Clever Hans seemed to be a true-blue math whiz because he could add and subtract even when von Osten wasn't posing the questions.

experimenter expectancy effect

phenomenon in which researchers' hypotheses lead them to unintentionally bias the outcome of a study

double-blind

when neither researchers nor participants are aware of who's in the experimental or control group

"IT WAS MORE OF A 'TRIPLE-BLIND' TEST. THE PATIENTS DIDN'T KNOW WHICH ONES WERE GETTING THE REAL DRUG, THE DOCTORS DIDN'T KNOW, AND, I'M AFRAID, NOBODY KNEW."

SOURCE: © ScienceCartoonsPlus.com.

Fact vs. Fiction

It's impossible to conduct a double-blind study of whether psychotherapy is effective. (See bottom of page for answer.)

○ Fact

○ Fiction

Nevertheless, psychologist Oscar Pfungst was skeptical of just how clever Clever Hans really was, and in 1904 he launched a series of careful observations. In this case, Pfungst did something that previous psychologists didn't think to do: He focused not on the horse, but on the people asking him questions. When he did, he discovered that von Osten and others were cuing the horse *unintentionally* to produce correct answers. Pfungst found that Clever Hans's questioners almost invariably tightened their muscles immediately before the correct answer. When Pfungst prevented Clever Hans from seeing the questioner or anyone else who knew the correct answer, the celebrated horse did no better than chance, and no better than any ordinary horse. The puzzle was solved: Clever Hans was cleverly detecting subtle physical cues emitted by questioners.

The Clever Hans story shows that people can—even without their knowledge—give off cues that affect a subject's behavior, even when that subject is a horse. This story also reminds us that an extraordinary claim, in this case that a horse can perform arithmetic, requires extraordinary evidence. von Osten's claims were remarkable, but his evidence wasn't. Interestingly, in a play on words, some authors have referred to facilitated communication, which we encountered at the beginning of this chapter, as the "phenomenon of Clever Hands" (Wegner, Fuller, & Sparrow, 2003), because it too appeared to be the result of an experimenter expectancy effect.

Extraordinary Claims ▶

Is the evidence as strong as the claim?

Clever Hans performing in public. If one can observe powerful experimenter (in this case, owner) expectancy effects even in animals, how powerful might such effects be in humans?

demand characteristics

cues that participants pick up from a study that allow them to generate guesses regarding the researcher's hypotheses

You might have noticed that we also referred to the experimenter expectancy effect as the Rosenthal effect. That's because in the 1960s psychologist Robert Rosenthal conducted an elegant series of experiments that persuaded the psychological community that experimenter expectancy effects were genuine. In one of them, Rosenthal and Kermit Fode (1963) randomly assigned some psychology students a group of five so-called maze bright rats—rats bred over many generations to run mazes quickly—and other students a group of five so-called maze dull rats—rats bred over many generations to run mazes slowly. Note that this is an experiment, because Rosenthal and Fode randomly assigned students to groups and manipulated which type of rat the students supposedly received. They then asked students to run the rats in mazes and to record each rat's completion time. But there was a catch: Rosenthal and Fode had actually randomly assigned rats to the students rather than the other way around. The story about the "maze bright" and "maze dull" rats was all cooked up. Yet when Rosenthal and Fode tabulated their results, they found that students assigned the "maze bright" rats reported 29 percent faster maze running times than did students assigned the "maze dull" rats. In some unknown fashion, the students had influenced their rats' running times. That's why experimenters need to be kept blind to which condition is which; by shielding them from this knowledge, they can't unintentionally influence the results of the study.

Demand Characteristics. A final potential pitfall of psychological research can be difficult to eliminate. Research participants can pick up cues, known as **demand characteristics**, from an experiment that allow them to generate guesses regarding the researcher's hypotheses (Belongax & Bellizzi, 2015; Orne, 1962; Rosnow, 2002). In some cases, participants' guesses about what the experimenter is up to may be correct; in other cases, they may not. The problem is that when participants think they know how the experimenter wants them to act,

---

Answer: Fact. It's probably true that a double-blind study of psychotherapy is impossible. One almost certainly can't shield people from the knowledge of whether or not they're receiving psychotherapy. That's one factor that makes the effects of psychotherapy more difficult to study than the effects of medication.

they may alter their behavior accordingly. So whether they've guessed right or wrong, their beliefs can prevent researchers from getting an unbiased view of participants' thoughts and behaviors.

To combat demand characteristics, researchers may disguise the purpose of the study, perhaps by providing participants with a plausible "cover story" that differs from the investigation's actual purpose. Alternatively, they may include "distractor" tasks or "filler" items—measures unrelated to the question of interest. These items help to prevent participants from altering their responses in ways they think the experimenters are looking for.

2.3: Ethical Issues in Research Design

2.3a **Explain the ethical obligations of researchers toward their research participants.**

2.3b **Describe both sides of the debate on the use of animals as research subjects.**

When designing and conducting research studies, psychologists need to worry about more than their scientific value. The ethics of these studies also matter. Although psychology adheres to the same basic scientific principles as other sciences, let's face it: A chemist needn't worry about hurting his mineral's feelings, and a physicist needn't be concerned about the long-term emotional well-being of a neutron. The scientific study of people and their behavior raises distinctive concerns.

Many philosophers believe—and the authors of this text agree—that science itself is value-neutral. Because science is a search for the truth, it's neither inherently good nor bad. This fact doesn't imply, though, that scientific *research* is value-neutral because there are both ethical and unethical ways of searching for the truth. Moreover, we may not all agree on which ways of searching for the truth are ethical. We'd probably all agree that it's acceptable to learn about brain damage by studying the behavior of people with brain damage on laboratory tasks of learning, just so long as these tasks aren't overly stressful. We'd also all agree (we hope!) that it's unacceptable for us to learn about brain damage by hitting people over the head with baseball bats and then testing their motor coordination by measuring how often they fall down a flight of stairs. Nevertheless, we might not all agree on whether it's ethically acceptable to learn about brain damage by creating severe lesions (wounds) in the brains of cats and examining their effects on cats' responses to fear-provoking stimuli (such as scary dogs). In many cases, the question of whether research is ethical isn't clear-cut, and reasonable people will sometimes disagree on the answer.

Historical photo of the Tuskegee study. This study demonstrates the tragic consequences of ignoring crucial ethical considerations in research.

Tuskegee: A Shameful Moral Tale

Scientists have learned the hard way that their otherwise healthy thirst for knowledge can occasionally blind them to crucial ethical considerations. One deeply troubling example comes from the Tuskegee study performed by the U.S. Public Health Service, an agency of the U.S. government, from 1932 to 1972 (Jones, 1993). During this time, a number of researchers wanted to learn more about the natural course of syphilis, a sexually transmitted disease. What happens, they wondered, to syphilis over time if it is left untreated?

The "subjects" in this study were 399 African American men living in the poorest rural areas of Alabama who'd been diagnosed with syphilis. Remarkably, the researchers never informed these men that they had syphilis, nor that an effective treatment for syphilis, namely, antibiotics, had become available. Indeed, the subjects didn't even know they were subjects, as researchers hadn't informed them of that crucial piece of information. Instead, the researchers

Watch CLINTON'S APOLOGY

merely tracked the subjects' progress over time, withholding all important medical information and all available treatments.

By the end of the study, 28 men had died of syphilis, 100 had died of syphilis-related complications, 40 of the men's wives had been infected with syphilis, and 19 children had been born with syphilis. In 1997—25 years after the termination of this study—then-President Bill Clinton, on behalf of the U.S. government, offered a formal apology for the Tuskegee study to the study's eight remaining survivors (see video *Clinton's Apology*).

Ethical Guidelines for Human Research

If any good at all came out of the horrific Tuskegee study and other ethical catastrophes in scientific research, it was a heightened appreciation for protecting the rights of human subjects. Fortunately, researchers could never perform the Tuskegee study today, at least not in the United States. That's because every major American research college and university has at least one *institutional review board* (IRB), which evaluates all research carefully with an eye toward protecting participants against abuses. IRBs typically consist of faculty members drawn from various departments within a college or university, as well as one or more outside members, such as a person drawn from the nearby community.

informed consent

informing research participants of what's involved in a study before asking them to participate

The award for the most ethically questionable research on humans published in a psychology journal may go to a 1960s' study in which investigators wanted to determine the effects of extreme fear on attention. A pilot informed 10 U.S. soldiers on board what they assumed to be a routine training flight that the plane's propeller and landing gear were malfunctioning and that he was going to crash-land in the ocean. In fact, the pilot had deceived the soldiers: The plane was fine. The flight attendant, who was "in" on the deception, handed out questionnaires to soldiers and instructed them to place them in a water-proof container. Perhaps not surprisingly, these soldiers made more errors filling out the measures than did a control group of soldiers on the ground (Berkun et al., 1962; Boese, 2007). Needless to say, this bizarre investigation could never make it past a modern-day IRB.

INFORMED CONSENT. IRBs insist on a procedure called **informed consent**, that is, researchers must tell subjects what they're getting into before asking them to participate. During the informed consent process, participants can typically ask questions about the study and learn more about what will be involved. The Tuskegee subjects never received informed consent, and we can be certain they wouldn't have agreed to participate had they known they wouldn't be receiving treatment for a potentially fatal illness. One challenge to informed consent is that some participants, such as those with Alzheimer's disease or with psychotic disorders (conditions, such as schizophrenia, in which individuals lose partial touch with reality), may agree to certain research procedures without fully understanding them (Nishimura et al., 2013). So it's up to investigators to ensure that participants providing informed consent are truly informed.

Nevertheless, IRBs may occasionally allow researchers to forgo certain elements of informed consent, but only when doing so is deemed to be essential. In particular, some psychological research entails *deception.* When researchers use deception, they deliberately mislead participants about the study's design or purpose. In one of the most controversial studies in the history of psychology (see LO 13.2c), Stanley Milgram (1963), then at Yale University, invited volunteers to participate in a study of the "effects of punishment on learning." The experimenter deceived participants into believing they were administering painful electric shocks to another participant, who made repeated errors on a learning task. In reality, the other "participant" never received any shocks. He was actually a *confederate* of the experimenter, that is, a research assistant who played the part of a participant. Moreover, Milgram had no interest in the effects of punishment on learning; he was interested in the influence of authority figures on obedience. Many of the true participants experienced considerable distress during the procedure, and some were understandably troubled by the fact that they had delivered what they had believed to be extremely painful—even potentially fatal—electric shocks to an innocent person.

Was Milgram's elaborate deception justified? Milgram (1964) argued that the hoax was required to pull off the study because informing subjects of its true purpose would have generated obvious demand characteristics. He further noted that he went out of his way to later explain the study's true purpose to participants and assure them that their obedience wasn't a sign of cruelty or psychological disturbance. In addition, he sent a questionnaire to all subjects after the studies were completed and found that only 1.3 percent reported any negative emotional aftereffects. In contrast, Diana Baumrind (1964) argued that Milgram's study wasn't worth the knowledge or psychological distress it generated. Milgram's failure to provide subjects with full informed consent, she maintained, was ethically indefensible. Simply put, Milgram's subjects didn't know what they were getting into when they volunteered.

The debate concerning the ethics of Milgram's study continues (Blass, 2004). Although we won't try to resolve this controversy here, we'll point out that the ethical standards of the American Psychological Association (2002) affirm that deception is justified only when (a) researchers couldn't have performed the study without the deception and (b) the scientific knowledge to be gained from the study outweighs its costs (see Table 2.3). Needless to say, evaluating (b) isn't easy, and it's up to researchers—and ultimately, the IRB—to decide whether the potential scientific benefits of a study are sufficient to justify deception. Over the years, IRBs—which didn't exist in Milgram's day—have become more stringent about the need for informed consent.

DEBRIEFING: EDUCATING PARTICIPANTS. IRBs may also request that a full debriefing be performed at the conclusion of the research session. *Debriefing* is a process whereby researchers inform participants what the study was about. In some cases, researchers use debriefings to explain their hypotheses in nontechnical language. By administering a debriefing, the study becomes a learning experience for not only the investigator, but also the subject.

Table 2.3 APA Ethical Principles for Human Research.

Psychological researchers must carefully weigh the potential scientific benefits of their research against the potential danger to participants. In 2002, the American Psychological Association (APA) published a code of ethics to govern all research with human participants. The following is a summary of the key ethical principles.

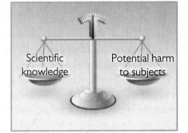

Informed Consent
- Research participants should be fully informed of the purpose of the research, its expected duration, and any potential risks, discomfort, or adverse effects associated with it.
- Participants should enter the study voluntarily and be informed of their right to withdraw from it at any time.
- A contact who can answer questions about the research and the participant's rights should be provided.

Protection from Harm and Discomfort
- Psychologists must take reasonable steps to avoid harm to research participants.

Deception and Debriefing
- When deceptive techniques are used in research, the participants should be informed of the deception as soon as possible after the deception takes place.
- Participants should not be deceived about research procedures that may cause them physical pain or emotional distress.
- Once the research study has concluded, participants should not only be informed of the deception but fully debriefed about the true nature of the research.

Ethical Issues in Animal Research

Few topics generate as much understandable anger and discomfort as animal research. This is especially true of *invasive* research, in which investigators cause physical harm to animals. In psychology departments, invasive research most often takes the form of producing lesions in animals' brains, usually by means of surgery, and observing their effects on animals' behavior. About 7 to 8 percent of published research in psychology relies on animals (American Psychological Association [APA], 2008) with the overwhelming majority of studies conducted on rodents (especially rats and mice) and birds. The goal of such research is to generate ideas about how the brain relates to behavior in animals—and how these findings generalize to humans—without having to inflict harm on people.

Many animal rights activists have raised useful concerns regarding the ethical treatment of animals and have underscored the need for adequate housing and feeding conditions (Beauchamp, Ferdowsian, & Gluck, 2014; Marino, 2009; Ott, 1995). In contrast, others have gone to extremes that could themselves be considered unethical, such as ransacking laboratories and liberating animals. In 1999, the Animal Liberation Front attacked several psychology laboratories at the University of Minnesota, releasing rats and pigeons and inflicting about $2 million worth of damage (Azar, 1999; Hunt, 1999). Incidentally, most

individuals on both sides of the animal rights debate agree that liberating animals is a dreadful idea, because many or most animals die shortly after being released.

These excessive tactics aside, the ethical issues here aren't easily resolved. Some commentators maintain that the deaths of approximately 100 million laboratory animals every year in medical and psychological research (Humane Society International, 2012) aren't worth the cost. For example, there are legitimate questions regarding how well animal models of psychological and medical disorders translate to human conditions (van der Worp et al., 2012). It's extremely unlikely, for instance, that "depression" is experienced in the same way by a rat as by a human. For other critics, the knowledge gleaned from animal research on aggression, fear, learning, memory, and related topics is of such doubtful external validity to humans as to be virtually useless (Ulrich, 1991).

This position has some merit but may be too extreme. Some animal research has contributed to direct benefits to humans, as well as useful knowledge in its own right. Many psychological treatments, especially those based on principles of learning, stemmed from animal research. Without animal research, we'd know relatively little about the physiology of the brain, or of how brain abnormalities are associated with risk for mental disorders (Domjan & Purdy, 1995; Stewart & Kalueff, 2015). Furthermore, to answer many critical psychological questions, there are often few or no good alternatives to using animals (Gallup & Suarez, 1985). For example, without animals we'd be unable to test the safety and effectiveness of many antidepressant or anti-anxiety medications.

None of this tells us when we should or shouldn't use animals in research. It's clear that animal research has yielded enormously important insights about the brain and behavior and that psychologists are likely to rely on such research for some time to come. At the same time, it's also clear that animal researchers must weigh carefully the potential scientific gains of their inquiries against the costs in death and suffering they produce. Because reasonable people will inevitably disagree about how to weigh these pros and cons, the intense controversy surrounding animal research is unlikely to subside anytime soon.

statistics

application of mathematics to describing and analyzing data

Journal Prompt

Animal research is ethically controversial, and many thoughtful people hold strongly differing viewpoints on its advantages and disadvantages. Describe some of the potential long-term benefits and costs of using animals in research.

2.4: Statistics: The Language of Psychological Research

2.4a Identify uses of various measures of central tendency and variability.

2.4b Explain how inferential statistics can help us to determine whether we can generalize from our sample to the full population.

2.4c Show how statistics can be misused for purposes of persuasion.

Up to this point, we've mostly spared you the gory mathematical details of psychological research. Aside from correlation coefficients, we haven't said much about how psychologists analyze their findings. Still, to understand psychological research and how to interpret it, we need to know at least a bit about **statistics**, which are the application of mathematics to describing and analyzing data. For you math phobics (or "arithmophobics," if you want to impress your friends with a technical term) out there, there's no cause for alarm. We promise to keep things simple and stress-free.

FORMULA APPRECIATION CLASS AT THE MATH MUSEUM

Descriptive Statistics: What's What?

At the risk of simplifying matters somewhat, psychologists use two major kinds of statistics. The first are **descriptive statistics**. They do exactly what the name implies: describe data. Using descriptive statistics on a sample of 100 men and 100 hundred women whose levels of extraversion we assess using a self-report measure, we could ask the following questions:

- What's the average level of extraversion in this sample?
- What's the average level of extraversion among men, and what's the average level of extraversion among women?
- How much do all of our participants, as well as men and women separately, vary in how extraverted they are?

To maintain our promise of keeping things simple, we'll discuss only two major types of descriptive statistics. The first is the **central tendency**, which gives us a sense of the "central" score in our data set or where the bulk of the group tends to cluster. In turn, there are three measures of central tendency: mean, median, and mode (known as the "three Ms"). Follow along with us on Table 2.4a (the left half of the table) as we calculate each.

The **mean**, also known as the average, is just the total score divided by the number of people. If our sample consists of five people as shown in the table, the mean IQ is simply the total of the five scores divided by five, which happens to be 102.

The **median**, not to be confused with the narrow strip of land in the middle of a highway, is the *middle* score in our data set. We obtain the median by lining up our scores in order and finding the middle one. So in this case, we'd line up the five IQ scores in order from lowest to highest, and find that 100 is the median because it's the score smack in the middle of the distribution.

The **mode** is the most *frequent* score in our data set. In this case, the mode is 120, because two people in our sample received scores of 120 on the IQ test and one person each received other scores.

As we can see, the three Ms sometimes tell us rather different things (Streiner, 2000). In this case, the mean and median were close to each other, but the mode was much higher than both. The mean is generally the best statistic to report when our data form a bell-shaped or "normal" distribution, as we can see in the top panel of Figure 2.6. But what happens when our distribution is "skewed," that is, tilted sharply to one side or the other, as in the bottom panels? Here the mean provides a misleading picture of the central tendency, so it's usually better to use the median or mode instead because these statistics are less affected by extreme scores at either the low or high end. In other cases, we need the mode to give us the most meaningful answer. Imagine that we asked 100 people drawn from the general population to name their top unlucky number, and that 90 of them said 13, 7 of them said 3, one of them said 25, and another said 1000. In this case, the mode would be 13—which correctly tells us the most common unlucky number—but the mean would be 22.16, which would be misleading.

Figure 2.6 Distribution Curves.

(*a*) a normal (bell-shaped) distribution, (*b*) a markedly negative skewed distribution, and (*c*) a markedly positive skewed distribution.

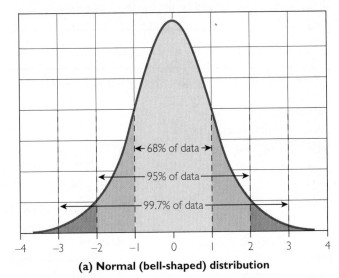

(**a**) **Normal (bell-shaped) distribution**

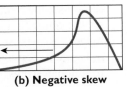

(**b**) **Negative skew**
Elongated tail at the **left**
More data in the tail than would be expected in a normal distribution

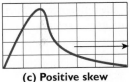

(**c**) **Positive skew**
Elongated tail at the **right**
More data in the tail than would be expected in a normal distribution

descriptive statistics

numerical characterizations that describe data

central tendency

measure of the "central" scores in a data set, or where the group tends to cluster

mean

average; a measure of central tendency

median

middle score in a data set; a measure of central tendency

mode

most frequent score in a data set; a measure of central tendency

Table 2.4 The Three Ms: Mean, Median, and Mode.

(a)	(b)
Sample IQ scores: 100, 90, 80, 120, 120	**Sample IQ scores:** 80, 85, 95, 95, 220
Mean: (100+90+80+120+120)/5=102	**Mean:** (80+85+95+95+220)/5=116
Median: order scores from lowest to highest: 80, 90, 100, 120, 120; middle score is 100	**Median:** 95
Mode: only 120 appears twice in the data set, so it's the most common score	**Mode:** 95
	Note: mean is affected by one extreme score, but median and mode aren't.

Figure 2.7 The Range versus the Standard Deviation.

These two number lines display data sets with the same *range* but different *standard deviations*. The variability is more tightly clustered in (a) than in (b), so the standard deviation in (a) will be smaller.

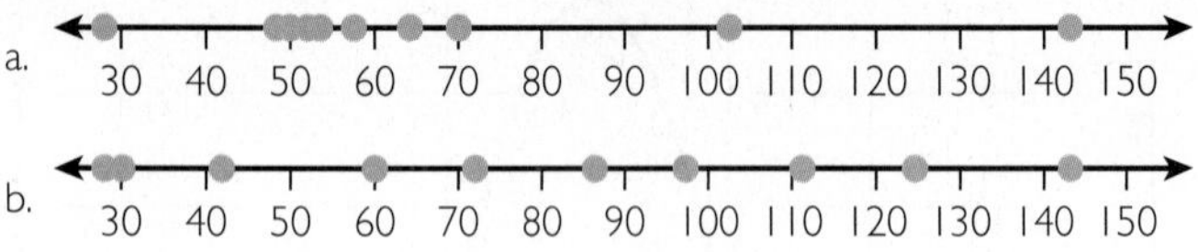

variability

measure of how loosely or tightly bunched scores are

range

measure of variability that consists of the difference between the highest and lowest scores

standard deviation

measure of variability that takes into account how far each data point is from the mean

To hammer home the point that the three Ms give us different answers, let's look at Table 2.4b to see what happens to our measures of central tendency. The mean of this distribution is 116, but four of the scores are much below 116, and the only reason the mean is this high is the presence of one person who scored 220 (who in technical terms is an *outlier*, because his or her score lies way outside the other scores). In contrast, both the median and mode are 95, which capture the central tendency of the distribution much better.

The second type of descriptive statistic is **variability** (sometimes called *dispersion*), which gives us a sense of how loosely or tightly bunched the scores are. Consider the following two sets of IQ scores from five people:

- 80, 85, 85, 90, 95
- 25, 65, 70, 125, 150

In both groups of scores, the mean is 87. But the second set of scores is much more spread out than the first. So we need some way of describing the differences in variability in these two data sets.

The simplest measure of variability is the **range**. The range is the difference between the highest and lowest scores. In the first set of IQ scores, the range is only 15, whereas in the second set the range is 125. So the range tells us that although the two sets of scores have a similar central tendency, their variability is wildly different (as in Figure 2.7a). Although the range is the easiest measure of variability to calculate, it can be deceptive because, as shown in Figure 2.7b, two data sets with the same range can be associated with a very different distribution of scores.

To compensate for this problem, psychologists often use another measure called the **standard deviation** to depict variability (this index is a bit complicated to calculate, so we'll spare you the trouble of that here). This measure is less likely to be deceptive than the range because it takes into account how far *each* data point is from the mean, rather than simply how widely scattered the most extreme scores are.

Statistics Quiz

Answer the following questions about the two small data sets below:

Data set A: 23, 32, 45, 45, 80
Data set B: 22, 35, 45, 58, 58

1) Which data set has the smaller mean?
   a. Data set A
   b. Data set B
   c. They are the same

   Feedback: Data set A mean = 45, Data set B mean = 43.6

2) Which data set has the smaller median?
   a. Data set A
   b. Data set B
   c. They are the same

   Feedback: Data set A median = 45, Data set B median = 45

3) Which data set has the smaller mode?
   a. Data set A
   b. Data set B
   c. They are the same

   Feedback: Data set A mode = 45, Data set B mode = 58

1) b, 2) c, 3) a.

Inferential Statistics: Testing Hypotheses

In addition to descriptive statistics, psychologists use **inferential statistics**, which allow us to determine how much we can generalize findings from our sample to the full population. When using inferential statistics, we're asking whether we can draw "inferences" (conclusions) regarding whether the differences we've observed in our sample apply to similar samples. Previously, we mentioned a study of 100 men and 100 women who took a self-report measure of extraversion. In this study, inferential statistics allow us to find out whether the differences we've observed in extraversion between men and women are believable, or if they're just a fluke occurrence in our sample. Let's imagine that we calculated the means for men and women (we first verified that the distribution of scores in both men and women approximated a bell curve). After doing so, we found that men scored 10.4 on our extraversion scale (the scores range from 0 to 15) and that women scored 9.9. So, *in our sample*, men are more extraverted, or at least say they are, than women. Can we now conclude that men are more extraverted than women in general? How can we rule out the possibility that this small sex difference in our sample is a result of chance? That's where inferential statistics enter the picture.

What's wrong with this (fake) newspaper headline?

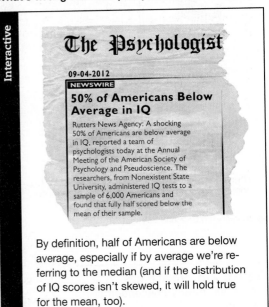

The Psychologist

09-04-2012

NEWSWIRE

50% of Americans Below Average in IQ

Rutters News Agency: A shocking 50% of Americans are below average in IQ, reported a team of psychologists today at the Annual Meeting of the American Society of Psychology and Pseudoscience. The researchers, from Nonexistent State University, administered IQ tests to a sample of 6,000 Americans and found that fully half scored below the mean of their sample.

By definition, half of Americans are below average, especially if by average we're referring to the median (and if the distribution of IQ scores isn't skewed, it will hold true for the mean, too).

STATISTICAL SIGNIFICANCE.   To figure out whether the difference we've observed in our sample is a believable (real) one, we need to conduct statistical tests to determine whether we can generalize our findings to the population. To do so, we can use a variety of statistics depending on the research design. But regardless of which test we use, we generally use a 0.05 level of confidence when deciding whether a finding is trustworthy. This minimum level—5 in 100—is taken as the probability that the finding occurred by chance. When the finding would have occurred by chance less than 5 in 100 times, we say that it's *statistically significant*. A statistically significant result is believable; it's probably a real difference in our sample. In psychology journals, we'll often see the expression "$p < 0.05$," meaning roughly that the probability (the lowercase p stands for probability) that our finding would have occurred by chance alone is less than 5 in 100, or 1 in 20 (that's a little bit of an oversimplification, but it's one we can live with for now).

inferential statistics

mathematical methods that allow us to determine whether we can generalize findings from our sample to the full population

PRACTICAL SIGNIFICANCE.   Writer and former psychology graduate student Gertrude Stein said that "a difference is a difference that makes a difference." Stein's quotation reminds us not to confuse statistical significance with *practical significance*, that is, real-world importance. A finding can be statistically significant yet not make much, if any, difference in the real world. To understand this point, we need to understand that a major determinant of statistical significance is sample size. The larger the sample size, the greater the odds (all else being equal) that a result will be statistically significant (Meehl, 1978; Schmidt, 1992). With huge sample sizes, virtually all findings—even tiny ones—will become statistically significant.

If we were to find a correlation of $r = 0.06$ between IQ and nose length in a sample of 500,000 people, this correlation would be statistically significant at the $p < 0.05$ level. Yet it's so minuscule in magnitude that it would be essentially useless for predicting anything.

How People Lie With Statistics

Humorist Mark Twain is often credited with writing that there are three kinds of untruths: "lies, damned lies, and statistics." Because many people's eyes glaze over when they see lots of numbers, it's easy to fool them with statistical sleight of hand. Here, we'll provide three examples of how people can misuse statistics and, just as important, how people can use them correctly. Our goal, of course, isn't to encourage you to lie with statistics, but to equip you with scientific thinking skills for spotting statistical abuses (Huck, 2008; Huff, 1954, Levitin, 2016).

EXAMPLE 1

Your Congressional Representative, Ms. Dee Section, is running for reelection. As part of her platform, she's proposed a new tax plan for everyone in your state. According to the "fine print" in Ms. Section's plan, 99 percent of people in your state will receive a $100 tax cut this year.

"There are lies, damn lies, and statistics. We're looking for someone who can make all three of these work for us."

Figure 2.8 Arrest Rates Before and After Transcendental Meditation.

Arrest rates per month in Pancake before (*left*) and after (*right*) introduction of transcendental meditation.

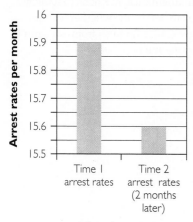

The remaining 1 percent, who make more than $3 million per year, will receive a tax cut of $500,000 (according to Ms. Seption, this large tax cut for the richest people is necessary because she gets her biggest campaign contributions from them).

Based on this plan, Ms. Dee Seption announces at a press conference, "If I'm elected and my tax plan goes through, the average person in our state will receive a tax cut of $5,099." Watching this press conference on television, you think, "Wow … what a deal! I'm definitely going to vote for Dee Seption. If she wins, I'll have more than $5,000 extra bucks in my bank account."

Question: *Why should you be skeptical of Dee Seption's claim?*

Answer: Ms. Dee Seption has engaged in a not-especially-subtle deception, suggesting that she's aptly named. She assures us that under her plan the "average person" in her state will receive a tax cut of $5,099. In one respect she's right, because the *mean* tax cut is indeed $5,099. But in this case, the mean is highly misleading, because under Seption's plan virtually everyone in her state will receive only a $100 tax cut. Only the richest of the rich will receive a tax cut of $500,000, making the mean highly unrepresentative of the central tendency. Dee Seption should have instead reported the median or mode, which are both only $100, as measures of central tendency. As we learned previously, the median and mode are less affected by extreme scores than the mean.

EXAMPLE 2

A researcher, Dr. Faulty Conclusion, conducts a study to demonstrate that transcendental meditation (TM), a form of relaxation that originated in East Asian cultures, reduces crime rates. According to Dr. Conclusion, towns whose citizens are taught to practice TM will experience a dramatic drop in arrests. He finds a small town, Pancake, Iowa (population 300), and teaches all citizens of Pancake to practice TM. For his control group, he identifies a small neighboring town in Iowa, called Waffle (population also 300), and doesn't introduce them to TM. According to Dr. Conclusion, Waffle is a good control group for Pancake, because it has the same population, ethnic makeup, income, and initial arrest rates.

Two months after the introduction of TM to Pancake, Dr. Conclusion measures the arrest rates in Pancake and Waffle. At a major conference, he proudly announces that although the arrest rates in Waffle stayed exactly the same, the arrest rates in Pancake experienced a spectacular plunge. To demonstrate this astonishing effect, he directs the audience to a graph (see Figure 2.8). As he does, the audience gasps in astonishment. "As you can see from this graph," Conclusion proclaims, "the arrest rates in Pancake were initially very high. But after I taught Pancake's citizens TM, their arrest rates two months later were much, much lower." Dr. Conclusion concludes triumphantly, "Our findings show beyond a shadow of a doubt that TM reduces crime rates."

Question: *What's wrong with Dr. Conclusion's conclusion?*

Answer: Dr. Conclusion's graph in Figure 2.8 sure looks impressive, doesn't it? The arrest rates have indeed gone down from the beginning to the end of the study. But let's take a good close look at the *y* axis (that's the vertical axis) of the graph. Can we see anything suspicious about it?

Dr. Conclusion has tricked us, or perhaps he's tricked himself. The *y* axis starts at 15.5 arrests per month and goes up to 16 arrests per month. In fact, Dr. Conclusion has demonstrated only that the arrest rate in Pancake declined from 15.9 arrests per month to 15.6 arrests per month—a grand total of less than one-third of an arrest per month! That's hardly worth writing home about, let alone mastering TM for.

Dr. Conclusion used what's termed a *truncated line graph*. That kind of graph is typically a real "no-no" in statistics, although many researchers still use it (Huff, 1954; Smith, 2001). In this kind of graph, the *y* axis starts not at the lowest possible score, where it should start (in this case, it should start at zero, because that's the lowest possible number of arrests per month), but somewhere close to the highest possible score. By using a truncated line graph, Dr. Conclusion made the apparent effects of TM appear huge when in fact they were pitifully small. Next time, he'd be better off using the full range of possible scores on his graph.

EXAMPLE 3

Ms. Representation conducts a study to determine the association between nationality and drinking patterns. According to Professor Representation's new "Grand Unified Theory of Drinking Behavior," people of German descent are at higher risk for alcoholism than are people of Norwegian descent. To test this hypothesis, she begins with a randomly selected sample of 10,000 people from the city of Inebriated, Indiana. She administers a survey to all participants inquiring about their drinking habits and national background. When she analyzes her data, she finds that 1,200 citizens of Inebriated meet official diagnostic criteria for alcohol use disorder (alcoholism). Of these 1,200 individuals, 450 are of German descent, whereas only 30 are of Norwegian descent—a 15-fold difference! She conducts a statistical test (we won't trouble you with the precise mathematics) and determines that this amazingly large difference is statistically significant at $p < 0.05$. At the annual convention of the International Society of Really, Really Smart Alcoholism Researchers, Ms. Representation asserts, "My bold hypothesis has been confirmed. I can conclude confidently that Germans are at higher risk for alcoholism than Norwegians."

Question: *Why are Ms. Representation's conclusions about drinking all washed up?*

Answer: Remember the *base rate fallacy* we introduced in this chapter? When interpreting findings, it's easy to forget about base rates. That's because base rates often "lurk in the distance" of our minds and aren't especially vivid. In this case, Ms. Representation forgot to take a crucial fact into account: In Inebriated, Indiana, the base rate of people of German descent is 25 times higher than the base rate of people of Norwegian descent. As a result, the fact that there are 15 times more German than Norwegian alcoholics in Inebriated doesn't support her hypothesis. In fact, given there are 25 times more Germans than Norwegians in Inebriated, the data actually run *opposite* to Ms. Representation's hypothesis: The percentage of alcoholic Norwegians is higher than the percentage of alcoholic Germans!

The bottom line: *Don't trust all of the statistics you read in a newspaper.*

Bear in mind that we've focused here on misuses and abuses of statistics. That's because we want to immunize you against statistical errors you're likely to encounter in the newspaper, on TV, as well as on the Internet and social media. But you shouldn't conclude from our examples that we can *never* trust statistics. As we'll learn throughout this text, statistics are a wonderful set of tools that can help us to understand behavior. When evaluating statistics, it's best to steer a middle course between dismissing them out of hand and accepting them uncritically. As is so often the case in psychology, remember that we should keep our minds open, but not so open that our brains fall out.

2.5: Evaluating Psychological Research

2.5a   Identify flaws in research designs and how to correct them.
2.5b   Identify skills for evaluating psychological claims in the popular media.

Every day, the Internet, newspapers, and television bombard us with the results of psychological and medical studies. Some of these studies are trustworthy, yet many others aren't. How can we sort out which are which?

Becoming a Peer Reviewer

Nearly all psychological journals send submitted articles to outside reviewers, who screen the articles carefully for quality control. As we'll recall, this often ego-bruising process is called *peer review*. One crucial task of peer reviewers is to identify flaws that could undermine a study's findings and conclusions, as well as to tell researchers how to do the study better next time. Now that we've learned the key ingredients of a psychological experiment and the pitfalls that can lead experiments to go wrong, let's try our hands at becoming peer reviewers. Doing so will allow us to become better consumers of real-world research.

We'll present descriptions of two studies, modeled after actual published investigations, both of which contain at least one hidden flaw. Read each study and try to figure out what's wrong with it. Once you have, try to suggest a way of fixing the flaw. Then, read the paragraph after it to see how close you came.

Ready? Here goes.

"THAT'S IT? THAT'S PEER REVIEW?"

SOURCE: © ScienceCartoonsPlus.com.

STUDY 1

An investigator, Dr. Sudo Sigh-Ents, sets out to test the hypothesis that subliminal self-help tapes increase self-esteem. She randomly selects 50 college freshmen from the subject pool to receive a commercially available subliminal self-help tape, which contains the words "You will feel better about yourself." She asks them to play the tape for two months each night for one hour before going to sleep (which is consistent with the standard instructions on the tape). Dr. Sigh-Ents measures participants' self-esteem at the start of the study and again after two months. She finds that their self-esteem has increased significantly over these two months, and concludes that "subliminal self-help tapes increase self-esteem."

Question: *What's wrong with this experiment and how would you fix it?*

Answer: What's wrong with this "experiment" is that it's not even an experiment. There's no random assignment of participants to experimental and control groups; in fact, there's no control group at all. There's also no manipulation of an independent variable. Remember that a variable is something that varies. In this case, there's no independent variable because all participants received the same manipulation, namely, playing the subliminal self-help tape every night. As a result, we can't know whether the increase in self-esteem was really the result of the tape. It could have been because of any number of other factors, such as placebo effects or increases in self-esteem that might often occur over the course of one's freshman year.

Next time, Dr. Sigh-Ents would be better off randomly assigning some participants to receive the subliminal self-help tape designed to increase self-esteem and other participants to receive a different subliminal self-help tape, maybe one with neutral instructions (like "You will feel the same about yourself.").

Ruling Out Rival Hypotheses

Have important alternative explanations for the findings been excluded?

STUDY 2

A researcher, Dr. Art E. Fact, is interested in determining whether a new treatment, Anger Expression Therapy, is effective in treating anxiety. He randomly assigns 100 individuals with anxiety disorders to two groups. The experimental group receives Anger Expression Therapy (which is administered by Dr. Fact himself), whereas the control group is placed on a waiting list and receives no treatment. At the conclusion of six months, Dr. Fact interviews his patients and finds that the rate of anxiety disorders is significantly lower in the experimental group than in the control group. He concludes, "Anger Expression Therapy is helpful in the treatment of anxiety disorders."

Question: *What's wrong with this experiment and how would you fix it?*

Answer: On its surface, this experiment looks okay. There's random assignment of participants to experimental and control groups, and manipulation of an independent variable, namely, the presence versus absence of Anger Expression Therapy. But Dr. Fact hasn't controlled for two crucial pitfalls. First, he hasn't controlled for the placebo effect because people receiving Anger Expression Therapy know they're receiving a treatment, and people in the control group know they're not.

To control for this problem, Dr. Fact should probably have built in an *attention-placebo control condition:* A condition in which a counselor provides attention, but no formal psychotherapy, to patients (Baskin et al., 2003). For example, the counselor might chat with her patients once a week for the same length of time as the patients who receive Anger Expression Therapy.

Second, Dr. Fact hasn't controlled for the experimenter expectancy effect. He knows which patients are in which group and could subtly influence patients who are receiving Anger Expression Therapy to improve or report better results. To control for this effect and minimize conformation bias, it might be better to ask the same therapist—someone other than Dr. Fact—to administer both the treatment and control conditions and to keep Dr. Fact blind to the group assignment when he interviews the patients at the conclusion of the study.

Anger Therapy

In an experiment on marital therapy for anger problems, a researcher could examine whether individuals who receive a specific treatment show less anger than people who don't receive this treatment. In such a study, the independent variable is whether the client receives marital therapy for anger. The dependent variable is the level of the client's anger at the end of the study.

Most Reporters Aren't Scientists: Evaluating Psychology in the Media

Few major American newspapers hire reporters with any formal psychological training—the *New York Times* is a notable exception—so we shouldn't assume that people who write news stories about psychology are trained to distinguish psychological fact from fiction, because most of them aren't (Stanovich, 2009a). This means that news stories are prone to faulty conclusions because reporters rely on the same heuristics and biases that we all do.

When evaluating media claims, we often need to consider the source.
SOURCE: Grizelda/CartoonStock Ltd.

When evaluating the accuracy of psychological reports in the media, it's worth keeping a few tips in mind. First, we should *consider the source* (Fritch & Cromwell, 2001; Gilovich, 1991). We should generally place more confidence in a finding reported in a reputable science magazine (like *Scientific American* or *Discover*) than in a supermarket tabloid (like the *National Enquirer*) or a popular magazine (like *People* or *Us*). This "consider the source" principle also applies to websites. Moreover, we should place more trust in findings from primary sources, such as the original journal articles themselves (if we can look them up in the library or on the Internet) than from secondary sources, such as newspapers, magazines, or websites that merely report findings from primary sources.

Second, we need to be on the lookout for excessive *sharpening* and *leveling* (Gilovich, 1991; Hornik et al., 2015). *Sharpening* refers to the tendency to exaggerate the gist, or central message, of a study, whereas *leveling* refers to the tendency to minimize the less central details of a study. Sharpening and leveling often result in a "good story," because they end up bringing the most important facts of a study into sharper focus. Of course, secondary sources in the news media need to engage in a certain amount of sharpening and leveling when reporting studies, because they can't possibly describe every minor detail of an investigation. Still, too much sharpening and leveling can result in a misleading picture. If an investigator discovers that a new medication is effective for 35 percent of people with anxiety disorders, but that a placebo is effective for 33 percent of people with anxiety disorders, the newspaper editor may lead off the story with this eye-popping headline: "Breakthrough: New Medication Outperforms Other Pills in Treating Anxiety." This headline isn't literally wrong, but it oversimplifies greatly what the researcher found.

Third, we can easily be misled by seemingly "balanced" coverage of a story. There's a crucial difference between genuine scientific controversy and the kind of balanced coverage that news reporters create by ensuring that representatives from both sides of the story receive equal air time. When covering a story relating to psychology, the news media usually try to include comments from "experts" (we place this term in quotation marks, because they're not always genuine experts) on opposing sides of an issue to make the story appear more balanced.

The problem is that "balanced coverage" sometimes creates *pseudosymmetry* (Dixon & Clark, 2013; Park, 2002): the appearance of a scientific controversy where none exists. A newspaper might feature a story about a study that provides scientific evidence against extrasensory perception (ESP). They might devote the first four paragraphs to a description of the study but the last four paragraphs to impassioned critiques of the study from ESP advocates. This coverage may create the impression that the scientific evidence for ESP is split right down the middle, with about half of the research supporting it and about half disputing it. It's easy to overlook the fact that there was no scientific evidence in the last four paragraphs, only criticisms of the evidence against ESP. Moreover, the article might fail to note that the scientific evidence regarding ESP is largely negative (Hines, 2003; Wagenmakers et al., 2011).

One reason why most of us find it difficult to think scientifically about research evidence is that we're continually bombarded with media reports that (unintentionally) provide us with poor role models for interpreting research (Lilienfeld, Ruscio, & Lynn, 2008; Stanovich, 2009a). Bearing these tips in mind should help us become better consumers of psychological science in everyday life and to make better real-world decisions.

Evaluating Claims HAIR-LOSS REMEDIES

Imagine yourself working for a federal agency that's received a complaint from a customer regarding potential false advertising. He was entirely bald 1 month ago, and he spent several hundred dollars purchasing weekly bottles of a new hair growth remedy, "Mane-Gro." He's still entirely bald. Your job is to evaluate whether the company's advertisement, which starts with "Grow back a full head of hair in only 3 weeks" is accurate and if so why, and if not, why not. The ad goes on to assert: "We've received confirmation of this remarkable claim from dozens of satisfied customers. Try it yourself and see!"

"Grow back a full head of hair in only 3 weeks!" sounds great (for those of us who've experienced hair loss, that is), but is it too good to be true? Let's evaluate this claim, which isn't terribly different from that found in actual ads for hair-loss remedies.

Consider how the six principles of scientific thinking are relevant as you evaluate this claim.

1. **Ruling Out Rival Hypotheses**

   Have important alternative explanations for the findings been excluded?

   The claim in the ad is open to a host of alternative explanations. For example, perhaps "the dozens of satisfied customers" were merely a tiny subset of customers who were satisfied; the company understandably may not have wanted to promote the experiences of its hundreds or thousands of dissatisfied customers. Also, the company may be exaggerating the claims; for example, perhaps a handful of customers noticed what appeared to be a slight return of their hair growth rather than a return of a full head of hair. It's also possible that the satisfied customers were using other hair growth products at the same time, and that these other products, not Mane-Gro, were causing the hair growth.

2. **Correlation vs. Causation**

   Can we be sure that A causes B?

   This critical thinking principle isn't especially relevant to the scenario.

3. **Falsifiability**

   Can the claim be disproved?

   In principle, the claim that the product allows customers to grow back a full head of hair could be falsified, ideally by conducting multiple well-controlled experiments in which some participants receive Mane-Gro and others receive a pla-

cebo. But the company apparently didn't conduct these experiments; or, if they did, they're not telling us what they found.

4. **Replicability**

   Can the results be duplicated in other studies?

   It's not even clear that the company conducted a controlled study in the first place, let alone attempted to replicate it. In any case, there's no evidence that the claim is backed up by independently replicated results.

5. **Extraordinary Claims**

   Is the evidence as strong as the claim?

   Even the ad itself acknowledges that the claim is "remarkable." Yet the evidence for the assertion is quite feeble; it's based entirely on anecdotes, which are almost always a weak source of scientific support.

6. **Occam's Razor**

   Does a simpler explanation fit the data just as well?

   There may well be far simpler explanations for the company's claim. For example, it's plausible that the company is presenting only the testimonials of people for whom the product worked—or at least appeared to work.

Summary

In summary, the claim that the product results in rapid and dramatic hair regrowth should be viewed with considerable skepticism. It's an extraordinary claim that it isn't supported by much evidence, and it's open to a host of rival explanations.

Journal Prompt

Why might journalists provide "balanced coverage" of a controversial story on psychological research? What are some problems with using this approach in journalism?

Summary: Research Methods

2.1: The Beauty and Necessity of Good Research Design

2.1a   Identify two modes of thinking and their applications controversial to scientific reasoning.

Increasing evidence suggests that there are two major modes of thinking. System 1 thinking, or "intuitive thinking," tends to be rapid and to rely on gut hunches, whereas System 2 thinking, or "analytical thinking," tends to be slow and to rely on a thoughtful examination of issues. Research designs make use of analytical thinking because scientific reasoning often requires us to question and at times override our intuitions about the world.

2.2: Scientific Methodology: A Toolbox of Skills

2.2a   Describe the advantages and disadvantages of naturalistic observation, case studies, self-report measures, and surveys.

Naturalistic observation, case studies, self-report measures, and surveys are all important research designs. Naturalistic observation involves recording behaviors in real-world settings but is often not carefully controlled. Case studies involve examining one or a few individuals over long periods of time; these designs are often useful in generating hypotheses but are typically limited in testing them rigorously. Self-report measures and surveys ask people about themselves; they can provide a wealth of useful information, but have certain disadvantages, especially response sets.

2.2b   Describe the role of correlational designs and distinguish correlation from causation.

Correlational studies allow us to establish the relations among two or more measures but do not allow for causal conclusions. Illusory correlation occurs when we mistakenly perceive a statistical association in its absence; correlational designs help to compensate for this error.

2.2c   Identify the components of an experiment, the potential pitfalls that can lead to faulty conclusions, and how psychologists control for these pitfalls.

Experimental designs involve random assignment of participants to conditions and manipulation of an independent variable, and when conducted properly, permit us to draw conclusions about the causes of a psychological intervention. Placebo effects and experimenter expectancy effects are examples of pitfalls in experimental designs that can lead us to draw false conclusions.

2.3: Ethical Issues in Research Design

2.3a   Explain the ethical obligations of researchers toward their research participants.

Concerns about ethical treatment of research participants have led research facilities, such as colleges and universities, to establish institutional review boards review all research involving human participants and require informed consent by participants. In some cases, they may also require a full debriefing at the conclusion of the research session.

2.3b   Describe both sides of the debate on the use of animals as research subjects.

Animal research has led to clear benefits in our understanding of human learning, brain physiology, and psychological treatment, to mention only a few advances. To answer many critical psychological questions, there are simply no good alternatives to using animals. Nevertheless, many critics have raised useful questions about the treatment of laboratory animals and emphasized the need for adequate housing and feeding conditions. Many protest the large number of laboratory animals killed each year and question whether animal research offers sufficient external validity to justify its use.

2.4: Statistics: The Language of Psychological Research

2.4a   Identify uses of various measures of central tendency and variability.

Three measures of central tendency are the mean, median, and mode. The mean is the average of all scores. The median is the middle score. The mode is the most frequent score. The mean is the most widely used measure but is the most sensitive to extreme scores. Two measures of variability are the range and standard deviation. The range is a more intuitive measure of variability, but it can yield a deceptive picture of how spread out individual scores are. The standard deviation is a better measure of variability, although it's more difficult to calculate.

2.4b   Explain how inferential statistics can help us to determine whether we can generalize from our sample to the full population.

Inferential statistics allow us to determine how much we can generalize findings from our sample to the full population. Not all statistically significant findings are large enough in magnitude to make a real-world difference, so we must also consider practical significance when evaluating the implications of our results.

2.4c   Show how statistics can be misused for purposes of persuasion.

Reporting measures of central tendency that are nonrepresentative of most participants, creating visual representations that exaggerate effects, and failing to take base rates into account are all frequent methods of manipulating statistics for the purposes of persuasion.

2.5: Evaluating Psychological Research

2.5a   Identify flaws in research designs and how to correct for them.

Good experimental design requires not only random assignment and manipulation of an independent variable but also inclusion of an appropriate control condition to rule out placebo effects. Most important, it requires careful attention to the possibility of alternative explanations of observed effects.

2.5b   Identify skills for evaluating psychological claims in the popular media.

To evaluate psychological claims in the news and elsewhere in the popular media, we should bear in mind that few reporters have formal psychological training. When considering media claims, we should consider the source, beware of excessive sharpening and leveling, and be on the lookout for pseudosymmetry.

endorphin

chemical in the brain that plays a specialized role in pain reduction

Some drugs work in the opposite way, functioning as *antagonists*, meaning they decrease receptor site activity (think of the word *antagonistic*). In essence, antagonists act as "fake neurotransmitters," fooling receptors into thinking they are dopamine without exerting the effects of this neurotransmitter. Imagine if you'd jammed a fake key into your neighbor's door lock, one that was shaped almost exactly like the correct key but that didn't open the door. Your neighbor would be locked out, not to mention rather annoyed. Antagonists work in much the same way.

Most medications used to treat the severe mental disorder of schizophrenia block dopamine receptors by binding to them, thereby preventing dopamine from binding to the receptors themselves (Bennett, 1998; Compton & Broussard, 2009). Another example of an antagonist is the Botulinum toxin, known as the cosmetic agent Botox™, which causes paralysis by blocking acetylcholine's actions on muscles. This paralysis temporarily decreases small wrinkles, such as those on our foreheads and around our eyes, by relaxing those muscles (Mukherjee, 2015).

Neural Plasticity: How and When the Brain Changes

plasticity

ability of the nervous system to change

We'll conclude our guided tour of neurons by looking at the ability of the nervous system to change. Nature—our genetic makeup—influences what kind of changes are possible and when they'll occur during the long and winding road from birth to old age. Nurture, consisting of learning, life events, injuries, and illnesses, affects our genetically influenced course. Scientists use the term **plasticity** to describe the nervous system's ability to change over time, such as in response to damage. Some scientists speak of brain circuits being "hardwired" when they don't change much, if at all.

But despite what the popular media often implies, precious few human behaviors are truly hardwired. So when we hear claims about language, jealousy, morality, or other human capacities being "hardwired," we should be skeptical (Lilienfeld et al., 2015). We're genetically predisposed toward these abilities, but they aren't fixed, let alone predetermined. The nervous system is continually changing, by leaps and bounds, as in early development, or more subtly, as with learning. Unfortunately, the nervous system often doesn't change enough following injury or stroke, which can lead to permanent paralysis and disability.

NEURAL PLASTICITY OVER DEVELOPMENT. Typically, our brain is most flexible during early development, when much of our nervous system has yet to be set in stone. That's because our brains don't mature fully until late adolescence or early adulthood. Some brain structures mature more rapidly than others. So some parts of the brain are quite plastic throughout childhood, but others lose their extreme plasticity in infancy.

The network of neurons in the brain changes over the course of development in four primary ways:

1. *growth* of dendrites and axons;
2. *synaptogenesis*, the formation of new synapses;
3. *pruning*, consisting of the death of certain neurons and the retraction of axons to remove connections that aren't useful; and
4. *myelination*, the insulation of axons with a myelin sheath.

Of these four steps, pruning is perhaps the most surprising. During pruning, as many as 70 percent of all neurons die off. This process is helpful, though, because it streamlines neural organization, thereby enhancing communication among brain structures (Oppenheim, 1991). In a real sense, less is more, because our brains can often process information more efficiently with fewer neurons, much as a committee can often make decisions more efficiently with fewer members. One theory of autism spectrum disorder, often referred to more simply as autism, suggests that this condition is caused by inadequate pruning (Hill & Frith, 2003), which may explain why individuals with autism tend to have unusually large brains (Herbert, 2005). It's an intriguing story, but some researchers aren't persuaded (Thomas et al., 2016).

NEURAL PLASTICITY AND LEARNING. Our brains change as we learn. These changes can result from the formation of new synapses, generating increased connections and communication among neurons. They can also result from the strengthening of existing synaptic connections, so that the neurotransmitters released into synapses produce a stronger and more prolonged response from neighboring neurons. Researchers call this second phenomenon *potentiation* (see LO 7.3a).

Many scientists believe that structural plasticity, that is, changes in the shape of neurons, is critical for learning (Woolf, 2006). In one study, researchers trained rats to swim to a platform hidden in a tub of milky water. By the time the rats became adept at doing so, axons entering a part of their brains relevant to spatial ability had expanded (Holahan et al., 2006). Exposure to enriched environments also changes the structure of dendrites. For example, rats exposed to an enriched environment—such as large cages with multiple animals, toys, and running wheels—develop more elaborate dendrites with more branches than do rats exposed to a standard environment of a cage with only two animals and no objects (Freire & Cheng, 2004; Leggio et al., 2005; see Figure 3.5).

NEURAL PLASTICITY FOLLOWING INJURY AND DEGENERATION.
The human brain and spinal cord display only limited regeneration following injury or serious illness. Still, certain brain regions can sometimes take over the functions previously performed by others, just as some members of a sports team can often take over for an injured player. For example, in blind people, the capacity to read Braille (a system of raised dots that correspond to letters in the alphabet) with the fingers is taken over by brain regions associated with vision in sighted people (Hamilton & Pascual-Leone, 1998; Sathian, 2005).

Scientists are trying to find ways to enhance the brain and spinal cord's abilities to repair themselves following injury (Maier & Schwab, 2006). Because neurodegenerative disorders, such as Alzheimer's disease, Parkinson's disease, and amytrophic lateral sclerosis ([ALS] or "Lou Gehrig's disease," after the Hall of Fame baseball player who died from it), pose enormous challenges to society, scientists are actively investigating ways of preventing damage or enabling the brain to heal itself.

Adult Neurogenesis. **Neurogenesis** is the creation of new neurons in the adult brain. Fewer than 20 years ago, most scientists were sure that we're born with all the neurons we'll ever have. Then, Fred Gage (interestingly, believed to be a descendant of Phineas Gage, whom we'll meet later in the chapter), Elizabeth Gould, and their colleagues discovered that in adult monkeys, neurogenesis occurs in certain brain areas (Gage, 2002; Gould & Gross, 2002). The odds are good that neurogenesis sometimes occurs in adult human brains too, although this issue remains scientifically controversial (Dennis et al., 2016). By triggering neurogenesis, scientists may one day be able to induce the adult nervous system to heal itself (Kozorovitskiy & Gould, 2003; Lie et al., 2004). Neurogenesis may also play a useful role in learning (Aimone, Wiles, & Gage, 2006).

Stem Cells. Many of us have heard or read about research on stem cells, especially embryonic stem cells, in the news. One reason they've garnered so much attention is that **stem cells** haven't yet committed themselves to a specific function, so they have the potential to become a wide variety of specialized cells (see Figure 3.6). This is akin to being a first-year undergraduate who's yet to declare a major: He or she could become nearly anything. Once the cell begins to specialize, though, the cell type becomes more permanently cast, much like an undergraduate who's spent three years taking pre-med courses. Stem cells offer several ways of treating diseases marked by neural degeneration (Fukuda & Takahashi, 2005; Miller, 2006; Muller, Snyder, & Loring, 2006). For example, researchers can implant stem cells directly into the host's nervous system and induce them to grow and replace damaged cells. In addition, researchers can genetically engineer stem cells to provide gene therapy—that is, provide the patient with replacement genes.

Yet stem-cell research is exceedingly controversial for ethical reasons. Although its advocates champion its potential for treating serious diseases, including Alzheimer's, diabetes, and some cancers, its opponents point out that such research requires investigators to create and then extract lab-created balls of cells that are four or five days old (which at that stage are smaller than the period at the end of this sentence). For opponents of stem-cell research, these cells are an early form of human life. As we learned

Figure 3.5 Neurons in Standard and Enriched Conditions.

Neurons of rats reared in enriched conditions (*bottom*) show more branching and extensions of dendrites than do neurons of rats reared in standard conditions (*top*).

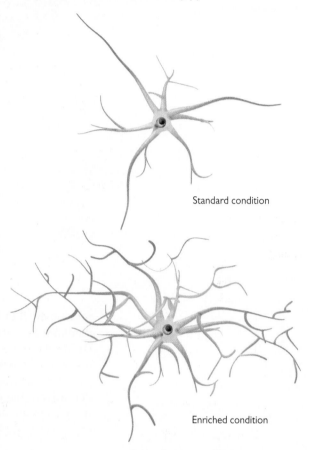

Standard condition

Enriched condition

neurogenesis

creation of new neurons in the adult brain

stem cell

a cell, often originating in embryos, having the capacity to differentiate into a more specialized cell

Senile plaques (large yellow/black splotch on lower left) and neurofibrillary tangles (smaller yellow spots) in the brain of a patient with Alzheimer's disease. The degeneration in several brain regions may contribute to the memory loss and intellectual decline associated with this disorder.

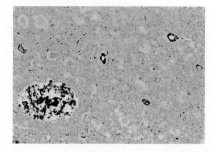

Figure 3.6 Stem Cells and Growth Factors.

Stem cells have the capacity to become many different cell types depending on the growth factors to which they're exposed.

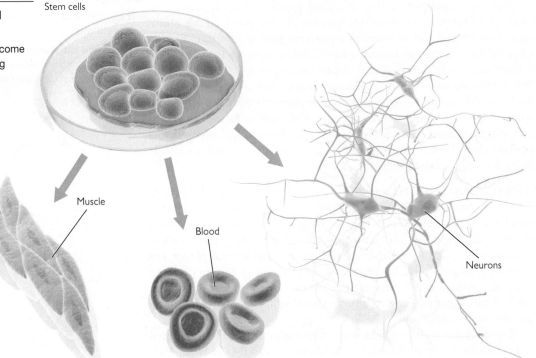

Stem cells

Muscle

Blood

Neurons

previously (LO 1.1b), certain profoundly important questions are metaphysical and therefore lie outside the boundaries of science: Science deals only with testable claims within the realm of the natural world (Gould, 1997). The question of whether stem-cell research may one day cure diseases falls within the scope of science, but the question of whether such research is ethical doesn't. Nor, in all likelihood, can science ever resolve definitively the question of when human life begins (Buckle, Dawson, & Singer, 1989). As a consequence, reasonable people will continue to disagree on whether stem-cell research should be performed.

3.2: The Brain–Behavior Network

3.2a Identify what roles different parts of the central nervous system play in behavior.

3.2b Clarify how the somatic and autonomic nervous systems work in emergency and everyday situations.

The trillions of connections among our neurons provide the physiological bases of our thoughts, emotions, and observable behaviors. But how do we get from electrical charges and the release of neurotransmitters to complex behaviors, like writing a term paper or asking someone out for a date? Let's say we decide to walk to a vending machine to buy a can of soda. How does our brain, this motley collection of tens of billions of neurons, accomplish this feat? First, our brain "decides" to do so—or at least so it seems. Second, our nervous system propels our body into action. Third, we need to locate and operate the vending machine. We must accurately identify the machine based on how it looks and feels, insert the right amount of money, and retrieve our soda to take a well-deserved sip. Communication among neurons in the vast network of connections we call our nervous system allows us to take these complex actions for granted.

We can think of our nervous system as a superhighway with a two-way flow of traffic. Sensory information comes into—and decisions to act come out of—the **central nervous system (CNS)**. The CNS is composed of the brain and spinal cord, whereas the **peripheral nervous system (PNS)** (see Figure 3.7) is composed of all the nerves that extend outside of the CNS. The PNS is further divided into the *somatic nervous*

central nervous system (CNS)

part of nervous system containing the brain and spinal cord that controls the mind and behavior

peripheral nervous system (PNS)

nerves in the body that extend outside the central nervous system (CNS)

Figure 3.7 The Nervous System Exerts Control over the Body.

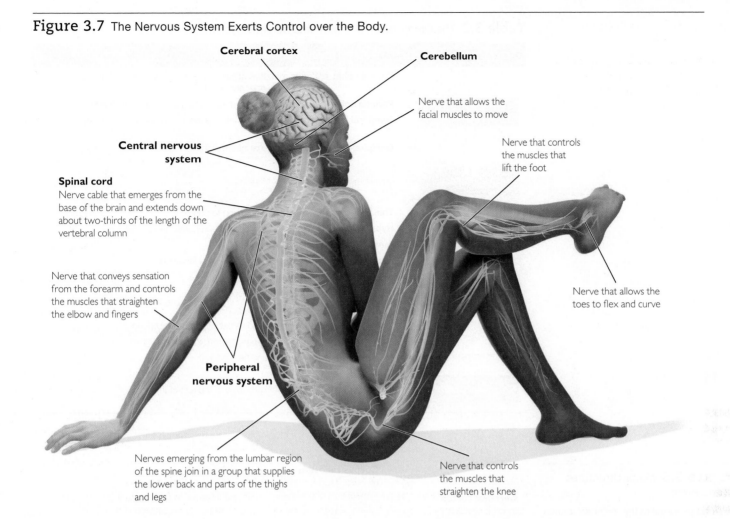

Cerebral cortex

Cerebellum

Nerve that allows the facial muscles to move

Central nervous system

Nerve that controls the muscles that lift the foot

Spinal cord
Nerve cable that emerges from the base of the brain and extends down about two-thirds of the length of the vertebral column

Nerve that conveys sensation from the forearm and controls the muscles that straighten the elbow and fingers

Nerve that allows the toes to flex and curve

Peripheral nervous system

Nerves emerging from the lumbar region of the spine join in a group that supplies the lower back and parts of the thighs and legs

Nerve that controls the muscles that straighten the knee

system, which controls voluntary behavior, and the *autonomic nervous system*, which controls nonvoluntary functions of the body. When you see the word *autonomic* before the words *nervous system*, think of the similar word *automatic*, because the autonomic nervous system controls behaviors that occur automatically, that is, outside of our conscious awareness.

The Central Nervous System: The Command Center

Scientists divide the CNS into six distinct sections or systems (see Table 3.2). The brain and spinal cord are protected by *meninges*, three thin layers of membranes. Further protection is afforded by the **cerebral ventricles**, fluid-filled pockets that extend throughout the brain and spinal cord. A clear liquid, called *cerebrospinal fluid* (CSF), runs through these ventricles and bathes our brain and spinal cord, providing nutrients and cushioning us against injury. This fluid is the CNS's shock absorber, allowing us to move our heads rapidly in everyday life without sustaining brain damage.

As we review different brain regions, bear in mind that although they serve different functions, they cooperate seamlessly to generate our thoughts, feelings, and observable behaviors (see Figure 3.8). We'll begin our guided tour of the brain with the part of the brain studied most extensively by psychologists.

THE CEREBRAL CORTEX. The **cerebral cortex** analyzes sensory information, helping us to perform complex brain functions, including reasoning and language. It's the largest component of the *cerebrum* or **forebrain**, the most highly developed area of the human brain, containing some 12 to 20 billion neurons, and accounting for about

cerebral ventricles

pockets in the brain that contain cerebrospinal fluid (CSF), which provide the brain with nutrients and cushion against injury

cerebral cortex

outermost part of forebrain, responsible for analyzing sensory processing and higher brain functions

forebrain (cerebrum)

forward part of the brain that allows advanced intellectual abilities

Table 3.2 The Organization of the Central Nervous System.

Central Nervous System	
Cortex	**Frontal Lobe:** performs executive functions that coordinate other brain areas, motor planning, language, and memory **Parietal Lobe:** processes touch information; integrates vision and touch **Temporal Lobe:** processes auditory information, language, and autobiographical memory **Occipital Lobe:** processes visual information
Basal Ganglia	control movement and motor planning
Limbic system	**Thalamus:** conveys sensory information to cortex **Hypothalamus:** oversees endocrine and autonomic nervous system **Amygdala:** regulates arousal and fear **Hippocampus:** processes memory for spatial locations
Cerebellum	controls balance and coordinated movement
Brain Stem	**Midbrain:** tracks visual stimuli and reflexes triggered by sound **Pons:** conveys information between the cortex and cerebellum **Medulla:** regulates breathing and heartbeats
Spinal Cord	conveys information between the brain and the rest of the body

Figure 3.8 Major Structures of the Brain.

A broad overview of the major structures of the human brain, including the cerebral cortex.

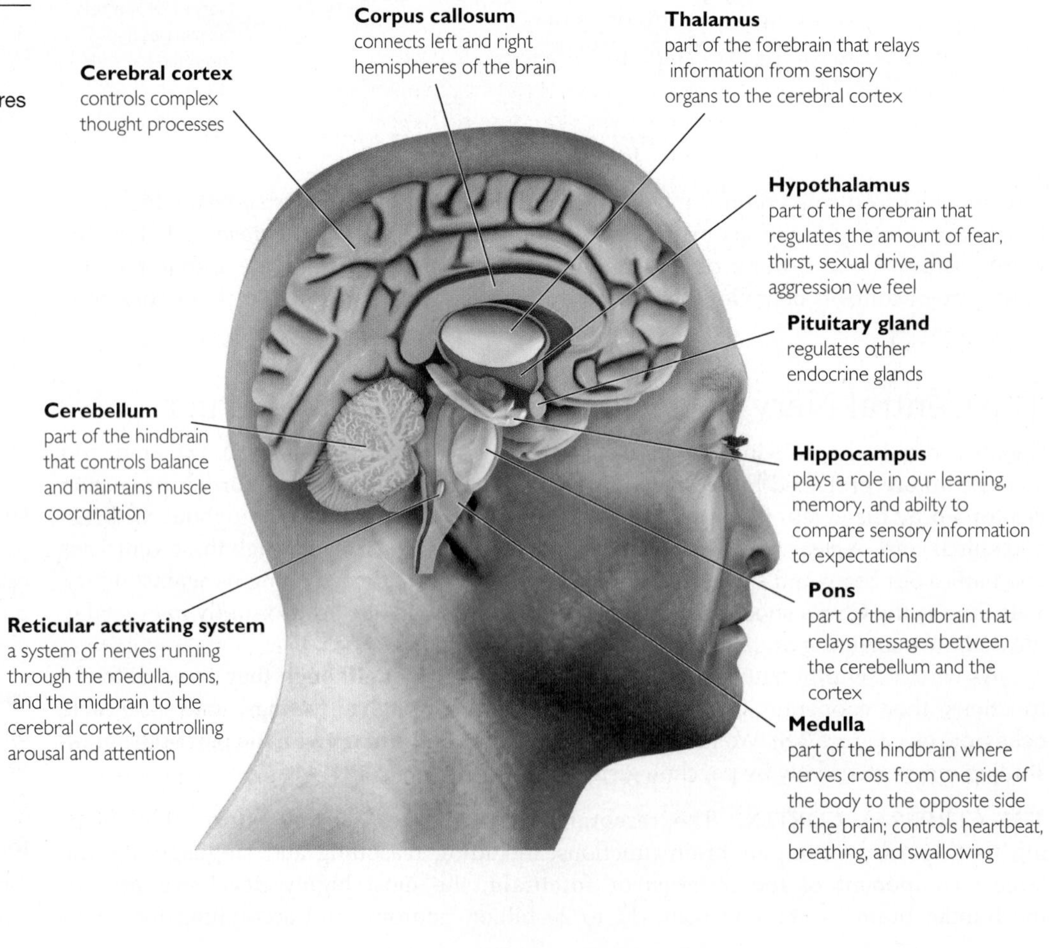

Corpus callosum
connects left and right hemispheres of the brain

Thalamus
part of the forebrain that relays information from sensory organs to the cerebral cortex

Cerebral cortex
controls complex thought processes

Hypothalamus
part of the forebrain that regulates the amount of fear, thirst, sexual drive, and aggression we feel

Pituitary gland
regulates other endocrine glands

Cerebellum
part of the hindbrain that controls balance and maintains muscle coordination

Hippocampus
plays a role in our learning, memory, and abilty to compare sensory information to expectations

Pons
part of the hindbrain that relays messages between the cerebellum and the cortex

Reticular activating system
a system of nerves running through the medulla, pons, and the midbrain to the cerebral cortex, controlling arousal and attention

Medulla
part of the hindbrain where nerves cross from one side of the body to the opposite side of the brain; controls heartbeat, breathing, and swallowing

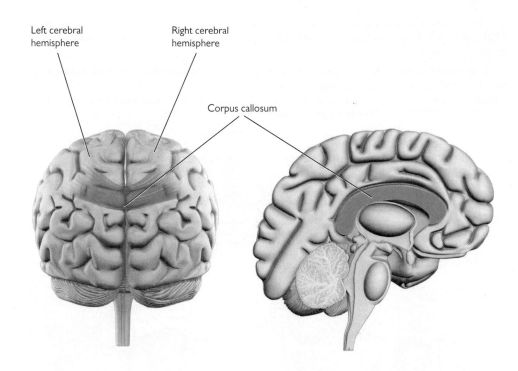

Left cerebral hemisphere

Right cerebral hemisphere

Corpus callosum

Figure 3.9 The Cerebral Hemispheres and the Corpus Callosum.

The corpus callosum connects the two cerebral hemispheres.

cerebral hemispheres

two halves of the cerebral cortex, each of which serve distinct yet highly integrated functions

corpus callosum

large band of fibers connecting the two cerebral hemispheres

40 percent of its volume. The cerebrum gives us our advanced intellectual abilities—which explains why it's of such keen interest to psychologists. The cerebrum consists of two **cerebral hemispheres** (see Figure 3.9). These hemispheres look alike but serve somewhat different functions. Nevertheless, like two figure skaters in a pairs competition, they communicate and cooperate continually. A huge band of fibers called the **corpus callosum**, meaning *colossal body* in Latin, connects the two hemispheres and permits them to communicate (see Figure 3.10).

The cerebral cortex is the outermost part of the cerebrum. It's aptly named, because "cortex" means *bark*, as the cortex surrounds the hemispheres much like bark on a tree. In turn, the cortex contains four regions called *lobes*, each associated with somewhat different functions (see Figure 3.10). Each of our hemispheres contains the same four lobes; they are the next stops in our tour.

Frontal Lobes. The **frontal lobes** lie in the forward part of the cerebral cortex. If you touch your forehead right now, your fingers are less than an inch away from your frontal lobes. The frontal lobes assist us in motor function (movement), language, and memory. They also oversee and organize most other brain functions, a process called *executive functioning*. Just as the U.S. president exerts control over the members of his or her cabinet, the brain's executive function provides a kind of top-level governance over other cognitive functions (Alvarez & Emory, 2006; Miyake & Friedman, 2012).

In most people's brains, a deep groove, called the *central sulcus*, separates the frontal lobe from the rest of the cortex. The **motor cortex** is the part of the frontal lobe that lies next to the central sulcus. Each part of the motor cortex controls a specific part of the body, with regions requiring more precise motor control, like our fingers, consuming more cortical space (see Figure 3.11).

Figure 3.10 The Four Lobes of the Cerebral Cortex.

The cerebral cortex consists of four interacting lobes: frontal, parietal, temporal, and occipital.

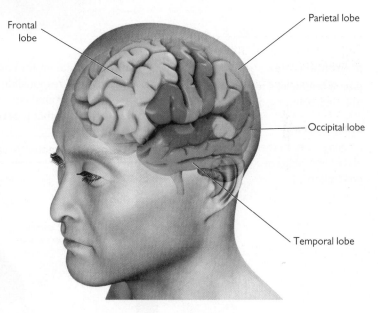

Frontal lobe

Parietal lobe

Occipital lobe

Temporal lobe

frontal lobe

forward part of cerebral cortex responsible for motor function, language, memory, and planning

motor cortex

part of frontal lobe responsible for body movement

Figure 3.11 Representation of the Body Mapped on to the Motor and Sensory Areas of the Cerebral Cortex.

The brain networks with the body in a systematic way, with specific regions of both the motor and primary sensory cortex mapping onto specific regions of the body.

SOURCE: Marieb, Elaine N.; Hoehn, Katja, Human Anatomy and Physiology, 7th Ed., c.2007. Reprinted and Electronically reproduced by permission of Pearson Education, Inc., Upper Saddle River, New Jersey.

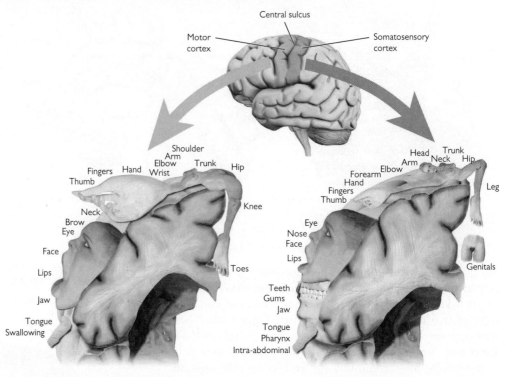

prefrontal cortex

part of frontal lobe responsible for thinking, planning, and language

Broca's area

language area in the prefrontal cortex that helps to control speech production

In front of the motor cortex lies a vast expanse of the frontal lobe called the **prefrontal cortex**, which is responsible for thinking, planning, and language (see Figure 3.12). One region of the prefrontal cortex, **Broca's area**, is named after French surgeon Paul Broca, who promoted the idea that it plays a key role in language production (Broca, 1861). Broca found

Figure 3.12 Selected Areas of the Cerebral Cortex.

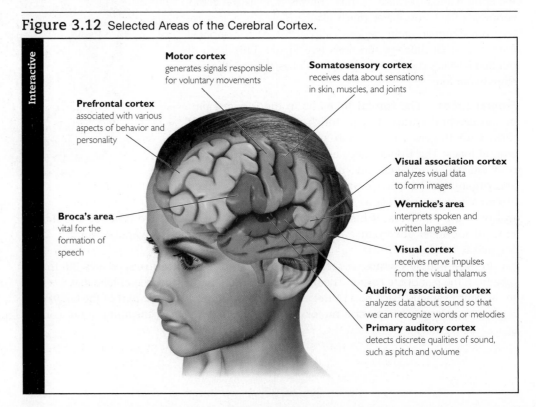

that this site was damaged in many patients who were having trouble generating speech. His first patient with this strange condition, known by the name of "Tan," responded only with the word *Tan* when asked questions. Broca and his colleagues soon recognized that brain damage in Tan and other patients with this speech disorder was almost always confined to the left cerebral hemisphere (Kean, 2014), a finding replicated by many researchers.

Replicability

Can the results be duplicated in other studies?

The prefrontal cortex, which receives information from many other regions of the cerebral cortex, also contributes to mood, personality, and self-awareness (Chayer & Freedman, 2001; Fuster, 2000). For example, damage to this region often boosts people's risk for impulsive or even criminal behaviors (Glenn & Raine, 2014). The famous story of Phineas Gage demonstrates the role of the prefrontal cortex in personality.

Gage was a railroad foreman who experienced a horrific accident in 1848. His job was to build railroad tracks running through rural Vermont. Gage was performing his usual task of filling holes with gunpowder to break up stubborn rock formations. He was pressing gunpowder into one hole with a tamping iron when an explosion suddenly propelled the iron with great velocity through his head. The iron pierced Gage's face under his cheekbone and destroyed much of his prefrontal cortex. Later computer analyses suggested that the rod passed largely or entirely through his left frontal lobes (Ratiu et al., 2004). Remarkably, Gage survived but he was a changed man. His physician, J. M. Harlow (1848), described Gage's personality after the accident as

> fitful, irreverent, indulging at times in the grossest profanity (which was not previously his custom)…his mind was radically changed, so decidedly that his friends and acquaintances said he was "no longer Gage."

Nevertheless, there's growing historical evidence that Gage's personality changes may not have been as drastic or as long-lasting as sometimes assumed. For example, for years following the accident, Gage worked as a successful stage coach driver in Chile, and a doctor who examined him around this time found him to be largely normal (Griggs, 2015; MacMillan, 2000; MacMillan & Lena, 2010). Hence, the Gage story, sad as it is, may have something of a happier ending that most psychologists have believed. Moreover, this ending reminds us of the brain's plasticity, and its often astounding ability to recover at least some of its function even in the face of devastating damage.

History tragically repeated itself in August 2012, when the frontal lobe of an Argentinian construction worker named Eduardo Leite was impaled by a six-foot pole. Amazingly, Leite survived and appears to be doing well, but it's too early to tell whether he'll emerge free of personality difficulties (MacKinnon, 2012).

Parietal Lobe. The **parietal lobe** is the upper middle part of the cerebral cortex lying behind the frontal lobe (refer to Figure 3.11). The back region of the parietal lobe, positioned just behind the motor cortex, is the primary sensory cortex, which is sensitive to touch, including pressure and pain, and temperature (Figure 3.12). The parietal lobe helps us track objects' locations (Nachev & Husain, 2006; Shomstein & Yantis, 2006), shapes, and orientations. It also helps us process others' actions and represents numbers (Gobel & Rushworth, 2004). The parietal lobe relays visual and touch information to the motor cortex every time we reach, grasp, and move our eyes (Culham & Valyear, 2006). If you close your eyes right now and try to imagine how the pillow on your bed feels, you can conjure up a mental image of that soft, fluffy, sensation. That's your parietal lobe at work.

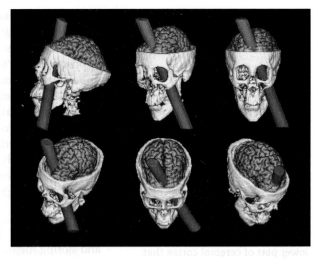

A computerized reconstruction of the tamping iron that passed through Phineas Gage's head. As we can see, the iron apparently passed through his left frontal lobes.

In 2009, this photograph of a man believed by historians to be Phineas Gage surfaced (Wilgus & Wilgus, 2009). One can clearly see (a) Gage holding the huge tamping rod that passed through his frontal lobes, (b) his missing left eye, which was destroyed by the rod, and (c) a tuft of hair on the left side of his head, presumably covering the region of his scalp from which the rod exited.

parietal lobe

upper middle part of the cerebral cortex lying behind the frontal lobe that's specialized for touch and perception

Figure 3.13 The Limbic System.
The limbic system consists mainly of the thalamus, hypothalamus, amygdala, and hippocampus.

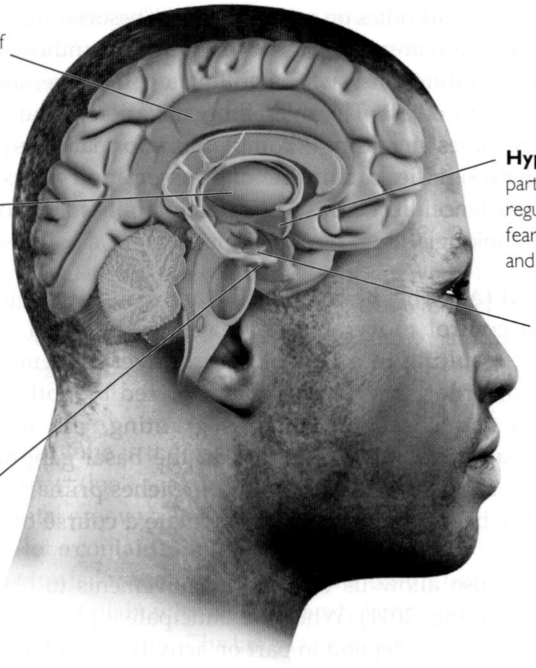

Cingulate cortex
primary cortical component of the limbic system, involved in emotional and cognitive processing

Thalamus
part of the forebrain that relays information from sensory organs to the cerebral cortex

Hippocampus
plays a role in our learning, memory, and ability to compare sensory information to expectations

Hypothalamus
part of the forebrain that regulates the amount of fear, thirst, sexual drive, and aggression we feel

Amygdala
influences our motivation, emotional control, fear response, and interpretations of nonverbal emotional expressions

thalamus

gateway from the sense organs to the primary sensory cortex

hypothalamus

part of the brain responsible for maintaining a constant internal state

amygdala

part of limbic system that plays key roles in fear, excitement, and arousal

hippocampus

part of the brain that plays a role in spatial memory

Replicability

Can the results be duplicated in other studies?

We'll next explore four especially crucial areas of the limbic system: the thalamus, the hypothalamus, the amygdala, and the hippocampus (see Figure 3.13).

The **thalamus** contains many areas, each of which connects to a specific region of the cerebral cortex. We can think of the thalamus as a sensory relay station. The vast majority of sensory information first passes through its doors, undergoing some initial processing, before traveling on to the cortex (refer again to Figure 3.13).

The **hypothalamus** (meaning "below the thalamus"), located on the floor of the brain, regulates and maintains constant internal bodily states. Different areas of the hypothalamus play various roles in emotion and motivation. Some are intimately involved with key psychological drives, helping to regulate hunger, thirst, sexual motivation, or other emotional behaviors. An old joke, relayed to generations of psychology students, is that the hypothalamus plays a key role in the "Four Fs": feeding, fighting, fleeing, and sexual activity (Lambert, 2011). The hypothalamus also assists with controlling our body temperature, acting much like a thermostat that adjusts our home's temperature in response to indoor changes in temperature.

The **amygdala** which is shaped like an almond (indeed, the term *amygdala* is derived from the Greek word for almond), is responsible for excitement, arousal, and especially fear. In studies of teenagers, the amygdala kicks into high gear when people play violent video games (Mathews et al., 2006), or when we view fearful faces (Killgore & Yergelun-Todd, 2005). It also plays a key role in fear conditioning, a process by which animals, including humans, learn to predict when something scary is about to happen (Davis & Shi, 2000; LeDoux, 2000). Ralph Adolphs and colleagues verified the role of the amygdala in fear in a 30-year-old woman, S. M., whose left and right amygdalas were almost entirely destroyed by a a rare disease. Although she had no difficulty identifying faces, she was markedly impaired in detecting fear in these faces (Adolphs et al., 1994). In addition, she displayed no fear when asked to handle a snake in a pet store and was not at all frightened during horror movies, like *The Blair Witch Project* (Feinstein et al., 2011; Lilienfeld et al., 2015). Still, as we've learned previously in the text (LO 2.2a) we need to take isolated case studies with a grain of salt, so replication of these findings in other individuals with amygdala damage will be important.

The **hippocampus** plays crucial roles in memory, especially spatial memory—the memory of the physical layout of things in our environment. When we make a mental map of how to get from one place to another, we're in part using our hippocampus. This may explain why a portion of the hippocampus is larger in London taxi drivers than in non–taxi drivers and is especially large in experienced taxi drivers (Maguire et al., 2000). This correlation could mean either that people with greater amounts of experience navigating complex environments develop larger hippocampi or that people with larger hippocampi seek out occupations, such as taxi driving, which rely on spatial navigation (or both). One study that could help us figure out what's causing what would be to examine whether cab drivers' hippocampi become larger as they acquire more driving experience. Although researchers haven't yet conducted such an investigation, they've looked at this issue in people who've recently learned to juggle. Sure enough, they've found evidence for short-term increases in the size of the hippocampus, suggesting that this brain area can indeed change in size following learning (Boyke et al., 2008).

Correlation vs. Causation

Can we be sure that A causes B?

The hippocampi of taxi drivers seem to be especially large, although the causal direction of this finding is unclear.

Damage to the hippocampus causes problems with forming new memories, but leaves old memories intact. One hypothesis is that the hippocampus houses memories temporarily before transferring them to other sites, such as the cortex, for permanent storage (Sanchez-Andres, Olds, & Alkon, 1993). The multiple trace theory is a rival hypothesis of memory storage in the hippocampus (Moscovitch et al., 2005). According to this theory, memories are initially stored at multiple sites. Over time, storage becomes stronger at some sites but weaker at others. The multiple trace theory implies that memories aren't transferred from the hippocampus to the cortex. Instead, memories are already stored in the cortex and merely strengthen over time.

Ruling out Rival Hypotheses

Have important alternative explanations for the findings been excluded?

THE CEREBELLUM. The **cerebellum** is Latin for "little brain," and in many respects it's a miniature version of the cortex. Part of the hindbrain, the cerebellum plays a predominant role in our sense of balance and enables us to coordinate movement and learn motor skills. Among other things, it helps prevent us from falling down. Not surprisingly, when humans experience damage to the cerebellum, they frequently suffer from serious balance problems (Fredericks, 1996). But in recent years, scientists have come to realize that the cerebellum does much more than stabilize our movements: It also contributes to executive, memory, spatial, and linguistic abilities (Schmahmann, 2004; Swain, Kerr, & Thompson, 2011).

cerebellum

brain structure responsible for our sense of balance

THE BRAIN STEM. The **brain stem**, housed inside the cortex and located at the very back of our brains, contains the *midbrain, pons,* and the *medulla* (see Figure 3.14).

brain stem

part of the brain between the spinal cord and cerebral cortex that contains the midbrain, pons, and medulla

Figure 3.14 The Brain Stem.

The brain stem is located at the top of the spinal cord, below the cortex.

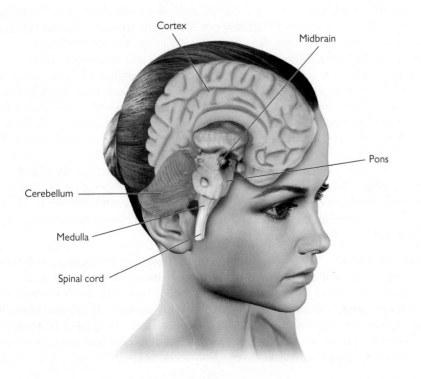

Cortex

Midbrain

Pons

Cerebellum

Medulla

Spinal cord

midbrain

part of the brain stem that contributes to movement, tracking of visual stimuli, and reflexes triggered by sound

reticular activating system (RAS)

brain area that plays a key role in arousal

Ruling Out Rival Hypotheses ▶

Have important alternative explanations for the findings been excluded?

---

hindbrain

region below the midbrain that contains the cerebellum, pons, and medulla

pons

part of the brain stem that connects the cortex with the cerebellum

medulla

part of the brain stem involved in basic functions, such as heartbeat and breathing

spinal cord

thick bundle of nerves that conveys signals between the brain and the body

The brain stem performs some of the basic bodily functions that keep us alive. The **midbrain**, in turn, plays an important role in movement. It also controls the tracking of visual stimuli and reflexes triggered by sound, like jumping after we're startled by a car backfiring.

Reticular Activating System. The **reticular activating system (RAS)** connects with the forebrain and cerebral cortex; this system plays a key role in arousal. Damage to the RAS can result in a coma. Some scientists even believe that many knockdowns in boxing result from a temporary compression of the RAS following a powerful punch (Weisberg, Garcia, & Strub, 1996).

The pathways emanating from the RAS activate the cortex by jacking up the *signal-to-noise ratio* among neurons in the brain (Gu, 2002). When it's working well, a cell phone produces sound with a high signal-to-noise ratio so that each caller can understand the other's messages. But when there's a great deal of background static—resulting in a low signal-to-noise ratio—callers find it difficult to understand each other.

We may see this problem in action in attention-deficit/hyperactivity disorder (ADHD), a disorder originating in childhood. ADHD is marked by extreme levels of inattention, over-activity, and impulsivity. Stimulant drugs used to treat ADHD, such as methylphenidate (often marketed under the brand names Ritalin™ or, in extended release form, Concerta™) appear to increase the signal-to-noise ratio in the prefrontal cortex (Devilbiss & Berridge, 2006). One hypothesis is that these drugs mimic activity in the RAS and neighboring brain regions, but other explanations are possible. For example, methylphenidate boosts levels of the neurotransmitter dopamine, which may help to explain why it improves attention and impulse control (Volkow et al., 2005).

The Pons and Medulla. The *pons* and *medulla* lie below the midbrain in the region of the brain called the **hindbrain**. The **pons**, which as we'll learn later (see LO 5.1c) plays a crucial role in triggering dreams, connects the cortex to the cerebellum.

The **medulla** regulates breathing, heartbeat, and other vital functions. Interestingly, it also controls nausea and vomiting (Hesketh, 2008), which explains why you may have had the distinctly unpleasant experience of wanting to throw up if you've experienced a hard hit to the back of your head. Serious damage to the medulla can cause *brain death*, which scientists define as irreversible coma. People who are brain dead are totally unaware of their surroundings and unresponsive, even to ordinarily very painful stimuli. They show no signs of spontaneous movement, respiration, or reflex activity.

People often confuse a *persistent vegetative state*, or cortical death, with brain death, but the two differ. Terri Schiavo made headlines in 2005 as the woman who had lain in a persistent vegetative state for 15 years. Schiavo collapsed in her Florida home in 1990 following temporary cardiac arrest, depriving her brain of oxygen and resulting in severe brain damage. The deep structures in her brain stem that control breathing, heart rate, digestion, and certain reflexive responses were still operating, so Schiavo wasn't brain dead, as much of the news media reported incorrectly. Nevertheless, her higher cerebral structures, necessary for awareness of herself and her environment, were damaged permanently. Her doctors knew that much of her cortex had withered away, and an autopsy later showed that she'd lost about half of her brain.

Those who believe that death of the higher brain centers, which are essential for consciousness, is equivalent to actual death felt that Schiavo had, in fact, died 15 years previously. Nevertheless, her death raises difficult questions that science can't fully resolve: Should brain death be the true criterion for death, or should this criterion instead be the permanent loss of consciousness?

THE SPINAL CORD. The **spinal cord** extends from our brain stem and runs down the middle of our backs, conveying information between the brain and the rest of the body. *Nerves* extend from neurons to the body, traveling in two directions much like the traffic on a two-lane highway. Sensory information is carried from the body to the brain by way of *sensory nerves*; motor commands are carried from the brain to the body by way of *motor nerves*. The spinal cord also contains sensory neurons that contact **interneurons**, neurons that send messages to other neurons located nearby. Interneurons connect sensory nerves with motor nerves within the spinal cord without having to report back to the brain. Interneurons explain how **reflexes**, automatic motor responses to sensory stimuli, can occur.

Consider an automatic behavior called the stretch reflex, which relies only on the spinal cord. We're carrying our laptop on our way to class, but over time our grasp over it releases ever so slightly without our even noticing. Our sensory nerves detect the muscle stretch and relay this information to the spinal cord. Interneurons intervene and motor neurons automatically send messages that cause our arm muscles to contract. Without our ever knowing it, a simple reflex causes our arm muscles to tighten, preventing us from dropping our beloved computer (see Figure 3.15).

The Peripheral Nervous System

Thus far, we've explored the inner workings of the CNS—the central nervous system. Now let's peer into the peripheral nervous system (PNS), the part of the nervous system consisting of the nerves that extend outside of the CNS. The PNS itself contains two branches, somatic and autonomic.

THE SOMATIC NERVOUS SYSTEM.   The **somatic nervous system** carries messages from the CNS to muscles throughout the body, controlling movement (look back to Figure 3.8). Whenever we stabilize or move our many joints, the CNS cooperates with the somatic nervous system to regulate our posture and bodily movement.

Let's revisit what happens when we decide to stroll over to the vending machine to purchase a can of soda. Sensory inputs of all types reach the cortex. Then all parts of the cortex send information to the basal ganglia. The basal ganglia contribute to our decision about what to do and relay that information to the motor cortex. Next up, the motor cortex sends commands to the spinal cord, activating motor neurons. These motor neurons send messages through nerves that reach muscles throughout the body and trigger muscle contractions. We walk, reach, touch, and grasp. Our brain triggers all of these movements, but our somatic nervous system carries them out. After we finish our drink, our somatic nervous system keeps working, enabling us to walk away—ideally, to the nearest recycling container.

THE AUTONOMIC NERVOUS SYSTEM.   The brain and spinal cord interact with our somatic nervous system to bring about sensation and behavior. In much the same way, the brain, especially the limbic system, interacts with the **autonomic nervous system** to control emotion and internal physical states. The autonomic nervous system is the part of the nervous system that controls the involuntary actions of our organs and glands; along with the limbic system, it regulates our emotions.

The autonomic nervous system, in turn, consists of two divisions: sympathetic and parasympathetic (see Figure 3.16). These two divisions work in opposing directions, so that when one is active, the other is passive.

The **sympathetic nervous system**, so called because its neurons tend to fire together ("in sympathy"), is active during emotional arousal, especially during crises. This system mobilizes the *fight-or-flight response*, described by Walter Cannon in 1929 (see LO 12.2a). Cannon noticed that when we encounter threats, like the sight of a huge predator charging toward us, our sympathetic nervous system becomes aroused and prepares us for fighting or fleeing. In extreme cases, when we can't avoid the threat, we may simply freeze (Maack, Buchanan, & Young, 2015), an odd evolutionary adaptation that probably stems from the fact that some predators lose interest in prey when these prey stop moving (you've probably observed this response in squirrels, who sometimes freeze when a car is coming right at them). Sympathetic activation triggers a variety of physical responses helpful for reacting in a crisis, including increased heart rate (allowing more blood to flow into our extremities, thereby preparing us to fight or flee), respiration, and perspiration. The **parasympathetic nervous system**, in contrast, is active during rest and digestion. This system kicks into gear when there's no threat on our mental radar screens. So you can think of your sympathetic nervous system as your anxious, stressed-out friend who reacts intensely whenever danger is lurking,

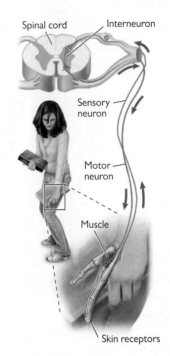

Figure 3.15 The Spinal Reflex.
We detect even small amounts of muscle stretch and compensate by contraction. In this way, we can maintain balance or keep from losing our grip.

interneuron

neuron that sends messages to other neurons nearby

reflex

an automatic motor response to a sensory stimulus

somatic nervous system

part of the nervous system that conveys information between the central nervous system and the body, controlling and coordinating voluntary movement

autonomic nervous system

part of the nervous system controlling the involuntary actions of our internal organs and glands, which (along with the limbic system) participates in emotion regulation

sympathetic nervous system

division of the autonomic nervous system engaged during a crisis or after actions requiring fight or flight

parasympathetic nervous system

division of autonomic nervous system that controls rest and digestion

Figure 3.16 The Autonomic Nervous System. (Male Shown)

The sympathetic and parasympathetic divisions of the autonomic nervous system control the internal organs and glands.

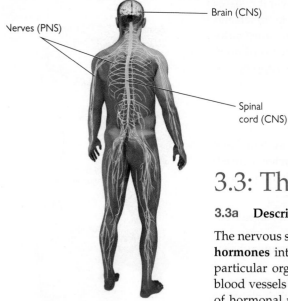

Nerves (PNS)

Brain (CNS)

Spinal cord (CNS)

endocrine system

system of glands and hormones that controls secretion of blood-borne chemical messengers

hormone

chemical released into the bloodstream that influences particular organs and glands

pituitary gland

master gland that, under the control of the hypothalamus, directs the other glands of the body

and of your parasympathetic nervous system as your mellow, relaxed friend who encourages everyone to "chill" whenever they're worried (Burnett, 2016).

> ## Journal Prompt
>
> Some students might think that this chapter belongs better in a biology or anatomy class than in a psychology class. Why do you think it essential to become familiar with the structure and functions of the brain and the remainder of the nervous system in a psychology class?

3.3: The Endocrine System

3.3a   Describe what hormones are and how they affect behavior.

The nervous system interfaces with the **endocrine system**, a network of glands that releases **hormones** into the bloodstream (see Figure 3.17). Hormones are molecules that influence particular organs. They differ from neurotransmitters in that they're carried through our blood vessels rather than our nerves, so they're much slower in their actions. We can think of hormonal messages as a bit like snail mail (regular mail, that is) and neurotransmitter messages as a bit like e-mail. Hormones tend to outlast neurotransmitters in their effects, so their impact tends to be more enduring.

The Pituitary Gland and Pituitary Hormones

The **pituitary gland** controls the other glands in the body. For this reason, it was once called the "master gland," although scientists now realize that it depends heavily on the actions of other glands too. It, in turn, is controlled by the hypothalamus. The pituitary gland releases a variety of hormones that serve numerous functions, ranging all the way from regulating physical growth, controlling blood pressure, and determining how much water we retain in our kidneys.

One pituitary hormone, *oxytocin*, has received substantial attention in recent years. It's responsible for several reproductive functions, including stretching the cervix and vagina during birth and aiding milk flow in nursing mothers. Oxytocin also plays essential roles in maternal and romantic love (Esch & Stefano, 2005), so much so that it's even been called the "love molecule" (Zak, 2012) or "cuddle hormone" (Griffiths, 2014). Scientists have identified two closely related species of voles (a type of rodent) that differ in their pair bonding: The males of one species are promiscuous, flitting from one attractive partner to another, whereas the males of the other remain faithfully devoted to one partner for life. Only in the brains of the loyal voles are oxytocin receptors linked to the dopamine system, which as we've learned influences the expectation of reward (Young & Wang, 2004). For male voles, at least, remaining faithful isn't a chore; it's literally a labor of love.

Oxytocin also seems to influence how much we trust others. In one study, men exposed to a nasal spray containing oxytocin were more likely than men exposed to a placebo spray to hand over money to their team partners in a risky investment game (Kosfeld et al., 2005; Rilling, King-Cassas, & Sanfey, 2008).

At the same time, though, the effects of oxytocin on trust and attachment aren't simple (Walum, Waldman, & Young, 2016), suggesting that the phrases "love molecule" and "cuddle hormone" are grossly oversimplified (Lilienfeld et al., 2015). In fact, oxytocin may well have earned the dubious title of the most overhyped molecule in all of psychology. For example, although oxytocin makes us treat people within our favored groups better, it makes us treat outsiders worse (Beery, 2015; De Drue, Greer, Van Kleef, Shalvi, & Handgraff 2011). Among people who are already aggressive, oxytocin seems to increase the risk of intimate violence toward romantic partners (DeWall et al., 2014). Scientists' best guess is that oxytocin boosts our sensitivity to social cues, both for good and for bad.

Figure 3.17 The Major Endocrine Glands of the Body.

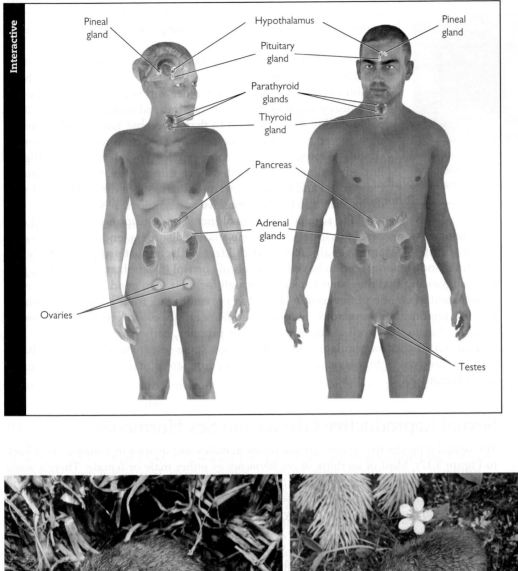

Although these two vole species (the prairie vole on the left and the montane vole on the right) look quite similar, they differ in their "personalities," at least when it comes to romance. The male prairie vole stays loyal to one partner, but the male montane vole doesn't. The difference lies in their oxytocin systems.

The Adrenal Glands and Adrenaline

Psychologists sometimes call the **adrenal glands** the emergency centers of the body. Located atop of the kidneys, they manufacture the hormones *adrenaline* and *cortisol*. Adrenaline boosts energy production in muscle cells, thrusting them into action, while conserving as much energy as possible. Nerves of the sympathetic nervous system signal the adrenal glands to release adrenaline. Adrenaline triggers many actions, including (1) contraction of our heart muscle and constriction of our blood vessels to provide more blood to the body, (2) opening the bronchioles (tiny airways) of the lungs to allow inhalation of more air, (3) breakdown of fat into fatty acids, providing us with more fuel to run toward potential prey or away from potential predators, (4) breakdown of glycogen (a carbohydrate) into glucose (a sugar) to energize our muscles, and (5) opening

adrenal gland

tissue located on top of the kidneys that releases adrenaline and cortisol during states of emotional arousal

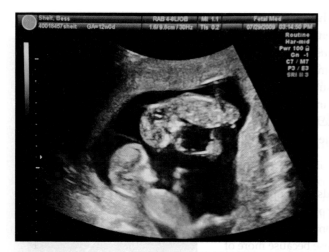

Identical twin fetuses developing in utero. Behavior geneticists compare identical with fraternal twins to estimate the magnitude of genetic and environmental influences on psychological traits.

adoption study

analysis of how traits vary in individuals raised apart from their biological relatives

epigenetics

a field that examines how environmental influences affect the expression of genes

Adoption Studies. As we've seen, studies of intact family members are limited because they can't disentangle genetic from environmental influences. To address this shortcoming, psychologists have turned to **adoption studies**, which examine the extent to which children adopted into new homes resemble their adoptive as opposed to their biological parents. Children adopted into other homes share genes, but not environment, with their biological relatives. As a consequence, if adopted children resemble their biological parents on a psychological characteristic, we can typically assume that it's genetically influenced.

One potential confound in adoption studies is *selective placement:* Adoption agencies frequently place children in homes similar to those of their biological parents (DeFries & Plomin, 1978). This confound can lead investigators to mistakenly interpret the similarity between adoptive children and their biological parents as a genetic effect. In adoption studies, researchers try to control for selective placement by correcting statistically for the correlation between biological and adoptive parents in their psychological characteristics.

As we'll discover in later chapters, psychologists have come to appreciate that genetic and environmental influences intersect in complex ways to shape our nervous systems, thoughts, feelings, and behaviors. For example, they've learned that people with certain genetic makeups tend to seek out certain environments (Plomin, DeFries, & McClearn, 1977; Ridley, 2003) and react differently than people with other genetic makeups to certain environments (Kim-Cohen et al., 2006). They've also learned that many environmental influences, like life stressors and maternal affection, actually work in part by turning certain genes on or off (Weaver et al., 2004). An exciting and increasingly influential field, **epigenetics** (Nigg, 2016), is examining how environmental factors affect the expression of genes, and how such expression influences our behavior. Nature and nurture, although different sources of psychological influence, are turning out to be far more intertwined than we'd realized.

Summary: Biological Psychology

3.1: Nerve Cells: Communication Portals

3.1a Distinguish the parts of neurons and what they do.

The neuron has a cell body, which contains a nucleus, where proteins that make up our cells are manufactured. Neurons have dendrites, long extensions that receive messages from other neurons and an axon, which extends from the cell body of each neuron and is responsible for sending messages.

3.1b Describe electrical responses of neurons and what makes them possible.

Neurons exhibit excitatory and inhibitory responses to inputs from other neurons. When excitation is strong enough, the neuron generates an action potential, which travels all the way down the axon to the axon terminal. Charged particles crossing the neuronal membrane are responsible for these events.

3.1c Explain how neurons use neurotransmitters to communicate with each other.

Neurotransmitters are chemical messengers neurons use to communicate with each other or to cause muscle contraction.

The axon terminal releases neurotransmitters at the synapse. This process produces excitatory or inhibitory responses in the receiving neuron.

3.1d Describe how the brain changes as a result of development, learning, and injury.

The brain changes the most before birth and during early development. Throughout the life span the brain demonstrates some degree of plasticity, which plays a role in learning and memory. Later in life, healthy brain plasticity decreases and neurons can show signs of degeneration.

3.2: The Brain–Behavior Network

3.2a Identify what roles different parts of the central nervous system play in behavior.

The cerebral cortex consists of the frontal, parietal, temporal, and occipital lobes. Cortex involved with vision lies in the occipital lobe, cortex involved with hearing in the temporal lobe, and cortex involved with touch in the parietal lobe. Association areas throughout the cortex analyze and reanalyze sensory inputs to build up our perceptions. The motor cortex in the frontal lobe, the basal ganglia, and the spinal cord work together with the somatic nervous system to bring about movement and action. The somatic nervous system has a sensory as well as a motor component, which enable touch and feedback from the muscles to guide our actions.

3.2b Clarify how the somatic and autonomic nervous systems work in emergency and everyday situations.

The somatic nervous system carries messages from the central nervous to the body's muscles. The autonomic nervous system consists of the parasympathetic and sympathetic divisions. Whereas the parasympathetic nervous system is active during rest and digestion, the sympathetic division propels the body into action during an emergency or crisis. Sympathetic arousal also occurs in response to everyday stressors.

3.3: The Endocrine System

3.3a Describe what hormones are and how they affect behavior.

Hormones are chemicals released into the bloodstream that trigger specific effects in the body. Activation of the sympathetic nervous system stimulates the release of adrenaline and cortisol by the adrenal glands, which energize our bodies. Sex hormones control sexual responses.

3.4: Mapping the Mind: The Brain in Action

3.4a Identify the different brain-stimulating, recording, and imaging techniques.

Electrical stimulation of the brain can elicit vivid imagery or movement. Methods such as electroencephalography (EEG) and magnetoencephalography (MEG) enable researchers to record brain activity. Imaging techniques provide a way to see the brain's structure or function. The first imaging techniques included computed tomography (CT) and magnetic resonance imaging (MRI). Imaging techniques that allow us to see how the brain's activity changes in response to psychological stimuli include positron emission tomography (PET) and functional MRI (fMRI).

3.4b Evaluate results demonstrating the brain's localization of function.

Stimulating, recording, and imaging techniques have shown that specific brain areas correspond to specific functions. Although these results provide valuable insight into how our brains delegate the many tasks we perform, many parts of the brain contribute to each specific task. Because individual brain areas participate in multiple functions, many cognitive functions cannot be neatly localized.

3.5: Nature and Nurture: Did Your Genes—or Parents—Make You Do It?

3.5a Describe genes and how they influence psychological traits.

Genes are composed of deoxyribonucleic acid (DNA), which is arranged on chromosomes. We inherit this genetic material from our parents. Each gene carries a code to manufacture a specific protein. These proteins influence our observable physical and psychological traits.

3.5b Explain the concept of heritability and the misconceptions surrounding it.

Heritability refers to how differences in a trait across people are influenced by their genes as opposed to their environments. The heritability of traits can sometimes change within individuals and over time within a population.

Chapter 4
Sensation and Perception

How We Sense and Conceptualize the World

Learning Objectives

4.1a Identify the basic principles that apply to all senses.

4.1b Discuss the role of attention and the nature of the binding problem.

4.2a Explain how the eye starts the visual process.

4.2b Identify the different kinds of visual perception.

4.2c Describe different visual problems.

4.3a Explain how the ear starts the auditory process.

4.3b Identify the different kinds of auditory perception.

4.4a Identify how we sense and perceive odors and tastes.

4.5a Describe the three different body senses.

4.5b Explain how pain perception differs from touch perception.

4.5c Describe the field of psychology called *human factors*.

4.6a Track how our minds build up perceptions.

4.6b Describe how we perceive people, objects, and sounds in our environments.

4.6c Distinguish subliminal perception from subliminal persuasion.

4.6d Analyze the scientific evidence for and against the existence of extrasensory perception (ESP).

Challenge Your Assumptions

Do some people "taste" shapes or "hear" colors?

Can our eyes detect only a single particle of light?

Can certain blind people still "see" some of their surroundings?

Can we perceive invisible stimuli?

Can we "read" someone else's thoughts?

Watch CAN YOU SELECT THE ITEM THAT'S AN ILLUSION?

Sensation and perception are the underlying processes operating in the visual illusions in the video that we hope delights and amazes you. They're called **illusions** because the way you perceived the stimuli doesn't match their physical reality. Your brain—not your eyes—perceived the anamorphic drawings as realistic three-dimensional objects, even though when viewed from different angles, it became obvious that they were actually nothing more than flat two-dimensional drawings. **Sensation** refers to the detection of physical energy by our sense organs, including our eyes, ears, skin, nose, and tongue, which then relay information to the brain. **Perception** is the brain's *interpretation* of these raw sensory inputs. Simplifying things just a bit, sensation first allows us to pick up the signals in our environments, and perception then allows us to assemble these signals into something meaningful.

We often assume that our sensory systems are infallible and that our perceptions are perfect representations of the world around us. We term these beliefs naive realism (see LO 1.1b). We'll discover in this chapter that naive realism is wrong, because, as the anamorphic illusions vividly illustrate, the world isn't precisely as we see it—a simple shift in visual perspective can tweak our perception to mind-boggling effect.

One way that we make sense of our often confusing and chaotic perceptual worlds is by filling in information about objects we encounter on an everyday basis. This process often occurs entirely without our awareness (Weil & Rees, 2011). Perception researchers showed participants incomplete objects on computer screens and determined which *pixels*, or picture elements, participants rely on to make perceptual judgments about the object (Gold et al., 2000). The pixels that participants used to perceive images were often located next to regions where there was no sensory information, demonstrating that we use available sensory information to make sense of what's missing and thereby identify incomplete objects. In other words, we often blend the real with the imagined, going beyond the information given to us. By doing so, we simplify the world and often make better sense of it in the process.

illusion

perception in which the way we perceive a stimulus doesn't match its physical reality

sensation

detection of physical energy by sense organs, which then send information to the brain

perception

the brain's interpretation of raw sensory inputs

4.1: Two Sides of the Coin: Sensation and Perception

4.1a Identify the basic principles that apply to all senses.
4.1b Discuss the role of attention and the nature of the binding problem.

How do signals that make contact with our sense organs—like our eyes, ears, and tongue—become translated into information that our brains can interpret and act on? And how does the raw sensory information delivered to our brains become integrated with what we

already know about the world, allowing us to recognize objects, avoid accidents, and find our way out the door each morning?

Here's how: Our brain picks and chooses among the types of sensory information it uses, often relying on expectations and prior experiences to fill in the gaps and simplify processing. The end result often differs from the sum of its parts—and sometimes it's a completely wrong number! Errors in perception, like the anamorphic illusions depicted in the video at the beginning of this chapter, and others we'll examine in this chapter, are often informative, not to mention fun. They show us which parts of our sensory experiences are accurate and which parts our brains fill in for us.

We'll first discover what our sensory systems can accomplish and how they manage to transform physical signals in the outside world into neural activity in the "inside world"—our brains. Then we'll explore how and when our brains flesh out the details, moving beyond the raw sensory information available to us.

Sensation: Our Senses as Detectives

Our senses enable us to see majestic scenery, hear glorious music, feel a loving touch, maintain balance as we walk across a stage, and taste wonderful food. Despite their differences, all of our senses rely on a mere handful of basic principles.

TRANSDUCTION: GOING FROM THE OUTSIDE WORLD TO WITHIN.   The first step in sensation is converting external energies or substances into a "language" the nervous system understands. **Transduction** is the process by which the nervous system converts an external stimulus, like light or sound, into electrical signals within neurons. A specific type of **sense receptor**, or specialized cell, transduces a specific stimulus. As we'll learn, specialized cells at the back of the eye transduce light, cells in a spiral-shaped organ in the ear transduce sound, odd-looking endings attached to axons embedded in deep layers of the skin transduce pressure, receptor cells lining the inside of the nose transduce airborne odorants, and taste buds transduce chemicals containing flavor.

For all of our senses, activation is greatest when we first detect a stimulus. After that, our response declines in strength, a process called **sensory adaptation**. What happens when we sit on a chair? After a few seconds, we no longer notice it, unless it's an extremely hard seat, or worse, has a thumbtack on it. The adaptation takes place at the level of the sense receptor. This receptor reacts strongly at first and then tamps down its level of responding to conserve energy and attentional resources. If we didn't engage in sensory adaptation, we'd be attending to just about everything around us, all of the time.

PSYCHOPHYSICS: MEASURING THE BARELY DETECTABLE.   Back in the 19th century, when psychology was gradually distinguishing itself as a science apart from philosophy, many researchers focused on sensation and perception. In 1860, German scientist Gustaf Fechner published a landmark work on perception. Out of his efforts grew **psychophysics**, the study of how we perceive sensory stimuli based on their physical characteristics.

Absolute Threshold.   Imagine that a researcher fits us with a pair of headphones and places us in a quiet room. She asks repeatedly if we've heard one of many very faint tones. Detection isn't an all-or-none state of affair because human error increases as stimuli become weaker in magnitude. Psychophysicists study phenomena like the **absolute threshold** of a stimulus—the lowest level of a stimulus we can detect on 50 percent of the trials when no other stimuli of that type are present. Absolute thresholds demonstrate how remarkably sensitive our sensory systems are. On a clear night, our visual systems can detect a single candle from 30 miles away. We can detect a smell from as few as 50 airborne odorant molecules; the salamander's exquisitely sensitive sniffer can pull off this feat with only one such molecule (Menini, Picco, & Firestein, 1995).

Just Noticeable Difference.   Just how much of a difference in a stimulus makes a difference? The **just noticeable difference (JND)** is the smallest change in the intensity of a stimulus that we can detect. The JND is relevant to our ability to distinguish a stronger from a weaker stimulus, like a soft noise from a slightly louder noise. Imagine we're playing

transduction

the process of converting an external energy or substance into electrical activity within neurons

sense receptor

specialized cell responsible for converting external stimuli into neural activity for a specific sensory system

sensory adaptation

activation is greatest when a stimulus is first detected

psychophysics

the study of how we perceive sensory stimuli based on their physical characteristics

absolute threshold

lowest level of a stimulus needed for the nervous system to detect a change 50 percent of the time

just noticeable difference (JND)

the smallest change in the intensity of a stimulus that we can detect

a song on an iPod, but the volume is turned so low that we can't hear it. If we nudge the volume dial up to the point at which we can *just* begin to make out the song, that's a JND. **Weber's law** states that there's a constant proportional relationship between the JND and the original stimulus intensity (see Figure 4.1). In plain language, the stronger the stimulus, the bigger the change needed for a change in stimulus intensity to be noticeable. Imagine how much light we'd need to add to a brightly lit kitchen to notice an increase in illumination compared with the amount of light we'd need to add to a dark bedroom to notice a change in illumination. We'd need a lot of light in the first case and only a smidgeon in the second.

Signal Detection Theory. David Green and John Swets (1966) developed **signal detection theory** to describe how we detect stimuli under uncertain conditions, as when we're trying to figure out what a friend is saying on a cell phone when there's a lot of static in the connection—that is, when there's high background noise. We'll need to increase the signal by shouting over the static or else our friend won't understand us. If we have a good connection, however, our friend can easily understand us without our shouting. This example illustrates the *signal-to-noise ratio*: It becomes harder to detect a signal as background noise increases.

Green and Swets were also interested in *response biases*, or tendencies to make one type of guess over another when we're in doubt about whether a weak signal is present or absent under noisy conditions. They developed a clever way to take into account some people's tendency to say "yes" when they're uncertain and other people's tendency to say "no" when they're uncertain. Instead of always delivering a sound, they sometimes presented a sound, sometimes not. This procedure allowed them to detect and account for participants' response biases. As we can see in Table 4.1, participants can report that they heard a sound when it was present (a *true positive*, or hit), deny hearing a sound when it was present (a *false-negative*, or miss), report hearing a sound that wasn't there (a *false-positive*, or false alarm), or deny hearing a sound that wasn't there (a *true negative*, or correct rejection). The frequency of false-negatives and false-positives helps us measure how biased participants are to respond "yes" or "no" in general.

Sensory Systems Stick to One Sense—Or Do They? Back in 1826, Johannes Müller proposed the doctrine of *specific nerve energies*, which states that even though there are many distinct stimulus energies—like light, sound, or touch—the sensation we experience is determined by the nature of the sense receptor, not the stimulus. To get a sense of this principle in action, the next time you rub your eyes shortly after waking up, try to notice phosphenes—vivid sensations of light caused by pressure on your eye's receptor cells. Many phosphenes look like sparks, and some even look like multicolored shapes in a kaleidoscope. Some people have speculated that phosphenes may explain certain reports of ghosts and UFOs (Neher, 1990).

Why do phosphenes occur? In the cerebral cortex, different areas are devoted to different senses. It doesn't matter to our brain whether light or touch activated the sense receptor: Our brains react the same way in either case. That is, once our visual sense receptors send

Figure 4.1 Just Noticeable Differences (JNDs) Adhere to Weber's Law.

In this example, changes in light are shown measured in lumens, which are units equaling the amount of light generated by one candle standing one foot away. Weber's law states that the brighter the light, the more change in brightness is required for us to be able to notice a difference.

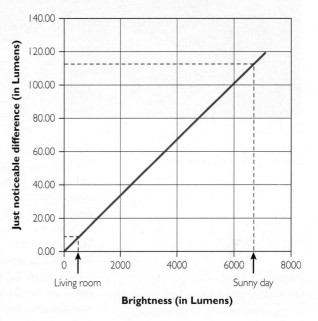

Brightness (in Lumens)

Weber's law

there is a constant proportional relationship between the JND and original stimulus intensity

signal detection theory

theory regarding how stimuli are detected under different conditions

Table 4.1 Distinguishing Signals from Noise.

In signal detection theory there are true positives, false-negatives, false-positives, and true negatives. Subject biases affect the probability of "yes" and "no" responses to the question "Was there a stimulus?"

	Respond "YES"	Respond "NO"
Stimulus present	True positive	False-negative
Stimulus absent	False-positive	True negative

John Medina
Author, "Brain Rules"

Ruling Out Rival Hypotheses

Have important alternative explanations for the findings been excluded?

---

synesthesia

a condition in which people experience cross-modal sensations

---

their signals to the cortex, the brain interprets their input as visual, regardless of how our receptors were stimulated in the first place.

Most areas of the cortex are connected to cortical areas devoted to the same sense: Vision areas tend to be connected to other vision areas, hearing areas to other hearing areas, and so on. Yet scientists have found many examples of cross-modal processing that produce different perceptual experiences than either modality provides by itself. One striking example is the *McGurk effect* depicted in the video (McGurk & MacDonald, 1976; Nahorna, Berthommier, & Schwartz, 2012). This effect demonstrates that we integrate visual and auditory information when processing spoken language, and our brains automatically calculate the most probable sound given the information from the two sources. In the McGurk effect, hearing the audio track of one syllable (such as "ba") spoken repeatedly while seeing a video track of a different syllable being spoken (such as "ga") produces the striking illusion of a different third sound (such as "da"). This third sound is the brain's best "guess" at integrating the two conflicting sources of information.

Another fascinating example is an illusion that shows how our senses of touch and sight interact to create a false perceptual experience (Erhsson, Spence, & Passingham, 2004; Knox, Coppieters, & Hodges, 2006). This illusion involves placing a rubber hand on top of a table with the precise positioning that a participant's hand would have if she were resting it on the table. The participant's hand is placed under the table, out of his or her view. A researcher simultaneously strokes the participant's hidden hand and rubber hand gently with a paintbrush. When the strokes match each other, the participant experiences an eerie illusion: The rubber hand seems to be his or her own hand.

As we've seen, these cross-modal effects may reflect "cross-talk" among different brain regions. But there's an alternative explanation: In some cases, a single brain region may serve double duty, helping to process multiple senses. For example, neurons in the auditory cortex tuned to sound also respond weakly to touch (Fu et al., 2003). Visual stimuli enhance touch perception in the somatosensory cortex (Taylor-Clarke, Kennett, & Haggard, 2002). The reading of Braille by people blind from birth activates their visual cortex (Beisteiner et al., 2015; Gizewski et al., 2003), the visual cortex responds to spoken language in blind children (Bedny, Richardson, & Saxe, 2015), and monkeys viewing videos with sound display increased activity in their primary auditory cortex compared with exposure to sound alone (Kayser et al., 2007).

Sir Francis Galton (1880), a cousin of Charles Darwin whom we've discussed in other chapters of this text, was the first to describe **synesthesia**, a remarkable condition in which people experience cross-modal sensations, like hearing sounds when they see colors—sometimes called "colored hearing"—or even tasting or smelling colors (Cytowic & Eagleman, 2009; Marks, 2014). In Table 4.2, we present a handful of the 60 types of synesthesia identified to date (Day, 2013).

Table 4.2 Examples of Different Types of Synesthesia.

Mirror-touch synesthesia	A person experiences the same sensation that another person experiences, such as touch.
Lexical-gustatory synesthesia	Words are associated with specific tastes or textures.
Chromesthesia	Sounds trigger the experience of color; in cases of misophonia, sounds trigger strong emotions such as anger or fear.
Personification	Numbers, letters, or days of the week take on personality characteristics and sometimes have a characteristic appearance. For example, the number 6 might be experienced as a king, or the number 8 a sorcerer.
Number-form synesthesia	Numbers are imagined as mental maps.
Spatial sequence synesthesia	Certain sequences of numbers, dates, or months are perceived as closer or farther in space.

Synesthesia may be an extreme version of the cross-modal responses that most of us experience from time to time, such as associating high tones with lighter colors and low tones with darker colors (Rader & Tellegen, 1987; Ward, Huckstep, & Tsakanikos, 2006). No one knows for sure how widespread synesthesia is. An early estimate put it at no higher than about 1 in 2,000 people (Baron-Cohen et al., 1993). However, a more recent survey of 500 British university students estimated the prevalence to be about 4 percent, implying that it might not be as rare as once thought (Simner et al., 2006).

In the past, some scientists questioned the authenticity of synesthesia, yet research demonstrates that the condition is genuine (Johnson, Allison, & Baron-Cohen, 2013; van Leeuwen, Singer, & Nikolić, 2015; Ward, 2013). Figure 4.2 illustrates a clever test that detects grapheme-color synesthesia. Specific parts of the visual cortex become active during most synesthesia experiences, verifying that these experiences are associated with brain activity (Paulesu et al., 1995; Rouw, Scholte, & Colizoli, 2011).

The Role of Attention

In a world in which our brains are immersed in a sea of sensory input, flexible attention is critical to our survival and well-being. To zero in on a video game we play in the park, for example, we must ignore that speck of dust on our shirt, the shifting breeze, and the riot of colors and sounds in the neighborhood. Yet at any moment we must be prepared to use sensory information that signals a potential threat, such as an approaching thunderstorm. Fortunately, we're superbly well equipped to meet the challenges of our rich and ever-changing sensory environments.

SELECTIVE ATTENTION: HOW WE FOCUS ON SPECIFIC INPUTS.   If we're constantly receiving inputs from all our sensory channels, like a TV set with all channels switched on at once, how do we keep from becoming hopelessly bewildered? **Selective attention** allows us to select one channel and turn off the others, or at least turn down their volume.

Donald Broadbent's (1957) *filter theory of attention* views attention as a bottleneck through which information passes. This mental filter enables us to pay attention to important stimuli and ignore others. Broadbent tested his theory using a task called *dichotic listening*—in which participants hear two different messages, one delivered to the left ear and one to the right ear. When Broadbent asked participants to ignore messages delivered to one of the ears, they seemed to know little or nothing about these messages. Anne Treisman (1960) replicated these findings, elaborating on them by asking participants to repeat the messages they heard. Although participants could only repeat the messages to which they'd attended, they'd sometimes mix in some of the information they were supposed to ignore, especially if it made sense to add it. If the attended ear heard, "I saw the girl…song was wishing," and the unattended ear heard, "me that bird…jumping in the street," a participant might hear "I saw the girl jumping in the street," because the combination forms a meaningful sentence. The information we've supposedly filtered out of our attention is still being processed at some level—even when we're not aware of it (Beaman, Bridges, & Scott, 2007).

An attention-related phenomenon called the *cocktail party effect* refers to our ability to pick out an important message, like our name, in a conversation that doesn't involve us. We don't typically notice what other people are saying in a noisy restaurant or at a party unless it's relevant to us—and then suddenly, we perk up. This finding tells us that the filter inside our brain, which selects what will and won't receive our attention, is more complex than just an "on" or "off" switch. Even when seemingly "off," it's ready to spring into action if it perceives something significant.

INATTENTIONAL BLINDNESS.   Before reading on, try the extrasensory perception (ESP) trick in Figure 4.3 on the next page. We're going to try to read your mind. Then come back and read the next paragraph.

We're surprisingly poor at detecting stimuli in plain sight when our attention is focused elsewhere (Henderson & Hollingworth, 1999; Levin & Simons, 1997; McConkie & Currie, 1996). That principle helps to explain why drivers sometimes strike a bicyclist who is clearly in their field of vision. In an astonishing demonstration of this phenomenon, called **inattentional blindness**, Daniel Simons and Christopher Chabris (1999, 2011) asked subjects to watch a video of people tossing a basketball back and forth quickly, and required

Figure 4.2 Are You Synesthetic?

Although most of us see the top image as a bunch of jumbled numbers, some grapheme-color synesthetes, who "see" certain numbers as colors, perceive it as looking like the image on the bottom. Synesthesia makes it much easier to identify the 2s embedded within the 5s.

SOURCE: Synesthesia: A window into perception, thought and language. Journal of Consciousness Studies, 8, 33–34.

▸ **Replicability**

Can the results be duplicated in other studies?

selective attention

process of selecting one sensory channel and ignoring or minimizing others

inattentional blindness

failure to detect stimuli that are in plain sight when our attention is focused elsewhere

Figure 4.3 An ESP Trick? Try It and Find Out.

Try this "ESP trick," adapted from a demonstration by Clifford Pickover. This remarkable trick will demonstrate that we—the authors of this text—can read your mind!

Select one of the six cards and be sure to recall it. To help you remember it, repeat its name out loud several times. Once you're sure you have the card in mind, turn to page 128.

them to keep track of the number of passes. Then, smack in the middle of the video, a woman dressed in a gorilla suit strolled across the scene for a full nine seconds. Remarkably, about half the viewers failed to notice the hairy misfit even though she paused to face the camera and thumped her chest. This and other findings demonstrate that we often need to pay close attention to pick out even dramatic changes in our environments (Koivisto & Revonsuo, 2007; Rensink, O'Regan, & Clark, 1997).

A closely related phenomenon, called *change blindness*, is a failure to detect obvious changes in one's environment (if you've tried the ESP trick we mentioned, you'll know what we mean). Change blindness is a particular concern for airplane pilots, who may fail to notice another plane taxiing across the runway as they're preparing to land (Podczerwinski, Wickens, & Alexander, 2002). You may be relieved to hear that industrial/organizational psychologists are working actively with aviation agencies to reduce the incidence of this problem.

Even experts sometimes fail to see the "obvious:" Eighty-three percent of 24 radiologists who performed a familiar task of detecting a lung nodule in a computer tomography (CT) scan failed to notice a gorilla image with a white outline that was inserted in the final case in a series. These findings were all the more impressive (or scary) because the gorilla image in this photograph was about the size of a matchbook—in this case 48 times larger than the average nodule. Fortunately, experts were much better at detecting real lung nodules than untrained observers (Drew, Vo, & Wolfe, 2013).

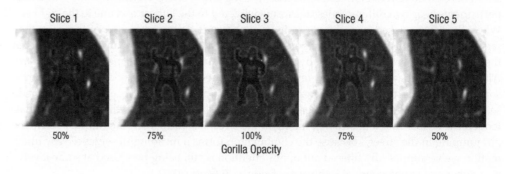

Slice 1	Slice 2	Slice 3	Slice 4	Slice 5
50%	75%	100%	75%	50%

Gorilla Opacity

Journal Prompt
Researchers believe that change blindness contributes to many car accidents. Why do you think this is the case? Why might change blindness be especially likely to occur when we're driving?

The Binding Problem: Putting the Pieces Together

The *binding problem* is one of the great mysteries of psychology. When we perceive an apple, different regions of our brains process different aspects of it. Yet somehow—we don't really know how—our brains manage to combine or "bind" these diverse pieces of information into a unified whole. An apple looks red and round, feels smooth, tastes sweet and tart, and smells, well, like an apple. Any one of its characteristics in isolation isn't an apple or even a part of an apple. One hypothesis is that rapid, coordinated activity across multiple cortical areas assists in binding (Engel & Singer, 2001). Binding may explain many aspects of perception and attention. When we see the world, we rely on shape, motion, color, and depth cues, each of which requires different amounts of time to detect individually (Bartels & Zeki, 2006). Yet our minds seamlessly and often unconsciously combine these visual cues into a unified perception of a scene (Keizer, Hommel, & Lamme, 2015). To better understand how perception and attention work together, we'll next discuss the different senses we rely on to make our way in the world, starting with the visual system.

Mysteries of Psychological Science
How Does Magic Work?

When you think of the astonishing tricks of stage magicians, does psychological science come to mind? Probably not. Yet in the past decade, psychologists and neuroscientists have partnered with famous magicians, including the Amazing Randi and Teller (of Penn & Teller fame) (Macknik et al., 2008), to establish a "science of magic." This science promises to unravel the psychological mechanisms of the reality-bending illusions that magicians create (Kuhn, Amlani, & Rensink, 2008; Stone, 2012). Magic tricks that confound and astound us can yield their secrets (only a few spoilers here) to researchers, and contribute to our understanding of perception.

Many of us have heard the old saying, "The hand is quicker than the eye," with regard to the ability of stage magicians to create mind-boggling stunts involving sleight of hand. Yet this adage actually reflects a popular misconception because most magic tricks are carried out at a normal speed (Kuhn, Amlani, & Rensink, 2008). Researchers have discovered that a more accurate phrase to capture how magicians fool us is, "The hand is quicker than the brain."

Consider the following example. A stage magician can get people to believe that a coin has disappeared after it's seemingly transferred from his right to left hand, because the audience can't tell that he secretly concealed (palmed) the coin in the right hand. The magician takes advantage of a little-known fact: Viewers don't consciously register information for a small fraction of second after it arrives in the brain, making it appear that the coin is still in the left hand, when it actually has been removed and hidden in the right hand (Stone, 2012). Because the onlooker's visual neurons keep firing for one-hundredth of a second after the coin is transferred (Libet et al., 1983), it ensures that the coin will appear to be in the left hand just long enough to fool observers. So when the magician opens his left hand, to the amazement of the stunned audience, the coin appears to have vanished!

Researchers have studied the vanishing ball illusion to understand how mental predictions and expectancies, rather than reality, affect perception. Here's how this fascinating illusion works. The magician throws two balls into the air, one at a time, and catches each in his hand. On both throws, his head and eyes look up to track the flight of the ball. The third time, the magician pretends to throw the ball, but secretly palms it in his hand as he moves his head up to follow the imaginary ball. In one study of this illusion (Kuhn & Land, 2006), two-thirds of the observers who viewed this trick perceived the ball to leave the magician's hand and disappear in mid-flight. In a second condition, rather than move his head to follow the flight of the imaginary ball, the magician looked at the hand that concealed the ball.

Apollo Robbins, a famed Las Vegas "close in" magician, can pick people's pockets, remove watches from their hands, and even take rings off their fingers without their having a clue. He accomplishes these astonishing feats by misdirecting their attention by coming close to them, often touching them in multiple places other than where the item to be pilfered is located. Researchers who have collaborated with Robbins to discover the neuroscience behind how he pulls off his stunts, have determined that people are more likely to follow the motion of his hands and be misdirected when they're moving in an arc or curve than when they're moving in a straight line, once again showing that magicians have something to teach scientists (Otero-Millan et al., 2011).

When this occurred, less than a third of the participants said the ball vanished. The success of the trick depended on the head direction of the magician, a social cue that created the expectation that the ball was in flight, which never actually happened.

Stage magicians also trick people by other means, such as by misdirecting attention and awareness. This technique fools us because we're consciously aware of and attend to only a tiny part of the information that enters our eyes (Kuhn, Amlani, & Rensink, 2008; Rensink, O'Regan, & Clark, 1997). By riveting the audience's attention to a grand theatrical movement, such as pulling the proverbial rabbit out of a hat, the performer distracts onlookers from noticing a less obvious movement related to a secret prop that's essential to the next trick. So the next time you witness the likes of "The Fabulous Fabrini" performing captivating feats of magic on stage or screen, don't be surprised if scientists are studying him to sleuth how attention, awareness, and perception can play tricks on our minds.

Figure 4.4 The Visible Spectrum Is a Subset of the Electromagnetic Spectrum.

Visible light is electromagnetic energy between ultraviolet and infrared. Humans are sensitive to wavelengths ranging from slightly less than 400 nanometers (violet) to slightly more than 700 nanometers (red).

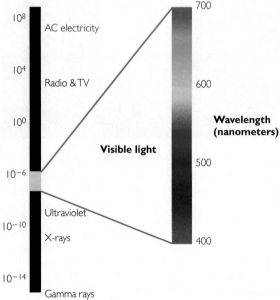

hue

color of light

Figure 4.5 Additive and Subtractive Color Mixing.

Additive color mixing of light differs from subtractive color mixing of paint.

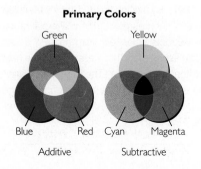

4.2: Seeing: The Visual System

4.2a Explain how the eye starts the visual process.
4.2b Identify the different kinds of visual perception.
4.2c Describe different visual problems.

The first thing we see after awakening is typically unbiased by any previous image. If we're on vacation and sleeping somewhere new, we may not recognize our surroundings for a moment or two. Building up an image involves many external elements, such as light, biological systems in the eye and brain that process images for us, and our past experiences.

Light: The Energy of Life

One of the central players in our perception of the world is light, a form of electromagnetic energy—energy composed of fluctuating electric and magnetic waves. Visible light has a *wavelength* in the hundreds of nanometers (a nanometer is one billionth of a meter). As we can see in Figure 4.4, we respond only to a narrow range of wavelengths of light; this range is the human visible spectrum. Each animal species detects a specific visible range, which can extend slightly above or below the human visible spectrum. Butterflies are sensitive to all of the wavelengths we detect in addition to ultraviolet light, which has a shorter wavelength than violet light. We might assume that the human visible spectrum is fixed, but increasing the amount of vitamin A in our diets can increase our ability to see infrared light, which has a longer wavelength than red light (Rubin & Walls, 1969).

When light reaches an object, part of that light gets reflected by the object and part gets absorbed. Our perception of an object's *brightness* is influenced directly by the intensity of the reflected light that reaches our eyes. Completely white objects reflect all of the light shone on them and absorb none of it, whereas black objects do the opposite. So white and black aren't really "colors"; white is the presence of all colors, black the absence of them. The brightness of an object depends not only on the amount of reflected light, but also on the overall lighting surrounding the object.

Psychologists call the color of light **hue**. We're maximally attuned to three primary colors of light: red, green, and blue. The mixing of varying amounts of these three colors—called *additive color mixing*—can produce any color (see Figure 4.5). Mixing equal amounts of red, green, and blue light produces white light. This process differs from the mixing of colored pigments in paint or ink, called *subtractive color mixing*. As we can see in most printer color ink cartridges, the primary colors of pigment are yellow, cyan, and magenta. Mixing them produces a dark color because each pigment absorbs certain wavelengths. Combining them absorbs most or all wavelengths, leaving little or no color (see Figure 4.5).

The Eye: How We Represent the Visual Realm

Without our eyes we couldn't sense or perceive much of anything about light, aside from the heat it generates. Keep an "eye" on Figure 4.6 as we tour the structures of the eye.

Figure 4.6 The Key Parts of the Eye.

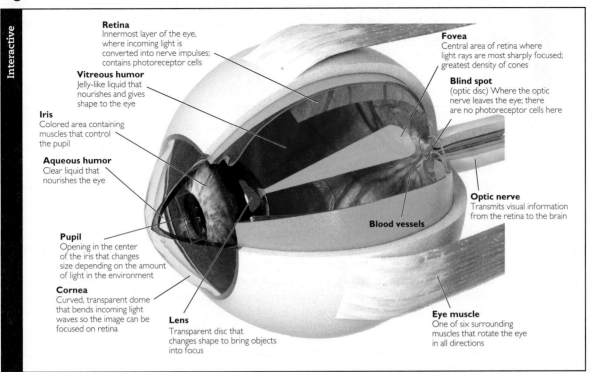

Retina
Innermost layer of the eye, where incoming light is converted into nerve impulses; contains photoreceptor cells

Vitreous humor
Jelly-like liquid that nourishes and gives shape to the eye

Iris
Colored area containing muscles that control the pupil

Aqueous humor
Clear liquid that nourishes the eye

Pupil
Opening in the center of the iris that changes size depending on the amount of light in the environment

Cornea
Curved, transparent dome that bends incoming light waves so the image can be focused on retina

Lens
Transparent disc that changes shape to bring objects into focus

Fovea
Central area of retina where light rays are most sharply focused; greatest density of cones

Blind spot
(optic disc) Where the optic nerve leaves the eye; there are no photoreceptor cells here

Optic nerve
Transmits visual information from the retina to the brain

Blood vessels

Eye muscle
One of six surrounding muscles that rotate the eye in all directions

HOW LIGHT ENTERS THE EYE. Different parts of our eye allow in varying amounts of light, permitting us to see either in bright sunshine or in a dark theater. Structures toward the front of the eyeball influence how much light enters our eye, and they focus the incoming light rays to form an image at the back of the eye.

The Sclera, Iris, and Pupil. Although poets have told us that the eyes are the windows to the soul, when we look people squarely in the eye all we can see is their sclera, iris, and pupil. The sclera is simply the white of the eye. The iris is the colored part of the eye, and is usually blue, brown, green, or hazel. Like the shutter of a camera, the iris controls how much light enters our eyes.

The **pupil** is a circular hole through which light enters the eye. The closing of the pupil is a reflex response to light or objects coming toward us. If we walk out of a building into bright sunshine, our eyes respond with the pupillary reflex to decrease the amount of light allowed into them. This reflex occurs simultaneously in both eyes (unless there's neurological damage), so shining a flashlight into one eye triggers it in both.

The dilation (expansion) of the pupil also has psychological significance. Our pupils dilate when we're trying to process complex information, like difficult math problems (Beatty, 1982; Karatekin, 2004). They also dilate when we view someone we find physically attractive, and reflect sexual interest of homosexual as well as heterosexual individuals (Rieger & Savin-Williams, 2012; Tombs & Silverman, 2004). These findings may help to explain why people find faces with large pupils more attractive than faces with small pupils, even when they're oblivious to this physical difference (Hess, 1965; Tomlinson, Hicks, & Pelligrini, 1978).

The Cornea, Lens, and Eye Muscles. The **cornea** is a curved, transparent layer covering the iris and pupil. Its shape bends light to focus the incoming visual image at the back of the eye. The **lens** also bends light, but unlike the cornea the lens changes its curvature, allowing us to fine-tune the visual image. The lens consists of some of the most unusual cells in the body: They're completely transparent, allowing light to pass through them.

In a process called **accommodation**, the lenses change shape to focus light on the back of the eyes; in this way, they adapt to different perceived distances of objects. So, nature has generously supplied us with a pair of "internal" corrective lenses, although they're often far from perfect. Accommodation can either make the lens "flat" (that is, long and skinny) enabling us to see distant objects, or "fat" (that is, short and wide) enabling us to

Research demonstrates that men tend to find the faces of women with larger pupils (in this case, the face on the left) more attractive than those with smaller pupils, even when they're unaware of the reason for their preference.

SOURCE: Hess, 1965; Tombs & Silverman, 2004.

pupil
circular hole through which light enters the eye

cornea
part of the eye containing transparent cells that focus light on the retina

lens
part of the eye that changes curvature to keep images in focus

accommodation
changing the shape of the lens to focus on objects near or far

Fact vs. Fiction

In the fertile phase of their menstrual cycles, women are especially prone to prefer men with large pupils (See bottom of page for answer.)

○ Fact

○ Fiction

focus on nearby objects. For nearby objects, a fat lens works better because it more effectively bends the scattered light and focuses it on a single point at the back of the eye.

The Shape of the Eye. How much our eyes need to bend the path of light to focus properly depends on the curve of our corneas and overall shape of our eyes. Nearsightedness, or *myopia*, results when images are focused in front of the rear of the eye due to our cornea being too steep or our eyes too long (see Figure 4.7a). Nearsightedness, as the name implies, is an ability to see close objects well coupled with an inability to see far objects well. Farsightedness, or *hyperopia*, results when our cornea is too flat or our eyes too short (see Figure 4.7b). Farsightedness, as the name implies, is an ability to see far objects well coupled with an inability to see near objects well. Our vision tends to worsen as we become older. That's because our lens can accommodate and overcome the effects of most mildly misshapen eyeballs until it loses its flexibility due to aging. This explains why only a few first-graders need eyeglasses, whereas most senior citizens do.

retina

membrane at the back of the eye responsible for converting light into neural activity

fovea

central portion of the retina

acuity

sharpness of vision

rods

receptor cells in the retina allowing us to see in low levels of light

dark adaptation

time in dark before rods regain maximum light sensitivity

THE RETINA: CHANGING LIGHT INTO NEURAL ACTIVITY. The **retina**, which according to many scholars is technically part of the brain, is a thin membrane at the back of the eye. The **fovea** is the central part of the retina and is responsible for **acuity**, or sharpness of vision. We need a sharp image to read, drive, sew, or do just about anything requiring fine detail. We can think of the retina as a "movie screen" onto which light from the world is projected. It contains 100 million sense receptor cells for vision, along with cells that process visual information and send it to the brain.

Rods and Cones. Light passes through the retina to sense receptor cells located in its outermost layer. The retina contains two types of receptor cells. The far more plentiful **rods**, which are long and narrow, enable us to see basic shapes and forms. We rely on rods to see in low levels of light. When we enter a dimly lit room, like a movie theater, from a bright environment, **dark adaptation** occurs. Dark adaptation takes about 30 minutes, or about the time it takes rods to regain their maximum sensitivity to light (Lamb & Pugh, 2004). Some have even speculated that pirates of old, who spent many long, dark nights at sea, might have worn eye patches to facilitate dark adaptation. There are no rods in the fovea, which explains why we should tilt our heads slightly to the side to see a dim star at night. Paradoxically, we can see the star better by *not* looking at it directly. By relying on our peripheral vision, we allow more light to fall on our rods.

Figure 4.7 Nearsighted and Farsighted Eyes.

Nearsightedness or farsightedness results when light is focused in front of or behind the retina.

SOURCE: Adapted from St. Luke's Cataract & Laser Institute

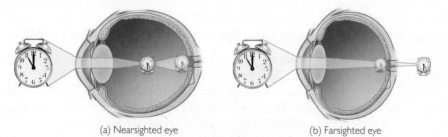

(a) Nearsighted eye   (b) Farsighted eye

Answer: Fact. Researchers found that when they're in the fertile phase of their menstrual cycles, women are especially prone to prefer men with large pupils (Caryl et al., 2009). For centuries European women applied a juice from a poisonous plant called *belladonna* (Italian for "beautiful woman"), sometimes also called *deadly nightshade*, to their eyes to dilate their pupils, and thereby make themselves more attractive to men. Today, magazine photographers often enlarge the pupils of models, reasoning it will increase their appeal.

The less numerous **cones**, which are shaped like—you guessed it—small cones, give us our color vision. We put our cones to work when reading because they're sensitive to detail; however, cones also require more light than do rods. That's why most of us have trouble reading in a dark room.

Different types of receptor cells contain *photopigments,* chemicals that change following exposure to light. The photopigment in rods is *rhodopsin.* Vitamin A, found in abundance in carrots, is needed to make rhodopsin. This fact led to the urban legend that eating carrots is good for our vision. Unfortunately, the only time vitamin A improves vision is when vision is impaired due to vitamin A deficiency.

The Optic Nerve. The *ganglion cells,* cells in the retinal circuit that contain axons, bundle all their axons together and depart the eye to reach the brain. The **optic nerve**, which contains the axons of ganglion cells, travels from the retina to the rest of the brain. After the optic nerves leave both eyes, they come to a fork in the road called the *optic chiasm.* Half of the axons cross in the optic chiasm and the other half stay on the same side. Within a short distance, the optic nerves enter the brain, turning into the optic tracts. The optic tracts send most of their axons to the visual part of the thalamus and then to the primary visual cortex—called V1—the primary route for visual perception (see Figure 4.8). The remaining axons go to structures in the midbrain, particularly the *superior colliculus* (LO 3.4d). These axons play a key role in reflexes, like turning our heads to follow something interesting.

The place where optic nerve connects to the retina is a **blind spot**, a part of the visual field that we can't see. It's a region of the retina containing no rods or sense receptors (refer to Figure 4.8). We have a blind spot because the axons of ganglion cells push everything else aside.

Before you read any further, try the exercise in Figure 4.9. This exercise makes use of the blind spot, which comes into play here when we move our face a certain distance from the white X, to generate an illusion. Our blind spot is actually there all of the time, creating perhaps the most remarkable of all visual illusions—one we experience every moment of our seeing lives. Our brain fills in the gaps created by the blind spot, and because each of

Figure 4.8 Perception and the Visual Cortex.

Visual information from the retina travels to the visual thalamus. Next, the visual thalamus sends inputs to the primary visual cortex (V1), then along two visual pathways to the secondary visual cortex (V2). One pathway leads to the parietal lobe, which processes visual form, position, and motion; and one to the temporal lobe, which processes visual form and color.

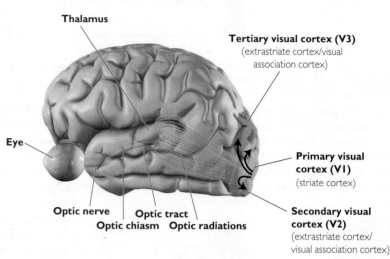

cones

receptor cells in the retina allowing us to see in color

optic nerve

nerve that travels from the retina to the brain

blind spot

part of the visual field we can't see because of an absence of rods and cones

Figure 4.9 Separating Sensation from Perception.

Position yourself about 10 inches from the page. Close your right eye and keep focusing on the white circle. Can you see the white *X*? Now slowly move your face toward the page and then away from it; at some point the white *X* will disappear and then reappear. Surprisingly, your brain supplies an illusory background pattern that fills in the white space occupied by the *X*.

Were you surprised that the white "X" disappeared from view? Were you even more surprised that you filled the missing space occupied by the "X" with a mental image exactly matching the fancy background pattern?

Fact vs. Fiction

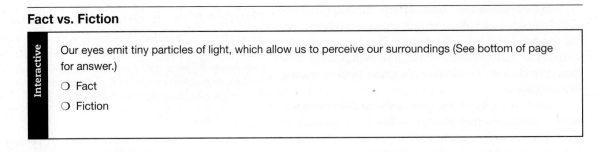

Our eyes emit tiny particles of light, which allow us to perceive our surroundings (See bottom of page for answer.)

○ Fact

○ Fiction

Figure 4.10 Cells Respond to Slits of Light of a Particular Orientation.

Top: Hubel and Wiesel studied activity in the visual cortex of cats viewing slits of light on a screen. *Bottom:* Visual responses were specific to slits of dark on light (minuses on pluses—a) or light on dark (pluses on minuses—b) that were of particular orientations, such as horizontal, oblique, or vertical—(c). Cells in the visual cortex also detected edges.

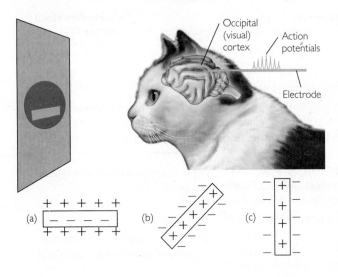

feature detector cell

cell that detects lines and edges

our eyes supplies us with a slightly different picture of the world, we don't ordinarily notice it.

HOW WE PERCEIVE SHAPE AND CONTOUR. In the 1960s, David Hubel and Torsten Wiesel sought to unlock the secrets of how we perceive shape and form; their work eventually garnered them a Nobel Prize. They used cats as subjects because their visual systems are much like ours. Hubel and Wiesel recorded electrical activity in the visual cortexes of cats while presenting them with visual stimuli on a screen (see Figure 4.10). At first, they were unaware of which stimuli would work best, so they tried many types, including bright and dark spots. At one point, they put up a different kind of stimulus on the screen, a long slit of light. As the story goes, one of their slides jammed in the slide projector slightly off-center, producing a slit of light (Horgan, 1999). Cells in the brain area V1 suddenly went haywire, firing action potentials at an amazingly high rate when the slit moved across the screen. Motivated by this surprising result, Hubel and Wiesel devoted years to figuring out which types of slits elicited such responses.

Here's what they found (Hubel & Wiesel, 1962; 1963). Many cells in V1 respond to slits of light of a specific orientation, for example, vertical, horizontal, or oblique lines or edges (refer again to Figure 4.10). Some cells in the visual cortex, *simple cells*, display "yes–no" responses to slits of a specific orientation, but these slits need to be in a specific location. Other cells, *complex cells*, are also orientation specific, but their responses are less restricted to one location. This feature makes complex cells much more advanced than simple cells.

Feature Detection. Our ability to use certain minimal patterns to identify objects is called *feature detection*. Although simple and complex cells are **feature detector cells** in that they detect lines and edges, there are more complex feature detector cells at higher, that is, later levels of visual processing. They detect lines of specific lengths, complex shapes, and even moving objects. We use our ability to detect edges and corners to perceive many human-made objects, like furniture, laptops, and even the corners of the screen you're reading at this moment.

As we saw in Figure 4.8, visual information travels from V1 to higher visual areas, called V2, along two major routes, one of which travels to the upper parts of the parietal lobe, and the other of which travels to the lower part of the temporal lobe (see LO 3.2a). Numerous researchers have proposed a model of visual processing in which successively higher cortical regions process more and more complex shapes (Riesenhuber & Poggio, 1999). The many visual processing areas of the cortex enable us to progress from perceiving basic shapes to the enormously complex objects we see in our everyday worlds.

HOW WE PERCEIVE COLOR. Color delights our senses and stirs our imagination, but how does the brain perceive it? Scientists have discovered that we use the lower visual pathway leading to the temporal lobe to process color (refer back to Figure 4.8), but it hardly starts there. Different theories of color perception explain different aspects of our ability to detect color, enabling us to see the world, watch TV, and enjoy movies, all in vibrant color.

Answer: Fiction. Many children and about 50 percent of college students (including those who've taken introductory psychology classes) harbor this belief, often called "emission theory" (Winer et al., 2002). Nevertheless, there's no scientific evidence for this theory, and there is considerable evidence against it.

Trichromatic Theory. **Trichromatic theory** proposes that we base our color vision on three primary colors—blue, green, and red. Trichromatic theory dovetails with our having three kinds of cones, each maximally sensitive to different wavelengths of light. Given that the three types of cones were discovered in the 1960s (Brown & Wald, 1964), it's perhaps surprising that Thomas Young and Hermann von Helmholtz described trichromatic theory more than a century earlier. Young (1802) suggested that our vision is sensitive to three primary colors of light, and von Helmholtz (1850) replicated and extended his proposal by examining the colors that color-blind individuals could see. The Young-Helmholtz trichromatic theory of color vision was born.

Persons with **color blindness** can't see all colors. Color blindness is most often due to the absence or reduced number of one or more types of cones stemming from genetic abnormalities. Still another cause is damage to a brain area related to color vision. Contrary to a popular misconception, *monochromats*—who have only one type of cone and thereby lose all color vision—are extremely rare, making up only about 0.0007 percent of the population. Most color-blind individuals can perceive a good deal of their world in color because they're *dichromats*, meaning they have two cones and are missing only one. Red–green dichromats see considerable color but can't distinguish reds as well as can people with normal color vision. We can find a test for red–green color blindness in Figure 4.11; many males have this condition but don't know it because it doesn't interfere much with their everyday functioning.

Humans, apes, and some monkeys are *trichromats*, meaning we and our close primate relatives possess three kinds of cones. Most other mammals, including dogs and cats, see the world with only two cones, much like people with red–green color blindness (the most frequent form of color blindness). Trichromatic vision evolved about 35 million years ago, perhaps because it allowed animals to easily pick ripe fruit out of a green background. Recent fossil evidence suggests an alternative hypothesis, namely, that trichromatic vision may have enabled primates to find young, reddish, tender leaves that were nutritionally superior (Simon-Moffat, 2002). All scientists agree that seeing more colors gave our ancestors a leg up in foraging for food. There's preliminary evidence that a small proportion of women are *tetrachromats*, meaning their eyes contain four types of cones: the three cone types most of us possess plus an additional cone for a color between red and green (Jameson, Highnote, & Wasserman, 2001).

Opponent Process Theory. Trichromatic theory accounts nicely for how our three cone types work together to detect the full range of colors. But further research revealed a phenomenon that trichromatic theory can't explain—afterimages. Afterimages occur when we've stared at one color for a long time and then look away. We'll often see a different colored replica of the same image, as in Figure 4.12. Trichromatic theory doesn't easily explain why looking at one color consistently results in seeing another color in the afterimage, such as afterimages for red always appearing green. It turns out that afterimages arise from the visual cortex's processing of information from our rods and cones.

Some people occasionally report faint negative afterimages surrounding objects or other individuals. This phenomenon may have given rise to the paranormal idea that we're all encircled by mystical "auras" consisting of psychical energy (Neher, 1990). Nevertheless, because no one's been able to photograph auras under carefully controlled conditions, there's no support for this extraordinary claim (Nickel, 2000).

Extraordinary Claims

Is the evidence as strong as the claim?

Ruling Out Rival Hypotheses

Have important alternative explanations for the findings been excluded?

A competing model, which provides an explanation for afterimages, **opponent process theory**, holds that we perceive colors in terms of three pairs of opponent cells: red or green, blue or yellow, or black or white. Afterimages, which appear in complementary colors, illustrate opponent processing. Ganglion cells of the retina and cells in the visual area of the thalamus that respond to red spots are inhibited by green spots. Other cells show the opposite responses, and still others distinguish yellow from blue spots. Our nervous system uses both trichromatic and opponent

trichromatic theory

idea that color vision is based on our sensitivity to three primary colors

▶ **Replicability**

Can the results be duplicated in other studies?

color blindness

inability to see some or all colors

opponent process theory

theory that we perceive colors in terms of three pairs of opponent colors: either red or green, blue or yellow, or black or white

◀ **Ruling Out Rival Hypotheses**

Have important alternative explanations for the findings been excluded?

Figure 4.11 The Ishihara Test for Red–Green Color Blindness.

If you can't see the two-digit number, you probably have red–green color blindness. This condition is common, especially among males.

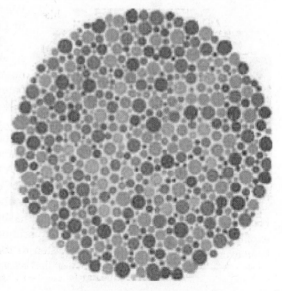

Figure 4.12 Afterimages: Opponent Processes in Action.

Find a patch of blank white wall or place a blank sheet of white paper nearby before you begin. Then relax your eyes and fix your gaze on the center of the skull for at least 30 seconds without looking around or away. Afterward, stare at the white wall or paper for a few seconds. What do you see?"

Replicability

Can the results be duplicated in other studies?

Ben Underwood has developed an amazing ability to use human echolocation to overcome many of the limitations of his blindness. Humans don't usually rely much on echolocation, although many whales do.

Ruling Out Rival Hypotheses

Have important alternative explanations for the findings been excluded?

processing principles during color vision, but different neurons rely on one principle more than the other. There's a useful lesson here that applies to many controversies in science: Two ideas that seem contradictory are sometimes both partly correct—they're merely describing differing aspects of the same phenomenon.

> ## Journal Prompt
>
> First, describe the opponent process theory of color vision and the trichromatic theory of color vision. Next, describe several ways in which the two competing models differ in their explanation of color perception.

When We Can't See or Perceive Visually

We've learned how we see, and how we don't always see exactly what's there. Yet some 39 million people worldwide can't see at all (World Health Organization, 2012).

BLINDNESS. Blindness is the inability to see, or more specifically, the presence of vision less than or equal to 20/200 on the familiar Snellen eye chart, on which 20/20 is perfect vision. For people with 20/200 vision, objects at 20 feet appear as they would at 200 feet in a normally sighted person. The majority of cases of blindness—from cataracts, a clouding of the lens of the eye, and glaucoma, a disease that causes pressure on the eye and damages the optic nerve—are treatable, and are most likely to occur as people age.

The blind cope with their loss of vision in various ways—often relying more on other senses, including touch. This issue has been controversial over the years, with studies both replicating and contradicting a heightened sense of touch in the blind. Recent studies suggest that tactile (touch) sensitivity is indeed heightened in blind adults, giving them the same sensitivity as someone 23 years younger (Goldreich & Kanics, 2003). It's further known that the visual cortex of blind persons undergoes profound changes in function, rendering it sensitive to touch inputs (Sadato, 2005). This means they can devote more cortex—somatosensory cortex and visual cortex—to a touch task, such as reading Braille. This phenomenon illustrates brain plasticity, in which some brain regions gradually take over the jobs previously assigned to others.

BLINDSIGHT: HOW ARE SOME BLIND PEOPLE ABLE TO NAVIGATE THEIR WORLDS? Recently, researchers (de Gelder et al., 2008) reported that a blind person, known by the initials TN, was able to walk around an obstacle course, with no assistance at all, side-stepping office equipment, boxes, and a variety of smaller objects. With normal eyes, TN is cortically blind—following several strokes, his brain fails to register sensory input. TN's rare ability may be the most impressive demonstration to date of a remarkable phenomenon called *blindsight*—the ability of blind people with damage to their cortex to make correct guesses about the appearance of things around them (Hamm et al., 2003; Weiskrantz, 1986). In TN's case, researchers used high-tech brain imaging to show that he was able to recognize facial expressions in angry, fearful, or joyous faces.

Because blindsight operates outside the bounds of conscious activity, some non-scientists have suggested that it may be a paranormal phenomenon. Yet there's a parsimonious natural explanation: People with blindsight have suffered damage to V1, the primary visual cortex, so that route of information flow to visual association areas is blocked. Coarser visual information still reaches the visual association cortex through an alternative pathway and bypasses V1. This visual information probably accounts for blindsight (Moore et al., 1995; Stoerig & Cowey, 1997; Weiskrantz, 1986).

Occam's Razor

Does a simpler explanation fit the data just as well?

Because TN was not deprived of auditory cues, the question arises of whether he might have been able to pull of his navigation feat with another equally amazing ability—echolocation. Certain animals, such as bats, dolphins, and many whales, emit sounds and listen to their echoes to determine their distance from a wall or barrier, a phenomenon called *echolocation*.

Remarkably, there's evidence that humans are capable of a crude form of echolocation. Echolocation might account for the fact that blind persons can sometimes detect objects a few feet away from them (Buckingham et al., 2015; Schörnich, Nagy, & Wiegrebe, 2012; Teng, Puri, & Whitney, 2011) and for TN's stumble free-walk. Ben Underwood, who was blinded at age three by retinal cancer, learned to make clicking noises that bounced off surfaces and clued him in to his surroundings. He rides his skateboard and plays basketball and video games. Recently, scientists have discovered that when blind people expert in echolocation use their ability to navigate in their environments, the same parts of the brain associated with visual images in sighted people become highly active (Thaler, Arnott, & Goodale, 2011).

Although the echolocation explanation can't be ruled out completely, the researchers who studied TN argue that echolocation is unlikely in that it's not a particularly effective way to detect the small objects TN successfully avoided. What's clear is that blindsight and echolocation are remarkable examples of how even subtle signals from neural pathways can impact our rich sensory experience of the world.

VISUAL AGNOSIA. *Visual agnosia* is a deficit in perceiving objects. A person with this condition can tell us the shape and color of an object but can't recognize or name it. At a dinner party, such a person might say, "please pass that eight-inch silver thing with a round end" rather than, "please pass the serving spoon." Oliver Sacks's 1985 book *The Man Who Mistook His Wife for a Hat* includes a case study of a man with visual agnosia who did exactly as the title suggests; he misperceived his wife as a fashion accessory.

4.3: Hearing: The Auditory System

4.3a **Explain how the ear starts the auditory process.**
4.3b **Identify the different kinds of auditory perception.**

If a tree falls in the forest and no one is around to hear it, does it make a sound? Ponder that age-old question while we explore our sense of hearing: **audition**. Next to vision, hearing is probably the sensory modality we rely on most to acquire information about our world.

audition
our sense of hearing

Sound: Mechanical Vibration

Sound is vibration, a kind of mechanical energy traveling through a medium, usually air. The disturbance created by vibration of molecules of air produces sound waves. Sound waves can travel through any gas, liquid, or solid, but we hear them best when they travel through air. In a perfectly empty space (a vacuum), there can't be sound because there aren't any airborne molecules to vibrate. That should help us answer our opening question: Because there are air molecules in the forest, a falling tree most definitely makes a loud thud even if nobody can hear it.

PITCH. Sounds have *pitch*, which corresponds to the frequency of the wave. Higher frequency corresponds to higher pitch, lower frequency to lower pitch. Scientists measure pitch in cycles per second, or hertz (Hz) (see Figure 4.13). The human ear can pick up frequencies ranging from about 20 to 20,000 Hz (see Figure 4.14).

When it comes to sensitivity to pitch, age matters. Younger people are more sensitive to higher pitch tones than older adults. A ring tone for cell phones has ingeniously exploited this simple fact of nature, allowing teenagers to hear their cell phones ring while many of their parents or teachers can't (Vitello, 2006).

LOUDNESS. The amplitude—or height—of the sound wave corresponds to *loudness*, measured in decibels (dB) (refer again to Figure 4.14). Loud noise results in increased wave amplitude because there's more mechanical disturbance, that is, more vibrating airborne molecules. Table 4.3 lists various common sounds and their typical loudness.

Figure 4.13 Sound Wave Frequency and Amplitude.

Sound wave frequency (cycles per second) is the inverse of wavelength (cycle width). Sound wave amplitude is the height of the cycle. The frequency for middle C (a) is lower than that for middle A (b).

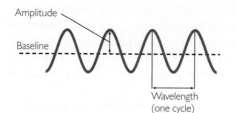

(a) Long-wavelength (low-frequency) sound

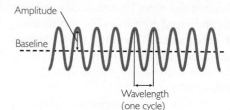

(b) Short-wavelength (high-frequency) sound

timbre

complexity or quality of sound that makes musical instruments, human voices, or other sources sound unique

Figure 4.14 The Audible Spectrum (in Hz).

The human ear is sensitive to mechanical vibration from about 20 to 20,000 Hz.

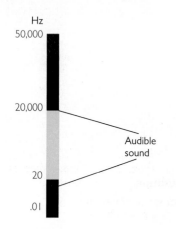

TIMBRE. **Timbre** refers to the quality or complexity of the sound. Different musical instruments sound different because they differ in timbre, and the same holds for human voices.

The Structure and Function of the Ear

Just as sense receptors for vision transduce light into neural activity, sense receptors for hearing transduce sound into neural activity. The ear has three parts: Outer, middle, and inner, each of which performs a different job (see Figure 4.15). The *outer ear*, consisting of the *pinna* (the part of the ear we see, namely, its skin and cartilage flap) and ear canal, has the simplest function; it funnels sound waves onto the *eardrum*.

On the other side of the eardrum lies the *middle ear*, containing the *ossicles*—the three tiniest bones in the body—named the hammer, anvil, and stirrup, after their shapes. These ossicles vibrate at the frequency of the sound wave, transmitting it from the eardrum to the inner ear.

Table 4.3 Common Sounds.

This decibel (dB) table compares some common sounds and shows how they rank in potential harm to hearing.

Sound	Noise Level (DB)	Effect
Jet engines (near) Rock concerts (varies)	140 110–140	We begin to feel pain at about 125 dB.
Thunderclap (near) Power saw (chainsaw)	120 110	Regular exposure to sound greater than 100 dB for more than 1 minute risks permanent hearing loss.
Garbage truck/cement mixer	100	No more than 15 minutes of unprotected exposure is recommended for sounds between 90 and 100 dB.
Motorcycle (25 ft) Lawn mower	88 85–90	Very annoying; 85 dB is the level at which hearing damage (after 8 hours) begins.
Average city traffic	80	Annoying; interferes with conversation; constant exposure may cause damage.
Vacuum cleaner	70	Intrusive; interferes with telephone conversation.
Normal conversation	50–65	Comfortable hearing levels are less than 60 dB.
Whisper Rustling leaves	30 20	Very quiet Just audible

SOURCE: NIDCD, 1990.

Figure 4.15 The Human Ear and Its Parts.

A cutaway section through the human ear and a close-up diagram of the hair cells.

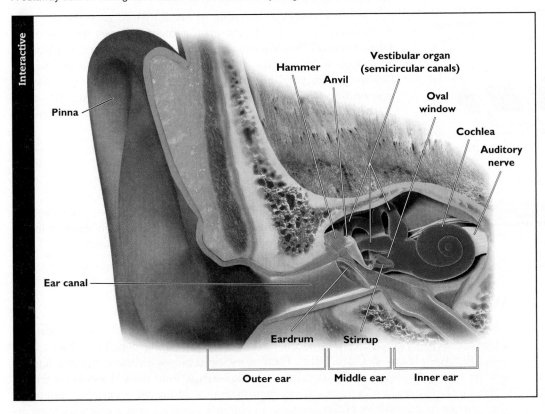

Once sound waves enter the *inner ear*, the **cochlea** converts vibration into neural activity. The outer part of the spiral-shaped cochlea is bony, but its inner cavity is filled with a thick fluid. Vibrations from sound waves disturb this fluid and travel to the base of the cochlea, where pressure is released and transduction occurs.

Also located in the inner ear, the **organ of Corti** and **basilar membrane** are critical to hearing because *hair cells* are embedded within them (see Figure 4.15). Hair cells are where transduction of auditory information takes place: They convert acoustic information into action potentials. Here's how: Hair cells contain cilia (hairlike structures) that protrude into the fluid of the cochlea. When sound waves travel through the cochlea, the resulting pressure deflects these cilia, exciting the hair cells (Roberts, Howard, & Hudspeth, 1988). That information feeds into the *auditory nerve*, which travels to the brain, through the thalamus, which is a sensory relay station.

Once the auditory nerve enters the brain, it makes contact with the brain stem, which sends auditory information higher—all the way up the auditory cortex. At each stage, perception becomes increasingly complex. In this respect, auditory perception is like visual perception.

The primary auditory cortex processes different tones in different places (see Figure 4.16). That's because each place receives information from a specific place in the basilar membrane. Hair cells located at the base of the basilar membrane are most excited by high-pitched tones, whereas hair cells at the top of the basilar membrane are most excited by low-pitched tones. Scientists call this model of pitch perception **place theory**, because a specific place along the basilar membrane—and in the auditory cortex, too—matches a tone with a specific pitch (Békésy, 1949). Place theory accounts only for our perception of high-pitched tones, namely those from 5,000 to 20,000 Hz.

There are two routes to perceiving low-pitched tones. We'll discuss the simpler way first. In **frequency theory**, the rate at which neurons fire action potentials faithfully reproduces the pitch. This method works well up to 100 Hz, because many neurons have maximal firing rates near that limit. *Volley theory* is a variation of frequency theory that works for

cochlea

bony, spiral-shaped sense organ used for hearing

organ of Corti

tissue containing the hair cells necessary for hearing

basilar membrane

membrane supporting the organ of Corti and hair cells in the cochlea

place theory

specific place along the basilar membrane matches a tone with a specific pitch

frequency theory

rate at which neurons fire the action potential reproduces the pitch

Figure 4.16 The Tone-Based Organization of the Basilar Membrane.

Hair cells at the base of the basilar membrane respond to high-pitched tones, whereas hair cells at the top of the basilar membrane respond to low-pitched tones.

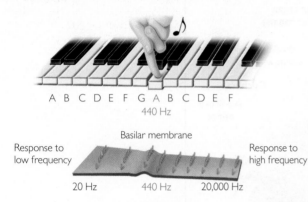

tones between 100 and 5,000 Hz. According to volley theory, sets of neurons fire at their highest rate, say 100 Hz, slightly out of sync with each other to reach overall rates up to 5,000 Hz.

When it comes to listening to music, we're sensitive not only to different tones, but to the arrangement of tones into melodies (Weinberger, 2006). We react differently to pleasant and unpleasant melodies. In one study, music that literally provoked feelings of "chills" or "shivers" boosted activity in the same brain regions corresponding to euphoric responses to sex, food, and drugs (Blood & Zatorre, 2001). So there may be a good reason why "sex," "drugs," and "rock and roll" often go together.

> ## Journal Prompt
>
> First, briefly describe the place theory and the frequency theory of sound perception. Next, contrast these two theories in terms of how we perceive high and low pitched sounds.

When We Can't Hear

About one in 1,000 people are deaf: They suffer from a profound loss of hearing. Approximately 15 percent of U.S. adults have detectable hearing deficits in one or both ears (Blackwell, Lucas, & Clark, 2014). There are several causes of deafness, some largely genetic, others deriving from disease, injury, or exposure to loud noise (Pascolini & Smith, 2009). *Conductive deafness* is the result of a malfunctioning of the ear, especially a failure of the eardrum or the ossicles of the inner ear. In contrast, *nerve deafness* is due to damage to the auditory nerve.

If your grandmother warns you to "Turn down the sound on your iPod, or you'll go deaf by the time you're my age," there's more than a ring of truth in her warning. Loud sounds, especially those that last a long time or are repeated, can damage our hair cells and lead to *noise-induced hearing loss* (Le Prell et al., 2012). This type of hearing loss is often accompanied by tinnitus, a ringing, roaring, hissing, or buzzing sound in the ears that can be deeply disturbing (Baguley, McFerran & Hall, 2013). Hearing loss can also occur after exposure to one extremely loud sound, such as an explosion. But most of us lose some hearing ability as we age—especially for high-frequency sounds—as a by-product of the loss of sensory cells and degeneration of the auditory nerve, even if we've never attended a rock concert without earplugs (Ohlemiller & Frisina, 2008).

4.4: Smell and Taste: The Sensual Senses

4.4a   Identify how we sense and perceive odors and tastes.

Without smell and taste, many of our everyday experiences would be bland. Cuisines of the world feature characteristic spices that enliven their dishes. Similarly, smell and taste stimulate our senses and elevate our spirits. The term *comfort food* refers to familiar dishes that we crave because of the warm memories they evoke.

Smell is also called **olfaction**, and taste **gustation**. These senses work hand in hand, enhancing our liking of some foods and our disliking of others. Smell and taste are the chemical senses because we derive these sensory experiences from chemicals in substances.

Animals use their sense of smell for many purposes—tracking prey, establishing territories, and recognizing the opposite sex, to name but a few. We humans aren't the most smell-oriented of creatures. The average dog is at least 100,000 times more sensitive to smell than we are, which explains why police use trained dogs rather than nosy people to sniff for bombs. To

olfaction

our sense of smell

gustation

our sense of taste

their surprise, researchers discovered that trained dogs, commonly Labrador retrievers, appeared to use their superior sense of smell to identify people with a high degree of accuracy with cancers of the lung, prostate, bladder, skin, and colon by detecting odors from organic compounds in samples of their breath, urine, or tissue scraps (Brooks et al., 2015; Jezierski et al., 2015). Nevertheless, there's a great deal of variability in the ability to dogs to correctly identify cancer specimens, even after extensive training, and an alternative explanation for positive findings is that dogs latch onto subtle responses of their handlers that unconsciously signal correct responses based on their beliefs regarding the presence or absence of cancer in samples (Lit, Schweitzer, & Oberbauer, 2011). If the dogs are, indeed, sniffing chemical compounds, it's not clear exactly which chemical compounds or combination of compounds the dogs sniff out to accomplish what may be an amazing feat. No doubt, researchers will continue to doggedly (pun intended) pursue the question of whether our "best friends" can truly detect cancer.

> **▶ Ruling Out Rival Hypotheses**
>
> Have important alternative explanations for the findings been excluded?

The most critical function of our chemical senses is to sample our food before swallowing it. The smell and taste of sour milk are powerful stimuli that few of us can ignore even if we want to. An unfamiliar bitter taste may signal dangerous bacteria or poison in our food. We develop food preferences for "safe" foods and base them on a combination of smell and taste. One study of young French women found that only those who already liked red meat—its smell and its taste—responded favorably to pictures of it (Audebert, Deiss, & Rousset, 2006). We like what smells and tastes good to us.

Culture also shapes what we perceive as delicious or disgusting. The prospect of eating sacred cow meat (as in a hamburger) would be as off-putting to Hindus as eating fried tarantulas, a delicacy in Cambodia, or Casu Marzu, a Sardinian cheese filled with insect larvae, would be to most Americans. Even within a society there are pronounced differences in food choices, as American meat lovers and vegans enjoy vastly different diets. We can acquire food preferences by means of learning, including modeling of eating behaviors, parental approval of food choices, and availability of foods (Rozin, 2006).

What Are Odors and Flavors?

Odors are airborne chemicals that interact with receptors in the lining of our nasal passages. Our noses are veritable smell connoisseurs, capable of detecting between 2,000 and 4,000 different odors. Not everything, though, has an odor. Clean water, for example, has no odor or taste. Not all animals smell airborne molecules. The star-nosed mole, named for its peculiarly shaped snout, can detect odors underwater (Catania, 2006). The animal blows out air bubbles and "sniffs" them back in to find food underwater and underground.

taste bud

sense receptor in the tongue that responds to sweet, salty, sour, bitter, umami, and perhaps fat

In contrast, we can detect only a few tastes. We're sensitive to five basic tastes—sweet, salty, sour, bitter, and umami, the last of which is a recently uncovered "meaty" or "savory" taste. There's preliminary evidence for a sixth taste, one for fatty foods (Besnard, Passilly-Degrace, & Khan, 2016; Gilbertson et al., 1997). Most recently, evidence has emerged for a seventh possible taste, one for starch, which researchers have called (surprise!) "starchy" (Lapis, Penner, & Lim, 2016)

Sense Receptors for Smell and Taste

We humans have more than 1,000 olfactory (smell) genes, 347 of which code for olfactory receptors (Buck & Axel, 1991). Each olfactory neuron contains a single type of olfactory receptor, which "recognizes" an odorant on the basis of its shape. This lock-and-key concept is similar to how neurotransmitters bind to receptor sites. When olfactory receptors come into contact with odor molecules, action potentials in olfactory neurons are triggered.

We detect taste with **taste buds** on our tongues. Bumps on the tongue called *papillae* contain numerous taste buds (Figure 4.17). There are separate taste buds for sweet, salty, sour, bitter, and umami (Chandrashekar et al., 2006).

Figure 4.17 How We Detect Taste.

The tongue contains many taste buds, which transmit information to the brain through nerve fibers as shown in this close-up.

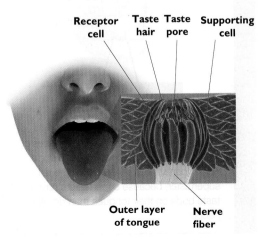

Receptor cell   Taste hair   Taste pore   Supporting cell

Outer layer of tongue   Nerve fiber

use the *vomeronasal organ*, located in the bone between the nose and the mouth, to detect pheromones. The vomeronasal organ doesn't develop in humans (Witt & Wozniak, 2006), causing some to suggest that humans are insensitive to pheromones. An alternative hypothesis is that humans detect pheromones via a different route. This idea is supported by the discovery of human pheromones (Pearson, 2006). A nerve that's only recently received attention, called "nerve zero," may step in to enable pheromones to trigger responses in the "hot-button sex regions of the brain" (Fields, 2007).

Still, we should be cautious about shelling out sizable chunks of our salaries on pheromone-based products that promise to stir up romance. Scientific evidence suggests they probably won't work. Pheromones are large molecules, so although it's easy to transfer a pheromone from one person to another during a passionate kiss, sending them across a restaurant table is definitely a stretch. Moreover, there's far more to human romance than physical chemistry; psychological chemistry matters, too.

Smells other than pheromones may contribute to human sexual behavior. Remarkably, human sperm cells may contain smell receptors that help them to find their way to female eggs (Spehr et al., 2003). Sometimes truth *is* stranger than fiction.

> ### Journal Prompt
>
> Smell is important in triggering memories in addition to stirring sexual feelings and behaviors. Sometimes a smell can connect us to a memory from long ago. Do you associate a certain smell with a special memory? Why do think the smell and the memory are linked?

When We Can't Smell or Taste

About 2 million Americans suffer from disorders of taste, smell, or both. Gradual loss of taste and smell can be a part of normal aging, as the number of taste buds, routinely replaced when we're younger, declines. But these losses can also result from diseases, such as diabetes and high blood pressure.

There are many disorders of olfaction (Hirsch, 2003). Although not as serious as blindness or deafness, they can pose several dangers, such as an inability to detect gas leaks and smell spoiled food before we eat it. Damage to the olfactory nerve, along with brain damage caused by such disorders as Parkinson's and Alzheimer's diseases can damage our sense of smell and ability to identify odors (Haehner, Hummel, & Reichmann, 2014; Zou et al., 2016). Losing our sense of taste can also produce negative health consequences. Patients with cancer who lose their sense of taste have a worse prognosis than other patients, because they can suffer from malnutrition; are less able to tolerate the side effects of chemotherapy, surgeries, and other treatments; and have less energy to recover quickly. Adding flavor enhancers to the diet in the elderly can improve their immune and health status. So taste may add an essential "zest" to life: a psychological flavoring that can help to ward off disease by boosting appetite.

4.5: Our Body Senses: Touch, Body Position, and Balance

4.5a Describe the three different body senses.
4.5b Explain how pain perception differs from touch perception.
4.5c Describe the field of psychology called *human factors*.

Using only the chalk on his hands and climbing shoes, Alain Roberts, nicknamed "The French Spiderman," has scaled the world's tallest skyscrapers. To do so, he must rely on his senses of touch, body position, and balance. One miscalculation, one slip of his foot or his hand, and he would plummet from the heights of buildings more than 80 stories tall.

Advocates of aromatherapy claim that essential oils derived from plants have special healing powers. Many claim that such oils can cure depression, anxiety disorders, insomnia, and other ailments. Although the pleasant smells of such plants can no doubt lift our moods a bit, there's little evidence that they possess magical curative power (McCutcheon, 1996).

Perfume manufacturers have long advertised fragrances as increasing attraction and romance. But at least in nonhuman animals, the chemicals that produce the most potent effects on sexual behaviors are actually odorless pheromones.

Fortunately for Roberts, he, like the rest of us, has three body senses that work in tandem. The system we use for touch and pain is the **somatosensory** (*somato-*, for "body") system. We also have a body position sense, called *proprioception*, or kinesthetic sense, and a sense of equilibrium or balance, called the *vestibular sense*.

The Somatosensory System: Touch and Pain

The stimuli that activate the somatosensory system come in a variety of types. In this respect, this sense differs from vision and audition, each of which is devoted mainly to a single stimulus type.

PRESSURE, TEMPERATURE, AND INJURY. Our somatosensory system responds to stimuli applied to the skin, such as light touch or deep pressure, hot or cold temperature, or chemical or mechanical (touch-related) injury that produces pain. Somatosensory stimuli can be very specific, such as the embossed patterns of a letter written in Braille, or generalized to a large area of the body. Damage to internal organs sometimes causes "referred pain"—pain in a different location—such as an ache felt throughout the left arm and shoulder during a heart attack.

SPECIALIZED AND FREE NERVE ENDINGS IN THE SKIN. We sense light touch, deep pressure, and temperature with specialized nerve endings located on the ends of sensory nerves in the skin (see Figure 4.20). We also sense touch, temperature, and especially pain with *free nerve endings*, which are far more plentiful than specialized nerve endings. Nerve endings of all types are distributed unevenly across our body surface. Most of them are in our fingertips (which explains why it really stings when we cut our finger, say, in a paper cut), followed by our lips, face, hands, and feet. We have the fewest in the middle of our backs, perhaps explaining why even a strenuous deep back massage rarely makes us scream in agony.

HOW WE PERCEIVE TOUCH AND PAIN. Information about body touch, temperature, and painful stimuli travels in our somatic nerves before entering the spinal cord. Touch

Alain Roberts, nicknamed "The French Spiderman," relies on his senses of touch, body position, and balance to scale skyscrapers with only chalk and climbing shoes.

somatosensory

our sense of touch, temperature, and pain

Figure 4.20 The Sense of Touch.

The skin contains many specialized and free nerve endings that detect mechanical pressure, temperature, and pain.

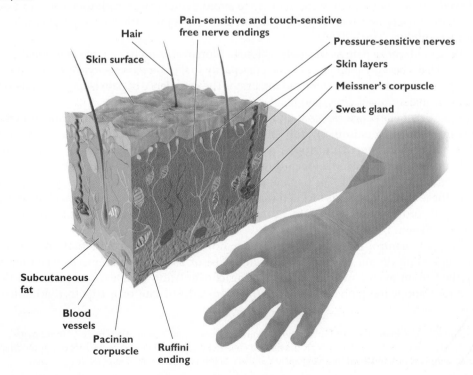

Fact vs. Fiction

Consuming ice cream or other cold substances too quickly causes pain in our brains. (See bottom of page for answer.)

○ Fact

○ Fiction

information travels more quickly than information about pain stimuli. Many of us have discovered this fact when stubbing our toes on a piece of furniture: We first feel our toes hitting the furniture but don't experience the stinging pain (ouch!) until a second or two later. That's because touch and pain have different functions. Touch informs us of our immediate surroundings and keys us into urgent matters, such as when something feels hot to avoid a serious burn, whereas pain alerts us to take care of injuries, which can often wait a little while.

Often touch and pain information activate local spinal reflexes before traveling to brain sites dedicated to perception. In some cases, painful stimuli trigger the withdrawal reflex. When we touch a fire or hot stove, we pull away immediately to avoid getting burned.

After activating spinal reflexes, touch and pain information travels upward through parts of the brain stem and thalamus to reach the somatosensory cortex (Bushnell et al., 1999). Additional cortical areas are active during the localization of touch information, such as association areas of the parietal lobe.

As we've all discovered, pain comes in many varieties: sharp, stabbing, throbbing, burning, and aching. Many of the types of pain perception relate to the pain-causing stimulus—thermal (heat-related), chemical, or mechanical pain can also be acute, that is, short-lived, or chronic, that is, enduring, perhaps even lasting years. Each kind of pain-producing stimulus has a *threshold*, or point at which we perceive it as painful. People differ in their pain thresholds. Surprisingly, one study showed that people with naturally red hair require more anesthetic than do people with other hair (Liem et al., 2004). Of course, this correlational finding doesn't mean that red hair causes lower pain thresholds. Instead, some of the differences in people's thresholds are probably due to genetic factors that happen to be associated with hair color. People with the genetic variation associated with red hair are more than twice as likely to avoid dental care, which they come to associate with anxiety and fear of pain, compared with people with no comparable genetic variation (Binkley et al., 2009).

Correlation vs. Causation

Can we be sure that A causes B?

We can't localize pain as precisely as touch. Moreover, pain has a large emotional component. That's because pain information goes partly to the somatosensory cortex and partly to limbic centers in the brain stem and forebrain. The experience of pain is frequently associated with anxiety, uncertainty, and helplessness.

Scientists believe we can control pain in part by controlling our thoughts and emotions in reaction to painful stimuli (Bushnell, Čeko, & Low, 2013; Moore, 2008). This belief has been bolstered by stories of people withstanding excruciating pain during combat or natural childbirth. According to the **gate control model** of Ronald Melzack and Patrick Wall (1965, 1970) depicted in the video *Gate Control Theory of Pain*, pain under these circumstances is blocked from consciousness because neural mechanisms in the spinal cord function as a "gate," controlling the flow of sensory input to the central nervous system.

gate control model

idea that pain is blocked or gated from consciousness by neural mechanisms in spinal cord

The gate control model can account for how pain varies from situation to situation depending on our psychological state. Most of us have experienced becoming so absorbed in an event, such as an interesting conversation or television program, that we forgot about the pain we were feeling from a headache or a trip to the dentist's

Answer: Fiction. Consuming ice cream or other cold substances too quickly doesn't cause pain in our brains. "Brain freeze," as it's sometimes called, doesn't affect the brain at all. It's produced by a constriction of blood vessels in the roof of our mouths in response to intense cold temperatures, followed by an expansion of these blood vessels, producing pain.

office. The gate control model proposes that the stimulation we experience competes with and blocks the pain from consciousness. Because pain demands attention, distraction is an effective way of short-circuiting painful sensations (Eccleston & Crombez, 1999; McCaul & Malott, 1984). For example, scientists discovered that they could relieve the pain of patients with burns undergoing physical therapy, wound care, and painful skin grafts by immersing them in a virtual environment populated by snowmen and igloos (Hoffman & Patterson, 2005). On the flip side, when people dwell on catastrophic thoughts about pain (such as "I won't be able to bear it") it can open the floodgates of distress.

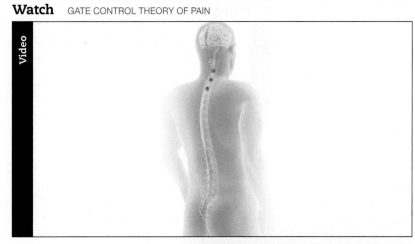

Watch GATE CONTROL THEORY OF PAIN

Video

What's the evidence for the involvement of the spinal cord in the gate control model? Patrick Wall (2000) showed that the brain controls activity in the spinal cord, enabling us to turn up, damp down, or in some cases ignore pain. The placebo effect exerts a strong response on subjective reports of pain. Falk Eippert and his colleagues (Eippert et al., 2009) used brain imaging to demonstrate that pain-related activity in the spinal cord is sharply reduced when participants receive an application of a placebo cream they're told would alleviate pain. Placebos may also stimulate the body's production of its natural painkillers: endorphins (see LO 3.1a) (Glasser & Frishman, 2008). Scientists are investigating ways of boosting endorphins while deactivating glial cells in the spinal cord that amplify pain (Bartley, 2009; Watkins & Maier, 2002).

Why do you think the designers of this virtual world chose imagery of snowmen and igloos for patients with burns? What imagery would you choose and why?

> **Ruling Out Rival Hypotheses**
>
> Have important alternative explanations for the findings been excluded?

Are there ethnic differences in how people experience pain? There's indeed evidence that people of certain cultural backgrounds, such as American Indians, Cambodians, Chinese, and Germans, are more reserved and less likely to communicate openly about pain, whereas South and Central Americans consider it more acceptable to moan and cry out when in pain (Ondeck, 2003). An alternative hypothesis is that healthcare professionals treat certain ethnic groups differently. African Americans and Hispanics are less likely than Caucasians to receive analgesic (anti-pain) medication during emergency department visits (Bonham, 2001), which could account for some of the differences in reports of pain. Although African Americans exhibit lower pain tolerance in experimental situations compared with non-Hispanic Whites (Rahim-Williams et al., 2012), patients who are African Americans may be more likely to encounter negative stereotypes among physicians that underestimate their pain intensity more than other sociodemographic groups, leading to inadequate pain management and needless suffering (Stanton et al., 2007; Tait & Chibnall, 2014).

Are there any unusual activities for which a stoic mindset may come in handy? Some popular psychology gurus certainly think so. Firewalkers, popular in India, Japan, North Africa, and the Polynesian islands, have walked 20- to 40-foot-long beds of burning embers. Although the practice has been around since as early as 1200 BC, there's recently been a glut of "Firewalking Seminars" in California, New York, and other states. These motivational classes promise ordinary people everything from heightened self-confidence to spiritual enlightenment—all by walking down an 8- to 12-foot-long path of burning embers. Contrary to what we might learn at these seminars, success in firewalking has nothing to do with pain sensitivity and everything to do with physics. The type of coal or wood used in firewalking has a low rate of heat exchange, such that it burns red hot in the center while remaining less hot on the outside (Kurtus, 2000). So any of us can firewalk successfully just so long as we walk (or even better, run) over the burning embers quickly enough. Still, accidents can occur if the fire isn't prepared properly or if the firewalker walks too slowly. Case in point: Thirty firewalkers who participated in a Tony Robbins motivational seminar in Dallas, Texas, suffered mild foot burns, and five were hospitalized (Page, 2016).

Although firewalking seminars are extremely popular, there's nothing magical or mysterious about firewalking—but don't try it at home.

Fact vs. Fiction

Trying to "tough it out" and ignore and suppress chronic pain is the best way to cope with pain in the long run. (See bottom of page for answer.)

○ Fact

○ Fiction

phantom pain

pain or discomfort felt in an amputated limb

PHANTOM LIMB ILLUSION. Persons with amputated limbs often experience the eerie phenomenon of **phantom pain**, pain or discomfort in the missing limb. About 90 percent of amputees experience phantom limb sensations (Chan et al., 2007). The missing limb often feels as if it's in an uncomfortably distorted position.

Vilayanur Ramachandran and colleagues developed a creative treatment for phantom limb pain called the *mirror box* (Ramachandran & Rogers-Ramachandran, 1996). Patients with phantom limb pain position their other limb so that it's reflected in exactly the position that the amputated limb would assume. Then the patient performs the "mirror equivalent" of the exercise the amputated limb needs to relieve a cramp or otherwise get comfortable. For the mirror box to relieve pain or discomfort in the

Psychomythology
Psychic Healing of Chronic Pain

Many people believe in the power of mind over pain, but some individuals claim to possess supernatural abilities or "gifts" that enable them to reduce others' pain. Is this fact or fiction? In the summer of 2003, the Australian television show *A Current Affair* approached psychologists at the University of Bond to conduct a double-blind, randomized, controlled test of psychic healing powers.

Using a newspaper advertisement, the researchers located volunteers suffering from pain caused by cancer, chronic back conditions, and fibromyalgia (a chronic condition of muscle, joint, and bone pain and fatigue) (Lyvers, Barling, & Harding-Clark, 2006). The researchers assigned half of the participants with chronic pain to a group that received psychic healing and the other half to a control condition that didn't. Neither the participants nor those interacting with them knew who was assigned to which group. In the healing condition, the psychic healer viewed and touched photographs of the participants with chronic pain in another room. The healer was given all the time deemed necessary.

The researchers used the McGill Pain Questionnaire (Melzack, 1975) to test participants' levels of discomfort before and after the trial. Then, researchers compared their before and after scores. On average, the scores showed no change before

and after treatment, with half the participants reporting more pain and half reporting less pain regardless of whether psychic healing occurred.

These results agreed with previous findings obtained by British researchers on spiritual healing (Abbot et al., 2001). In a study of 120 chronic pain sufferers, they similarly used the McGill Pain Questionnaire. These researchers compared pain reports before and after face-to-face versus distant spiritual healing compared with no spiritual healing. The results suggested that despite the popularity of spiritual healing in England, this method lacks scientific support. A different research team, however, reported an improvement in neck pain following spiritual healing (Gerard, Smith, & Simpson, 2003). But because their study lacked a placebo treatment or blinding of the therapist, these authors couldn't rule out a placebo effect.

Lyvers and colleagues (2006) addressed the placebo effect with a double-blind design and rated their participants with chronic pain on a five-point scale that assessed the degree to which they believed in psychic phenomena. They found no correlation between psychic healing and decreased pain; however, they found that decreases in reported pain correlated with increased belief in psychic phenomena. So beliefs in the paranormal may create reality, at least psychological reality.

Answer: Fiction. For many years, the scientific consensus has been that we can ignore pain, or at least withstand it, with a stoic mindset (Szasz, 1989). With chronic pain, this strategy doesn't work particularly well. In fact, practicing mindfulness meditation, in which meditators are instructed to accept pain nonjudgmentally, rather than ignoring or suppressing it, is effective for many individuals in reducing pain and accompanying distress (Baer, 2015; Kabat-Zinn, 1982). In one approach, practitioners mindfully observe pain sensations, emotions, and attitudes surrounding such sensations and mentally shuttle back and forth between painful and neutral or pleasant body sensations (Smalley & Winston, 2010).

amputated limb, the illusion must be realistic. Seventeen out of 18 patients were successfully treated for phantom limb pain with the mirror box following amputation of one or more lower limbs resulting from injuries suffered as a result of the 2010 earthquake in Haiti (Miller, Seckel, & Ramachandran, 2012).

The mirror box consists of a two-chamber box with a mirror in the center. When the participant looks at her right hand in the box, it creates the illusion that the mirror image of her right hand is her left hand. This box can sometimes alleviate the discomfort of phantom limb pain by positioning the intact limb as the phantom limb appears to be positioned, and then moving it to a more comfortable position.

> ## Journal Prompt
> Psychic healing for chronic pain appears to reduce pain by way of a placebo effect. If a placebo effect is responsible, but the person feels less pain, are there any dangers or costs to the patient in using this method?

WHEN WE CAN'T FEEL PAIN. Just as some people are blind or deaf, others experience disorders that impair their ability to sense pain. Although pain isn't fun, research on pain insensitivity shows that pain serves an essential function. Pain insensitivity present from birth is an extremely rare condition that's sometimes inherited (Victor & Ropper, 2001). For the most part, children with this condition are completely unable to detect painful stimuli. Lacking any awareness of pain, they may chew off parts of their bodies, like their fingertips or the ends of their tongues, or suffer bone fractures without realizing it. Needless to say, this condition can be exceedingly dangerous. Other individuals show an indifference to painful stimuli: They can identify the type of pain but experience no significant discomfort from it.

Proprioception and Vestibular Sense: Body Position and Balance

Right at this moment you're probably sitting somewhere. You may not be thinking about body control or keeping your head and shoulders up, because your brain is kindly taking care of all that for you. If you decided to stand up and grab a snack, you'd need to maintain posture and balance, as well as navigate bodily motion. **Proprioception**, also called our *kinesthetic sense*, helps us keep track of where we are and move efficiently. The **vestibular sense**, also called our *sense of equilibrium*, enables us to sense and maintain our balance as we move about. Our senses of body position and balance work together.

Ashlyn Blocker has congenital insensitivity to pain with anhidrosis (CIPA). *Congenital* means "present at birth," and *anhidrosis* means "inability to sweat." CIPA is a rare disorder that renders people unable to detect pain or temperature; those affected also can't regulate body temperature well because of an inability to sweat. Her parents and teachers need to monitor her constantly because she's prone to eating scalding hot food without the slightest hesitation. She may badly injure herself on the playground and continue to play.

PROPRIOCEPTORS: TELLING THE INSIDE STORY. We use *proprioceptors* to sense muscle stretch and force. From these two sources of information we can tell what our bodies are doing, even with our eyes closed. There are two kinds of proprioceptors: stretch receptors embedded in our muscles and force detectors embedded in our muscle tendons. Proprioceptive information enters the spinal cord and travels upward through the brain stem and thalamus to reach the somatosensory and motor cortexes (Naito, 2004). There, our brains combine information from our muscles and tendons, along with a sense of our intentions, to obtain a perception of our body's location (Proske, 2006).

THE VESTIBULAR SENSE: A BALANCING ACT. In addition to the cochlea, the inner ear contains three **semicircular canals** (see Figure 4.21). These canals, which are filled with fluid, sense equilibrium and help us maintain our balance. Vestibular information reaches parts of the brain stem that control eye muscles and triggers reflexes that coordinate eye and head movements (Highstein, Fay, & Popper, 2004). Vestibular information also travels to the cerebellum, which controls bodily responses that enable us to catch our balance when we're falling.

The vestibular sense isn't heavily represented in our cerebral cortex, so our awareness of this sense is limited. We typically become aware of this sense only when we lose our sense of balance or experience dramatic mismatches between our vestibular and visual inputs, which occur when our vestibular system and our eyes tell us different

proprioception

our sense of body position

vestibular sense

our sense of equilibrium or balance

semicircular canals

three fluid-filled canals in the inner ear responsible for our sense of balance

Figure 4.21 How We Sense Motion.

The semicircular canals of the inner ear detect movement and gravity.

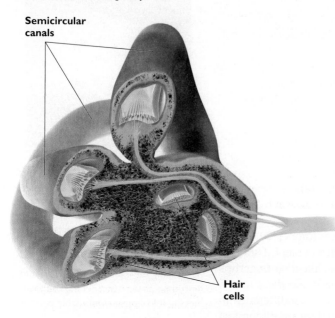

Semicircular canals

Hair cells

things. We commonly experience dizziness and nausea following these mismatches, such as when we're moving quickly in a car while not looking outside at the road whizzing past us.

Ergonomics: Human Engineering

How do our bodies interact with new technologies? A field of psychology called *human factors* optimizes technology to better suit our sensory and perceptual capabilities. We can use what we know about human psychology and sensory systems—ranging from our body position sense to vision—to build more *ergonomic*, or worker-friendly, gadgets and tools of the trade (Dul et al., 2012).

As Donald Norman (1998) pointed out, many everyday objects are designed without the perceptual experiences of users in mind. As a result, they can be extremely difficult to figure out how to operate. Have you ever tried to repeatedly push open a door that needed to be pulled open, or spent several minutes trying to figure out how to turn on a shower in an apartment or hotel room? Poor design kept the United States in limbo for 5 weeks following the 2000 presidential election between George W. Bush and Al Gore, when a bewildering election ballot in some Florida counties left state officials unable to figure out which candidate voters picked.

Fortunately, human factors psychologists have applied their extensive knowledge of sensation and perception to improve the design of many everyday devices. To take just one example, many people hold jobs that require them to sit at a computer terminal most of the day. This means that a new design for a computer screen, keyboard, or mouse that enables them to better reach for their computers or see their screens can increase their efficiency. Human factors psychologists design not only computer components, but also devices that assist surgeons in performing delicate operations, workstations to improve comfort and decrease injuries on the job, and control panels on aircraft carriers, to make them safer and easier to use. The psychology of human factors reminds us that much of what we know about sensation and perception has useful applications to many domains of everyday life.

Interactive

Psychologist Donald Norman, posing in his office behind a teapot. Can you figure out what makes this teapot design a poor one? The handle is directly underneath the spout, which would cause hot tea to pour directly onto your hand.

4.6: Perception: When Our Senses Meet Our Brains

4.6a **Track how our minds build up perceptions.**

4.6b **Describe how we perceive people, objects, and sounds in our environments.**

4.6c **Distinguish subliminal perception from subliminal persuasion.**

4.6d **Analyze the scientific evidence for and against the existence of extrasensory perception (ESP).**

Now that we've learned how we process sensory information, we'll embark on an exciting voyage into how our minds organize the bits of sensory data into more meaningful concepts. What's so remarkable about our brain's ability to bring together so much data is that it doesn't rely only on what's in our sensory field. Our brain pieces together (a) what's in the sensory field, along with (b) what was just there a moment ago, and (c) what we remember from our past. When we perceive the world, we sacrifice small details in favor of crisp and often more meaningful representations. In most cases, the trade-off is well worth it, because it helps us make sense of our surroundings.

Parallel Processing: The Way Our Brain Multitasks

We can attend to many sense modalities simultaneously, a phenomenon called **parallel processing** (Rumelhart & McClelland, 1987). Two important concepts that go along with parallel processing are **bottom-up processing** and **top-down processing** (see LO 8.1a). In bottom-up processing, we construct a whole stimulus from its parts. An example is perceiving an object on the basis of its edges. Bottom-up processing starts with the raw stimuli we perceive and ends with our synthesizing them into a meaningful concept. This kind of processing begins with activity in the primary visual cortex, followed by processing in the association cortex (see LO 3.2a). In contrast, top-down processing starts with our beliefs and expectations, which we then impose on the raw stimuli we perceive. Top-down processing starts with processing in the association cortex, followed by processing in the primary visual cortex.

Some perceptions rely more heavily on bottom-up processing (Koch, 1993), others on top-down processing (McClelland & Plaut, 1993). In most cases, though, these two kinds of processing work hand in hand (Patel & Sathian, 2000). We can illustrate this point by how we process ambiguous figures (see Figure 4.22). Depending on our expectations, we typically perceive these figures differently. The top-down influence that we're thinking of a jazz musician biases our bottom-up processing of the shapes in Figure 4.22 and increases the chances we'll perceive a saxophone player. In contrast, if our top-down expectation were of a woman's face, our sensory-based bottom-up processing would change accordingly. Can you see both figures?

Perceptual Hypotheses: Guessing What's Out There

Because our brains rely so much on our knowledge and experiences, we can usually get away with economizing in our sensory processing and making educated guesses about what sensory information is telling us. Moreover, a pretty decent guess with fewer neurons is more efficient than a more certain answer with a huge number of neurons. As cognitive misers, we generally try to get by with as little neural firepower as we can.

PERCEPTUAL SETS. We form a **perceptual set** when our expectations influence our perceptions—an example of top-down processing. We may perceive a misshapen letter as an "H" or as an "A" depending on the surrounding letters and the words that would result from our interpretation (see Figure 4.23).

We also tend to perceive the world in accord with our preconceptions. An ambiguous cartoon drawn by W. E. Hill raises the question: Is it a young woman or an old witch? Participants placed in the perceptual set of a young woman by viewing a version of the cartoon exaggerating those features (see Figure 4.24) reported seeing a young woman. In contrast, participants placed in the perceptual set of an old woman by viewing a version of the cartoon exaggerating those features reported seeing an old woman (Boring, 1930).

PERCEPTUAL CONSTANCY. The process by which we perceive stimuli consistently across varied conditions is **perceptual constancy**. Without perceptual constancy, we'd be hopelessly confused, because we'd be seeing our worlds as continually changing. Yet our brain allows us to correct from these minor changes. There are several kinds of perceptual constancy: shape, size, and color constancy. Consider a door we view from differing perspectives (see Figure 4.25, Slide 1). Because of *shape constancy*, we still see a door as a door whether it's completely shut, barely open, or more fully open, even though these shapes look almost nothing like each other.

Or take *size constancy*, our ability to perceive objects as the same size no matter how far away they are from us (see Figure 4.25, Slide 2). When a friend walks away from us, her image becomes smaller. But we almost never realize this is happening, nor do we conclude that our friend is mysteriously shrinking. Outside of our conscious awareness, our brains mentally enlarge figures far away from us so that they appear more like similar objects in the same scene.

Figure 4.22 What Do You See?

Because of the influence of top-down processing, reading the caption "saxophone player" beneath this ambiguous figure tends to produce a different perception than reading the caption "woman."

parallel processing

the ability to attend to many sense modalities simultaneously

bottom-up processing

processing in which a whole is constructed from parts

top-down processing

conceptually driven processing influenced by beliefs and expectancies

perceptual set

set formed when expectations influence perceptions

perceptual constancy

the process by which we perceive stimuli consistently across varied conditions

Figure 4.23 Context Influences Perception.

Depending on the perceptual set provided by the context of the surrounding letters, the middle letter can appear as an "H" or as an "A." Most of us read this phrase as "THE BAT" because of the context.

Monocular Cues of Depth

This painting depicts a scene that provides monocular cues to depth.

1. Relative size: The house is drawn approximately as high as the fence post, but we know the house is much bigger, so it must be considerably farther away.
2. Texture gradient: The grasses in front of the fence are drawn as individual blades but those in the field behind are shown with almost no detail.
3. Interposition: The tree at the corner of the house is blocking part of the house, so we know that the tree is closer to us than the house is.

Gisela Leibold is unable to detect motion. She's understandably concerned about important information she might miss riding down an escalator in Munich.

The visual cliff tests infants' ability to judge depth.

when you switch to the other eye. Each eye sees the world a bit differently, and our brains ingeniously make use of this information to judge depth.

- **Binocular convergence:** When we look at nearby objects, we focus on them reflexively by using our eye muscles to turn our eyes inward, a phenomenon called *convergence*. Our brains are aware of how much our eyes are converging and use this information to estimate distance.

Depth Perception Appears in Infancy. We can judge depth as soon as we learn to crawl. Eleanor Gibson established this phenomenon in a classic setup called the *visual cliff* (Gibson, 1991; Gibson & Walk, 1960). The typical visual cliff consists of a table and a floor several feet below, both covered by a checkered cloth. A clear glass surface extends from the table out over the floor, creating the appearance of a sudden drop. Infants between 6 and 14 months of age hesitate to crawl over the glass elevated several feet above the floor, even when their mothers beckon. The visual cliff demonstrates that depth cues present soon after birth are probably partly innate, although they surely develop with experience.

HOW WE PERCEIVE WHERE SOUNDS ARE LOCATED. Cues play an important role as well in localizing (locating) sounds. We use various brain centers to localize sounds with respect to our bodies. When the auditory nerve enters the brain stem, some of its axons connect with cells on the same side of the brain, but the rest cross over to the other side of the brain. This clever arrangement enables information from both ears to reach the same structures in the brain stem. Because the two sources of information take different routes, they arrive at the brain stem slightly out of sync with each other. Our brains compare this difference between our ears—a so-called *binaural cue*—to localize sound sources (Figure 4.30). There's also a loudness difference between our ears, because the ear closest to the sound source is in the direct path of the sound wave, whereas the ear farthest away is in a sound shadow, created by our head. We rely mostly on binaural cues to detect the source of sounds. But we also use monaural cues, heard by one ear only. The cues help us distinguish sounds that are clear from those that are muffled due to obstruction by the ear, head, and shoulders, allowing us to figure out where sounds are coming from.

When Perception Deceives Us

Sometimes the best way to understand how something works is to see how it doesn't work—or works in unusual circumstances. We've already examined some illusions that illustrate principles of sensation and perception. Now we'll examine further how illusions and other unusual phenomena shed light on everyday perception.

- The *moon illusion*, which has fascinated people for centuries, is the illusion that the moon appears larger when it's near the horizon than high in the sky. Scientists have put forth several explanations for this illusion, but none is universally accepted. A common misconception is that the moon appears larger near the horizon due to a magnification effect caused by Earth's atmosphere. But we can easily refute this hypothesis.

Falsifiability

Can the claim be disproved?

Ruling Out Rival Hypotheses

Have important alternative explanations for the findings been excluded?

Although Earth's atmosphere does alter the moon's color at the horizon, it doesn't enlarge it. Let's contrast this common misconception with a few better-supported explanations. The first is that the moon illusion is due to errors in perceived distance. The moon is some 240,000 miles away, a huge distance we've little experience judging. When the moon is high in the sky, there's nothing else around for comparison. In contrast, when the moon is near the horizon, we may perceive it as farther away because we can see it next to things we know to be far away, like buildings, mountains, and trees. Because we know these things are large, we perceive the moon as larger still. Another explanation is that we're mistaken about the three-dimensional space in which we live, along with the moon. For example, many people have the misperception that the sky is shaped like a flattened dome, leading us to see the moon as farther away on the horizon than at the top of the sky (Rock & Kaufman, 1962; Ross & Plug, 2002).

- The startling *Ames room illusion*, developed by Adelbert Ames, Jr. (1946), is shown in Figure 4.31. This distorted room is actually trapezoidal; the walls are slanted and the

Figure 4.30 How We Locate Sounds.

When someone standing to our left speaks to us, the sound reaches our left ear slightly earlier than it reaches our right. Also, the intensity detected by the left ear is greater than the intensity detected by the right ear, because the right ear lies in a sound shadow produced by the head and shoulders.

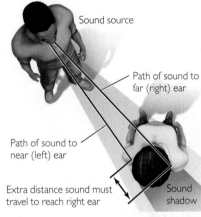

Sound source

Path of sound to far (right) ear

Path of sound to near (left) ear

Extra distance sound must travel to reach right ear

Sound shadow

The moon illusion causes us to perceive the moon as larger near the horizon than high in the sky.

Figure 4.31 The Ames Room.

Viewed through a small peephole, the Ames room makes small people look impossibly large and large people look impossibly small. Who is the younger and smaller child in this picture?

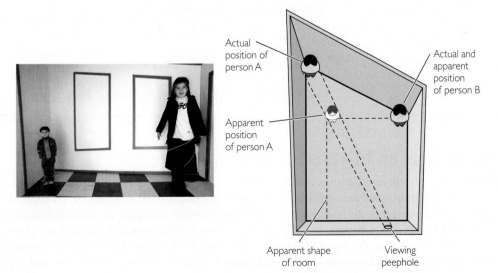

Actual position of person A

Actual and apparent position of person B

Apparent position of person A

Apparent shape of room

Viewing peephole

ceiling and floor are at an incline. Insert two people of the same size and the Ames room creates the bizarre impression of a giant person on the side of the room where the ceiling is lower (but doesn't appear to be) and of a tiny person on the side of the room where the ceiling is higher. This illusion is due to the relative size principle. The height of the ceiling is the key to the illusion, and the other distortions in the room are only necessary to make the room appear normal to the observer. Hollywood special effects wizards have capitalized on this principle in movies such as the *Lord of the Rings* and *Charlie and the Chocolate Factory* to make some characters appear gargantuan and others dwarf-like.

Figure 4.32 How Well Can You Judge Relative Size.

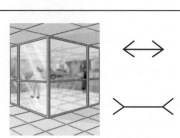

(a) Which horizontal line is longer?

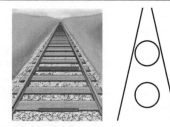

(b) Which line above is longer, and which circle is bigger?

Slide 1:
In the *Müller-Lyer illusion*, a line of identical length appears longer when it ends in a set of arrowheads pointing inward than in a set of arrowheads pointing outward. That's because we perceive lines as part of a larger context. Three researchers (Segall, Campbell, & Herskovitz, 1966) found that people from different cultures displayed differing reactions to the Müller-Lyer illusion. The Zulu, who live in round huts and plow their fields in circles rather than rows, are less susceptible to the Müller-Lyer illusion, probably because they have less experience with linear environments (McCauley & Henrich, 2006).

Slide 2:
In the *Ponzo illusion*, also called the *railroad tracks illusion*, converging lines enclose two objects of identical size, leading us to perceive the object closer to the converging lines as larger. Our brain "assumes" that the object closer to the converging lines is farther away—usually it would be correct in this guess—and compensates for this knowledge by making the object look bigger.

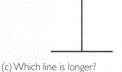

(c) Which line is longer?

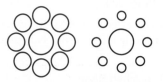

(d) Which center circle is bigger?

Slide 3:
The *horizontal–vertical illusion* causes us to perceive the vertical part of an upside-down "T" as longer than the horizontal part, because the horizontal part is divided in half by the vertical part.

Slide 4:
The *Ebbinghaus–Titchener illusion* leads us to perceive a circle as larger when surrounded by smaller circles and smaller when surrounded by larger circles. Although this illusion fools our eyes, it doesn't fool our hands! Studies in which participants have to reach for the center circle indicate that their grasp remains on target (Milner & Goodale, 1995), although some scientists have recently challenged this finding (Franz, Bulthoff, & Fahle, 2003).

Subliminal and Extrasensory Perception

We've seen numerous examples of our ability to be cognitive misers. One way we scrimp and save our attentional resources is to process many of the sensory inputs to which we're exposed unconsciously. In fact, many of our actions occur with little or no forethought or deliberation (Hassin, Uleman, & Bargh, 2005). Consider that our lives would grind to a standstill if we had to think carefully before uttering every word, typing every sentence, or making the minor corrections in steering needed to drive a car safely. Under ordinary circumstances, we don't direct our attention consciously to these activities, yet we constantly adjust to the flow of sensory experience. Might some sensory inputs be so subtle that they aren't registered consciously, yet still affect our everyday lives? Put another way, if we can detect stimuli without our knowing it, does that affect our behavior?

SUBLIMINAL PERCEPTION AND PERSUASION. You're home on a Sunday afternoon, curled up on your couch watching a movie on TV. Suddenly, within a span of a few minutes you see three or four extremely quick flashes of light on the screen. Only a few minutes later, you're seized with an uncontrollable desire to eat a cheeseburger. Did the advertiser fiendishly insert several photographs of a cheeseburger in the midst of the film, so rapidly you couldn't detect them?

The American public has long been fascinated with the possibility of **subliminal perception**—the processing of sensory information that occurs below the limen, that is, the level of conscious awareness (Cheesman & Merikle, 1986; Rogers & Smith, 1993). To study subliminal perception, researchers typically present a word or photograph very quickly, say at 50 milliseconds (one-twentieth of a second). They frequently follow this stimulus immediately with another stimulus (like a pattern of dots or lines) that blocks out mental processing of the subliminal stimulus. When participants can't correctly identify the content of the stimulus at better-than-chance levels, researchers deem it subliminal. The claim for subliminal perception may seem extraordinary, but there's considerable evidence for the phenomenon (Seitz & Watanabe, 2003).

When investigators subliminally trigger emotions by exposing participants to words related to anger, these participants are more likely to rate other people as hostile (Bargh & Pietromonaco, 1982). In one study, researchers subliminally presented participants with words such as church, saint, and preacher, and then provided them with an opportunity to cheat on a different task. None of the participants who subliminally received religious words cheated, compared with 20 percent of those who subliminally received neutral, nonreligious words (Randolph-Seng & Nielsen, 2007). For unclear reasons, the effects of subliminal information often vanish when participants become aware of or even suspect attempts to influence them subliminally, and even these effects are typically very short-lived (Glaser & Kihlstrom, 2005; Kihlstrom, 2015).

Even though we're subject to subliminal perception, that doesn't mean we numbly succumb to *subliminal persuasion*, that is, subthreshold influences over our votes in elections, product choices, and life decisions (Newell & Shanks, 2014). Subliminally presented words related to thirst, such as "drink," may slightly influence how much people drink, but specific words related to brand names, such as "cola," don't influence beverage choice (Dijksterhuis, Aarts, & Smith, 2005). This may be because we can't engage in much, if any, in-depth processing of the *meaning* of subliminal stimuli (Rosen, Glasgow, & Moore, 2003). As a result, these stimuli probably can't produce large-scale or enduring changes in our attitudes, let alone our decisions.

Still, subliminal self-help CDs, DVDs, and podcasts are a multimillion-dollar-a-year industry in the United States alone. They purportedly contain repeated subliminal messages (such as "Feel better about yourself") designed to influence our behavior or emotions. Scores of studies show that subliminal self-help tapes are ineffective (Eich & Hyman, 1991; Moore, 1992). Nevertheless, those who listen to them believe they have improved, even when there's no evidence to support improvement (Greenwald et al., 1991). Phil Merikle (1988) uncovered another reason why subliminal self-help tapes don't work: His auditory analyses revealed that many of these tapes contain no message at all!

Some people even claim that *reversed* subliminal messages influence behavior. In 1990, the then popular rock band Judas Priest was put on trial for the suicide of a teenager and the attempted suicide of another. While listening to a Judas Priest song, the boys supposedly heard the words "Do it" played backward. The prosecution claimed that this reversed message led the boys to shoot themselves. In the end, the members of Judas Priest were acquitted (Moore, 1996). As the expert witnesses noted, forward subliminal messages can't produce major changes in behavior, so it's even less likely that backward

subliminal perception

perception below the limen or threshold of conscious awareness

◀ **Extraordinary Claims**

Is the evidence as strong as the claim?

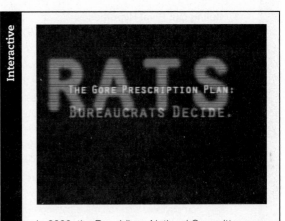

In 2000, the Republican National Committee ran this ad criticizing Al Gore's health care plan in which the word "RATS" appears for a fraction of a second. This subliminal message would not persuade viewers that Gore's plan is bad, because even if viewers were subject to subliminal perception they wouldn't have engaged in in-depth processing of the meaning of the word "RATS."

Evaluating Claims PACKAGING SUBLIMINAL PERSUASION FOR THE CONSUMER

Interactive

The Internet is chock-full of advertisements for subliminal self-help DVDs, CDs, and podcasts that promise to change your life. Manufacturers claim that these life-transforming self-help tools are easy to use in the comfort and privacy of your own home and can perform miraculously because they send messages to your unconscious mind to influence your actions and attitudes. But is there evidence for these extravagant claims?

A few days ago, you read a sci-fi novel about how a ruthless leader wielded devious methods of subliminal persuasion to manipulate a colony of humans to do his bidding on a planet in a galaxy far far away. The plot seemed far-fetched, but you found yourself wondering: Could subliminal persuasion be used to personal advantage? You did the mandatory Google Search and read about subliminal self-help tools in the following paragraph. They seemed plausible—like they might be worth a shot, but worth $40 for each DVD?

"More than one million people have discovered the power of our DVDs, and you can too. Browse our long list of DVDs tailored to address what *you* need NOW. Our patented DVDs will improve all aspects of your life. You may not notice changes right away, but after a few weeks, with the confidence that increases with each passing day, you probably won't recognize your old self in the mirror. Fueled with SUBLIMINAL POWER, you'll learn to increase your emotional intelligence, conquer your fears, lose weight, and even attract a mate, if that's what you need NOW. Don't take our word for it, here's what Andrew from Atlanta had to say, 'Your DVDs are the best I've ever tried—they changed my life!'"

Scientific skepticism requires us to evaluate all claims with an open mind but to insist on compelling evidence before accepting them. How do the principles of scientific thinking help us to evaluate this claim about subliminal persuasion self-help tools?

Consider how the six principles of scientific thinking are relevant as you evaluate this claim.

1. Ruling Out Rival Hypotheses

Have important alternative explanations for the findings been excluded?

Important alternative explanations haven't been excluded. To date, scientists have failed to document the ability of subliminal persuasion to produce minor, much less profound, personal changes. Still, to the extent that changes are evident while using the DVDs, the placebo effect might be at play. Moreover, the DVDs may spur people to be more aware than usual of positive thoughts and valued actions (such as limiting portions to promote weight loss) and feel better and more self-confident as a result. Also, if people purchase the DVDs when they're particularly demoralized, with the mere passage of time and with the advent of positive life experiences, consumers may come away with the illusory impression that subliminal messages caused the positive changes.

2. Correlation vs. Causation

Can we be sure that A causes B?

We can't be sure that personal changes supposedly associated with the DVDs are caused by subliminal persuasion, as the ad doesn't describe controlled research that

isolates the effects of the messages. But we can be reasonably certain, based on past research, that subliminal persuasion isn't effective, contrary to the claims in the ad.

3. Falsifiability

Can the claim be disproved?

Researchers haven't found support for subliminal persuasion, certainly not on the order of the personal changes touted in the ad. Nevertheless, it would be possible for researchers to evaluate the effectiveness of the DVDs, as advertised, and the exact role of subliminal messages, by including the subliminal messages in some of the DVDs and comparing their effectiveness with the DVDs minus the messages. If the DVDs didn't produce the claimed positive effects, and if differences failed to surface as a function of whether the messages were included, it would refute the claims regarding subliminal persuasion.

4. Replicability

Can the results be duplicated in other studies?

There's no evidence that the claim is derived from research using the DVDs advertised. We should be skeptical of claims that are based on only a single study, especially when the results contradict decades of previously replicated research.

5. Extraordinary Claims

Is the evidence as strong as the claim?

Extraordinary claims regarding subliminal persuasion require extraordinary evidence, and the ad provides no such evidence. Scientists have failed to document the ability of subliminal persuasion to produce meaningful personal changes. The sheer number of people who purchase a product provides no evidence pertinent to the effectiveness of the product. Additionally, the testimonial and anecdotal evidence provided by one "satisfied customer" isn't sufficient to conclude that the product works.

6. Occam's Razor

Does a simpler explanation fit the data just as well?

Yes. Simpler explanations for any positive changes associated with the DVDs center on placebo effects, increased self-observation and attention to positive changes, and changes associated with naturally occurring life events.

Summary

There's no scientific support for the extraordinary claim that subliminal persuasion can produce profound life changes. The claims in the ad aren't based on well-replicated research, although they could be tested and perhaps falsified in rigorous studies. There are much simpler explanations than subliminal persuasion for any positive changes associated with the advertised DVDs.

messages can do so. In some cases, extraordinary claims remain just that—extraordinary claims with no scientific support.

EXTRASENSORY PERCEPTION (ESP): FACT OR FICTION? Proponents of **extra sensoryperception (ESP)** argue that we can perceive events outside of the known channels of sensation, like seeing, hearing, and touch. Before we examine the evidence for this extraordinary claim, we first address the question…

What's ESP, Anyway? *Parapsychologists*—investigators who study ESP and related psychic phenomena—have subdivided ESP into three major types (Hines, 2003; Hyman, 1989):

1. **Precognition:** acquiring knowledge of future events before they occur through paranormal means, that is, mechanisms that lie outside of traditional science. (You knew we were going to say that, didn't you?);

2. **Telepathy:** reading other people's minds; and

3. **Clairvoyance:** detecting the presence of objects or people that are hidden from view.

Is There Scientific Evidence for ESP? In the 1930s, Joseph B. Rhine, who coined the term *extrasensory perception,* launched the full-scale study of ESP. Rhine used a set of stimuli called *Zener cards,* which consist of five standard symbols: squiggly lines, star, circle, plus sign, and square. He presented these cards to participants in random order and asked them to guess which card would appear (precognition), which card another participant had in mind (telepathy), and which card was hidden from view (clairvoyance). Rhine (1934) initially reported positive results, as his participants averaged about 7 correct Zener card identifications per deck of 25, where 5 cards would be chance performance.

But there was a problem, one that has dogged ESP research for well more than a century: Try as they might, other investigators couldn't replicate Rhine's findings. Moreover, scientists later pointed out serious flaws in Rhine's methods. Some of the Zener cards were so worn down or poorly manufactured that participants could see the imprint of the symbols through the backs of the cards (Alcock, 1990; Gilovich, 1991). In other cases, scientists found that Rhine and his colleagues hadn't properly randomized the order of the cards, rendering his analyses essentially meaningless. Eventually, enthusiasm for Zener card research dried up.

Beginning in 1972, the U.S. government invested $20 million in the Stargate program to study the ability of "remote viewers" to acquire useful military information in distant places, like the locations of nuclear facilities in enemy countries through clairvoyance. The government discontinued the program in 1995, apparently because the remote viewers provided no useful information and sometimes were wildly wrong (Hyman, 1996).

The problem with replication has come up more recently with research using the *Ganzfeld technique* in which the experimenter covers participants' eyes with goggles that look like the halves of ping-pong balls to create a uniform visual field when a red floodlight is directed toward the eyes. Another person (the "sender") attempts to mentally transmit a target picture while the participant reports mental images that come to mind. The participant then rates each of four pictures for how well it matches the mental imagery experienced. Only one of the pictures is the target the sender tried to transmit.

Studies have found that the size of Ganzfeld effects was small and corresponded to chance differences in performance (Bem & Honorton, 1994; Milton & Wiseman, 1999). Other ESP paradigms have proven equally disappointing. For example, research conducted more than three decades ago suggested that people could mentally transmit images to dreaming individuals (Ullman, Krippner, & Vaughn, 1973). Yet later investigators couldn't replicate these results, either.

The latest concern about replication stems from studies of precognition in which Cornell University researcher Daryl Bem (2011) recently claimed that 9 out of 10 experiments he conducted indicated that people's ability to acquire knowledge of future events affects their present behavior. Each of Bem's studies reversed the typical order of presentation of stimuli and responses by exposing participants to stimuli *after,* rather than before they respond to an experimental task. For example, in many psychology studies, researchers have found that when participants rehearse words (i.e., the stimuli) their recall is

> ◄ **Extraordinary Claims**
>
> Is the evidence as strong as the claim?

extrasensory perception (ESP)

perception of events outside the known channels of sensation

The Zener cards, named after a collaborator of Joseph B. Rhine, have been used widely in ESP research.

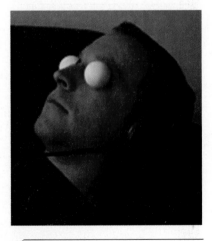

A participant in a Ganzfeld experiment attempting to receive images from a sender. The uniform sensory field he's experiencing is designed to minimize visual and auditory "noise" from the environment, supposedly permitting him to detect otherwise weak ESP signals.

> ◄ **Replicability**
>
> Can the results be duplicated in other studies?

improved (i.e., the responses) relative to non-studied words. However, what if participants rehearse words *after* a recall test, and their memory for the rehearsed words improves on the previous test, relative to the non-rehearsed words? This astonishing finding would throw a monkey wrench into the idea that causes precede effects and imply that people can somehow "see into the future" to affect their prior responses. Yet this is exactly what Bem found. Future events (i.e., rehearsing words after the test) seemed to predict past behaviors (i.e., test performance).

Even before Bem's study saw the light of publication in a prestigious psychology journal, it set ablaze a firestorm of criticism based on methodological and statistical concerns (Francis, 2012; Wagenmakers et al., 2011). Still, scientists' mantra regarding whether a finding is reliable is *replication, replication, replication*. So Stuart Ritchie, Richard Wiseman, and Christopher French—scientists at three different universities—jumped at the opportunity to replicate Bem's memory rehearsal study, the one that claimed to provide the strongest evidence of all for reverse causality. The result? All three researchers failed to replicate Bem's findings: There was no recall difference across studied and non-studied words.

Other recent attempts to replicate Bem's controversial work have yielded similarly disconfirming results, but other attempts will surely follow (Barušs, & Rabier, 2014; Galak et al., 2012). Although a recent meta-analysis of 90 experiments provided statistical support for Bem's claims (Bem et al., 2015), many scientists remain extremely skeptical and suspect that the positive results are due to publication bias—the tendency of journals to not publish failures to replicate previous findings. If some studies repeat Bem's findings but others don't, it will be important to figure out why this is the case. But for now, the commonsense view of causes preceding effects seems not to be under serious threat. The many non-replications of ESP findings underscore the absence of a feature that's a hallmark of mature sciences: an "experimental recipe" that yields replicable results across independent laboratories (Hyman, 1989).

In the absence of scientific supporting evidence, many ESP proponents have come up with ad-hoc hypotheses for explaining away negative findings. Already the failures to replicate Bem (2011) have been attributed to the skepticism of the experimenters, an attitude claimed to inhibit ESP and dubbed the experimenter effect. Psi missing refers to significantly worse than chance performance on ESP tasks (Gilovich, 1991). Some ESP proponents have even argued that psi missing demonstrates the existence of ESP, because below chance performance indicates that individuals with ESP are deliberately selecting incorrect answers! Such ad-hoc hypotheses render claims about ESP extremely difficult to falsify.

Replicability

Can the results be duplicated in other studies?

Falsifiability

Can the claim be disproved?

Replicability

Can the results be duplicated in other studies?

Why People Believe in ESP. The extraordinary claim of ESP isn't matched by equally extraordinary evidence. Yet surveys indicate that 41 percent of American adults believe in ESP (Haraldsson & Houtkooper, 1991; Moore, 2005). Moreover, two-thirds of Americans say they've had a psychic experience, like a dream foretelling the death of a loved one or a premonition about a car accident that came true (Greeley, 1987). In light of more than 150 years of failed replications, it's reasonable to ask why our beliefs in ESP are so strong given that the research evidence for it is so weak.

Extraordinary Claims

Is the evidence as strong as the claim?

Illusory correlation (see LO 2.2b) offers one likely answer. We attend to and recall events that are striking coincidences and ignore or forget events that aren't; as a result, we perceive a statistical association when it's not there. Imagine we're in a new city and thinking of an old friend we haven't seen in years. A few hours later, we run into that friend on the street. "What a coincidence!" we tell ourselves. This remarkable event is evidence of ESP, right? Perhaps. But we're forgetting about the thousands of times we've been in new cities and thought about old friends whom we never encountered (Presley, 1997).

Further contributing to belief in ESP is our tendency to underestimate the frequency of coincidences. Most of us don't realize just how probable certain seemingly "improbable" events are. Take a crack at this question: *How large must a group of people be before the probability of two people sharing the same birthday exceeds 50 percent?*

Many participants respond with answers like 365, 100, or even 1,000. To most people's surprise, the correct answer is 23. That is, in a group of 23 people it's more likely than not that at least two people have the same birthday (see Figure 4.33). Once we get up to a group of 60 people, the odds exceed 99 percent. Because we tend to underestimate the likelihood of coincidences, we may be inclined to attribute them incorrectly to psychic phenomena.

Psychic Predictions. For many years, science journalist Gene Emery tracked failed psychic predictions. In 2005, he found that psychics predicted that an airplane would crash into the Egyptian pyramids, astronauts would discover a Nazi flag planted on the moon, Earth's magnetic field would reverse, and a participant on a television reality show would cannibalize one of the contestants, none of which have occurred. Conversely, no psychic predicted any of the significant events that *did* occur in 2005, like Hurricane Katrina, which inflicted terrible loss of life and property damage on New Orleans and neighboring areas (Emery, 2005).

Many psychic forecasters make use of *multiple end points*, meaning they keep their predictions so open-ended that they're consistent with almost any conceivable set of outcomes (Gilovich, 1991). A psychic may predict, "A celebrity will get caught in a scandal this year." But aside from being vague, this prediction is extremely open-ended. What counts as a "celebrity?" Sure, we'd all agree that Beyoncé and Brad Pitt are celebrities, but does our congressional representative count? What about a local television newscaster? Similarly, what counts as a "scandal?"

What about psychics, like John Edward or James von Pragh, who claim to tell us things about ourselves or our dead relatives that they couldn't possibly have known? Most of these psychics probably rely on a set of skills known as *cold reading*, the art of persuading people we've just met that we know all about them (Hines, 2003; Hyman, 1977). If you want to impress your friends with a cold reading, Table 4.4 contains some tips to keep in mind.

Cold reading works for one major reason: We humans seek meaning in our worlds and often find it even when it's not there. So in many respects we're reading into the cold reading at least as much as the cold reader is reading into us.

You might try this for the fun of it. To persuade people you have ESP, try the following demonstration in a large group of friends. Tell them, "I want you to think of an odd two-digit number that's less than 50, the only catch being that the two digits must be

Figure 4.33 The "Birthday Paradox".

As we reach a group size of 23 people, the probability that at least 2 people share the same birthday exceeds 0.5, or 50 percent. Research demonstrates that most people markedly underestimate the likelihood of this and other coincidences, sometimes leading them to attribute these coincidences to paranormal events.

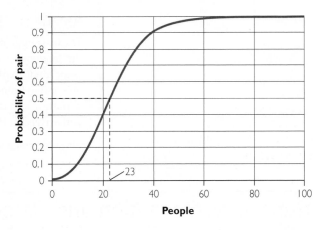

Crystal ball readers claim to be able to tell us a great deal about ourselves and our futures. Yet many of them probably rely on cold-reading techniques that most of us could duplicate with relatively little training.

Table 4.4 Cold-Reading Techniques.

Technique	Example
Let the person know at the outset that you won't be perfect.	"I pick up a lot of different signals. Some will be accurate, but others may not be."
Start off with a *stock spiel*, a list of general statements that apply to just about everyone.	"You've recently been struggling with some tough decisions."
Fish for details by peppering your reading with vague probes.	"I'm sensing that someone with the letter *M* or maybe *N* has been important in your life lately."
Use the technique of *sleight of tongue*, meaning that you toss out so many guesses in rapid-fire fashion that at least a few of them are bound to be right.	"Has your father been ill?"; "How about your mother?"; "Hmmm…I sense that someone in your family is ill or worried about getting ill."
Use a prop.	A crystal ball, set of tarot cards, or horoscope convey the impression that you're basing your reading on mystical information.
Make use of *population stereotypes*, responses or characteristics reported by many or even most people.	"I believe you have a piece of clothing, like an old dress or blouse, that you haven't worn in years but have kept for sentimental value."
Look for physical cues to the individual's personality or life history.	A traditional manner of dress often suggests a conventional and proper person, a great deal of shiny jewelry often suggests a flamboyant person, and so on.
Remember that "flattery will get you everywhere."	Tell people what they want to hear, like "I see a great romance on the horizon."

SOURCE: Hines, 2003; Hyman, 1977; Rowland, 2001.

different—because that would make it too easy for me." Give them a few moments, and say, "I get the sense that some of you were thinking of 37." Then pause and say, "I was initially thinking of 35, but changed my mind. Was I close?" Research shows that slightly more than half of people will pick either 37 or 35, which are population stereotypes that can convince many people you possess telepathic powers (French, 1992; Hines, 2003).

Journal Prompt

The text suggests that some people might believe in ESP because of illusory correlations—the tendency to perceive statistical associations between events that aren't objectively associated. Explain how illusory correlations might promote belief in ESP. Think about one or two times in your life when you concluded that an event might be "extrasensory" in nature, and describe how the phenomenon of illusory correlation might explain how you arrived at that conclusion.

Summary: Sensation and Perception

4.1: Two Sides of the Coin: Sensation and Perception

4.1a Identify the basic principles that apply to all senses.

Transduction is the process of converting an external energy, such as light or sound vibration, into electrical activity within neurons. The doctrine of specific nerve energies refers to how each of the sensory modalities is handled by specific regions of the brain. Even though most connections in the brain are faithful to one sense modality, brain regions often respond to information from a different sense.

4.1b Discuss the role of attention and the nature of the binding problem.

To adapt to the challenges of an ever-changing environment, flexible attention is critical to survival and well-being. Yet attention must also be selective so that we're not overwhelmed by sensory inputs. One of the great mysteries of psychology is how we are able to bind different pieces of sensory information and cues together into a unified whole.

4.2: Seeing: The Visual System

4.2a Explain how the eye starts the visual process.

The lens in the eye accommodates to focus on images both near and far by changing from "fat" to "flat." The lens optimally focuses light on the retina, which lies at the rear of the eye. The retina contains rods and cones filled with pigments. Additional cells in the retina transmit information about light to ganglion cells, and the axons of these cells combine to form the optic nerve.

4.2b Identify the different kinds of visual perception.

Our visual system is sensitive to shape and color. We use different parts of the visual cortex to process these different aspects of visual perception. V1 cells are sensitive to lines of a particular orientation. Color perception involves a mixture of trichromatic and opponent processing.

4.2c Describe different visual problems.

Blindness is a worldwide problem, especially in underdeveloped countries. There are several types of color blindness, the most common being red–green. The phenomenon of blindsight demonstrates that some blind people can make decent guesses about the location of objects in their environments.

4.3: Hearing: The Auditory System

4.3a Explain how the ear starts the auditory process.

Sound waves created by vibration of air molecules are funneled into the outer ear. These vibrations perturb the eardrum, causing the three small bones in the middle ear to vibrate. This process creates pressure in the cochlea, which contains the basilar membrane and organ of Corti, in which hair cells are embedded. The hair cells then bend, thereby exciting them. The message is relayed through the auditory nerve.

4.3b Identify the different kinds of auditory perception.

Place theory is pitch perception based on where along the basilar membrane hair cells are maximally excited. Frequency theory is based on hair cells reproducing the frequency of the pitch in their firing rates. In volley theory, groups of neurons stagger their responses to follow a pitch.

4.4: Smell and Taste: The Sensual Senses

4.4a Identify how we sense and perceive odors and tastes.

The tongue contains taste receptors for sweet, sour, bitter, salty, umami, and perhaps fat and starchy. Our ability to taste foods relies largely on smell. Olfactory receptors in our noses are sensitive to hundreds of different airborne molecules. We react to extremely sour tastes, which may be due to food spoilage, with disgust. We also appear sensitive to pheromones, odorless molecules that can affect sexual responses.

4.5: Our Body Senses: Touch, Body Position, and Balance

4.5a Describe the three different body senses.

The three body senses are called "somatosensory" for body sensation, "proprioception" for muscle position sense, and "vestibular sense" for the sense of balance and equilibrium. The somatosensory system responds to light touch, deep pressure, hot and cold temperature, and tissue damage. Our muscles contain sense receptors that detect stretch and others that detect force. We calculate where our bodies are located from this information. We're typically unaware of our sense of equilibrium.

4.5b Explain how pain perception differs from touch perception.

There's a large emotional component to pain perception that's not present with touch. This is because pain information activates parts of the limbic system in addition to the somatosensory cortex.

4.5c Describe the field of psychology called *human factors*.

The field of human factors starts with what psychologists have learned about sensation and perception, and then designs user-friendly devices, like computer keyboards and airplane cockpits, with this knowledge in mind.

4.6: Perception: When Our Senses Meet Our Brains

4.6a Track how our minds build up perceptions.

Information travels from primary sensory to secondary sensory cortex and then on to association cortex. Along the way, perception becomes increasingly complex. We also process many different inputs simultaneously, a phenomenon called *parallel processing*. In addition to sensory inputs, our perceptual sets and expectations influence our perceptions. Perceptual constancy allows us to perceive stimuli across varied conditions.

4.6b Describe how we perceive people, objects, and sounds in our environments.

Many neurons assembled in vast neural networks are probably responsible for face recognition. We perceive motion based on comparing visual frames like those in a movie, and we perceive depth by using both monocular and binocular cues. Cues also play an important role in locating sounds. Sometimes perception deceives us and we experience illusions.

4.6c Distinguish subliminal perception from subliminal persuasion.

Subliminal perception refers to the processing of sensory information that occurs below the limen or threshold of conscious awareness. Subliminal persuasion refers to subthreshold influences over our attitudes, choices, or behaviors.

4.6d Analyze the scientific evidence for and against the existence of extrasensory perception (ESP).

Most people accept the existence of ESP without the need for scientific evidence, in part because they greatly underestimate how likely it is that a coincidence occurs by chance. The evidence for ESP is weak and often not replicable across independent laboratories.

Chapter 5
Consciousness

Expanding the Boundaries of Psychological Inquiry

5.1a Explain the role of the circadian rhythm and how our bodies react to a disruption in our biological clocks.

5.1b Identify the different stages of sleep and the neural activity and dreaming behaviors that occur in each.

5.1c Identify the features and causes of sleep disorders.

5.2a Describe Freud's theory of dreams.

5.2b Explain three major modern theories of dreaming.

5.3a Determine how scientists explain unusual and seemingly "mystical" alterations in consciousness.

5.3b Distinguish myths from realities concerning hypnosis.

5.4a Identify possible influences on substance use.

5.4b Distinguish different types of drugs and their effects on consciousness.

Challenge Your Assumptions

Can we trust people's reports that they've been abducted by aliens?

Does a person's consciousness leave the body during an out-of-body experience?

Are people who have a near-death experience only imagining their glimpse of the afterlife?

Does hypnosis produce a trance state?

Is alcohol a depressant drug?

Watch ABDUCTED BY ALIENS?

Nearly one-fifth of college students in one survey endorsed the belief that extraterrestrials (ETs) can visit us in dreams, and 10 percent claimed to have "experienced or met an extraterrestrial" (ET) (Kunzendorf et al., 2007–2008). But did they *really* encounter ETs? As depicted in the video, the answer to this question is a resounding "No." Yet why do people report such strange occurrences? Susan Clancy (2005), in her landmark interview study of people who come to believe they were kidnapped by aliens (Clancy et al., 2002; McNally & Clancy, 2005), happened on a startling discovery that may explain the abduction reports.

Many of the people they interviewed shared a history of **sleep paralysis**—a strange experience of being unable to move just after falling asleep or immediately on awakening. This puzzling phenomenon is surprisingly common. One-third to one-half of college students have had at least one episode of sleep paralysis, which typically is no cause for concern (Fukuda et al., 1998). Sleep paralysis is caused by a disruption in the sleep cycle and is often associated with anxiety or even terror, feelings of vibrations, humming noises, and the eerie sense of menacing figures close to or on top of the immobile person. There are cultural differences in how people interpret this strange experience. In Thailand, people attribute it to a ghost, but in Newfoundland, people attribute it to an "old hag"—an elderly witch sitting on the person's chest. According to Susan Blackmore (2004), the "latest sleep paralysis myth may be alien abduction" (p. 315).

Clancy found that some people who suspect they've experienced an alien visitation consult with therapists who don't consider sleep paralysis as an alternative explanation, and some of these patients reported that their therapists used hypnosis to assist them in recovering memories of their interactions with aliens. Yet hypnosis isn't a trustworthy method for unearthing accurate memories. In fact, we'll soon learn that hypnosis can often help to create false memories. In many of the cases Clancy reported, it's not a big leap for people who suspect they were abducted to elaborate on their story during hypnosis and to imagine that aliens performed medical experiments on them, as many filmmakers and science fiction writers would have us believe.

Sleep paralysis is only one of many remarkable sleep-related experiences we'll encounter in this chapter, along with other fascinating examples of alterations in **consciousness**. Consciousness encompasses our ever-changing awareness of thoughts, emotions, bodily sensations, events, and actions. By one definition, "Consciousness is what you lose when you fall into a deep sleep at night and what you gain when you wake up in the morning" (Sanders, 2012, p. 22). Yet we'll see that even when we sleep, some of us retain self-awareness and know we're dreaming on occasion.

sleep paralysis

state of being unable to move just after falling asleep or right before waking up

◀ **Ruling Out Rival Hypotheses**

Have important alternative explanations for the findings been excluded?

consciousness

our subjective experience of the world, our bodies, and our mental perspectives

Sleep paralysis has been reported in many cultures, with the terrifying nighttime visitors ranging from an "old hag" to demonlike entities, as depicted in this painting, *The Nightmare,* by Henry Fuseli.

Our sleeping and waking experiences shade subtly into one another. On average, we spend 30–50 percent of our waking hours mind-wandering, fantasizing, and flitting from one task-irrelevant or dream-like thought to another (Killingsworth & Gilbert, 2010; Klinger, 2013; Smallwood & Schooler, 2015). Some so-called *fantasy-prone personalities* (about 2–4 percent of the population) say they spend at least half of their waking lives caught up in vivid daydreams and fantasies (Lynn & Rhue, 1988; Wilson & Barber, 1981). A common view is that fantasy is an unhealthy escape from reality. However, fantasies and daydreams are perfectly normal and can help us plan for the future, solve problems, express our creativity, and reinvigorate us by providing a break from routine and boring tasks (Klinger, 1971; Schooler et al., 2011).

Honed by hundreds of thousands of years of natural selection, most of us can easily focus our attention when needed to respond to virtually any situation or threat efficiently, seamlessly, and often unconsciously (Kirsch & Lynn, 1998; Wegner, 2004). Alterations in awareness and the ability to control awareness are adaptive for members of the animal kingdom as well. Dolphins and some other aquatic animals (such as seals and sea lions) "sleep" with one of their brain's hemispheres asleep and the other awake. The eye on the side opposite the sleeping hemisphere typically remains shut, with the other eye remaining open. After a few hours, the other hemisphere and eye take over as sleep continues. This remarkable arrangement permits these animals to sleep while remaining on the lookout for predators and obstacles, as well as to rise periodically to the surface of the water to breathe (Ridgway, 2002). Recently, researchers have discovered that great frigate birds, during up to 10-day non-stop transatlantic flights, sleep with both hemispheres switched off simultaneously, or only one hemisphere of the brain active at a time, allowing them to keep one eye open to be alert to threats (Rattenborg et al., 2016).

In this chapter, we'll encounter numerous examples of how the spotlight of our awareness and level of alertness changes continually and how consciousness is sensitively attuned to changes in our brain chemistry, expectations, and culture. As we consider the critical question of how our subjective experience of the world and ourselves develops and morphs on a moment-to-moment basis, we'll come to appreciate how scientists are taking advantage of high-tech tools to measure neural events and explore the most basic biological processes that sculpt our stream of consciousness (Chalmers, 1995; Crick & Koch, 2003).

We'll also examine how the unity of consciousness can break down in unusual and sometimes fascinating ways, such as during sleepwalking, when we're unconscious yet move about as if awake, and déjà vu, when we feel as though we're reliving an event we've never experienced (Voss, Baym, & Paller, 2008). In the extremely rare condition called *locked-in syndrome*, people may be misdiagnosed as being in a coma, yet actually be awake and alert. They can appear unconscious to onlookers because virtually all of their voluntary muscles are paralyzed, rendering them unable to speak or move. The famous Parisian journalist Jean-Dominique Bauby could control only his left eyelid after he suffered a stroke. Nevertheless, he wrote a memoir using a special alphabet code devised by his therapist and blinking his eye to dictate one letter at a time, underscoring the ability of people to adapt under the most trying of circumstances. As in many cases in psychology, abnormalities in functioning can often shed light on normal functioning (Cooper, 2003; Harkness, 2007).

5.1: The Biology of Sleep

5.1a Explain the role of the circadian rhythm and how our bodies react to a disruption in our biological clocks.

5.1b Identify the different stages of sleep and the neural activity and dreaming behaviors that occur in each.

5.1c Identify the features and causes of sleep disorders.

We spend as much as one-third or more of our lives in one specific state of consciousness. No, we don't mean zoning out during a boring lecture. We're referring to sleep. Although it's clear that sleep is of central importance to our health and daily functioning, psychologists still don't know for sure why we sleep. Some theories suggest that sleep plays a critical role in new learning, storing memories, and remembering emotional information (Gómez & Edgin, 2015; Payne & Kensinger, 2010); others suggest that it's critical for the immune system. Other models emphasize the possible role of sleep in promoting insight and problem solving (Wagner, et al., 2004) as well as neural development and neural connectivity more generally (Bushey et al., 2011; Frank & Cantera, 2014; Mignot, 2008). J. Allan Hobson (2009) suggested that brain activation during sleep is essential to waking consciousness and our ability to plan, reason, and function to the best of our ability. Alternatively, some evolutionary theorists have proposed that sleep contributes to our survival by conserving our energy, taking us out of circulation at times when we might be most vulnerable to unseen predators, and restoring our strength to fend them off (Siegel, 2005). There may be considerable truth to several or even all of these explanations.

The Circadian Rhythm: The Cycle of Everyday Life

Long before scientists began to probe the secrets of sleep in the laboratory, primitive hunters were keenly aware of daily cycles of sleep and wakefulness. **Circadian rhythm** is a fancy term (*circadian* is Latin for "about a day") for changes that occur on a roughly 24-hour basis in many of our biological processes, including hormone release, brain waves, body temperature, and drowsiness. Popularly known as the brain's **biological clock**, a meager 20,000 neurons located in the hypothalamus make us feel drowsy at different times of the day and night. Many of us have noticed that we feel like taking a nap at around three or four in the afternoon. Indeed, in many European and Latin American countries, a midafternoon nap (a *siesta* in Spanish) is part of the daily ritual. This sense of fatigue is triggered by our biological clocks. The urge to snooze comes over us at night as well because levels of the hormone *melatonin*, which triggers feelings of sleepiness, increase after dark.

The biological clock even ticks in marine algae and red blood cells too (Edgar et al., 2012). When humans' biological clocks are disrupted, such as when we work late shifts, or travel across time zones and experience jet lag, it disturbs sleep and increases the risk of injuries, fatal accidents, and health problems, including obesity, diabetes, and heart disease (Åkerstedt et al., 2002; Kirkcaldy, Levine, & Shephard, 2000; Parsons et al., 2015). Scientists are hot on the trail of drugs that target melatonin receptors in the brain to resync our brain's biological clock (Rajaratnam et al., 2009). That's because melatonin plays a key role in regulating circadian rhythms.

How much sleep do people obtain in a 24-hour period? A recent survey of more than 320,000 respondents revealed that the average U.S. adult sleeps 7.18 hours, although 29.2 percent reported that they slept less than 6 hours a night (Ford, Cunningham, & Croft, 2015), an amount considerably less than the 7 to 10 hours that most of us need. Newborns are gluttons for sleep and need about 16 hours over the course of a day. At the other extreme are the lucky few—less than 1 percent of the population—who carry a mutation in a gene called DEC2 that allows them to get away with sleeping six hours or less a night without "crashing" the next day (He et al., 2009). College students may need as many as nine hours of sleep a night, although most sleep no more than six hours (Maas, 1999), creating a powerful urge to nap the next day (Rock, 2004). One common misconception is that the elderly need less sleep than the rest of us, only six or seven hours a night. In reality, they probably need just as much sleep, but they sleep more fitfully (Ohayon, 2002).

Ordinarily, there don't seem to be many negative consequences of losing one night's sleep other than feeling edgy, irritable, and unable to concentrate well the next day. Yet after a few nights of sleep deprivation, we feel more "out of it" and begin to accumulate a balance of "sleep debt," which can require at least several nights of sleeping a few extra hours to pay off. People deprived of multiple nights of sleep, or who cut back drastically on sleep, often experience mild depression; difficulties in learning new information and paying attention; problems in thinking clearly, solving problems, and making decisions; increased emotional reactivity; and slowed reaction times (Cohen, et al., 2010; Gangswisch et al., 2010; Rosales-Lagarde et al., 2012). After

circadian rhythm

cyclical changes that occur on a roughly 24-hour basis in many biological processes

biological clock

term for the area of the hypothalamus that's responsible for controlling our levels of alertness

The tragic crash of Colgan Air Flight 3409 outside of Buffalo, New York, has been blamed on sleep deprivation, as both the pilot and copilot had been sleep-deprived before the flight.

more than four days of severe sleep deprivation, we may even experience brief hallucinations, such as hearing voices or seeing things (Wolfe & Pruitt, 2003). Sleep deprivation is associated with a variety of adverse health outcomes: weight gain (we burn off a lot of calories just by sleeping); increased risk for high blood pressure, diabetes, and heart problems; and a less vigorous immune response to viral infections (Dement & Vaughan, 1999; Motivala & Irwin, 2007). This last effect probably explains why you're more likely to get a cold after going for several days to a week with little sleep (Prather et al., 2015). Some researchers even believe that the massive increase in obesity and diabetes in the United States over the past few decades is largely as a result of Americans' chronic sleep deprivation (Buxton et al., 2012; Hasler et al., 2004), although this claim is scientifically controversial. Loss of sleep has also been tied to friendly-fire incidents in the 1991 Persian Gulf War, in which soldiers mistook their comrades for the enemy, resulting in senseless casualties (Kennedy, 2009).

Recent data point to a racial dimension to sleep loss as well: Minorities, African Americans in particular, appear to sleep less—and less well—than Caucasians. The reasons for this difference aren't clear. It remains even after taking into account differences between African Americans and Caucasians in social class and education, so other factors, like race differences in everyday life stressors, appear to be at play (Carnethon et al., 2012; Quenqua, 2012).

In keeping with what many of our parents wisely counseled—"everything in moderation"—too much sleep can pose problems as well. Moms and dads typically worry about their sleep-deprived teenagers. But the parents of 15-year-old Louisa Ball, who lives in south England, were concerned for another reason; their daughter routinely slept for two weeks straight without interruptions, unless she received medication. Louisa suffers from a rare neurological condition called Kleine-Levin Syndrome, aptly nicknamed "Sleeping Beauty Disorder." Her parents need to wake her every 22 hours to feed her and take her to the bathroom, after which she falls asleep immediately.

Stages of Sleep

For much of human history, people believed there was something like a switch in our brains that turned consciousness on when we were awake and off when we snoozed. But one night in 1951, a discovery in Nathaniel Kleitman's sleep laboratory at the University of Chicago changed how we think about sleep and dreaming. Eugene Aserinsky, Kleitman's graduate student, monitored his eight-year-old son's eye movements and brain waves while he slept. Aserinsky was astonished to observe that his son's eyes danced periodically back and forth under his closed lids. Whenever the eye movements occurred, the boy's brain pulsed with electrical activity, as measured by an electroencephalogram (EEG), much as it did when he was awake (Aserinsky, 1996).

The fledgling scientist had the good sense to know that he was onto something of immense importance. The slumbering brain was hardly an inert tangle of neurons; rather, it was abuzz with activity, at least at various intervals. Aserinsky further suspected that his son's eye movements reflected episodes of dreaming. Aserinsky and Kleitman (1953) confirmed this hunch when they awakened participants while they were displaying **rapid eye movement (REM)**. In almost all cases, they reported vivid dreams. In contrast, participants were much less likely to report vivid dreams when researchers awakened them from sleep when they weren't displaying REM, although later research showed that vivid dreams occasionally happened then, too.

In landmark research using all night-recording devices, Kleitman and William Dement (Dement & Kleitman, 1957) went on to discover that during sleep we pass repeatedly through five stages every night. Each cycle lasts about 90 minutes, and each stage of sleep is clearly distinguishable from awake states, as shown in Figure 5.1.

STAGE 1 SLEEP. Has someone ever nudged you to wake up, and you weren't even sure whether you were awake or asleep? Perhaps you even replied, "No, I wasn't really sleeping," but your friend insisted, "Yes, you were. You were starting to snore." If so, you were probably in stage 1 sleep. In this light stage of sleep, which lasts for

rapid eye movement (REM)

darting of the eyes underneath closed eyelids during sleep

5 to 10 minutes, our brain activity powers down by 50 percent or more, producing *theta* waves, which occur four to seven times per second. These waves are slower than the *beta* waves of 13 or more times per second produced during active alert states, and the alpha waves of 8 to 12 times per second when we're quiet and relaxed. As we drift off to deeper sleep, we become more relaxed, and we may experience *hypnagogic imagery*—scrambled, bizarre, and dreamlike images that flit in and out of consciousness. We may also experience sudden jerks (sometimes called *myoclonic jerks*) of our limbs as if being startled or falling. In this state of sleep, we're typically quite confused. Some scientists speculate that many reports of ghosts and other spirits stem from hypnagogic imagery that sleepers misinterpret as human figures (Hines, 2003).

STAGE 2 SLEEP. In stage 2 sleep, our brain waves slow down even more. Sudden intense bursts of electrical activity called sleep spindles of about 12–14 cycles a second, and occasional sharply rising and falling waves known as K-complexes, first appear in the EEG (Aldrich, 1999). K-complexes appear only when we're asleep. As our brain activity decelerates, our heart rate slows, our body temperature decreases, our muscles relax even more, and our eye movements cease. We spend as much as 65 percent of our sleep in stage 2.

STAGES 3 AND 4 SLEEP. After about 10 to 30 minutes, light sleep gives way to much deeper slow-wave sleep, in which we can observe *delta waves*, which are as slow as one to two cycles a second, in the EEG. In stage 3, delta waves appear 20 to 50 percent of the time, and in stage 4, they appear more than half the time. In recent years, researchers have tended to conceptualize sleep stages 3 and 4 in terms of a single, consolidated stage of sleep, marked by slow wave, deep sleep (Iber et al., 2007). To feel fully rested in the morning, we need to experience deeper sleep throughout the night. In this context, a common myth is that drinking alcohol is a good way to catch up on sleep. Not quite. Having several drinks before bed usually puts us to bed sooner, but it usually makes us feel more tired the next day because alcohol suppresses delta wave sleep. Children are famously good sleepers because they spend as much as 40 percent of their sleep time in "deep sleep" and are difficult to awaken. In contrast, adults spend only about one-quarter of their sleep "sleeping like a baby," in deep sleep.

STAGE 5: REM SLEEP. After 15 to 30 minutes, we return to stage 2 before our brains shift dramatically into high gear, with high frequency, low-amplitude waves resembling those of wakefulness. We've entered stage 5, known commonly as **REM sleep**. In contrast, stages 1–4 are known as **non-REM (NREM) sleep**.

Our hyped brain waves during REM sleep are accompanied by increased heart rate and blood pressure, as well as rapid and irregular breathing, a state that occupies about 20 to 25 percent of our night's sleep. After 10 to 20 minutes of REM sleep, the cycle starts up again, as we glide back to the early stages of sleep and then back into deeper sleep yet again. Each night, we circle back to REM sleep five or six times (see Figure 5.2). Contrary to a belief held by Sigmund Freud and others, dreams occur for more than a few seconds. In fact, our later REM periods toward the early morning typically last for half an hour or more, compared with the 10 to 20 minutes we spend in REM after falling asleep. So if it seems like one of your dreams has lasted for 45 minutes, that's often because it has.

Figure 5.1 The Stages of Sleep.

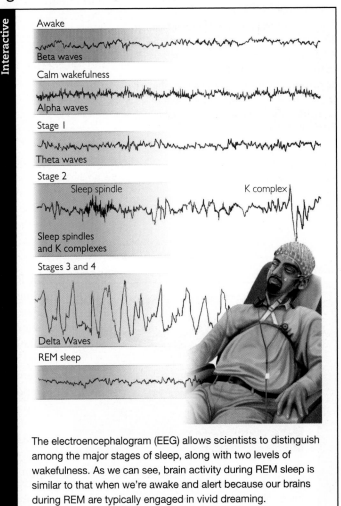

The electroencephalogram (EEG) allows scientists to distinguish among the major stages of sleep, along with two levels of wakefulness. As we can see, brain activity during REM sleep is similar to that when we're awake and alert because our brains during REM are typically engaged in vivid dreaming.

REM sleep

stage of sleep during which the brain is most active and during which vivid dreaming most often occurs

non-REM (NREM) sleep

stages 1 through 4 of the sleep cycle, during which rapid eye movements do not occur and dreaming is less frequent and vivid

Figure 5.2 Stages of Sleep in a Typical Night.

The graph shows the typical progression through the night of stages 1–4 and REM sleep. Stages 1–4 are indicated on the *y*-axis, and REM stages are represented by the green curves on the graph. The REM periods occur about every 90 minutes throughout the night (Dement, 1974).

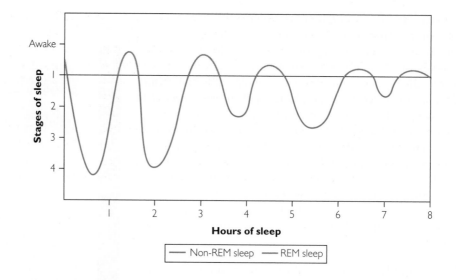

REM Sleep

Research demonstrates that REM and non-REM dreams tend to differ in content. The dream image above would be more likely in a REM dream.

We don't dream *only* during REM sleep, although we dream *more* in REM sleep (Domhoff, 1996, 1999). Many REM dreams are emotional, illogical, and prone to sudden shifts in plot (Foulkes, 1962; Hobson, Pace-Schott, & Stickgold, 2000). In contrast, non-REM dreams often are shorter (Antrobus, 1983; Foulkes & Rechtschaffen, 1964), more thought-like and repetitive, and deal with everyday topics of current concern to us, like homework, shopping lists, or taxes (Hobson, 2002; Rechtschaffen, Verdone, & Wheaton, 1963). Nevertheless, as the night wears on, dream reports from NREM sleep (starting with stage 2) resemble REM dream reports, leading some researchers to suggest that REM and NREM dreams aren't as distinct as once believed (Antrobus, 1983; Foulkes & Schmidt, 1983; McNamara et al., 2005).

REM sleep is biologically important and probably essential. Depriving rats of REM sleep typically leads to their deaths within a few weeks (National Institute on Alcohol Use and Alcoholism, 1998), although rats die even sooner from total sleep deprivation (Rechtschaffen, 1998). When we humans are deprived of REM for a few nights, we experience *REM rebound*: The amount and intensity of REM sleep increases, suggesting that REM serves a critical biological function (Ocampo-Garces et al., 2000). Many of us have observed REM rebound when we haven't slept much for a few nights in a row. When we finally get a good night's sleep, we often experience much more intense dreams, even nightmares, probably reflecting a powerful lack of REM sleep. Yet scientists are still debating the biological functions of REM sleep.

Some researchers once believed that the darting movements of REM sleep served to scan the images of dreams (Dement, 1974; Siegel, 2005). William Dement once observed a person during REM engaging in a striking pattern of back-and-forth horizontal eye movements. When Dement awakened him, he reported dreaming of a Ping-Pong match. Nevertheless, the evidence for this "scanning hypothesis" of REM is mixed, and the fact that individuals who are blind from birth engage in REM calls it into question (Gross, Byrne, & Fisher, 1965). During REM the muscles of our middle ears become active, almost as though they're assisting us to hear sounds in the dream (Pessah & Roffwarg, 1972; Slegel et al., 1991).

During REM sleep, our supercharged brains are creating dreams, but our bodies are relaxed and, for all practical purposes, paralyzed. For this reason, scientists sometimes call REM sleep *paradoxical sleep* because the brain is active at the same time the body is inactive. If REM didn't paralyze us, we'd act out our dreams, something that people with a strange—and fortunately rare—condition called *REM behavior disorder (RBD)* do on occasion. In one case of RBD, for 20 years a 77-year-old minister acted out violent dreams in his sleep and occasionally injured his wife (Mahowald & Schenck, 2000). Fortunately, only about 1 person in 200 has symptoms of RBD, but the percentage of RBD climbs as high as 2 percent for people older than the age of 60 and as high as 6 percent for people older than the age of 70. Raters of videos of sleeping people who experienced episodes of RBD successfully matched the movements they observed with the content of dreams that participants reported 39.5 percent of the time, strongly suggesting that people with RBD are acting out their dreams. (Peever, Luppi, & Montplaisir, 2014).

In RBD, the brain stem structures that ordinarily prevent us from moving during REM sleep don't function properly. Recently, it's come to light that RBD may be a very early marker of dementia and Parkinson's disease, with RBD emerging an average of 14 to 25 years before major symptoms of neurodegenerative diseases first appear (Boeve, 2010; Schenck, Boeve, & Mahowald, 2013).

Classic work by Michel Jouvet (1962) showed that lesioning a brain-stem region called the *locus coeruleus*, which is responsible for keeping us paralyzed during REM, leads cats to act out their dreams. If Jouvet gave cats a ball of yarn to play with during the day, they'd often reenact this play behavior in their dreams.

Journal Prompt

Do you sleep with your cell phone on and often get calls, texts, or other alerts in the middle of the night? Even if you don't, how do you think this would affect the quality of sleep knowing how the stages of sleep tend to progress?

Lucid Dreaming

We've been talking about sleeping and waking as distinct stages, but they may blend gradually into one another (Antrobus, Antrobus, & Fisher, 1965; Voss et al., 2009a). A phenomenon that challenges the idea that we're either totally asleep or totally awake is described in the following example: "I briefly looked back. The person following me did not look like an ordinary human being; he was as tall as a giant... Now it was fully clear to me that I was undergoing a dream...Then it suddenly occurred to me that I did not have to escape but was capable of doing something else... So...I turned around, and allowed the pursuer to approach me. Then I asked him what it actually was that he wanted. His answer was: "How am I supposed to know?! After all, this is your dream and, moreover, you studied psychology and not me" (Tholey, 1987, p. 97 translated in Metzinger, 2009, p. 146).

If, like this slumberer, you've ever dreamed and known you were dreaming, you've experienced **lucid dreaming** (Blackmore, 1991; LaBerge, 2014; Van Eeden, 1913). Most of us have experienced at least one lucid dream. One-fifth of Americans report dreaming lucidly on a monthly basis (Saunders et al., 2016; Snyder & Gackenbach, 1988), and less than 5 percent report that they dream lucidly on a weekly basis (Dresler et al., 2011). Many lucid dreamers become aware they're dreaming when they see something so bizarre or improbable that they conclude (correctly) that they're having a dream.

Using brain imaging, researchers (Dresler et al., 2012) recently discovered that when participants experience a lucid dream, parts of their cerebral cortex associated with self-perceptions and evaluating thoughts and feelings rev up with activity. Another study (Voss et al., 2009a), which measured electrical activity in the brain, suggested that lucid dreams are a hybrid or mixed state of consciousness with features of both waking and REM sleep. If these studies can be replicated, it would imply that it's possible to remain asleep yet self-aware, and that we don't merely report that dreams have a lucid quality after we awaken.

Lucid dreaming opens up the possibility of controlling our dreams (Kunzendorf et al., 2006–2007). The ability to become lucid during a nightmare usually improves the dream's outcome (Levitan & LeBerge, 1990; Spoormaker & Van den Bout, 2006). Nevertheless, there's no good evidence that changing our lucid dreams can help us to overcome depression, anxiety, or other adjustment problems, despite the claims of some popular psychology books, Internet sites, and even telephone applications that claim to increase dream lucidity (Mindell, 1990).

lucid dreaming

experience of becoming aware that one is dreaming

▸ **Replicability**

Can the results be duplicated in other studies?

To ensure that the effects of sleeping pills don't carry over to when we're awake, it's important to monitor how we react to them and ensure that we have plenty of time to sleep before needing to be active again.

insomnia

difficulty falling and/or staying asleep

Correlation vs. Causation

Can we be sure that A causes B?

narcolepsy

disorder characterized by the rapid and often unexpected onset of sleep

Lucas Carlton suffers from narcolepsy and sleeps 20 hours a day. He's shown here at home in England in one of his narcoleptic states.

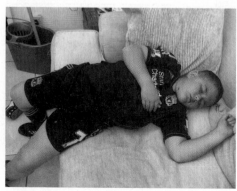

Disorders of Sleep

Nearly all of us have trouble falling asleep or staying asleep from time to time. When sleep problems recur, interfere with our ability to function at work or school, or affect our health, they can exact a dear price. The cost of sleep disorders in terms of lost work productivity alone amounts to as much as $63 billion per year in the United States (Kessler et al, 2011). We can also gauge the cost in terms of human lives, with an estimated 1,500 Americans who fall asleep at the wheel killed each year (Fenton, 2007). These grim statistics are understandable given that 30 to 50 percent of people report some sort of sleep problem (Althius et al., 1998; Blay, Andreoli, & Gastal, 2008).

INSOMNIA. The most common sleep disturbance is insomnia. **Insomnia** can take the following forms: (a) having trouble falling asleep (regularly taking more than 30 minutes to doze off), (b) waking too early in the morning, and (c) waking up during the night and having trouble returning to sleep. An estimated 9 to 15 percent of people report severe or longstanding problems with insomnia (Morin & Edinger, 2009).

In a survey of more than 7,600 patients in a healthcare system, a diagnosis of insomnia was associated with 46 percent higher healthcare costs a year after diagnosis compared with patients without an insomnia diagnosis (Anderson et al., 2014). Additionally, 7.2 percent of costly workplace accidents and errors are estimated to be associated with insomnia (Shahly et al., 2012). We must be careful in interpreting these findings, however, because insomnia may be correlated but not causally related to these negative outcomes, as other disorders or conditions that often accompany insomnia, such as depression, continual pain, or a variety of medical conditions, might be responsible for increased healthcare costs (Katz & McHorney, 2002; Smith & Haythornthwaite, 2004).

Brief bouts of insomnia are often the result of stress and relationship problems, medications and illness, working late or variable shifts, jet lag, drinking caffeine, or napping during the day. Insomnia can become recurrent if we become frustrated and anxious when we can't fall asleep right away (Spielman, Conroy, & Glovinsky, 2003). Many people don't realize that even most "good sleepers" take 15 to 20 minutes to fall asleep. If you have trouble drifting off to sleep and counting sheep doesn't help, James Maas (1999) recommends that you try the following: hide clocks to avoid becoming preoccupied with the inability to fall asleep quickly; sleep in a cool room; go to sleep and wake up at regular times; and avoid caffeine, naps during the day, reading in bed, and watching television or surfing the Web right before bedtime.

Sleeping pills can be effective in treating insomnia. Still, researchers have discovered that brief psychotherapy is more effective than Ambien, a popular sleeping pill (Jacobs et al., 2004), although psychotherapy and medications for insomnia can be effectively combined (Sudak, Kloss, & Zamzow, 2014). Recently, it's come to light that in rare instances, people who use Ambien engage in odd and even dangerous behaviors, including preparing food and eating raw food, walking, making phone calls, and even driving while asleep. Like Ambien, another popular sleeping medication, Lunesta, can cause amnesia for events that occur after taking it (Schenck, 2006). More serious are indications that Ambien is associated with an increased risk of developing dementia, with higher doses associated with increased risk (Shih et al., 2015).

Longstanding use of many sleeping pills can create dependency and make it more difficult to sleep once people stop taking them. So, in an ironic twist, sleeping pills can actually cause insomnia (Bellon, 2006).

NARCOLEPSY. **Narcolepsy** is a dramatic disorder in which people experience bouts of sudden sleep lasting anywhere from a few seconds to several minutes and, less frequently, as long as an hour. The overwhelming urge to sleep can strike at any moment, as in the case of a patient with narcolepsy who fell asleep in all sorts of situations: during his favorite movies, in the shower, and while driving. He was a prison guard, but he couldn't stay awake on the job. He feared his boss would fire him and stifled many a yawn in his presence.

As this striking example reveals, the symptoms of narcolepsy can interfere with day-to-day functioning and be quite disturbing, so it's not surprising that nearly 20 percent of people with narcolepsy suffer from serious depression or social anxiety disorder (Ohayon, 2013). Surprise, elation, or other strong emotions—even those associated with laughing at a joke or engaging in sexual intercourse—can lead some people with narcolepsy to experience *cataplexy*, a complete loss of muscle tone. During cataplexy, people can fall because their muscles become limp as a rag doll. Cataplexy occurs in healthy people during REM sleep. But in narcolepsy, people experiencing cataplexy remain alert, even though they can't move. Ordinarily, sleepers don't enter REM sleep for more than an hour after they fall asleep. But when people who experience an episode of narcolepsy doze off, they plummet into REM sleep immediately, suggesting that it results from a sleep–wake cycle that's badly off-kilter. Vivid hypnagogic hallucinations often accompany the onset of narcoleptic episodes, raising the possibility that REM intrusions are one cause of brief waking hallucinations.

Watch MABEL THE NARCOLEPTIC DOG

Genetic abnormalities boost the risk of narcolepsy, and some people develop narcolepsy after a brain tumor or an accident that causes brain damage (Kanbayashi et al., 2015). The hormone *orexin* plays a key role in triggering sudden attacks of sleepiness (Mieda & Sakurai, 2016). Indeed, people with narcolepsy have abnormally few brain cells that produce orexin. Medications that either replace orexin or mimic its effects in the brain may one day cure narcolepsy. Some dogs also suffer from narcolepsy. The video of Mabel depicts her brief narcoleptic episode, after which she recovers and achieves full wakefulness.

SLEEP APNEA.   In 2008, a 53-year-old Go Airlines captain and his copilot fell asleep during the flight, failed to respond to air traffic controllers for nearly 20 minutes, and overshot the runway by about 30 miles before they woke up (CNN, August 3, 2009). What happened? The captain suffered from **sleep apnea**, a serious sleep disorder that afflicts between 2 and 20 percent of the general population, depending on how broadly or narrowly it's defined (Peppard et al., 2013; Shamsuzzaman, Gersh, & Somers, 2003; Strohl & Redline, 1996). Apnea is caused by a blockage of the airway during sleep, as shown in Figure 5.3. This problem causes people with apnea to snore loudly, gasp, and sometimes stop breathing for more than 20 seconds. Struggling to breathe rouses the person many times—often several hundred times—during the night and interferes with sleep, causing fatigue the next day. Yet most people with sleep apnea have no awareness of these multiple awakenings.

A lack of oxygen and the buildup of carbon dioxide can lead to many problems, including night sweats, weight gain, fatigue, hearing loss, an irregular heartbeat (Sanders & Givelber, 2006) and can increase the risk for dementia or other cognitive impairments (Yaffe et al., 2011). A 10-year study of 6,441 men and women underscored the dangerous effects of sleep apnea. The researchers found that the disorder raised the overall risk of death by 17 percent; in men 40–70 years old with severe apnea, the increase in risk shot up to 46 percent compared with healthy men of the same age (Punjabi et al., 2009).

Because apnea is associated with being overweight, doctors typically recommend weight loss as a first treatment option. Many people benefit from wearing a facemask attached to a machine that blows air into their nasal passages, forcing the airway to remain open. Nevertheless, adjusting to this rather uncomfortable machine can be challenging (Wolfe & Pruitt, 2003).

NIGHT TERRORS.   Night terrors are often more disturbing to onlookers than to sleepers. Parents who witness a child's night terrors can hardly believe that the child has no recollection of what occurred. Screaming, crying, perspiring, confusion, and wide-eyed, the child may thrash about before falling back into a deep sleep. Such episodes usually last for only a few minutes, although they may seem like an eternity to a distraught parent.

Despite their dramatic nature, **night terrors** are typically harmless events that occur almost exclusively in children. Parents often learn not to overreact

sleep apnea

disorder caused by a blockage of the airway during sleep, resulting in daytime fatigue

A person using a device to combat sleep apnea at home.

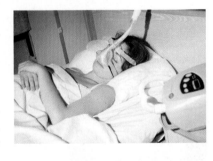

Figure 5.3 Flow of Air and Quality of Sleep. When the flow of air is blocked, as in sleep apnea, the quality of sleep can be seriously disrupted.

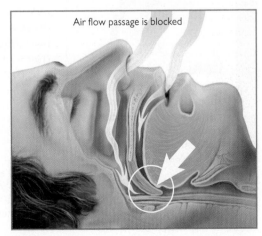

Air flow passage is blocked

Fact vs. Fiction

We can fall asleep with our eyes open. (See bottom of page for answer.)

○ Fact

○ Fiction

night terms

sudden waking episodes characterized by screaming, perspiring, and confusion followed by a return to a deep sleep

and even ignore the episodes if the child isn't in physical danger. Night terrors occasionally occur in adults, especially when they're under intense stress. Despite what most people believe, night terrors aren't associated with vivid dreaming; in fact, they occur exclusively in non-REM sleep.

SLEEPWALKING AND SEXSOMNIA. For many of us, the image of a "somnambulist," or sleepwalker, is a person with eyes closed, arms outstretched, and both hands at shoulder height, walking like a zombie. In actuality, a sleepwalking person often acts like any fully awake person, although a sleepwalker may be somewhat clumsier. Some 15 to 30 percent of children and 4 to 5 percent of adults sleepwalk occasionally (Mahowald & Bornemann, 2005; Petit et al., 2015). **Sleepwalking** often involves relatively little activity, but sleepwalkers have been known to drive cars and turn on computers while asleep (Underwood, 2007). In fact, a few people who committed murder have used sleepwalking as a legal defense. In one controversial case, a young man drove almost 20 miles, removed a tire iron from a car, and used it to kill his mother-in-law. He also strangled his father-in-law to unconsciousness and stabbed them both with a knife. The man was declared innocent because he had slept through the whole event and wasn't responsible for his behavior (McCall, Smith, & Shapiro, 1997).

sleepwalking

walking while fully asleep

In a strange condition known as sleep sex or *sexsomnia*, people engage in sexual acts while asleep and don't remember what occurred after they awaken. In a number of controversial legal cases, people have been found not guilty of sexual assault by claiming they suffered from sexsomnia (Bothroyd, 2010).

Contrary to popular misconception, sleepwalkers aren't acting out their dreams because sleepwalking almost always occurs during non-REM (especially stage 3 or 4) sleep. For most people, sleepwalking is harmless, and sleepwalkers rarely remember their actions after awakening. If someone is sleepwalking, it's perfectly safe to wake him or her up, despite what we may have seen or heard in movies (Wolfe & Pruitt, 2003).

Sleepwalking

The photo above incorrectly captures how a sleepwalking person would appear to an onlooker. Sleepwalkers typically walk just like regular people, not like zombies.

5.2: Dreams

5.2a Describe Freud's theory of dreams.

5.2b Explain three major modern theories of dreaming.

Dreaming is a virtually universal experience. Some people insist they never dream, but research shows this phenomenon is almost always a result of a failure to recall dreams rather than a failure to experience them. When brought into a sleep laboratory, just about everyone reports vivid dreaming when awakened during a REM period (Dement, 1974; Domhoff & Schneider, 2004), although a mysterious handful of people don't (Butler & Watson, 1985; Pagel, 2003). Even people who are blind dream. But whether their dreams contain visual imagery depends on when they became blind. People blinded before age four don't experience visual dream imagery, whereas those blinded after age seven do so, suggesting that between ages four to six is the window

Answer: Fact. Amazing, but it's actually the case that we can fall asleep with our eyes open! In a 1960 study, an investigator taped the eyes of three volunteers—one of them severely sleep-deprived—wide open while flashing bright lights at them, blasting loud music into their ears, and administering periodic electric shocks to their legs. They fell sound asleep within 12 minutes (Boese, 2007).

Fact vs. Fiction

We're most likely to believe that our negative dreams are meaningful when they're about a friend. (See bottom of page for answer.)

○ Fact

○ Fiction

within which the ability to generate visual imagery develops (Kerr, 1993; Kerr & Domhoff, 2004).

Whether we're researchers in Timbuktu or New York City, we'll find cross-culturally consistent patterns in dreaming. Virtually all of us experience dreams that contain more aggression than friendliness, more negative than positive emotions, and more misfortune than good fortune. At least a few differences in dreams are associated with cultural factors. For example, the dreams of people in more technologically advanced societies feature fewer animals than those in small, traditional societies (Domhoff, 1996, 2001).

Scientists still don't know for sure why we dream, but evidence from a variety of sources suggests that dreams are involved in (a) processing emotional memories (Malinoski & Horton, 2015; Maquet & Franck, 1997); (b) integrating new experiences with established memories to make sense of and create a model of the world, including one's social reality (Hobson, 2009; Revonsuo, Tuominen, & Valli, 2015; Stickgold, James, & Hobson, 2002); (c) learning new strategies and ways of doing things, like swinging a golf club (Walker et al., 2002); (d) simulating threatening events so we can better cope with them in everyday life (Revonsuo, 2000; Robert & Zadra, 2014); and (e) reorganizing and consolidating memories (Crick & Mitchison, 1983; Diekelmann & Born, 2010). Still, the function of dreams remains a puzzle because research evidence concerning the role of learning and memory in dreams is mixed. We'll discuss four major theories of dreams, beginning with the granddaddy of them all: Sigmund Freud.

Freud's Dream Protection Theory

Humans have been trying to decipher the meaning of dreams for thousands of years. The Babylonians believed that dreams were sent by the gods, the Assyrians thought that dreams contained signs or omens, the Greeks built dream temples in which visitors awaited prophecies sent by the gods during dreams, and North American Indians believed that dreams revealed hidden wishes and desires (Van de Castle, 1994).

Sigmund Freud sided with the Native Americans. In his landmark book, *The Interpretation of Dreams* (1900), Freud described dreams as the guardians of sleep. During sleep, the ego, which acts as a sort of mental censor, is less able than when awake to keep sexual and aggressive instincts at bay by repressing them. If not for dreams, these instincts would bubble up, disturbing sleep. The *dream-work* disguises and contains the threatening sexual and aggressive impulses by transforming them into symbols that represent *wish fulfillment*—how we wish things could be.

According to Freud, dreams don't surrender their secrets easily; they require interpretation to reverse the dream-work and reveal their true meanings. He distinguished between the details of the dream itself, which he called the *manifest content*, and it's true, hidden meaning, which he called the *latent content*. For example, a dream about getting a flat tire (manifest content) might signify anxiety about the loss of status at our job (latent content).

Nightmares are most frequent in children but are also common in adults.

Most Frequent Dream Themes

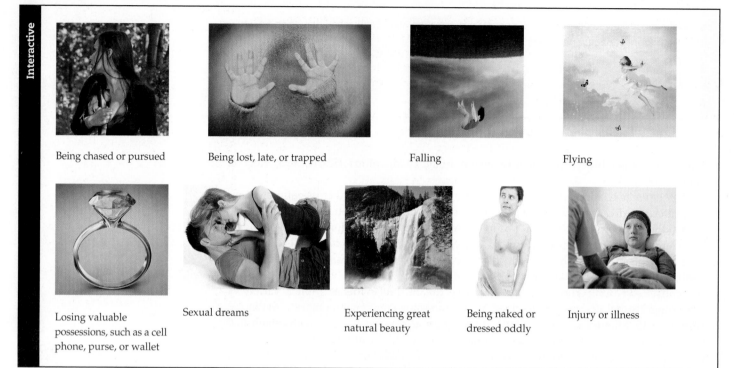

Being chased or pursued

Being lost, late, or trapped

Falling

Flying

Losing valuable possessions, such as a cell phone, purse, or wallet

Sexual dreams

Experiencing great natural beauty

Being naked or dressed oddly

Injury or illness

Falsifiability

Can the claim be disproved?

Ruling Out Rival Hypotheses

Have important alternative explanations for the findings been excluded?

Most scientists have rejected the dream protection and wish fulfillment theories of dreams (Domhoff, 2001). Contrary to Freud's dream protection theory, some patients with brain injuries report that they don't dream, yet sleep soundly (Jus et al., 1973). If, as Freud claimed, "wish fulfillment is the meaning of each and every dream" (Freud, 1900, p. 106), we'd expect dream content to be mostly positive. Yet although most of us have occasional dreams of flying, winning the lottery, or being with the object of our wildest fantasies, these themes are less frequent than dreams of misfortune. Freud also believed that many or most dreams are sexual in nature. But sexual themes account for as little as 10 percent of the dreams we remember (Domhoff, 2003). Of course, though a determined Freudian might argue that we're merely forgetting about many sexual dreams, this hypothesis has never been tested.

Another challenge to Freud's dream theory is that many dreams don't appear to be disguised, as he contended. As many as 90 percent of dream reports are straightforward descriptions of everyday activities and problems, like talking to friends (Domhoff, 2003; Dorus, Dorus, & Rechtschaffen, 1971). But nightmares clearly aren't wish fulfillments, and they aren't at all uncommon in either adults or children. So, if you have an occasional nightmare, rest assured: It's perfectly normal.

Nevertheless, recurrent nightmares can be disturbing. Contrary to what Freud believed, it's possible to change nightmares with psychotherapy. Imagery rehearsal therapy combats nightmares by rehearsing—thinking and imagining—a new more positive dream at different times during the day (Krakow et al., 2001). A recent meta-analysis (mathematical synthesis) of studies of people with trauma-related nightmares yielded evidence that people who write down the new dream and rehearse it every day report sharp reductions in the frequency of their nightmares, improvements in sleep quality, and decreases in symptoms of posttraumatic stress disorder (Casement & Swanson, 2012).

Activation–Synthesis Theory

activation–synthesis theory

theory that dreams reflect inputs from brain activation originating in the pons, which the forebrain then attempts to weave into a story

Starting in the 1960s and 1970s, Alan Hobson and Robert McCarley developed **activation–synthesis theory** (Hobson & McCarley, 1977; Hobson et al., 2000), which proposes that dreams reflect brain activation in sleep, rather than repressed unconscious wishes, as Freud claimed. Far from having deep, universal meaning, Hobson and McCarley maintained that dreams reflect the activated brain's attempt to make sense of random and internally generated neural signals during REM sleep.

Throughout the day and night, the balance of neurotransmitters in the brain shifts continually. REM sleep is turned on by surges of the neurotransmitter acetylcholine, as the neurotransmitters serotonin and norepinephrine are shut down. Acetylcholine activates nerve cells in the pons, located at the base of the brain, while dwindling levels of serotonin and norepinephrine decrease reflective thought, reasoning, attention, and memory. The activated pons sends incomplete signals to the thalamus, which is a relay station for sensory information, to the language and visual areas of the forebrain, as shown in Figure 5.4. That's the activation part of the theory. The forebrain does its best to cobble together the signals it receives into a meaningful story. That's the synthesis part of the theory. Nevertheless, the bits of information it receives are haphazard and chaotic, so the narrative is rarely coherent or logical. The amygdala is also ramped up, adding the emotional colors of fear, anxiety, anger, sadness, and elation to the mix. According to activation–synthesis theory, the net result of these complex brain changes is what we experience as a dream, which may bear slim to no relation to our everyday lives.

Hobson (2009) most recently proposed that dreams reflect what he calls "protoconsciousness," which he described as a primitive or primary state of brain organization that starts to develop even before birth in the uterus and is a building block of consciousness (p. 808). In this dream state, raw emotions and perceptions become dominant. While our ability to reason shrinks, the brain is free to generate a working virtual reality model of the world, which assists the person in making accurate predictions in everyday life. The dreamer explores new hypotheses and possibilities of what could be experienced. Such exploration is made possible when critical judgment, self-reflection, and memory are suspended when we're shut off from sensory input from the environment and our sense of reality is "internally activated." In short, Hobson argues that dreaming helps us to navigate the demands of everyday life and make sense of the world, even though the content of our dreams rarely parallels closely what's happening in our lives currently or mirrors our past experiences. Given these circumstances, the dream is typically not subject to clear-cut and meaningful interpretation as the product of wish fulfillment, as Freud claimed (Fosse et al., 2003; Hobson & Friston, 2012).

Dreaming and the Forebrain

An alternative to the activation–synthesis theory emphasizes the role of the forebrain in dreaming. Mark Solms (1997; Solms & Turnbull, 2002) surveyed 332 cases of patients with brain damage from stroke, tumors, and injury. From this gold mine of data, he determined that damage to the parietal lobes and to the deep frontal white matter—which connects different parts of the cortex to the lower parts of the brain—can lead to a complete loss of dreaming. It's likely that the damaged brain areas are pathways that allow brain centers involved in dreaming to communicate. When they're disconnected, dreaming stops.

Thus, damage to the forebrain can eliminate dreams entirely, even when the brain stem is working properly. This finding seems to refute the claim of activation–synthesis theory that the brain stem plays an exclusive role in producing dreams and underscores the role of the forebrain in dreaming. According to Solms, dreams are driven largely by the motivational and emotional control centers of the forebrain as the logical "executive" parts of the brain snooze.

Neurocognitive Perspectives on Dreaming

Scientists who've advanced a **neurocognitive theory** of dreaming argue that explaining dreams only in terms of neurotransmitters and random neural impulses doesn't tell the full story. Instead, they contend, dreams are reflections of waking life and are a meaningful product of our cognitive capacities, which shape what we dream about. For example, children younger than age 7 or 8 recall dreaming on only 20 to 30 percent of occasions when awakened from REM sleep compared with 80 to 90 percent of adults (Foulkes, 1982, 1999). Until they reach the age of 9 or 10, children's dreams tend to be simple, lacking in

Figure 5.4 Activation-Synthesis Theory.

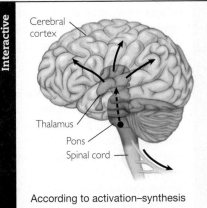

Cerebral cortex

Thalamus

Pons

Spinal cord

According to activation–synthesis theory, the pons transmits random signals to the thalamus, which relays information to the forebrain of the cerebral cortex. The forebrain in turn attempts to create a story from the incomplete information it receives.

Ruling Out Rival Hypotheses

Have important alternative explanations for the findings been excluded?

Falsifiability

Can the claim be disproved?

neurocognitive theory

theory that dreams are a meaningful product of our cognitive capacities, which shape what we dream about

Evaluating Claims DREAM INTERPRETATIONS

For some time, you've been curious about what, if anything, your dreams mean. You've come across Web sites and books that claim dreams are trying to tell us something and can be subject to analysis through their symbols, but you're not sure you buy this claim fully.

Recently, while surfing the Internet to learn more about dreams, the following claim grabs your attention.

"Your dreams are *hidden messages* sent from your subconscious to help guide your life. Using the *ancient art of dream analysis*, you can uncover hidden meanings in your dreams. For example, through the dream analysis that anyone can learn, you'll discover that *seeing a coconut in your dreams* means that you'll receive an unexpected sum of money."

Scientific skepticism requires us to evaluate all claims with an open mind but to insist on compelling evidence before accepting them. How do the Principles of Scientific thinking help us to evaluate this claim about dream analysis and the meaning of the dreams?

Consider how the six principles of scientific thinking are relevant as you evaluate this claim.

1. Ruling Out Rival Hypotheses

Have important alternative explanations for the findings been excluded?

Scientific evidence doesn't support the claim that specific symbols in our dreams possess a deeper meaning from the unconscious or predict something in our lives. Many dreams have no special meaning at all, and some dreams reflect everyday preoccupations. Still, different people interpreting the dream could come up with many different interpretations of what a coconut might mean in a dream. No evidence is provided for why we should give any weight to this particular interpretation or why it's more valid than any other of many possible interpretations.

2. Correlation vs. Causation

Can we be sure that A causes B?

Readers might infer that a causal connection exists between seeing a coconut in a dream and later receiving a large sum of money. Nevertheless, an association between seeing a coconut and receiving money might be purely coincidental.

3. Falsifiability

Can the claim be disproved?

It's difficult, if not impossible to disprove this claim. The claim is so vague that any number of circumstances could be taken as evidence for the truth of the claim. For example, it doesn't indicate whether the sum of money would be

forthcoming the next day or years later, which would make the claim difficult to falsify. Also, the claim doesn't specify what "unexpected" means. Does what is unexpected refer to the amount of money received or the mere fact that money comes your way that wasn't anticipated?

4. Replicability

Can the results be duplicated in other studies?

There's no evidence that the claim is derived from research. We should be skeptical of claims that aren't based on even a single study or don't provide suggestions regarding how the claim could be evaluated with carefully controlled research.

5. Extraordinary Claims

Is the evidence as strong as the claim?

This claim is extraordinary because most dream reports are actually straightforward descriptions of everyday activities and problems rather than hidden or disguised messages. Also, the fact that dream interpretations have been around a long time doesn't mean they're valid.

6. Occam's Razor

Does a simpler explanation fit the data just as well?

A simpler explanation might be that the images are not hidden messages from the unconscious, have no special meaning, and reflect nothing more than complex brain activity and images cobbled together to form a meaningful narrative during sleep.

Summary

There's no scientific support for the claim that dreams have special meanings that can be revealed through the interpretation of the supposed symbolic content of dreams, which are open to many possible interpretations.

movement, and apart from an occasional nightmare, less emotional and bizarre than adult dreams (Domhoff, 1996). A typical five-year-old's dream may be of a pet or animal in a zoo. According to the neurocognitive perspective, complex dreams are cognitive achievements that parallel the gradual development of visual imagination and other advanced cognitive abilities. We begin to dream like adults when our brains develop the "wiring" to do so (Domhoff, 2001).

According to the neurocognitive perspective, the fact that dreams are often rather ordinary and dramatize concerns that are important to us when we're not in slumberland implies that they reflect more than random neural impulses generated by the brain stem (Domhoff, 2011; Foulkes, 1985; Revonsuo, 2000). Content analyses of tens of thousands of adult dreams (Hall & Van de Castle, 1966) reveal that many are associated with everyday activities, emotional concerns, and preoccupations (Domhoff, 1996; Hall & Nordby, 1972; Smith & Hall, 1964), including playing sports, preparing for tests, feeling self-conscious about our appearance, and being single (Pano, Hilscher, & Cupchik, 2008–2009). Moreover, dream content is surprisingly stable over long time periods. In a journal containing 904 dreams that a woman kept for more than five decades, six themes (eating or thinking of food, the loss of an object, going to the bathroom, being in a small or messy room, missing a bus or train, doing something with her mother) accounted for more than three-fourths of the content of her dreams (Domhoff, 1993). Additionally, 50 to 80 percent of people report recurrent dreams, like missing a test, over many years (Cartwright & Romanek, 1978; Zadra, 1996).

The **dream continuity hypothesis** holds that dreams mirror our life circumstances (Domhoff, 1996). This hypothesis would be supported if the dreams of people with disabilities were different from those of individuals with no disabilities. But when Hobson and his colleagues (Voss et al., 2011) examined the dreams of people who were either deaf-mute or paraplegic from the time of birth, they found that the form and content of their dreams were no different from those of people without disabilities. Clearly, dreams often take on a life of their own, far removed from everyday reality.

As we've seen, there are sharp disagreements among scientists about the role of the brain stem and REM sleep, and the role that development plays in dreaming. Nevertheless, scientists generally agree that (1) acetylcholine turns on REM sleep and (2) the forebrain plays an important role in dreams.

dream continuity hypothesis
hypothesis that there is continuity between sleeping and waking experiences and that dreams can mirror life circumstances

Journal Prompt
Describe how the activation–synthesis theory of dreaming and the neurocognitive theory of dreaming are similar and how they are not.

5.3: Other Alterations of Consciousness and Unusual Experiences

5.3a Determine how scientists explain unusual and seemingly "mystical" alterations in consciousness.

5.3b Distinguish myths from realities concerning hypnosis.

As the stages of sleep demonstrate, consciousness is far more complicated than just "conscious" versus "unconscious." Moreover, there are other variations on the theme of consciousness besides sleep and waking. Some of the more radical alterations in consciousness include hallucinations, as well as out-of-body, near-death, and déjà vu experiences.

Hallucinations: Experiencing What Isn't There

Hallucinations, ranging from seeing ghost-like apparitions or scenes of splendid beauty, to hearing voices in the head commanding people to engage in unspeakable acts of violence, to feeling bugs marching on the skin, can seem amazingly real. Hallucinations are realistic perceptual experiences in the absence of any external stimuli, and they can occur in any sensory modality. Brain scans reveal that when people report visual hallucinations, their visual cortex becomes active, just as it does when they see a real object

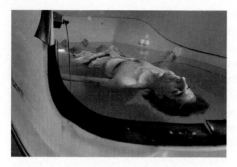

People who float in lukewarm saltwater in dark and silent sensory deprivation tanks often hallucinate to compensate for the lack of sensory stimulation (Smith, 2009).

out-of-body experience (OBE)

sense of our consciousness leaving our body

As real as an out-of-body experience seems to the person having it, research has found no evidence that consciousness exists outside the body.

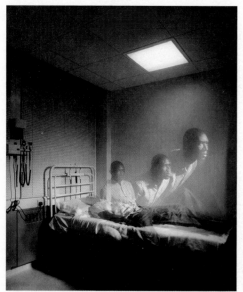

(Allen et al., 2008; Bentall, 2014). The same correspondence holds true for other senses, like hearing and touch, underscoring the link between our perceptual experiences and brain activity.

A frequent misconception is that hallucinations occur only in psychologically disturbed individuals (Aleman & Laroi, 2008). Yet surveys reveal that between 10 and 14 percent (Tien, 1991) to as many as 39 percent (Ohayon, 2000; Posey & Losch, 1983) of college students and people in the general population report having hallucinated during the day at least once—even when not taking drugs or experiencing psychological problems (Ohayon, 2000). Some non-Western cultures, including some in Africa, value hallucinations as gifts of wisdom from the gods and incorporate them into their religious rituals. People in these societies may even go out of their way to induce hallucinations by means of prayer, fasting, and hallucinogenic drugs (Al-Issa, 1995; Bourguignon, 1970).

Visual hallucinations can also be brought about by oxygen and sensory deprivation, epilepsy, fever, dementia, and migraine headaches (Manford & Andermann, 1998). Auditory hallucinations (those involving sound) can occur when patients mistakenly attribute their thoughts, or inner speech, to an external source (Bentall, 2014; Frith, 1992). The auditory verbal hallucinations of psychotic and well-functioning nonpsychotic individuals are similar in many respects. But they differ in that the voices that psychotic individuals hear are much more negative and perceived to be less controllable (Daalman et al., 2010). Psychological interventions that teach patients skills to help them to notice and accept disturbing hallucinations and view them as nothing more than passing mental events have shown promise, both in decreasing belief in their reality and in improving functioning among individuals with psychotic disorders, which are conditions marked by a partial loss of content with reality (Khoury et al., 2013; Thomas et al., 2014).

Out-of-Body and Near-Death Experiences

Carlos Alvarado (2000) described a 36-year-old police officer's account of an **out-of-body experience (OBE)** when she pursued an armed suspect on her first night on patrol. "When I and three other officers stopped the vehicle and started getting (to) the suspect...I was afraid. I promptly went out of my body and up into the air maybe 20 feet above the scene. I remained there, extremely calm, while I watched the entire procedure—including myself—do exactly what I had been trained to do." Alvarado reported that "[s]uddenly, [she] found herself back in her body after the suspect had been subdued" (p. 183).

OBEs are surprisingly common: About 25 percent of college students and 10 percent of the general population report having experienced one or more of them (Alvarado, 2000). In many cases, individuals describe themselves as floating above their bodies, calmly observing themselves from above, implying that our sense of ourselves need not be subjectively locked into our bodies (Smith, 2009). People who are prone to OBEs frequently report other unusual experiences, including vivid fantasies, lucid dreams, hallucinations, perceptual distortions, and strange body sensations in everyday life (Blackmore, 1984, 1986; Cardeña & Alverado, 2014). Some people also experience OBEs when they're medicated, using psychedelic drugs, experiencing migraine headaches or seizures, or either extremely relaxed or under extreme stress.

Yet are people really able to roam outside their bodies during an OBE? Laboratory studies have compared what's reported during an OBE against sights and sounds known to be present in a given location, like a hidden ledge 10 feet above a bed. Interestingly, even though many participants report they can see or hear what's occurring at a distant place, their reports are generally inaccurate or, at best, a "good guess" when they're accurate. When researchers have reported positive results, these results have virtually never been replicated (Alvarado, 2000). So there's no good evidence that people are truly floating above their bodies during an OBE, although it certainly seems that way to them (Cheyne & Girard, 2009). These findings appear to falsify the claim that people genuinely emerge from their bodies during OBEs.

Replicability

Can the results be duplicated in other studies?

Falsifiability

Can the claim be disproved?

What, then, are some possible explanations for these dramatic changes in consciousness? Our sense of self depends on a complex interplay of sensory information. Research suggests that when our senses of touch and vision are scrambled, the result is a disruption of our experience of our physical body with striking similarities to an OBE (Ehrsson, 2007; Lenggenhager et al., 2007). The "club drug," ketamine (widely known as "Special K"), which users often report produces bizarre OBEs and feelings of detachment from the physical world, disrupts patterns of brain activity that bring about a unified sense of the self and body by reducing transmission of the neurotransmitter glutamate (Wilkins, Girard, & Cheyne, 2011). OBEs remind us that one of the human brain's great achievements is its ability to integrate sensory information from different pathways into a unified experience. Yet when this ability is disrupted, it can trick us into thinking our physical selves are separate from our bodies (Cheyne & Girard, 2009; Terhune, 2009).

OBEs also sometimes occur in **near-death experiences (NDEs)** reported by people who've nearly died or thought they were going to die. In fact, about one quarter of patients with NDEs experience their consciousness outside their bodies (van Lommel et al., 2001). Ever since Raymond Moody (1975) cataloged them more than 40 years ago, Americans have become familiar with the classical elements of the NDE that are widely circulated in books and movies—passing through a dark tunnel; experiencing a white light as a spiritual being, such as a deceased loved one or angel; the life review (seeing our lives pass before our eyes); and meeting spiritual beings or long-dead relatives, all before "coming back into the body" (see Table 5.1). Not all reports of NDEs follow this exact script, but most are close, as the case that follows illustrates. Dr. Elizabeth Kübler-Ross (1973) reported the tale of a man who was critically injured by a large truck and then observed the accident scene from above his body. He then saw his family, surrounded by an aura of light. Experiencing the family's wondrous, unconditional love, he decided to return to his body to share his experiences with others.

Roughly 6 to 33 percent of people who've been close to death report NDEs (Blanke & Dieguez, 2009; Greyson, 2014; Ring, 1984; Sabom, 1982; van Lommel et al., 2001). NDEs differ across people and cultures, suggesting they don't provide a genuine glimpse of the afterlife, but are constructed from prevalent beliefs about the hereafter in response to the threat of death (Ehrenwald, 1974; Noyes & Kletti, 1976). People from Christian and Buddhist cultures frequently report the sensation of moving through a tunnel, but native people in North America, the Pacific Islands, and Australia rarely do (Kellehear, 1993).

It's tempting to believe that NDEs prove that when we die, we'll all be ushered into the afterlife by friends or loved ones. Nevertheless, the evidence is insufficient to support this extraordinary claim. Scientists have offered alternative explanations for NDEs based on changes in the chemistry of the brain associated with cardiac arrest, anesthesia, and other physical traumas (Blackmore, 1993). For example, a feeling of complete peace that can

Although there are many variations of a "near-death experience," most people in our culture believe it involves moving through a tunnel and toward a white light.

near-death experience (NDE)

experience reported by people who've nearly died or thought they were going to die

> **Extraordinary Claims**
>
> Is the evidence as strong as the claim?

Table 5.1 Common Elements in Adult Near-Death Experiences.

- Difficulty describing the experience in words
- Hearing ourselves pronounced dead
- Feelings of peace and quiet
- Hearing unusual noises
- Meeting "spiritual beings"
- Experiencing a bright light as a "being of light"
- Panoramic "life review," that is, seeing our entire life pass before our eyes
- Experiencing a realm in which all knowledge exists
- Experiencing cities of light
- Experiencing a realm of ghosts and spirits
- Sensing a border or limit
- Coming back "into the body"

BASED ON: Greyson, 2000; Moody, 1975, 1977.

sociocognitive theory

approach to explaining hypnosis based on people's attitudes, beliefs, expectations, and responsiveness to waking suggestions

dissociation theory

approach to explaining hypnosis based on a separation between personality functions that are normally well integrated

---

Correlation vs. Causation ▶

Can we be sure that A causes B?

Ruling Out Rival Hypotheses ▶

Have important alternative explanations for the findings been excluded?

Researchers have used the Poggendorf illusion, shown above, to study the effects of hypnotic age regression. Adults tend to see the two segments of the black line as misaligned (in reality, they're perfectly aligned), whereas children don't. When adult participants are age-regressed to childhood, they still see the two segments of the black line as misaligned, suggesting that hypnotic age regression doesn't make adults' perceptions more childlike (Ascher, Barber, & Spanos, 1972; Nash, 1987).

THEORIES OF HYPNOSIS. Researchers have attempted to explain hypnosis in terms of unconscious drives and motivations, a willingness to overlook logical inconsistencies, enhanced receptivity to suggestion, and an inhibition of the brain's frontal lobes (Lynn & Rhue; 1991; Nash & Barnier, 2008; Sheehan & McConkey, 1982). Each of these theories has contributed valuable insights into hypnotic phenomena. Nevertheless, two other models, the sociocognitive theory and the dissociation theory, have received the lion's share of attention.

Sociocognitive Theory. Sociocognitive theorists (Barber, 1969; Coe & Sarbin, 1991; Lynn, Kirsch, & Hallquist, 2008; Spanos, 1986) reject the idea that hypnosis is a trance state or unique state of consciousness. Instead, they explain hypnosis in the same way they explain everyday social behaviors. According to **sociocognitive theory**, people's attitudes, beliefs, motivations, and expectations about hypnosis, as well as their ability to respond to waking imaginative suggestions, shape their responses to hypnosis.

Consistent with sociocognitive theory, peoples' expectations of whether they'll respond to hypnotic suggestions are correlated with how they respond (Kirsch & Council, 1992). Still, this correlation doesn't necessarily mean that people's expectations cause them to be susceptible to hypnosis. Studies in which participants' responses vary as a function of what they're told about hypnosis provide more convincing evidence of causality. For example, participants told that hypnotized people can resist suggestions find themselves able to resist, whereas those told that hypnotized people can't resist suggestions often fail to resist (Lynn et al., 1984; Spanos, Cobb, & Gorassini, 1985).

Studies show that a training program that increases people's positive beliefs and expectancies about hypnosis and their willingness to imagine along with suggestions increases their ability to respond to hypnosis (Gorassini & Spanos, 1998). About half of participants who initially scored at the lowest range of suggestibility tested at the top range after training. These findings both challenge the idea that hypnotic suggestibility is a stable trait that can't be modified (Piccione, Hilgard, & Zimbardo, 1989) and offer support for sociocognitive theory.

Dissociation Theory. Ernest Hilgard's (1977, 1986, 1994) **dissociation theory** is an influential alternative to sociocognitive theories of hypnosis (Kihlstrom, 1992, 1998; Woody & Sadler, 2008). Hilgard (1977) defined *dissociation* as a division of consciousness, in which attention, effort, and planning are carried out without awareness. He hypothesized that hypnotic suggestions result in a separation between personality functions that are normally well integrated.

Hilgard (1977) happened on a discovery that played a key role in the development of his theory. During a demonstration of hypnotically suggested deafness, a student asked whether some part of the person could hear. Hilgard then told the participant that when he touched the participant's arm he'd be able to talk to the part that could hear if such a part existed. When Hilgard placed his hand on the participant's arm, the participant described what people in the room said. However, when Hilgard removed his hand, the participant was again "deaf." Hilgard invented the metaphor of the *hidden observer* to describe the dissociated, unhypnotized "part" of the mind that he could access on cue.

Later researchers suggested an alternative explanation for the hidden observer phenomenon (Kirsch & Lynn, 1998; Spanos, 1986, 1991). Nicholas Spanos (1991) believed that the hidden observer arises because the hypnotist suggests it directly or indirectly. That is, participants pick up on the fact that the instructions used to bring forth the hid-

◀ **Ruling Out Rival Hypotheses**

Have important alternative explanations for the findings been excluded?

---

den observer imply they should act as though a separate, nonhypnotized part of the person can communicate with the hypnotist. Spanos hypothesized that changing the instructions should change what the hidden observer reports. That's exactly what he found. Changing the instructions led hidden observers to experience more pain or less pain, or to perceive a number normally or in reverse (Spanos & Hewitt, 1980). In short, the hidden observer appears to be no different from any other suggested hypnotic response: It's shaped by what we expect and believe.

According to a revision of Hilgard's dissociation theory (Woody & Bowers, 1994), hypnosis bypasses the ordinary sense of control we exert over our behaviors. Thus, suggestions directly bring about responses with little or no sense of effort or conscious control (Jamieson & Sheehan, 2004; Sadler & Woody, 2010). This theory does a good job of describing what people experience during hypnosis and fits nicely with sociocognitive theories that emphasize the unconscious, automatic nature of most behaviors both within and apart from the context of hypnosis (Lynn & Green, 2011).

Psychomythology

Age Regression and Past Lives

One of the most popular myths of hypnosis is that it can help people retrieve memories of events as far back in time as birth. A televised documentary (Bikel, 1995) showed a group therapy session in which a woman was age-regressed through childhood, to the womb, and eventually to being trapped in her mother's fallopian tube. The woman provided a highly emotional demonstration of the discomfort that one would experience if one were indeed stuck in such an uncomfortable position. Although the woman may have believed in the reality of her experience, we can be quite certain that it wasn't memory based (after all, she didn't have a brain yet, because she wasn't even a fertilized egg at this point). Instead, age-regressed participants behave the way they think children should behave. Age-regressed adults don't show the expected patterns on many indices of development. For example, when regressed to childhood, they exhibit the brain waves (EEGs) typical of adults rather than of children. No matter how compelling, age-regressed experiences aren't exact mental replicas of childhood experiences (Nash, 1987).

Some therapists believe that they can trace their patients' current problems to previous lives and practice **past-life regression therapy** (Weiss, 1988). Typically, they hypnotize and age-regress patients to "go back to" the source of their present-day problems. For example, some practitioners of past-life regression therapy claim that neck and shoulder pains may be signs of having been executed by hanging or by a guillotine in a previous life.

With rare exceptions (Stevenson, 1974), researchers believe that reports of a past life are the products of imagination and what hypnotized participants know about a given time period. When checked against known facts (such as whether the country was at war or peace, the face on the coin of the time), participants' descriptions of the historical circumstances of their supposed past lives are rarely accurate. When they are, we can often explain this accuracy by "educated guesses" and knowledge of history (Spanos et al., 1991). For example, one participant regressed to ancient times claimed to be Julius Caesar, emperor of Rome, in 50 BC, even though the designations of BC and AD weren't adopted until centuries later and even though Julius Caesar died decades before the first Roman emperor came to power.

past-life regression therapy

therapeutic approach that uses hypnosis to supposedly age-regress patients to a previous life to identify the source of a present-day problem

Journal Prompt

Provide some examples of the circumstances in which you encountered one of the myths of hypnosis (either in a movie, TV, book, or from someone you know). Why do you think these myths persist in the absence of scientific evidence?

5.4: Drugs and Consciousness

5.4a Identify possible influences on substance use.
5.4b Distinguish different types of drugs and their effects on consciousness.

Virtually every culture has discovered that certain plants can alter consciousness, often dramatically. Knowledge of the mind-bending qualities of fermented fruits and grains, the juice of the poppy, boiled coffee beans and tea leaves, the burning of tobacco or marijuana leaf, certain molds that grow on crops, and the granulated extract of the coca leaf has been handed down to us from ancient times. We now know that these **psychoactive drugs** contain chemicals similar to those found naturally in our brains and that their molecules alter consciousness by changing chemical processes in neurons. Some psychoactive drugs are used to treat physical and mental illness, but others are used almost exclusively for recreational purposes. The precise psychological and physical effects depend on the type of drug and dosage, as we've summarized in Table 5.2.

But as we'll see, the effects of drugs depend on far more than their chemical properties. *Mental set*—beliefs and expectancies about the effects of drugs—the settings in which people take these drugs, and their cultural heritage and genetic endowment all play a part in accounting for the highs and lows of drug use.

psychoactive drug

substance that contains chemicals similar to those found naturally in our brains that alter consciousness by changing chemical processes in neurons

Substance Use Disorders

Drugs are substances that change the way we think, feel, or act. It's easy to forget that alcohol and nicotine are drugs because they're typically commonplace and legal. Still, the misuse of both legal and illegal drugs is a serious societal problem. According to a national

Table 5.2 Major Drug Types and Their Effects.

Drug Type	Examples	Effect on Behavior
Depressants	Alcohol, barbiturates, Quaaludes, Valium	Decreased activity of the central nervous system (initial high followed by sleepiness, slower thinking, and impaired concentration)
Stimulants	Tobacco, cocaine, amphetamines, methamphetamine	Increased activity of the central nervous system (sense of alertness, well-being, energy)
Opioids	Heroin, morphine, codeine, oxycodone	Sense of euphoria, decreased pain
Psychedelics	Marijuana, LSD, Ecstasy, psilocybin	Dramatically altered perception, mood, and thoughts

survey (Johnston et al., 2015), 70 percent of young people (ages 29–30) reported having tried marijuana, and 54 percent report having tried other illegal drugs, like cocaine, opioids such as heroin, and hallucinogens.

DIAGNOSIS OF SUBSTANCE USE DISORDER.   Generally speaking, people qualify for a diagnosis of *substance use disorder* when they experience recurrent significant impairment or distress associated with one or more drugs (APA, 2013). Substance use disorder is a relatively new diagnostic category that appeared in the latest (fifth) edition of the American Psychiatric Association's diagnostic manual. The new diagnosis combines the previous diagnostic categories of substance abuse, which encompasses recurrent problems with substances in the home, work, school, or with the law, and substance dependence, which includes symptoms of tolerance and withdrawal. The new diagnostic scheme considers the full range of alcohol-related problems and emphasizes the severity of these problems, rather than a sharp distinction between the former categories of substance abuse and dependence.

tolerance

reduction in the effect of a drug as a result of repeated use, requiring users to consume greater quantities to achieve the same effect

withdrawal

unpleasant effects of reducing or stopping consumption of a drug that users had consumed habitually

physical dependence

dependence on a drug that occurs when people continue to take it to avoid withdrawal symptoms

psychological dependence

non-physiological dependence on a drug that occurs when continued use of the drug is motivated by intense cravings

Tolerance, a key feature of substance use disorders, occurs when people need to consume an increased amount of a drug to achieve intoxication. Alternatively, people who develop tolerance may not obtain the same reaction or "kick" from a drug after using it for some time. Tolerance is often associated with increases in the amount of drugs people consume. When people use drugs for long periods of time and then either stop or cut down on their use, they're likely to experience **withdrawal** symptoms that vary with the drug they use. Alcohol withdrawal symptoms, for example, can range from insomnia and mild anxiety to more severe symptoms such as seizures, confusion, and bizarre visual hallucinations (Bayard et al., 2004; Schuckit, 2015). People exhibit **physical dependence** on a drug when they continue to take it to avoid withdrawal symptoms. In contrast, people can develop **psychological dependence** when their continued use of a drug is motivated by intense cravings, even though use of the drug creates problems in relationships or at work. According to one survey (Knight, Maines, & Robinson, 2002), within a 12-month period, 6 percent of college students reported severe symptoms of alcohol use, including tolerance and withdrawal, and 31 percent reported significant problems with alcohol that met criteria for substance abuse. Overall, about 10 percent of excessive drinkers meet criteria for alcohol dependence (Esser et al., 2014).

EXPLANATIONS FOR SUBSTANCE USE.   People often begin using drugs when they become available, when their family or peers approve of them, and when they don't anticipate serious consequences from their use (Pihl, 1999). Illegal drug use typically starts in early adolescence, peaks in early adulthood, and declines sharply thereafter. Fortunately, later in life, pressures to be employed and establish a family often counteract earlier pressures and attitudes associated with drug use (Newcomb & Bentler, 1988). In the sections to come, we'll focus on the causes of alcohol use disorders because they're the forms of drug misuse that scientists best understand.

Sociocultural Influences.   Cultures or groups in which drinking is strictly prohibited, such as Muslims or Mormons, exhibit low rates of alcoholism (substance use disorder, with tolerance and withdrawal symptoms; Chentsova-Dutton & Tsai, 2007). In Egypt, the annual rate of alcohol dependence is only 0.2 percent (World Health Organization, 2004), whereas in France and Italy, where they view drinking as a healthy part of daily life, the rates are considerably higher. In Poland, the annual rate is 11.2 percent. Some researchers attribute these differences to cultural differences in attitudes toward alcohol and its abuse. Nevertheless, these differences could also be due in part to genetic influences, and the cultural attitudes themselves may reflect these differences.

Is There an Addictive Personality? Important as they are, sociocultural factors don't easily explain individual differences *within* cultures. We can find alcoholics in societies with strong sanctions against drinking and teetotalers in societies in which drinking is widespread. To explain these facts, popular and scientific psychologists alike have long wondered whether certain people have an "addictive personality" that predisposes them to abuse alcohol and other drugs (Shaffer, 2000). On the one hand, research suggests that common wisdom to the contrary, there's no single addictive personality profile (Rozin & Stoess, 1993). On the other hand, researchers have found that certain personality traits predispose to alcohol and drug abuse. In particular, studies have tied substance abuse to impulsivity (Baker & Yardley, 2002; Kanzler & Rosenthal, 2003; Khurana et al., 2013); the tendency to seek high levels of novel and stimulating sensory experiences (Leeman et al, 2014); sociability (Wennberg, 2002); a propensity to experience negative emotions, like anxiety and hostility (Jackson & Sher, 2003); and a tendency to find the effects of the drug to be particularly rewarding (like it, want it) (King et al., 2014). But some of these traits may partly result from, rather than cause, substance misuse. Also, as we'll soon learn, genetic influences appear to account at least in part for both antisocial behavior and alcoholism risk (Slutske et al., 1998).

Learning and Expectancies. According to the tension reduction hypothesis (Cappell & Herman, 1972; Sayette, 1999; Sher, 1987), people consume alcohol and other drugs to relieve anxiety. Such self-medication reinforces drug use, increasing the probability of continued use. Alcohol affects brain centers involved in reward (Koob, 2000) as well as dopamine, which plays a crucial role in reward. Nevertheless, people are most likely to drink to relieve anxiety when they believe alcohol is a stress reducer (Goldsmith et al., 2012; Greeley & Oei, 1999), so expectancies almost certainly play a role, too. But once individuals become dependent on alcohol, the discomfort of their withdrawal symptoms can motivate drug-seeking behavior and continued use.

Genetic Influences. Alcoholism tends to run in families (Sher, Grekin, & Williams, 2005). But this doesn't tell us whether this finding is the result of genes, shared environment, or both. Twin and adoption studies have resolved the issue: They show that genetic factors play a key role in the vulnerability to alcoholism (McGue, 1999; Verhulst, McNeale, & Kendler, 2015). Multiple genes are probably involved (Enoch, 2013; Rietschel & Treutlein, 2013), but what's inherited? No one knows for sure, but researchers have uncovered a genetic link between people's response to alcohol and their risk of developing alcoholism (Li, Zhao, & Gelernter, 2012). A strong negative reaction to alcohol use decreases the risk of alcoholism, whereas a weak response increases this risk (Schuckit, 1994). A mutation in the aldehyde 2 (ALDH2) gene causes a distinctly unpleasant response to alcohol: facial flushing, heart palpitations (feeling one's heart beating), and nausea (Higuchi et al., 1995). This gene is present in about 40 percent of people of Asian descent, who are at low risk for alcoholism and drink less alcohol than people in most other ethnic groups (Cook & Wall, 2005).

> **Ruling Out Rival Hypotheses**
>
> Have important alternative explanations for the findings been excluded?

> **Correlation vs. Causation**
>
> Can we be sure that A causes B?

Increased or Decreased Risk?

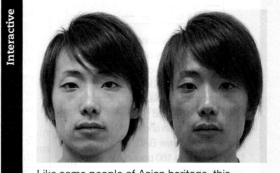

Like some people of Asian heritage, this person shows a pronounced flushing response after having a drink, as seen in this before and after panel. Based on the research literature, is he likely to be at increased or decreased risk for alcohol problems in later life compared with most people?

Depressants

Alcohol and sedative-hypnotics (barbiturates and benzodiazepines) are depressant drugs, so-called because they depress the effects of the central nervous system. By the way, **sedative** means "calming," and **hypnotic** means "sleep-inducing" (despite its name, it doesn't mean "hypnosis-inducing"). In contrast, stimulant drugs, like nicotine and cocaine, which we'll review in the next section, rev up our central nervous systems. We'll learn that the effects of alcohol are remarkably wide ranging, varying from stimulation at low doses to sedation at higher doses.

sedative

drug that exerts a calming effect

hypnotic

drug that exerts a sleep-inducing effect

ALCOHOL. Humanity has long had an intimate relationship with alcohol. Some scientists speculate that a long-forgotten person from the late Stone Age, perhaps 10,000 years ago, accidentally consumed of a jar of honey that had been left out too long (Vallee, 1988). He or

 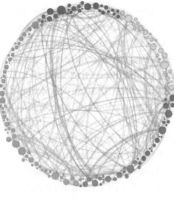

This picture shows the remarkable "cross talk" among brain networks that occurs after participants ingest psilocybin (*right*) that is not evident under ordinary circumstances after participants ingest a placebo (*left*).

among neural networks—especially those related to the visual cortex. These brain changes were correlated with the drug's hallucinatory effects. As connections of brain areas with the visual cortex were ramped up, brain circuits in other areas of the brain were damped down, creating a feeling of "ego dissolution," that is, a dissolving of the sense of "self," a finding also seen after participants ingested psilocybin in another study (Lebedev, 2015). In studies of LSD and psilocybin, researchers have observed increased levels of communication among brain networks that ordinarily don't "speak to each other," providing a tentative explanation for the rich, multisensory experiences associated with potent psychedelic drugs (Petri et al., 2014; Tagliazucchi et al., 2016).

Unlike LSD, Ecstasy, also known as MDMA (technically called methylenedioxymethamphetamine, and *now* you can understand why people abbreviate it), has both stimulant and hallucinogenic properties. It produces cascades of the neurotransmitter serotonin in the brain, which increases self-confidence and well-being, and produces powerful feelings of empathy for others. Given the mind-opening properties of potent hallucinogens, including Ecstasy, LSD, psilocybin, and ketamine, it's not surprising that they've attracted the attention of psychologists interested in treating a variety of conditions, including depression, drug addiction, posttraumatic stress disorder, obsessive-compulsive disorder, and anxiety related to advanced stage cancer.

Under tightly controlled conditions in the lab, initial findings in treating these conditions have been encouraging. Still, positive effects often quickly disappear after a few days, and much more research is necessary to evaluate the risks versus rewards of powerful interventions with unpredictable effects on consciousness (Barrau-Alonso et al., 2013). For example, LSD and other hallucinogens can produce typically short-lived panic, paranoid delusions, confusion, depression, and bodily discomfort—the so-called "bad trip." An interesting historical tidbit is that LSD's subjective effects proved so fascinating to the Central Intelligence Agency (CIA) that in 1953 it launched a research program called MKULTRA to explore LSD's potential as a mind-control drug. This secret program involved administering LSD to unsuspecting individuals, including army scientists. After one of the scientists experienced a psychotic reaction and jumped to his death from a hotel window, the CIA turned to testing the effects of LSD on drug-dependent people and prostitutes. The full scope of this operation came to light only after the program was discontinued in 1972. The researchers didn't find LSD to be a promising mind-control agent because its subjective effects were so unpredictable.

Still, persistent psychotic or negative reactions triggered by LSD and other hallucinogens are probably rare events in individuals with no history of prior mental disorders, although *flashbacks*—recurrences of one or more element of a psychedelic experience—do occur on occasion. Flashbacks are generally not particularly troubling, and large scale studies in the United States have found no evidence that the use of psychedelic drugs (such as LSD and psilocybin) is associated with psychological problems such as anxiety, depression, suicidal behaviors, or psychosis (Johansen & Krebs, 2015; Krebs, & Johansen, 2013). Nevertheless, in another survey, about 4 percent of people who ingested a hallucinogen reported later drug-free experiences that were so disturbing that they contemplated seeking treatment (Baggott et al., 2011). Consuming hallucinogenic drugs carries some risk, and psychological scientists will need to carry out long-term studies to accurately evaluate whether it's safe to use these as medications in treatment.

Drugs, like other means of altering consciousness, remind us that the "brain" and the "mind" are merely different ways of looking at the same phenomenon. They also illustrate the fluid way we experience the world and ourselves. Although a precise grasp of consciousness eludes us, appreciating the nuances of consciousness and their neurological correlates bring us closer to understanding the biological and psychological underpinnings of our waking and sleeping lives.

All-night dance parties termed "raves," in which Ecstasy and other psychedelic drugs are widely available, became popular in the mid-1990s in the United States.

Summary: Consciousness

5.1: The Biology of Sleep

5.1a Explain the role of the circadian rhythm and how our bodies react to a disruption in our biological clocks.

5.1b Identify the different stages of sleep and the neural activity and dreaming behaviors that occur in each.

In the 1950s, researchers identified five stages of sleep that include periods of dreaming in which participants' eyes move rapidly back and forth (rapid eye movement, or REM, sleep). Although vivid, bizarre, and emotional dreams are most likely to occur in REM sleep, dreams occur in non-REM sleep as well. In stage 1 sleep, we feel drowsy and quickly transition to stage 2 sleep, during which our brain waves slow down, heart rate slows, body temperature decreases, and muscles relax. In stages 3 and 4 sleep ("deep sleep"), large amplitude delta waves (one to two cycles/second) become more frequent. In stage 5, REM sleep, the brain is activated much as it is during waking life.

5.1c Identify the features and causes of sleep disorders.

Insomnia (problems falling asleep, waking in the night, or waking early) is the most common sleep disorder and is costly to society in terms of fatigue, missed work, and accidents. Episodes of narcolepsy, which can last as long as an hour, are marked by the rapid onset of sleep. Sleep apnea is also related to daytime fatigue and is caused by a blockage of the airways during sleep. Night terrors and sleepwalking, both associated with deep sleep, are typically harmless and are not recalled by the person on awakening.

5.2: Dreams

5.2a Describe Freud's theory of dreams.

Freud theorized that dreams represent disguised wishes. However, many dreams involve unpleasant or undesirable experiences, and many involve uninteresting reviews of routine daily events. Thus, Freud's dream theory hasn't received much empirical support.

5.2b Explain three major modern theories of dreaming.

According to activation–synthesis theory, the forebrain attempts to interpret meaningless signals from the brain stem (specifically, the pons). Another theory of dreaming suggests that reduction of activity in the prefrontal cortex results in vivid and emotional, but logically disjointed, dreams. Neurocognitive theories hold that our dreams depend in large part on our cognitive and visuospatial abilities.

5.3: Other Alterations of Consciousness and Unusual Experiences

5.3a Determine how scientists explain unusual and seemingly "mystical" alterations in consciousness.

Hallucinations and mystical experiences are associated with fasting, sensory deprivation, hallucinogenic drugs, prayer, and like near-death experiences, vary considerably in content across cultures. During out of body experiences, people's consciousness doesn't actually exit their bodies, and some NDEs are experienced by people who aren't near death. Déjà vu experiences don't represent a memory from a past life, but may be triggered by small seizures in the temporal lobe or when a present experience resembles an earlier one that's forgotten.

5.3b Distinguish myths from realities concerning hypnosis.

Contrary to popular belief, hypnosis isn't a sleeplike state, participants generally don't report having been in a "trance," people are aware of their surroundings and don't forget what happened during hypnosis, the type of induction has little impact, and hypnosis doesn't improve memory. In fact, hypnosis can lead to more false memories that are held with confidence, regardless of their accuracy. According to the sociocognitive model of hypnosis, the often dramatic effects associated with hypnosis may be attributable largely to pre-existing expectations and beliefs about hypnosis. The dissociation model is another influential explanation for hypnosis. This model emphasizes divisions of consciousness during hypnosis or the automatic triggering of responses by hypnotic suggestion.

5.4: Drugs and Consciousness

5.4a Identify possible influences on substance use.

Substance use disorder is associated with recurrent problems related to the drug and may be associated with symptoms of tolerance and withdrawal. Cultures that prohibit drinking, such as Muslim cultures, generally exhibit low rates of alcoholism. Many people take drugs and alcohol in part to reduce tension and anxiety.

5.4b Distinguish different types of drugs and their effects on consciousness.

The effects of drugs are associated with the dose of the drug, as well as with users' expectancies, personality, and culture. Nicotine, a powerful stimulant, is responsible for the effects of tobacco on consciousness. Smokers often report feeling stimulated as well as tranquil, relaxed, and alert. Cocaine is the most powerful natural stimulant, with effects similar to those of amphetamines. Cocaine is highly addictive. Alcohol is a central nervous system depressant, like sedative-hypnotic drugs such as Valium. Sedative-hypnotic drugs reduce anxiety at low doses and induce sleep at moderate doses. Expectancies influence how people react to alcohol. Heroin and other opiates are highly addictive. Heroin withdrawal symptoms range from mild to severe. The effects of marijuana, sometimes classified as a mild hallucinogen, include mood changes, alterations in perception, and disturbances in short-term memory. LSD is a potent hallucinogen. Although flashbacks are rare, LSD can elicit a wide range of positive and negative reactions.

habituation

process of responding less strongly over time to repeated stimuli

---

Figure 6.1 Habituation in a Simple Animal.

Aplysia californicus is a sea slug about five inches long that retracts its gill when pricked, but then it habituates (stops retracting its gill) if pricked repeatedly.

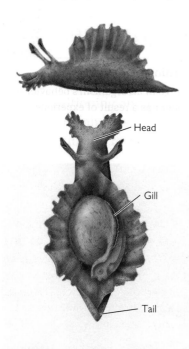

Head

Gill

Tail

Habituating to background noise while studying can be difficult, especially if the noise is loud.

Psychologists have long debated how many distinct types of learning there are. We won't try to settle this controversy here. Instead, we'll review several types of learning that psychologists have studied in depth, starting with the most basic.

Before we do, place your brain on pause, close your eyes, and attend to several things that you almost never notice: the soft buzzing of the lights in the room, the feel of your clothing against your skin, the sensation of your tongue on your teeth or lips. Unless someone draws our attention to these stimuli, we don't even realize they're there, because we've learned to ignore them. **Habituation** is the process by which we respond less strongly over time to repeated stimuli. It helps explain why loud snorers can sleep peacefully through the night while keeping their irritated roommates wide awake. Chronic snorers have become so accustomed to the sound of their own snoring that they no longer notice it.

Habituation is the simplest and probably earliest form of learning to emerge in humans. Fetuses display habituation as early as 32 weeks. When researchers apply a gentle vibrator to the mother's stomach, the fetus first jerks around in response to the stimulus but stops moving after repeated vibrations (Morokuma et al., 2004). What was first a jolt to the fetus's system later became a mere annoyance that it could safely ignore.

In research that earned him the Nobel Prize in 2000, neurophysiologist Eric Kandel uncovered the biological mechanism of habituation of *Aplysia californicus*, a five-inch-long sea slug. Prick *Aplysia* on a certain part of its body, and it retracts its gill in a defensive maneuver. Touch *Aplysia* in the same spot repeatedly, and it begins to ignore the stimulus. This habituation, Kandel found, is accompanied by a progressive decrease in release of the neurotransmitter serotonin (LO 3.1c) at *Aplysia*'s synapses (Siegelbaum, Camardo, & Kandel, 1982). This discovery helped psychologists unravel the neural bases of learning (see Figure 6.1).

Psychologists have studied habituation by measuring—of all things—sweat. Because perspiration on our fingertips is generally a good indicator of anxiety (Fowles, 1980; Rosebrock et al., 2016), scientists measure it by using an electrical conductivity measure called *the skin conductance response*. Most research shows that our hands stop sweating sooner for weak stimuli than they do for strong stimuli, meaning that weak stimuli stop producing anxiety fairly quickly compared with strong stimuli. In the case of very strong stimuli, like painful electric shocks, we often see no habituation at all—people continue to sweat anxiously at the same high levels—even across many trials (Lykken et al., 1988).

This research suggests that habituation makes good sense from an evolutionary standpoint. We wouldn't want to attend to every tiny sensation that comes across our mental radar screens, because most pose no threat. Yet we wouldn't want to habituate to stimuli that could be dangerous. Fortunately, not all repeated stimuli lead to habituation, only those that we deem safe or worth ignoring do.

Some cases of repeated exposure to stimuli don't lead to habituation but to *sensitization*—that is, responding *more strongly* over time (Blumstein, 2016). Sensitization is most likely when a stimulus is dangerous, irritating, or both. Many organisms, from *Aplysia* to humans, show sensitization as well as habituation. Have you ever tried to study when the person next to you was whispering, and the whispering kept getting more annoying to the point that you couldn't concentrate? If so, you've experienced sensitization.

6.1: Classical Conditioning

6.1a Describe Pavlov's model of classical conditioning and discriminate conditioned stimuli and responses from unconditioned stimuli and responses.

6.1b Explain the major principles and terminology associated with classical conditioning.

6.1c Explain how complex behaviors can result from classical conditioning and how they emerge in our daily lives.

The story of habituation could hardly be more straightforward. We experience a stimulus, respond to it, and then stop responding after repeated exposure. We've learned something significant, namely, what *doesn't* matter. But we haven't learned what *does* matter. Specifically, we haven't learned to forge connections between two stimuli. Yet a great deal of learning depends on associating one thing with another. If we never learned to connect one stimulus, like the appearance of an apple, with another stimulus, like its taste, our everyday life would be a world of disconnected sensory experiences.

In the 19th century, a school of thinkers called the *British Associationists* believed that we acquire virtually all of our knowledge by *conditioning*, that is, by forming associations among stimuli (Goodwin, 2015). Once we form these links, like the connection between our mothers' voices with their faces, we need only recall one element of the pair to retrieve the other. Back in the 18th and 19th centuries, the British Associationists believed that simple connections provided the mental building blocks for all of our more complex ideas. At least some of their armchair conjectures were to be confirmed by a pioneering Russian physiologist who demonstrated these processes of association in the laboratory.

The rock band Barenaked Ladies accurately described classical conditioning in their song, "Brian Wilson." They sing about Pavlov and how a bell sound comes to trigger salivation. Not too shabby for a group of nonpsychologists!

Pavlov's Discovery of Classical Conditioning

That physiologist's name was Ivan Pavlov. Pavlov's primary research was on digestion in dogs—in fact, his discoveries concerning digestion, not classical conditioning, earned him the Nobel Prize in 1904 (Todes, 2014). Pavlov placed a dog in a harness and inserted a cannula—a collection tube—into its salivary glands to study its digestive responses to meat powder. In doing so, he observed something unexpected: The dog began salivating (more informally, it started to drool), not only to the meat powder itself, but to previously neutral stimuli that had become associated with it, such as research assistants who brought in the powder. Indeed, the dog even salivated to the sound of these assistants' footsteps as they approached the laboratory. The dog seemed to be anticipating the meat powder and responding to stimuli that signaled its arrival.

Today, we call this process of association **classical conditioning** (or **Pavlovian conditioning**): a form of learning in which animals come to respond to a previously neutral stimulus that had been paired with another stimulus that elicits an automatic response. Yet Pavlov's initial observations were merely anecdotal, so like any good scientist he soon put his informal observations to a more rigorous test.

classical (Pavlovian) conditioning

form of learning in which animals come to respond to a previously neutral stimulus that had been paired with another stimulus that elicits an automatic response

unconditioned response (UCR)

automatic response to a nonneutral stimulus that does not need to be learned

unconditioned stimulus (UCS)

stimulus that elicits an automatic response

The following video illustrates how Pavlov first demonstrated classical conditioning systematically.

1. He started with an initially neutral stimulus, one that didn't elicit any particular response. In this case, Pavlov used a metronome, a clicking pendulum that keeps time (in other studies, Pavlov used a tuning fork or whistle; contrary to popular belief, he didn't use a bell).

2. He then paired the neutral stimulus again and again with an **unconditioned stimulus (UCS)**, a stimulus that elicits an automatic—that is, a reflexive—response. In the case of Pavlov's dogs, the unconditioned stimulus is the meat powder, and the automatic, reflexive response it elicits is the **unconditioned response (UCR)**.

Watch THE BASICS OF CLASSICAL CONDITIONING

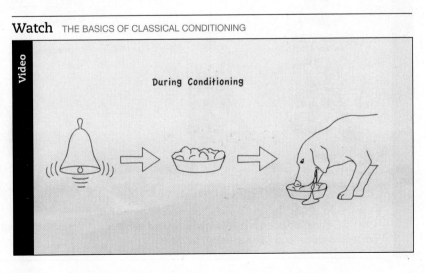

During Conditioning

For Pavlov's dogs, the unconditioned response was salivation. The key point is that the animal doesn't need to learn to respond to the unconditioned stimulus with the unconditioned response: Dogs naturally drool in response to food. The animal generates the unconditioned response without any training at all, because the response is a product of nature (genes), not nurture (experience).

3. As Pavlov repeatedly paired the neutral stimulus with the unconditioned stimulus, he observed something remarkable. If he now presented the metronome alone, it elicited a response, namely, salivation. This new response is the **conditioned response (CR)**: a response previously associated with a nonneutral stimulus that comes to be elicited by a neutral stimulus. Lo and behold, learning has occurred. The metronome had become a **conditioned stimulus (CS)**—a previously neutral stimulus that comes to elicit a conditioned response as a result of its association with an unconditioned stimulus. The dog, which previously did nothing when it heard the metronome, except perhaps turn its head toward it, now salivates when it hears the metronome. The conditioned response, in contrast to the unconditioned response, is a product of nurture (experience), not nature (genes).

In most cases, the CR is fairly similar to the UCR, but it's rarely identical to it. For example, Pavlov found that dogs salivated less in response to the metronome (the CS) than to the meat powder (the UCS).

conditioned response (CR)

response previously associated with a nonneutral stimulus that is elicited by a neutral stimulus through conditioning

conditioned stimulus (CS)

initially neutral stimulus that comes to elicit a response as a result of association with an unconditioned stimulus

Figure 6.2 Pavlov's Classical Conditioning Model.

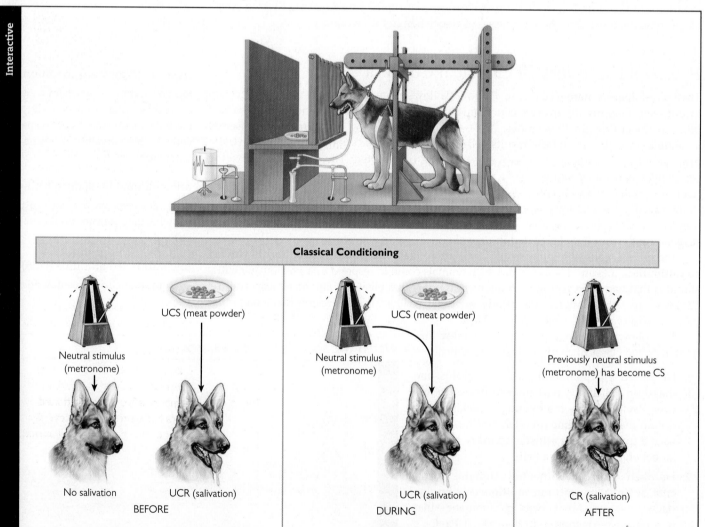

The UCS (meat powder) is paired with a neutral stimulus (metronome clicking) and produces UCR (salivation). Then the metronome is presented alone, and CR (salivation) occurs.

Interestingly, classical conditioning may not even require the animal to be conscious. Classical conditioning can occur even among people who are in a vegetative state. In one study, researchers repeatedly delivered a musical note followed by a puff of air to the eyes—a UCS that produces a UCR of blinking—to 22 patients in vegetative or minimally conscious states (Bekinschtein et al., 2009). Eventually, the musical note became a CS, producing eye blinking even in these largely or entirely unconscious individuals.

Although questions have recently arisen about the replicability of some psychological findings (LO 1.2a), we need not have this concern about classical conditioning. Indeed, few findings in psychology are as replicable as classical conditioning. We can apply the classical conditioning paradigm to just about any animal with an intact nervous system and demonstrate it repeatedly without fail. If only all psychological findings were so dependable!

◀ **Replicability**

Can the results be duplicated in other studies?

Principles of Classical Conditioning

We'll next explore the major principles underlying classical conditioning. Pavlov noted, and many others have since confirmed, that classical conditioning occurs in three phases—acquisition, extinction, and spontaneous recovery. In addition, as we'll see, once classical conditioning to a stimulus occurs, it often extends to a host of related stimuli, making its everyday life influence surprisingly powerful.

ACQUISITION. In **acquisition**, we gradually learn—or acquire—the CR. If we look at Figure 6.3a, we'll see that as the CS and UCS are paired over and over again, the CR increases progressively in strength. The steepness of this curve varies somewhat depending on how close together in time we present the CS and UCS. In general, the closer in time the pairing of CS and UCS, the faster learning occurs, with about a half-second delay typically being the optimal pairing for learning. Longer delays usually decrease the speed and strength of the organism's response. That makes good evolutionary sense because a stimulus that immediately precedes a second stimulus is more likely to have caused it than a stimulus that came a long time before it.

Incidentally, backward conditioning—in which the UCS is presented *before* the CS—is extremely difficult to achieve (Alexander, 2013). So, if we repeatedly present a dog with meat power, and then a metronome sound a second or two later, the metronome won't later trigger much, if any, salivation on its own. For conditioning to work efficiently, the CS must forecast the appearance of the UCS. Again, that makes good evolutionary sense, because a stimulus that came after a second stimuli cannot have caused it.

EXTINCTION. In a process called **extinction**, the CR decreases in magnitude and eventually disappears when the CS is repeatedly presented alone, that is, without the UCS (see Figure 6.3b). After numerous presentations of the metronome without meat powder, Pavlov's dogs eventually stopped salivating. Most psychologists once believed that extinction was similar to forgetting: The CR fades away over repeated trials, just as many memories gradually decay (see LO 7.1b). Yet the truth is more complicated and interesting

Classical Conditioning

Interactive

Like many people, this girl found her first ride on a roller coaster to be terrifying. Now, all she needs to do is to see a photograph of a roller coaster for her heart to start pounding. Describing this scenario using classical conditioning terms (a) her first roller coaster ride is the UCS, (b) a photograph of a roller coaster is a CS, and (c) her heart pounding in response to this photograph is a CR.

Figure 6.3 Acquisition and Extinction.

Acquisition results from the repeated pairing of UCS and CS, increasing the CR's strength (a). In extinction, the CS is presented again and again without the UCS, resulting in the gradual disappearance of the CR (b).

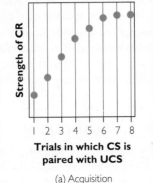

(a) Acquisition

(b) Extinction

acquisition

learning phase during which a conditioned response is established

extinction

gradual reduction and eventual elimination of the conditioned response after the conditioned stimulus is presented repeatedly without the unconditioned stimulus

The renewal effect: A person hiking through the woods may experience fear when she approaches an area if she's previously spotted a dangerous animal there.

spontaneous recovery

sudden reemergence of an extinct conditioned response after a delay in exposure to the conditioned stimulus

renewal effect

sudden reemergence of a conditioned response following extinction when an animal is returned to the environment in which the conditioned response was acquired

stimulus generalization

process by which conditioned stimuli similar, but not identical, to the original conditioned stimulus elicit a conditioned response

stimulus discrimination

process by which organisms display a less pronounced conditioned response to conditioned stimuli that differ from the original conditioned stimulus

Figure 6.4 Generalization Gradient.

The more similar to the original CS the new CS is, the stronger the CR will be. Pavlov used a tone pitched close to the original tone's pitch.

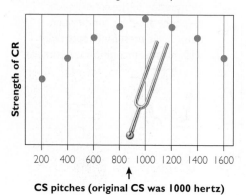

CS pitches (original CS was 1000 hertz)

than that. Extinction is an active, rather than passive, process. During extinction, a new response, which in the case of Pavlov's dogs was the *absence* of salivation, gradually "writes over" or inhibits the CR, namely, salivation. The extinguished CR doesn't vanish completely; it's merely overwritten by the new behavior (Vervliet, Craske, & Hermans, 2013). This contrasts with some forms of traditional forgetting, in which the memory itself disappears. Interestingly, Pavlov had proposed this hypothesis in his writings, although few people believed him at the time. How do we know he was right? Read on.

SPONTANEOUS RECOVERY. In a phenomenon called **spontaneous recovery**, a seemingly extinct CR reappears (often in somewhat weaker form) if we present the CS again, say, hours or even days later. It's as though the CR were lurking in the background, waiting to emerge following another presentation of the CS. In a classic study, Pavlov (1927) presented the CS (tone from a metronome) alone again and again and extinguished the CR (salivation) because there was no UCS (meat powder) following it. Two hours later, he presented the CS again and the CR returned. The animal hadn't really forgotten the CR; it had just suppressed it.

A related phenomenon is the **renewal effect**, which occurs when we extinguish a response in a setting different from the one in which the animal acquired it. When we restore the animal to the original setting, the extinguished response reappears (Bouton, 1994; Vervliet et al., 2013). The renewal effect may help to explain why people with *phobias*—intense, irrational fears—who've overcome their phobias often experience a reappearance of their symptoms when they return to the environment in which they acquired their fears (Denniston, Chang, & Miller, 2003). Even though it may sometimes lead to a return of phobias, the renewal effect is often adaptive. If we've been bitten by a snake in one part of a forest, it makes sense to experience fear when we find ourselves there again, even years later. That same snake or his slithery descendants may still be lying in wait in the same spot.

STIMULUS GENERALIZATION. Pavlov found that following classical conditioning, his dogs salivated not merely to the original metronome sound, but to sounds similar to it. This phenomenon is called **stimulus generalization**: the process by which CSs that are similar, but not identical, to the original CS elicit a CR. Stimulus generalization occurs along a *generalization gradient:* The more similar to the original CS the new CS is, the stronger the CR will be (see Figure 6.4). Pavlov found that his dogs showed their largest amount of salivation to the original sound, with progressively less salivation to sounds that were less and less similar to it in pitch. Stimulus generalization is typically adaptive because it allows us to transfer what we've learned to new things. For example, once we've learned to drive our own car, we can borrow a friend's car without needing a full tutorial on how to drive it.

STIMULUS DISCRIMINATION. The flip side of the coin to stimulus generalization is **stimulus discrimination**; it occurs when we exhibit a less pronounced CR to CSs that differ from the original CS. Stimulus discrimination helps us understand why we can enjoy scary movies. Although we may hyperventilate a bit while watching television footage of a ferocious tornado tearing through a small town, we'd respond much more strongly if the tornado were headed straight for our home. Thankfully, we've learned to discriminate between a televised stimulus and the real-world version of it, and to modify our response as a result. Like stimulus generalization, stimulus discrimination is usually adaptive, because it allows us to distinguish among stimuli that share some similarities but that differ in important ways. Without it, we'd be scared to pet a new dog if we were bitten by a similar-looking dog last week.

Higher-Order Conditioning

Taking conditioning a step further, organisms learn to develop conditioned associations to previously neutral stimuli that come to be associated with the original CS. If after conditioning a dog to salivate to a tone, we pair a picture of a circle with that tone, a dog eventually salivates to the circle as well as to the tone, although usually somewhat less strongly. That's **higher-order conditioning**: the process by which organisms develop classically conditioned responses to previously neutral stimuli that later become associated with the original CS (Gewirtz & Davis, 2000; Onuma & Sakai, 2016). With higher-order conditioning, each progressive level results in weaker conditioning, just as a verbal message becomes less accurate as it's passed from one person to another. So second-order conditioning—in which a new CS is paired with the original CS—tends to be weaker than garden-variety classical conditioning, and third-order conditioning—in which a third CS is in turn paired with the second-order CS—is even weaker. Fourth-order conditioning and beyond is typically difficult or impossible to achieve.

Higher-order conditioning allows us to extend classical conditioning to a host of new stimuli. It helps explain why we may suddenly feel hungry after seeing a mere photograph of a mouth-watering food, whether it be a steak, a fruit, or dessert on a roadside billboard. We've already come to associate the sight, sound, and smell of our favorite foods with satisfying our hunger, and we eventually came to associate a visual image of them with these CSs.

Many addictions are also shaped in part by higher-order conditioning, with the context or setting in which people take the drugs serving as higher-order CSs (Lewis, 2016; Sullum, 2003). One research team (Robins, Helzer, & Davis, 1975) examined 451 Vietnam veterans who returned to the United States with serious heroin addictions. Many mental health experts confidently predicted that they and other addicted veterans would remain hooked upon returning to America. Surprisingly, 86 percent of them lost their addiction shortly after returning to the United States. Because the context had changed from Vietnam to the United States, the veterans' classically conditioned responses to heroin extinguished.

Applications of Classical Conditioning to Daily Life

Without classical conditioning, we couldn't develop physiological associations to stimuli that signal biologically important events, such as things we want to eat—or that want to eat us. Many of the physiological responses we display in classical conditioning contribute to our survival. Salivation, for instance, helps us to digest food. Skin conductance responses probably were important to our primate ancestors (Stern, Ray, & Davis, 1980), who found that sticky fingers and toes came in handy for grasping tree limbs while fleeing from predators. Slightly moist fingertips help us adhere to things, as you'll discover if you moisten the tip of your index finger while turning to the next page of a book.

Classical conditioning isn't limited to salivating dogs in old Russian laboratories; it applies to daily life too. One of our favorite examples is that words beginning with the letter "z," like zany, and "k," like kooky, are especially likely to make us laugh (Wiseman, 2009). The explanation may very well be classical conditioning. Saying these letters makes us contort our faces so that we smile a bit; these smiling expressions may in turn become conditioned stimuli for positive moods. We'll next consider four everyday applications of classical conditioning here: advertising, the acquisition of fears and phobias, the acquisition of fetishes, and disgust reactions.

CLASSICAL CONDITIONING AND ADVERTISING. Few people grasp the principles of classical conditioning, especially higher-order conditioning, better than advertisers do. By repeatedly pairing the sights and sounds of products with photographs of handsome hunks and scantily clad beauties, marketing whizzes aim to establish classically conditioned connections between their brands and positive emotions. They do so for a good reason: Research shows that it works. So does another favorite trick of advertisers: repeatedly pairing pictures of products with pictures of our favorite celebrities (Till, Stanley, & Priluck, 2008). Even companies marketing medications to consumers on television routinely pair information about antidepressants, Viagra, and other drugs with pleasurable stimuli, such as sunsets, sensual music, and images of attractive individuals (Biegler & Vargas, 2013).

higher-order conditioning

developing a conditioned response to a conditioned stimulus by virtue of its association with another conditioned stimulus

Higher-order conditioning helps explain the seemingly mysterious "power of suggestion." Merely hearing "Want a Coke?" on a hot summer day can make us feel thirsty.

One researcher (Gorn, 1982) paired slides of either blue or beige pens (the CSs) with music that participants had rated as either enjoyable or not enjoyable (the UCSs). Then he gave participants the opportunity to select a pen upon departing the lab. Whereas 79 percent of participants who heard music they liked picked the pen that had been paired with music; only 30 percent of those who heard music they disliked picked the pen that had been paired with music.

Not all researchers who've paired products, like familiar brands of cereal, with pleasurable stimuli have successfully replicated classical conditioning effects (Gresham & Shimp, 1985; Smith, 2001). But many of these negative findings are open to a rival explanation: latent inhibition. **Latent inhibition** refers to the fact that when we've experienced a CS alone many times, it's difficult to classically condition it to another stimulus (Palsson et al., 2005; Vaitl & Lipp, 1997). Because some investigators who failed to obtain classical conditioning effects for products relied on brands with which participants were already familiar, their negative findings may be attributable to latent inhibition. Indeed, when researchers have used novel brands, they've generally been able to show classical conditioning effects (Stuart, Shimp, & Engle, 1987).

Ruling Out Rival Hypotheses

Have important alternative explanations for the findings been excluded?

THE ACQUISITION OF FEARS AND PHOBIAS: THE STRANGE TALE OF LITTLE ALBERT.

Can classical conditioning help explain how we come to fear or avoid stimuli? John B. Watson, the founder of behaviorism (LO 1.4a), answered this question in 1920 when he and his graduate student, Rosalie Rayner, performed what's often regarded as one of the most ethically questionable studies in the history of psychology.

Watson and Rayner (1920) set out in part to falsify the Freudian view (LO 1.4a and 14.2a) of phobias, which proposes that phobias stem from deep-seated conflicts buried in the unconscious. To do so, they recruited a nine-month-old infant who'll be forever known in the psychological literature as Little Albert. At that time, Little Albert was fond of little creatures, like white rats. But Watson and Rayner were about to change that.

Two months later, Watson and Rayner first allowed Little Albert to play with a white rat. But only seconds afterward, Watson snuck up behind Little Albert and struck a gong with a steel hammer, creating an earsplitting noise, startling him out of his wits, and making him cry. After seven such pairings of the rat and UCS (the loud sound from the gong), Little Albert displayed a CR (crying) to the rat alone, demonstrating that the rat had now become a CS. That conditioned response was still present when Watson and Rayner exposed Little Albert to the rat five days later. Little Albert also displayed stimulus generalization, crying not only in response to rats, but also to a rabbit, a dog, a furry coat, and, to a lesser extent, a Santa Claus mask and John B. Watson's hair. Fortunately for him, Little Albert also demonstrated at least some stimulus discrimination, as he didn't display much fear toward cotton balls or the hair of Dr. Watson's research assistants. Needless to say, because inducing a phobia-like condition in an infant raises a host of troubling ethical questions, Watson and Rayner's Little Albert study would never get past a modern-day college or university institutional review board (see LO 2.3a).

Incidentally, no one knows for sure what became of poor Little Albert. His mother withdrew him from the study about a month after it began, never to be heard from again. One team of psychologists has recently claimed that Little Albert was actually Douglas Merritte, who was born to a nurse in 1919 at Johns Hopkins University Hospital and tragically died at age six due to a build-up of fluid in his brain (Beck, Levinson, & Irons, 2009). In contrast, several other psychologists believe that Little Albert was instead William Barger, whose childhood nickname was Albert. In contrast to Merritte, Barger lived to the ripe old age of 87 (Digdon, Powell, & Harris, 2014; Powell, 2010; Reese, 2010). The debate continues.

Stimulus generalization, like that experienced by Little Albert, allows our learning to be remarkably flexible—which is often, although not always, a good thing. It allows us to develop fears of many stimuli. Certain phobias, such as those of snakes, spiders, heights, water, and blood, are considerably more

---

Replicability

Can the results be duplicated in other studies?

Falsifiability

Can the claim be disproved?

latent inhibition

difficulty in establishing classical conditioning to a conditioned stimulus we've repeatedly experienced alone, that is, without the unconditioned stimulus

Advertisers use higher-order classical conditioning to get customers to associate their products with an inherently enjoyable stimulus.

widespread than are others (American Psychiatric Association, 2013). And some are downright strange, as Table 6.1 illustrates.

The good news is that if classical conditioning can contribute to our acquiring phobias, it can also contribute to our overcoming them. Mary Cover Jones, a student of Watson, treated a three-year-old named Little Peter, who had a phobia of rabbits. Jones (1924) treated Peter's fear successfully by gradually introducing him to a white rabbit while giving him a piece of his favorite candy. As she moved the rabbit increasingly close to him, the sight of the rabbit eventually came to elicit a new CR: pleasure rather than fear. Modern-day psychotherapists, although rarely feeding their clients candy, use similar practices to eliminate phobias. They may pair feared stimuli with relaxation or other pleasurable stimuli (Wolpe, 1990).

Watch CLASSICAL CONDITIONING IN HUMANS: LITTLE ALBERT

Applying Principles of Learning to Humans

FETISHES. On the flip side of the coin from phobias, **fetishism**—sexual attraction to nonliving things—may also arise in part from classical conditioning (Akins, 2004; Hoffmann, Peterson, & Gamer, 2012). Like phobias, fetishes come in a bewildering variety of forms: shoes, stockings, dolls, stuffed animals, automobile engines (yes, that's right), and just about anything else (Lowenstein, 2002).

In a series of studies, Michael Domjan and his colleagues classically conditioned fetishes in male Japanese quails. For example, they presented male quails with a cylindrical object made of terrycloth, followed by a female quail with which they happily mated. After 30 such pairings, about half of the male quails attempted to mate with the cylindrical object when it appeared alone (Köksal et al., 2004). Although the generalizability of these findings to humans is unclear, at least some people appear to develop fetishes by the repeated pairing of neutral objects with sexual activity (Rachman & Hodgson, 1968; Weinberg, Williams, &

fetishism

sexual attraction to nonliving things

Table 6.1 Phobias Galore.

This sampling of phobias—a few relatively common, most quite rare—illustrates just how enormously varied people's fears can be. Many of these phobias may be acquired at least partly by classical conditioning.

Phobia	Fear of
Alliumphobia	garlic
Arachibutyrophobia	peanut butter sticking to the roof of one's mouth
Aulophobia	flutes
Brontophobia	thunderstorms
Bufonaophobia	toads
Catoptrophobia	mirrors
Coulrophobia	clowns
Epistaxiaophobia	nosebleeds
Lachanophobia	vegetables
Melissophobia	bees
Peladophobia	bald people
Pogonophobia	beards
Pteronophobia	being tickled by feathers
Rhytiphobia	getting wrinkles
Samhainophobia	Halloween
Taphephobia	being buried alive
Xyrophobia	razors

Michael Domjan and his colleagues used classical conditioning to instill a fetish in male quails.

Calhan, 1995). Interestingly, in humans, males are much more prone to fetishes of all kinds than are women (Dawson, Bannerman, & Lalumière, 2016), perhaps because males tend to be more visually oriented than females when it comes to sexual stimuli. As a consequence, they're more likely to develop classically conditioned reactions to them.

DISGUST REACTIONS. Imagine that a researcher asked you to eat a piece of fudge. No problem, right? Well, now imagine the fudge were shaped like dog feces. If you're like most subjects in the studies of Paul Rozin and his colleagues, you'd hesitate (D'Amato, 1998; Rozin & Haidt, 2013; Rozin, Millman, & Nemeroff, 1986) Hence, the Toronto woman who intends to open a dessert bar in which all food items will be shaped like feces and served in toilet-shaped dishes (no, we're not making this up) may want to think twice about her plans (Romm, 2016).

Rozin (who's earned the nickname "Dr. Disgust") and his colleagues have found that we acquire disgust reactions with surprising ease. In most cases, these reactions are probably a product of classical conditioning. CSs—like a photograph of rotten eggs—that are associated with disgusting UCSs—like the smell and taste of rotten eggs in our mouths—may themselves come to elicit disgust. In many cases, disgust reactions are tied to stimuli that are biologically important to us, like animals or objects that are dirty or potentially poisonous (Connolly et al., 2008; Rozin & Fallon, 1987).

In another study, Rozin and his collaborators asked participants to drink from two glasses of water, both of which contained sugar (sucrose). In one case, the sucrose came from a bottle labeled "Sucrose"; in another, it came from a bottle labeled "Sodium Cyanide, Poison." The investigators told subjects that both bottles were completely safe. They even asked subjects to select which label went with which glass, proving the labels were meaningless. Even so, subjects were hesitant to drink from the glass that contained the sucrose labeled as poisonous (Rozin, Markwith, & Ross, 1990). Participants' responses in this study were irrational, but perhaps understandable: They were probably relying on the heuristic "better safe than sorry." Classical conditioning helps keep us safe, even if it goes too far on occasion (Engelhard, Olatunji, & de Jong, 2011).

Psychomythology
Are We What We Eat?

Many of us have heard that "we are what we eat," but in the 1950s the psychologist James McConnell took this proverb quite literally. McConnell became convinced he'd discovered a means of chemically transferring learning from one animal to another. Indeed, for many years psychology textbooks informed undergraduates that scientists could chemically transfer learning across animals.

McConnell's animal of choice was the planaria, a flatworm that's typically no more than a few inches long. Using classical conditioning, McConnell and his colleagues exposed planaria to a light, which served as the CS, while pairing it with a one-second electric shock, which served as the UCS. When planaria receive an electric shock, they contract reflexively. After numerous pairings between light and shock, the light itself causes planaria to contract (Thompson & McConnell, 1955).

McConnell wanted to find out whether he could chemically transfer the memory of this classical conditioning experience to another planaria. His approach was brutally simple. Relying on the fact that many planaria are miniature cannibals, he chopped up the trained planaria and fed them to their fellow worms. Remarkably, McConnell (1962) reported that planaria who'd gobbled up classically conditioned planaria acquired classically conditioned reactions to the light more quickly than planaria who hadn't.

James McConnell and his colleagues paired a light with an electric shock, which caused the planaria worm to contract reflexively.

Understandably, McConnell's memory transfer studies generated enormous excitement. Imagine if McConnell were right! You could sign up for your introductory psychology class, swallow a pill containing all of the psychological knowledge you'd need to get an A, and...voila, you're now an expert psychologist. Indeed, McConnell went directly to the general public with his findings, proclaiming in *Time*, *Newsweek*, and other popular magazines that scientists were on the verge of developing a "memory pill" (Rilling, 1996).

Yet it wasn't long before the wind went out of McConnell's scientific sails: Although researchers at more than 50 labs tried to replicate his findings, many couldn't (Stern, 2010). What's more, researchers brought up a host of alternative explanations for his results. For one, McConnell hadn't ruled out the possibility that his findings were attributable to *pseudoconditioning*, which occurs when the CS by itself triggers the UCR. That is, he hadn't excluded the possibility that the light itself caused the planaria to contract (Collins & Pinch, 1993), perhaps leading him to the false conclusion that the cannibalistic planaria had acquired a classically conditioned reaction to the light. Eventually, after years of intense debate and mixed or negative results, the scientific community concluded that McConnell may have fooled himself into seeing something that was never there: He'd become a likely victim of confirmation bias (see LO 1.1b). His planaria lab closed its doors in 1971, and was never heard from again.

Still, McConnell may yet have the last laugh. Even though his studies may have been flawed, some scientists have conjectured that memory may indeed be chemically transferrable in some cases (Smalheiser, Manev, & Costa, 2001). As is so often the case in science, the truth will win out.

Journal Prompt

Think of a stimulus to which you believe you have been classically conditioned. Perhaps you experienced an especially positive or negative emotional reaction to certain foods, a fear of a type of animal, or a pleasurable response whenever you see a photograph of someone. In each case, identify the UCS, UCR, CS, and CR and describe how you believe you acquired the CR.

6.2: Operant Conditioning

6.2a   **Distinguish operant conditioning from classical conditioning.**

6.2b   **Describe Thorndike's law of effect.**

6.2c   **Describe reinforcement and its effects on behavior, and distinguish negative reinforcement from punishment.**

6.2d   **Identify the four schedules of reinforcement and the response pattern associated with each.**

6.2e   **Describe some applications of operant conditioning.**

operant conditioning
learning controlled by the consequences of the organism's behavior

What do the following four examples have in common?

- Using bird feed as a reward, a behavioral psychologist teaches a pigeon to distinguish paintings by Monet from paintings by Picasso. By the end of the training, the pigeon is a veritable art aficionado.

- Using fish as a treat, a trainer teaches a dolphin to jump out of the water, spin three times, splash in the water, and propel itself through a hoop.

- In his initial attempt at playing tennis, a frustrated 12-year-old hits his opponent's serve into the net the first 15 times. After two hours of practice, he returns his opponent's serve successfully more than half the time.

- A hospitalized patient with dissociative identity disorder (formerly known as multiple personality disorder) displays features of an "alter" personality whenever staff members pay attention to him. When they ignore him, his alter personality seemingly vanishes.

The answer: All are examples of operant conditioning. The first, incidentally, comes from an actual study (Watanabe, Sakamoto, & Wakita, 1995). **Operant conditioning** is learning controlled by the consequences of the organism's behavior (McSweeney & Murphy, 2014; Staddon & Cerutti, 2003). In each of these examples, superficially different as they are, the organism's behavior is shaped by what comes after it, namely, reward. Psychologists also refer to operant conditioning as *instrumental conditioning*, because the organism's response serves an instrumental function. The organism "gets something" out of the response, like food, sex, attention, or avoiding something unpleasant.

Animal trainers use operant conditioning techniques to teach animals to perform tricks, like jumping through hoops.

Table 6.2 Comparing Operant and Classical Conditioning.

	Classical Conditioning	**Operant Conditioning**
Target behavior is …	Elicited automatically	Emitted voluntarily
Reward is …	Provided unconditionally	Contingent on behavior
Behavior depends primarily on …	Autonomic nervous system	Skeletal muscles

Behaviorists refer to the behaviors produced by the animal to receive a reward as *operants*, because the animal "operates" on its environment to get what it wants. Dropping a dollar into a soda machine is an operant, as is asking out an attractive classmate. In the first case, our reward is a refreshing drink and in the second, a hot date—if we're lucky.

Distinguishing Operant Conditioning from Classical Conditioning

Operant conditioning differs from classical conditioning in three important ways, which we've highlighted in Table 6.2.

1. In classical conditioning, the organism's response is *elicited*, that is, "pulled out" of the organism by the UCS, and later the CS. Remember that in classical conditioning the UCR is a reflexive and automatic response that doesn't require training. In operant conditioning, the organism's response is *emitted*, that is, generated by the organism in a seemingly voluntary fashion.

2. In classical conditioning, the organism's reward is independent of what it does. Pavlov gave his dogs meat powder regardless of whether, or how much, they salivated. In operant conditioning, the animal's reward is contingent—that is, dependent—on what it does. If the animal doesn't emit a response, it comes out empty-handed (or in the case of a dog, empty-pawed).

3. In classical conditioning, the organism's responses depend primarily on the autonomic nervous system (LO 3.2b). In operant conditioning, the organism's responses depend primarily on the skeletal muscles. In contrast to classical conditioning, in which learning involves changes in heart rate, breathing, perspiration, and other bodily systems, in operant conditioning learning involves changes in voluntary motor behavior.

law of effect

principle asserting that if a stimulus followed by a behavior results in a reward, the stimulus is more likely to give rise to the behavior in the future

The Law of Effect

The famous **law of effect**, put forth by psychologist E. L. Thorndike, forms the basis of much of operant conditioning: *If a response, in the presence of a stimulus, is followed by a satisfying state of affairs, the bond between stimulus and response will be strengthened.* This statement isn't as complicated as it appears. It means that if we're rewarded for a response to a stimulus, we're more likely to repeat that response to the stimulus in the future. Psychologists sometimes refer to early forms of behaviorism as S-R psychology (*S* stands for *stimulus*, *R* for *response*). According to S-R theorists, most of our complex behaviors reflect the progressive accumulation of associations between stimuli and responses: the sight of a close friend and saying hello, or the smell of a delicious hamburger and reaching for it on our plate. S-R theorists maintain that almost everything we do voluntarily—driving a car, eating a sandwich, or planting a kiss on someone's lips—results from the gradual buildup of S-R bonds due to the law of effect. Thorndike (1898) discovered the law of effect in a classic study of cats and puzzle boxes. Here's what he did.

Thorndike placed a hungry cat in a box and put a tantalizing piece of fish just outside. To escape from the box, the cat needed to hit upon (literally) the right solution, which was pressing on a lever or pulling on a string inside the box (see Figure 6.5).

Figure 6.5 Thorndike's Puzzle Box.

Thorndike's classic puzzle box research seemed to suggest that cats solve problems solely through trial and error.

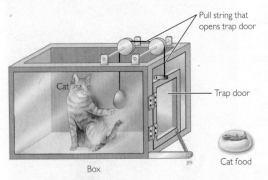

Pull string that opens trap door

Cat

Trap door

Cat food

Box

When Thorndike first placed the cat in the puzzle box, it typically flailed around aimlessly in a frantic effort to escape. Then, by sheer accident, the cat eventually found the correct solution, scurried out of the box, and gobbled up its delectable treat. Thorndike wanted to find out what would happen to the cat's behavior over time. Once it figured out the solution to the puzzle, would it then get it right every time?

Thorndike found that the cat's time to escape from the puzzle box decreased *gradually* over 60 trials. There was no point at which the cat abruptly realized what it needed to do to escape. According to Thorndike, his cats were learning by trial and error through the steady buildup of S-R associations. Indeed, Thorndike and many other S-R theorists went so far as to conclude that all learning, including all human learning, occurs only by trial and error. For them, S-R bonds are gradually "stamped into" the organism by reward.

These findings, Thorndike concluded, provide a crushing blow to the hypothesis that cats learn by **insight**, that is, by grasping the underlying nature of the problem. Had his cats possessed insight into the nature of the problem, the results presumably would have looked like what we see in Figure 6.6. This figure illustrates what psychologists term the *aha reaction:* "Aha—I got it!" (Luo, Niki, & Phillips, 2004). Once the animal solves the problem, it gets it correct just about every time after that. Yet Thorndike never found an Aha! moment: The time to a correct solution decreased only gradually.

B. F. Skinner and Reinforcement

Thorndike's pioneering discoveries on the law of effect laid the groundwork for research on operant conditioning. B. F. Skinner then kicked it up a notch using electronic technology.

Skinner found Thorndike's experimental setup unwieldy because the researcher needed to stick around to place the unhappy cat back into the puzzle box following each trial. This limitation made it difficult to study the buildup of associations in ongoing operant behavior over hours, days, or weeks. So he developed what came to be known informally as a **Skinner box** (more formally, an operant chamber), which electronically records an animal's responses and prints out a graph (technically called a cumulative record) of the animal's activity. A Skinner box typically contains a bar that delivers food when pressed, a food dispenser, and often a light that signals when reward is forthcoming (see Figure 6.7).

With this setup, Skinner studied the operant behavior of rats, pigeons, and other animals and mapped out their responses to reward. By allowing a device to record behavior without any direct human observation, Skinner ran the risk of missing some important behaviors that the box wasn't designed to record. Nonetheless, his discoveries forever altered the landscape of psychology.

Terminology of Operant Conditioning

To understand Skinner's research, we need to make our way through a bit of psychological jargon. Here we'll discuss three key concepts in Skinnerian psychology: reinforcement, punishment, and discriminative stimulus.

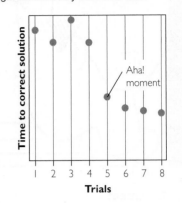

Figure 6.6 "Aha Reaction."

Insight learning: Once an individual solves the problem, he or she gets the answer right almost every time after that.

insight

grasping the underlying nature of a problem

Skinner box

small animal chamber constructed by Skinner to allow sustained periods of conditioning to be administered and behaviors to be recorded unsupervised

"Oh, not bad. The light comes on, I press the bar, they write me a check. How about you?"

Figure 6.7 Rat in Skinner Box and Electronic Device for Recording the Rat's Behavior.

B. F. Skinner devised a small chamber (the Skinner box) containing a bar that the rat presses to obtain food, a food dispenser, and often a light that signals when reward is forthcoming. An electronic device graphs the rat's responses in the researcher's absence.

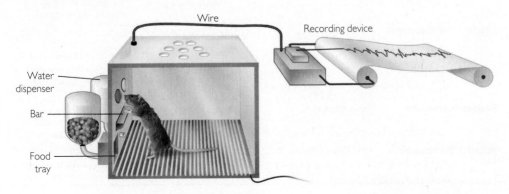

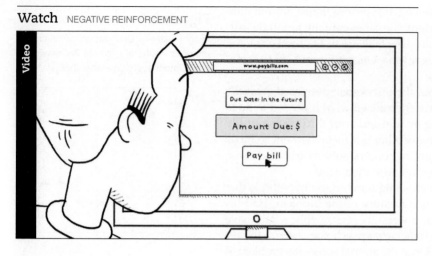

Watch NEGATIVE REINFORCEMENT

reinforcement

outcome or consequence of a behavior that strengthens the probability of the behavior

positive reinforcement

presentation of a stimulus that strengthens the probability of the behavior

negative reinforcement

removal of a stimulus that strengthens the probability of the behavior

punishment

outcome or consequence of a behavior that weakens the probability of the behavior

REINFORCEMENT. Up to this point, we've used the term *reward* to refer to any consequence that makes a behavior more likely to occur. Yet Skinner found this term imprecise, because it doesn't tell us how the organism's behavior changes in response to the reward. He preferred the term **reinforcement**, meaning any outcome that strengthens the probability of a response (Skinner, 1953, 1971).

Skinner distinguished **positive reinforcement**, when we administer a stimulus, from **negative reinforcement**, when we remove a stimulus (see video *Negative Reinforcement*).

Both forms of reinforcement, though, increase the likelihood of the behavior. Positive reinforcement could be giving a child a Hershey's Kiss when he picks up his toys; negative reinforcement could be ending a child's time-out for bad behavior once she's stopped whining. In both cases, the most frequent outcome is an increase or strengthening of the response. Note, though, that Skinner would call these actions "reinforcements" *only* if they make the response more likely to occur in the future.

Hundreds of psychology students over the years have demonstrated the power of positive reinforcement using unconventional participants: their professors. In the game Condition Your Professor (Vyse, 2013), a class of introductory psychology students agrees to provide positive reinforcement—such as smiling or nodding their heads—to their professor whenever he or she moves in a particular direction, such as to the far left side of the room. Your authors know of one famous introductory psychology teacher who spent almost all of his time lecturing from behind his podium. During one class, his students smiled profusely and nodded their heads whenever he ventured out from behind the podium. Sure enough, by the end of class the professor was spending most of his time away from the podium. You and your classmates might want to attempt a similar stunt with your introductory psychology professor: Just don't mention we suggested it.

PUNISHMENT. We shouldn't confuse negative reinforcement with **punishment**, which is any outcome that *weakens* the probability of a response. Like reinforcements, punishments can be either positive or negative. If a punishment involves administering a stimulus, then it's positive; if it's taking away a stimulus, then it's negative (see Table 6.3).

Positive punishment typically involves administering a stimulus that the organism wants to avoid, such as a physical shock or a spanking, or an unpleasant social outcome, such as laughing at someone. Negative punishment involves the removal of a stimulus that the organism wishes to experience, such as a favorite toy or article of clothing.

Table 6.3 Distinguishing Reinforcement From Punishment.

	Procedure	Effect on behavior	Typical Example
Positive Reinforcement	Presenting a stimulus	Increases target behavior	Giving a gold star on homework, resulting in a student studying more
Negative Reinforcement	Removing a stimulus	Increases target behavior	Static on phone subsides when you stand in a specific spot in your room, causing you to stand there more often to decrease the static
Positive Punishment	Presenting a stimulus	Decreases target behavior	Scolding by a pet owner, reducing a dog's habit of chewing on shoes
Negative Punishment	Removing a stimulus	Decreases target behavior	Taking away a favorite toy, stopping a child from throwing future tantrums

We also shouldn't confuse punishment with the disciplinary practices often associated with it; discipline is punishment only if it decreases the probability of the behavior. Skinner, who insisted on precision in language, argued that certain actions that might superficially appear to be punishments are actually reinforcers. He defined reinforcers and punishments solely in terms of their consequences. Consider this scenario: A mother rushes into her three-year-old son's bedroom and yells "Stop that!" each time she hears him kicking the wall. Is she punishing his demanding behavior? There's no way to tell without knowing the effect on his behavior. If he kicks the wall more often following the scolding, then the mother is actually reinforcing his behavior—strengthening the probability of a response. If his kicking decreases or stops altogether after he was scolded, then the mother's scolding is a punishment—weakening the probability of a response.

Does punishment work in the long run? Popular wisdom tells us that it usually does: "Spare the rod, spoil the child." Yet Skinner (1953) and most of his followers argued against the routine use of punishment to change behavior. They believed that reinforcement alone could shape most human behaviors for the better.

According to Skinner and others (Azrin & Holz, 1966), punishment has several disadvantages:

1. Punishment tells the organism only what *not* to do, not what *to* do. A child who's punished for throwing a tantrum won't learn how to deal with frustration more constructively.

2. Punishment often creates anxiety, which can interfere with future learning.

3. Punishment may encourage subversive behavior, prompting people to become sneakier about the situations in which they can and can't display forbidden behavior. A child who's punished for grabbing his brother's toys may learn to grab his brother's toys only when his parents aren't looking.

4. Punishment from parents may provide a model for children's aggressive behavior (Straus, Sugarman, & Giles-Sims, 1997). A child whose parents slap him when he misbehaves may "get the message" that slapping is acceptable.

Numerous researchers have reported that the use of physical punishment by parents is positively correlated with aggressive behavior in children (Fang & Corso, 2007; Gershoff, 2002), although scientists disagree about the size of this correlation (Paolucci & Violato, 2004). Across many studies, Murray Straus and his colleagues (for example, Straus & McCord, 1998) found that physical punishment is associated with more behavioral problems in children. In a study of 1,575 subjects drawn from the general population, Cathy Widom further found that physically abused children are at heightened risk for aggressiveness in adulthood (Widom, 1989a, 1989b). Many researchers interpreted this finding as implying that early physical abuse causes aggression.

Widom (1989a) concluded that her findings reveal the operation of a "cycle of violence," whereby parental aggression begets childhood aggression. When these children become parents, many become abusers themselves. Similarly, Elizabeth Gershoff (2002) reviewed 88 studies of corporal punishment based on a whopping 39,309 participants. Although she found that corporal punishment is sometimes associated with short-term improvements in children's behavior, she also found that a history of such punishment in childhood is associated with an increased probability of becoming an abuser in adulthood. These findings have led some scholars to argue that childhood spanking should be banned (Gershoff, 2013).

Yet let's remember that these studies are correlational and don't demonstrate causality. Other interpretations are possible (Jaffee, Strait, & Odgers, 2012). For example, because children share half of their genes with each parent, and because aggression is partly heritable (Krueger, Hicks, & McGue, 2001; Niv et al., 2013), the correlation between parents' physical aggression and their children's aggression may be the result of parents who are physically aggressive passing on this genetic predisposition to their children (Boutwell et al., 2011; DiLalla & Gottesman, 1991; Lynch et al., 2006). It's also conceivable that the causal arrow is reversed: Aggressive children may be difficult to control and therefore evoke physical abuse from their parents. This hypothesis doesn't in any way

Forcing a student to see the principal is typically a form of punishment; nevertheless, it can instead serve as a negative reinforcement if it allows the student to escape from an unpleasant class.

Correlation vs. Causation

Can we be sure that A causes B?

excuse physical abuse or imply that it's acceptable, but it may help to explain why it occurs. In addition, it's possible that mild levels of punishment are effective, but that severe forms of punishment, including abuse, aren't (Baumrind, Larzelere, & Cowan, 1992; Lynch et al., 2006).

Making matters more complicated, the association between physical punishment and childhood behavior problems may vary by race and culture. In some studies, spanking and other forms of physical discipline have correlated positively with childhood behavior problems in Caucasian families, but correlated negatively in African American families (Lansford et al., 2004). Still, not all researchers have replicated these findings, so the issue requires further investigation (Gershoff et al., 2012). Moreover, spanking tends to be more predictive of higher levels of childhood aggression and anxiety in countries in which spanking is rare, like China and Thailand, than in countries in which it's common, such as Kenya and India (Lansford et al., 2005). The reasons for this difference aren't clear, although children who are spanked in countries in which spanking is more culturally accepted may feel less stigmatized than children in countries in which it's culturally condemned.

Still, that's not to say that we should never use punishment, only that we should use it sparingly (as illustrated in the video *Alternatives to Punishment*).

Most research suggests that punishment works best when it's delivered consistently and follows the undesired behavior promptly (Brennan & Mednick, 1994). In particular, immediate punishment sometimes tends to be effective, whereas delayed punishment is often useless (Church, 1969; McCord, 2006; Moffitt, 1983). Punishment of an undesired behavior also works best when we simultaneously reinforce a desired behavior (Azrin & Holz, 1966), probably because doing so tells people not only what *not to* do, but what *to* do.

DISCRIMINATIVE STIMULUS.   Another critical term in operant conditioning lingo is the **discriminative stimulus**, any stimulus that signals the presence of reinforcement (be careful not to confuse this term with *stimulus discrimination*). When we snap our fingers at a dog in the hopes of having it come over to us, the dog may approach us for a much-appreciated petting. For the dog, our finger snapping is a discriminative stimulus: It's a signal that if it approaches us, it will receive reinforcement (Neuringer, 2014). According to behaviorists, we're responding to discriminative stimuli virtually all the time, even if we're not aware of it. A friend's waving at us from across campus is another common discriminative stimulus: It often signals to us that our friend wants to chat with us, thereby reinforcing us for responding to her wave.

SAME SONG, SECOND VERSE.   *Acquisition, extinction, spontaneous recovery, stimulus generalization*, and *stimulus discrimination* are all terms with which we've crossed paths in our discussion of classical conditioning. These terms apply just as much to operant conditioning too. We can find their definitions in Table 6.4. Here, we'll examine how three of these concepts apply to operant conditioning.

Extinction.   In operant conditioning, extinction occurs when we stop delivering reinforcers following a previously reinforced behavior. Gradually, this behavior declines in frequency and disappears. If parents give a screaming child a toy to quiet her, they may be inadvertently reinforcing her behavior, because she's learning to scream to get something. If parents buy earplugs and stop placating the child by giving toys, the screaming behavior gradually extinguishes. In such cases we often see an *extinction burst*. That is, shortly after withdrawing the reinforcer the undesired behavior initially increases in intensity, probably because the child is trying harder to get reinforced. So there's some truth to the old saying that things sometimes need to get worse before they get better.

Replicability

Can the results be duplicated in other studies?

Skinner and his followers believed that reinforcement is generally much more effective than punishment in shaping children's behavior.

discriminative stimulus

stimulus that signals the presence of reinforcement

Watch ALTERNATIVES TO PUNISHMENT

Video

Table 6.4 Definition Reminders of Key Concepts in Classical and Operant Conditioning.

Term	Definition
Acquisition	Learning phase during which a response is established
Extinction	Gradual reduction and eventual elimination of a response after a stimulus is presented repeatedly
Spontaneous recovery	Sudden reemergence of an extinguished response after a delay
Stimulus generalization	Displaying a response to stimuli similar to but not identical to the original stimulus
Stimulus discrimination	Displaying a less pronounced response to stimuli that differ from the original stimulus

Stimulus Discrimination. As we mentioned previously, one group of investigators used food reinforcement to train pigeons to distinguish paintings by Monet from those of Picasso (Watanabe et al., 1995). That's stimulus discrimination, because the pigeons learned to tell the difference between two different types of stimuli.

Stimulus Generalization. Interestingly, these investigators found that their pigeons also displayed stimulus generalization. Following operant conditioning, they distinguished paintings by impressionist artists whose styles were similar to Monet's, such as Renoir, from paintings by cubist artists similar to Picasso, such as Braque.

Schedules of Reinforcement

Skinner (1938) found that animals' behaviors differ depending on the **schedule of reinforcement**, that is, the pattern of delivering reinforcement. In the simplest pattern, **continuous reinforcement**, we reinforce a behavior every time it occurs. **Partial reinforcement**, sometimes called *intermittent reinforcement*, occurs when we reinforce responses only some of the time.

Try answering this question: If we want to train a dog to perform a trick, like catching a Frisbee, should we reinforce it for (a) each successful catch or (b) only some of its successful catches? If you're like most people, you'd answer (a), which seems to match our common-sense notions regarding the effects of reinforcement. At first blush, it seems logical to assume that the more consistent the reinforcement, the more consistent will be the resulting behavior.

Nevertheless, Skinner's principle of partial reinforcement shows that our commonplace intuitions about reinforcement are backward. According to the principle of partial reinforcement, behaviors we reinforce only occasionally are slower to extinguish than those we reinforce continuously, that is, every time. Does this idea seem counterintuitive? Think of it this way: If the dog has learned that he'll be rewarded for catching the Frisbee only occasionally, he's more likely to continue trying to catch it in the hopes of getting reinforcement.

So if we want an animal to maintain a trick for a long time, we should actually reinforce it for correct responses only every once in a while. Skinner (1969) noted that continuous reinforcement allows animals to learn new behaviors more quickly, but that partial reinforcement leads to a greater resistance to extinction. This principle may help to explain why some people remain trapped for years in terribly dysfunctional, even abusive, relationships (Dutton & Painter, 1993). Some relationship partners provide intermittent reinforcement to their significant others, treating them miserably most of the time but treating them well on rare occasions. This pattern of partial reinforcement may keep individuals "hooked" in relationships that aren't working—and aren't likely to work in the long run.

Although there are numerous schedules of reinforcement, we'll discuss the four major ones here. Remarkably, the effects of these reinforcement schedules are consistent across species as diverse as cockroaches, pigeons, rats, and humans. That's awfully impressive replicability.

The principal reinforcement schedules vary along two dimensions:

1. *The consistency of administering reinforcement.* Some reinforcement contingencies are *fixed*, whereas others are *variable*. That is, in some cases reinforcement occurs on a

When parents stop giving this boy his favorite toy when he screams, he'll initially scream harder to get what he wants. Eventually he'll realize it won't work and give up the screaming behavior.

schedule of reinforcement

pattern of reinforcing a behavior

continuous reinforcement

reinforcing a behavior every time it occurs, resulting in faster learning but faster extinction than only occasional reinforcement

partial reinforcement

occasional reinforcement of a behavior, resulting in slower extinction than if the behavior had been reinforced continually

▶ **Replicability**

Can the results be duplicated in other studies?

Reinforcement

If we want this dog to retain this dancing trick in the future, we should reinforce it some of the time it performs the trick.

fixed ratio (FR) schedule

pattern in which we provide reinforcement following a regular number of responses

variable ratio (VR) schedule

pattern in which we provide reinforcement after a specific number of responses on average, with the number varying randomly

regular (fixed) basis, whereas in others it occurs on an irregular (variable) basis.

Variable schedules tend to yield more consistent rates of responding than do fixed schedules. This finding makes intuitive sense. If we never know when our next treat is coming, it's in our best interests to keep emitting the response to ensure we've emitted it enough times to earn the reward.

2. *The basis of administering reinforcement.* Some reinforcement schedules operate on *ratio* schedules, whereas others operate on *interval* schedules. In ratio schedules, the animal is reinforced on the basis of the *number of responses* it's emitted. In interval schedules, it's reinforced on the basis of the *amount of time* elapsed since the last reinforcement.

Ratio schedules tend to yield higher rates of responding than do interval schedules. This finding also makes intuitive sense. If a dog gets a treat every 5 times he rolls over, he's going to roll over more often than if he gets a treat every 5 minutes, regardless of whether he rolls over once or 20 times during that interval.

We can combine these two dimensions to arrive at four major schedules of reinforcement, each of which yields a distinctive pattern of responding (see Figure 6.8).

1. In a **fixed ratio (FR) schedule**, we provide reinforcement after a regular number of responses. For example, we could give a rat a pellet after it presses the lever in a Skinner box 15 times.

2. In a **variable ratio (VR) schedule**, we provide reinforcement after a specific number of responses on average, but the precise number of responses required during any given period varies randomly. A pigeon on a variable ratio schedule with an average ratio of 10 might receive a piece of bird feed after 6 pecks, then after 12 pecks, then after 1 peck, then after 21 pecks, with the average of these ratios being 10.

Variable ratio (VR) schedules usually yield the highest rates of responding of all. It's for this reason that there's one place where we can be guaranteed to find a VR schedule: a casino (Rachlin, 1990). Roulette wheels, slot machines, and other casino devices deliver cash rewards on an irregular basis, and they do so based on the

Figure 6.8 Four Major Reinforcement Schedules and Their Response Patterns.

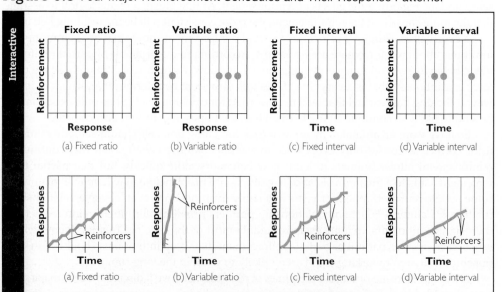

The four major reinforcement schedules are (a) fixed ratio, (b) variable ratio, (c) fixed interval, and (d) variable interval. Note the "scalloped" pattern in (c), the fixed interval response pattern. The subject decreases the reinforced behavior immediately after receiving a reinforcer, then increases the behavior in anticipation of reinforcement as the time for reinforcement approaches.

gambler's responses. Sometimes the gambler has to pull the arm of the slot machine (the "one-armed bandit") hundreds of times before receiving any money at all. At other times, the gambler pulls the arm only once and makes out like a bandit himself, perhaps walking away with thousands of dollars for a few seconds of work. The extreme unpredictability of the VR schedule is precisely what keeps gamblers hooked, because a huge reinforcement can come at any time. In 2007, one man managed to blow nearly $127 million dollars in two Las Vegas casinos over a span of a year, ruining him financially. On occasion, he would stay up for 24 hours straight playing at blackjack tables, losing five dollars at a time (Berzon, 2009).

VR schedules keep pigeons hooked too. Skinner (1953) found that pigeons placed on VR schedules sometimes continue to peck on a disk for food after more than 150,000 nonreinforced responses. In some cases, they literally ground down their beaks in the process. Much like desperate gamblers in a Las Vegas casino hoping for a huge payoff, they don't give up despite repeated disappointments.

3. In a **fixed interval (FI) schedule**, we provide reinforcement for producing the response at least once after a specified amount of time has passed. For example, a worker in a clock factory might get paid every Friday for the work she's done, as long as she's generated at least one clock during that one-week interval.

Fixed interval schedules are especially distinctive in the behaviors they yield; they're associated with a "scalloped" pattern of responding (refer back to Figure 6.8). This pattern reflects the fact that the animal "waits" for a time after it receives reinforcement, and then increases its rate of responding just before the interval is up as it begins to anticipate reinforcement (Groskreutz, 2013).

4. In a **variable interval (VI) schedule**, we provide reinforcement for producing the response after an average time interval, with the actual interval varying randomly. For example, we could give a dog a treat for performing a trick on a variable interval schedule with an average interval of 8 minutes. This dog may have to perform the trick sometime during a 7-minute interval the first time, then a 1-minute interval the second time, then a 20-minute interval, and then a 4-minute interval, with the average of these intervals being 8 minutes (to review these four schedules, see the video *Schedule of Reinforcement*).

Schedules of Reinforcement

Interactive

If this football player received a salary bonus for every five touchdowns he scored, he would be on a fixed ratio reinforcement schedule.

Watch SCHEDULES OF REINFORCEMENT

Video

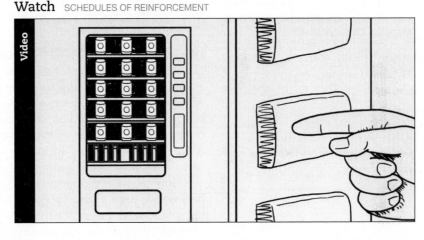

fixed interval (FI) schedule

pattern in which we provide reinforcement for a response at least once following a specified time interval

variable interval (VI) schedule

pattern in which we provide reinforcement for a response at least once during an average time interval, with the interval varying randomly

Applications of Operant Conditioning to Daily Life

Operant conditioning plays a role in a surprising number of everyday experiences and in some special circumstances, as well. As we've noted, operant conditioning is central to some parenting practices. It's also relevant to a wide array of other situations ranging from animal training to weight-loss plans—and even to learning to master a video game. Here we'll explore a few well-studied examples of operant conditioning in action.

ANIMAL TRAINING. If you've ever seen animals perform at a circus, zoo, or aquarium, you might wonder how on earth they learned such elaborate routines. There's an old joke that just as magicians pull rabbits out of hats, behaviorists pull habits out of rats—and other animals too. They typically do so by means of a procedure called shaping by successive approximations, or **shaping**, for short. Using shaping, we reinforce behaviors that aren't exactly the target behavior but that are progressively closer versions of it (Murphy & Lupfer, 2014). Typically, we shape an organism's response by initially reinforcing most or all

shaping

conditioning a target behavior by progressively reinforcing behaviors that come closer and closer to the target

The *gambler's fallacy* describes the common error of believing that random events have "memories." After losing 10 roulette spins in a row, the gambler often concludes that he's now "due" to win. Yet his or her odds of winning on the 11th spin are no higher than they were on his first 10 spins. Along with VR schedules, this fallacy is a potent recipe for addictive gambling.

Correlation vs. Causation

Can we be sure that A causes B?

responses that are close to the desired behavior, and then gradually *fading* (that is, decreasing the frequency of) our reinforcement for the not-exactly-right behaviors over time (see the video *Using Shaping to Train a Dog to Jump Through a Hoop*).

Animal trainers often combine shaping with a technique called *chaining*, in which they link a number of interrelated behaviors to form a longer series. Each behavior in the chain becomes a cue for the next behavior in the chain, just as A becomes a cue for B, B for C, and so on when we're learning the alphabet.

By means of shaping and chaining, Skinner taught pigeons to play Ping-Pong, although they weren't exactly Olympic-caliber table tennis players. To do so, he first reinforced them for turning toward the paddles, then approaching the paddles, then placing the paddles in their beaks, then picking up the paddles with their beaks, and so on. Then, he chained later behaviors, like swinging the paddle and then hitting the ball, to the earlier behaviors. Skinner began his training by reinforcing initial approximations to the desired response. As we might imagine, shaping and chaining complex animal behaviors requires patience, as the process can take days or weeks. Still, the payoff can be substantial, because we can train animals to engage in numerous behaviors that lie well outside their normal repertoires. Indeed, all contemporary animal trainers rely on Skinnerian principles.

OVERCOMING PROCRASTINATION: I'LL GET TO THAT LATER. Be honest: Did you put off reading this chapter until the last moment? If so, don't feel ashamed, because procrastination is one of the most frequent study problems that college students report. Although widespread, procrastination may not be harmless. The stress it causes may be bad for our physical and psychological health. Moreover, procrastinators tend to perform more poorly in their classes than do early birds (Kim & Seo, 2015; Tice & Baumeister, 1997). Although these findings are correlational and don't establish that procrastination causes bad grades, they certainly suggest that putting things off isn't ideal.

How can we overcome procrastination? Don't put off reading the rest of this paragraph, because we have a possible remedy for dilly-dallying. Although there are several potential solutions for procrastination, among the best is probably the one discovered by David Premack (1965). In his research on monkeys, Premack found that we can positively reinforce a less frequently performed behavior with a more frequently performed behavior (Danaher, 1974). Although not a foolproof rule (Knapp, 1976), this principle typically works surprisingly well. Research suggests this approach may help people to stop putting off things they've long avoided, like going to the dentist (Ramer, 1980).

If you find yourself putting off a reading or writing task, think of behaviors you'd typically perform if given the chance—perhaps hanging out with a few close friends, watching a favorite TV program, or treating yourself to an ice cream cone. Then, reinforce yourself with these higher frequency behaviors *only* after you've completed your homework.

THERAPEUTIC APPLICATIONS OF OPERANT CONDITIONING. We can apply operant conditioning to clinical settings as well. One of the most successful applications of operant conditioning has been the *token economy*. Token economies are systems, often set up in psychiatric hospitals, for reinforcing appropriate behaviors and extinguishing inappropriate ones (Carr, Frazier, & Roland, 2005; Doll, McLaughlin, & Barretto, 2013; Kazdin, 1982). Typically, psychologists who construct token economies begin by identifying target behaviors, that is, actions they hope to make more frequent. Staff members reinforce patients who exhibit these behaviors using tokens, chips, points, or other **secondary reinforcers**. Secondary

Watch USING SHAPING TO TRAIN A DOG TO JUMP THROUGH A HOOP

secondary reinforcer

neutral object that becomes associated with a primary reinforcer

Mysteries of Psychological Science
Why Are We Superstitious?

How many of the following behaviors do you perform?

- Never opening an umbrella indoors
- Not walking under a ladder
- Crossing the street whenever you see a black cat
- Carrying a lucky charm or necklace
- Going out of your way not to step on cracks in the sidewalk
- Knocking on wood
- Crossing your fingers
- Avoiding the number 13 (like not stopping on the 13th floor of a building)

If you've engaged in several of these actions, you're at least somewhat superstitious. You're also in good company (Lindeman & Svedholm, 2012). Twelve percent of Americans are afraid of walking under a ladder, and 14 percent are afraid of crossing paths with a black cat (Vyse, 2013). So many people are afraid of the number 13 (a fear called *triskaidekaphobia*) that the floor designations in many tall buildings skip directly from 12 to 14 (Hock, 2002). In Paris, triskaidekaphobics who are going out to dinner with 12 other people can hire a *quatorzième,* a person paid to serve as a fourteenth guest. As many as 90 percent of college students engage in one or more superstitious rituals before taking an exam, such as using a "lucky" pen or wearing a "lucky" piece of jewelry (Vyse, 2013).

How do superstitions arise? In a famous operant conditioning study, B. F. Skinner (1948) placed 8 food-deprived pigeons in a Skinner box while delivering reinforcement (bird feed) every 15 seconds *independent of their behavior.* That is, the birds received reinforcement regardless of what they did. After a few days, Skinner observed something surprising. He found that six of the eight pigeons had acquired remarkably strange and varied behaviors, like making two or three turns between reinforcements or swinging their heads from right to left.

You may have observed similarly odd behaviors in pigeons that people are feeding in city parks; some may prance around or walk rapidly in circles in anticipation of reinforcement. According to Skinner, his pigeons had developed *superstitious behavior:* actions linked to reinforcement by sheer coincidence (Morse & Skinner, 1957). There's no actual association between superstitious behavior and reinforcement, although the animal acts as though there is. The behavior that the pigeon just happened to be performing immediately prior to being reinforced was strengthened—remember that reinforcement increases the probability of a response—so the pigeon kept on doing it (this kind of accidental operant conditioning is sometimes called *superstitious conditioning*).

Not all studies have replicated these findings in pigeons (Staddon & Simmelhag, 1971), although at least some animal—and human—superstitions probably develop in the fashion Skinner described (Bloom et al., 2007; Garcia-Montes et al., 2008). So if we happened to be wearing

So many people are afraid of the number 13 that many buildings don't have a 13th floor.

a certain pair of socks prior to a big test and got an A, we may develop the false belief that these socks somehow contributed to our good performance. We might then wear that same pair of socks before our next exam. Over time, we may become dependent on superstitions. Some researchers have found that relying on "lucky" objects, like a favorite charm, actually improves performance on such skills as golfing and memory tasks, probably because doing so boosts our self-confidence (Damisch, Stoberock, & Mussweiler, 2010). Nevertheless, other researchers have failed to replicate these findings (Calin-Jageman & Caldwell, 2014), so it's not clear whether superstitious behaviors actually "work."

Athletes are notoriously superstitious (Ofori, Biddle, & Lavalee, 2012). Interestingly, the prevalence of superstitions in sports depends on the extent to which the outcomes are due to chance (Vyse, 2013). That's exactly what Skinner would have predicted, because partial reinforcement schedules are more likely to produce enduring behaviors than are continuous reinforcement schedules. In baseball, hitting is much less under players' control than is fielding: Even the best hitters succeed only about 3 out of 10 times, whereas the best fielders succeed 9.8 or even 9.9 out of 10 times. So hitting is controlled by a partial reinforcement schedule, whereas fielding is controlled by something close to a continuous reinforcement schedule. As we might expect, baseball players have far more hitting-related superstitions—like drawing a favorite symbol in the sand in the batter's box—than fielding-related superstitions (Gmelch, 1971; Vyse, 2013).

To be certain, human superstitions aren't due entirely to operant conditioning. Many superstitions are spread partly by word-of-mouth (Herrnstein, 1966). If our mother tells us over and over again that black cats bring bad luck, we may become wary of them. Still, for many superstitions, operant conditioning probably plays an important role.

---

reinforcers are neutral objects that become associated with **primary reinforcers**—things, like a favorite food or drink, that naturally increase the target behavior.

As an advanced graduate student, the first author of your text worked in a psychiatric hospital unit consisting of children with serious behavior problems, including yelling and cursing. In this unit, one target behavior was being polite to staff members. So whenever a child was especially polite to a staff member, he was rewarded with points,

primary reinforcer

item or outcome that naturally increases the target behavior

Fact vs. Fiction

Interactive

Stressful life events tend to increase superstitions.

○ Fact

○ Fiction

The token economy is one of the most successful applications of operant conditioning. Some teachers use a variation of the token economy, the point chart, to reinforce pupils' positive behaviors.

Ruling Out Rival Hypotheses

Have important alternative explanations for the findings been excluded?

which he could trade in for something he wanted, like ice cream or attending a movie with staff members. Whenever a child was rude to a staff member, he was punished with a loss of points.

Research suggests that token economies are often effective in improving behavior in hospitals, group homes, and juvenile detention units (Ayllon & Milan, 2002; Paul & Lentz, 1977). Nevertheless, token economies are controversial, because the behaviors learned in institutions don't always transfer to the outside world (Carr et al., 2005; Wakefield, 2006). That's especially likely if the patients return to settings, such as deviant peer groups, in which they're reinforced for socially inappropriate behaviors.

Operant conditioning has also been helpful in the treatment of individuals with autism spectrum disorder (autism), especially in improving their language deficits. *Applied behavior analysis* (ABA) for autism makes extensive use of shaping techniques; mental health professionals offer food and other primary reinforcers to individuals with autism as they reach progressively closer approximations to certain words and, eventually, complete sentences (Matson, Hather, & Belva, 2012).

Ivar Lovaas and his colleagues have pioneered the best-known ABA program for autism (Lovaas, 1987; McEachin, Smith, & Lovaas, 1993). The results of Lovaas's work have been promising. Children with autism who undergo ABA training emerge with better language and intellectual skills than do control groups of children with autism who don't undergo such training (Green, 1996; Matson et al., 1996; Romanczyk et al., 2003).

Nevertheless, because Lovaas didn't randomly assign children with autism to experimental and control groups, his findings are vulnerable to a rival explanation: Perhaps the children in the experimental group had higher levels of functioning to begin with. Indeed, there's evidence this was the case (Schopler, Short, & Mesibov, 1989). The current consensus is that ABA isn't a miracle cure for the language deficits of autism—there are few, if any, miracle cures in psychological treatment—but that it can be extremely helpful in many cases (Herbert, Sharp, & Gaudiano, 2002).

Putting Classical and Operant Conditioning Together

Up to this point, we've discussed classical and operant conditioning as though they were two entirely independent processes. Yet the truth is almost certainly more complicated. The similarities between classical and operant conditioning, including the fact that we find acquisition, extinction, stimulus generalization, and so on, in both, have led some theorists to argue that these two forms of learning aren't as different as traditionally believed (Brown & Jenkins, 1968; Staddon & Cerutti, 2003).

Answer: Fact. For example, in one study, Israeli civilians exposed to missile attacks during the 1991 Gulf War became more superstitious than did other Israelis ((Keinan, 1994). For many people, superstitions appear to be a means of regaining control over unpredictable environments.

Although there are certainly important similarities between classical and operant conditioning, brain-imaging studies demonstrate that these two forms of learning are associated with activations in different brain regions. Classically conditioned fear reactions are often based largely in the amygdala (LeDoux, 1996; Likhtik et al., 2008; Veit et al., 2002), whereas operantly conditioned responses are based largely in brain areas rich in dopamine, which are linked to reward (Robbins & Everitt, 1998; Simmons & Neill, 2009; LO 3.1c).

These two types of conditioning often interact. We've already discovered that certain phobias arise in part by classical conditioning: A previously neutral stimulus (the CS)—say, a dog—is paired with an unpleasant stimulus (the UCS)—a dog bite—resulting in the CR of fear. So far, so good.

But this tidy scheme doesn't answer an important question: Why doesn't the CR of fear eventually extinguish? Given what we've learned about classical conditioning, we might expect the CR of fear to fade away over time with repeated exposure to the CS of dogs. Yet this often doesn't happen (Rachman, 1977). Many people with phobias remain deathly afraid of their feared stimulus for years, even decades. Indeed, only about 20 percent of untreated adults with phobias ever get over their fears (American Psychiatric Association, 2013). Why?

Enter *two-process theory* to the rescue as an explanation (Mowrer, 1947; Schactman & Reilly, 2011). According to this theory, we need both classical and operant conditioning to explain the persistence of anxiety disorders. Here's how: First, people acquire phobias by means of classical conditioning. Then, once they develop phobias, they start to avoid their feared stimuli whenever they encounter them. If they have a dog phobia, they may cross the street whenever they see someone walking toward them with a large German shepherd. When they do, they experience a reduction in anxiety, which *negatively reinforces* their fear. Recall that negative reinforcement involves the removal of a stimulus, in this case anxiety, that makes the behavior associated with it more likely. So, by avoiding dogs whenever they see them, people with a dog phobia are negatively reinforcing their fear, although they are almost surely doing so without realizing it. Ironically, they're operantly conditioning themselves to make their fears more likely to persist. They're exchanging short-term gain for long-term pain. Two-factor theory points the way to an effective treatment for anxiety disorders: force people to confront, rather than avoid, their anxiety. Indeed, as we'll learn later in the text, this is the precise recipe for exposure therapy, the best-supported treatment approach for anxiety disorders (LO 16.4a).

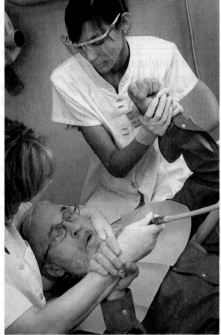

Fears of dental procedures are often reinforced by avoidance behavior over many years, such as a refusal to go to the dentist until it's absolutely necessary.

Journal Prompt

Think of a bad habit that you want to break. Create an imaginary behavioral modification program using operant conditioning to help you change this bad habit into a good one. Be sure to identify what is reinforcing the bad habit, how to extinguish it, how to reinforce the new habit, and what schedule of reinforcement you might use.

6.3: Cognitive Models of Learning

6.3a Outline the evidence that supports latent learning and observational learning.
6.3b Identify evidence of insight learning.

Thus far, we've largely omitted one word when discussing how we learn: *thinking.* That's not accidental, because early behaviorists didn't believe that thought played much of a causal role in learning. Skinner (1953) was an advocate of what he called *radical behaviorism,* so-called because he believed that observable behavior, thinking, and emotion are all governed by the same laws of learning, namely, classical and operant conditioning. For radical behaviorists, thinking and emotion *are* behaviors, they're just not observable.

Observational Learning

observational learning

learning by watching others

According to some psychologists, one important variant of latent learning is **observational learning**: learning by watching others (Bandura, 1965; Singer-Dudek, Cho, & Lyons, 2013). In many cases, we learn by watching *models:* parents, teachers, and others who are influential to us. Many psychologists regard observational learning as a form of latent learning because it allows us to learn without reinforcement. We can merely watch someone else being reinforced for doing something and take our cues from them.

Observational learning spares us the expense of having to learn everything firsthand (Bandura, 1977). Most of us aren't experts in skydiving, but from our observations of people who've gone skydiving we learn that it's generally a wise idea to have a parachute on before jumping out of a plane. Note that we didn't need to learn this useful tidbit of advice by trial and error, or else we wouldn't be here to talk about it. Observational learning can spare us from serious, even life-threatening, mistakes. But it can also contribute to our learning of maladaptive habits.

Children acquire a great deal of their behavior by observational learning of adults, especially their parents.

OBSERVATIONAL LEARNING OF AGGRESSION. In classic research in the 1960s, Albert Bandura and his colleagues demonstrated that children can learn to act aggressively by watching aggressive role models (Bandura, Ross, & Ross, 1963).

These researchers asked preschool boys and girls to watch an adult (the model) interact with a large Bobo doll, a wobbly doll that bounces back to its original upright position after being hit (Bandura, Ross, & Ross, 1961). The experimenters randomly assigned some children to watch the adult model playing quietly and ignoring the Bobo doll, and others to watch the adult model punching the Bobo doll in the nose, hitting it with a mallet, sitting on it, and kicking it around the room. As though that weren't enough, the aggressive model shouted out insults and vivid descriptions of his actions while inflicting violence: "Sock him in the nose," "Kick him," "Pow!"

Bandura and his coworkers then brought the children into a room with an array of appealing toys, including a miniature fire engine, a jet fighter, and a large doll set. Just as children began playing with these toys, the experimenter interrupted them, informing them that they needed to move to a different room. This interruption was intentional because the investigators wanted to frustrate the children to make them more likely to behave aggressively. Then the experimenter brought them into a second room, which contained a Bobo doll identical to the one they'd seen.

On a variety of dependent measures, Bandura and his colleagues found that previous exposure to the aggressive model triggered significantly more aggression against the Bobo doll than did exposure to the nonaggressive model. The children who'd watched the aggressive model yelled at the doll much as the model had done, and they even imitated many of his verbal insults. In a later study, Bandura and his colleagues (Bandura, Ross, & Ross, 1963) replicated these results when they displayed the aggressive models to children on film rather than in person.

Replicability

Can the results be duplicated in other studies?

MEDIA VIOLENCE AND REAL-WORLD AGGRESSION. The Bandura studies and scores of later studies of observational learning led psychologists to examine a theoretically and socially important question: Does exposure to media violence, such as in films, movies, or video games, contribute to real-world violence? The research literature addressing this question is as vast as it is confusing, and could easily occupy an entire book by itself. So we'll only briefly touch on some of the research highlights here.

Hundreds of investigators using correlational designs have reported that children who watch many violent television programs are more aggressive than are other children (Wilson & Herrnstein, 1985). But do these findings demonstrate that media violence causes real-world violence? If you answered "No," give yourself a favored reinforcer. They could indicate merely that highly aggressive children are more likely than other children to tune in to aggressive television programs (Freedman, 1984). Alternatively, these findings could be the result of a third variable, such as children's initial levels of aggressiveness. That is, highly aggressive children may be more likely than other children to both watch violent television programs *and* to act aggressively.

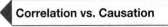

Correlation vs. Causation

Can we be sure that A causes B?

Investigators have tried to get around this problem by using longitudinal designs (see LO 10.1a), which track individuals' behaviors over time. Longitudinal studies show that children who choose to watch many violent television shows commit more aggressive acts years later than do children who choose to watch fewer violent television shows, even when researchers have equated children in their initial levels of aggression (Huesmann et al., 2003) (see Figure 6.10).

These studies offer somewhat more compelling evidence for a causal link between media violence and aggression than do traditional correlational studies. But even they don't demonstrate a causal association, because they're not true experiments (LO 2.2c). Participants in these studies aren't randomly assigned to conditions, but instead select

Watch OBSERVATIONAL LEARNING: BANDURA'S BOBO DOLL STUDY

Video

Bandura's Bobo Doll: Observational Learning

which television shows to watch. As a consequence, unmeasured personality variables, like impulsivity, or social variables, like weak parental supervision, might account for these findings. Moreover, just because variable *A* precedes variable *B* doesn't mean that variable *A causes* variable *B*. For example, if we found that most common colds start with a scratchy throat and a runny nose, we shouldn't conclude that scratchy throats and runny noses cause colds, only that they're early signs of a cold.

Ruling Out Rival Hypotheses

Have important alternative explanations for the findings been excluded?

Still other investigators have examined whether the link between media models and later aggression holds up under the tightly controlled conditions of the laboratory. In most of these studies, researchers have exposed subjects to either violent or nonviolent media presentations and seen whether subjects in the former groups behaved more aggressively, such as by yelling at the experimenter or delivering electric shocks to another subject when provoked. In general, these studies strongly suggest a causal association between media violence and laboratory aggression (Wood, Wong, & Chachere, 1991). The same conclusion may hold for the relation between violent video games and aggression (Anderson, Gentile, & Buckley, 2007; Bushman & Anderson, 2001), although the causal link here is controversial and less well established (Ferguson, 2009; Ferguson, 2015). In particular, some researchers argue that the link between violent video games and real-world violence is attributable to alternative explanations, such as the tendency of aggressive children to both watch these games and to engage in physical aggression (Ferguson, 2013).

Ruling Out Rival Hypotheses

Have important alternative explanations for the findings been excluded?

Finally, some investigators have conducted *field studies* of the link between media violence and aggression (Anderson & Bushman, 2002). In field studies, researchers examine the relation between naturally occurring events and aggression in the real world. For example, one investigator (Williams, 1986) conducted a field study of a small, isolated mountain town in Canada that had no television before 1973. She called it "Notel," short for "*no television.*" Compared with school-age children in two other Canadian towns that already had television, children in Notel showed a marked increase in physical and verbal aggression two years later. Nevertheless, these findings are difficult to interpret in light of a potential confound: At around the same time that Notel received television, the Canadian government constructed a large highway that connected Notel to nearby towns. This highway might have introduced the children in Notel to negative outside influences, including crime from other cities.

Ruling Out Rival Hypotheses

Have important alternative explanations for the findings been excluded?

Figure 6.10 Longitudinal Study of Individuals Who Watched Violent TV as Children.

In both females and males, there's a positive correlation between viewing violent television in childhood and violent behavior in adulthood. But this correlation doesn't demonstrate causality. Why?

SOURCE: Based on Huesmann et al., 2003.

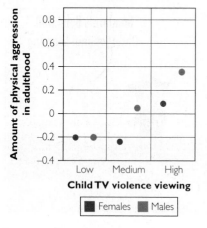

mirror neuron

cell in the prefrontal cortex that becomes activated when an animal performs an action or observes it being performed

Mirror neurons become active when we watch someone similar to us performing a behavior.

So what can we make of all of the research on media violence and aggressive behaviors? We're confronted with four lines of evidence—correlational studies, longitudinal studies, laboratory studies, and field studies—each with its own strengths and weaknesses. Correlational, longitudinal, and field studies tend to be strong in *external validity*, that is, generalizability to the real world, but weak in *internal validity*, that is, the extent to which they permit cause-and-effect inferences (LO 2.2a). Laboratory studies, in contrast, tend to be weak in external validity but strong in internal validity. Yet despite their shortcomings, all four types of studies point in the same direction: at least some causal relation between media violence and aggression (Anderson et al., 2003; Carnagay, Anderson, & Bartholow, 2007). Scientific conclusions tend to be the most convincing when we base them on findings from different research designs, each with a slightly different set of imperfections (Shadish, Cook, & Campbell, 2002). As a result, most—but by no means all—psychological scientists agree that media violence contributes to aggression in at least some circumstances (Anderson & Bushman, 2002a; Bushman & Anderson, 2001; Gentile, 2015).

At the same time, it's equally clear that media violence is only one tiny piece of a multifaceted puzzle. We can't explain aggression by means of media violence alone because the substantial majority of individuals exposed to high levels of such violence don't become aggressive (Freedman, 2002; Wilson & Herrnstein, 1985). Moreover, the relations between media violence and aggression tend to be at best modest in size, suggesting that far more than the media is at work in the causes of violence.

Mirror Neurons and Observational Learning

You find yourself alone in a new city standing in line behind someone using an ATM. Like so many other cash machines, this one is slightly—and annoyingly—different from all the other ones you've seen. You watch as the person in front of you inserts her card, pushes a few buttons, and grabs her money from the slot at the bottom of the machine. Now it's your turn, and you know exactly what to do. You learned by watching. But how? Although the question of how our brains engage in observational learning is still shrouded in mystery, neuroscientists have recently begun to pinpoint a potential physiological basis for it.

When a monkey watches another monkey perform an action, such as reaching for an object, a group of neurons in its prefrontal cortex, near its motor cortex (LO 3.1c), becomes active (Rizzolatti et al., 1996). These cells are called **mirror neurons** because they're the same cells that would have become active had the monkey performed the same movement. It's as though these neurons are "imagining" what it would be like to perform the behavior.

Mirror neurons appear to be remarkably selective. They don't become active when a monkey sees another monkey that remains stationary or sees a piece of food that another monkey grabbed. Instead, they become active only when a monkey sees another monkey engaging in an action, like grabbing. Moreover, these neurons seem tuned to extremely specific behaviors. Investigators have found one mirror neuron in monkeys that fires only when the monkey itself or a person it's observing grabs a peanut, and a different mirror neuron that fires only when the monkey itself or a person it's observing eats a peanut (Winerman, 2005). Using brain-imaging techniques, researchers have identified what appears to be a similar mirror neuron system in humans (Gallese & Goldman, 1998; Molenberghs, Cunnington, & Mattingley, 2012), but they've yet to identify individual mirror neurons, as they have in monkeys. No one knows for sure what mirror neurons do or why they're in our brains. But some neuroscientists have conjectured that such neurons play a central role in empathy (Azar, 2005; Iacoboni, 2009; Ramachandran, 2000), including feeling others' emotional states and emulating their movements (Fabbri-Destro & Rizzolatti, 2008). Some psychologists have gone further to speculate that mirror neuron abnormalities play a key role in autism spectrum disorder (autism), which is often associated with difficulties in adopting the perspectives of others (Dingfelder, 2005; Kana, Wadsworth, & Travers, 2011).

In recent years, though, the nature and function of mirror neurons have become scientifically controversial. For example, it's not clear whether these neurons play a role in empathy or psychological conditions characterized by deficient empathy, such as autism and psychopathic personality. The findings, which are limited, are at best correlational (Dinstein et al., 2008; Fecteau, Pascual-Leone, & Théoret, 2008). It's quite possible, for example, that empathy deficits contribute to mirror neuron abnormalities rather than the other way around. Making matters more complicated, research has called into question whether mirror neuron deficits are even correlated with autism (Hickok, 2014; Jarrett, 2014; Sowden et al., 2015). So the role of mirror neurons in humans continues to be something of a mystery.

Insight Learning

Latent learning and observational learning were by no means the only holes poked in behaviorist theory. Another serious challenge came from a German psychologist during World War I: Wolfgang Köhler.

Around the same time that psychologists were conducting the first latent learning studies, Köhler (1925), one of the founders of Gestalt psychology (LO 4.6a), was posing assorted problems to four chimpanzees in the Canary Islands off the coast of Africa. His favorite of the four was a genius of an ape named Sultan, who was especially adept at solving puzzles. In one case, Köhler placed a tempting bunch of bananas outside of the cage, well out of Sultan's reach, along with two bamboo sticks inside the cage. Neither stick was long enough to reach the bananas. After what appeared to be some heavy-duty pondering, Sultan suddenly hit upon the solution: Stick one bamboo stick inside the other, creating one extra-long bamboo stick.

What was notable, argued Köhler, was that his chimpanzees seemed to experience the "Aha reaction" we discussed previously. Their solutions to his problems didn't appear to reflect trial and error, as it did with Thorndike's cats, but rather *insight*, the sudden understanding of the solution to a problem. That is, their solutions resembled what we saw back in Figure 6.6. The chimps seemed to suddenly "get" the solution to the problem, and from then on they got it right just about every time.

Still, Köhler's findings and conclusions weren't without shortcomings. His observations were anecdotal and unsystematic. Because Köhler videotaped only some of his chimpanzees' problem solving, it's difficult to rule out the possibility that at least some of his chimps had engaged in trial and error before figuring out each problem (Gould & Gould, 1994). Moreover, because the chimps were often in the same cage, they might have engaged in observational learning. Still, Köhler's work suggests that at least some smart animals can learn through insight rather than trial and error. There's good evidence that humans can too (Dawes, 1994).

> ◀ **Correlation vs. causation**
>
> Can we be sure that A causes B?

Köhler's apes also figured out how to get to a banana suspended well above their heads: Stack a bunch of boxes atop each other, and climb to the top box.

> ◀ **Ruling Out Rival Hypotheses**
>
> Have important alternative explanations for the findings been excluded?

6.4: Biological Influences on Learning

6.4a **Explain how biological predispositions can facilitate learning of some associations.**

For many decades, most behaviorists regarded learning as distinct from biology. The animal's learning history and genetic makeup were like two ships passing in the night. Yet we now understand that our biology influences the speed and nature of our learning in complex and fascinating ways. Here are three powerful examples.

Conditioned Taste Aversions

One night in the 1970s, psychologist Martin Seligman went out to dinner with his wife. He ordered a filet mignon steak flavored with sauce béarnaise, his favorite topping. About six hours later, while at the opera, Seligman felt nauseated and became violently ill. He and his stomach recovered, but his love of sauce béarnaise didn't. From then on, Seligman couldn't even think of, let alone taste, sauce béarnaise without feeling like throwing up (Seligman & Hager, 1972).

The *sauce béarnaise syndrome*, also known as *conditioned taste aversion*, refers to the fact that classical conditioning can lead us to develop avoidance reactions to the taste of food (Kohut & Riley, 2015). Before reading on, ask yourself a question: Does Seligman's story contradict the other examples of classical conditioning we've discussed, like that of Pavlov and his dogs?

In fact, it does in at least three ways (Garcia & Hankins, 1977):

1. In contrast to most classically conditioned reactions, which require repeated pairings between CS and UCS, conditioned taste aversions typically require *only one trial* to develop.
2. The delay between CS and UCS in conditioned taste aversions can be as long as six or even eight hours (Rachlin & Logue, 1991).

3. Conditioned taste aversions tend to be remarkably specific and display little evidence of stimulus generalization. One of the earliest childhood memories of one of your text's authors is that of eating a delicious piece of lasagna and then becoming violently ill several hours later. For more than 20 years, he avoided lasagna at all costs while thoroughly enjoying spaghetti, manicotti, veal parmigiana, and virtually every other Italian dish despite its similarity to lasagna. He finally forced himself to get over his lasagna phobia, but not without a momentous struggle.

These differences make good sense from an evolutionary standpoint (O'Donnell, Webb, & Shine, 2010). We wouldn't want to have to experience horrific food poisoning again and again to learn a conditioned association between taste and illness. Doing so would not only be incredibly unpleasant, but we'd sometimes be dead after the first trial. The long lag time between eating and illness violates typical classical conditioning because close timing between the CS and UCS is usually necessary for learning. But in this case, the delayed association between CS and UCS is adaptive, because it teaches us to avoid dangerous foods we might have ingested hours earlier.

Conditioned taste aversions are a particular problem among patients with cancer undergoing chemotherapy, which frequently induces nausea and vomiting. As a result, they often develop an aversion to any food that preceded chemotherapy, even though they realize it bears no logical connection to the treatment. Fortunately, health psychologists have developed a clever way around this problem. Capitalizing on the specificity of conditioned taste aversions, they ask patients with cancer to eat an unfamiliar *scapegoat food*—a novel food of which they aren't fond—before chemotherapy. In general, the taste aversion becomes conditioned to the scapegoat food rather than to patients' preferred foods (Andresen, Birch, & Johnson, 1990).

John Garcia and one of his colleagues helped to demonstrate biological influences on conditioned taste aversions. They found that rats exposed to X-rays, which make them nauseated, developed conditioned aversions to a specific taste but not to a specific visual or auditory stimulus presented after the X-rays (Garcia & Koelling, 1966). In other words, the rats more readily associated nausea with taste than with other sensory stimuli after a single exposure (see Figure 6.11). Conditioned taste aversions aren't much fun, but they're often adaptive. In the real world, poisoned drinks and foods, not sights and sounds, make animals feel sick. As a consequence, animals more easily develop conditioned aversions to stimuli that tend to trigger nausea in the real world.

This finding contradicts the assumption of *equipotentiality*—the claim that we can classically condition all CSs equally well to all UCSs—a belief held by many traditional behaviorists (Plotkin, 2004). Garcia and others had found that certain CSs, such as those associated with taste, are easily conditioned to certain UCSs, such as those associated with nausea (Rachman, 1977; Thorndike, 1911). Recall that following his night out with his wife, Martin Seligman felt nauseated at the thought of sauce béarnaise, but not at the thought of the opera or—thankfully, for his marriage—his wife.

> ## Journal Prompt
>
> Do you have a conditioned taste aversion to a specific food or class of foods? Describe the event or events that might have led to this aversion.

Psychological science has helped many patients with cancer who are undergoing chemotherapy to minimize conditioned taste aversions to their favorite foods.

Preparedness and Phobias

A second challenge to the equipotentiality assumption comes from research on phobias. If we look at the distribution of phobias in the general population, we'll find something curious: People aren't always afraid of things with which they've had the most frequent unpleasant experiences. Phobias of the dark, heights, snakes, spiders, deep water, and blood are commonplace, even though many people who fear these stimuli have never had a frightening encounter with them. In contrast, phobias of razors, knives, the edges of furniture, ovens, and electrical outlets are extremely rare, although many of us have been cut, bruised, burned, or otherwise hurt by them.

Figure 6.11 Conditioned Taste Aversion.

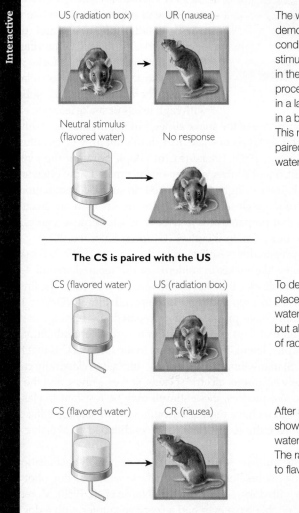

US (radiation box)   UR (nausea)

Neutral stimulus (flavored water)   No response

The work of John Garcia and his colleagues demonstrated that animals tend to develop conditioned taste aversions only to certain stimuli, namely, those that trigger nausea in the real world. Here you can see the process for conditioning a taste aversion in a laboratory rat. First, the rat is placed in a box where there is radiation (USC). This naturally triggers nausea (UCR). When paired with a neutral stimulus (flavored water) the rat shows no response.

The CS is paired with the US

CS (flavored water)   US (radiation box)

To develop a taste aversion the rat is then placed in a radiation box with the flavored water. The rats drink the flavored water, but also gets sick from being in a box of radiation.

CS (flavored water)   CR (nausea)

After several acquisition trials, the rat will show nausea and aversion to the flavored water, even when it is not in a radiation box. The rat has now developed a taste aversion to flavored water.

Seligman (1971) proposed that we can explain the distribution of phobias in the population by means of **preparedness**: We're evolutionarily predisposed to fear certain stimuli more than others (McNally, 2015). According to Seligman, that's because certain stimuli, like steep cliffs and poisonous animals, posed a threat to our early human ancestors (Hofmann, 2008; Ohman & Mineka, 2001). In contrast, household items and appliances didn't, because they weren't around back then. In the words of Susan Mineka (1992), prepared fears are "evolutionary memories": emotional legacies of natural selection.

Mineka and Michael Cook (1993) showed lab-reared rhesus monkeys, who had no previous exposure to snakes, a videotape of fellow monkeys reacting in horror to snakes. Within less than half an hour, the monkeys acquired a fear of snakes by observational learning (surprisingly, rhesus monkeys who've never been exposed to snakes show no fear of them). The researchers then edited the videotapes to make it appear that the same monkeys were reacting in horror, but this time in response to flowers, a toy rabbit, a toy snake, or a toy crocodile. They then showed these doctored videotapes to different groups of monkeys who had no experience with flowers, rabbits, snakes, or crocodiles. The monkeys who observed these altered videotapes acquired fears of the toy snake and toy crocodile, but not the flowers or toy rabbit. From the standpoint of preparedness, this finding is understandable. Snakes and crocodiles were dangerous to our primate ancestors, but flowers and rabbits weren't (Ohman & Mineka, 2003).

Preparedness may render us likely to develop *illusory correlations* between fear-provoking stimuli and negative consequences (Fiedler, Freytag, & Meiser, 2009; Tomarken, Mineka, & Cook, 1989). Recall (LO 2.2b) that an illusory correlation is a statistical mirage; it's the perception of a nonexistent association between two variables (Watts, Smith, & Lilienfeld, 2015).

preparedness

evolutionary predisposition to learn some pairings of feared stimuli over others owing to their survival value

This coyote, eating from a sheep carcass that's been tainted with a mild poison, will become sick several hours later. The coyote will avoid sheep from then on. Ranchers have made use of this technique to keep coyotes from attacking their livestock.

Replicability

Can the results be duplicated in other studies?

Ruling Out Rival Hypotheses

Have important alternative explanations for the findings been excluded?

Mineka and Cook (1993) showed that monkeys can acquire fears of snakes by means of observational learning. Nevertheless, these monkeys didn't acquire fears of nondangerous stimuli, like flowers, suggesting a role for evolutionary predispositions in the development of fears.

instinctive drift

tendency for animals to return to innate behaviors following repeated reinforcement

One team of investigators administered intermittent electrical shocks to subjects—some of whom feared snakes and some of whom didn't—while they watched slides of snakes and damaged electrical outlets. The pairings of the slide stimuli with the shocks were random, so that the actual correlation between them was zero. Yet subjects with high levels of snake fear perceived a marked correlation between the occurrence of the snake slides, but not the electrical outlets, with the electric shocks. Subjects with low levels of snake fear didn't fall prey to this illusory correlation (Tomarken, Sutton, & Mineka, 1995). Snake-fearful people were on the lookout for any threatening stimuli that might signal snakes, so they overestimated how often snake slides co-occurred with electric shock. Interestingly, they showed no such overestimation for electrical outlets, even though they're more closely linked in our minds than are snakes to electric shock. This finding suggests that preparedness may be at work, because snakes, but not electrical outlets, posed threats to our primate ancestors (Grupe & Nitschke, 2011).

Still, the laboratory evidence for preparedness isn't completely consistent. When researchers have paired either prepared stimuli—like snakes or spiders—or unprepared stimuli—such as flowers or mushrooms—with electric shocks, they haven't invariably replicated the finding that subjects more rapidly acquire fears to prepared than unprepared stimuli (Davey, 1995; McNally, 1987). Moreover, some authors have proposed that preparedness findings may be the result of an alternative explanation that isn't evolutionary in nature: latent inhibition. As we'll recall from previously in the chapter, latent inhibition refers to the fact that CSs that have appeared alone (that is, without a UCS) many times are especially difficult to classically condition to a stimulus. Because we routinely encounter electric sockets, stoves, knives, and the like, without experiencing any negative consequences, these stimuli may be resistant to classical conditioning. In contrast, because few of us have regular encounters with snakes, cliffs, deep water, and so on, these stimuli may be more easily classically conditioned to aversive outcomes (Bond & Siddle, 1996).

Aside from preparedness, genetic influences probably play a role in the acquisition of certain phobias. Individuals with a dog phobia don't differ from those without a dog phobia in their number of negative experiences with dogs, such as bites (DiNardo et al., 1988). Moreover, only about half of people with a dog phobia have ever had a scary encounter with a dog; the same holds for people with many other phobias. These results make it unlikely that classical conditioning alone can explain all cases of phobia. Instead, some people appear to be predisposed genetically to develop phobias *given* a history of certain classical conditioning experiences (Czajkowski et al., 2011; Kendler et al., 1992; van Houtem et al., 2013).

Instinctive Drift

Animal trainers Marian and Keller Breland taught pigeons, chickens, raccoons, pigs, and a host of other creatures to perform a variety of tricks for circuses and television advertisers. As students of B. F. Skinner at Harvard, they relied on traditional methods of operant conditioning to shape their animals' behavior. So do virtually all contemporary animal trainers.

In the process of their animal training adventures, the Brelands discovered that their little charges didn't always behave as anticipated. In one case, they tried to train raccoons to drop tokens into a piggy bank. Although they successfully trained the raccoons to pick up the coins using food reinforcement, they soon ran headfirst into a surprising problem. Despite repeated reinforcement for dropping the coins into the piggy bank, the raccoons began rubbing the coins together, dropping them, and rubbing them together again instead.

The raccoons had reverted to an innate behavior, namely, rinsing. They were treating the tokens like pieces of food, like the small hard shells they extract from the beds of ponds and streams (Timberlake, 2006). Breland and Breland (1961) referred to this phenomenon as **instinctive drift**: the tendency for animals to return to innate behaviors following repeated reinforcement (Burgos, 2015). Researchers have observed instinctive drift in other animals, including rats (LeFrancois, 2012; Powell & Curley, 1984). Psychologists don't fully understand the reasons for such drift. Nevertheless, instinctive drift suggests that we can't fully understand learning without taking into account innate biological influences, because these influences place limits on what kinds of behaviors we can train through reinforcement.

6.5: Learning Fads: Do They Work?

6.5a   Evaluate popular techniques marketed to enhance learning.

If you've made it all the way to this point in the chapter (congratulations!), you know that learning new information is hard work. Perhaps because learning new things requires so much time and effort on our part, many mental health professionals have marketed a motley assortment of techniques that supposedly help us to learn more quickly, or more easily, than we currently do. Do these newfangled methods work? We'll find out by examining three popular techniques.

Sleep-Assisted Learning

Imagine that you could master all of the information in this book while getting a few nights of sound sleep. You could pay someone to audio-record the entire book, play the recording over the span of several weeknights, and you'd be all done. You could say goodbye to those late nights in the library or dorm room reading about psychology.

As in many areas of psychology, hope springs eternal. Many proponents of *sleep-assisted learning*—learning new material while asleep—have made some extraordinary claims regarding this technique's potential. For example, on scores of websites, we can download various audio clips that can purportedly help us to learn languages, stop procrastinating, lose weight, or boost our self-confidence, all while we're comfortably catching up on our zzzs.

These assertions are certainly quite remarkable. Does the scientific evidence for sleep-assisted learning stack up to its proponents' impressive claims?

As is so often the case in life, things that sound too good to be true often are. Admittedly, the early findings on sleep-assisted learning were encouraging. One group of investigators exposed sailors to Morse code (a shorthand form of communication that radio operators sometimes use) while asleep. These sailors mastered Morse code three weeks faster than did other sailors (Simon & Emmons, 1955). Other studies from the former Soviet Union seemingly provided support for the claim that people could learn new material, such as tape-recorded words or sentences, while asleep (Aarons, 1976).

Nevertheless, these early positive reports neglected to rule out a crucial alternative explanation: The recordings may have awakened the subjects. The problem is that almost all of the studies showing positive effects didn't monitor subjects' electroencephalograms (EEGs); to ensure they were even asleep while listening to the tapes (Druckman & Bjork, 1994; Druckman & Swets, 1988; Lilienfeld et al., 2010). Better controlled studies that monitored subjects' EEGs to make sure they were asleep offered little evidence for sleep-assisted learning. So to the extent that sleep-learning recordings "work," it's probably because subjects hear snatches of them while drifting in and out of sleep. As for that quick fix for reducing stress, we'd recommend skipping the audio recordings and just getting a good night's rest.

Still, that's not to say that sleep can't help with learning. For example, evidence suggests that, compared with staying awake, sleeping between study sessions focused on learning a new language helps students to retain more information about this language, even up to half a year later (Mazza et al., 2016). There's a little catch to doing so, though: In contrast to what advocates of sleep-assisted learning insist, participants need to be awake while learning the new words!

Accelerated Learning

Still other companies promise consumers ultrafast techniques for learning. These methods, known as Superlearning or Suggestive Accelerative Learning and Teaching Techniques (SALTT), supposedly allow people to pick up new information at anywhere

Instinctive drift is the tendency to return to an evolutionarily selected behavior.

> **Extraordinary Claims**
>
> Is the evidence as strong as the claim?

> **Ruling Out Rival Hypotheses**
>
> Have important alternative explanations for the findings been excluded?

Evaluating Claims: STUDY SKILLS COURSES

At many colleges and universities, new students are understandably overwhelmed. They haven't yet learned how to study for college-level examinations, and they're not prepared for the enormous volume of reading assigned in their courses (such as having to read lengthy chapters on learning in their introductory psychology textbook). So it's not surprising that study skills courses and workshops have become popular, especially among freshmen.

Imagine that, as a first-semester freshman at "Princetown" University, you find yourself falling hopelessly behind in your coursework. You've just had your first round of exams and despite studying for about 20 hours for each of them, you received a D+ in introductory psychology, an F in introductory physics and, to add insult to injury, a C– in introductory basketweaving. While having coffee at a shop near campus, you come across an ad for a study skills course. The ad reads:

"Weekend study skills course for Princetown students … only $50. Makes use of well-tested learning methods, such as those based on operant conditioning and distributed practice. Several studies show that these techniques can improve your test performance by up to 10 percent. They don't work for everyone, but they may be worth a try for you."

Scientific skepticism requires us to evaluate all claims with an open mind but to insist on compelling evidence before accepting them. How do the principles of scientific thinking help us to evaluate this claim about the effectiveness of a study skills course?

Consider how the six principles of scientific thinking are relevant as you evaluate this claim.

1. Ruling Out Rival Hypotheses

Have important alternative explanations for the findings been excluded?

It's not clear from the advertisement whether rival hypotheses have been excluded. It's indeed possible that the study skills course has worked in the past, but it's also possible that some of the reported improvements resulted from the mere passage of time, to placebo effects, to practice effects (that is, to students taking exams multiple times), or to other artifacts. We'd need to know whether researchers had compared the study skills course with an alternative, non study-based, intervention as a control group.

2. Correlation vs. Causation

Can we be sure that A causes B?

This principle isn't especially relevant to the scenario described.

3. Falsifiability

Can the claim be disproved?

Yes, in principle, the claim could be falsified. If the study skills course were compared against alternative interventions

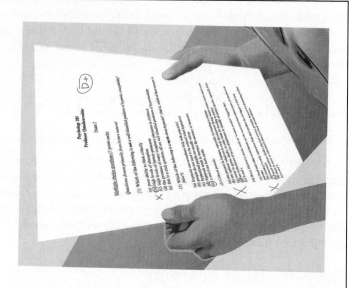

that didn't involve study skills and consistently did no better than these interventions in enhancing study skills, it would refute the claim that it's effective.

4. Replicability

Can the results be duplicated in other studies?

The ad does refer to "several studies," which is encouraging. Nevertheless, we'd need to know more to be able to evaluate whether these investigations were genuine replications of the original study, and to ensure that they were rigorously conducted.

5. Extraordinary Claims

Is the evidence as strong as the claim?

The ad appears to refrain from making extraordinary claims; it asserts only that the study skills course improves test performance by "up to 10 percent" and acknowledges that the course doesn't work for everyone. It also refers to operant conditioning and distributed practice (see LO 7.5b), both are which are well-supported learning principles.

6. Occam's Razor

Does a simpler explanation fit the data just as well?

This principle isn't especially relevant to the scenario described.

Summary

The advertisement makes several claims about the study skills course that may or may not be adequately supported, and that would need to be verified by an inspection of the original studies. At the same time, the ad refers to well-established learning principles and avoids making excessive claims of effectiveness. The course might well be worth checking out with an appropriately skeptical mind-set.

from 25 to several hundred times their normal learning speeds (Wenger, 1983). SALTT relies on a mixture of several techniques, such as generating expectations for enhanced learning (telling students they'll learn more quickly), getting students to visualize information they're learning, playing classical music during learning, and breathing in a regular rhythm while learning (Lozanov, 1978). When combined, these techniques supposedly allow learners to gain access to intuitive aspects of their minds that otherwise remain inaccessible. One recent book on accelerated learning purports to allow students to "double your learning capabilities in 10 minutes or less" and to "release your inner genius and become the student you were always meant to be" (McCullough, 2014).

Nevertheless, the evidence for the effectiveness of accelerated learning methods doesn't come close to matching the extraordinary claims (Della Sala, 2007). Almost all studies show that these methods don't produce enhanced learning (Dipamo & Job, 1990; Druckman & Swets, 1988). Even when researchers have reported positive results for such techniques, these findings have been open to rival explanations. That's because many of the studies conducted on accelerated learning compared this method with a control condition in which students did little or nothing. As a result, the few positive results reported for accelerated learning could be attributable to placebo effects, especially because one of the major components of accelerated learning is boosting learners' expectations (Druckman & Swets, 1988).

Discovery Learning

As we've discovered throughout this text, learning how to *rule out rival explanations* for findings is a key ingredient of scientific thinking. But science educators haven't always agreed on how to teach this crucial skill.

One increasingly popular way of imparting this knowledge is *discovery learning*: giving students experimental materials and asking them to figure out the scientific principles on their own (Klahr & Nigram, 2004). For example, a psychology professor who's teaching operant conditioning might set her students up with a friendly rat, a maze, and a plentiful supply of cheese and ask them to figure out which variables affect the rat's learning. For instance, does the rat learn the maze most quickly when we reinforce it continuously or only occasionally?

Nevertheless, as David Klahr and others have shown, the old-fashioned method of *direct instruction*, in which we simply tell students how to solve problems, is usually more effective and efficient than discovery learning (Alfieri et al., 2011). In one study, investigators examined third- and fourth-graders' ability to isolate the variables that influence how quickly a ball rolls down a ramp, such as the ramp's steepness or length. Only 23 percent of students assigned to a discovery learning condition later solved a slightly different problem on their own, whereas 77 percent of students assigned to a direct instruction condition did (Klahr & Nigram, 2004).

That's not to say that discovery learning has no role in education, because in the long term it may encourage students to learn how to pose scientific questions on their own (Alferink, 2007; Kuhn & Dean, 2005). But because many students may never figure out how to solve certain scientific problems independently, it's ill-advised as a stand-alone approach (Kirschner, Sweller, & Clark, 2006; Mayer, 2004). Moreover, discovery learning may be an especially bad idea for people with weak overall cognitive skills, whom data suggest are often slow to learn new tasks on their own (DeDonno, 2016).

Learning Styles

Few claims about learning are as widespread as the belief that all individuals have distinctive **learning styles**—their preferred means of acquiring information. According to proponents of this view, some students are "analytical" learners who excel at breaking down problems into different components, whereas others are "holistic" learners who excel at viewing problems as a whole. Still others are "verbal" learners who prefer to talk through problems, whereas others are "spatial" learners who prefer to visualize problems in their heads (Cassidy, 2004; Desmedt & Valcke, 2004). Some educational psychologists have claimed to boost learning dramatically by matching different methods of instruction to students' learning styles. According to them, children who are verbal learners should learn much faster and better with written material, children who are spatial learners should learn much faster and better with visual material, and so on. These beliefs about learning styles are remarkably prevalent: In one survey conducted across five countries, between 93 percent and 97 percent of teachers believed that matching instruction styles to students learning styles increased students' learning (Howard-Jones, 2014).

Extraordinary Claims

Is the evidence as strong as the claim?

Ruling Out Rival Hypotheses

Have important alternative explanations for the findings been excluded?

Ruling Out Rival Hypotheses

Have important alternative explanations for the findings been excluded?

---

learning style

an individual's preferred or optimal method of acquiring new information

Fact vs. Fiction

Using PowerPoint® in lectures enhances student learning.

○ Fact

○ Fiction

Learning Styles

The view that students with certain learning styles benefit from specific types of instructional materials is popular in education. Research doesn't support this "matching theory" of learning styles. If the claim were true, then "visual learners" would perform significantly better on material presented visually than do "spatial learners." However, researchers rarely, if ever, find this effect.

Appealing as these assertions are, they haven't stood the test of careful research (Lilienfeld et al., 2009; Rohrer & Paschler, 2012; Willingham, Hughes, & Doboloyi, 2015). For one thing, it's difficult to assess learning style reliably (Snider, 1992; Stahl, 1999). As we'll recall from previously in the text (LO 2.2a), *reliability* refers to consistency in measurement. In this case, different measures designed to assess people's learning styles often yield very different answers about their preferred mode of learning. In part, that's probably because few of us are purely analytical or holistic learners, verbal or spatial learners, and so on; most of us are a blend of multiple styles. Moreover, studies have generally revealed that tailoring different methods to people's learning styles doesn't result in enhanced learning (Kavale & Forness, 1987; Kratzig & Arbuthnott, 2006; Tarver & Dawson, 1978). Instead, most research shows that certain teaching approaches, like setting high standards for students and providing them with the motivation and skills to reach these standards, work best regardless of students' learning styles (Geake, 2008; Zhang, 2006). Like a number of other fads in popular psychology, the idea of learning styles seems to be more fiction than fact (Alferink, 2007; Holmes, 2016; Pashler et al., 2009; Stahl, 1999).

Journal Prompt

Have you ever tried one of the fad learning methods described in this section? If so, was the improvement in your learning that you may have noticed due to the technique itself? Generate two or three alternative explanations for why this improvement might have been due to factors other than the technique.

Answer: Fiction. Although students may experience the illusion of learning more from PowerPoint®-based lectures than from other lectures—and may enjoy such lectures more—the evidence that they actually learn more is weak (Holmes, 2016; Nouri & Shahid, 2005). This illusion of learning may be a major contributor to a variety of learning fads.

Summary: Learning

6.1: Classical Conditioning

6.1a **Describe Pavlov's model of classical conditioning and discriminate conditioned stimuli and responses from unconditioned stimuli and responses.**

In classical conditioning, animals come to respond to a previously neutral stimulus that had been paired with another stimulus (the CS) that elicits a reflexive, automatic response. After repeated pairings with the UCS, which elicits an automatic, reflexive response (the UCR) from the organism, the CS comes to elicit a conditioned response (CR).

6.1b Explain the major principles and terminology associated with classical conditioning.

Acquisition is the process by which we gradually learn the CR. Extinction is the process whereby following repeated presentation of the CS alone, the CR decreases in magnitude and eventually disappears. Extinction appears to involve an "overwriting" of the CR by new information rather than a forgetting of this information.

6.1c Explain how complex behaviors can result from classical conditioning and how they emerge in our daily lives.

Higher-order conditioning occurs when organisms develop classically conditioned responses to CSs associated with the original CS. Such conditioning allows us to expand our learning to a host of different, but related, stimuli in everyday life.

6.2: Operant Conditioning

6.2a Distinguish operant conditioning from classical conditioning.

Operant conditioning is learning controlled by its consequences. Operant conditioning involves many of the same processes, including acquisition and extinction, as does classical conditioning. Nevertheless, in operant conditioning, responses are emitted rather than elicited, the reinforcement is contingent on behavior, and responses mostly involve skeletal (voluntary) muscles rather than the autonomic nervous system.

6.2b Describe Thorndike's law of effect.

Thorndike's law of effect tells us that if a response, in the presence of a stimulus, is followed by a reward, it's likely to be repeated, resulting in the gradual "stamping in" of S-R (stimulus-response) connections.

6.2c Describe reinforcement and its effects on behavior and distinguish negative reinforcement from punishment.

Reinforcement can be either positive (presentation of an outcome) or negative (withdrawal of an outcome). Negative reinforcement increases the rate of a behavior, whereas punishment decreases it. One disadvantage of punishment is that it tells the organism only what *not* to do, not what *to* do.

6.2d Identify the four schedules of reinforcement and the response pattern associated with each.

There are four major schedules of reinforcement: fixed ratio, fixed interval, variable ratio, and variable interval. These four schedules differ along two dimensions: consistency of administering reinforcement (fixed or variable) and the basis of administering reinforcement (ratio or interval).

6.2e Describe some applications of operant conditioning.

Operant conditioning has a number of applications to everyday life, including shaping—which is a fundamental technique of animal training—and overcoming procrastination. Psychologists have also harnessed operant conditioning principles to develop token economies and other therapeutically useful applications. Operant conditioning principles probably also help to explain certain irrational behaviors in everyday life, including superstitions.

6.3: Cognitive Models of Learning

6.3a Outline the evidence that supports latent learning and observational learning.

S-O-R psychologists believe that the organism's interpretation of stimuli plays a central role in learning. Tolman's work on latent learning, which showed that animals can learn without reinforcement, challenged the radical behaviorists' view of learning. Research suggests that individuals can acquire aggressive behavior by observational learning. Correlational studies, longitudinal studies, laboratory studies, and field studies suggest that media violence contributes to aggression, although questions regarding the strength of this relationship remain.

6.3b Identify evidence of insight learning.

Köhler's work suggested that apes can learn through insight, and later work with humans suggests the same conclusion. This research calls into question Thorndike's conclusion that all learning occurs through trial and error.

6.4: Biological Influences on Learning

6.4a Explain how biological predispositions can facilitate learning of some associations.

Psychologists have increasingly recognized that our genetic endowment influences learning. Conditioned taste aversions refer to the phenomenon whereby classical conditioning can lead us to develop avoidance reactions to the taste of food. John Garcia and his colleagues showed that conditioned taste aversions violate the principle of equipotentiality, because they demonstrate that certain CSs are more easily conditioned than others to certain UCSs. Research on preparedness suggests that we are evolutionarily predisposed to learn to fear some stimuli more easily than others.

6.5: Learning Fads: Do They Work?

6.5a Evaluate popular techniques marketed to enhance learning.

Proponents of sleep-assisted learning claim that individuals can learn new material while asleep. Nevertheless, early reports of successful learning during sleep appear attributable to a failure to carefully monitor subjects' EEGs to ensure that they were asleep. Studies of accelerated learning techniques also show few or no positive effects, and positive results appear attributable to placebo effects and other artifacts. Although popular in science education, discovery learning approaches are often less effective and efficient than direct instruction. Some educational psychologists claim to be able to boost learning by matching individuals' learning styles with different teaching methods, but studies that have matched learning styles with teaching methods have typically yielded negative results.

Chapter 7
Memory

Constructing and Reconstructing Our Pasts

 Learning Objectives

7.1a Identify the ways that memories do and don't accurately reflect experiences.

7.1b Explain the function, span, and duration of each of the three memory systems.

7.1c Differentiate the subtypes of long-term memory.

7.2a Identify methods for connecting new information to existing knowledge.

7.2b Identify the role that schemas play in the storage of memories.

7.2c Distinguish ways of measuring memory.

7.2d Describe how the relation between encoding and retrieval conditions influences remembering.

7.3a Describe the role of long-term potentiation in memory.

7.3b Distinguish different types of amnesia and the relevance of amnesia to the brain's organization of memory.

7.3c Identify the key impairments of Alzheimer's disease.

7.4a Identify how children's memory abilities change with age.

7.5a Identify factors that influence people's susceptibility to false memories and memory errors.

7.5b Describe some of the real-world implications of false memories and memory errors.

Challenge Your Assumptions

Interactive

Do we really remember everything that's ever happened to us?

Do memory aids like "ROY G. BIV" (for the colors of the rainbow) really help us to remember?

Do people recall events they no longer believe happened to them?

Can people recover repressed memories of traumatic experiences?

Watch THE MEMORY GAME

This video conveys a powerful message: Our memories are far from perfect and are sometimes far off the mark. Now test yourself and try your hand (or your memory, that is) at a similar exercise that requires only a pen or pencil and a sheet of paper (for maximum effect, you may want to try this demonstration along with a group of friends). Read the list of words below, taking about a second per word. Read the left column first, then the middle column, then the right. Ready? Okay, begin.

Bed	Cot	Sheets
Pillow	Dream	Rest
Tired	Snore	Yawn
Darkness	Blanket	Couch

Now, turn away and take a minute or so to jot down as many of these words as you can recall. Did you remember *couch*? If so, give yourself a point. How about *snore*? If so, good—give yourself another point. Okay, how about *sleep*? If you're like about a third of typical people, you "remembered" seeing the word *sleep*. But now take a close look at the list. The word *sleep* isn't there. Now you have a good grasp of the amazement that some of the people interviewed in the video experienced when they were confronted with the imperfections of their memories.

If you or your friends remembered seeing *sleep* on the list, you experienced a **memory illusion**: a false but subjectively compelling memory (Brainerd, Reyna, & Zember, 2011; Deese, 1959; Roediger & McDermott, 1995, 1999). Like visual illusions, most memory illusions are byproducts of our brain's generally adaptive tendency to go beyond the information available to it. By doing so, our brain helps us make sense of the world, but it sometimes leads us astray (Gilovich, 1991; Kida, 2006). As the interviewer explained in the video, you may have remembered seeing the word *sleep* because it was linked closely in meaning to the other words on the list—such as, bed, dream, and rest. As a consequence, you may have been fooled into remembering that the word *sleep* was there. By relying on the *representativeness heuristic* (see LO 8.1a)—like goes with like—we simplify things to make them easier to remember. In this case, though, our use of this handy heuristic comes with a modest price: a memory illusion.

memory illusion
false but subjectively compelling memory

Interactive

Human memory works like a video camera, accurately recording the events we see and hear. (See bottom of page for answer.)

○ Fact

○ Fiction

7.1: How Memory Operates: The Memory Assembly Line

7.1a   **Identify the ways that memories do and don't accurately reflect experiences.**

7.1b   **Explain the function, span, and duration of each of the three memory systems.**

7.1c   **Differentiate the subtypes of long-term memory.**

memory

retention of information over time

We can define **memory** as the retention of information over time. We have memories for many kinds of information, ranging from our 16th birthday party, to how to ride a bike, to the shape of a pyramid. Our memories work pretty well most of the time. Odds are high that tomorrow you'll find your way into school or work just fine and that, with a little luck, you'll even remember some of what you read in this chapter. Yet in other cases, our memories fail us, often when we least expect it. How many times have you misplaced your keys or cell phone or forgotten the names of people you've met over and over again? We call this seeming contradiction the *paradox of memory:* Our memories are surprisingly good in some situations and surprisingly poor in others.

The Paradox of Memory

Salvador Dali's classic painting *The Persistence of Memory* is a powerful reminder that our memories are much more like melting wax than hardened metal. They often change over time, far more than we realize.

To a large extent, this chapter is the story of this paradox. As we'll see, the answer to the paradox of memory hinges on a crucial fact: *The same memory mechanisms that serve us well in most circumstances can sometimes cause us problems in others.*

WHEN OUR MEMORIES SERVE US WELL.   Research shows that our memories are often astonishingly accurate. Most of us can recognize our schoolmates decades later and recite the lyrics to dozens, even hundreds, of songs. Consider a study in which college students viewed 2,560 photographs of objects or scenes for a few seconds each. Three days later, the researchers showed these students each original photograph paired with a new one. Remarkably, the students correctly picked out the original photographs 93 percent of the time (Standing, Conezio, & Haber, 1970). In another case, a researcher contacted participants 17 years(!) after they'd viewed more than 100 line drawings for 1 to 3 seconds in a laboratory study. They identified these drawings at better-than-chance rates compared with participants who'd never seen the drawings (Mitchell, 2006).

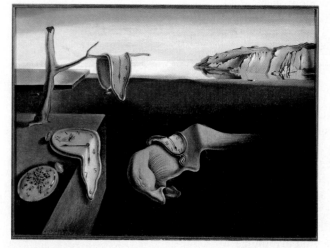

The memories of a small subset of individuals with a condition known as autism spectrum disorder (autism) are even more astonishing. Contrary to popular misconception (Stone & Rosenbaum, 1988), most individuals with autism lack specialized memory abilities, but

Answer: Fiction. A survey of the general public revealed that 64 percent of Americans agreed with this statement (Simons & Chabris, 2011), and about the same percentage of law enforcement officers in another survey endorsed this same belief (Wise et al., 2011). In the former survey, 38 percent of respondents said that once a memory is formed, it never changes. Even most psychotherapists believe that everything we learn is permanently stored in the mind (Loftus & Loftus, 1980; Yapko, 1994). Yet research contradicts this mistaken yet popular belief: Memories, although often accurate, can be spotty, replete with errors, and change over time.

there are impressive exceptions. Take the case of Kim Peek, who was the inspiration for the 1998 Academy Award–winning film *Rain Man* (Peek died in 2009). Peek's IQ was 87, noticeably below the average of approximately 100. Yet Peek memorized about 12,000 books word for word, the ZIP codes of every town in the United States, and the number of every highway connecting every city in the United States (Foer, 2007a; Treffert & Christensen, 2005). Kim Peek was also a *calendar calculator:* If you gave him any past or future date, like October 17, 2094, he'd give you the correct day of the week in a matter of seconds. Not surprisingly, Kim earned the nickname of "Kim-puter" among researchers who studied his astonishing memory feats.

Kim Peek, the "real Rain Man" (who passed away in 2009), exhibited phenomenal memory despite low overall intelligence.

Yet it's not only people with autism who possess remarkable memory capacities. Consider the case of Rajan Mahadevan (better known simply as Rajan), now a lecturer in the psychology department of the University of Tennessee. Rajan's memory feats are so spectacular that they were spoofed on an episode of the cartoon show *The Simpsons*. Rajan had somehow managed to memorize the number *pi*—the ratio of a circle's diameter to its radius—to a remarkable 38,811 digits (see Figure 7.1). When he recited them, it took him three hours at a rate of more than three digits per second (by the way, if you're curious, the world record for remembering pi is now up to more than 80,000 digits) (Foer, 2007a). How did Rajan pull off this amazing feat? We'll find out later in the chapter. Yet Rajan also provides a wonderful illustration of the paradox of memory. Despite finding pi to be a piece of cake, he kept forgetting the location of the men's restroom at the University of Minnesota psychology department even though it was just down the hall from where he'd been tested repeatedly (Biederman et al., 1992).

What would it be like if we could somehow remember almost everything we ever experienced? Would this talent be a blessing? A curse? Or perhaps a mix of both? Consider the fascinating case of a woman in her 40s, known only by the initials A. J., who has such an astounding memory that she's left even seasoned psychological researchers shaking their heads in bewilderment. Although emotionally quite normal, A. J. is markedly abnormal in one way: She remembers just about everything she's ever experienced. When given a date, like March 17, 1989, she can report precisely what she was doing on that day—taking a test, eating dinner with a good friend, or traveling to a new city. The claims here are extraordinary, but they've now been confirmed by research. Scientists have confirmed that she's almost always right. Moreover, she remembers on what day of the week that date fell. In 2003, a team of investigators asked A. J. to remember all of the dates of Easter over the past 24 years. She got all but two correct and reported accurately what she'd done each day (Parker, Cahill, & McCaugh, 2006).

> ◄ **Extraordinary Claims**
>
> Is the evidence as strong as the claim?

A. J., like about a dozen other people identified thus far, "suffers" from an exceedingly rare condition called *hyperthymestic syndrome*: memory of life events that's too good. Or does she really suffer? It's not entirely clear, because she regards her remarkable memory as both a curse and a blessing (Price & Davis, 2008). A. J. says that she sometimes remembers painful events that she'd prefer to forget, but also that she'd never want to give up her special memory "gift." As to the causes of hyperthymestic syndrome, scientists are baffled (Foer, 2007b). Nevertheless, recent research suggests subtle differences in brain structure between people with and without this condition, especially involving brain regions involved in autobiographical memory (LePort et al., 2012).

In a very real sense, we *are* our memories. Our memories define not only our past, but also our sense of identity. For A. J., life is like "a movie in her mind that never stops," as she puts it. Her recollections of her life and interactions with friends are remarkably vivid and emotionally intense. A. J.'s memory has shaped her personality in profound ways.

WHEN OUR MEMORIES FAIL US. In some exceedingly rare cases, as with A. J., memory is virtually perfect. Many others of us have extremely good memories in one or two narrow domains, like art history, baseball batting averages, or Civil War trivia. Yet memory can be surprisingly malleable and prone to error, as we learned from the video and the memory exercise we completed.

Figure 7.1 Rajan's Demonstration Sheet of Digits of Pi.
Rajan's feats demonstrate the uppermost end of the capacity of human memory.

Pi=3.					
1415926535	8979323846	2643383279	5028841971	6939937510	(50)
5820974944	5923078164	0628620899	8628034825	3421170679	(100)
8214808651	3282306647	0938446095	5058223172	5359408128	(150)
4811174502	8410270193	8521105559	6446229489	5493038196	(200)
4428810975	6659334461	2847564823	3786783165	2712019091	(250)
4564856692	3460348610	4543266482	1339360726	0249141273	(300)
7245870066	0631558817	4881520920	9628292540	9171536436	(350)
7892590360	0113305305	4882046652	1384146951	9415116094	(400)
3305727036	5759591953	0921861173	8193261179	3105118548	(450)
0744623799	6274956735	1885752724	8912279381	8301194912	(500)
9833673362	4406566430	8602139494	6395224737	1907021798	(550)
6094370277	0539217176	2931767523	8467481846	7669405132	(600)
0005681271	4526356082	7785771342	7577896091	7363717872	(650)
1468440901	2249534301	5654958537	1050792279	6892589235	(700)
4201995611	2129021960	8640344181	5981362977	4771309960	(750)
5187072113	4999999837	2978049951	0597317328	1609631859	(800)
5024459455	3469083026	4252230825	3344685035	2619311881	(850)
7101000313	7838752886	5875332083	8142061717	7669147303	(900)
5982534904	2875546873	1159562863	8823537875	9375195778	(950)
1857780532	...8065	...	661...	...	(1000)

When you picture yourself taking a recent walk on the beach, do you see yourself as an outside observer would? If so, such a recollection provides compelling evidence that memory can be reconstructive.

The Reconstructive Nature of Memory

These two demonstrations drive home a crucial point: Our memories frequently fool us and fail us. Indeed, a central theme of this chapter is that our memories are far more reconstructive than reproductive. When we try to recall an event, we *actively reconstruct* our memories using the cues and information available to us. We don't *passively reproduce* our memories, as we would if we were downloading information from the Internet. Remembering is largely a matter of patching together our often-fuzzy recollections with our best hunches about what really happened. When we recall our past experiences, we rarely, if ever, reproduce precise replicas of them (Neisser & Hyman, 1999; Lynn et al., 2015; Mori, 2008). We should therefore be skeptical of claims that certain vivid memories or even dreams are exact "photocopies" of past events (van der Kolk et al., 1984).

In fact, it's easy to show that our memories are often reconstructive. After reading this sentence, close your eyes for a few moments and picture your most recent walk along a beach, lake, or pond. Then, after opening your eyes, ask yourself what you "saw."

Did you see yourself as if from a distance, as an outside observer would? Many people report this visual perspective. As Sigmund Freud noted well over a century ago, such memories provide an existence proof (see LO 2.2a) that at least some of our memories are reconstructive (Schacter, 1996). You couldn't possibly have *seen* yourself from a distance, because you don't see yourself when you look at your surroundings: You must have constructed that memory rather than recalled it in its original form (Nigro & Neisser, 1983). Interestingly, Asians are more likely than European Americans to see themselves at a distance in such memories (Cohen & Gunz, 2002; Martin & Jones, 2012). This result fits with findings that members of many Asian cultures are more likely than members of Western cultures to adopt others' perspectives (see LO 1.1a). So our memories are probably shaped by not only our hunches and expectations, but also by our cultural backgrounds.

How can our memories be so good in some cases and so bad in others? How can we explain both the astonishing memories of people like A. J. and Rajan and the far from perfect memories of most of us? To grasp the paradox of memory, we need to figure out how some of our experiences make it into our memories, whereas so many others never do. To do so, let's embark on a guided tour of the factory assembly line inside our heads.

The Three Systems of Memory

Up to this point, we've been talking about memory as though it were a single thing. It isn't. Traditionally, most psychologists have distinguished among three major *systems* of memory: sensory memory, short-term memory, and long-term memory, as depicted in Figure 7.2 (Atkinson & Shiffrin, 1968; Norman, 2013; Waugh & Norman, 1965). These systems serve different purposes and vary along at least two important dimensions: *span*—how much information each system can hold—and *duration*—over how long a period of time that system can hold information.

In reality, the distinctions among these three memory systems aren't always clear-cut. Moreover, many modern researchers suspect that there are more than three memory systems (Baddeley, 1993; Hasson, Chen, & Honey, 2015; Healy & McNamara, 1996). For the sake of simplicity, we'll begin by discussing the three-systems model, although we'll point out some ambiguities along the way.

We can think of these three systems much like different factory workers along an assembly line. The first system, *sensory memory*, is tied closely to the raw materials of our experiences, our perceptions of the world; it holds these perceptions for just a few seconds or less before passing *some* of them on to the second system. This second system, *short-term memory*, works actively with the information handed to it, transforming it into more meaningful material before passing *some* of it on to the third system.

Figure 7.2 The Three-Memory Model.

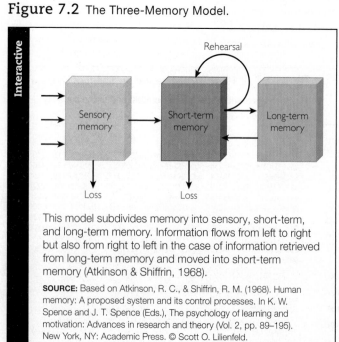

This model subdivides memory into sensory, short-term, and long-term memory. Information flows from left to right but also from right to left in the case of information retrieved from long-term memory and moved into short-term memory (Atkinson & Shiffrin, 1968).

SOURCE: Based on Atkinson, R. C., & Shiffrin, R. M. (1968). Human memory: A proposed system and its control processes. In K. W. Spence and J. T. Spence (Eds.), The psychology of learning and motivation: Advances in research and theory (Vol. 2, pp. 89–195). New York, NY: Academic Press. © Scott O. Lilienfeld.

Short-term memory holds on to information longer than sensory memory does, but not much longer. The third and final system, *long-term memory*, permits us to retain important information for minutes, days, weeks, months, or even years. In some cases, the information in long-term memory lasts for a lifetime. The odds are high, for example, that you'll remember your first kiss and your high school graduation for many decades, perhaps until the last day of your life. As you can tell from our use of the word *some* in the previous sentences, we almost always lose a great deal of information at each relay station in the memory assembly line.

SENSORY MEMORY.   If you're anywhere near a television set, turn it on for 10 seconds or so (alternatively, on your computer or smartphone, watch the first 10 seconds of a video). What did you see?

Regardless of what program or video you were watching, you almost certainly experienced a steady and uninterrupted stream of visual information. In reality, that continuous stream of images was an illusion, because television programs and movies consist of a series of disconnected frames, each separated by an extremely brief interlude of darkness you can't perceive. Yet your brain sees these frames as blending together into a seamless whole, in part because it continues to detect each frame for an extremely brief period of time after it disappears.

That is, our brains retain each frame in our **sensory memory**, the first factory worker in the assembly line of memory. Sensory memory briefly maintains our perceptions in a "buffer" area before passing them on to the next memory system, which is short-term memory. Sensory memory is a helpful system, because it buys our brains a bit of extra time to process incoming sensations. It also allows us to "fill in the blanks" in our perceptions and see the world as an unbroken stream of events.

Psychologists believe that each sense, including vision, hearing, touch, taste, and smell, uses its own form of sensory memory. In the case of television, film, or YouTube clips, for example, we experience an **iconic memory**, the type of sensory memory that applies to vision (Persuh, Genzer, & Melara, 2012). Iconic memories last for only about a second, and then they're gone forever.

Psychologist George Sperling (1960) conducted a pioneering study that demonstrated the existence of iconic memory. He quickly flashed participants a display of 12 letters, with 4 letters arranged in three rows, as shown in Figure 7.3. The display lasted only about one-twentieth of a second, and participants had to recall as many letters within the display as they could. Sperling found that most participants could recall only four or five letters. Surprisingly, different participants remembered different letters. This finding suggested to Sperling that all 12 letters had an equal chance of being recalled but that no one person could recall them all. This finding was puzzling. After all, if participants had remembered the whole visual display, why could they recall only a handful of letters and no more?

To find out, Sperling experienced a "flash" of insight, pun intended. Immediately after he flashed the 12 letters, he presented a tone (high, medium, or low) to signal participants which of the three rows (top, middle, or bottom) to report. Then he randomly instructed participants to report only one of the three rows. When he used this technique, he found that virtually all participants now got almost all letters in that row correct. This finding confirmed Sperling's hunch: Participants had access to all 12 letters in their memories. Sperling concluded that our iconic memories fade so quickly that we can't access all the information before it disappears. So Sperling's participants were able to take in all of the information but retained it in memory only long enough to read off a few letters.

Iconic memory may help to explain the remarkable, and exceedingly rare, phenomenon of *eidetic imagery*, popularly called "photographic memory." People with eidetic memory, most of them children, can supposedly hold a visual image in their minds with such clarity that they can describe it perfectly or almost perfectly (see Figure 7.4). Some psychologists believe that eidetic memory reflects an unusually long persistence of the iconic image in some fortunate people. Nevertheless, it's not clear that any memories are truly photographic, because even these memories often contain minor errors, such as information that wasn't in the original visual stimulus (Minsky, 1986; Rothen, Meier, & Ward, 2012). More likely, people with eidetic memories are blessed with excellent, although not perfect, recollections.

Iconic memory: After a lightning strike, we retain a visual image of it for about one second.

SOURCE: © Ralph Wetmore

sensory memory

brief storage of perceptual information before it is passed to short-term memory

iconic memory

visual sensory memory

Figure 7.3 Display of 12 Letters as Used in Sperling's 1960 Study.

Sperling's partial report method demonstrated that all displayed letters were held in sensory memory but decayed rapidly before all of them could be transferred to short-term memory (Sperling, 1960).

SOURCE: Based on Sperling, G. (1960). The information available in brief visual presentations. Psychological Monographs: General and Applied, 74 (11, Whole No. 498), 1–29. © Scott O. Lilienfeld.

Figure 7.4 Alice with Cheshire Cat.
Memory psychologists have used variations of this drawing from Lewis Carroll's *Alice's Adventures in Wonderland* to test for eidetic imagery. To find out if you have eidetic memory, look at the drawing for no longer than 30 seconds. Do that now before reading on. Now, without looking back at the drawing, can you remember how many stripes were on the cat's tail? Few adults can remember such details (Gray & Gummerman, 1975), although eidetic memory is much more prevalent among elementary school children (Haber, 1979).

echoic memory

auditory sensory memory

short-term memory

memory system that retains information for limited durations

> **Ruling Out Rival Hypotheses**

Have important alternative explanations for the findings been excluded?

decay

fading of information from memory over time

interference

loss of information from memory because of competition from additional incoming information

Sensory memory applies to hearing too. Now read that last sentence aloud: "Sensory memory applies to hearing too." If you pause for a few moments after saying it, you'll be able to replay the words precisely as you heard them for a few seconds, much like a soft echo reverberating from a mountaintop. That's why psychologists call this form of sensory memory **echoic memory** (Neisser, 1967). In contrast to iconic memories, echoic or auditory memories can last as long as 5 to 10 seconds (Cowan, Lichty, & Grove, 1990), conveniently permitting you to take notes on your psychology professor's most recent sentence even after he or she has finished saying it. Interestingly, there's also some evidence of eidetic memories for hearing, in which a few fortunate individuals report that their echoic memories persist for unusually long periods of time. Now, wouldn't that make taking lecture notes a breeze?

SHORT-TERM MEMORY. Once information makes it past our sensory buffers, it moves into our **short-term memory**, a second system for retaining information in our memories for brief periods of time. Short-term memory is the second factory worker in our memory assembly line. One key component of short-term memory is what psychologists call *working memory*, which refers to our ability to hold on to information we're currently thinking about, attending to, or processing actively (Baddeley, 2012; Baddeley & Hitch, 1974; Unsworth & Engle, 2007). If sensory memory is what feeds raw materials into the assembly line, short-term memory is the workspace where construction happens. After construction takes place, we either move the product into the warehouse for long-term storage or, in some cases, scrap it altogether.

The Duration of Short-Term Memory. If short-term memory is a short stop on the assembly line, just how brief is it? In the late 1950s, a husband-and-wife team decided to find out. Lloyd and Margaret Peterson (1959) presented participants with lists of three letters each, such as MKP or ASN, and then asked them to recall these three-letter strings. In some cases, they made participants wait only 3 seconds before recalling the letters; in other cases, they made them wait up to 18 seconds. Each time, they asked participants to count backward by threes while they were waiting.

Many psychologists were surprised by the Petersons' results, and you may be too. They found that after about 10 or 15 seconds, most participants *did no better than chance*. So the duration of short-term memory is quite brief; it's probably no longer than about 20 seconds. Some researchers believe it's even shorter than that, perhaps even less than five seconds, because some participants in the Peterson and Peterson study may have been able to silently rehearse the letters even when counting backward (Sebrects, Marsh, & Seamon, 1989).

Incidentally, many people misuse the term *short-term memory* in everyday language. For example, they may say that their "short-term memory isn't working" because they forgot what they had for dinner yesterday. As we've seen, the duration of short-term memory is far briefer than that.

Memory Loss from Short-Term Memory: Decay versus Interference. Why did the Petersons' participants lose their short-term memories so quickly, just as we quickly lose our memories of names of people we've just met or phone numbers we've just heard? The most obvious explanation is that short-term memories **decay**, that is, fade away over time. The longer we wait, the less is left. Yet there's a competing explanation for the loss of information from short-term memory: **interference**. According to this view, our memories get in the way of each other. That is, our memories are very much like radio signals. They don't change over time, but they're harder to detect if they're jammed by other signals.

As it turns out, there's evidence for both decay and interference. Recent physiological evidence for decay comes from research suggesting that the birth of new neurons in the hippocampus leads to the decay of memories in that brain region (Kitamura et al., 2009). As we create new memories, our old ones gradually fade away. Nevertheless, there's even stronger evidence for the role of interference in memory loss. For example, two investigators (Waugh & Norman, 1965) presented participants with many different lists of 16 digits, such as 6 2 7 1 8 5 3 4 2 6 9 7 4 5 8 3. Right after participants saw each list, the researchers gave them one "target" digit to focus on and then asked participants which digit came after this target digit. In all cases, this target digit appeared twice in the list, and participants had to remember the digit that came after its *first* presentation in the list. In the preceding digit list, the target item might be "8," so we'd search for the first 8 in the list—and the correct response would be 5.

Ruling Out Rival Hypotheses

Have important alternative explanations for the findings been excluded?

As an ingenious means of ruling out alternative hypotheses, the experimenters manipulated two variables to figure out which of them influenced forgetting. Specifically, they manipulated (1) where in the list the target digit appeared (early or late) and (2) how rapidly they presented digits to participants—either quickly (one digit every second) or slowly (one digit every 4 seconds). They told participants to listen carefully to each digit but not to rehearse it mentally. Now, if decay were the principal culprit in forgetting, participants' performance should become worse when researchers read the list slowly because more time had passed between digits. In contrast, if interference were the principal culprit, participants' performances should become worse when the target digit appeared later rather than earlier in the list, regardless of speed, because memory for later digits is hampered by memory for earlier digits.

The results showed that interference is the major contributor to forgetting. Participants' forgetting is due almost entirely to where in the list the target digit appears, rather than to the speed of presentation (Keppel & Underwood, 1962). Still, most researchers believe that both decay and interference play some role in short-term memory loss (Altmann & Schunn, 2002; Hardt, Nader, & Nadel, 2013).

We're not quite done with our examination of interference yet, because it turns out that there are two different kinds of interference (Ebert & Anderson, 2009; Underwood, 1957). One kind, **retroactive interference**, occurs when learning something new hampers earlier learning: The new interferes with the old (think of the prefix *retro-*, because retroactive interference works in a reverse direction). If you've learned one language, say Spanish, and then later learned a somewhat similar language, perhaps Italian, you probably found that you started making mistakes in Spanish you'd never made before. Specifically, you may have found yourself using Italian words, like *buono*, for Spanish words, like *bueno* (both *buono* and *bueno* mean "good").

In contrast, **proactive interference** occurs when earlier learning gets in the way of new learning: The old interferes with the new. For example, knowing how to play tennis might interfere with our attempt to learn to play racquetball, which requires a much smaller racquet. Not surprisingly, both retroactive and proactive interference are more likely to occur when the old and new stimuli that we've learned are similar. Learning a new language doesn't much affect our ability to master a new spaghetti recipe.

Interference

Interactive

This player is actively engaged in a racquetball match. If she was an experienced tennis player before attempting racquetball, the odds are high that her tennis swings would initially get in the way of her learning how to swing a racquetball racquet properly. That is, it will take her a while to "unlearn" her tennis swings. She is experiencing proactive interference (the old interfering with the new).

retroactive interference

interference with retention of old information due to acquisition of new information

proactive interference

interference with acquisition of new information due to previous learning of information

---

Journal Prompt

Give an example of a time when retroactive interference prevented you from remembering or doing something correctly. Next, describe a time when proactive interference prevented you from remembering or doing something correctly.

The Capacity of Short-Term Memory: The Magic Number. We've already seen that short-term memory doesn't last very long. Twenty seconds, or even less, and—poof—the memory is gone, unless we've made an extra-special effort to retain it. But how large is the *span* of short-term memory?

Try reading each of the following rows of numbers, one row at a time, at a rate of one number per second. Once you're done with each row, close your eyes and try writing down what you remember. Ready? Okay, begin.

$$9 - 5 - 2$$
$$2 - 9 - 7 - 3$$
$$5 - 7 - 4 - 9 - 2$$
$$6 - 2 - 7 - 3 - 8 - 4$$
$$2 - 4 - 1 - 8 - 6 - 4 - 7$$
$$3 - 9 - 5 - 7 - 4 - 1 - 8 - 9$$
$$8 - 4 - 6 - 3 - 1 - 7 - 4 - 2 - 5$$
$$5 - 2 - 9 - 3 - 4 - 6 - 1 - 8 - 5 - 7$$

You've just taken a test of "digit span." How did you make out? Odds are that you breezed through three digits, started to find four digits a bit tricky, and maxed out at somewhere between five and nine digits. It's unlikely you got the 10-digit list completely right; if you did, you've earned the right to call yourself a memory superstar.

That's because the digit span of most adults is between five and nine digits, with an average of seven digits. Indeed, this finding is so consistent that psychologist George Miller (1956) referred to seven plus or minus two pieces of information as the **Magic Number**.

According to Miller, the Magic Number is the universal limit of short-term memory, and it applies to just about all information we encounter: numbers, letters, people, vegetables, and cities. Because it's hard to retain much more than seven plus or minus two pieces of information in our short-term memory, it's almost surely not a coincidence that telephone numbers in North America are exactly seven digits long, not counting the area code (some European phone numbers are slightly longer, but few exceed nine, the typical upper limit for the Magic Number). Some psychologists have since argued that Miller's Magic Number overestimates the capacity of short-term memory, and that the true Magic Number is as low as three or four (Cowan, 2001; Cowan, 2010; Mathy & Feldman, 2011). Regardless of who's right, it's clear that the capacity of short-term memory is extremely limited.

Chunking. If our short-term memory capacity is no more than nine digits, and perhaps much less, how do we manage to remember much larger amounts of information than this for brief periods of time? Read the following sentence; then wait a few seconds and recite it back to yourself: Harry Potter's white owl Hedwig flew off into the dark and stormy night. Were you able to remember most or even all of it? The odds are high that you were. Yet this sentence contained 13 words, which exceeds the Magic Number. How did you accomplish this feat?

We can expand our ability to remember things in the short term by using a technique called **chunking**: organizing material into meaningful groupings (Gobet et al., 2001; Yamaguchi & Logan, 2016). For example, look at the following string of 15 letters for a few seconds, and then try to recall them:

K A C F J N A B I S B C F U I

How did you do? Odds are you didn't do too well, probably right around the Magic Number, that is, only a subset of the letters listed. Okay, now try this 15-letter string.

C I A U S A F B I N B C J F K

Did you do any better this time? It's the same 15 letters, but you probably noticed something different about this group than the first group: They consisted of meaningful abbreviations. So you probably "chunked" these 15 letters into five meaningful groups of three letters each: CIA, USA, FBI, NBC, JFK. In this way, you reduced the number of items you needed to remember from 15 to only 5. In fact, you might have gotten this number down to less than five by combining CIA and FBI (both the initials of U.S. government intelligence agencies) into one chunk.

Consider this amazing feat. After two years of training, one man named S. F. was able to get his digit span memory up to 79 digits using chunking (Chase & Ericcson, 1981; Foer, 2011). Among other tricks, S. F., who was a runner, memorized enormous numbers of world record times for track events and used them to chunk numbers into bigger units. Yet S. F. hadn't really increased his short-term memory capacity at

Magic Number

the span of short-term memory, according to George Miller: seven plus or minus two pieces of information

chunking

organizing information into meaningful groupings, allowing us to extend the span of short-term memory

Master chess players recall realistic chess positions, like the one shown, better than do beginners. But they do no better than beginners at recalling unrealistic chess positions. So the experts' edge stems not from raw memory power, but from chunking.

all, only his chunking ability. His memory span for letters was only a measly six, well within the range of the Magic Number achieved by the rest of us memory slackers.

Chunking also explains how Rajan performed his remarkable pi memorization feats. He memorized enormous numbers of area codes, dates of famous historical events, and other meaningful numbers embedded within the list of pi digits to effectively reduce more than 30,000 digits to a much smaller number.

Experts rely on chunking to help them recall complicated information. For example, chess masters recall *realistic* chess positions far better than do novices, yet do no better than novices at recalling random chess positions, suggesting that experts organize meaningful chess positions into broader patterns (Chase & Simon, 1973; Gobet & Simon, 1998).

Rehearsal. Whereas chunking increases the span of short-term memory, a strategy called rehearsal extends the duration of information in short-term memory. **Rehearsal** is repeating the information mentally, or even aloud. In that way, we keep the information "alive" in our short-term memories, just as jugglers keep a bunch of bowling pins "alive" by continuing to catch them and toss them back into the air. Of course, if they pause for a second to scratch their nose, the bowling pins come crashing to the ground. Similarly, if we stop rehearsing and shift our attention elsewhere, we'll quickly lose material from our short-term memory.

There are two major types of rehearsal. The first, **maintenance rehearsal**, simply involves repeating the stimuli in their original form; we don't attempt to change the original stimuli in any way. We engage in maintenance rehearsal whenever we hear a phone number and keep on repeating it—either aloud or in our minds—until we're ready to dial the number. In this way, we keep the information "alive" in our short-term memory. Of course, if someone interrupts us while we're rehearsing, we'll forget the number.

The second type of rehearsal, **elaborative rehearsal**, usually takes more effort. In this type of rehearsal, we "elaborate" on the stimuli we need to remember by linking them in some meaningful way, perhaps by visualizing them or trying to understand their interrelationship (Craik & Lockhart, 1972; Mora & Campbell, 2015).

To grasp the difference between maintenance and elaborative rehearsal, let's imagine that a researcher gave us a *paired-associate task*. In this task, the investigator presents us with various pairs of words, such as *dog–shoe, tree–pipe, key–monkey,* and *kite–president*. Then, he or she presents us with the first word in each pair—*dog, tree,* and so on—and asks us to remember the second word in the pair. If we used maintenance rehearsal, we'd simply repeat the words in each pair over and over again as soon as we heard it—*dog–shoe, dog–shoe, dog–shoe,* and so on. In contrast, if we used elaborative rehearsal, we'd try to link the words in each pair in a meaningful way. One effective way of accomplishing this goal is to come up with a meaningful, perhaps even absurd, visual image that combines both stimuli (Ghetti et al., 2008; Paivio, 1969) (see Figure 7.5).

Research shows that we're especially likely to remember the two stimuli if we picture them interacting in some fashion (Blumenfeld et al., 2010; Wollen, Weber, & Lowry, 1972). That's probably because doing so allows us to chunk them into a single integrated stimulus. So to remember the word pair *dog–rocket*, for example, we could picture a dog piloting a rocket ship or a rocket ship barking like a dog.

Elaborative rehearsal usually works better than maintenance rehearsal (Harris & Qualls, 2000). This finding demolishes a widely held misconception about memory: that rote memorization is typically the best means of retaining information (Holmes, 2016). There's a take-home lesson here when it comes to our study habits. To remember complex information, it's almost always better to connect that information with things we already know than to merely keep repeating it.

Depth of Processing. This finding is consistent with a **levels of processing** model of memory (see video). According to this model, the more deeply we process information, the better we tend to remember it.

This model identifies three levels of processing of verbal information (Craik & Lockhart, 1972): visual, phonological (sound-related), and semantic (meaning-related). Visual processing is the most shallow; phonological, somewhat less shallow; and semantic, the

Figure 7.5 Word Pairs

Using elaborative rehearsal helps us recall the word pair *dog–shoe* (Paivio, 1969).

SOURCE: Based on Paivio, A. (1969). Mental imagery in associative learning and memory. Psychological Review, 76, 341–363. © Scott O. Lilienfeld.

rehearsal

repeating information to extend the duration of retention in short-term memory

maintenance rehearsal

repeating stimuli in their original form to retain them in short-term memory

elaborative rehearsal

linking stimuli to each other in a meaningful way to improve retention of information in short-term memory

levels of processing

depth of transforming information, which influences how easily we remember it

Watch DEPTH OF PROCESSING

deepest. To understand the differences among these three levels, try to remember the following sentence:

ALL PEOPLE CREATE THEIR OWN
MEANING OF LIFE.

If you relied on *visual* processing, you'd hone in on how the sentence looks. For example, you might try to focus on the fact that the sentence consists entirely of capital letters. If you relied on *phonological* processing, you'd focus on how the words in the sentence sound. Most likely, you'd repeat the sentence again and again until it began to sound boringly familiar. Finally, if you relied on *semantic* processing, you'd emphasize the sentence's meaning. You might elaborate on how you've tried to create your own meaning of life and how doing so has been helpful to you. Research shows that deeper levels of processing, especially semantic processing, tend to produce more enduring long-term memories (Craik & Tulving, 1975; Lindsay & Norman, 2013).

Still, some psychologists have charged the levels-of-processing model with being largely unfalsifiable (Baddeley, 1993). According to them, it's virtually impossible to determine how deeply we've processed a memory in the first place, so we could never independently test the claim that more deeply processed memories are better remembered. Moreover, critics claim that proponents of the levels-of-processing model are merely equating "depth" with how well participants later remember. There may well be some truth to this criticism. Still, it's safe to say that the more meaning we can supply to a stimulus, the more likely we are to recall it in the long term.

Falsifiability

Can the claim be disproved?

long-term memory

relatively enduring (from minutes to years) retention of information stored regarding our facts, experiences, and skills

permastore

type of long-term memory that appears to be permanent

LONG-TERM MEMORY.   Now that the second factory assembly line worker—short-term memory—has finished her construction job, what does she pass on to the third and final worker? And how does what the third worker receives differ from what the second worker started out with? **Long-term memory**, the third worker, is our relatively enduring store of information. It includes the facts, experiences, and skills we've acquired over our lifetimes.

Differences Between Long-Term and Short-Term Memory.   Long-term memory differs from short-term memory in several important ways. First, in contrast to short-term memory, which can typically hold at most seven to nine stimuli in hand at a single time, the capacity of long-term memory is huge. Just how huge? No one knows for sure. Some scientists estimate that a typical person's memory holds about as much information as 500 huge online encyclopedias, each about 1,500 pages long (Cordón, 2005). So if someone praises you on your "encyclopedic memory," accept the compliment. They're probably right.

Second, although information in short-term memory vanishes after only about 20 seconds at most and probably less, information in long-term memory often endures for years, even decades—and sometimes permanently. Consider the work of psychologist Harry Bahrick, who has studied individuals' memory for languages they learned in school over many decades. In Figure 7.6, we can see that people's memory declines markedly about two to three years after taking a Spanish course. Yet after about two years, the decline becomes quite gradual. Indeed, it begins to level out after a while, with almost no additional loss for up to 50 years after they took the course (Bahrick & Phelps, 1987). Bahrick referred to this kind of long-term memory, which remains "frozen" over time, as **permastore**, as an analogy to the permafrost found in the Arctic or Antarctic that never melts.

Third, the types of mistakes we commit in long-term memory usually differ from those we make in short-term memory. Long-term memory errors tend to be *semantic*, that is, based on the meaning of the information we've received. So we might misremember a "poodle" as a "terrier." In contrast, short-term memory errors tend to be *acoustic*, that is, based on the sound of the information we've received (Conrad, 1964; Wickelgren, 1965). So we might misremember hearing "noodle" rather than "poodle."

Figure 7.6 Long-Term Memory Retention.

The classic work of Harry Bahrick (1984) shows that retention of a foreign language remains remarkably constant for spans of almost 50 years after an initial drop.

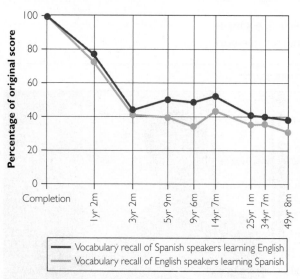

Vocabulary recall of Spanish speakers learning English
Vocabulary recall of English speakers learning Spanish

SOURCE: Adapted from Bahrick, 1984, Figure 3

Primacy and Recency Effects.   When we try to remember a large number of items, such as a grocery list or a schedule of events, we often forget some of them. To some extent, psychologists can predict which items we're more likely to forget and which we're more likely to remember.

To demonstrate this point, read the list of 20 words, either to yourself or aloud. Read the left column first, then the middle column, then the right one. Then, turn away and take a few minutes to try to recall as many of these words as you can in any order you'd like. Ready? Begin.

Ball	Sky	Store
Shoe	Desk	Pencil
Tree	Car	Grass
Dog	Rope	Man
Paper	Dress	Cloud
Bird	Xylophone	Hat
House	Knife	Vase

If you're like most people, you probably did a bit better with the early words, like *ball, shoe,* and *tree,* than with the words in the middle of the list. That's the **primacy effect**: The tendency to remember stimuli, like words, early in a list. Also, you may have done a bit better with the later words, like *cloud, hat,* and *vase.* That's the **recency effect**: The tendency to remember stimuli later in a list. As an aside, there's a decent chance you remembered the word *xylophone,* which seems to be something of an oddball in the list. That's because we tend to remember stimuli that are distinctive in some way (Hunt, 2012; Neath & Surprenant, 2003; Radvansky, Gibson, & McNerny, 2011).

If we averaged your results along with those of a few hundred other participants, we'd end up with the graph depicted in Figure 7.7, called the **serial position curve**. As we can see, this curve clearly displays the primacy and recency effects.

Most researchers agree that primacy and recency effects reflect the operation of different memory systems. Because the last few words in the list were probably lingering in your short-term memory, you were probably especially likely to recall them. So, the recency effect seems to reflect the workings of short-term memory.

What explains the primacy effect? This one is trickier, but there's good evidence that you were more likely to recall the earlier words in the list because you had more opportunity to rehearse them silently—and perhaps even to chunk them. As a consequence, these words were more likely to be transferred from short-term memory into long-term memory. So the primacy effect seems to reflect the operation of long-term memory.

Types of Long-Term Memory. As we mentioned earlier, some psychologists argue that there are actually more than three memory systems. In particular, they claim that long-term memory isn't just one system, but many.

To find out why, try your hand at the following four questions.

1. In what year did the United States become independent from Great Britain?
2. What Republican candidate for president did Barack Obama defeat in the 2012 U.S. election?
3. How old were you when you first tried to ride a bicycle?
4. Where did you celebrate your last birthday?

Figure 7.7 The Serial Position Curve.

Most psychologists believe that the primacy and recency effects in this curve are the telltale signs of two different memory systems: long-term and short-term memory, respectively.

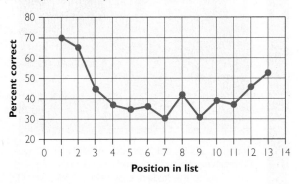

primacy effect

tendency to remember words at the beginning of a list especially well

recency effect

tendency to remember words at the end of a list especially well

serial position curve

graph depicting both primacy and recency effects on people's ability to recall items on a list

---

Fact vs. Fiction

There's a serial position curve for U.S. presidents. (See bottom of page for answer.)

○ Fact

○ Fiction

Interactive

Answer: Fact. There's even a serial position curve for U.S. presidents. If given the chance to name as many presidents as they can, most people list early presidents, like Washington, Jefferson, and Adams, and recent presidents, like Clinton, Bush, and Obama more than middle presidents, with good old Abe Lincoln being a striking exception (Roediger & Crowder, 1976; Roediger & DeSoto, 2014). The same effect holds for recall of Canadian prime ministers (Neath & Saint-Aubin, 2011).

Errors in Long-Term Memory

During a 2009 rock concert in Michigan, Bruce Springsteen referred repeatedly to being in Ohio (and even greeted the audience by yelling "Hello Ohio!"). "The Boss" committed an error in semantic memory, which is a subtype of long-term memory.

semantic memory

our knowledge of facts about the world

episodic memory

recollection of events in our lives

explicit memory

memories we recall intentionally and of which we have conscious awareness

implicit memory

memories we don't deliberately remember or reflect on consciously

procedural memory

memory for how to do things, including motor skills and habits

priming

our ability to identify a stimulus more easily or more quickly after we've encountered similar stimuli

According to Endel Tulving (1972) and many other memory researchers (Renoult et al., 2012), our answers to the first two questions rely on different memory systems than our answers to the last two. Our answers to the first two questions (1776 and Mitt Romney) depend on **semantic memory**, our knowledge of facts about the world. In contrast, our answers to the last two questions, which are unique to us, depend on **episodic memory**, our recollection of events in our lives. A. J., whom we discussed at the beginning of the chapter, experiences remarkably accurate episodic memories. There's good evidence that these two types of memory are housed in different brain regions. Semantic memory tends to activate the left frontal cortex more than the right frontal cortex and vice versa for episodic memory (Cabeza & Nyberg, 1997). Still, common neural pathways may bring together semantic and episodic memories regardless of their content (Burianova, McIntosh, & Grady, 2010).

Semantic and episodic memory both require conscious effort and awareness. Whether we're trying to recall the definition of "chunking" from earlier in this chapter or our first kiss, we *know* we're trying to remember. Moreover, when we recall this information, we have a conscious experience of accessing it. That is, both semantic and episodic memory are examples of **explicit memory** the process of recalling information intentionally. (Some researchers refer to the information recalled by explicit memory as *declarative memory*.)

Explicit memory differs from **implicit memory**, the process of recalling information we don't remember deliberately. Implicit memories don't require conscious effort on our part (Gopie, Craik, & Hasher, 2011; Roediger, 1990). For example, each of us can go through the steps of unlocking our front doors without consciously recalling the sequence of actions required to do so. In fact, we probably can't tell without reenacting it in our heads or actually standing in front of our doors which way the key turns in the lock and how we hold the key in our hands while unlocking the door.

Studies of people with brain damage provide remarkable *existence proofs* (see LO 2.2a) for the distinction between implicit and explicit memory. Antonio Damasio (2000) has studied a patient named David, whose left and right temporal lobes were largely obliterated by a virus. David has virtually no explicit memory for anyone he's met; when Damasio shows him photographs of people with whom he's recently interacted, he can't recognize any of them. Yet when Damasio asks David which of these people he'd ask for help if he needed it, he points to those who've been kind to him, utterly clueless of who they are. David has no explicit memory for who's helped him, but his implicit memory remains intact.

To make matters still more complicated, there are several subtypes of implicit memory. We'll focus on two here: *procedural memory* and *priming*. However, according to most psychologists, implicit memory also includes habituation, classical conditioning, and other basic forms of learning, as shown in Figure 7.8.

One subtype of implicit memory, **procedural memory**, refers to memory for motor skills and habits. Whenever we ride a bicycle or open a soda can, we're relying on procedural memory. In contrast to semantic memory, which is "know what" memory, procedural memory is "know how" memory. Our procedural and semantic memories for the same skills are sometimes surprisingly different. For those of you who are avid typists, find a keyboard and type the word *the*. That's a breeze, right? Now turn away from the keyboard for a moment, and try to remember where the *t*, *h*, and *e* are located, but without moving your fingers. If you're like most people, you'll draw a blank. You may even find that the only way to remember their location is to use your fingers to type the imaginary letters in midair. Although your procedural memory for locating letters on a keyboard is effortless, your semantic memory for locating them is a different story.

A second subtype of implicit memory, **priming**, refers to our ability to identify a stimulus more easily or more quickly when we've previously encountered similar

(a) (b)

Is the drawing at the bottom a duck or a rabbit? This illusion, originally concocted by psychologist Joseph Jastrow around the turn of the century, affords a good illustration of priming you can try on your friends. Show some of your friends only Photograph A (covering up Photograph B) then show other friends only Photograph B (covering up Photograph A). Ask them what they see in the drawing. Your friends primed with Photograph A will be more likely to "see" the related image of a duck, and your friends primed with Photograph B will be more likely to "see" the related image of a rabbit (see LO 4.6a).

Procedural memory is memory for how to do things, even things we do automatically without thinking about how to do them.

stimuli. Imagine that a researcher flashes the word *QUEEN*, interspersed with a few hundred other words, very quickly on a computer screen. An hour later, she asks you to perform a task that requires you to fill in the missing letters of a word. In this case, the stem completion task is K _ _ _. Research shows that having seen the word *QUEEN*, you're more likely to complete the stem with *KING* (as opposed to *KILL* or *KNOW*, for example) than are participants who haven't seen *QUEEN* (Neely, 1976). This is true, incidentally, even for participants who insist they can't even remember having seen the word *QUEEN*. This memory is implicit because it doesn't require any deliberate effort on our part (Yeh, He, & Cavanagh, 2012).

If you're having a hard time keeping all of these subtypes of long-term memory straight, Figure 7.8 summarizes the major subtypes of explicit and implicit memory, including those we've discussed.

Figure 7.8 The Many Subtypes of Memory.

A summary of the subtypes of explicit and implicit memory.

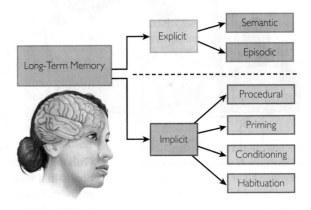

7.2: The Three Processes of Memory

7.2a Identify methods for connecting new information to existing knowledge.
7.2b Identify the role that schemas play in the storage of memories.
7.2c Distinguish ways of measuring memory.
7.2d Describe how the relation between encoding and retrieval conditions influences remembering.

How do we transfer information into our long-term memories? Memory psychologists agree that there are three major *processes* of memory: *encoding, storage,* and *retrieval*. By the way, we shouldn't confuse these three processes with the three *systems* of memory we've just discussed (sensory, short-term, and long-term). Whereas the three systems refer to the *what* of memory, the three processes we're about to discuss refer to the *how* of memory. They explain how information passes into long-term memory and gets back out again when we need it (see Figure 7.9).

together to achieve the claimed effect. In addition, the precise quantity of each ingredient is neither specified nor standardized, making disproving the claim challenging based on the information in the ad.

4. Replicability
Can the results be duplicated in other studies?

There's no evidence that the claim is derived from research using the product advertised, and no mention of the relative strength of the ingredients, how they were processed, in what proportions they were combined, and so forth, making rigorous replication impossible. We should be skeptical of claims regarding the effectiveness of the formula based on nothing more than a statement that the product is "scientifically proven to improve memory" with no reference to published, peer-reviewed studies, not to mention successful replications. The ad uses the term "proven," yet scientific knowledge is rarely, if ever, conclusive.

5. Extraordinary Claims
Is the evidence as strong as the claim?

The claim that this product is a cure for absentmindedness and imperfect memory is extraordinary, but the ad provides no evidence to support this claim. The fact that "75 percent of Americans are turning to complementary and alternative medicine to improve their memory" has no bearing on whether this product is effective. Moreover, don't be misled by appeals that press the idea that a product is effective merely because it's "natural." Just because a product contains natural ingredients doesn't mean it's safe and effective.

6. Occam's Razor
Does a simpler explanation fit the data just as well?

Yes. Simpler explanations for positive changes associated with the product include increased self-observation, mindfulness, and attention to positive changes independent of the ingredients contained in the product.

Summary
There's no scientific support for the extraordinary claim that the product can improve absentmindedness and memory. The assertions in the ad can't be readily falsified and aren't based on well-replicated research. Furthermore, the ad establishes no causal link between the product and claimed positive outcomes. Finally, simpler explanations could account for any positive changes associated with the advertised product.

Retrieval: Heading for the "Stacks"

To remember something, we need to fetch it from our long-term memory banks. This is **retrieval**, the third and final process of memory. Yet, as we mentioned earlier, this is where our metaphor of a library begins to break down, because what we retrieve from our memory often doesn't match what we put into it. Our memories are reconstructive, often transforming our recollections to fit our beliefs and expectations.

Many types of forgetting result from failures of retrieval: Our memories are still present, but we can't access them. It's pretty easy to demonstrate this point. If a friend is nearby, try the following demonstration, courtesy of psychologist Endel Tulving (even if you don't have a friend handy, you can still follow along). Read each category in Table 7.1 to your friend, followed by the word that goes along with it. Tell your friend that after you're done reading all of the categories and their corresponding words, you'll ask him or her to recall just the words—in any order—not the categories.

After you read the list to your friend, ask him or her to take a few minutes to write down as many words as he or she can remember. Almost certainly, your friend missed some of them. For those missing words, prompt your friend with the category. So if your friend missed *Finger*, ask, "Do you remember the word that went with 'A part of the body'?" You'll probably find that these prompts help your friend to remember some of the forgotten words. In psychological lingo, the category names serve as **retrieval cues**: hints that make it easier for us to recall information. So your friend's long-term memory contained these missing words, but he or she needed the retrieval cues to remember them.

MEASURING MEMORY. Psychologists assess people's memory in three major ways: recall, recognition, and relearning. Think of them as the three Rs (another mnemonic device, by the way).

Recall and Recognition. What kind of exam do you find the toughest: essay or multiple choice? For sure, we've all taken multiple-choice tests that are "killers." Still, all else being equal, essay tests are usually harder than multiple-choice tests. That's because **recall**, that is, generating previously remembered information on our own, tends to be more difficult than **recognition**, selecting previously remembered information from an array of options (Bahrick, Bahrick, & Wittlinger, 1975). To demonstrate what we mean, try recalling the

retrieval
reactivation or reconstruction of experiences from our memory stores

retrieval cue
hint that makes it easier for us to recall information

recall
generating previously remembered information

recognition
selecting previously remembered information from an array of options

sixth president of the United States. Unless you're an American history buff, you may be stumped. If so, try this question instead.

The sixth president of the United States was:

(a) George Washington   (c) Bill Clinton

(b) John Quincy Adams   (d) Carly Fiorina

With a bit of thought, you probably figured out that (b) was the correct answer. You could safely eliminate (a) because you know George Washington was the first president, (c) because you know Bill Clinton was a much more recent president, and (d) because you know Carly Fiorina hasn't been president. Moreover, you may well have recognized John Quincy Adams as an early U.S. president, even if you didn't know he was number six.

Why is recall usually harder than recognition? In part, it's because recalling an item requires two steps—generating an answer and then determining whether it seems correct—whereas recognizing an item takes only one step: determining which item from a list seems most correct (Haist, Shimamura, & Squire, 1992).

Relearning. A third way of measuring memory is **relearning**: how much more quickly we learn information when we study something we've already studied relative to when we studied it the first time. For this reason, psychologists often call this approach the method of *savings*: Now that we've studied something, we don't need to take as much time to refresh our memories of it (that is, we've "saved" time by studying it).

The concept of relearning originated with the pioneering work of German researcher Hermann Ebbinghaus (1885) well over a century ago. Ebbinghaus used hundreds of "nonsense syllables," like ZAK and BOL, to test his own recollection across differing time intervals. As we can see in Figure 7.12, he found that most of our forgetting occurs almost immediately after learning new material, with less and less forgetting after that. Nevertheless, he also found that when he attempted to relearn the nonsense syllables he'd forgotten after a delay, he learned them much more quickly the second time around.

Imagine you learned to play the guitar in high school but haven't played it for several years. When you sit down to strum an old song, you're rusty at first. Although you need to go back to your notes to remind yourself the first couple of times you sit down to play, you'll probably find that it doesn't take you nearly as long to get the hang of the song the second time around. That's relearning. Relearning shows that a memory for this skill was still lurking in your brain—somewhere.

Relearning is a more sensitive measure of memory than either recall or recognition. That's because relearning allows us to assess memory using a relative amount (how much faster was material learned the second time?) rather than the simple "right" or "wrong" we obtain from recall or recognition (MacLeod, 2008; Nelson, 1985). It also allows us to measure memory for procedures, like driving a car or playing a piano piece, as well as for facts and figures.

When memorizing his nonsense syllables, Ebbinghaus happened on a crucial principle that applies to most forms of learning: the law of **distributed versus massed practice** (Donovan & Radosevich, 1999; Willingham, 2002). Simply put, this law tells us that we tend to remember things better in the long run when we spread our learning over long intervals than when we pack it

Table 7.1 Demonstration of Retrieval Cues.

Read each category and corresponding word to a friend. Then, ask your friend to recall only the words in any order. For each word your friend forgot, ask whether he or she remembers something from that word's category. As you'll see, this demonstration helps to make a simple point: Many memory failures are actually failures of retrieval.

Category	Word
A metal	Silver
A precious stone	Pearl
A relative	Niece
A bird	Canary
Type of reading material	Journal
A military title	Major
A color	Violet
A four-legged animal	Mouse
A piece of furniture	Dresser
A part of the body	Finger
A fruit	Cherry
A weapon	Cannon
A type of dwelling	Mansion
An alcoholic beverage	Brandy
A crime	Kidnapping
An occupation	Plumber
A sport	Lacrosse
An article of clothing	Sweater
A musical instrument	Saxophone
An insect	Wasp

relearning

reacquiring knowledge that we'd previously learned but largely forgotten over time

distributed versus massed practice

studying information in small increments over time (distributed) versus in large increments over a brief amount of time (massed)

Figure 7.12 Ebbinghaus's Curve of Forgetting.

This graph from Ebbinghaus's classic memory research shows the percent "savings," or how much faster information he relearned the second time following various delays (plotted in hours).

SOURCE: Based on Ebbinghaus, H. (1885). Memory: A contribution to experimental psychology. New York, NY: Teachers College, Columbia University. © Scott O. Lilienfeld.

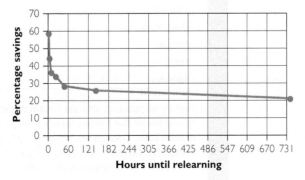

The Role of the Amygdala.

The amygdala is where the emotional components of these and other memories, especially those governing fear, are stored. The amygdala interacts with the hippocampus during the formation of memory, but each structure contributes different information (refer again to Figure 7.16). Researchers uncovered the specific roles of the amygdala and hippocampus in a study of two patients identified by their initials, S. M. and W. S. The first suffered damage to the amygdala; the second, to the hippocampus (LeBar & Phelps, 2005). The patient with amygdala damage (S. M.), who is featured in the chapter-opening video for Chapter 11, remembered facts about the fear-producing experience but did not experience the fear itself. In contrast, the patient with hippocampal damage (W. S.) experienced the fear, but not the facts surrounding the fear-producing experience. So the amygdala and hippocampus play distinctive roles in memory, with the amygdala helping us recall the emotions associated with fear-provoking events and the hippocampus helping us recall the events themselves (Fitzgerald et al., 2011; Marschner et al., 2008).

Erasing Painful Memories.

What if it were possible to erase or take the sting out of traumatic or painful memories, like witnessing someone's death or experiencing the devastating breakup of a relationship? As we've learned, emotional memories can persist, even if they often become distorted over time. The hormones adrenaline and norepinephrine (see LO 3.3a) are released in the face of stress and stimulate protein (beta-adrenergic) receptors on nerve cells, which solidify emotional memories.

Lawrence Cahill and James McGaugh (1995) demonstrated the staying power of emotional memories in an elegant study. They created two stories regarding 12 slides they showed to participants. They told half of the participants an emotionally neutral story about a boy's visit to a hospital where his father works. They told the other half a far more disturbing story about the same slides; in the middle of the story, they informed participants that the boy was injured and operated on at a hospital to reattach his severed legs. Participants returned for a memory test 24 hours later, and Cahill and McGaugh asked them what they remembered. Participants who heard the emotionally arousing story displayed the best recall for the part of the story about the boy's trauma. In contrast, participants who heard the neutral story recalled the same amount of detail for all parts of the story.

Cahill and his colleagues (Cahill et al., 1994) conducted a similar experiment with an interesting twist. This time, they gave some participants a drug called *propranolol*, which blocks the effects of adrenaline on beta-adrenergic receptors (doctors also use it to treat high blood pressure). When participants' adrenaline was inhibited by propranolol, they didn't display especially good recall for the emotionally arousing part of the story. In fact, their recall was no different from that of individuals who listened to the emotionally neutral story.

Psychiatrist Roger Pitman reasoned that propranolol might blunt the memories of real-life traumas, such as automobile accidents. Pitman and his colleagues (Pitman et al., 2002) administered propranolol to people for 10 days after they experienced a traumatic event, such as a car accident and, a month later, examined their physical reactions to individually prepared tapes that replayed key aspects of the event. Forty-three percent of participants who received a placebo showed a physical response to the tape that recreated their traumatic experience. Yet none of the people who received the drug did. Researchers have suggested that propranolol be used in combination with psychotherapy soon after a traumatic event to prevent the development of long-lasting stress reactions, such as those in posttraumatic stress disorder (Giustino, Fitzgerald, & Maren, 2016).

Pitman's pill only dampened the effects of traumatic memories; it didn't erase them. Other investigators have replicated these findings using different designs (Brunet et al., 2011; Kindt, Soeter, & Vervliet, 2009; Menzies, 2012). Still, this research hasn't laid to rest difficult questions about whether such procedures are ethical, much less desirable. After all, if we could choose to forget every negative experience, would we learn and grow from our mistakes? The mere fact that we *can* do something doesn't mean we *should*, so the debate continues.

Replicability

Can the results be duplicated in other studies?

Journal Prompt

The hippocampus and the amygdala appear to play important roles in memory formation. Describe the memory processes associated with each brain structure and how the case studies discussed in this chapter provide evidence for these processes.

The Biology of Memory Deterioration

As we humans pass the ripe old age of 65, we often begin to experience memory problems and some degeneration in the brain. Yet despite what many people believe (Erber & Szuchman, 2014; Lilienfeld et al., 2010), senility isn't an unavoidable part of aging, and some manage to make it past 100 with only modest amounts of everyday forgetfulness. But scientists disagree as to how much memory loss is "normal" during the advanced years. Some argue that we needn't accept any memory impairment as normal. Nevertheless, a longitudinal study of participants aged 59 to 84 years at baseline showed small but consistent reductions in the overall area of the cortex at 2- and 4-year intervals (Resnick et al., 2003). We might assume that subtle cognitive decline would accompany these tissue losses, but alternative hypotheses are possible. For example, cognition may be fully preserved until a critical amount of tissue loss occurs.

Many people equate senility with one cause: Alzheimer's disease. Yet Alzheimer's disease is only the most frequent cause of senility, accounting for about 50 to 60 percent of cases of *dementia*, that is, severe memory loss. Two other common causes of senility are the accumulation of multiple small strokes in the brain and deterioration in the frontal and temporal lobes. Alzheimer's disease occurs at alarming rates as people age—by 2050, one American will develop Alzheimer's disease every 33 seconds (Alzheimer's Association, 2016). The risk for Alzheimer's disease is 11 percent for those older than 65 years of age, but a whopping 42 percent for those older than 85 years of age. With the "graying" (aging) of the U.S. population, Alzheimer's disease is expected to become even more of a concern in coming decades, with 14 to 16 million Americans projected to develop the disease by mid-century if a cure can't be found (Alzheimer's Association, 2016).

The cognitive impairments of Alzheimer's disease are both memory- and language-related, which corresponds to the patterns of cortical loss in this illness (see Figure 7.17). The memory loss begins with recent events, with memories of the distant past being the last to go. Patients with Alzheimer's forget their grandchildren's names well before forgetting their children's names. They also experience disorientation and are frequently at a loss as to where they are, what year it is, or who the current president is.

The Alzheimer's brain contains many senile plaques and neurofibrillary tangles (see LO 3.1d). These abnormalities contribute to the loss of synapses and death of cells in the hippocampus and cerebral cortex. They may also contribute to memory loss and intellectual decline. Loss of synapses is correlated with intellectual status, with greater loss as the disease progresses (Scheff et al., 2007). But this result doesn't necessarily

Correlation vs. Causation

Can we be sure that A causes B?

mean that the reduction in synapses causes the memory decline. Along with loss of synapses comes degeneration and death of acetylcholine neurons in the forebrain. Accordingly, the most common treatments for Alzheimer's disease today are drugs, like Donepezil (whose genetic name is *Aricept*), that boost the

Ruling Out Rival Hypotheses

Have important alternative explanations for the findings been excluded?

Figure 7.17 Changes in the Brain of Patients with Alzheimer's Disease.

Changes include enlargement of the ventricles and severe loss of the cortex in areas involved in language and memory.

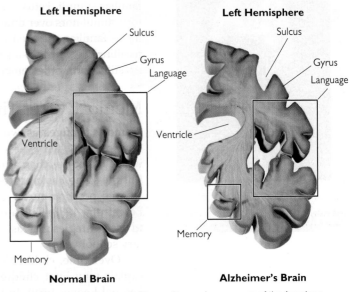

SOURCE: Courtesy of Alzheimer's Disease Research, a program of the American Health Assistance Foundation

Chapter 8
Thinking, Reasoning, and Language

Getting Inside Our Talking Heads

 Learning Objectives

8.1a Identify methods for achieving cognitive economy.

8.1b Describe what factors affect our reasoning about the world.

8.2a Discover what influences our decision-making.

8.2b Describe some common problem-solving strategies and challenges.

8.2c Describe various models of the human mind.

8.3a Describe the four levels of analysis that make up language.

8.3b Trace the development of language acquisition in children.

8.3c Identify the pros and cons of bilingualism.

8.3d Distinguish human language from nonhuman animal communication.

8.4a Identify the skills required to learn to read.

8.4b Analyze the relationship between reading speed and reading comprehension.

Challenge Your Assumptions

Are in-depth analyses generally more effective than first impressions?

Do nonhuman animals have language?

Are children who learn two languages at a disadvantage relative to other children?

Does speed-reading work?

Watch PROBLEM SOLVING: THINKING OUTSIDE THE BOX

One of the most valuable lessons psychology can teach us is to appreciate mental capacities we normally take for granted. Take thinking and language, for example. We rely on them almost every second of our waking hours but rarely notice the unfathomable complexity that goes into them. It's only when we encounter problems we have to solve or when we need to struggle to express new ideas that we notice ourselves thinking at all. The video above describes one example of the kind of challenges we face when solving problems as we navigate our way through the world.

In this chapter we'll explore the whys and hows of our thinking and communicating. First, we'll examine our thinking and reasoning processes in everyday life and discover how we make decisions and solve problems. We'll discover how our thinking and reasoning go right—which they do much of the time—and how they go wrong. Then we'll examine how we communicate and comprehend meaning using words, and the enormous challenges we face—and overcome—while doing so.

8.1: Thinking and Reasoning

8.1a Identify methods for achieving cognitive economy.
8.1b Describe what factors affect our reasoning about the world.

Nearly all of the chapters of this text thus far, and more still to come, describe aspects of thinking. Generally speaking, we can define **thinking** as any mental activity or processing of information. It includes learning, remembering, perceiving, communicating, believing, and deciding. All are fundamental aspects of what psychologists call cognition.

As we discovered previously in the text (LO 1.4a), behaviorists attempted to explain mental activity in terms of stimulus and response, reinforcement and punishment. Yet psychologists have long known that our minds often go beyond the available information, making leaps of insight and drawing inferences. Our minds fill in the gaps to create information that isn't present in its environmental inputs. Behaviorism, at least traditional forms of it, can't easily account for this phenomenon.

Cognitive Economy—Imposing Order on Our World

Given the complexity of the cognitive tasks we must perform every day, our brains have adapted by finding ways to streamline the process. That's where cognitive economy enters the picture. As some psychologists (Fiske & Taylor, 2013) have noted, we're all *cognitive misers*; just as a miser is cheap with his or her money, a cognitive miser invests as little mental energy as possible unless it's necessary to do so. We economize mentally in a

thinking

any mental activity or processing of information, including learning, remembering, perceiving, communicating, believing, and deciding

variety of ways that reduce our mental effort but enable us to get things right most of the time. Yet cognitive economy can occasionally get us in trouble, especially when it leads us not merely to simplify, but *over*simplify.

Our minds use a variety of heuristics, or mental shortcuts, to increase our thinking efficiency (Ariely, 2008; Herbert, 2010; Kahneman, 2011). From an evolutionary perspective, heuristics have probably enhanced our survival. For example, the heuristic "avoid strangers" kept humans safe from marauders and enemy tribes since before recorded history. But in some cases, heuristics can get in our way. Avoiding strangers might lead to missed opportunities, such as the chance to meet a potential mate or someone who has unique skills and knowledge to help us solve a problem. Even though our mental short-cuts can backfire if we're not careful, we've developed them for a reason: They're often useful in everyday life (Gigerenzer, 2007; Gilovich, Griffin, & Kahneman, 2002).

We process an enormous amount of information every waking moment of every day. From the moment we wake up, we must take into account what time it is, notice if there are any obstacles on the floor (like a roommate's shoes) between us and the shower, plan what time we need to get to class or work, and collect everything we need to take with us. Of course, that's all before we've even stepped out the door. If we were to attend to and draw conclusions about every aspect of our experience all the time, we'd be so overwhelmed that we'd be paralyzed psychologically.

We draw inferences that provide mental shortcuts many times a day, and most of the time, they steer us right. If a roommate's keys are lying on the coffee table, we might infer that our roommate is home. We might conclude that the stressed-looking woman walking briskly by staring at her phone might not be the best person to stop and ask for directions. Without actually tasting it (or better yet, conducting a microscopic bacterial analysis), we typically can decide that the three-week-old milk in our refrigerator has gone bad based on its smell alone. Each of these conclusions is unwarranted under rigorous standards of evidence-based reasoning. Yet most of these guesses (what we've called "intuitive" or System 1 thinking; see LO 2.1a) are probably accurate enough to be safe bets most of the time.

Cognitive economy allows us to simplify what we attend to and keep the information we need for decision-making to a manageable minimum (Kusev & van Schaik, 2013). Gerd Gigerenzer and his colleagues (Gigerenzer & Goldstein, 1996; Gigerenzer, Hertwig, & Pachur, 2011) referred to this type of cognitive economy as "fast and frugal" thinking. He argued that it serves us well most of the time. In fact, in many cases, the heuristics we use are more valid than an exhaustive (and exhausting!) analysis of all potential factors (Gladwell, 2005; Hafenbrädl et al., 2016).

One study revealed that untrained observers can make surprisingly accurate judgments about people on the basis of limited information. Samuel Gosling and his colleagues asked a group of untrained observers to make personality judgments about students by viewing their dorm rooms or bedrooms for only a few minutes. The researchers gave observers no instructions about what features of the room to focus on and covered all photos in the rooms so that observers couldn't determine the sex, race, or age of the rooms' occupants. Yet observers accurately gauged several aspects of the occupants' personalities, such as their emotional stability, openness to new experiences, and conscientiousness (Gosling, 2008). Presumably, observers were relying on mental shortcuts to draw conclusions about occupants' personalities because they had no firsthand experience with them. Recent research has shown that people's personalities, such as their levels of extraversion, can be detected to some extent from their Facebook profiles (Back et al., 2010). Interestingly, people are less able to intuit people's personality traits from online gamers' avatars and player names than from their social media accounts (Graham & Gosling, 2012) suggesting that gamers' online presence may reflect how they want to be perceived more strongly than how they really are.

Nalini Ambady and Robert Rosenthal (1993) provided another remarkable example of how cognitive economy serves us well. They showed participants 30-second silent clips of instructors teaching and asked them to evaluate the instructors' nonverbal behaviors. Participants' ratings on the basis of only 30 seconds of exposure were correlated significantly with the teachers' end-of-course evaluations by their students; in fact, their ratings were still predictive of course evaluations even when the clips were only six seconds long. Ambady and Rosenthal referred to our ability to extract useful information from small bits of behavior as "thin slicing."

Research by Samuel Gosling and his collaborators suggests that observers can often infer people's personality traits at better-than-chance levels merely by inspecting their rooms. What might you guess about the level of conscientiousness of this room's occupant?

John Gottman and his colleagues also showed that after observing just 15 minutes of a couple's videotaped interaction, they could predict with more than 90 percent accuracy which couples would divorce within the next 15 years. It turns out that the emotion of contempt—perhaps surprisingly, not anger—is one of the best predictors (Carrère & Gottman, 1999).

But cognitive economy is a mixed blessing, because it can also lead us to faulty conclusions (Lehrer, 2009; Myers, 2002). Although our snap judgments are usually accurate (or at least accurate enough to get by), we can occasionally be wildly wrong (Gigerenzer, 2007; Krueger & Funder, 2004; Shepperd & Koch, 2005). For example, people with psychopathic personality, a condition marked by dishonesty, callousness, and lack of guilt, along with self-confidence and superficial charisma, often come across to others as quite appealing at first (Babiak, 1995). It's not until we get to know them better than we realize how badly we were fooled.

Heuristics and Biases: Double-Edged Swords

Psychologists have identified many more heuristics and **cognitive biases**, predispositions and default expectations that we use to interpret our experiences that operate in our everyday lives. We'll examine a few of them here.

REPRESENTATIVENESS HEURISTIC. The **representativeness heuristic** involves judging the probability of an event based on how prevalent that event has been in past experience (Kahneman, Slovic, & Tversky, 1982; Tversky & Kahneman, 1974). If we meet someone who is shy, awkward, and a tournament chess player, we might guess that he is more likely to be a computer science major than a communications major. If so, we relied on a representativeness heuristic, because this person matched our stereotype of a computer science major.

Stereotyping is a form of cognitive economy, and it's often a result of our overgeneralizing from experiences with individuals in a minority group (such as African Americans or Muslim Americans) to all individuals in that group. So the representativeness heuristic can sometimes lead us to incorrect conclusions. Imagine we met another student who is Asian American, is bilingual in English and Chinese, and is vice president of the college's Chinese Students Association. We might judge that she's more likely to be an Asian American Studies major than a psychology major. In this case, though, the representativeness heuristic may have misled us. Although this student's characteristics may be consistent with those of many Asian American Studies majors, we also need to consider the fact that even within the broad group of Asian American students, there are many more psychology majors than there are Asian American Studies majors. So the odds would predict that she's actually more likely to be a psychology major.

The challenge to our reasoning in this example is that we're poor at taking into account *base rate* information. **Base rate** is a fancy term for how common a behavior or characteristic is in general (Finn & Kamphuis, 1995; Meehl & Rosen, 1955). When we say that alcoholism has a base rate of about 5 percent in the U.S. population (American Psychiatric Association, 2000), we mean that about 1 in 20 Americans experiences alcoholism on average. When evaluating the probability that a person belongs to a category (for example, Asian American Studies major), we need to consider not only how similar that person is to other members of the category, but also how prevalent that category is overall, the base rate (see Figure 8.1).

Many people neglect base rates when evaluating medical information (Gigerenzer et al., 2007). For example, in the experience of your textbook authors, many students who have a grandparent with schizophrenia become extremely concerned when they learn that that the risk of schizophrenia is increased fivefold—that's 500 percent—among grandchildren of people with this condition. Yet, because the base rate of schizophrenia in the general population is only about 1 percent or bit less, this means that the odds are 95 percent or greater that these students will never develop schizophrenia.

cognitive bias

systematic error in thinking

representativeness heuristic

heuristic that involves judging the probability of an event by its superficial similarity to a prototype

base rate

how common a characteristic or behavior is in the general population

---

Figure 8.1 A Floral Demonstration of Base Rates.

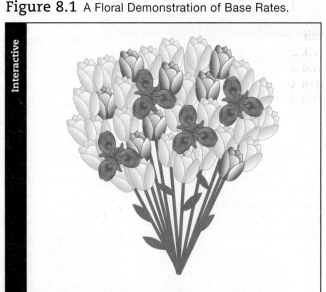

This bouquet includes purple irises and yellow and purple tulips. If we were to choose a purple flower at random, would it be more likely to be an iris or a tulip?

Did you say iris? This is a common response but it fails to take base rates into account. It's true that all of the irises are purple and most of the tulips are yellow. So it may seem like a purple flower drawn at random is likely to be an iris. But there are actually twice as many purple tulips as there are purple irises. That means that the base rate of purple tulips in this bouquet is higher than the base rate of purple irises.

Fact vs. Fiction

It's easier to think of words that start with the letter k than words that have a k as the third letter (even though there are many more words with k as the third letter in English) because of the availability heuristic. (See bottom of page for answer.)

○ Fact

○ Fiction

Our mental images of Michigan (*top*) and Detroit, Michigan (*bottom*), conjure up markedly different estimates of violent crime. In this case, the availability heuristic can lead us to faulty conclusions.

availability heuristic

heuristic that involves estimating the likelihood of an occurrence based on the ease with which it comes to our minds

AVAILABILITY HEURISTIC. We also rely heavily on the **availability heuristic** in our everyday lives. Based on this heuristic, we estimate the likelihood of an occurrence based on how easily it comes to our minds—on how "available" (accessible) it is in our memories (Kahneman et al., 1982). Like representativeness, availability often works well. If we ask you whether there's a higher density of trees (a) on your college campus or (b) in the downtown area of the nearest major city, you're likely to answer (a). Odds are you'd be right (unless, of course, your college campus is *in* a downtown area). When you answered the question, it's unlikely you actually calculated the precise proportion of trees you've observed in each place. Instead, you probably called to mind mental images of your campus and of a downtown area and observed that the examples of the campus that came to mind more often had trees in them than the examples of downtown areas that came to mind.

But now consider this example, which you may want to try on your friends (Jaffe, 2004). Ask half of your friends to guess the number of murders per year in Michigan and the other half to guess the number of murders per year in Detroit, Michigan. If you average the answers for each group, based on the availability heuristic, you will probably find that your friends give higher estimates for the number of murders in Detroit, Michigan, than for the entire state of Michigan! In one study, people who were asked about the state of Michigan estimated about 100 murders per year, but those asked about Detroit estimated 200 murders per year (Kahneman, 2011).

This paradoxical outcome is almost certainly a result of our reliance on the availability heuristic. When we imagine the state of Michigan, we conjure up images of sprawling farms and peaceful suburbs. Yet when we imagine the city of Detroit, we conjure up images of dangerous inner-city areas and run-down buildings. So thinking of Detroit makes the idea of murder more readily available to us.

Journal Prompt

Recently a couple was in legal trouble for allowing their 6- and 10-year-old children to walk about a mile from a park to home. Many parents believe that today's world is more dangerous for children than was the case for previous generations, so they do not allow their kids to walk places or play outdoors unsupervised. However, the actual rates of child abduction have not risen and the risk for getting in a car accident is much greater than the probability that a child will be kidnapped. Explain why parents tend to worry more about child abduction than about their child being injured or killed in a car accident.

hindsight bias

our tendency to overestimate how well we could have predicted something after it has already occurred

HINDSIGHT BIAS. **Hindsight bias**, sometimes also known as the "I knew it all along" effect, refers to our tendency to overestimate how accurately we could have predicted something happening once we know the outcome (Fischoff, 1975; Kunda, 1999). As the

Answer: Fact. When thinking of words with 'k' in the them, words starting with 'k' more easily come to mind. It's more difficult to generate words with 'k' as the third letter, even though we know lots of them, such as poke, take, like, wok, joke, hike, elk, ink, awkward, etc.

Hindsight Bias

Interactive

Nostradamus was a 16th-century prophet whose four-line poems supposedly foretold the future. Here's a famous one:

Beasts ferocious with hunger will cross the rivers, The greater part of the battlefield will be against the Hister. Into a cage of iron will the great one be drawn, When the child of Germany observes nothing.

After reading it, can you guess what historical event it supposedly predicted? Odds are high you won't. Yet after discovering that it's about Hitler's rise to power, you're likely to find that the poem fits the event quite well. This is an example of hindsight bias.

old saying goes, "Hindsight is 20/20." This is also where the term "Monday Morning Quarterbacking" comes from—when commentators and spectators of a football game played Sunday evening point out after the fact that a different strategy would have worked better. Even if they are correct, it's much easier to say "It would have worked better if …" once you already know that the action taken hasn't worked. For example, right before the United States invaded Iraq in 2003, many American politicians were in strong support of the military intervention. Yet only a few years later, when it became evident that the invasion wasn't going well, many American politicians insisted that that it was "obvious" that invading Iraq was a dreadful idea. Just about everything seems obvious—once we know the outcome, that is (Watts, 2011).

As we discussed previously (see LO 1.1b) we're also prone to a powerful cognitive error called *confirmation bias*, which is our tendency to seek out evidence that supports our hypotheses or beliefs and to deny, dismiss, or distort evidence that doesn't (Nickerson, 1998). As we've also learned, scientific methods help us compensate for this bias in research. Yet, as we'll discover later in this chapter, confirmation bias can also have consequences for our real-world decision-making.

Top-Down Processing

Our brains have evolved to streamline processing in other ways besides heuristics and biases. One key example is that we fill in the gaps of missing information using our experience and background knowledge. Psychologists call this phenomenon top-down processing (LO 4.6A). We can contrast top-down processing with bottom-up processing, in which our brain processes only the information it receives, and constructs meaning from it slowly and surely by building up understanding through experience. Previously in the text (LO 4.1a), we saw how perception differs from sensation because

An example of top-down processing comes from mondegreens—commonly misheard song lyrics. A recent high-profile example of this phenomenon was a line from Taylor Swift's song "Blank Space." Do you remember hearing her sing "Gotta lot of Starbucks lovers"? The real line is "Got a long list of ex-lovers," but our top-down processing leads us to think "lot of Starbucks" is a more logical parsing of the words (especially if we're frequent coffee drinkers).

our perceptual experiences rely not only on raw sensory input, but also on stored knowledge that our brains access to interpret those experiences. We also learned that chunking (LO 7.1B), another form of top-down processing, is a memory aid that relies on our ability to organize information into larger units, expanding the span and detail of our memories. Each of these examples highlights our brain's tendency to simplify our cognitive functioning by using pre-existing knowledge to spare us from reinventing the wheel.

CONCEPTS AND SCHEMAS.   One common source of top-down processing that helps us to think and reason is our use of concepts and schemas. **Concepts** are our knowledge and ideas about objects, actions, and characteristics that share core properties. We have concepts of the properties that all motorcycles share or what feature unifies all purple things. Schemas are concepts we've stored in memory about how certain actions, objects, and ideas relate to each other. They help us to mentally organize *events* that share core features, say, going to a restaurant, cleaning the house, or visiting the zoo. As we acquire knowledge, we create schemas that enable us to know roughly what to expect in a given situation and to draw on our knowledge when we encounter something new.

A concept allows us to have all of our general knowledge about dogs, for example, at our disposal when dealing with a new dog, Rover. We don't need to discover from scratch that Rover barks, pants when he's hot, and has a stomach. All of these things come "for free" once we recognize Rover as a dog. Similarly, when we go to a new doctor's office, no one has to tell us to check in with the receptionist and sit in the waiting room until someone calls us to enter an examining room, because our schema for doctors' visits tells us that this is the standard script. Of course, our concepts and schemas don't apply to all real-world situations. For example, some high-end restaurants have begun violating the dining-out schema by collecting payment from diners by credit card before arrival, so that no money changes hands after the meal. Yet most of the time, our concepts and schemas safely allow us to exert less cognitive effort over basic knowledge, freeing us to engage in more complex reasoning and emotional processing.

HOW DOES LANGUAGE INFLUENCE OUR THOUGHTS?   We've all had times when we realized we were conversing with ourselves mentally; we may have even started talking aloud to ourselves. Clearly, we sometimes think in words. But can putting our thoughts into words change our thinking? For example, if we mentally label someone as "hysterical" as opposed to "distressed," might that not influence our thinking about his or her behaviors?

There's an extreme view on the role of language in thought suggesting that we cannot experience thought without language. This view, called **linguistic determinism**, provides an extreme version of top-down processing in which no ideas can be generated without linguistic knowledge (Figure 8.2). But there are several reasons to doubt linguistic determinism.

First, children can perform many complex cognitive tasks long before they can talk about them. Second, neuroimaging studies show that although language areas often become activated when people engage in certain cognitive tasks, such as reading, those brain regions aren't especially active during other cognitive tasks, such as spatial tests and visual imagery (Gazzaniga, Ivry, & Mangun, 2002). These studies strongly suggest that thought can occur without language.

Clearly, linguistic determinism—at least in its original form—doesn't have much going for it. Nevertheless, there's some promise for a less radical perspective, called **linguistic relativity**. Proponents of this view maintain that characteristics of language shape our thought processes.

---

concept

our knowledge and ideas about a set of objects, actions, and characteristics that share core properties

linguistic determinism

view that all thought is represented verbally and that, as a result, our language defines our thinking

linguistic relativity

view that characteristics of language shape our thought processes

---

Fact vs. Fiction

Concepts are a form of cognitive economy because they don't rely on any specific knowledge or experience. (See bottom of page for answer.)

○ Fact

○ Fiction

Answer: Fiction. The fact that we have concepts that carry prior knowledge and experience with them is what enables us to be economical in our thinking, we don't have to start from scratch every time we encounter a new object, event, or situation.

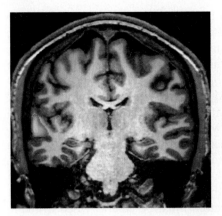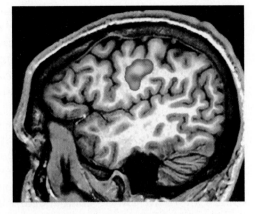

The brain scan on the left shows left temporal lobe activity, resulting from a participant listening to speech. The brain scan on the right shows the frontal and parietal lobes being activated when the participant is engaging in motor activity that is non-linguistic. Note that the right image shows no temporal activation, demonstrating that cognitive processing doesn't always involve linguistic processing.

This idea is also called the *Sapir-Whorf hypothesis*, named after the two scholars who proposed it (Sapir, 1929; Whorf, 1956). There's evidence both for and against linguistic relativity.

Several studies suggest that language can affect thinking (Majid, 2010; McDonough, Choi, & Mandler, 2003). Two researchers examined the memories of Russians who moved to the United States and achieved fluency in English. These participants recalled events that happened in Russia more accurately when speaking Russian and recalled events that happened in the United States more accurately when speaking English, even though they were in the United States when they recalled both sets of events (Marian & Neisser, 2000).

Yet in other cases, language doesn't appear to influence thought. One example is color categorization (Lenneberg, 1967). Different languages contain different numbers of basic

Fact vs. Fiction

The language of the Dani people from Papua New Guinea only has words for *dark* and *bright*, but not for individual colors. However, Dani people can distinguish colors just as we do. (See bottom of page for answer.)

○ Fact

○ Fiction

Figure 8.2 Could Helen Keller Think Before She Learned to Communicate?

Helen Keller, who lost her hearing and sight at 19 months as a result of illness, eventually learned to communicate through signs performed against the palm of her hand. After learning to communicate through sign and writing, she described her experience of the world before learning language:

"I did not know that I am. I lived in a world that was a no-world… I did not know that I knew aught [anything] or that I lived or acted or desired. I had neither will nor intellect." (Keller, 1910, pp. 113–114)

Answer: Fact. The fact that people who don't have color terms still have distinct categories of colors such as red and blue provides convincing evidence that language doesn't necessarily always influence thought.

color terms. In English, we generally use a set of 11 basic color terms: red, blue, green, yellow, white, black, purple, orange, pink, brown, and gray. In contrast, other languages have fewer terms, some as few as three. Regardless of how many terms for colors cultures have, most people around the world still perceive colors as dividing into roughly the same color categories (Rosch, 1973).

So does this mean that speakers of all languages think in precisely the same ways? No, because evidence suggests that language shapes some, but not all, aspects of perception, memory, and thought. Nevertheless, when researchers identify language-related differences in thought, it's not easy to disentangle the influences of language from those of culture. Different language communities also have different priorities, emphases, and values that shape how they think about the world. Because nearly all cross-linguistic comparisons are correlational rather than experimental, language and culture are nearly always confounded. We therefore must be careful when drawing causal conclusions about the impact of language on thinking.

> **Correlation vs. Causation** ▶
>
> Can we be sure that A causes B?

> ### Journal Prompt
>
> The Sapir-Whorf hypothesis suggests that the language we use to describe something can affect our thinking about it. Can you think of an example from your own life when language influenced the way in which you thought about an event?

8.2: Thinking at Its Hardest: Decision-Making and Problem Solving

8.2a Discover what influences our decision-making.
8.2b Describe some common problem-solving strategies and challenges.
8.2c Describe various models of the human mind.

Probably the most difficult and effortful thinking we do is that involved in making decisions and solving problems. Psychologists call these aspects of thinking "higher-order" cognition because they require us to take all of the more basic aspects of cognition, such as perception, knowledge, memory, language, and reasoning, and integrate them to generate a plan of action.

Decision-Making: Choices, Choices, and More Choices

decision-making

the process of selecting among a set of possible alternatives

Decision-making is the process of selecting among a set of alternatives. Should I order fries or a salad with my sandwich? Should I major in philosophy or physics? Which interview outfit looks more professional?

Each decision we make seems deceptively simple: It's an either–or choice. But many factors enter into most decisions. Let's take the seemingly straightforward question of whether to order a salad or fries. Such a choice often depends on a variety of factors, such as whether we're watching our weight, whether we like the type of salad dressings and fries available at the restaurant, and maybe even what everyone else at our table is ordering. For many of these small decisions, we often weigh the considerations quickly and implicitly, that is, below conscious awareness. As we learned previously (see LO 2.1a), this process typically involves System 1 thinking, which is rapid and intuitive (Kahneman, 2011). But for some other decisions, such as where to go to college or whether to get married, the decisions have much larger consequences and require more careful deliberation. In these cases, decision-making often becomes more explicit and deliberate. We mull over the options; sometimes identify and list the pros and cons of each, and may solicit the advice and opinions of friends, family, and trusted advisers. Here, we rely on System 2 thinking, which is slow and analytical.

Is explicitly analyzing the situation before making a decision a good idea? It depends (Lehrer, 2009). Timothy Wilson and his colleagues gave female college students a choice among five art posters to take home. The investigators asked half of the students to just "go with their gut" and pick the poster they liked and the other half to carefully list each of the pros and cons of each poster. When the researchers recontacted the participants a few weeks later, those who went with their guts reported that they were much happier with their choices (Wilson et al., 1993). When it comes to emotional preferences, such as which art we like or which people we find attractive, thinking too much may get us in trouble. Ironically, this may be especially true for complex, emotionally laden decisions, such as which car to buy, because our brains can easily become overwhelmed by excessive information (Dijksterhuis et al., 2006). In such cases, listing all of the pros and cons can sometimes confuse us, producing a "paralysis by analysis."

Yet when it comes to evaluating scientific claims in the laboratory and in real life, such careful analysis may be the better bet (Lilienfeld et al., 2010; Myers, 2002). In cases in which there are objectively more optimal and less optimal outcomes, such as in chess playing or business negotiations, slower and more deliberative decision-making tends to result in better outcomes (Moxley et al., 2012). In fact, business communities are increasingly encouraging managers to be more strategic in their decision-making about personnel, resources, and organizational structure. The new field of "decision management" attempts to bring scientific evidence into the business world to help organizations prosper through sound decision-making and avoid bias (Yates & Potworowski, 2012).

Marketing researchers, advertising executives, and political pollsters have long known that an additional factor influences our decision-making: **framing**, that is, how a question is formulated or presented (Tversky & Kahneman, 1986).

framing

the way a question is formulated that can influence the decisions people make

The fact that our decisions are so readily influenced by framing has important societal implications. For example, decision-making about retirement savings, medical healthcare plan selection, and student loan repayment plans is heavily influenced by framing, often leading people to make irrational decisions that aren't in their best interest. In fact, these effects have been powerful enough that in 2015, U.S. President Barack Obama issued an executive order instructing government agencies to take framing and other behavioral science considerations into account when developing materials for U.S. citizens. Richard Thaler and Cass Sunstein wrote a controversial book called *Nudge* (2008) in which they outlined the irrational decisions that people often make, the reasons they make them, and some of the ways that framing can be used to "nudge" people toward decisions that are better for them and for society as a whole. For example, something as simple as asking people to opt *out* of contributing to retirement rather than opting *in* significantly increases the number of people who save for retirement.

Researchers in a recently established field called *neuroeconomics* have become interested in how the brain works while making financial decisions (Glimcher et al., 2008; Hasler, 2012). By using fMRI to identify brain areas that become active in specific decision-making situations—such as when interacting with a person who's stingy or selfish—researchers hope to better predict and understand how emotion, reasoning, and arousal influence our decisions (Kato et al., 2009). For example, decision-making activates areas of the brain involved in processing rewards as well as areas involved in attending carefully to the relative merits of different options. Although the brain's reward areas are important for motivating good decision-making, heightened activation of areas involved in attentional control is associated with better choices (Laureiro-Martínez et al., 2015). Neuroeconomics has the potential to help us understand why decision-making goes wrong some of the time and in some people. For example, clinical psychologists have recently begun exploring how to use neuroeconomics to diagnose psychological disorders (Sharp, Monterosso, & Read Montague, 2012).

Framing

Interactive

Imagine you've been diagnosed with lung cancer and your doctor gives a choice of treatments:

1) Surgery which has a 90 percent post-procedure survival rate and a 34 percent 5-year survival rate.

2) Radiation, which has a 100 percent post-procedure survival rate and a 22 percent 5-year survival rate.

Which would you pick?

Now imagine you've been diagnosed with a brain tumor. Your doctor again gives you a choice between treatments:

1) Surgery, which has a 10 percent post-procedure fatality rate and a 66 percent 5-year fatality rate.

2) Radiation which has a 0 percent post-procedure fatality rate and a 78 percent 5-year fatality rate.

Which would you pick?

If you chose:

Surgery-Radiation: You picked surgery in the first scenario but radiation in the second. This is actually the most common response. But if you look closely, you'll discover that the two scenarios actually contain the exact same information, just presented differently. For example, 90 percent survival is the same as 10 percent fatality. But the different framing leads us to think differently about the prospect of imminent death when considering our options.

Surgery-Surgery: You picked surgery in both scenarios even though the second scenario gave you a one in ten chance of dying. Maybe you noticed that the first scenario gave you the exact same odds, just presented differently. Congratulations, you resisted the framing bias that influences a lot of people's thinking; you realized that although the scary chance of dying post-procedure was present, your long-term odds of survival would be higher with surgery than with radiation.

Radiation-Radiation: You picked radiation in both scenarios, which means you were not influenced by the framing when making a decision; many people are more likely to pick surgery in the first scenario because it offers a 90 percent post-procedure survival rate, but are scared off by surgery in the second scenario because it emphasizes fatalities rather than survival. However, you may have been showing a slightly different bias. In both cases, the 5-year survival rate would have been higher with surgery. So you may have been overemphasizing immediate survival when choosing a treatment plan rather than thinking long term.

Radiation-Surgery: Interesting! You chose the exact opposite treatment plans of most people. Most people choose surgery in the first scenario but radiation in the second. Just like the people who picked surgery first and radiation second, you were influenced by the framing of the question because both of the scenarios presented the exact same information, just presented differently. For example, 90 percent survival in the first scenario is the same as 10 percent fatality in the second. But the different framing led you to think differently about the options. Perhaps in the first scenario you were thinking about immediate survival being at 100 percent but in the second scenario you realized that long-term prognosis should also be taking into account.

Problem Solving: Accomplishing Our Goals

Many times a day, we're faced with problems to solve. Some are as simple as figuring out where we left our favorite pair of shoes, but others involve attempting to recover a corrupted computer file or figuring out how to fit luggage for a week-long trip into an overnight bag. **Problem solving** is generating a cognitive strategy to accomplish a goal.

APPROACHES TO SOLVING PROBLEMS. We've encountered a variety of heuristics, like availability and representativeness, that we use to draw conclusions and solve problems in a fast and frugal way. Although these heuristics are often effective, we can draw on a variety of more deliberate solutions too. In particular, we can solve many problems following step-by-step learned procedures known as **algorithms**. Algorithms come in handy for problems that depend on the same basic steps for arriving at a solution every time the solution is required, such as replacing the starter on a car, performing a tonsillectomy, or making a peanut-butter-and-jelly sandwich. Algorithms ensure that we address all steps when we solve a problem, but they're pretty inflexible. Imagine that you had an algorithm for cooking a mushroom omelet that includes melting some butter, but that you ran out of butter. You'd be stuck. As a result, you could either give up—or, instead, "use your head" to engage in a more flexible solution.

Another more flexible approach is to break down a problem into subproblems that are easier to solve. If we're trying to construct a doghouse, we might break down the problem into identifying the size and dimensions of the doghouse, purchasing the materials, constructing the floor, and so on. By breaking down the problem into chunks, we can often solve it more quickly and easily. Another effective approach involves reasoning from related examples, such as realizing that because oil is often substituted for butter in

problem solving

generating a cognitive strategy to accomplish a goal

algorithm

step-by-step learned procedure used to solve a problem

baking recipes, it might work for an omelet too (Gentner et al., 2009). Many breakthroughs in scientific problems in the laboratory and real world have come from drawing *analogies* between two distinct topics. These analogies solve problems with similar structures. For example, after observing how burrs stuck to his dog's fur by using a series of tiny hooks that attached to individual strands of fur, George de Mestral invented Velcro in 1948.

Distributed cognition is another approach to generating creative solutions to problems. *Distributed cognition* refers to group problem solving in which multiple minds work together, bouncing ideas off of each other and each contributing different ideas, knowledge, and perspectives. In other words, the thinking is distributed across multiple coordinated brains. Often people think of solutions that wouldn't have occurred to them after hearing someone else generate an idea. Psychological scientists have used this approach to optimize outcomes in everything from medical treatment planning to sports team performance to air traffic control (Krieger et al., 2016; Walker et al., 2010; Williamson & Cox, 2014). There can be downsides to group problem solving, especially when everyone gets stuck in the same mindset. Still, as long as everyone is willing to share a unique perspective, distributed problem solving can be highly effective.

OBSTACLES TO PROBLEM SOLVING.   Although we use a variety of effective strategies to solve problems, we also face a variety of hurdles—cognitive tendencies that can interfere with the use of effective problem-solving strategies. We'll consider three such obstacles: salience of surface similarities, mental sets, and functional fixedness.

Salience of Surface Similarities.   Salience refers to how attention-grabbing something is. We tend to focus our attention on the surface-level (superficial) properties of a problem, such as the topic of an algebra word problem, and try to solve problems the same way we solved problems that exhibited similar surface characteristics. When one algebra word problem calls for subtraction and another calls for division, the fact that both deal with trains isn't going to help us. Ignoring the surface features of a problem and focusing on the underlying reasoning needed to solve it can be challenging.

Try your hand at the two problems described below.

Surface Similarities

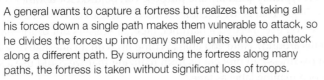

A general wants to capture a fortress but realizes that taking all his forces down a single path makes them vulnerable to attack, so he divides the forces up into many smaller units who each attack along a different path. By surrounding the fortress along many paths, the fortress is taken without significant loss of troops.

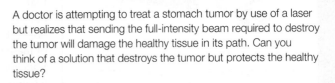

A doctor is attempting to treat a stomach tumor by use of a laser but realizes that sending the full-intensity beam required to destroy the tumor will damage the healthy tissue in its path. Can you think of a solution that destroys the tumor but protects the healthy tissue?

Solution: Did you figure out a solution to the second problem? Hint: It involves the same reasoning process as the first. Sending in lots of low-intensity beams from many directions would work for the tumor problem as well as the fortress scenario. In one study, only 20 percent of students who saw the fortress problem figured out the tumor problem (Gick & Holyoak, 1983). But when researchers told students that the fortress problem could help them solve the tumor problem, their success shot up to 92 percent. The students hadn't noticed that the fortress solution was relevant.

consequence of his own exceptional intelligence, he was fascinated by the question of what makes some people especially smart.

Galton proposed a radical hypothesis: Intelligence is the by-product of sensory capacity. He reasoned that most knowledge first comes through the senses, especially vision and hearing. Therefore, he assumed, people with superior sensory capacities, such as better eyesight, should acquire more knowledge than will other people. Even today, we sometimes refer to smart people as "perceptive."

For a six-year period beginning in 1884, Galton set up a laboratory at a museum in London, England. There, he administered a battery of 17 sensory tests to more than 9,000 visitors (Gillham, 2001). He measured just about everything under the sun potentially related to sensory ability: the highest and lowest pitch of sounds that individuals could detect; their reaction times to various stimuli; and their abilities to discriminate the weights of similar objects. James McKeen Cattell, who worked under Galton (and who became the first professor of psychology in the United States at the University of Pennsylvania), imported Galton's tests to America, administering them to thousands of college students to find out what they were measuring. Like his teacher, Cattell assumed that intelligence was a matter of raw sensory ability.

Yet later research showed that one exceptional sense, like heightened hearing, doesn't bear much of a relation to other exceptional senses, like heightened vision (Acton & Schroeder, 2001). Nor are measures of sensory ability highly correlated with overall intelligence (Li, Jordanova, & Lindenberger, 1998). These findings falsify Galton's claim that intelligence equals sensory ability. Whatever intelligence is, it's more than just good eyesight, hearing, and smell. A moment's reflection reveals that this must be the case: According to Galton, Helen Keller, the blind and deaf woman who became a brilliant author and social critic, would almost by definition have been classified as intellectually disabled. Galton's definition can't be entirely right.

Still, as we'll learn later, Galton may have been onto something. Recent research suggests that some forms of sensory ability relate modestly to intelligence, although these two concepts clearly aren't identical.

Falsifiability

Can the claim be disproved?

intelligence test

diagnostic tool designed to measure overall thinking ability

abstract thinking

capacity to understand hypothetical concepts

Galton's laboratory on display at the International Health Exhibition in London in 1884. The exhibit later moved to the South Kensington Museum where, between 1886 and 1890, thousands of visitors took a battery of 17 sensory tests.

Intelligence as Abstract Thinking

Early in the 20th century, the French government wanted to find a way to identify children in need of special educational assistance. In 1904, the Minister of Public Instruction in Paris tapped two individuals, Alfred Binet (pronounced "Bee-NAY") and Théodore Simon (pronounced "See-MOAN"), to develop an objective psychological test that would separate "slower" learners from other children without having to rely on the subjective judgments of teachers.

Binet and Simon experimented with many different items (an item is a question on a measure, including an intelligence or personality test) designed to distinguish students whom teachers perceived as plodding learners from other students. In 1905, they developed what most psychologists regard as the first **intelligence test**, a diagnostic tool designed to measure overall thinking ability.

Their items were remarkably diverse in content. They involved naming objects, generating the meanings of words, drawing pictures from memory, completing incomplete sentences ("The man wrote a letter using his _____."), determining the similarities between two objects ("In what way are a dog and a rose alike?"), and constructing a sentence from three words (*woman, house,* and *walked*). Despite the superficial differences among these items, they had one thing in common that Binet and Simon (1905) recognized: *higher mental processes.* These processes included reasoning, understanding, and judgment (Siegler, 1992). In this respect, their items differed sharply from those of Galton, which had relied solely on sensation. Virtually all items on modern intelligence tests have followed Binet and Simon's lead.

Indeed, most experts agree that whatever intelligence is, it has something to do with **abstract thinking**: the capacity to understand hypothetical concepts, rather than concepts in the here and now (Gottfredson, 1997; Sternberg, 2003b). In 1921, a panel of 14 American experts generated a list of definitions of intelligence.

They didn't succeed in hammering out a single definition, but they mostly agreed that intelligence consists of the abilities to:

- reason abstractly;
- learn to adapt to novel environmental circumstances;
- acquire knowledge; and
- benefit from experience.

Interestingly, research on how laypeople view intelligence yields similar conclusions, at least in the United States. If there's a commonality across experts in what intelligence is, it's the ability to *learn* (Matzel, Sauce, & Wass, 2013), especially when it comes to mastering complex skills (Lubinski, 2004). Intelligent people are "quick studies": They acquire complicated knowledge and abilities and do so with relative ease.

Still, there are cross-cultural differences in how people conceptualize intelligence. Most Americans view intelligence as consisting of the capacity to reason well and reason quickly ("to think on one's feet"), as well as to amass large amounts of knowledge in brief periods of time (Sternberg et al., 1981). In contrast, in some non-Western countries, laypersons view intelligence as reflecting wisdom and judgment more than intellectual brilliance (Baral & Das, 2003). For example, in China people tend to view intelligent individuals as those who perform actions for the greater good of the society and are humble (Yang & Sternberg, 1997). Geniuses who "toot their own horns" might be showered with fame and fortune in the United States, but they might be viewed as hopeless braggarts in the eyes of many Chinese. This difference is consistent with findings that Chinese culture tends to be more focused on group harmony than is American culture (Ma, Hu, & Gocłowska, 2016; Triandis, 2001) (see LO 10.4a).

Intelligence as General versus Specific Abilities

There was one other crucial way that Binet and Simon's items differed from Galton's. When researchers looked at the correlations among these items, they were in for a surprise. Even though Binet and Simon's items differed enormously in content, the correlations among them were all positive: People who got one item correct were more likely than chance to get the others correct. Admittedly, most of these correlations were fairly low, say 0.2 or 0.3 (as we learned previously in the text, correlations have a maximum value of 1.0; see LO 2.2b), but they were almost never zero or negative. Interestingly, this finding has held up with items on modern IQ tests (Alliger, 1988; Carroll, 1993; Lubinski, 2004; MacDonald, 2013). Given that some of Binet and Simon's items assessed vocabulary, others assessed spatial ability, and still others assessed verbal reasoning; this finding was puzzling.

This curious phenomenon of positive correlations among intelligence test items caught the attention of psychologist Charles Spearman (1927). To account for these correlations, Spearman hypothesized the existence of a single shared factor across all these aspects— *g* **(general intelligence)**—that explained the overall differences in intellect among people. All intelligence test items are positively correlated, he believed, because they reflect the influence of overall intelligence. Even rodents appear to exhibit *g*, or at least something very much like it. For example, in mice the capacities to master mazes easily, to learn to avoid punishment, and to distinguish among different odors are all positively correlated (Matzel et al., 2013).

Spearman wasn't sure what produces individual differences in *g*, although he speculated that it has something to do with "mental energy" (Sternberg, 2003b). For Spearman, *g* corresponds to the strength of our mental engines. Just as some cars possess more powerful engines than others, he thought, some people have more "powerful"—more effective and efficient—brains than others. They have more *g*.

The meaning of *g* remains exceedingly controversial (Gould, 1981; Herrnstein & Murray, 1994; Jensen, 1998; van der Maas et al., 2006). All because of this little letter, some intelligence researchers are barely on speaking terms. Why? Because *g* implies that some people are just plain smarter than others. Many people understandably find this view distasteful, because it smacks of elitism. Others, like the late Stephen Jay Gould, have argued that *g* is merely a statistical artifact. In his influential and still widely assigned book *The Mismeasure of Man*, Gould (1981) maintained that the idea that all people can be ranked along a single dimension of general intelligence is mistaken. Gould's critics have correctly responded that *g* is unlikely to be a statistical illusion, because scientists have consistently

Ken Jennings *(top)*, who broke the record for winnings on the game show *Jeopardy!*, would be regarded as especially intelligent by most individuals in Western culture. In contrast, a village elder *(bottom)* who can impart wisdom would be regarded as especially intelligent by many individuals in Chinese culture.

Replicability

Can the results be duplicated in other studies?

g (general intelligence)

hypothetical factor that accounts for overall differences in intellect among people

Figure 9.1 Which of These Two Puzzles Is Solvable.

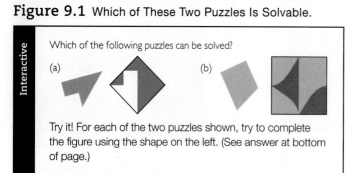

Interactive

Which of the following puzzles can be solved?

(a)   (b)

Try it! For each of the two puzzles shown, try to complete the figure using the shape on the left. (See answer at bottom of page.)

found that intelligence test items are positively correlated with each other regardless of their content (Gottfredson, 2009).

Moreover, Spearman (1927) didn't believe that g tells the whole story about intelligence. For every intelligence test item, he also proposed the existence of a factor called **s (specific abilities)**, that's unique to each item. According to Spearman, how well we perform on a given mental task depends not only on our general smarts (g), but also on our particular skills in narrow domains (s). For example, our ability to solve the spatial problem in Figure 9.1 is due not only to our general problem-solving abilities, but also to our specific talents with spatial tests, tasks examining the location of objects in physical space. Even if we're really smart—high in overall g—we might flunk this item because we have a specific deficiency when it comes to spatial problems. That deficiency may mean either that we're not inherently adept at spatial tasks or that we haven't had much experience with them. To understand this distinction, think of sports as an analogy. Some people are almost surely better overall athletes than others, but some athletes excel in certain domains (some are best at running, others at swimming, and others at throwing, for example) as a function of their specific athletic skills, not to mention their practice in these domains.

s (specific abilities)

particular ability level in a narrow domain

Fluid and Crystallized Intelligence

Later researchers found that although Spearman's g was real, it wasn't as uniform as he'd believed (Carroll, 1993; Vernon, 1971). In the 1930s, Louis Thurstone (1938) discovered that some intelligence test items relate more highly to each other than do other items: These items form clumps corresponding to different intellectual capacities. Later, Raymond Cattell (no relation to James McKeen Cattell) and John Horn distinguished fluid from crystallized intelligence, arguing that what we call "intelligence" is actually a mixture of two related but somewhat different capacities.

Fluid intelligence refers to the ability to learn new ways of solving problems. We depend on our fluid intelligence the first time we try to solve a puzzle we've never seen or the first time we try to operate an apparatus, such as a new type of cell phone, we've never used. In contrast, **crystallized intelligence** refers to the accumulated knowledge of the world we acquire over time (Cattell, 1971; Ghisletta et al., 2012; Horn, 1994). We rely on our crystallized intelligence to answer questions such as, What's the capital of Italy? or How many justices sit on the U.S. Supreme Court? According to Cattell and Horn, knowledge from newly learned tasks "flows" into our long-term memories, "crystallizing" into lasting knowledge (see Figure 9.2). Most modern researchers don't believe that the existence of fluid and crystallized intelligence undermines the existence of g. Instead, they view them as "facets" or more specific aspects of g (Bowden et al., 2004; Messick, 1992).

There's reasonably impressive evidence for the fluid–crystallized distinction. Fluid abilities are more likely to decline with age than are crystallized abilities (Nisbett et al., 2012). In fact, some researchers have found that crystallized abilities often increase with age, including old age (Salthouse, 1996; Schaie, 1996; Schroeders, Schipolowski, & Wilhelm, 2015). In addition, fluid abilities tend to be more highly related to g than are crystallized abilities (Blair, 2006; Gustafsson, 1988). This finding suggests that of the two abilities, fluid intelligence may better capture the power of the "mental engine" to which Spearman referred.

Crystallized intelligence, but not fluid intelligence, is moderately and positively associated (a correlation of about 0.3) with a personality trait we'll encounter later in the text (LO 14.5a), namely, *openness to experience* (Ackerman & Heggestad, 1997; DeYoung, Peterson, & Higgins, 2005; Gignac, Stough, & Loukomitis, 2004). People with high levels of openness to experience are imaginative; intellectually curious; and excited about exploring new ideas, places, and things (Goldberg, 1993; Nusbaum & Silvia, 2011).

fluid intelligence

capacity to learn new ways of solving problems

crystallized intelligence

accumulated knowledge of the world acquired over time

Figure 9.2 Knowledge "Flowing" into a Flask.

According to Cattell and Horn's model, there are two kinds of intelligence, fluid and crystallized. Fluid intelligence "flows" into crystallized intelligence over time.

Fluid IQ

Crystallized IQ

Correlation vs. Causation

Can we be sure that A causes B?

We don't fully understand the causal direction of this intriguing correlation. Higher crystallized intelligence could give rise to greater openness to experience because people who know more things to begin with may find learning new things to be easier and therefore more enjoyable. Alternatively, greater openness to experience could give rise to greater crystallized intelligence, as people who are intellectually curious may expose themselves to more knowledge and learn more things (Ziegler et al., 2012).

Multiple Intelligences: Different Ways of Being Smart

Up to this point, we've been talking about "intelligence" as though it were only one overarching intellectual ability. But in recent decades, several prominent psychologists have argued for the existence of **multiple intelligences**: entirely different domains of intellectual skill. According to them, the concept of *g* is wrong, or at least incomplete. For them, we need multiple intelligences to explain the story of people who are extremely successful in some intellectual domains yet unsuccessful in others.

Take, for example, Chris Langan, regarded by many as one of the smartest human beings on the planet. Langan received a perfect score of 1600 on his SAT, a widely used college admissions test, and he dropped out of two colleges in part because he felt that he knew more than his professors—he may have been right. In 2008, Langan won $250,000 on NBC's game show *1 vs. 100*. In his spare time, he wrote a book introducing his "Cognitive-Theoretical Model of the Universe," a comprehensive theory linking the mind to reality, which contains sentences like, "No matter what else happens in this evolving universe, it must be temporally embedded in this dualistic self-inclusion operation" (no, we don't understand it, either).

You can be forgiven if you'd assumed that Chris Langan is now a world-renowned scientist. In fact, for about two decades, Chris Langan has worked as a bar bouncer while holding other assorted jobs, including construction worker and firefighter. Today, he works on a farm in Missouri with his wife. Even though Langan long yearned to earn a doctoral degree and to become a great scientist, he never got close. Why? He seemed to have a knack for offending others, including his college professors, without intending to. Moreover, he appeared unwilling to tolerate the minor bureaucratic frustrations of academic life. To this day, Langan's grand theory remains obscure because he's never submitted it to a peer-reviewed journal.

The Langan story reminds us that people can be smart in different ways. (Guilford, 1967; Sternberg, 2015a). Even Spearman's concept of *s* is a partial acknowledgement of the existence of multiple intelligences, because it recognizes that people with equal levels of *g* can have different intellectual strengths and weaknesses. But in contrast to Spearman, most proponents of multiple intelligences insist that *g* is only one component of intelligence.

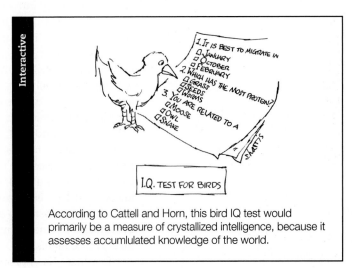

According to Cattell and Horn, this bird IQ test would primarily be a measure of crystallized intelligence, because it assesses accumlulated knowledge of the world.

multiple intelligences

idea that people vary markedly in their ability levels across different domains of intellectual skill

According to Gardner, individuals vary in the types of intelligence at which they excel. (a) Martin Luther King, Jr., was a great orator with high linguistic (and probably interpersonal) intelligence; (b) Taylor Swift is a musician with renowned musical intelligence; and (c) professional tennis player Serena Williams has impressive bodily-kinesthetic intelligence.

(a)

(b)

(c)

FRAMES OF MIND.   Howard Gardner's (1983, 1999) theory of multiple intelligences has been enormously influential in educational practice and theory over the past two decades. According to Gardner, there are numerous "frames of mind," or different ways of thinking about the world. For him, each frame of mind is a different and fully independent intelligence in its own right.

Gardner (1983) outlined a number of criteria for determining whether a mental ability is a separate intelligence. Among other things, researchers must demonstrate that different intelligences can be isolated from one another in studies of people with brain damage; people with damage to a specific brain region must show deficits in one intelligence but not others. In addition, different intelligences should be especially pronounced in people with exceptional talents. For example, Gardner believed that the existence of *autistic savants* provides evidence for multiple intelligences. These individuals, who have autism spectrum disorder (autism), show remarkable abilities in one or two narrow domains, such as knowing the precise batting averages of all active baseball players, but not in most other domains. Gardner also suggested that different intelligences should make sense from an evolutionary standpoint: They should help organisms survive or make it easier for them to meet future mates.

Gardner (1999) proposed eight different intelligences ranging from linguistic and spatial to musical and interpersonal, as described in Table 9.1. He also tentatively proposed the existence of a ninth intelligence, called *existential* intelligence: the ability to grasp deep philosophical ideas like the meaning of life.

Gardner's model has inspired thousands of teachers around the world to tailor their lesson plans around children's individual profiles of multiple intelligences (Armstrong, 2009; Lai & Yap, 2016). For example, in a class of students with high levels of bodily-kinesthetic intelligence but low levels of logico-mathematical intelligence, a teacher might encourage students to learn arithmetic problems like $3 + 4 = 7$ by dividing them into groups of three and four, having them stand in front of the class, and all join hands to form a bigger group of seven.

Yet this approach may not be a good idea, and even Gardner himself has said he isn't entirely comfortable with it (Willingham, 2004). After all, if a child has a weakness in a specific skill domain like vocabulary or mathematics, it may make more sense to try to teach "to" that domain rather than "away" from it. Otherwise, we may allow the child's already poor skills to decay, much like a weak muscle we choose not to exercise. In addition, as we learned earlier in the text (LO 6.5a), research hasn't consistently supported the claim that matching teaching styles to students' learning styles enhances learning outcomes (Reiner & Willingham, 2010; Stahl, 1999).

The scientific reaction to Gardner's model has been mixed. All researchers agree with Gardner that we vary in our intellectual strengths and weaknesses. Gardner also deserves credit for highlighting the point that all intelligent people aren't smart in the same way. But much of Gardner's model is vague and difficult to test. In particular, it's not clear why certain mental abilities, but not others, qualify as multiple intelligences. According to Gardner's criteria, there should probably also be "humor" and "memory" intelligences (Willingham, 2004). Or given Gardner's emphasis on evolutionary adaptiveness, why not

Table 9.1 Howard Gardner's Multiple Intelligences.

Intelligence Type	Characteristics of High Scorers
Linguistic	Speak and write well
Logico-mathematical	Use logic and mathematical skills to solve problems such as scientific questions
Spatial	Think and reason about objects in three-dimensional space
Musical	Perform, understand, and enjoy music
Bodily-kinesthetic	Manipulate the body in sports, dance, or other physical endeavors
Interpersonal	Understand and interact effectively with others
Intrapersonal	Understand and possess insight into oneself
Naturalistic	Recognize, identify, and understand animals, plants, and other living things

SOURCE: Based on Gardner, H. (1999). Intelligence reframed: Multiple intelligences for the 21st century. New York, NY: Basic Books. © Scott O Lilienfeld.

"romantic" intelligence, the ability to attract sexual partners? It's also not clear that all of Gardner's "intelligences" are genuinely related to intelligence. Some, such as bodily-kinesthetic intelligence, seem much closer to talents that depend heavily on nonmental abilities like athletic skills (Scarr, 1985; Sternberg, 1988b).

Moreover, because Gardner hasn't developed formal tests to measure his intelligences, his model is difficult to falsify (Ekinci, 2014; Klein, 1998). In particular, there's no good evidence that his multiple intelligences are truly independent, as he claims (Lubinski & Benbow, 1995). If measures of these intelligences were all positively correlated, that could suggest that they're all manifestations of *g*, just as Spearman argued. Even research on autistic savants doesn't clearly support Gardner's model, because autistic savants tend to score higher on measures of general intelligence than do other individuals with autism (Miller, 1999). This finding suggests that their highly specialized abilities are due at least partly to *g*.

THE TRIARCHIC MODEL.   Like Gardner, Robert Sternberg has argued that there's more to intelligence than *g*. Sternberg's (1983, 1988b) **triarchic model** posits the existence of three largely distinct intelligences (see Figure 9.3).

Moreover, in conjunction with the College Board, he's been developing measures of the second and third intelligence, which he believes are largely unrepresented in standard IQ tests (Gillies, 2011; Hunt 2010). These three intelligences are:

1. **Analytical intelligence:** the ability to reason logically. In essence, analytical intelligence is "book smarts." It's the kind of intelligence we need to do well on traditional IQ tests and college admissions exams, the kind possessed by Chris Langan. According to Sternberg, this form of intelligence is closely related to *g*. But for him, it's only one component of intelligence and not necessarily the most crucial. Indeed, Sternberg has long complained about a "*g*-ocentric" view of intelligence, one in which school-related smarts is the only kind of intelligence that psychologists value (Sternberg & Wagner, 1993).

2. **Practical intelligence:** also called *tacit intelligence*, the ability to solve real-world problems, especially those involving other people. In contrast to analytical intelligence, this form of intelligence is akin to "street smarts." It's the kind of smarts we need to "size up" people we've just met or figure out how to get ahead on the job. Practical intelligence also relates to what some researchers call *social intelligence*, or the capacity to understand others (Guilford, 1967). Sternberg and his colleagues have developed measures of practical intelligence to assess how well employees and bosses perform in business settings, how well soldiers perform in military settings, and so on.

3. **Creative intelligence:** also called *creativity*, our ability to come up with novel and effective answers to questions. It's the kind of intelligence we need to find new and effective solutions to problems, like composing an emotionally moving poem or exquisite piece of music. Sternberg argues that practical and creative intelligences predict outcomes, like job performance, that analytical intelligence doesn't (Sternberg & Wagner, 1993; Sternberg et al., 1995).

Our intuitions tell us that these three types of intellect don't always go hand in hand. We can all think of people who are extremely book smart but who possess all of the social skills of a block of concrete. Similarly, we can think of people who have high levels of street smarts but who do poorly on school-related tests.

Yet, like virtually all anecdotes, such examples have their limitations. Indeed, some scientists have questioned Sternberg's claims. In particular, Sternberg has yet to demonstrate that practical intelligence is independent of *g* (Gottfredson, 2003; Jensen, 1993). Like crystallized intelligence, it may merely be one specialized subtype of *g*. Furthermore, Sternberg's work-related measures of practical intelligence may actually be measures of job knowledge. Not surprisingly, people who know the most about a job tend to perform it the best (Schmidt & Hunter, 1993). Moreover, the causal direction of this correlation isn't clear. Although more practical knowledge may lead to better job performance, better job performance may lead to more practical knowledge (Brody, 1992). Even creative intelligence is probably not independent of *g*. As we'll learn later in the chapter,

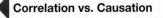

◀ **Falsifiability**

Can the claim be disproved?

triarchic model

model of intelligence proposed by Robert Sternberg positing three distinct types of intelligence: analytical, practical, and creative

Figure 9.3 Sternberg's Triarchic Model of Intelligence.

Sternberg's model proposes three kinds of intelligence: analytical, practical, and creative.

SOURCE: Based on Sternberg, R. J., & Wagner, R. K. (1993). Thinking styles inventory. Unpublished instrument. © Scott O Lilienfeld.

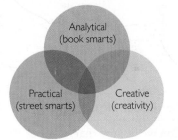

◀ **Correlation vs. Causation**

Can we be sure that A causes B?

measures of these two constructs tend to be at least moderately correlated (Preckel, Holling, & Wiese, 2006).

Thus, the concept of multiple intelligences remains scientifically controversial. Unquestionably, we all possess different intellectual strengths and weaknesses, but it's not clear that they're as independent of each other as Gardner and Sternberg assert. So there may still be a general intelligence dimension after all (Chooi, Long, & Thompson, 2014). At the same time, Gardner and Sternberg deserve credit for reminding us of an undeniable truth noticed decades earlier by Spearman, namely, that there's much more to intelligence than g, and that all of us possess specific intellectual strengths and weaknesses.

Journal Prompt

Sternberg proposed that there are three types of intelligence. Describe each of these three types. For each one, give an example from your life illustrating how you used it, and also give one example of how you could have benefited from more of it.

Biological Bases of Intelligence

One popular notion about intelligence is that it's related positively to brain size; we often speak of smart people as "brainy" or "big-brained." But to what extent is intelligence related to the brain's size and efficiency?

INTELLIGENCE AND BRAIN STRUCTURE AND FUNCTION. For years, almost all psychology textbooks informed students that although brain size correlates with intelligence *across* species, it's uncorrelated with intelligence *within* species, including humans. Yet several studies demonstrate that brain volume, as measured by structural magnetic resonance-imaging (MRI) scans (LO 3.4a), correlates positively—between 0.3 and 0.4—with measured general intelligence (Brouwer et al., 2014; McDaniel, 2005; Willerman et al., 1991). So when we refer to the super-smart kid in class as a "brain,"—the one who gets 100s on all of his or her exams without studying—we may not be entirely off base. Still, the correlation between brain volume and IQ is complicated and may hold more for verbal than for spatial abilities (Witelson, Beresh, & Kiger, 2006).

Correlation vs. Causation

Can we be sure that A causes B?

Moreover, we don't know whether these findings reflect a direct causal association. Perhaps bigger brains contribute to higher intelligence. Or perhaps some third variable, like better nutrition before or shortly after birth, leads to both. In addition, a correlation of less than 0.4 tells us that the association between brain size and intelligence is far less than perfect. For example, Albert Einstein's brain actually weighed about 1,230 grams, slightly less than the average brain. Interestingly, though, the lower part of Einstein's parietal cortex, an area that becomes active during spatial reasoning tasks, was 15 percent wider than normal (Witelson, Kigar, & Harvey, 1999). This finding may help to explain Einstein's remarkable capacity for visual imagery (Falk, 2009). In addition, Einstein's brain also had an unusually high density of neurons and glial cells (see LO 3.1a), suggesting that his brain packed more mass than the average brain (Anderson & Harvey, 1996).

Recent studies on brain development suggest that there may be more to the story. A study using structural MRI revealed that highly intelligent (IQs in the top 10 percent) seven-year-olds have a *thinner* cerebral cortex than do other children. The cortexes of these children then thicken rapidly, peaking at about age 12 (Shaw et al., 2006). We don't yet know what these findings mean, and independent investigators haven't replicated them. But they may indicate that, like fine wines, intelligent brains take longer to mature than others.

Replicability

Can the results be duplicated in other studies?

Functional brain imaging and laboratory studies of information processing offer intriguing clues regarding what intelligence is and where in the brain it resides. Over the span of about a month, Richard Haier and his colleagues (Haier et al., 1992) taught a group of eight undergraduates to play the computer video game Tetris. All participants improved over time, and those with the highest scores on a measure of intelligence improved the most. Surprisingly, participants with higher levels of intelligence exhibited *less* brain activity in many areas than participants with lower levels of intelligence (Haier., 2009). Haier's explanation? The brains of the more intelligent students were especially efficient. Much like well-conditioned athletes who barely break a sweat while running a five-mile race, they could afford to slack off a bit while learning the task (Haier, 2009). Admittedly, not all researchers have

---

Replicability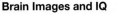

Can the results be duplicated in other studies?

---

replicated Haier's results (Fidelman, 1993) and still others have raised questions about whether the findings generalize to new tasks (Nussbaumer, Grabner, & Stern, 2015). Still, these findings raise the intriguing possibility that intelligence in part reflects efficiency of mental processing (Langer et al., 2012).

THE LOCATION OF INTELLIGENCE. Where in the brain is intelligence located? This may seem like a silly question because it's unlikely that a neurosurgeon can point to a specific region of the brain and say "Right there…That's what makes us smart." Yet intelligence is more localized to certain areas of the cortex than others. One group of investigators administered a number of reasoning tasks that are highly "*g*-loaded"—substantially related to general intelligence (see Figure 9.4).

These tasks all activated the prefrontal cortex (Duncan et al., 2000), a brain region that plays key roles in planning, impulse control, and short-term memory. The link seems to be especially marked for fluid intelligence (Cole, Ito, & Braver, 2015). Other evidence demonstrates that intelligence is associated with the density of neural connections between the prefrontal cortex (especially on the left side of the brain) and other brain regions, suggesting that the prefrontal cortex may be a "command and control center" that pulls together information from other parts of the brain to help us think (Cole, Yarkoni, Repovs, Anticevic, & Braver, 2012).

Nevertheless, the prefrontal cortex doesn't tell the whole story when it comes to intelligence. For example, regions of the parietal lobe, which is intimately involved in spatial abilities (see L.O. 3.2a), also appear to be associated with intelligence (Haier, 2009; Jung & Haier, 2007).

INTELLIGENCE AND REACTION TIME. When speaking loosely, we sometimes refer to people who don't seem as intelligent as other people as "slow." Psychologists have transported this folk belief to the laboratory by studying the relation of intelligence to *reaction time*, or the speed of responding to a stimulus (Jensen, 2006). Perhaps surprisingly, fluid intelligence appears to slightly predict how quickly people respond to a simple stimulus, such as light suddenly turning on (Woods, Wyma, Yund, Herron, & Reed, 2015).

Imagine being seated in front of the reaction time box shown in Figure 9.5 (Hick, 1952), which features a semicircle of eight buttons, with lights alongside them.

On each trial, anywhere from one to eight of the lights turn on, and then one of them suddenly turns off. Your job is to hit the button next to the light that turned off—and to do so as quickly as possible. The results of numerous studies indicate that measured intelligence correlates negatively and moderately (about −0.3 to −0.4) with reaction time on this task

Brain Images and IQ

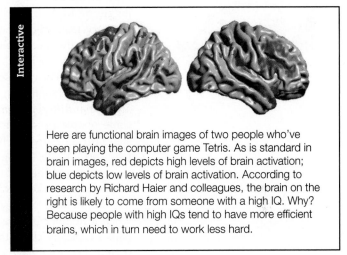

Here are functional brain images of two people who've been playing the computer game Tetris. As is standard in brain images, red depicts high levels of brain activation; blue depicts low levels of brain activation. According to research by Richard Haier and colleagues, the brain on the right is likely to come from someone with a high IQ. Why? Because people with high IQs tend to have more efficient brains, which in turn need to work less hard.

Figure 9.4 Sample Task (a Highly *g*-Loaded Item)

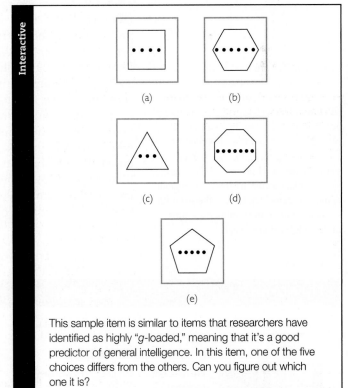

This sample item is similar to items that researchers have identified as highly "*g*-loaded," meaning that it's a good predictor of general intelligence. In this item, one of the five choices differs from the others. Can you figure out which one it is?

Answer to Figure 9.4: d. It's the only choice for which the number of dots within the figure doesn't equal the number of sides of the figure.

Figure 9.5 Reaction-Time Apparatus.

Psychologists have used a reaction-time box to study the relation between intelligence and response to simple stimuli. Typically, the red lights turn on, and then as soon as one turns off, the participant tries as quickly as possible to press the blue button next to the unlit light.

In 2016, the U.S. Federal Trade Commission ordered the popular brain-training company *Lumosity* to pay $2 million dollars because of deceptive advertising. *Lumosity* claimed that its brain-training programs, designed to boost working memory, also increase performance at school and at work and slow mental decline arising from normal aging and dementia. In fact, the scientific evidence that brain-training programs increase IQ is at best weak.

lumosity

About Lumosity

At Lumos Labs, we believe in helping people keep their brains challenged. That's why we created a simple online tool to allow anyone to train core cognitive abilities.

We're scientists and designers working together

From neuroscience to visual art, we combine many diverse disciplines to create our engaging brain training program — making cognitive research available to everyone.

(Deary, Der, & Ford, 2001; Detterman, 1987): People with higher intelligence react more quickly than other people do when the light turns off (Brody, 992; Schubert et al., 2015). They also appear to be somewhat more consistent in their reaction times (Doebler & Scheffler, 2015). So Galton may not have been completely wrong in believing that speed of sensory processing contributes to intelligence, although these two concepts clearly aren't identical.

INTELLIGENCE AND MEMORY. Intelligence also bears an intimate connection to memory capacity. Many researchers have examined the relation of tasks that assess "working memory" to intelligence. As we learned previously in the text (LO 7.1b), this type of memory is closely related to short-term memory, and it reflects our ability to juggle multiple bits of information in our minds at the same time. A typical working memory task might require participants to perform a test of digit span while trying to figure out the meaning of a proverb (such as "What does the saying 'A bird in the hand is worth two in the bush' mean?"). Scores on working memory tasks are moderately correlated (about .05) with scores on intelligence tests (Ackerman, Beier, & Boyle, 2005; Engle, 2002; Kane, Hambrick, & Conway, 2005). Indeed, an increasing number of researchers argue that differences among people in their working memory may help to explain why some people process information more quickly than others, and hence score better on standard measures of IQ (Conway et al., 2011; Duggan & Garcia-Barrera, 2015; Redick, Unsworth, Kelly, & Engle, 2012).

In light of the findings we've just reviewed, numerous commercial companies, such as *Lumosity*, market enormously popular computerized products, such as *BrainTwister* and *BrainFitness Pro*, to boost working memory. For example, they may teach users to recognize when a number in a sequence matches a previous number in that sequence. These companies typically claim that by doing so they can increase working memory and IQ; some, such as *Lumosity*, have even purported to be able to reverse cognitive decline arising from Alzheimer's disease and other forms of dementia.

Controlled studies suggest that although these products might increase working memory on the same tasks that have been trained, it's not clear that these increases extend to new working memory tasks, that is, those that differ from the original tasks (Simons et al., 2016). Put a bit differently, brain-training games appear to improve performing on brain-training games, but perhaps not much more. Most importantly, despite their company's claims, these products probably don't increase IQ (Makin, 2016; Redick et al., 2012; Shipstead, Redick, & Engle, 2012). So although working memory and IQ are correlated, these findings remind us that one can't assume that improving working memory will *cause* increases in general intelligence. Finally, as noted earlier in the text (LO 2.2c) many of the supposed effects of brain-training games on intelligence may be the result of placebo effects (Boot et al., 2013). In one study, investigators recruited participants for a brain-training intervention with a flyer that promoted the likely cognitive benefits arising from brain training, but recruited other participants with a flyer than didn't mention these benefits. Only the first group showed any improvements on a standard IQ test (Foroughi et al., 2016).

◀ **Correlation vs. Causation**

Can we be sure that A causes B?

PULLING IT ALL TOGETHER. If there's one central theme to these diverse findings, it's that intelligence is related to efficiency or speed of information processing (Schmiedek et al., 2007; Vernon, 1987). So here, common sense may be partly correct: People who are rapid thinkers tend to be especially intelligent. Still, the associations are far less than a perfect correlation of 1.0, which tells us that whatever intelligence, it's more than quickness of thinking. These results also suggest that the capacity to retrieve short-term information—and to keep this information active while we process it online—is related to intelligence, although the causal direction of this association isn't clear.

9.2: Intelligence Testing: The Good, the Bad, and the Ugly

9.2a Determine how psychologists calculate IQ.

9.2b Explain the history of misuse of intelligence tests in the United States.

9.2c Describe tests of intelligence used today and evaluate the reliability and validity of IQ scores.

9.2d Distinguish the unique characteristics of intellectual disability and genius.

Psychologists have long struggled with the thorny question of how to measure people's intelligence. The simplest way to do so, of course, would be to ask them "How smart are you?" Tempting as this approach might be, it's unlikely to work. Self-estimates of IQ correlate only about 0.3 with objective measures of intelligence (Freund & Kasten, 2012; Hansford & Hattie, 1982; Paulhus, Lysy, & Yik, 1998).

Making matters more complicated, evidence suggests that people with poor cognitive skills are especially likely to overestimate their intellectual abilities (Dunning, Heath, & Suls, 2004; Kruger & Dunning, 1999). This "double curse of incompetence," as psychologists sometimes term it, may explain why some people perform poorly in school and on the job, even though they're convinced they're performing well. As Shakespeare observed, "a fool thinks himself to be wise, but the wise man knows himself to be a fool." This curse may also help to explain the embarrassing behavior of some singers and dancers on television talent shows, who seem utterly oblivious of the fact that they're no more skilled (and sometimes much less so) than the average person off the street. *Metacognitive skills* probably play a key role in this phenomenon (Koriat & Bjork, 2005). Metacognition refers to knowledge of our own knowledge. People with poor metacognitive skills in a given domain may overestimate their performance, because they don't know what they don't know (Dunning, Heath, & Suls, 2004; Dunning & Helzer, 2014; Sinkavich, 1995).

These findings confirm the intuitions of Binet, Simon, and other psychologists that we need systematic tests to measure intelligence, because self-assessments of intelligence won't do. When Binet and Simon created the first intelligence test more than a century ago, however, they had no inkling that they'd forever alter the landscape of psychology. Yet their invention has changed how we select people for schools, jobs, and the military; it's changed schooling and social policies; and it's changed how we think about ourselves. The history of intelligence testing begins where Binet and Simon left off.

How We Calculate IQ

Not long after Binet and Simon introduced their test to France, Lewis Terman of Stanford University developed a modified and translated version called the **Stanford-Binet IQ test**, first published in 1916 and still used today in its revised fifth edition. Originally developed for children but since extended to adults, the Stanford-Binet consists of a wide variety of tasks like those Binet and Simon used, such as measures that involve testing vocabulary and memory for pictures, naming familiar objects, repeating sentences, and following commands (Janda, 1998). Terman's great achievement was to establish a set of *norms*, baseline scores in the general population from which we can compare each individual's score. Using norms, we can ask whether a given person's score on intelligence test items is above or below those of similar-aged people and by how much. All modern intelligence tests contain norms for different age groups, such as adults between 30 and 54 and between 55 and 69.

Shortly before World War I, German psychologist Wilhelm Stern (1912) invented the formula for the **intelligence quotient**, which will forever be known by two letters: *IQ*. Stern's formula for computing IQ was simple: Divide *mental age* by *chronological age* and multiply the resulting number by 100. **Mental age**, a concept introduced by Binet, is the age corresponding to the average person's performance on an intelligence test. A girl who takes an IQ test and does as well as the average 6-year-old has a mental age of 6, regardless of her actual age. Her chronological age is simply her actual age in years. So if a 10-year-old child does as well on an IQ test as the average 8-year-old, his or her IQ according to Stern's formula would be 80 (a mental age of 8, divided by a chronological age of 10, multiplied by 100).

Stanford-Binet IQ test

intelligence test based on the measure developed by Binet and Simon, adapted by Lewis Terman of Stanford University

intelligence quotient (IQ)

systematic means of quantifying differences among people in their intelligence

mental age

age corresponding to the average individual's performance on an intelligence test

Conversely, if an 8-year-old child does as well on an IQ test as the average 10-year-old, his or her IQ according to Stern's formula would be 125 (a mental age of 10, divided by a chronological age of 8, multiplied by 100).

Although Stern's formula does a respectable job of estimating intelligence for children and young adolescents, it soon became evident that the formula contains a critical flaw. Mental age scores increase progressively in childhood, but start to level off at around age 16 (Eysenck, 1994). Once we hit 16 or so, our performance on IQ test items doesn't increase by much. Because our mental age levels off but our chronological age increases with time, Stern's formula would result in everyone's IQ getting lower as they get older. By the time people turned 30, virtually all of them would be intellectually disabled, and by the fact they turned 80, they'd barely be capable of doing anything that required mental effort. Of course, that isn't the case. That's why almost all modern intelligence researchers rely on a statistic called **deviation IQ** when computing IQ for adults (Wechsler, 1939). Basically, using a statistical measure of variability called the *standard deviation* (see LO 2.4a), the deviation IQ expresses each person's IQ relative to the norms for his or her age group. An IQ of 100, which is average, means that a person's IQ is exactly typical of people of his or her age group. An IQ of 80 is a standard amount below average for any age group, and an IQ of 120 is a standard amount above. In this way, the deviation IQ gets rid of the problem posed by Stern's formula, because it doesn't result in IQs decreasing after age 16.

deviation IQ

expression of a person's IQ relative to his or her same-aged peers

The Eugenics Movement: Misuses and Abuses of IQ Testing

Soon after French psychologists Binet and Simon had developed their test, researchers in other countries began translating it into various languages. Among the first was American psychologist Henry Goddard, who translated it into English in 1908. In only a matter of years, IQ testing became a booming business in the United States. It was no longer merely a vehicle for targeting schoolchildren in need of special help, however, but a means of identifying adults deemed intellectually inferior.

The IQ testing movement quickly spiraled out of control. Examiners frequently administered these tests in English to new American immigrants who barely knew the language. It's hardly surprising, then, that about 40 percent of these immigrants were classified as having mental retardation (today termed intellectual disability). Moreover, Goddard and others adapted childhood tests for use in testing adults, without fully understanding how the IQ scores applied to adults (Kevles, 1985). As a consequence, legions of adults given his tests, including prison inmates and delinquents, scored in the range of mental retardation.

Figure 9.6 Popularity of the Name Eugene Over Time.

In the early part of the 20th century, the name "Eugene" (along with similar names, such as Eugenio and Gene) was enormously popular for boys, reflecting the powerful influence of eugenics on popular culture.

SOURCE: Retrieved from http://www. thinkbabynames.com/graph/1/0/Eugene/ Eugene_Eugenio_Ewan_Gene_Geno. © Scott O Lilienfelda.

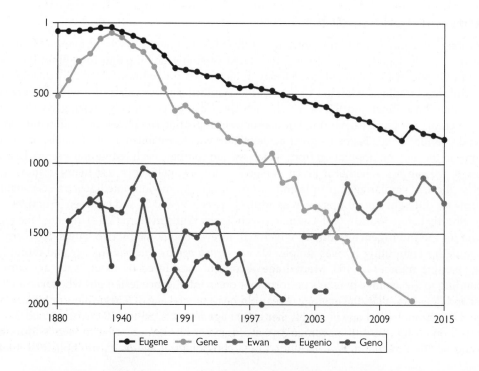

Eventually, concern with the low IQs of many immigrants and some Americans led to a social movement called **eugenics** (meaning "good genes"), a term coined by none other than Sir Francis Galton (Gillham, 2001). Eugenics was the effort to improve a population's "genetic stock" by encouraging people with "good genes" to reproduce by discouraging people with "bad genes" from reproducing, or both. Galton had been a proponent of only the first type of eugenics, but many later psychologists advocated both.

Although eugenics was by no means unique to America (Kuntz & Bachrach, 2006), it became immensely popular there in the early 20th century, especially from 1910 to 1930. Dozens of universities, including several Ivy League schools, offered courses in eugenics (Selden, 1999). Most high school and college biology texts presented eugenics as a scientific enterprise. One intriguing piece of trivia is that the popularity of the eugenics movement in the early 20th century led the name Eugene to become of one of the most frequently used boy's names in the United States (Gottesman & McGue, 2015).

Acceptance of eugenics gave rise to some deeply disturbing practices. Beginning in the 1920s, the U.S. Congress passed laws designed to restrict immigration from other countries supposedly marked by low intelligence, especially those in eastern and southern Europe (Gould, 1981). Even worse, 33 U.S. states passed laws requiring the sterilization of low-IQ individuals with the aim of halting the supposed deterioration of the population's intelligence (see Figure 9.7). When all was said and done, about 66,000 North Americans, many of them African Americans and other poor minorities, underwent forced sterilizations (Reynolds, 2003).

Disturbingly, the U.S. Supreme Court supported these sterilization practices in 1927 in the case *Buck v. Bell* (Cohen, 2016; Nourse, 2016). Ruling to uphold the sterilization of 18-year-old Carrie Buck, who'd come from two generations of purportedly "feeble-minded" ancestors, Supreme Court Justice Oliver Wendell Holmes wrote that "three generations of imbeciles are enough." Fortunately, the practice of sterilization slowed in the 1940s and had subsided almost completely by the early 1960s, although involuntary sterilization laws remained on the books in the United States for years. Virginia became the last state to repeal them in 1974.

We can still feel the enduring impact of the eugenics movement today. Many people are understandably suspicious of claims regarding IQ and its genetic bases, as these claims remind them of the efforts by eugenics advocates to "purge" low-IQ individuals from the gene pool. Still, we must be careful not to confuse a claim's validity with the people who advocate it, otherwise known as the logical error of "guilt by association." It's true that many eugenics supporters were strong proponents of IQ testing and research on the genetic bases of IQ. But this fact doesn't, by itself, imply that we should dismiss the science of IQ testing or research on genetic bases of IQ. Although it's entirely appropriate to be dismayed by the tragic history of the eugenics movement in the United States, the two issues are logically separable.

IQ Testing Today

Today, the IQ test stands as one of psychology's best-known, yet most controversial, accomplishments. In 1989, the American Academy for the Advancement of Science listed the IQ test as one of the 20 greatest scientific achievements of the 20th century (Henshaw, 2006). Whether we agree with this assessment, there's no question that IQ testing has been remarkably influential. Although psychologists have developed dozens of IQ tests, a mere handful have come to dominate the modern testing scene. We'll discuss these tests next, along with standardized tests like the SAT and measures of infant intelligence.

COMMONLY USED ADULT IQ TESTS. The IQ test administered most widely to assess intelligence in adults is the **Wechsler Adult Intelligence Scale (WAIS)** (Watkins et al., 1995). Ironically, David Wechsler, a psychologist who developed this test, was a Romanian immigrant to the United States who was among those classified as

Figure 9.7 A Sterilization Map of the United States.

Between 1905 and 1979, many U.S. states had mandatory sterilization laws, a legacy of the eugenics movement.

SOURCE: Based on data from http://www.uvm.edu/~lkaelber/eugenics/. © Scott O Lilienfeld.

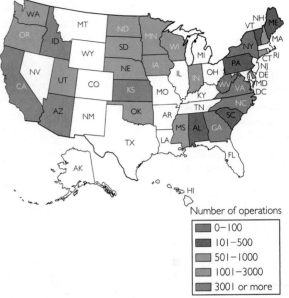

Number of operations
- 0–100
- 101–500
- 501–1000
- 1001–3000
- 3001 or more

eugenics

movement in the early 20th century to improve a population's genetic stock by encouraging those with good genes to reproduce, preventing those with bad genes from reproducing, or both

Lee Anderson, 87, shown August 8, 2006, at her home in Fayetteville, North Carolina, was involuntarily sterilized in 1950 by the Eugenics Board of North Carolina after the birth of her last child.

Wechsler Adult Intelligence Scale (WAIS)

most widely used intelligence test for adults today, consisting of 15 subtests to assess different types of mental abilities

feebleminded by early flawed IQ tests. Perhaps not surprisingly, Wechsler's negative experience led him to construct an IQ test based on more than verbal abilities. The most recent version of his test, the WAIS-IV (Wechsler, 2008), consists of 15 "subtests," or specific tasks, designed to assess such varied mental abilities as vocabulary, arithmetic, spatial ability, reasoning about proverbs, and general knowledge about the world (data collection for the WAIS 5 is currently in progress). We can find sample items from several of these subtests in Figure 9.8. The WAIS-IV yields five major scores: (1) overall IQ, (2) verbal comprehension, (3) perceptual reasoning, (4) working memory, and (5) processing speed. Verbal comprehension relates primarily to crystallized intelligence,

Figure 9.8 Sample Items from WAIS.

Eleven of the 15 subtests of the WAIS-IV (the newest version), along with items similar to those on the test.

*Note: For copyright reasons, we can't present the items on the actual test.

Wechsler Adult Intelligence Scale (WAIS) Sample Items*		
Test	Description	Example
Information	Taps general range of information	On which continent is France?
Comprehension	Tests understanding of social conventions and ability to evaluate past experiences	Why do people need birth certificates?
Arithmetic	Tests arithmetic reasoning through verbal problems	How many hours will it take to drive 150 miles at 50 miles per hour?
Similarities	Asks in what way certain objects or concepts are similar; measures abstract thinking	How are a calculator and a typewriter alike?
Digit span	Tests attention and rote memory by orally presenting series of digits to be repeated forward or backward	Repeat the following numbers backward: 2 4 3 5 1 8 6
Vocabulary	Tests ability to define increasingly difficult words	What does *repudiate* mean?
Digit symbol	Tests speed of learning through timed coding tasks in which numbers must be associated with marks of various shapes	Shown: Fill in:
Picture completion	Tests visual alertness and visual memory through presentation of an incompletely drawn figure; the missing part must be discovered and named	Tell me what is missing:
Block design	Tests ability to perceive and analyze patterns by presenting designs that must be copied with blocks	Assemble blocks to match this design:
Visual puzzles	Tests ability to organize parts of a figure into a larger spatial array	Which three of these pieces go together to make this puzzle?
Figure weights	Tests ability to reason logically about numbers	Which one of these goes here to balance the scale?

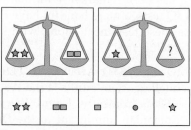

whereas perceptual reasoning, working memory, and processing speed relate primarily to fluid intelligence.

COMMONLY USED CHILDHOOD IQ TESTS. Two widely used IQ tests for children are the Wechsler Intelligence Scale for Children (WISC) and the Wechsler Primary and Preschool Scale of Intelligence (WPPSI; pronounced "WHIP-see"), the former in its fifth edition and the latter in its third edition. Both measures are versions of the WAIS adapted for older children and adolescents (the WISC-V) or younger children aged $2\frac{1}{2}$ to 7 years old (the WPPSI-IV) (Kaplan & Saccuzzo, 2012).

CULTURE-FAIR IQ TESTS. One longstanding criticism of IQ tests has been their heavy reliance on language. Test takers who aren't fluent in the native language may do poorly on IQ tests largely because they don't comprehend the test instructions or the questions themselves. Moreover, cultural factors can affect people's familiarity with test materials—and in turn their performances on intellectual tasks (Neisser et al., 1996). In one study, a researcher asked schoolchildren in England and Zambia (a country in southern Africa) to reproduce a series of visual patterns using both paper and pencil—a medium with which British children tend to be familiar—and wire—a medium with which Zambian children tend to be familiar. The British children did better than the Zambian children when using paper and pencil, but the Zambian children did better than the British children when using wire (Serpell, 1979).

As a consequence of these problems, psychologists have developed a variety of **culture-fair IQ tests**, which consist of abstract-reasoning items that don't depend on language (Cattell, 1949; van de Vijver & Hambleton, 1996). The developers of these tests typically presume they are less influenced by cultural differences than are standard IQ tests, although this conjecture has rarely been tested.

Perhaps the best-known culture-fair test is Raven's Progressive Matrices, used widely in Great Britain as a measure of intelligence, especially fluid intelligence (Raven, Raven, & Court, 1998). As Figure 9.9 shows, this test requires examinees to pick out the final geometrical pattern in a sequence (the matrices are "progressive" because they start off easy and become increasingly difficult). Raven's Progressive Matrices is an excellent measure of *g* (Neisser et al., 1996; Nisbett et al., 2012).

College Admissions Tests: What Do They Measure?

The odds are high that you've taken at least one, and perhaps many, college admissions tests in your life. In fact, to get into college you may have endured the misery of the SAT, once called the *Scholastic Assessment Test*, and before that, the *Scholastic Aptitude Test* (oddly enough, the initials "SAT" no longer stand for anything) or the ACT (which formerly stood for the *American College Test*, which also no longer stands for anything). The SAT now consists of three sections—Mathematics, Critical Reading, and Writing—with scores on each ranging from 200 to 800.

COLLEGE ADMISSIONS TESTS AND IQ. College admissions tests are designed either to test overall competence in a specific domain or to predict academic success. For many years, the Educational Testing Service apparently collected data on the correlation between the SAT and IQ, but didn't release them until about 15 years ago (Seligman, 2004). When Murphy Frey and Douglas Detterman (2004) analyzed these data, they found that the SAT correlates highly (between about 0.7 and 0.8) with two standard measures of intelligence, including the Raven's Progressive Matrices. So the SAT is clearly linked to measured intelligence.

culture-fair IQ test

abstract reasoning measure that doesn't depend on language and is often believed to be less influenced by cultural factors than other IQ tests are

Figure 9.9 Item Similar to That on Raven's Progressive Matrices.

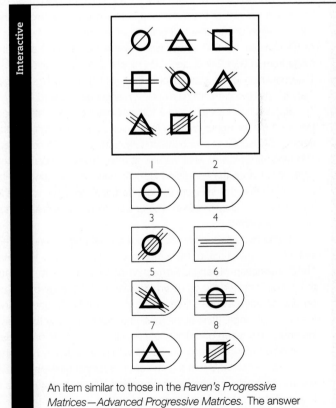

An item similar to those in the *Raven's Progressive Matrices—Advanced Progressive Matrices*. The answer is at the bottom of the page.

SOURCE: Based on Raven, J., Raven, J. C., & Court, J. H. (1998). Manual for Raven's Advanced Progressive Matrices. Oxford, England: Oxford Psychologists Press. © Scott O Lilienfeldr.

Answer to Figure 9.9: 6.

Psychomythology

Do College Admissions Tests Predict Grades?

Psychologists designed the SAT, ACT, Graduate Record Exam (GRE), and other admissions tests to forecast performance in undergraduate and graduate courses. Yet the correlations between these tests and college grades are often below 0.5 and in a few cases close to zero (Morrison & Morrison, 1995). Moreover, although SATs and GREs tend to predict first-year grades at reasonable levels, they generally do a worse job of predicting performance in later years of college (Kuncel & Hezlett, 2007).

These low correlations have prompted many critics to conclude that the SAT and GRE aren't helpful for making predictions about grades (Oldfield, 1998; Sternberg & Williams, 1997). More than one-fourth of major liberal arts colleges in the United States no longer require the SAT, and these numbers are growing (Lewin, 2006). In 2001, the chancellor of the University of California State system, Richard Atkinson—himself a prominent psychologist—argued that the SAT is only weakly predictive of students' actual achievement (Atkinson, 2001). Since then, many colleges and universities have dropped the SAT and other standardized tests as admission requirements.

Are these colleges right to do so? Yes and no. They're right that the SAT and GRE are highly imperfect predictors and that they don't correlate highly with future grades. But they're wrong that this fact renders the tests largely useless. To understand why, let's look at the graph in Figure 9.10a. We call this graph a *scatterplot* (see L.O. 2.2b), because it's a plot of the correlation between two variables, in this case between SAT scores and grade point average (GPA) in college. As we can see, the SAT scores (combined across all three subtests) range from 700 to 2,300, and GPA ranges from 1.5 to almost 4.0. The correlation in this scatterplot is 0.65, which is fairly high. Recall that high positive correlations display a pronounced upward tilt.

But let's now look at Figure 9.10b, which is a close-up of the dots that are 1,500 or higher on the x (horizontal) axis. As we can see, the range of SAT scores is now between only 1,500 and 2,300 combined. This range is typical of what we find at many highly competitive colleges. What does the correlation look like now? As we can see, it's much lower than that in Figure 9.10a; in fact, the correlation is close to zero (it's even slightly negative). The upward tilt of the correlation has clearly disappeared.

These two scatterplots illustrate a crucial phenomenon overlooked by many critics of the SAT and GRE (Sternberg & Williams, 1997): restriction of range. *Restriction of range* refers to the fact that correlations tend to go down when we limit the range of scores on one or both variables (Alexander et al., 1987). To understand restriction of range, think of the relation of height to basketball playing ability. In a group of ordinary people playing a pickup basketball game on a Saturday afternoon, height will correlate highly with who scores more points. But in a game of professional basketball players, height barely matters, because almost everyone who makes it to a professional basketball team is tall.

Restriction of range helps to explain why the SAT and GRE aren't highly predictive of scores in college and graduate school: Colleges and graduate schools rarely admit low scorers (Camara, 2009). Indeed, when two researchers examined the validity of the

Figure 9.10 Scatterplot of Correlation between SAT Scores and College GPA.

In the graph depicted in (a), SAT scores are clearly correlated with GPA. We can see an upward slant to the data points as we move from lower to higher scores. In the graph depicted in (b), the same data are depicted but only for the narrow range of higher SAT scores (1,500–2,300). As we can see, there is no clear correlation between SAT scores and GPA in this range.

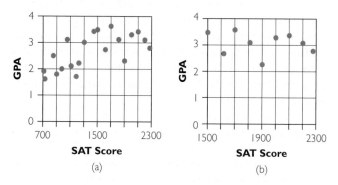

SAT Score
(a)

SAT Score
(b)

GRE in a graduate department that admitted applicants regardless of their GRE score, the GRE correlated highly (between 0.55 and 0.70) with measures of graduate GPA (Huitema & Stein, 1993). So when we remove restriction of range, the GRE and other standardized tests indeed become highly predictive of later grades.

Among professional basketball players, height isn't an especially good predictor of who scores the most points, because the range of heights is dramatically restricted.

COACHING ON COLLEGE ADMISSIONS TESTS. You've probably heard of companies such as Princeton Review and Kaplan that prepare students for the SAT and other college admissions tests. Many of these companies guarantee whopping increases of 100 points or more when taking the tests a second time (Powers & Rock, 1999).

Nevertheless, the actual benefits of these courses aren't entirely clear (DerSimonian & Laird, 1983). There's definitely a positive *correlation* between whether people take coaching courses and their SAT scores, but this association may be due to a third variable: Students who take coaching courses tend to be more educated and better prepared for these tests to begin with (Camara, 2009). Still, the evidence suggests that commercial coaching improves SAT scores slightly, probably by 10 to 15 points on average per section (Kulik, Bangert-Drowns, & Kulik, 1984; Powers, 1993).

In addition, the companies are probably neglecting to consider an alternative explanation for their advertised increases in test scores: practice effects (Shadish, Cook, & Campbell, 2002). By *practice effects*, we mean that people frequently improve on tests as a result of practice alone. So the companies may be concluding mistakenly that people who take their courses are improving *because* of these courses rather than merely *after* them. When researchers have controlled for practice effects by including a control group of people who take the SAT a second time but haven't taken an SAT preparation course, the improvements resulting from these courses have been much smaller than the companies claimed (Camara, 2009; Powers & Rock, 1999).

◀ **Correlation vs. Causation**

Can we be sure that A causes B?

◀ **Ruling Out Rival Hypotheses**

Have important alternative explanations for the findings been excluded?

Reliability of IQ Scores: Is IQ Forever?

We often think of people's IQ scores in much the same way we think of their Social Security numbers: as sticking with them for life. Joe's a 116, Maria's a 130, and Bill's a 97. Yet IQ scores aren't fixed. They almost never remain the same over time; in fact, they occasionally shift for the same person by as much as 10 points or more over a matter of months.

STABILITY OF IQ IN ADULTHOOD. IQ scores usually remain reasonably stable in adulthood. As noted earlier in the text (LO 2.2a), *reliability* refers to consistency of measurement. As we also learned, one important type of reliability is *test–retest reliability*, which refers to the extent to which scores on a measure remain stable over time. For adult IQ tests like the WAIS-IV, test-retest reliabilities tend to be about 0.95 over an interval of several weeks (Wechsler, 1997). As you may recall, 0.95 is an extremely high correlation, nearly but not quite perfect. Even across long stretches of time, IQ scores tend to be reasonably stable (Deary & Brett, 2015; Gow et al., 2011). In one study of 101 Scottish schoolchildren followed up over time, IQ scores obtained at age 11 correlated 0.73 with their IQ scores at age 77 (Deary et al., 2000).

STABILITY OF IQ IN INFANCY AND CHILDHOOD. There's a key exception to the rule regarding the high test-retest reliability of IQ tests. Before ages two or three in children, IQ tests aren't stable over time. In fact, IQ measured in the first six months of life correlates just about zero with adult IQ (Brody, 1992). Nor do IQ scores obtained in the first few years of life do a good job of forecasting long-term outcomes, unless they're extremely low, such as under 50; such scores tend to be predictive of later mental retardation. IQ tests designed for very young children assess the sensory abilities that Galton emphasized, which bear little association with intelligence. In contrast, IQ tests designed for older children and beyond assess the abstract reasoning emphasized by Binet and Simon. This reasoning, as we've discovered, lies at the heart of what we call *intelligence*.

Some measures of infant intelligence are slightly more promising when it comes to predicting later IQ. One is speed of habituation. As we discovered earlier in the text (LO 6.1a), habituation refers to the tendency to stop responding to repeated presentations of the same stimulus. Infants who habituate to a visual stimulus (like a red circle) more quickly—as measured by how long they stare at it—turn out to have higher IQs in later childhood and adolescence than do other children. Most of the correlations are the 0.3 to 0.5 range (McCall & Carriger, 1993; Slater, 1997), although some researchers maintain that they are lower (Bakker, van Dijk, & Wicherts, 2012).

◀ **Correlation vs. Causation**

Can we be sure that A causes B?

Correlation vs. Causation

Can we be sure that A causes B?

It's not entirely clear why habituation measures predict later IQ. Perhaps this correlation reflects a direct causal association between intelligence and habituation: Infants who are smart "take in" information from novel stimuli quickly, so they're ready to move on to new things. Alternatively, this correlation may reflect the influence of a third variable, such as interest in new stimuli (Colombo, 1993). Maybe infants who are more interested in new things habituate more quickly *and* learn more things, resulting in higher intelligence later on.

A related approach presents babies with pairs of pictures, like photos of faces. For many trials, the two faces are the same. Then, suddenly a novel face appears along with the familiar face. Infants who attend more to the new face later tend to have higher IQs in childhood and adolescence than other infants (DiLalla et al., 1990; Rose et al., 2012; Smith, Fagan, & Ulvund, 2002). Still, this measure has its problems. In particular, its test–retest reliability is fairly low (Benasich & Bejar, 1992).

It remains to be seen whether researchers will develop even better measures of infant intelligence. Ultimately, these measures may yield clues regarding how intelligence develops and perhaps even what intelligence is.

Validity of IQ Scores: Predicting Life Outcomes

Whatever we think of IQ tests, there's little question that they're valid for at least some purposes. As we learned earlier in the text (LO 2.2a), *validity* refers to the extent to which a test measures what it purports to measure. One important indicator of a test's validity is its ability to relate to outcomes measured at about the same time the test is administered, or what psychologists call *concurrent* validity (think of the word *current*). Modern IQ tests possess strong concurrent validity; for example, they correlate moderately to highly with other IQ tests given during the same session (Wechsler, 1988).

Another important indicator of a test's validity is its capacity to forecast future outcomes, or what psychologists call *predictive* validity. IQ scores do a good job of predicting academic success; they correlate about 0.5 with grades in high school and college (Neisser et al., 1996). Still, because this correlation is considerably lower than 1.0, it tells us there's more to school success than IQ. Motivation, intellectual curiosity, effort, and *mental energy*—the ability to focus on difficult problems for long periods of time (Lykken, 2005)—also play crucial roles. IQ scores also forecast other important life behaviors; for example, people with high IQs tend to be more politically active regardless of their views (Deary, Batty, & Gale, 2008).

Seated comfortably on mom's lap, a baby takes an experimental measure of infant intelligence that assesses response to novelty. The baby had previously viewed a number of identical pairs of photos of two people playing with toys and is now viewing two different photos of people playing with different toys. The extent to which infants look at the novel photo modestly predicts their adult intelligence.

How typical are people like Chris Langan, who have extremely high IQs but unremarkable occupational success? Less than we might think. IQ scores predict performance across a wide variety of occupations, with the average correlation again being about 0.5 (Cheng & Furnham, 2012; Ones, Viswesvaran, & Dilchert, 2005; Sackett, Borneman, & Connelly, 2008). By comparison, the correlation between ratings of how well people do in job interviews and job performance is only about 0.15, which is ironic given that many employers place heavier weight on interviews than on IQ when selecting job applicants (Dawes, Faust, & Meehl, 1989; Hunter & Hunter, 1984). The correlation between IQ and job performance is higher in more mentally demanding occupations, such as physician and lawyer, than in less mentally demanding occupations, such as clerk and newspaper delivery person (Salgado et al., 2003). IQ scores predict other aspects of job performance too. For example, they are moderately correlated (about 0.2) with whether people are "good citizens" in the workplace (Gonzalez-Mulé, Mount, & Oh, 2014).

Perhaps the link between IQ and achievement is more complex than we've implied. Some people, like journalist Malcolm Gladwell, author of the best-selling book *Outliers* (2008), claim that the correlation between high IQ and life accomplishments holds up to only a moderate IQ level, after which the correlation becomes essentially nonexistent. This phenomenon, which psychologists call a *threshold effect*, implies that above a certain level of IQ, intelligence is no longer predictive of important real-world accomplishments. Yet the evidence doesn't support that assertion: The correlation

Fact vs. Fiction

Interactive

Intelligence is essentially unrelated to job performance among politicians, especially at high levels of office. (See bottom of page for answer.)

○ Fact

○ Fiction

a.

b.

c.

between IQ and life achievements remains essentially identical even at extremely high levels of IQ (Kuncel, Ones, & Sackett, 2010; Lubinksi, 2009; Sackett, Borneman, & Connelly, 2008).

IQ also predicts a variety of important real-world behaviors outside the classroom and workplace. For example, IQ is negatively associated with risk for crime (Lubinski, 2004). As one illustration of this principle, the IQs of delinquent adolescents are about seven points lower than those of other adolescents (Wilson & Herrnstein, 1985). In addition, low IQ is associated with later health-related outcomes, including sickness and car accidents (Gottfredson, 2004; Johnson et al., 2011; Lubinski & Humphreys, 1992). Remarkably, low IQ in childhood even predicts risk for premature death in adulthood (Wraw et al., 2015). At least some of the negative correlation between IQ and illness may be attributable to *health literacy*, the ability to understand health-related information such as instructions from doctors and on drug labels. People with low health literacy may have difficulty maintaining good health behaviors, such as getting enough exercise, eating the right foods, or taking the right dosage of their medications.

But there's a potential confound here. IQ is positively associated with social class, as poorer people tend to have lower IQs (Strenze, 2007). So poverty, rather than IQ, may explain at least some of the associations we've discussed. Researchers have tried to address this rival hypothesis by determining whether the correlations hold up even when accounting for social class. In most cases, including the association between IQ and both health outcomes and crime, they do (Herrnstein & Murray, 1994; Johnson et al., 2011; Neisser et al., 1996). Still, to some extent, the causal arrow probably runs in both directions. Poverty may contribute to low IQs, but low IQs may also contribute to poverty, because people with low IQs may lack some of the cognitive abilities that allow them to obtain and keep well-paying jobs.

Low levels of health literacy, which are associated with IQ, can lead to dangerous misunderstandings of medication instructions. Some participants in a study interpreted these warning labels to mean: (a) you need to chew the pill before swallowing; (b) you should use caution when taking the medication; and (c) you shouldn't leave the medication in the sun (Davis et al., 2006).

▶ **Ruling Out Rival Hypotheses**

Have important alternative explanations for the findings been excluded?

▶ **Correlation vs. Causation**

Can we be sure that A causes B?

Journal Prompt

The text discusses several cases in which IQ tests may or may not be good predictors of later real-world behaviors. For what variables might IQ be a good predictor of later outcomes, and for what variables might it be a poor predictor? Why?

A Tale of Two Tails: From Intellectual Disability to Genius

Within the population, IQ scores are distributed in a **bell curve**. In this distribution, discovered by the German mathematician Karl Friedrich Gauss (1777–1855), the bulk of the scores fall toward the middle, with progressively fewer scores toward the "tails" or extremes, forming the shape of a bell.

bell curve

distribution of scores in which the bulk of the scores fall toward the middle, with progressively fewer scores toward the "tails" or extremes

Answer: Fiction. Intelligence makes a difference even among the U.S. presidents. Presidents' estimated scores are positively correlated with historians' ratings of overall presidential excellence (Simonton, 2006).

Figure 9.11 Distribution of IQ Scores in the General Population.

The bell curve roughly approximates the distribution of IQ scores in the general population.

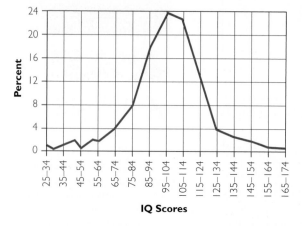

intellectual disability

condition characterized by an onset before adulthood, an IQ below about 70, and an inability to engage in adequate daily functioning

Most individuals with Down syndrome have mild or moderate intellectual disability, formerly called *mental retardation*. Nevertheless, many have been successfully mainstreamed into traditional classrooms.

Figure 9.11 shows that the bell curve fits the distribution of IQ scores in the population fairly well, with one minor exception. Most of the scores fall in the broad middle of the distribution; about 95 percent of us have IQs between 70 and 130. The curve contains a small bump on the left, indicating that there are more very low IQ scores than we'd expect from a perfect bell curve. These extreme scores are probably a consequence of *assortative mating* (Mackintosh, 1998): the tendency of individuals with similar genes to bear children together. In this case, individuals with intellectual disabilities of various sorts are especially likely to parent a child with other individuals with such disabilities, probably because they frequent the same locations (such as special schools), then develop a relationship and have children.

Let's now look at what we know about the two tails of the IQ score distribution: intellectual disability and genius.

INTELLECTUAL DISABILITY Psychologists define **intellectual disability**, once called *mental retardation*, by means of three criteria, *all* of which must be present: (1) onset prior to adulthood; (2) IQ below approximately 70; and (3) inadequate adaptive functioning, as assessed by difficulties with dressing and feeding oneself, communicating with others, and managing other basic life skills (Greenspan & Switzky, 2003). The adaptive functioning criterion largely explains why about two-thirds of children with intellectual disability lose this diagnosis in adulthood (Grossman, 1983); as individuals acquire life-functioning skills, they no longer qualify for this diagnosis. The definition of intellectual disability has taken on new importance over the past decade with the 2002 Supreme Court decision of *Atkins v. Virginia*, which ruled that criminals with what the court then termed "mental retardation" can't be executed.

Some experts also emphasize *gullibility* (the susceptibility to being duped by others) as a criterion for intellectual disability, in part for social policy reasons. A diagnosis of intellectual disability qualifies individuals for additional government services. For this reason, the inability to protect oneself from being taken advantage of by others should be weighted heavily in determining whether a person is intellectually disabled (Greenspan, Loughlin, & Black, 2001; Greenspan & Woods, 2014).

About 1 percent of persons in the United States, most of them males, fulfill the criteria for intellectual disability (American Psychiatric Association, 2013). The current system of psychiatric diagnosis classifies intellectual disability into four categories: mild (once called *educable*), moderate (once called *trainable*), severe, and profound. Contrary to popular conception, most individuals with intellectual disability—at least 85 percent—fall into the "mild" category. In most cases, children with mild disability can be integrated or *mainstreamed* into regular classrooms. Contrary to what we might expect, the more severe the intellectual disability, the *less* likely it is to run in families (Reed & Reed, 1965). Mild forms of intellectual disability are typically due to a mix of genetic and environmental influences that parents pass on to their children. In contrast, severe forms of intellectual disability are more often the result of rare genetic mutations or accidents during birth, neither of which tend to be transmitted within families.

There are at least 200 different causes of intellectual disability. Two of the most common genetic conditions associated with intellectual disability are fragile X syndrome, which is produced by a mutation on the X chromosome (females have two copies of this chromosome; males, only one), and Down syndrome, which is the result of an extra copy of chromosome 21. Most children with Down syndrome have either mild or moderate intellectual disability. Nevertheless, a subset of individuals with Down syndrome known as *mosaics* (so called because only some of their cells contain an extra chromosome 21) have relatively normal IQs. People with Down syndrome typically exhibit a distinctive pattern of physical features, including a flat nose, upwardly slanted eyes, a protruding tongue, and a short neck. The prevalence of Down syndrome rises sharply with the birth mother's age; at age 30, it's less than 1 in 1,000, but by age 49, it's about 1 in 12 (Hook & Lindsjo, 1978).

Fact vs. Fiction

The terms *moron, imbecile,* and *idiot,* today used in everyday language as insults, once referred to differing levels of intellectual disability: mild (moron), moderate to severe (imbecile), and profound (idiot). (See bottom of page for answer.)

○ Fact

○ Fiction

Fortunately, societal attitudes toward individuals with intellectual disabilities have improved dramatically over the past century. The Americans with Disabilities Act (ADA), passed in 1990, outlawed job and educational discrimination on the basis of mental and physical disabilities, and the Individuals with Disabilities Education Act (IDEA), passed in 1996, provided federal aid to states and local educational districts for accommodations for youth with mental and physical disabilities. Both ADA and IDEA have helped bring those with intellectual disabilities out of institutions and into our workplaces and schools. As we increase our regular contact with these individuals, such laws may further erode the lingering stigma that some Americans feel toward these members of society. In 2010, U.S. President Barack Obama signed into law "Rosa's Bill" (named after Rosa Marcellino, an intellectually disabled girl in Maryland with Down syndrome), which officially changed the term *mental retardation* to *intellectual disability.* Because *retarded* means "slow," this new terminology should hopefully alleviate some of the unwarranted stigma associated with intellectual disability.

GENIUS AND EXCEPTIONAL INTELLIGENCE. Let's now turn to the opposite tail of the bell curve. If you're fortunate enough to score in the top 2 percent of the IQ range, you'll qualify for membership in an organization called Mensa. A large proportion of individuals with IQs at or near this range populate certain occupations, such as physician, lawyer, engineer, and professor (Herrnstein & Murray, 1994; Sorjonen et al., 2012) (see Figure 9.12). Yet we know relatively little about the psychological characteristics of individuals with high

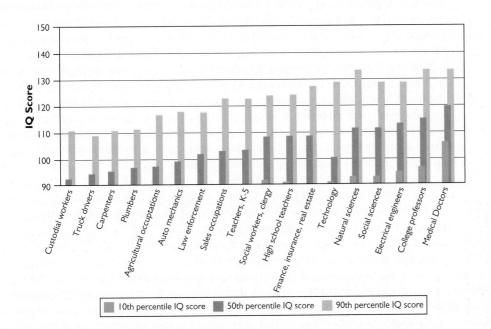

Figure 9.12 IQ Scores among Select Professions.

A study of IQ scores reveals that among a range of professions, medicine, college-level teaching, and engineering attract those with the highest average IQs. However, at least 50 percent of those in every profession score above 90 on IQ tests. There are highly intelligent people in every profession.

SOURCE: Based on Hauser, 2002.

Answer: Fact. Sadly, these words have persisted in everyday language as insults, adding to the needless stigma often experienced by individuals with intellectual disability (Scheerenberger, 1983).

Figure 9.13 The Trajectories of Highly Gifted Students.

In the Johns Hopkins University data (which were later transferred to Vanderbilt University), students who scored in the top 1 percent of the SAT Mathematics Section at age 13 (shown there as "Q4") exceeded almost all other students in their percentage of doctoral degrees, science, technology, engineering, and math (STEM) doctoral degrees and publications, patents for new inventions, and income as adults.

SOURCE: How to raise a genius: lessons from a 45-year study of super-smart children. 2016. © Nature Publishing Group. Reproduced with permission via CCC.

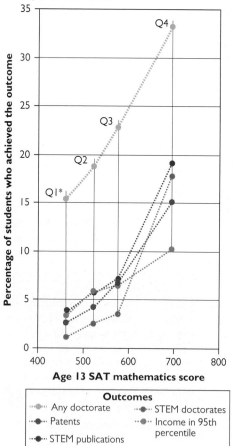

Top of the charts

Long-term studies of gifted students—those who scored in the top 1 percent as adolescents on the mathematics section of the SAT—reveal that people at the very top of the range went on to outperform the others.

Outcomes
- Any doctorate
- Patents
- STEM publications
- STEM doctorates
- Income in 95th percentile

*Students were split into quartiles (Q1–4) on the basis of their maths SAT score at age 13.

IQs or their academic, occupational, and social performance over time. Several studies offer tantalizing clues.

In the 1920s, Lewis Terman and his colleagues (Terman & Oden, 1959) initiated one of the classic studies of intellectually gifted individuals. From some 250,000 junior high school students in California, Terman selected about 1,500 who had IQs of about 135 or higher. He tracked these individuals, known affectionately as Terman's "Termites," for several decades (some are still alive today). Although Terman's study was flawed, in part because he didn't recruit a control group of individuals with average or low IQs, it refuted two common misconceptions regarding people with high IQs.

First, contradicting the common belief that almost all child prodigies "burn out" in adulthood, Terman's participants became a highly distinguished group: 97 earned doctoral degrees, 57 earned medical degrees, and 92 earned law degrees. These numbers are all much higher than what we'd expect from the general population (Leslie, 2000). A later study, initiated at Johns Hopkins University in Baltimore, examined an even more select group—young adolescents who scored in the top 0.001 percent (that's 1 in 10,000) on tests of verbal or mathematical ability. As discussed in the video opening this chapter, the results were similar. By their early 20s, these individuals were attending graduate school at a rate more than 50 times higher than that in the general population and many had already published scientific or literary articles (Lubinski, 2009; Lubinski et al., 2006; Makel, Kell, Lubinski, Putallaz, & Benbow, 2016). A related study, also conducted at Johns Hopkins, similarly found high rates of artistic and other achievements among individuals who scored in the top 1 percent of college entrance exams. One of these individuals was an aspiring young artist named Stefani Germanotta. You know her today as Lady Gaga (Clynes, 2016). Why some exceedingly talented individuals excel whether others do not, however, remains a fascinating scientific mystery.

Second, Terman's results disputed the popular notion that there's an intimate link between genius and madness. Although the absence of a control group makes it difficult to know for certain, his findings pointed to slightly lower rates of mental illness and suicide among his adult Termites compared with the general population. Later researchers have found broadly similar results (Simonton & Song, 2009), although a few have reported that exceedingly intelligent children, such as those with IQs above 180, may be at heightened risk for selected mental health problems, especially loneliness and depression (Janos & Robinson, 1985; Winner, 1999). These negative outcomes may stem from the greater ridicule and isolation that these children experience. Still, there's scant evidence that high intelligence is associated with high levels of severe mental illness.

What's the recipe for creating a genius? We don't know, although as we'll soon discover, genetic factors almost certainly play a significant role. Still, as the brilliant inventor Thomas Edison said famously, "Genius is 1 percent inspiration, 99 percent perspiration." Here common wisdom, which tells us that "practice makes perfect," is partly, although not entirely, correct: One of the best predictors of exceptional career success in violin, piano, ballet, chess, and sports is the sheer amount of time we spend in practice. The most talented musicians practice twice as much as the less talented ones (Ericsson, Krampe, & Tesch-Römer, 1993; Gladwell, 2008).

Still, the causal arrow here isn't clear. Greater amounts of practice could be causing greater success, or greater levels of initial talent could be causing greater amounts of practice. We won't

◀ **Correlation vs. Causation**

Can we be sure that A causes B?

spend 10 hours a day perfecting our guitar playing unless we're decent at it to begin with. In addition, research suggests that across many domains, such as science, art, and music, individuals rarely attain remarkable intellectual accomplishments until they've dedicated themselves intensely for a lengthy period of time. Indeed, some people even refer to the "10,000-hour rule," meaning that outstanding achievements in a specific domain aren't possible until people have practiced in it for at least 10,000 hours, or about 10 years on average. (Gladwell, 2008; Simonton, 1997). So the familiar Hollywood stereotype of the teenager or young adult who achieves astonishing intellectual brilliance with virtually no effort is exceedingly unrealistic.

Still, we shouldn't exaggerate the role of practice. Practice is probably necessary, but not sufficient, to achieve excellence. Recent analyses indicate that across many disciplines, including music, art, and athletics, deliberate practice accounts for only a minority of the success across individuals (Macnamara, Hambrick, & Oswald, 2014). For example, in both sports and music, it probably counts for about 20 percent. So although practice certainly matters, it may not matter much unless we're blessed with innate talent in our chosen domains.

9.3: Genetic and Environmental Influences on IQ

9.3a Explain how genetic influences can be determined from family, twin, and adoption studies.

9.3b Identify potential environmental influences on IQ.

Up to this point, we've talked at length about what intelligence is and how we measure it. But we've said little about its causes or about the relative roles of nature and nurture in its development. Over the past few decades, psychologists have obtained a better handle on the genetic and environmental contributors to IQ. As we'll discover, however, significant flash points of controversy remain.

Movie Portrayal of Geniuses

Hollywood movies like the 1997 movie *Good Will Hunting* are not accurate in their portrayal of childhood or adolescent geniuses exerting minimal effort to make astonishing discoveries. Research shows that such discoveries almost always require a decade or more of hard, concentrated work in specific areas.

Exploring Genetic Influences on IQ

As we learned earlier in the text (LO 3.5b), scientists can study genetic influences on psychological characteristics in three major ways: family studies, twin studies, and adoption studies. They've done so for intelligence, and with surprisingly consistent results.

FAMILY STUDIES. *Family studies*, as you'll recall, allow us to determine the extent to which a trait "runs" or goes together in intact families, those in which all family members live in the same home. Sir Francis Galton, who coined the phrase *nature and nurture* (Galton, 1876), conducted one of the first family studies of intelligence. He gathered data on the extent to which persons renowned for their intellectual accomplishments had biological relatives who were also renowned for their intellectual accomplishments. He found that the proportion of relatives who'd achieved intellectual greatness declined steadily with increasing biological distance. Intellectually brilliant individuals had many first-degree relatives (parents, siblings, and children) who were also brilliant, but fewer second-degree relatives (such as cousins) and still fewer third-degree relatives (such as second cousins) who were brilliant. Later studies have confirmed that IQ runs in families: The correlation of IQ for brothers and sisters raised in the same family is about 0.45, whereas for cousins it's about 0.15 (Bouchard & McGue, 1981; Plomin & Petrill, 1997). Galton (1869) concluded that these findings demonstrated a genetic basis to intellectual greatness, but he overlooked a crucial limitation that applies to all family studies: *Studies of intact families don't allow us to distinguish the effects of genes from those of the environment.* As a consequence, when a trait runs in families, we don't know whether it's for genetic reasons, environmental reasons, or a mix of both.

TWIN STUDIES. Because family studies don't permit investigators to disentangle the effects of nature from those of nurture, they've turned to more informative research designs. Among them are *twin studies*, which typically compare correlations in a trait in two types of twins: identical (monozygotic) and fraternal (dizygotic).

The logic of the twin design is straightforward. Because identical twins share twice as many of their genes on average as fraternal twins, we can compare the correlations in IQ in these two twin types. Given a handful of assumptions we won't bother with here, higher identical than fraternal twin correlations strongly suggest genetic influence on a trait. In almost all cases, studies of twins reared together have offered evidence of

Twin studies of intelligence typically compare the mental performance of identical (*top*) versus fraternal (*bottom*) twins.

considerably higher identical than fraternal twin correlations for IQ (Bouchard & McGue, 1981; Loehlin, Willerman, & Horn, 1988; Shakeshaft et al., 2015; Toga & Thompson, 2005). In typical studies of IQ, identical twin correlations have been in the 0.7- to 0.8-range, whereas fraternal twin correlations have been in the 0.3- to 0.4-range. Nevertheless, in all studies of twins raised together, identical twin correlations have been considerably lower than 1.0.

These findings tell us two things. First, the much higher identical than fraternal twin correlations tell us that IQ is influenced by genetic factors. The best estimate for the heritability of IQ falls somewhere between 40 and 70 percent (Brody, 1992; Devlin, Daniels, & Roeder, 1997). Interestingly, the heritability of IQ seems to increase from about only 20 percent in infancy to about 80 percent in adulthood (McClearn et al., 1997; Plomin & Deary, 2015), perhaps because people become less influenced by their environments, especially their parents, as they move away from home.

The twin findings don't tell us which genes are relevant to intelligence, and investigators have tried with mixed success to pinpoint genes specific to intelligence (Chabris et al., 2012). Whatever these genes are, they appear to slice across multiple domains of mental ability, including attention, working memory, and perhaps even risk for Alzheimer's disease (Plomin & Kovas, 2005; Plomin & Deary, 2015; Posthuma & de Gues, 2006). Moreover, it's clear that intelligence isn't due to only one or even a small number of genes; instead, it appears to be tied to enormous numbers of genes, each probably exerting tiny effects on brain functioning (Davies et al., 2011). Hence, it's clear that there's no "gene" for intelligence, or even just a few genes.

There appears to be one notable exception to the moderate to high heritability of IQ. Increasing evidence suggests that the heritability of IQ may be very low in individuals, especially children, at or below the poverty line (Deary, Spinath, & Bates, 2006; Nisbett et al., 2012; Rowe, Jacobson, & Van den Oord, 1999; Turkheimer et al., 2003). These findings raise the possibility that at high levels of environmental deprivation, the effects of environment on intelligence may largely swamp out the effects of genes. In contrast, when environments are optimal, they may allow people to actualize their genetic potential toward learning and seeking out new information, thereby boosting their intelligence (Tucker-Drob, Briley, & Harden, 2013). These intriguing findings also remind us that heritability isn't a fixed number, because it can be influenced by the range of environments in our sample (see LO 3.5b). In this case, because people in poor neighborhoods often have restricted access to environmental resources like books and computers, there's less opportunity for them to realize their genetic potential for intelligence (Nisbett et al., 2012).

Second, twin findings provide convincing evidence for environmental influences on IQ, because the identical twin correlations for IQ are always far less than perfect. Given that identical twins share 100 percent of their genes, they would correlate 1.0 if genetic influences alone were operative (assuming the IQ tests are highly reliable). The fact that they correlate less than 1.0 tells us that environmental influences also play a role, although the studies don't tell us what these influences are.

Ruling Out Rival Hypotheses

Have important alternative explanations for the findings been excluded?

Thus far, we've discussed only studies of twins raised together. These studies are vulnerable to a rival hypothesis: Perhaps identical twins are more similar than fraternal twins because they spend more time together. To exclude this possibility, investigators have conducted studies of identical and fraternal twins reared apart since birth or shortly after birth. During the 1980s and 1990s, Thomas Bouchard and his colleagues at the University of Minnesota conducted the landmark study of twins reared apart. Remarkably, the results of this study revealed that a sample of more than 40 identical twin pairs reared apart were just as similar on three measures of IQ (including the WAIS and Raven's Progressive Matrices) as were identical twins reared together (Bouchard et al., 1990). Other investigators have replicated these findings (Pederson et al., 1992); although because twins reared apart are extremely rare, the sample sizes of these studies are relatively low.

Replicability

Can the results be duplicated in other studies?

ADOPTION STUDIES. As we've seen, studies of intact family members are limited because they can't disentangle genetic from environmental influences. To address this shortcoming, psychologists have turned to *adoption studies*, which examine the extent to which children adopted into new homes resemble their adoptive versus their biological parents. Adoption studies allow us to separate environmental from genetic effects on IQ, because adoptees are raised by parents with whom they share an environment but not genes. One potential confound in adoption studies is *selective placement*: Adoption agencies frequently place children in homes similar to those of the biological parents (DeFries & Plomin, 1978; Tully, Iacono, & McGue, 2008). This confound can lead investigators to mistakenly interpret the similarity between adoptive children and adoptive parents as an environmental effect. In adoption studies of IQ, researchers often try to control for selective placement by correcting statistically for the correlation in IQ between biological and adoptive parents.

Adoption studies have established a clear contribution of the environment to IQ. For example, adopted children who come from extremely deprived environments show an increase in IQ when adopted into homes that provide more enriched environments (Capron & Duyme, 1989). In one study of French children raised in a very poor environment, children who were adopted showed an average 16-point IQ edge over children who weren't (Schiff et al., 1982).

But do adopted children's IQs resemble their biological parents' IQs? The results of adoption studies indicate that the IQs of adopted children tend to be similar to the IQs of their biological parents, offering evidence of genetic influence. As young children, adoptees tend to resemble the adoptive parents in IQ, but this resemblance dissipates once these children become older and approach adolescence (Loehlin, Horn, & Willerman, 1989; Phillips & Fulker, 1989; Plomin et al., 1997).

Many children adopted from environments of severe deprivation, such as this orphanage in Romania, show increases in IQ after immersion in a healthier and more attentive adoptive environment.

Exploring Environmental Influences on IQ

So twin and adoption studies paint a consistent picture: Both genes and environment affect IQ scores. But these studies leave a mysterious question unanswered: What exactly are these environmental factors? Psychologists don't know for sure, although they've made significant inroads toward identifying promising candidates. As we'll see, environmental influences can include not only the *social* environment, such as school and parents, but also the *biological* environment, such as the availability of nutrients and exposure to toxic substances (lead, for instance). We'll also discover that the evidence for some of these environmental influences is more compelling than for others.

DOES HOW WE THINK ABOUT INTELLIGENCE AFFECT IQ? Recent research suggests that how we conceptualize intelligence—our "mind-set" about intelligence—may actually influence our intelligence. Carol Dweck (2002, 2006) showed that people who believe that intelligence is a fixed entity that doesn't change tend to take fewer academic risks, such as enrolling in challenging classes. According to Dweck, they think, "If I do really poorly in a class, it probably means I'm stupid, and I can't do anything about that." After failing on a problem, they tend to become discouraged and give up, probably because they assume they can't boost their intelligence. In contrast, people who believe that intelligence is a flexible process that can increase over time tend to take more academic risks; they think, "If I do really poorly in a class, I can still do better next time." They tend to persist after failing on a problem, probably because they believe that effort can pay off (Dweck, 2015). As a consequence, they may perform better in the long run on challenging intellectual tasks (Salekin, Lester, & Sellers, 2012). Nevertheless, because not all researchers have found that mind-sets regarding intelligence are associated with performance on mental tests, these claims require further investigation (Glenn, 2010).

BIRTH ORDER: ARE OLDER SIBLINGS WISER? In the 1970s, Robert Zajonc (whose name, oddly enough, rhymes with *science*), created a stir by arguing that later-born children tend to be less intelligent than earlier-born children (Zajonc, 1976). According to Zajonc, IQ declines steadily with increasing numbers of children in a family. He even authored an article in the popular magazine *Psychology Today* entitled "Dumber by the Dozen" (Zajonc, 1975).

In one respect, Zajonc was right: Later-born children tend to have very slightly lower IQs (on the order of a few points at most) than do earlier-born children (Damian & Roberts, 2015; Kristensen & Bjerkedal, 2007). But it's not clear that he interpreted this weak correlation correctly. Here's the problem: Parents with lower IQs are slightly more likely to have many children than are parents with higher IQs. As a consequence, when we look across families, birth order is associated with IQ, but only because low-IQ families have a larger number of later-born children than do high-IQ

> ◀ **Replicability**
>
> Have important alternative explanations for the findings been excluded?

> ◀ **Correlation vs. Causation**
>
> Can we be sure that A causes B?

families. In contrast, when we look *within* families, the relationship between birth order and IQ becomes smaller and may even vanish (Michalski & Shackelford, 2001; Rodgers et al., 2000). So a more accurate way to state the correlation is that children who come from larger families have slightly lower IQs than do children who come from smaller families.

DOES SCHOOLING MAKE US SMARTER?   Autopsy studies show that educated people have more synapses, that is, neural connections, than do less-educated people (Orlovskaya et al., 1999). In addition, the number of years of schooling correlates between 0.5 and 0.6 with IQ scores (Neisser et al., 1996). Although some authors have interpreted this correlation as meaning that schooling leads to higher IQ and perhaps even more synapses—it's equally possible that the causal arrow is reversed. Indeed, there's evidence that individuals with high IQ scores enjoy taking classes more than do individuals with low IQ scores (Rehberg & Rosenthal, 1978). As a consequence, they may be more likely to stay in school and go on to college and beyond. This wouldn't be terribly surprising given that individuals with high IQ scores tend to do better in their classes.

Correlation vs. Causation

Can we be sure that A causes B?

Children's IQs tend to drop significantly during summer vacations, suggesting an environmental influence on IQ.

Still, several lines of evidence suggest that schooling exerts a causal influence on IQ (Ceci, 1991; Ceci & Williams, 1997; Nisbett, 2009; Nisbett et al., 2012):

1. Researchers have examined pairs of children who are almost exactly the same age, but in which one child attended an extra year of school because he or she was born just a few days earlier (say, August 31 as opposed to September 2). This can occur because public schools often have hard-and-fast cutoff dates for how old children must be to begin school. In such cases, children who've attended an extra year of school tend to have higher IQs, despite being nearly identical in chronological age.

2. Children's IQs tend to drop significantly during summer vacations.

3. Students who drop out of school end up with lower IQs than do students who stay in school, even when they start out with the same IQ.

BOOSTING IQ BY EARLY INTERVENTION.   In a controversial article in the late 1960s, psychologist Arthur Jensen contended that IQ is highly heritable and therefore difficult to modify by means of environmental intervention (Jensen, 1969). In making this argument, Jensen fell prey to a logical error we debunked previously in this text (see LO 3.5b), namely, that heritability implies that a trait can't be changed. Yet he raised an important question: Can we boost IQ with early educational interventions?

Some of the best evidence comes from studies of *Head Start*, a preschool program launched in the 1960s to give disadvantaged children a "jump-start" by offering them an enriched educational experience. The hope was that this program would allow them to catch up intellectually to other children. Dozens of studies of Head Start programs have yielded consistent results, and they've been somewhat disappointing. On the positive side, these programs produce short-term increases in IQ, especially among children from deprived environments (Ludwig & Phillips, 2008). Nevertheless, these increases don't typically persist after the programs end (Caruso, Taylor, & Detterman, 1982; Royce, Darlington, & Murray, 1983). Similar results emerge from studies of other early-intervention programs (Brody, 1992; Herrnstein & Murray, 1994). Moreover, even

The federal Head Start program was launched in the 1960s to give disadvantaged preschoolers a jump-start on their education. Studies show that Head Start programs typically produce short-term increases in IQ, but that these increases fade with time.

when short-term boosts in IQ are found, they may be due largely to "teaching to the test" given that the increases don't extend to the IQ test items most linked to general intelligence (Nijenhuis, Jongeneel-Grimen, & Kirkegaard, 2014).

At the same time, these early intervention programs appear to produce lasting and at times large increases in *school achievement*, which is hardly a meaningless accomplishment. Several studies indicate that Head Start and similar early-intervention programs result in lower rates of dropping out of high school and of being held back a grade compared with control conditions (Campbell & Ramey, 1995; Darlington, 1986; Neisser et al., 1996). They may also yield higher levels of early literacy and understanding of others' emotions (Bierman et al., 2008). In addition, there's preliminary evidence that they boost certain executive functions, which as we learned earlier in the text include the ability to inhibit and modify one's impulses (Bierman et al., 2010) and improve children's social and emotional functioning, including their ability to inhibit aggression, gain acceptance from peers, and develop close relationships with their teachers (Nix et al., 2016).

A SELF-FULFILLING PROPHECY: EXPECTANCY EFFECTS ON IQ. In the 1960s, Robert Rosenthal and Lenore Jacobson wanted to examine the effects of teacher expectancies on IQ. As we saw earlier in the text (LO. 2.2c), the *experimenter expectancy effect* refers to the tendency of researchers to unintentionally influence the outcome of studies. In this case, Rosenthal and Jacobson (1966) looked at the expectancies of teachers rather than of researchers. They administered an IQ test to students in the first through sixth grades, disguising it with a fake name ("The Harvard Test of Inflected Acquisition"). Then they gave teachers the results, which indicated that 20 percent of their students would display remarkable gains in intelligence during the subsequent 8 months: These students were "bloomers" who'd soon reach their full intellectual potential. But Rosenthal and Jacobson misled the teachers. They had *randomly* assigned these 20 percent of students to be classified as bloomers, and these students' initial scores didn't differ from those of other students. Yet when Rosenthal and Jacobson retested all students a year later with the same IQ test, the 20 percent labeled as bloomers scored about four IQ points higher than the other students. Expectations had become reality.

This effect has since been replicated in a number of studies, although the size of the effect is usually only modest (Rosenthal, 1994; Smith, 1980). Moreover, interventions designed to improve teachers' expectations of their students' intellectual performance seem to improve students' achievement, especially in mathematics (Rubie-Davies & Rosenthal, 2016). We don't know how this effect occurs, although there's evidence that teachers more often smile at, make eye contact with, and nod their heads toward students they incorrectly believe are smart compared with other students (Chaiken, Sigler, & Derlega, 1974). As a consequence, they may positively reinforce these students' learning.

Still, the effects of expectancy on IQ and achievement may have their limits. These effects are substantial only when teachers don't know their students well; when teachers have worked with students for at least a few weeks, the effects often disappear (Raudenbush, 1984). Once teachers form firm impressions of how smart their students are, it's hard to persuade them that their impressions are off base.

> **Replicability**
>
> Can the results be duplicated in other studies?

POVERTY AND IQ: SOCIOECONOMIC AND NUTRITIONAL DEPRIVATION. It's difficult to put an exact number on the effects of poverty, but there's reason to believe that social and economic deprivation can adversely affect IQ. Arthur Jensen (1977) studied a group of families in an extremely poor area of rural Georgia. For African American (but not Caucasian) children, he found evidence for cumulative declines, that is, differences that increase over time. Older siblings consistently had lower IQs than did younger siblings, with a steady decrease of about 1.5 IQ points per year. Jensen's explanation was that siblings in this impoverished region experienced progressively more intellectual deprivation as they aged, leading them to fall further behind other children (Willerman, 1979). Moreover, because the environments of African-American children were even more impoverished than those of white children, the former children may have been especially likely to suffer this ill effect.

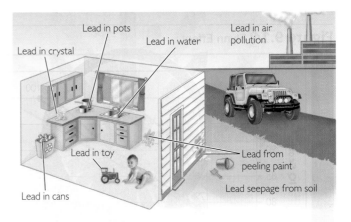

Lead exposure can arise from many sources in everyday life and may contribute to decreased IQ. Nevertheless, the causal association between lead intake and IQ remains controversial.

Along with poverty often comes inadequate diet. Studies from poor areas in Central America suggest that malnutrition in childhood, especially if prolonged, can lower IQ (Eysenck & Schoenthaler, 1997). In one investigation, researchers gave nutritional (protein) supplements to preschool children from an impoverished region of Guatemala. These children's school-related test scores were significantly higher than those of similar children who didn't receive supplements (Pollitt et al., 1993). The intake of high-fat and high-sugar foods in childhood is also linked to slightly lower IQ scores several years later, although these data are only correlational (Northstone & Emmett, 2010) and could be due to unmeasured factors, like the extent to which parents play an active role in their children's upbringing. Poor children are also especially likely to be exposed to lead as a result of drinking lead-contaminated water, breathing lead-contaminated dust, or eating lead paint chips. Such exposure is also associated

> **Ruling Out Rival Hypotheses**
>
> Can the results be duplicated in other studies?

Figure 9.20 Two Scatterplots Representing Test Bias.

These two scatterplots display a hypothetical example of test bias. In (a), IQ scores correlate highly with GPA for Caucasians (0.7 correlation), whereas in (b), correlations between IQ scores and GPA are much lower for Asian Americans (0.25). Even though Asian Americans display higher IQs on average in this example, the test is biased against them because it's a weaker predictor of GPA in that group.

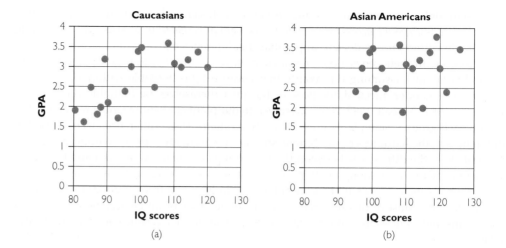

(a) (b)

college grade point average (GPA) in Caucasians is 0.7, as shown in Figure 9.20a, but only 0.25 for Asian Americans, as shown in Figure 9.20b. This finding implies that IQ is a better predictor of GPA in Caucasians than in Asian Americans. In this hypothetical case, the IQ test is biased *against* Asian Americans, even though the average IQ scores for that group are higher than those of Caucasians. Thus, average differences between groups *do not* necessarily indicate test bias.

So are IQ tests racially biased? The answer isn't entirely resolved, but the answer seems to be "generally no" (Brody, 1992; Lilienfeld et al., 2010; Neisser et al., 1996). In almost all studies, researchers have found that the correlations between IQ tests and both academic and occupational achievement are about equal across races (Brown, Reynolds, & Whitaker, 1999; Gottfredson, 2009; Hunter, Schmidt, & Hunter, 1979; Reynolds, 2013). There may be a few exceptions on specific IQ test items (Aguinis, Culpepper, & Pierce, 2010), but they aren't sufficiently large or frequent to account for overall differences across races in IQ.

The finding of little or no race bias in IQ tests leads to the conclusion that IQ differences among races go hand in hand with differences in average *achievement* among races. Unfortunately, in U.S. society, some races tend to do better in school and have higher-ranking and higher-paying jobs than other races do. According to some psychologists, the most likely explanation for this state of affairs is that *society* itself is biased, leading to differences in IQ test performance and to differences in grades and career achievement among races. For example, African Americans and Hispanic Americans may receive lower scores on IQ tests because of prejudice, inferior schooling, and other environmental disadvantages. These disadvantages, in turn, leave many African and Hispanic Americans less prepared to compete in higher education and the job market. Nevertheless, the finding that IQ tests are also equally correlated with reaction time measures across races suggests that this explanation may not tell the whole story, because these measures are unlikely to be affected by social disadvantage (Jensen, 1980).

stereotype threat

fear that we may confirm a negative group stereotype

Watch INTELLIGENCE TESTS AND STEREOTYPES

STEREOTYPE THREAT. One other environmental trigger that may affect how individuals perform and achieve, especially on IQ measures and standardized tests, is **stereotype threat**. As the video *Intelligence Tests and Stereotypes* notes, stereotype threat refers to the fear that we may confirm a negative group stereotype, such as a view of our group as being less intelligent or less athletic than other groups. Stereotype threat creates a self-fulfilling prophecy in which those who are anxious about confirming a negative stereotype actually increase their likelihood of doing so. According to psychologist Claude Steele, stereotype threat can impair individuals' performances on IQ tests and standardized tests like the SAT. Here's his reasoning: If we're members of a group that has a reputation for doing poorly on IQ tests, the mere thought that we're taking an IQ test will arouse stereotype threat. We think, "I'm supposed to do really badly on this test." This belief, Steele (1997, 2011) contends, can itself influence behavior, leading some people who would otherwise do well to display reduced performance.

Steele and his colleagues have shown that stereotype threat can depress African Americans' IQ scores, at least in the laboratory. When researchers gave African Americans items from an IQ test but told them the items were measuring something other than IQ, like "the ability to solve puzzles," they performed better than when the researchers told them the items were measuring IQ (Nguyen & Ryan, 2008; Steele & Aronson, 1995; Walton & Spencer, 2009). Stereotype threat manipulations may cause African American participants to become stressed, preoccupied, or overly self-conscious, thereby impeding their performance (Logel et al., 2009; Schmader, Johns, & Forbes, 2008). Stereotype threat, incidentally, also seems to depress women's scores on measures of mathematical (but not spatial) ability relative to those of men (Doyle & Voyer, 2016).

In addition, in some but not all studies, giving African Americans and Caucasians an in-class writing assignment designed to boost their personal identity—by asking them to identify their most important personal value, such as their friends, their family, or their need to express themselves through art—reduced the racial gap in academic performance by 40 percent (Cohen et al., 2006). The meaning of these intriguing findings isn't clear. One possibility is that thinking about what's important to us, or focusing on ourselves as individuals rather than as members of a group, renders us less vulnerable to stereotype threat. Because recent evidence suggest that these effects may be difficult to replicate and may be considerably smaller than once believed, we'll need to await the next edition of this textbook to sort out whether these results are believable (Hanselman, Rozek, Grigg, & Borman, 2016).

More broadly, there's reason for caution in interpreting the findings from stereotype threat studies. Some recent evidence suggests that the size of stereotype threat findings may have been overestimated, perhaps because researchers in this field have been more likely to publish positive than negative findings (Flore & Wicherts, 2014), which is a widespread bias in scientific research. In addition, almost all stereotype threat findings come from the tightly controlled world of the psychological laboratory and therefore may be of limited external validity (see LO 2.2a). So the extent to which stereotype threat findings generalize to the real world remains an active area of investigation and debate (Danaher & Crandall, 2008; Stricker & Ward, 2004).

Some researchers (McCarty, 2001) and writers in the popular media (Chandler, 1999) have gone so far as to suggest that racial differences between African Americans and Caucasians on IQ tests are due completely to stereotype threat and self-fulfilling prophecies (Brown & Day, 2006). Nevertheless, most studies suggest that the effects of stereotype threat aren't large enough to account fully for this gap, although they may account for some of it (Jussim, Crawford, Anglin, Stevens, & Duarte, 2016; Sackett, Hardison, & Cullen, 2004).

So where does all of this leave us? Although the literature is somewhat mixed and confusing, our discussion leads us to the conclusion that broader societal differences in resources, opportunities, attitudes, and experiences are likely to be responsible for much, if not all, of the racial differences in IQ. The encouraging news, however, is that nothing in the research literature implies that racial differences in IQ are unchangeable. If environmental disadvantages can contribute to IQ differences, eradicating the disadvantages may reduce or eliminate those differences.

Research suggests that stereotype threat can lead African American students to perform worse on tests on which they believe members of their race tend to do poorly.

> **Replicability**
>
> Can the results be duplicated in other studies?

Journal Prompt

The field of intelligence testing has long had a controversial history of finding apparent differences between the sexes and even among certain races. Aside from those discussed in the text, what are some potential environmental explanations for these reported differences?

more chatty. Hart and Risley's finding provides evidence for a powerful environmental influence on children's vocabulary, right? Those who talk less have kids who learn fewer words. Well, not so fast. In intact families, parents and children share not only environment, but genes too. So there's an alternative explanation for Hart and Risley's findings: Perhaps they reflect the fact that parents who speak a lot to their children are genetically predisposed to have higher vocabularies themselves (Stromswold, 2001). So these parents may merely be passing on their genetic predisposition for better vocabularies to their children. More recent studies have found that much of the influence on children's vocabulary *is* environmental, or at least can be altered by a change in environment (Suskind, 2015).

GENE–ENVIRONMENT INTERACTION.   Nature and nurture sometimes *interact* over the course of development, meaning that the effect of one depends on the contribution of the other. For example, some, but not all, studies show that people who possess a gene that results in low production of an enzyme called *monoamine oxidase* (MAO) are at somewhat heightened risk for developing into violent criminals (Moore, Scarpa, & Raine, 2002). In 2002, Avshalom Caspi and his colleagues conducted a longitudinal study of children who possessed this gene, some of whom committed violent crimes and some of whom didn't. The researchers discovered that whether this genetic risk factor is associated with violent behavior depends on whether children were exposed to a specific environmental factor. Specifically, children with *both* the low MAO gene *and* a history of maltreatment (such as physical abuse) were at heightened risk for antisocial behaviors like stealing, assault, and rape. Children with the low MAO gene alone weren't at heightened risk, and neither were those with the high MAO gene, even when they were maltreated (Caspi et al., 2002; Kim-Cohen et al., 2006). This finding illustrates **gene–environment interaction**: In many cases, the effects of genes depend on the environment and vice versa.

NATURE VIA NURTURE.   Nature can impact what kind of environment children experience. In particular, children with certain genetic predispositions often seek out and create their own environments, a phenomenon termed **nature via nurture** (Lykken, 1995; Ridley, 2003). In this way, nurture affords children the opportunity to express their genetic tendencies (Scarr & McCartney, 1983). For example, as they grow older, highly fearful children tend to seek out environments that protect them from their anxieties (Rose & Ditto, 1983). Because highly fearful children select safer environments, it may appear that growing up in safe environments helps to create fearfulness, when in fact the environment is a consequence of children's genetic predispositions.

GENE EXPRESSION.   Strange as it may sound, environmental experiences actually turn genes on and off. This phenomenon of **gene expression** indicates that having the genes that predispose us to have particular traits or characteristics doesn't make activation of those traits automatic (Champagne & Mashoodh, 2009; Plomin & Crabbe, 2000). Yes, every one of the 100 trillion or so (give or take a few trillion) cells in our bodies contains every one of our genes. Yet only some of these genes are active, and it sometimes takes environmental experiences to flip their switches to "on." For example, children with genes that predispose them to anxiety may never become anxious unless a highly stressful event (for example, the death of a parent early in development) triggers these genes to become active.

One of the most surprising aspects of gene expression to be discovered in recent years is that genetic expression is in a state of constant fluctuation—genes that are turned on don't necessarily stay on. Instead, environmental factors may result in month-by-month or even day-by-day adjustments in which genes are actively impacting development and behavior at any given time. This phenomenon is known as epigenetics and has been important in understanding physical and mental health. Research on how epigenetics impact children's behavioral development is just getting rolling, so the field will be learning much more about how epigenetics influences behaviors in the coming years. Epigenetic effects remind us that nurture affects nature. In turn, nature affects how we react to nurture and so on (Akbarian & Nestler, 2013).

Ruling Out Rival Hypotheses

Have important alternative explanations for the findings been excluded?

---

gene–environment interaction

situation in which the effects of genes depend on the environment in which they are expressed

nature via nurture

tendency of individuals with certain genetic predispositions to seek out and create environments that permit the expression of those predispositions

gene expression

activation or deactivation of genes by environmental experiences throughout development

Table 10.1 Intersections of Nature and Nurture.

Nature and nurture are hard to disentangle—it's easy to mistake an environmental effect for a genetic effect and vice versa. Here are some of the ways that genes and environment can intersect, making it difficult to separate out the influence of each.

Nature–Nurture Intersections	Definitions
Gene–environment interactions	The impact of genes on behavior depends on the environment in which the behavior develops.
Nature via nurture	Genetic predispositions can drive us to select and create particular environments that influence our behavior, leading to the mistaken appearance of a pure effect of nature.
Gene expression	Some genes "turn on" only in response to specific environmental triggers.
Epigenetics	Whether genes are active is regulated day-by-day and moment-by-moment environmental conditions.

The Mystique of Early Experience

There's no doubt that early life experiences sometimes shape later development in powerful ways. Indeed, early input from the outside world exerts a significant impact on brain development. Yet these influences on brain and behavior don't stop after the first few years but operate throughout the life span. Therefore, we shouldn't make the mistake of overestimating the impact of experiences during infancy on long-term development. Although such experiences are influential, they can often be reversed (Bruer, 1999; Clarke & Clarke, 1976; Kagan, 1998; Paris, 2000).

In fact, most children are more resilient than we often believe. For example, contrary to popular psychology sources, separating an infant from its mother during the first few hours after birth has no negative consequences for children's emotional adjustment (Klaus & Kennell, 1976). There's no question that early experience plays an important role in children's physical, cognitive, and social development. But there's no reason to believe that later experiences play any less of a role in development than do early experiences. In fact, later positive experiences can often counteract the negative effects of early deprivation (Kagan, 1975; McGoron, Gleason, Smyke,… Zeanah, 2012). We know that the infant brain undergoes massive growth and changes during pregnancy and the first year of life. But neuroscience research also shows that the brain changes in important ways in response to experience throughout childhood and well into early adulthood (Greenough, 1997), supporting the notion that later experiences in life can be as influential as those in early childhood. Most children are also remarkably capable of withstanding stress and trauma, emerging from potentially traumatic experiences, including kidnappings and even sexual abuse, in surprisingly good shape (Bonanno, 2004; Cicchetti & Garmezy, 1993; Garmezy, Masten, & Tellegen, 1984; Rind, Tromovitch, & Bauserman, 1998; Salter et al., 2003). It's not uncommon for these children to show some short-term negative effects, including changes in behavior or sleep routines, and certainly some children experience long-term negative outcomes. But fortunately, most children bounce back from these events with little permanent damage to their well-being.

Keeping an Eye on Cohort Effects

Imagine we conduct a study designed to examine how people's knowledge of computers changes with age. Our hypothesis is simple: People's knowledge of computers should increase steadily from adolescence until early adulthood, after which it should level off at about age 30. After about age 30, we predict, knowledge of computers should remain about the same or increase slightly. To test our hypothesis, we sample 100,000 people in the U.S. population, with a broad age range from 14 to 80. We carefully screen out people with dementia or other forms of brain damage to ensure that we're not accidentally including people with cognitive impairment. However, contrary to our hypothesis, we find that people's knowledge of computers declines dramatically with age, especially between the ages of 60 and 80. Where did we go wrong?

Ruling Out Rival Hypotheses

Have important alternative explanations for the findings been excluded?

cross-sectional design

research design that examines people of different ages at a single point in time

cohort effect

effect observed in a sample of participants that results from individuals in the sample growing up at the same time

longitudinal design

research design that examines development in the same group of people on multiple occasions over time

Ruling Out Rival Hypotheses

Have important alternative explanations for the findings been excluded?

Older adults may be less comfortable or skilled with technology because it wasn't around when they were growing up, limiting our ability to compare performance of older adults with younger adults in a cross-sectional study.

It turns out that we forgot to consider an alternative explanation for our findings. We started out by asking a perfectly sensible question. But in science, we also must make sure that the design we select is the right one to answer the question. In this case, it wasn't. We used a **cross-sectional design**, a design in which researchers examine people who are of different ages at a single point in time (Achenbach, 1982; Raulin & Lilienfeld, 2008). In a cross-sectional design, we obtain a "snapshot" of each person at a single age; we assess some people when they're 24, some when they're 47, others when they're 63, and so on.

The major problem with cross-sectional designs is that they don't control for **cohort effects**: effects due to the fact that sets of people who lived during one time period, called *cohorts*, can differ in some systematic way from sets of people who lived during a different time period. In the study we've described, cohort effects are a serious shortcoming, because before the late 1980s, few Americans used computers. So those older than 60 years of age may not be as computer savvy as younger folks for reasons that have nothing to do with aging, but everything to do with the era in which they grew up.

A **longitudinal design** is the only sure way around this problem. In a longitudinal design, psychologists track the development of the same group of participants over time (Shadish, Cook, & Campbell, 2002). Rather than obtaining a snapshot of each person at only one point in time, we obtain the equivalent of a series of home movies taken across multiple ages. This design allows us to examine true *developmental* effects: changes over time within individuals as a consequence of growing older (Adolph & Robinson, 2011). Without longitudinal designs, we can be tricked into drawing faulty conclusions. For example, much of the pop psychology literature warns us that divorce results in children engaging in disruptive behaviors such as throwing tantrums, breaking rules, defying authority figures, and committing crimes (Wallerstein, 1989). Yet a longitudinal study that tracked a sample of boys over several decades revealed otherwise: Boys whose parents divorced exhibited these behaviors *years before* the divorce occurred (Block & Block, 2006; Block, Block, & Gjerde, 1986). This raises some interesting unanswered questions about why parents with male children who engage in problem behaviors are more likely than other parents to get divorced. The key point is that the longitudinal nature of the design enabled us to rule out the plausible—but in this case incorrect—explanation that the boys' behaviors are a reaction to the divorce.

Although longitudinal designs are ideal for studying change over time, they can be costly and time-consuming and in some cases nearly impossible. For example, our study of computer literacy would take more than six decades to complete. Such studies also can result in *attrition*—participants dropping out of the study before it is completed. Attrition can be a particular problem when the participants who drop out differ in important ways from those who stay in. When longitudinal designs aren't feasible, we should interpret the results of cross-sectional studies with caution, bearing in mind that cohort effects may account for any observed changes at different ages. Nevertheless, there are many research questions for which cross-sectional designs are more useful than longitudinal designs. For example, when comparing the performance of two-year-olds with two-and-a-half-year-olds on a memory test, the potential for cohort effects seems low. In fact, in such a study, a longitudinal design could be problematic because administering the same memory task to the same children twice so close together would probably result in better performance on the second test simply because the task was familiar. We should also bear in mind that most longitudinal studies use observational rather than experimental designs, because we typically can't randomly assign individuals to conditions. As a result, we can't use most of these studies to infer cause-and-effect relationships.

Post Hoc Fallacy

There are a few other unique challenges that arise when investigating psychological development. Understanding these challenges, along with the scientific thinking principles we've encountered throughout this text, will provide us with the equipment we need to evaluate the causes of physical, cognitive, emotional, and social changes from childhood to old age.

First, we've learned throughout the text that a correlation between two variables measured at the same time doesn't mean that one causes the other. But when it comes to development, where things happen progressively over time, this logical fallacy can become particularly tempting. It's easy to assume that things that occur early in development cause things that come later. For example, if we learned that children who are shy are more likely to become engineers as adults, we could easily imagine plausible arguments for how shyness might lead to interests in engineering. But now imagine we learned that nearly 100 percent of serial killers drank milk as children. It would be silly to conclude that milk drinking creates

---

Correlation vs. Causation

Can we be sure that A causes B?

---

mass murderers. We wouldn't have grounds for inferring causation from this linkage, because many factors could have influenced both behaviors. This logical error—the mistake of assuming that because A comes before B, A must cause B—is called the **post hoc fallacy** (*post hoc* is Latin for "after this").

Bidirectional Influences

Human development is almost always a two-way street: Developmental influences are bidirectional. Children's experiences influence their development, but their development also influences what they experience. Psychological traffic from parents to children runs in both directions: Parents influence their children's behavior, which in turn influences parents' reactions and so on (Bell, 1968; Collins et al., 2000; O'Connor et al., 1998). Children also change their environments by acting in ways that create changes in the behaviors of their siblings, friends, and teachers (Plomin, DeFries, & Loehlin, 1977; Steele, Rasbash, & Jenkins, 2012). Furthermore, as children grow older, they play an increasingly active role in selecting their own environments.

It's crucial to keep bidirectional influences in mind, because pop psychology is chock full of *unidirectional* explanations: those that attempt to explain development in terms of a one-headed arrow. Parents fight with each other → their children react negatively. Children witness violence at school → they become more aggressive. There's probably a kernel of truth in each of those explanations. Yet they typically tell only part of the story. That's why so many arrows in psychology contain two heads (↔), not one. In the study of human development, two "heads" are almost always better—or least more accurate—than one, at least as far as arrows are concerned.

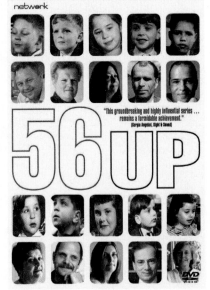

Longitudinal designs track the lives of the same groups of people over time. The classic *Up Series* directed by Michael Apted used the same technique by tracing the lives of 14 British people from age 7 all the way up through age 56.

post hoc fallacy

false assumption that because one event occurred before another event it must have caused that event

Environmental and Genetic Explanations

Interactive

Can you think of both an environmental and genetic explanation for why adolescents in gangs become trouble makers? Environmental explanation—kids who hang out with troublemakers can be persuaded to engage in troubled behaviors themselves. Genetic explanation—kids who are genetically predisposed to engage in destructive acts are driven to seek out other like-minded kids.

10.2: The Developing Body: Physical and Motor Development

10.2a Track the trajectory of prenatal development, and identify barriers to normal development.

10.2b Describe how infants learn to coordinate motion and achieve major motor milestones.

10.2c Describe physical maturation during childhood and adolescence.

10.2d Explain which aspects of physical ability decline during aging.

The human body begins to take shape long before birth, as does the ability to perform coordinated movements. Learning, memory, and even preferences—for certain sounds or body positions, for example—are also well under way in unborn infants. Nevertheless, the form and structure of the body, including the brain, undergo radical changes throughout the life span, shaping the range of behaviors exhibited across development.

Figure 10.1 The Journey of a Fertilized Egg from Ovary to Uterus

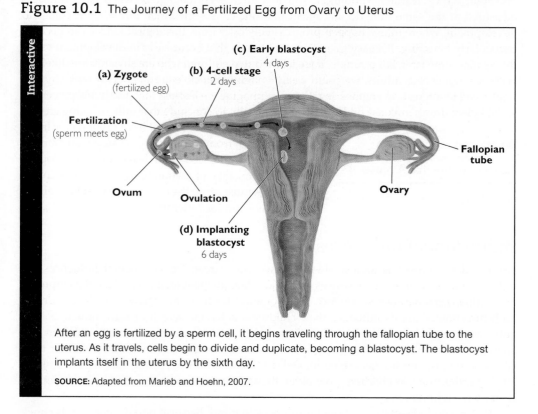

After an egg is fertilized by a sperm cell, it begins traveling through the fallopian tube to the uterus. As it travels, cells begin to divide and duplicate, becoming a blastocyst. The blastocyst implants itself in the uterus by the sixth day.

SOURCE: Adapted from Marieb and Hoehn, 2007.

Conception and Prenatal Development: From Zygote to Baby

During the **prenatal** (before birth) period of development, the human body acquires its basic form and structure.

The most dramatic changes in prenatal development occur in the earliest stages of pregnancy. Following conception, when a sperm cell fertilizes an egg to produce a **zygote**, prenatal physical development unfolds in three stages. In the *germinal stage*, the zygote begins to divide and double, forming a **blastocyst**—a ball of identical cells that haven't yet begun to take on any specific function in a body part. The blastocyst keeps growing as cells continue to divide for the first week and a half or so after fertilization (see Figure 10.1). Around the middle of the second week, the cells begin to differentiate, taking on different roles as the organs of the body begin to develop.

Once cells start to assume different functions, the blastocyst becomes an **embryo**. The *embryonic stage* continues from the second to the eighth week of development, during which limbs, facial features, and major organs (including the heart, lungs, and brain) begin to take shape. During this stage, many things can go wrong in fetal development. Spontaneous miscarriages often occur when the embryo doesn't form properly (Roberts & Lowe, 1975), frequently without the mother even knowing she was pregnant.

By the ninth week, the major organs are established, and the heart begins to beat. This final milestone is called the *fetal stage* because it's the point at which the embryo becomes a **fetus**. The fetus's "job" for the rest of the pregnancy is physical maturation. This phase is more about fleshing out what's already there than establishing new structures. The last third of pregnancy in particular is devoted almost entirely to "bulking up."

BRAIN DEVELOPMENT: 18 DAYS AND BEYOND. The human brain begins to develop a mere 18 days after fertilization. Unlike most organs, which are completely formed by birth and continue to grow only in size, our brains continue to develop well into adolescence and probably even early adulthood (Caviness et al., 1996).

Between the 18th day of pregnancy and the end of the 6th month, neurons begin developing at an astronomical rate, a process called *proliferation*. Some estimates place the rate of

prenatal
prior to birth

zygote
fertilized egg

blastocyst
ball of identical cells early in pregnancy that haven't yet begun to take on any specific function in a body part

embryo
second to eighth week of prenatal development, during which limbs, facial features, and major organs of the body take form

fetus
period of prenatal development from ninth week until birth after all major organs are established and physical maturation is the primary change

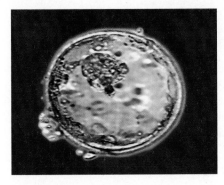

A blastocyst is a mass of identical cells, the earliest stage of cell division after fertilization.

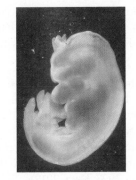

The embryo stage is when cells begin to differentiate into preliminary structures such as the skeleton, organs, and limbs.

The fetus has a recognizable human form and a heartbeat by nine weeks into the pregnancy.

neural development as high as an astonishing 250,000 brain cells per minute at peak times. The fetus ends up manufacturing far more neurons than it will need as an infant. In addition to producing all of these cells, the brain must organize them to perform coordinated functions. Starting in the fourth month and continuing throughout pregnancy, migration of cells begins to occur. Neurons start to sort themselves out, moving to their final positions in specific structures of the brain, such as the hippocampus and cerebellum.

OBSTACLES TO NORMAL FETAL DEVELOPMENT.   Although most babies are born healthy and fully intact, fetal development can be disrupted in four ways: (1) premature birth, (2) low birth weight, (3) exposure to hazardous environmental influences, and (4) biological influences resulting from genetic disorders or errors in cell duplication during cell division.

Premature Birth.   A full-term baby is born after 40 weeks of pregnancy—actually closer to 9½ months than 9 months, as is commonly believed. Premature infants ("preemies") are those born at fewer than 36 weeks gestation. The *viability* point, the point in pregnancy at which infants can typically survive on their own, is around 25 weeks. In rare cases, fetuses as young as 22 weeks have survived, but only with serious physical and cognitive impairments. Preemies have underdeveloped lungs and brains and are often unable to engage in basic physiological functions such as breathing and maintaining a healthy body temperature. They often experience serious delays in cognitive and physical development. With each week of pregnancy, the odds of fetal survival increase and the odds of developmental disorders decrease (Hoekstra et al., 2004). Many premature babies who are otherwise healthy manage to "catch up" and suffer few long-term consequences, especially those born later than 32 weeks' gestation.

Low Birth Weight.   Premature babies typically do not weigh as much as full-term infants because they didn't have the chance to bulk up before being born. However, other babies are carried for a full 40 weeks but are still born with a low birth weight. Low-birth-weight babies are defined as less than 5½ pounds for a full-term baby (compared with an average birth weight of about 7½ pounds) (Pringle et al., 2005; Windham et al., 2000). Low birth weight is linked to a high risk of death, infection, developmental delays, and even psychological disorders such as depression and anxiety (Boyle et al., 2011; Copper et al., 1993; Schothorst & van Engeland, 1996). Nevertheless, it is unknown how many of these associations are due directly to low birth weight because low birth weight may itself be a reflection of other difficulties during pregnancy. In general, full-term low-birth-weight babies tend to have more pronounced difficulties than otherwise healthy premature infants—those who had the chance to bulk up but failed to do so probably had other risk factors that led to the low birth weight in the first place. For example, babies who have low birth weights are more often born to single moms, to young moms, to women with lower education levels and fewer financial

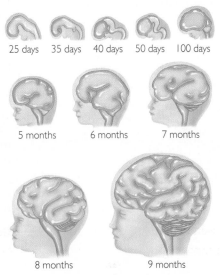

25 days   35 days   40 days   50 days   100 days

5 months   6 months   7 months

8 months   9 months

The fetal brain begins as a long tube that develops into a variety of different structures, with the brain stem (which controls basic functions like breathing and digestion) developing first, followed by cortical structures later in pregnancy.

SOURCE: Based on Restak, 1984.

Correlation vs. Causation

Can we be sure that A causes B?

resources, and to those who did not receive much prenatal medical care (Defo & Partin, 1993; Gebremedhin et al., 2015). Most experts believe that low birth weight can be minimized by providing broader access to prenatal education and healthcare among expectant mothers.

teratogen

an environmental factor that can exert a negative impact on prenatal development

fetal alcohol syndrome

condition resulting from high levels of prenatal alcohol exposure, causing learning disabilities, physical growth retardation, facial malformations, and behavioral disorders

Hazardous Environmental Influences. Most women don't even realize they're pregnant until after the fetus's body and brain development are well under way. As a result, women often engage unknowingly in activities that are potentially harmful to the fetus. **Teratogens** are environmental factors that can affect prenatal development negatively. They run the gamut from drugs and alcohol to chicken pox and X-rays. Even anxiety and depression in the mother are potential teratogens because they alter the fetus's chemical and physiological environment (Bellamy, 1998; Katz, 2012).

Alcohol exposure can result in **fetal alcohol syndrome**, which includes a host of symptoms, such as learning disabilities, delays in physical growth, facial malformations, and behavioral disorders (Abel, 1998). Cigarette smoking during pregnancy is one of the most prevalent teratogens. Mothers who smoke cigarettes or marijuana or who use other recreational drugs during pregnancy are particularly likely to deliver low-birth-weight babies. Healthcare professionals have become increasingly sensitive to the adverse effects that mental health factors in the mother can have on fetal development. Chronic stress in mothers, for example, has adverse effects on prenatal development (DiPietro, 2012; Glover, 1997). Expectant mothers who are taking antidepressants prior to pregnancy face a dilemma. Most psychologists assume that pharmaceuticals are likely to have teratogenic effects, so women will often decide to stop taking their depression medications during pregnancy. However, the return of depression symptoms also puts the fetus at risk. Women and their healthcare providers in these cases must decide which is likely to have the least adverse effects on the developing infant. Some teratogens can influence how specific parts of the brain develop, depending on which teratogen and when the embryo or fetus is exposed to it. Other teratogens exert a more general impact on brain development. Because the brain has such a long period of maturation relative to most other organs, it's particularly vulnerable to teratogens.

Genetic Disorders. Genetic disorders or random errors in cell division are another set of adverse influences on prenatal development. Often, a single cell, including the egg or sperm cell prior to fertilization, or even a family of cells, is copied with some error or break in the genetic material. Like a page with a smudge that keeps being photocopied with that smudge preserved, these cells replicate with the error retained, resulting in impaired development of organs or organ systems. Any number of irregularities can result, some as minor as a birthmark and others as major as intellectual disability and disorders that prevent blood clotting or result in degeneration of muscle tissues.

Infant Motor Development: How Babies Get Going

Starting at birth, infants begin to learn how to make use of their bodies through movement and how to coordinate interactions with their environment. Some aspects of motor coordination are evident even at birth, but others develop gradually throughout infancy and early childhood.

SURVIVAL INSTINCTS: INFANT REFLEXES. Infants are born with a large set of automatic motor behaviors—or *reflexes*—that are triggered by specific types of stimulation. Reflexes fulfill important survival needs (Swaiman & Ashwal, 1999). One example is the *sucking reflex*, an automatic response to oral stimulation. If we put something in a baby's mouth (including a finger—try it sometime … with the parents' permission, of course!), she'll clamp down and begin sucking. A related reflex is the *rooting reflex*, which serves the same survival need: eating. If we softly stroke a hungry infant's cheek, she'll automatically turn her head toward our hand and begin casting about with her mouth, eagerly seeking a nipple to suck. These reflexes help keep infants alive; if they needed to learn through trial and error that sucking on an object yields nourishment, they might starve trying to get the hang of it.

Figure 10.2 The Progression of Motor Development

Different children typically achieve major motor milestones in the same order, although each milestone requires an entirely new set of motor coordination skills. For example, cruising, walking, and running look similar but require different muscle groups and shifts in weight to accomplish movement.

Sitting without support
6 months

Crawling
9 months

Standing
11 months

Cruising
12 months

Walking without assistance
13 months

Running
18–24 months

LEARNING TO GET UP AND GO: COORDINATING MOVEMENT. But reflexes can get babies only so far; they must learn other motor behaviors through trial and error. **Motor behaviors** are bodily motions that occur as a result of self-initiated force that moves the bones and muscles. The major motor milestones during development include sitting up, crawling, standing unsupported, and walking. The age at which different children reach these milestones varies enormously, although almost all children acquire them in the same order (see Figure 10.2).

We take for granted how easy it is to reach for a cup of coffee sitting on a table, yet the calculations our body makes—the physical adjustments that control our body's positioning and the direction and speed of our movements—to accomplish that act are incredibly complex. They're also customized to fit each situation, or we'd end up knocking our coffee to the floor most of the time (Adolph, 1997). As novices, babies haven't yet learned to perform the lightning-quick calculations needed for good hand-eye coordination and motor planning. Crawling and walking are even more complicated than reaching, because they involve supporting the infant's weight, coordinating all four limbs, and somehow keeping track of where the baby is heading.

motor behavior

bodily motion that occurs as a result of self-initiated force that moves the bones and muscles

Fact vs. Fiction

Experienced crawlers are good at navigating their way through tight openings and down slopes. When these crawlers learn to walk, their navigation skills transfer readily to moving through their environment in an upright position. (See bottom of page for answer.)

○ Fact

○ Fiction

Many cultural parenting practices seem extreme to those from other cultures. For example, many Americans see swaddling infants throughout their first year as limiting early physical development. Although cultural variability in parenting practices influences the rate of motor development, none of these early physical experiences result in long-term advantages or impairments.

FACTORS INFLUENCING MOTOR DEVELOPMENT. There's a wide range in the rate and manner in which children achieve motor milestones. Some crawl and walk much earlier than others do, and a few skip the crawling stage entirely. These findings suggest that these skills don't necessarily build on each other in a causal fashion, as the post hoc fallacy might lead us to believe. What remains to be explained, then, is why all children acquire motor milestones in the same order.

Physical maturation of both the body and the brain plays a key role in allowing children to become increasingly steady and flexible in their movements. Some motor developments may be a consequence of innately programmed patterns of motion that become activated in response to stimuli. Many motor achievements, such as crawling and walking, also depend on the physical maturation of the body, allowing children to acquire the necessary strength and coordination. Differences among children in the rate at which motor development unfolds are also tied to their body weight. Heavier babies tend to achieve milestones more gradually than lighter babies do because they need to build up their muscles more before they can support their weight (Thelen & Ulrich, 1991).

Cultural and parenting practices also play crucial roles in motor development (Thelen, 1995). Considerable variability exists in the timing of developmental milestones across cultures. In Peru and China, infants are tightly swaddled in blankets that provide warmth and a sense of security but prevent free movement of the limbs (Li et al., 2000). Swaddled babies tend to cry less and sleep more soundly, but prolonged swaddling over the first year of life slows down their motor development. In contrast, many African and West Indian mothers engage in a variety of stretching, massage, and strength-building exercises with their infants. This practice, which looks harmful to American eyes, speeds up infants' motor development (Hopkins & Westra, 1988). Even things as basic as cloth or disposable diapers, which are prevalent only in industrialized societies, slow down walking (Cole, Lingeman, & Adolph, 2012).

Journal Prompt

If possible, speak to a person who raised you when you were a baby and have him or her describe your motor development. When did you first roll over, sit, crawl, pull up, and walk? Did you follow the typical developmental milestones described in the text? Did you skip any stages?

Growth and Physical Development Throughout Childhood

Our bodies continue to change dramatically through early childhood and adolescence. Careful inspection of an infant reveals that he has no apparent neck, a head almost half the size of his torso, and arms that don't even reach the top of his head. Over the course of childhood, different parts of the body grow at different rates and the ultimate proportions of the

Answer: Fiction. Once babies start walking, they have to relearn what kinds of spaces their bodies will fit through as well as how to handle slopes and stairs. Walking not only uses different types of motor coordination than crawling, but it also changes their perspective and how the baby's body takes up space as she moves.

body are quite different than at birth. For example, the absolute size of the head continues to increase with development, but it grows at a slower pace than the torso or legs. As a result, an adolescent or young adult has a smaller head-size-to-body-size ratio than an infant (see Figure 10.3).

Throughout this text, we've sprinkled numerous examples of popular psychology wisdom that are false. Well, here's some common knowledge that's *true*: Growth spurts are real. Michael Hermanussen and his colleagues found "mini growth spurts" occurring every 30 to 55 days in children ages 3 to 16, followed by lulls during which growth was much slower (Hermanussen, 1998; Hermanussen et al., 1988). One study that measured three infants daily found that infants' growth occurs more suddenly. They showed no growth at all for days at a time, followed by overnight increases of as much as an inch (Lampl, Veldhuis, & Johnson, 1992)! Nevertheless, other studies have failed to replicate this finding, suggesting instead that growth is actually more gradual, with shifts in the *rate* of growth at various points in development (Heinrichs et al., 1995; Hermanussen & Geiger-Benoit, 1995; Lampl, 2012). The evidence suggests that there are spurts, but that the periods between them aren't marked by a total absence of growth. Although all infants experience growth spurts, the timing of these spurts appears to be at least somewhat predicted by characteristics of the mother during pregnancy (such as her weight and whether she had high blood pressure) as well as whether this was her first or a later pregnancy (Pizzi et al., 2014). Interestingly, infants sleep longer and take more frequent naps during growth periods (Lampl & Johnson, 2011), although the direction of causality between sleep and growth isn't clear. In all likelihood, both sleep and growth are the result of a third variable, such as metabolism or gene expression.

Replicability

Can the results be duplicated in other studies?

Figure 10.3 Changes in Body Proportions During Development

This figure displays the proportional size of the head, torso, and limbs across the life span when scaled to the same overall height. The size of the head relative to the body decreases dramatically over the course of development, whereas the relative length of the legs increases dramatically.

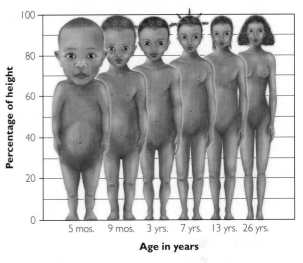

Age in years

Correlation vs. Causation

Can we be sure that A causes B?

Physical Maturation in Adolescence: The Power of Puberty

Our bodies don't reach full maturity until **adolescence**—the transitional period between childhood and adulthood commonly associated with the teenage years. Adolescence is a time of profound physical changes, many of them hormonal. The pituitary gland stimulates physical growth, and the reproductive system releases sex hormones—estrogens and androgens (see LO 3.1c) into the bloodstream, triggering growth and other physical changes. Many people think of androgens, such as testosterone, as male hormones and estrogens as female hormones. In fact, both types of hormones are present in both sexes in varying proportions. In boys, testosterone promotes increases in muscle tissue, growth of facial and body hair, and broadening of the shoulders. In girls, estrogens promote breast growth, uterus and vaginal maturation, hip broadening, and the onset of menstruation. Androgens in girls also induce physical growth and the growth of pubic hair (see Figure 10.4 on next page). Boys' muscle strength begins to exceed girls' in adolescence, and boys undergo a variety of changes in lung function and blood circulation. These changes result in greater average physical strength and endurance in boys than in girls, explaining the divergence between boys' and girls' athletic ability that emerges in adolescence (Beunen & Malina, 1996; Malina & Bouchard, 1991).

A crucial component of hormonal changes in adolescence is **puberty**, or *sexual maturation*—the attainment of physical potential for reproduction. Maturation includes changes in **primary sex characteristics**, which include the reproductive organs and genitals. Maturation also includes changes in **secondary sex characteristics**, which are sex-differentiating characteristics that don't relate directly to reproduction, such as breast enlargement in girls, deepening voices in boys, and pubic hair in both genders. In girls, **menarche**—the onset of menstruation—tends not to begin until they've achieved full physical maturity. Menarche is the body's insurance plan against allowing girls to become pregnant before their bodies can carry an infant to term and give birth safely (Tanner, 1990).

adolescence

the transition between childhood and adulthood commonly associated with the teenage years

puberty

the achievement of sexual maturation resulting in the potential to reproduce

primary sex characteristic

a physical feature such as the reproductive organs and genitals that distinguish the sexes

secondary sex characteristic

a sex-differentiating characteristic that doesn't relate directly to reproduction, such as breast enlargement in women and deepening voices in men

menarche

start of menstruation

Figure 10.4 Physical and Sexual Maturation During the Preteen and Teenage Years

Hormones result in rapid growth to full adult height. They also trigger changes in the reproductive system and in secondary sex characteristics such as increased breast size and broader hips in girls and broader shoulders in boys.

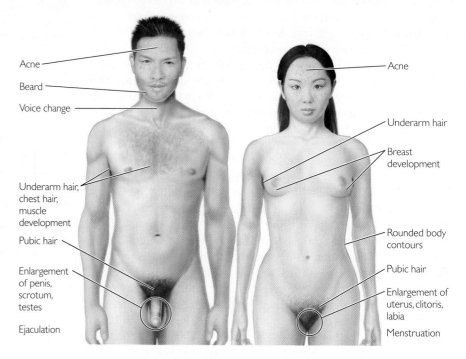

Acne
Beard
Voice change
Underarm hair, chest hair, muscle development
Pubic hair
Enlargement of penis, scrotum, testes
Ejaculation

Acne
Underarm hair
Breast development
Rounded body contours
Pubic hair
Enlargement of uterus, clitoris, labia
Menstruation

These seventh-grade students vary in physical height, but the girl (on the right) is the tallest of the bunch. Girls tend to mature earlier and more rapidly than boys do. The girl is probably close to reaching her adult height, whereas the boys still have a great deal of growing to do.

spermarche

boys' first ejaculation

There's variability in when menstruation begins because girls reach full physical maturity at different ages.

Spermarche, the first ejaculation, is the comparable milestone in boys; it occurs, on average, at around 13 years of age. Because boys need not be fully physically mature to bear children, spermarche isn't as closely tied to physical maturity as is menarche. In fact, boys often take much longer to mature fully than girls do, which is why we often see sixth- and seventh-grade girls towering above their male counterparts. The first signs of sexual maturation in boys are enlargement of the testicles and penis and growth of pubic hair (Graber, Petersen, & Brooks-Gunn, 1996). Later, boys begin to see signs of facial and body hair, and their voices deepen.

The timing of puberty in boys and girls is genetically influenced; identical twins tend to begin menstruating within a month of each other, whereas fraternal twins average about a year's difference in onset (Tanner, 1990). Still, a variety of environmental factors, some relating to physical and mental health, affect when adolescents reach puberty. Adolescents from higher socioeconomic status households generally have access to better nutrition and health care and reach puberty earlier as a result (Eveleth & Tanner, 1976). Girls from wealthier countries tend to begin menstruating earlier than those from poorer countries. Girls in Japan and the United States usually start menstruating between 12½ and 13½ years of age, whereas girls in the poorest regions of Africa don't usually start menstruating until between the ages of 14 and 17 (Eveleth & Tanner, 1990).

On average, the age of menarche in girls has decreased over the past 100 years, moving from around 15 to around 13 years of age on average. Researchers have also found signs of puberty in American boys up to 2 years earlier than previously reported—age 9 on average for blacks, age 10 for whites and Hispanics (Herman-Giddens et al., 2012). These changes are probably due primarily to better nutrition and health care (Tanner, 1998), although other factors, such as increased exposure to hormones fed to livestock, may also contribute (Soto et al., 2008). Although younger onset of puberty has been attributed to positive increases in health, experiencing an especially early menarche (age 11 or younger) appears to have some negative associations. For example, according to Henrichs and her colleagues (Henrichs et al., 2014), girls who experience early menarche tend to have been exposed to multiple early adversities such as abuse, parental neglect, or exposure to community violence earlier in development.

Unfortunately, an early onset of menarche is actually associated with a variety of negative long-term health outcomes such as cardiovascular disease and cancer in adulthood (Jacobson et al., 2009) as well as increased incidence of sexually risky behaviors (Vaughan et al., 2015). Of course, it's difficult to tell whether the early onset of menarche actually causes these other health risks or if, instead, it is a marker of predisposition for these negative outcomes.

Physical Development in Adulthood

After reaching full physical and sexual maturation during puberty, most of us reach our physical peaks in our early twenties (Larsson, Grimby, & Karlsson, 1979; Lindle et al., 1997). Strength, coordination, speed of cognitive processing, and physical flexibility also attain their highest levels in early adulthood.

PHYSICAL CHANGES IN MIDDLE ADULTHOOD. Americans spend millions of dollars each year on products and gimmicks marketed to make them look younger as they attempt to stave off the inevitable ravages of aging. Unfortunately, some of the effects of age on physical appearance and functioning are inescapable facts of life. As we age, we experience a decline in muscle tone and an increase in body fat. Basic sensory processes such as vision and hearing tend to decline too. Even our sense of smell becomes less sensitive when we reach our 60s and 70s.

Fertility in women declines sharply during their 30s and 40s (see Figure 10.5), which has become a challenge for many women in contemporary society who opt to delay child-bearing until they achieve career success. As a result, fertility treatments have been on the rise. The bad news is that the risks of serious birth defects in babies increase substantially among women who become pregnant in their 30s and 40s.

One of the major milestones of physical aging in women is **menopause**—the termination of menstruation, signaling the end of a woman's reproductive potential. Menopause is triggered by a reduction in estrogen, which can result in "hot flashes" marked by becoming incredibly hot, sweaty, and dry-mouthed. Many women report mood swings, sleep disruption, and temporary loss of sexual drive or pleasure. Interestingly, the prevalence of these effects varies across cultures. Although about 50 percent of North American women report hot flashes, less than 15 percent of Japanese women do (Lock, 1998). Moreover, the meaning of menopause for women also differs across cultures. Whereas more than half of Australian women fear menopause as a sign of aging, more than 80 percent of Laotian women say menopause symptoms have no personal significance for them (Sayakhot, Vincent, & Teede, 2012). A common misconception is that menopause is a period of heightened depression. Research suggests that women in menopause are no more prone to depression than are women at other phases of life (Busch, Zonderman, & Costa, 1994; Dennerstein, Lehert, & Guthrie, 2002).

Men experience nothing comparable to menopause; they can continue to reproduce well into old age. Still, there's a gradual decline in sperm production and testosterone levels with age, and maintaining an erection and achieving ejaculation can become a challenge—as the popularity of Viagra and Cialis television ads targeted toward aging males attests. Like older women, older men are at heightened risk for having children with developmental disorders, including autism (Callaway, 2012). Despite changes in the reproductive equipment of aging adults, most senior citizens continue to experience healthy sex drives.

CHANGES IN AGILITY AND PHYSICAL COORDINATION WITH AGE. There are individual and task-specific differences in the effects of aging on motor coordination. Complex tasks show greater effects of age than do simpler ones (Luchies et al., 2002; Welford, 1977); simple motor tasks, such as tapping a finger to a beat, display relatively small declines (Ruff & Parker, 1993). Elderly adults also find it more difficult to learn new motor skills like learning to drive a new car (Guan & Wade, 2000).

Some individuals display greater age-related decreases than others. Strength training and increased physical activity may minimize some of these declines and increase life span (Fiatarone et al., 1990; Frontera et al., 1988; Hurley, Hanson, & Sheaff, 2011). Many of the changes we typically associate with aging are actually due not to aging itself, but to diseases that are correlated with age, like heart disease and arthritis. Although chronological age and physical health are negatively correlated, the great variability in how people age refutes the popular notion that old age invariably produces physical decline.

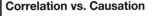

Correlation vs. Causation

Can we be sure that A causes B?

Figure 10.5 Fertility Peaks in the Twenties and Declines Thereafter

Women reach peak fertility between the ages of 20 and 25. The likelihood of a woman becoming pregnant drops dramatically between 30 and 50. This figure shows how the success of women becoming pregnant during one year's time declines with age.

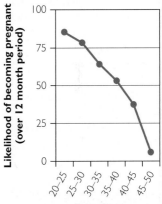

menopause

the termination of menstruation, marking the end of a woman's reproductive potential

Research suggests that physical activity and strength training are valuable in minimizing age-related declines.

Correlation vs. Causation

Can we be sure that A causes B?

Evaluating Claims ANTI-AGING TREATMENTS

Many people are in search of a "fountain of youth"—a quick, easy, and affordable way to reduce or even reverse the signs of aging. A variety of products and procedures purport to do exactly this, yet it's difficult to discern which of them—if any—are effective.

You're sitting with your appearance-conscious aunt watching TV when a commercial featuring a famous 40-something actress appears. Her skin is flawless and youthful-looking. She says to the camera, "You think I've had plastic surgery, don't you? No one's skin can look this good naturally at my age! Well, I'm here to tell you that there's an all-natural, effective way to achieve such youthful skin." The commercial cuts to a clip of her applying skin cream to her face. The voice-over makes the following claims:

- "Research at Harold University Medical School shows that this product is highly effective at reversing the appearance of wrinkles and blemishes, and preventing new ones. In a *randomized, double-blind human study* our product showed a significant effect on the signs of aging relative to several popular market competitors."

- "See how natural looking and youthful our product will make you. We offer *no overnight miracles or quick-fixes*, but have found gradual results over time for those who stick to the program."

- "We hold *exclusive worldwide rights* to this highly refined formula and are making it *available to the public for a limited time* only, so act now!"

Your aunt seems intrigued and is seriously considering placing an order. What do you think?

Scientific skepticism requires us to evaluate all claims with an open mind but to insist on compelling evidence before accepting them. How do the principles of scientific thinking help us to evaluate this claim about the effectiveness of this anti-aging product?

Consider how the six principles of scientific thinking are relevant as you evaluate this claim.

1. Ruling Out Rival Hypotheses
Have important alternative explanations for the findings been excluded?

The commercial mentions use of a double-blind randomized study that directly compares their product to other popular ones. The double-blind design minimizes the possibility of placebo effects. It would be important to find out what the comparison products are and whether they were appropriate competitors, but the fact that the design was mentioned as well as the specific university where the work was conducted makes the claims more convincing than those in most product advertisements.

2. Correlation vs. Causation
Can we be sure that A causes B?

Yes, we can be fairly certain assuming the study was conducted properly. The use of a randomized experimental design implies that the effects observed can be attributed to the product.

3. Falsifiability
Can the claim be disproved?

The claims can be disproved and the use of a randomized double-blind research study conducted at a medical school provided opportunity for the claims to be disproved. If the product had the same or fewer effects on aging skin than the competitors, the claims would have been disconfirmed

4. Replicability
Can the results be duplicated in other studies?

Assuming that the methodology and results of the study were made available, other researchers could indeed replicate the study and confirm that the findings can be duplicated. Until there are multiple replications, though, these findings should be interpreted with caution.

5. Extraordinary Claims
Is the evidence as strong as the claim?

By explaining that the results may take time, the commercial avoids exaggerated claims. It also doesn't promise any specific quantifiable results, only that your appearance will be more "natural looking" and "youthful."

6. Occam's Razor
Does a simpler explanation fit the data just as well?

The commercial claims that the product works but doesn't really offer an explanation of *why* it works. As a result, there are a variety of potential explanations, both simple and complex, for the product's apparent success. Before purchasing the product, it might be wise to explore how and why the researchers or manufacturers explain the data.

Summary

In general, this commercial does a fairly good job of providing the kind of information that a consumer would need to be able to make an informed decision about whether to buy the product. Reporting experimental research conducted by a reputable institution and making modest claims about effectiveness are both strengths. It would be useful to look into greater details about how they measured the outcomes of the study and which competing products they used, but they're definitely on the right track. The only problematic practice they employed was the use of the *scarcity heuristic*—attempting to pressure consumers to make a purchase by creating the impression that the opportunity to acquire the product is limited.

10.3: The Developing Mind: Cognitive Development

10.3a Understand major theories of how children's thinking develops.

10.3b Explain how children acquire knowledge in important cognitive domains.

10.3c Describe how attitudes toward knowledge change during adolescence.

Cognitive development—how we acquire the ability to learn, think, communicate, and remember over time—sheds light on the mystery of how we come to understand our worlds. Over the past 50 or 60 years, psychologists have constructed a variety of systematic theories to explain cognitive development across the life span.

cognitive development
study of how children acquire the ability to learn, think, reason, communicate, and remember

Theories of Cognitive Development

Psychologists have generated a variety of theoretical perspectives to explain how our thinking develops. Cognitive developmental theories differ in three core ways:

1. Some propose *stagelike* changes in understanding (sudden spurts in knowledge followed by periods of stability); others, more *continuous* (gradual, incremental) changes in understanding.
2. Some adopt a *domain-general* account of development; others, a *domain-specific* account. Domain-general accounts propose that changes in children's cognitive skills affect most or all areas of cognitive function in tandem. In contrast, domain-specific accounts propose that children's cognitive skills develop independently and at different rates across different domains, such as reasoning, language, and counting.
3. They differ in their views of the main source of learning. Some models emphasize physical experience (moving around in the world); others, social interaction (how parents and peers engage with them); and still others, biological maturation (innate programming of certain mental capacities).

PIAGET'S THEORY: HOW CHILDREN CONSTRUCT THEIR WORLDS. The Swiss psychologist Jean Piaget (1896–1980) was the first person to present a comprehensive account of cognitive development. He attempted to identify the stages that children pass through on their way to adultlike thinking. Piaget's theory led to the formation of cognitive development as a distinct discipline, and for decades, most research in this field focused on substantiating—or more recently, refuting—his claims.

Perhaps Piaget's greatest contribution was his insight that children aren't miniature adults. He showed that children's understanding of the world differs fundamentally from adults' but is perfectly rational given their limited experience with the world. For example, children often believe that their teachers live at school, a reasonable assumption given that's the only place they've seen their teachers. Piaget also demonstrated that children aren't passive observers of their worlds but rather active learners who seek information and observe the consequences of their actions.

Piaget was a *stage theorist*. He proposed that children's development is marked by radical reorganization of thinking at specific transition points—stages—followed by periods during which their understanding of the world stabilizes. He also believed that the end point of cognitive development is the achievement of the ability to reason logically about hypothetical problems. As outlined in the box on the next page Piaget identified four stages, each of which is characterized by a certain level of abstract reasoning capacity, with the ability to think beyond the here and now increasing at each stage. Piaget's stages are domain general, slicing across all areas of cognitive capacity. Thus, a child capable of a certain level of abstract reasoning in mathematics can also achieve this level in a spatial problem-solving task.

Piaget proposed that cognitive change is a result of children's need to achieve *equilibration:* maintaining a balance between their experience of the world and their understanding of it. Children, he argued, are motivated to match their thinking about reality with their observations. When the child experiences something new, she checks whether that experience fits with her understanding of how the world works. If the information is inconsistent, as when a child experiences the world as flat but learns in school that the earth is round, something must give way. Piaget

Jean Piaget was the first scientist to develop a comprehensive theory of cognitive development. His ideas rested on the assumption that children's thinking was not just an immature form of adult thinking but was fundamentally different from that of adults.

Piaget's Stages of Development

STAGE	TYPICAL AGES	DESCRIPTION
Sensorimotor	**Birth to 2 years**	**No thought beyond immediate physical experiences**
Children's main source of knowledge, thinking, and experience in this stage is their physical interactions with the world. They acquire all information through perceiving and observing the physical consequences of their actions. The major milestone of this stage is *mental representation*—the ability to think about things that are absent from immediate surroundings, such as remembering previously encountered objects.		
Preoperational	**2 to 7 years**	**Able to think beyond the here and now, but egocentric and unable to perform mental transformations**
Children can use symbols such as language and drawings as representations of ideas in this stage. When a child holds a banana and pretends it's a phone, he's displaying symbolic behavior. He has a mental representation that differs from his physical experience. This stage is called "preoperational" because children are unable to perform what Piaget referred to as *mental operations*. Although they have mental representations, they can't perform mental transformations ("operations") on them.		
Concrete Operations	**7 to 11 years**	**Able to perform mental transformations but only on concrete physical objects**
In this stage, children have the ability to perform mental operations, but only for actual physical events. For example, they can sort coins by size or set up a battle scene with toy soldiers. But they can't perform mental operations in abstract or hypothetical situations. They need physical experience as an anchor to which they can tether their mental operations.		
Formal Operations	**11 years to adulthood**	**Able to perform hypothetical and abstract reasoning**
Children can now perform what Piaget regarded as the most sophisticated type of thinking: hypothetical reasoning beyond the here and now. Children at this stage can understand logical concepts, such as if–then statements ("If I'm late for school, then I'll get sent to the principal's office"). They can also begin to think about abstract questions like the meaning of life.		

SOURCE: Based on Jean Piaget, The Psychology Of The Child, 2008. © Scott O.Lilienfeld.

suggested that children use two processes—assimilation and accommodation—to keep their thinking about the world in tune with their experiences.

assimilation

Piagetian process of absorbing new experience into current knowledge structures

Assimilation and Accommodation. The process of absorbing new experience into our current understanding is **assimilation**. Children use assimilation to acquire and integrate new knowledge within a stage. During assimilation, the child's cognitive skills and worldviews remain unchanged. So when she learns new information that conflicts with her existing knowledge, she reinterprets new experiences to fit with what she already knows.

The assimilation process can continue for only so long. Eventually, the child can no longer reconcile what she believes with what she experiences. When a child can no longer assimilate experiences into her existing knowledge structures, something has to budge. She's forced to engage in accommodation.

accommodation

Piagetian process of altering a belief to make it more compatible with experience

Accommodation is the process of altering beliefs about the world to make them more compatible with experience. Stage changes are the result of accommodation, because accommodation forces children to accept a new way of looking at the world. This process of assimilating and accommodating in tandem ensures a state of harmony between the world and mind of the child—equilibration.

Figure 10.6 An Example of Assimilation and Accommodation in Action

(a) Initial Belief   (b) Assimilation   (c) Accommodation

(a) A child who believes the earth is flat faces a challenge to her understanding when she learns that the earth is round. (b) She might assimilate this new knowledge by picturing a flat disk, like a coin. This adjustment allows her to absorb this fact without changing her belief that the earth is flat. However, a child confronted with a globe will have a difficult time assimilating this information into her conception of the earth as flat. (c) When the child's existing beliefs can no longer assimilate new information, her beliefs undergo accommodation to more accurately reflect the new information.

Pros and Cons of Piaget's Theory. Piaget's theory was a significant landmark in psychology because it helped us understand how children's thinking evolves into more adultlike thinking. Nevertheless, his theory turned out to be inaccurate in several ways. Subsequent research has revealed that much of development is more continuous than stagelike (Flavell, 1992; Klahr & MacWhinney, 1998; Siegler, 1995). Developmental change is also less domain-general than Piaget proposed.

Another criticism of Piaget's theory is that some phenomena he observed appeared to be at least partly a product of task demands. He often relied on children's ability to reflect and report on their reasoning processes. As a result, he probably underestimated children's abilities. Investigators using tasks that are less dependent on language have often failed to

Different Cognitive Tasks Used to Illustrate Piaget's Stages

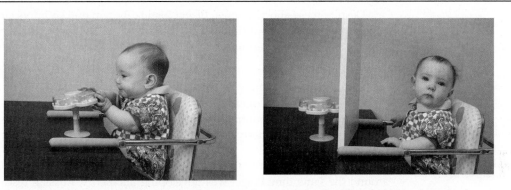

This child appears to have forgotten that the toy continues to exist after it's been hidden from view, demonstrating the lack of the Piagetian concept Mental Representation.

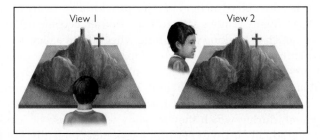

Piaget's three mountain task requires children to look at a display from one perspective (View 1) and infer what someone would see if viewing the mountains from a different perspective (View 2). Piaget argued that egocentric reasoning in the preoperational stage prevents children from succeeding at this task.

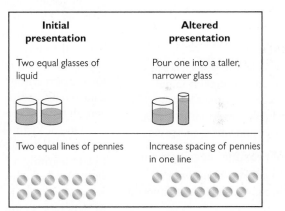

	Initial presentation	Altered presentation
	Two equal glasses of liquid	Pour one into a taller, narrower glass
	Two equal lines of pennies	Increase spacing of pennies in one line

Piaget's conservation tasks ask the child to examine two equal amounts and then watch as the researcher manipulates one of the two amounts in some way. The researcher then asks the child to compare the two quantities. The conservation of liquid task is on the top; the conservation of number task, on the bottom. To succeed at the conservation task, children need to say that the amounts remain the same even though they appear unequal.

Piaget's pendulum task requires children to answer the question: "What makes a pendulum swing faster or slower?" Children have the opportunity to construct a pendulum using longer and shorter strings with heavier and lighter weights. Children in the formal operations stage can systematically manipulate various combinations of weights and lengths to observe how they influenced the speed of the swing.

Replicability

Can the results be duplicated in other studies?

replicate Piaget's findings. In fact, many researchers have found that children can achieve important milestones such as hypothesis testing at considerably earlier ages than reported by Piaget (Baillargeon, 1987; Gopnik, 2012).

Piaget's methodologies may also have been culturally biased in that they elicited more sophisticated responses from children in Westernized societies with formal education than from children in non-Westernized societies. Indeed, non-Westernized children often reveal sophisticated insights when interviewed in a more culturally sensitive manner (Cole, 1990; Gellatly, 1987; Luria, 1976; Rogoff & Chavajay, 1995). Meanwhile, even in Western societies, a significant proportion of adolescents and even adults fail some formal operational tasks (Byrnes, 1988; Kuhn et al., 1995), suggesting that Piaget may have been overly optimistic about the typical course of cognitive development. Perhaps he based his conclusions on a particularly educated sample that skewed his estimates of the typical developmental trajectory. Piaget's observations themselves may also have been biased because many were based on tests of his own three children.

Despite these shortcomings, Piaget justifiably remains an important figure in the field of cognitive development (Lourenco & Machado, 1996). As a result of his legacy, psychologists today have reconceptualized cognitive development by:

1. Viewing children as different in kind rather than degree from adults.
2. Characterizing learning as an active rather than passive process.
3. Exploring general cognitive processes that may cut across multiple domains of knowledge, thereby accounting for cognitive development in terms of fewer—and more parsimonious—underlying processes.

Occam's Razor

Does a simpler explanation fit the data just as well?

VYGOTSKY'S THEORY: SOCIAL AND CULTURAL INFLUENCES ON LEARNING. At around the same time Piaget was developing his theory, Russian researcher Lev Vygotsky (1896–1934) was developing a different but equally comprehensive theory of cognitive development.

Vygotsky was particularly interested in how social and cultural factors influence learning. He noted that parents and other caretakers tend to structure the learning environment for children in ways that guide them to behave as if they've learned something before they have. This process is now known as **scaffolding**, a term borrowed from building construction (Wood, Bruner, & Ross, 1976). Just as builders provide external scaffolds for support while a building is under construction, parents provide a structure to aid their children. Over time, parents gradually remove structure as children become better able to complete tasks on their own, much like taking off training wheels from a bicycle.

One of Vygotsky's most influential notions was developmental readiness for learning. He identified the **zone of proximal development** as the phase when children are receptive to learning a new skill but aren't yet successful at it. He suggested that for any given skill, children move from a phase when they can't learn it, even with assistance, to the zone of proximal development, during which they're ready to make use of scaffolding. In Vygotsky's view, children gradually learn to perform a task independently, but require guidance when getting started. Vygotsky also believed that different children can acquire skills and master tasks at different rates. For him, there were no domain-general stages.

Vygotsky's work has had a substantial impact on European, British, and American researchers and remains influential today, especially in educational settings, where guided learning and peer collaboration are popular (Gredler, 2012; Jaramillo, 1996; Rogoff, 1995; Tomasello, 2008). Whereas Piaget emphasized physical interaction with the world as the primary source of learning, Vygotsky emphasized social interaction.

scaffolding

Vygotskian learning mechanism in which parents provide initial assistance in children's learning but gradually remove structure as children become more competent

zone of proximal development

phase of learning during which children can benefit from instruction

CONTEMPORARY THEORIES OF COGNITIVE DEVELOPMENT. Theoretical accounts today are more diverse than when the field of cognitive development got off the ground, and few are strictly Piagetian or Vygotskian. Still, we can trace the roots of each theory to one of these two theorists.

General Cognitive Accounts. Several modern theories resemble Piaget's theories in that they emphasize general cognitive abilities and acquired rather than innate knowledge (Bloom, 2000; Elman, 2005). Contemporary theorists share Piaget's commitment to general cognitive processes and experience-based learning. Nevertheless, they differ from Piaget in that they regard learning as gradual rather than stagelike.

The term *scaffolding* is used to refer to the way parents structure the learning environment for their children. Here, the father is instructing his child on how to fit the shape onto a peg, but allowing the child to insert the shape herself.

Fact vs. Fiction

Piaget's and Vygotsky's theories differed in their predictions about whether developmental growth in children's ability would be more gradual or more abrupt. Piaget argued for stagelike change whereas Vygotsky posited that change would be more incremental. (See bottom of page for answer.)

○ Fact

○ Fiction

Lev Vygotsky (pictured here with his daughter) developed a theory of cognitive development that emphasized social and cultural information as the key sources of learning. Although Vygotsky's scholarly career was shortened by an early death (he died of tuberculosis at age 37), his theory is still extremely influential.

Sociocultural Accounts. These theories emphasize the social context and the ways in which interactions with caretakers and other children guide children's understanding of the world (Rogoff, 1998; Tomasello, 2000). Some sociocultural theorists emphasize experience-based learning; others, innate knowledge. But along with Vygotsky, they share a focus on the child's interaction with the social world as the primary source of development.

Modular Accounts. Like Vygotsky's theory, this class of theories emphasizes the idea of domain-specific learning, that is, separate spheres of knowledge in different domains (Carey, 1985; Waxman & Booth, 2001). For example, the knowledge base for understanding language may be independent of the ability to reason about space, with no overlapping cognitive skills between them.

Journal Prompt

Using Vygotsky's idea of zone of proximal development, describe a time when (a) something was very easy and you did not need help, (b) something was so difficult you could not do it even with help, and (c) a time when you were able to do something with some help from another person. In which situation did you learn the most?

Cognitive Landmarks of Early Development

We've already learned about some of the major cognitive developmental accomplishments within the realms of perception, memory, and language. But children must attain a variety of other cognitive skills to make sense of their worlds. Here, we'll review a few of the important milestones.

PHYSICAL REASONING: FIGURING OUT WHICH WAY IS UP. To understand their physical worlds, children must learn to reason about them. Children need to learn that objects are solid, they fall when dropped, and one object can disappear behind another and reappear on the other side. Adults take all of these concepts for granted, but they aren't obvious to novice experiencers of the world.

Piaget proposed that sensorimotor children don't understand that objects continue to exist when they're out of view—an ability known as *object permanence.* He based his conclusions on the finding that infants don't search for an object if it's hidden under a cloth. Nevertheless, Renee Baillargeon (1987) showed that by five months and possibly younger, infants display an understanding of object permanence if given a task that doesn't require a physically coordinated search for the object. Baillargeon based her conclusions on

Answer: Fact. Piaget argued that there are sweeping changes that happen in which children take a step forward in their ability to mentally represent their experiences. For Vygotsky, change took place gradually over time based on experience with parents and other caretakers.

Figure 10.7 Children Learn Gradually That Unsupported Objects Will Fall

As early as four-and-a-half months, infants expect objects that are completely unsupported, as in (a) to fall and objects that are completely supported, as in (e) not to fall. An understanding of how much support must be present to prevent an object from falling develops over time. Early on, infants expect that any contact with a support surface will prevent the object from falling, as in (b), (c), and (d). With experience, infants learn to expect that only those in (d) and (e), in which the majority of the weight is on the support surface, won't fall.

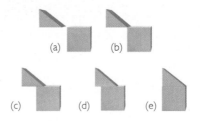

(a) (b) (c) (d) (e)

Children acquire concepts of events as well as objects. For example, young children rapidly learn what's likely to occur during routine events such as birthday parties, visits to the doctor's office, and trips to fast-food restaurants. Children depend so heavily on their expectations of events that they sometimes incorrectly recall a typical feature of an event that didn't occur (Fivush & Hudson, 1990; Nelson & Hudson, 1988).

studies of how long infants look at displays that are either consistent or inconsistent with object permanence. She hypothesized that young children failed Piaget's object permanence task not because they lacked object permanence, but because they lacked the ability to plan and perform a physical search for the hidden toy. When Baillargeon eliminated these task demands by relying on a looking-based measure, an earlier mastery of object permanence emerged. Infants possess a basic understanding of some other aspects of how physical objects behave. For example, they know that unsupported objects should fall (Spelke, 1994). This knowledge becomes more refined with experience (see Figure 10.7) (Baillargeon & Hanko-Summers, 1990; Needham & Baillargeon, 1993). In particular, as we age, we become less reliant on intuitions and more reliant on evidence of how things actually work.

One major barrier to developing an ability to reason about the physical world is that children (and often even adults) experience some interference from what has sometimes been called "naïve" or "folk" psychology, much of which derives from our common sense about how the world works. For example, children frequently fail to accurately predict the trajectory of a moving object because they attribute intentions or goals to the object that violate basic physics principles (Bloom & Weisberg, 2007). Anyone who has ever hit a golf ball or billiard ball and has yelled at it for failing to move in the direction it was supposed to go can almost certainly relate.

Folk psychology can interfere with our reasoning about physical objects in other ways. For example, children often suggest that clouds exist for the purpose of making it rain or that trees grow to provide homes for birds (Kelemen, Rottman, & Seston, 2012). Over time, especially with formal science education, many children can learn to stop attributing physical events and observations to human-like goals or intentions (Opfer & Gelman, 2011). But even college students, when caught unaware in an unfamiliar situation, can allow their folk psychology to interfere with their physical reasoning (McCloskey, 1983). Not only is formal science education only partially successful, it doesn't appear to be necessary to overcome these assumptions. Indigenous cultures, such as the Itza Maya in Guatemala, who are more connected to the natural world than are industrialized societies, seem to overcome these reasoning biases without any formal education (Medin & Atran, 2004). As we've discussed throughout this text, scientific reasoning is not especially intuitive (McCauley, 2012), which is why we've worked so hard to help you understand and apply it. Practice doesn't make perfect, but it sure helps!

CONCEPTS AND CATEGORIES: CLASSIFYING THE WORLD. One of the most fundamental cognitive accomplishments is learning to categorize objects by kind. Children learn to recognize dogs even though dogs come in all shapes, sizes, and colors. They also learn to distinguish dogs from cats, horses, and goats. Categorization is crucial because it frees us from having to explore every object to find out what it is and does (see LO 8.1a). Imagine if every time a baby were given a new bottle, she had to discover through trial and error what it was. Children, not to mention adults, wouldn't get very far without categories.

Even infants possess basic abilities to categorize. When shown a series of pictures of birds, infants eventually get bored with them and look away, but they exhibit fresh interest when shown a picture of a dinosaur. This finding implies that they've categorized birds as all of the same kind and therefore no longer new, but the dinosaur as belonging to a different category (Arterberry & Bornstein, 2012; Quinn & Eimas, 1996).

Over the course of development, conceptual knowledge becomes richer, more detailed, and more flexible (Nelson, 1977). Children learn how objects are thematically related to each other, such as a dog and a bone being related because dogs eat bones. They also learn more about aspects of categories that explain how members of categories connect, such as that fruits taste sweet and grow on trees. This increased conceptual knowledge about categories assists them in reasoning about the world.

SELF-CONCEPT AND THE CONCEPT OF "OTHER": WHO WE ARE AND WHO WE AREN'T. Developing a sense of self as distinct from others is critical for children's development. Their ability to understand themselves as possessing unique identities mostly develops during the toddler and preschool years (Harter, 2012).

Psychomythology

Creating "Superbabies" One App at a Time

For years, parents have yearned for a quick and easy educational method to boost their infants' intelligence. After all, in today's cutthroat world, what parents wouldn't want to place their child at a competitive advantage? To get a jump-start, of course, parents must begin early, ideally soon after birth. In the 1980s, thousands of parents bombarded their newborn infants with activities designed to teach them foreign languages and advanced math in an effort to create "superbabies" (Clarke-Stewart, 1988). In the 1990s, the press reported on a research finding dubbed the "Mozart Effect." The actual finding was quite a modest—but interesting—discovery that college students performed better on a spatial reasoning task if they'd heard classical music immediately beforehand (Rauscher, Shaw, & Ky, 1993). The finding was exaggerated in the media which touted it as a sure-fire way to increase intelligence, leading hundreds of thousands of parents to begin playing classical music to their babies. Unfortunately, there's no evidence that listening to classical music has any lasting impact on intelligence (Chabris, 1999; Steele, Bass, & Crook, 1999). In fact, the transient effects observed doesn't appear to be specific to music at all. Instead, the most parsimonious explanation turns out to be that emotional arousal temporarily boosts performance in general, and the classical music is just one way to influence people's emotions (Thompson, Schellenberg, & Husain, 2001).

As technology has evolved, infant-oriented multimedia educational tools have become a huge industry including videos, interactive toys, and smartphone and tablet apps. Parents and grandparents have spent hundreds of millions of dollars on products such as Baby Einstein videos and Leapfrog toys to improve their babies' intelligence (Minow, 2005; Quart, 2006). Yet there's limited evidence that these products work. In fact, research suggests that babies learn less from videos than from playing actively for the same time period (Anderson & Pempek, 2005; Zimmerman, Christakis, & Meltzoff, 2007). One reason for this deficit in learning from videos may be that they are often solitary activities that don't actively involve parental support for learning. When parents participate in the learning process, learning from videos and other media is somewhat more successful (Dayanim & Namy, 2015). As discussed in the video that follows, many experts believe that technology-free learning opportunities are the most natural and most effective ones.

Watch   SMART BABIES BY DESIGN

Video

Kathy Hirsh-Pasek
Temple University

But even by three months of age, infants possess some ability to distinguish themselves from others. Babies at this age who view videos of themselves side by side with another baby prefer to look at the image of the other baby (Bahrick, Moss, & Fadil, 1996; Rochat, 2001), suggesting that they recognize the other baby as being different from them. Even if all they can see is their legs and another infant's legs, they still prefer to watch the video of the other baby's legs. This finding demonstrates that babies' preference for another baby's face isn't merely a result of having seen their own face in the mirror or in photographs.

As early as their first birthdays, children can recognize their images in a mirror (Amsterdam, 1972; Priel & deSchonen, 1986). By two years, they can recognize pictures of themselves and refer to themselves by name (Lewis & Brooks-Gunn, 1979). These accomplishments appear to be tied to development in a specific brain region, namely, the junction of the left temporal and parietal lobes (Lewis & Carmody, 2008; Grossman, 2015). A further milestone is children's ability to understand that others' perspectives can differ from theirs—a capacity called **theory of mind** (Premack & Woodruff, 1978). Theory of mind refers to children's ability to reason about what other people believe. The big challenge for children on this front is to realize that "other people may not know what I know." In some sense, children know this fact by the time they're one or two years old, because they ask their parents questions like "Where's Daddy?" and "What's this?" revealing that they expect parents to know things they don't. Yet it's particularly challenging for children to realize that sometimes *they* know things that others don't.

A classic test of theory of mind is the *false-belief task* (Birch & Bloom, 2007; Wimmer & Perner, 1983), which evaluates children's

theory of mind

ability to reason about what other people know or believe

Infants who view a video image of their own legs side by side with a videotape of another infant's legs will look longer at the video of the other baby. This finding suggests that infants recognize the correspondence between the video images and their own bodies (Bahrick & Watson, 1985) and find their own actions less interesting to watch.

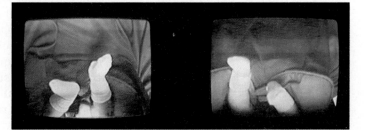

Figure 10.8 The False-Belief Task

In the false-belief task, the child participant knows something about which someone else is unaware. (a) The child learns about a scenario in which a little boy, Joey, is helping his mom put away groceries. (b) His mom lets him put his candy bar in the cabinet. (c) Then Joey walks away. (d) While Joey is out of the room, his mom moves the candy bar to the refrigerator.

The child participant now knows where the candy bar really is. The question is whether she recognizes that Joey doesn't know. When asked where Joey thinks the candy is, will the child respond with her own knowledge of the true location, or will she realize that Joey is unaware of this change and still believes the candy bar is in the cabinet?

(a)   (b)   (c)   (d)

ability to understand that someone else believes something they know to be wrong. In this task, children hear a story (often accompanied by illustrations like those in Figure 10.8) about a child who stores a special treat in one place, but a third party (such as the child's mother), unbeknownst to the child, moves the treat to another place. Researchers then ask the child where the child in the story will look for the treat when he returns. Children who pass this task understand that although they know where the treat is actually hidden, the child in the story holds an incorrect belief about the treat's location. Those who fail the task believe that if they know where the treat is, the child in the story must know too.

Children typically don't succeed at this task until around age four or five. Yet how early children succeed on false-belief tasks varies depending on seemingly minor variations in the task, such as whether it's a story-book or real-world situation (Wellman, Cross, & Watson, 2001). Also, if researchers tell children the reason for the change was to "trick" someone, they're more successful at an earlier age. Thus, the age at which children pass the false-belief task is due partially to aspects of the task in addition to their understanding of others' knowledge (Dalke, 2011). Still, it's clear that the ability to understand others' perspectives increases with age.

Ruling Out Rival Hypotheses

Have important alternative explanations for the findings been excluded?

NUMBERS AND MATHEMATICS: WHAT COUNTS. Counting and math are relatively recent achievements in human history. Humans developed the first counting system only a few thousand years ago. Unlike many cognitive skills that children acquire, counting and mathematics don't inevitably develop. In fact, in a few nonindustrialized cultures such as the Pirahã, a tribe in Brazil, conventional counting and mathematics appear not to exist (Gordon, 2004; Everett & Madora, 2012).

Learning to count is much more complex than it seems. Of course, many children learn to "count to 10" at a very early age, reciting "1-2-3-4-5-6-7-8-9-10" in rapid succession and waiting for applause to follow. But children must also learn a variety of more complex aspects of numbers, such as that (1) numbers are about amount, (2) number words refer to specific quantities (and not just "a bunch" or "a few"), and (3) numbers are ordered from smallest to largest in quantity (Gelman & Gallistel, 1978). Children must also master the idea that two elephants are the same number as two grains of rice—that the *size* of entities isn't relevant to quantity. Kelly Mix and her colleagues showed that this insight is extremely difficult for children (Mix, 1999; Mix, Huttenlocher, & Levine,

Fact vs. Fiction

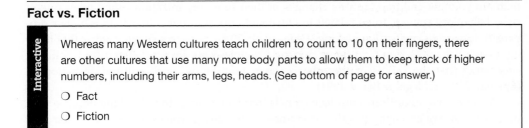

Whereas many Western cultures teach children to count to 10 on their fingers, there are other cultures that use many more body parts to allow them to keep track of higher numbers, including their arms, legs, heads. (See bottom of page for answer.)

○ Fact

○ Fiction

Figure 10.9 Children Find It Easier to Match Quantities When the Objects Resemble Each Other

In Mix's studies, children match the display on the left with one of the displays on the right. Children find this much easier in the top figure (a), in which the disks resemble the dots, than in the bottom figure (b), in which the stimuli are different.

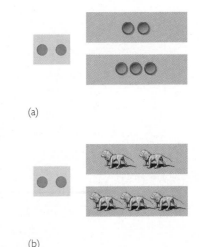

(a)

(b)

SOURCE: Based on Mix, 1999.

1996). Children find it easier to match two sets of the same quantity when the objects to be counted closely resemble each other than when they look different (see Figure 10.9). When similarity among the objects is high, children master this task at three years of age, but when the objects look different, children don't succeed until three-and-a-half years. And when they have to match the quantity of a visual set with sets of sounds, they don't succeed until after age four.

Counting and other mathematical skills in preschool- and school-aged children develop at different rates across cultures. Cross-cultural differences in how parents and teachers introduce counting to children seem to account, at least in part, for these differences. Differences in how linguistic counting systems are structured also play a role. For example, the English word *twelve* doesn't convey any information about what quantity it represents, whereas in Chinese, it's literally translated as "one ten, two," which appears to help children understand what quantity it represents (Gladwell, 2008; Miller et al., 1995).

Cognitive Changes in Adolescence

As Piaget noted, it's not until adolescence that we achieve our most abstract levels of reasoning ability. There are many reasons that cognitive development continues well into the teenage years. Part of the story here is about brain development, and part of it is about the kinds of problems, opportunities, and experiences we encounter for the very first time during adolescence.

Although most brain maturation occurs prenatally and in the first few years of life, the frontal lobes don't mature fully until late adolescence or early adulthood (Casey, Giedd, & Thomas, 2000; Johnson, 1998) as discussed in LO 3.1b. The frontal lobes are largely responsible for planning, decision making, and impulse control. The fact that the frontal lobes are still maturing during adolescence may explain some of the impulsive behaviors, like skateboarding down a steep incline, for which teens are notorious (Weinberger, Elvevag, & Giedd, 2005). Even on the simplest tasks, such as suppressing the impulse to look at a flashing light, teens have a more difficult time and require more brain processing than do adults (Luna & Sweeney, 2004). In addition, during adolescence, limbic structures of the brain involved in social rewards become more active, probably rendering teens susceptible to peer group influences, which can lead to further risk-taking (Steinberg, 2007). There are also significant changes in connectivity across different brain systems during adolescence. Some areas become more connected during adolescence, whereas others become more functionally independent. Both types of changes have an impact on adolescents' behaviors including learning, motivation, motor coordination, and inhibitory control (Stevens, 2016; van Duijvenvoorde et al., 2016).

Adolescents routinely encounter new adultlike opportunities to engage in potentially harmful activities, even though their brains aren't ready to make well-reasoned decisions. For example, they're often faced with decisions such as whether to have sex, engage in vandalism, or drive drunk. Adolescents must negotiate these choices without a "full deck" of decision-making cards. Nevertheless, there's debate over whether we can blame teen behavioral problems entirely on the "teen brain." Teens are no more prone to risk taking

Answer: Fact. Some counting systems have enough designated body parts to allow for counting up to as high as 74.

than are younger children, despite changes in their brain organization—the higher rate of risky behaviors appears to be related to enhanced opportunities rather than a higher propensity toward risky decision making (Defoe et al., 2015). Some researchers argue that these impulsive behaviors don't routinely appear in adolescents in non-Westernized cultures, suggesting that the causes of this phenomenon may be as much cultural as biological (Epstein, 2007; Schlegel & Barry, 1991).

A common assumption about teenagers is that they engage in risk-taking because they possess a sense of invincibility—they don't believe bad things can ever happen to them. But research calls this notion into question (Vartanian, 2000). Most adolescents don't actually underestimate the risks of such behaviors as driving fast or having early or unprotected sex (they're often aware they're taking chances, but believe they're willing to accept the consequences) (Albert, Chein, & Stein, 2013; Reyna & Farley, 2006).

ATTITUDES TOWARD KNOWLEDGE IN ADOLESCENTS AND YOUNG ADULTS. Another critical cognitive change that takes place during the late high school and college years is in adolescents' and young adults' perspectives toward knowledge. Students starting college are often frustrated to find few black-and-white answers to questions, including questions in their psychology courses. One of the hardest things for them to appreciate is that the answer to questions like "Which theory is better?" is often "It depends." William Perry (1970) cataloged the transitions that students undergo during the college years as they discover that their professors have few absolute answers to offer. He noted that over the course of their college years, students pass through a variety of "positions," or perspectives, on knowledge.

Students who expect clear right or wrong answers to all questions may initially resist changing their views and instead try to reconcile their expectations with what they're learning in the classroom (recall Piaget's assimilation process). They may understand that the "it depends" perspective is the one their professors want them to embrace. So they'll often say the "right things" on exams to get good grades, but believe deep down that there's a right and a wrong answer to most questions. With time and experience, students relax their expectations for absolute answers and construe knowledge as relative. Ultimately, students typically come to realize that they can't abandon the idea of "truth" or "reality" completely, but recognize that they can appreciate and respect differing points of view. Although the past three decades have witnessed minor modifications to Perry's stages, his overall model has withstood the test of time (Cano, 2005; Cano & Cardelle-Elawar, 2004).

Cognitive Function in Adulthood

There are minuses and pluses to growing older. On the downside, many aging adults complain that they just can't remember things they used to. They're right: Many aspects of cognitive function *do* decline as people get older (Ghisletta et al., 2012). Our ability to recall information, especially the names of people, objects, and places, begins to decrease after age 30. Still, there's considerable variability in how much memory declines, with most people experiencing only modest decreases with age (Shimamura et al., 1995). People's overall speed of processing also declines, which is why teenagers can regularly beat older adults at video games and other speed-sensitive tasks (Cerella, 1985; Salthouse, 2004). These age-related declines are probably a result of brain changes that occur with age, because overall brain matter decreases over the course of adulthood. Age-related declines in brain volume are particularly pronounced in certain brain areas (Scahill et al., 2003), including the cortex (see LO 3.1b) and the hippocampus, which plays a key role in memory (see LO 7.1c). Aging brains also become less efficient at "emptying the trash"—removing waste proteins, which also contributes to cognitive decline (Kress et al., 2014)

On the upside, some aspects of cognitive function are largely spared from age-related decline, and others actually improve with age:

- Although free recall (being asked to generate items from memory) declines with age, cued recall and recognition remain intact (Schonfield & Robertson, 1966).
- Aging adults show relatively little decline when asked to remember material that's pertinent to their everyday lives, as opposed to the random lists of words often used in memory research (Graf, 1990; Perlmutter, 1983).

Ruling Out Rival Hypotheses

Have important alternative explanations for the findings been excluded?

Replicability

Can the results be duplicated in other studies?

When we consider that older adults have decades of accumulated knowledge and crystallized intelligence outstripping that of younger adults, we can see why many of the world's cultures honor and revere the elderly.

- Older adults perform better on most vocabulary and knowledge tests than do younger adults (Cattell, 1963). Crystallized intelligence, our accumulated knowledge and experience, tends to stay the same or increase with age (Baltes, Saudinger, & Lindenberger, 1999; Beier & Ackerman, 2001; Horn & Hofer, 1992). Here's a case in which common sense is true: Older *is* wiser!

10.4: The Developing Personality: Social and Moral Development

10.4a Describe how and when children establish emotional bonds with their caregivers.

10.4b Explain the environmental and genetic influences on social behavior and social style in children.

10.4c Determine how morality and identity develop during adolescence and emerging adulthood.

10.4d Identify developmental changes during major life transitions in adults.

10.4e Summarize different ways of conceptualizing old age.

We humans are inherently social beings. Our work lives, school lives, romantic lives, and family lives all involve interaction with others. Because social relationships are so central to our everyday functioning, it's not surprising that our interpersonal relations change as we develop.

Social Development in Infancy and Childhood

Soon after birth, infants begin to take a keen interest in others. Infants prefer looking at faces over just about all other visual information. As early as four days after birth, infants show a marked preference for Mommy's face over that of other people (Pascalis et al., 1995). Infants' interest in others is a good thing because people—particularly familiar people like their parents—are valuable sources of information and provide the love and support infants need to flourish.

Infants become increasingly socially engaged and interactive with others over the first six or seven months. But then something changes dramatically. The same infant who was giggling on the floor with a perfect stranger at six months may scream in terror if approached by that same stranger only a few months later. This phenomenon, known as **stranger anxiety**, manifests itself in a fear of strangers beginning at about eight or nine months of age (Greenberg, Hillman, & Grice, 1973; Konner, 1990). It generally increases up until about 12 to 15 months of age and then declines steadily (see Figure 10.10). Stranger anxiety makes good evolutionary sense, because it occurs around the age most infants begin to crawl around on their own (Boyer & Bergstrom, 2011). As a result, it's the age at which infants can—and usually do—find a way to get themselves into trouble. So this anxiety may be an adaptive mechanism for keeping infants away from dangers, including unknown adults. Interestingly, the onset of stranger anxiety appears to be virtually identical across all cultures (Kagan, 1976). Although stranger anxiety is a virtually universal across most infants, babies who exhibit more extreme or more prolonged stranger anxiety also tend to be more inhibited later in childhood (Brooker et al., 2013).

TEMPERAMENT AND SOCIAL DEVELOPMENT: BABIES' EMOTIONAL STYLES. As anyone who's spent time with infants can attest, babies vary widely in their social interaction styles. Some are friendly, others are shy and wary, and still others ignore most people altogether. These individual differences in children's social and emotional styles reflect differences in **temperament** (Mervielde et al., 2005). Temperament can be distinguished from other later appearing personality characteristics because it emerges early and appears to be largely genetically influenced, although there's some evidence that maternal stress levels during pregnancy may also impact infant temperament (Baibazarova et al., 2013; van den Heuvel et al., 2015).

In their studies of American children, Alexander Thomas and Stella Chess (1977) identified three major temperamental styles. *Easy* infants (about 40 percent of babies) are adaptable and relaxed, *difficult* infants (about 10 percent of babies) are fussy and easily frustrated,

stranger anxiety

a fear of strangers developing at eight or nine months of age

temperament

basic emotional style that appears early in development and is largely genetic in origin

Figure 10.10 Stranger Anxiety

As we can see in this graph, infants' wariness when confronted with a stranger first begins at around eight or nine months and continues to increase. Typically, stranger anxiety reactions declines between 12 and 15 months of age.

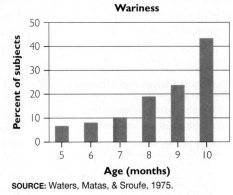

Wariness

SOURCE: Waters, Matas, & Sroufe, 1975.

▶ **Ruling Out Rival Hypotheses**

Have important alternative explanations for the findings been excluded?

The majority of children fall into one of three temperament categories: (a) easy, (b) difficult, and (c) slow to warm up

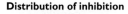

Figure 10.11 Behaviorally Inhibited Children

About 10 percent of children are behaviorally inhibited, with the majority either uninhibited or somewhere in between.

Distribution of inhibition

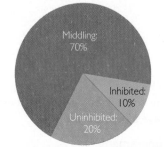

Middling: 70%

Inhibited: 10%

Uninhibited: 20%

SOURCE: Kagan, Reznick, & Snidman, 1988.

and *slow-to-warm-up* infants (about 15 percent of babies) are disturbed by new stimuli at first but gradually adjust to them. The remaining 35 percent of children don't fit neatly into any of these three categories.

Temperament remains largely stable across infancy (Bornstein et al., 2015). Although temperament is largely genetically influenced, an infant's temperament influences how parents and caregivers interact with their infants (Dunn & Kendrick, 1980; Lee & Bates, 1985). In turn, parents' and caregivers' behavior probably shapes infants' temperament. This finding illustrates the concept discussed previously in this chapter that nature can shape nurture. Temperament can even influence how cute adults perceive babies as being. For example, all else being equal, parents perceive infants who laugh a lot as cuter than other babies (Parsons et al., 2014).

Based initially on research with cats, Jerome Kagan identified another temperamental style he termed *behavioral inhibition* (Kagan et al., 2007). Like "scaredy cats," who crawl under the nearest bed at the sight of a new person or moving object, behaviorally inhibited human infants become frightened at the sight of novel or unexpected stimuli like unfamiliar faces, loud tones, or little moving robots (Kagan, Reznick, & Snidman, 1988). Their hearts pound, their bodies tense up, and their amygdalae become active (Schwartz et al., 2003). This last finding makes sense, because we'll recall from earlier in the text that the amygdala plays a key role in processing fear. According to Kagan and his colleagues, we can find this temperamental style in about 10 percent of children (see Figure 10.11).

Infants with high levels of behavioral inhibition are at heightened risk for shyness and anxiety disorders in childhood, adolescence, and adulthood (Biederman et al., 2001; Rotge et al., 2011; Turner, Beidel, & Wolff, 1996). Still, behavioral inhibition isn't all bad. Infants with extremely *low* levels of behavioral inhibition may be at increased risk for impulsive behaviors in later childhood (Burgess et al., 2003), so a certain amount of behavioral inhibition may be healthy. Like other temperaments, behavioral inhibition is genetically influenced but can still be shaped by environmental factors. For example, behaviorally inhibited children placed in daycare settings often adapt to this social environment by becoming less inhibited (Martin & Fox, 2006).

Certain cultural differences in temperament are evident even in newborns (Freedman & DeBoer, 1979; Farkas Farkas & Valloton, 2016). Daniel Freedman (1978; Freedman & Freedman, 1969) compared how Chinese American and European American four-day-old infants reacted when researchers placed a cloth over their faces. Chinese American infants were considerably calmer than were European American infants, many of whom struggled mightily to remove the offending cloths. These findings seem to suggest the presence of genetic differences across ethnicities. Nevertheless, there are several rival explanations. For example, different cultural practices in pregnant women (such as exercise and diet) could change the infant's prenatal environment. There are also cultural differences in how early temperament relates to later adjustment (Gartstein et al., 2013), illustrating how genetic predispositions can be expressed differently in different cultural or family environments. Alternatively, mothers of different cultures may differ in their patterns of hormone release during pregnancy, in turn altering their intrauterine (within the womb) environment.

ATTACHMENT: ESTABLISHING BONDS. Virtually all infants forge close emotional bonds with significant adults, usually their parents. This emotional connection we share with those to whom we feel closest is called **attachment**. There may be a good evolutionary reason for the attachment bond. As psychiatrist John Bowlby (1973) noted, it ensures that infants and children don't stray too far from the caretakers who feed and protect them. To understand the origins of attachment, we need to begin with the story of an Austrian zoologist and his birds.

Ruling out Rival Hypotheses ▶

Have important alternative explanations for the findings been excluded?

attachment

the strong emotional connection we share with those to whom we feel closest

Imprinting. In the 1930s, Konrad Lorenz—who went on to win a Nobel Prize for the work we're about to describe—was observing the behaviors of geese. By sheer accident, he discovered that goslings (young geese) seemed to follow around the first large moving object they saw after hatching, which, in 99 percent or more of cases, turns out to be none other than Mother Goose. Although Lorenz (1937) referred to this phenomenon as "stamping in" in German; it's come to be known in English as *imprinting*. Once a gosling has imprinted on something or someone, it becomes largely fixated on it and is unlikely to follow or bond with anything else. What happens when the mother goose isn't around? Goslings will imprint on whatever large moving object they see first, including large white bouncing balls, boxes on wheels, and even Lorenz himself.

As Nobel Prize–winning biologist Konrad Lorenz goes for a swim, he's followed by three geese who imprinted on him almost immediately after they hatched.

We humans don't imprint onto our mothers the way geese do: We don't bond automatically to the first moving thing we see. Still, human infants and most mammalian infants exhibit a "softer" form of imprinting in which they forge strong bonds with those who tend to them shortly after birth.

Lorenz discovered that imprinting occurs only during a *critical period* (Almli & Finger, 1987): a specific window of time during which an event must occur. Lorenz reported that this critical period was about 36 hours. If the goslings didn't see their mothers until after that window closed, they never imprinted on her or on anything else for that matter. It turns out that critical periods rarely end as abruptly as Lorenz reported (Bruer, 1999). That's especially true of intelligent mammals like cats, dogs, and humans, whose behaviors are more flexible than those of geese. That's why psychologists typically use the term *sensitive period* to refer to developmental windows in creatures with a greater range of behaviors.

Do humans have sensitive periods for the development of healthy interpersonal relationships? Although the question is controversial, early and prolonged separation from attachment figures may produce detrimental effects on psychological adjustment, including social bonding.

Some of the best evidence for this possibility comes from a longitudinal study of infants adopted from Romanian orphanages. In the 1970s and 1980s, all forms of birth control were banned in Romania, resulting in catastrophic numbers of unplanned pregnancies and babies whose parents couldn't support them. Romanian orphanages were overwhelmed by vast numbers of infants for whom they had to provide care. As a result, these orphanages offered little social interaction or emotional care, and infants were often left in their cribs all day and night. These infants had no opportunity to develop bonds with adult caretakers until much later, when thousands of them were adopted by families in the United States and England. This tragic "natural experiment" presented a unique opportunity to study and test the predictions of John Bowlby's Attachment Theory. Bowlby first developed an interest in how young children were affected by early separation from their parents during World War II. Because Germany was frequently bombing London, thousands of London families decided to send their children away into the countryside for safety. Bowlby predicted and found some compelling evidence that children who were separated from their primary caretakers before the age of five were significantly more likely to become delinquents and engage in criminal behavior later in their lives.

The situation in Romania led to opportunities to investigate more systematically exactly how children were affected by the lack of attachment figures, as well as the sensitive period during which attachment figures appear to be especially important. Sir Michael Rutter and his colleagues, among others, found results consistent with Bowlby's. Infants from the Romanian orphanages adopted before six months of age fared well later, but those who were older than six months of age when they were adopted often exhibited what appeared to be negative psychological effects of their early environment, including inattention, hyperactivity, difficulties becoming attached to their adult caregivers, and difficulty in establishing new friendships (Almas et al., 20154; O'Connor & Rutter, 2000; Rutter et al., 2012). Nevertheless, there may be another explanation for these findings: The children who were adopted later may have had more emotional difficulties to begin with. As a consequence, they may have been more difficult to place in adoptive families. Nevertheless, the finding that early

Ruling out Rival Hypotheses

Have important alternative explanations for the findings been excluded?

"IT'S AN INTERESTING PSYCHOLOGICAL PHENOMENON. THEY THINK HE'S THEIR MOTHER. SO DOES HE."

institutionalization is associated with later emotional problems has been replicated in numerous studies using different methodologies (Ames, 1997; Kreppner, O'Connor, & Rutter, 2001).

Contact Comfort: The Healing Touch. Given that human infants don't imprint onto attachment figures, on what basis do they bond to their parents? For decades, psychologists assumed that the primary basis for the attachment bond is survival. Children bond to those who provide them with milk and food, and in most cases this happens to be Mommy. This view fit with a behaviorist account, which proposes that reinforcement is the primary influence on our preferences.

Harry Harlow overturned this assumption in the 1950s with his research on infant rhesus monkeys, which are close genetic relatives of humans (Blum, 2002). Harlow (1958) separated baby monkeys from their mothers only a few hours after birth. He then placed them in a cage with two "surrogate" mothers, both inanimate. One—the "wire mother"—consisted of an angular face and a cold, mangled mesh of uncomfortable metal wires. This wire mother did have one thing going for her, though: nourishment. She sported a little bottle of milk from which the baby monkey could drink. In sharp contrast, the second mother, the "terry cloth mother," had a round face and was made of foam rubber overlaid with a comfortable layer of terry cloth and heated with a light bulb. Harlow found that although baby monkeys routinely went to wire mothers for milk, they spent much more of their time with terry cloth mothers. In addition, when Harlow exposed monkeys to a scary stimulus, like a toy robot playing a drum, they were much more likely to run to the terry cloth mother and cling to her for reassurance. Harlow termed this phenomenon **contact comfort**: the positive emotions afforded by touch. Contact comfort may help us understand why we human primates find simple touch, like holding the hand of a romantic partner, so reassuring. Indeed, direct touch with a caretaker helps babies to thrive, which is the basis for skin-to-skin contact sometimes known as *kangaroo care* in which infants lie skin-to-skin with a parent or caretaker (as if in a kangaroo's pouch). This practice is widely encouraged in maternity wards and birthing center and helps babies gain weight, sleep better, and bond more closely with their parents than does attention alone (Field, 2003)

Attachment Styles: The Strange Situation. Although virtually all infants attach to their parents, different children exhibit this attachment in different ways. Some are cuddly and affectionate, some are clingy, and some seem almost angry with their parents. To investigate whether there are distinct styles of attachment between infants and caregivers, Mary Ainsworth and her colleagues (1978) developed the *Strange Situation*. The Strange Situation is a laboratory procedure designed to evaluate attachment style by observing one-year-olds' reactions to being separated from and then reunited with their primary caregivers, usually their mothers. The Strange Situation starts out by placing the infant and mother in an unfamiliar room loaded with all kinds of interesting toys the infant is free to explore. The researchers observe (1) how comfortable the infant is exploring on his or her own, (2) the infant's emotional reaction when a stranger enters the room, (3) the infant's response to the mother leaving the infant alone with the stranger and (4) the infant's behavior when the mother returns (see Figure 10.12). Based on the infant's behavior in these stages of the Strange Situation, researchers classify infants' attachment relationships into one of four categories.

Replicability

Can the results be duplicated in other studies?

Attachment

When frightened by a novel object, Harlow's infant monkeys almost always preferred the terry cloth mother over the wire mother. This finding tells us attachment is based on contact comfort, not nourishment.

contact comfort

positive emotions afforded by touch

Figure 10.12 Physical Setup of the Strange Situation
In the Strange Situation, both the mother and a stranger are present before the mother leaves the child with the stranger. The child's response to the mother's departure and reaction when she returns are used to determine the child's attachment style.

Mother   Stranger

1. **Secure attachment** (about 60 percent of U.S. infants). The infant explores the room but checks to make sure mom is watching, returns to mom when the stranger enters, reacts to mom's departure by becoming upset, but greets her return with joy. In essence, the infant uses mom as a *secure base:* a rock-solid source of support to which to turn in times of trouble (Bowlby, 1990).
2. **Insecure-avoidant attachment** (about 15–20 percent of U.S. infants). The infant explores the room independently without checking in with mom, is indifferent to the entry of the stranger, shows no distress at mom's departure, and displays little reaction upon her return.
3. **Insecure-anxious attachment** (about 15–20 percent of U.S. infants). The infant does not explore the toys without mom's assistance, shows distress when the stranger enters, reacts to mom's departure with panic, and shows a mixed emotional reaction upon her return, simultaneously reaching for her yet squirming to get away after she picks him or her up (for this reason, some psychologists refer to this style as "anxious-ambivalent").
4. **Disorganized attachment** (about 5–10 percent of U.S infants). This rarest of attachment styles wasn't included in the original classification, but was added later by Mary Main and her colleagues (Main & Cassidy, 1988). Children with this pattern react to the toys, the stranger, and mom's departure and return with an inconsistent and confused set of responses. They may appear dazed when reunited with their mom.

Note that we wrote "U.S. infants" in parentheses following each classification. That's because there are cultural differences in attachment style. For example, more infants in Japan than in the United States fall into the insecure-anxious category, whereas more infants in the United States than in Japan fall into the insecure-avoidant category (Rothbaum et al., 2000). These differences may stem in part from the fact that Japanese babies experience fewer separations from their mothers in everyday life than do American babies. As a consequence, Japanese babies may find the Strange Situation even "stranger"—and more stressful—than do American babies (van Ijzendoorn & Sagi, 1999).

The attachment styles derived from the Strange Situation predict children's later behavior. Infants with a secure attachment style tend to grow up to be more well-adjusted, helpful, and empathic than do infants with other attachment styles (LaFreniere & Sroufe, 1985; Sroufe, 1983). In contrast, infants with an anxious attachment style are more likely to be disliked and mistreated by their peers later in childhood than are infants with other attachment styles.

Infants can form multiple attachments, bonding with both mothers and fathers and with siblings, grandparents, and other caregivers. Their attachment style exhibited with one caregiver doesn't necessarily predict their attachment style with other caregivers (van Ijzendorn & De Wolff, 1997). Developing an attachment to one adult figure in the infant's life doesn't necessarily undermine the ability to form other attachments. Infants placed in daycare may establish secure attachment relationships with their caretakers, although secure attachments are more likely with parents. Moreover, the quality of attachment to daycare workers depends on the quality and type of daycare (Ahnert et al., 2006). In two-parent households, infants typically display a strong early preference for the primary caregiver (usually the mother) that disappears by around 18 months.

Today, most attachment researchers rely on the Strange Situation to measure infants' attachment styles. Although this makes it easier to compare results across studies and individuals, relying on a single measure over and over again has its limitations (Shadish, Cook, & Campbell, 2002). The Strange Situation is, after all, simply one indicator of attachment, and attachment bonds involve many more scenarios than just reactions to novel experiences. To address this concern, some researchers have begun to develop alternative measures of attachment, such as interviews in adulthood designed to assess bonding to one's parents (Hesse, 1999).

The Strange Situation also isn't especially *reliable*. Reliability, we'll recall (see L.O. 2.2a), refers to the consistency of a measuring instrument. If the Strange Situation were a highly reliable measure of attachment, babies who are securely attached at 12 months, for example, should also be securely attached at 14 months. Yet many infants switch their attachment classifications over brief time periods (Lamb et al., 1984; Paris, 2000). In general, attachment styles remain consistent only when the family environment stays the same. For example, if parents undergo a change in job status, their children's attachment style often changes as

"For the last time—don't throw him in the air so roughly!"

Correlation vs. Causation ▶

Can we be sure that A causes B?

Although the popular stereotype of a family includes a husband, a wife, and several children, a surprisingly small proportion of families fit this mold. Single-parent families, same-sex parents, unmarried co-parents, blended families following a second marriage, and childless couples are far more common than most people think.

The Role of the Father.   Fathers differ from mothers in several ways in their interactions with their children. First, fathers and infants tend to share less mutual attention and show less affection than do mothers and their babies (Colonnesi et al., 2012). Second, fathers spend less time with their babies than mothers do, even in households in which both mothers and fathers are at home (Golombok, 2000). Third, when fathers interact with their children, they spend more of their time than do mothers in physical play (Parke, 1996). Fourth, both boys and girls tend to choose their fathers over their mothers as playmates (Clarke-Stewart, 1980). Despite these differences between mothers and fathers, fathers exert an important influence on children's psychological well-being and adjustment. Children benefit from warm, close relationships with their fathers regardless of how much time they spend with him (Lamb & Tamis-LeMonda, 2003; Yogman, Garfield, & Committee on Psychosocial Aspects of Child and Family Health, 2016).

"Nontraditional" Families: Science and Politics.   Most child development research has been conducted on children in "traditional" families—those living in a household with two parents of opposite sex. But many children grow up in single-parent households or have same-sex parents. Politicians and the media have had much to say about the demise of the traditional American family and the need to protect traditional family values. What does research have to say about the effects of "nontraditional" parenting configurations?

The impact of single-parenthood on children is unclear. On the one hand, there's evidence that compared with children from two-parent families, children from single-parent families have more behavior problems, such as aggression and impulsivity (Golombok, 2000), and are at significantly higher risk for crime (Lykken, 1993, 2000). On the other hand, these data are only correlational, so we can't draw causal inferences from them. Single-parent households tend to differ from two-parent households in a variety of ways that may contribute to this correlation. For example, single mothers tend to be poorer, less educated, and marked by higher levels of life stress (Aber & Rappaport, 1994) than are married mothers. Single mothers also move more often, making it difficult for their children to form stable social bonds with peers (Harris, 1998).

Support for the idea that other variables explain child adjustment in single-parent households other than the absence of a second parent comes from research on widowed mothers. Even though these are also single-parent households, children in these families generally exhibit no higher rates of emotional or behavioral problems than do children from two-parent households (Felner et al., 1981; McLeod, 1991). This finding suggests that the apparent effects of single-mother parenting could be attributable to characteristics of the *father* or perhaps other unknown variables.

Of course, many single mothers do a fine job of raising their children, so being raised by a single mom doesn't necessarily doom children to later behavior problems. In addition, children raised by single fathers don't appear to differ in their behaviors from children

raised by single mothers (Golombok, 2000; Hetherington & Stanley-Hagan, 2002). Although compared with other parents some single parents have children with more behavioral problems, the causes of this difference are unknown.

The evidence regarding the impact of same-sex parents on children's development is clearer. Children raised by same-sex couples don't differ from those raised by opposite-sex couples in social adjustment outcomes, academic performance, or sexual orientation (Gottman, 1990; Perrin, Cohen, & Caren, 2013; Potter, 2012; Wainright, Russell, & Patterson, 2004). However, some researchers have argued that many of these studies are characterized by biased samples, potentially leading to inflated measures of well-being relative to children of same-sex parents in the general population (Regnarus, 2012). The bottom line is that having two parents who divide their roles into a primary caregiver and a secondary attachment figure who plays the rough-and-tumble role seen in fathers of traditional families is important for most children. But the gender composition of these caregivers may not especially matter.

Effects of Divorce on Children. Much of the popular psychology literature informs us that divorce often exacts a serious emotional toll on children. This belief was reinforced by the results of a widely publicized 25-year study of 60 families by Judith Wallerstein (1989), who reported that the negative effects of divorce were enduring: Many years later, the children of divorced parents had difficulties establishing career goals and stable romantic relationships. Yet Wallerstein didn't include a control group of families in which one or both parents had been separated from their children for other reasons, such as death or incarceration, so we can't tell whether the outcomes she observed were a consequence of divorce specifically.

> ◀ **Ruling Out Rival Hypotheses**
>
> Have important alternative explanations for the findings been excluded?

Better-designed studies indicate that the substantial majority of children survive their parents' divorce without long-term emotional damage (Cherlin et al., 1991; Hetherington, Cox, & Cox, 1985). In addition, the effects of divorce seem to depend on a variety of factors including the severity of conflict between parents before the divorce. When parents experience only mild conflict before the divorce, the seeming effects of divorce are actually *more* severe than when parents experience intense conflict before the divorce (Amato & Booth, 1997; Rutter, 1972). In the latter case, divorce typically produces no ill effects on children, probably because they find the divorce to be a welcome relief from their parents' incessant arguing. Education level of the parents also predicts children's well-being following divorce. Children with more educated mothers handle divorce better, whereas children with more educated fathers handle it worse (Mandemakers & Kalmijn, 2014). The most likely explanation for children with educated moms being better off is that the family tends to have more resources and therefore more stability post-divorce. The reasons for educated fathers resulting in worse outcomes are less clear.

One group of researchers investigated the effects of divorce on children by comparing the children of identical twins, only one of whom had been divorced. The design provides an elegant control for genetic effects, because these twins are genetically identical, so their offspring share 50 percent of their genes. The researchers found that children of identical twins who'd divorced had higher levels of depression and substance abuse, as well as poorer school performance, than did the children of identical twins who hadn't divorced (D'Onofrio et al., 2006). These findings suggest that divorce can exert negative effects on some children, although the findings don't rule out the possibility that parental conflict prior to and during the divorce, rather than divorce itself, accounts for the differences (Hetherington & Stanley-Hagan, 2002).

> ◀ **Ruling Out Rival Hypotheses**
>
> Have important alternative explanations for the findings been excluded?

SELF-CONTROL: LEARNING TO INHIBIT IMPULSES. A crucial ingredient of social development, and one that parents begin wishing for long before it emerges, is **self-control**: the ability to inhibit our impulses (Eigsti et al., 2006). We may be tempted to snag that unclaimed coffee at the Starbucks counter or tell our unbearably arrogant coworker what we really think of him, but we usually—and thankfully—restrain our desires to do so. Other times, we must put our desires on the back burner until we fulfill our obligations, such as putting off going to see a movie we're excited about until we've finished an important assignment.

self-control

ability to inhibit an impulse to act

Children are notoriously bad at delaying gratification, but some are better at it than others. As Walter Mischel and his colleagues discovered, children's early capacity to delay gratification is a good predictor of later social adjustment. To study delay of gratification,

mere exposure effect

phenomenon in which repeated exposure to a stimulus makes us more likely to feel favorably toward it

Correlation vs. Causation ▶

Can we be sure that A causes B?

Replicability ▶

Can the results be duplicated in other studies?

Figure 11.3 Which Polygon Do You Prefer?

Pairs of polygons used in the mere exposure research of Robert Zajonc and his colleagues are presented below. Participants exposed repeatedly to only one polygon within the pair prefer that polygon, even if they don't recall having seen it.

SOURCE: Science or Science Fiction?: Investigating the Possibility (and Plausibility) of Subliminal Persuasion, Laboratory Manual, Department of Psychology, Cornell University retrieved from http://www.csic.cornell.edu/201/subliminal/#appB.

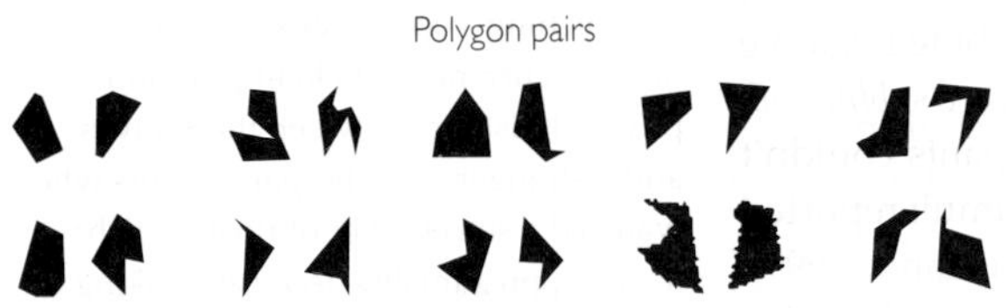

Polygon pairs

Popular wisdom would say no. It tells us that "familiarity breeds contempt": The more often we've seen or heard something, the more we come to dislike it. Yet research by Robert Zajonc and others on the **mere exposure effect** suggests that the opposite is more often the case; that is, familiarity breeds *comfort* (Zajonc, 1968). The mere exposure effect refers to the fact that repeated exposure to a stimulus makes us more likely to feel favorably toward it (Bornstein, 1989; Kunst-Wilson & Zajonc, 1980).

Of course, the finding that we like things we've seen many times before may not be terribly surprising. This correlation could be due merely to the fact that we repeatedly seek out things we like. If we love ice cream, we're likely to spend more time seeking ice cream than are people who hate ice cream, assuming such human beings actually exist. Better evidence for the mere exposure effect derives from experiments using meaningless material, for which individuals are unlikely to have any prior feelings (Zajonc, 2001). Experiments show that repeated exposure to various stimuli, such as nonsense syllables (like "zab" and "gar"), Chinese letters (to non-Chinese participants), and polygons of various shapes, results in greater liking toward these stimuli compared with little or no exposure (see Figure 11.3).

Multiple investigators have replicated these effects using quite different stimuli, including songs, attesting to their generality (Verrier, 2012). The mere exposure effect extends to faces too. We tend to prefer an image of ourselves as we appear in the mirror to an image of ourselves as we appear in a photograph (Mita, Dermer, & Knight, 1977), probably because we see ourselves in the mirror just about every day. Our friends, in contrast, generally prefer the photographic image. Advertisers are well aware of the mere exposure effect and capitalize on it mercilessly (W. E. Baker, 1999; Fang, Singh, & AhluWalia, 2007; Morgenstern, Isensee & Hanewinkel, 2013). Repetitions of a commercial tend to increase our liking for the product, especially if we're positively inclined toward it to begin with.

There's evidence that the mere exposure effect can operate unconsciously, because it emerges even when experimenters present meaningless stimuli subliminally, below the threshold of awareness (Bornstein, 1989; Zajonc, 2001). Even when people aren't aware of having seen a stimulus, such as a specific polygon, they report liking it better than stimuli, like slightly different polygons, they've never seen. Mere exposure effects may be even larger for subliminally than for *supraliminally* (consciously) presented stimuli (Bornstein, 1989). Still, there's scientific controversy about just how enduring the mere exposure effect is. It seems to influence short-term, but not long-term, preferences (Lazarus, 1984).

No one knows why mere exposure effects occur. These effects may reflect *habituation*, a primitive form of learning (see LO 6.1a). The more frequently we encounter a stimulus without anything bad happening, the more comfortable we feel in its presence. Alternatively, we may prefer things we find easier to process (Harmon-Jones & Allen, 2001; Mandler, Nakamura, & Van Zandt, 1987). The more often we experience something, the less effort it typically takes to comprehend it. In turn, the less effort something takes, the more we tend to like it—just as we generally prefer books that are easy to read over those that are hard to read (Herbert, 2011; Hertwig et al., 2008). Recall from earlier in the text that we're *cognitive misers:* In general, we prefer less mental work to more.

So now to the bottom line: All else being equal, you'll probably like this paragraph better after having read it a few times than after you read it the first time. That's a not-so-subtle hint to read it again!

Journal Prompt

Think back to something that you didn't like at first but ended up liking following repeated exposure to it. Describe how your feelings toward it changed over time. How might you use the mere exposure effect to your advantage in everyday life?

FACIAL FEEDBACK HYPOTHESIS. If no one is near you, and you're not afraid of looking foolish, make a big smile and hold it for a while, maybe for 15 seconds. How do you feel (other than silly)? Next, make a big frown, and again hold it for a while. How do you feel now?

According to the **facial feedback hypothesis**, you're likely to feel emotions that correspond to your facial features—first happy and then sad or angry (Adelmann & Zajonc, 1989; Goldman & de Vignemont, 2009; Niedenthal, 2007). This hypothesis originated with none other than Charles Darwin (1872), although Robert Zajonc revived it in the 1980s. Zajonc went beyond Darwin by proposing that changes in the blood vessels of the face "feed back" temperature information to the brain, altering our emotions in predictable ways. Like James and Lange, Zajonc argued that our emotions typically arise from our behavioral and physiological reactions. But unlike James and Lange, Zajonc viewed this process as purely biochemical and noncognitive, that is, as involving no thinking (Zajonc, Murphy, & Inglehart, 1989).

Most people prefer their mirror image to their image as taken by a photographer. In this case, this subject is more likely to prefer the photograph on the left, presumably because he's more accustomed to this view of himself.

There's at least some scientific support for the facial feedback hypothesis. In one study, experimenters asked participants to hold chopsticks in their mouths in one of three positions to which they were randomly assigned, one that produced a Duchenne (genuine) smile, one that produced a fake smile, and one that produced a neutral expression. Then, participants submerged their hands in ice water for a minute, a widely used laboratory technique for eliciting pain. Participants who engaged in smiles, especially Duchenne smiles, showed lower heart rates immediately following the task, suggesting that the smiles had tamped down their stress levels (Kraft & Pressman, 2012). Still, it's not clear that these effects work by means of facial feedback to the brain, as Zajonc claimed. An alternative hypothesis for these effects is classical conditioning (see LO 6.1a). Over the course of our lives, we've experienced countless conditioning "trials" in which we smile while feeling happy and frown while feeling unhappy. Eventually, smiles become conditioned stimuli for happiness; frowns for unhappiness.

Ruling Out Rival Hypotheses ▶

Have important alternative explanations for the findings been excluded?

---

facial feedback hypothesis

theory that blood vessels in the face feed back temperature information in the brain, altering our experience of emotions

Other evidence for the facial feedback hypothesis, however, is mixed. In one widely cited investigation, researchers asked participants to rate how funny they found various cartoons (Strack, Martin, & Stepper, 1988). They randomly assigned some participants to watch cartoons while holding a pen with their teeth and others to watch cartoons while holding a pen with their lips. If you try this at home, you'll discover that when you hold a pen with your teeth, you tend to smile; when you hold a pen with your lips, you tend to frown. Sure enough, participants who held a pen with their teeth rated the cartoons as funnier than did other participants. It's a clever study, and one that the first author of your text recounted in his introductory psychology course for many years. Yet a recent collaborative effort across 17 laboratories (based on nearly 1,900 participants) failed to replicate this finding (Wagenmakers et al., in press), again illustrating the importance of replication in psychological science. As of this writing, the authors of your textbook aren't sure whether this now-famous finding is genuine, but we'll hopefully know more by the time the next edition of this text is published.

Replicability ▶

Can the results be duplicated in other studies?

Injections of the chemical Botox, used to treat wrinkles by paralyzing the muscles surrounding them, results in diminished affective reactions to emotionally arousing film clips compared with injections of substances that don't affect facial muscles (Davis et al., 2010). This finding, along with others (Finzi & Rosenthal, 2014; Magid et al., 2015), is consistent with the facial feedback hypothesis, because Botox may dampen emotions by reducing facial movement.

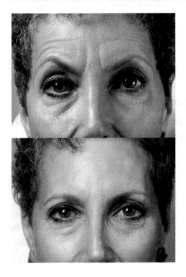

11.2: Nonverbal Expression of Emotion: The Eyes, Bodies, and Cultures Have It

11.2a Explain the importance of nonverbal expression of emotion.
11.2b Identify major lie detection methods and their pitfalls.

Much of our emotional expression is nonverbal. Not only do our facial expressions change frequently when we experience a strong emotion, but so do our gestures and postures. As the late baseball Hall of Famer Yogi Berra (known for his funny words of wisdom) said, "You can observe a lot just by watching." What's more, our nonverbal

eat a single item with the same total amount of chocolate (Van Kleef, Kavvouris, & van Trijp, 2014). We'd bet many readers would volunteer to participate in that study. A nifty trick to keep in mind is to eat food on a smaller plate: doing so will make portions appear bigger and limit the amount we eat.

internal–external theory

theory holding that obese people are motivated to eat more by external cues than internal cues

Stanley Schachter proposed the **internal–external theory**, which holds that relative to other people, people with obesity are motivated to eat more by external cues like portion size, as well as the taste, smell, and appearance of food, than by internal cues like a growling stomach or feelings of fullness (Canetti, Bachar, & Berry 2002; S. Schachter, 1968). According to this theory, individuals are at risk for obesity when they continue to eat even after being full and base their food choices on the appealing qualities of food, time of day, or social circumstances. In laboratory studies, people who are obese are more likely than other people to overeat after researchers manipulate clocks in the room to fool participants into thinking it's dinnertime (Schachter & Gross, 1968). Nevertheless, another possibility, which research favors, is that the oversensitivity to external cues is a consequence rather than a cause of eating patterns (Nisbett, 1972).

> **Correlation vs. Causation** ▶
>
> Can we be sure that A causes B?

A Surgical Option for Significant Weight Loss: Bariatric Surgery. Some people can't lose significant amounts of weight no matter how hard they try. Many people who are severely obese and whose weight jeopardizes their health have the option of participating in *bariatric surgical procedures* to achieve long-term and significant weight loss—often more than 25 percent of their presurgical weight—by restricting the amount of food their stomachs can hold (Adams et al., 2012; Chang et al., 2014). In the most common such surgery, called *gastric bypass surgery*, surgeons route food into a surgically created stomach pouch, roughly the size of an egg, which they connect to the small intestine, bypassing the rest of the stomach. The surgery is generally safe, but complications can occasionally arise. The procedure facilitates smaller meals because the "new stomach" is considerably smaller than the original stomach, and the process activates hormones that suppress hunger and promote feelings of fullness.

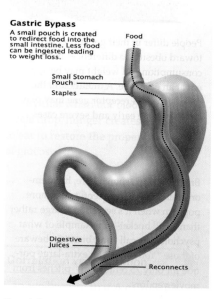

Gastric Bypass
A small pouch is created to redirect food into the small intestine. Less food can be ingested leading to weight loss.

Food

Small Stomach Pouch

Staples

Digestive Juices

Reconnects

Gastric bypass surgery, illustrated here, can help severely obese people achieve significant weight loss over the long run.

EATING DISORDERS: BULIMIA AND ANOREXIA. People with eating disorders are strongly motivated to stay thin or lose weight, while they often are preoccupied with food and experience guilt and other negative emotions during and after eating. The eating disorder of **bulimia nervosa** (better known simply as *bulimia*) is associated with a pattern of *bingeing*—eating large amounts of highly caloric foods in brief periods of time—followed by *purging*—vomiting or other means of drastic weight loss, like frantic exercise or extreme dieting. During a binge, some people gorge themselves with food equaling more than 10,000 calories in a 2-hour period and average about 3,500 calories per binge. That amounts to about six Big Macs (Walsh, 1993; Walsh et al., 1992).

Binge eating disorder is diagnosed when people binge on a recurrent basis—at least once a week for three months—but don't purge afterward (American Psychiatric Association [APA], 2013; Keel, 2007). Binge eating disorder is more common than bulimia and anorexia and afflicts slightly more than 3 percent of the population, whereas bulimia afflicts 1 to 3 percent of the population (Craighead, 2002; Kessler et al., 2013; Smink, Van Hoeken, & Hoek, 2013). These disorders are far more common among women than men (Hudson et al., 2007).

Some researchers have proposed a new disorder to be included in a future edition of the *Diagnostic and Statistical Manual (DSM)* that includes people who purge on a recurrent basis in the absence of bingeing (American Psychiatric Association [APA], 2013). In such cases, individuals often experience a loss of control after eating normal or small amounts of food and then purge to regulate negative emotions, after which they experience more positive emotions (Forney, Haedt-Matt, & Keel, 2014; Haedt-Matt & Keel, 2015).

bulimia nervosa

eating disorder associated with a pattern of bingeing and purging in an effort to lose or maintain weight

Bulimia literally means "ox hunger." Bingeing can be frightening because it's often accompanied by the feeling that it's impossible to stop eating. After a binge, most people with bulimia feel guilt and anxiety over the loss of control and the prospect of gaining weight. Frequently, their answer to this problem is to purge, which typically takes the form of self-induced vomiting, but sometimes involves abusing laxatives or diet pills or exercising excessively (Williamson et al., 2002).

Bingeing and purging set up a vicious cycle (Lavender et al., 2016; Marks, 2015). Purging is reinforcing because it relieves negative feelings such as guilt, fear, and sadness after overeating and sidesteps weight gain (Berg et al., 2013). But it sets the stage for bouts of overeating. For example, vomiting allows people with bulimia to "undo" the binge and negative feelings and rationalize later bouts of overeating ("I can always get rid of the ice cream").

After bingeing, they may resolve to go on a strict diet. Yet severe, medically unsupervised dieting often leads to hunger and increases preoccupation with food and the temptation to binge (Fairburn, 2008; Stice et al., 2005). When eating spirals out of control, concerns about dieting and the likelihood of another binge escalate, thereby completing the self-destructive circle (Fairburn, Cooper, & Shafran, 2003). This binge-purge cycle can be physically hazardous, resulting in heart problems, asthma, tears to the esophagus, menstrual problems, and wearing away of tooth enamel (Mehler, 2003; Olguin et al., 2016).

People with bulimia and binge eating disorder report high levels of body dissatisfaction and often see themselves as obese when they're of normal weight (Johnson & Wardle, 2005). In fact, the best predictor of any eating disorder is body dissatisfaction (Hudson et al., 2010; Keel & Forney, 2013). Still, twin studies suggest that eating disorders are influenced by genetic factors (Bulik et al., 2006; Mitchison & Hay, 2014; Root et al., 2010), although they're also probably triggered in part by sociocultural expectations concerning the ideal body image. In modern society, the media equate beauty with a slender female figure. Movies, sitcoms, and magazines feature extremely underweight females, typically 15 percent below women's average weight (Johnson, Tobin, & Steinberg, 1989). So it's no wonder that women who frequently view television programs featuring extremely thin women experience higher levels of body image dissatisfaction than do other women (Himes & Thompson, 2007; Thompson et al., 2004; Tiggemann & Pickering, 1996). It's possible that women who are already concerned about their body image may tend to watch television programs featuring idealized images of women, so the causal arrow could run in the opposite direction. Still, there's compelling circumstantial evidence for at least some causal effect of the media on eating disorders. Following the introduction of American and British television onto the remote Pacific island of Fiji, the symptoms of eating disorders in teenage girls increased fivefold within only four years (Becker et al., 2002). Bulimia is rarely or never present in cultures not exposed to the ideal of a thin body type (Keel, 2013; Keel & Klump, 2003).

Anorexia nervosa, or anorexia, is less common than bulimia, with rates ranging from 0.5 percent to 1 percent of the population (Craighead, 2002; Hudson et al., 2007). But like bulimia and binge eating disorder, anorexia usually begins in adolescence and is sometimes fueled by sociocultural pressures to be thin. Although anorexia is more common in girls than boys, as many as 25 percent of people diagnosed with anorexia are male adolescents (Wooldridge & Lytle, 2012). Whereas individuals with bulimia tend to be in the normal weight range, those with anorexia become emaciated in their relentless pursuit of thinness (Golden & Sacker, 1984). Along with a "fear of fatness," individuals with anorexia—like those with bulimia— have a distorted perception of their body size. Even those with bones showing through their skin may describe themselves as fat.

Psychologists diagnose anorexia when individuals display a refusal to maintain body weight at or above a healthy weight expected for age and height, with a significantly low body weight due to restriction of food or energy intake. Individuals with anorexia often lose between 25 percent and 50 percent of their body weight, even though they're often preoccupied with food. Starvation can actually produce symptoms of eating disorders. In the "starvation study," 36 healthy young men volunteered to restrict their food intake severely for half a year as an alternative to serving in the military (Keys et al., 1950). Their preoccupation with food increased dramatically. Some hoarded food or gulped it down. Some men broke the eating rules and binged, followed by intense guilt or self-induced vomiting.

With continued low weight, a loss of menstrual periods, hair loss, heart problems, life-threatening electrolyte imbalances, and fragile bones may result (Gottdiener et al., 1978; Katzman, 2005). A patient with anorexia treated by your text's second author broke her femur (the long bone in the thigh) during an ordinary game of tennis. Some researchers put the mortality rate for anorexia at 5–10 percent, making it one of the most life-threatening of all psychological conditions (Birmingham et al., 2005; Franko et al., 2013; P. F. Sullivan, 1995).

Anorexia is present not only in Western countries but also in regions that have had little exposure to Western media, including some Middle Eastern nations and parts of India (Keel & Klump, 2003; Pike, Hoek, & Dunne, 2014). Although anorexia appears to be more culturally and historically universal compared with bulimia, societal *explanations* for its causes have differed across time and place. For example, historical descriptions suggest that some young Catholic nuns in medieval times who starved themselves probably had anorexia. Yet they explained their fasting behaviors as efforts to purify their souls for God (Keel & Klump, 2003; Smith, Spillane, & Annus, 2006).

◀ **Correlation vs. Causation**

Can we be sure that A causes B?

anorexia nervosa

eating disorder associated with excessive weight loss and the irrational perception that one is overweight

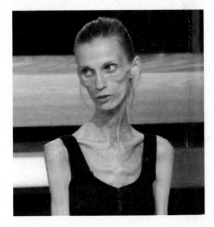

Anorexia isn't limited to women, although it's comparatively rare among men. It's associated with body image distortion, which contributes to a fear of being fat despite being severely underweight.

Evaluating Claims   DIET AND WEIGHT-LOSS PLANS

We Americans are always looking for a new, quicker way to lose weight and achieve our ideal body size and shape. The creators of weight-loss plans are only too happy to oblige. Some claim we can lose weight by avoiding carbohydrates; others, by drinking protein shakes; and still others, by consuming only one type of soup or grapefruit. You have a friend who seems to be on one diet or another most of the time, and he even has his own blog in which he recounts in great detail his daily challenges in losing the "final five" pounds to reach his "running weight." For some time now, he's been on the losing side of losing the final five, and you come across an ad on the Internet that might interest him, but you wonder: Should I suggest that he try one more weight loss program that might not be helpful at all, waste his time, and even demoralize him? Here's what you read:

"Our program helps you to lose weight by changing your everyday habits. Learn how to eat smaller portions and cut calories, choose more nutritious foods, and make exercise a part of your daily routine. We have worked in close collaboration with scientists to develop a revolutionary program that is easy to bring into the workplace and your home based on 10 time-tested principles of effective dieting. Our online video series takes you through each principle, one-by-one, and provides all the motivation you need to succeed! One of our most successful enrolees lost *98 pounds in only 4 months*. So what do *you* have to lose? Nothing, except those unwanted pounds for a slimmer, healthier you!"

Scientific skepticism requires us to evaluate all claims with an open mind but to insist on compelling evidence before accepting them. How do the principles of scientific thinking help us to evaluate this claim about losing weight?

Consider how the six principles of scientific thinking are relevant as you evaluate this claim.

1. Ruling Out Rival Hypotheses
Have important alternative explanations for the findings been excluded?

This ad doesn't make any promises about how much weight participants lose, and to its credit, notes that reducing calories (through smaller portions of nutritious foods) and exercise are necessary components of a sensible diet. Still, the testimonial in the ad implies that participants can achieve rapid and substantial weight loss. Yet the weight loss claimed might not be typical of gains achieved by the average person, and the report of massive weight loss might be exaggerated. Without research that follows participants over time, verifies their compliance with the program and weight lost, and compares their weight loss with that of people who don't participate in the program, it's impossible to evaluate the intervention and determine the average amount of weight lost. Enrollees may lose weight for reasons that have nothing to do with the program but are instead a consequence of their tendency to be more mindful of their food consumption and health and to change their eating behaviors and exercise more as a result. Also, weight loss could be due to naturally occurring fluctuations in weight rather than to the treatment itself.

2. Correlation vs. Causation
Can we be sure that A causes B?

This principle of scientific thinking is relevant to this scenario to the extent that weight loss may appear to be associated with participation in the program, but may not occur as a result of the interventions or the principles claimed to produce weight loss.

3. Falsifiability
Can the claim be disproved?

The claim that the program is effective could be disproved with controlled research in which some people are randomly assigned to receive the program and others are randomly assigned to a control intervention or to no intervention at all.

4. Replicability
Can the results be duplicated in other studies?

To be trusted, results should be replicated in independent studies. Not enough details about the program or the principles are provided in the ad to permit us to draw any conclusions about whether the claim is based on replicable findings.

5. Extraordinary Claims
Is the evidence as strong as the claim?

The anecdotal claim that someone lost almost 100 pounds in four months is extraordinary—that would be an average of nearly a pound per day! Note that the ad doesn't mention potential adverse health effects of such dramatic weight loss. In addition, no reason is given for the weight loss, so we can't assume that diet is the cause. Beware of claims based on "revolutionary" new studies. The principle of connectivity reminds us that science builds upon previous research. The ad doesn't state that the collaboration with scientists included rigorous evaluation of the claims. The ad suggests that participants have "nothing to lose," yet investing in an ineffective program can be a waste of time, demoralizing, and an opportunity lost to participate in a more scientifically grounded weight loss program.

6. Occam's Razor

Does a simpler explanation fit the data just as well?

Not much data are presented, and several simple explanations described earlier could account for at least some weight loss that occurred during or after the intervention.

Summary

The ad correctly specifies steps, such as eating smaller portions, that individuals could take to lose weight in a sensible manner. Nevertheless, the implication that participants can achieve rapid and substantial weight loss is not well supported by well-replicated research, alternative and simpler explanations for at least moderate weight loss are plausible, and potential consumers of the video series should be wary of claims of quick and extraordinary weight loss.

Sexual Motivation

Sexual desire—called *libido*—is a wish or craving for sexual activity and sexual pleasure (Regan & Berscheid, 1999). Sexual desire is deeply rooted in our genes and biology, but as we'll see, it's also influenced by social and cultural factors.

SEXUAL DESIRE AND ITS CAUSES.   The sex hormone testosterone can sometimes enhance sexual interest in the short term, particularly in males (see LO 3.3a), but other biological influences are also at play when it comes to sexual desire. For example, low levels of sexual desire are associated with high levels of the neurotransmitter serotonin (Houle et al., 2006). Researchers have discovered that variations in a gene that produces DRD4, a protein related to dopamine transmission, are correlated with students' reports of sexual desire and arousal (Zion et al., 2006). The scientists estimated that approximately 20 percent of the population possesses the mutation for increased sexual desire, whereas another 70 percent possesses a variant of the gene that depresses sexual desire. Variations in the gene are also associated with increased reports of promiscuity, such as "having a one night stand" and infidelity (Garcia et al., 2010). These findings dovetail with research showing that dopamine plays a key role in reward (see LO 3.1c). Medicines that block the release of serotonin and increase the release of dopamine and norepinephrine—two neurotransmitters critical for sexual desire—can be prescribed to treat low sexual desire in premenopausal women (Stahl, 2015).

Many people believe that men have a stronger desire for sex than do women. This stereotype may hold more than a kernel of truth (Baumeister, Catanese, & Vohs, 2001). Compared with women, men desire sex more frequently and experience more sexual arousal (Hiller, 2005; Klusmann 2002), have a greater number and variety of sexual fantasies (Laumann et al., 1994; Leitenberg & Henning, 1995), think about sex more often (Fisher, Moore, & Pittenger, 2012), masturbate more frequently (Oliver & Hyde, 1993), want to have more sexual partners (Buss & Schmitt, 1993), and desire sex earlier in a relationship (Sprecher, Barbee, & Schwartz, 1995). Women tend to experience greater variability than men in their sex drive (Lippa, 2009), and women, particularly those with high sex drives, tend to be attracted to both men and women and are more fluid in their sexual orientation (Bailey et al., 2016; Norris, Marcus, & Green, 2015). In contrast, men with high sex drives tend to be attracted to one sex or the other (Lippa, 2006). In contrast to men, women's appetite for sex—but not their need for romantic tenderness—appears to decline after they form a secure relationship (Murray & Milhausen, 2012). Of course, none of these findings about sex necessarily apply to any individual man or woman, and there's tremendous variability in sexual interest among men and women—indeed, at least as much variability as there is between men and women.

Socialization may help explain why men and women appear to differ in sexual desire. Women are socialized to be less assertive and aggressive in many spheres of life, including the expression of their sexual desires. So perhaps women and men actually experience comparable sexual drives, but women don't express or admit their desires as much (T. D. Fisher, 2009). Although the data tilt toward the conclusion that men have an inherently stronger sex drive than do women, the evidence isn't definitive.

THE PHYSIOLOGY OF THE HUMAN SEXUAL RESPONSE.   In 1954, the husband and wife team of William Masters and Virginia Johnson launched their pioneering investigations of sexual desire and the human sexual response. Their observations included sexual behaviors under virtually every imaginable condition—and some virtually unimaginable. Masters and

Ruling Out Rival Hypotheses

Have important alternative explanations for the findings been excluded?

Figure 11.12 Variations in Female Sexual Response Cycle.

This figure depicts the sexual arousal cycle for three different women, each represented by a different color. Two of the three women experienced at least one orgasm. The woman whose response is traced by the blue line experienced excitement but no orgasm.

SOURCE: Rathus, Spencer A.; Nevid, Jeffrey S.; Fichner-Rathus, Lois, Human Sexuality In A World Of Diversity, 7th Ed., ©2008, p. 149. Reprinted and Electronically reproduced by permission of Pearson Education, Inc., Upper Saddle River, New Jersey.

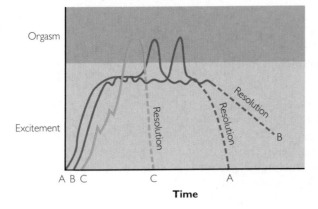

Correlation vs. Causation

Can we be sure that A causes B?

excitement phase

phase in human sexual response in which people experience sexual pleasure and notice physiological changes associated with it

plateau phase

phase in human sexual response in which sexual tension builds

orgasm (climax) phase

phase in human sexual response marked by involuntary rhythmic contractions in the muscles of genitals in both men and women

resolution phase

phase in human sexual response following orgasm, in which people report relaxation and a sense of well-being

Johnson's laboratory wasn't exactly a prescription for romantic intimacy: In addition to a bed, it contained monitoring equipment to measure physiological changes, cameras, and a probe that contained a camera to record changes in the vagina during intercourse. Yet most people who volunteered for their studies accommodated to the laboratory with surprising ease.

Masters and Johnson (1966) reported that the basic sexual arousal cycle was the same for men and women. Based on their research and other observations (H. S. Kaplan, 1977), scientists define the *sexual response cycle* in terms of four phases: (1) excitement, (2) plateau, (3) orgasm, and (4) resolution (see Figure 11.12).

The **excitement phase** is initiated by whatever prompts sexual interest. People often experience little sexual desire when they're tired, distracted, stressed out, in pain, or ill. Lack of attraction to a partner, depression, anxiety, and resentment can also inhibit sexual desire. In the excitement phase, people experience sexual pleasure and start to notice physiological changes, such as penile erection in men and vaginal swelling and lubrication in women. During the **plateau phase**, sexual tension builds, and if it continues, ultimately leads to orgasm. In the **orgasm (climax) phase**, sexual pleasure and physical changes peak, there are involuntary rhythmic contractions in the muscles of the genitals in men and women, and men ejaculate. After orgasm, people report relaxation and a sense of well-being in the **resolution phase**, as the body returns to its unstimulated state (Belliveau & Richter, 1970; Resnick & Ithman, 2009).

Masters and Johnson's groundbreaking efforts didn't capture a crucial fact: People's sexuality is deeply embedded in their relationships and feelings for each other. People experience more frequent and consistent orgasms when they love their partner and feel loved in return (Birnbaum, Glaubman, & Mikulincer, 2001) and feel satisfied in their relationship (Brody & Weiss, 2011; Young et al., 2000). But we can question the causal direction between relationship quality and the frequency and consistency of orgasms. Frequent orgasms may not merely reflect healthy relationships but contribute to them.

FREQUENCY OF SEXUAL ACTIVITIES AND AGING. Early in their marriage, couples have sex on average about twice a week (Laumann et al., 1994). As people age, the frequency of their sexual activities decreases but their sexual satisfaction doesn't. Perhaps people expect their sexual activity to decrease as they age, so they're not disappointed by this change.

Contrary to the myth that sexual activities virtually cease for senior citizens, many people are sexually active well into their 70s and 80s, especially when they're healthy, are not depressed, are in happy marriages, and perceive that their partner desires a sexual relationship (Erber & Szuchman, 2014; Waite et al., 2015). In a survey of 1,491 individuals aged 40–80 years, 79.4 percent of men and 69.3 percent of women reported having engaged in sexual intercourse during the year prior to the study (Laumann et al., 2009). Women experience complex and sometimes striking changes in hormones during menopause, although there's another explanation for the difference between older men's and women's sexual activities. By the age of 80, women have less opportunity to find male partners; for every 100 women, there are only 39 men (Meston, 1997).

Ruling Out Rival Hypotheses

Have important alternative explanations for the findings been excluded?

SEXUALITY AND CULTURE. People's expression of sexual desires is shaped by social norms and culture. Clellan Ford and Frank Beach's (1951) fascinating observations reveal how cultural norms influence people's ideas of what's sexually appropriate or inappropriate. When members of the Tsonga tribe in Africa first saw Europeans kissing, they laughed and remarked, "Look at them—they eat each other's saliva and dirt" (Ford & Beach, 1951). Admittedly, they have a point. Members of the Apinaly society in Brazil don't kiss, but women of the tribe may bite off their lovers' eyebrows and noisily spit them to one side. Women of the island Turk are even less kind, at least by Western standards: They customarily poke a finger into the man's ear when they're sexually excited.

David Buss (1989) found that residents of non-Western societies, including India, Iran, and China, place a much greater value on chastity in a potential partner than do individuals in Western European countries, including Sweden, Holland, and France. Americans are divided on whether they approve (58 percent) or disapprove (42 percent) of premarital sex (Twenge, Sherman, & Wells, 2015). This latter percentage stands at odds with the prevalence of premarital sex in the United States, with men reporting rates between 85 and 96 percent and women reporting rates of 80 to 94 percent (Finer, 2007; Laumann et al., 1994).

SEXUAL ORIENTATION: SCIENCE AND POLITICS. What motivates attraction to same versus opposite sex sexual partners? Same-sex romantic relationships develop in virtually all cultures and have done so since the dawn of recorded history. Biologists have documented homosexual behaviors in some 450 species (Bagemihl, 1999). People differ in their sexual orientation or interest in same (homosexual), opposite (heterosexual), or both (bisexual) sex sexual partners. We should keep in mind that sexual orientation isn't the same as sexual activity. For example, people may restrict their sexual partners to opposite sex individuals, yet be sexually attracted to same-sex individuals, or vice versa. People also differ in how they think and feel about their homosexuality. Many people who engage in occasional homosexual activities don't view themselves as gay, and many people participate in both homosexual and heterosexual activity and consider themselves bisexual (Bell & Weinberg, 1978; Savin-Williams & Ream, 2007).

Research indicates that gay people are as likely as heterosexual people to provide supportive environments for children.

Prevalence of Different Sexual Orientations. Research suggests that about 2.2 percent of males and 2.4 percent of females 18 or older identify themselves as gay, lesbian, or bisexual (Ward et al., 2014; Laumann et al., 1994; National Opinion Research Center, 2003). Nevertheless, even the best estimates may not represent the general population, because researchers often conduct surveys in prisons, college dorms, or military barracks or under the sponsorship of gay organizations, all of which may result in sampling bias.

Since Alfred Kinsey's famous "Kinsey Report" of the 1940s and 1950s, which presented his groundbreaking research on human sexuality, scientists have acquired a better understanding of homosexuality and challenged common misconceptions about gay men, lesbians, and bisexuals. Contrary to the stereotype that one person in a gay relationship adopts a masculine role whereas the other adopts a feminine role, less than a fourth of gay men and women fit neatly into those categories (Jay & Young, 1979; Lever, 1995). A good deal of media coverage also implies that gay individuals recruit others to become gay, are especially likely to sexually abuse children and adolescents, and are unfit to be parents. Yet scientific evidence supports none of these views (Bos, van Balen, & van den Boom, 2007; Freund, Watson & Rienzo, 1989; Patterson, 1992).

Can Sexual Orientation Be Changed? Is it possible to change the sexual orientation of gay men and women who wish to become heterosexual? Robert Spitzer (2003) evaluated 200 cases of people who underwent sexual reorientation therapy. He reported many instances in which people changed from a predominantly homosexual to heterosexual orientation for a five-year period or longer. In a striking published statement nearly a decade later, however, Spitzer (2012) acknowledged that a fatal flaw in the study was that he had no way to gauge the validity of participants' claims of changed sexual orientation. For example, the participants could have been lying to investigators or deceiving themselves about their sexual orientation. Going further, Spitzer apologized to the gay community for making unsubstantiated claims and to gay individuals who had wasted time and energy engaging in reparative therapy based on exaggerated reports of its effectiveness. The American Psychological Association (Association Psychological Association, 2009) affirmed that same-sex sexual and romantic attractions are normal variations of human sexuality and concluded that insufficient evidence supports the use of psychological interventions to change sexual orientation.

> **▸ Ruling Out Rival Hypotheses**
>
> Have important alternative explanations for the findings been excluded?

Prior to 1973, homosexuality was included in the American Psychiatric Association's formal list of mental disorders, the *DSM* (Bayer & Spitzer, 1985; see LO 15.1c), but scientific and social attitudes have changed markedly over the past three and a half decades, as the APA's recent statement indicates. Although gay men and women report relatively high rates of anxiety, depression, and suicide (Biernbaum & Ruscio, 2004; Ferguson, Horwood, & Beautrais, 1999; Wang et al., 2015), in many or most cases, gay individuals' psychological problems may reflect their reaction to social oppression and intolerance of their lifestyles and genetic factors, rather than preexisting mental disturbance (Zietsch et al., 2012). Accordingly, gay individuals who participate in reorientation therapy and don't achieve the changes they seek may become even more dissatisfied. There's growing consensus that evidence-based treatments that value cultural diversity are well-positioned to help many currently distressed people accept and live with their homosexuality, rather than change their sexual orientation (Bartoli & Gillem, 2008; Glassgold et al., 2009).

GENETIC AND ENVIRONMENTAL INFLUENCES ON SEXUAL ORIENTATION. Bearing in mind the caveat that heritability doesn't imply that a characteristic can't be changed, most scientists are skeptical about the ability of gay individuals to change their sexual orientation because there are indications of inborn differences between homosexual and heterosexual individuals. Because many gay men and women report they've felt different from others for as long as they can remember, it's plausible that biological differences are sometimes present even before birth; for example, gender nonconformity in childhood is a well replicated finding across different cultures (Bailey et al., 2016; Bailey & Zucker, 1995; Green, 1987; Zuger, 1988). Gay men report that they were often feminine boys and lesbians that they were often masculine girls, suggesting an early-emerging and potential genetic influence on childhood gender nonconformity. Support for this hypothesis comes from seven twin studies that demonstrated that genetic differences account for about a third of the variation in sexual orientation (Bailey et al., 2016). Nevertheless, the fact that a great deal of variation in sexual orientation can't be explained in terms of genetic differences tells us that environmental influences play a key role in homosexuality, although it doesn't tell us what these influences are.

Replicability

Can the results be duplicated in other studies?

Sex Hormones, Prenatal Influences, and Sexual Orientation. When the fetus develops, sex hormones (see LO 3.3a) influence whether the brain sets the child on a path toward more masculine than feminine characteristics, or vice versa. According to one theory, girls exposed to excessive testosterone in the womb develop masculinized brains, and boys exposed to too little testosterone develop feminized brains (Ellis & Ames, 1987; Hines, 2010). These hormonal influences affect temperament and set the stage for both childhood gender nonconformity and a homosexual orientation in later life (Bem, 1996).

Having older brothers increases the odds of male homosexuality by 33 percent for each older brother, amounting to an increase in the rate of homosexuality from about 3–5 percent (Blanchard & Bogaert, 1996). Most, but not all, researchers have succeeded in replicating this effect (Kishida & Rahmen, 2015; VanderLaan & Vasey, 2011; Zietsch et al., 2012). If this finding indeed proves to be replicable, one explanation is that male fetuses produce substances that trigger the mother's immune system to develop anti-male antibodies that affect the sexual differentiation of the fetus's brain, with the effect intensifying with the birth of each succeeding male child. Researchers recently qualified the original finding by showing that older brothers increase the odds of homosexuality in right-handed but not left-handed males (Blanchard, 2008). Perhaps left-handed fetuses may not be sensitive to the anti-male antibodies, or the mothers of left-handed fetuses may not produce these antibodies.

Replicability

Can the results be duplicated in other studies?

Fingerprints, finger length, and handedness are all determined largely before birth, and gay and heterosexual individuals differ with respect to each of these characteristics (Hall & Kimura, 1994; Lalumière, Blanchard, & Zucker, 2000; Williams et al., 2000). So there's some justification for pointing the finger (pun intended) at prenatal influences, even though we can't yet specify which influences, such as exposure to sex hormones, are most important.

Sexual Orientation: Brain Differences. In 1981, Simon LeVay created a stir among scientists and laypersons alike by reporting that a small cluster of neurons in the hypothalamus, no larger than a millimeter, was less than half the size in gay men compared with heterosexual men. The study is open to several criticisms: LeVay examined gay men's brains at autopsy, and the men died from AIDS-related complications. Still, it's unlikely that the differences LeVay uncovered are due entirely to AIDS, because a number of the heterosexual men also died of AIDS-related complications. The changes LeVay observed in the hypothalamus might also have been the result, rather than the cause, of homosexuality and differences in lifestyles between gay and heterosexual men. Yet another limitation was that LeVay's sample of gay men with AIDS wasn't representative of all gay men, so the fact that one study failed to fully replicate his findings casts doubt on the link between sexual orientation and neurons in the hypothalamus (Bailey et al., 2016; Byne et al., 2000)

Correlation vs. Causation

Can we be sure that A causes B?

Replicability

Can the results be duplicated in other studies?

Researchers have looked beyond the hypothalamus to find biological indicators of sexual orientation and discovered that the brain's corpus callosum is larger in homosexual than heterosexual men (Witelson et al., 2008). The scientists suggested that this finding implies that homosexuality is influenced by genetic factors,

Fact vs. Fiction

People can guess sexual orientation by looking at pictures of faces. (See bottom of page for answer.)

○ Fact

○ Fiction

because the size of the corpus callosum is inherited. Nevertheless, we should again bear in mind that both brain size and brain activity could be a consequence, rather than a cause, of sexual orientation.

Scientists have yet to discover a dependable biological marker of sexual orientation. For example, many gay men have more older sisters than older brothers, and the size of the hypothalamus is comparable in most gay and non-gay individuals. In all likelihood, social, environmental, and cultural influences that remain to be understood, in conjunction with genetic factors, play important roles in shaping people's sexual orientation.

11.5: Attraction, Love, and Hate: The Greatest Mysteries of Them All

11.5a Identify principles and factors that guide attraction and relationship formation.

11.5b Describe the major types of love and the elements of love and hate.

In 1975, psychologists Ellen Berscheid and Elaine Hatfield received a dubious distinction (Benson, 2006). They became the first individuals to receive the Golden Fleece Award, an "honor" (actually, a dishonor) bestowed on them by then–Wisconsin Senator William Proxmire. Proxmire had cooked up this award as a way of drawing public attention to projects that he regarded as colossal wastes of taxpayer money. Berscheid and Hatfield, it so happens, had won this award for their government-funded research on the psychological determinants of attraction and love (look for their names in the section you're about to read). Proxmire found the very idea of studying these topics scientifically to be absurd:

> "I'm strongly against this," he said, "not only because no one—not even the National Science Foundation—can argue that falling in love is a science; not only because I am sure that even if they spend 84 million or 84 billion they wouldn't get an answer that anyone would believe. I'm also against it because I don't *want* to know the answer!" (Hatfield & Walster, 1978, viii)

Of course, Proxmire was entitled not to know the answer. Yet more than three decades of research have since shown that Proxmire was woefully wrong in one crucial respect: Psychologists *can* study love scientifically. In this respect, we've come a long way from the 1970s. None of this takes away from the profound mysteries of falling in love, but it suggests that love may not be quite as unfathomable as we—or the thousands of poets who've written about it across the centuries—might believe.

Social Influences on Interpersonal Attraction

How can two people meet and become lovers in a world teeming with nearly 7 billion people? Of course, attraction is only the initial stage in a relationship, but we need to feel a twinkle of chemistry with someone before deciding whether we're compatible enough with him or her in our core values and attitudes before proceeding any further (Murstein, 1977). We might ascribe finding our true love to the fickle finger of destiny, but scientists suggest that friendship, dating, and mate choices aren't random. Three major principles guide attraction and relationship

The origins of love are remarkably old, even ancient. In 2007, archaeologists unearthed these skeletons of a male and female couple in Italy (coincidentally, only 25 miles from Verona, the site of Shakespeare's legendary *Romeo and Juliet*), frozen in an embrace over 5,000 years ago.

Answer: Fact. Researchers have found that college students who viewed equal numbers of homosexual and heterosexual women on Internet dating sites guessed correctly about 64 percent of the time (Rule, Amaday, & Hallett, 2009). A study with male faces confirmed this finding (Rule & Ambaday, 2008). It's unclear whether people perform above chance because of subtle social cues, biologically influenced differences in facial appearance, or differences in posed facial expressions.

Psychological research shows that physical proximity, such as being seated next to each other in a classroom or working on projects together, can set the stage for attraction and relationship formation.

proximity

physical nearness, a predictor of attraction

similarity

extent to which we have things in common with others, a predictor of attraction

Most commercial online dating sites capitalize on the principle of similarity: birds of a feather flock together. Nevertheless, most of the claims of these sites are poorly supported scientifically, in part because similarity is a better predictor of what people say they want in a prospective relationship partner than what they end up wanting.

formation: proximity, similarity, and reciprocity (Berscheid & Reis, 1998; Luo & Klohnen, 2005; Sprecher, 1998).

PROXIMITY: WHEN NEAR BECOMES DEAR. A simple truth of human relationships is that our closest friends often live, study, work, or play closest to us. Many years after high school, the second author of your textbook married the woman who sat in front of him in numerous classes. Because their last names started with the letter *L*, the fact that the seats were arranged alphabetically ensured they'd have an opportunity to become acquainted. After their 30-year high school reunion brought them together again, they fell in love and married.

This example illustrates how physical nearness—or **proximity**—affords relationship formation. Like reunited schoolmates, people in classrooms with alphabetically assigned seats tend to have friends with last names that start with the same letter or a letter close in the alphabet (Segal, 1974). We're most likely to be attracted to and befriend people nearby whom we see on a regular basis (Nahemow & Lawton, 1975). Leon Festinger, Stanley Schachter, and Kurt Back (1950) asked individuals living in apartments for married students at the Massachusetts Institute of Technology to name three of their closest friends. Of these friends, 65 percent lived in the same building, and 41 percent lived next door.

The effects of mere exposure we encountered earlier in the chapter may explain why seeing someone on a frequent basis, whether in the supermarket or workout room, heightens attraction. In a study conducted in a college classroom, four women with similar appearances posed as students and attended 0, 5, 10, or 15 sessions (Moreland & Beach, 1992). At the end of the semester, the experimenters showed participants slides of the women and asked them to rate attendees' attractiveness. Although the posers didn't interact with any of the students, participants judged women who attended more classes as more attractive.

SIMILARITY: LIKE ATTRACTS LIKE. Would you rather be stranded on a desert island with someone very much like yourself or very different? Perhaps if you like Mozart and your island mate prefers rap, you'd have a lot to talk or at least debate about. Yet with little in common, you might find it difficult to establish a personal connection. This point brings us to our next principle: **similarity**, the extent to which we have things in common with others.

Scientists have found that there's more truth to the adage "Birds of a feather flock together" than the equally well-worn proverb "Opposites attract." Whether it's art, music, food preferences, educational level, physical attractiveness, or values, we're attracted to people who are similar to us (Byrne, 1971; Montoya & Horton, 2013; Swann & Pelham, 2002). We're also more likely to befriend, date, and marry compatible people (Curran & Lippold, 1975; Knox, Zusman, & Nieves, 1997). There's even evidence that pet owners tend to select dogs who resemble them (Nakajima, Yamamoto, & Yoshimoto, 2009; Roy & Christenfeld, 2004), although not all researchers are persuaded by these findings (Levine, 2005).

Online dating services have caught on to the fact that similarity breeds content (Finkel et al., 2012; Hill, Rubin & Peplau, 1976). One service, eHarmony.com, matches prospective partners on the basis of personality similarity, although there's little evidence that they're successful at doing so (Epstein, 2007). In addition, the claims of most online dating sites are overstated, in part because similarity better predicts what people *say* they like in relationship partner than what they actually like (Finkel et al., 2012). Still, actual similarity generally pays off in the long run. Married couples that share similar traits are more likely to stay together than are dissimilar couples (Meyer & Pepper, 1977).

Similarity greases the wheels of social interaction for a few reasons. First, when people's interests and attitudes overlap, the foundation is paved for mutual understanding. Second, we assume we'll be readily accepted and liked by others who see eye to eye with us. Similar people may share common goals, and achieving shared goals, in turn, enhances attraction; likewise, attraction may bring people together to achieve common goals (Finkel & Eastwick, 2016; Montoya & Horton, 2014). Third, people who share our likes and dislikes provide validation for our views and help us feel good about ourselves. There may even be considerable truth to the saying "The enemy of my enemy is my friend" (Heider, 1958). Research demonstrates that a glue that binds friendships, especially in the early stages, is sharing negative impressions about others (Bosson et al., 2006). Negative gossip may foster feelings of familiarity with another person and permit us to elevate ourselves at the expense of others, thereby enhancing our self-esteem (Weaver & Bosson, 2011).

RECIPROCITY: ALL GIVE AND NO TAKE DOES NOT A GOOD RELATIONSHIP MAKE. For a relationship to move to deeper levels, the third principle of attraction—**reciprocity**, or the rule of give and take—is often crucial. Across cultures, there's a norm of reciprocity (Gouldner, 1960) that begins to kick into motion as early as 11 years of age (Rotenberg & Mann, 1986). That is, we tend to feel obligated to give what we get and maintain equity in a relationship (Walster, Berscheid, & Walster, 1973). Liking begets liking, and revealing personal information begets disclosure, regardless of whether the communication is an online chat, an email, or a conversation with a partner (Stocks, Mirghasemmi, & Oceja, 2016). When we believe people like us, we're inclined to feel attracted to them (Brehm et al., 2002; Carlson & Rose, 2007). When we believe that our partner finds us attractive or likable, we generally act more likable in response to this ego-boosting information (Curtis & Miller, 1986). Talking about meaningful things is a vital element of most friendships. In particular, disclosure about intimate topics often brings about intimacy. When one person talks about superficial topics or discusses intimate topics in a superficial way, low levels of disclosure often result (Lynn, 1978). Although a complete lack of reciprocity can put a relationship into the deep freeze, absolute reciprocity isn't required to make a relationship hum, especially when one partner responds to our disclosures with sympathy and concern (Berg & Archer, 1980).

reciprocity
rule of give and take, a predictor of attraction

PHYSICAL ATTRACTION: LIKE IT OR NOT, WE JUDGE BOOKS BY THEIR COVERS. Some important scientific discoveries arise from *serendipity*, that is, sheer luck. So it was with a study that Elaine Hatfield and her colleagues conducted more than 50 years ago (Hatfield et al., 1966). They administered a battery of personality, attitude, and interest measures to 725 incoming college men and women during freshman "Welcome Week." Hatfield and her coworkers paired these students randomly for a leisurely date and dance lasting two-and-a-half hours, giving them the chance to get acquainted. Which variables, the researchers wondered, would predict whether the partners were interested in a second date? Much to their surprise, the only variable that significantly predicted attraction was one the researchers had included only as an afterthought (Gangestad & Scheyd, 2005): people's level of physical attractiveness as rated by their partners (Hatfield et al., 1966).

Physically attractive people tend to be more popular than physically unattractive people (Dion, Berscheid, & Walster, 1972; Fehr, 2008). Yet what makes us find others attractive? Is it all merely a matter of "chemistry," an inexplicable process that lies beyond the grasp of science, as Senator Proxmire believed? Or is there a science to "love at first sight," or at least attraction at first sight?

> ## Journal Prompt
> Consider the common sayings "opposites attract," "birds of a feather flock together," and "beauty is in the eye of the beholder." Do any other common sayings regarding physical attractiveness come to mind? What can we learn about the accuracy of these statements from psychological research on interpersonal attraction? Which statements are supported by research and which aren't?

Public attention directed at male and female soccer stars, such as English footballer David Beckham and 2012 Olympic gold medal winner Alex Morgan, depends not only on their athletic performance but on their physical attractiveness as well. Athletes who are both strong performers and attractive garner by far the most public attention (Mutz & Meier, 2016).

SEX DIFFERENCES IN WHAT WE FIND ATTRACTIVE: NATURE, NURTURE, OR BOTH? Although physical attractiveness is important to both sexes when it comes to choosing our romantic partners, it's especially important to men (Buunk et al., 2002; Feingold, 1992). David Buss (1989) conducted a comprehensive survey of mate preferences among heterosexuals in 37 cultures across six continents, with countries as diverse as Canada, Spain, Finland, Greece, Bulgaria, Venezuela, Iran, Japan, and South Africa. Although he found that the importance people attach to physical attractiveness varies across cultures, men consistently place more weight on looks in women than women do in men. Men also prefer women who are somewhat younger than

Fact vs. Fiction

Interactive

Employers are more likely to call back attractive female job applicants with photographs included with their résumé, compared with both females with no photos and plain-looking females with photos accompanying their résumés. (See bottom of page for answer.)

○ Fact

○ Fiction

they are. Conversely, Buss found that women tend to place more emphasis than do men on having a partner with a high level of financial resources. In contrast with men, women prefer partners who are somewhat older than they are. Still, men and women value most of the same things. Both sexes put a premium on having a partner who's intelligent, dependable, and kind (Buss, 1994).

Evolutionary Models of Attraction. Putting aside these commonalities, how can we make sense of sex differences in mate preferences? Evolutionary theorists point out that because most men produce an enormous number of sperm—an average of about 300 million per ejaculation—they typically pursue a mating strategy that maximizes the chances that at least one of these sperm will find a receptive egg at the end of its long journey (Symons, 1979). As a consequence, evolutionary psychologists contend, men are on the lookout for cues of potential health and fertility such as physical attractiveness and youth. Women, in contrast, typically produce only one egg per month, so they must be choosy. In a study of speed dating—a technique invented by Los Angeles Rabbi Yaacov Deyo in 1998 to help Jewish singles get acquainted—men and women interacted with potential dates for three minutes (Kurzban & Weeden, 2005). Men chose to have further contact with half of the women they met, whereas women were decidedly pickier, selecting one in three men to meet again. Women tend to pursue a mating strategy that maximizes the chances that the man with whom they mate will provide well for their offspring. Hence, women prefer men who are well off monetarily and a bit more experienced in the ways of life (Buunk et al., 2002).

Social Role Theory. Some researchers have offered alternatives to evolutionary models of attraction. According to Alice Eagly and Wendy Wood's (1999) *social role theory*, biological variables play a role in men's and women's preferences, but not in the way that evolutionary psychologists contend. Instead, biological factors constrain the roles that men and women adopt (Eagly, Wood, & Johannesen-Schmidt, 2004). Because men tend to be bigger and stronger compared with women, they've more often ended up playing the roles of hunter, food provider, and warrior. Moreover, because men don't bear children, they have considerable opportunities to pursue high-status positions. In contrast, because women bear children, they've more often ended up playing the role of child care provider and have been more limited in pursuing high-status positions.

Men tend to be attracted to women who wear red or are surrounded by red. Researchers found that women are three times more likely to wear a pink or red shirt when they're at high rather than low risk for conceiving a child (Beall & Tracy, 2013).

Some of these differences in traditional roles may help to explain men's and women's different mate preferences. For example, because women have typically held fewer high-status positions than men have, they may have preferred men who are dependable financial providers (Eagly Wood, & Johannesen-Schmidt, 2004). Consistent with social role theory, men and women have become more similar in their mate preferences over the past half-century (Buss et al., 2001), perhaps reflecting the increasing social opportunities for women across that time period. So although nature may channel men and women into somewhat different roles and therefore different mate preferences, nurture may shape these roles and preferences in significant ways.

Answer: Fiction. Researchers sent résumés to potential employers with photos of either an attractive female, a plain-looking female, or a woman with no photo included with the résumé (Ruffle & Shtudiner, 2014). Women with no photo were more likely to be called back than attractive or plain looking women with a photo included. The researchers reported that female jealousy and envy were likely reasons for this finding. In contrast, attractive men with photos were called back at the highest rate, more than doubling that of the plain-looking men with photos and at a higher rate than men with no photos included.

IS BEAUTY IN THE EYE OF THE BEHOLDER?   Popular wisdom tells us that "beauty is in the eye of the beholder." To some extent, that saying is true. Yet it's also an oversimplification. People tend to agree at considerably higher-than-chance levels about who is and isn't physically attractive (Burns & Farina, 1992). This is the case not only within a race, but also across races; Caucasian and African American men tend to agree on which women are attractive, as do Caucasian and Asian American men (Cunningham et al., 1995). Even across vastly different cultures, men and women tend to agree on whom they find physically attractive (Langlois et al., 2000).

Although standards of beauty differ somewhat within and across cultures, research suggests that both most African American men and most Caucasian men agree on which Caucasian women (such as Jennifer Aniston, *left*) and African American women (such as Beyoncé, *right*) are physically attractive.

Furthermore, men and women prefer certain body shapes in members of the opposite sex. Men tend to be especially attracted to women with a waist-to-hip ratio of about 0.7, that is, with a waist about 70 percent as large as their hips (Pazhoohi & Liddle, 2012; Singh, 1993), although this ratio is often less important than other variables, like body weight (Furnham, Petrides, & Constantinides, 2005; Kościński, 2013). Men remember more details about a female target figure they viewed with a waist-hip ratio of 0.60 to 0.80, in contrast with female targets they viewed with waist hip ratios of 0.50 and 0.90 (Fitzgerald, Horgan, & Himes, 2016; Tassinary & Hansen, 1998). In contrast, women generally prefer men with a higher waist-to-hip ratio (Singh, 1995). According to evolutionary psychologist Donald Symons (1979), these findings imply that "beauty lies in the adaptations of the beholder." Women's waist-to-hip ratio tends to decline as they become older, so this ratio is a cue—although a highly imperfect one—to fertility.

Still, there are differences in physical preferences within and across cultures (Swami & Furnham, 2008). For example, men from African American and Caribbean cultures often find women with a large body size more physically attractive than do men of European cultures (Rosenblum & Lewis, 1999). Furthermore, preferences toward thinness have frequently shifted over historical time, as even a casual inspection of paintings of nude women over the past few centuries reveals.

WHEN BEING "JUST AVERAGE" IS JUST FINE.   Which person are we more likely to find attractive: (a) Someone who's exotic, unusual, or distinctive in some way or (b) someone who's just plain average? If you're like most people, you'd assume (a). Indeed, we sometimes insult people's appearance by calling women "plain Janes" and men "average Joes." Yet as Judith Langlois and Lori Roggman (1990) showed, being average has its pluses. By using a computer to digitize the faces of students and then combine them progressively, these researchers found that people generally prefer faces that are most average. In their study, people preferred average faces a whopping 96 percent of the time.

Replicability

Can the results be duplicated in other studies?

Ruling Out Rival Hypotheses

Have important alternative explanations for the findings been excluded?

Although some psychologists found these results difficult to believe, many investigators have replicated them for European, Japanese, and Chinese faces (Gangestad & Scheyd, 2005; Komori, Kawamura, & Ishihara, 2009; Rhodes, Halberstadt, & Brajkovich, 2001). Average faces are also more symmetrical than nonaverage faces, so our preferences for average faces might be due to their greater symmetry. Yet studies show that even when faces are symmetrical, people still prefer faces that are more average (Valentine, Darling, & Donnelly, 2004).

Evolutionary psychologists have speculated that "averageness" in a face tends to reflect an absence of genetic mutations, serious diseases, and other abnormalities. As a consequence, we could be drawn to people with such faces, as they're often better "genetic catches." Maybe. But studies show that people prefer not merely average faces, but average animals like birds and fish and even average objects like cars and watches (Halberstadt & Rhodes, 2003). In one study, investigators found that average voices tend to be perceived as more attractive than individual voices (Bruckert et al., 2010). So our preference for average faces may be due to an alternative mechanism, namely, a more general preference for anything that's average. Perhaps we find average stimuli to be more familiar and easier to process mentally, because they reflect stimuli we've seen before many times (Gangestad & Scheyd, 2005).

Ruling Out Rival Hypotheses

Have important alternative explanations for the findings been excluded?

It's not merely human faces that we find cute. Even cars that exhibit certain facial characteristics, such as large "eyes," a small, rounded "nose," and a large "head" relative to the rest of the body, tend to elicit the so-called "cute response" in most of us.

passionate love

love marked by powerful, even overwhelming, longing for one's partner

companionate love

love marked by a sense of deep friendship and fondness for one's partner

Companionate love is often the primary form of love among the elderly. It can be a powerful emotional bond between couples across the life span.

Love: Science Confronts the Mysterious

Elizabeth Barrett Browning wrote famously: "How do I love thee? Let me count the ways." According to some psychologists, we may not need to count all that high. We'll explain. Psychologists are no different from the rest of us. They've tried to understand the myriad varieties of love, with some concluding that there's only one type of love; others, that love comes in many shapes and sizes. According to Elaine Hatfield and Richard Rapson (1996), there are two major types of love: passionate and companionate. Robert Sternberg, as we'll soon see, puts the number at seven.

PASSIONATE LOVE: LOVE AS A HOLLYWOOD ROMANCE. Passionate love is marked by a powerful, even overwhelming, longing for one's partner. It's a strange mix of delirious happiness when we're around the object of our desire and utter misery when we're not. It's the stuff of which Hollywood movies are made. As Romeo and Juliet knew all too well, passionate love is fueled when obstacles, such as seemingly insurmountable physical distance or the strenuous objection of parents, are placed in the way of romance (Driscoll, Davis, & Lipetz, 1972). Such hurdles may heighten arousal, thereby intensifying passion, as Schachter and Singer's two-factor theory would predict (Kenrick, Neuberg, & Cialdini, 2005). In a study that followed participants for one month after a speed-dating event, individuals who experienced anxiety about a potential partner's romantic involvement expressed greater preference for a serious relationship than for a one-night stand (Eastwick & Finkel, 2008). Uncertainty about how relationships will unfold, combined with hope that romantic feelings will be reciprocated, fuel attachment and desire (Tennov, 1979). The good news is that long-term passionate love is possible: In one survey, 40 percent of couples assessed after 10 years or more of marriage reported that they were "very intensely in love" (O'Leary et al., 2012).

COMPANIONATE LOVE: LOVE AS FRIENDSHIP. Companionate love is marked by a sense of deep friendship and fondness for one's partner (Acevedo & Aron, 2009). Romantic relationships tend to progress over time from passionate to companionate love (Fehr, Harasymchuk, & Sprecher, 2014; Wojciszke, 2002), although most healthy relationships retain at least a spark of passion. In older couples, companionate love may be the overriding emotion in the relationship.

There's growing evidence that companionate and passionate love are psychologically independent. Studies indicate that people can "fall in love" with partners in the sense of caring deeply about them, yet experience little or no sexual desire toward them (Diamond, 2004). In addition, these two forms of love may be associated with different brain systems (Diamond, 2003; Gonzaga et al., 2006). Animal research suggests that emotional attachment to others is influenced largely by such hormones as oxytocin (see LO 3.3a), which plays a key role in pair bonding and interpersonal trust. In contrast, sexual desire is influenced by sex hormones such as testosterone and estrogen.

THE THREE SIDES OF LOVE. Robert Sternberg believes that the "two types of love" model is too simple. In his *triangular theory of love*, Sternberg (1986, 1988a) proposed three major elements of love: (1) intimacy ("I feel really close to this person"), (2) passion ("I'm crazy about this person"), and (3) commitment ("I really want to stay with this person"). These elements combine to form seven varieties of love (see Figure 11.13 on next page). Sternberg's model is more a description of love types than an explanation of why people fall in love, but it's a helpful road map toward understanding one of life's great mysteries.

Answer: Fact. Across the world, most people display a *cute response:* a positive emotional reaction to faces that display certain characteristics, especially (a) large eyes; (b) a small, round nose; (c) big, round ears; and (d) a large head relative to the body (Lorenz, 1971). These are the same facial features we find in infants, so natural selection may have predisposed us to find these features irresistibly adorable (Angier, 2006).

Hate: A Neglected Topic

Until recently, psychologists didn't want to have much to do with the topic of hate. Most introductory psychology textbooks don't even list the word *hate* in their indices. Yet with the horrific events of September 11, 2001, and the burgeoning problem of terrorism around the globe, it's clear that psychologists can no longer turn a blind eye to the question of why some people despise others, at times to the point of wanting to destroy them (Bloom, 2004; Sternberg, 2004). Of course, hate can assume a variety of less violent but still pernicious forms in everyday life, including extreme forms of racism, sexism, anti-Semitism, homophobia, and political partisanship. Without question, hatred toward individuals who differ markedly from us, such as people from other cultures, is fueled by the Internet and social media, which can create virtual communities of like-minded people who share similar hostile views (Post, 2010). This "echo chamber" of similar or identical views can fuel groupthink, confirmation bias, and other problematic ways of thinking we've encountered in previous chapters (Quattrociocchi, Scalia, & Sunstein, 2016).

Using his triangular theory of love as a starting point, Robert Sternberg (2003a) developed a theory of hate, with hatred consisting of three elements:

1. Negation of intimacy ("I would never want to get close to these people")
2. Passion ("I absolutely and positively despise these people.")
3. Commitment ("I'm determined to stop or harm these people.")

As in his theory of love, different forms of hate arise from combinations of these three elements, with "burning hate"—the most severe—reflecting high scores on all three. For Sternberg, the key to fueling hate is propaganda. Groups and governments that "teach" hatred of other groups are experts at portraying these groups as evil and worthy of disdain (Keen, 1986; Lilienfeld, Ammirati, & Landfield, 2009; Sternberg, 2003a).

The good news is that if we can learn hate, we can probably unlearn it. Teaching individuals to overcome their confirmation bias toward perceiving only the negative attributes of individuals or groups they dislike may be an essential first step (Harrington, 2004; Lilienfeld et al., 2009). Recognizing that "there's good and bad in everyone," as the saying goes, may help us combat our deep-seated animosity toward our enemies—and more broadly, members of other races, cultures, and groups whose views differ from our own.

Figure 11.13 What Is Love?

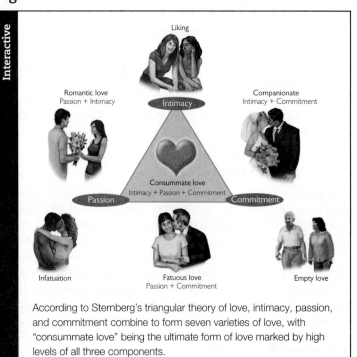

According to Sternberg's triangular theory of love, intimacy, passion, and commitment combine to form seven varieties of love, with "consummate love" being the ultimate form of love marked by high levels of all three components.

Summary: Emotion and Motivation

11.1: Theories of Emotion: What Causes Our Feelings?

11.1a Describe the major theories of emotion.

According to discrete emotions theory, people experience a small number (perhaps seven) of distinct biologically influenced emotions. According to cognitive theories, including the James–Lange theory, emotions result from our interpretation of stimuli or our bodily reactions to them. According to the Cannon–Bard theory, emotion-provoking events lead to both emotions and bodily reactions. Schachter and Singer's two-factor theory proposes that emotions are the explanations we attach to our general state of arousal following an emotion-provoking event.

11.1b Identify unconscious influences on emotion.

Many emotional experiences are generated automatically and operate unconsciously, as illustrated by research on the mere exposure effect and the facial feedback hypothesis.

11.2: Nonverbal Expression of Emotion: The Eyes, Bodies, and Cultures Have It

11.2a Explain the importance of nonverbal expression of emotion.

Much of emotional expression is nonverbal; gestures highlight speech (illustrators), involve touching our bodies (manipulators), or convey specific meanings (emblems). Nonverbal expressions are often more valid indicators of emotions than are words.

11.2b Identify major lie detection methods and their pitfalls.

The polygraph test measures physiological responses to questions designed to expose falsehoods. The Controlled Question Test (CQT) contains questions relevant and irrelevant to the crime and control questions that reflect presumed lies. Greater physiological reactivity in response to relevant questions supposedly suggests deception. Nevertheless, the CQT detects general arousal rather than guilt and results in numerous false-positives. False-negatives can result when individuals employ countermeasures (such as biting their tongue or curling their toes). The Guilty Knowledge Test (GKT) relies on the premise that criminals harbor concealed knowledge about the crime. The GKT has a low false-positive rate but a fairly high false-negative rate.

11.3: Happiness and Self-Esteem: Science Confronts Pop Psychology

11.3a Identify common myths and realities about happiness and self-esteem.

Myths: The prime determinant of happiness is what happens to us, money makes us happy, happiness declines in old age, and people on the West Coast are happiest. Realities: Happiness is associated with being married, having a college education, and being religious; voting Republican; exercising; being thankful; and immersing ourselves in what we're doing ("flow"). We tend to overestimate the long-term impact of events on our happiness. Myth: Low self-esteem is the root of all unhappiness. Reality: Self-esteem is only modestly associated with mental health but is associated with greater initiative, persistence, and positive illusions—the tendency to perceive ourselves more favorably than others do.

11.3b Describe the emerging discipline of positive psychology.

Positive psychology emphasizes strengths, love, and happiness. Nevertheless, some critics have argued that positive psychology's "look on the bright side of life" approach may have its downsides, in part because excessive happiness may sometimes be maladaptive.

11.4: Motivation: Our Wants and Needs

11.4a Explain basic principles and theories of motivation.

Motivation refers to the drives—especially our wants and needs—that propel us in specific directions. Drive reduction theory states that drives (such as hunger and thirst) pull us to act in certain ways. The Yerkes–Dodson law posits an inverted U-shaped relation between arousal and mood/performance. Approach and avoidance often drive conflict. According to incentive theories, positive goals are motivators. These motivators include primary (biological) and secondary (psychological desires/achievement, self-actualization) needs.

11.4b Describe the determinants of hunger, weight gain, and obesity.

The lateral hypothalamus has been called a "feeding center" and the ventromedial hypothalamus a "satiety center," although these descriptions oversimplify scientific reality. Hunger is also associated with hormones (ghrelin), low glucose levels, neurotransmitters (leptin, serotonin), a genetically programmed set point for body fat and muscle mass, specific genes (melanocortin-4 receptor gene, leptin gene), and sensitivity to food cues and expectations.

11.4c Identify the symptoms of bulimia, binge eating disorder, and anorexia.

Bulimia nervosa is marked by recurrent binge eating, followed by attempts to minimize weight gain. In binge-eating disorder, bingeing is recurrent but purging is absent. Anorexia nervosa is characterized by a refusal to eat, resulting in a significantly low body weight expected for age and height.

11.4d Describe the human sexual response cycle and factors that influence sexual activity.

Masters and Johnson described four stages of the sexual response cycle: excitement, plateau, orgasm, and resolution. Frequency of sexual activity decreases with age, but sexual satisfaction doesn't. Expression of sexual desire is shaped by social norms and culture.

11.4e Identify common misconceptions about and potential influences on sexual orientation.

Common myths include the notions that gay individuals (a) typically adopt a masculine or feminine role, (b) are especially likely to sexually abuse children and adolescents, and (c) are usually inadequate parents. Potential influences on sexual orientation are an inherited tendency toward childhood gender nonconformity, sex hormones, prenatal influences, and brain differences.

11.5: Attraction, Love, and Hate: The Greatest Mysteries of Them All

11.5a **Identify principles and factors that guide attraction and relationship formation.**

Factors guiding attraction and relationship formation are proximity (physical closeness), similarity (like attracts like), reciprocity (give what we get), physical attractiveness (more important to men than to women), evolutionary influences, social roles, and preference for "average" faces.

11.5b **Describe the major types of love and the elements of love and hate.**

The major love types are passionate and companionate. According to Sternberg's model of love, the major love elements are intimacy, passion, and commitment. The major hate elements are negation of intimacy, passion, and commitment.

Chapter 12
Stress, Coping, and Health

The Mind–Body Interconnection

 ## Learning Objectives

12.1a Explain how stress is defined and approached in different ways.

12.1b Identify different approaches to measuring stress.

12.2a Describe Selye's general adaptation syndrome.

12.2b Describe the diversity of stress responses.

12.3a Describe the role of social support and different types of control in coping with stress.

12.3b Explain how our attitudes, beliefs, and personality may influence our responses to stress.

12.4a Describe how the immune system is affected by stress.

12.4b Identify how physical disorders such as ulcers are related to stress.

12.4c Describe the role of personality, everyday experiences, and socioeconomic factors in coronary heart disease.

12.5a Identify four behaviors that contribute to a healthy lifestyle.

12.5b Identify why it is difficult to change our lifestyles.

12.5c Describe different alternative and complementary medical approaches and compare their effectiveness with placebos.

Challenge Your Assumptions

Do most people who encounter highly aversive events develop posttraumatic stress disorder?

Are some people more prone to heart attacks than other people are?

Are crash diets that promise quick and enduring weight loss effective?

Are acupuncture and other alternative medical treatments more effective than are traditional medical procedures?

Can placebos affect brain activity?

Watch   COPING IN THE FACE OF ADVERSITY

Video

Tuesday, September 11, 2001, is a day few Americans will forget. Across the country, people were glued to their television sets watching in horror as two loaded passenger planes flew into the Twin Towers of the World Trade Center (WTC) in New York City. In the worst terrorist attack in American history, more than 2,700 people were killed at the WTC alone. Hundreds more were killed when terrorists crashed two other planes—one into the Pentagon and one into a field in rural Pennsylvania, where passengers had attempted to regain control of the plane.

In the aftermath of this tragedy, inspiring stories emerged of courageous first responders—firefighters, paramedics, police, and emergency service workers—who risked their lives to save others. Nearly 400 people who participated in rescue operations died on 9/11. One of those heroes who died trying to save others was firefighter Jonathan Lelpi. The video memorializes his life and courage from the deeply personal perspective of his father, Lee Lelpi, who is a retired firefighter himself. Mr. Lelpi spent agonizing months searching every day for his son. He coped with the tragic loss of his son by "turning it around and doing something positive," establishing the National September 11 Memorial and Museum, an enduring tribute to those who perished on that day: In Mr. Lelpi's gripping words, "giving a voice to people who lost their voice."

Bob Small, an investment company executive, barely survived the devastation of the WTC, and suffered afterward with recurrent dreams of another plane hitting the building and dreams of himself or other people jumping off the Twin Towers, an unforgettable scene that he actually witnessed. To keep the memories of that day alive and remain a part of him—to never lose touch with the reality he experienced, give it meaning, and feel grounded—he has filled one of his rooms with mementos, pieces from the WTC, newspaper stories; small things yet imbued with huge personal significance.

These stories cannot help but stir questions in our minds. What happens after we experience a traumatic event like 9/11? How do people fare following a close brush with death or grapple with the horrific demise of a loved one? Do the effects reverberate long afterward, producing lasting psychological or physical illnesses? Or can many people manage to cope, even thrive, in the wake of harrowing circumstances?

The stories of Lee Lelpi and Bob Small give us a snapshot of a few of the myriad ways in which people contend with adversity. In this chapter, we'll take a much closer look at how people cope with trying experiences, from the annoyance of a computer crash to the terror of surviving a plane crash. We'll also examine the complex interplay between stress and physical health. Dean Kilpatrick and his colleagues (Kilpatrick et al., 2013) surveyed nearly 3,000 men and women in the general population and found that nearly 90 percent of respondents had experienced at least one potentially traumatic event, such as a sexual or physical assault or car accident, and that exposure to multiple types of highly adverse events was the norm. So it's actually the unusual person who doesn't experience severe stress in his or her

Firefighters and police officers who merely witness traumatic events often experience high levels of stress.

lifetime (de Vries & Olff, 2009; Ozer et al., 2003). Groups at especially high risk for stressful events include the young, the unmarried, and people of low socioeconomic status (Cohen & Janicki-Deverts, 2012; Luby et al., 2013; Miranda & Green, 1999; Turner, Wheaton, & Lloyd, 1995). Women are more likely than men to experience sexual assault and child abuse, but less likely to experience nonsexual assaults, accidents, disasters, fires, or wartime combat (Tolin & Foa, 2006). Interpersonal violence, such as sexual assault and combat exposure, is more likely to bring about long-term distressing aftereffects than are natural disasters, after which members of the community often band together to provide mutual support (Arnberg, Johannesson, & Michel, 2013; Hoge & Warner, 2014). Many people assume that individuals who live in rural areas or nonindustrialized countries experience minimal stress compared with residents of urban and more developed areas. Yet scientists have discovered little support for this popular belief: Stress-producing events are widespread among all sectors of society (Bigbee, 1990; Figley, 2013).

Fortunately, exposure to events like Hurricane Katrina, frontline combat in Afghanistan, the catastrophic flooding in Louisiana in 2016—or even the horrific 2012 school shooting in Newtown, Connecticut—doesn't guarantee that people will be traumatized for life. Herein lies another case in which scientific research contradicts popular psychology. Many self-help books inform us that most people require psychological help in the face of stressful circumstances (Sommers & Satel, 2005). Some companies dispense squadrons of grief counselors to help people cope with the upshot of stressful events; these companies often assume that without psychological help, most witnesses to trauma are doomed to serious psychological problems. In 2007, grief counselors arrived at the scene to help traumatized college students deal with the horrific shootings at Virginia Tech, and in 1998, counselors even traveled to the Boston Public Library to help librarians deal with their feelings of loss following the destruction of books in a flood.

Yet we'll discover in this chapter that even in the face of horrific circumstances like shootings and natural disasters, most of us are surprisingly resilient (Bonanno, 2004; Bonanno, Westphal, & Mancini, 2011; Maddi, 2013). Even most victims of child sexual abuse turn out to be psychologically healthy adults, although there are certainly exceptions (Rind, Tromovitch, & Bauserman, 1998). Because practicing psychologists tend to see only those people who react emotionally to stress—after all, the healthy people don't come for help—they probably overestimate most people's fragility and underestimate their resilience, an error sometimes called the *clinician's illusion* (Cohen & Cohen, 1984; Davidson et al., 2008).

Before we discuss why some people thrive and others nosedive when confronted with stressful life events, we'll consider the fundamental question of what stress is. We'll then explore competing views of stress, the mind–body link responsible for stress-related disorders, how we cope with stressful situations, and the rapidly growing fields of health psychology and alternative medicine.

12.1: What Is Stress?

12.1a Explain how stress is defined and approached in different ways.

12.1b Identify different approaches to measuring stress.

Before we proceed further, it's important to distinguish two terms—*stress* and *trauma*—that are commonly confused. **Stress**—a type of response—consists of the tension, discomfort, or physical symptoms that arise when a situation, called a *stressor*—a type of stimulus—strains our ability to cope effectively. A *traumatic* event is a stressor that's so severe that it can produce long-term psychological or health consequences.

The field's thinking about stress has evolved over the years (Cooper & Dewe, 2004). Before the 1940s, scientists rarely used the term *stress* outside the engineering profession (Hayward, 1960), where it referred to stresses on materials and building structures. A building was said to withstand stress if it didn't collapse under intense pressure. It wasn't until 1944 that the term *stress* found its way into the psychological literature (Jones & Bright, 2001). This engineering analogy highlights the notion that

stress

the tension, discomfort, or physical symptoms that arise when a situation, called a *stressor*—a type of stimulus—strains our ability to cope effectively

"if the body were like a machine and machines are subject to wear and tear then so too would be the body" (Doublet, 2000). But just as two buildings can withstand different amounts of stress before weakening and collapsing, people differ widely in their personal resources, the significance they attach to stressful events, and their abilities to grapple with them.

Stress in the Eye of the Beholder: Three Approaches

Researchers have approached the study of stress in three different, yet interrelated and complementary, ways (Kessler, Price, & Wortman, 1985). Each approach has yielded valuable insights and, when considered together, they illuminate the big and small events that generate distress and the ways we perceive and respond to stressful situations.

STRESSORS AS STIMULI.   The *stressors as stimuli* approach focuses on identifying different types of stressful events, ranging from job loss to combat. This approach has pinpointed categories of events that most of us find dangerous and unpredictable (Chu et al., 2013; Cohen, Gianaros, & Manuck, 2016). For example, pregnancy is often a joyous yet stressful event, fraught with uncertainties, including concerns about the child's health. Women who are highly anxious or experience negative life events during pregnancy are more likely to deliver their babies early—3–5 weeks before normal gestation of 40–42 weeks—compared with women who experience more typical worries (Dunkel-Schetter, 2009). When people retire, the combination of low income and physical disability can make matters worse, suggesting that stressful situations can produce cumulative effects (Smith et al., 2005). The stressors as stimuli approach also identifies the people who are most susceptible to stress following different events. For example, college freshmen show a greater response to such negative life events as the breakup of a relationship compared with older men or women (Jackson & Finney, 2002).

STRESS AS A RESPONSE.   Stress researchers also study *stress as a response*—they assess people's psychological and physical reactions to stressful circumstances. Typically, scientists expose participants to stress-producing stimuli in the laboratory; in other cases, they study people who've encountered real-life stressors. Then they measure a host of outcome variables: stress-related feelings such as depression, hopelessness, hostility, and physiological responses such as increases in heart rate and the release of stress hormones called **corticosteroids**.

Highly stressful life events, such as disasters, can exert positive as well as negative effects on people and communities. It might seem strange, but as many as two-thirds to three-quarters of people who've experienced a highly stressful event, such as a natural disaster, assault, or life-threatening illness, report some degree of **posttraumatic growth**: the perception of beneficial change or personal transformation in the struggle to overcome adversity (Cole & Lynn, 2010–2011, 1996; Linley & Joseph, 2004). Nevertheless, researchers have administered measures of perceived and actual growth over time and found that people's perception of growth overestimated their actual posttraumatic growth in areas of positive relationships, gratitude, life satisfaction, and meaning in life. Following adversity, people apparently reinterpret their lives more positively as a self-protective coping strategy (Frazier et al., 2009). Still, some people do experience positive, profound, and enduring personal transformations in the wake of highly aversive events.

Disasters can unify communities and bring out the best in us. Christopher Peterson and Martin Seligman (2003) conducted a survey of character strengths of 4,817 Americans before the 9/11 terrorist attacks and within two months afterward. After the attacks, kindness, teamwork, leadership, gratitude, hope, love, and spirituality increased. One team of researchers performed a linguistic analysis on the diaries of 1,084 users of an online journaling service two months before and two months after the 9/11 attacks. Forty-five percent of the entries after the attack dealt with a larger social group, such as the community and nation, in

Some researchers call the psychological and physical response to a stressor "strain," much as a material can be said to be strained when under stress.

corticosteroid

stress hormone that activates the body and prepares us to respond to stressful circumstances

posttraumatic growth

the perception of beneficial change or personal transformation in the struggle to overcome adversity

The stress of unemployment includes not only the frustration and despair of looking for a new job, but also the economic hardship of living on a sharply reduced income.

In 2005, Hurricaine Katrina, one of the most destructive hurricanes in U.S. history and the most costly natural disaster, devastated much of New Orleans and impacted other cities and towns across the Gulf Coast, killing 1,245 people, uprooting families, and leaving an estimated $108 billion in property damage in its wake.

primary appraisal

initial decision regarding whether an event is harmful

secondary appraisal

perceptions regarding our ability to cope with an event that follows primary appraisal

problem-focused coping

coping strategy by which we problem solve and tackle life's challenges head on

emotion-focused coping

coping strategy that features a positive outlook on feelings or situations accompanied by behaviors that reduce painful emotions

contrast with none of the entries before the attack (Cohen, Mehl, & Pennebaker, 2004). These findings suggest that stressful circumstances that touch the lives of an entire community can increase social awareness, cement interpersonal bonds, and enhance a variety of positive personal characteristics. Yet the effects of highly aversive events, for good or ill, are often temporary, with the most negative aftereffects seen in people with preexisting psychological problems or prior trauma exposure (Bonanno et al., 2010). Engaging in pleasurable activities, finding purpose in life, and establishing and taking comfort in close relationships can not only blunt the trying effects of stressful events, but also predicts life satisfaction more generally (Peterson, Park, & Seligman, 2013).

STRESS AS A TRANSACTION. Stress is a subjective experience; not all people react to the same stressful events in the same way. Some people are devastated by the breakup of a meaningful relationship, whereas others are optimistic about the opportunity to start afresh. Researchers who study *stress as a transaction* between people and their environments examine the interaction between potentially stressful life events and how people interpret and cope with them (Coyne & Holroyd, 1982; Lazarus & Folkman, 1984; Wethington, Glanz, & Schwartz, 2015). Richard Lazarus and his coworkers contended that a critical factor influencing whether we experience an event as stressful is our appraisal, that is, evaluation of the event. When we encounter a potentially threatening event, we initially engage in **primary appraisal**. That is, we first decide whether the event is harmful before making a **secondary appraisal** about how well we can cope with it (Lazarus & Folkman, 1984).

When we believe we can't cope, we're more likely to experience a full-blown stress reaction than when we believe we can (Lazarus, 1999). When we're optimistic and think we can achieve our goals, we're especially likely to engage in **problem-focused coping**, a strategy in which we tackle life's challenges head on (Carver & Scheier, 1999; Lazarus & Folkman, 1984). When we earn a disappointing grade on a test, we may analyze why we fell short and devise a workable plan to improve our performance on the next test. When situations arise that we can't avoid or control, we're more likely to adopt **emotion-focused coping**, a strategy in which we try to place a positive spin on our feelings or predicaments or seek emotional support to reduce painful emotions (Baker & Berenbaum, 2007; Carver, Scheier, & Weintraub, 1989; Lazarus & Folkman, 1984). After the breakup of a relationship, we may remind ourselves that we were unhappy months before it occurred and reenter the dating arena.

Journal Prompt

Think about a recent event that engendered major stress in your life. Describe your primary and secondary appraisals of the event and how your appraisals affected your response to the stressful event.

Emotion-focused coping may encourage people who've divorced to begin dating again.

No Two Stresses Are Created Equal: Measuring Stress

Measuring stress is a tricky business, largely because what's exceedingly stressful for one person, such as an argument with a boss, may be a mere annoyance for another. Two scales—the Social Readjustment Rating Scale and the Hassles Scale—endeavor to gauge the nature and impact of different stressful events.

MAJOR LIFE EVENTS. Adopting the view that stressors are stimuli, David Holmes and his colleagues developed the Social Readjustment Rating Scale (SRRS), the first of many efforts to measure life events systematically. The SRRS is based on 43 life events such as "jail term" and "personal injury or illness," ranked in terms of their stressfulness (Holmes & Rahe, 1967; Miller & Rahe, 1997). Studies using the SRRS and related measures indicate that the number of stressful events people report over the previous year or so is associated with a variety of physical disorders (Dohrenwend & Dohrenwend, 1974; Holmes & Masuda, 1974), psychological disorders like depression (Coyne, 1992; Holahan & Moos, 1991; Schmidt et al., 2004), and suicide attempts (Blasco-Fontecilla, et al., 2012).

Nevertheless, the sheer number of stressful life events is far from a perfect predictor of who'll become physically or psychologically ill (Coyne & Racioppo, 2000). That's because this approach to measuring stressors doesn't consider other crucial factors, including people's interpretation of events, coping behaviors and resources, and difficulty recalling events accurately (Coyne & Racioppo, 2000; Lazarus, 1999). In addition, it neglects to take into account some of the more chronic, or ongoing, stressors that many individuals experience. Even subtle forms of discrimination or differential treatment based on race, gender, sexual orientation, or religion, for example, can be a significant source of stress even though they rarely are prompted by or lead to a single stressful event we can check off a list (Berger & Sarnyai, 2015). This approach also neglects the fact that some stressful life events, like divorce and troubles with the boss, can be *consequences* rather than *causes* of people's psychological problems (Depue & Monroe, 1986). That's because people's psychological difficulties, such as severe depression and anxiety, can create a host of interpersonal problems, such as difficult interactions with loved ones and coworkers.

HASSLES: DON'T SWEAT THE SMALL STUFF. We've all had days when just about everything goes wrong and everybody seems to get on our nerves: Our daily lives are often loaded with **hassles**, minor nuisances that strain our ability to cope. But can lots of hassles–the wear and tear of daily life–add up to be as taxing as the monumental events that shake the foundations of our world?

Researchers developed the Hassles Scale to measure how stressful events, ranging from small annoyances to major daily pressures, impact our adjustment (DeLongis, Folkman, & Lazarus, 1988; Kanner et al., 1981). Both major life events and hassles are associated with poor general health, but the frequency and perceived severity of hassles are actually better predictors of physical health, depression, and anxiety than are major life events (Fernandez & Sheffield, 1996; Kanner et al., 1981). In fact, negative reactions to seemingly minor stressful events predict anxiety and depressive disorders 10 years later (Charles et al., 2013). Nevertheless, it's possible that this finding might reflect the fact that people who are prone to negative emotions react negatively to stressors at both the first and second time that stress is measured.

Researchers have questioned whether some items on the Hassles Scale, such as difficulties with relaxing and insomnia, may reflect symptoms of psychological disorders such as depression or anxiety, rather than hassles themselves (Monroe, 1983). To address this question, the scale developers (DeLongis et al., 1988) revised the scale by removing all words related to psychological symptoms and found that hassles were still associated with health outcomes.

Another possibility researchers have considered is that major, not minor, stressful events are the real culprits because they set us off when we already feel hassled or create hassles with which we then need to cope. To test this hypothesis, researchers have used statistical procedures to show that even when the influence of major life events is subtracted from the mix, hassles still predict psychological adjustment (Forshaw, 2002; Kanner et al., 1981). These findings suggest that everyday hassles do indeed contribute to stress.

Researchers have also devised interview-based methods to provide a more in-depth picture of life stress than self-report measures. Interviewers can identify the positive and negative events that people experience as stressful, distinguish ongoing from "one-shot"

To avoid losing his mobile phone George had it chained to the wall.

Misplacing cell phones and other possessions is one of many hassles we encounter in our daily lives. Research suggests that such hassles can be quite stressful over the long haul.

> **Correlation vs. Causation**
>
> Can we be sure that A causes B?

hassle

minor annoyance or nuisance that strains our ability to cope

> **Correlation vs. Causation**
>
> Can we be sure that A causes B?

> **Ruling Out Rival Hypotheses**
>
> Have important alternative explanations for the findings been excluded?

> **Ruling Out Rival Hypotheses**
>
> Have important alternative explanations for the findings been excluded?

stressors, and consider how events interact to produce physical and psychological problems (Dohrenwend, 2006; Monroe, 2008). Still, in assessing stress, researchers must balance the rich information yield from interviews with the ease of administration and efficiency of questionnaires.

12.2: How We Adapt to Stress: Change and Challenge

12.2a Describe Selye's general adaptation syndrome.
12.2b Describe the diversity of stress responses.

As any of us who have had to confront a harrowing event, like a car accident or high-pressure interview for a big job, knows, adapting to stress isn't easy. Yet natural selection has endowed us with a set of responses for coping with anxiety-provoking circumstances.

The Mechanics of Stress: Selye's General Adaptation Syndrome

In 1956, Canadian physician Hans Selye ignited the field of modern-day stress research by publishing *The Stress of Life*, a landmark book that unveiled his decades of study on the effects of prolonged stress on the body. Selye's genius was to recognize a connection between the stress response of animals, including stomach ulcers and increases in the size of the adrenal gland, which produces stress hormones, and that of physically ill patients, who showed a consistent pattern of stress-related responses. Dovetailing with the engineering analogy we've already discussed, Selye believed that too much stress leads to breakdowns. He argued that we're equipped with a sensitive physiology that responds to stressful circumstances by kicking us into high gear. He called the pattern of responding to stress the **general adaptation syndrome (GAS)**. According to Selye, all prolonged stressors take us through three stages of adaptation: *alarm, resistance,* and *exhaustion* (see Figure 12.1). To illustrate key aspects of the GAS and the extent to which our appraisals determine our reactions to stress, let's consider the experience of a hypothetical person, named Mark, who's terrified of flying.

THE ALARM REACTION. Selye's first stage, the *alarm reaction*, involves excitation of the autonomic nervous system, the discharge of the stress hormone adrenaline, and physical symptoms of anxiety. Joseph LeDoux (1996) and others have identified the seat of anxiety within the limbic system—sometimes dubbed the *emotional brain*—that includes the amygdala, hypothalamus, and hippocampus. Once in flight, Mark feels the plane moving through pockets of turbulence and his cold, clammy hands clutch the shaking seat. His mouth is dry. His heart pounds. His breathing is rapid and shallow. He feels lightheaded and dizzy. Images of plane crashes he's seen on television pop uncontrollably into his mind. Mark's swift emotional reaction to the turbulence is tripped largely by his amygdala, where vital emotional memories are stored and create gut feelings of a possible crash. The hypothalamus sits atop a mind–body link known as the *hypothalamus-pituitary-adrenal* (HPA) axis, shown in Figure 12.2 on the next page.

When the hypothalamus (H) receives signals of fear, the sympathetic nervous system activates the adrenal gland (A), which secretes the stress hormones epinephrine (adrenaline) and norepinephrine (noradrenalin). In a matter of moments, Mark's blood pressure rises, his pupils dilate, and his heart pumps blood to vital organs, readying Mark for the **fight-or-flight response** (see LO 3.2b). This response, first described by Walter Cannon in 1915, is a set of physiological and psychological reactions that mobilize us either to confront or leave a threatening situation. Cannon noted that when animals, including humans, face a threat, they have two options: *fight* (actively attack the threat or cope in the immediate situation) or *flee* (escape). Of course, Mark can't flee, so his fear escalates. The hypothalamus and pituitary gland (P)

general adaptation syndrome (GAS)

stress-response pattern proposed by Hans Selye that consists of three stages: alarm, resistance, and exhaustion

---

Figure 12.1 Selye's General Adaptation Syndrome.

According to Selye's general adaptation syndrome, our level of resistance to stress drops during the alarm phase, increases during the resistance phase, and drops again during the exhaustion phase.

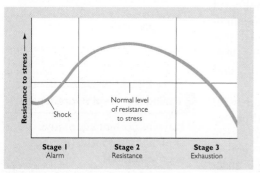

fight-or-flight response

physical and psychological reaction that mobilizes people and animals to either defend themselves (fight) or escape (flee) a threatening situation

orchestrate the adrenal gland's release of another stress hormone, cortisol, which floods Mark with energy, while his hippocampus retrieves terrifying images from news stories of planes going down in flames.

RESISTANCE.   After the initial rush of stress hormones, Mark enters Selye's second stage of the GAS: *resistance*. He adapts to the stressor and finds ways to cope with it. The instant Mark's hippocampus detected danger from the first jolt of rough air, it opened up a gateway to portions of his cerebral cortex, which neuroscientist Joseph LeDoux (1996) called the "thinking brain." At one point, Mark experiences a sudden impulse to bolt from his seat, but his basal ganglia, linked to the frontal cortex of his thinking brain, wisely leads him to think better of it. Mark slowly but surely gets a handle on his fears. He reminds himself that flying is statistically much safer than driving and that he's flown through choppy air in the past without being injured. He looks around and notices that most of the other passengers look calm. He reminds himself to breathe slowly, and with each breath his relaxation replaces tension.

EXHAUSTION.   Mark calms down and is able to get through his flight without panicking. But what happens when a stressor, such as wartime combat lasting months, is more prolonged and uncontrollable? Here's when the third stage of Selye's GAS—*exhaustion*—sets in. If our personal resources are limited and we lack good coping measures, our resistance may ultimately break down, causing our levels of activation to bottom out. The results can range from damage to an organ system, to depression and anxiety, to a breakdown in the immune system, which we'll discuss later in the chapter.

Still, Selye correctly recognized that stress could sometimes be advantageous. He coined the term *eustress* based on the Greek word *eu* meaning "good," to distinguish it from *distress*, or "bad" stress. Events that are challenging, yet not overwhelming, such as competing in an athletic event or giving a speech, can create "positive stress" and provide opportunities for personal growth. Short-term stress that lasts minutes to hours can also trigger a healthy immune response to help us fend off physical ailments (Dhabhar, 2014).

The Diversity of Stress Responses

Not all of us react to stressors with a fight-or-flight response. Our reactions vary from one stressor to another, and these reactions are shaped by gender.

FIGHT OR FLIGHT OR TEND AND BEFRIEND?   Shelley Taylor and her colleagues coined the catchy phrase **tend and befriend** to describe a common pattern of reacting to stress among women (Taylor et al., 2000; Taylor, 2006). The researchers observed that in times of stress, women generally rely on their social contacts and nurturing abilities—they *tend* to those around them and to themselves—more than men do, and they typically *befriend*, or turn to others for support.

That's not to say that women lack a self-preservation instinct or that they don't experience a fight-or-flight pattern when endangered. They certainly don't shrink from defending themselves and their children or from attempting to escape when physically threatened. Nevertheless, compared with men, women generally have more to lose—especially when they're pregnant, nursing, or caring for children—if they're injured or killed when fighting or fleeing. Therefore, over the course of evolutionary history, they've developed a tend-and-befriend response to threat, which, along with the fight-or-flight response, boosts the odds of their and their offspring's survival. Yet males, too, sometimes show a tend-and-befriend response. For example, they may respond with increased sharing, trust, and trustworthy behaviors when they participate in a stress-producing game with a partner in the laboratory, compared with participants in a non-stressful control condition (von Dawans et al., 2012).

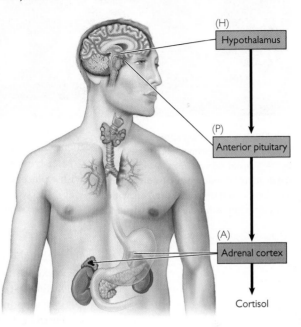

Figure 12.2 The Hypothalamus-Pituitary-Adrenal (HPA) Axis.

(H) Hypothalamus
(P) Anterior pituitary
(A) Adrenal cortex
Cortisol

tend and befriend

reaction that mobilizes people to nurture (tend) or seek social support (befriend) under stress

In stressful times, women often rely on friendships for support and comfort, a pattern that psychologist Shelley Taylor called "tend and befriend." Movies, such as the comedy *Bad Moms* (2016) and the now-classic female bonding flick, *Thelma and Louise* (1991), have parlayed dramatizations of this response to stressors into box office gold.

The 2012 tragic shooting spree at Sandy Hook Elementary School, perpetrated by 20-year-old Adam Lanza, resulted in the death of 20 children and 6 adult staff members, and it left some survivors with symptoms of posttraumatic stress disorder.

Oxytocin (see LO 3.7a), a hormone that plays key roles in love, trust, and emotional bonding, further counters stress and promotes the tend-and-befriend response (Kosfeld et al., 2005; Taylor & Master, 2011). Researchers discovered that women with high levels of oxytocin during pregnancy and in the first month after giving birth are more likely to touch their children affectionately, sing special songs to them, and bathe and feed them in special ways (Feldman et al., 2007). Laboratory studies also suggest that oxytocin promotes trust consistent with a tend-and-befriend response. For example, in one study, participants interacted with a conversational partner who dismissed, ignored, and interrupted them. Even when they experienced distress following the social rejection, they reported greater trust in their partner when they received oxytocin before their interaction compared with a placebo (Cardoso et al., 2013; Cardoso & Ellenbogen, 2014).

> ## Journal Prompt
>
> Write about a fight-or-flight reaction you experienced in response to a stressor. Next, write about a tend and befriend response to another stressful event. In this latter instance, what person or persons did you seek support from? How did you respond to the social support that was offered? Which of these two approaches to contending with stress did you find to be most useful, and why was the approach useful?

LONG-LASTING STRESS REACTIONS.   Bad things happen to all of us. For most of us, life goes on. But others experience long-lasting psychological repercussions, including posttraumatic stress disorder (Comijs et al., 2008; Meichenbaum, 1994). On April 16, 2007, 23-year-old Cho Seung-Hui, a student at Virginia Tech, went on a shooting rampage, killing 31 classmates and professors before taking his own life. When Marjorie Lindholm, 24, heard the news of the massacre, she immediately relived the terror she experienced as a student at Columbine High School on April 20, 1999. On that day, two students, Eric Harris and Dylan Klebold, shot 12 of her classmates and a teacher before turning the guns on themselves. In a television interview, she said, "I started crying, then shaking. I remembered everything I saw at Columbine. I got physically ill. There is no way I'm going to forget that day" (Stepp, 2007).

Marjorie displays some of the hallmark symptoms of *posttraumatic stress disorder* (PTSD), a condition that sometimes follows extremely stressful life events. Its telltale symptoms include vivid memories, feelings, and images of traumatic experiences, known commonly as *flashbacks*. Other symptoms of PTSD include efforts to avoid reminders of the trauma; feelings of detachment or estrangement from others; and symptoms of increased arousal, such as difficulty sleeping and startling easily. The severity, duration, and nearness to the stressor all affect people's likelihood of developing PTSD (American Psychiatric Association, 2013; Ozer et al., 2003).

Fact vs. Fiction

Interactive

Playing the popular computer game Tetris may help prevent flashbacks of disturbing events. (See bottom of page for answer.)

O Fact

O Fiction

Answer: Fact. Tetris may help prevent flashbacks of disturbing events. In one study, students watched a disturbing 12-minute film of horrible deaths and injuries. Students who played Tetris for 10 minutes a half-hour after the film recorded far fewer flashbacks in a diary they kept for a week after the study compared with students who didn't play the game (Holmes et al., 2009). Playing Tetris, which involves brightly colored moving shapes, may distract participants from dwelling on thoughts about upsetting scenes and interfere with the formation of disturbing memories. Researchers still need to determine whether playing Tetris or other video games prevents flashbacks, and perhaps PTSD, in people who experience real life traumas.

12.3: Coping With Stress

12.3a Describe the role of social support and different types of control in coping with stress.

12.3b Explain how our attitudes, beliefs, and personality may influence our responses to stress.

Clearly, some of us adapt better in the face of challenge and change than others. Why is this so, and what can we do to reduce stress, manage our lives, and stay healthy? We'll next take stock of how we can use social support and coping strategies to deal with stressful circumstances.

Support and comfort from others can buffer the effects of highly aversive situations.

Social Support

Imagine that you survived the 9/11 World Trade Center attack or a terrifying mass shooting. What would be helpful? When we ask our students this question, many say that the support of family, friends, neighbors, teachers, coworkers, and clergy would be invaluable. **Social support** encompasses interpersonal relations with people, groups, and the larger community. Social support can provide us with emotional comfort; financial assistance; and information to make decisions, solve problems, and contend with stressful situations (Schaefer, Coyne, & Lazarus, 1981; Stroebe, 2000; Wills & Fegan, 2001). Lisa Berkman and Leonard Syme (1979) conducted a landmark study of the hypothesis that social support buffers against the adverse effects of stress on health. They analyzed data from nearly 5,000 men and women in Alameda County, California, over a 9-year period. They honed in on four kinds of social ties: marriage, contact with friends, church membership, and formal and informal group associations. They then created a social network index reflecting the number of social connections and social supports available to each person.

During the 9-year period, Berkman and Syme found a strong relationship between the number of social connections and the probability of dying. But do these findings mean that isolation increases our chances of dying? A rival hypothesis is that poor health results in few social bonds, rather than the other way around. To rule out this possibility, the researchers surveyed participants when they started the study. People with high and low levels of support reported a comparable illness history, suggesting that poor initial health can't explain why people with the least social support are later more likely to die.

Still, people aren't necessarily accurate when they judge their health. To address this concern, James House, Cynthia Robbins, and Helen Metzner (1982) ensured that their 2,700 participants received a medical examination *before* their study got under way. This exam provided a more objective assessment of health status. The researchers replicated Berkman and Syme's (1979) findings: Even when they took initial health status into account, people with less social support had higher mortality rates.

Fortunately, the positive influence of social support isn't limited to health outcomes. Supportive and caring relationships can help us cope with short-term crises and life transitions and protect against depression, even when we encounter major stressors (Alloway & Bebbington, 1987; Gotlib & Hammen, 1992; Ibarra-Rovillard & Kuiper, 2011). But the breakup of close relationships through separation, divorce, discrimination, or bereavement ranks among the most stressful events we can experience (Gardner, Gabriel, & Deikman, 2000; Mancini, Sinan, & Bonanno, 2015).

social support

relationships with people groups, and the larger community that can provide us with emotional comfort and personal and financial resources

▷ **Ruling Out Rival Hypothesis**

Have important alternative explanations for the findings been excluded?

▷ **Replicability**

Can the results be duplicated in other studies?

Gaining Control

As mentioned previously, we can also relieve stress by acquiring control of situations. Next, we'll discuss five types of control we can use, either alone or in combination, in different situations (Sarafino, 2006).

BEHAVIORAL CONTROL. Behavioral control is the ability to step up and do something to reduce the impact of a stressful situation or prevent its recurrence. As you may recall, this type of active coping is *problem-focused* and is generally more effective in relieving stress than is *avoidance-oriented coping*—avoiding action to solve our

Psychomythology

Are Almost All People Traumatized by Highly Aversive Events?

A widespread view in popular psychology is that most people exposed to trauma develop posttraumatic stress disorder (PTSD) or other serious psychological disorders. Immediately following the 9/11 attacks, for example, many mental health professionals predicted an epidemic of PTSD across the United States (Sommers & Satel, 2005). Were they right?

George Bonanno and his colleagues conducted a study that underscores the remarkable resilience of survivors of extremely aversive events (Bonanno et al., 2006). Using a random digit dialing procedure, the researchers sampled 2,752 adults in the New York City area about 6 months after the 9/11 attacks. They conducted their assessments using a computer-assisted telephone interview system. People were judged to be resilient if they reported zero or one PTSD symptoms during the first 6 months after the attack. Bonanno's results offered surprising evidence for psychological adjustment: 65.1 percent of the sample was resilient. A quarter of the people who were in the World Trade Center at the time of the attack developed probable PTSD, although more than half of the people in this category were resilient. Other research indicates that although most Americans were profoundly upset for several days following the 9/11 attacks, nearly all quickly regained their equilibrium and returned to their previous levels of functioning (McNally, 2003). So when it comes to responses to trauma, resilience is the rule rather than the exception.

People who cope well in the aftermath of a serious stressor tend to display relatively high levels of functioning before the event (Bonanno et al., 2005), and people who don't cope so well often report a history of childhood adversities, depression, and other emotional problems (Berntsen, 2012; Bonanno et al., 2005). Yet resilience isn't limited to a few particularly well-adjusted, brave, or tough-minded people, nor to a single type or class of events. Instead, it's the most common response to traumatic events. Children, too, who are commonly regarded as fragile and vulnerable to stress, are typically resilient in the face of adversity (Sommers & Satel, 2005). Most people who take care of a partner dying of AIDS, suffer the death of a spouse, experience divorce, become unemployed, suffer a spinal cord injury, or survive a physical or sexual assault report few long-term psychological symptoms (Bonanno, 2004; Bonanno, Kennedy, et al., 2012; Galatzer-Levy, Bonanno, & Mancini, 2010).

In a fascinating study of Danish soldiers before, during, and after deployment to Afghanistan, some soldiers actually reported *decreases* in PTSD symptoms during or immediately after deployment, followed by *increases* in symptoms after they returned from Afghanistan (Berntsen et al., 2012). These findings challenge the idea that people invariably develop PTSD in the face of stressful circumstances like military deployment. These soldiers probably benefitted from the camaraderie and social support in their military units, which they didn't experience at home.

Although at some time most of us will experience a potentially traumatic stressor, the lifetime prevalence of PTSD is only 5 percent in men and 10 percent in women (Keane, Marshall, & Taft, 2006; Kessler et al., 1995). Even among military personnel who served in support of the wars in Iraq and Afghanistan, the rate of long-term posttraumatic reactions reported in the best-controlled studies hovers around 7–8 percent (Bonanno, et al., 2012; Wisco et al., 2014). These percentages again remind us that most of us are resilient, even in the face of extremely disturbing events.

---

problems or giving up hope (Lazarus & Folkman, 1984; Roth & Cohen, 1986). Research in the United States and Iceland shows that the more high school and college students use problem-focused coping techniques, the less likely they are to develop drinking problems (Rafnsson, Jonsson, & Windle, 2006). In another study, researchers followed patients with dementia and their caregivers for up to six years. The progression of dementia in patients was slower when their caregivers used problem-focused coping (Tschanz et al., 2012).

COGNITIVE CONTROL. Cognitive control is the ability to think differently about negative emotions that arise in response to stress-provoking events (Higgins & Endler, 1995; Lazarus & Folkman, 1984; Skinner et al., 2003). This type of control includes *emotion-focused coping*, which we introduced previously, a strategy that comes in handy when adjusting to uncertain situations or aversive events we can't control or change. In a novel study, Thomas Strentz and Stephen Auerbach (1988) exposed airline pilots and flight attendants to a simulated hijacking attempt and four days of captivity. Participants who had received instructions to use emotion-focused coping strategies before the hijacking reported less distress during captivity compared with those who had received instructions to use problem-focused coping because there were few options to change the actual circumstances for the better.

STRESS MANAGEMENT TECHNIQUES
1. ———
2. ———
3. ———
4. ———

GLASBERGEN

"Howl at an ambulance or fire siren every chance you get. Run around the room in circles with a sock in your mouth. Eat a messy meal without using your hands or utensils. Ask a friend to scratch your belly…"

SOURCE: © 2003 by Randy Glasbergen. www.glasbergen.com.

DECISIONAL CONTROL. Decisional control is the ability to choose among alternative courses of action (Sarafino, 2006). For example, we can gain control over the often stressful college experience by consulting with trusted friends about which classes to take and which professors to avoid, and we can gain control over our health by making decisions about which surgeon to consult to perform a high-stakes operation.

INFORMATIONAL CONTROL. Informational control is the ability to acquire information about a stressful event. Knowing what types of questions are on the SAT or GRE can help us prepare for them, as can knowing something about the person we're "fixed up with" on an upcoming date. We engage in **proactive coping** when we anticipate stressful situations and take steps to prevent or minimize difficulties before they arise (Greenglass, 2002; Karasek & Theorell, 1990; Zambianchi & Bitti, 2014). People who engage in proactive coping tend to perceive stressful circumstances as opportunities for growth (Greenglass, 2002).

EMOTIONAL CONTROL. Emotional control is the ability to suppress and express emotions. Writing in a diary, for example, can facilitate emotional control and has a host of long-lasting benefits (Pennebaker, 1997). In a now-classic study, James Pennebaker and his colleagues (Pennebaker, Kiecolt-Glaser, & Glaser, 1988) asked one group of college students to write for 4 consecutive days for 20 minutes a day about their deepest thoughts and feelings about past traumas. They asked another group of students to write about superficial topics. Six weeks after the study, students who "opened up" about their traumatic experiences made fewer visits to the health center and showed signs of improved immune functioning compared with the students who wrote about trivial topics. Replications in laboratories around the world have confirmed that writing about traumatic events can influence a variety of academic, social, and cognitive variables and improve the health and well-being of people ranging from arthritis sufferers to maximum security prisoners (Campbell & Pennebaker, 2003; Pennebaker & Graybeal, 2001; Smyth et al., 1999), although scientific debate regarding the size of these effects continues (Frisina, Borod, & Lepore, 2004).

> **Replicability**
>
> Can the results be duplicated in other studies?

IS CATHARSIS A GOOD THING? Contrary to the popular notion that expressing what we feel is always beneficial, disclosing painful feelings, called *catharsis*, is a double-edged sword. When it involves problem solving and constructive efforts to make troubling situations "right," it can be beneficial. But when catharsis reinforces a sense of helplessness, as when we voice our rage about something we can't or won't change, catharsis can actually be harmful (Littrell, 1998). This finding is worrisome, because a slew of popular psychotherapies rely on catharsis, encouraging clients to "get it out of your system," "get things off your chest," or "let it all hang out." Some of these therapies instruct clients to yell, punch pillows, or throw balls against a wall when they become upset (Bushman, Baumeister, & Phillips, 2001; Lewis & Bucher, 1992; Lohr et al., 2007). Yet research shows that these activities rarely reduce our long-term stress, although they may make us feel slightly better for a few moments. In other cases, they actually seem to heighten our anger or anxiety in the long run (Tavris, 1989), perhaps because emotional upset often generates a vicious cycle: We can become distressed about the fact that we're distressed.

DOES CRISIS DEBRIEFING HELP? Some therapists—especially those employed by fire, police, or other emergency services—administer a popular treatment called *crisis debriefing*, which is designed to ward off PTSD among people exposed to trauma. Several thousand crisis debriefers descended on lower Manhattan in the wake of the 9/11 attacks in a well-meaning effort to help traumatized witnesses of the attacks. Crisis debriefing is a single-session procedure, typically conducted in groups, that usually lasts three to four hours. Most often, therapists conduct this procedure within one or two days of a traumatic event, such as a terrible accident. It proceeds according to standardized steps, including strongly encouraging group members to discuss and

GRE preparation classes can be one useful source of informational control.

proactive coping

anticipation of problems and stressful situations that promotes effective coping

Expressing Anger

According to research on the expression of anger, cathartic release of anger, such as this girl repeatedly punching the pillow, actually heigtens long-term stress.

Aerobic exercise, including rowing, swimming, and biking, is an excellent way to lose weight, stay fit, and maintain or even improve cardiovascular health.

perhaps even the growth of neurons (Erickson & Kramer, 2009; Middleton et al., 2011), more sustained and vigorous exercise is typically needed to reach our fitness potential and live longer (Garatachea et al., 2014; Moore et al., 2012).

BUT CHANGING LIFESTYLES IS EASIER SAID THAN DONE.   Why do we have difficulty changing our lifestyles, even when we know that bad habits can endanger our health? As many as 30 to 70 percent of patients don't take their physician's medical advice (National Heart, Lung, and Blood Institute, 1998), and as many as 80 percent don't follow their physician's recommendations to exercise, stop smoking, change their diet, or take prescribed medications (Berlant & Pruitt, 2003). The extent of some medical noncompliance is truly staggering. Paula Vincent (1971) found that 58 percent of patients with glaucoma, a serious eye disease, didn't take their prescribed eye drops, even though they knew that their failure to do so could make them go blind!

Personal Inertia.   One reason for noncompliance is that it's difficult to overcome personal inertia—our reluctance to try something new. Many self-destructive habits relieve stress and don't create an imminent health threat, so it's easy for us to "let things be." Eating a heaping portion of ice cream doesn't seem terribly dangerous when we view heart disease as a distant and uncertain catastrophe. John Norcross and his colleagues found that only 19 percent of people who made a New Year's resolution to change a problem behavior, including changing their diet or exercising more, maintained the change when followed up two years later (Norcross, Ratzin, & Payne, 1989; Norcross & Vangarelli, 1989).

Misestimating Risk.   Another reason we maintain the status quo is that we underestimate certain risks to our health and overestimate others. To illustrate this point, try answering the following three questions before reading on:

In the United States, which causes more deaths?

1. All types of accidents combined or strokes

2. All motor vehicle (car, truck, bus, and motorcycle) accidents combined or digestive cancer

3. Diabetes or homicide

If we told you that four fully loaded jumbo jets were crashing every day in the United States, you'd be outraged. Yet the equivalent of that number—about 1,200 people—die each day in the United States from smoking-related causes (Centers for Disease Control and Prevention, 2005). How likely is it we'll actually die in a plane crash? Not likely at all. We'd need to fly in commercial airliners for about 10,000 years straight—that is, around the clock without any breaks—before the odds of our dying in a plane crash exceed 50 percent. But because plane crashes make big news, we overestimate their frequency.

The answers are (1) strokes (by about twofold), (2) digestive cancer (by about threefold), and (3) diabetes (by about fourfold). If you got one or more of these questions wrong (and most people do), the odds are that you relied on the *availability heuristic*—the mental shortcut by which we judge the likelihood of an event by the ease with which it comes to mind (Hertwig, Pachur, & Kurzenhauser, 2005; Tversky & Kahneman, 1974).

Because the news media provide far more coverage of dramatic accidents and homicides than strokes, digestive cancer, or diabetes, we overestimate the probability of accidents and homicides and underestimate the probability of many diseases. And because the media feature so many emotional and memorable stories of famous women who've developed breast cancer, we're likely to think of breast cancer as a more frequent and deadly illness compared with heart disease (Ruscio, 2000). Heart disease is less newsworthy precisely because it's more commonplace, and perhaps less terrifying, than cancer is with its troubling treatment-related side effects, including very obvious hair loss. In general, we underestimate the frequency of the most common causes of death, and overestimate the frequency of the least common causes of death (Lichtenstein et al., 1978). These errors in judgment can be costly: If women believe that heart disease isn't a threat, they may not change their lifestyle.

Many people are well aware of health risks but don't take them to "heart," pun intended. Smokers greatly overestimate their chances of living to the age of 75 (Schoenbaum, 1997). Other people rationalize their lifestyle choices by telling themselves, "Something's going to kill me anyway, so I might as well enjoy my life and do whatever I want."

Feeling Powerless.   Still, other people feel powerless to change, perhaps because their habits are so deeply ingrained. Consider a person who's smoked a pack of cigarettes a day for the last 15 years. She's inhaled cigarette smoke over a million times. It's no wonder she feels helpless to change her habit.

Journal Prompt

Reflect for a moment on the healthy behaviors discussed in your text. Which of these healthy behaviors do you engage in currently? How do you maintain these behaviors? Which healthy behaviors do you *not* engage in regularly or to your satisfaction? Why is this the case? Based on the text, why might it prove difficult to transform your unhealthy habits into healthy ones?

PREVENTION PROGRAMS.   Because modifying such deeply entrenched behaviors can be so difficult, we're best off not developing them in the first place. Prevention efforts should begin by adolescence, if not earlier, because the earlier in life we develop unhealthy habits, the more likely they'll create problems, like alcohol abuse, for us later in life (Hingson, Heeren, & Winter, 2006). Health psychologists have developed prevention programs that contain the following elements:

Despite its popularity, the DARE program isn't effective for preventing substance abuse or enhancing self-esteem.

- Educating young people about the risks and negative consequences of obesity, smoking, and excessive drinking, as well as positive health behaviors such as good nutrition and the importance of exercise

- Teaching young people to recognize and resist peer pressure to engage in unhealthy behaviors

- Exposing young people to positive role models who don't drink or smoke

- Teaching effective coping skills for daily living and dealing with stressful life events

But not all prevention efforts are successful. The Drug Abuse Resistance Education, or DARE, program is used in schools nationwide to teach students how to avoid getting into drugs, gangs, and violent activities (Ringwalt & Greene, 1993). The program uses uniformed police officers and targets fifth- and sixth-graders. It emphasizes the negative aspects of excessive drinking and substance abuse and the positive aspects of self-esteem and healthy life choices. The program is popular with school administrators and parents; there's a good chance you've seen DARE bumper stickers on cars in your neighborhood. Nevertheless, researchers have repeatedly found that the program doesn't produce positive long-term effects on substance abuse or boost self-esteem (Lynam et al., 1999). A few researchers have even found that it may occasionally backfire to produce increases in mild forms of substance abuse (Lilienfeld, 2007; Werch & Owen, 2002). Programs that focus on using coping skills and managing stress generally show better treatment and prevention outcomes (MacKillop & Gray, 2015). These findings remind us that we need to evaluate programs carefully before they're widely promoted based on their intuitive appeal alone (Wilson, 2011).

Complementary and Alternative Medicine

What do the following three practices have in common?

1. Consuming supplements of *gracinia cambogia*, a substance derived from the tamarind rind, to lose weight

2. Placing thin needles in the external ear to relieve nausea following an operation

3. Manipulating the spine to treat pain and prevent disease

Evaluating Claims STRESS REDUCTION AND RELAXATION TECHNIQUES

Interactive

You've been under a lot of stress lately, with finals coming up, spreading yourself too thin between your part-time job and juggling your academic work, and troubles with contending with your feelings about a very nasty supervisor at work.

You've been deep into music the past few days, seeking a way to chill out. In searching on the Internet for some tunes from your favorite groups, you come across the following ad that fuels your curiosity.

"Listeners agree that Trans-Cortex space-dimensional music CDs can relax up to 90 percent of overstressed listeners! Our music creates an immersive experience of deep peace and calm. As you are literally transported to new dimensions of space-time consciousness, all your stress will evaporate; You'll feel invigorated, ready to move forward and face challenges with supreme confidence. Listeners who responded to a survey based on 20 free samples of our top-selling selections reported that their experience of the music exceeded their expectations! Try it and see for yourself. If you're not more than satisfied, we'll refund your money, no questions asked."

Scientific skepticism requires us to evaluate all claims with an open mind but to insist on compelling evidence before accepting them. How do the principles of scientific thinking help us to evaluate this claim about stress reduction, relaxation, and listening to special music?

Consider how the six principles of scientific thinking are relevant as you evaluate this claim.

1. Ruling Out Rival Hypotheses
Have important alternative explanations for the findings been excluded?

Alternative explanations haven't been ruled out. It's possible that 90 percent of people reported that they experienced deep peace and calm after listening to the music because, with few exceptions, only those respondents that felt peaceful and calm were motivated to answer the questions. The other people who listened to the music and didn't feel relaxed and peaceful may not have bothered to fill it out! The ad doesn't tell us how many people were surveyed, and how many of those people surveyed answered the questions. So it's possible that very few of the total number of listeners experienced any relaxing effects at all. Also, because we don't know what the listener's expectations were before listening to the music, it's difficult to know how

to interpret the claim that the experience of the music exceeded expectations. Perhaps listeners' expectations were very low in the first place. We also don't know whether the people who responded to the survey were those who were particularly keen on the type of music advertised. Perhaps they were not at all representative of a general music audience and don't share the tastes of the great majority of potential customers. The terms *overstressed* and *relaxed* are too general and poorly defined to determine how the claim might apply to potential customers, and it's not clear that relaxation was associated with the music or perhaps just sitting quietly for a short period.

2. Correlation vs. Causation
Can we be sure that A causes B?

This principle of scientific thinking is not terribly relevant to this scenario.

3. Falsifiability
Can the claim be disproved?

Yes, the claim regarding relaxation can be disproved. At the very least, it would be necessary to carefully define and characterize the sample of listeners, assess stress and relaxation levels with well validated and reliable measures and make it plain what it means to be "overstressed" and "relaxed," determine listeners' expectations before exposure to the music, assess the effects of listening to the music under reasonably controlled or at least clearly specified conditions, and compare the effects of listening to the music with those of sitting quietly or with other types of music. The claim that the listener will be transported to new dimensions of space-time consciousness is impossible to disprove, because transport to a non definable and non measurable "dimension of space-time consciousness" lies outside the boundaries of science and cannot be falsified.

4. Replicability
Can the results be duplicated in other studies?

There's no evidence that the claim is derived from research that permits clear conclusions. We should be skeptical of claims based on studies that are not described in terms sufficiently specific to permit replication.

5. Extraordinary Claims
Is the evidence as strong as the claim?

This claim is extraordinary because it's highly improbable that 90 percent of people would experience complete relaxation and supreme confidence after listening to music. The evidence provided is not nearly as strong as the claim.

6. Occam's Razor
Does a simpler explanation fit the data just as well?

A simpler explanation is that the survey was biased such that the impressive statistic of 90 percent was based on the responses of an unrepresentative and small group of respondents who felt relaxed and confident after listening to the music samples.

The ad doesn't provide a sufficient basis for purchasing the music. Money back guarantees are lures to attract customers that benefit the seller. Many people who purchase products that fail to live up to their promise don't request their money back. It's a hassle to go to the trouble to do so and, in this case, it would be easy for consumers to attribute the music "not working" to their personal failings, such as being "too stressed" or "not confident enough" for the music to exert its claimed success.

Summary

In summary, the claim that the product produces relaxation in 90 percent of overstressed listeners should be viewed with considerable skepticism.

Table 12.2 Use of CAM Therapies Among American Adults During the Previous Year (2012).

Type of Therapy	Users During the Previous Year (%)
Natural products (e.g., nonvitamin, nonmineral dietary supplements)	17.7
Deep breathing	10.9
Yoga, tai chi, or qi gong	10.1
Chiropractic and related methods	8.4
Meditation	8.0
Massage	6.9
Special diets	3.0
Homeopathy	2.2
Progressive relaxation	2.1
Guided imagery	1.7
Acupuncture	1.5
Biofeedback	0.1

SOURCE: Statistics taken from National Health Interview Statistics Report (Clarke et al., 2015).

The answer: Each is an alternative or nonstandard treatment that falls outside the mainstream of modern medicine. **Alternative medicine** refers to healthcare practices and products used *in place of* conventional medicine, that is, medicine for which there's solid evidence of safety and effectiveness. **Complementary medicine or integrative health medicine**, in contrast, refers to products and practices that are used *together with* conventional medicine (National Center for Complementary and Integrative Health, 2016). Together, both forms of medicine are known as CAM (complementary and alternative medicine). What unites them is that they've not yet been shown to be safe and effective using scientific standards (Bausell, 2007; Singh & Ernst, 2008).

Each year, Americans fork out about $34 billion to CAM practitioners and to purchase CAM products (Saks, 2015). In a national survey, 33 percent of adults and 12 percent of children reported using some form of CAM over the preceding year (Black et al., 2015; Clarke et al., 2015). We can examine various CAM therapies in Table 12.2.

BIOLOGICALLY BASED THERAPIES: VITAMINS, HERBS, AND FOOD SUPPLEMENTS. An estimated 41 million U.S. adults spend more than $22 billion each year for herbal treatments and supplements of uncertain effectiveness (Gupta, 2007; Wu et al., 2014). Yet many herbal and natural preparations that some once viewed as promising have been found to be no more effective than a placebo (Bausell, 2007). Contrary to popular belief, scientific findings suggest that

- the herb St. John's Wort doesn't alleviate the symptoms of moderate to severe depression (Davidson et al., 2002);
- shark cartilage cannot cure cancer (Loprinzi et al., 2005);
- the widely used supplements glucosamine and chondroitin don't relieve mild arthritis pain (Reichenbach et al., 2007);

alternative medicine

healthcare practices and products used in place of conventional medicine

complementary medicine or integrative health medicine

healthcare practices and products used together with conventional medicine

Celebrities and Health Opinions

Some celebrities have expressed strong opinions against conventional medical practices. For example, Bill Maher has voiced strong opposition to the swine flu vaccine despite the medical establishment's call for preventive vaccination. Maher's opinion about vaccination could have consequences for public health. People could heed his "advice," not get vaccinated, and become ill with the flu. In turn, they may place others at risk for the flu.

Should we uncritically accept medical opinion and advice we encounter in the media or elsewhere? By now, you should be able to guess our answer: no! Conversely, should we conclude that all CAM treatments are worthless? Not at all. As we learned previously in the text (LO 1.3a), it's essential that we keep an open mind and not dismiss new treatments out of hand. Many drugs derive from plant and natural products, and many effective medicines surely remain to be discovered. Every year, drug companies screen thousands of natural products for disease-fighting properties, and a few prove worthy of further testing. For example, *taxol*, derived from the Pacific yew tree, has been shown to be effective as an anticancer drug. Although St. John's Wort isn't especially effective for severe depression, some evidence suggests that it is somewhat helpful for mild depression (Kasper et al., 2007; Wallach & Kirsch, 2003). Nevertheless, not all researchers have replicated these positive findings (Rapaport et al., 2011), so caution is needed, especially because St. John's Wort can interfere with the effectiveness of certain medications. At the same time, St. John's Wort and other herbal medicines may eventually become part of mainstream treatment if they turn out to be safe and effective.

◀ **Replicability**

Can the results be duplicated in other studies?

The same is true of psychological practices. Meditation, once regarded as an alternative approach, now appears to be an effective means of reducing stress and has increasingly blended into the spectrum of conventional approaches.

Barry Beyerstein (1997) recommended that we ask the following two questions before trying an alternative approach:

1. Does it lack a scientific rationale or contradict well-accepted scientific laws or principles?

2. Do carefully done studies show that the product or treatment is less effective than conventional approaches?

If the answer to both questions is "yes," we should be especially skeptical. When in doubt, it's wise to consult a physician about a CAM treatment. Doing so will give us confidence that the treatment we select, regardless of whether it's conventional, is genuinely a "good alternative."

Summary: Stress, Coping, And Health

12.1: What Is Stress?

12.1a Explain how stress is defined and approached in different ways.

Stress is a part of daily life. Most people experience one or more extremely stressful events in their lifetime. People experience stress when they feel physically threatened, unsafe, or unable to meet the perceived demands of life. Stress can be viewed as a stimulus, a response, or a transaction with the environment. Identifying specific categories of stressful events (unemployment, natural disasters) is the focus of the stressors as stimuli view of stress, whereas reactions to stressful events and their consequences are important in studying the response aspects of stress. The stress as a transaction view holds that the experience of stress depends on both primary appraisal (the decision regarding whether the event is harmful) and secondary appraisal (perceptions of our ability to cope with the event) of the potentially stressful event.

12.1b Identify different approaches to measuring stress.

Psychologists often assess life events that require major adaptations and adjustments, such as illness and unemployment. They also assess hassles—annoying, frustrating daily events that may be more related to adverse psychological and health outcomes than major stressors. Interview-based methods provide a more in-depth picture of life stress than do questionnaires.

12.2: How We Adapt to Stress: Change and Challenge

12.2a Describe Selye's general adaptation syndrome.

The GAS consists of three stages: (1) alarm: the autonomic nervous system is activated; (2) resistance: adaptation and coping occurs; and (3) exhaustion: resources and coping abilities are depleted, which can damage organs and contribute to depression and posttraumatic stress disorder (PTSD).

12.2b Describe the diversity of stress responses.

Our stress reactions vary from one stressor to another and may be shaped by gender. The tend-and-befriend response is more common in women than in men. In times of stress, women often rely more on their social contacts, nurture others, and befriend or turn to others for support. About 5 percent (men) to 10 percent (women) of people experience PTSD in the face of a potentially traumatic stressor. Yet as many as two-thirds of people are resilient in the face of powerful stressors.

12.3: Coping With Stress

12.3a Describe the role of social support and different types of control in coping with stress.

Social support and the following types of stress control are important: (1) behavioral control (taking action to reduce stress), (2) cognitive control (reappraising stressful events that can't be avoided), (3) decisional control (choosing among alternatives), (4) informational control (acquiring information about a stressor), and (5) emotional control (suppressing and expressing emotions at will). Flexible coping (adjusting coping strategies to specific situations) is also helpful.

12.3b Explain how our attitudes, beliefs, and personality may influence our responses to stress.

Hardy people view change as challenge, have a deep sense of commitment to their life and work, and believe they can control events. Optimism and spirituality boost stress resistance, whereas rumination is not an adaptive way of coping with stressful circumstances.

12.4: How Stress Impacts Our Health

12.4a Describe how the immune system is affected by stress.

The immune system is the body's defensive barrier against disease. Phagocytes and lymphocytes neutralize viruses and bacteria and produce proteins called antibodies that fight infection. Diseases of the immune system include AIDS and autoimmune diseases in which the immune system is overactive. Stress can decrease resistance to illness, delay healing, and impair the immune system.

12.4b Identify how physical disorders such as ulcers are related to stress.

Psychologists use the term *psychophysiological* to describe illnesses like ulcers in which emotions and stress contribute to, maintain, or aggravate physical conditions. Ulcers, which appear to be caused by the *H. pylori* bacterium and exacerbated by stress, can be understood in terms of a biopsychosocial perspective, which considers both physical and psychological factors.

12.4c Describe the role of personality, everyday experiences, and socioeconomic factors in coronary heart disease.

For many years, the Type A personality was thought to promote risk of CHD, but more recent work points to chronic hostility as a more central risk factor. Socioeconomic factors and everyday life experiences can set the stage for many physical problems, including coronary heart disease.

12.5: Promoting Good Health—and Less Stress!

12.5a Identify four behaviors that contribute to a healthy lifestyle.

Behaviors that can promote health include not smoking, curbing alcohol consumption, maintaining a healthy weight, and exercising.

12.5b Identify why it is difficult to change our lifestyle.

Reasons it's difficult to change our lifestyle include personal inertia, the tendency to misestimate risk, and feelings of powerlessness.

12.5c Describe different alternative and complementary medical approaches and compare their effectiveness with placebos.

Alternative medicine approaches include biologically based therapies (vitamins, herbs, and food supplements), manipulative and body-based methods (chiropractic medicine), mind–body medicine (biofeedback, yoga, and meditation), energy medicine (acupuncture), and whole medical systems (homeopathy). Complementary medicine or integrative health medicine refers to products and practices that are used *together with* conventional medicine. Many alternative approaches are no more effective than placebos. Alternative medical products and procedures can become part of conventional medicine when demonstrated to be safe and effective.

Chapter 13
Social Psychology
How Others Affect Us

Learning objectives

13.1a Identify the ways in which social situations influence the behavior of individuals.

13.1b Explain how the fundamental attribution error can cause us to misjudge others' behaviors.

13.2a Determine the factors that influence when we conform to others.

13.2b Recognize the dangers of group decision making, and identify ways to avoid mistakes common in group decisions.

13.2c Identify the factors that maximize or minimize obedience to authority.

13.3a Explain which aspects of a situation increase or decrease the likelihood of bystander intervention.

13.3b Describe the social and individual difference variables that contribute to human aggression.

13.4a Describe how attitudes relate to behavior.

13.4b Evaluate theoretical accounts of how and when we alter our attitudes.

13.4c Identify common and effective persuasion techniques and how they're exploited by pseudoscientists.

13.5a Distinguish prejudice and stereotypes as beliefs from discrimination as a behavior.

13.5b Identify some of the causes of prejudice and describe methods for combating it.

Challenge Your Assumptions

Interactive

Are conformity and obedience always psychologically unhealthy?

If an authority figure in a white lab coat ordered you to give a stranger a powerful electric shock, would you be likely do so?

If we're being assaulted while out on a walk, are we safer if many people are watching as opposed to only one person?

To persuade people of something, should we give them a large bribe to change their views?

Are prejudice and discrimination different phenomena?

Psychology imparts a powerful lesson: We're often influenced by the behavior of those around us, even when we don't realize it. In this video, you'll witness a powerful demonstration of a well-established phenomenon about which we'll learn much more in the chapter: *bystander nonintervention*.

Like some psychological research, work on bystander nonintervention turns common sense on its head: Surprisingly, we tend to be *less* likely to intervene in crises when other people are around than when we're alone. As the video notes, one reason is that when others are around, we feel less responsible for the potential consequences of not acting. Later in the chapter, we'll explore other reasons for this surprising effect, which underscores the point that social influence can produce powerful real-world consequences.

Watch   BYSTANDER NONINTERVENTION: THE POWER OF SOCIAL INFLUENCE

13.1: What Is Social Psychology?

13.1a   **Identify the ways in which social situations influence the behavior of individuals.**

13.1b   **Explain how the fundamental attribution error can cause us to misjudge others' behaviors.**

Social psychology helps us to understand not only why many of us are seemingly psychologically paralyzed during obvious emergencies, but also why many other forms of interpersonal influence are so powerful. **Social psychology** is the study of how people influence others' behavior, beliefs, and attitudes—for both good and bad (Lewin, 1951). Social psychology helps us understand not only why we sometimes act helpfully and even heroically in the presence of others, but also why we occasionally show our worst sides, caving in to group pressure or standing by idly while others suffer. It also sheds light on why we're prone to accept blindly irrational, even pseudoscientific, beliefs. There's a catch here, however. Research shows that we tend to believe that others are vulnerable to social influence, but we don't believe that we are (Pronin, 2008; see LO 1.2b). So we may initially resist some social psychological findings because they seem to apply to everyone else but us. In reality, they're relevant to us too.

social psychology

study of how people influence others' behavior, beliefs, and attitudes

In this chapter, we'll begin by examining the social animals we call human beings (Aronson, 2012) and discuss how and why we often underestimate the impact of social influence on others' behavior. We'll move on to examine two especially potent social influences—conformity and obedience—and then address the question of why we help people at some times and harm them at others. At the same time, we'll examine the factors that help us overcome strong influences on us to harm others. Then, we'll discuss our attitudes and how social pressure shapes them. We'll conclude by exploring the troubling question of how prejudice toward others arises and, more optimistically, how we can combat or least compensate for it.

Although all six scientific thinking principles we've presented throughout the text are extremely important, *replicability* is especially crucial when it comes to evaluating research in social psychology. Over the past few years in particular, a growing number of scholars—some within the discipline of social psychology itself—have raised significant challenges to the replicability of certain widely reported social psychological findings. Indeed, some widely reported social psychology findings haven't held up well under the scrutiny of replication (Earp & Trafinow, 2015; Open Science Collaboration, 2015). These replication difficulties are perhaps not terribly surprising, because as social creatures, we're exquisitely sensitive to subtle interpersonal cues. As a consequence, seemingly trivial changes in the experimental set-up—the instructions given to participants, the perceived attitudes and appearance of the research assistants, the friendliness of other participants, and so on—may influence the results of social psychological studies in unpredictable ways. In this chapter, we'll do our best to focus on the well-replicated findings of social psychology, but we'll also highlight instances in which there are unresolved questions regarding the dependability of the results.

Humans as a Social Species

Social psychology is important for one key reason: We humans are a highly social species. Most evidence suggests that as early hominids in Africa hundreds of thousands of years ago, we evolved in relatively small and tight social bands (Barchas, 1986). Even as modern-day humans, most of us gravitate to small groups. In forming cliques, or groups that include some people—in-group members—we by extension exclude others—out-group members.

GRAVITATING TO EACH OTHER—TO A POINT. Anthropologist Robin Dunbar (1993) became famous for a number: 150. This number is the approximate size of most human social groups, from the hunter-gatherers of days of yore to today's scientists working in a specialized research area (Gladwell, 2005). Dunbar argued that the size of our cortex relative to the rest of our brain places limits on how many people with whom we can closely associate. For animals with smaller cortices relative to the rest of their brains, such as chimpanzees and dolphins, the number of relations may be smaller (Dunbar, 1993; Marino, 2005). Whether 150 is the universal "magic number," Dunbar is probably right that our highly social brains are predisposed to forming intimate interpersonal networks that are large—but only so large.

THE NEED TO BELONG: WHY WE FORM GROUPS. When we're deprived of social contact for a considerable length of time, we usually become lonely. According to psychologists Roy Baumeister and Mark Leary's (1995) *need-to-belong theory*, we humans have a biologically based need for interpersonal connections. Stanley Schachter (1959) discovered the power of this social need in a small pilot study. He asked five male volunteers to live alone in separate rooms for an extended time period. All five were miserable. One participant with an especially low tolerance for isolation bailed out after only 20 minutes and three lasted only two days. The lone holdout, who reported feeling extremely anxious, made it to eight days. Research on inmates placed in solitary confinement suggests that they experience more psychological symptoms, especially mood and anxiety problems, than do other inmates (Andersen et al., 2000; Grassian, 2006). They even appear to be more prone to suicidal behaviors (Kaba et al., 2014). Still, because the inmates placed in solitary confinement may be more emotionally maladjusted to begin with than other inmates, this finding is challenging to interpret with certainty.

More systematic research shows that the threat of social isolation can lead us to behave in self-destructive ways and even impair our mental functioning. In a series of experiments, Jean Twenge and her colleagues asked undergraduates to complete a

---

Replicability

Can the results be duplicated in other studies?

Ruling Out Rival Hypotheses

Have important alternative explanations for the findings been excluded?

personality measure and gave them bogus feedback based on their test results: They told some of the participants "You're the type who will end up alone later in life" and others "You're likely to be accident prone later in life." The students who received feedback that they'd be isolated toward the end of their lives were significantly more likely than those in the other group to engage in unhealthy behaviors like eating a fattening snack and procrastinating on an assignment (Twenge, Catanese, & Baumeister, 2002). The same negative feedback is so upsetting that it may even impair students' performance on IQ tests (Baumeister, Twenge, & Nuss, 2002).

Although the data are only correlational, mounting evidence suggests that loneliness is associated with a heightened risk for later depression—a link that may be causal.

Brain-imaging research goes a step further, shedding light on the commonplace observation that being cut off from social contact "hurts," literally and figuratively. Kip Williams and his coworkers have developed a clever computerized ball-tossing game, "Cyberball," in which they interact with other players whom they are led to believe are real (in fact, these players don't exist). The researchers have rigged the game so that participants are eventually excluded from the game; as the game progresses, the other (nonexistent) players begin to toss the ball only to each other, ignoring the actual participant. (Eisenberger, Lieberman, & Williams, 2003). Most participants dislike the experience and often report feelings of rejection, social pain, sadness, and anger (Hartgerink et al., 2015). Research using Cyberball even suggests that the painkiller Tylenol—compared with a placebo—blunts the activity of the cingulate cortex, a brain region that becomes active in response to social rejection (DeWall et al., 2010). So the pain that we experience in response to social rejection may be similar in some ways to physical pain.

Work by John Cacioppo and his colleagues further suggests that long-term loneliness can exert negative, at times devastating, effects on our psychological adjustment (Cacioppo et al., 2015; Cacioppo & Patrick, 2009). Although 80 percent of teenagers and 40 percent of adults 65 years or older report occasional loneliness, for some people—between 15 and 30 percent depending on how loneliness is defined—loneliness is a way of life (Hawkley & Cacioppo, 2010). Increases in loneliness are tied to heightened rates of depression a year later (Cacioppo et al., 2006). Although these data are correlational and don't conclusively demonstrate a cause-and-effect relation, increases in depression don't predict increases in loneliness (Cacioppo, Hawkley, & Thisted, 2010), suggesting that loneliness may contribute to depression, rather than vice versa. Moreover, loneliness predicts early death (Holt-Lunstad et al., 2015), cognitive decline, and perhaps even heightened risk for Alzheimer's disease (Hawkley & Cacioppo, 2010), although it's unclear whether these linkages are directly causal.

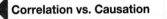

Correlation vs. Causation

Can we be sure that A causes B?

HOW WE CAME TO BE THIS WAY: EVOLUTION AND SOCIAL BEHAVIOR. Because we'll soon be examining many unhealthy forms of social influence, such as how unquestioning acceptance of authority figures can lead us to do foolish things, we might be tempted to conclude that almost all social influence is negative. That would be a serious mistake. Virtually all of the social influence processes we'll discuss are adaptive under most circumstances and help to regulate cultural practices. From the perspective of an evolutionary approach to social behavior, many social influence processes have been naturally selected, because they've generally served us well over the course of evolution (Buss & Kenrick, 1998; Tybur & Griskevicius, 2013). Even if we're skeptical of this view, we can still accept a core premise: Social influence processes work for us well most of the time, but they can occasionally backfire on us if we're not careful.

Orderly evacuation of a building in an emergency highlights how conformity and obedience can be constructive.

An evolutionary perspective on social behavior leads us to one crucial conclusion: *Conformity, obedience, and many other forms of social influence become maladaptive only when they're blind or unquestioning.* From this standpoint, irrational group behavior—like the disastrous obedience of thousands of German citizens during the Nazi regime of the 1930s and 1940s, the massive genocide in Sudan in the late 20th and early 21st centuries, and the terrorism of ISIS (the Islamic State of Iraq and Syria) in more recent years —are byproducts of basically adaptive processes that have gone terribly wrong. There's nothing wrong with looking to a persuasive leader for guidance, just as long as we don't stop asking tough questions. Once we accept social influence without evaluating it critically, though, we place ourselves at the mercy of powerful others.

SOCIAL COMPARISON: WHERE DO I STAND? One reason others affect us is that they often serve as a mirror of sorts, providing us with helpful information about ourselves (Cooley, 1902; Shrauger & Schoeneman, 1979). According to Leon Festinger's (1954) **social comparison theory**, we evaluate our abilities and beliefs by comparing them with those of others. Doing so helps us to understand ourselves and our social worlds better. If you want to find out if you're a good psychology student, it's only natural to compare your exam performance with that of your classmates (Kruglanski & Mayseless, 1990). Doing so gives you a better sense of how you stack up relative to them and can spur you on to make needed improvements in your study habits.

Social comparison comes in two different "flavors." In *upward social comparison*, we compare ourselves with people who seem superior to us in some way, as when a new member of the basketball team compares herself with the team's top two superstars. In *downward social comparison*, we compare ourselves with others who seem inferior to us in some way, as when the same basketball player compares herself with her clumsy friends who keep bouncing basketballs off of their feet.

Despite their differences, both upward and downward social comparison can boost our self-concepts (Buunk et al., 1990; Suls, Martin, & Wheeler, 2002). When we engage in upward social comparison, especially with people who aren't too different from us, we may feel better because we conclude that "If he can achieve that, I bet I can too." When we engage in downward social comparison, we often end up feeling superior to our peers who are less competent than us in an important domain of life. For example, we may convince ourselves that we're a "big fish in a small pond," such as being the brightest student in a class of poorly performing students (Marsh et al., 2015). Downward social comparison probably accounts in part for the popularity of televised reality shows, which often feature the daily lives of people who are unsuccessful in their romantic relationships or friendships. Interestingly, even when social comparison makes us look inferior relative to someone else, we may buffer our self-concepts by persuading ourselves that it's only because the other person is exceptionally talented (Alicke et al., 1997). In one study, participants learned—falsely—that another person had outperformed them on a test of intelligence. Relative to observers, these participants markedly overestimated that person's intelligence. By concluding that "the person who outperformed me is a genius" (p. 781), participants salvaged their self-esteem: "It's not that I'm dumb, it's that he's incredibly smart."

SOCIAL CONTAGION. Just as we often turn to others to better understand ourselves, we often look to them when a situation is ambiguous and we're not sure what to do. That's only natural, and it's often a pretty good idea. When we experience severe turbulence on an airplane, we often look to the faces of other passengers as cues for how to react. If they appear calm, we'll generally relax; if they appear nervous or panicked, we'll probably start looking around for the nearest emergency exit. But what if others are thinking and behaving irrationally? Then, we may do the same, because social behavior is often contagious.

Mass Hysteria: Irrationality at a Group Level. **Mass hysteria** is a contagious outbreak of irrational behavior that spreads much like a flu epidemic. Because we're most likely to engage in social comparison when a situation is ambiguous, many of us are prone to mass hysteria under certain circumstances. Many wild rumors spread the same way and are often fueled by anxiety. Such rumors can occasionally lead to problematic, even disastrous, consequences. On April 23, 2013, a single fake tweet proclaimed that President Barack Obama had been seriously injured following an attack on the White House. The U.S. financial markets quickly plunged by $130 billion, although they rebounded soon after it became evident that the tweet was false. (Bartholomew & Hassall, 2015).

In some cases, episodes of mass hysteria lead to *collective delusions*, in which many people simultaneously become convinced of bizarre things that are false. Consider how the frequency of unidentified flying object (UFO) sightings shot up at times when societal consciousness of space travel was heightened (see Figure 13.1).

This trend started on June 24, 1947, when pilot Kenneth Arnold spotted nine mysterious shiny objects while flying over the ocean near Mount Rainier

social comparison theory

theory that states we seek to evaluate our abilities and beliefs by comparing them with those of others

mass hysteria

outbreak of irrational behavior that is spread by social contagion

---

Figure 13.1 Graph of UFO Sightings

In the 1950s and 1960s, the number of UFO sightings shot up dramatically following the launches of *Sputnik I* and *II* (the Russian satellites that were the first objects launched into space) and following the U.S. launch of the space probe *Mariner 4*. Although these data don't permit definite cause-and-effect conclusions, they're consistent with the possibility that UFO sightings are of social origin.

SOURCE: Hartmann, W. K. (1992). Astronomy: The cosmic journey. Belmont, CA: Wadsworth. Reprinted with permission from William K. Hartmann.

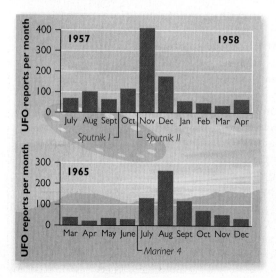

in Washington State. Interestingly, Arnold told reporters that these objects were shaped like *sausages*. Nevertheless, he also made the offhand observation that they'd "skipped over the water like saucers."

Within days, the phrase *flying saucers* appeared in more than 150 newspapers across the United States (Bartholomew & Goode, 2000). And within only a few years, thousands of people were claiming to see saucer-shaped objects in the sky. Had the newspapers been more accurate in their coverage of Arnold's words, we might today be hearing UFO reports of flying sausages rather than flying saucers. But once the media introduced the term *flying saucers*, the now familiar circular shape of UFOs took hold in the American consciousness and never let go. Even today, scores of people misinterpret such phenomena as lenticular cloud formations (which resemble saucers), the planet Venus, meteors, airplanes, satellites, weather balloons, and even swarms of glowing insects as indications of extraterrestrial visitation (T. Hines, 2003)

People sometimes misinterpret lenticular cloud formations as flying saucers. Such erroneous interpretations are especially likely when other people report similar perceptions.

Another collective delusion occurred in the spring of 1954, when the city of Seattle, Washington, experienced an epidemic of "windshield pitting." Thousands of residents became alarmed by tiny indentations, or pits, in their car windshields that they suspected were the result of secret nuclear tests performed by the federal government (Bartholomew & Goode, 2000). Although the residents of Seattle hadn't realized it, the windshield pits had been there all along, as they are on most cars. The windshield-pitting epidemic offers another illustration of how shared societal beliefs can influence our interpretations of reality. When confronted with two explanations for the pitting—a secret nuclear explosion or the impact of dirt particles hitting the windshield—Seattle residents would have been better off picking the simpler one.

▶ **Occam's Razor**

Does a simpler explanation fit the data just as well?

Urban Legends.   Another demonstration of the power of social contagion comes from *urban legends:* false stories repeated so many times that people believe them to be true (Brunvand, 1999). As Gordon Allport and Leo Postman (1945) noted more than six decades ago, rumors tend to grow less accurate with repeated retellings, often becoming oversimplified to make for a good story. With the increasing popularity of the Internet, YouTube, and social media of many kinds, urban legends and other erroneous rumors can now spread "virally," becoming virtual overnight sensations in the absence of any objective evidence (Fernback, 2003; Sunstein, 2009). How many of the urban legends in Figure 13.2 have you heard?

All of the stories in Figure 13.2 are false, yet scores of people believe them. Urban legends are convincing in part because they're surprising, yet plausible (Gilovich, 1991). They also make for good stories because they tug on our emotions, especially negative ones (Heath & Heath, 2007; Rosnow, 1980). Research shows that the most popular urban legends contain a heavy dose of material relevant to the emotion of disgust, perhaps because they arouse our perverse sense of curiosity (Eriksson, & Coultas, 2014). Because they provoke our interest and concern, they often spread like wildfire. It's perhaps not coincidental that many feature rats and other animals that most of us don't find especially appealing (Heath, Bell, & Sternberg, 2001).

The Positive Effect of Others' Presence

The presence of others enhances our performance on simple or familiar tasks. These cyclists will probably ride faster together than either would alone due to the phenomenon of social facilitation.

Journal Prompt

Think of an urban legend about which you've heard or read recently. First describe it, and then offer an explanation for why so many intelligent people appear to believe it.

SOCIAL FACILITATION: FROM BICYCLISTS TO COCKROACHES.

Because we're social creatures, even the mere presence of others can enhance our performance in certain situations, a phenomenon that Robert Zajonc

Figure 13.2 Urban Legend?

Some popular urban legends: All are widely known, yet all are false. Incidentally, if you ever want to find out whether a remarkable rumor from the Internet or media is true, check the high-quality websites www.snopes.com, which continually tracks the accuracy of urban legends.

A woman heated her poodle in a microwave oven in a well-meaning attempt to dry it off following a rainstorm. It exploded.

While still alive, Walt Disney arranged to have his body frozen after his death so that it could be unfrozen at a future date when advanced technology will permit him to live again.

Outside her home, a woman found a stray Chihuahua. She cared for the pet for several weeks and eventually brought it to a veterinarian, who informed her that her cute little "dog" was actually a giant rat.

Many gang members drive around late at night without their car lights on and then shoot people who flash their lights at them.

A woman on a transatlantic flight was trapped in the bathroom for over two hours after flushing the toilet created a vacuum, binding her to the seat.

social facilitation

enhancement of performance brought about by the presence of others

attribution

process of assigning causes to behavior

fundamental attribution error

tendency to overestimate the impact of dispositional influences on other people's behavior

called **social facilitation**. In what might have been the world's first social psychological study, Norman Triplett (1897) found that bicycle racers obtained faster speeds when racing along with other bicyclists than when racing against only the clock. The difference—8.6 miles per hour on average—was substantial. Zajonc (1965) reported that social facilitation applies to birds, fish, and even insects. In what's surely one of the most creative studies in the history of psychology, Zajonc and two colleagues randomly assigned cockroaches to two conditions: one in which they ran a maze alone and another in which they ran a maze while being observed by an audience of fellow cockroaches from a "spectator box." Compared with the lone cockroaches, cockroaches in the second condition ran the maze significantly faster and committed fewer errors (Zajonc, Heingartner, & Herman, 1969).

Yet the impact of others on our behavior isn't always positive (Bond & Titus, 1983). Social facilitation occurs only on tasks we find easy, whereas *social disruption*—a worsening of performance in the presence of others—occurs on tasks we find difficult. You've probably happened upon this effect if you've ever "choked" in the company of others while singing a difficult song or telling a joke with a complicated punch line. One team of five researchers watched people playing pool (Michaels et al., 1982). The experienced pool players did better in the presence of others, but the inexperienced pool players did worse. So the effects of social influence can be positive or negative depending on the situation. We're especially likely to "choke" on a difficult task when we're distracted—such as by the knowledge that others are watching us—which can limit the working memory (see LO 7.1b) we can devote to solving the problem (Beilock, 2008; Beilock & Carr, 2005).

The Fundamental Attribution Error: The Great Lesson of Social Psychology

When we try to figure out why people, ourselves included, did something, we're forming **attributions**, or assigning causes to behavior. Some attributions are internal (inside the person), such as when we conclude that Joe Smith robbed a bank because he's impulsive. Other attributions are external (outside the person), such as when we conclude that Bill Jones robbed a bank because his family was broke (Kelley, 1973). We can explain a great deal of our everyday behavior by invoking situational factors that are external to us, such as social pressure.

When we read about the frenzied behavior of people during collective delusions, such as the Seattle windshield pitting epidemic, we may laugh and pat ourselves on the back with the confident reassurance that we would never have acted this way. Yet if the field of social psychology imparts one lesson that we should take with us for the rest of our lives (Myers, 1993a), it's that we tend to attribute too much of people's behavior to who they are. This mistake is known as the **fundamental attribution error**. Coined by social psychologist Lee Ross (1977), this term refers to the tendency to overestimate the impact of *dispositional influences* on others' behavior. By dispositional influences, we mean enduring characteristics, such as personality traits, attitudes, and intelligence.

Because of the fundamental attribution error, we also tend to underestimate the impact of *situational influences* on others' behavior, meaning that we attribute too little of their behavior to what's going on around them. For instance, we may assume incorrectly that a boss in a failing company who fired several of his loyal employees to save money must be callous, when in fact he was under enormous pressure to spare the jobs of hundreds of other loyal employees. No one knows for sure why we commit the fundamental attribution error, but one likely culprit is the fact that we're rarely aware of all of the situational factors impinging on others' behavior at a given moment (Gilbert & Malone, 1995; Pronin, 2008). When we witness a senator caving into political influence on a vote, we may think to ourselves, "What a coward!" because we may not recognize—or appreciate—the intense social pressure he was experiencing. Interestingly, we're less likely to commit the fundamental attribution error if we've been in the same situation ourselves (Balcetis & Dunning, 2008) or have been encouraged to feel empathic toward those we're observing (Regan & Totten, 1975). Perhaps taking a walk in others' shoes helps us grasp what they have to contend with.

Mysteries of Psychological Science
Why are Yawns Contagious?

One vivid illustration of the power of social influence comes from the phenomenon of contagious yawning. Both everyday observation and systematic research bear out the fact that once someone in a group starts yawning, others do too (Provine, 2012). Yawning doesn't spread merely from person to person; it even spreads from written material to people (Platek et al., 2003; Provine, 2005). Indeed, as you're reading this paragraph, you may find yourself starting to yawn (hopefully not because you're bored!). Between 40 and 60 percent of adults yawn soon after seeing another person yawn, and many yawn even after reading the word *yawn* (Platek, Mohamed, & Gallup, 2005). Yet the psychological and physiological functions of yawning, and contagious yawning in particular, remain mysterious.

Although yawning emerges in fetuses as early as three months following conception, contagious yawning doesn't typically emerge until about age four (Helt et al., 2010). This developmental trend may reflect the emergence of empathy and theory of mind in children (see LO 10.3b); as we become better able to identify with others' mental states, we become more likely to mimic their actions. Interestingly, individuals with autism spectrum disorder (autism), who tend to exhibit theory of mind deficits, are less likely than other individuals to engage in contagious yawns (Helt et al., 2010). People prone to schizophrenia, as well as those with psychopathic personality traits, especially an absence of empathy, may exhibit the same absence of contagious yawning (Haker & Rössler, 2009; Rundle, Vaughan, & Stanford, 2015). Recent research has also examined the existence of contagious yawning in animals. Although most species don't display contagious yawning, chimpanzees do (Anderson, Myowa-Yamokowshi, & Matso-zawa, 2004). Interestingly, chimpanzees exhibit contagious yawning more to members of their own social groups than to other chimpan-

Psychological research bears out our everyday observation that yawning is contagious.

zees, again suggesting a tie to empathy (Campbell & de Waal, 2011). In some studies, dogs, who've co-evolved closely with humans for thousands of years and have grown highly attuned to our social signals (Hare & Woods, 2013), have been found to yawn in response to other people's yawns (Provine, 2012).

Still, none of this tells us why yawning is contagious. The truth is that psychologists don't know. Some psychologists argue that contagious yawning promotes the social bonding of individuals within groups. Because people often yawn when they're drowsy or underaroused (Guggisberg et al., 2010), contagious yawning may have evolved to foster alertness within a group (Gallup, 2011), which might in turn protect group members against threats. Of course, it's also possible that contagious yawning has no actual function itself. It may merely be an indirect consequence of the fact that natural selection has shaped us to become social beings who are exquisitely attuned to the behaviors of others.

This explanation dovetails with a curious finding that emerges in some, but not all, studies. We tend to commit the fundamental attribution error only when explaining *others'* behavior; when explaining the causes of our *own* behavior, we're often a bit more likely to invoke situational influences, probably because we're well aware of all of the situational factors affecting us (Jones & Nisbett, 1972). For example, if we ask you why your best friend in college chose to attend this school, you'll most likely mention dispositional factors: "She's a really motivated person and likes to work hard." In contrast, if we ask *you* why you chose to attend this school, you'll most likely mention situational factors: "When I visited the college, I really liked the campus and was impressed by what I heard about the professors." Still, this difference isn't large in size and usually holds only when we're describing people we know well (Malle, 2006).

EVIDENCE FOR THE FUNDAMENTAL ATTRIBUTION ERROR. Edward E. Jones and Victor Harris (1967) conducted the first study to demonstrate the fundamental attribution error. They asked undergraduates to serve as "debaters" in a discussion of U.S. attitudes toward Cuba and its controversial leader Fidel Castro, who died in 2016. In full view of the other debaters, they randomly assigned students to read aloud debate speeches that adopted either a pro-Castro or an anti-Castro position.

After hearing these speeches, the researchers asked the other debaters to evaluate each debater's *true* attitudes toward Castro. That is, putting aside the speech he or she read, what do you think each debater *really* believes about Castro? Students fell prey to the fundamental attribution error; they assumed that what debaters said reflected their true position

Figure 13.3 Participants' Performance in Jones & Harris (1967) Castro Study

Participants inferred that debaters' pro-Castro positions reflected their actual attitudes even though debaters couldn't choose which position to adopt—an example of the fundamental attribution error.

SOURCE: Data from Jones, E. E., & Harris, V. A. (1967). The attribution of attitudes. Journal of Experimental Social Psychology, 3, 1–24. © Scott O. Lilienfeld.

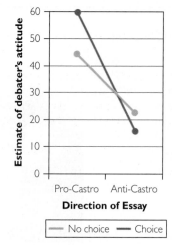

The 1960s television show *Candid Camera*, which placed ordinary people in absurd situations, illustrates the *fundamental attribution error* (Maas & Toivanen, 1978). Viewers laugh at people's often silly reactions, underestimating how likely most of us are to fall victim to situational influences—in this case, group pressure. In one classic episode (shown here), an unsuspecting person enters an elevator filled with *Candid Camera* staff (a and b). Suddenly and for no reason, all of the staff turn to the right (c). Sure enough, the bewildered person turns to the right also (d).

conformity

tendency of people to alter their behavior as a result of group pressure

regarding Castro *even though they knew that the assignment to conditions was entirely random* (see Figure 13.3). They forgot to take the situation—namely, the random assignment of participants to the experimental condition—into account when evaluating debaters' attitudes (Ross, Amabile, & Steinmetz, 1977).

THE FUNDAMENTAL ATTRIBUTION ERROR: CULTURAL INFLUENCES. Like many psychological phenomena, the fundamental attribution error is influenced by culture. Although almost everyone is prone to this error, Japanese and Chinese people seem to be less so (Mason & Morris, 2010; Nisbett, 2003). That may be because they're more likely than people in Western cultures to view behaviors in context (see LO 1.1a). As a result, they may be more prone to seeing others' behavior as a complex stew of both dispositional and situational influences.

For example, after reading newspaper descriptions of mass murderers, Chinese participants are less likely to invoke dispositional explanations for their behavior ("He must be an evil person") and more likely to invoke situational explanations ("He must have been under terrible stress in his life"). In contrast, U.S. participants show the opposite pattern (Morris & Peng, 1994). This cultural difference even extends to inanimate objects. When shown a circle moving in various directions, Chinese students are more likely to say that the circle's movement is due to situational factors ("Something is pushing on the circle") than to dispositional factors ("The circle wants to move to the right"). We again find the opposite pattern among U.S. students (Nisbett, 2003). Yet, even within Western cultures, there are intriguing differences in the tendency to commit the fundamental attribution error. For example, Protestants are more prone to make dispositional attributions than are Catholics, perhaps because they're especially likely to believe in a soul, a spiritual entity within each of us that survives even after our deaths (Li et al., 2012).

13.2: Social Influence: Conformity and Obedience

13.2a Determine the factors that influence when we conform to others.
13.2b Recognize the dangers of group decision making, and identify ways to avoid mistakes common in group decisions.
13.2c Identify the factors that maximize or minimize obedience to authority.

Think of an organization or group to which you've belonged, like a club, school committee, sports team, fraternity, or sorority. Have you ever just gone along with one of the group's ideas even though you knew it was bad, perhaps even unethical? If so, you're in good company. **Conformity** refers to the tendency of people to alter their behavior as a result of group pressure (Kiesler & Kiesler, 1969; Pronin, Berger, & Molouki, 2007; Sherif, 1936). We all conform to social pressure from time to time. Yet as we'll soon see, we occasionally take this tendency too far.

Conformity: The Asch Studies

Solomon Asch conducted the classic study of conformity in the 1950s. Asch's (1955) research design was as straightforward as it was elegant. In some social psychological studies such as Asch's, participants are lured in by a cover story that conceals the study's true goal. Often, other "participants" in the study are actually *confederates*, or undercover agents of the researcher. But the actual participants aren't aware of that deception.

In this chapter, we'll ask you to imagine yourself as a participant in several classic social psychological studies. Let's begin with Asch's: Read the description in the box before continuing.

Figure 13.4 Asch's Conformity Study

Interactive

THE SETUP

Standard line   Comparison lines
1 2 3

Asch invites participants to a "study of perceptual judgments" that asks eight participants—including you—to compare a standard line with three comparison lines: 1, 2, and 3. Unbeknownst to you, the other "participants" are actually confederates. A researcher explains your job is to say aloud which of three comparison lines matches the standard line. The researcher starts with the person across the table, so you're always the fifth to be called.

Which of the "comparison lines" is the same length as the "standard line"? If several other participants said it was line 3, would you go along with them?

SOURCE: Adapted from Asch, S. E. (1955). Opinions and social pressure. Scientific American, 193, 31–35. © Scott O. Lilienfeld

THE STUDY

On the first trial, the correct answer is clearly "1." You listen intently as the first few participants call out their answers. Participant 1: "1." Participant 2: "1." Participant 3: "1." Participant 4: "1." As Participant 5, you simply follow and say "1." The three participants following you give the same answer: 1. "This study's going to be a breeze," you say to yourself. The second trial displays a similar problem, just as easy to answer, in which the correct answer is clearly "2" (see above). Again you listen while the participants call out their answers. Participant 1: "3." Participant 2: "3." Participant 3: "3." Participant 4: "3." You can hardly believe your eyes. It seems obvious that "2" is the correct answer, but everyone is calling "3." What on Earth is going on? Are your eyes deceiving you? What are you going to do?

THE RESULTS

(Graph: y-axis "% of trials in which subjects conformed" from 0 to 40; x-axis "Number of opponents" from 0 to 12.)

If you're like 75 percent of participants in the original Asch study, you'd conform to the incorrect norm on at least 1 of the 12 trials. Across all 12 trials in the Asch study, participants conformed to the wrong answer 37 percent of the time. Some conformed even when the comparison line differed from the standard line by more than 6 inches! Understandably, participants reported being confused and even distressed because they experienced a sharp conflict between their perceptions and what they believed to be others' perceptions.

SOURCE: Adapted from Asch, S. E. (1955). Opinions and social pressure. Scientific American, 193, 31–35. © Scott O. Lilienfeld

SOCIAL INFLUENCES ON CONFORMITY.   Asch (1955) and later researchers went on to pinpoint some of the social factors that influence how likely we are to conform. They concluded that conformity was influenced by the following independent variables:

1. **Uniformity of Agreement:** If all confederates gave the wrong answer, the participant was more likely to conform. Nevertheless, if one confederate gave the correct response, the level of conformity plummeted by three-fourths.
2. **Difference in the Wrong Answer:** Knowing that someone else in the group differed from the majority—*even if that person held a different view from that of the participant*—made the participant less likely to conform.
3. **Size:** The size of the majority made a difference, but only up to about five or six confederates. People were no more likely to conform in a group of 10 than in a group of 5 (see Figure 13.4).

Asch also tried to rule out alternative hypotheses for his findings. To determine whether group norms affected participants' *perceptions* of the lines, he repeated his original study but asked participants to write, rather than call out, their responses. In this condition, their answers were right more than 99 percent of the time, suggesting that such norms affect only people's expressed behavior, not their perceptions of reality.

We should be careful not to draw the wrong conclusions from Asch's classic findings. His data demonstrate that many or most of us conform blindly to group pressure from time to time. Nevertheless, his data also show that many of us can and do resist the power of the

▶ Ruling Out Rival Hypotheses

Have important alternative explanations for the findings been excluded?

group (Griggs, 2015a). Indeed, Asch's participants went against the norm almost two-thirds of the time. The lesson here is that group pressure can powerful, but it's hardly irresistible.

IMAGING STUDIES: PROBING FURTHER INFLUENCES. Although Asch concluded that group norms affected only participants' observable behavior, brain-imaging data raise the possibility that social pressure may at times influence perception too. Gregory Berns and his colleagues (Berns et al., 2005) placed participants in a functional magnetic resonance imaging (fMRI) scanner and showed them two figures. They asked participants to determine whether the figures were the same or different. To do so, they had to mentally rotate one or both of them. The researchers led participants to believe that four other people were making the same judgments along with them; in fact, these judgments were preprogrammed into a computer.

On some trials, the other "participants" gave unanimously correct answers; on others, they gave unanimously incorrect answers. Like Asch, Berns and his collaborators found high levels of conformity: Participants went along with others' wrong answers 41 percent of the time. Their conforming behavior was associated with activity in the amygdala, which tends to trigger anxiety in response to danger cues (see LO 3.2a). This finding suggests that conformity may come with a price tag of negative emotions, particularly anxiety. Berns and his colleagues also found that conformity was associated with activity in the parietal and occipital lobes, the areas of the brain responsible for visual perception. This finding suggests that social pressure might sometimes affect how we perceive reality, although activity in these brain areas may have instead reflected participants' tendency to doubt and then recheck their initial perceptions.

> **Ruling Out Rival Hypotheses**
>
> Have important alternative explanations for the findings been excluded?

INDIVIDUAL, CULTURAL, AND GENDER DIFFERENCES IN CONFORMITY. People's responses to social pressure are also associated with individual and cultural differences, underscoring the point that not all of us conform all of the time. People with low self-esteem are especially prone to conformity (Hardy, 1957), almost certainly because they fear disapproval. Most Asians are also more likely to comply to group norms than are Americans (Bond & Smith, 1996; S. H. Oh, 2013), probably because most Asian cultures are more collectivist than is American culture (Oyserman, Coon, & Kemmelmeier, 2002). This greater collectivism probably leads many Asians to be more concerned about peer opinion than are Americans. In addition, people in individualistic cultures like the United States generally prefer to stand out from the crowd, whereas those in collectivist cultures prefer to blend in. In one study, researchers presented American and Asian participants with a bunch of orange and green pens that contained a majority of one color and a minority of the other. Americans tended to pick the minority-colored pens, whereas Asians tended to pick the majority-colored pens (Kim & Markus, 1999).

In contrast, gender doesn't seem to matter much when it comes to conformity. Early studies suggested that women were more likely to conform than men are (Eagly & Carli, 1981). But because the experimenters were all male, this difference may have been due to an alternative explanation: Perhaps male experimenters had unknowingly provoked submissive behavior in female participants. When later studies were conducted by female experimenters, the sex difference in conformity largely vanished (Feldman-Summers et al., 1980; Javornisky, 1979).

> **Ruling Out Rival Hypotheses**
>
> Have important alternative explanations for the findings been excluded?

Deindividuation

Research on deindividuation suggests that irresponsible behavior would probably be more likely to occur in the setting on the bottom, because (1) people aren't wearing name tags, therefore they aren't easily identifiable, and (2) the room is dark and may foster greater anonymity.

Deindividuation: Losing Our Typical Identities

One process that can make us more vulnerable to conformity is **deindividuation**: the tendency of people to engage in atypical behavior when stripped of their usual identities (Festinger, Pepitone, & Newcomb, 1952). Several factors contribute to deindividuation, but the most prominent are a feeling of anonymity and a lack of personal responsibility (Dipboye, 1977; Postmes & Spears, 1998). When we're deindividuated, we become more vulnerable to social influences, including the impact of social roles.

The advent of e-mail, text messaging, and other largely impersonal forms of communication may contribute to deindividuation, in turn leading to a heightened risk of "flaming"—sending insulting messages to others (Kato, Kato, & Akahori, 2007). Indeed, once people start posting nasty anonymous online comments on YouTube videos, others quickly pile on (Moor, Heuvelman, & Verleur, 2010), a phenomenon that scholars term the *online disinhibition effect*. The face painting of warriors and the masks donned by the Ku Klux Klan may also fuel deindividuation by fostering anonymity (R. I. Watson, 1973). In one study, children asked to wear masks were more likely than other children to help themselves to forbidden Halloween candy (Miller & Rowold, 1979). In another study, participants were more likely to cheat in a dimly lit than in a fully lit room. They were even more likely to behave selfishly—helping themselves to more than their fair share of money—when asked to wear sunglasses, even though they were no less anonymous than when not wearing sunglasses (Zhong, Bohns, & Gino, 2010). Apparently, even the mere illusion of anonymity can foster deindividuation.

Every day, we play multiple social roles: student, son, or daughter; roommate; and club member, to name but a few. What happens when we temporarily lose our typical social identities and are forced to adopt different ones?

STANFORD PRISON STUDY: CHAOS IN PALO ALTO.   Philip Zimbardo and his colleagues first approached this question four decades ago (Haney, Banks, & Zimbardo, 1973). Zimbardo knew about the dehumanizing conditions in many prisons and wondered whether they stemmed from peoples' personalities or from the roles they're required to adopt. The roles of prisoner and guard, which are inherently antagonistic, may carry such powerful expectations that they generate self-fulfilling prophecies. What would happen if ordinary people played the roles of prisoner and guard? Would they begin to assume the identities assigned to them? To find out, carefully read the description of Zimbardo prison study in the box below.

deindividuation

tendency of people to engage in uncharacteristic behavior when they are stripped of their usual identities

---

Stanford Prison Study

Interactive

The Setup:
Zimbardo and his colleagues advertised for volunteers for a 2-week "psychological study of prison life." Using a coin toss, they randomly assigned 24 male undergraduates, prescreened for normal adjustment using personality tests, to be either prisoners or guards.

The Study:

Zimbardo and his collaborators transformed the basement of the Stanford psychology department in Palo Alto, California, into a simulated prison, complete with prison cells. To add to the realism, actual Palo Alto police officers arrested the would-be prisoners at their homes and transported them to the simulated prison. The prisoners and guards were forced to dress in clothes befitting their assigned roles. Zimbardo, who acted as the prison "superintendent," instructed guards to refer to prisoners only by numbers, not by names.

The Results:

The first day passed without incident, but something soon went horribly wrong. Guards began to treat prisoners cruelly and to subject them to harsh punishments. Guards forced prisoners to perform humiliating lineups, do push-ups, sing, strip naked, and clean filthy toilets with their bare hands. In some cases, they even placed bags over prisoners' heads.

By day 2, the prisoners mounted a rebellion, which the guards quickly quashed. Things went steadily downhill from there. The guards became increasingly sadistic, using fire extinguishers on the prisoners and forcing them to simulate sodomy. Soon, many prisoners began to display signs of emotional disturbance, including depression, hopelessness, and anger. Zimbardo released two prisoners from the study because they appeared to be on the verge of a psychological breakdown. One prisoner went on a hunger strike in protest.

At day 6, Zimbardo—after some prodding from one of his former graduate students, Christina Maslach—ended the study 8 days early. Although the prisoners were relieved at the news, some guards were disappointed (Haney, Banks, & Zimbardo, 1973). Perhaps Zimbardo was right; once prisoners and guards had been assigned roles that deemphasized their individuality, they adopted their designated roles more easily than anyone might have imagined. Yet because of the fundamental attribution error, which leads us to underestimate the power of the situation, most of us find the results of the Stanford Prison Study startling (Haney & Zimbardo, 2009).

Zimbardo's study, although enormously influential, has been the target of considerable criticism in recent years (Bartels, 2015). In particular, this study wasn't carefully controlled: In many respects, it was more of a demonstration than an experiment. In particular, his prisoners and guards may have experienced demand characteristics (see LO 2.3a) to behave in accord with their assigned roles. Among other things, they may have assumed that the investigators wanted them to play the parts of prisoners and guards and obliged. These demand characteristics may have been inadvertently amplified by the researchers. Indeed, there's evidence that during the study, Zimbardo referred to himself and the prison guards collectively as "we"—perhaps implying that he allied himself with the guards—and at times encouraged the guards to create a hostile atmosphere for the prisoners (Griggs & Whitehead, 2014).

Replicability

Can the results be duplicated in other studies?

Moreover, at least one attempt to replicate the Stanford prison study, sponsored by the British Broadcasting Corporation, was unsuccessful, suggesting that the effects of deindividuation aren't inevitable (Reicher & Haslam, 2006). The results of another study raise the possibility that the results of the Stanford Prison Study may have been due at least partly to biases in participant selection. Researchers recruited potential participants with an advertisement containing virtually identical wording to that used by Zimbardo and his colleagues for the Stanford Prison Study. Participants who volunteered for the study displayed high scores on measures of aggressiveness, manipulativeness, narcissism, and dominance and low scores on measures of altruism and empathy (Carnahan & McFarland, 2007)—all characteristics one might expect to be linked to sadistic behavior. So perhaps participants in the Stanford Prison Study weren't so average after all. Just as important, people's responses to deindividuation almost surely is shaped in part by their personality traits. Walk through the description in the box below before reading on.

The Real World: Chaos in Abu Ghraib

Interactive

The Stanford prison study was almost certainly not an isolated event (Zimbardo, 2007). In 2004, the world witnessed disturbingly similar images in the now-infamous Iraqi prison of Abu Ghraib. There, we saw guards—this time, U.S. soldiers—placing bags over Iraqi prisoners' heads, leading them around with dog leashes, pointing mockingly at their exposed genitals, and arranging them in human pyramids for the soldiers' amusement. These similarities weren't lost on Zimbardo (2004b, 2007), who maintained that the Abu Ghraib fiasco was a product of situational forces. According to Zimbardo, the dehumanization of prisoners and prison guards made it likely they'd lose themselves in the social roles to which superiors assigned them.

That said, the overwhelming majority of U.S. prison guards during the Iraqi War didn't engage in abuse, so the reasons for such abuse don't lie entirely in the situation. As research on Asch's studies reminds us, individual differences in personality play a key role in conformity. Indeed, several guards who perpetrated the Abu Ghraib abuses had a long history of irresponsible and arguably even psychopathic behavior (Saletan, 2004). Behavior is a function of both situations and persons.

Furthermore, deindividuation doesn't necessarily make us behave badly; it makes us more likely to conform to whatever norms are present in the situation (Postmes & Spears, 1998). A loss of identity actually makes people more likely to engage in prosocial, or helping, behavior when others are helping out (Johnson & Downing, 1979). Moreover, being anonymous sometimes makes us more, not less, likely to assist others. For example, when people can't be identified, they're especially likely to help strangers by pointing out fashion gaffes that could embarrass them, such as the fact that their zippers are open (Hirsch, Galinsky, & Zhong, 2011). For good, bad, and often both, deindividuation makes us behave more like a member of the group and less like an individual.

CROWDS: MOB PSYCHOLOGY IN ACTION. Deindividuation helps explain why crowd behavior is so unpredictable: The actions of people in crowds depend largely on whether others are acting prosocially or antisocially (against others). A myth that's endured for centuries is that crowds are always more aggressive than individuals. In the late 19th century, sociologist Gustav Le Bon (1895) argued that crowds are a recipe for irrational and even destructive behavior. According to Le Bon, people in crowds are more anonymous and therefore more likely to act on their impulses than are individuals.

In some cases, Le Bon was right. In November 2008, a Long Island, New York, Walmart employee was trampled to death by a stampeding crowd of more than 200 people after the doors opened for Black Friday shopping. Four other people, including a pregnant woman, were injured. Some shoppers, eager to get good deals on discounted products, ran over emergency workers assisting the victims.

Yet in other cases, crowds are less aggressive than individuals (de Waal, 1989; de Waal, Aureli, & Judge, 2000). Depending on prevailing social norms, deindividuation can make us either more or less aggressive. Moreover, people in crowds typically limit their social interactions to minimize conflict (Baum, 1987). For example, people on crowded buses and elevators generally avoid staring at one another. This behavior is probably adaptive, because people are less likely to say or do something that could offend others. Even the online disinhibition effect is more complex than originally believed, because in some cases it contributes to *prosocial* comments on blogs. For example, online self-disclosure regarding one person's emotionally painful experiences, such as struggles with depression or eating disorders, is often followed by online expressions of sympathy and self-disclosure by others (Lapidot-Lefler & Barak, 2015).

Groupthink

Closely related to conformity is a phenomenon that social psychologist Irving Janis (1972) termed **groupthink**: an emphasis on group unanimity at the expense of critical thinking. Groups sometimes become so intent on ensuring that everyone agrees with everyone else that they lose their capacity to evaluate issues objectively (Sunstein & Hastie, 2015). To be sure, groups, including juries and presidential cabinets, often make good decisions, especially when group members are free to contribute opinions that aren't influenced—and potentially contaminated—by peer pressure (Surowiecki, 2004). Yet groups sometimes make poor, even terrible, decisions, especially when members' judgments aren't independent of each other. When groups combine information from members, they typically rely on "common knowledge"—information that group members share—rather than unique knowledge, resulting in no net gain in new information (Stasser & Titus, 2003). As we've learned throughout this text, widely held knowledge is sometimes incorrect.

GROUPTHINK IN THE REAL WORLD. Janis arrived at the concept of groupthink after studying the reasoning processes behind the failed 1961 invasion of the Bay of Pigs in Cuba. Following lengthy discussions with cabinet members, President John F. Kennedy recruited 1,400 Cuban immigrants to invade Cuba and overthrow its dictator, Fidel Castro. But the invasion was ineptly planned, and nearly all of the invaders were captured or killed.

Although the members of Kennedy's cabinet were uncommonly brilliant, their actions were astonishingly foolish. After the failed invasion, Kennedy asked, "How could I have been so stupid?" (Dallek, 2003). The Bay of Pigs invasion wasn't the last time groupthink led intelligent people to make catastrophic decisions. In 1986, the space shuttle *Challenger* exploded, killing the 7 astronauts aboard a mere 73 seconds after takeoff. Following group discussions, project managers of the *Challenger* agreed to launch it after a series of bitterly cold days in January, despite warnings from NASA engineers that the shuttle might explode because rubber rings on the rocket booster could fail in freezing temperatures (Esser & Lindoerfer, 1989).

Perhaps ironically, some critics have recently charged the discipline of social psychology—which itself spawned the concept of groupthink—with groupthink. Specifically, they've argued that the social psychology field, which tends to be politically liberal, largely excludes politically conservative perspectives on such controversial topics as affirmative action, capital punishment, and abortion (Duarte al., 2015; Redding, 2012). In any case, it's clear that *viewpoint diversity*—valuing a range of different perspectives—is a crucial antidote to groupthink, both within and outside academia.

Table 13.1 depicts some of the "symptoms" identified by Janis (1972) that render groups vulnerable to groupthink. Nevertheless, some psychologists have pointed out that Janis's descriptions of groupthink derived from anecdotal observations, which we've learned are often flawed as sources of evidence. Moreover, groupthink doesn't always lead to bad decisions, just overconfident ones (Tyson, 1987). Seeking group consensus isn't always a bad idea, but doing so before all of the relevant evidence is available is (Longley & Pruitt, 1980).

Groupthink, like all social psychological processes, isn't inevitable. Janis (1972) noted that the best way to avoid groupthink is to encourage dissent within an organization. He recommended that all groups appoint a "devil's advocate"—a person whose role is to voice doubts about the wisdom of the group's decisions. Studies show that including a devil's advocate in groups tends to reduce groupthink and to result in better decisions (Schwenk, 1989). A related

Although crowds *sometimes* engage in irrational, even violent, behavior, research suggests that compared with individuals, crowds aren't necessarily more aggressive. The January 2013 inauguration of President Barack Obama, shown here, was marked by only one reported arrest despite an estimated crowd size of more than one million people.

groupthink

emphasis on group unanimity at the expense of critical thinking

Table 13.1 Symptoms of Groupthink.

Symptom	Example
An illusion of the group's invulnerability	"We can't possibly fail!"
An illusion of the group's unanimity	"Obviously, we all agree."
An unquestioned belief in the group's moral correctness	"We know we're on the right side."
Conformity pressure—pressure on group members to go along with everyone else	"Don't rock the boat!"
Stereotyping of the out-group—a caricature of the enemy	"They're all morons."
Self-censorship—the tendency of group members to keep their mouths shut even when they have doubts	"I suspect the group leader's idea is stupid, but I'd better not say anything."
Mindguards—self-appointed individuals whose job it is to stifle disagreement	"Oh, you think you know better than the rest of us?"

effective approach is to encourage splitting the group up into smaller teams and asking them to debate alternative courses of action (Lunenberg, 2012). In addition, Janis suggested having independent experts on hand to evaluate whether the group's decisions make sense. Holding a follow-up meeting to evaluate whether the decision reached in the first meeting still seems reasonable can serve as a helpful check against errors in reasoning. Although not explicitly recommended by Janis, research suggests that increasing racial and cultural diversity within groups can result in better decisions, partly because it may lead to consideration of alternative perspectives. For example, in studies of jury decision making, including at least two African Americans in predominantly white juries is associated with fewer factual mistakes on the part of jurors, more detailed consideration of the facts of the case, and fairer verdicts (Sommers, 2006).

group polarization

tendency of group discussion to strengthen the dominant positions held by individual group members

cult

group of individuals who exhibit intense and unquestioning devotion to a single individual or cause

GROUP POLARIZATION: GOING TO EXTREMES. Related to groupthink is **group polarization**, which occurs when group discussion strengthens the dominant position held by individual group members (Isenberg, 1986; Myers & Lamm, 1976; Paulus, 2015). In one study, a group of students who were slightly unprejudiced became less prejudiced after discussing racial issues, whereas a group that was slightly prejudiced became *more* prejudiced after discussing racial issues (Myers & Bishop, 1970). Group polarization can be helpful if it leads to efficient decisions. Yet in other cases, it can be destructive, as when juries rush to unanimous decisions before they've considered all the evidence (Daftary-Kapur, Dumas, & Penrod, 2010; Myers & Kaplan, 1976).

There's evidence that the American electorate is becoming increasingly polarized, with left-leaning citizens becoming more liberal, and right-leaning citizens becoming more conservative (Abramowitz & Saunders, 2008; Persily, 2015). Indeed, in the United States, prejudice toward people in opposing parties now equals or exceeds prejudice against people of different races (Iyengar & Westwood, 2015). Needless to say, these negative attitudes make it challenging for reasonable people of good faith to find common ground on social and political issues. At least some of this polarization may be due to the increasing accessibility of Internet blogs, continually updated news websites, social media of all kinds, radio talk shows, and cable television, which provide political partisans on both sides with a steady diet of information that supports their views—and fuels their confirmation bias (Jamieson & Cappella, 2007; Lilienfeld, Ammirati, & Landfield, 2009; Sunstein, 2002). Moreover, research on book-buying habits shows that liberals almost exclusively read liberal books and conservatives almost exclusively read conservative books (Eakin, 2004). Few people on either extreme of the political spectrum regularly expose themselves to information that challenges their views, probably generating further polarization.

CULTS AND BRAINWASHING. In extreme forms, groupthink can lead to **cults**: groups that exhibit intense and unquestioning devotion to a single individual or cause.

Groupthink

Interactive

"All those in favor say 'Aye.'"
"Aye."   *"Aye."*   *"Aye."*
"Aye."   *"Aye."*   *"Aye."*

This cartoon illustrates self-censorship, which is a common symptom of groupthink.

SOURCE: © *The New Yorker Collection 1979 Henry Martin from cartoonbank.com. All Rights Reserved.*

Cult membership involves following the cult's practices without question. Reverend Sun Yung Moon of the Unification Church has united thousands of total strangers in mass wedding ceremonies. The couples are determined by pairing photos of prospective brides and grooms. They meet for the first time during the week leading up to the wedding day, or often on the day of the ceremony itself.

Although most cults aren't dangerous (Bridgestock, 2009), they can occasionally produce disastrous consequences. Consider Heaven's Gate, a Southern California–based group founded in 1975 by Marshall Applewhite, a former psychiatric patient. Cult members believed that Applewhite was a reincarnated version of Jesus Christ. Applewhite, they were convinced, would take them to a starship in their afterlives. In 1997, a major comet approached Earth, and several false reports circulated in the media that a spaceship was tailing it. The Heaven's Gate members believed that this was their calling. Virtually all of the cult members—39 of them—committed suicide by drinking a poisoned cocktail.

Because cults are secretive and difficult to study, we know relatively little about them. But evidence suggests that cults promote groupthink in four major ways (Lalich, 2004): having a persuasive leader who fosters loyalty; disconnecting group members from the outside world; discouraging questioning of the group's assumptions; and establishing training practices that gradually indoctrinate members (Galanter, 1980).

Despite what many people believe, most cult members are psychologically normal (Aronoff, Lynn, & Malinowski, 2000; Lalich, 2004), although many cult *leaders* probably suffer from serious mental illness. This erroneous belief probably stems from the fundamental attribution error. In trying to explain why people join cults, we overestimate the role of personality traits and underestimate the role of social influences. We may make the same error, incidentally, when evaluating the personality traits of many or most terrorists. Despite what many people believe, the evidence suggests that most suicide bombers in the Middle East, including the September 11 hijackers and most Al-Qaeda and ISIS members, aren't seriously mentally disordered (Gordon, 2002); in this respect, they appear to be similar to the majority of cult members. Moreover, most suicide bombers are relatively well off and well educated (Sageman, 2004). Instead, many or most of these individuals are largely normal people who've been indoctrinated into a warped ideology.

One widespread misconception is that all cult members are *brainwashed*, or transformed by group leaders into unthinking zombies. The concept of brainwashing originated during the Korean War, when American troops were subjected to indoctrination by Chinese captors. Although some psychologists have argued that many cults use brainwashing techniques (Singer, 1979), the existence of brainwashing is scientifically controversial (Reichert, Richardson, & Thomas, 2015). There's not much evidence that brainwashing permanently alters victims' beliefs (Melton, 1999). In addition, brainwashing is probably far less effective than most people assume. For example, during the Korean War, few of the approximately 3,500 American political prisoners captured by the Chinese falsely confessed to war crimes. Moreover, an even smaller number (probably less than 1 percent) displayed any signs of adherence to Communist ideologies following their return to the United States (Spanos, 1996). Finally, there's reason to doubt whether brainwashing is a unique means of changing people's behavior. Instead, the persuasive techniques of brainwashing probably aren't all that different from those used by effective political leaders and salespeople (Zimbardo, 1997).

How can we best resist the indoctrination that leads to cults? Here, the psychological research is clear, although counterintuitive: First expose people to information consistent with cult beliefs and then debunk it. In his work on the **inoculation effect**, social psychologist William McGuire (1964) demonstrated that the best way of immunizing people against an undesirable belief is to gently introduce them to reasons this belief seems to be correct, which gives them the chance to generate their own counterarguments against those reasons. In this way, they'll be more resistant to arguments for this belief—and more open to arguments against it—in the future (Compton & Pfau, 2005). This approach works much like a vaccine, which inoculates people against a virus by presenting them with a small dose of it, thereby activating the body's defenses (McGuire, 1964; McGuire & Papageorgis, 1961; Richards & Banas, 2015). For example, if we want to persuade someone to purchase a used car, we might list all of the reasons why buying this car seems like a bad idea and then point out why these reasons aren't as convincing as they seem.

inoculation effect

approach to convincing people to change their minds about something by first introducing reasons why the perspective might be correct and then debunking these reasons

Obedience: The Psychology of Following Orders

In the case of conformity, we go along to get along. The transmission is "horizontal"—the group influence originates from our peers. In the case of **obedience**, though, we take our marching orders from people above us in the hierarchy of authority, such as a teacher, parent, or boss. Here the transmission is "vertical"—the group influence springs not from our peers, but from our leaders (Loevinger, 1987). Also, in contrast to conformity, in which the social influence is typically implicit (unspoken), in obedience, it's almost always explicit: An authority figure tells us to do something, and we comply. Many groups, such as cults, acquire their influence from a potent combination of both conformity and obedience.

obedience

adherence to instructions from those of higher authority

OBEDIENCE: A DOUBLE-EDGED SWORD. Obedience is a necessary, even essential, ingredient in our daily lives. Without it, society couldn't run smoothly. You're reading this text in part because your professor told you to, and you'll obey the traffic lights and stop signs on your next trip to school or work because you know you're expected to. Yet like conformity, obedience can produce troubling consequences when people stop asking questions about *why* they're behaving as others want them to. As British writer C. P. Snow wrote, "When you look at the dark and gloomy history of man, you will find that more hideous crimes have been committed in the name of obedience than have ever been committed in the name of rebellion." Let's look at one infamous example.

During the Vietnam War, U.S. Lieutenant William Calley commanded a platoon of a division named Charlie Company that had encountered heavy arms fire for weeks. Understandably, the members of Charlie Company were on edge during the morning of March 16, 1968, as they entered the village of My Lai (pronounced "Me Lie"), expecting to find a hideout for North Vietnamese soldiers. Although the platoon located no enemy soldiers in My Lai, Calley ordered soldiers to open fire on villagers, none of whom had initiated combat. They bludgeoned several old men to death with the butts of their rifles and shot praying children and women in the head. When all was said and done, the American platoon had brutally slaughtered about 500 innocent Vietnamese ranging in age from 1 to 82.

Calley insisted that he was merely taking orders from his superiors and bore no direct responsibility for the massacre: "I was ordered to go in there and destroy the enemy. That was my job that day. That was the mission I was given" (Calley, 1971). In turn, the soldiers in Calley's platoon claimed they were merely taking orders from Calley. In 1971, Calley was convicted of murder and sentenced to life in military prison, but President Richard Nixon reduced his sentence.

In sharp contrast to Calley's behavior, Officer Hugh Thompson, Jr., attempted to halt the massacre by landing his U.S. Army helicopter between Calley's troops and the innocent villagers. Risking their lives, Thompson and his two crewmen ordered the troops to stop shooting, saving scores of innocent lives.

As inexplicable as the My Lai massacre seems, it's only one instance of the perils of unthinking obedience. How can we make sense of this behavior?

Two sides of the coin of obedience: Lt. William Calley (*left*) was charged with murder by the Army for ordering his platoon to massacre unarmed civilians in the My Lai massacre in 1968. Calley was the only one in the platoon to be charged with a crime. Hugh Thompson (*right*) and his fellow crew members landed their helicopter between their fellow Army platoon and the civilians in the My Lai massacre in an effort to save the lives of the unarmed villagers. Thompson and crew were awarded the Soldier's Medal for bravery.

STANLEY MILGRAM: SOURCES OF DESTRUCTIVE OBEDIENCE. Stanley Milgram was a graduate student of Solomon Asch's who sought to understand the principles underlying irrational group behavior. The child of Jewish parents who grew up during World War II, Milgram was preoccupied with the profoundly troubling question of how the Holocaust could have occurred. The prevailing wisdom in the late 1940s and 1950s was that the Holocaust was primarily the product of twisted minds that had perpetuated dastardly deeds. Yet Milgram suspected that the truth was subtler, and in some ways more frightening, as he came to believe that the psychological processes that give rise to destructive obedience are surprisingly commonplace.

THE MILGRAM PARADIGM.   In the early 1960s, Milgram began to tinker with a laboratory paradigm (a model experiment) that could provide a window into the causes of obedience (Blass, 2004). After a few years of pilot testing, Milgram finally hit on the paradigm he wanted, not knowing that it would become one of the most influential in the history of psychology (Cialdini & Goldstein, 2004; Slater, 2004). To find out about Milgram's paradigm and his now famous findings, carefully read the description of his study in the box below.

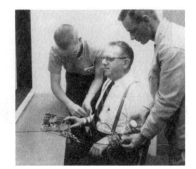

In Milgram's study, a participant is shown being strapped to a shock plate.

Milgrim Study of Obedience

The Setup:

You spot an advertisement in a local New Haven, Connecticut, newspaper, asking for volunteers for a study of memory. The ad notes that participants will be paid $4.50, a hefty chunk of change in the 1960s. You arrive at the laboratory at Yale University, where a tall and imposing man in a white lab coat, Mr. Williams, greets you. Mr. Williams is obviously the experimenter. You also meet another friendly, middle-aged participant, Mr. Wallace, who unbeknownst to you is actually a confederate. The cover story is that you and Mr. Wallace will be participating in a study of the effects of "punishment on learning," with one of you being the teacher and the other the learner. Drawing lots to see who'll play which role, you get the piece of paper that says "teacher" (in fact, the lots are rigged). From here on, Mr. Williams refers to you as the "teacher" and to Mr. Wallace as the "learner."

As the teacher, Mr. Williams explains, you'll present Mr. Wallace with what psychologists call a *paired-associate task*. In this task, you'll read a long list of word pairs, like *strong–arm* and *black–curtain*. Then you'll present the learner with the first word in each pair (such as *strong*) and ask him to select the second word (*arm*) from a list of four words. Now here's the surprise: To evaluate the effects of punishment on learning, you'll be delivering a series of painful electric shocks to the learner. With each wrong answer, you'll move up one step on a shock generator. The shocks range from 15 to 450 volts and are accompanied by labels ranging from "Slight Shock" and "Moderate Shock" to "Danger: Severe Shock" and, finally and most ominously, "XXX."

The Study:

You watch as Mr. Williams brings the learner into a room and straps his arm to a shock plate. The learner, Mr. Williams explains, will push a button corresponding to his answer to the first word in each pair. His answer will light up in an adjoining room where you sit. For a correct answer, you'll do nothing. But for an incorrect answer, you'll give the learner an electric shock, with the intensity increasing with each mistake. At this point, the learner mentions to Mr. Williams that he has "a slight heart condition" and asks anxiously how powerful the shocks will be. Mr. Williams responds curtly that although the shocks will be painful, they "will cause no permanent tissue damage."

You're led into the adjoining room and seated in front of the shock generator. Following Milgram's plan, the learner makes a few correct responses, but soon begins to make errors. If at any time you turn to Mr. Williams to ask if you should continue, he responds with a set of prearranged prompts that urge you to go on ("Please go on." or "The experiment requires that you continue." or "You have no other choice; you *must* go on."). Milgram standardized the verbal statements of the learner, which also unbeknownst to you, have been prerecorded on audiotape (Milgram, 1974). At 75 volts, the learner grunts "Ugh!" and by 330 volts, he frantically yells "Let me out of here!" repeatedly and complains of chest pain. From 345 volts onward, there's nothing—only silence. The learner stops responding to your items, and Mr. Williams instructs you to treat these nonresponses as incorrect answers and to keep administering increasingly intense shocks.

The Results:

When Milgram first designed this study, he asked 40 psychiatrists at Yale University to forecast the outcome. Most participants, they predicted, would break off at 150 volts. Only 0.1 percent (that's 1 in 1,000), representing a "pathological fringe" (Milgram, 1974), would go all the way to 450 volts, they guessed. Before reading on, you may want to ask yourself what you would have done had you been a participant in Milgram's study. Would you have delivered any shocks? If so, how far would you have gone?

In fact, in the original Milgram study, *all* participants administered at least some shocks. Most went up to at least 150 volts, and a remarkable 62 percent displayed complete compliance, going all the way up 450 volts. This means that the Yale psychiatrists were off by a factor of several hundred.

These results were, well, shocking. Milgram himself was startled by them (Blass, 2004). Before Milgram's study, most psychologists assumed that the overwhelming majority of normal people would disobey what were obviously cruel and outrageous orders. But like the Yale psychiatrists, they committed the fundamental attribution error: They underestimated the impact of the situation on participants' behaviors.

There were other surprises. Many participants showed uncontrollable tics and fits of nervous laughter. Yet few appeared to be sadistic. Even those who complied until the bitter end seemed reluctant to deliver shocks, asking or begging the experimenter to allow them to stop. Yet most participants still followed Mr. Williams' orders despite these pleas, often assuming no responsibility for their actions. One person's responses were illustrative; after the study was over he claimed, "I stopped, but he [the experimenter] made me go on" (Milgram, 1974).

that the situation is really an emergency. Imagine that on your way to class tomorrow, you see a student in dirty clothing slumped across a bench. As you stroll by, thoughts whiz through your mind: Is he asleep? Is he drunk? Could he be seriously ill, even dead? Could my psychology professor be conducting a study to examine my responses to emergencies? Here's where pluralistic ignorance comes into play. We look around, notice that nobody is responding, and assume—perhaps mistakenly—that the situation isn't an emergency. We assume we're the only one who thinks the situation might be an emergency. Reassured that the coast is clear and there's nothing to worry about, we continue on our merry way.

An example of pluralistic ignorance familiar to all college students is the "silent classroom scenario," which often occurs after a professor has delivered a lecture that has left everyone in the class thoroughly bewildered. Following the lecture, the professor asks "Are there are any questions?" and no one responds. Each student in the class looks nervously at the other students, all of whom are sitting quietly, and each assumes mistakenly that he or she is the only one who didn't understand the lecture (Wardell, 1999).

Pluralistic ignorance is relevant when we're trying to figure out whether an ambiguous situation is really an emergency. But it doesn't fully explain the behavior of bystanders in the Kitty Genovese; Richmond, California, gang rape; or Delhi, India, rickshaw tragedies, because those situations were clearly emergencies. Even once we've recognized that the situation is an emergency, the presence of others still tends to inhibit helping.

Diffusion of Responsibility: Passing the Buck. A second step is required for us to intervene in an emergency. We need to feel a burden of responsibility for the consequences of *not* intervening. Here's the catch: The more people present at an emergency, *the less each person feels responsible for the negative consequences of not helping.* Darley and Latané called this phenomenon **diffusion of responsibility**: The presence of others makes each person feel less responsible for the outcome. If you don't assist someone in a crowded park who's having a heart attack and that person dies, you can always say to yourself, "Well, that's a terrible tragedy, but it wasn't really *my* fault. After all, plenty of other people could have helped too." The participants in Milgram's study who complied with the experimenter's commands when instructing someone else to deliver shocks probably experienced diffusion of responsibility: They could reassure themselves "Well, I wasn't the only one who did it."

So we can experience pluralistic ignorance, which prevents us from interpreting a situation as an emergency, *and* we can experience diffusion of responsibility, which discourages us from offering assistance in an emergency. From this perspective, it's perhaps surprising that any of us helps in emergencies, because the obstacles to intervening are considerable.

Studies of Bystander Nonintervention. To get at the psychological roots of the bystander effect, Darley, Latané, and their colleagues tested the effect of bystanders on participants' willingness to (1) report that smoke was filling a room (Darley & Latané, 1968b); (2) react to what sounded like a woman falling off a ladder and injuring herself (Latané & Rodin, 1969); and (3) respond to what sounded like another student experiencing an epileptic seizure (Darley & Latané, 1968a). In the video that opened this chapter, you watched a simulation of the second study using a man rather than a woman. In all of these studies, participants were significantly more likely to seek or offer help when they were alone than in a group (see Figure 13.7).

Researchers have replicated these findings many times using slightly different designs. In an analysis of almost 50 studies of bystander intervention involving close to 6,000 participants, Bibb Latané and Steve Nida (1981) found that people were more likely to help when alone than in groups about 90 percent of the time. That's an impressive degree of replicability. Even *thinking* about being in a large group makes us less likely to help in an emergency (Garcia et al., 2002).

> **Replicability**
>
> Can the results be duplicated in other studies?

Still, there are a few grounds for optimism. Research suggests that when an emergency is physically dangerous for victims, bystanders may be somewhat more likely to intervene than when it's not especially dangerous (Fischer et al., 2011). Also, the bystander effect can apparently be eliminated when people know they might be watched. For example, placing a camera in public spaces seems to reverse this effect, probably because people know they might be held accountable for the consequences of not acting (van Bommel et al., 2012). Finally, there's reason to believe that exposure to research on bystander effects may boost the chances of intervening

diffusion of responsibility

reduction in feelings of personal responsibility in the presence of others

Figure 13.7 Bystander Intervention

Across three classic experiments on bystander intervention, the percentage of people helping when in groups was markedly lower than the percentage of people helping when alone.

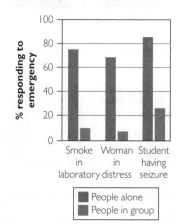

in emergencies. This finding illustrates what Kenneth Gergen (1973) called an **enlightenment effect**: Learning about psychological research can change real-world behavior for the better (Katzev & Brownstein, 1989). One group of investigators (Beaman et al., 1978) presented the research literature on bystander intervention effects to one psychology class—containing much of the same information you've just read—but didn't present this literature to a very similar psychology class. Two weeks later, the students, accompanied by a confederate, came upon a person slumped over on a park bench. Compared with 25 percent of students who hadn't received the bystander intervention lecture, 43 percent of students who'd received the lecture intervened to help. This study worked, probably because it imparted new knowledge about bystander intervention and perhaps also because it made people more aware of the importance of helping. So the very act of reading this chapter may have made you more likely to become a responsive bystander.

Social Loafing: With a Little Too Much Help From My Friends

Have you ever been a member of a group that got virtually nothing accomplished? (All of your text authors regularly attend meetings of university faculty members, so we're particular experts on this topic.) If so, you may have been a victim of **social loafing**, a phenomenon in which people slack off when they're working in groups (Latané, Williams, & Harkins, 1979; North, Linley, & Hargreaves, 2000; Simms & Nichols, 2014). As a consequence of social loafing, the whole is less than the sum of its parts.

Some psychologists believe that social loafing is a variant of bystander nonintervention. That's because social loafing appears to be due in part to diffusion of responsibility: People working in groups typically feel less responsible for the outcome of a project than they do when working alone. As a result, they don't invest as much effort.

Psychologists have demonstrated social loafing in numerous experiments (Ohlert & Kleinert, 2012). In one, a researcher placed blindfolds and headphones on six participants and asked them to clap or yell as loudly as possible. When participants thought they were making noise as part of a group, they were less loud than when they thought they were making noise alone (Williams, Harkins, & Latané, 1981). Cheerleaders also cheer less loudly when they believe they're part of a group than when they believe they're alone (Hardy & Latané, 1986). Investigators have also identified social loafing effects in studies of rope-pulling (tug-of-war), navigating mazes, identifying radar signals, and evaluating job candidates (Karau & Williams, 1995). Like many other social psychological phenomena, social loafing may be influenced by cultural factors. People in individualistic countries like the United States are more prone to social loafing than are people in collectivist countries like China, probably because people in the latter countries feel more responsible for the outcomes of group successes or failures (Earley, 1989).

One of the best antidotes to social loafing is to ensure that each person in the group is identifiable, for example, by guaranteeing that managers and bosses can evaluate each individual's performance (Lount & Walk, 2014; Voyles, Bailey, & Durik, 2015). By doing so, we can help "diffuse" the diffusion of responsibility that often arises in groups.

Man on Ground

Pluralistic ignorance (people walking by may assume the man is drunk or asleep rather than injured) and diffusion of responsibility (the presence of numerous people present makes each person feel less responsible for the consequences of not helping) are two social psychological principles that help explain why these people don't stop to help the man lying on the ground.

Studies of social loafing demonstrate that in large groups, individuals often work (or in this case, pull) less hard than they do when alone.

enlightenment effect

learning about psychological research can change real-world behavior for the better

social loafing

phenomenon whereby individuals become less productive in groups

Journal Prompt

Many students (and non-students) dislike group work because of the fear that their fellow group members will not pull their weight. What are some ways of avoiding this phenomenon of social loafing in group work (other than avoiding group work altogether)?

Psychomythology

Is Brainstorming in Groups A Good Way to Generate Ideas?

Imagine that you've been hired by an advertising firm to cook up a new marketing campaign for Mrs. Yummy's Chicken Noodle Soup. The soup hasn't been selling well as of late, and your job is to come up with an advertising jingle that will instill in every American an uncontrollable urge to reach for the nearest cup of chicken noodle soup.

Although you initially plan to come up with slogans on your own, your boss walks into your cubicle and informs you that you'll be participating in a "group brainstorming" meeting later that afternoon in the executive suite. There, you and 12 other firm members will let your imaginations run wild, saying whatever comes to mind in the hopes of hitting on a winning chicken noodle soup advertising formula. Indeed, companies across the world regularly use group brainstorming as a means of generating novel ideas. They assume that several heads generating a flurry of ideas are better than one. In a book titled *Applied Imagination*, which influenced many companies to adopt brainstorming, Alex Osborn (1957) argued that "the average person can think up twice as many ideas when working with a group than when working alone" (p. 229).

Although the idea behind group brainstorming is intuitively appealing, it turns out to be wrong. Numerous studies demonstrate that group brainstorming is less effective than individual brainstorming (Brown & Paulus, 2002; Byron, 2012; Diehl & Stroebe, 1987). When brainstorming, groups tend to come up with fewer ideas, and often fewer good ones, than do individuals (Paulus, 2004; Putman & Paulus, 2009). Group brainstorming also generally results in ideas that are less creative than those generated by individual brainstorming. Making matters worse, groups often overestimate how successful they are at producing new ideas, which may help to explain brainstorming's popularity (Paulus, Larey, & Ortega, 1995).

There are at least two reasons group brainstorming tends to be less effective than individual brainstorming. One is that group members may be anxious about being evaluated by others, leading them to hold back potentially good ideas. The second is social loafing. When brainstorming in groups, people frequently engage in what's called "free riding": They sit back and let others do the hard work (Diehl & Stroebe, 1987; Hall & Buzwell, 2012). Whatever the reason, research suggests that when it comes to brainstorming, one brain may be better than two—or many more—at least when the brains can communicate with each other.

Psychological research suggests that we sometimes engage in genuine altruism—helping largely out of empathy.

altruism

helping others for unselfish reasons

Prosocial Behavior and Altruism

Even though there's usually danger rather than safety in numbers when it comes to others helping us, many of us do help in emergencies even when others are around (Fischer et al., 2006). In the Kitty Genovese tragedy, at least one person and perhaps more apparently did call the police (Manning, Levine, & Collins, 2007). Indeed, there's good evidence that many of us engage in **altruism**, that is, helping others for unselfish reasons (Batson, 1987; Dovidio et al., 2006; Penner et al., 2005).

ALTRUISM: HELPING SELFLESSLY. Over the years, some scientists have argued that we help others entirely for egoistic (self-centered) reasons, such as relieving our own distress, experiencing the joy of others we've helped (Hoffman, 1981), or anticipating that people we've helped will be more likely to reciprocate by helping us later (Gintis et al., 2003). From this perspective, we help others only to benefit ourselves. Yet in a series of experiments, Daniel Batson and his colleagues showed that we sometimes engage in genuine altruism. That is, in some cases, we help others in discomfort primarily because we feel empathic toward them; that is, we sympathize with their feelings (Batson et al., 1991; Batson & Shaw, 1991; Fischer et al., 2006). In some studies, they exposed participants to a female victim (actually a confederate) who was receiving painful electric shocks and gave them the option of either (a) taking her place and receiving shocks themselves or (b) turning away and not watching her receive shocks. When participants were made to feel empathic toward the victim (for example, by learning that their values and interests were similar to hers), they generally offered to take her place and receive shocks rather than turn away (Batson et al., 1981). In some cases, we seem to help not only to relieve our distress, but also to relieve the distress of others.

Along with empathy, a number of psychological variables increase the odds of helping. Let's look at some of the most crucial ones.

HELPING: SITUATIONAL INFLUENCES. People are more likely to help in some situations than in others. They're more likely to help others when they can't easily escape the situation—for example, by running or driving away. They're also more likely to help someone who collapses on a crowded subway than on the sidewalk. Characteristics of the victim also matter. In one study, bystanders helped a person with a cane 95 percent of the time, but helped an

Americans triggers activa
(Cunningham, Nezlek, &
duration (525 millisecond
well as higher levels of ac
et al., 2002). This provoca
negative reaction to black
default to prejudiced beli
undergraduates drank le
Splenda (the control cond
male named Sam. Glucos
ter at inhibiting our impu
glucose wrote essays that
about Sam than did stude
of us hold stereotyped bel
mental effort (Gailliot et a

The Nature of Pr

It's safe to say that we a
(Aronson, 2000). Some ha
in the human species. Fro
ing close alliances with in
This is part of a broader
1985; Mineka, 1992): Bett
skin conductance respons
have been paired repeatec
ily, and perhaps quite nat

Still, notice that we v
an evolutionary predispo
prejudice is inevitable. Tw
with people similar to us.

The first is **in-group l**
members outside our grои
emerge in children as earl
sporting event, you've ob
fans (the word *fan*, incider
ing the visiting team with
in the game's outcome—a
is their "tribe," and they'll

In-group bias may be
out-group members. In or
students while they pond
similar to themselves—a l
dissimilar from themselve
medial prefrontal cortex,
when we feel empathy to
when participants though
less active when they tho
vative (Mitchell, Macrae,
The second bias is **o**
dency to view all peop
similar (Park & Rothbart
makes it easy for us to d
such as different races, ir
simply tell ourselves that
sirable characteristic—su
people of Race X act the
similar"). In this way, we

obviously drunk person only 50 percent of the time (Piliavin, Rodin, & Piliavin, 1969). Being in a good mood also makes us more likely to help (Isen, Clark, & Schwartz, 1976). So does exposure to role models who help others (Bryan & Test, 1967; Rushton & Campbell, 1977).

One striking study examined seminary students who were on their way across campus to deliver a sermon on the Biblical story of the Good Samaritan, which describes the moral importance of assisting injured people (Darley & Batson, 1973). The investigators led some students to believe that they needed to rush over to give the lecture; others believed they had some extra time. While walking across campus, the students came across a man (actually a confederate) who was slumped over in a doorway and who twice coughed and moaned loudly. The seminary students were significantly less likely to offer assistance to the man if they were in a hurry (only 10 percent) than if they had time to spare (63 percent). Some of the students simply stepped over him on their way to the lecture. So much for the Good Samaritan!

Helping: Individual and Gender Differences. Individual differences in personality also influence the likelihood of helping, again reminding us that interpersonal behavior is a function of both person and situation. Participants who are less concerned about social approval are more likely to go against the grain and intervene in emergencies even when others are present (Latané & Darley, 1970). Extraverted people are also more prone to help others than are introverted people (Krueger, Hicks, & McGue, 2001). Not surprisingly, even when they're off duty, people with lifesaving skills, such as trained medical workers, are more likely to offer assistance to others in emergencies than are other people (Huston et al., 1981; Patton, Smith, & Lilienfeld, 2016). Some people may not help on certain occasions simply because they don't know what to do.

Some researchers have reported a slight tendency for men to help more than women (Eagly & Crowley, 1986). This difference isn't especially consistent across studies (Becker & Eagly, 2004), and it seems to be accounted for by an alternative explanation, namely, the tendency of men to help more than women only in situations involving physical or social risk. Moreover, men are especially likely to help women rather than other men, especially if the women are physically attractive (Eagly & Crowley, 1986).

> ◀ **Ruling Out Rival Hypotheses**
>
> Have important alternative explanations for the findings been excluded?

Aggression: Why We Harm Others

Like our primate cousins, the chimpanzees, we occasionally engage in violence toward others. And like them, we're a war-waging species; as we write this chapter, there are at least nine full-scale wars, often defined as conflicts that kill more than 1,000 people per year, raging across the globe. The good news, if there is any, is that the world today is probably safer than it's ever been. For example, the proportion of people killed in wars, as high as it is, is lower now that it's been in the past several centuries (Pinker, 2011). This positive trend probably reflects the growing democratization of the world, because democratic countries rarely attack each other. Across more than 50 countries examined, the rates of homicide have also been steadily declining over the past six decades (LaFree, Curtis, & McDowall, 2015). Yet, even with these encouraging caveats in mind, large pockets of the world remain terribly dangerous places, and the threat of violent extremism continues to loom large, even in Western countries.

Psychologists define **aggression** as behavior intended to harm others, either verbally or physically. To account for aggressive behavior on both large and small scales, we need to examine the role of both situational and dispositional factors.

aggression

behavior intended to harm others, either verbally or physically (or both)

SITUATIONAL INFLUENCES ON AGGRESSION. Using both laboratory and naturalistic designs (see LO 2.2a), psychologists have pinpointed a host of situational influences—some short term, others long term—on human aggression. Here are some of the best-replicated findings.

> ◀ **Replicability**
>
> Can the results be duplicated in other studies?

- **Interpersonal Provocation:** Not surprisingly, we're especially likely to strike out aggressively against those who have provoked us, say, by insulting, threatening, or hitting us (Geen, 2001; Vasquez et al., 2013).
- **Frustration:** We're especially likely to behave aggressively when frustrated, that is, thwarted from reaching a goal (Anderson & Bushman, 2002b; Berkowitz, 1989; Pawliczek et al., 2013). In one study, a research assistant asked participants to perform a difficult paper-folding (origami) task at an unreasonably rapid rate and either apologized for moving participants along too quickly or told them to pick up the pace ("I would like to

Figure 13.10 The Da[nger?]
of Stereotypes

Gordon Allport and Leo Postm[an]
drawing similar to this one to s[how?]
stereotypes can distort the tra[nsmission of?]
information across people. The[y asked a?]
white participant to look at the [drawing, which?]
clearly depicts a white man wi[th a razor pointed?]
at an African American man—[and then to describe?]
the scene to a string of five or [more?]
participants in a "game of telep[hone." As the?]
story was passed from particip[ant to participant,?]
it became progressively warpe[d. In more?]
than half of the retellings of the [scene, subjects placed?]
the African American man as h[olding the razor.?]

SOURCE: Based on Pelham, B. V[...]
& Jones, J. T. (2002). Why Susie [sells?]
seashore: Implicit egotism and [...]
Journal of Personality and Social [...]
487. © Scott O. Lilienfeld,

explicit prejudice

unfounded negative belief of
which we're aware regarding the
characteristics of an out-group

implicit prejudice

unfounded negative belief of
which we're unaware regarding the
characteristics of an out-group

ultimate attribution err[or]

assumption that behavior[s by?]
individual members of a g[roup are?]
due to their internal dispo[sitions?]

extrinsic religiosity, who view religion as a means to an end, such as obtaining friends or social support, tend to have high levels of prejudice (Batson & Ventis, 1982). In contrast, people with high levels of *intrinsic religiosity*—for whom religion is a deeply ingrained part of their belief system—tend to have equal or lower levels of prejudice than do nonreligious people (Gorsuch, 1988; Pontón & Gorsuch, 1988).

Prejudice "Behind the Scenes"

Most surveys demonstrate that interracial prejudice has declined substantially in the United States over the past four to five decades (Dovidio & Gaertner, 2000), although at least some evidence points to an uptick in prejudice over the past few years (Pasek et al., 2014). Despite the overall apparent decrease in prejudice in America, some scholars contend that a good deal of prejudice, particularly that of Caucasians toward African Americans, has merely "gone underground"—that is, become subtler (Dovidio et al., 1997; Fiske, 2002; Hackney, 2005; Sue et al., 2007).

One approach to studying subtle prejudice is to measure implicit (unconscious) prejudice (Fazio & Olson, 2003; Vanman et al., 2004). In contrast to **explicit prejudices**, which are biases of which we're aware, **implicit prejudices** are biases of which we're unaware. Implicit prejudice became an issue in the 2016 presidential campaign, when then Democratic candidate Hillary Clinton argued that a better understanding of implicit bias is needed to improve race relations, including relations between majority police officers and minority citizens (Merica, 2016). Increasingly, psychologists have tried to capture implicit prejudice in the laboratory. For example, one research team asked whites to cooperate with blacks on a task. Although white participants claimed to like their black partners, sensitive measures of their facial activity implied otherwise: Their forehead muscles involved in frowning became active (Vanman et al., 1997).

One implicit prejudice technique that's received substantial attention over the past decade or so is the Implicit Association Test (IAT) developed by Anthony Greenwald and Mahzarin Banaji. As shown in Figure 13.12, researchers might ask a participant to press a key on the computer keyboard with his left hand if he sees a photograph of an African American or a positive word (like *joy*) and to press a different key with his right hand if he sees a photograph of a Caucasian or a negative word (like *bad*). After performing this task for a number of trials, researchers ask participants to again press the left and right keys, but this time for the reverse pairing (that is, to press the left key for a photograph of either an African American or a negative word and the right key for a photograph of either a Caucasian or a positive word) (Greenwald, McGhee, & Schwartz, 1998).

Many studies demonstrate that most Caucasian participants respond more quickly to pairings in which African American faces are paired with negative words and Caucasian faces are paired with positive words (Banaji, 2001; De Houwer et al., 2009). According to proponents of the IAT, this interesting finding suggests that many whites hold implicit (unconscious) prejudice against African Americans (Gladwell, 2005; Greenwald & Nosek, 2001). Perhaps surprisingly, about 40 percent of African Americans display the same bias on the IAT (Banaji & Greenwald, 2013), suggesting that even some African Americans might harbor subtle biases against members of their own race. Investigators have expanded the IAT to detect a variety of forms of subtle prejudice, including racism, sexism, homophobia, religious discrimination, and ageism (prejudice against older individuals). If you want to

Answer: Fact. In one study, a researcher found that people who were prejudiced against Jews and African Americans also expressed dislike of the Pireneans, Danireans, and Wallonians—all of which are nonexistent ethnic groups (Hartley, 1946).

try out the IAT, check out the following website, which features many versions of the test designed to assess implicit prejudice toward various groups: http://implicit.harvard.edu/implicit/demo.

Nevertheless, the IAT is scientifically controversial (De Houwer et al., 2009). It's clear that it measures something interesting, but exactly what it measures isn't entirely clear. For one thing, the IAT often displays quiet low correlations with measures of explicit prejudice, such as questionnaire measures of racist attitudes (Arkes & Tetlock, 2004; Oswald et al., 2015). Proponents of the IAT sometimes argue that this absence of a correlation actually supports the IAT's validity, because the IAT supposedly measures unconscious rather than conscious racial attitudes. Yet this reasoning raises questions regarding the falsifiability of the IAT because IAT proponents could presumably interpret a positive or zero correlation as evidence for the IAT's validity. Moreover, it's unclear whether the IAT measures prejudice as much as *awareness* of, or familiarity with, stereotypes (Kaufman, 2011). Unprejudiced persons may correctly perceive that much of mainstream American society links Muslims, for example, with many negative characteristics and Christians with many positive characteristics, yet they may reject these associations as biased (Arkes & Tetlock, 2004; Levitin, 2013; Redding, 2004).

Falsifiability

Can the claim be disproved?

Another problem is that at least some positive findings linking the IAT to real-world racism may stem from only a handful of participants with extreme scores; as a result, the IAT may not measure implicit prejudice for the substantial majority of people (Blanton et al., 2009). Scholars continue to debate whether the IAT and similar implicit measures genuinely assess prejudice and, if so, how well (Blanton & Jaccard, 2008, 2015; De Houwer et al., 2009; Gawronski, LeBel, & Peters, 2007; Greenwald, Banaji, & Nosek, 2015).

A final important avenue of implicit prejudice research examines minority members' similarity to majority group members' racial stereotypes. Majority individuals may be subtly biased against individuals who fit their implicit stereotypes of how minority individuals "look." For example, even when examining crimes of equal severity, African Americans who fit White's views of a "steoretypical" African American male are more likely to be sentenced to death than are other African Americans (Eberhardt et al., 2006). These troubling findings point to subtle but important potential biases in the criminal justice system that will require close attention in the coming years.

Figure 13.12 The Implicit Association Test

The Implicit Association Test (IAT) is the most widely researched measure of implicit or unconscious prejudice. This is a rendered example: Most white participants associate negative words more readily with African American than white faces, and many African American participants display the same effect. But does the test really measure unconscious prejudice, or does it measure something else? The debate continues.

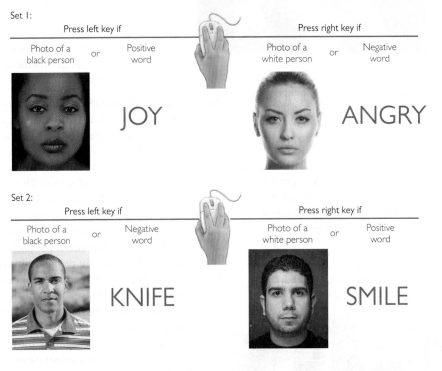

Combating Prejudice: Some Remedies

Having traversed some pretty depressing ground—blind conformity, destructive obedience, bystander nonintervention, social loafing, and now prejudice—we're pleased to close our chapter with a piece of good news: We can overcome prejudice, at least to some extent (Aboud et al., 2012). But how?

ROBBERS CAVE STUDY. We can find some clues in a study that Muzafer Sherif and his colleagues conducted in Robbers Cave, Oklahoma (so named because robbers once used these caves to hide from law enforcement authorities). Sherif split 22 well-adjusted fifth grade students into two groups, the Eagles and the Rattlers, and sent them packing to summer camp. After giving the boys within each group the chance to form strong bonds, Sherif introduced the groups to each other and engaged them in a four-day sports and games tournament. When he did,

Chapter 14
Personality

How We Become Who We Are

Learning Objectives

14.1a Describe how twin and adoption studies shed light on genetic and environmental influences on personality.

14.2a Describe the core assumptions of psychoanalytic theory.

14.2b Describe key criticisms of psychoanalytic theory and the central features of neo-Freudian theories.

14.3a Identify the core assumptions of behavioral and social learning theories of personality.

14.3b Describe key criticisms of behavioral and social learning approaches.

14.4a Explain the concept of self-actualization and its role in humanistic models.

14.4b Describe key criticisms of humanistic approaches.

14.5a Describe trait models of personality, including the Big Five.

14.5b Identify key criticisms of trait models.

14.6a Describe structured personality tests such as the MMPI-2 and their methods of construction.

14.6b Describe projective tests, particularly the Rorschach, and their strengths and weaknesses.

14.6c Identify common pitfalls in personality assessment.

Challenge Your Assumptions

Does a similar upbringing lead to similarities in our personalities?

Can we reduce the enormous variation in people's personalities to a mere handful of underlying factors?

Is our behavior highly consistent across situations?

Can we use responses to inkblots to infer people's personality traits?

Is criminal profiling scientific?

Watch IDENTICAL TWINS: A VALUABLE WINDOW INTO PERSONALITY

Video

As this video illustrates, genes influence our personalities in powerful ways. Yet, as the video further demonstrates, environmental factors can shape our genetic propensities in intriguing ways, leading to differences even between genetically identical individuals.

In this chapter, we'll address a host of fascinating questions regarding how our personalities emerge and develop over time. The answers to those questions, we'll soon learn, aren't simple. Although most of us believe we can explain why people act as they do, we're wrong at least as often as we're right (Hamilton, 1980; Nisbett & Wilson, 1977).

Few are more confident in their abilities to explain behavior than radio and television "advice experts" and pop psychologists featured on television variety shows, many of whom liberally sprinkle their shows with off-the-cuff psychological accounts for people's behavior (Furnham, 2016; Heaton & Wilson, 1995; Williams & Ceci, 1998). Consider the following statements typical of those offered by talk show psychologists: "He murdered all of those people because he had an unhappy childhood." "She overeats because she has low self-esteem." Intuitively appealing as those explanations are, we must beware of *single-cause explanations* of human behavior. When trying to uncover the root causes of people's actions, we must keep in mind that personality is multiply determined. Indeed, personality is the unimaginably complicated outcome of hundreds or even thousands of causal factors: genetic, prenatal, parenting, peer influences, life stressors, and plain old luck, both good and bad.

Radio and talk show personalities such as Dr. Phil McGraw ("Dr. Phil") often provide single-cause explanations for complex, multiply determined psychological problems.

14.1: Personality: What Is It and How Can We Study It?

14.1a Describe how twin and adoption studies shed light on genetic and environmental influences on personality.

Earlier in the text (see LO 13.1a), we learned how our social context can influence our behavior in profound ways. There, we met up with the *fundamental attribution error*, the tendency to attribute too much of others' behavior to their dispositions, including their personalities, and consequently not enough to the situations they confront.

Even bearing this error in mind, most psychologists agree that there *is* such a thing as **personality**—people's typical ways of thinking, feeling, and behaving. We aren't exclusively a product of the social factors that affect us at any given moment, although we're certainly influenced by them. Most also agree broadly with the American psychologist Gordon Allport's (1966) definition of personality as consisting of relatively enduring predispositions that influence our behavior across many situations (Funder, 1991; John, Robins, & Pervin, 2008; Tellegen, 1991). These predispositions, also called **traits**—such as introversion,

personality

people's typical ways of thinking, feeling, and behaving

trait

relatively enduring predisposition that influences our behavior across many situations

nomothetic approach

approach to personality that focuses on identifying general laws that govern the behavior of all individuals

idiographic approach

approach to personality that focuses on identifying the unique configuration of characteristics and life history experiences within an individual

---

Falsifiability

Can the claim be disproved?

---

aggressiveness, and conscientiousness—account in part for consistencies in our behavior across both time and situations.

There are two major approaches to studying personality (Scurich, Monahan, & John, 2012). A **nomothetic approach** strives to understand personality by identifying general laws that govern the behavior of all individuals. Most modern personality research, including most of the research we'll examine in this chapter, is nomothetic because it aims to derive principles that explain the thinking, emotions, and behaviors of all people. This approach typically allows for generalization across individuals but limited insight into the unique patterning of attributes within one person.

In contrast, an **idiographic approach** (think of the word *idiosyncratic*) strives to understand personality by identifying the unique configuration of characteristics and life history experiences within a person. Most case studies are idiographic. Gordon Allport (1965) presented a classic example of the idiographic approach in his book *Letters from Jenny*, which features an analysis of 301 letters written by one woman over 12 years. In these letters, Allport uncovered themes that characterized Jenny's attitudes toward her son, Ross. When Jenny wrote about Ross in positive terms, themes of her early life often emerged; when she wrote about him in negative terms, themes of her unappreciated sacrifices for him often emerged. The idiographic approach reveals the richly detailed tapestry of one person's life, but allows for limited generalizability to other people. Moreover, it generates hypotheses that are often difficult to falsify, because these hypotheses are frequently post hoc ("after the fact") explanations about events that have already occurred.

How do personality traits originate? We'll first approach this deceptively complex question from the vantage point of behavior-genetic studies of personality and move on to specific theories of personality, including Freudian, behavioral, and humanistic models, that offer competing answers to this question. As we'll discover, all of these theories aim to explain *both commonalities and differences* among people in their personalities. For example, they try to account for not only how we develop a conscience, but also why some of us have a stronger conscience than others.

Behavior-genetic methods, with which we first crossed paths previously in the text (see LO 3.5a), help psychologists disentangle the following three broad sets of influences on personality:

- *Genetic* factors.
- *Shared environmental* factors—experiences that make individuals within the same family more alike. If parents try to make all of their children more outgoing by reinforcing them with attention and succeed in doing so, their parenting in this case is a shared environmental factor.
- *Nonshared environmental* factors—experiences that make individuals within the same family less alike. If a parent treats one child more affectionately than another and as a consequence this child ends up with higher self-esteem than the other child, the parenting in this case is a nonshared environmental factor.

Investigating the Causes of Personality: Overview of Twin and Adoption Studies

To distinguish among these three sets of influences, behavior geneticists have applied twin studies and adoption studies (see LO 3.5b) to personality. Because identical (monozygotic) twins are more similar genetically than are fraternal (dizygotic) twins, a higher correlation of traits among identical than fraternal twins—assuming that the environmental influences on both sets of twins are comparable—suggests a genetic influence. In contrast, identical twin correlations that are equal to or less than fraternal twin correlations suggest the absence of a genetic component and instead point to nonshared environmental influences—those that make people within a family (including twins) different.

REARED-TOGETHER TWINS: GENES OR ENVIRONMENT? From the findings of one landmark twin study of personality, we can see that numerous personality traits—including anxiety proneness, impulse control, and traditionalism (the extent to which people believe in well-established social values, such as the importance of obeying one's

Table 14.1 Comparison of Correlations of Twins Reared Together and Apart for Selected Personality Traits.

	Twins Reared Together		Twins Reared Apart	
	Identical Twin Correlation	Fraternal Twin Correlation	Identical Twin Correlation	Fraternal Twin Correlation
Anxiety proneness	0.52	0.24	0.61	0.27
Aggression	0.43	0.14	0.46	0.06
Alienation	0.55	0.38	0.55	0.38
Impulse control	0.41	0.06	0.50	0.03
Emotional well-being	0.58	0.23	0.48	0.18
Traditionalism	0.50	0.47	0.53	0.39
Achievement orientation	0.36	0.07	0.36	0.07

SOURCE: Based on data from Tellegen et al., 1988

parents and teachers)—are influenced substantially by genetic factors (see the left side of Table 14.1).

This study examined identical twin pairs raised together and fraternal twins who were either both male or both female (Tellegen et al., 1988). A number of researchers have replicated these findings in twin samples from intact families (Kendler et al., 2009; Loehlin, 1992; Plomin, 2004).

The results in Table 14.1 impart another lesson that's easy to overlook. All of the identical twin correlations are substantially less than 1.0. This finding demonstrates that nonshared environment, that is, environmental influences that differ within families, plays an important role in personality (Krueger, 2000; Plomin & Daniels, 1987; Turkheimer, 2000). If heritability were 1.0 (that is, 100 percent), the identical twin correlations would also be 1.0. Because they're considerably less than 1.0, nonshared environmental influences must play a key role in personality. Regrettably, these twin findings don't tell us what these nonshared environmental influences are.

REARED-APART TWINS: SHINING A SPOTLIGHT ON GENES. Table 14.1 might tempt us to conclude that the similarities between identical twins are primarily a result of their similar upbringing rather than their shared genes. But this explanation is refuted by studies of identical and fraternal twins raised apart.

In an extraordinary investigation, researchers at the University of Minnesota spent more than two decades accumulating the largest ever sample of identical and fraternal twins reared apart—about 130 in total (Bouchard et al., 1990). Many had been separated almost immediately after birth, raised in different states and sometimes different countries, and reunited for the first time decades later in the Minneapolis–St. Paul airport.

Before psychologists conducted these studies, some prominent social scientists predicted confidently that identical twins reared apart would barely resemble each other in personality (Mischel, 1981). Were they right? The right side of Table 14.1 displays some of the principal findings from the Minnesota Twins study, as it came to be called in honor of the city's beloved baseball team. Two findings in the right side of this table stand out. First, identical twins reared apart tend to be strikingly similar in their personality traits. They're also far more similar than fraternal twins who are reared apart (Tellegen et al., 1988). A more convincing case for the role of genetic influences on personality would be hard to come by.

Second, when comparing the results in the left and right sides of Table 14.1, it's evident that identical twins reared apart are about as similar as identical twins reared together. This remarkable finding suggests that shared environment, the sum total of environmental influences shared by members of the same family, plays little or no role in the causes of adult personality. Behavior-genetic researchers have replicated this result in other twin samples (Loehlin, 1992; Pedersen et al., 1988; Vernon et al., 2008).

This finding is sufficiently surprising that it bears repeating: *Shared environment plays little or no role in adult personality*. In many respects, this may be the

Replicability

Can the results be duplicated in other studies?

Falsifiability

Can the claim be disproved?

These identical twin brothers, Gerald Levey and Mark Newman, were separated at birth. Remarkably, both became firefighters despite being unaware of each other's existence (one in New Jersey and the other in Queens, New York).

Most dream dictionaries available in bookstores imply that there are universal meanings for dream symbols. Even most psychoanalysts reject this claim.

denial

refusal to acknowledge current events in our lives

regression

the act of returning psychologically to a younger, and typically simpler and safer, age

---

Ruling Out Rival Hypotheses ▶

Have important alternative explanations for the findings been excluded?

---

reaction-formation

transformation of an anxiety-provoking emotion into its opposite

projection

unconscious attribution of our negative characteristics to others

displacement

directing an impulse from a socially unacceptable target onto a safer and more socially acceptable target

rationalization

providing a reasonable-sounding explanation for unreasonable behaviors or for failures

sublimation

transforming a socially unacceptable impulse into an admired goal

- Whereas repression deals with past events, **denial** is the refusal to acknowledge current events in our lives, such as a serious problem in our marriage. We most often observe denial in people with psychotic disorders such as schizophrenia, although individuals undergoing extreme stress occasionally engage in denial too. It's not uncommon, for example, for the relatives of individuals who've recently died in a tragic accident to insist that their loved ones must somehow, somewhere, be alive.

- **Regression** is the act of returning psychologically to a younger age, typically early childhood, when life was simpler and safer. Older children who've long since stopped sucking their thumbs sometimes suddenly resume thumb sucking under stress.

- **Reaction-formation** is the transformation of an anxiety-provoking emotion into its opposite. The observable emotion we see actually reflects the opposite emotion the person feels unconsciously. Freud contended that we can infer the presence of reaction-formation by the intensity with which the person expresses the emotion, as this emotion displays an exaggerated or "phony" quality.

In a remarkable study, Henry Adams and his colleagues found that males with high levels of *homophobia*—a dislike (not technically a fear, as the word implies) of homosexuals—showed significantly *greater* increases in penile circumference than did males with low levels of homophobia in response to sexually explicit videotapes of homosexual stimuli, such as men engaging in sex with other men (Adams, Wright, & Lohr, 1996). This finding is tantalizingly consistent with the Freudian concept of reaction-formation; some homophobics may harbor unconscious homosexual impulses they find unacceptable and transform them into a conscious dislike of homosexuals. Still, there's an alternative explanation: Anxiety can increase sexual arousal and perhaps trigger penile erections (Barlow, Sakheim, & Beck, 1983). So future investigators will need to rule out this rival hypothesis.

- **Projection** is the unconscious attribution of our negative characteristics to others. According to psychoanalysts, people with paranoia are projecting their unconscious hostility onto others. Deep down they want to harm others, but because they can't accept these impulses, they perceive others as wanting to harm them.

- Closely related to projection is **displacement**, in which we direct an impulse from a socially unacceptable target onto a safer and more socially acceptable target. After a frustrating day at work, we may pound our fist against the punching bag at the gym rather than into the faces of our annoying coworkers.

- **Rationalization** provides a reasonable-sounding explanation for our unreasonable behaviors or for failures. Some people who receive *posthypnotic suggestions* (see LO 5.3b) to perform bizarre actions engage in rationalizations to explain these actions. A participant given a posthypnotic suggestion to bark like a dog after emerging from hypnosis may do so. When the hypnotist asks him why he barked, he may rationalize his behavior: "Hmmm...I was just thinking about how much I missed my dog, so I felt like barking" (see Figure 14.3). A related defense mechanism, *intellectualization*, allows us to avoid anxiety by thinking about abstract and interpersonal ideas (refer to Table 14.4).

- **Sublimation** transforms a socially unacceptable impulse into an admired goal. George Vaillant's (1977) book *Adaptation to Life*, which is a 40-year longitudinal study of Harvard University graduates, features several striking examples of sublimation. Among them is the story of a man who set fires in childhood and went on to become chief of his local fire department.

Journal Prompt

Selecting three of Sigmund Freud's defense mechanisms, give an example from your own life of when you believe that you might have used these defense mechanisms to reduce anxiety.

Stages of Psychosexual Development

No aspect of Freud's theory is more controversial than his model of psychosexual development. Nor has any aspect of his theory been more widely criticized as pseudoscientific (Cioffi, 1998; Craddock, 2013). According to Freud, personality development proceeds through a series of stages. He termed these stages *psychosexual* because each focuses on a different sexually arousing zone of the body. Although we're accustomed to thinking of our genitals as our primary sexual organs, Freud believed that other bodily areas are sources of sexual gratification in early development. Contrary to prevailing wisdom at the time, Freud insisted that sexuality begins in infancy. He maintained that the extent to which we resolve each stage successfully bears crucial implications for later personality development. He further believed that individuals can become *fixated*, or "stuck," in an early stage of development. Fixations can occur because children were deprived of sexual gratification they were supposed to receive during that stage or were excessively gratified during that stage. In either case, they experience difficulty moving ahead to the next stage. Let's examine the five psychosexual stages as Freud conceptualized them, again bearing in mind that most modern critics don't share his views.

THE ORAL STAGE.   The first stage of psychosexual development, the **oral stage**, which generally lasts from birth to 12–18 months, focuses on the mouth. During this stage, infants obtain sexual pleasure primarily by sucking and drinking. Freud believed that adults who are orally fixated tend to react to stress by becoming intensely dependent on others for reassurance—a form of regression, according to Freud—just as infants depend on their mother's breast as a source of satisfaction. These adults also are prone to unhealthy "oral" behaviors like overeating, drinking excessively, or smoking.

THE ANAL STAGE.   At the **anal stage**, which lasts from about 18 months to 3 years, children first come face to face with psychological conflict. During this stage, children want to alleviate tension and experience pleasure by moving their bowels, but soon discover they can't do so whenever nature calls. Instead, they must learn to inhibit their urges and wait to move their bowels in a socially appropriate place—ideally, the toilet. If children's toilet training is either too harsh or too lenient, they'll become fixated and prone to regressing to this stage during anxiety-provoking circumstances. Freudians believe that anally fixated individuals—*anal personalities*—tend toward excessive neatness, stinginess, and stubbornness in adulthood.

THE PHALLIC STAGE.   The **phallic stage**, which lasts from approximately three to six years, is of paramount importance to Freudians in explaining personality. During this stage, the penis (for boys) and clitoris (for girls) become the primary sexual zone for pleasure. Simultaneously, children enter into a love triangle involving their parents. According to Freud, whether we resolve this love triangle successfully bears enormous implications for our later personality development. In boys, the phallic stage is termed the **Oedipus complex**, after the tragic Greek character who unknowingly killed his father and married his mother (in girls it's sometimes called the *Electra complex*). In girls, the phallic stage supposedly takes the form of *penis envy*, in which the girl desires to possess a penis, just like Daddy has. For reasons that Freud never clearly explained, girls believe themselves inferior to boys because of their "missing" organ, an inferiority that persists beyond childhood for years or even decades. Penis envy is probably Freud's most ridiculed concept—and with good reason, largely because there's no research support for it.

During the Oedipus complex, the child wants the opposite-sex parent all for himself or herself and wants to eliminate the same-sex parent as a rival. Ultimately, though, reality sets in, leading children to abandon their love for the opposite-sex parent. The children then identify with their same-sex parent and adopt that parent's characteristics: Like father, like son; like mother, like daughter. Nevertheless, if children don't fully resolve the Oedipus complex, claimed Freud, the stage is set for psychological problems later in life.

THE LATENCY AND GENITAL STAGES.   The fourth psychosexual stage, the **latency stage**, is a period of calm following the stormy phallic stage. During the latency stage, which lasts from about 6 to 12 years, sexual impulses are submerged into the

Figure 14.3 "Sour Grapes"

According to psychoanalysts, rationalization often involves a psychological minimization of previously desired outcomes. This etching from Aesop's fables illustrates one example of rationalization, namely, the famous "sour grapes" phenomenon: The fox, who can't reach the previously desired grapes, tells himself, "These grapes are much too green and sour. Even if I could reach them, I would not eat them."

oral stage

psychosexual stage that focuses on the mouth

Defense Mechanisms

Interactive

In this photograph from a 2008 game, frustrated player Prince Fielder throws his bat to the ground after popping out. Freudians would say that Fielder is engaging in displacement.

anal stage

psychosexual stage that focuses on toilet training

phallic stage

psychosexual stage that focuses on the genitals

Oedipus complex

conflict during phallic stage in which boys supposedly love their mothers romantically and want to eliminate their fathers as rivals

latency stage

psychosexual stage in which sexual impulses are submerged into the unconscious

genital stage

psychosexual stage in which sexual impulses awaken and typically begin to mature into romantic attraction toward others

Falsifiability

Can the claim be disproved?

Table 14.5 Freud's Stages of Psychosexual Development.

Stage	Approximate Age	Primary Source of Sexual Pleasure
Oral	Birth to 12–18 months	Sucking and drinking
Anal	18 months to 3 years	Alleviating tension by expelling feces
Phallic*	3 years to 6 years	Genitals (penis or clitoris)
Latency	6 years to 12 years	Dormant sexual stage
Genital	12 years and beyond	Renewed sexual impulses; emergence of mature romantic relationships

*Includes Oedipus and Electra complexes

unconscious. Consistent with this belief, most boys and girls during this stage find members of the opposite sex to be "yucky" and utterly unappealing.

During the fifth and final psychosexual stage, the **genital stage**—which generally begins at around age 12—sexual impulses reawaken. If development up to this point has proceeded without major glitches, this stage witnesses the emergence of mature romantic relationships. In contrast, if serious problems weren't resolved at previous stages, difficulties with establishing intimate love attachments are likely.

Psychoanalytic Theory Evaluated Scientifically

Freud's psychoanalytic theory has greatly influenced our thinking about personality, and for that reason alone, his ideas merit careful examination (Kramer, 2007). Even Freud's most vocal detractors acknowledge that he was an ingenious thinker. But ingenuity shouldn't be confused with scientific support, and many authors have raised troubling questions concerning the scientific status of psychoanalytic theory. Here we'll examine five major criticisms.

UNFALSIFIABILITY.   Critics have noted that many hypotheses derived from Freudian theory are difficult or impossible to refute (Shermer, 2011). To take just one example, the concept of the defense mechanism of reaction-formation offers a convenient escape hatch that allows many psychoanalytic hypotheses to evade falsification. If we were to find evidence that most five-year-old boys report being sexually repulsed by their mothers, would this observation refute the existence of the Oedipus complex? Superficially, the answer would seem to be yes, but Freudians could respond that these boys are engaging in reaction-formation and are attracted to their mothers at an unconscious level.

Indeed, Freud often used *ad hoc maneuvers* (see LO1.2a) to protect his pet hypotheses from refutation (Boudry, 2013; Cioffi, 1998). One of Freud's patients intensely disliked her mother-in-law and took pains to ensure that she wouldn't spend a summer vacation with her. Yet while in therapy with Freud, she dreamt of spending a summer vacation with her mother-in-law. This dream seemingly falsifies Freud's theory that all dreams are wish fulfillments (see LO 5.2a). Yet Freud argued that her dream *supported* his theory because her underlying wish was to prove Freud incorrect (Dolnick, 1998). Although we might marvel at Freud's ingenuity, this "heads I win, tails you lose" reasoning renders psychoanalytic theory difficult to falsify.

FAILED PREDICTIONS.   Although much of Freudian theory is difficult to falsify, those portions of the theory that can be falsified often have been (Grunbaum, 1984). For example, Freud claimed that children exposed to overly harsh toilet training would grow up to be rigid and perfectionistic. Yet most investigators have found no association between toilet training practices and adult personality (Fisher & Greenberg, 1996). Similarly, despite various promising attempts to measure them (Cramer, 2015), there's little scientific support for many Freudian defense mechanisms, including repression (McNally, 2003). In particular, laboratory research shows that people are no more likely to forget negative life experiences than equally arousing but positive life experiences (Holmes,

1974, 1990). Freud also predicted that his preferred method of treatment, namely psychoanalysis, was the only route to improvement. Yet, although psychotherapies based on Freudian principles tend to be more effective than no treatment at all (Shedler, 2010), there's no compelling evidence that they're more effective than a variety of other psychological interventions, including those focused on the present rather than on early childhood (Anestis, Anestis, & Lilienfeld, 2011).

QUESTIONABLE CONCEPTION OF THE UNCONSCIOUS. There's increasing reason to accept Freud's claim that much of our behavior is performed unconsciously. Nevertheless, there's increasing reason to doubt Freud's specific conceptualization of the unconscious. In fairness to Freud, he was almost surely right about two important things: We're often unaware of why we do things, and we then convince ourselves after the fact of plausible, but often erroneous explanations for why we did them. Richard Nisbett and Timothy Wilson (1977) reviewed a broad range of studies demonstrating that we often convince ourselves that we behave for reasons that are plausible but incorrect. For example, in the context of a memory study, investigators randomly exposed some participants but not others to the word pair *ocean–moon* embedded in a list of word pairs. When later asked to name their favorite laundry detergent, the former participants were significantly more likely than the latter to name "Tide." Yet when asked the reasons for their choice, none came up with the correct explanation, namely, that the words *ocean* and *moon* triggered an association to *tide*. Instead, participants came up with presumably false but plausible explanations (such as "I recently saw a Tide commercial on television").

Recent evidence suggests that subliminally presented stimuli (see LO 4.6c), that is, stimuli presented below the threshold for awareness, can sometimes affect our behavior in subtle ways (Keith & Beins, 2017; Mlodinow, 2012). Other highly controversial evidence derives from priming paradigms, in which researchers observe the effects of subtle stimuli on people's behavior (see LO 7.1c). In one sensational and widely discussed study, researchers primed some participants but not others with words relevant to old age (like *Florida* and *wrinkle*) in the context of a language task. Remarkably, after the study was over, primed participants walked down the hallway more slowly than did unprimed participants (Bargh & Chartrand, 1999). Nevertheless, several research teams have failed to replicate this and similar priming findings (Doyen et al., 2012; LeBel & Paunonen, 2011), so there's ample reason to be skeptical of them.

Some of the positive results we've described may seem to support Freudian theory because they suggest that factors of which we're unaware influence our behavior (Westen, 1998). Still, they don't provide evidence for *the* unconscious: A massive reservoir of impulses and memories submerged beneath awareness (Wilson, 2002). Freud viewed the unconscious as a "place" where sexual and aggressive energies, along with repressed memories, are housed. Research doesn't support the existence of this place, let alone tell us where it's located (Kihlstrom, 1987).

RELIANCE ON UNREPRESENTATIVE SAMPLES. Many authors have charged that Freud based his theories on atypical samples but generalized them to the rest of humanity. Most of Freud's patients were upper-class neurotic Viennese women, a far cry from the average Nigerian man or Malaysian woman. Freud's theories may therefore possess limited *external validity*, that is, generalizability (see LO 2.2a), for people from other cultural backgrounds. Moreover, although Freud's methods of inquiry were idiographic, his theory was nomothetic: He studied a relatively small number of individuals in depth, but applied his theories to virtually all of humanity.

FLAWED ASSUMPTION OF SHARED ENVIRONMENTAL INFLUENCE. Many Freudian hypotheses presume that shared environment plays a key role in molding personality. For example, Freudians claim that the child emerging from the phallic stage assumes the personality characteristics of the same-sex parent. Nevertheless, as behavior-genetic studies have shown, shared environment plays scant role in adult personality (Lewis & Bates, 2014; Loehlin, 2011), contradicting a key proposition of Freudian theory.

One of Freud's best-known patients, known as "Anna O.," was Bertha Pappenheim, who later became the founder of social work in Germany (she was even honored with her own postage stamp). Because many of Freud's patients, like Pappenheim, were relatively wealthy Viennese women, critics have questioned the generalizability of his conclusions to other cultures.

◄ **Replicability**

Can the results be duplicated in other studies?

In summary, Freudian theory has had a profound influence on modern conceptions of the mind, but much of it is problematic from a scientific standpoint. The one insight of Freud that's best stood the test of time is that we're often unaware of why we do what we do. But this insight wasn't original to Freud (Crews, 1998), and as we'll learn later in the chapter, it's consistent with other models of personality, including behaviorism. Finally, several scholars have tried to argue that Freud's insights are consistent with recent findings from neuroscience (Schwartz, 2015). For example, brain-imaging studies show that during dreams, our frontal lobes (which play key roles in tamping down undesirable thoughts and behaviors) become deactivated, broadly consistent with the Freudian idea that our normally inhibited drives and impulses become unleashed during dreams (Solms, 2013). Still, it's not at all clear that such findings offer especially compelling support for psychoanalytic views; for example, the notion that we suspend rational analysis during dreams is hardly unique to Freud. So, it's far too early to tell whether neuroscience will vindicate most, if any, of Freud's key claims.

Freud's Followers: The Neo-Freudians

Largely in reaction to criticisms of Freudian theory, a number of theorists—many of them Freud's own students—broke from their mentor to forge their own models of personality. Because these thinkers modified Freud's views in significant ways, they're typically referred to as neo-Freudians.

NEO-FREUDIAN THEORIES: CORE FEATURES. Most neo-Freudian theories share with Freudian theory an emphasis on (a) unconscious influences and (b) the importance of early experience in shaping personality. Nevertheless, **neo-Freudian theories** differ from Freudian theory in two key ways:

1. Compared with Freudian theory, Neo-Freudian theories place less emphasis on sexuality as a driving force in personality and more emphasis on social drives, such as the need for approval.
2. Compared with Freudian theory, most neo-Freudian theories are more optimistic concerning the prospects for personality growth throughout the life span. Freud was notoriously pessimistic about the possibility of personality change after childhood; he once wrote that the primary goal of psychoanalysis was to transform neurotic misery into ordinary, everyday unhappiness (Breuer & Freud, 1895).

ALFRED ADLER: THE STRIVING FOR SUPERIORITY. The first major follower of Freud to defect from the fold was Viennese psychiatrist Alfred Adler (1870–1937). According to Adler (1931), the principal motive in human personality is not sex or aggression, but the *striving for superiority*. Our overriding goal in life, said Adler, is to be better than others. We aim to accomplish this goal by crafting our distinctive **style of life**, or long-standing pattern of achieving superiority over our peers. People may try to satisfy their superiority strivings by becoming famous entertainers, great athletes, or outstanding parents.

Adler (1922) maintained that neurotic difficulties stem from early childhood; children who are either pampered or neglected by their parents are at later risk for an **inferiority complex**, a popular term inspired by Adler. People with an inferiority complex are prone to low self-esteem and tend to overcompensate for this feeling. As a result, they often attempt to demonstrate their superiority to others at all costs, even if it means dominating them. For Adler, most forms of mental illness are unhealthy attempts to overcompensate for the inferiority complex.

Adler's hypotheses, like most of Freud's, are difficult to falsify (Popper, 1965). Critics once asked Adler to explain how someone's decision to become a homeless person with alcoholism supported his theory that people always try to attain superiority over others. He responded that such a person has selected a lifestyle that affords a convenient excuse for being unable to achieve greatness. In effect, he can tell himself or herself, "If only I didn't drink, I would have become successful." As we can see, with a little creativity, we can cook up an Adlerian explanation after the fact for almost any behavior.

---

neo-Freudian theories

theories derived from Freud's model but with less emphasis on sexuality as a driving force in personality and more optimism regarding the prospects for long-term personality growth

style of life

according to Alfred Adler, each person's distinctive way of achieving superiority

inferiority complex

feelings of low self-esteem that can lead to overcompensation for such feelings

Jung believed that the collective unconscious is our shared storehouse of ancestral memories. He even claimed that episodes of synchronicity, which involve the simultaneous occurrence of thoughts and events, reflect the actions of the collective unconscious. Is this claim falsifiable?

SOURCE: © ScienceCartoonPlus.com

Falsifiability

Can the claim be disproved?

CARL JUNG: THE COLLECTIVE UNCONSCIOUS. Another pupil of Freud who parted ways with his mentor was Swiss psychiatrist Carl Gustav Jung (1875–1961). Although Freud originally anointed Jung to be the standard-bearer of the next generation of psychoanalysts, Jung became disenchanted with Freud's overemphasis on sexuality. Jung's views have become enormously influential in popular psychology, and Jung is something of a cult figure in pop psychology circles.

Jung (1936) argued that in addition to Freud's version of the unconscious—which Jung termed the *personal unconscious*—there's also a **collective unconscious**. For Jung, the collective unconscious comprises the memories that ancestors have passed down to us across the generations. It's our shared storehouse of ancestral memories that accounts for cultural similarities in myths and legends. We recognize our mothers immediately after birth, Jung argued, because the memories of thousands of generations of individuals who've seen their mothers after birth have been passed down to us genetically.

Jung further believed that the collective unconscious contains numerous **archetypes**, or cross-culturally universal symbols, which explain the similarities among people in their emotional reactions to many features of the world. Archetypes include the mother, the goddess, the hero, and the mandala (circle), which Jung believed symbolized a desire for wholeness or unity (Campbell, 1988; Jung, 1950). Jung (1958) even speculated that the modern epidemic of flying saucer reports stems from an unconscious desire to achieve a sense of unity with the universe, because flying saucers are shaped like mandalas. Some psychotherapists even use *Jungian sandplay therapy* (Steinhardt, 1998) to uncover children's deep-seated conflicts. These practitioners try to infer children's archetypes on the basis of shapes that they draw in sand and use them as a springboard for therapy. Nevertheless, there's no evidence that Jungian sandplay therapy is effective (Lilienfeld, 1999b), even though it's probably a lot of fun for children, not to mention therapists.

Provocative as it is, Jung's theory suffers from some of the same shortcomings as those of Freud and Adler. It's difficult to falsify, as it generates few clear-cut predictions (Gallo, 1994; Monte, 1995). For example, it's hard to imagine what evidence could falsify Jung's claim that flying saucer sightings stem from an underlying wish for wholeness with the universe. In addition, although Jung hypothesized that archetypes are transmitted to us from our ancestral past, he may not have sufficiently considered a rival explanation. Perhaps archetypes are cross-culturally universal because they reflect crucial elements of the environment—mothers, wise elders, the sun, and the moon (the sun and moon are, after all, shaped like mandalas)—that people across all cultures experience. Shared experiences rather than shared genes may account for commonalities in archetypes across the world (McGowan, 1994).

KAREN HORNEY: FEMINIST PSYCHOLOGY. German physician Karen Horney (1885–1952) was the first major feminist personality theorist. Although not departing drastically from Freud's core assumptions, Horney (1939) took aim at those aspects of his theory that she saw as gender biased. She viewed Freud's concept of penis envy as especially misguided. Horney maintained that women's sense of inferiority stems not from their anatomy but from their excessive dependency on men, which society has ingrained in them from an early age. She similarly objected to the Oedipus complex on the grounds that it's neither inevitable nor universal. This complex, she maintained, is a *symptom* rather than a cause of psychological problems, because it arises only when the opposite-sex parent is overly protective and the same-sex parent is overly critical.

FREUD'S FOLLOWERS EVALUATED SCIENTIFICALLY. Many neo-Freudian theorists tempered some of the excesses of Freudian theory. They pointed out that anatomy isn't always destiny when it comes to the psychological differences between the sexes, and they argued that social influences must be reckoned with in the development of personality. By and large, they also recognized that personality is less fixed over time than Freud had assumed. Nevertheless, as we've seen, falsifiability remains a serious concern for neo-Freudian theories, especially those of Adler and Jung. As a consequence, their scientific standing remains almost as controversial as that of Freudian theory.

Jung believed that the mandala was an archetype, or cross-culturally universal symbol. Jung might have taken the notion too far, neglecting to consider the fact that many other archetypes are also circular.

collective unconscious

according to Carl Jung, our shared storehouse of memories that ancestors have passed down to us across generations

archetype

cross-culturally universal symbol

Falsifiability

Can the claim be disproved?

Ruling Out Rival Hypotheses

Have important alternative explanations for the findings been excluded?

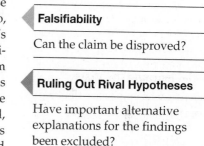
Karen Horney, the first major feminist psychological theorist, believed that Freud greatly underemphasized social factors as causes of inferiority feelings in many women.

Falsifiability

Can the claim be disproved?

14.3: Behavioral and Social Learning Theories of Personality

14.3a Identify the core assumptions of behavioral and social learning theories of personality.

14.3b Describe key criticisms of behavioral and social learning approaches.

We've already encountered behavioral models, including radical behaviorism, previously in the text (see LO 6.2b). So why are we again crossing paths with behaviorism? After all, behaviorism is a theory of learning rather than a theory of personality, isn't it?

Actually, behaviorism is both. Radical behaviorists like B. F. Skinner believe that differences in our personalities stem largely from differences in our learning histories. Unlike Freudians, radical behaviorists reject the notion that the first few years of life are especially critical in personality development. Childhood certainly matters, but our learning histories continue to mold our personalities throughout the life span.

For radical behaviorists, our personalities are bundles of habits acquired by classical and operant conditioning. In contrast to other personality theorists, radical behaviorists don't believe that personality *causes* behavior. For them, personality *consists of* behaviors. These behaviors are both overt (observable) and covert (unobservable), such as thoughts and feelings. A radical behaviorist wouldn't have much trouble accepting the idea that some people are extraverted or that extraverted people tend to have many friends and attend many parties. But a radical behaviorist would strongly dispute the conclusion that certain people have many friends and attend many parties *because* they're extraverted.

Behavioral Views of the Causes of Personality

Radical behaviorists view personality as under the control of two major influences: (a) genetic factors and (b) *contingencies* in the environment, that is, reinforcers and punishers. Together, these influences explain why our personalities differ.

BEHAVIORAL VIEWS OF DETERMINISM. Like psychoanalysts, radical behaviorists are determinists: They believe all of our actions are products of preexisting causal influences. This is one of the precious few issues on which Freud and Skinner would likely have agreed if we could magically bring them back to life for a debate, one that most modern psychologists would probably pay a sizable chunk of their life savings to witness. For radical behaviorists, free will is an illusion (see LO 1.4c). We may believe we're free to continue reading this sentence or to stop to grab a long-awaited bowl of ice cream, but we're fooling ourselves. We're convinced that we're free to select our behaviors only because we're usually oblivious to the situational factors that trigger them (Skinner, 1974).

BEHAVIORAL VIEWS OF UNCONSCIOUS PROCESSING. Both Freudians and Skinnerians agree that we often don't understand the reasons for our behavior (Overskeid, 2007), but their views of why this is the case differ sharply. For Skinner, we're "unconscious" of many things because we're often unaware of immediate situational influences on our behavior (Skinner, 1974). We may have had the experience of suddenly humming a song to ourselves and wondering why we were doing so, until we realized that this song had been playing softly on a distant radio. According to Skinner, we were initially unaware of the external cause of this behavior, in this case, the song in the background.

Yet such unawareness is a far cry from the Freudian unconscious, which is a vast storehouse of inaccessible thoughts, memories, and impulses. For radical behaviorists, there's no such storehouse because the unconscious variables that play a role in causing behavior lie *outside*, not inside, us.

Social Learning Theories of Personality: The Causal Role of Thinking Resurrected

Although initially influenced by radical behaviorists, **social learning theorists** (also sometimes called *social cognitive theorists*) believed that Skinner had gone too far in his wholesale

social learning theorists

theorists who emphasize thinking as a central cause of personality

Although this person may perceive her decision to eat or not eat a piece of candy as under her control, radical behaviorists would regard her perception as an illusion.

rejection of the influence of thoughts on behavior. Spurred on by Edward Chase Tolman and others who believed that learning depends on our plans and goals (see LO 6.3a), these theorists emphasized thinking as a cause of personality. How we interpret our environments affects how we react to them; if we perceive others as threatening, we'll typically be hostile and suspicious in return. According to social learning theorists, classical conditioning and operant conditioning are not automatic or reflexive processes; they're the products of cognition. That is, as we acquire information in classical and operant conditioning, we're actively thinking about and interpreting what this information means. For example, in classical conditioning, the organism is gradually building up expectancies regarding the relation between conditioned and unconditioned stimuli (Mischel, 1973).

SOCIAL LEARNING VIEWS OF DETERMINISM. Most social learning theorists hold a more complex view of determinism than do radical behaviorists. As we learned earlier in the text (LO 1.1a), Albert Bandura (1986) made a compelling case for **reciprocal determinism**, a form of causation whereby personality and cognitive factors, behavior, and environmental variables mutually influence one another. Our high levels of extraversion may motivate us to introduce ourselves to our introductory psychology classmates and thereby make new friends. In turn, our newfound friends may reinforce our extraversion, encouraging us to attend parties we'd otherwise skip. Attending these parties may result in our acquiring additional friends who further reinforce our extraversion, and so on.

OBSERVATIONAL LEARNING AND PERSONALITY. Social learning theorists proposed that much of learning occurs by watching others. As we learned previously in the text (LO 6.3a), *observational learning* appears to be a key form of learning neglected by traditional behaviorists (Bandura, 1965; Nadel et al., 2011). Observational learning greatly expands the range of stimuli from which we can benefit. It also means that our parents and teachers can play significant roles in shaping our personalities, because we acquire both good and bad habits by watching and later emulating them. For example, through observational learning, we can learn to behave altruistically by seeing our parents donate money to charities.

SENSE OF PERCEIVED CONTROL. Social learning theorists emphasized individuals' sense of control over life events. Julian Rotter (1966) introduced the concept of **locus of control** to describe the extent to which we believe that reinforcers and punishers lie inside or outside our control. People with an internal locus of control ("internals") believe that life events are due largely to their own efforts and personal characteristics. In contrast, people with an external locus of control ("externals") believe that life events are largely a product of chance and fate. For example, an "internal" would be likely to respond "true" to a statement such as *If I set my mind to it, I can accomplish just about anything I want*, whereas an "external" would be likely to respond "false."

Rotter hypothesized that internals are less prone than externals to emotional upset following life stressors, because they're more likely to believe they can remedy problems on their own. Indeed, almost all forms of psychological distress, including depression and anxiety, are associated with an external locus of control (Benassi, Sweeney, & Dufour, 1988; Carton & Nowicki, 1996; Coyne & Thompson, 2011). It's not clear, though, whether these correlational findings reflect a causal relationship between external locus of control and mental disorders, as Rotter supposed. Perhaps once people develop depression or anxiety, they begin to feel their lives are spiraling out of control. Or perhaps people who doubt their abilities are prone to an external locus of control, on the one hand, and depression and anxiety, on the other.

In observational learning, parents, teachers, and other adults play significant roles in shaping children's personalities: Children learn good and bad habits by watching and later emulating adults. This child may learn early that charitable giving is a worthy endeavor.

reciprocal determinism

tendency for people to mutually influence each other's behavior

locus of control

extent to which people believe that reinforcers and punishers lie inside or outside their control

▶ **Correlation vs. Causation**

Can we be sure that A causes B?

Journal Prompt

Give an example of a time in your life of a time when you relied on an external locus of control and another when you relied on an internal locus of control. Of the two (internal and external locus of control), which do you tend to use more often?

How much of the daughter's personality and mannerisms are due to social learning from her mother? The scientific jury is still out.

Replicability

Can the results be duplicated in other studies?

Behavioral and Social Learning Theories Evaluated Scientifically

B. F. Skinner and his fellow radical behaviorists agreed with Freud that our behavior is determined and that free will is an illusion, but they maintained that the primary causes of our behavior—contingencies—lie outside rather than inside us. Even critics of radical behaviorism acknowledge that Skinner and his followers placed the field of psychology on firmer scientific footing. Many of them charged, however, that the claim of radical behaviorists that our thoughts play no causal role in our behavior is implausible from an evolutionary perspective. Natural selection has endowed us with an enormous cerebral cortex, which is specialized for problem solving, planning, reasoning, and other high-level cognitive processes. It seems difficult to comprehend why our huge cortexes would have evolved if our thoughts were merely byproducts of contingencies.

Social learning theorists rekindled psychologists' interests in thinking and argued that observational learning is a crucial form of learning in addition to classical and operant conditioning. Nevertheless, social learning theory isn't immune to criticism. In particular, the claim that observational learning exerts a powerful influence over our personalities implies an important causal role of shared environment. After all, if we learn largely by modeling the behaviors of our parents and other relatives, we should become like them. Yet as we've learned, behavior-genetic studies have shown that the effects of shared environment on adult personality are weak or nonexistent (Harris, 2002).

Although social learning theorists believe that learning processes depend on cognition (thinking); scientists have observed these processes in animals with tiny cerebral cortexes and even with no cortexes at all. For example, they've documented classical conditioning in honeybees (Alcock, 1999) and starfish (McClintock & Lawrence, 1985). There's even evidence that classical conditioning occurs in such microscopic organisms as protozoa (Bergstrom, 1968) and hydra (Tanaka, 1966), although not all researchers have replicated these findings (Applewhite et al., 1971). There have also been reports of observational learning in the octopus (Fiorito & Scotto, 1993), although these findings are controversial.

The fact that learning occurs in animals with quite simple nervous systems implies any one of three things. First, perhaps social learning theorists are wrong that basic forms of learning depend on cognition. Second, perhaps the thinking processes involved in these forms of learning are primitive in certain cases, although we might justifiably question whether a starfish, let alone a protozoan, is capable of genuine "thought." Third, the learning processes of simple animals may rely on different mechanisms from those of humans. At this point, the scientific evidence doesn't permit a clear answer.

14.4: Humanistic Models of Personality: The Third Force

14.4a Explain the concept of self-actualization and its role in humanistic models.
14.4b Describe key criticisms of humanistic approaches.

Psychoanalytic theory, along with behavioral and social learning models, dominated personality psychology throughout the first half of the 20th century. In the 1950s and 1960s, however, *humanistic models* emerged as a "third force" in personality psychology. Humanistic psychologists rejected the strict determinism of psychoanalysts and behaviorists and embraced the notion of free will. We're perfectly free, they maintained, to choose either socially constructive or destructive paths in life.

Most humanistic psychologists propose that the core motive in personality is **self-actualization**: the drive to develop our innate potential to the fullest possible extent (see LO 11.4a). Most Freudians would say that self-actualization would be disastrous for society because our innate drives, housed in the id, are selfish and potentially harmful if not controlled. For Freudians, a society of self-actualized people would result in sheer pandemonium, with citizens expressing their sexual and aggressive urges with reckless abandon. Humanistic theorists, in contrast, view human nature as inherently constructive, so they see self-actualization as a worthy goal.

self-actualization

drive to develop our innate potential to the fullest possible extent

Rogers and Maslow: Self-Actualization Realized and Unrealized

The best-known humanistic theorist was Carl Rogers (1902–1987), who used his personality theory as a point of departure for an influential form of psychotherapy that we'll discuss later the text. Ever the optimist, Rogers believed that we could all achieve our full potential for emotional fulfillment if only society allowed it.

ROGERS'S MODEL OF PERSONALITY.   According to Rogers (1947), our personalities consist of three major components: organism, self, and conditions of worth.

1. The *organism* is our innate—and substantially genetically influenced—blueprint. In this regard, it's like the Freudian id, except that Rogers viewed the organism as inherently positive and helpful toward others. Rogers wasn't terribly specific, however, about the makeup of the organism.
2. The *self* is our self-concept, the set of beliefs about who we are.
3. **Conditions of worth** are the expectations we place on ourselves for appropriate and inappropriate behavior. Like the Freudian superego, they emanate from our parents and society, and eventually we internalize them. Conditions of worth arise—typically in childhood—when others make their acceptance of us conditional (that is, dependent) on certain behaviors but not others. As a result, we accept ourselves only if we act in certain ways. A child who enjoys writing poetry may develop conditions of worth if taunted by peers. "When I'm teased for writing poetry, I'm not worthwhile. When I stop, I'm not teased; so I become worthwhile." For Rogers, individual differences in personality stem largely from differences in the conditions of worth that others impose on us. Although in his idealistic moments Rogers envisioned a world in which conditions of worth no longer existed, he reluctantly acknowledged that in modern society, even the best adjusted among us inevitably harbor certain conditions of worth. Conditions of worth result in **incongruence** between self and organism. Incongruence means that our personalities are inconsistent with our innate dispositions: We're no longer our genuine selves, because we're acting in ways that are inconsistent with our genuine potentialities.

MASLOW: THE CHARACTERISTICS OF SELF-ACTUALIZED PEOPLE.   Whereas Rogers focused largely on individuals whose tendencies toward self-actualization were thwarted and therefore ended up with psychological problems, Abraham Maslow (1908–1970) focused on individuals who were self-actualized, especially historical figures. He regarded full self-actualization as a rare feat, one accomplished by only about 2 percent of people. Among those whom Maslow considered self-actualized were Thomas Jefferson, Abraham Lincoln, Martin Luther King, Jr., Helen Keller, and Mahatma Gandhi.

According to Maslow (1971), self-actualized people tend to be creative, spontaneous, and accepting of themselves and others. They're self-confident but not self-centered. They focus on real-world and intellectual problems and have a few deep friendships rather than many superficial ones. Contrary to what we might expect, self-actualized individuals typically crave privacy and can come off as aloof or even difficult to deal with, because they've outgrown the need to be popular. As a consequence, they're not afraid to "rock the boat" when necessary or express unpopular opinions. They're also prone to **peak experiences**—transcendent moments of intense excitement and tranquility marked by a profound sense of connection to the world.

Carl Rogers, pioneer of humanistic psychology, held an optimistic view of human nature, although some critics have accused him of being naive in minimizing the dark side of human nature.

conditions of worth

according to Carl Rogers, expectations we place on ourselves for appropriate and inappropriate behavior

incongruence

inconsistency between our personalities and innate dispositions

peak experience

transcendent moment of intense excitement and tranquility marked by a profound sense of connection to the world

Mahatma Gandhi is one of the historical figures whom Abraham Maslow considered to be self-actualized.

Journal Prompt

Your text provides several historical examples of people that Abraham Maslow considered to have achieved self-actualization. Describe the characteristics of a self-actualized person in your own words, and provide an example of a person you know whom you believe meets most or all of these characteristics. Why do you believe that this person is self-actualized in Maslow's terms?

Humanistic Models Evaluated Scientifically

Humanistic models of personality boldly proclaimed the importance of free will and personal choice and appealed to a generation of young people disenchanted with the determinism of psychoanalysis and behaviorism. Yet investigators in *comparative psychology*, the branch of psychology that compares behavior across species, have challenged Rogers's claim that human nature is entirely positive. Their research suggests that the capacity for aggression is inherent in our close primate cousins, the chimpanzees (Goodall & van Lawick, 1971; Wrangham & Glowacki, 2012). There's also compelling evidence from twin studies that aggression is part of humans' genetic heritage (Anholt, 2012; Krueger, Hicks, & McGue, 2001; Porsch et al., 2016). Therefore, actualization of our full genetic potential is unlikely to bring about the state of eternal bliss that Rogers imagined. At the same time, research suggests that the capacity for altruism is intrinsic to both chimpanzees and humans (de Waal, 1990, 2009; Wilson, 1993). Human nature, it seems, is a complex mix of selfish and selfless motives.

Rogers's research demonstrated that the discrepancy between people's descriptions of their actual versus ideal selves is greater for emotionally disturbed than for emotionally healthy individuals. This difference decreases over the course of psychotherapy (Rogers & Dymond, 1954). Rogers interpreted this finding as reflecting a lessening of conditions of worth. Yet these results are hard to interpret, because the people who showed decreases in incongruence following therapy weren't the same people who improved (Loevinger, 1987).

Maslow's research on the characteristics of self-actualized individuals paved the way for today's influential but controversial "positive psychology" movement (see LO 11.3b). Indeed, although he rarely receives credit for it, Maslow (1954) introduced this term. Yet his work is problematic on methodological grounds. In beginning with the assumption that self-actualized individuals tend to be creative and spontaneous, Maslow may have limited his search to historical figures who displayed these traits. As such, he may have fallen prey to confirmation bias (Aronson, 2011; LO 1.1b): Because he wasn't blind to his hypothesis concerning the personality features of self-actualized individuals, he had no sure way of guarding against this bias.

Falsifiability

Can the claim be disproved?

Humanistic models are also difficult to falsify. If a study of the general population showed that many people were self-actualized, humanistic psychologists could interpret this finding as evidence that self-actualization is a key influence on personality. But if this study showed that virtually no one was self-actualized, humanistic psychologists could explain away this finding by saying that most individuals' drives toward self-actualization had been stifled. Although the claim that self-actualization is the central motive in personality may not be testable scientifically, the principle that we should develop our potential to the fullest may have considerable value as a philosophy of life.

14.5: Trait Models of Personality: Consistencies in Our Behavior

14.5a Describe trait models of personality, including the Big Five.
14.5b Identify key criticisms of trait models.

In contrast to most personality theorists we've reviewed, proponents of trait models are interested primarily in describing and understanding the *structure* of personality. That is, they examine the question of what makes up our personality, rather than the question of what causes it. Much like early chemists who strove to identify the elements of the periodic table, trait theorists aim to pinpoint the major elements—in psychological terms, traits—of personality, which, as we've learned, are relatively enduring dispositions that affect our behaviors across situations. Moreover, whereas the personality theories we've reviewed are interested primarily in commonalities among people, trait psychologists are interested largely in *individual differences* (see LO 1.1a). They strive to answer the question: Why do we differ from each other in our tendencies to act, think, and feel in characteristic ways?

Identifying Traits: Factor Analysis

Invoking personality traits as causes of behavior has its challenges. To start with, we must avoid the *circular reasoning fallacy* (see LO 1.2b). We might conclude that a child who kicks others on the playground is aggressive. But in asking how we know that the child is aggressive, we might respond "because he kicks other children on the playground." Note that this answer merely restates the same evidence we used to infer that the child was aggressive in the first place, so we're just reasoning in a big circle. To avoid this error in logic, we need to demonstrate that personality traits predict behaviors in novel situations or correlate with biological or laboratory measures.

From there, we need to narrow down the pool of possible traits. That's much easier than it sounds. As the pioneering personality theorist Gordon Allport observed, there are more than 17,000 terms in the English language referring to personality traits: shy, stubborn, impulsive, greedy, cheerful, and on and on (Allport & Odbert, 1936). To reduce this enormous diversity of traits to a much smaller number of underlying traits, trait theorists commonly use a statistical technique called **factor analysis**. This method analyzes the correlations among responses on personality measures to identify the underlying "factors" that give rise to these correlations. Let's start with an example.

Table 14.6 presents the correlations among six different variables—sociability, popularity, liveliness, risk-taking, sensation seeking, and impulsivity—in a hypothetical correlation matrix: a table of correlations. As we look over this correlation matrix, we'll notice that only some of the cells contain numbers; that's because correlation matrixes present each correlation only once. (That's why, for example, the matrix displays the correlation between variables 1 and 4 only once.) We can see that variables 1 through 3 are highly correlated, as are variables 4 through 6 (recall that the maximum correlation between two variables is 1.0). But these two sets of variables aren't correlated much with one another, so the correlation matrix suggests the presence of two factors. We might tentatively call the factor comprising variables 1 through 3 (in bold) "extraversion," and we might call the factor comprising variables 4 through 6 (non-bold) "fearlessness." The formal technique of factor analysis uses more rigorous statistical criteria to accomplish the same goal as the "eyeball method" we just walked you through.

The Big Five Model of Personality: The Geography of the Psyche

Although there's no universal consensus among trait theorists regarding the most scientifically supported model of personality structure, one model has amassed an impressive body of research evidence. This model, often called the **Big Five**, consists of five traits that have surfaced repeatedly in factor analyses of reasonably comprehensive personality measures.

Circular Reasoning

Concluding that a child is "aggressive" merely because he or she engages in aggressive behavior is an example of circular reasoning. To be meaningful, personality traits must do more than simply describe behaviors we've already observed.

factor analysis

statistical technique that analyzes the correlations among responses on personality inventories and other measures

Big Five

five traits that have surfaced repeatedly in factor analyses of personality measures

---

Table 14.6 An "Eyeball" Factor Analysis of Six Variables.

Follow along as we describe this correlation matrix of six personality measures (the 1.00s on the diagonal represent the correlation of each variable with itself, which is a perfect correlation).

	Measures					
	Variable 1 Sociability	**Variable 2 Popularity**	**Variable 3 Liveliness**	**Variable 4 Risk-Taking**	**Variable 5 Sensation Seeking**	**Variable 6 Impulsivity**
Variable 1	1.00	**0.78**	**0.82**	0.12	0.07	−0.03
Variable 2		1.00	**0.70**	0.08	0.02	0.11
Variable 3			1.00	0.05	0.11	0.18
Variable 4				1.00	**0.69**	**0.85**
Variable 5					1.00	**0.72**
Variable 6						1.00

Figure 14.4 Sheldon's Body Types

According to William Sheldon, three major body types are associated with different personality traits. Yet research hasn't borne out most of Sheldon's claims. Because Sheldon wasn't blind to body type when rating people's personality traits, his findings may have been due largely to confirmation bias.

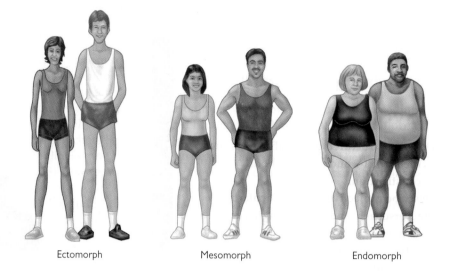

Ectomorph Mesomorph Endomorph

Reliability, we'll recall, refers to consistency of measurement and *validity* to the extent to which a test measures what it purports to measure. We'll keep these dual criteria in mind as we survey the two major types of personality tests: structured and projective.

Structured Personality Tests

structured personality test

paper-and-pencil measure consisting of questions that respondents answer in one of a few fixed ways

The best-known personality instruments are **structured personality tests**. Psychologists sometimes also call them "objective" tests, although this term is somewhat misleading, because responses to structured test items are often still open to interpretation on the part of examiners. Most structured personality tests are paper-and-pencil measures consisting of questions that respondents answer in one of a few fixed ways. By fixed ways, we mean choosing between true and false answers or by selecting options on a scale with, for example, 1 being "always true," 2 being "somewhat true," and so on, until 5, which is "always false" (these numerical scales are called *Likert* formats). Structured personality tests have several advantages: They're typically easy to administer and score, and they allow researchers to collect data from many participants simultaneously.

Minnesota Multiphasic Personality Inventory (MMPI)

widely used structured personality test designed to assess symptoms of mental disorders

MMPI AND MMPI-2: DETECTING ABNORMAL PERSONALITY. The **Minnesota Multiphasic Personality Inventory (MMPI)** (Hathaway & McKinley, 1940) is the most extensively researched of all structured personality tests. Psychologists across the world use the MMPI to detect symptoms of major mental disorders. Developed in the early 1940s by psychologist Starke Hathaway and neurologist J. Charnley McKinley of the University of Minnesota, the MMPI was revised in the 1980s by James Butcher and his colleagues (Butcher et al., 1989). This revised test, the MMPI-2, consists of 567 true-false items.

MMPI and MMPI-2: Construction and Content. The MMPI-2, like its predecessor, consists of 10 *basic* scales, 8 of which are designed to detect symptoms of several major mental disorders, such as paranoia, depression, and schizophrenia. Hathaway and McKinley developed these scales by means of an **empirical method of test construction**. Using an empirical (or data-based) approach, researchers begin with two or more criterion groups, such as a group of people with a specific psychological disorder and a group of people with no psychological disorder, and examine which items best distinguish these groups. For example, the items on the MMPI depression scale are those that best differentiate persons with clinical depression from those with no diagnosed mental disorder.

empirical method of test construction

approach to building tests in which researchers begin with two or more criterion groups and examine which items best differentiate them

face validity

extent to which respondents can tell what the items are measuring

One consequence of the empirical method of test construction is that many MMPI and MMPI-2 items possess low **face validity**. Face validity is the extent to which respondents can tell what the items are measuring. In a face-valid test, we can take the items on "face value": They assess what they seem to assess. Face validity is actually a misnomer, because it isn't really a form of validity at all. Because Hathaway and McKinley were concerned only with *whether*, not *why*, the MMPI items differentiated among criterion groups, they ended up with many items that bear little obvious connection with the disorder they supposedly

Fact vs. Fiction

Interactive

Informal (unstructured) interviews (interviews that lack standardized questions and scoring criteria), which are used widely to select job applicants and college students for admissions purposes, are a highly reliable and valid method of assessing personality. (See bottom of page for answer.)

○ Fact

○ Fiction.

assess. As an example of an item with low face validity from another widely used structured personality test, can you guess which personality trait the following item assesses: "I think newborn babies look very much like little monkeys"? The answer is nurturance, that is, a tendency to care for others—with a "True" answer reflecting low nurturance and a "False" answer reflecting high nurturance—although few test-takers can figure that out (Jackson, 1971, p. 238).

Researchers can't agree on whether low face validity is an overall advantage or disadvantage. Some believe that items with low face validity assess key aspects of personality that are subtle or lie outside respondents' awareness (Meehl, 1945). Moreover, such items have the advantage of being difficult for respondents to fake. In contrast, other researchers believe that these items don't add to the MMPI's diagnostic capacity (Jackson, 1971; Weed, Ben-Porath, & Butcher, 1990).

The MMPI-2 contains three major *validity* scales. These scales detect various *response sets*, which are tendencies to distort responses to items (see LO 2.2a). Response sets, which can diminish the validity of psychological tests, include *impression management*—making ourselves look better than we really are—and *malingering*—making ourselves appear psychologically disturbed even when we're not. The MMPI L (Lie) Scale consists of items assessing the denial of trivial faults (such as "I occasionally become angry"). If you deny a large number of such faults, it's likely that you're either (a) engaging in impression management or (b) a promising candidate for sainthood. Given that (a) is more likely than (b), psychologists typically use scores on the L scale to detect a dishonest approach to test-taking. The F (Frequency) Scale consists of items that people in the general population rarely endorse (such as "I have a cough most of the time"). High scores on F can indicate malingering, although they can also reflect serious psychological disturbance or carelessness in responding to items. The K (Correction) Scale consists of items that are similar to, although subtler than, those on the L scale; this scale measures defensive or guarded responding (Graham, 2011).

As we can see in Figure 14.5, psychologists plot the 10 basic scales and 3 validity scales of the MMPI-2 in profile form, which displays the pattern of each person's scale scores. Although many clinicians enjoy interpreting MMPI-2 profiles, research demonstrates that simple statistical formulas that can be programmed into a computer yield interpretations that are equally, if not more, valid than those of experienced clinicians (Fokkema et al., 2015; Garb, 1998; Goldberg, 1969). Nevertheless, these findings, which hold not only for the MMPI-2, but also for most or even all personality tests, seem not to have exerted an appreciable impact on clinical practice (Dawes, Faust, & Meehl, 1989; Vrieze & Grove, 2009).

The MMPI and MMPI-2 Evaluated Scientifically. Extensive research supports the reliability of most MMPI-2 scales, as well as their validity for differentiating among mental disorders (Graham, 2011; Greene, 2000; Nichols, 2011). For example, the MMPI-2 schizophrenia scale distinguishes individuals with schizophrenia from those with other severe disorders, like clinical depression (Walters & Greene, 1988).

Answer: Fiction Different interviewers frequently disagree on their impressions of interviewees (McDaniel et al., 1994; Weisner & Cronshaw, 1988). Moreover, the predictive validity of unstructured interview tends to be low. Most interviewers are convinced that such interviews are extremely valid for inferring personality even though they are mistaken (Dana, Dawes, & Peterson, 2013).

Like graphologists, the students in the Chapmans' study probably relied on the representativeness heuristic: Like goes with like (Kahneman, 2011). As a result, they were fooled, because things that seem similar on the surface don't always go together in real life. These students probably also relied on availability heuristic (see LO 8.1b), recalling the cases in which drawing signs correspond to personality traits and forgetting the cases in which they don't. Clinicians, being mere mortals like the rest of us, can easily fall victim to these heuristics too, which may explain why some of them are convinced that certain personality tests are more valid than the scientific evidence indicates.

These commonplace errors in thinking remind us of a theme we've underscored throughout this book: Personal experience, although useful in generating hypotheses, can be misleading when it comes to testing them. But there's good news here too.

Scientific methods, which are essential safeguards against human error, can allow us to determine whether we should trust our personal experience or disregard it in favor of evidence to the contrary. In this way, these methods can help us reduce the risk of error and help us to better measure and understand personality.

Summary: Personality

14.1: Personality: What Is It and How Can We Study It?

14.1a Describe how twin and adoption studies shed light on genetic and environmental influences on personality.

Twin and adoption studies suggest that many personality traits are heritable and point to a key role for nonshared environment, but not shared environment, for adult personality.

14.2: Psychoanalytic Theory: The Controversial Legacy of Sigmund Freud and His Followers

14.2a Describe the core assumptions of psychoanalytic theory.

Freud's psychoanalytic theory rests on three core assumptions: psychic determinism, symbolic meaning, and unconscious motivation. According to Freud, personality results from the interactions among id, ego, and superego. The ego copes with threat by deploying defense mechanisms. Freud's five psychosexual stages are oral, anal, phallic, latency, and genital.

14.2b Describe key criticisms of psychoanalytic theory and the central features of neo-Freudian theories.

Psychoanalytic theory has been criticized on several grounds, including unfalsifiability, failed predictions, questionable conception of the unconscious, lack of evidence, and a flawed assumption of shared environmental influence. Neo-Freudians shared with Freud an emphasis on unconscious influences and the importance of early experience, but placed less emphasis on sexuality as a driving force in personality.

14.3: Behavioral and Social Learning Theories of Personality

14.3a Identify the core assumptions of behavioral and social learning theories of personality.

Radical behaviorists view personality as under the control of two major influences: genetic factors and contingencies in the environment. Radical behaviorists, like psychoanalysts, are determinists and believe in unconscious processing, but deny the existence of "the" unconscious. In contrast to radical behaviorists, social learning theorists accord a central role to thinking in the causes of personality and argue that observational learning and a sense of personal control play key roles in personality.

14.3b Describe key criticisms of behavioral and social learning approaches.

Critics have accused radical behaviorists of going too far in their exclusion of thinking as a cause of personality. The social learning theory claim that observational learning plays a crucial role in personality runs counter to findings that shared environmental influence on adult personality is minimal.

14.4: Humanistic Models of Personality: The Third Force

14.4a Explain the concept of self-actualization and its role in humanistic models.

Most humanistic psychologists argue that the core motive in personality is self-actualization. According to Carl Rogers, unhealthy behavior results from the imposition of conditions of worth, which block drives toward self-actualization. According to Abraham Maslow, self-actualized individuals are creative, spontaneous, accepting, and prone to peak experiences.

14.4b Describe key criticisms of humanistic approaches.

Critics have attacked humanistic models for being naive about human nature and for advancing theories that are difficult to falsify.

14.5: Trait Models of Personality: Consistencies in Our Behavior

14.5a Describe trait models of personality, including the Big Five.

Trait theories use factor analysis to identify groups of personality features that tend to correlate with each other. These groupings often correspond to broader traits such as extraversion and agreeableness. One influential model of personality is the Big Five, which predicts many important aspects of real-world behavior, including job performance. Nevertheless, the Big Five may be limited as a model of personality structure because people may not have conscious access to all important features of personality.

14.5b Identify key criticisms of trait models.

In the late 1960s, Walter Mischel pointed out that personality traits rarely predict isolated behaviors with high levels of accuracy; later research vindicated his claim, but demonstrated that personality traits are often helpful in predicting long-term behavioral trends. Some models of personality structure, including the Big Five, are more descriptive than explanatory.

14.6: Personality Assessment: Measuring and Mismeasuring the Psyche

14.6a Describe structured personality tests such as the MMPI-2 and their methods of construction.

Structured personality tests consist of questions that people can answer in only one of a few fixed ways. Some, like the MMPI-2 and CPI, were developed empirically; others, like the NEO-PI-R, were developed rationally/theoretically.

14.6b Describe projective tests, particularly the Rorschach, and their strengths and weaknesses.

Projective tests consist of ambiguous stimuli that the examinee must interpret. Many of these tests lack adequate levels of reliability, validity, and incremental validity.

14.6c Identify common pitfalls in personality assessment.

Two common pitfalls in personality assessment are the P. T. Barnum effect and illusory correlation. Both errors highlight the need for scientific methods as safeguards against human error.

Chapter 15
Psychological Disorders

When Adaptation Breaks Down

Learning Objectives

15.1a Identify criteria for defining mental disorders.

15.1b Describe conceptions of diagnoses across history and cultures.

15.1c Identify common misconceptions about psychiatric diagnoses and the strengths and limitations of the current diagnostic system.

15.2a Describe the many ways people experience anxiety.

15.3a Identify the characteristics of different mood disorders.

15.3b Describe major explanations for depression and how life events can interact with characteristics of the individual to produce depression symptoms.

15.3c Identify common myths and misconceptions about suicide.

15.4a Identify the characteristics of borderline and psychopathic personality disorders.

15.4b Explain the controversies surrounding dissociative disorders, especially dissociative identity disorder.

15.5a Recognize the characteristic symptoms of schizophrenia.

15.5b Explain how psychosocial, neural, biochemical, and genetic influences create the vulnerability to schizophrenia.

15.6a Describe the symptoms and debate surrounding disorders diagnosed in childhood.

Challenge Your Assumptions

Are psychiatric diagnoses just labels for undesirable behaviors?

Is the insanity defense usually unsuccessful?

Does virtually everyone who attempts suicide want to die?

Is schizophrenia different from multiple personality disorder?

Are most people with psychopathic personalities violent?

The videos of the three patients you just watched bring into bold relief the different ways in which psychological disorders touch the lives of people and often interfere with their ability to work, play, and live life to the fullest.

Martha, a middle-aged Asian woman has been diagnosed with depression. Her bleak mood has taken a severe toll on her eating and sleeping habits to the point that she "barely eats or sleeps." Even when she does eat, she does so without gusto, unable to taste her favorite foods. Her energy is sapped, she feels weak, and she experiences trembling in her arms and bones.

Dave, a white man in his late 30s, has been diagnosed with obsessive-compulsive disorder. He feels compelled to engage in repetitive behaviors that serve no purpose other than to temporarily alleviate his anxiety and uncertainty. For example, he can lock his own front door and walk away, no problem. But when it comes to someone else's front door, it's quite a different story; it sometimes takes him 20 times to lock the door and feel satisfied that it's locked. He's even broken keys in locks while trying to reassure himself that the door is closed securely. Unfortunately, his relief is only short-lived.

Larry, a white man in his early 40s, has been diagnosed with schizophrenia. He speaks in a flat voice, revealing little emotion, his speech punctuated with pauses. He occasionally hears voices in his head and he talks to himself. His voices are companions, some fictional and some nonfictional. The first sign of his mental disorder emerged when he was very young. He drew charts of fictional baseball players and gave each player a name that he invented. Although this passion for baseball and mental games might not be all that unusual for a child, it fore-shadowed far more serious problems later in life confusing fantasy with reality.

These are only a few of the examples of mental disorders that we'll encounter in this chapter. We'll explore how psychologists have conceptualized and diagnosed mental illness historically and right up to the present, describe the symptoms of psychological disorders, and discuss researchers' increasingly sophisticated efforts to understand the causes of mental conditions.

15.1: Conceptions of Mental Illness: Yesterday and Today

15.1a **Identify criteria for defining mental disorders.**

15.1b **Describe conceptions of diagnoses across history and cultures.**

15.1c **Identify common misconceptions about psychiatric diagnoses and the strengths and limitations of the current diagnostic system.**

These brief sketches don't do justice to the extraordinarily rich and complex lives of these three people, but they give us some sense of the broad scope of *psychopathology*, or mental illness. But what do Martha, Dave, and Larry have in common? Putting it differently, what distinguishes psychological abnormality from normality?

What Is Mental Illness? A Deceptively Complex Question

The answer to this question isn't as simple as we might assume because the concept of *mental disorder* doesn't lend itself to a clear-cut dictionary definition (McNally, 2011). Instead, psychologists and psychiatrists have proposed a host of criteria for what mental disorder is. We'll review five of them here. Each criterion captures something important about mental disorder, but each has its shortcomings (Gorenstein, 1984; Wakefield, 1992).

STATISTICAL RARITY. Many mental disorders such as schizophrenia are uncommon. Yet we can't rely on statistical rarity to define mental disorder because not all infrequent conditions—such as extraordinary creativity—are pathological or indicative of mental illness, and many mental disorders—such as mild depression—are quite common (Kendell, 1975).

SUBJECTIVE DISTRESS. Most mental disorders produce emotional pain for individuals afflicted with them, but not all of them do. For example, during the manic phases of bipolar disorder, people frequently feel better than normal and perceive nothing wrong with their behaviors. Similarly, many adults with antisocial personality disorder experience less distress than the typical person.

IMPAIRMENT. Most mental disorders interfere with people's ability to function in everyday life. These disorders can destroy marriages, friendships, and jobs. Yet the presence of impairment by itself can't define mental illness because some conditions, such as laziness, can produce impairment but aren't mental disorders.

SOCIETAL DISAPPROVAL. Nearly 50 years ago, Thomas Szasz (1960) argued famously that "mental illness is a myth" and that "mental disorders" are nothing more than conditions that society dislikes. He even proposed that psychologists and psychiatrists use diagnoses as weapons of control; by attaching negative labels to people whose behaviors they find objectionable, they're putting these people "in their place." Szasz was both right and wrong. He was right that our negative attitudes toward those with serious mental illnesses are often deep-seated and widespread. Szasz was also right that societal attitudes shape our views of abnormality.

Indeed, psychiatric diagnoses have often mirrored the views of the times. For centuries, some psychiatrists invoked the diagnosis of *masturbational insanity* to describe individuals whose compulsive masturbation supposedly drove them mad (Hare, 1962). Homosexuality was classified as a mental illness until members of the American Psychiatric Association voted to remove it from their list of disorders in 1973 (Bayer, 1981; see Chapter 11). As society became more accepting of homosexuality, mental health professionals came to reject the view that such behavior is pathological.

But Szasz was wrong that society regards all disapproved conditions as mental disorders (Wakefield, 1992). For example, racism is justifiably deplored by society, but isn't considered a mental disorder (Yamey & Shaw, 2002). Neither is messiness nor rudeness, even though they're both considered undesirable by society.

Psychiatric diagnoses are often shaped by the views—and biases—of the historical period. In the mid-1800s, some psychiatrists applied the diagnosis of *drapetomania* to describe the "disorder" of slaves who attempted repeatedly to escape from their masters. One physician even prescribed whipping and toe amputation as "treatments" for this condition (Cartwright, 1851).

BIOLOGICAL DYSFUNCTION. Many mental disorders probably result from breakdowns or failures of physiological systems. For example, we'll learn that schizophrenia is often marked by an underactivity in the brain's frontal lobes. In contrast, some mental disorders, such as specific phobias, which are intense and irrational fears, appear to be acquired largely through learning experiences and often require only a weak genetic predisposition to trigger them.

In fact, it's unlikely that any one criterion distinguishes mental disorders from normality (McNally, 2011; Stein et al., 2010). As a consequence, some authors have argued for a *family resemblance view* of mental disorder (Kirmayer & Young, 1999;

Lilienfeld & Marino, 1995; Rosenhan & Seligman, 1989). From this perspective, mental disorders don't all have one thing in common. Just as brothers and sisters within a family look similar but don't all possess the same eyes, ears, or noses, mental disorders share a loose set of features. These features include those we've described—statistical rarity, subjective distress, impairment, societal disapproval, and biological dysfunction—as well as others, such as a need for treatment, irrationality, and loss of control over one's behavior (Bergner, 1997).

The infamous "dunking test" for witches was popular during the witch scares of the 16th and 17th centuries. According to the dunking test, if a woman drowned, it meant she wasn't a witch. In contrast, if she floated to the top of the water, it meant she was a witch and needed to be executed. Either way, she died.

Historical Conceptions of Mental Illness: From Demons to Asylums

Throughout history, people have recognized certain behaviors as abnormal. Yet their explanations and treatments for these behaviors have shifted in tune with prevailing cultural conceptions. The history of society's evolving views of mental illness tells the fascinating story of a bumpy road from nonscience to science.

CONCEPTIONS OF MENTAL DISORDERS: FROM THE DEMONIC TO THE MEDICAL MODEL. During the Middle Ages, many people in Europe and later in America viewed mental illnesses through the lens of a **demonic model**. They attributed hearing voices, talking to oneself, and behaving oddly to the actions of evil spirits infesting the body (Hunter & Macalpine, 1963). The often bizarre "treatments" of the day, including exorcisms, flowed directly from the demonic model. Yet the legacy of the demonic model lives on today in the thousands of exorcisms still performed in Italy, Mexico, and other countries (Harrington, 2005).

As the Middle Ages faded and the Renaissance took hold, views of those with mental illness became more enlightened. More people came to perceive mental illness primarily as a physical disorder requiring medical treatment—a view sometimes called the **medical model** (Blaney, 1975). Beginning in the 15th century, European governments began to house these individuals in **asylums**—institutions for those with mental illness (Gottesman, 1991).

Yet the medical treatments of that era were scarcely more scientific than those of the demonic era, and several were equally barbaric. Treatments included "bloodletting" (the draining of "excessive" blood, then believed to cause mental illness) and frightening patients "out of their diseases" by tossing them into a snake pit, hence the term *snake pit* as a synonym for an insane asylum (Szasz, 2006).

Not surprisingly, most patients of this era deteriorated, and in the case of bloodletting, some died. Even those who improved in the short term may have merely been responding to the *placebo effect*—improvement resulting from the expectation of improvement (Horowitz, 2012). Yet few physicians of the day considered the placebo effect as a rival explanation for these treatments' seeming effectiveness (Lilienfeld et al., 2014). Although most of these treatments seem preposterous today, it's crucial to recognize that psychological and medical treatments are products of the times. Society's beliefs about the causes of mental illness shape its interventions.

Fortunately, reform was on the way. Thanks to the heroic efforts of Phillippe Pinel (1745–1826) in France and Dorothea Dix (1802–1887) in America, an approach called **moral treatment** gained a foothold in Europe and America. Advocates of moral treatment insisted that those with mental illness be treated with dignity, kindness, and respect. Before moral treatment, patients in asylums were often bound in chains; following moral treatment, they were free to roam the halls of hospitals, get fresh air, and interact freely with staff and other patients. Still, effective treatments for mental illnesses were virtually nonexistent, so many people continued to suffer for years with no hope of relief.

THE MODERN ERA OF PSYCHIATRIC TREATMENT. It wasn't until the early 1950s that a dramatic change in the treatment of mental illness arrived on the scene. It was then that psychiatrists introduced a medication imported from France called *chlorpromazine* (its brand name is Thorazine) into mental hospitals. Chlorpromazine wasn't a miracle cure, but it offered a modestly effective treatment for some symptoms of schizophrenia and similar

demonic model

view of mental illness in which behaving oddly, hearing voices, or talking to oneself was attributed to evil spirits infesting the body

medical model

view of mental illness as a result of a physical disorder requiring medical treatment

asylum

institution for people with mental illnesses created in the 15th century

> **Ruling Out Rival Hypotheses**
>
> Have important alternative explanations for the findings been excluded?

moral treatment

Approach to mental illness calling for dignity, kindness, and respect for those with mental illness

Dorothea Dix was a Massachusetts school-teacher whose lobbying efforts resulted in the establishment of more humane psychiatric facilities in the 1800s.

deinstitutionalization

the governmental policy of the 1960s and 1970s that focused on releasing hospitalized psychiatric patients into the community and closing mental hospitals

disorders marked by a partial loss of contact with reality. Many patients with these conditions became able to function independently, and some returned to their families and jobs.

By the 1960s and 1970s, the advent of chlorpromazine and similar medications (see LO 16.6a) became the primary impetus for a governmental policy called **deinstitutionalization**, which allowed the release of hospitalized psychiatric patients into the community and contributed to the closure of many mental hospitals (Torrey, 2013) (see Figure 15.1). But deinstitutionalization was a mixed blessing. Some patients returned to a semblance of a regular life, but tens of thousands of others spilled into cities and rural areas without adequate follow-up care. Many went off their medications and wandered the streets aimlessly. Some of the homeless people we can see today on the streets of major American cities are a tragic legacy of deinstitutionalization (Dear & Wolch, 2014). Today, psychologists, social workers, and other mental health professionals are working to improve the quality and availability of community care for psychiatric patients. Among the consequences of these efforts are *community mental health centers* and *halfway houses,* free or low-cost care facilities in which people can obtain treatment.

Psychiatric Diagnoses Across Cultures

Psychiatric diagnoses are shaped not only by history, but also by culture (Chentsova-Dutton & Tsai, 2007; Watters, 2010). Psychologists have increasingly recognized that certain conditions are *culture-bound*, that is, specific to one or more societies (see Table 15.1) (Kleinman, 1988; Simons & Hughes, 1986).

CULTURE-BOUND SYNDROMES. For example, some parts of Malaysia and several other Asian countries, including China and India, have witnessed periodic outbreaks of a strange condition known as *koro* (Crozier, 2012). The victims of *koro*, most of whom are male, typically believe that their penis and testicles are disappearing and receding into their abdomen (female victims of *koro* sometimes believe that their breasts are disappearing). *Koro* is spread largely by social contagion. Once one man begins to experience its symptoms, others often follow suit, triggering widespread panic. In one region of India in 1982, the *koro* epidemic spun so out of control that the local government took to the streets with loudspeakers to reassure terrified civilians that their genitals weren't vanishing. Government officials even measured male residents' penises with rulers in an attempt to prove their fears unfounded (Bartholomew, 1994).

Another disorder specific to Malaysia, the Philippines, and some African countries is *amok*. This condition is marked by episodes of intense sadness and brooding followed by uncontrolled behavior and unprovoked attacks on people or animals (American Psychiatric Association [APA], 2013). This condition gave rise to the popular phrase *running amok*, meaning "going wild." More recently, in Japan, a growing number of men appear to have developed a condition known as "2-D love," which is characterized by an attraction to two-dimensional imaginary characters such as cartoon women; one man with the disorder has collected more than 150 pillow covers featuring drawings of young women (Katayama, 2009).

Other culture-bound syndromes seem to be variants of conditions in Western culture. In Japan, for example, social anxiety is typically expressed as a fear of offending others (called *taijin kyofushu*), such as by saying something offensive or giving off a terrible body odor (Kleinknecht et al. 1994; Vriends et al., 2013). But in the United States, social anxiety is

Figure 15.1 Decline in Psychiatric Inpatients.

Over the past several decades, the number of hospitalized psychiatric patients has gradually declined.

SOURCE: www.ahrq.gov/legacy/about/annualconf09/vandivort_mark_owens/slide4.jpg

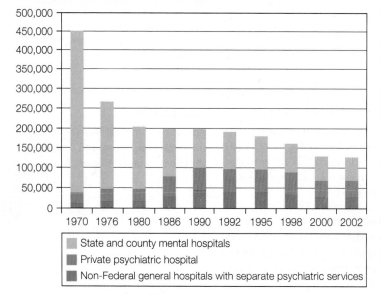

	State and county mental hospitals
	Private psychiatric hospital
	Non-Federal general hospitals with separate psychiatric services

Table 15.1 A Sampling of Common Culture-Bound Syndromes Not Discussed in the Text.

Syndrome	Region/Population Affected	Description
arctic hysteria	Alaska Natives (Inuit)	Abrupt episode accompanied by extreme excitement and frequently followed by convulsive seizures and coma.
ataque de nervios	Latin America	Symptoms include uncontrollable shouting, attacks of crying, trembling, heat in the chest rising to the head, and verbal or physical aggression.
brain fog	West Africa	Symptoms include difficulties in concentrating, remembering, and thinking.
latah	Malaysia and Southeast Asia	Found mostly among women; marked by an extreme startle reaction, followed by a loss of control, cursing, and mimicking of others' actions and speech.
windigo	Native Americans in Central and Northeastern Canada	Morbid state of anxiety with fears of becoming a cannibal.

SOURCE: Based on Simons, 2001

more commonly generated by fear of public embarrassment. Culture may influence how people express interpersonal anxiety. Because Japanese culture is more collectivistic compared with Western culture, Japanese tend to be more concerned about their impact on others than are Westerners.

In contrast, some conditions may be considerably more frequent in Western than non-Western cultures. Some eating disorders are largely specific to the United States and Europe, where the media bombard viewers with images of thin models, probably making already self-conscious women even more self-conscious (Keel & Klump, 2003; McCarthy, 1990). Body integrity identity disorder, in which people experience persistent desires to undergo operations to amputate their limbs or body parts, has thus far been reported only in the United States and Europe (Littlewood, 2004). Although responsible physicians won't perform such operations, many patients with body integrity identity disorder have found doctors willing to amputate their limbs (Blom, Hennekam, & Denys, 2012; First, 2004).

CULTURAL UNIVERSALITY. Still, many mental disorders appear to exist in most and perhaps all cultures. Jane Murphy (1976) examined two isolated societies—a group of Yorubas in Nigeria and a group of Inuit Eskimos near the Bering Strait—that had experienced essentially no contact with Western culture. These cultures possessed terms for disorders that are strikingly similar to schizophrenia, alcoholism, and psychopathic personality. For example, in Inuit, *kunlangeta* describes a person who lies, cheats, steals, is unfaithful to women, and doesn't obey elders—a description that fits almost perfectly the Western concept of psychopathic personality. When Murphy asked one of the Inuit how they dealt with such individuals, he replied "somebody would have pushed him off the ice when no one was looking." Apparently, Inuit aren't much fonder of psychopaths than we are.

Mal de ojo, or the "evil eye," is a culture-bound syndrome common in many Mediterranean and Latin countries. Believed by its victims to be brought on by the glance of a malicious person, *mal de ojo* is marked by insomnia, nervousness, crying for no reason, and vomiting. Here, customers in Egypt select pendants for warding off the evil eye.

Special Considerations in Psychiatric Classification and Diagnosis

Because there are so many ways in which psychological adaptation can go awry, we'd be hopelessly lost without some system of diagnostic classification. Psychiatric diagnoses serve at least two crucial functions. *First,* they help us pinpoint the psychological problem a person is experiencing. Once we've identified this problem, it's often easier to select a treatment. *Second,* psychiatric diagnoses make it easier for mental health professionals to communicate. When a psychologist diagnoses a patient with schizophrenia, he or she can be reasonably certain that other psychologists know the patient's principal symptoms. Diagnoses operate as forms of mental shorthand, simplifying complex descriptions of problematic behaviors into convenient summary phrases.

Fact vs. Fiction

Most psychotic people in non-Western societies would be viewed as "shamans" (See bottom of page for answer.)

○ Fact

○ Fiction

Still, there are a host of misconceptions regarding psychiatric diagnosis; we'll examine four of them here.

Misconception 1: *Psychiatric diagnosis is nothing more than pigeonholing, that is, sorting people into different "boxes."* According to this criticism, when we diagnose people with a mental disorder, we deprive them of their uniqueness; we imply that all people within the same diagnostic category are alike in all important respects.

Reality: A diagnosis implies only that all people with a particular diagnosis are alike in at least *one* important respect (Lilienfeld, Watts, & Smith, 2015). Psychologists recognize that even within a diagnostic category such as schizophrenia or bipolar disorder, people differ dramatically in their other psychological difficulties, race and cultural background, personality traits, interests, and cognitive skills. People are far more than their disorders.

Misconception 2: *Psychiatric diagnoses are unreliable. Reliability* refers to consistency of measurement. In the case of psychiatric diagnoses, the form of reliability that matters most is *interrater reliability:* the extent to which different raters (such as different psychologists) agree on patients' diagnoses.

Reality: For major mental disorders such as schizophrenia, mood disorders, anxiety disorders, and alcoholism, interrater reliabilities are typically about as high—correlations between raters of .8 or above out of a maximum of 1.0—as for most medical disorders (Kraemer et al., 2012; Matarazzo, 1983). Still, the picture isn't entirely rosy. For many personality disorders—a class of disorders we'll discuss later—interrater reliabilities tend to be lower (Freedman et al., 2013; Zimmerman, 1994).

Misconception 3: *Psychiatric diagnoses are invalid.* From the standpoint of Thomas Szasz (1960) and other critics, psychiatric diagnoses are largely useless because they don't provide us with much, if any, new information. They're merely descriptive labels for behaviors we don't like.

Reality: When it comes to some pop psychology labels, Szasz probably had a point. Consider the explosion of diagnostic labels that are devoid of scientific support, such as codependency, sexual addiction, Internet addiction, road rage disorder, chocoholism (chocolate addiction), and compulsive shopping disorder (Kessler et al., 2006; Koran et al., 2006; McCann et al., 2013; Winiarski, Smith, & Lilienfeld, 2015). Although frequently used in talk shows, television programs, movies, and self-help books, these labels aren't recognized as formal psychiatric diagnoses.

Yet there's now considerable evidence that many psychiatric diagnoses *do* tell us something new about the person. In a classic paper, psychiatrists Eli Robins and

Trials involving "dueling expert witnesses" may contribute to the erroneous public perception that psychologists can't agree on the diagnoses of individuals with suspected mental disorders.

Samuel Guze (1970) outlined several criteria for determining whether a psychiatric diagnosis is valid. According to Robins and Guze, a valid diagnosis

1. distinguishes that diagnosis from other similar diagnoses.
2. predicts diagnosed individuals' performance on laboratory tests, including personality measures, neurotransmitter levels, and brain imaging findings (Andreasen, 1995).
3. predicts diagnosed individuals' family history of psychiatric disorders.
4. predicts diagnosed individuals' *natural history*—that is, what tends to happen to them over time.

In addition, some authors have argued that a valid diagnosis ideally

5. predicts diagnosed individuals' response to treatment (Waldman, Lilienfeld, & Lahey, 1995).

There's good evidence that unlike most pop psychology labels, many mental disorders fulfill Robins and Guze's criteria for validity. Table 15.2 illustrates these criteria using the example of *attention-deficit/hyperactivity disorder (ADHD)*, a disorder we'll encounter later in the chapter that's characterized by inattention, impulsivity, and overactivity.

Misconception 4: *Psychiatric diagnoses stigmatize people.* According to **labeling theorists**, psychiatric diagnoses exert powerful negative effects on people's perceptions and behaviors (Scheff, 1984; Slater, 2004). Labeling theorists argue that once a mental health professional diagnoses us, others perceive us differently. Suddenly, we're "weird," "strange," even "crazy." This diagnosis leads others to treat us differently, in turn often leading us to behave in weird, strange, or crazy ways.

Reality: In a famous study, David Rosenhan (1973) asked eight individuals with no symptoms of mental illness (himself included) to pose as fake patients in 12 psychiatric hospitals. These "pseudopatients" (fake patients) presented themselves to admitting psychiatrists with a single complaint: They were hearing a voice saying "empty, hollow, and thud." In all 12 cases, the psychiatrists admitted these pseudopatients to the hospital, almost always with diagnoses of schizophrenia (one received a diagnosis of manic depression, or what would today be called bipolar disorder). Remarkably, they remained there for an average of three weeks despite displaying no further symptoms of mental illness. The diagnosis of schizophrenia, Rosenhan concluded, became a self-fulfilling prophecy, leading doctors and nursing staff to view these individuals as disturbed. For example, the nursing staff interpreted one pseudopatient's note taking as "abnormal writing behavior."

labeling theorists

scholars who argue that psychiatric diagnoses exert powerful negative effects on people's perceptions and behaviors

---

Table 15.2 Criteria for Validity: The Case of ADHD.

Although controversial in many respects, the diagnosis of attention-deficit/hyperactivity disorder (ADHD) largely satisfies the Robins and Guze criteria for validity.

Robins and Guze Criteria	Findings Concerning the ADHD Diagnosis
1. Distinguishes a particular diagnosis from other similar diagnoses	The child's symptoms can't be accounted for by other diagnoses, such as bipolar disorder and anxiety disorders.
2. Predicts performance on laboratory tests (personality measures, neurotransmitter levels, brain imaging findings)	The child is likely to perform poorly on laboratory measures of attention.
3. Predicts family history of psychiatric disorders	The child has a higher probability than the average child of having biological relatives with ADHD.
4. Predicts what happens to the individual over time	The child is likely to show continued difficulties with inattention in adulthood but improvements in impulsivity and hyperactivity in adulthood.
5. Predicts response to treatment	The child has a good chance of responding positively to stimulant medications such as Ritalin.

It's true that there's still stigma attached to some psychiatric diagnoses. If someone tells us that a person has schizophrenia, for instance, we may be wary of the individual at first or misinterpret his or her behavior as consistent with the diagnosis. Yet the negative effects of labels last only so long. Even in Rosenhan's study, all pseudopatients were released from the hospital with diagnoses of either schizophrenia or manic depression "in remission" ("in remission" means without any symptoms) (Spitzer, 1975). These discharge diagnoses tell us that psychiatrists eventually recognized that these individuals were behaving normally. Overall, there's not much evidence that most psychiatric diagnoses themselves generate long-term negative effects (Ruscio, 2003).

Psychiatric Diagnosis Today: *DSM-5*

Diagnostic and Statistical Manual of Mental Disorders (DSM)

diagnostic system containing the American Psychiatric Association (APA) criteria for mental disorders

The official system for classifying individuals with mental disorders in the United States and much of the world is the ***Diagnostic and Statistical Manual of Mental Disorders (DSM)***, which originated in 1952 and is now in its fifth edition, called *DSM-5* (APA, 2013). There are 18 different classes of disorders in the *DSM-5*, several of which we'll be discussing in the pages to come. A related system, the *International Classification of Diseases* (ICD-10; World Health Organization, 2010) is used in many countries outside the United States, although we'll not discuss it in detail here.

DIAGNOSTIC CRITERIA AND DECISION RULES. *DSM-5* contains a list of criteria for diagnosing each condition and a set of decision rules for deciding how many of these criteria need to be met. For example, to diagnose a person with major depressive disorder, *DSM-5* requires that the person exhibit at least five of nine symptoms, including fatigue, insomnia, problems concentrating, and significant weight loss over a two-week period, with the requirement that the person experience either depressed mood, diminished interest or pleasure in everyday activities, or both.

THINKING ORGANIC. *DSM-5* warns diagnosticians about physical—or "organic," that is, medically induced—conditions that can simulate certain psychological disorders (Schildkraut, 2011). *DSM-5* notes that certain substance use or medical disorders can mimic the clinical picture of depression. For example, it informs readers that *hypothyroidism*, a disorder marked by underactivity of the thyroid gland (in our lower necks), can produce depressive symptoms (Tallis, 2011). If a patient's depression appears as a result of hypothyroidism, the psychologist shouldn't diagnose major depression. It's essential to "think organic," or to first rule out medical causes of a disorder, when diagnosing psychological conditions.

prevalence

percentage of people within a population who have a specific mental disorder

THE DSM-5: OTHER FEATURES. *DSM-5* is also a valuable source of information concerning the characteristics, such as the **prevalence**, of many mental disorders. Prevalence refers to the percentage of people in the population with a disorder. In the case of major depression, the lifetime prevalence is at least 10 percent among women and at least 5 percent among men (some estimates are even higher). That means that for a woman, the odds are at least 1 in 10 she'll experience an episode of major depression at some point in her life; for a man, the odds are at least 1 in 20 (APA, 2013).

A clinical psychologist would probably perceive cutting oneself as pathological, but *DSM-5* reminds clinicians that in some cultures, such practices are used to produce tribal scars and should be regarded as normal.

DSM-5 adopts a *biopsychosocial approach,* which acknowledges the interplay of biological (like hormonal abnormalities), psychological (like irrational thoughts), and social (interpersonal interactions) influences. Specifically, it reminds diagnosticians to attend carefully to patients' ongoing life stressors, past and present medical conditions, and overall level of functioning when evaluating their psychological status. It also reminds clinicians to take culture into account when assigning diagnoses.

THE DSM-5: CRITICISMS. There's little dispute that *DSM-5* is a helpful system for slicing up the enormous pie of psychopathology into more meaningful and manageable pieces. Yet it and previous versions of the manual have received more than their share of criticism (Frances & Widiger, 2012; Greenberg, 2013; Widiger & Clark, 2000).

There are more than 300 diagnoses in *DSM-5*, not all of which meet the Robins and Guze criteria for validity. To take only one example, the *DSM-5* diagnosis of "Mathematics Disorder" describes little more than difficulties with performing arithmetic or math reasoning problems. It seems to be more of a label for learning problems than a diagnosis that tells us something new about the person. In addition, although the diagnostic criteria and decision rules for many *DSM-5* disorders are based primarily on scientific findings, others are based largely on subjective committee decisions. Another problem with *DSM-5* is the high level of **comorbidity** among many of its diagnoses (Cramer et al., 2010; Friborg et al., 2014; Lilienfeld, Waldman, & Israel, 1994), meaning that individuals with one diagnosis frequently have one or more additional diagnoses. For example, it's extremely common for people with major depression to meet criteria for one or more anxiety disorders. This extensive comorbidity raises the troubling question of whether *DSM-5* is diagnosing genuinely independent conditions as opposed to slightly different variations of one underlying condition (Cramer et al., 2010).

Watch DCM-5 CONTROVERSIES

Another criticism of *DSM-5* is its substantial reliance on a **categorical model** of psychopathology (Trull & Durett, 2005). In a categorical model, a mental disorder—such as major depression—is either present or absent, with no in-between. Pregnancy fits a categorical model, because a woman is either pregnant or she's not. Yet many and perhaps most disorders in *DSM-5* better fit a **dimensional model**, meaning they differ from normal functioning in degree, not kind (Haslam, Holland, & Kuppens, 2012; Krueger & Piasecki, 2002). Height fits a dimensional model, because although people differ in height, these differences aren't all or none. The same may be true of many forms of depression and anxiety, which most research suggests lie on a continuum with normality (Kollman et al., 2006; Slade & Andrews, 2005). These findings square with our everyday experience, because we all feel at least a bit depressed and anxious from time to time.

Some authors have proposed that the Big Five, a system of personality dimensions we encountered earlier in the text, may better capture the true "state of nature" than many of the categories in *DSM-5* (Widiger & Clark, 2000; Wright et al., in press). For example, depression is typically characterized by high levels of neuroticism and introversion. Indeed, *DSM-5* includes a system of personality dimensions similar to the Big Five in a secondary section of the manual dedicated to future research (Skodol et al., 2013). Indeed, many psychologists and psychiatrists have resisted a dimensional model, perhaps because they, like the rest of us, are *cognitive misers*; they strive to simplify the world. Most of us find it easier to think of the world in terms of black and white categories than complex shades of gray (Lilienfeld & Waldman, 2004; Macrae & Bodenhausen, 2000).

A particular concern regarding *DSM-5* is its tendency to "medicalize normality," that is, to classify relatively mild psychological disturbances as pathological (Frances, 2013; Haslam, 2016). For example, in a sharp break from previous versions of the *DSM*, *DSM-5* now allows individuals to be diagnosed with major depressive disorder following the loss of a loved one (assuming they meet the pertinent *DSM-5* criteria), including the death of a spouse. Although this change may be justified by research (Pies, 2012), critics worry that it will open the floodgates to diagnosing many people with relatively normal grief reactions as disordered (Wakefield & First, 2012).

Like virtually all documents crafted by human beings, *DSM-5* is vulnerable to political influences (Kirk & Kutchins, 1992; Wakefield, 2015). For example, some researchers have

comorbidity

co-occurrence of two or more diagnoses within the same person

categorical model

model in which a mental disorder differs from normal functioning in kind rather than degree

dimensional model

model in which a mental disorder differs from normal functioning in degree rather than kind

Like some psychological disorders, blood pressure better fits a dimensional than a categorical model because there's no sharp dividing line between normal and high blood pressure.

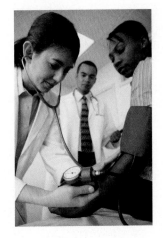

In medicine, doctors recognize that a fever is a nonspecific symptom of hundreds of different diseases, so they try to identify the underlying disease causing the fever. Similarly, RDoC strives to classify mental disorders not in terms of the symptoms of psychopathology, but in terms of dysfunctions in brain circuitry. This approach is controversial, and it's unclear how successful it will be.

Research Domain Criteria

a recently launched program of research designed to classify mental disorders in terms of deficits in brain circuitry.

lobbied successfully for the inclusion of their "favorite" disorder or area of specialty. But like all scientific endeavors, the system of psychiatric classification tends to be self-correcting. Just as homosexuality was stricken from the *DSM* in the 1970s, science will continue to weed out invalid disorders, ensuring that future editions of the *DSM* will be based on better evidence.

THE RESEARCH DOMAIN CRITERIA (RDoC). Although the *DSM* has been an important scientific achievement (Lieberman, 2015), it's been a disappointment in one crucial respect. Specifically, in the time since the first edition of the *DSM* appeared more than six decades ago, there's no evidence that it's made much of a dent in the prevalence of mental disorders, nor on the risk of suicide stemming from these disorders (Insel, 2009). So even though the rigor of psychiatric diagnosis has improved, this rigor hasn't translated into lower mental disorder rates, let alone lower death rates.

In addition, growing evidence suggests that many or most *DSM-5* diagnoses are not as distinguishable as researchers had assumed. For example, recent work suggests that many *DSM* diagnoses such as schizophrenia, major depressive disorder, obsessive compulsive disorder, and several other conditions we'll learn about in this chapter are moderately correlated and linked by an underlying tendency toward psychological distress (Caspi et al., 2014). Moreover, some brain imaging research raises the possibility that different psychological disorders share dysfunctions in similar brain circuits (Goodkind et al., 2015).

In response to the perceived failures of *DSM*, a growing chorus of researchers called for an alternative to the *DSM* model. In 2009, the U.S. National Institute of Mental Health launched a major scientific endeavor, the **Research Domain Criteria** (RDoC), as part of a long-term effort to substitute for, or at least supplement, the *DSM*. In contrast to the *DSM*, which focuses almost exclusively on the symptoms of mental disorders, RDoC aims to develop a broad framework for studying and classifying mental disorders that incorporates multiple dimensions: from genetics and neuroscience to the nature of social interactions. For example, one of the pivotal ways of conceptualizing mental illnesses in RDoC is to view them as disorders of brain circuits (Cuthbert & Insel, 2013). That is, unlike *DSM-5*, RDoC strives to "get under the hood" of patients' mental disorders to develop a system of classification based on what has gone awry in their brains. Among these circuits are brain systems linked to threat processing, as well as those linked to reward processing.

Let's take major depressive disorder as an example. *DSM-5* approaches this condition from the standpoint of its symptoms, such as depressed mood, fatigue, guilt, and sleeping problems. The problem with this system is that major depressive disorder may be much like fever. A fever isn't really a disease in its own right; instead, it's only a symptom of hundreds of different underlying diseases (Kihlstrom, 2002). Similarly, depression may not be a single disease, but instead a grouping of symptoms that can result from any number of different diseases.

In sharp contrast to the *DSM*, RDoC tries to understand major depressive disorder from the standpoint of deficits in brain circuits, such as those linked to reward processing. It might conceptualize depression as a disorder characterized by deficits in the capacity to experience reward, and it might try to pinpoint promising "markers," such as brain imaging findings or performance on laboratory tasks, that reflect inadequate reward processing in the brain. In this way, RDoC could one day dispense with *DSM* diagnoses, such as those discussed in this chapter, and instead classify mental illnesses largely or entirely in terms of the nature and degree of dysfunction in people's brain circuits. This would be supplemented by information about how genes and patterns of social interactions shape the likelihood of developing depression and the way symptoms of depression are expressed in everyday life.

RDoC is an exciting new direction for psychopathology research. At the same time, though, it may have its limitations. For one thing, we don't yet know whether most or all

Evaluating Claims ONLINE TESTS FOR MENTAL DISORDERS

Interactive

Lately, ever since your friend shared that he has suffered from attention deficit-hyperactivity disorder (ADHD) since childhood, you've been wondering whether you might also qualify for a diagnosis of ADHD. You sometimes have a difficult time concentrating when something doesn't engage your attention, and your mind often wanders when you're trying to read your psychology text (even though it's fascinating). After working for an hour or so on your schoolwork, you feel the need to stretch, walk around, or take an Internet break. You've always thought of yourself as a fidgety person. You've done fine in your classes and carry a high grade point average, but your conversation with your friend has piqued your curiosity about ADHD.

You've been doing a little reading on the Internet over the past few days to see whether the diagnosis of ADHD might apply to you. On a website called "Diagnose Yourself," you come across the following claim regarding a brief self-test for adult ADHD and puzzle over whether you should purchase it. Choose which of the six principles of scientific thinking are most relevant as you evaluate this claim.

"This 20-question self-test is *the most valid and reliable* screening measure for adult ADHD available on the Internet! This test is the only test you will need to self-screen for a diagnosis of ADHD, as it does a superior job of providing a diagnosis while screening out anxiety disorders and bipolar disorder."

Scientific skepticism requires us to evaluate all claims with an open mind but to insist on compelling evidence before accepting them. How do the principles of scientific thinking help us to evaluate this claim about the ability of the test to screen for a diagnosis of ADHD?

Consider how the six principles of scientific thinking are relevant as you evaluate this claim.

1. Ruling Out Rival Hypotheses
Have important alternative explanations for the findings been excluded?

The ad claims that the test can exclude anxiety disorders and bipolar disorder, conditions that could potentially account for some symptoms of ADHD. Nevertheless, this is a very tall order, and the ad provides no scientifically-based reason to believe that this test can live up to the claim. To arrive at a valid diagnosis and to distinguish ADHD from other disorders—that is, to rule out rival explanations– it's necessary to consider historical information and current behaviors and performance in different settings (such as school, workplace, and home), as well as tests of attention and input from different professionals (such as physicians, teachers, and family members). The test is therefore unlikely to be well-equipped to rule out rival hypotheses.

2. Correlation vs. Causation
Can we be sure that A causes B?

This principle of scientific thinking is not particularly relevant to this claim, as the ad does not address potential causal determinants of ADHD.

3. Falsifiability
Can the claim be disproved?

It would be very difficult, if not impossible, to falsify the claim that the "self-test is *the most valid and reliable* screening measure for adult ADHD available on the Internet." To evaluate this claim, it would be necessary to evaluate the test in comparison with every other test on the Internet. To do so would prove beyond the reach and resources of any researcher. The information on the Internet is not only vast, but it would be virtually impossible to identify all such tests, and the information on the Internet is constantly subject to change, representing a continually moving target.

4. Replicability
Can the results be duplicated in other studies?

There's no evidence that the claim is derived from systematic research, let alone from multiple replicated studies. We should be skeptical of claims regarding tests for psychological diagnoses in which reference is not made to how the research was conducted or whether independent researchers have been able to reproduce it.

5. Extraordinary Claims
Is the evidence as strong as the claim?

The claim that the test is the "most valid and reliable" is extraordinary because it includes all self-tests on the Internet that screen for adult ADHD, and it's put forward with no supportive evidence. It's difficult to evaluate because of the vast and constantly changing nature of information presented on the Internet. Moreover, most online diagnostic tests have never been evaluated in peer-reviewed studies.

6. Occam's Razor
Does a simpler explanation fit the data just as well?

Let's say that you take the test and score in the high range. Your high score might simply be due to the fact that you endorse experiences common to many people; after all, most people's minds wander from time to time and many people fidget. Unless the test can accurately discriminate common experiences from experiences specific to ADHD, it will probably misclassify many people as having "ADHD." Given that the experiences the person in the example describes don't interfere with daily functioning, it's unlikely that an ADHD diagnosis would be appropriate.

Summary

There's no scientific support for the claim that the test advertised is superior to all others and that it can provide a diagnosis that excludes other possible diagnoses with overlapping symptoms.

mental disorders stem from dysfunctions in brain circuits (Lilienfeld & Treadway, 2016). For example, specific phobias, which as we'll learn later in this chapter are intense and irrational fears, often result largely from adverse environmental experiences, such as a nasty dog bite (which can sometimes produce a dog phobia) or a scary plane ride (which can sometimes produce a flying phobia). Also, it's likely that a comprehensive understanding of mental illness will require scientists to develop models of psychopathology that integrate biological with sociocultural influences. It's not yet clear whether or how RDoC can pull off this feat (Berenbaum, 2013).

NORMALITY AND ABNORMALITY: A SPECTRUM OF SEVERITY. As you read case histories or descriptions in this chapter, you may wonder, "Is my behavior abnormal?" or "Maybe my problems are more serious than I thought." At times like this, it's useful to be aware of *medical students' syndrome* (Howes & Salkovskis, 1998). As medical students first become familiar with the symptoms of specific diseases, they often begin to focus on their bodily processes. Soon they find it hard to stop wondering whether a slight twinge in their chest might be an early warning of heart trouble or a mild headache the first sign of a brain tumor. Similarly, as we learn about psychological disorders, it's only natural to "see ourselves" in some patterns of behavior, largely because in meeting the complex demands of daily life, we all experience disturbing impulses, thoughts, and fears from time to time. So don't become alarmed as you learn about these conditions because many are probably extremes of psychological difficulties we all experience on occasion. Of course, if you experience a psychological problem that's disturbing and persistent you may want to consider consulting a mental health professional.

MENTAL ILLNESS AND THE LAW: A CONTROVERSIAL INTERFACE. Psychological problems not only affect our mental functioning, but also can place us at risk for legal problems. There are few topics about which the general public is certain it knows more, yet actually knows less, than the controversial interface between mental illness and the law. The last few years have witnessed horrific acts of mass violence perpetrated by individuals who apparently suffer from severe mental illness, including the 2012 theater shooting in Aurora, Colorado, and the 2012 Sandy Hook school shooting in Newtown, Connecticut. These tragic events raise complex questions regarding how, if at all, *DSM-5* disorders relate to violence and how society should deal with mentally ill people who've committed violence.

Mental Illness and Violence. One of the most pervasive myths in psychology is that people with mental illness are at greatly heightened risk for violence (Corrigan et al., 2012). In fact, the overwhelming majority of people with schizophrenia and other psychotic disorders aren't physically aggressive toward others; moreover, people with these conditions are much more likely to be victims than perpetrators of violence (Friedman, 2006; Steadman et al., 1998; Teplin, 1985). One might have hoped that the seemingly endless parade of "real crime" shows on television would have helped to combat this misconception, but it's probably done the opposite. Although only a small percentage of people with mental disorders commit aggressive acts, about 75 percent of televised characters with mental illness are violent (Owen, 2012; Wahl, 1997).

Still, like many misconceptions, this one contains a kernel of truth. Although most people with mental illness aren't at increased risk for violence, a subset—especially those who are convinced they're being persecuted (by the government, for example) and those with substance abuse—is (Douglas, Guy, & Hart, 2009; Monahan, 1992; Steadman et al., 1998).

involuntary commitment

procedure of placing some people with mental illnesses in a psychiatric hospital or another facility based on their potential danger to themselves or others or their inability to care for themselves.

Involuntary Commitment. We're all familiar with *criminal commitment*, which is just a fancy term for putting someone in jail or prison. Yet society possesses another mechanism for committing individuals against their will. Known as **involuntary commitment** or civil commitment, it's a procedure for protecting us from certain people with mental disorders and protecting them from themselves. Most U.S. states specify that individuals with mental illness can be committed against their will only if they (1) pose a clear and present threat to themselves or others or (2) are so psychologically impaired that they can't care

Psychomythology

The Insanity Defense: Controversies and Misconceptions

In courts of law, mental illnesses and the law occasionally collide head-on, often with unpredictable consequences. The best-known example of this clash is the **insanity defense**, which is premised on the idea that we shouldn't hold people legally responsible for their crimes if they weren't of "sound mind" when they committed them. The insanity defense comes in many forms, which differ across state and federal courts. As of 2016, 46 U.S. states use some version of this defense, with four—Utah, Montana, Idaho, and Kansas—opting out of it.

Most contemporary forms of this defense are based loosely on the *M'Naghten rule*, formulated during an 1843 British trial. This rule requires that to be declared insane, persons must either have (1) not known what they were doing at the time of the crime or (2) not known that what they were doing was wrong (Melton et al., 1997). A defendant (accused person) who was so disoriented during an epileptic seizure that he didn't realize he was attacking a police officer might fulfill the first prong of M'Naghten; a defendant who believed he was actually murdering Adolf Hitler when he shot his next-door neighbor might fulfill the second. Several other versions of the insanity defense strive to determine whether defendants were incapable of controlling their impulses at the moment of the crime. Because this judgment is exceedingly difficult (how can we know whether a man who murdered his wife *could* have controlled his temper had he really tried?), some courts ignore it.

The insanity defense is controversial, to put it mildly. To its proponents, this defense is necessary for defendants whose mental state is so deranged that it impairs their freedom to decide whether to commit a crime (Morse & Bonney, 2013; Sadoff, 1992). To its critics, this defense is nothing more than a legal cop-out that excuses criminals of responsibility (Lykken, 1982; Thompson & Cockerham, 2014). These divergent perspectives reflect a more deep-seated disagreement about free will versus determinism. The legal system assumes that our actions are freely chosen, whereas scientific psychology assumes that our actions are completely determined by prior variables, including our genetic makeup and learning history. So lawyers and judges tend to view the insanity defense as a needed exception for the small minority of defendants who lack free will. In contrast, many psychologists view this defense as illogical, because they see all crimes, including those committed by people with severe mental disorders, as equally "determined."

There are numerous misconceptions regarding the insanity verdict (Daftary-Kapur et al., 2011; see Table 15.3). For example, although most people believe that a sizable proportion, perhaps 15–20 percent, of criminals is acquitted (found innocent) on the basis of the insanity verdict, the actual percentage is less than 1 percent (Morse & Bonney, 2013). This erroneous belief probably stems from the *availability heuristic*: Because we hear a great deal about a few widely publicized cases of defendants acquitted on the grounds of insanity, we overestimate this verdict's prevalence (Butler, 2006). A better appreciation of the facts surrounding the insanity defense may help to dispel unwarranted public views regarding its use.

Diagnosed with postpartum depression, Andrea Yates drowned her five young children in the bathtub, apparently following orders from Satan. In 2006, Yates was acquitted on the basis of an insanity verdict. The intense publicity surrounding this and several other trials involving the insanity verdict has probably contributed to public misperceptions regarding the verdict's prevalence.

Table 15.3 Myth vs. Reality: The Insanity Defense.

Myth	Reality
Insanity is a psychological or psychiatric term.	Insanity is a purely legal term that refers only to whether the person was responsible for the crime; it does not refer to the nature of his or her psychiatric disorder.
The determination of insanity rests on a careful evaluation of the person's current mental state.	The determination of insanity rests on a determination of the person's mental state at the time of the crime.
The insanity defense requires a judgment of the defendant's incompetence to stand trial.	Competence to stand trial bears on defendant's ability to assist in his or her own defense.
A large proportion of criminals escape criminal responsibility by using the insanity defense.	The insanity defense is raised in only about 1 percent of criminal trials and is successful only about one-fourth of the time.
Most people acquitted on the basis of an insanity defense quickly go free.	The average insanity acquittee spends close to three years in a psychiatric hospital, often longer than the length of a criminal sentence for the same crime.
Most people who use the insanity defense are faking mental illness.	The rate of faking mental illness among insanity defendants appears to be low.

Based on Butler, 2006; Grisso, 2003; Pasewark & Pantle, 1979; Perlin, 2016; Phillips, Wolf, & Coons, 1998; Silver, Cirincione, & Steadman, 1994

Watch PANIC ATTACKS

that are repeated and unexpected and when they either experience persistent concerns about panicking or change their behavior to avoid future attacks (for example, change jobs) (APA, 2013). Panic attacks typically peak within 10 minutes and can include sweating, dizziness, lightheadedness, a racing or pounding heart, shortness of breath, feelings of unreality, and fears of going crazy or dying (Craske et al., 2010). Because many patients experiencing their initial panic attack believe they're having a heart attack, many first go to the emergency room, only to be sent home and told "it's all in your head." Some panic attacks are associated with specific situations, such as riding in elevators or shopping in supermarkets, whereas others come entirely without warning, often generating fears of the situations in which they occur.

> **First-Person Account: Panic Disorder**
>
> "For me, a panic attack is almost a violent experience. I feel disconnected from reality. I feel like I'm losing control in a very extreme way. My heart pounds really hard, I feel like I can't get my breath, and there's an overwhelming feeling that things are crashing in on me."
>
> (DICKEY, 1994)

Panic attacks can occur in every anxiety disorder, as well as in mood and eating disorders. About 20–25 percent of college students report at least one panic attack in a one-year period, with about half that number reporting unexpected attacks (Lilienfeld, 1997; Sharkin, 2013). Panic disorder often develops in late adolescence and early adulthood (Kessler et al., 2012) and is associated with a history of fears of separation from a parent during childhood (Lewinsohn et al., 2008). It's unclear, though, whether this correlation means that separation fears predispose to later panic disorder or whether such fears are merely an early reflection of the same underlying condition that gives rise to panic disorder.

Correlation vs. Causation

Can we be sure that A causes B?

Phobias: Irrational Fears

phobia

intense fear of an object or a situation that's greatly out of proportion to its actual threat.

A **phobia** is an intense fear of an object or a situation that's greatly out of proportion to its actual threat. Many of us have mild fears—of things like spiders and snakes—that aren't severe enough to be phobias. For a fear to be diagnosed as a phobia, it must restrict our life, create considerable distress, or do both.

Phobias are the most common of all anxiety disorders. One in eight of us has a phobia of an animal, blood or injury, or a situation like a thunderstorm. Social fears are almost as common (Kessler et al., 2012). Agoraphobia, which we'll examine next, is the most debilitating of the phobias and occurs in about 1 in 20 of us (Keller & Craske, 2008; Kessler et al., 2006).

AGORAPHOBIA. Some 2,700 years ago in the city-states of ancient Greece, agoraphobia acquired its name as a condition in which certain fearful citizens couldn't pass through the central city's open-air markets (*agoras*). A common misconception is that agoraphobia is a fear of crowds or public places. But **agoraphobia** actually refers to a fear of being in a place or situation in which escape is difficult or embarrassing or in which help is unavailable in the event of a panic attack (APA, 2013).

agoraphobia

fear of being in a place or situation from which escape is difficult or embarrassing or in which help is unavailable in the event of a panic attack.

Agoraphobia typically emerges in the midteens and is often a direct outgrowth of panic disorder. In fact, most people with panic disorder develop at least some agoraphobic symptoms (Cox & Taylor, 1998; Sanderson & Dublin, 2010) and become apprehensive in a host of

Fact vs. Fiction

Most people with agoraphobia can't leave their houses. (See bottom of page for answer.)

○ Fact

○ Fiction

settings outside the home, such as stores, movie theaters, lines of people, public transportation, crowds, bridges, and wide-open spaces. The expression of agoraphobia seems to differ across cultures. For example, some Eskimos in Greenland suffer from a condition called "kayak angst," marked by a pronounced fear of going out to sea by oneself in a kayak (Barlow, 2000; Thomason, 2014).

In some cases, agoraphobia reaches extreme proportions. Two clinicians saw a 62-year-old woman with agoraphobia who hadn't left her house—even once—for 25 years (Jensvold & Turner, 1988). Having experienced severe panic attacks and terrified by the prospect of still more, she spent almost all of her waking hours locked away in her bedroom with curtains drawn. The therapists attempted to treat her agoraphobia by encouraging her to take short trips out of her house, but she repeatedly refused to walk even a few steps past her front door.

Some of the most common fears involve insects and animals such as spiders and snakes.

SPECIFIC PHOBIA AND SOCIAL ANXIETY DISORDER. Phobias of objects, places, or situations—called *specific phobias*—commonly arise in response to animals, insects, thunderstorms, water, elevators, and darkness. Many of these fears, especially of animals, are widespread in childhood but disappear with age (APA, 2013).

Surveys show that most people rank public speaking as a greater fear than dying (Wallechinsky, Wallace, & Wallace, 1977). Given that statistic, imagine how people with **social anxiety disorder**—sometimes also called social phobia—must feel. They experience an intense fear of negative evaluation in social situations, such as while eating, giving a speech, conversing with others, and performing in public. Their social fears can even extend to swimming, swallowing, and signing their checks in the presence of others (Mellinger & Lynn, 2003). Their anxiety goes well beyond the stage fright that most of us feel occasionally (Morrison & Heimberg, 2013).

social anxiety disorder

intense fear of negative evaluation in social situations.

> *First-Person Account:* **Social Anxiety Disorder**
>
> "When I would walk into a room full of people, I'd turn red and it would feel like everybody's eyes were on me. I was embarrassed to stand off in a corner by myself, but I couldn't think of anything to say to anybody. It was humiliating. I felt so clumsy, I couldn't wait to get out."
>
> (Dickey, 1994)

Fact vs. Fiction

Most phobias can't be traced directly to negative experiences with the object of the fear. (See bottom of page for answer.)

○ Fact

○ Fiction

Answer 1: Fiction. Being housebound occurs only in cases of severe agoraphobia (Rapp, 1984).

Answer 2: Fact. Most people with phobias report no direct traumatic experiences with the object of their fear (Field, 2006).

Figure 15.3 The Shuttle Box.

Using an apparatus like this, Martin Seligman found that dogs that were first prevented from escaping the shock gave up trying to escape electric shocks even when they were free to do so. He called this phenomenon "learned helplessness."

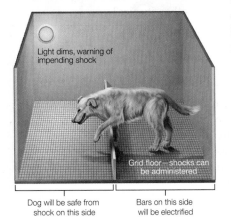

Light dims, warning of impending shock

Grid floor—shocks can be administered

Dog will be safe from shock on this side

Bars on this side will be electrified

Ruling Out Rival Hypotheses

Have important alternative explanations for the findings been excluded?

Correlation vs. Causation

Can we be sure that A causes B?

learned helplessness

tendency to feel helpless in the face of events we can't control.

Replicability

Can the results be duplicated in other studies?

Yet Seligman found something surprising. Dogs first restrained in a hammock and exposed to shocks they couldn't escape later often made no attempt to escape shocks in the shuttle box, even when they could easily get away from them. Some of the dogs just sat there, whimpering and crying, passively accepting the shocks as though they were inescapable. They'd learned to become helpless.

Bruce Overmier and Seligman (1967) described **learned helplessness** as the tendency to feel helpless in the face of events one can't control and argued that it offers an animal model of depression. Seligman noted striking parallels between the effects of learned helplessness and depressive symptoms: passivity, appetite and weight loss, and difficulty learning that one can change circumstances for the better. But we must be cautious in drawing conclusions from animal studies because many psychological conditions, including depression, may differ in animals and humans (Raulin & Lilienfeld, 2008).

Provocative as it is, Seligman's model can't account for all aspects of depression. It doesn't explain why people with depression make internal attributions (explanations) for failure. In fact, the tendency to assume personal responsibility for failure contradicts the notion that people with depression regard negative events as beyond their control. The original model also doesn't acknowledge that the mere expectation of uncontrollability isn't sufficient to induce depression. After all, people don't become sad when they receive large amounts of money in a lottery, even though they've no control over that event (Abramson, Seligman, & Teasdale, 1978).

When data don't fit a model, good scientists revise it. Seligman and his colleagues (Abramson et al., 1978) altered the learned helplessness model to account for the attributions people make to explain their worlds. They argued that people prone to depression attribute failure to *internal* as opposed to external factors and success to *external* as opposed to internal factors. A person with depression might blame a poor test grade on a lack of ability, an internal factor, and a good score on the ease of the exam, an external factor. The researchers also observed that depression-prone people make attributions that are *global* and *stable*; they tend to see their failures as general and fixed aspects of their personalities. Still, internal, global, and stable attributions may be more a consequence than a cause of depression (Harvey & Weary, 1984). The depression brought on by undesirable life events may skew our thinking, leading us to make negative attributions, a tendency that may be evident as early as the primary grades (Fincham, Diener, & Hokoda, 2011; Gibb & Alloy, 2006).

Whether we develop depression depends not only on our attributions of outcomes, but also on the difference between how we feel and how we want to feel (Tsai, 2007). Jeanne Tsai and her colleagues found that cultural factors influence people's ideal emotion (Tsai, Knutson, & Fung, 2006). Compared with Hong Kong Chinese, European Americans and Asian Americans value excitement, whereas compared with European Americans, Hong Kong Chinese and Asian Americans value calm. Yet across all three cultural groups, the size of the gap between ideal and actual emotion is positively correlated with depression.

DEPRESSION: THE ROLE OF BIOLOGY. Twin studies indicate that genes exert a moderate effect on the risk of major depression (Kendler et al., 1993; Kendler Gatz, Gardner, & Pedersen, 2006). Some researchers have suggested that specific variations in the serotonin transporter gene (which affects the rate of reuptake of serotonin) play a role in depression, especially in conjunction with life experiences. Scientists first reported that people who inherit two copies of this stress-sensitive gene are two and a half times more likely to develop depression following four stressful events than people with another version of the gene that isn't sensitive to stress (Caspi et al., 2003). The stress-sensitive gene appears to affect people's ability to dampen negative emotions in the face of stress (Kendler, Gardner, & Prescott, 2003). Nevertheless, there are serious concerns about the replicability and strength of these findings, which have been inconsistent across laboratories (Karg et al., 2011; Risch et al., 2009; Rutter, 2009; Sharpley et al., 2014). To resolve questions regarding the role of gene-life events interactions in depression, researchers will need to conduct well-designed studies in which stressful life events are carefully defined to determine whether the positive findings are replicable. The hope is that these studies will clarify whether any genetic irregularities that surface are specific to depression; they may be associated with anxiety, too (Hariri et al., 2002).

Depression also appears linked to low levels of the neurotransmitter norepinephrine (Leonard, 1997; Robinson, 2007) and diminished neurogenesis (growth of new neurons), which brings about reduced hippocampal volume (Pittinger & Duman, 2008; Videbech & Ravnkilde, 2004). Many patients with depression have problems in the brain's reward and stress-response systems (Depue & Iacono, 1989; Forbes, Shaw, & Dahl, 2007; Treadway & Zald, 2013) and decreased levels of dopamine, the neurotransmitter most closely tied to reward (Martinot et al., 2001). This finding may help to explain why depression is often associated with an inability to experience pleasure.

Researchers are pursuing the exciting possibility that inflammation—whether brought about by an infection or a hyped-up immune response due to other causes—may trigger some cases of depression and other mental disorders such as schizophrenia (Liu, Ho, & Mak, 2012). The discovery of previously unknown lymphatic vessels linking the immune system to the brain may both provide a means for understanding how a dysfunctional immune system could impact the brain and produce or worsen mental disorders (Louveau et al., 2015) and open the door to the treatment of psychological conditions with medicines, such as low dose aspirin, that reduce inflammation (Köhler et al., 2015).

> ◀ **Ruling Out Rival Hypotheses**
>
> Have important alternative explanations for the findings been excluded?

Journal Prompt

Your text provides several possible explanations (loss of reinforcement, learned helplessness) for the causes of depression. Select one of these explanations and propose a study that would help to evaluate this explanation.

Bipolar Disorder: When Mood Goes to Extremes

We've all experienced good moods, but **manic episodes** are in a class by themselves. Manic episodes are typically marked by dramatically elevated mood (feeling "on top of the world"), decreased need for sleep, greatly heightened energy and activity, inflated self-esteem, increased talkativeness, and irresponsible behavior. People in a manic episode often display "pressured speech," as though they can't get their words out quickly enough, and are difficult to interrupt (APA, 2013). Their ideas often race through their heads quickly, which may account for the heightened rate of creative accomplishments in some individuals with bipolar disorder. Symptoms of a manic episode typically begin with a rapid increase over only a few days. People usually experience their first manic episode after their early 20s (Kessler et al., 2005).

Bipolar disorder, formerly called manic-depressive disorder, is diagnosed when there's a history of at least one manic episode (APA, 2013). In contrast to major depression, bipolar disorder is equally common in men and women. In the great majority of cases—up to 90 percent—people who've had one manic episode experience at least one more (Alda, 1997; Geddes & Miklowitz, 2013). Some have episodes separated by many years and then have a series of episodes, one rapidly following the other. More than half the time, a major depressive episode precedes or follows a manic episode (Solomon et al., 2010). Manic episodes often produce serious problems in social and occupational functioning, such as substance abuse and unrestrained sexual behavior. People in the midst of manic episodes frequently go on uncontrolled spending sprees. Ed Bazinet, one of New York's wealthiest people, who made millions selling miniature ceramic houses, experienced a manic episode at the New York International Gift Fair. Bazinet ordered more than $20 million worth of body and home goods, including soaps, clothes hanger covers, furniture, throw pillows, and wall art, after which he checked into a psychiatric facility (James & Patinkin, 2012). As this example illustrates, during a manic episode, judgment is often severely impaired. One of your book's authors treated a manic patient who

manic episode

experience marked by dramatically elevated mood, decreased need for sleep, increased energy, inflated self-esteem, increased talkativeness, and irresponsible behavior.

bipolar disorder

condition marked by a history of at least one manic episode.

passed himself off to a financial company as his own father, gained access to his father's savings for retirement, and gambled away his entire family fortune. Another frittered away most of his life's savings by purchasing more than 100 bowling balls, none of which he needed. The negative effects of a manic episode, including loss of employment, family conflicts, and divorce, can persist for many years (Coryell et al., 1993).

> ### First-Person Account: Bipolar Disorder
>
> "When I start going into a high, I no longer feel like an ordinary housewife. Instead I feel organized and accomplished and I begin to feel I am my most creative self. I can write poetry easily … melodies without effort … paint … I feel a sense of euphoria or elation…. I don't seem to need much sleep … I've just bought six new dresses … I feel sexy and men stare at me. Maybe I'll have an affair, or perhaps several…. However, when I go beyond this state, I become manic…. I begin to see things in my mind that aren't real…. One night I created an entire movie…. I also experienced complete terror … when I knew that an assassination scene was about to take place…. I went into a manic psychosis at that point. My screams awakened my husband…. I was admitted to the hospital the next day."
>
> (Fieve, 1975, p. 17)

Bipolar disorder is among the most genetically influenced of all mental disorders (Miklowitz & Johnson, 2006). Twin studies suggest that its heritability ranges from about 60 percent to as high as 85 percent (Alda, 1997; Lichtenstein et al., 2009; McGuffin et al., 2003). Many genes appear to be culprits in increasing the risk of bipolar disorder, and there's at least some genetic overlap between psychotic symptoms in bipolar disorder and schizophrenia (Craddock, O'Donovan, & Owen, 2005; Lichtenstein et al., 2009; Purcell et al., 2009).

Brain imaging studies suggest that people with bipolar disorder experience increased activity in structures related to emotion, including the amygdala (Chang et al., 2004; Thomas et al., 2013), and decreased activity and decreased gray matter in areas associated with planning, such as the prefrontal cortex (Kruger et al., 2003; Phillips & Swartz, 2014). Still, the cause–effect relationship between physiological findings and mood disorders isn't clear. For example, the high levels of norepinephrine and differences in brain activity observed in people with bipolar disorder may be an effect rather than a cause of the disorder (Thase, Jindal, & Howland, 2002).

Correlation vs. Causation

Can we be sure that A causes B?

Bipolar disorder is influenced by more than biological factors. Stressful life events are associated with an increased risk of manic episodes, more frequent relapse, and a longer recovery from manic episodes (Johnson & Miller, 1997; Yan-Meier et al., 2011). Interestingly, some manic episodes appear to be triggered by *positive* life events associated with striving for and achieving goals, such as job promotions or winning poetry contests (Johnson et al., 2000; Johnson et al., 2008). Once again, we can see that psychological disorders arise from the intersection of genetic and sociocultural forces.

Suicide: Facts and Fictions

Major depression and bipolar disorder are associated with a higher risk of suicide than are most other disorders (Chesney, Goodwin, & Fazel, 2014; Miklowitz & Johnson, 2006). More than a third of people with bipolar disorder have attempted suicide, and the suicide rate of people with bipolar disorder is about 15 times higher than that of the general population (Harris & Barraclough, 1997; Novick, Swartz, & Frank, 2010). Some anxiety disorders, such as panic disorder and social anxiety disorder, as well as substance abuse, are also associated with heightened suicide risk (Spirito & Esposito-Smythers, 2006). As of 2013, scientists ranked suicide as the 10th-leading cause of death in the United States and the eighth-leading cause of death among Native Americans (Centers for Disease Control and Prevention (CDC), Suicide Facts at a Glance, 2015).

Typically, more than 40,000 people commit suicide in the United States each year, a number that surely underestimates the problem because relatives report many suicides as accidents. For each completed suicide, there are an estimated 8 to 25 attempts. Contrary to what many believe, most people are more of a threat to themselves than

Table 15.4 Common Myths and Misconceptions About Suicide.

Myth	Reality
Talking to people with depression about suicide often makes them more likely to commit the act.	Talking to people with depression about suicide makes them more likely to obtain help.
Suicide is almost always completed with no warning.	Many or most individuals who commit suicide communicate their intent to others, which gives us an opportunity to seek help for a suicidal person.
As a severe depression lifts, people's suicide risk decreases.	As a severe depression lifts, the risk of suicide may actually increase, in part because individuals possess more energy to attempt the act.
Most people who threaten suicide are seeking attention.	Although attention seeking motivates some suicidal behaviors, most suicidal acts stem from severe depression and hopelessness.
People who talk a lot about suicide almost never commit it.	Talking about suicide is associated with a considerably greater risk of suicide.

others. For every two people who are victims of homicide, three take their own lives (National Institute of Mental Health [NIMH], 2015). In Table 15.4, we present a number of other common myths and misconceptions about suicide, along with correct information in each case.

It's essential to try to predict suicide attempts because most people are acutely suicidal for only a short window of time (Joiner, 2010; Schneidman, Farberow, & Litman, 1970; Simon, 2006), and intervention during that time can be critical. Unfortunately, the prediction of suicide poses serious practical problems. First, we can't easily conduct longitudinal studies to determine which people will attempt suicide. It would be unethical to allow people believed to be at high suicide risk to go through with attempts to allow us to pinpoint predictors of suicide. Second, it's difficult to study the psychological states associated with suicide because the period of high risk for a suicide attempt is often brief. Third, the low prevalence of suicide makes predicting it difficult (Finn & Kamphuis, 1995; Meehl & Rosen, 1955). Most estimates put the rate of completed suicide at 12 or 13 out of 100,000 people in the general population. So if only about one-hundredth of 1 percent of the population completes a suicide, our best guess—with about 99.9 percent accuracy—is that no one will commit suicide. Nevertheless, the social costs of failing to predict a suicide are so great that efforts to accurately predict suicide attempts continue (see Figure 15.4).

Fortunately, research has taught us a great deal about risk factors for suicide. The single best predictor of suicide is a previous attempt because 30–40 percent of all people who kill themselves have made at least one prior attempt (Maris, 1992; Pelkonen & Marttunen, 2003). With increased number of attempts comes a greater likelihood of an eventual fatal attempt (Tidemalm et al., 2014). About three times as many men as women commit suicide, but nearly three times as many women try it (NIMH, 2015). Recent research suggests that *psychache*—agonizing psychological pain—is one of the best predictors of suicide attempts (Troister, D'Agata, & Holden, 2015). Intense agitation is also a powerful predictor of suicide risk (Fawcett, 1997). Major suicide risk factors include:

1. Depression
2. Hopelessness
3. Intense agitation

Figure 15.4 Suicides by Location.

The famed Golden Gate Bridge in San Francisco has been the site of more than 1,200 suicides. One inch on each of the blue lines equates to about 20 suicides.

SOURCE: SFGate.com

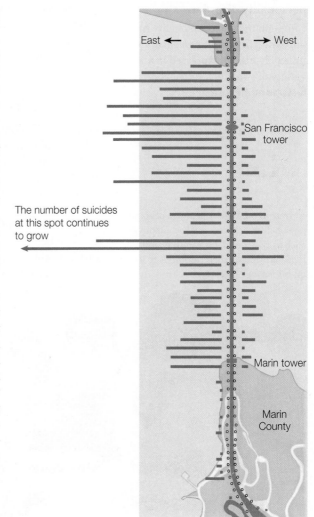

East ← → West

San Francisco tower

The number of suicides at this spot continues to grow

Marin tower

Marin County

4. Substance abuse
5. Schizophrenia
6. Homosexuality, probably because of social stigma
7. Unemployment
8. Chronic, painful, or disfiguring physical illness
9. Recent loss of a loved one; being divorced, separated, or widowed
10. Family history of suicide
11. Personality disorders, such as borderline personality disorder
12. Anxiety disorder, such as panic disorder and social anxiety disorder
13. Old age, especially in men
14. Recent discharge from a hospital

15.4: Personality and Dissociative Disorders: The Disrupted and Divided Self

15.4a **Identify the characteristics of borderline and psychopathic personality disorders.**

15.4b **Explain the controversies surrounding dissociative disorders, especially dissociative identity disorder.**

Most of us are accustomed to thinking of ourselves as one coherent unified identity. But some individuals—especially those with personality and dissociative disorders—experience a serious disruption in their thoughts or behaviors that prevents them from experiencing a healthy, consistent identity. Identifying personality disorders can be especially challenging because we all experience variations in personality and sense of self from time to time.

personality disorder

condition in which personality traits, appearing first in adolescence, are inflexible, stable, expressed in a wide variety of situations, and lead to distress or impairment.

Personality Disorders

Of all psychological conditions, personality disorders are historically among the least reliably diagnosed (Fowler, O'Donohue, & Lilienfeld, 2007; Perry, 1984; Zimmerman, 1994). That's because clinicians sometime disagree about whether a given patient exhibits certain personality disturbances, such as excessive impulsivity or identity problems. *DSM-5* states that we should diagnose a **personality disorder** only when personality traits first appear by adolescence; are inflexible, stable, and expressed in a wide variety of situations; and lead to distress or impairment (APA, 2013). But more than most patterns of behavior we've described, whether we perceive someone with a personality disorder as abnormal depends on the situational or cultural context in which their behavior occurs (Price & Bouffard, 1974). The suspiciousness of a person with a paranoid personality disorder may be a liability in a cooperative work group, but an asset in a private investigator.

Although the 10 personality disorders in *DSM-5* are distinguishable from each other, they often exhibit substantial comorbidity with each other and with other mental disorders, such as major depression and generalized anxiety disorder (Lenzenweger, McLachlan, & Rubin, 2007), leading some to question whether they're truly distinct from one another and from other psychological conditions (Harkness & Lilienfeld, 1997). Two of these disorders, in particular, have been extensively studied and produce profound impairment both for affected individuals and those around them. Therefore, in this section we'll consider in detail the two most widely investigated personality disorders—*borderline personality disorder* and *psychopathic personality*. In many respects, the fascinating issues raised by these two disorders highlight the

At least in mild doses, features of some personality disorders may be adaptive, such as when students carefully and repeatedly check their responses to test questions for mistakes

complexities involved in diagnosing and understanding personality disorders in general.

BORDERLINE PERSONALITY DISORDER: STABLE INSTABILITY. Estimates suggest that between 2 and 6 percent of adults, most of them women (Swartz et al., 1990; Zanarini et al., 2011), develop **borderline personality disorder**, a condition marked by instability in mood, sense of self, and impulse control. Individuals with borderline personality disorder tend to be extremely impulsive and unpredictable, although many are married and hold down good jobs. Their interests and life goals frequently shift dramatically. Their relationships and friendships frequently alternate from extremes of worshipping others from one day to hating them the next. Some scholars have aptly described this disorder as a pattern of "stable instability" (Grinker & Werble, 1977).

Watch BORDERLINE PERSONALITY DISORDER

The name *borderline personality* stems from the now outmoded belief that this condition lies on the border between psychotic and "neurotic"—relatively normal, yet mildly disabled—functioning (Stern, 1938). Instead, researcher Marsha Linehan has argued that a better name for this condition is emotional dysregulation disorder.

Borderline Personality: A Volatile Blend of Traits. Borderline personality symptoms have an impulsive and self-destructive quality and often include drug abuse; sexual promiscuity; overeating; and even self-mutilation, such as cutting oneself when upset (Salsman & Linehan, 2012). People with this condition may threaten and even attempt suicide to manipulate others, reflecting the chaotic nature of their relationships (Leichsenring et al., 2011). Because many experience intense feelings of abandonment, extreme loneliness, and feelings of emptiness when alone, they may jump frantically from one unhealthy relationship to another, as the video *Borderline Personality Disorder* illustrates.

Explanations of Borderline Personality Disorder. Psychoanalyst Otto Kernberg (1967, 1973) traced the roots of borderline personality to childhood problems with developing a sense of self and bonding emotionally to others. According to Kernberg, individuals with borderline personality disorder can't integrate differing perceptions of people, themselves included. This defect supposedly arises from an inborn tendency to experience intense anger and frustration from living with a cold, unempathetic mother. Kernberg argued that borderline individuals experience the world and themselves as unstable because they tend to "split" people and experiences into either all good or all bad. Although influential, Kernberg's model of borderline personality remains inadequately researched.

According to Linehan's (1993; Crowell, Beauchaine, & Linehan, 2009) sociobiological model, individuals with borderline personality disorder inherit a tendency to overreact to stress and experience lifelong difficulties with regulating their emotions. Indeed, twin studies suggest that borderline personality traits are substantially heritable (Carpenter et al., 2013; Torgersen et al., 2000). Difficulties in controlling emotions may be responsible for the rejection many individuals with borderline personality disorder encounter, as well as their excessive concerns about being validated, loved, and accepted.

Edward Selby and Thomas Joiner's emotional cascade model holds that intense rumination about negative events or emotional experiences may result in uncontrolled "emotional cascades," which prompt self-injurious actions such as cutting. Although these impulsive and desperate actions succeed in providing brief distraction from rumination, they often fuel further bouts of rumination, creating a vicious cycle of problems with regulating emotions (Gardner, Dodsworth, & Selby, 2014; Selby et al., 2009; Selby & Joiner, 2009).

borderline personality disorder
condition marked by extreme instability in mood, identity, and impulse control.

Psychologist Marsha Linehan of the University of Washington is the world's leading expert on the treatment of borderline personality disorder. In 2011, she surprised many people by acknowledging publicly that she had been diagnosed with the condition earlier in life. Linehan's courageous admission may help to dispel some of the unjustified stigma surrounding this personality disorder.

For many years, psychologists believed that borderline personality was a lifelong condition that never improved over time. In contrast, data suggests that of treatment-seeking adults that meet criteria for borderline personality disorder, only 7 percent still do a decade later (Durbin & Klein, 2006; Lilienfeld & Arkowitz, 2012).

PSYCHOPATHIC PERSONALITY: DON'T JUDGE A BOOK BY ITS COVER. We don't intend to alarm you. Yet the odds are high that in your life, you've met—perhaps even dated—at least one person whom psychologists describe as a **psychopathic personality**, which used to be known informally as a *psychopath* or *sociopath*.

> ### First-Person Account: Psychopathic Personality
>
> "In my lifetime I have murdered 21 human beings. I have committed thousands of burglaries, robberies, larcenies, arsons, and last but not least I have committed sodomy on more than 1,000 male human beings. For all of these things I am not the least bit sorry. I have no conscience so that does not worry me."
>
> (KING, 1997, P. 169). QUOTE FROM CARL PANZRAM, A SERIAL KILLER, BURGLAR, AND ARSONIST.

Psychopathic personality is not formally a psychological disorder and is not listed as a separate condition in *DSM-5*. Nevertheless, it overlaps moderately with the *DSM-5* diagnosis of **antisocial personality disorder (ASPD)**. In contrast to ASPD, which is marked by a lengthy history of illegal and irresponsible actions dating back to childhood or adolescence, psychopathic personality is marked by a distinctive set of personality traits (Lilienfeld, 1994). Because much more psychological research has concentrated on psychopathic personality than on ASPD (Hare, 2003; Patrick, 2016), we focus on psychopathy here because the latter condition is far better understood.

Psychopathic Personality: A Dangerous Mixture of Traits. Those with psychopathic personality—most of them male—are guiltless, dishonest, manipulative, callous, and self-centered (Cleckley, 1941/1988; Lykken, 1995). Moreover, many people with this condition have a history of *conduct disorder*, marked by lying, cheating, and stealing in childhood and adolescence. Recently, increasing data suggest that many adults with psychopathic personality exhibited a distinctive constellation of personality traits as children, perhaps as early as when they were five or even three years old. This constellation of features, termed *callous-unemotional traits*, is characterized by emotional coldness, along with a lack of guilt and empathy (Frick et al., 2014). As you might imagine, children with these traits aren't exactly "teachers' pets," and they often get into more than their share of trouble at school, not to mention at home. Growing evidence suggests that such children are at heightened risk for psychopathic personality traits in adolescence and perhaps adulthood (Frick & White, 2008). At the same time, labeling children with callous-emotional traits is scientifically and ethically controversial, especially because some of them "grow out" of these traits and don't develop psychopathic personality features later on (Edens et al., 2001). Because of psychopathic individuals' distinctly unpleasant personality traits, one might assume we'd all go out of our way to avoid individuals with this disorder—and we'd probably be better off if we did. However, many of us seek out people with psychopathic personality as friends and even romantic partners because they tend to be superficially charming, personable, and engaging (Dutton, 2012; Hare, 1993).

If the traits we've described fit someone you know to a T, there's no need to panic. Despite popular conception, most people with psychopathic personality aren't physically aggressive. Nevertheless, they're at somewhat heightened risk for crime compared with the average person, and a handful—probably a few percent—are habitually violent (Leistico et al., 2008). Notorious serial killer Ted Bundy, a charming ex-psychology major and law school student who raped and brutally murdered as many as several dozen women, almost certainly met the criteria for psychopathic personality disorder, as do about 25 percent of prison inmates (Hare, 2003; Poythress et al., 2010). Also, despite scores of movie portrayals of crazed serial killers, people with this disorder typically aren't psychotic. To the contrary, most are entirely rational. They know full well that their irresponsible actions are morally wrong; they just don't care (Cima, Tonnaer, & Hauser, 2010).

There's reason to suspect that people with this condition populate not only much of the criminal justice system, but also positions of leadership in corporations and politics

---

psychopathic personality

condition marked by superficial charm, dishonesty, manipulativeness, self-centeredness, and risk taking.

antisocial personality disorder (ASPD)

condition marked by a lengthy history of irresponsible or illegal actions.

(Babiak & Hare, 2006). For example, among the U.S. presidents, higher estimated levels of a constellation of traits called fearless dominance, which captures the boldness and adventurousness often found in psychopaths, are linked to superior leadership as rated by expert historians (Lilienfeld, Watts, & Smith, 2012). Indeed, some psychopathic traits, such as interpersonal skills, superficial likability, ruthlessness, and risk taking, may give people with this disorder a leg up for getting ahead of the rest of the pack. Still, there's surprisingly little research on "successful psychopaths"—people with high levels of psychopathic traits who function well in society (Hall & Benning, 2006; Lilienfeld et al., 2015; Widom, 1977).

Causes of Psychopathic Personality. Despite more than six decades of research, the causes of psychopathic personality remain largely unknown (Skeem et al., 2011). Classic research shows that individuals with this disorder don't show much classical conditioning to unpleasant unconditioned stimuli such as electric shock (Lykken, 1957). Similarly, when asked to sit patiently in a chair for an electric shock or a loud blast of noise, their levels of skin conductance—an indicator of arousal—increase only about one-fifth as much as those without psychopathic personality (Hare, 1978; Lorber, 2004). These abnormalities probably stem from a deficit in fear, which may give rise to some of the key features of the disorder (Fowles & Dindo, 2009; Lykken, 1995; Patrick, 2016). Consistent with these laboratory findings, functional brain imaging studies demonstrate that individuals with pronounced psychopathic traits tend to exhibit underactivity of the amygdala in response to fear-related stimuli, such as faces of terrified people (Moul, Kilcross, & Dadds, 2012). The amygdala is an almond-shaped brain structure that plays a key role in fear processing. Perhaps partly as a consequence of this dearth of fear, people with psychopathic personality aren't especially motivated to learn from punishment and tend to repeat the same mistakes in life (Newman & Kosson, 1986; Zeier et al., 2012).

An alternative explanation is that individuals with this disorder are underaroused. The *Yerkes–Dodson law* describes a well-established psychological principle: an inverted U-shaped relationship between arousal on the one hand and mood and performance on the other. As this law reminds us, people who are habitually underaroused experience *stimulus hunger*; they're bored and seek out excitement. The underarousal hypothesis may help to explain why those with psychopathic personality tend to be risk takers (Zuckerman, 1989), as well as why they frequently get in trouble with the law and abuse all manner of substances (Taylor & Lang, 2006). Nevertheless, the causal arrow between underarousal and psychopathy may run in the opposite direction: If people with psychopathic traits are fearless, they may experience little arousal in response to stimuli (Lykken, 1995).

> **Ruling Out Rival Hypotheses**
>
> Have important alternative explanations for the findings been excluded?

> **Correlation vs. Causation**
>
> Can we be sure that A causes B?

Dissociative Disorders

When speaking about ourselves, we use the words *me* and *I* without giving it a second thought. That's not the case in most **dissociative disorders**, which involve disruptions in the ordinarily seamless integration of consciousness, memory, identity, or perception (APA, 2013).

dissociative disorder

condition involving disruptions in consciousness, memory, identity, or perception

---

Fact vs. Fiction

Individuals with psychopathic personality disorder are "hopeless cases" who can't be rehabilitated.

○ Fact

○ Fiction

Interactive

Answer: Fiction At least some people with this disorder may improve as a consequence of psychotherapy, especially when treatment is prolonged and intensive (Salekin, 2002; Skeem, Monahan, & Mulvey, 2002).

The idea that one person can have more than one identity—let alone more than a hundred, as in a number of reported cases (Acocello, 1999)—is an extraordinary claim. So it's no wonder that dissociative identity disorder (DID) is one of the most controversial of all diagnoses. Before we consider the debate that swirls around this condition, we'll consider several other dissociative disorders.

DEPERSONALIZATION/DEREALIZATION DISORDER. If you've ever felt detached from yourself, as though you're living in a movie or dream or observing your body from the perspective of an outsider, you've experienced *depersonalization*. More than half of adults have experienced one brief episode of depersonalization, and such experiences are especially common among adolescents and college students (APA, 2013; Simeon et al., 1997). Derealization, the sense that the external world is strange or unreal, often accompanies both depersonalization and panic attacks. Only if people experience multiple episodes of depersonalization, derealization, or both, do they qualify for a diagnosis of **depersonalization/derealization disorder**.

depersonalization/derealization disorder

condition marked by multiple episodes of depersonalization, derealization, or both.

Sleep disturbances may play a prominent role in depersonalization/derealization. When people are deprived of sleep for 24 hours, they report more dissociative-like symptoms, and when they're taught sleep hygiene techniques (e.g., not drinking caffeine close to bedtime) to improve their sleep, they report fewer dissociative symptoms (van der Kloet et al., 2012). Some researchers propose that a disturbed sleep-wake cycle produces dreamlike thoughts during the daytime that cause or at least fuel dissociative experiences.

> ## Journal Prompt
>
> Have you ever experienced an episode of what you believe to be depersonalization/derealization? Write a detailed description of your experience. If you've never experienced such an episode, what do you think it would be like for you? Why do you think depersonalization/derealization commonly occurs during panic attacks?

dissociative amnesia

inability to recall important personal information—most often related to a stressful experience—that can't be explained by ordinary forgetfulness.

DISSOCIATIVE AMNESIA. In **dissociative amnesia**, people can't recall important personal information—most often following a stressful experience—that isn't as a result of ordinary forgetting. Their memory loss is extensive and can include suicide attempts or violent outbursts (Sar et al., 2007). More commonly, psychologists diagnose dissociative amnesia when adults report gaps in their memories for child abuse.

This diagnosis has proven controversial for several reasons. First, memory gaps regarding nontraumatic events are common in healthy individuals and aren't necessarily stress-related or indicative of dissociation (Belli et al., 1998). Second, most people may not be especially motivated to think about or recall child abuse or other upsetting events. As Richard McNally (2003) pointed out, not thinking about something isn't the same as being *unable* to remember it, which is amnesia. Third, careful studies have turned up no convincing cases of amnesia that can't be explained by other factors, like disease, brain injury, normal forgetting, or an unwillingness to think about disturbing events (Kihlstrom, 2005; Pope et al., 2007). Fourth, individuals with high levels of dissociation are *less* likely to forget supposedly threatening (sexual) words, which experimenters direct them to forget (Elzinga et al., 2000; Giesbrecht et al., 2008).

dissociative fugue

sudden, unexpected travel away from home or the workplace, accompanied by amnesia for significant life events.

At times, we've all felt like running away from our troubles. In **dissociative fugue**, a subtype of dissociative amnesia, people not only forget significant events in their lives, but also flee their stressful circumstances (*fugue,* which has the same root as fugitive, is Latin for "flight"). In some cases, they move to another city or another country, assuming a new identity. Fugues can last for hours or, in unusual cases, years. Dissociative fugue is rare, occurring in about 2 of every 1,000 people (American

Psychiatric Association [APA], 2000), with more prolonged fugue states even rarer (Karlin & Orne, 1996).

In 2006, a 57-year-old husband, father, and Boy Scout leader from New York was found living under a new name in a homeless shelter in Chicago after he left his garage near his office and disappeared. When a tip to the television program *America's Most Wanted* uncovered his true identity six months later, his family contacted him, but he claimed to have no memory of who they were (Brody, 2007).

In this and other cases, it's essential to find out whether the fugue resulted from a head injury, a stroke, or another neurological cause. Moreover, some people merely claim amnesia to avoid responsibilities or stressful circumstances, relocate to a different area, and get a fresh start in life (Marcopulos & Hedjar, 2014). Even when fugues occur shortly after a traumatic event, it's difficult to know whether the trauma caused the amnesia or other factors such as the desire to avoid responsibilities or keep out of trouble are at work. Scientists don't fully understand the role trauma, psychological factors, and neurological conditions play in fugue states (Kihlstrom, 2005).

> **Ruling Out Rival Hypotheses**
>
> Have important alternative explanations for the findings been excluded?

Jeffrey Ingram, aged 40, experienced a dissociative fugue in which he claimed for more than a month that he couldn't remember anything about his life. He was reunited with his fiancée in 2006 only after he appeared on television shows asking the public to identify him.

DISSOCIATIVE IDENTITY DISORDER: MULTIPLE PERSONALITIES, MULTIPLE CONTROVERSIES. **Dissociative identity disorder (DID)** is characterized by the presence of two or more distinct personality states that markedly disrupt the person's usual sense of identity and may be observed by others or reported by the individual. These personality states or "alters," as they're sometimes called, are often different from the primary or "host" personality and may be of different names, ages, genders, races, and even species. In some cases, these features are the opposite of those exhibited by the host personality. For example, if the host personality is shy and retiring, one or more alters may be outgoing or flamboyant. Psychologists have reported the number of alters to range from one (the so-called split personality) to hundreds or even thousands, with one reported case of 4,500 personalities (Acocella, 1999). In general, women are more likely to receive a DID diagnosis and report more alters than men (APA, 2013).

Researchers have identified intriguing differences among alters in their respiration rates, brain wave activity (Ludwig et al., 1972), eyeglass prescriptions, handedness, skin conductance responses, voice patterns, and handwriting (Lilienfeld & Lynn, 2013). Fascinating as these findings are, they don't provide conclusive evidence for the existence of alters. These differences could stem from changes in mood or thoughts over time or to bodily changes, such as muscle tension, that people can produce on a voluntary basis (Allen & Movius, 2000; Merckelbach, Devilly, & Rassin, 2002; Paris, 2012). Moreover, scientists have falsified claims that alters are truly distinct. When psychologists have used objective measures of memory, they've typically found that information presented to one alter is available to the other, providing no evidence for amnesia across alters (Allen & Moravius, 2000; Huntjens, Verschuere, & McNally, 2012).

> **Ruling Out Rival Hypotheses**
>
> Have important alternative explanations for the findings been excluded?

dissociative identity disorder (DID) condition characterized by the presence of two or more distinct personality states that recurrently take control of the person's behavior.

> **Falsifiability**
>
> Can the claim be disproved?

The primary controversy surrounding DID revolves around one question: Is DID a response to early trauma, or is it a consequence of social and cultural factors (Merskey, 1992)? According to the *posttraumatic model* (Dalenberg et al., 2012; Gleaves, May, & Cardeña, 2001; Ross, 1997), DID arises from a history of severe abuse—physical, sexual, or both—during childhood. This abuse leads individuals to "compartmentalize" their identity into distinct alters as a means of coping with intense emotional pain. In this way, the person can feel as though the abuse happened to someone else.

Advocates of the posttraumatic model claim that 90 percent or more of individuals with DID were severely abused in childhood (Gleaves, 1996). Nevertheless, many studies that reported this association didn't check the accuracy of abuse claims against objective information such as court records of abuse (Coons, Bowman, & Milstein, 1988). Moreover, researchers haven't shown that early abuse is specific to DID because it's present in many other disorders (Pope & Hudson, 1992). These considerations don't exclude a role for early trauma in DID, but they suggest that researchers must conduct further controlled studies before drawing strong conclusions (Gleaves, 1996; Gleaves et al., 2001).

"I HAVE 25 PATIENTS IN MY COUNSELING GROUP -- MRS. SHERMAN, MR. MARTIN, AND MR. MARTIN'S 23 OTHER PERSONALITIES."

SOURCE: Dan Rosandich, www.CartoonStock.com

Sheri Storm was diagnosed with dissociative identity disorder but later became convinced that a therapist had inadvertently implanted her alter personalities using suggestive techniques. This painting—completed by Storm during therapy—depicts the seemingly endless parade of her alters emerging in treatment.

According to advocates of the competing *sociocognitive model*, the claim that some people have hundreds of personalities is extraordinary, but the evidence for it is unconvincing (Lilienfeld et al., 1999; McHugh, 1993; Merskey, 1992; Spanos, 1996). According to this model, people's expectancies and beliefs—shaped by certain psychotherapeutic procedures and cultural influences and a tendency to fantasize and misremember events, rather than early traumas—account for the origin and maintenance of DID. Advocates of this model claim that some therapists use procedures like hypnosis and repeated prompting of alters that suggest to patients that their puzzling symptoms are the products of indwelling identities (Lilienfeld & Lynn, 2013; Lilienfeld et al., 1999). The following observations and findings support this hypothesis:

- Many or most DID patients show few or no clear-cut signs of this condition, such as alters, prior to psychotherapy (Kluft, 1984).

- Mainstream treatment techniques for DID reinforce the idea that the person possesses multiple identities. These techniques include using hypnosis to "bring forth" hidden alters, communicating with alters and giving them different names, and encouraging patients to recover repressed memories supposedly housed in dissociated selves (Lynn, Condon, & Colletti, 2013).

- The number of alters per DID individual tends to increase substantially when therapists use these techniques (Piper, 1997).

- Researchers have reported a link between dissociation and the tendency to fantasize in everyday life (Giesbrecht et al., 2008), which may be related to the production of false memories, although the interpretation of these findings has proven controversial (Dalenberg et al., 2011).

As of 1970, there were 79 documented cases of DID in the world literature. As of 1986, the number of DID cases had mushroomed to approximately 6,000 (Lilienfeld et al., 1999), and some estimates in the early 21st century are in the hundreds of thousands. The sociocognitive model holds that the popular media have played a pivotal role in the DID epidemic (Elzinga, van Dyck, & Spinhoven, 1998). Indeed, much of the dramatic increase in DID's prevalence followed closely on the release of the best-selling book *Sybil* (Schreiber, 1973) in the mid-1970s, later made into an Emmy Award–winning television movie starring Sally Field. The book and later film told the heartbreaking story of a young woman with 16 personalities who reported a history of sadistic child abuse. Interestingly, subsequently released audiotapes of Sybil's therapy sessions suggested that she had no alters or memories of child abuse prior to treatment and that her therapist had urged her to behave in dramatically differently ways on different occasions (Nathan, 2011; Rieber, 1999).

Over the past two decades, media coverage of DID has skyrocketed (Showalter, 1997; Spanos, 1996; Wilson, 2003). Sensationalized portrayals of DID have appeared regularly in television programs (*The United States of Tara, Mr. Robot*) and movies (*Fight Club, Secret Window, Raising Cain, Split*). Many of these media portrayals perpetuate myths regarding the disorder, such as the idea that individuals with DID have multiple indwelling personalities. Moreover, some celebrities, like comedian Roseanne Barr and football star Hershel Walker, have claimed to suffer from the disorder. Although DID is virtually nonexistent in Japan and India, it's now diagnosed with considerable frequency in some countries, such as Holland, in which it has recently received more publicity (Lilienfeld & Lynn, 2013). In summary, there's considerable support for the sociocognitive model and the claim that therapists, along with the media, are creating alters rather than discovering them. The dissociative disorders provide a powerful, although troubling, example of how social and cultural forces can shape psychological disorders.

15.5: The Enigma of Schizophrenia

15.5a Recognize the characteristic symptoms of schizophrenia.

15.5b Explain how psychosocial, neural, biochemical, and genetic influences create the vulnerability to schizophrenia.

Psychiatrist Daniel Weinberger has called **schizophrenia** the "cancer" of mental illness: It's perhaps the most severe of all disorders—and the most mysterious (Levy-Reiner, 1996). As we'll discover, it's a devastating disorder of thought and emotion associated with a loss of contact with reality.

The Daily News, June 1 2013 — Page 1

Study Shows American Public Has Schizophrenic Views on Taxes

Staff writer, Caroline Beimford

A recently published study shows that Americans are very divided on the issue of taxes. While some are opposed to any tax increases, others see the necessity of

The headline of this newspaper story, which refers to American's divided views on taxes, confuses schizophrenia with split personality.

Symptoms of Schizophrenia: The Shattered Mind

Even today, many people confuse schizophrenia with DID (Taylor & Kowalski, 2012). Swiss psychiatrist Eugen Bleuler gave us the modern term *schizophrenia* in 1911. The term literally means "split mind," which no doubt contributed to the popular myth that the symptoms of schizophrenia stem from a split personality. You may have even heard people refer to a "schizophrenic attitude" when explaining that they're "of two minds" regarding an issue. Don't be misled. As Bleuler recognized, the difficulties of individuals with schizophrenia arise from disturbances in attention, thinking, language, emotion, and relationships with others. In contrast to DID, which is supposedly characterized by multiple intact personalities, schizophrenia is characterized by one personality that's shattered.

schizophrenia

severe disorder of thought and emotion associated with a loss of contact with reality.

More than half of people with schizophrenia suffer from serious disabilities, such as an inability to hold a job and maintain close relationships (Harvey, Reichenberg, & Bowie, 2006). More than 10 percent of homeless people, with some estimates ranging as high as 45 percent, qualify for a diagnosis of schizophrenia (Folsom & Jeste, 2008). Individuals who experience schizophrenia comprise less than 1 percent of the population, with most estimates ranging from 0.4 to 0.7 percent (Saha et al., 2005). Yet they make up half of the patients in state and county mental institutions in the United States. But

there's some good news. Today, more than ever, people with schizophrenia can function in society, even though they may need to return periodically to hospitals for treatment (Lamb & Bachrach, 2001; Mueser & McGurk, 2004). As many as one-half to two-thirds of people with schizophrenia improve significantly, although not completely, and a small percentage may even recover completely after a single episode (Harrow et al., 2005; Robinson et al., 2004). Researchers found that 20 high-functioning people with schizophrenia—which included doctors, an attorney, and a chief executive—used such strategies as taking medication, getting exercise and adequate sleep, avoiding alcohol and crowds, and seeking social support to manage their illness successfully (Marder et al., 2008).

Watch SCHIZOPHRENIA

Video

The **Negative Symptoms** of Schizophrenia include:

Flat or Blunted Affect. This is where the patient's internal mood state is not communicated through non-verbal behavior. Their facial expressions seem to show a lack of emotion.

Researchers have struggled with the problem of describing schizophrenia since the 18th century, when Emil Kraepelin first outlined the features of patients with *dementia praecox,* meaning psychological deterioration in youth. But Kraepelin didn't get it quite right. Even though the typical onset of schizophrenia is in the mid-20s for men and the late 20s for women, schizophrenia can also strike after age 45 (APA, 2013).

First-Person Account: **Schizophrenia**

"The reflection in the store window—it's me, isn't it? I know it is, but it's hard to tell. Glassy shadows, polished pastels, a jigsaw puzzle of my body, face, and clothes, with pieces disappearing whenever I move…. Schizophrenia is painful, and it is craziness when I hear voices, when I believe people are following me, wanting to snatch my very soul. I am frightened, too, when every whisper, every laugh is about me; when newspapers suddenly contain cures, four-letter words shouting at me; when sparkles of light are demon eyes."

(MᴄGRATH, 1984)

---

delusion

strongly held fixed belief that has no basis in reality.

psychotic symptom

psychological problem reflecting serious distortions in reality.

hallucination

sensory perception that occurs in the absence of an external stimulus.

DELUSIONS: FIXED FALSE BELIEFS. Among the hallmark symptoms of schizophrenia are **delusions**—strongly held fixed beliefs that have no basis in reality. Delusions are **psychotic symptoms** because they represent a serious distortion of reality.

Delusions commonly involve themes of persecution. One of your book's authors treated a man who believed that coworkers tapped his phone and conspired to get him fired. Another was convinced that a helicopter in the distance beamed the Beatles song "All You Need Is Love" into his head to make him feel jealous and inadequate. The authors of your book have also treated patients who reported delusions of grandeur (greatness), including one who believed that she'd discovered the cure for cancer even though she had no medical training. John Hinckley, the man who nearly assassinated then–President Ronald Reagan in 1981, was convinced that murdering the president would gain him the affection of actress Jodie Foster. In Table 15.5 you'll find a sampling of other unusual delusions, which may be associated with schizophrenia or neurological conditions such as traumatic brain injury and dementia.

HALLUCINATIONS: FALSE PERCEPTIONS. Among the other serious symptoms of schizophrenia are **hallucinations**, sensory perceptions that occur in the absence of an external stimulus (Bentall, 2013). They can be auditory (involving hearing), olfactory (involving smell), gustatory (involving taste), tactile (involving the sense of feeling), or visual. Most hallucinations in schizophrenia are auditory, usually consisting of voices. Hallucinated voices may express disapproval or carry on a running commentary about the person's thoughts or actions. *Command hallucinations*, which tell patients what to do ("Go over to that man and tell him to shut up!"), may be associated with a heightened risk

Table 15.5 A Sampling of 10 Unusual Delusions.

Name of Delusion	Description
Capgras syndrome	Belief that a familiar person has been replaced by an imposter
Fregoli delusion	Belief that different people are actually the same person in disguise
Mirrored self misidentification	Belief that one's reflection in the mirror is that of another person
Erotomania	Belief that another person, often a celebrity, is in love with the patient, who may then repeatedly call or send unwelcome love letters
Clinical lycanthropy	Belief that one has turned into a wolf or has the ability to do so
Cervanthropy	Belief that one has turned into a deer
Truman Show delusion	Belief that one is being filmed and the films are being viewed by others, as depicted in the 1998 movie *The Truman Show* starring Jim Carrey
Folie à deux	French for the "folly of two" a person in a close relationship induces the same delusion in his or her partner (e.g., the government is poisoning their food). Rare cases of *folie a deux* in identical twins, *folie a trois* (involving three people), and *folie a famille* (involving an entire family) have also been reported
Somatoparaphrenia	Unawareness of a body part, such as a limb (or an entire side of the body), or the belief that it belongs to another person.
Cotard delusion	Belief that one is dead

In the 2001 film *A Beautiful Mind*, actor Russell Crowe (*left*) portrays Nobel Prize–winning mathematician John Nash, who was diagnosed with schizophrenia. In this scene, Nash is shown talking to a friend whom he sees—but does not exist. What's scientifically unrealistic about this scene? See answer at the bottom of the page.

of violence toward others (Bucci et al., 2013; McNiel, Eisner, & Binder, 2000). Incidentally, extremely vivid or detailed visual hallucinations—especially in the absence of auditory hallucinations—are usually signs of an organic (medical) disorder or substance abuse rather than schizophrenia (Shea, 2013).

Do your thoughts sound like voices in your head? Many people experience their thoughts as inner speech, which is entirely normal. Some researchers suggest that auditory hallucinations occur when people with schizophrenia believe mistakenly that their inner speech arises from a source outside themselves (Bentall, 2013; Frith, 1992; Thomas, 1997). Brain scans reveal that when people experience auditory hallucinations, brain areas associated with speech perception and production become activated (Jardri et al., 2011; McGuire, Shah, & Murray, 1993).

DISORGANIZED SPEECH. Consider this example of the speech of a patient with schizophrenia: "It was shockingly not of the best quality I have known all such evildoers coming out of doors with the best of intentions" (Grinnell, 2008). We can see that this patient skips from topic to topic in a disjointed way. Most researchers believe that this peculiar language results from thought disorder (Meehl, 1962; Stirk et al., 2008). The usual associations that we forge between two words, such as *mother–child*, are considerably weakened or highly unusual for individuals with schizophrenia (for example, *mother–rug*) (Kuperberg et al., 2006).

Bleuler (1911/1915) famously observed, "in some cases, all the threads between thought are torn." (p. 20). In severe forms, the resulting speech is so jumbled it's almost impossible to understand, leading some psychologists to describe it as *word salad*. Language problems, like thought disorder, point to fundamental impairments in schizophrenia in the ability to shift and maintain attention, which influence virtually every aspect of affected individuals' daily lives (Cornblatt & Keilp, 1994; Fuller et al., 2006).

GROSSLY DISORGANIZED BEHAVIOR AND CATATONIA. When people develop schizophrenia, self-care, personal hygiene, and motivation often deteriorate. They may avoid conversation; laugh, cry, or swear inappropriately; or wear a warm coat on a sweltering summer day.

Answer: Extremely vivid or detailed visual hallucinations are rare in schizophrenia.

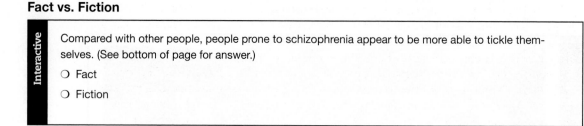

Fact vs. Fiction

Compared with other people, people prone to schizophrenia appear to be more able to tickle themselves. (See bottom of page for answer.)

O Fact

O Fiction

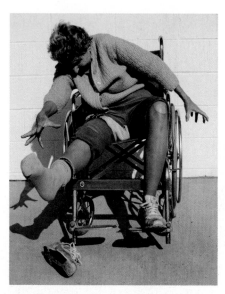

Catatonic individuals, like the one shown here, may permit their limbs to be moved to any position and maintain this posture for lengthy periods of time, a condition called *waxy flexibility*.

Ruling Out Rival Hypotheses ▶

Have important alternative explanations for the findings been excluded?

catatonic symptom

motor problem, including holding the body in bizarre or rigid postures, curling up in a fetal position, and resisting simple suggestions to move.

Correlation vs. Causation ▶

Can we be sure that A causes B?

Catatonic symptoms involve motor (movement) problems, including holding the body in bizarre or rigid postures, curling up in a fetal position, resisting simple suggestions to move or speak, and pacing aimlessly. Catatonic individuals may also repeat a phrase in conversation in a parrotlike manner, a symptom called *echolalia*. At the opposite extreme, they may occasionally engage in bouts of frenzied, purposeless motor activity.

Explanations for Schizophrenia: The Roots of a Shattered Mind

Today, virtually all scientists believe that psychosocial factors play some role in schizophrenia. Nevertheless, they also agree that these factors probably trigger the disorder only in people with a genetic vulnerability.

THE FAMILY AND EXPRESSED EMOTION. Early theories of schizophrenia mistakenly laid the blame for the condition on mothers, with so-called *schizophrenogenic* (schizophrenia-producing) mothers being the prime culprits. Based on informal observations of families of children with schizophrenia, some authors described such mothers as overprotective, smothering, rejecting, and controlling (Arieti, 1959; Lidz, 1973). Other theorists pointed the finger of blame at the interactions among all family members (Dolnick, 1998).

But as important as clinical experience can be in generating hypotheses, it doesn't provide an adequate arena for testing them. These early studies were severely flawed, largely because they lacked control groups of people without schizophrenia. A now widely accepted rival hypothesis is that family members' responses aren't the cause of schizophrenia, but instead are typically a response to the stressful experience of living with a severely disturbed person.

It's widely acknowledged that parents and family members don't "cause" schizophrenia (Gottesman, 1991; Walker et al., 2004). Still, families may influence whether patients with the disorder relapse. After leaving hospitals, patients experience more than twice the likelihood of relapse (50–60 percent) when their relatives display high *expressed emotion* (EE)—that is, criticism, hostility, and overinvolvement (Brown et al., 1962; Butzlaff & Hooley, 1998; Kuipers, 2011). Criticism is especially predictive of relapse (Halweg et al., 1989; McCarty et al., 2004), even over 20 years, and may result in part from relatives' frustrations in living with a person with schizophrenia who displays disruptive behaviors (Cechnicki et al., 2012). Indeed, EE may reflect family members' reactions to their loved one's schizophrenia as much as contribute to their loved one's relapse (King, 2000). If so, the direction of causation may run more from patients to family members than from family members to patients.

The apparent effects of EE vary across ethnic groups (Singh, Harley, & Suhail, 2013). Critical comments from family members may undermine recovering patients' confidence

Answer: Fact. Recent evidence suggests that people with mild features of schizophrenia or who experience the auditory hallucinations typical of schizophrenia are especially good self-ticklers (Lematre, Loyat, & Lafargue, 2014), potentially pointing to deficits in a sense of self in this disorder.

and sense of independence, which are valued in Caucasian-American culture (Chentsova-Dutton & Tsai, 2007). In contrast, in Mexican-American culture, independence isn't as highly valued, so criticism doesn't predict relapse. Nevertheless, a lack of family warmth, which is prized in Mexican-American families, does predict relapse (Lopez et al., 2004). Moreover, in Africa-American families, results of one study suggest that high levels of EE predict *better* outcomes among individuals with schizophrenia, perhaps because family members perceive EE as an expression of openness, honesty, and caring (Rosenfarb, Bellack, & Aziz, 2006). Although EE often predicts relapse, well-controlled studies don't support the hypothesis that child rearing directly *causes* schizophrenia, any more than does extreme poverty, childhood trauma, or parental conflict, all of which are correlated with schizophrenia (Cornblatt, Green, & Walker, 1999; Schofield & Balian, 1959).

SCHIZOPHRENIA: BRAIN, BIOCHEMICAL, AND GENETIC FINDINGS.   Research using a variety of technologies has uncovered intriguing biological clues to the causes of schizophrenia. We'll focus on three such clues: brain abnormalities, neurotransmitter differences, and genetic influences.

Brain Abnormalities.   Research indicates that one or more of four fluid-filled structures called *ventricles*, which cushion and nourish the brain, are typically enlarged in individuals with schizophrenia. This finding is important for two reasons. First, these brain areas frequently expand when others shrink, suggesting that schizophrenia is a disorder of brain deterioration (DeLisi, 2008). Second, deterioration in these areas is associated with thought disorder (Vita et al., 1995).

Other brain abnormalities in schizophrenia include increases in the size of the *sulci*, or spaces between the ridges of the brain (Cannon, Mednick, & Parnas, 1989) and decreases in (a) the size of the temporal lobes (Boos et al., 2007; Haijma et al., 2013), (b) activation of the amygdala and hippocampus (Hempel et al., 2003;Pankow et al., 2013), and (c) the symmetry of the brain's hemispheres (Luchins, Weinberger, & Wyatt, 1982; Zivotofsky et al., 2007). Functional brain imaging studies show that the frontal lobes of people with schizophrenia are less active than those of non-patients when engaged in demanding mental tasks (Andreasen et al., 1992; Knyazeva et al., 2008), a phenomenon called *hypofrontality*. Still, it's not clear whether these findings are causes or consequences of the disorder. For example, hypofrontality could be the result of the tendency of patients with schizophrenia to concentrate less on tasks compared with other individuals. Researchers also need to rule out alternative explanations for brain underactivity that could arise from patients' diet, drinking and smoking habits, and medication use (Hanson & Gottesman, 2005).

Some studies have suggested that marijuana use in adolescence can bring about schizophrenia and other psychotic disorders in genetically vulnerable individuals (Compton et al., 2009; Degenhardt et al., 2009; Kelley et al., 2016). Nevertheless, it's difficult to pin down a causal relationship between marijuana use and schizophrenia for three reasons: (1) People who use marijuana are likely to use a variety of other drugs; (2) individuals with schizophrenia may be more likely to use marijuana, so the causal arrow may be reversed; and (3) the rates of schizophrenia remained stable between 1970 and 2005 in the United Kingdom, although marijuana use increased over this period (Frisher et al., 2009). Still, people with a personal or family history of psychotic disorders, including schizophrenia, would be particularly ill advised to use marijuana.

Neurotransmitter Differences.   The biochemistry of the brain is one of the keys to unlocking the mystery of schizophrenia. One early explanation was the *dopamine hypothesis* (Carlsson, 1995; Keith et al., 1976; Nicol & Gottesman, 1983). The evidence for the role of dopamine in schizophrenia is mostly indirect. First, most antischizophrenic drugs block dopamine receptor sites. To put it crudely, the drugs "slow down" nerve impulses by partially blocking the action of dopamine. Second, amphetamine, a stimulant that blocks the reuptake of dopamine, tends to worsen the symptoms of schizophrenia (Lieberman & Koreen, 1993; Snyder, 1975).

Nevertheless, the hypothesis that a simple excess of dopamine creates the symptoms of schizophrenia doesn't seem to fit the data (Kendler & Schaffner, 2011). A better-supported

Correlation vs. Causation

Can we be sure that A causes B?

In one identical twin with schizophrenia, the fluid-filled ventricles of the brain (*see red arrows*) are enlarged relative to his or her co-twin without schizophrenia. Such enlargement probably reflects a deterioration in brain tissue surrounding the ventricles, which expand to fill the missing space.

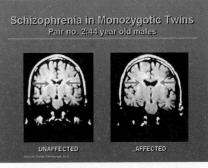

Schizophrenia in Monozygotic Twins
Pair no. 2:44 year old males

UNAFFECTED   AFFECTED

Correlation vs. Causation

Can we be sure that A causes B?

Ruling Out Rival Hypotheses

Have important alternative explanations for the findings been excluded?

Correlation vs. Causation

Can we be sure that A causes B?

Ruling Out Rival Hypotheses ▶

Have important alternative explanations for the findings been excluded?

Ruling Out Rival Hypotheses ▶

Have important alternative explanations for the findings been excluded?

Replicability ▶

Can the results be duplicated in other studies?

diathesis-stress model

perspective proposing that mental disorders are a joint product of a genetic vulnerability, called a diathesis, and stressors that trigger this vulnerability.

---

rival hypothesis is that abnormalities in dopamine *receptors* produce these symptoms. Receptor sites in the brain appear to be highly specific for dopamine transmission. These sites respond uniquely to drugs designed to reduce psychotic symptoms and are associated with difficulties in attention, memory, and motivation (Busatto et al., 1995; Keefe & Henry, 1994; Reis et al., 2004). These findings provide evidence for a direct tie between dopamine pathways and symptoms of schizophrenia, such as paranoia. Still, dopamine is probably only one of several neurotransmitters that play a role in schizophrenia; other likely candidates are norepinephrine, glutamate, and serotonin (Cornblatt et al., 1999; Grace, 1991; Moghaddam & Javitt, 2012).

Genetic Influences. Still unresolved is the question of which biological deficits are present before schizophrenia and which appear after the disorder begins (Seidman et al., 2003). The seeds of schizophrenia are often sown well before birth and lie partly in individuals' genetic endowment. As we can see in Figure 15.5 on the next page, being the offspring of someone diagnosed with schizophrenia greatly increases one's odds of developing the disorder. If we have a sibling with schizophrenia, we have about a 1 in 10 chance of developing the disorder; these odds are about 10 times higher than those of the average person. As genetic similarity increases, so does the risk of schizophrenia.

Still, it's possible the environment accounts for these findings because siblings not only share genes, but also grow up in the same family. To eliminate this ambiguity, researchers have conducted twin studies, which provide convincing support for a genetic influence on schizophrenia. If we have an identical twin with schizophrenia, our risk rises to about 50 percent. An identical twin of a person with schizophrenia is about 3 times more likely than a fraternal twin of a person with schizophrenia to develop the disorder and about 50 times more likely than an average person (Gottesman & Shields, 1972; Kendler & Diehl, 1993; Meehl, 1962). Adoption data also point to a genetic influence. Even when children who have a biological parent with schizophrenia are adopted by parents with no hint of the disorder, their risk of schizophrenia is greater than that of a person with no biological relative with schizophrenia (Gottesman, 1991). Interestingly, scientists have identified structural brain abnormalities, like ventricular enlargement and decreases in brain volume, in the healthy close relatives of patients with schizophrenia, further suggesting that genetic influences produce a vulnerability to schizophrenia (Staal et al., 2000).

Researchers have long sought answers to the questions of what, exactly, is inherited that predisposes a person to the symptoms of schizophrenia and why the number of synapses is often dramatically reduced in people with this condition. We now seem to be a step closer to answering these important questions. To search for genes associated with schizophrenia, Sekar and colleagues (Sekar et al., 2016) recently combed through a vast genetic database of more than 60,000 people with schizophrenia and healthy people. The scientist's painstaking work paid off: People with schizophrenia were much more likely to have inherited a variant in a gene called C4, which is intimately associated with the immune system and with the process of pruning or reducing the number of synapses, which are essential to normal brain development and neural plasticity. This finding supports the hypothesis that the symptoms of schizophrenia arise in part when the C4 gene triggers "overpruning" or eliminating needed synapses in areas of the brain associated with the ability to think, plan, and organize thoughts (Whalley, 2016). At the same time, it's unlikely that any single gene can account for the broad range of symptoms associated with schizophrenia, and the C4 gene is only a modest predictor of schizophrenia risk, so it is unlikely to tell the full story of the causes of this devastating disorder. The next challenge researchers face is to replicate this fascinating finding and to determine how the reduction in synapses contributes to the enormously diverse symptoms of schizophrenia.

One thing is for sure—the search for genes associated with schizophrenia will continue. In one recent study (Ripke et al., 2013), a team of researchers identified 22 different gene sites associated with schizophrenia and estimated that 8,300 independent genetic variations contribute to the risk for schizophrenia

VULNERABILITY TO SCHIZOPHRENIA: DIATHESIS-STRESS MODELS. Diathesis-stress models incorporate much of what we know about schizophrenia (Meehl, 1962). Such models propose that schizophrenia, along with many other mental disorders, is a joint product of a genetic vulnerability, called a *diathesis*, and stressors that trigger this vulnerability (Salomon & Jin, 2013; Walker & DiForio, 1997; Zubin & Spring, 1977).

Paul Meehl (1990) suggested that approximately 10 percent of the population has a genetic predisposition to schizophrenia. What are people with this predisposition like? During adolescence and adulthood, they may strike us as "odd ducks." They may seem socially uncomfortable, and their speech, thought processes, and perceptions may impress us as unusual. They're likely to endorse items on psychological tests such as "Occasionally, I have felt as though my body did not exist" (Chapman, Chapman, & Raulin, 1978). Such individuals display symptoms of psychosis-proneness or *schizotypal personality disorder*. Most people with schizotypal personality disorder don't develop full-blown schizophrenia (Corcoran, First, & Cornblatt, 2010), perhaps because they've a weaker genetic vulnerability or because they've experienced fewer stressors.

Well before people experience symptoms of schizophrenia, we can identify "early warning signs" or markers of vulnerability to this condition. People with schizotypal personality disorder display some of these markers, which include social withdrawal, thought and movement abnormalities, and learning and memory deficits (Ryan, MacDonald, & Walker, 2013; Volgmaier et al., 2000). Their difficulties begin early in life. Elaine Walker and Richard Lewine (1990) found that people who viewed home movies of siblings interacting could identify which children later developed schizophrenia at better-than-chance levels. Even at an early age, vulnerable children's lack of emotions and decreased eye contact and social responsiveness tipped off observers. This design is valuable because it gets around the retrospective bias introduced by asking adults to report on their childhood experiences.

But most people with a vulnerability to schizophrenia don't develop it. Whether someone ends up with the disorder depends, in part, on the impact of events that interfere with normal development. More people with schizophrenia are born in the winter and spring than at other times of the year (Davies et al., 2003; Torrey et al., 1997). The reason for this strange finding doesn't appear to lie in astrology: Certain viral infections that affect pregnant women and that may trigger schizophrenia in vulnerable fetuses are most common in winter months. Children of women who had the flu during their second trimester of pregnancy (Brown et al., 2004; Mednick et al., 1988), suffered starvation early in pregnancy (Kirkbride et al., 2012; Susser & Lin, 1992), or experienced complications while giving birth (Bersani et al., 2012; Weinberger, 1987) are at a somewhat heightened risk of schizophrenia. Viral infections in the uterus may also play a key role in triggering certain cases of schizophrenia (Khandaker et al., 2013; Walker & DiForio, 1997). But the great majority of people exposed to infection or trauma before birth never show signs of schizophrenia. So these events probably create problems only for people who are genetically vulnerable to begin with (Cornblatt et al., 1999; Verdoux, 2004).

Figure 15.5 Schizophrenia Risk and the Family.

The lifetime risk of developing schizophrenia is largely a function of how closely an individual is genetically related to a person with schizophrenia.

SOURCE: Based on data from Gottesman, I.I. (1991) Schizophrenia genesis: The Origins of Madness. New York: W.H. Freeman

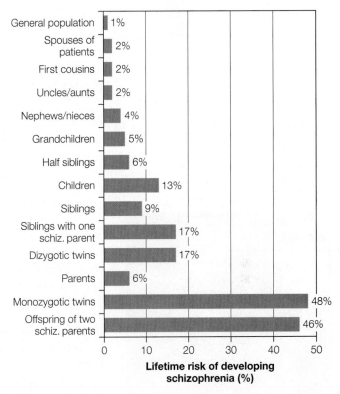

15.6: Childhood Disorders: Recent Controversies

15.6a Describe the symptoms and debate surrounding disorders diagnosed in childhood.

Although in this chapter we've focused primarily on disorders of adulthood, we'll now close with a few words about childhood disorders, especially those that have been front and center in the public eye. Each of the disorders we'll consider—autism spectrum disorders, attention-deficit/hyperactivity disorder, and early onset bipolar disorder—have garnered their share of controversy in the popular media and the scientific community.

Fact vs. Fiction

Most individuals with autism spectrum disorders have a particular talent for generating prime numbers. (See bottom of page for answer.)

○ Fact

○ Fiction

Autism Spectrum Disorders

autism spectrum disorder (ASD)

DSM-5 category that includes autistic disorder and Asperger's disorder.

One in 68. According to the Centers for Disease Control (CDC, 2016) that's the proportion of individuals with **autism spectrum disorder (ASD)**, a category in *DSM-5* that includes autistic disorder (better known as autism) and Asperger's disorder, formerly a separate condition that's now regarded as a less severe form of autism. *DSM-5* contends that the symptoms of autism can best be described as on a continuum of severity, rather than in categorical terms, with many children with Asperger's disorder being able to function effectively in a school or occupational setting.

Although the proportion of people with ASD may not seem all that high, it's remarkably high compared with the figure of 1 in 2,000 to 2,500, which researchers had accepted for many years (Wing & Potter, 2002). Across a mere 10-year period—from 1993 to 2003—statistics from the U.S. Department of Education revealed a 657 percent increase in the rates of autism (technically called *infantile autism*) across the country (see Figure 15.6). In Wisconsin, the increase was a staggering 15,117 percent (Rust, 2006). These dramatic upsurges in the prevalence of autism have led many researchers and educators, and even some politicians, to speak of an autism "epidemic" (Kippes & Garrison, 2006). But is the epidemic real? We'll soon see.

Individuals with ASD are marked by persistent deficits in communication, social bonding, and imagination, sometimes accompanied by intellectual impairment (APA, 2013). The *DSM-5* breaks down the symptoms of ASDs into social impairments and repetitive or restrictive behaviors, which can include repetitive speech or movements, resistance to change, and highly specialized and limited interests and preoccupation with certain foods or unusual objects such as light bulbs.

Tens of thousands of parents remain convinced that vaccines trigger autism, despite scientific evidence to the contrary.

Figure 15.6 The Autism Epidemic in America from 1992 to 2008.

The fact that autism diagnoses have been skyrocketing isn't controversial—but the reasons for the increase are.

SOURCE: U.S. Department of Education

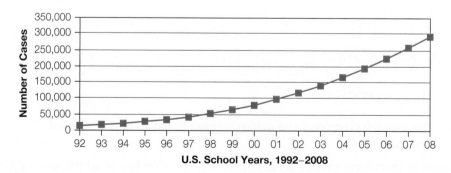

Answer: Fiction. There's no good support for this claim, which derives from a few widely publicized examples (Welling, 1994).

The causes of ASDs remain mysterious, although twin studies suggest that genetic influences play a prominent role (Hallmayer et al., 2011; Rutter, 2000). Still, genetic influences alone can't easily account for an astronomical rise in a disorder's prevalence over the span of a decade. It's therefore not surprising that researchers have looked to environmental variables to explain this bewildering increase. In particular, some investigators have pointed their fingers squarely at one potential culprit: vaccines (Rimland, 2004).

Much of the hype surrounding the vaccine–autism link was triggered by a study of only 12 children in the late 1990s (Wakefield et al., 1998) demonstrating an apparent linkage between autistic symptoms and the MMR vaccine, the vaccine for mumps, measles, and rubella (also known as German measles). The journal *Lancet*, which published the study, officially retracted it in 2010, saying that Wakefield never received ethical clearance for the investigation and that the article contained false claims about participant recruitment. The symptoms of autism usually become most apparent shortly after the age of two, not long after infants have received MMR and other vaccinations for a host of diseases. Indeed, tens of thousands of parents insist that their children developed autism following the MMR vaccine or following vaccines containing a preservative known as *thimerosol*, which is present in many mercury-bearing vaccines.

Nevertheless, studies in the United States, Europe, and Japan failed to replicate the association between the MMR vaccine and autism, strongly suggesting that the seeming correlation between vaccinations and autism was a mirage (Dees & Berman, 2013; Offit, 2008). The results of several large American, European, and Japanese studies show that even as the rate of MMR vaccinations remained constant or declined, the rate of autism diagnoses continued to soar (Herbert, Sharp, & Gaudiano, 2002; Honda, Shimizu, & Rutter, 2005). Moreover, even after the Danish government stopped administering thimerosol-containing vaccines, the prevalence of autism still skyrocketed (Madsen et al., 2002).

Many parents of children with autism probably fell prey to *illusory correlation*; they'd "seen" a statistical association that didn't exist. Their error was entirely understandable. Given that their children had received vaccines and developed autistic symptoms at around the same time, it was only natural to perceive an association between the two events.

Making matters more complex, recent research calls into question the very existence of the autism epidemic (Grinker, 2007; Russell, 2012; Wilson, 2005). Most previous investigators had neglected to take into account an alternative explanation—changes in diagnostic practices over time, which have expanded the autism diagnosis to include more mildly affected children, including those formerly diagnosed with Asperger's disorder. Evidence suggests that more liberal diagnostic criteria rather than vaccines can account for most, if not all, of the reported autism epidemic (Gernsbacher, Dawson, & Goldsmith, 2005; Lilienfeld & Arkowitz, 2007). In addition, the Americans with Disabilities Act and Individuals with Disabilities Education Act, both passed in the 1990s, indirectly encouraged school districts to classify more children as having autism and other developmental disabilities because these children could now receive more extensive educational accommodations.

Of course, at least a small part of the epidemic might be genuine, and some still unidentified environmental cause could account for the increase. But in evaluating the evidence, we should ask ourselves a critical question. Which is more plausible as an explanation of a 657 percent increase within one decade, a vaccine that's yet to be shown to produce any increase in the symptoms of autism or a simple change in diagnostic practices?

> ◀ **Replicability**
>
> Can the results be duplicated in other studies?

> ◀ **Ruling Out Rival Hypotheses**
>
> Have important alternative explanations for the findings been excluded?

> ◀ **Occam's Razor**
>
> Does a simpler explanation fit the data just as well?

Attention-Deficit/Hyperactivity Disorder and Early-Onset Bipolar Disorder

Even the best-adjusted children often appear overactive, energetic, and restless. But children with **attention-deficit/hyperactivity disorder (ADHD)** often behave like caricatures of the exuberant child. You probably know or have known someone with ADHD: 5 percent of school-age children satisfy the diagnostic criteria for the disorder (APA, 2013). Boys are anywhere from

attention-deficit/hyperactivity disorder (ADHD)

childhood condition marked by excessive inattention, impulsivity, and activity.

One of the first descriptions of ADHD came from a 1845 children's book by Heinrich Hoffman, which featured "Fidgety Philip," a boy who was so restless he was unable to sit still at the dinner table and caused a huge mess.

two to four times more likely than girls to develop ADHD, and between 30 and 80 percent of children with ADHD continue to display ADHD symptoms into adolescence and adulthood (Barkley, 2006; Monastra, 2008). The ADHD diagnosis subsumes two subtypes: (1) with hyperactivity and (2) without hyperactivity, in which inattention is predominant (APA, 2013).

SYMPTOMS OF ADHD. The first signs of ADHD may be evident as early as infancy. Parents often report that children with ADHD are fussy, cry incessantly, and frequently move and shift their position in the crib (Wolke, Rizzo, & Woods, 2002). By three years of age, they're constantly walking or climbing and are restless and prone to emotional outbursts. But it's not until elementary school that their behavior patterns are likely to be labeled "hyperactive" and a treatment referral made. Teachers complain that such children won't remain in their seats, follow directions, or pay attention and that they display temper tantrums with little provocation. Such children often struggle with learning disabilities, difficulties with processing verbal information, and poor balance and coordination (Jerome, 2000; Mangeot et al., 2001). By middle childhood, academic problems and disruptive behavior are frequently evident.

Many children with ADHD can concentrate when sufficiently motivated. Sit with a child with ADHD playing his or her favorite computer game, and you'll probably be impressed with the child's intense concentration. This curious phenomenon occurs because children with ADHD can sometimes "hyperfocus" when something captures their attention; however, they experience difficulty shifting their attention to focus on tasks that *aren't* attention-grabbing, like homework and chores (Barkley, 1997).

A high level of physical activity often diminishes as children with ADHD mature and approach adolescence. Nevertheless, by adolescence, impulsiveness, restlessness, inattention, problems with peers, delinquency, and academic difficulties comprise a patchwork of adjustment problems (Barkley, 2006; Hoza, 2007; Kelly, 2009). Alcohol and substance abuse are frequent, and many adolescents with ADHD appear in juvenile court as a result of running away from home, skipping school, and stealing. Adults with ADHD are at increased risk for accidents and injuries, divorce, unemployment, and contact with the legal system (Monastra, 2008).

ADHD appears to be genetically influenced in many cases, with estimates of its heritability as high as 0.80 (Larsson et al., 2014). What may be inherited are abnormalities in genes that influence (a) serotonin, dopamine, and norepinephrine; (b) a smaller brain volume; and (c) decreased activation in the frontal areas of the brain (Monastra, 2008).

People with ADHD can be treated successfully with stimulant medications. Nevertheless, these medications occasionally have serious side effects, making accurate diagnosis a serious public health issue. Yet an accurate diagnosis of ADHD can be dicey. A host of conditions that can cause problems in attention and behavioral control, including traumatic brain injuries, diabetes, thyroid problems, vitamin deficiencies, anxiety, and depression, must first be ruled out (Goodman et al., 2016; Monastra, 2008). Some scholars have expressed concerns that ADHD is overdiagnosed in some settings (LeFever, Arcona, & Antonuccio, 2003; Francis, 2013), although others point to evidence that some children with ADHD are actually overlooked by many diagnosticians (Sciutto & Eisenberg, 2007).

THE CONTROVERSY OVER EARLY-ONSET BIPOLAR DISORDER. Perhaps the most controversial diagnostic challenge is distinguishing children with ADHD from children with bipolar disorder (Meyer & Carlson, 2008). The diagnosis of early-onset bipolar disorder was once rare, but ballooned from only 0.42 percent of cases of outpatient mental health visits in the early 1990s to 6.67 percent of such visits in 2003 (Moreno et al., 2007), raising concerns about its overdiagnosis. Children are particularly likely to receive a diagnosis of early-onset bipolar disorder when they show rapid mood changes, reckless behavior, irritability, and aggression (McClellan, Kowatch, & Findling, 2007). Popular books like *My Bipolar Child* (Freeman, 2016), which list these and other symptoms, catch the eye of many parents with troubled children and raise concerns about bipolar disorder. Yet a moment's reflection suggests that many children fit this description, and surely many children with ADHD can be so characterized. Because 60–90 percent of children with bipolar disorder share an ADHD diagnosis, an alternative hypothesis to consider is that many children diagnosed with bipolar disorder are merely those with severe symptoms of ADHD, such as extreme temper outbursts and mood swings (Kim & Miklowitz, 2002; Marangoni, De Chiara, & Faedda, 2015). To address concerns about the overdiagnosis of bipolar disorder in children, *DSM-5* developed a new category of *disruptive mood dysregulation disorder* to diagnose children with persistent irritability and frequent behavior outbursts (APA, 2013). Nevertheless, the validity of this condition remains controversial, and some experts have expressed concerns that it may result in labeling children with repeated temper tantrums as pathological (Frances, 2012). A thorough evaluation involving parents, teachers, and mental health professionals is essential to an accurate diagnosis of early-onset bipolar disorder, as well as ADHD.

> ◀ **Ruling Out Rival Hypotheses**
>
> Have important alternative explanations for the findings been excluded?

Journal Prompt

There is debate about whether the increase in ADHD diagnoses in recent decades reflects a genuine increase in the disorder's prevalence. What evidence would help to inform this debate?

Summary: Psychological Disorders

15.1: Conceptions of Mental Illness: Yesterday and Today

15.1a Identify criteria for defining mental disorders.

The concept of mental disorder is difficult to define. Nevertheless, criteria for mental disorders include statistical rarity, subjective distress, impairment, societal disapproval, and biological dysfunction. Some scholars argue that mental illness is best captured by a family resemblance view.

15.1b Describe conceptions of diagnoses across history and cultures.

The demonic model of mental illness was followed by the medical model of the Renaissance. In the early 1950s, medications to treat schizophrenia led to deinstitutionalization. Some psychological conditions are culture specific. Still, many mental disorders, such as schizophrenia, can be found in most or all cultures.

15.1c Identify common misconceptions about psychiatric diagnoses and the strengths and limitations of the current diagnostic system.

Misconceptions include the ideas that a diagnosis is nothing more than pigeonholing and that diagnoses are unreliable, invalid, and stigmatizing. The *Diagnostic and Statistical Manual of Mental Disorders* (*DSM-5*) is a valuable tool, but its limitations include high levels of comorbidity and an assumption of a categorical model in the absence of compelling evidence. The recently proposed Research Domain Criteria (RDoC), which conceptualizes mental disorders as dysfuntions in brain circuitry, may eventually emerge as an alternative to the *DSM*.

15.2: Anxiety-Related Disorders: The Many Faces of Worry and Fear

15.2a Describe the many ways people experience anxiety.

Panic attacks involve intense yet brief rushes of fear that are greatly out of proportion to the actual threat. People with generalized anxiety disorder spend much of their day worrying. In phobias, fears are intense and highly focused. In posttraumatic stress disorder, extremely stressful events produce enduring anxiety. Obsessive-compulsive and related disorders are marked by repetitive and distressing thoughts and behaviors. Learning theory proposes that fears can be learned via classical and operant conditioning and observation. Anxious people tend to catastrophize or exaggerate the likelihood of negative events. Many anxiety and anxiety-related disorders are genetically influenced.

15.3: Mood Disorders and Suicide

15.3a Identify the characteristics of different mood disorders.

The sad mood of major depression is the mirror image of the expansive mood associated with a manic episode, seen in bipolar disorder. Depression can be recurrent or, more rarely, chronic. Manic episodes are often preceded or followed by bouts of depression. Bipolar disorder is among the most genetically influenced of all mental disorders.

15.3b Describe major explanations for depression and how life events can interact with characteristics of the individual to produce depression symptoms.

Stressful life events are linked to depression. Depressed people may face social rejection, which can amplify depression. According to Lewinsohn's behavioral model, depression results from a low rate of response-contingent positive reinforcement. Beck's cognitive model holds that negative schemas play an important role in depression, whereas Seligman's model emphasizes learned helplessness. Genes exert a moderate effect on the risk of developing depression.

15.3c Identify common myths and misconceptions about suicide.

Myths about suicide include the misconception that talking to depressed people about suicide makes them more likely to commit the act, suicide is almost always completed with no warning, suicide risk decreases as severe depression lifts, most people who threaten suicide are seeking attention, and people who talk a lot about suicide almost never commit it.

15.4: Personality and Dissociative Disorders: The Disrupted and Divided Self

15.4a Identify the characteristics of borderline and psychopathic personality disorders.

Borderline personality disorder is marked by instability in mood, identity, and impulse control. People with psychopathic personality are guiltless, dishonest, callous, and self-centered.

15.4b Explain the controversies surrounding dissociative disorders, especially dissociative identity disorder.

Dissociative disorders involve disruptions in consciousness, memory, identity, or perception. The role of severe child abuse in dissociative identity disorder (DID) is controversial. The sociocognitive model holds that social influences, including the media and suggestive procedures in psychotherapy, shape symptoms of DID.

15.5: The Enigma of Schizophrenia

15.5a Recognize the characteristic symptoms of schizophrenia.

The symptoms of schizophrenia include delusions, hallucinations, disorganized speech, and grossly disorganized behavior or catatonia.

15.5b Explain how psychosocial, neural, biochemical, and genetic influences create the vulnerability to schizophrenia.

Scientists have discovered brain abnormalities in patients with schizophrenia. Individuals with schizophrenia are prone to relapse when their relatives display high expressed emotion (criticism, hostility, and overinvolvement).

15.6: Childhood Disorders: Recent Controversies

15.6a Describe the symptoms and debate surrounding disorders diagnosed in childhood.

Autism spectrum disorder is a category in DSM-5 that includes autistic disorder and Asperger's disorder. Children with ADHD experience problems with inattention, impulsivity, and hyperactivity and often struggle with learning disabilities, difficulties processing verbal information, and poor balance and coordination. Some scholars have expressed concerns that ADHD is overdiagnosed in some settings, although others point to evidence that some children with ADHD are actually overlooked by many diagnosticians. One of the most controversial diagnostic challenges is distinguishing children with ADHD from children with bipolar disorder.

Chapter 16
Psychological and Biological Treatments

Helping People Change

Learning Objectives

16.1a Describe who seeks treatment, who benefits from psychotherapy, and who practices psychotherapy.

16.1b Describe what it takes to be an effective therapist.

16.2a Describe the core beliefs and criticisms of psychodynamic therapies.

16.2b Describe and evaluate the effectiveness of humanistic therapies.

16.3a List the advantages of group methods.

16.3b Describe the research evidence concerning the effectiveness of Alcoholics Anonymous.

16.3c Identify different approaches to treating the dysfunctional family system.

16.4a Describe the characteristics of behavior therapy and identify different behavioral approaches.

16.4b Describe the features of cognitive-behavioral therapies (CBT) and third-wave therapies.

16.5a Evaluate the claim that all psychotherapies are equally effective.

16.5b Explain how ineffective therapies can sometimes appear to be effective.

16.6a Recognize different types of drugs and cautions associated with drug treatment.

16.6b Outline key considerations in drug treatment.

16.6c Identify misconceptions about biomedical treatments.

Challenge Your Assumptions

Are inexperienced therapists as effective as more experienced therapists?

Do all psychotherapies require people to achieve insight to improve?

Is Alcoholics Anonymous better than other types of treatment for alcoholism?

Are some psychotherapies harmful?

Does electroshock treatment produce long-term brain damage?

Watch   MODELS OF PSYCHOTHERAPY: THREE PERSPECTIVES

Before reading on, picture a typical psychotherapy session. What's the person in therapy—often called the *client*—doing? How about the therapist? What does the room look like? Perhaps your first thought is of the proverbial client on a couch, with the therapist sitting behind him or her, pen and pad in hand, intent on unearthing long-forgotten memories, analyzing dreams, and encouraging the client to vent painful feelings.

If this scenario comes to mind, it's no wonder. From the early days of psychotherapy (often simply called *therapy*), these images have been etched into our cultural consciousness. But we'll discover that this picture doesn't begin to tell the story of the vast array of psychotherapeutic approaches that encompass individual therapy; treatments conducted in groups and with families; and even art, dance, and music therapies. Nor does the scenario capture the powerful biological treatments that have transformed the lives of people with psychological disorders by directly targeting the brain's functioning. In this chapter, we'll examine a broad spectrum of therapies, both psychological and biological, that are designed to alleviate emotional suffering. In the video, you'll witness three such approaches: behavioral activation, designed to increase engagement in activities to promote positive mood; cognitive therapy, geared to identify and change patterns of thinking related to negative emotions; and mindfulness-based therapy, developed to help clients gain psychological distance from distressing thoughts, feelings, and other personal experiences and open up space to make positive life changes. We'll also take a close look at the research evidence for these and other psychotherapies. Although the improvements yielded by effective psychotherapies, such as more positive emotions and thoughts, are often subjective, the good news is that psychologists have found ways to investigate these changes systematically.

Like many concepts in psychology, *psychotherapy* isn't easy to define. More than a half-century ago, one pioneer in psychotherapy wrote, half-jokingly, "Psychotherapy is an undefined technique applied to unspecified problems with unpredictable outcomes. For this technique, we recommend rigorous training" (Raimy, 1950, p. 63). Some might well contend that things haven't changed much since then. Still, for our purposes, we can define **psychotherapy** as a psychological intervention designed to help people resolve emotional, behavioral, and interpersonal problems and improve the quality of their lives (Engler & Goleman, 1992). Although the popular media often speak of therapy as though it were one thing, there are more than 600 "brands" of psychotherapy (McKay & Lilienfeld, 2015), at least three times as many as there were in the 1970s. As we'll learn, research demonstrates that many of these therapies are effective, but scores of others haven't been tested. In the pages to come, we'll offer critical thinking tools to help us distinguish scientifically supported psychological and biomedical therapies from therapies that are either ineffective or promising but scientifically unsupported.

psychotherapy

psychological intervention designed to help people resolve emotional, behavioral, and interpersonal problems and improve the quality of their lives

16.1: Psychotherapy: Clients and Practitioners

16.1a Describe who seeks treatment, who benefits from psychotherapy, and who practices psychotherapy.

16.1b Describe what it takes to be an effective therapist.

We'll begin by considering several questions: Who seeks and benefits from psychotherapy? How is psychotherapy practiced? What makes a psychotherapist effective?

Who Seeks and Benefits From Treatment?

According to surveys of the U.S. public, about 20 percent of Americans have received psychological treatment at some point, and about 3 to 4 percent are currently in outpatient psychotherapy (Adler, 2006; Olfson & Marcus, 2010). People grapple with specific problems in psychotherapy, but they also contend frequently with generalized feelings of helplessness, social isolation, not feeling validated by others, and a sense of failure (Bedi & Duff, 2014; Garfield, 1978; Lambert, 2003). Still others turn to therapy to expand their self-awareness, learn better ways of relating to others, and consider lifestyle changes.

GENDER, ETHNIC, AND CULTURAL DIFFERENCES IN ENTERING TREATMENT. Some people are more likely to enter psychotheapy than others. Women are more likely to seek treatment than are men (Addis & Mahalik, 2003; DuBrin & Zastowny, 1988), who may not seek services because of social norms of traditional masculinity that discourage help-seeking (Möller-Leimkühler, 2002). Still, both sexes benefit equally from psychotherapy (Petry, Tennen, & Affleck, 2000). Members of many racial and ethnic minority groups, particularly African Americans, Asian Americans, and Hispanic Americans, are less likely to seek mental health services than are Caucasian Americans (Hunt et. al., 2015; Lee et al., 2014; Sue & Lam, 2002), perhaps because of the lingering stigma surrounding psychotherapy in these groups. Nevertheless, when individuals hailing from diverse cultural and ethnic backgrounds obtain psychotherapy, they're likely to benefit from it (Navarro, 1993; Prochaska & Norcross, 2007).

Culturally sensitive psychotherapists maximize their effectiveness by tuning their interventions to clients' cultural values and the difficulties they encounter in adapting to a dominant culture that may differ vastly from their own (Benish, Quintana, & Wampold, 2011; Norcross & Wampold, 2011a; Sue & Sue, 2003). Although ethnic minorities prefer therapists with a similar ethnic background (Coleman, Wampold, & Casali, 1995), there's no consistent evidence that client-therapist ethnic (Cabral & Smith, 2011; Shin et al., 2005) or gender (Bowman et al., 2001) matches enhance therapy outcome. Still, when clients are relative newcomers to a culture and not well acquainted with its traditions, therapist–client ethnic match may play a greater role in therapy's effectiveness (Sue, 1998). The good news is that people can be helped by therapists who differ from them in significant ways, including ethnicity and gender (Cardemil, 2010; Whaley & Davis, 2007).

REAPING BENEFITS FROM TREATMENT. The effectiveness of therapy depends on a host of individual differences. Clients who are most likely to improve are better adjusted to begin with, realize they may be contributing to their problems, and are motivated to work on those problems (Prochaska & DiClemente, 1982; Prochaska & Norcross, 2013). Clients who experience some anxiety do better in psychotherapy than other clients—probably because their distress fuels their motivation to make life changes (Frank, 1974; Miller et al., 1995)—as do clients with temporary or situational problems, such as relationship upheavals (Gasperini et al., 1993; Steinmetz, Lewinsohn, & Antonuccio, 1983). When clients have a say in the type of therapy they receive, they're

Popular portrayals of psychotherapy have a long history in the media.

more satisfied with their treatment and experience better outcomes than when they don't choose a treatment or get to participate in treatment selection (Lindhiem et al., 2014).

Who Practices Psychotherapy

Licensed professionals, especially clinical psychologists, psychiatrists, mental health counselors, and clinical social workers are the mainstays of the mental health profession. But unlicensed religious, vocational, and rehabilitation counselors, as well as art and music therapists, also provide psychological services. Not all therapists are the same; mental health consumers are often unaware of the substantial differences in education, training, and roles of different psychotherapists. Table 16.1 provides some guidance.

PROFESSIONALS VERSUS PARAPROFESSIONALS.   Contrary to the myth that all psychotherapists have advanced degrees in mental health, volunteers and **paraprofessionals**, helpers who have no formal professional training, often provide psychological services in such settings as crisis intervention centers and other social service agencies. Settings in which paraprofessionals serve even extend to beauty salons, where hair stylists trained to assess anxiety and depression symptoms refer patrons to services in their communities, although we don't yet know whether these new approaches are effective (Hanlon, 2011).

In most states, the term *therapist* isn't legally protected, so virtually anyone can hang up a shingle and offer treatment. Many paraprofessionals obtain agency-specific training and attend workshops that enhance their educational backgrounds. They may also be trained to recognize situations that require consultation with professionals with greater expertise.

Do most therapists need to be professionally trained or have many years of experience to be effective (Blatt et al., 1996; Christensen & Jacobson, 1994; Montgomery et al., 2010)? Again, contrary to popular belief, most studies reveal few or no differences in effectiveness between more and less experienced or professional therapists (Dawes, 1994; McFall, 2006; Richards et al., 2016; Tracey et al., 2014). Why is this so? As psychiatrist Jerome Frank (1961)

paraprofessional

person with no professional training who provides mental health services

Table 16.1 Occupations, Degrees, Roles, and Work Settings of Mental Health Professionals.

Degree Key: BSN, bachelor of science in nursing; BSW, bachelor of social work; DNP, doctorate nurse practitioner; DO, doctor of osteopathy; DSW, doctor of social work; EdD, doctor of education; EdS, specialist in education; LCSW, licensed clinical social worker; MA, master of arts; MC, master of counseling; MD, doctor of medicine; MEd, master of education; MS, master of science; MSN, master of science in nursing; MSW, master of social work; PhD, doctor of philosophy; PsyD, doctor of psychology.

Occupation	Degree/License	Settings/Role
Clinical Psychologist	PhD/PsyD, MA, MS	Private practice, hospitals, schools, community agencies, medical settings, academic, other
Psychiatrist	MD or DO	Physicians, private practice, hospitals, medical centers, schools, academic, other
Counseling Psychologist	PhD, EdD, MA, MS, MC	University clinics, mental health centers; treat people with less severe psychological problems
School Psychologist	PhD, PsyD, EdD, EdS, MA, MS, MEd	In-school interventions, assessment, prevention programs; work with teachers, students, parents
Clinical Social Worker	Training varies widely; BSW, MSW, DSW, LCSW	Private practice following supervised experience, psychiatric facilities, hospitals/community agencies, schools, case managers; help with social and health problems
Mental Health Counselor	MSW, MS, MC	Private practice, community agencies, hospitals, other; career counseling, marriage issues, substance abuse
Psychiatric Nurse	Training varies widely; associate degree, BSN, MSN, DNP, PhD	Hospitals, community health centers, primary care facilities, outpatient mental health clinics; manage medications; with advanced degrees can diagnose, treat mental patients
Pastoral Counselor	Training varies; from bachelor's degree to more advanced degrees	Counseling; support in spiritual context; wellness programs; group, family, and couples therapy

noted, regardless of level of professional training, people who fulfill the role of therapist may provide clients with hope, empathy, advice, support, and opportunities for new learning experiences (Frank & Frank, 1991; Lambert & Ogles, 2004).

Even if there are few or no differences in therapy outcome as a function of professional training, there are several advantages to consulting with a professional. Professional helpers (1) understand how to operate effectively within the mental health system; (2) appreciate complex ethical, professional, and personal issues; and (3) can select treatments of demonstrated effectiveness (Garske & Anderson, 2003).

MEETING THE NEEDS FOR PSYCHOLOGICAL SERVICES: HOW WELL ARE WE DOING?
Still, paraprofessionals serve a vital function: They help to compensate for a sizable gap between the high demand for, and meager supply of, licensed practitioners (den Boer et al., 2005). Paraprofessionals provide services to some of the many people who need psychological services yet don't receive them, mostly because they simply don't have access (Layard & Clark, 2015). Roughly 700,000 mental health professionals are tasked with providing services for approximately 75 million people, which amounts to a serious shortfall of professional help for those in need (Kazdin & Blasé, 2011). As many as 70 percent of people suffering from psychological conditions, such as anxiety and mood disorders, don't use or have access to psychological services (Kazdin & Rabbitt, 2013). Up to 80 percent of children don't receive adequate treatment for mental health issues (Kataoka, Zhang, & Wells, 2002), only 13 percent of low-income adults with PTSD receive psychological interventions that target trauma (Davis et al., 2009), and 60–90 percent of Latinos don't receive adequate psychological services (Alegría et.al., 2008; Kataoka et al., 2002). As serious as the problem of unmet mental health needs is in the United States and Europe, it's even worse in third world countries. In the United States and Great Britain, for example, 67 percent and 69 percent of adults with mental disorders, respectively, go untreated; yet in low- and middle-income countries, such as most African nations, the percentage rises to 91 percent (Layard & Clark, 2015).

Socioeconomic and geographical factors also predict who receives treatment. Low income is a barrier to receiving effective services. Therapy can be costly for those without health insurance or whose health plans don't include mental health coverage (Olfson & Marcus, 2010; Santiago, Kaltman, & Miranda, 2012). An estimated 87 percent of uninsured children don't receive psychological services (Kataoka et al., 2002). People in rural settings often lack easy access to professional care, which is more readily available to people in urban areas and in cities with universities and medical facilities (Health Resources and Services Administration, 2010). Deinstitutionalization (see LO 15.1b) has created a vast sea of homeless people with severe mental illnesses who typically receive minimal or no psychological services (Horvitz-Lennon et al., 2009). What's more, many of the 10 million or so individuals in prison worldwide suffer from serious mental disorders and lack viable treatment options (Fazel & Danesh, 2002, Fazel & Seewald, 2012).

Still, efforts are underway to provide low-cost services to a broader clientele, and new models of service delivery, including treatment by smartphone apps along with close therapist supervision, are being developed and implemented (Kazdin & Blase, 2011; Kazdin & Rabbitt, 2013). Increasingly, psychotherapy is conducted by way of telephone and consultation on the Internet, making cost-effective treatment available to increasing numbers of people who seek help—a trend that psychotherapy experts predict will increase over the coming years (Anderrson, 2016; Hedman, Ljótsson, & Lindefors, 2012; Norcross, Pfund, & Prorchaska, 2013). To facilitate mental health, individuals can be encouraged to use social media, which increasingly provides access to valuable information regarding healthy lifestyles and methods to cope with stress, anxiety, and depression, as well as access to a potentially wider base of social support. Still, the Internet isn't always a reliable source of information, so be sure to apply the principles of scientific thinking to evaluate the claims that you encounter.

We've seen that psychological services and "psychotherapy" have expanded to include a wider spectrum of interventions and service providers that can contribute to the mental health of broader segments of the population (Kazdin & Rabbitt, 2013). It's still too early to tell how effective these alternative methods and models of providing

Fact vs. Fiction

All mental health professionals are average or above average in clinical skills. (See bottom of page for answer.)

○ Fact

○ Fiction

treatment will be, although they ultimately have the potential to reach millions of people in need.

WHAT DOES IT TAKE TO BE AN EFFECTIVE PSYCHO-THERAPIST? Given that training and years of experience aren't critical determinants of what makes a good therapist, what does make a good therapist? Effective therapists are likely to be warm, direct, empathic, and enjoy their work; establish a positive working relationship with clients; and tend not to contradict clients (Garske & Anderson, 2003; Heinonen et al., 2012; Kazdin, Marciano, & Whitley, 2005; Luborsky et al., 1997; Moyers & Miller, 2013). Effective therapists also select important topics on which to focus in sessions (Goldfried, Raue, & Castonguay, 1998), match their treatments to the needs and characteristics of clients (Beutler & Harwood, 2002), and collect feedback from their clients (Norcross & Wampold, 2011b). Still, sizable differences in therapist characteristics and abilities may overshadow the relatively small differences in the effectiveness of the types of treatments they provide (Ahn & Wampold, 2001; Luborsky et al., 1986). So when it comes to the success of psychotherapy, the choice of *therapist* is every bit as important as the choice of *therapy* (Blow, Sprenkle, & Davis, 2007).

What makes a good therapist from the client's point of view? The composite view of the "good" therapist is that of an expert who's warm, respectful, caring, and engaged (Littauer, Sexton, & Wyan, 2005; Strupp, Fox, & Lessler, 1969). In Table 16.2, we present some tips for both selecting good therapists and avoiding bad ones.

In the HBO television series *In Treatment*, Laura (played by Melissa George) develops sexual feelings for her therapist, Paul (played by Gabriel Byrne). Paul doesn't have a sexual relationship with her because he experiences a panic attack. A sexual relationship with a client is highly unethical. Which of the following behaviors is also unethical?

(A) Revealing a client's plan to commit suicide to a family member to prevent the suicide.

(B) Revealing a client's plan to assault another person to prevent the assault.

(C) Informing a client's elderly father that she harbors hateful feelings toward him.

Answer: (C) With few exceptions, therapists keep all information confidential. However, therapists can share information without the client's written permission when the client is at serious risk for suicide or endangering others.

Journal Prompt

List two or three reasons why some people are more likely than others to seek psychological treatment? You may wish to consider such factors as gender, race/ethnic, and cultural differences. Describe several approaches that can be implemented to decrease people's reluctance to seek treatment.

Answer: Fiction. When you think about it, all mental health professionals cannot be average or above average in clinical skills; some must be below average as well. Nevertheless, based on a multidisciplinary survey of mental health professionals (e.g., psychologists, psychiatrists, clinical social workers) surveyed, one would believe that the statement is true: Walfish et al. (2012) reported that 25 percent of mental health professionals placed their clinical skills in the top 10 percent compared with their peers, and none reported that his or her skills were below average. Psychotherapists are not alone in inflating their competence—"self-assessment bias" seems to reflect a general tendency to not consider oneself as incompetent and to inflate one's competence (Dunning, Health, & Suls 2003).

Table 16.2 What Should I Look for in a Therapist, and What Type of Therapist Should I Avoid?

Tens of thousands of people call themselves therapists, and it's often hard to know what kind of therapist to seek out or avoid. This checklist may help you, your friends, or your loved ones to select a good therapist—and to steer clear of a bad one.

1. I can talk freely and openly with my therapist.
2. My therapist listens carefully to what I say and understands my feelings.
3. My therapist is warm, direct, and provides useful feedback.
4. My therapist explains up front what he or she will be doing and why and is willing to answer questions about his or her qualifications and training, my diagnosis, and our treatment plan.
5. My therapist encourages me to confront challenges and solve problems.
6. My therapist uses scientifically based approaches and discusses the pros and cons of other approaches.
7. My therapist regularly monitors how I'm doing and is willing to change course when treatment isn't going well.

If your answer is yes to one or more of the following statements, the therapist may *not* be in a good position to help you and even may be harmful.

1. My therapist gets defensive and angry when challenged.
2. My therapist has a one-size-fits-all approach to all problems.
3. My therapist spends considerable time each session making "small talk," telling me exactly what to do, and sharing personal anecdotes.
4. My therapist isn't clear about what is expected of me in the treatment plan, and our discussions lack any focus and direction.
5. My therapist doesn't seem willing to discuss the scientific support for what he or she is doing.
6. There are no clear professional boundaries in my relationship with my therapist; for example, my therapist talks a lot about his or her personal life or asks me for personal favors.

16.2: Insight Therapies: Acquiring Understanding

16.2a Describe the core beliefs and criticisms of psychodynamic therapies.
16.2b Describe and evaluate the effectiveness of humanistic therapies.

insight therapies

psychotherapies, including psychodynamic, humanistic, existential, and group approaches, with the goal of expanding awareness or insight

In much of the chapter that lies ahead, we'll examine some of the more prominent therapeutic approaches and evaluate their scientific status. We'll begin with **insight therapies**, which aim to cultivate insight, that is, expanded self-awareness and knowledge. The psychodynamic and humanistic therapies we'll review are two prominent schools of insight therapy.

Psychodynamic therapies are treatments inspired by classical psychoanalysis and influenced by Freud's techniques. Compared with psychoanalysis, which tends to be expensive and lengthy (often lasting years or even decades) and often involves meeting most days of the week, psychodynamic therapy is typically less costly, is briefer—weeks or months or open-ended—and involves meeting only once or twice a week (Shedler, 2010). After we examine Freud's techniques, we'll consider a group of therapists called *neo-Freudians*, who adopted Freud's psychodynamic perspective but modified his approach in distinctive ways.

humanistic therapies

therapies that emphasize the development of human potential and the belief that human nature is basically positive

Under the umbrella of **humanistic therapies**, we can find a variety of approaches rooted in the humanistic perspective on personality. Therapies within this orientation share an emphasis on insight, self-actualization, and the belief that human nature is basically positive (Maslow, 1954; Rogers, 1961; Shlien & Levant, 1984). Humanistic therapists reject the interpretive techniques of psychoanalysis. Instead, they strive to understand clients' inner worlds through empathy and focus on clients' thoughts and feelings in the present moment.

Psychoanalytic and Psychodynamic Therapies: Freud's Legacy

Psychodynamic therapists share the following three approaches and beliefs, which form the core of their approach (Blagys & Hilsenroth, 2000; Shedler, 2010):

1. They believe the causes of abnormal behaviors, including unconscious conflicts, wishes, and impulses, stem from traumatic or other adverse childhood experiences.
2. They strive to analyze (a) distressing thoughts and feelings clients avoid, (b) wishes and fantasies, (c) recurring themes and life patterns, (d) significant past events, and (e) the therapeutic relationship.
3. They believe that when clients achieve insight into previously unconscious material, the causes and the significance of symptoms will become evident, often causing symptoms to disappear.

PSYCHOANALYSIS: KEY INGREDIENTS. Freud's psychoanalysis was one of the first forms of psychotherapy. According to Freud, the goal of psychoanalysis is to decrease guilt and frustration and *make the unconscious conscious* by bringing to awareness previously repressed impulses, conflicts, and memories (Bornstein, 2001; Lionells et al., 2014). Psychoanalytic therapists, sometimes called *analysts*, attempt to fill this tall order using six primary approaches.

The Freudian concept of free association is a bit like a magician pulling kerchiefs out of a hat, with one thought leading to the next, in turn leading to the next, and so on.

1. **Free Association.** As clients lie on a couch in a comfortable position, therapists instruct them to say whatever thoughts come to mind, no matter how meaningless or nonsensical they might seem. This process is called **free association** because clients are permitted to express themselves without censorship. An interesting tidbit of information is that before Freud developed the technique of free association, he brought forth associations in a different way. He told his clients to close their eyes and concentrate while he pressed his hand on their forehead. He then suggested that their repressed memories would return to consciousness (Ellenberger, 1970). Today, many therapists would rightly regard this procedure as carrying a risk of generating false memories.

   free association

   technique in which clients express themselves without censorship of any sort

2. **Interpretation.** From the client's string of free associations, analysts form hypotheses regarding the origin of the client's difficulties and share them with him or her as the therapeutic relationship evolves. Therapists also formulate *interpretations*—explanations—of the unconscious bases of a client's dreams, emotions, and behaviors. They point out the supposedly disguised expression of a repressed idea, impulse, or wish, as in the following interpretation of a client's repeated "accidents" resulting in injury: "Having these accidents perhaps served an unconscious purpose; they assured you of getting the attention you felt you could not get otherwise." As in comedy, timing is everything: If the therapist offers the interpretation before the client is ready to accept it, psychoanalysts maintain, anxiety may derail the flow of new associations.

3. **Dream Analysis.** According to Freud, dreams express unconscious themes that influence the client's conscious life. The therapist's task is to interpret the relation of the dream to the client's waking life and the dream's symbolic significance. Thus, the therapist might interpret the appearance of an ogre in a dream as representing a hated and feared parent.

4. **Resistance.** As treatment progresses and people become aware of previously unconscious and often feared aspects of themselves, they often experience **resistance**; they try to avoid further confrontation. Clients express resistance in many ways, including skipping therapy sessions or drawing a blank when the therapist asks a question about painful moments in their past, but all forms of resistance can stall their progress. To minimize resistance, most psychoanalysts express empathy for clients' personal struggles, while they attempt to make them aware that they're unconsciously blocking therapeutic efforts and make clear *how* and *what* they're resisting (Agosta, 2015; Anderson & Stewart, 1983).

   resistance

   attempts to avoid confrontation and anxiety associated with uncovering previously repressed thoughts, emotions, and impulses

transference

act of projecting intense, unrealistic feelings and expectations from the past onto the therapist

5. **Transference.** As analysis continues, clients begin to experience **transference**; they project intense, unrealistic feelings and expectations from their past onto the therapist. The ambiguous figure of the analyst supposedly becomes the focus of emotions once directed at significant persons from the client's childhood. In one example, a client brought a gun into treatment and pointed it at the therapist. The therapist replied: "This is what I meant about your murderous feelings toward your father (Laughs). Do you see it now?" (Monroe, 1955). Freud believed that transference provides a vehicle for clients to understand their irrational expectations and demands of others, including the therapist.

Research suggests that we indeed often react to people in our present life in ways similar to people in our past (Berk & Andersen, 2000; Luborsky, et al., 1985). These findings may suggest that Freud was right about the transference; alternatively, they may mean that our stable personality traits lead us to react to people in similar ways over time. These lingering questions aside, therapists' interpretations of the transference may be helpful for some clients (Ogrodniczuk & Piper, 1999).

6. **Working Through.** In the final stage of psychoanalysis, therapists help clients *work through*, or process, their problems. The insight gained in treatment is a helpful starting point, but it's not sufficient. As a consequence, therapists must repeatedly address conflicts and resistance to achieving healthy behavior patterns and help clients confront old and ineffective coping responses as they reemerge in everyday life (Menninger, 1958; Wachtel, 1997).

This client began crying after her therapist gently suggested that she take more risks in life. "That's exactly what my father used to tell me as a child," she said, and "Now I feel criticized by you the same way I felt criticized by my father." According to psychoanalysts, the client is experiencing transference.

interpersonal therapy (IPT)

treatment that strengthens social skills and targets interpersonal problems, conflicts, and life transitions

DEVELOPMENTS IN PSYCHOANALYSIS: THE NEO-FREUDIAN TRADITION. Freud's ideas spawned new therapeutic approaches in the psychodynamic tradition (Ellis, Abrams, & Abrams, 2008). In contrast to Freudian therapists, neo-Freudian therapists are more concerned with conscious aspects of the client's functioning. For example, according to neo-Freudian Carl Jung, the goal of psychotherapy is *individuation*—the integration of opposing aspects of the personality, like passive versus aggressive tendencies, into a harmonious "whole," namely, the self. To help clients achieve individuation, Jung considered their future goals as well as past experiences. Neo-Freudians also emphasize the impact of cultural and interpersonal influences, such as close friendships and loving relationships, on behavior across the life span (Adler, 1938; Mitchell & Black, 1995). Beyond Freud's emphasis on sexuality and aggression, neo-Freudians acknowledge the impact of other needs, including love, dependence, power, and status. They're also more optimistic than Freud was regarding people's prospects for achieving healthy functioning.

The emphasis on interpersonal relationships is the hallmark of Harry Stack Sullivan's *interpersonal psychotherapy*. According to Sullivan (1954), psychotherapy is a collaborative undertaking between client and therapist. Sullivan contended that the analyst's proper role is that of *participant observer*. Through ongoing observations, the analyst discovers and communicates to clients their unrealistic attitudes and behaviors in everyday life.

Sullivan's work influenced the contemporary approach of **interpersonal therapy (IPT)**. Originally a treatment for depression (Klerman et al., 1984; Santor & Kusumakar, 2001), IPT is a short-term intervention (12–16 sessions) designed to strengthen people's social skills and assist them in coping with interpersonal problems, conflicts (such as disputes with family members), and life transitions (such as childbirth and retirement). In addition to effectively treating depression (Barth et al., 2013; Klerman et al., 1984; Hinrichsen, 2008), IPT has demonstrated success in treating substance abuse and eating disorders comparable with that of cognitive-behavioral therapies (Klerman & Weissman, 1993; Murphy et al., 2012).

Is Insight Necessary? As we've seen, psychodynamic therapies rely heavily on insight. Many Hollywood films, such as *Good Will Hunting* (1997) and *Analyze This* (1999), reinforce the impression that insight—especially into the childhood origins of problems—is the crucial ingredient in therapeutic change. Yet extensive research demonstrates that understanding our emotional history, however deep and gratifying, isn't required to relieve psychological distress (Weisz et al., 1995). To improve, clients typically need to practice new and more adaptive behaviors in everyday life—that is, to engage in *working through* (Wachtel, 1977).

Some psychodynamic concepts, including therapeutic interpretations, are difficult to falsify. How can we demonstrate that a person's dream of his father scowling at him, for example, points to repressed memories of child abuse, as a therapist might infer? A client might respond, "Aha, that's it!" but this reaction could reflect transference or an attempt to please the therapist. If the client improves, the therapist might conclude that the interpretation is accurate, but the timing could be coincidental rather than causal (Grunbaum, 1984).

The failure to rule out rival hypotheses may lead both therapist and client to mistakenly attribute progress to insight and interpretation when other influences, like placebo effects, are responsible (Meyer, 1981). Research supports this caution. In one long-term study of psychoanalytic treatment (Bachrach et al., 1991), half of 42 clients improved but failed to show insight into their "core conflicts." Yet patients attributed improvement more to the support the therapist provided than to insight.

> ### Falsifiability
> Can the claim be disproved?

> ### Correlation vs. Causation
> Can we be sure that A causes B?

> ### Ruling Out Rival Hypotheses
> Have important alternative explanations for the findings been excluded?

Are Traumatic Memories Repressed?   Although many psychodynamic therapists believe that current difficulties often stem from the repression of traumatic events such as childhood abuse (Frederickson, 1992; Levis, 1995), research doesn't bear out this claim (Lynn et al., 2004; McHugh, 2008). Try this thought experiment. Which event would you be more likely to forget: an instance when your peers ridiculed you and beat you up in third grade for being the class know-it-all or a time when the teacher praised you in class for your participation? Odds are you thought you'd be better able to recall the unsettling event, and you'd be right. Disturbing events are actually *more* memorable and *less* subject to being forgotten than are everyday occurrences (Loftus, 1993; Porter & Peace, 2007).

David Rubin and Dorthe Berntsen (2009) found that a whopping 61 percent of participants who reported that they would likely seek psychotherapy sometime in the future believed that they might have been victims of childhood sexual abuse they'd forgotten. The authors contended that memory recovery techniques could create false memories of abuse in such patients, because they find the idea that they were abused plausible (Rubin & Boals, 2010).

After reviewing the research evidence, Richard McNally (2003) concluded that the scientific support for repressed memories is weak and that many memories, especially those that stretch to the distant past, are often subject to distortion. Nevertheless, the issue remains controversial (Brewin & Andrews, 2016; Erdelyi, 2006; Patihis et al., 2014).

It's always the same dream. I'm in therapy, analyzing my recurring dream.

Psychodynamic Therapies Evaluated Scientifically.   Valuable as they've been, classical psychodynamic therapies are questionable from a scientific standpoint. Freud and Jung based their therapeutic observations largely on small samples of wealthy, intelligent, and successful people, rendering their external validity unclear. Their clinical sessions weren't observed by others or conducted on a systematic basis that permitted replication by others, as would be the case with rigorously controlled research.

The concerns we've raised aside, research indicates that interpersonal therapies have generally, but not consistently, fared well in comparisons with scientifically supported treatments such as cognitive-behavioral therapy (Luty et al., 2010; Murphy et al., 2012; Vos et al., 2012). Brief versions of psychodynamic therapy are better than no treatment (Leichsenring, Rabung, & Leibing, 2004; Shedler, 2010), although they may be somewhat less effective than or comparable with cognitive-behavioral therapies, which don't emphasize insight (Grawe, Donati, & Bernauer, 1998; Shapiro & Shapiro, 1982; Watzke et al., 2014). Moreover, psychodynamic therapy isn't especially effective for psychotic disorders like schizophrenia (Buckley et al., 2015; Jauhar et al., 2014).

> ### Replicability
> Can the results be duplicated in other studies?

Humanistic Therapies: Achieving Our Potential

Humanistic therapists share a desire to help people overcome the sense of alienation so prevalent in our culture; to develop their sensory and emotional awareness; and to express their creativity and help them become loving, responsible, and authentic. Humanistic therapists stress the importance of assuming responsibility for decisions, not attributing our problems to the past, and living fully and finding meaning in the present.

person-centered therapy

nondirective therapy centering on the client's goals and ways of solving problems

PERSON-CENTERED THERAPY: ATTAINING ACCEPTANCE.   No therapist better exemplifies the practice of humanistic therapy than Carl Rogers. Rogers developed a therapy called **person-centered therapy** (formerly called *client-centered therapy*) in which therapists don't tell clients how to solve their problems and clients can use the therapy hour however they choose (Rogers, 1942). Person-centered therapy is *nondirective* because therapists encourage clients to direct the course of therapy and don't define or diagnose clients' problems or try to get at the root cause of their difficulties. To ensure a positive outcome, the therapist must satisfy three conditions:

1. The therapist must be an authentic, genuine person who reveals his or her own reactions to what the client is communicating.

   Client: I think I'm beyond help.

   Therapist: Huh? You feel as though you're beyond help. I know. You feel just completely hopeless about yourself. I can understand that. I don't feel hopeless, but I realize you do (Meador & Rogers, 1979, p. 157).

2. The therapist must express *unconditional positive regard*, that is, a nonjudgmental acceptance of all feelings the client expresses. Rogers was convinced that unconditional positive regard elicits a more positive self-concept. He maintained that it allows clients to reclaim aspects of their "true selves" that they disowned previously in life as a result of others placing conditions of worth on them.

3. The therapist must relate to clients with empathic understanding. In Rogers's words: "To sense the patient's world as if it were our own, but without ever losing the 'as if' quality. This is empathy" (Rogers, 1957, p. 98).

One way to communicate empathy is by way of *reflection*, that is, mirroring back the client's feelings—a technique for which Rogers was famous. Here's an example:

   Client: I was small and I envied people who were large. I was—well, I took beatings by boys and I couldn't strike back… .

   Therapist: You've had plenty of experience in being the underdog (Rogers, 1942, pp. 145–146).

With increased awareness and heightened self-acceptance, people hopefully come to think more realistically, become more tolerant of others, and engage in more adaptive behaviors (Rogers, 1961). Some researchers have developed computer programs that attempt to simulate Rogers's person-centered therapy, especially Rogers's method of reflection (see Figure 16.1).

Person-centered interviewing techniques, including showing warmth, empathy, and unconditional acceptance; using reflective listening; and avoiding confrontation, lie at the heart of *motivational interviewing* (Miller & Rollnick, 2002; Miller & Rose, 2009). This one- to two-session procedure recognizes that many clients are ambivalent about changing long-standing behaviors and is geared toward clarifying and bringing forth their reasons for changing—and not changing—their lives. Motivational interviewing, initially shown to be helpful in treating alcohol-related problems (Project MATCH Research Group, 1997), has been successful in modifying a variety of psychological conditions, such as obsessive-compulsive disorder and posttraumatic stress disorder, and health-related behaviors, including exercising, dieting, and complying with medical therapies (Arkowitz, Miller, & Rollnick, 2015; Burke, Arkowitz, & Menchola, 2003; Olsen et al., 2012).

Interactive

According to Rogers, if a father gives his child love only when he receives a good grade, but not when he receives a poor grade, the father is expressing conditional regard.

Journal Prompt

In your own words, describe the concept of "unconditional positive regard." Discuss why it's an important aspect of person-centered therapy, including the potential impact of unconditional positive regard on the client and the psychotherapy relationship.

Figure 16.1 Simulated Conversation between Client and Computer Therapist, Eliza.

Some researchers have developed computer programs that attempt to simulate Rogers's person-centered therapy, especially Rogers's method of reflection. Here, we can read excerpts from a conversation between a client and the computer therapist, Eliza, developed by computer scientist Joseph Weizenbaum. Would Eliza make a good therapist?

Eliza: Hi, I am Eliza.

Client: Hi Eliza.

Eliza: How are you today? What would you like to discuss?

Client: My girlfriend.

Eliza: Tell me more.

Client: I don't know how I feel about her.

Eliza: Why don't you know how you feel about her?

Client: Sometimes she is nice, other times she is not.

Eliza: What does that suggest to you?

Client: She has psychological problems.

Eliza: Come come, elucidate your thoughts.

Client: She changes all the time.

Eliza: I see.

Client: She can be very mean.

Eliza: I see.

Client: But I still love her.

Eliza: I'm not sure I understand you fully.

Client: I don't understand myself.

Eliza: Does that trouble you?

GESTALT THERAPY: BECOMING WHOLE. Fritz Perls, the flamboyant founder of **Gestalt therapy**, was trained as a psychodynamic therapist, but imported some concepts from Gestalt psychology into a new brand of therapy. The word *gestalt* (configuration) means an organized whole. Gestalt therapists believe that people with psychological difficulties are "incomplete gestalts" because they've excluded from their awareness experiences and aspects of their personalities that trigger anxiety. As a consequence, Gestalt therapists aim to integrate different and sometimes opposing aspects of clients' personalities into a unified sense of self.

For Gestalt therapists, the key to personal growth is accepting responsibility for one's feelings and maintaining contact with the here and now, rather than getting stuck in the past or imagining the future. Gestalt therapy was the first of many therapies that recognize the importance of awareness, acceptance, and expression of feelings. In the *two-chair technique*, Gestalt therapists ask clients to move from chair to chair, creating a dialogue with two conflicting aspects of their personalities (see Figure 16.2). The "good boy" versus the "spoiled brat" may serve as the focal point for such an interchange. Gestalt therapists believe this procedure allows a synthesis of the opposing sides to emerge. For example, the good boy, always eager to please others, may learn from a conversation with the spoiled brat that it's acceptable in certain instances to be assertive, even demanding. Thus, the "good brat" may be more effective and authentic than either personality aspect alone.

EXISTENTIAL THERAPY. Existential therapy falls within the tradition of humanistic psychotherapies. Unlike person-centered therapy, which highlights the importance of self actualization, and Gestalt therapy, which touts the value of awareness and expression of feelings, existential therapists contend that human beings construct meaning and that mental illness stems from a failure to find meaning in life (Maddi, 1985; Schneider, 2003). Psychiatrist Victor Frankl's views—influenced by his experiences in the dehumanizing environment of four Nazi concentration camps where he lost his parents, his brother, and his wife—beautifully capture the core tenets of existential therapy (Frankl, 1965). Out of the unspeakable suffering he experienced and witnessed, Frankl came to believe that human beings can preserve spiritual freedom and independence of mind even under conditions of enormous psychological and physical stress (Frankl, 1965). For example, he relates the story of feeling utterly hopeless while being ordered to march along with his fellow concentration camp survivors. Yet, after Frankl somehow managed to summon the mental image of his new wife, he found inner strength. For Frankl, the freedom to find meaning in existence permits one to retain hope and dignity, even in a concentration camp. This freedom lends life significance and allows us to courageously confront our inescapable confrontation with death.

Gestalt therapy

therapy that aims to integrate different and sometimes opposing aspects of personality into a unified sense of self

Figure 16.2 The Two-Chair Technique.

Gestalt therapy's two-chair technique aims to integrate opposing aspects of the client's personality, such as the "good boy" and the "spoiled brat."

Frankl developed *logotherapy*, which he defined as the treatment of the patient's attitudes toward his or her existence. Frankl found attitudinal treatment effective in his work with prison inmates facing the gas chamber and with terminal cancer patients (Frankl, 1965). Like other existentialists (May, 1969; Merleau-Ponty, 1962), Frankl stressed responsibility and the need to rise to life's challenges. Irwin Yalom (1980), another influential existentialist therapist, observed that examining thoughts and feelings regarding responsibility, isolation, freedom, meaninglessness, and death can be painful in the short run. Nevertheless, confronting them head-on can lead to broadened awareness, self-acceptance, and an enhanced sense of control over one's life in the long run. Therapists of different theoretical orientations commonly integrate existential themes into their practices (Schneider, 2015; Wolfe, 2016).

HUMANISTIC THERAPIES EVALUATED SCIENTIFICALLY.   The core concepts of humanistic therapies, such as meaning and self-actualization, are difficult to measure and falsify. For example, at exactly what point can we say a person is self-aware and authentic?

Falsifiability

Can the claim be disproved?

To his credit, however, Rogers specified three conditions for effective psychotherapy that could be falsified. Research has shown that he was largely on the mark when it comes to the therapeutic relationship. Establishing a strong alliance is helpful to the ultimate success of therapy (Horvath et al., 2011; Laska, Gurman, & Wampold, 2014). In fact, the therapeutic relationship is typically a stronger predictor of success in therapy than the use of specific techniques (Bohart et al., 2002). But Rogers was wrong in one key respect: The three core conditions he specified aren't "necessary and sufficient" for improvement (Bohart, 2003; Norcross & Beutler, 1997). Although he overstated their impact, empathy and positive regard are modestly related to therapy outcome (Bohart et al., 2002; Farber & Lane, 2002). Some studies have revealed a positive relation between genuineness and therapeutic outcome, but others haven't (Klein et al., 2002; Orlinsky, Grawe, & Parks, 1994). As we'll learn later, some people can derive considerable benefits from self-help programs that don't even involve therapists (Gould & Clum, 1993), so the therapeutic relationship isn't necessary for improvement. Moreover, research suggests that the causal direction of the relation between the therapeutic alliance and improvement may often be the reverse of what Rogers proposed; clients may first improve and then develop a stronger emotional bond with the therapist as a result (DeRubeis & Feeley, 1990; Kazdin, 2007).

Correlation vs. Causation

Can we be sure that A causes B?

Person-centered therapy is more effective than no treatment (Greenberg, Elliot, & Lietaer, 1994). But findings concerning the effectiveness of person-centered therapy are inconsistent, with some suggesting it may not help much more than a placebo treatment such as merely chatting for the same amount of time with a nonprofessional (Smith, Glass, & Miller, 1980). In contrast, other studies suggest that person-centered therapies often result in substantial improvement and may be comparable in effectiveness to the cognitive-behavioral therapies we'll encounter later (Elliott, 2002; Greenberg & Watson, 1998). Existential therapy has not been studied extensively to date, although researchers have reported that therapy geared to cultivate a sense of meaning holds promise in alleviating symptom-related distress in patients suffering with advanced cancer (Breitbart et al., 2012)

16.3: Group Therapies: The More the Merrier

16.3a List the advantages of group methods.
16.3b Describe the research evidence concerning the effectiveness of Alcoholics Anonymous.
16.3c Identify different approaches to treating the dysfunctional family system.

group therapy

therapy that treats more than one person at a time

Since the early 1920s, when Viennese psychiatrist Jacob Moreno introduced the term **group therapy**, helping professionals have appreciated the value of treating more than one person at a time. The popularity of group approaches has paralleled the increased demand for psychological services in the general population. Group therapies, which typically range in size from 3 to as many as 20 clients, are efficient, time-saving, and less costly than individual treatments and span all major schools of psychotherapy (Levine, 1979; McRoberts, Burlingame, & Hoag, 1998). In a safe group environment, participants can provide and receive support, exchange information and feedback, model effective behaviors and practice new skills, and recognize that they're not alone in struggling with adjustment problems (Yalom, 1985).

Today, psychologists conduct group sessions in a variety of settings, including homes, hospitals, inpatient and residential settings, community agencies, and professional offices. They reach people who are divorced, experiencing marital problems, struggling with gender identity, and experiencing problems with alcoholism and eating disorders, among many other problems in living (Dies, 2003; Lynn & Frauman, 1985). The most recent trend is for self-help groups to form over the Internet, especially for people with problems that may be embarrassing to share in face-to-face encounters (Davison, Pennebaker, & Dickerson, 2000; Golkaramnay et al., 2007). Research suggests that group procedures are effective for a wide range of problems and are about as helpful as individual treatments (McEvoy, 2007; Fuhriman & Burlingame, 1994).

Group therapy procedures are efficient, time-saving, and less costly than many individual treatment methods.

Alcoholics Anonymous

Self-help groups are composed of peers who share a similar problem; often they don't include a professional mental illness specialist. Over the past several decades, these groups, of which **Alcoholics Anonymous** (AA) is the best known, have become remarkably popular. AA was founded in 1935 and is now the largest organization for treating people with alcoholism, with more than 2.1 million members and an estimated 114,000 groups worldwide (Galanter, Dermatis, & Santucci, 2012; MacKillop & Gray, 2014). At AA meetings, people share their struggles with alcohol, and new members are "sponsored" or mentored by more senior members, who've often achieved years of sobriety.

Alcoholics Anonymous
twelve-step self-help program that provides social support for achieving sobriety

The program is organized around the famous "12 steps" toward sobriety and is based on the assumptions that alcoholism is a physical disease and "once an alcoholic, always an alcoholic," which require that members never drink another drop after entering treatment. Several of the 12 steps ask members to place their trust in a "higher power" and to acknowledge their powerlessness over alcohol. AA also offers a powerful social support network (Vaillant & Milofsky, 1982). Groups based on the 12-step model have been established for drug users (Narcotics Anonymous), gamblers, overeaters, spouses and children of alcoholics, "shopaholics" (compulsive shoppers), sexual addicts, and scores of others experiencing problems with impulse control. Nevertheless, there's virtually no research on the effectiveness of these other 12-step approaches.

Although AA appears to be helpful for some people, many claims regarding its success aren't supported by data. People who attend AA meetings or receive treatment based on the 12 steps fare about as well as, but no better than, people who receive other treatments, including cognitive-behavioral therapy (Brandsma, Maultsby, & Welsh, 1980; Ferri, Amoto, & Davoli, 2006; Project MATCH Research Group, 1997). Moreover, AA members who end up in studies are usually the most active participants and have received prior professional help, resulting in an overestimate of how well AA works. Also, as many as 68 percent of participants drop out within three months of joining AA (Emrick, 1987), and those who remain in treatment are probably those who've improved (MacKillop et al., 2003). A study that followed AA members for 16 years found that attendance in the first and third years each predicted abstinence and fewer drinking problems (Moos & Moos, 2006).

Alcoholics Anonymous has been in existence since the 1930s and provides self-help to people of all ages and backgrounds.

A key factor in who improves in AA is the ability to participate in an adaptive social network (Kelly et al., 2012). Involvement in AA predicted abstinence and decreased alcohol consumption in individuals who participated in Network Support treatment, which encourages adults with alcohol problems to develop networks of friends and associates who support their abstinence (Litt et al., 2016).

Controlled Drinking and Relapse Prevention

Contrary to the AA philosophy, the behavioral view assumes that excessive drinking is a learned behavior that therapists can modify and control without total abstinence (Marlatt, 1983). There's bitter controversy about whether *controlled drinking*, that is, drinking in moderation, is even an appropriate treatment goal. Nevertheless, there's considerable evidence that treatment programs that encourage people with alcoholism to set limits, drink moderately, and reinforce their progress can be effective for many clients (MacKillop, et al., 2003; Miller & Hester, 1980; Sobell & Sobell, 1973, 1976). Programs that teach people skills to cope with stressful life circumstances and tolerate negative emotions (Monti, Gulliver, & Myers, 1994) are at least as effective as 12-step programs (Project MATCH Research Group, 1997).

Bucking the popular belief, sometimes repeated in the AA community, of "one drink, one drunk," *relapse prevention* (RP) treatment assumes that many people with alcoholism will at some point experience a lapse, or slip, and resume drinking (Larimer, Palmer, & Marlatt, 1999; Marlatt & Gordon, 1985). RP teaches people not to feel ashamed, guilty, or discouraged when they lapse. Negative feelings about a slip can lead to continued drinking, called the *abstinence violation effect* (Marlatt & Gordon, 1985; Polivy & Herman, 2002). Once someone slips up, he or she figures, "Well, I guess I'm back to drinking again" and goes back to drinking at high levels. RP therapists teach people to rebound after a lapse and avoid situations in which they're tempted to drink. Thus, they learn that a *lapse* doesn't mean a *relapse*. Research suggests that relapse prevention programs are often effective (Bowen et al., 2014; Irvin et al., 1999). Still, total abstinence is probably the best goal for people with severe dependence on alcohol or for whom controlled drinking has failed (Rosenberg, 1993).

Journal Prompt

The text describes two contrasting approaches to alcohol dependency: total abstinence (typically embraced by Alcoholics Anonymous, or AA) and controlled and moderate drinking. In the United States, the AA approach of encouraging total abstinence seems more popular than controlled drinking. Why do you think this is the case? What are the pros and cons of each approach to problem drinking?

strategic family intervention

family therapy approach designed to remove barriers to effective communication

Where's the problem? According to the strategic family therapy approach, families often single out one family member as "the problem" when the problem is actually rooted in the interactional patterns of all family members.

Family Therapies: Treating the Dysfunctional Family System

Family therapists see most psychological problems as rooted in a dysfunctional family system. For them, treatment must focus on the family context out of which conflicts presumably arise. In *family therapy*, the "patient"—the focus of treatment—isn't one person with the most obvious problems, but rather the family unit itself. Family therapists therefore focus on interactions among family members.

STRATEGIC FAMILY THERAPY. **Strategic family interventions** are designed to remove barriers to effective communication. According to strategic therapists, including Virginia Satir (1964), Jay Haley (1976), and Paul Watzlawick (Watzlawick, Weakland, & Fisch, 1974), the real source of psychological problems of one or more family members often lies in the dysfunctional ways in which they communicate, solve problems, and relate to one another.

Strategic therapists invite family members to carry out planned tasks known as *directives*, which shift how family members solve problems and interact. They often involve *paradoxical requests*, which many of us associate with the concept of "reverse psychology." Some researchers (Beutler, Clarkin, & Bongar, 2000; Weeks & L'Abate, 2013) have found that therapists often achieve success when they command their "resistant" or uncooperative clients to intentionally produce the thought, feeling, or behavior that troubled them.

Consider a therapist who "reframed" (cast in a positive light) a couple's arguments by interpreting them as a sign of their emotional closeness. The therapist gave the couple the paradoxical directive to *increase* their arguing to learn more about their love for each other. To show the therapist they were "not in love," they stopped arguing, which was, of course, the therapist's goal in the first place. Once their arguments ceased, their relationship improved (Watzlawick, Beavin, & Jackson, 1967).

STRUCTURAL FAMILY THERAPY. In **structural family therapy** (Minuchin, 1974), the therapist actively immerses himself or herself in the everyday activities of the family to make changes in how they arrange and organize interactions. Salvatore Minuchin and his colleagues successfully treated a 14-year-old girl named Laura who obtained her father's attention by refusing to eat. Eventually, Laura could express in words the message that her refusal to eat conveyed indirectly, and she no longer refused to eat to attain affection (Aponte & Hoffman, 1973). Research indicates that family therapy is more effective than no treatment (Hazelrigg, Cooper, & Borduin, 1987; Vetere, 2001) and at least as effective as individual therapy (Gurman & Kniskern, 2014; Shadish, 1995).

structural family therapy

treatment in which therapists deeply involve themselves in family activities to change how family members arrange and organize interactions

16.4: Behavioral and Cognitive-Behavioral Approaches: Changing Maladaptive Actions and Thoughts

16.4a Describe the characteristics of behavior therapy and identify different behavioral approaches.

16.4b Describe the features of cognitive-behavioral therapies (CBT) and third-wave therapies.

In sharp contrast to psychotherapists who hold that insight is the key to improvement, **behavior therapists** are so named because they focus on the specific behaviors that lead the client to seek therapy and address the current variables that maintain problematic thoughts, feelings, and behaviors (Antony & Roemer, 2003). Because behavior therapies focus primarily on contending with identified problems rather than their supposed "root causes," many psychoanalysts once predicted that they would result in *symptom substitution*. That is, following behavior therapy, the client's underlying conflict, such as early aggression toward parents, would merely manifest itself as a different symptom. Yet data show that behavior therapies rarely, if ever, produce symptom substitution (Kazdin & Hersen, 1980; Tryon, 2008). For example, clients whose phobias are eliminated by behavioral therapy don't tend to develop other problems, like depression.

Behavior therapists assume that behavior change results from the operation of basic principles of learning, especially classical conditioning (see LO 6.1a), operant conditioning (see LO 6.2a), and observational learning (see LO 6.3a). For example, a client with a dog phobia may reinforce his problematic behaviors by crossing the street whenever he sees a dog. Avoiding the dog helps him obtain negative reinforcement—in this case, escaping anxiety—although he is probably unaware of this function.

Behavior therapists use a wide variety of *behavioral assessment* techniques to pinpoint environmental causes of the person's problem, establish specific and measurable treatment goals, and devise therapeutic procedures. Behavior therapists may use direct observations of current and specific behaviors, verbal descriptions of the nature and dimensions of the problem, scores on paper-and-pencil tests, standardized interviews (First et al., 1996), and physiological measures (Yartz & Hawk, 2001) to plan treatment and monitor its progress. With recent technological innovations, clients today can use portable cell phones, computers, tablet devices, and fitness trackers to record their thoughts, feelings, behaviors, and even physiological responses, such as heart rate, as they arise in real-life situations. Clinicians have used such monitoring techniques, called **ecological momentary assessment,** to (a) increase clients' awareness of the frequency and circumstances associated with a behavior

behavior therapist

therapist who focuses on specific problem behaviors and current variables that maintain problematic thoughts, feelings, and behaviors

ecological momentary assessment

assessment of thoughts, emotions, and behaviors that arise in the moment in situations in which they occur in everyday life.

A behavior therapist treating a bad habit, like nail biting, would try to determine the situations in which nail biting occurs, as well as the consequences of nail biting for the person, such as distraction from anxiety.

they hope to change, such as pathological alcohol use, and (b) to assist therapists with assessment and treatment planning (Kirchner & Shiffman, 2013; Piasecki et al., 2014).

A complete assessment considers clients' gender, race, socioeconomic class, culture, sexual orientation, and ethnic factors (Hays, 2008; Ivey, Ivey, & Simek-Morgan, 1993), as well as information about their interpersonal relationships and drug use (Lazarus, 2003). Evaluation of treatment effectiveness is integrated seamlessly into all phases of therapy, and therapists encourage clients to apply their newly acquired coping skills to everyday life. Let's now examine the nuts and bolts of several behavioral approaches.

Systematic Desensitization and Exposure Therapies: Learning Principles in Action

systematic desensitization

clients are taught to relax as they are gradually exposed to what they fear in a stepwise manner

exposure therapy

therapy that confronts clients with what they fear with the goal of reducing the fear

Systematic desensitization is an excellent example of how behavior therapists apply learning principles to treatment. Psychiatrist Joseph Wolpe developed systematic desensitization (SD) in 1958 to help clients manage phobias. SD gradually exposes clients to anxiety-producing situations through the use of imagined scenes. This technique was the earliest **exposure therapy**, a class of procedures that aims to reduce clients' fears by confronting them directly with the source of their fears. Exposure therapies have been widely applied in the treatment of obsessive-compulsive disorder, posttraumatic stress disorder, and other anxiety-related conditions, such as social phobia (Foa & McLean, 2016).

HOW DESENSITIZATION WORKS: ONE STEP AT A TIME.   SD is based on the principle of *reciprocal inhibition*, which says that clients can't experience two conflicting responses simultaneously. If a client is relaxed, he or she can't be anxious at the same time. Wolpe described his technique as a form of classical conditioning and called it *counterconditioning*. By pairing an incompatible relaxation response with anxiety, we condition a more adaptive response to anxiety-arousing stimuli.

A therapist begins SD by teaching the client how to relax by alternately tensing and relaxing his or her muscles (Bernstein, Borkovec, & Hazlett-Stevens, 2000; Jacobson, 1938). Next, the therapist helps the client to construct an *anxiety hierarchy*—a "ladder" of situations that climbs from least to most anxiety provoking. We can find a hierarchy used to treat a person with a phobia of dogs in Figure 16.3. The therapy proceeds in a stepwise manner. The therapist asks the client to relax and imagine the first scene, moving to the next, more anxiety-producing scene only after the client reports feeling relaxed while imagining the first scene.

Consider the following example of how a client moves stepwise up the anxiety hierarchy, from the least to most anxiety-producing scene.

> **Therapist:** "Soon I shall ask you to imagine a scene. After you hear a description of the situation, please imagine it as vividly as you can, through your own eyes, as if you were actually there. Try to include all the details in the scene. While you're visualizing the situation, you may continue feeling as relaxed as you are now… . After 5, 10, or 15 seconds, I'll ask you to stop imagining the scene … and to just relax. But if you begin to feel even the slightest increase in anxiety or tension, please signal this to me by raising your left forefinger … I'll step in and ask you to stop imagining the situation and then will help you get relaxed once more" (Goldfried & Davison, 1976, pp. 124–125).

If the client reports anxiety at any point, the therapist interrupts the process and helps him or her relax again. Then, the therapist reintroduces the scene that preceded the one that caused anxiety. This process continues until the client can confront the most frightening scenes without anxiety.

Desensitization can also occur in vivo, that is, in "real life." In vivo SD involves gradual exposure to what the client actually fears, rather than imagining the anxiety-provoking situation. SD is effective for a wide range of phobias, insomnia, speech disorders, asthma attacks, nightmares, and some cases of problem drinking (Spiegler & Guevremont, 2003).

The Effectiveness of Systematic Desensitization.   Behavior therapists strive to discover not only what works, but also why it works. Researchers can evaluate many therapeutic procedures by isolating the effects of each component and comparing these effects with that

In vivo desensitization: clients gradually approach and handle any fears, as these clients are doing as they overcome their fear of flying.

Figure 16.3 A Systematic Desensitization Hierarchy of a Person With a Fear of Dogs.

1. You are looking at pictures of dogs in magazines.

2. You are looking at a video of a dog playing with another dog.

3. You are looking at a video of a dog playing with a person.

4. From 100 feet away, you are watching an Irish Setter playing with the therapist.

5. You are approaching the dog and observing the interaction with the therapist from a distance of 50, 25, 10, and 5 feet in successive trials.

6. You are petting the dog.

7. You are playing with the dog.

8. You are allowing the dog to lick you.

dismantling

research procedure for examining the effectiveness of isolated components of a larger treatment

of the full treatment package (Wilson & O' Leary, 1980). This approach is called **dismantling** because it enables researchers to examine the effectiveness of isolated components of a broader treatment. Dismantling helps rule out rival hypotheses about the effective mechanisms of SD and other treatments.

Dismantling studies show that no single component of desensitization (relaxation, imagery, an anxiety hierarchy) is essential: We can eliminate each without affecting treatment outcome. Therefore, the door is open to diverse interpretations for the treatment's success (Kazdin & Wilcoxon, 1976; Lohr, DeMaio, & McGlynn, 2003). One possibility is that the credibility of the treatment creates a strong placebo effect (Mineka & Thomas, 1999). Interestingly, desensitization may fare no better than a placebo procedure designed to arouse an equivalent degree of positive expectations (Lick, 1975). Alternatively, when therapists expose clients to what they fear, clients may realize that their fears are irrational, or their fear response may extinguish following repeated uneventful contact with the feared stimulus (see LO 6.1b)(Casey, Oei, & Newcombe, 2004; Foa & McLean, 2016; Rachman, 1994).

Ruling Out Rival Hypotheses

Have important alternative explanations for the findings been excluded?

Ruling Out Rival Hypotheses

Have important alternative explanations for the findings been excluded?

FLOODING AND VIRTUAL REALITY EXPOSURE. Flooding therapies provide a vivid contrast to SD. Flooding therapists jump right to the top of the anxiety hierarchy and expose clients to images of the stimuli they fear the most for prolonged periods, often for an hour or even several hours. Flooding therapies are based on the idea that fears are maintained by avoidance. For example, because individuals with a height phobia continually avoid high places, they never learn that the disastrous consequences they envision won't occur. Ironically, their avoidance only perpetuates their fears by means of negative reinforcement (see LO 6.2c). The flooding therapist repeatedly provokes anxiety in the absence of actual negative consequences so that extinction of the fear can proceed.

Like SD, flooding can be conducted in vivo. To paraphrase the Nike slogan ("Just do it"): "If you're afraid to do it, do it!" During the first session, a therapist who practices in vivo flooding might accompany a person with a height phobia to the top of a skyscraper and look down for an hour—or however long it takes for anxiety to dissipate. Remarkably, many people with specific phobias—including those who were in psychodynamic therapy for decades with no relief—have been essentially cured of their fears after only a single session (Antony & Barlow, 2002; Williams, Turner, & Peer, 1985). Therapists have successfully used flooding with numerous anxiety disorders, including obsessive-compulsive disorder (OCD), social phobia, posttraumatic stress disorder, and agoraphobia.

A crucial component of flooding is **response prevention** (more recently called *ritual prevention* in the case of obsessive-compulsive disorder), in which therapists prevent clients from performing their typical avoidance behaviors (Spiegler, 1983). A therapist may treat a person with a hand-washing compulsion by exposing her to dirt and preventing her from washing her hands (Franklin & Foa, 2002). Research demonstrates that this treatment is effective for OCD and closely related conditions (Chambless & Ollendick, 2001; Gillihan et al., 2015).

Virtual reality exposure therapy is the "new kid on the block" of exposure therapies. With high-tech equipment, which provides a "virtually lifelike" experience of fear-provoking situations, therapists can treat many anxiety-related conditions, including height phobia (Emmelkamp et al., 2001), thunderstorm phobia (Botella et al., 2006), flying phobia (Emmelkamp et al., 2002; Opris et al., 2012), social anxiety disorder (Anderson et al., 2013), and posttraumatic stress disorder (Reger et al., 2011; Rothbaum et al., 2001). Virtual reality exposure not only rivals the effectiveness of traditional in vivo exposure, and generalizes to real life situations, but also provides repeated exposure to situations that often aren't feasible in real life, like flying in airplanes (Morina et al., 2015).

In 2005, researchers discovered that the antibiotic D-cycloserine, used for many years to treat tuberculosis, facilitates long-term extinction of fear of heights when administered several hours before people undergo exposure riding in a "virtual glass elevator" (Davis et al., 2005). D-cycloserine works by boosting the functioning of a receptor in the brain that enhances fear-extinction learning in both animals and humans. Today, D-cycloserine is recognized as a promising adjunct to treatments for anxiety-related conditions, including obsessive-compulsive disorder (Norberg, Krystal, & Tolin, 2008) and possibly posttraumatic stress disorder (de Kleine et al., 2012). Still, D-cyclocerine does not always outperform placebos (Litz et al., 2012; Rothbaum et al., 2014; Scheeringa & Weems, 2014), so the verdict regarding its specific effects on psychological disorders is not settled.

EXPOSURE: FRINGE AND FAD TECHNIQUES. Traditionally, behavior therapists have been careful not to exaggerate claims of the effectiveness of exposure therapies and promote them to the public as cure-alls. We can contrast this cautious approach with that of recent proponents of fringe therapeutic techniques, some of who've made extraordinary claims that don't stack up well against the evidence.

Roger Callahan, who developed *Thought Field Therapy* (TFT), claimed that his procedure could cure phobias in as little as five minutes (Callahan, 1995, 2001) and cure not only human fears, but also fears in horses and dogs. In TFT, the client thinks of a distressing problem while the therapist taps specific points on the client's body in a predetermined order. Meanwhile, the client hums parts of "The Star Spangled Banner," rolls his or her eyes, or counts (how TFT therapists accomplish these feats with animals is unknown). These decidedly strange procedures supposedly remove invisible "energy blocks" associated with a specific fear. There's no research evidence for the assertion that the technique cures anxiety by manipulating energy fields, which have never been shown to exist, or for the implausible claim of virtually instantaneous cures for the vast majority of phobia sufferers

---

response prevention

technique in which therapists prevent clients from performing their typical avoidance behaviors

Thought field therapists claim that touching body parts in a set order can play a role in treating long-standing phobias resistant to treatment by other means.

Extraordinary Claims

Is the evidence as strong as the claim?

(Lohr et al., 2003; Pignotti & Thyer, 2015). Because the "energy blocks" of TFT aren't measurable, the theoretical claims of TFT are unfalsifiable.

Some other exposure-based therapies feature numerous "bells and whistles" that provide them with the superficial veneer of science. Take *eye movement desensitization and reprocessing* (EMDR), which has been marketed widely as a "breakthrough" treatment for anxiety disorders (Shapiro, 1995; Shapiro & Forrest, 1997). As of 2016, more than 100,000 therapists have been trained in EMDR (EMDR Institute, 2016). EMDR proponents claim that clients' lateral eye movements, made while they imagine a past traumatic event, enhance their processing of painful memories. Yet systematic reviews of research demonstrate that the eye movements of EMDR play no role in this treatment's effectiveness. Moreover, EMDR is no more effective than standard exposure treatments (Davidson & Parker, 2001; Lohr, Tolin, & Lilienfeld, 1998; Rubin, 2003). Accordingly, a parsimonious hypothesis is that the active ingredient of EMDR isn't the eye movements for which it's named, but rather the exposure the technique provides.

> ◀ **Falsifiability**
>
> Can the claim be disproved?

> ◀ **Occam's Razor**
>
> Does a simpler explanation fit the data just as well?

Modeling in Therapy: Learning by Watching

Clients can learn many things by observing therapists model positive behaviors. Modeling is one form of *observational learning,* also called *vicarious learning.* Albert Bandura (1971, 1977) has long advocated **participant modeling**, a technique in which the therapist models a calm encounter with the client's feared object or situation and then guides the client through the steps of the encounter until he or she can cope unassisted.

participant modeling

technique in which the therapist first models a problematic situation and then guides the client through steps to cope with it unassisted

ASSERTION TRAINING. Modeling is an important component of assertion and social skills training programs designed to help clients with social anxiety. The primary goals of assertion training are to facilitate the expression of thoughts and feelings in a forthright and socially appropriate manner and to ensure that clients aren't taken advantage of, ignored, or denied their legitimate rights (Alberti & Emmons, 2001). In assertion training, therapists teach clients to avoid extreme reactions to others' unreasonable demands, such as submissiveness, on the one hand, and aggressiveness, on the other. Assertiveness, the middle ground between these extremes, is the goal.

In EMDR, the client focuses on the therapist's fingers as they move back and forth. Nevertheless, studies indicate that such eye movements play no useful role in EMDR's effectiveness.

BEHAVIORAL REHEARSAL. Therapies commonly use behavioral rehearsal in assertion training and other participant modeling techniques. In behavioral rehearsal, the client engages in role-playing with a therapist to learn and practice new skills. The therapist plays the role of a relevant person such as a spouse, parent, or boss. The client reacts to the character enacted by the therapist, and in turn, the therapist offers coaching and feedback. To give the client an opportunity to model assertive behaviors, therapist and client reverse roles, with the therapist playing the client's role. By doing so, the therapist models not only what the client might say, but also how the client might say it.

To transfer what clients learn to everyday life, therapists encourage them to practice their newfound skills outside therapy sessions. Modeling and social skills training can make valuable contributions to treating (although not curing) schizophrenia, autism, depression, attention-deficit/hyperactivity disorder (ADHD), and social anxiety (Antony & Roemer, 2003; Scattone, 2007; Monastra, 2008).

Operant and Classical Conditioning Procedures

Psychologists have used operant conditioning procedures to good effect among children with autism and a host of other childhood disorders. As we'll recall from previously in the text, operant conditioning is learning in which behavior is modified by its consequences. An example of an operant procedure is the **token economy**, widely used in treatment programs in institutional and residential settings, as well as the home (Kazdin, 2012). In token economies, certain behaviors, like helping others, are consistently rewarded with tokens that clients can later exchange for more tangible rewards, whereas other behaviors, like screaming at hospital staff, are ignored or punished. In this way, such programs shape, maintain, or alter behaviors by the consistent application of operant conditioning principles (Boerke & Reitman, 2011; Kazdin, 1978). Critics of token economies argue that the benefits don't necessarily generalize to other settings and that they're difficult and impractical to administer (Corrigan, 1995; Doll, McLaughlin, & Barretto, 2013). Nevertheless, token economies have

token economy

method in which desirable behaviors are rewarded with tokens that clients can exchange for tangible rewards

shown some success in the classroom (Boniecki & Moore, 2003), in treating children with ADHD at home and at school (Mueser & Liberman, 1995), and in treating clients with schizophrenia who require long-term hospitalization (Dixon et al., 2010; Paul & Lentz, 1977).

aversion therapy

treatment that uses punishment to decrease the frequency of undesirable behaviors

Aversion therapies are based primarily on classical conditioning and pair undesirable behaviors with stimuli that most people experience as painful, unpleasant, or even revolting. For example, therapists have used medications such as disulfiram—better known as Antabuse—to make people vomit after drinking alcohol (Brewer, 1992), electric shocks to treat psychologically triggered recurrent sneezing (Kushner, 1968), and verbal descriptions of feeling nauseated while people imagine smoking cigarettes (Cautela, 1971).

Research provides, at best, mixed support for the effectiveness of aversive procedures (Spiegler & Guevremont, 2003). For example, people with alcoholism often simply stop taking Antabuse rather than stop drinking (MacKillop & Gray, 2014). In general, therapists attempt minimally unpleasant techniques before moving on to more aversive measures. The decision to implement aversion therapies should be made only after carefully weighing their costs and benefits relative to alternative approaches.

Cognitive-Behavioral and Third-Wave Therapies: Learning to Think and Act Differently

cognitive-behavioral therapy

treatment that attempts to replace irrational cognitions and maladaptive behaviors with more rational cognitions and adaptive behaviors

Advocates of **cognitive-behavioral therapies** hold that beliefs play the central role in our feelings and behaviors. These therapies share three core assumptions: (1) cognitions are identifiable and measureable; (2) cognitions are the key players in both healthy and unhealthy psychological functioning; and (3) irrational beliefs or catastrophic thinking such as "I'm worthless and will never succeed at anything" can be replaced with more rational and adaptive cognitions, or viewed in a more accepting light.

THE ABCs OF RATIONAL EMOTIVE BEHAVIOR THERAPY. Beginning in the mid-1950s, pioneering therapist Albert Ellis (Ellis, 1958, 1962) advocated *rational emotive therapy* (RET), later renamed *rational emotive behavior therapy* (REBT). In many respects, REBT is a prime example of a cognitive-behavioral approach. It's cognitive in its emphasis on changing how we think (that's the "cognitive" part), but it also focuses on changing how we act (that's the "behavioral" part).

Ellis argued that we respond to an unpleasant activating (internal or external) event (A) with a range of emotional and behavioral consequences (C). As we all know, people often respond differently to the same objective event; some students respond to a 75 on an exam by celebrating, whereas others respond by berating themselves for not getting a 90 or even a 100. For Ellis, the differences in how we respond to the same event stem largely from differences in (B) our belief systems (see Figure 16.4). The ABCs Ellis identified lie at the heart of most, if not all, cognitive-behavior therapies.

Some beliefs are rational: They're flexible, logical, and promote self-acceptance. In contrast, others are irrational: They're associated with unrealistic demands about the self ("I must be perfect"), others ("I must become worried about other people's problems"), and life conditions ("I must be worried about things I can't control"). Ellis also maintained that psychologically unhealthy people frequently "awfulize," that is, engage in catastrophic thinking about their problems ("If I don't get this job, it would be the worst thing that ever happened to me"). Albert Ellis identified 12 irrational beliefs ("The Dirty Dozen") listed here that are widespread in our culture. You may find it interesting to see which of these beliefs you've entertained at some point in your life. Because these ideas are so much a part of many people's thinking, don't be surprised if you hold a number of

Figure 16.4 The ABCs of Rational Emotive Behavior Therapy.

How people feel about an event is influenced in powerful ways by their beliefs about the event.

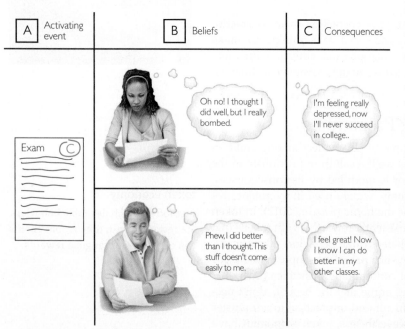

Fact vs. Fiction

Interactive

There's no evidence that therapists' theoretical orientation is correlated with their personality traits. (See bottom of page for answer.)

○ Fact

○ Fiction

them. According to Ellis, our vulnerability to psychological disturbance is a product of the frequency and strength of our irrational beliefs (David, Lynn, & Ellis, 2010).

1. You must have nearly constant love and approval from everyone who is important to you.
2. You must prove yourself highly adequate and successful, or at least extremely competent or talented at some valued activity.
3. People who hurt you or treat you poorly are bad, evil, and blameworthy, and they deserve to be punished harshly for their actions.
4. When things don't go your way, it's an awful, horrible, or terrible catastrophe.
5. External factors, such as life events, are responsible for your misery; you have little ability to control or eliminate your negative feelings, including sadness and anger.
6. You must become upset and preoccupied with frightening or dangerous situations or people.
7. It's easier to avoid confronting many of life's challenges and responsibilities than it is to become self-disciplined.
8. The past must continue to dominate your feelings and behavior because previous experiences once exerted a strong impact on you.
9. If you can't cope with or resolve everyday hassles quickly, it's terrible; things and relationships should work out better than they do.
10. Being passive with no commitment to accomplish anything other than "enjoying oneself" is a good way to achieve happiness.
11. To feel comfortable, you must be highly organized or certain about how things will turn out.
12. Your worth and acceptance depend on your performance and how others rate you. Rather than evaluate your performance in specific areas of functioning, you should give yourself a global rating ("I'm good," "I'm bad," and so on).

(Based on: Ellis, 1977)

To his ABC scheme, Ellis added a (D), (E), and (F) component to describe how therapists treat clients. REBT therapists encourage clients to actively *dispute* (D) their irrational beliefs, adopt more *effective* (E) and rational beliefs to increase adaptive responses, and experience new and desired *feelings* (F) and behaviors in relation to (A). To modify clients' irrational beliefs, the therapist forcefully encourages them to rethink their assumptions and personal philosophy. REBT therapists often assign "homework" designed to falsify clients' maladaptive beliefs. For example, they may give shy clients an assignment to talk to an attractive man or woman to falsify their belief that "If I'm rejected by someone I like, it will be absolutely terrible."

Falsifiability

Can the claim be disproved?

Journal Prompt

Carefully review Ellis's "Dirty Dozen" irrational beliefs. Which of these beliefs do you hold to at least some extent? Describe the personal and interpersonal impact of each of the beliefs you identified.

Answer: Fiction. Several, although not all, studies suggest that compared with other therapists, psychoanalytic therapists tend to be especially insecure and serious, behavior therapists tend to be especially assertive and self-confident, and cognitive-behavioral therapists tend to be especially rational (Keinan, Almagor, & Ben-Porath, 1989; Walton, 1978).

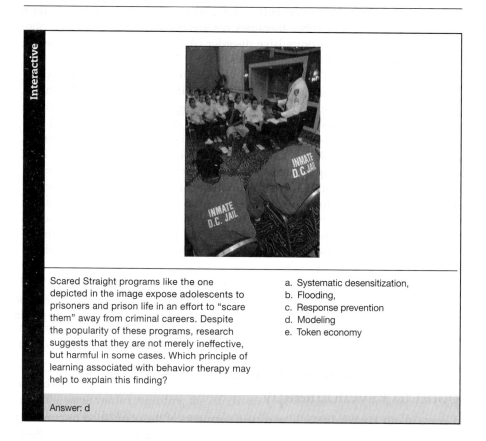

Interactive

Scared Straight programs like the one depicted in the image expose adolescents to prisoners and prison life in an effort to "scare them" away from criminal careers. Despite the popularity of these programs, research suggests that they are not merely ineffective, but harmful in some cases. Which principle of learning associated with behavior therapy may help to explain this finding?

a. Systematic desensitization,
b. Flooding,
c. Response prevention
d. Modeling
e. Token economy

Answer: d

2007; Petry, Tennen, & Affleck, 2000; Rabinowitz & Renert, 1997; Schmidt & Hancey, 1979). Still, we must be tentative in our conclusions because researchers haven't studied these variables in depth. Many controlled studies of psychotherapy don't report participants' race, ethnicity, disability status, or sexual orientation, nor do they analyze whether the effectiveness of psychotherapy depends on these variables (Cardemil, 2010; Sue & Zane, 2006). So we can't be completely confident that therapies effective for Caucasians are equally effective for other populations.

Nonspecific Factors

One probable reason many therapies are comparable in effectiveness is that certain *nonspecific factors*—those that cut across many or most therapies—are responsible for improvement across diverse treatments. As Jerome Frank (1961) noted in his classic book *Persuasion and Healing*, these nonspecific factors include listening with empathy, instilling hope, establishing a strong emotional bond with clients, providing a clear theoretical rationale for treatment, and implementing techniques that offer new ways of thinking, feeling, and behaving (Del Re et al., 2012; Lambert & Ogles, 2004; Miller, Duncan, & Hubble, 2005). Frank observed that these nonspecific factors are also shared by many forms of faith healing, religious conversion, and interpersonal persuasion over the centuries and that they extend across most, if not all, cultures. Additional common factors include the therapist assisting the client in making sense of the world, exerting influence and mastery through social means and connecting with others, and developing positive treatment expectancies (Wampold, 2007, 2015).

Although we might be tempted to dismiss nonspecific factors as "placebos," this would miss the crucial point that they're essential in instilling in clients the motivation to change. Indeed, studies show that common factors typically account for a hefty chunk of improvement in therapy (Cuijpers et al., 2008; Laska et al., 2014; Wampold & Imel, 2015).

Psychomythology
Are Self-Help Books Always Helpful?

Each year Americans can choose from about 3,500 newly published self-help books that promise everything from achieving everlasting bliss and expanded consciousness to freedom from virtually every human failing and foible imaginable. Self-help books are only one piece of the massive quilt of the self-improvement industry that extends to Internet sites; magazines; radio and television shows; CDs; DVDs; lectures; workshops; advice columns; and, most recently, smartphone applications and computerized delivery of evidence-based treatments (Abroms et al., 2011; Craske et al., 2011).

It's no mystery why self-help books are so popular that Americans spend $650 million a year on them, and at least 80 percent of therapists recommend them to their clients (Arkowitz & Lilienfeld, 2007). Researchers have studied the effects of reading self-help books, known in psychology lingo as "bibliotherapy." The relatively small number of studies conducted on self-help books suggests that bibliotherapy and psychotherapy often lead to comparable improvements in depression, anxiety, and other problems, or that self-help promotes improvements relative to no exposure to self-help materials (Gould & Clum, 1993; Ritzert et al., 2016).

Still, we should bear in mind three points. First, we can't generalize the limited findings to all the books on the shelves of our local bookstore, because the overwhelming majority of self-help books are untested (Rosen et al., 2014). Second, people who volunteer for research on self-help books may be more motivated to read the entire book and benefit from it compared with the curious person who purchases the book under more casual circumstances. Third, many self-help books address relatively minor problems, like everyday worries and public speaking. When researchers (Menchola, Arkowitz, & Burke, 2007) have examined more serious problems, like major depression and panic disorder, psychotherapy has fared better than bibliotherapy, although both do better than no treatment.

Some people don't respond at all to self-help books (Febbraro et al., 1999), and many self-help books promise far more than they can deliver. Readers who fall short of how the promotional information on the cover assures them they'll respond may feel like failures and be less likely to seek professional help or make changes on their own. Bearing this possibility in mind, Hal Arkowitz and Scott Lilienfeld (2007) offered the following recommendations about selecting self-help books:

- Use books that have research support and are based on valid psychological principles of change (Gambrill, 1992). Make sure the author refers to published research that supports the claims made. Books that have shown positive effects in studies include *Feeling*

The "secret" to the 2007 best seller *The Secret* by Rhonda Byrne is the so-called *law of attraction*—good thoughts attract good things, and bad thoughts attract bad things. Yet there's no evidence that merely wishing for something good to happen without taking concrete steps to accomplish it is effective. We should be skeptical of self-help books that promise simple answers to complex problems.

Good by David Burns, *Mind Over Mood* by Dennis Greenberger and Christine Padesky, and *Coping with Panic* by George Clum.
- Evaluate the author's credentials. Does he or she have the professional training and expertise to write on the topic at hand?
- Be wary of books that make far-fetched promises, such as curing a phobia in five minutes. The 2007 blockbuster best seller *The Secret* (Byrne, 2007), popularized by Oprah Winfrey, informs readers that positive thinking alone can cure cancer, help one become a millionaire, or achieve just about any goal one wants. Yet there's not a shred of research evidence that this kind of wishful thinking is helpful (Smythe, 2007).
- Beware of books that rely on a one-size-fits-all approach. A book that tells us to always express anger to our relationship partner fails to take into account the complexity and specifics of the relationship.
- Serious problems like clinical depression, obsessive-compulsive disorder, and schizophrenia warrant professional help rather than self-help alone.

In contrast, *specific factors* characterize only certain therapies: They include meditating, challenging irrational beliefs, and social skills training. In some cases, specific factors may be key ingredients in psychotherapeutic change; in other cases, they may not enhance treatment effectiveness beyond common factors (Stevens, Hynan, & Allen, 2000). Psychologists are divided about the extent to which common versus specific factors influence the outcome

psychotherapy is effective because most clients enter psychotherapy when their symptoms are most extreme.

Many "jinxes" probably stem from a failure to consider regression to the mean (Kruger, Savitsky, & Gilovich, 1999). If we've been doing far better than we had expected in a sports tourna- ment and a friend says "Wow, you're doing great," we may fear that our friend has jinxed us. In fact, we *are* likely to do worse after our friend says that, but because of regression to the mean, not because of a jinx. Recall from the post hoc fallacy (see LO 10.1a) that because A comes before B doesn't mean that A causes B.

Fact vs. Fiction

Interactive

Even when patients are told that a placebo is physiologically inactive, it still appears to be effective for some conditions. (See bottom of page for answer.)

○ Fact

○ Fiction

Fact vs. Fiction

Interactive

Only a minority of therapists use empirically supported treatments. (See bottom of page for answer.)

○ Fact

○ Fiction

authors of your text find the latter argument more compelling, because the burden of proof for selecting and administering a treatment should always fall on therapists. Therefore, if there's reasonable evidence that certain treatments are better than others for certain disorders, therapists should be guided by that evidence (Lilienfeld et al., 2013).

16.6 Biomedical Treatments: Medications, Electrical Stimulation, and Surgery

16.6a **Recognize different types of drugs and cautions associated with drug treatment.**

16.6b **Outline key considerations in drug treatment.**

16.6c **Identify misconceptions about biomedical treatments.**

Biomedical treatments—including medications, electrical stimulation techniques, and brain surgery—directly alter the brain's chemistry or physiology. Just as the number of psychotherapy approaches has more than tripled since the 1970s, antidepressant prescriptions have quadrupled from 1988–1994 to 2005–2008. Today, antidepressants are the most

Answer 1: Fact. The expectation of improvement can be so powerful that people with the digestive disorder of irritable bowel syndrome still respond positively to a sugar placebo pill even when a physician informs them it's a placebo (Kaptchuk et al., 2010).

Answer 2: Fact. Survey data suggest that only a minority of therapists use empirically supported treatments (Baker et al., 2009; Freiheit et al., 2004). For example, a survey of practitioners who treat clients with eating disorders (especially anorexia and bulimia) indicated that most of them don't regularly administer either cognitive-behavioral or interpersonal therapies, the primary interventions found to be helpful for these conditions (Lilienfeld et al., 2013; Pederson et al., 2000).

Evaluating Claims PSYCHOTHERAPIES

Interactive

Your close friend, Ava, comes to you and shares her recent struggles with depression. She reports feeling sad, losing interest in life, feeling guilty about minor things, and experiencing fleeting thoughts of hurting herself. She says that she's felt this way before, and she shares that she's tried medication in the past, but prefers to be treated without meds this time around. You suggest that consulting a therapist might be helpful.

You and Ava search the Internet and review the websites of therapists in your city who claim to be experts in treating depression. You and Ava are intrigued by the following description on the "Cognitve-Behavioral Therapy Treatment Institute" Web site.

"Cognitive-behavioral therapy, which I use in my practice, may not be effective in all cases, but several studies have shown that CBT is equally as effective in the treatment of depression as anti-depressant medication. I am pleased to offer CBT as a treatment because research from independent laboratories indicates that the effects of CBT extend beyond psychotherapy, whereas the effects of medication typically last only for as long as the medication is used."

Scientific skepticism requires us to evaluate all claims with an open mind but to insist on compelling evidence before accepting them. How do the principles of scientific thinking help us to evaluate this claim about the relative effectiveness of CBT and medication and the persistence of effects of these different treatments?

Consider how the six principles of scientific thinking are relevant as you evaluate this claim.

1. **Ruling Out Rival Hypotheses**

   Have important alternative explanations for the findings been excluded?

   It's not clear that all alternative explanations for the findings have not been excluded, such as regression toward the mean, retrospective reworking of the past, and spontaneous remission. Another possible explanation is the operation of placebo effects (Kaptchuk & Miller, 2015). For example, it's possible that both treatments are effective because they produce positive expectations for change (i.e., a placebo effect), which, as you'll recall, can lead to significant relief of symptoms of depression (Kirsch, 2010). The fact that the effects persist beyond treatment for psychotherapy might be because patients expect that the effects of psychotherapy will be more enduring, and patients are more optimistic after psychological treatment than after they take medication, accounting for the more lasting effects of psychotherapy. A study that includes a comparison condition in which a placebo is used would be helpful to address the role of placebo effects, as would matching psychotherapy and medication for positive treatment expectancies and seeing if psychotherapy still outperforms medication in the long run.

2. **Correlation vs. Causation**

   Can we be sure that A causes B?

   This principle of scientific thinking is not terribly relevant to this scenario.

3. **Falsifiability**

   Can the claim be disproved?

   The claims in the ad could be disproved by studies that don't support the findings. For example, if a number of large studies randomly assigned some people with depression to receive cognitive-behavioral therapy and others to receive only emotional support, and these studies showed no differences whatsoever in depression scores between the groups, that would begin to call the claim into serious question.

4. **Replicability**

   Can the results be duplicated in other studies?

   The fact that the findings were duplicated in independent laboratories is noteworthy and indicates that the results are reliable. Additional large-scale studies that follow men and women over time would increase confidence that the results are reliable and generalize across genders.

5. **Extraordinary Claims**

   Is the evidence as strong as the claim?

   The claim avoids exaggerating the benefits of CBT by noting that it may not be effective in all cases. The ad notes correctly that CBT is about as effective as antidepressant medication for clinical depression and that the effects of psychotherapy can be more enduring than the effects of medication.

6. **Occam's Razor**

   Does a simpler explanation fit the data just as well?

   It's possible that regression to the mean, spontaneous remission, retrospective reworking of the past and the presence of a placebo effect are alternative explanations, but, absent additional research, it's premature to claim that another explanation provides a better or simpler explanation.

Summary

The information in the ad is measured and generally appropriate, given what's known about the effects of psychotherapy and medication in the treatment of major depression. In cases of serious depression, it might be helpful to combine psychotherapy and medication.

tardy, means late-appearing), but it occasionally begins after only a few months of therapy at low dosages (Simpson & Kline, 1976). Newer antipsychotic medicines such as Risperdal, generally produce fewer serious adverse effects. But they too occasionally produce serious side effects, including sudden cardiac deaths, and the verdict is out regarding whether they're more effective compared with previous and less-costly medications (Correll & Schenk, 2008; Lieberman et al., 2005; Schneeweiss & Avorn, 2009).

One Dose Doesn't "Fit All": Differences in Responses to Medication. People don't all respond equally to the same dose of medication. Weight, age, and even racial differences often affect drug response. African Americans tend to require lower doses of certain anti-anxiety and antidepressant drugs and have a faster response than do Caucasians, and Asians metabolize (break down) these medications more slowly than do Caucasians (Baker & Bell, 1999; Campinha-Bacote, 2002; Strickland et al., 1997). Because some people become physically and psychologically dependent on medications such as the widely prescribed antianxiety medications Valium and Xanax (known as benzodiazepines), physicians must proceed with caution and determine the lowest dose possible to achieve positive results and minimize unpleasant side effects (Wigal et al., 2006). Discontinuation of certain drugs, such as those for anxiety and depression, should be performed gradually to minimize withdrawal reactions, including anxiety and agitation (Dell'Osso & Lader, 2013; Fava et al., 2015).

Medications on Trial: Harmful and Overprescribed? Some psychologists have raised serious questions about the effectiveness of the SSRIs, especially among children and adolescents (Healy, 2004; Kendall, Pilling, & Whittington, 2005). There also are widely publicized indications that SSRIs increase the risk of suicidal thoughts in people younger than 18 years of age, although there's no clear evidence that they increase the risk of *completed* suicide (Goldstein & Ruscio, 2009). For this reason, the U.S. Food and Drug Administration (FDA) now requires drug manufacturers to include warnings on the labels of SSRIs of possible suicide risk. Following these "black box" warnings (so called because they're enclosed in a box with black borders on the medication label) in 2004, antidepressant prescriptions dropped by more than 30 percent among adolescents within two years, although this trend reversed somewhat after 2008 (Friedman, 2014).

Scientists don't understand why antidepressants increase suicidal thoughts in some children and adolescents. These drugs sometimes produce agitation, so they may make already depressed people even more distressed and possibly suicidal (Brambilla et al., 2005). Yet the risk of suicide attempts and completions among people prescribed SSRIs remains very low.

Another area of public concern is overprescription. Parents, teachers, and helping professionals have expressed particular alarm that psychostimulants for attention-deficit/hyperactivity disorder (ADHD), such as Ritalin (methylphenidate), are overprescribed and may substitute for teaching effective coping strategies for focusing attention (LeFever et al., 2003; Safer, 2000). Since the early 1990s, the number of prescriptions for ADHD has increased fourfold. Although little is known about the long-term safety of Ritalin with children younger than six, the number of prescriptions for children ages two (!) to four nearly tripled between 1991 and 1995 alone (Bentley & Walsh, 2006).

Critics of psychostimulants have pointed to their potential for abuse. Moreover, their adverse effects include decreased appetite, gastrointestinal pain, headache, insomnia, irri-

Parenting a child with attention-deficit/hyperactivity disorder (ADHD) can be challenging and often requires support from teachers and medical professionals.

tability, heart-related complications, and stunted growth (Aagaard & Hansen, 2011). A recent survey indicated that only a fifth of children with ADHD received stimulants for the disorder (Merikangas et al., 2013), suggesting that these medications aren't generally overprescribed. Nevertheless, stimulant overprescription clearly occurs in some cases (Smith & Farah, 2011). Children should be diagnosed with ADHD and placed on stimulants only after they've been evaluated with input from parents and teachers. The good news is that 70–80 percent of children with ADHD can be treated effectively with stimulants (Steele et al., 2006), which can sometimes be combined to good advantage with behavior therapy (Jensen et al., 2005). Moreover, more recently developed nonstimulant medications for ADHD, such as Strattera, hold promise for improving concentration and attention.

Fad treatments and diets are poor alternatives to medications and psychological treatments of ADHD. For example, there's no convincing scientific evidence that reducing the amount of sugar in the diet improves symptoms of ADHD. Other dietary changes, like eliminating artificial food colors or flavors, also have little or no impact on ADHD symptoms (Waschbusch & Hill, 2003).

A final area of concern is *polypharmacy:* prescribing many medications—sometimes five or more—at the same time. This practice can be hazardous if not carefully monitored, because certain medications may interfere with the effects of others or interact with them in dangerous ways. Polypharmacy is a particular problem among the elderly, who tend to be especially susceptible to drug side effects (Fulton & Allen, 2005).

EVALUATING PSYCHOPHARMACOTHERAPY. To medicate or not to medicate, that is the question. In many instances, psychotherapy, with no added medications, can successfully treat people with many disorders. CBT is at least as effective as antidepressants, even for severe depression, and perhaps more effective than antidepressants are in preventing relapse (Cuijpers et al., 2013; DeRubeis et al., 2005; Hollon et al., 2002). Psychotherapy alone is also effective for a variety of anxiety disorders, mild and moderate depression, bulimia, and insomnia (Otto, Smits, & Reese, 2005; Thase, 2000).

Scientists are finding that when patients benefit from psychotherapy, this change is reflected in the workings of their brain. In some cases, psychotherapy and medication produce similar brain changes, suggesting that different routes to improvement share similar mechanisms (Kumari, 2006) and reminding us that "mind" and "brain" describe the same phenomena at different levels of explanation. Yet although medication and psychotherapy may both normalize brain function, they may also do so in different ways. In a review of 63 studies investigating psychotherapy or pharmacotherapy effects in patients with anxiety and major depressive disorders, medications decreased activity in the limbic system, the seat of emotion and reaction to threat. In contrast, psychotherapy produced changes mostly in the frontal areas of the brain, perhaps reflecting its success at transforming maladaptive to adaptive thoughts (Quidé et al, 2012).

This research cautions us against a widespread logical error, namely, inferring a disorder's optimal treatment from its cause (Ross & Pam, 1995). Many people believe mistakenly that a condition that's largely biological in its causes, like schizophrenia, should be treated with medication and that a condition that's largely environmental in its causes, such as a specific phobia, should be treated with psychotherapy. Yet the research we've reviewed shows that this logic is erroneous because psychological treatments affect our biology, just as biomedical treatments affect our psychology. Still, some researchers suggest that one day it may be possible to use brain-imaging techniques to predict who will respond to psychotherapy versus medication. In this way, they may be able to guide clinical practice by tailoring interventions to treat or repair dysfunctions in specific brain circuitry (Ball, Stein, & Paulus, 2014; Phillips et al., 2015; Yang, Kircher, & Straube, 2014). Indeed, this goal of **personalized medicine** is one of the most promising frontiers in contemporary psychology and psychiatry (Ahaji & Nemeroff, 2015).

Critics of pharmacotherapy claim that medications are of little value in helping patients learn social skills, modify self-defeating behaviors, or cope with conflict. For example, when patients with anxiety disorders discontinue their medications, half or more may relapse (Marks et. al., 1993). Over the long haul, psychotherapy may be much less expensive than medications, so it often makes sense to try psychotherapy first (Arkowitz & Lilienfeld, 2007).

Still, there are often clear advantages of combining medication with psychotherapy (Thase, 2000). If people's symptoms interfere greatly with their functioning or if psychotherapy alone hasn't worked for a two-month period, adding medication is frequently justified. Generally, research suggests that combining medication with psychotherapy is warranted for schizophrenia, bipolar disorder, major depression with and without psychotic symptoms, panic disorder, and obsessive-compulsive disorder (Cuijpers et al., 2014; Hollon et al., 2014; Thase, 2000; Uher & Pavlova, 2016). As of 2007, 61 percent of physicians prescribed medications to patients while the patients participated in psychotherapy, reflecting a national trend toward combining medical and psychological treatments (Olfson & Marcus, 2010).

Polypharmacy—the practice of prescribing multiple medications at the same time—can increase the risk of infrequent yet serious side effects produced by interactions among drugs. The tragic death of actor Heath Ledger in 2008 highlights the possibility of overdose by taking multiple medications that aren't carefully monitored by medical professionals.

personalized medicine

medical practice that customizes interventions to maximize success in treating patients with specific psychological or medical disorders and conditions

Psychosurgery has a long history, as this photo of a 2,000-plus-year-old skull from Peru shows. As we can see, this skull contains a huge hole produced by a procedure called *trephining*. Scientists believe that trephining may have been performed in an effort to heal mental disorders or to relieve brain diseases like epilepsy and tumors (Alt et al., 1997).

Watch PSYCHOSURGERY

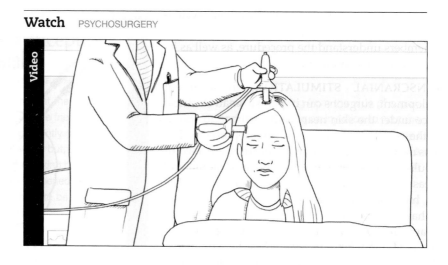

Ruling Out Rival Hypotheses

Have important alternative explanations for the findings been excluded?

Critics also noted that the motives for conducting psychosurgery weren't always benign (Valenstein, 1973). Social goals such as the control of behavior of violent sexual criminals, homosexual child abusers, and prison inmates who received lobotomies were occasionally confused with therapeutic goals (Mashour et al., 2005).

In the 1960s, surgeons ushered new forms of psychosurgery to the forefront. Surgeons replaced primitive procedures with ultrasound, electricity, freezing of tissues, and implants of radioactive materials. Automated surgical devices added precision to delicate brain surgery. With the advent of modern psychosurgical techniques, negative physical side effects became less frequent.

Today, surgeons sometimes perform psychosurgery as a last resort for patients with a handful of conditions, such as severe OCD, major depression, and bipolar disorder. There are few well-controlled long-term studies of psychosurgery and an absence of data about which patients respond best. Even when psychosurgery appears successful, we can generate alternative explanations, including placebo effects and self-serving biases, to account for apparent treatment gains (Dawes, 1994).

Recognizing the need to protect patient interests, institutional review boards (IRBs) in hospitals where surgeons perform psychosurgery must approve each operation. IRBs help ensure that (1) there's a clear rationale for the operation, (2) the patient has received an appropriate preoperative and postoperative evaluation, (3) the patient has consented to the operation, and (4) the surgeon is competent to conduct the procedure (Mashour et al., 2005). Scientific research may one day lead to more effective forms of psychosurgery, but the scientific and ethical debates surrounding such surgery are likely to endure.

Summary: Psychological and Biological Treatments

16.1: Psychotherapy: Clients and Practitioners

16.1a Describe who seeks treatment, who benefits from psychotherapy, and who practices psychotherapy.

Therapists treat people of all ages and social, cultural, and ethnic backgrounds. Individuals with anxiety and those with minor and temporary problems are most likely to benefit from therapy. Unlicensed paraprofessionals with no formal training, as well as licensed professionals, can be equally effective as trained therapists. Socioeconomic status, gender, and ethnicity predict who will seek psychotherapy.

16.1b Describe what it takes to be an effective therapist.

Showing warmth, selecting important topics to discuss, not contradicting clients, and establishing a positive relationship are more important determinants of a therapist's effectiveness than is being formally trained or being licensed.

16.2: Insight Therapies: Acquiring Understanding

16.2a Describe the core beliefs and criticisms of psychodynamic therapies.

The core beliefs of psychodynamic therapies are the importance of (a) analyzing unconscious conflicts, wishes, fantasies, impulses, and life patterns; (b) childhood experiences, including traumatic and adverse life events; (c) the therapeutic relationship; and (d) acquiring insight. Evidence for psychodynamic therapies is based largely on small and highly select patient samples, anecdotal studies, and the questionable curative value of insight, although controlled studies suggest that these therapies may be helpful in some cases.

16.2b Describe and evaluate the effectiveness of humanistic therapies.

Humanistic therapies hold that self-actualization is a universal human drive and adopt an experience-based approach in which clients work to fulfill their potential. Research suggests that genuineness, unconditional positive regard, and empathic understanding are related to improvement but not necessary and sufficient conditions for effective psychotherapy. Existential therapists contend that human beings construct meaning and that mental illness stems from a failure to find meaning in life. Existential therapy has not been studied extensively to date.

16.3: Group Therapies: The More the Merrier

16.3a List the advantages of group methods.

Group methods span all schools of psychotherapy and are efficient, time-saving, and less costly than individual methods. Participants learn from others' experiences, benefit from feedback and modeling others, and discover that problems and suffering are widespread.

16.3b Describe the research evidence concerning the effectiveness of Alcoholics Anonymous.

AA is helpful for some clients, but it appears to be no more effective than other treatments, including CBT. Research suggests that controlled drinking approaches can be effective with some people with alcoholism.

16.3c Identify different approaches to treating the dysfunctional family system.

Family therapies treat problems in the family system. Strategic family therapists remove barriers to effective communication, whereas structural family therapists plan changes in the way family interactions are structured.

16.4: Behavioral and Cognitive-Behavioral Approaches: Changing Maladaptive Actions and Thoughts

16.4a Describe the characteristics of behavior therapy and identify different behavioral approaches.

Behavior therapy is grounded in the scientific method and based on learning principles. Exposure therapies confront people with their fears. Exposure can be gradual and stepwise or start with the most frightening scenes imaginable. Modeling techniques, based on observational learning principles, include behavioral rehearsal and role-playing to foster assertiveness. Token economies and aversion therapies are based on operant conditioning and classical conditioning principles, respectively.

16.4b Describe the features of cognitive-behavioral therapies (CBT) and third-wave therapies.

Cognitive-behavioral therapists modify irrational and negative beliefs and distorted thoughts that contribute to unhealthy feelings and behaviors. Ellis's rational emotive behavior therapy, Beck's cognitive therapy, and Meichenbaum's stress inoculation training are influential variations of CBT. So-called third wave CBT approaches include mindfulness and acceptance-based psychotherapies.

16.5: Is Psychotherapy Effective?

16.5a Evaluate the claim that all psychotherapies are equally effective.

Many therapies are effective. Nevertheless, some therapies, including behavioral and cognitive-behavioral treatments, are more effective than other treatments for specific problems such as anxiety disorders. Still other treatments, like crisis debriefing, appear to be harmful in some cases.

16.5b Explain how ineffective therapies can sometimes appear to be effective.

Ineffective therapies can appear to be helpful because of spontaneous remission, the placebo effect, self-serving biases, regression to the mean, and retrospective rewriting of the past.

16.6: Biomedical Treatments: Medications, Electrical Stimulation, and Surgery

16.6a Recognize different types of drugs and cautions associated with drug treatment.

Medications are available to treat psychotic conditions (neuroleptics/antispsychotics or major tranquilizers), bipolar disorder (mood stabilizers), depression (antidepressants), anxiety (anxiolytics), and attentional problems (psychostimulants).

16.6b Outline key considerations in drug treatment.

People who prescribe drugs must be aware of side effects, must not overprescribe medications, and must carefully monitor the effects of multiple medications (polypharmacy).

16.6c Identify misconceptions about biomedical treatments.

Contrary to popular belief, electroconvulsive therapy (ECT) is not painful or dangerous and doesn't invariably produce memory loss, personality changes, or brain damage. Psychosurgery may be useful as a treatment of absolute last resort.

Glossary

absolute refractory period   time during which another action potential is impossible; limits maximal firing rate

absolute threshold   lowest level of a stimulus needed for the nervous system to detect a change 50 percent of the time

abstract thinking   capacity to understand hypothetical concepts

accommodation   changing the shape of the lens to focus on objects near or far

accommodation   piagetian process of altering a belief to make it more compatible with experience

acquired immune deficiency syndrome (AIDS)   a life-threatening, incurable, and yet treatable condition in which the human immunodeficiency virus (HIV) attacks and damages the immune system

acquisition   learning phase during which a conditioned response is established

action potential   electrical impulse that travels down the axon triggering the release of neurotransmitters

activation–synthesis theory   theory that dreams reflect inputs from brain activation originating in the pons, which the forebrain then attempts to weave into a story

acuity   sharpness of vision

acupuncture   ancient Chinese practice of inserting thin needles into one or more of 2,000 points in the body to alter energy forces believed to run through the body

ad hoc immunizing hypothesis   escape hatch or loophole that defenders of a theory use to protect their theory from falsification

adaptive conservatism   evolutionary principle that creates a predisposition toward distrusting anything or anyone unfamiliar or different

adolescence   the transition between childhood and adulthood commonly associated with the teenage years

adoption study   analysis of how traits vary in individuals raised apart from their biological relatives

adrenal gland   tissue located on top of the kidneys that releases adrenaline and cortisol during states of emotional arousal

aerobic exercise   exercise that promotes the use of oxygen in the body

affective forecasting   ability to predict our own and others' happiness

aggression   behavior intended to harm others, either verbally or physically (or both)

agoraphobia   fear of being in a place or situation from which escape is difficult or embarrassing or in which help is unavailable in the event of a panic attack

Alcoholics Anonymous   twelve-step self-help program that provides social support for achieving sobriety

algorithm   step-by-step learned procedure used to solve a problem

alternative medicine   healthcare practices and products used in place of conventional medicine

altruism   helping others for unselfish reasons

amygdala   part of limbic system that plays key roles in fear, excitement, and arousal

anal stage   psychosexual stage that focuses on toilet training

anorexia nervosa   eating disorder associated with excessive weight loss and the irrational perception that one is overweight

anorexia nervosa   psychiatric condition marked by extreme weight loss and the perception that one is overweight even when one is massively underweight

anterograde amnesia   inability to encode new memories from our experiences

antisocial personality disorder (ASPD)   condition marked by a lengthy history of irresponsible or illegal actions

anxiety sensitivity   fear of anxiety-related sensations

applied research   research examining how we can use basic research to solve real-world problems

archetype   cross-culturally universal symbols

assimilation   Piagetian process of absorbing new experience into current knowledge structures

association cortex   regions of the cerebral cortex that integrate simpler functions to perform more complex functions

asylum   institution for people with mental illnesses created in the 15th century

attachment   the strong emotional connection we share with those to whom we feel closest

attention-deficit/hyperactivity disorder (ADHD)   childhood condition marked by excessive inattention, impulsivity, and activity

attitude   belief that includes an emotional component

attribution   process of assigning causes to behavior

audition   our sense of hearing

autism spectrum disorder (ASD)   *DSM-5* category that includes autistic spectrum disorder and Asperger's disorder

autonomic nervous system   part of the nervous system controlling the involuntary actions of our internal organs and glands, which (along with the limbic system) participates in emotion regulation

availability heuristic   heuristic that involves estimating the likelihood of an occurrence based on the ease with which it comes to our minds

average expectable environment   environment that provides children with basic needs for affection and discipline

aversion therapy   treatment that uses punishment to decrease the frequency of undesirable behaviors

axon   portion of neuron that sends signals

babbling   intentional vocalization that lacks specific meaning

basal ganglia   structures in the forebrain that help to control movement

base rate   how common a characteristic or behavior is in the general population

basic research   research examining how the mind works

basilar membrane   membrane supporting the organ of Corti and hair cells in the cochlea

behavior therapist   therapist who focuses on specific problem behaviors and current variables that maintain problematic thoughts, feelings, and behaviors

behaviorism   school of psychology that focuses on uncovering the general laws of learning by looking at observable behavior

belief perseverance   tendency to stick to our initial beliefs even when evidence contradicts them

bell curve   distribution of scores in which the bulk of the scores fall toward the middle, with progressively fewer scores toward the "tails" or extremes

between-group heritability   extent to which differences in a trait between groups is genetically influenced

Big Five five traits that have surfaced repeatedly in factor analyses of personality measures

bilingual proficient and fluent at speaking and comprehending two distinct languages

binocular depth cues stimuli that enable us to judge depth using both eyes

biofeedback feedback by a device that provides almost an immediate output of a biological function, such as heart rate or skin temperature

biological clock term for the area of the hypothalamus that's responsible for controlling our levels of alertness

biopsychosocial perspective the view that an illness or a medical condition is the product of the interplay of biological, psychological, and social factors

bipolar disorder condition marked by a history of at least one manic episode

blastocyst ball of identical cells early in pregnancy that haven't yet begun to take on any specific function in a body part

blind spot part of the visual field we can't see because of an absence of rods and cones

blind unaware of whether one is in the experimental or control group

borderline personality disorder condition marked by extreme instability in mood, identity, and impulse control

bottom-up processing processing in which a whole is constructed from parts

brain stem part of the brain between the spinal cord and cerebral cortex that contains the midbrain, pons, and medulla

broaden and build theory theory proposing that happiness predisposes us to think more openly

Broca's area language area in the prefrontal cortex that helps to control speech production

bulimia nervosa eating disorder associated with a pattern of bingeing and purging in an effort to lose or maintain weight

"but you are free" technique persuasive technique in which we convince someone to perform a favor for us by telling them that they are free not to do it

Cannon-Bard theory theory proposing that an emotion-provoking event leads simultaneously to an emotion and to bodily reactions

case study research design that examines one person or a small number of people in depth, often over an extended time period

catatonic symptom motor problem, including holding the body in bizarre or rigid postures, curling up in a fetal position, and resisting simple suggestions to move

categorical model model in which a mental disorder differs from normal functioning in kind rather than degree

central nervous system (CNS) part of nervous system containing the brain and spinal cord that controls the mind and behavior

central tendency measure of the "central" scores in a data set, or where the group tends to cluster

cerebellum brain structure responsible for our sense of balance

cerebral cortex outermost part of forebrain, responsible for analyzing sensory processing and higher brain functions

cerebral hemispheres two halves of the cerebral cortex, each of which serve distinct yet highly integrated functions

cerebral ventricles pockets in the brain that contain cerebrospinal fluid (CSF), which provide the brain with nutrients and cushion against injury

chromosome slender thread inside a cell's nucleus that carries genes

chunking organizing information into meaningful groupings, allowing us to extend the span of short-term memory

circadian rhythm cyclical changes that occur on a roughly 24-hour basis in many biological processes

classical (Pavlovian) conditioning form of learning in which animals come to respond to a previously neutral stimulus that had been paired with another stimulus that elicits an automatic response

cochlea bony, spiral-shaped sense organ used for hearing

cognitive bias systematic error in thinking

cognitive development study of how children acquire the ability to learn, think, reason, communicate, and remember

cognitive dissonance unpleasant mental experience of tension resulting from two conflicting thoughts or beliefs

cognitive map mental representation of how a physical space is organized

cognitive model of depression theory that depression is caused by negative beliefs and expectations

cognitive neuroscience relatively new field of psychology that examines the relation between brain functioning and thinking

cognitive psychology school of psychology that proposes that thinking is central to understanding behavior

cognitive theories of emotion theories proposing that emotions are products of thinking

cognitive-behavioral therapies treatments that attempt to replace irrational cognitions and maladaptive behaviors with more rational cognitions and adaptive behaviors

cohort effect effect observed in a sample of participants that results from individuals in the sample growing up at the same time

collective unconscious according to Carl Jung, our shared storehouse of memories that ancestors have passed down to us across generations

color blindness inability to see some or all colors

comorbidity co-occurrence of two or more diagnoses within the same person

companionate love love marked by a sense of deep friendship and fondness for one's partner

complementary medicine or integrative health medicine healthcare practices and products used together with conventional medicine

compulsion repetitive behavior or mental act performed to reduce or prevent stress

computed tomography (CT) a scanning technique using multiple X-rays to construct three-dimensional images

concept our knowledge and ideas about a set of objects, actions, and characteristics that share core properties

concrete operations stage stage in Piaget's theory characterized by the ability to perform mental operations on physical events only

conditioned response (CR) response previously associated with a nonneutral stimulus that is elicited by a neutral stimulus through conditioning

conditioned stimulus (CS) initially neutral stimulus that comes to elicit a response as a result of association with an unconditioned stimulus

conditions of worth according to Carl Rogers, expectations we place on ourselves for appropriate and inappropriate behavior

cones receptor cells in the retina allowing us to see in color

confirmation bias tendency to seek out evidence that supports our beliefs and to deny, dismiss, or distort evidence that contradicts them

conformity tendency of people to alter their behavior as a result of group pressure

consciousness our subjective experience of the world, our bodies, and our mental perspectives

contact comfort positive emotions afforded by touch

context-dependent learning   superior retrieval of memories when the external context of the original memories matches the retrieval context

continuous reinforcement   reinforcing a behavior every time it occurs, resulting in faster learning but faster extinction than only occasional reinforcement

control group   in an experiment, the group of participants that does not receive the manipulation

convergent thinking   capacity to generate the single best solution to a problem

cornea   part of the eye containing transparent cells that focus light on the retina

coronary heart disease (CHD)   damage to the heart from the complete or partial blockage of the arteries that provide oxygen to the heart

corpus callosum   large band of fibers connecting the two cerebral hemispheres

correlation–causation fallacy   error of assuming that because one thing is associated with another, it must cause the other

correlational design   research design that examines the extent to which two variables are associated

corticosteroid   stress hormone that activates the body and prepares us to respond to stressful circumstances

critical thinking   set of skills for evaluating all claims in an open-minded and careful fashion

cross-sectional design   research design that examines people of different ages at a single point in time

cryptomnesia   failure to recognize that our ideas originated with someone else

crystallized intelligence   accumulated knowledge of the world acquired over time

cult   group of individuals who exhibit intense and unquestioning devotion to a single individual or cause

culture-fair IQ test   abstract reasoning measure that doesn't depend on language and is often believed to be less influenced by cultural factors than other IQ tests are

dark adaptation   time in dark before rods regain maximum light sensitivity

decay   fading of information from memory over time

decision-making   the process of selecting among a set of possible alternatives

decline effect   fact that the size of certain psychological findings appears to be shrinking over time

defense mechanisms   unconscious maneuvers intended to minimize anxiety

defensive pessimism   strategy of anticipating failure and compensating for this expectation by mentally overpreparing for negative outcomes

deindividuation   tendency of people to engage in uncharacteristic behavior when they are stripped of their usual identities

deinstitutionalization   The governmental policy of the 1960s and 1970s that focused on releasing hospitalized psychiatric patients into the community and closing mental hospitals

déjà vu   strong feeling of familiarity regarding a new experience

delusion   strongly held fixed belief that has no basis in reality

demand characteristics   cues that participants pick up from a study that allow them to generate guesses regarding the researcher's hypotheses

demonic model   view of mental illness in which behaving oddly, hearing voices, or talking to oneself was attributed to evil spirits infesting the body

dendrite   portion of neuron that receives signals

denial   refusal to acknowledge current events in our lives

dependent variable   variable that an experimenter measures to see whether the manipulation produces an effect

depersonalization/derealization disorder   condition marked by multiple episodes of depersonalization, derealization, or both

depth perception   ability to judge distance and three-dimensional relations

descriptive statistics   numerical characterizations that describe data

developmental psychology   study of how behavior changes over the life span

deviation IQ   expression of a person's IQ relative to his or her same-aged peers

Diagnostic and Statistical Manual of Mental Disorders (DSM)   diagnostic system containing the American Psychiatric Association (APA) criteria for mental disorders

dialect   language variation used by a group of people who share geographic proximity or ethnic background

diathesis-stress model   perspective proposing that mental disorders are a joint product of a genetic vulnerability, called a diathesis, and stressors that trigger this vulnerability

diffusion of responsibility   reduction in feelings of personal responsibility in the presence of others

dimensional model   model in which a mental disorder differs from normal functioning in degree rather than kind

discrete emotions theory   theory that humans experience a small number of distinct emotions that are rooted in their biology

discrimination   negative behavior toward members of out-groups

discriminative stimulus   stimulus that signals the presence of reinforcement

dismantling   research procedure for examining the effectiveness of isolated components of a larger treatment

displacement   directing an impulse from a socially unacceptable target onto a safer and more socially acceptable target

display rules   cross-cultural guidelines for how and when to express emotions

dissociation theory   approach to explaining hypnosis based on a separation between personality functions that are normally well integrated

dissociative amnesia   inability to recall important personal information—most often related to a stressful experience—that can't be explained by ordinary forgetfulness

dissociative disorder   condition involving disruptions in consciousness, memory, identity, or perception

dissociative fugue   sudden, unexpected travel away from home or the workplace, accompanied by amnesia for significant life events

dissociative identity disorder (DID)   condition characterized by the presence of two or more distinct personality states that recurrently take control of the person's behavior

distributed versus massed practice   studying information in small increments over time (distributed) versus in large increments over a brief amount of time (massed)

divergent thinking   capacity to generate many different solutions to a problem

dominant gene   gene that masks other genes' effects

door-in-the-face technique   persuasive technique involving making an unreasonably large request before making the small request we're hoping to have granted

double-blind   when neither researchers nor participants are aware of who's in the experimental or control group

dream continuity hypothesis   hypothesis that there is continuity between sleeping and waking experiences and that dreams can mirror life circumstances

drive reduction theory theory proposing that certain drives, like hunger, thirst, and sexual frustration, motivate us to act in ways that minimize aversive states

durability bias belief that both our good and bad moods will last longer than they do

echoic memory auditory sensory memory

ecological momentary assessment evaluation of thoughts, emotions, and behaviors that arise in the moment in situations in which they occur in everyday life

ego psyche's executive and principal decision maker

elaborative rehearsal linking stimuli to each other in a meaningful way to improve retention of information in short-term memory

electroconvulsive therapy (ECT) treatment for serious psychological problems in which patients receive brief electrical pulses to the brain that produce a seizure

electroencephalograph (EEG) recording of brain's electrical activity at the surface of the skull

embryo second to eighth week of prenatal development, during which limbs, facial features, and major organs of the body take form

emerging adulthood period of life between the ages of 18 and 25 when many aspects of emotional development, identity, and personality become solidified

emotion-focused coping coping strategy that features a positive outlook on feelings or situations accompanied by behaviors that reduce painful emotions

emotion mental state or feeling associated with our evaluation of our experiences

emotional intelligence ability to understand our own emotions and those of others and to apply this information to our daily lives

empirical method of test construction approach to building tests in which researchers begin with two or more criterion groups and examine which items best differentiate them

empirically supported treatment (EST) intervention for specific disorders supported by high-quality scientific evidence

empty-nest syndrome alleged period of depression in mothers following the departure of their grown children from the home

encoding specificity phenomenon of remembering something better when the conditions under which we retrieve information are similar to the conditions under which we encoded it

encoding process of getting information into our memory banks

endocrine system system of glands and hormones that controls secretion of blood-borne chemical messengers

endorphin chemical in the brain that plays a specialized role in pain reduction

enlightenment effect learning about psychological research can change real-world behavior for the better

epigenetics a field that examines how environmental influences affect the expression of genes

episodic memory recollection of events in our lives

eugenics movement in the early 20th century to improve a population's genetic stock by encouraging those with good genes to reproduce, preventing those with bad genes from reproducing, or both

evolutionary psychology a field that seeks to explain psychological traits as naturally selected adaptations.

excitement phase phase in human sexual response in which people experience sexual pleasure and notice physiological changes associated with it

existence proof demonstration that a given psychological phenomenon can occur

experiment research design characterized by random assignment of participants to conditions and manipulation of an independent variable

experimental group in an experiment, the group of participants that receives the manipulation

experimenter expectancy effect phenomenon in which researchers' hypotheses lead them to unintentionally bias the outcome of a study

explicit memory memories we recall intentionally and of which we have conscious awareness

explicit prejudice unfounded negative belief of which we're aware regarding the characteristics of an out-group

exposure therapy therapy that confronts clients with what they fear with the goal of reducing the fear

external validity extent to which we can generalize findings to real-world settings

extinction gradual reduction and eventual elimination of the conditioned response after the conditioned stimulus is presented repeatedly without the unconditioned stimulus

extralinguistic information elements of communication that aren't part of the content of language but are critical to interpreting its meaning

extrasensory perception (ESP) perception of events outside the known channels of sensation

face validity extent to which respondents can tell what the items are measuring

facial feedback hypothesis theory that blood vessels in the face feed back temperature information in the brain, altering our experience of emotions

factor analysis statistical technique that analyzes the correlations among responses on personality inventories and other measures

falsifiable capable of being disproved

family study analysis of how characteristics run in intact families

feature detector cell cell that detects lines and edges

fetal alcohol syndrome condition resulting from high levels of prenatal alcohol exposure, causing learning disabilities, physical growth retardation, facial malformations, and behavioral disorders

fetishism sexual attraction to nonliving things

fetus period of prenatal development from ninth week until birth after all major organs are established and physical maturation is the primary change

fight-or-flight response physical and psychological reaction that mobilizes people and animals to either defend themselves (fight) or escape (flee) a threatening situation

fitness organisms' capacity to pass on their genes

fixed interval (FI) schedule pattern in which we provide reinforcement for a response at least once following a specified time interval

fixed ratio (FR) schedule pattern in which we provide reinforcement following a regular number of responses

flashbulb memory emotional memory that is extraordinarily vivid and detailed

fluid intelligence capacity to learn new ways of solving problems

Flynn effect finding that states average IQ scores have been rising at a rate of approximately three points per decade

foot-in-the-door technique persuasive technique involving making a small request before making a bigger one

forebrain (cerebrum) forward part of the brain that allows advanced intellectual abilities

formal operations stage stage in Piaget's theory characterized by the ability to perform hypothetical reasoning beyond the here and now

fovea central portion of the retina

framing the way a question is formulated that can influence the decisions people make

free association technique in which clients express themselves without censorship of any sort

frequency theory rate at which neurons fire the action potential reproduces the pitch

frontal lobe forward part of cerebral cortex responsible for motor function, language, memory, and planning

functional fixedness difficulty conceptualizing that an object typically used for one purpose can be used for another

functional MRI (fMRI) technique that uses magnetic fields to visualize brain activity using changes in blood oxygen level

functionalism school of psychology that aimed to understand the adaptive purposes of psychological characteristics

fundamental attribution error tendency to overestimate the impact of dispositional influences on other people's behavior

***g* (general intelligence)** hypothetical factor that accounts for overall differences in intellect among people

gate control model idea that pain is blocked or gated from consciousness by neural mechanisms in spinal cord

gender identity individuals' sense of being male or female

gender role a set of behaviors that tend to be associated with being male or female

gene expression activation or deactivation of genes by environmental experiences throughout development

gene–environment interaction situation in which the effects of genes depend on the environment in which they are expressed

gene genetic material, composed of deoxyribonucleic acid (DNA)

general adaptation syndrome (GAS) stress-response pattern proposed by Hans Selye that consists of three stages: alarm, resistance, and exhaustion

generalized anxiety disorder (GAD) continual feelings of worry, anxiety, physical tension, and irritability across many areas of life functioning

generative allowing an infinite number of unique sentences to be created by combining words in novel ways

genital stage psychosexual stage in which sexual impulses awaken and typically begin to mature into romantic attraction toward others

genotype our genetic makeup

Gestalt therapy therapy that aims to integrate different and sometimes opposing aspects of personality into a unified sense of self

glial cell cell in nervous system that plays a role in the formation of myelin and the blood–brain barrier, responds to injury, removes debris, and enhances learning and memory

glucostatic theory theory that when our blood glucose levels drop, hunger creates a drive to eat to restore the proper level of glucose

graphology psychological interpretation of handwriting

group polarization tendency of group discussion to strengthen the dominant positions held by individual group members

group therapy therapy that treats more than one person at a time

groupthink emphasis on group unanimity at the expense of critical thinking

guilty knowledge test (GKT) alternative to the polygraph test that relies on the premise that criminals harbor concealed knowledge about the crime that innocent people don't

gustation our sense of taste

habituation process of responding less strongly over time to repeated stimuli

hallucination sensory perception that occurs in the absence of an external stimulus

hallucinogenic causing dramatic alterations of perception, mood, and thought

hardiness set of attitudes marked by a sense of control over events, commitment to life and work, and courage and motivation to confront stressful events

hassle minor annoyance or nuisance that strains our ability to cope

health psychology field of psychology, also called *behavioral medicine*, that integrates the behavioral sciences with the practice of medicine

hedonic treadmill tendency for our moods to adapt to external circumstances

heritability percentage of the variability in a trait across individuals that is the result of genes

heuristic mental shortcut or rule of thumb that helps us to streamline our thinking and make sense of our world

hierarchy of needs model developed by Abraham Maslow proposing that we must satisfy physiological needs and needs for safety and security before progressing to more complex needs

higher-order conditioning developing a conditioned response to a conditioned stimulus by virtue of its association with another conditioned stimulus

hindbrain region below the midbrain that contains the cerebellum, pons, and medulla

hindsight bias our tendency to overestimate how well we could have predicted something after it has already occurred

hippocampus part of the brain that plays a role in spatial memory

homeopathic medicine remedies that feature a small dose of an illness-inducing substance to activate the body's own natural defenses

homeostasis equilibrium

homesign system of signs invented by children who are deaf and born of hearing parents and therefore receive no language input

hormone chemical released into the bloodstream that influences particular organs and glands

hue color of light

humanistic therapies therapies that emphasize the development of human potential and the belief that human nature is basically positive

hypnosis set of techniques that provides people with suggestions for alterations in their perceptions, thoughts, feelings, and behaviors

hypnotic drug that exerts a sleep-inducing effect

hypothalamus part of the brain responsible for maintaining a constant internal state

hypothesis testable prediction derived from a scientific theory

iconic memory visual sensory memory

id reservoir of our most primitive impulses, including sex and aggression

identity our sense of who we are, as well as our life goals and priorities

ideological immune system our psychological defenses against evidence that contradicts our views

idiographic approach approach to personality that focuses on identifying the unique configuration of characteristics and life history experiences within an individual

illness anxiety disorder condition marked by intense preoccupation with the possibility of a serious undiagnosed illness

illusion perception in which the way we perceive a stimulus doesn't match its physical reality

illusory correlation   perception of a statistical association between two variables where none exists

immune system   our body's defense system against invading bacteria, viruses, and other potentially illness-producing organisms and substances

implicit memory   memories we don't deliberately remember or reflect on consciously

implicit prejudice   unfounded negative belief of which we're unaware regarding the characteristics of an out-group

impression management theory   theory that we don't really change our attitudes, but report that we have so that our behaviors appear consistent with our attitudes

in-group bias   tendency to favor individuals within our group over those from outside our group

inattentional blindness   failure to detect stimuli that are in plain sight when our attention is focused elsewhere

incentive theories   theories proposing that we're often motivated by positive goals

incongruence   inconsistency between our personalities and innate dispositions

incremental validity   extent to which a test contributes information beyond other more easily collected measures

independent variable   variable that an experimenter manipulates

individual differences   variations among people in their thinking, emotion, personality, and behavior

infantile amnesia   inability of adults to remember personal experiences that took place before an early age

inferential statistics   mathematical methods that allow us to determine whether we can generalize findings from our sample to the full population

inferiority complex   feelings of low self-esteem that can lead to overcompensation for such feelings

informed consent   informing research participants of what is involved in a study before asking them to participate

inoculation effect   approach to convincing people to change their minds about something by first introducing reasons why the perspective might be correct and then debunking them

insanity defense   legal defense proposing that people shouldn't be held legally responsible for their actions if they weren't of "sound mind" when committing them

insight therapies   psychotherapies, including psychodynamic, humanistic, existential, and group approaches, with the goal of expanding awareness or insight

insight   grasping the underlying nature of a problem

insomnia   difficulty falling and/or staying asleep

instinctive drift   tendency for animals to return to innate behaviors following repeated reinforcement

integrity test   questionnaire that presumably assesses workers' tendency to steal or cheat

intellectual disability   condition characterized by an onset before adulthood, an IQ below about 70, and an inability to engage in adequate daily functioning

intelligence quotient (IQ)   systematic means of quantifying differences among people in their intelligence

intelligence test   diagnostic tool designed to measure overall thinking ability

interference   loss of information from memory because of competition from additional incoming information

internal validity   extent to which we can draw cause-and-effect inferences from a study

internal–external theory   theory holding that obese people are motivated to eat more by external cues than internal cues

interneuron   neuron that sends messages to other neurons nearby

interpersonal therapy (IPT)   treatment that strengthens social skills and targets interpersonal problems, conflicts, and life transitions

introspection   method by which trained observers carefully reflect and report on their mental experiences

involuntary commitment   Procedure of placing some people with mental illnesses in a psychiatric hospital or another facility based on their potential danger to themselves or others or their inability to care for themselves

James-Lange theory of emotion   theory proposing that emotions result from our interpretations of our bodily reactions to stimuli

jigsaw classroom   educational approach designed to minimize prejudice by requiring all children to make independent contributions to a shared project

just noticeable difference (JND)   the smallest change in the intensity of a stimulus that we can detect

just-world hypothesis   claim that our attributions and behaviors are shaped by a deep-seated assumption that the world is fair and all things happen for a reason

labeling theorists   scholars who argue that psychiatric diagnoses exert powerful negative effects on people's perceptions and behaviors

language acquisition device   hypothetical organ in the brain in which nativists believe knowledge of syntax resides

language   largely arbitrary system of communication that combines symbols (such as words and gestural signs) in rule-based ways to create meaning

latency stage   psychosexual stage in which sexual impulses are submerged into the unconscious

latent inhibition   difficulty in establishing classical conditioning to a conditioned stimulus we've repeatedly experienced alone, that is, without the unconditioned stimulus

latent learning   learning that's not directly observable

lateralization   cognitive function that relies more on one side of the brain than the other

law of effect   principle asserting that if a stimulus followed by a behavior results in a reward, the stimulus is more likely to give rise to the behavior in the future

learned helplessness   tendency to feel helpless in the face of events we can't control

learning style   an individual's preferred or optimal method of acquiring new information

learning   change in an organism's behavior or thought as a result of experience

lens   part of the eye that changes curvature to keep images in focus

leptin   hormone that signals the hypothalamus and brain stem to reduce appetite and increase the amount of energy used

levels of analysis   rungs on a ladder of analysis, with lower levels tied most closely to biological influences and higher levels tied most closely to social influences

levels of processing   depth of transforming information, which influences how easily we remember it

lexical approach   assumption that the most crucial features of personality are embedded in our language

limbic system   emotional center of brain that also plays roles in smell, motivation, and memory

linguistic determinism   view that all thought is represented verbally and that, as a result, our language defines our thinking

linguistic relativity   view that characteristics of language shape our thought processes

locus of control   extent to which people believe that reinforcers and punishers lie inside or outside their control

long-term memory   relatively enduring (from minutes to years) retention of information stored regarding our facts, experiences, and skills

long-term potentiation (LTP)   gradual strengthening of the connections among neurons from repetitive stimulation

longitudinal design   research design that examines development in the same group of people on multiple occasions over time

low-ball technique   persuasive technique in which the seller of a product starts by quoting a low sales price and then mentions all of the add-on costs once the customer has agreed to purchase the product

lucid dreaming   experience of becoming aware that one is dreaming

Magic Number   the span of short-term memory, according to George Miller: seven plus or minus two pieces of information

magnetic resonance imaging (MRI)   technique that uses magnetic fields to indirectly visualize brain structure

magnetoencephalography (MEG)   technique that measures brain activity by detecting tiny magnetic fields generated by the brain

maintenance rehearsal   repeating stimuli in their original form to retain them in short-term memory

major depressive episode   state in which a person experiences a lingering depressed mood or diminished interest in pleasurable activities, along with symptoms that include weight loss and sleep difficulties

manic episode   experience marked by dramatically elevated mood, decreased need for sleep, increased energy, inflated self-esteem, increased talkativeness, and irresponsible behavior

mass hysteria   outbreak of irrational behavior that is spread by social contagion

mean   average; a measure of central tendency

median   middle score in a data set; a measure of central tendency

medical model   view of mental illness as a result of a physical disorder requiring medical treatment

meditation   a variety of practices that train attention and awareness

medulla   part of brain stem involved in basic functions, such as heartbeat and breathing

memory illusion   false but subjectively compelling memory

memory   retention of information over time

menarche   start of menstruation

menopause   the termination of menstruation, marking the end of a woman's reproductive potential

mental age   age corresponding to the average individual's performance on an intelligence test

mental set   phenomenon of becoming stuck in a specific problem-solving strategy, inhibiting our ability to generate alternatives

mere exposure effect   phenomenon in which repeated exposure to a stimulus makes us more likely to feel favorably toward it

meta-analysis   statistical method that helps researchers interpret large bodies of psychological literature

meta-memory   knowledge about our own memory abilities and limitations

metalinguistic   awareness of how language is structured and used

metaphysical claim   assertion about the world that is not testable

midbrain   part of the brain stem that contributes to movement, tracking of visual stimuli, and reflexes triggered by sound

midlife crisis   supposed phase of adulthood characterized by emotional distress about the aging process and an attempt to regain youth

Minnesota Multiphasic Personality Inventory (MMPI)   widely used structured personality test designed to assess symptoms of mental disorders

mirror neuron   cell in the prefrontal cortex that becomes activated when an animal performs an action or observes it being performed

misinformation effect   creation of fictitious memories by providing misleading information about an event after it takes place

mnemonic   a learning aid, strategy, or device that enhances recall

mode   most frequent score in a data set; a measure of central tendency

molecular genetic study   investigation that allows researchers to pinpoint genes associated with specific characteristics, including personality traits

monocular depth cues   stimuli that enable us to judge depth using only one eye

moral treatment   approach to mental illness calling for dignity, kindness, and respect for those with mental illness

morpheme   smallest meaningful unit of speech

motivation   psychological drives that propel us in a specific direction

motor behavior   bodily motion that occurs as result of self-initiated force that moves the bones and muscles

motor cortex   part of frontal lobe responsible for body movement

multiple intelligences   idea that people vary markedly in their ability levels across different domains of intellectual skill

multiply   determined caused by many factors

myelin sheath   glial cells wrapped around axons that act as insulators of the neuron's signal

mystical experience   feelings of unity or oneness with the world, often with strong spiritual overtones

naive realism   belief that we see the world precisely as it is

narcissism   a personality trait marked by extreme self-centeredness.

narcolepsy   disorder characterized by the rapid and often unexpected onset of sleep

narcotic   drug that relieves pain and induces sleep

nativist   account of language acquisition that suggests children are born with some basic knowledge of how language works

natural selection   principle that organisms that possess adaptations survive and reproduce at a higher rate than do other organisms

naturalistic observation   watching behavior in real-world settings without trying to manipulate the situation

nature via nurture   tendency of individuals with certain genetic predispositions to seek out and create environments that permit the expression of those predispositions

near-death experience (NDE)   experience reported by people who've nearly died or thought they were going to die

negative reinforcement   removal of a stimulus that strengthens the probability of the behavior

neo-Freudian theories   theories derived from Freud's model but with less emphasis on sexuality as a driving force in personality and more optimism regarding the prospects for long-term personality growth

neurocognitive theory   theory that dreams are a meaningful product of our cognitive capacities, which shape what we dream about

neurogenesis   creation of new neurons in the adult brain

neuron   nerve cell specialized for communication

neurotransmitter   chemical messenger specialized for communication from neuron to neuron

night terrors   sudden waking episodes characterized by screaming, perspiring, and confusion followed by a return to a deep sleep

nomothetic approach   approach to personality that focuses on identifying general laws that govern the behavior of all individuals

non-REM (NREM) sleep   stages 1 through 4 of the sleep cycle, during which rapid eye movements do not occur and dreaming is less frequent and vivid

nonverbal leakage   unconscious spillover of emotions into nonverbal behavior

obedience   adherence to instructions from those of higher authority

observational learning   learning by watching others

obsession   persistent idea, thought, or urge that is unwanted, causing marked distress

obsessive-compulsive disorder (OCD)   condition marked by repeated and lengthy (at least one hour per day) immersion in obsessions, compulsions, or both

occipital lobe   back part of cerebral cortex specialized for vision

Oedipus complex   conflict during phallic stage in which boys supposedly love their mothers romantically and want to eliminate their fathers as rivals

olfaction   our sense of smell

one-word stage   early period of language development when children use single-word phrases to convey an entire thought

operant conditioning   learning controlled by the consequences of the organism's behavior

operational definition   a working definition of what a researcher is measuring

opponent process theory   theory that we perceive colors in terms of three pairs of opponent colors: either red or green, blue or yellow, or black or white

optic nerve   nerve that travels from the retina to the brain

oral stage   psychosexual stage that focuses on the mouth

organ of Corti   tissue containing the hair cells necessary for hearing

orgasm (climax) phase   phase in human sexual response marked by involuntary rhythmic contractions in the muscles of genitals in both men and women

out-group homogeneity   tendency to view all individuals outside our group as highly similar

out-of-body experience (OBE)   sense of our consciousness leaving our body

P. T. Barnum effect   tendency of people to accept descriptions that apply to almost everyone as applying specifically to them

panic attack   brief, intense episode of extreme fear characterized by sweating, dizziness, light-headedness, racing heartbeat, and feelings of impending death or going crazy

panic disorder   repeated and unexpected panic attacks, along with either persistent concerns about future attacks or a change in personal behavior in an attempt to avoid them

parallel processing   the ability to attend to many sense modalities simultaneously

paraprofessional   person with no professional training who provides mental health services

parasympathetic nervous system   division of autonomic nervous system that controls rest and digestion

parietal lobe   upper middle part of the cerebral cortex lying behind the frontal lobe that is specialized for touch and perception

partial reinforcement   occasional reinforcement of a behavior, resulting in slower extinction than if the behavior had been reinforced continually

participant modeling   technique in which the therapist first models a problematic situation and then guides the client through steps to cope with it unassisted

passionate love   love marked by powerful, even overwhelming, longing for one's partner

past-life regression therapy   therapeutic approach that uses hypnosis to supposedly age-regress patients to a previous life to identify the source of a present-day problem

patternicity   the tendency to perceive meaningful patterns in their absence

peak experience   transcendent moment of intense excitement and tranquility marked by a profound sense of connection to the world

perception   the brain's interpretation of raw sensory inputs

perceptual constancy   the process by which we perceive stimuli consistently across varied conditions

perceptual set   set formed when expectations influence perceptions

peripheral nervous system (PNS)   nerves in the body that extend outside the central nervous system (CNS)

permastore   type of long-term memory that appears to be permanent

person-centered therapy   nondirective therapy centering on the client's goals and ways of solving problems

personality disorder   condition in which personality traits, appearing first in adolescence, are inflexible, stable, expressed in a wide variety of situations, and lead to distress or impairment

personality   people's typical ways of thinking, feeling, and behaving

personalized medicine   medical practice that customizes interventions to maximize success in treating patients with specific psychological or medical disorders and conditions

phallic stage   psychosexual stage that focuses on the genitals

phantom pain   pain or discomfort felt in an amputated limb

phenotype   our observable traits

pheromone   odorless chemical that serves as a social signal to members of one's species

phobia   intense fear of an object or a situation that's greatly out of proportion to its actual threat

phoneme   category of sounds our vocal apparatus produces

phonetic decomposition   reading strategy that involves sounding out words by drawing correspondences between printed letters and sounds

physical dependence   dependence on a drug that occurs when people continue to take it to avoid withdrawal symptoms

Pinocchio response   supposedly perfect physiological or behavioral indicator of lying

pituitary gland   master gland that, under the control of the hypothalamus, directs the other glands of the body

place theory   specific place along the basilar membrane matches a tone with a specific pitch

placebo effect   improvement resulting from the mere expectation of improvement

plasticity   ability of the nervous system to change

plateau phase   phase in human sexual response in which sexual tension builds

pleasure principle   tendency of the id to strive for immediate gratification

pluralistic ignorance   error of assuming that no one in a group perceives things as we do

pons   part of the brain stem that connects the cortex with the cerebellum

positive illusions   tendencies to perceive ourselves more favorably than others do

positive psychology   discipline that has sought to emphasize human strengths

positive reinforcement   presentation of a stimulus that strengthens the probability of the behavior

positivity effect tendency for people to remember more positive than negative information with age

positron emission tomography (PET) imaging technique that measures consumption of glucose-like molecules, yielding a picture of neural activity in different regions of the brain

post hoc fallacy false assumption that because one event occurred before another event, it must have caused that event

posttraumatic growth the perception of beneficial change or personal transformation in the struggle to overcome adversity

posttraumatic stress disorder (PTSD) Marked emotional disturbance after experiencing or witnessing a severely stressful event

prefrontal cortex part of frontal lobe responsible for thinking, planning, and language

prefrontal lobotomy surgical procedure that severs fibers connecting the frontal lobes of the brain from the underlying thalamus

prejudice the drawing of negative conclusions about a person, group of people, or situation prior to evaluating the evidence

prenatal prior to birth

preoperational stage stage in Piaget's theory characterized by the ability to construct mental representations of experience but not yet perform operations on them

preparedness evolutionary predisposition to learn some pairings of feared stimuli over others owing to their survival value

prevalence Percentage of people within a population who have a specific mental disorder

primacy effect tendency to remember words at the beginning of a list especially well

primary appraisal initial decision regarding whether an event is harmful

primary emotions small number (perhaps seven) of emotions believed by some theorists to be cross-culturally universal

primary reinforcer item or outcome that naturally increases the target behavior

primary sensory cortex regions of the cerebral cortex that initially process information from the senses

primary sex characteristic a physical feature such as the reproductive organs and genitals that distinguish the sexes

priming our ability to identify a stimulus more easily or more quickly after we've encountered similar stimuli

proactive coping anticipation of problems and stressful situations that promotes effective coping

proactive interference interference with acquisition of new information due to previous learning of information

problem solving generating a cognitive strategy to accomplish a goal

problem-focused coping coping strategy by which we problem solve and tackle life's challenges head on

procedural memory memory for how to do things, including motor skills and habits

projection unconscious attribution of our negative characteristics to others

projective hypothesis hypothesis that in the process of interpreting ambiguous stimuli, examinees project aspects of their personality onto the stimulus

projective test test consisting of ambiguous stimuli that examinees must interpret or make sense of

proprioception our sense of body position

proxemics study of personal space

proximity physical nearness, a predictor of attraction

pseudoscience set of claims that seems scientific but isn't

psychic determinism the assumption that all psychological events have a cause

psychoactive drug substance that contains chemicals similar to those found naturally in our brains that alter consciousness by changing chemical processes in neurons

psychoanalysis school of psychology, founded by Sigmund Freud, that focuses on internal psychological processes of which we're unaware

psychological dependence nonphysical dependence on a drug that occurs when continued use of the drug is motivated by intense cravings

psychology the scientific study of the mind, brain, and behavior

psychoneuroimmunology study of the relationship between the immune system and central nervous system

psychopathic personality condition marked by superficial charm, dishonesty, manipulativeness, self-centeredness, and risk taking

psychopharmacotherapy use of medications to treat psychological problems

psychophysics the study of how we perceive sensory stimuli based on their physical characteristics

psychophysiological illnesses such as asthma and ulcers in which emotions and stress contribute to, maintain, or aggravate the physical condition

psychosocial crisis dilemma concerning an individual's relations to other people

psychosurgery brain surgery to treat psychological problems

psychotherapy psychological intervention designed to help people resolve emotional, behavioral, and interpersonal problems and improve the quality of their lives

psychotic symptom psychological problem reflecting serious distortions in reality

puberty the achievement of sexual maturation resulting in the potential to reproduce

punishment outcome or consequence of a behavior that weakens the probability of the behavior

pupil circular hole through which light enters the eye

random assignment randomly sorting participants into two groups

random selection procedure that ensures every person in a population has an equal chance of being chosen to participate

range measure of variability that consists of the difference between the highest and lowest scores

rapid eye movement (REM) darting of the eyes underneath closed eyelids during sleep

rational/theoretical method of test construction approach to building tests that requires test developers to begin with a clear-cut conceptualization of a trait and then write items to assess that conceptualization

rationalization providing a reasonable-sounding explanation for unreasonable behaviors or for failures

reaction-formation transformation of an anxiety-provoking emotion into its opposite

reality principle tendency of the ego to postpone gratification until it can find an appropriate outlet

recall generating previously remembered information

recency effect tendency to remember words at the end of a list especially well

receptor site location that uniquely recognizes a neurotransmitter

recessive gene gene that is expressed only in the absence of a dominant gene

reciprocal determinism tendency for people to mutually influence each other's behavior

reciprocity   rule of give and take, a predictor of attraction

recognition   selecting previously remembered information from an array of options

reflex   an automatic motor response to a sensory stimulus

regression   the act of returning psychologically to a younger, and typically simpler and safer, age

rehearsal   repeating information to extend the duration of retention in short-term memory

reinforcement   outcome or consequence of a behavior that strengthens the probability of the behavior

relational aggression   form of indirect aggression prevalent in girls, involving spreading rumors, gossiping, and using nonverbal putdowns for the purpose of social manipulation

relearning   reacquiring knowledge that we'd previously learned but largely forgotten over time

reliability   consistency of measurement

REM sleep   stage of sleep during which the brain is most active and during which vivid dreaming most often occurs

renewal effect   sudden reemergence of a conditioned response following extinction when an animal is returned to the environment in which the conditioned response was acquired

replicability   when a study's findings are able to be duplicated, ideally by independent investigators

representativeness heuristic   heuristic that involves judging the probability of an event by its superficial similarity to a prototype

repression   motivated forgetting of emotionally threatening memories or impulses

Research Domain Criteria   a recently launched program of research designed to classify mental disorders in terms of deficits in brain circuitry

resistance   attempts to avoid confrontation and anxiety associated with uncovering previously repressed thoughts, emotions, and impulses

resolution phase   phase in human sexual response following orgasm, in which people report relaxation and a sense of well-being

response prevention   technique in which therapists prevent clients from performing their typical avoidance behaviors

response set   tendency of research participants to distort their responses to questionnaire items

resting potential   electrical charge difference (−60 millivolts) across the neuronal membrane, when the neuron is not being stimulated or inhibited

reticular activating system (RAS)   brain area that plays a key role in arousal

retina   membrane at the back of the eye responsible for converting light into neural activity

retrieval cue   hint that makes it easier for us to recall information

retrieval   reactivation or reconstruction of experiences from our memory stores

retroactive interference   interference with retention of old information due to acquisition of new information

retrograde amnesia   loss of memories from our past

reuptake   means of recycling neurotransmitters

rods   receptor cells in the retina allowing us to see in low levels of light

Rorschach Inkblot Test   projective test consisting of 10 symmetrical inkblots

s **(specific abilities)**   particular ability level in a narrow domain

scaffolding   Vygotskian learning mechanism in which parents provide initial assistance in children's learning but gradually remove structure as children become more competent

scapegoat hypothesis   claim that prejudice arises from a need to blame other groups for our misfortunes

scatterplot   grouping of points on a two-dimensional graph in which each dot represents a single person's data

schedule of reinforcement   pattern of reinforcing a behavior

schema   organized knowledge structure or mental model that we've stored in memory

schizophrenia   severe disorder of thought and emotion associated with a loss of contact with reality

scientific skepticism   approach of evaluating all claims with an open mind but insisting on persuasive evidence before accepting them

scientific theory   explanation for a large number of findings in the natural world

secondary appraisal   perceptions regarding our ability to cope with an event that follows primary appraisal

secondary reinforcer   neutral object that becomes associated with a primary reinforcer

secondary sex characteristic   a sex-differentiating characteristic that doesn't relate directly to reproduction, such as breast enlargement in women and deepening voices in men

sedative   drug that exerts a calming effect

selective attention   process of selecting one sensory channel and ignoring or minimizing others

self-actualization   drive to develop our innate potential to the fullest possible extent

self-control   ability to inhibit an impulse to act

self-esteem   evaluation of our worth

self-monitoring   personality trait that assesses the extent to which people's behavior reflects their true feelings and attitudes

self-perception theory   theory that we acquire our attitudes by observing our behaviors

semantic memory   our knowledge of facts about the world

semantics   meaning derived from words and sentences

semicircular canals   three fluid-filled canals in the inner ear responsible for our sense of balance

sensation   detection of physical energy by sense organs, which then send information to the brain

sense receptor   specialized cell responsible for converting external stimuli into neural activity for a specific sensory system

sensorimotor stage   stage in Piaget's theory characterized by a focus on the here and now without the ability to represent experiences mentally

sensory adaptation   activation is greatest when a stimulus is first detected

sensory memory   brief storage of perceptual information before it is passed to short-term memory

serial position curve   graph depicting both primacy and recency effects on people's ability to recall items on a list

set point   value that establishes a range of body and muscle mass we tend to maintain

shaping   conditioning a target behavior by progressively reinforcing behaviors that come closer and closer to the target

short-term memory   memory system that retains information for limited durations

sign language   language developed by members of a deaf community that uses visual rather than auditory communication

signal detection theory   theory regarding how stimuli are detected under different conditions

similarity   extent to which we have things in common with others, a predictor of attraction

Skinner box   small animal chamber constructed by Skinner to allow sustained periods of conditioning to be administered and behaviors to be recorded unsupervised

sleep apnea   disorder caused by a blockage of the airway during sleep, resulting in daytime fatigue

sleep paralysis   state of being unable to move just after falling asleep or right before waking up

sleepwalking   walking while fully asleep

social anxiety disorder   intense fear of negative evaluation in social situations

social comparison theory   theory that states we seek to evaluate our abilities and beliefs by comparing them with those of others

social facilitation   enhancement of performance brought about by the presence of others

social learning theorists   theorists who emphasize thinking as a central cause of personality

social loafing   phenomenon whereby individuals become less productive in groups

social pragmatics   account of language acquisition that proposes that children infer what words and sentences mean from context and social interactions

social psychology   study of how people influence others' behavior, beliefs, and attitudes

social support   relationships with people and groups that can provide us with emotional comfort and personal and financial resources

sociocognitive theory   approach to explaining hypnosis based on people's attitudes, beliefs, expectations, and responsiveness to waking suggestions

somatic marker theory   theory proposing that we use our "gut reactions" to help us determine how we should act

somatic nervous system   part of the nervous system that conveys information between the central nervous system and the body, controlling and coordinating voluntary movement

somatic symptom disorder   condition marked by excessive anxiety about physical symptoms with a medical or purely psychological origin

somatosensory   our sense of touch, temperature, and pain

source monitoring confusion   lack of clarity about the origin of a memory

spermarche   boys' first ejaculation

spinal cord   thick bundle of nerves that conveys signals between the brain and the body

spirituality   search for the sacred, which may or may not extend to belief in God

split-brain surgery   procedure that involves severing the corpus callosum to reduce the spread of epileptic seizures

spontaneous recovery   sudden reemergence of an extinct conditioned response after a delay in exposure to the conditioned stimulus

standard deviation   measure of variability that takes into account how far each data point is from the mean

Stanford-Binet IQ test   intelligence test based on the measure developed by Binet and Simon, adapted by Lewis Terman of Stanford University

state-dependent learning   superior retrieval of memories when the organism is in the same physiological or psychological state as it was during encoding

statistics   application of mathematics to describing and analyzing data

stem cell   a cell, often originating in embryos, having the capacity to differentiate into a more specialized cell

stereotype threat   fear that we may confirm a negative group stereotype

stereotype   a belief—positive or negative—about the characteristics of members of a group that is applied generally to most members of the group

stimulant   drug that increases activity in the central nervous system, including heart rate, respiration, and blood pressure

stimulus discrimination   process by which organisms display a less pronounced conditioned response to conditioned stimuli that differ from the original conditioned stimulus

stimulus generalization   process by which conditioned stimuli similar, but not identical, to the original conditioned stimulus elicit a conditioned response

storage   process of keeping information in memory

stranger anxiety   a fear of strangers developing at eight or nine months of age

strategic family intervention   family therapy approach designed to remove barriers to effective communication

stress   the tension, discomfort, or physical symptoms that arise when a situation, called a *stressor*—a type of stimulus—strains our ability to cope effectively

structural family therapy   treatment in which therapists deeply involve themselves in family activities to change how family members arrange and organize interactions

structuralism   school of psychology that aimed to identify the basic elements of psychological experience

structured personality test   paper-and-pencil measure consisting of questions that respondents answer in one of a few fixed ways

style of life   according to Alfred Adler, each person's distinctive way of achieving superiority

sublimation   transforming a socially unacceptable impulse into an admired goal

subliminal perception   perception below the limen or threshold of conscious awareness

suggestive memory technique   procedure that encourages patients to recall memories that may or may not have taken place

superego   our sense of morality

sympathetic nervous system   division of the autonomic nervous system engaged during a crisis or after actions requiring fight or flight

synapse   space between two connecting neurons through which messages are transmitted chemically

synaptic cleft   a gap into which neurotransmitters are released from the axon terminal

synaptic vesicle   spherical sac containing neurotransmitters

synesthesia   a condition in which people experience cross-modal sensations

syntax   grammatical rules that govern how words are composed into meaningful strings

systematic desensitization   clients are taught to relax as they are gradually exposed to what they fear in a stepwise manner

taste bud   sense receptor in the tongue that responds to sweet, salty, sour, bitter, umami, and perhaps fat

temperament   basic emotional style that appears early in development and is largely genetic in origin

temporal lobe   lower part of cerebral cortex that plays roles in hearing, understanding language, and memory

tend-and-befriend   reaction that mobilizes people to nurture (tend) or seek social support (befriend) under stress

teratogen   an environmental factor that can exert a negative impact on prenatal development

terror management theory   theory proposing that our awareness of our death leaves us with an underlying sense of terror with which we cope by adopting reassuring cultural worldviews

test bias   tendency of a test to predict outcomes better in one group than in another

thalamus   gateway from the sense organs to the primary sensory cortex

Thematic Apperception Test (TAT)   projective test requiring examinees to tell a story in response to ambiguous pictures

theory of mind   ability to reason about what other people know or believe

thinking   any mental activity or processing of information, including learning, remembering, perceiving, communicating, believing, and deciding

threshold   membrane potential necessary to trigger an action potential

timbre   complexity or quality of sound that makes musical instruments, human voices, or other sources sound unique

tip-of-the-tongue (TOT) phenomenon   experience of knowing that we know something but being unable to access it

token economy   method in which desirable behaviors are rewarded with tokens that clients can exchange for tangible rewards

tolerance   reduction in the effect of a drug as a result of repeated use, requiring users to consume greater quantities to achieve the same effect

top-down processing   conceptually driven processing influenced by beliefs and expectancies

trait   relatively enduring predisposition that influences our behavior across many situations

transcranial magnetic stimulation (TMS)   technique that applies strong and quickly changing magnetic fields to the surface of the skull that can either enhance or interrupt brain function

transduction   the process of converting an external energy or substance into electrical activity within neurons

transference   act of projecting intense, unrealistic feelings and expectations from the past onto the therapist

triarchic model   model of intelligence proposed by Robert Sternberg positing three distinct types of intelligence: analytical, practical, and creative

trichromatic theory   idea that color vision is based on our sensitivity to three primary colors

twin study   analysis of how traits differ in identical versus fraternal twins

two-factor theory   theory proposing that emotions are produced by an undifferentiated state of arousal along with an attribution (explanation) of that arousal

Type A personality   personality type that describes people who are competitive, driven, hostile, and ambitious

ultimate attribution error   assumption that behaviors among individual members of a group are due to their internal dispositions

unconditioned response (UCR)   automatic response to a nonneutral stimulus that does not need to be learned

unconditioned stimulus (UCS)   stimulus that elicits an automatic response

validity   extent to which a measure assesses what it purports to measure

variability   measure of how loosely or tightly bunched scores are

variable interval (VI) schedule   pattern in which we provide reinforcement for a response at least once during an average time interval, with the interval varying randomly

variable ratio (VR) schedule   pattern in which we provide reinforcement after a specific number of responses on average, with the number varying randomly

variable   anything that can vary

vestibular sense   our sense of equilibrium or balance

Weber's law   there is a constant proportional relationship between the JND and original stimulus intensity

Wechsler Adult Intelligence Scale (WAIS)   most widely used intelligence test for adults today, consisting of 15 subtests to assess different types of mental abilities

Wernicke's area   part of the temporal lobe involved in understanding speech

whole word recognition   reading strategy that involves identifying common words based on their appearance without having to sound them out

wisdom   application of intelligence toward a common good

withdrawal   unpleasant effects of reducing or stopping consumption of a drug that users had consumed habitually

within-group heritability   extent to which the variability of a trait within a group is genetically influenced

Yerkes–Dodson law   inverted U-shaped relation between arousal on the one hand and mood and performance on the other

yoga   physical, mental, and spiritual practices that include postures, meditation, breathing techniques, mental concentration, visualization or guided imagery, and relaxation exercises

zone of proximal development   phase of learning during which children can benefit from instruction

zygote   fertilized egg

Anderson, C. A., & Anderson, K. B. (1996). Violent crime rate studies in philosophical context: A destructive testing approach to heat and southern culture of violence effects. *Journal of Personality and Social Psychology, 70,* 740–756.

Anderson, C. A., & Bushman, B. J. (2002a). The effects of media violence on society. *Science, 295,* 2377–2378.

Anderson, C. A., & Bushman, B. J. (2002b). Human aggression. *Annual Review of Psychology, 53,* 27–51.

Anderson, C. A., Berkowitz, L., Donnerstein, E., Huesmann, L. R., Johnson, J. D., Linz, D., … Wartella, E. (2003). The influence of media violence on youth. *Psychological Science in the Public Interest, 4,* 81–110.

Anderson, C. A., Bushman, B. J., & Groom, R. W. (1997). Hot years and serious and deadly assault: Empirical tests of the heat hypothesis. *Journal of Personality and Social Psychology, 73,* 1213–1223.

Anderson, C. A., Gentile, D. A., & Buckley, K. E. (2007). Violent video game effects on children and adolescents: Theory, research, and public policy. Oxford, England: Oxford University Press.

Anderson, C. A., Shibuya, A., Ihiri, N., Swing, E. L., Bushman, B. J., Sakamoto, A., … Saleem, M. (2010). Violent video game effects on aggression, empathy, and prosocial behavior in Eastern and Western countries. *Psychological Bulletin, 136,* 151–173.

Anderson, C. M., & Stewart, S. (1983). *Mastering resistance.* New York, NY: Guilford Press.

Anderson, D. R., & Pempek, T. A. (2005). Television and very young children. *American Behavioral Scientist, 48,* 505–522.

Anderson, G. M. (2012). Twin studies in autism: What they might say about genetic and environmental influences. *Journal of Autism and Developmental Disorders, 42,* 1526–1527.

Anderson, J. R., Myowa-Yamakoshi, M., & Matsuzawa, T. (2004). Contagious yawning in chimpanzees. *Proceedings of the Royal Society B: Biological Sciences, 271,* S468.

Anderson, K. J., Revelle, W., & Lynch, M. J. (1989). Caffeine, impulsivity, and memory scanning: A comparison of two explanations for the Yerkes-Dodson effect. *Motivation and Emotion, 13,* 1–20.

Anderson, K. W., Taylor, S., & McLean, P. (1996). Panic disorder associated with blood-injury-reactivity: The necessity of establishing functional relationships among maladaptive behaviors. *Behavior Therapy, 27,* 463–472.

Anderson, L. H., Whitebird, R. R., Schultz, J., McEvoy, C. E., Kreitzer, M. J., & Gross, C. R. (2014). Healthcare utilization and costs in persons with insomnia in a managed care population. *The American Journal of Managed Care, 20*(5), e157-65.

Anderson, P. L., Price, M., Edwards, S. M., Obasaju, M. A., Schmertz, S. K., Zimand, E., & Calamaras, M. R. (2013). Virtual reality exposure therapy for social anxiety disorder: A randomized controlled trial. *Journal of Consulting and Clinical Psychology, 81*(5), 751.

Andersson, G. (2016). Internet-delivered psychological treatments. *Annual Review of Clinical Psychology, 12,* 157–179.

Andrasik, F. (2012). Behavioral treatment of headaches: Extending the reach. *Neurological Sciences, 33,* 127–130.

Andreasen, N. C. (1987). Creativity and mental illness: Prevalence rates in writers and their first-degree relatives. *American Journal of Psychiatry, 144,* 1288–1292.

Andreasen, N. C. (1995). The validation of psychiatric-diagnosis: New models and approaches. *American Journal of Psychiatry, 152,* 161–162.

Andreasen, N. C., O'Leary, D. S., Flaum, M., Nopoulos, P., Watkins, G. L., Boles Ponto, L. L., & Hichwa, R. D, (1997). Hypofrontality in schizophrenia: Distributed dysfunctional circuits in neuroleptic-naive patients. *Lancet, 349,* 1730–1734.

Andreasen, N. C., Rezai, K., Alliger, R., Swayze, V. W. II, Flaum, M., Kirchner, P., … O'Leary D. S., (1992). Hypofrontality in neuroleptic-naive patients and in patients with chronic schizophrenia: Assessment with xenon 133 single-photon emission computed tomography and the Tower of London. *Archives of General Psychiatry, 49,* 943–958.

Andresen, G. V., Birch, L. L., & Johnson, P. A. (1990). The scapegoat effect on food aversions after chemotherapy. *Cancer, 66,* 1649–1653.

Andrews-McClymont, J., Lilienfeld, S. O., & Duke, M. P. (2013). Evaluating an animal model of compulsive hoarding in humans. *Review of General Psychology, 17,* 399–419.

Andrews, G., Hobbs, M. J., Borkovec, T. D., Beesdo, K., Craske, M. G., Heimberg, R. G., … Stanley, M. A. (2010). Generalized worry disorder: A review of DSM-IV generalized anxiety disorder and options for DSM-V. *Depression and Anxiety, 27*(2), 134–147.

Anestis, M. D., Anestis, J. C., & Lilienfeld, S. O. (2011). When it comes to evaluating psychodynamic therapy, the devil is in the details. *American Psychologist, 66,* 149–151.

Angier, N. (2006, January 3). The cute factor. *New York Times.* Retrieved from http://www.nytimes.com/2006/01/03/science/03cute.html?ex=1293944400&en=9942fdaf51f1211c&ei=5090&partner=rssuserland&emc=rss

Angier, N. (2009, June 22). When an ear witness decides the case. *New York Times.* Retrieved from http://www.nytimes.com/2009/06/23/science/23angi.html

Angrosino, M. V. (2007). *Naturalistic observation* (Vol. 1). Walnut Creek, CA: Left Coast Press.

Angst, J., Cui, L., Swendsen, J. J., Rothen, S., Cravchik, A., Kessler, R., & Merikangas, K. (2010). Major depressive disorder with sub-threshold bipolarity in the National Comorbidity Survey Replication. *The American Journal of Psychiatry, 167*(10), 1194.

Anholt, R. R. (2012). Genetics of aggression. *Annual Review of Genetics, 46,* 145–164.

Antonovsky, A. (1967). Social class, life expectancy and overall mortality. *Milbank Memorial Fund Quarterly, 45,* 31–73.

Antony, M. A., & Barlow, D. H. (2002). Specific phobia. In D. H. Barlow (Ed.), *Anxiety and its disorders: The nature and treatment of anxiety and panic* (2nd ed., pp. 380–417). New York, NY: Guilford Press.

Antony, M. A., & Roemer, L. (2003). Behavior therapy. In A. S. Gurman & S. B. Messer (Eds.), *Essential psychotherapies: Theory and practice* (2nd ed., pp. 182–223). New York, NY: Guilford Press.

Antrobus, J. S. (1983). REM and NREM sleep reports: Comparison of word frequencies by cognitive classes. *Psychophysiology, 20,* 562–568.

Antrobus, J. S., Antrobus, J. S., & Fisher, C. (1965). Discrimination of dreaming and nondreaming sleep. *Archives of General Psychiatry, 12,* 395–401.

Aponte, H., & Hoffman, L. (1973). The open door: A structural approach to a family with an anorectic child. *Family Process, 12,* 1–44.

Appelbaum, P. S. (1997). Almost a revolution: An international perspective on the law of involuntary commitment. *Journal of the American Academy of Psychiatry and Law, 25,* 135–147.

Appelle, S., Lynn, S. J., & Newman, L. (2000). The alien abduction experience: Theoretical and empirical issues. In E. Cardeña, S. J. Lynn, & S. Krippner (Eds.), *The varieties of anomalous experience: Examining the scientific evidence* (pp. 253–283). Washington, DC: American Psychological Association.

Applewhite, P. B., Gardner, F., Foley, D., & Clendenin, M. (1971). Failure to condition tetrahymena. *Scandinavian Journal of Psychology, 12,* 65–67.

Archer, D. (1997). *A world of differences: Understanding cross-cultural communication* [Video]. Berkeley, CA: University of California, Extension Center for Media and Independent Learning.

Archer, J. (2004). Sex differences in aggression in real-world settings: A meta-analytic review. *Review of General Psychology, 8*(4), 291–322.

Ardhanareeswaran, K. (2015). Diphenhydramine HCl. *Journal of the American Medical Association, 177,* 665–670.

Ariely, D. (2008). *Predictably irrational: The hidden forces that shape our decisions.* New York, NY: HarperCollins.

Arieti, S. (1959). Manic-depressive psychosis. In S. Arieti (Ed.), *American handbook of psychiatry* (pp. 439–444). New York, NY: Basic Books.

Arkes, H. R. (1993). Some practical judgment and decision-making research. In N. J. Castellan (Ed.), *Individual and group decision making: Current issues* (pp. 3–19). Hillsdale, NJ: Erlbaum.

Arkes, H. R., & Tetlock, P. E. (2004). Attributions of implicit prejudice or "Would Jesse Jackson 'fail' the Implicit Association Test?" *Psychological Inquiry, 15,* 257–278.

Arkowitz, H., & Lilienfeld, S. O. (2006). Psychotherapy on trial. *Scientific American Mind, 3,* 42–49.

Arkowitz, H., & Lilienfeld, S. O. (2007). A pill to fix your ills? *Scientific American Mind, 18,* 80–81.

Arkowitz, H., & Lilienfeld, S. O. (2009, January). Why science tells us not to rely on eyewitness accounts. *Scientific American Mind.* http://www.scientificamerican.com/article.cfm?id=do-the-eyes-have-it

Arkowitz, H., Miller, W. R., & Rollnick, S. (Eds.). (2015). *Motivational interviewing in the treatment of psychological problems.* New York, NY: Guilford Publications.

Armstrong, T. (2009). *Multiple intelligences in the classroom.* Alexandria, VA: Association for Supervision and Curriculum Development.

Arnberg, F. K., Johannesson, K. B., & Michel, P. O. (2013). Prevalence and duration of PTSD in survivors 6 years after a natural disaster. *Journal of Anxiety Disorders, 27*(3), 347–352.

Arnett, J. J. (1995). The young and the reckless: Adolescent reckless behavior. *Current Directions in Psychological Science, 4,* 67–71.

Arnett, J. J. (1999). Adolescent storm and stress, reconsidered. *American Psychologist, 4,* 317–326.

Arnett, J. J. (2004). *Emerging adulthood: The winding road frm the late teens through the twenties.* Oxford, England: Oxford University Press.

Arnold, L. M. (1999). A case series of women with postpartum-onset obsessive-compulsive disorder. *Primary Care Companion Journal of Clinical Psychiatry, 1,* 103–108.

Arnold, O., & Kaiser, F. G. (2016). Understanding the foot-in-the-door effect as a pseudo-effect from the perspective of the Campbell paradigm. *International Journal of Psychology.* Awaiting volume and page numbers.

Aronoff, J., Barclay, A. M., & Stevenson, L. A. (1988) The recognition of threatening facial stimuli. *Journal of Personality and Social Psychology, 54,* 647–655.

Aronoff, J., Lynn, S. J., & Malinowski, P. (2000). Are cultic environments psychologically harmful? *Clinical Psychology Review, 20,* 91–111.

Aronson, E. (2000). The jigsaw strategy: Reducing prejudice in the classroom. *Psychology Review, 7,* 2–5.

Aronson, E. (2004). Reducing hostility and building compassion: Lessons from the jigsaw classroom. In A. G. Miller (Ed.), *The social psychology of good and evil* (pp. 469–488). New York, NY: Guilford Press.

Aronson, E. (2011). *Not by chance alone: My life as a social psychologist.* New York, NY: Basic Books.

Aronson, E. (2012). *The social animal* (11th ed.). New York, NY: Worth.

Aronson, E., & Mills, J. (1959). The effect of severity of initiation on liking for a group. *Journal of Abnormal and Social Psychology, 59,* 177–181.

Aronson, E., Blaney, N., Stephan, C., Sikes, J., & Snapp, M. (1978). *The jigsaw classroom.* Beverly Hills, CA: Sage.

Arterberry, M. E., & Bornstein, M. H. (2012). Categorization of real and replica objects by 14- and 18-month-old infants. *Infant Behavior and Development, 35*, 606–612.

Asch, S. E. (1955). Opinions and social pressure. *Scientific American, 193*, 31–35.

Ascher, L. M., Barber, T. X., & Spanos, N. P. (1972). Two attempts to replicate the Parrish-Lundy-Leibowitz experiment on hypnotic age regression. *American Journal of Clinical Hypnosis, 14*, 178–185.

Asendorpf, J. B., Conner, M., De Fruyt, F., De Houwer, J., Denissen, J. J. A., Fiedler, K., … Wicherts, J. M. (2013). Replication is more than hitting the lottery twice. *European Journal of Personality, 27*, 138–144.

Aserinsky, E. (1996). Memories of famous neuropsychologists: The discovery of REM sleep. *Journal of the History of the Neurosciences, 5*, 213–227.

Aserinsky, E., & Kleitman, N. (1953). Regularly occurring periods of ocular motility and concomitant phenomena during sleep. *Science, 118*, 361–375.

Ashton, S. G., & Goldberg, L. W. (1973). In response to Jackson's challenge: The comparative validity of personality scales constructed by the external (empirical) strategy and scales developed intuitively by experts, novices, and laymen. *Journal of Research in Personality, 7*, 1–20.

Assendelft, W. J. J., Morton, S. C., Yu, E. I., Suttorp, M. J., & Shekelle, P. G. (2003). Spinal manipulative therapy for low back pain: A meta-analysis of effectiveness relative to other therapies. *Annals of Internal Medicine, 138*, 871–881.

Astin, J. A., & Ernst, E. (2002). The effectiveness of spinal manipulation for the treatment of headache disorders: A systematic review of randomized clinical trials. *Cephalalgia, 22*, 617–623.

Atkinson, R. C. (2001, February 18). *Standardized tests and access to American universities.* The 2001 Robert H. Atwell Distinguished Lecture delivered at the 83rd Annual Meeting of the American Council on Education, Washington, DC. Retrieved from http://www.ucop.edu/news/sat/speech.html

Atkinson, R. C., & Shiffrin, R. M. (1968). Human memory: A proposed system and its control processes. In K. W. Spence and J. T. Spence (Eds.), *The psychology of learning and motivation: Advances in research and theory* (Vol. 2, pp. 89–195). New York, NY: Academic Press.

Atri, A., Sharma, M., & Cottrell, R. (2006). Role of social support, hardiness, and acculturation as predictors of mental health among international students of Asian Indian origin. *International Quarterly of Community Health Education, 27*, 59–73.

Audebert, O., Deiss, V., & Rousset, S. (2006). Hedonism as a predictor of attitudes of young French women towards meat. *Appetite, 46*, 239–247.

Aveyard, M. E. (2012). Some constants sound curvy: Effects of sound symbolism on object recognition. *Memory & Cognition, 40*, 83–92.

Ax, A. F. (1953). The physiological differentiation between fear and anger in humans. *Psychosomatic Medicine, 55*, 433–442.

Axsom, D., & Cooper, J. (1985). Cognitive dissonance and psychotherapy: The role of effort justification in inducing weight loss. *Journal of Experimental Social Psychology, 21*, 149–160.

Axtell, R. E. (1997). *Do's and taboos of body language around the world.* New York, NY: Wiley.

Ayllon, T., & Milan, M. (2002). Token economy: Guidelines for operation. In M. Hersen & W. Sledge, *Encyclopedia of psychotherapy* (pp. 829–833). New York, NY: Academic Press.

Azar, B. (1999, July/August). Destructive lab attack sends a wake-up call. *APA Monitor, 30* (7), 16.

Azar, B. (2005, October). How mimicry begat culture. *American Psychological Association Monitor, 36*(9). Retrieved from http://www.apa.org/monitor/oct05/mimicry.aspx

Azevedo, F. A., Carvalho, L. R. B., Grinberg, L. T., Farfel, J. M., Ferretti, R. E. L., Leite, R. E. P., … Herculano-Houzel, S. (2009). Equal numbers of neuronal and nonneuronal cells make the human brain an isometrically scaled-up primate brain. *Journal of Comparative Neurology, 513*, 532–541.

Azrin, N. H., & Holz, W. C. (1966). Punishment. In W. K. Honig (Ed.), *Operant behavior: Areas of research and application* (pp. 380–447). New York, NY: Appleton-Century-Crofts.

Babiak, P. (1995). When psychopaths go to work: A case study of an industrial psychopath. *Applied Psychology, 44*, 171–188.

Babiak, P., & Hare, R. D. (2006). *Snakes in suits: When psychopaths go to work.* New York, NY: Regan Books.

Babyak, M. A., Blumenthal, J. A., Herman, S., Khatri, P., Doraiswamy, P. M., Moore, K. A., … Ranga Krishnan, K. (2000). Exercise treatment for major depression: Maintenance of therapeutic benefit at 10 months. *Psychosomatic Medicine, 62*, 633–638.

Bachrach, H., Galatzer-Levy, R., Skolnikoff, A., & Waldron, S. (1991). On the efficacy of psychoanalysis. *Journal of the American Psychoanalytic Association, 39*, 871–916.

Back, M. D., Stopfer, J. M., Vazire, S., Gaddis, S., Schmukle, S. C., Egloff, B., & Gosling, S. D. (2010). Facebook profiles reflect actual personality, not self-idealization. *Psychological Science, 21*, 372–374.

Back, M. D., Stopfer, J. M., Vazire, S., Gaddis, S., Schmukle, S. C., Egloff, B., & Gosling, S. D. (2010). Facebook profiles reflect actual personality, not self-idealization. *Psychological Science, 21*, 372–374.

Baddeley, A. (2012). Working memory: Theories, models, and controversies. *Annual Review of Psychology, 63*, 1–29.

Baddeley, A. D. (1993). *Your memory: A user's guide* (2nd ed.). London, England: Lifecycle Publications.

Baddeley, A. D., & Hitch, G. J. (1974). Working memory. In G. A. Bower (Ed.), *Recent advances in learning and motivation* (Vol. 8, pp. 47–90). New York, NY: Academic Press.

Badman, M. K., & Flier, J. S. (2005). The gut and energy balance: Visceral allies in the obesity wars. *Science, 307*, 1909–1914.

Baer, R. A. (2003). Mindfulness training as a clinical intervention: A conceptual and an empirical review. *Clinical Psychology: Science and Practice, 10*, 125–143.

Baer, R. A. (Ed.). (2015). *Mindfulness-based treatment approaches: Clinician's guide to evidence base and applications.* Cambridge, MA: Academic Press.

Baer, R. A. (Ed.). (2015). *Mindfulness-based treatment approaches: Clinician's guide to evidence base and applications.* New York, NY: Academic Press.

Bagby, R. M., Joffe, R. T., Parker, J. D., Kalemba, V., & Harkness, K. L. (1995). Major depression and the five-factor model of personality. *Journal of Personality Disorders, 9*, 224–234.

Bagemihl, B. (1999). *Biological exuberance, animal homosexuality and natural diversity.* London, England: Profile Books.

Baggott, M. J., Coyle, J. R., Erowid, E., Erowid, F., & Robertson, L. C. (2011). Abnormal visual experiences in individuals with histories of hallucinogen use: A web-based questionnaire. *Drug and Alcohol Dependence, 114*(1), 61–67.

Baggott, M. J., Coyle, J. R., Erowid, E., Erowid, F., & Robertson, L. C. (2011). Abnormal visual experiences in individuals with histories of hallucinogen use: A Web-based questionnaire. *Drug and Alcohol Dependence, 114*(1), 61–67.

Bagnardi, V., Blangiardo, M., LaVecchia, C. L., & Corrado, G. (2001). *Alcohol consumption and the risk of cancer: A meta-analysis.* Bethesda, MD: National Institute on Alcohol Abuse and Alcoholism.

Baguley, D., McFerran, D., & Hall, D. (2013). Tinnitus. *Lancet, 382*(9904), 1600–1607.

Bahrick, H. P. (1984). Semantic memory content in permastore: Fifty years of memory for Spanish learning in school. *Journal of Experimental Psychology: General, 113*, 1–29.

Bahrick, H. P., & Phelps, E. (1987). Retention of Spanish vocabulary over 8 years. *Journal of Experimental Psychology: Learning, Memory, & Cognition, 13*, 344–349.

Bahrick, H. P., Bahrick, P. O., & Wittlinger, R. P. (1975). Fifty years of memory for names and faces: A cross-sectional approach. *Journal of Experimental Psychology: General, 104*, 54–75.

Bahrick, L. E., & Watson, J. S. (1985). Detection of intermodal proprioceptive visual contingency as a potential basis of self-perception in infancy. *Developmental Psychology, 21*, 963–973.

Bahrick, L. E., Moss, L., & Fadil, C. (1996). The development of self recognition in infancy. *Ecological Psychology, 8*, 189–208.

Baibazarova, E., van de Beek, C., Cohen-Kettenis, P. T., Buitelaar, J., Shelton, K. H., & van Goozen, S. H. (2013). Influence of prenatal maternal stress, maternal plasma cortisol and cortisol in the amniotic fluid on birth outcomes and child temperament at 3 months. *Psychoneuroendocrinology, 38*(6), 907–915.

Bailey, J. M., & Zucker, K. J. (1995). Childhood sex-typed behavior and sexual orientation: A conceptual analysis and quantitative review. *Developmental Psychology, 31*, 43–55.

Bailey, J. M., Vasey, P. L., Diamond, L. M., Breedlove, S. M., Vilain, E., & Epprecht, M. (2016). Sexual orientation, controversy, and science. *Psychological Science in the Public Interest, 17*(2), 45–101.

Baillargeon, R. (1987). Object permanence in 3 ½ and 4 ½ month olds. *Developmental Psychology, 23*, 655–664.

Baillargeon, R., & Hanko-Summers, S. (1990). Is the top object adequately supported by the bottom object? Young infants' understanding of support relations. *Cognitive Development, 5*, 29–53.

Baker, F. M., & Bell, C. C. (1999). Issues in the psychiatric treatment of African Americans. *Psychiatry Services, 50*, 362–368.

Baker, J. P., & Berenbaum, H. (2007). Emotional approach and problem-focused coping: A comparison of potentially adaptive strategies. *Cognition & Emotion, 21*(1), 95–118. doi:10.1080/02699930600562276

Baker, J. R., & Yardley, J. K. (2002). Moderating effect of gender on the relationship between sensation-seeking impulsivity and substance use in adolescents. *Journal of Child and Adolescence Substance Abuse, 12*, 27–43.

Baker, S. C., & MacIntyre, P. D. (2000). The role of gender and immersion in communication and second language orientations. *Language Learning, 50*, 311–341.

Baker, T. B., McFall, R. M., & Shoham, V. (2009). Current status and future prospects of clinical psychology toward a scientifically principled approach to mental and behavioral health care. *Perspectives on Psychological Science, 9*, 67–103.

Baker, W. E. (1999). When can affective conditioning and mere exposure directly influence brand choice? *Journal of Advertising, 28*, 31–47.

Bakker, M., van Dijk, A., & Wicherts, J. M. (2012). The rules of the game called psychological science. *Perspectives on Psychological Science, 7*, 543–554.

Balcetis, E., & Dunning, D. A. (2008). A mile in moccasins: How situational experience diminishes dispositionism in social inference. *Personality and Social Psychology Bulletin, 34*, 102–144.

Ball, J. D., Archer, R. P., & Imhoff, E. A. (1994). Time requirements of psychological testing: A survey of practitioners. *Journal of Personality Assessment, 63*, 239–249.

Ball, T. M., Stein, M. B., & Paulus, M. P. (2014). Toward the application of functional neuroimaging to individualized treatment for anxiety and depression. *Depression and Anxiety, 31*(11), 920–933.

Baltes, P. B., Staudinger, U. M., & Lindenberger, U. (1999). Lifespan psychology: Theory and application to intellectual functioning. *Annual Review of Psychology, 50,* 471–507.

Banaji, M. R. (2001). Implicit attitudes can be measured. In H. D. Roediger, III, J. S. Naime, I. Neath, & A. Surprenant (Eds.), *The nature of remembering: Essays in honor of Robert G. Crowder* (pp. 117–150). Washington, DC: American Psychological Association.

Banaji, M. R., & Greenwald, A. G. (2013). *Blindspot: Hidden biases of good people.* New York, NY: Delacorte Press.

Bancaud, J., Brunet-Bourgin, F., Chauvel, P., & Halgren, E. (1994). Anatomical origin of déjà vu and vivid "memories" in human temporal lobe epilepsy. *Brain, 117,* 71–90.

Bancroft, J. (2005). The endocrinology of sexual arousal. *Journal of Endocrinology, 186,* 411–427.

Bandura, A. (1965). Vicarious processes: A case of no-trial learning. In L. Berkowitz (Ed.), *Advances in experimental social psychology* (Vol. 2, pp. 3–55). New York, NY: Academic Press.

Bandura, A. (1971). *Psychological modeling.* Chicago, IL: Aldine-Atherton.

Bandura, A. (1973). *Aggression: A social learning analysis.* Oxford, England: Prentice Hall.

Bandura, A. (1977). Self-efficacy: Toward a unifying theory of behavioral change. *Psychological Review, 84,* 191–215.

Bandura, A. (1986). *Social foundations of thought and action: A social-cognitive theory.* Englewood, Cliffs, NJ: Prentice Hall.

Bandura, A., Ross, D., & Ross, S. A. (1961). Transmission of aggression through imitation of aggressive models. *Journal of Abnormal and Social Psychology, 63,* 575–582.

Bandura, A., Ross, D., & Ross, S. A. (1963). Imitation of film mediated aggressive models. *Journal of Abnormal and Social Psychology, 66,* 3–11.

Bányai, E. I., & Hilgard, E. R. (1976). A comparison of active-alert hypnotic induction with traditional relaxation induction. *Journal of Abnormal Psychology, 85,* 218–224.

Bar-On, R. (2004). The Bar-On Emotional Quotient Inventory (EQ-i): Rationale, description, and psychometric properties. In G. Geher (Ed.), *Measuring emotional intelligence: Common ground and controversy* (pp. 115–145). Hauppauge, NY: Nova Science.

Baral, B. D., & Das, J. P. (2003). Intelligence: What is indigenous to India and what is shared? In R. J. Sternberg (Ed.), *International handbook of intelligence* (pp. 270–301). Cambridge, England: Cambridge University Press.

Barber, T. X. (1969). *Hypnosis: A scientific approach.* New York, NY: Van Nostrand Reinhold.

Barbour, K. A., Houle, T. T., & Dubbert, P. M. (2003). Physical inactivity as a risk factor for chronic disease. In L. M. Cohen, D. E. McCargie, & F. L. Collins (Eds.), *The health psychology handbook* (pp. 146–168). Thousand Oaks, CA: Sage.

Barchas, P. (1986). A sociophysiological orientation to small groups. In E. Lawler (Ed.), *Advances in group processes* (Vol. 3, pp. 209–246). Greenwich, CT: JAI Press.

Bard, P. (1942). Neural mechanisms in emotional and sexual behavior. *Psychosomatic Medicine, 4,* 171–172.

Bargh, J. (2008). Free will is unnatural. In J. Baer, J. Kaufmann, and R. Baumeister (Eds), *Are we free: Psychology and free will* (pp. 128–154). New York, NY: Oxford University Press.

Bargh, J. A., & Chartrand, T. L. (1999). The unbearable automaticity of being. *American Psychologist, 54,* 462–479.

Bargh, J. A., & Pietromonaco, P. (1982). Automatic information processing and social perception: The influence of trait information presented outside of conscious awareness on impression formation. *Journal of Personality and Social Psychology, 43,* 437–449.

Bargh, J. A., Schwader, K. L., Hailey, S. E., Dyer, R. L., & Boothby, E. J. (2012). Automaticity in social-cognitive processes. *Trends in Cognitive Sciences, 16,* 593–605.

Barkley, R. A. (1997). *ADHD and the nature of self-control.* New York, NY: Guilford Press.

Barkley, R. A. (2006). *Attention-deficit-hyperactivity disorder: A handbook for diagnosis and treatment.* New York, NY: Guilford Press.

Barkow, J. H., Cosmides, L., & Tooby, J. (1992). *The adapted mind: Evolutionary psychology and the generation of culture.* New York, NY: Oxford University Press.

Barlett, C., & Coyne, S. M. (2014). A meta-analysis of sex differences in cyber-bullying behavior: The moderating role of age. *Aggressive Behavior, 40,* 474–488.

Barlow, D. (2004). Psychological treatments. *The American Psychologist, 59*(9), 869–78.

Barlow, D. H. (2000). Unraveling the mysteries of anxiety and its disorders from the perspective of emotion theory. *American Psychologist, 55,* 1247–1263.

Barlow, D. H. (2002). *Anxiety and its disorders: The nature and treatment of anxiety and panic.* New York, NY: Guilford Press.

Barlow, D. H. (2010). Negative effects from psychological treatment: A perspective. *American Psychologist, 65,* 13–20.

Barlow, D. H., Allen, L. B., & Choate, M. L. (2004). Toward a unified treatment for emotional disorders. *Behavior Therapy, 35*(2), 205–230.

Barlow, D. H., Farchione, T. J., Fairholme, C. P., Ellard, K. K., Boisseau, C. L., Allen, L. B., & May, J. T. E. (2010). *Unified protocol for transdiagnostic treatment of emotional disorders: Therapist guide.* New York, NY: Oxford University Press.

Barlow, D. M., Sakheim, D. K., and Beck, J. G. (1983). Anxiety increases sexual arousal. *Journal of Abnormal Psychology, 92,* 49–54.

Barnes, C. D., Brown, R. P., & Tamborski, M. (2012). Living dangerously: Culture of honor, risk-taking, and the non-randomness of 'accidental' deaths. *Social Psychological and Personality Science, 3,* 100–107.

Barnes, P. M., Bloom, B., & Nahin, R. (2008). CDC National Health Statistics Report #12. *Complementary and alternative medicine use among adults and children: United States, 2007.* Retrieved from http://www.ncbi.nlm.nih.gov/pubmed/19361005

Barnes, P. M., Powell-Griner, E., McFann, K., & Nahin, R. L. (2004). *Complementary and alternative medicine use among adults: United States, 2002.* CDC Advance Data Report #343.

Barnett, R. C., & Rivers, C. (2004, October 13). The persistence of gender myths in math. *Education Week, 24*(7), 39.

Baron-Cohen, S., Harrison, J., Goldstein, L. H., & Wyke, M. (1993). Coloured speech-perception: Is synaesthesia what happens when modularity breaks down? *Perception, 22,* 419–426.

Barrau-Alonso, V. M., Sendra-Lopez, J., Benítez-Álvarez, N., Vera-Barrios, E., Hernández-Dorta, A., Díaz-Marrero, G., ... & Gracia-Marco, R. (2013). 2179–Psychedelic drugs in psychotherapy. A revival?. *European Psychiatry, 28,* Supplement 1.

Barrick, M. R., & Mount, M. K. (1991). The Big Five personality dimensions and job performance: A meta-analysis. *Personnel Psychology, 44,* 1–26.

Barron, F. (1969). *Creative person and creative process.* New York, NY: Holt, Rinehart and Winston.

Barsalou, L. W. (2008). Cognitive and neural contributions to understanding the conceptual system. *Current Directions in Psychological Science, 17,* 91–95.

Bartels, A., & Zeki, S. (2006). The temporal order of binding visual attributes. *Vision Research, 46,* 2280–2286.

Bartels, J. M. (2015). The Stanford prison experiment in introductory psychology textbooks: A content analysis. *Psychology Learning & Teaching, 14,* 36–50.

Barth, J., Munder, T., Gerger, H., Nüesch, E., Trelle, S., Znoj, H., ... & Cuijpers, P. (2013). Comparative efficacy of seven psychotherapeutic interventions for patients with depression: A network meta-analysis. *PLoS Med, 10*(5), e1001454.

Bartholomew, R. E. (1994). The social psychology of "epidemic" koro. *International Journal of Social Psychiatry, 40,* 46–60.

Bartholomew, R. E., & Goode, E. (2000). Mass delusions and hysterias: Highlights from the past millennium. *Skeptical Inquirer, 24,* 20–28.

Bartholomew, R.E., & Hassall, P. (2015). *A colourful history of popular delusions.* Amherst, N.Y.: Prometheus Books.

Bartlett, T. (2013). Power of suggestion. *Chronicle Review.* Retrieved from http://chronicle.com/article/Power-of-Suggestion/136907

Bartley, J. (2009). Could glial activation be a factor in migraine? *Medical Hypotheses, 72,* 255–257.

Bartoli, E., & Gillem, A. R. (2008). Continuing to depolarize the debate on sexual orientation and religious identity and the therapeutic process. *Professional Psychology: Research and Practice, 39,* 202–209.

Bartone, P. T. (1999). Hardiness protects against war-related stress in army reserve forces. *Consulting Psychology Journal, 51,* 72–82.

Bartoshuk, L. M. (2004). Psychophysics: A journey from the laboratory to the clinic. *Appetite, 43,* 15–18.

Bartz, W. R. (2002, September/October). Teaching skepticism via the CRITIC acronym. *Skeptical Inquirer, 17,* 42–44.

Baruss, I., & Rabier, V. (2014). Failure to replicate retrocausal recall. *Psychology of Consciousness: Theory, Research, and Practice, 1*(1), 82–91.

Bashore, T. T., & Rapp, P. E. (1993). Are there alternatives to traditional polygraph procedures? *Psychological Bulletin, 113,* 2–22.

Basil, J. A., Kamil, A. C., Balda, R., & Fite, K. V. (1996). Differences in hippocampal volume among food storing corvids. *Brain Behavior and Evolution, 47,* 156–154.

Baskin T. W., Tierney S. C., Minami T., & Wampold B. E. (2003). Establishing specificity in psychotherapy: A meta-analysis of structural equivalence of placebo controls. *Journal of Clinical Psychology, 71,* 973–979.

Batson, C. D. (1987). Prosocial motivation: Is it ever truly altruistic? In L. Berkowitz (Ed.), *Advances in experimental social psychology* (Vol. 20, pp. 65–122). New York, NY: Academic Press.

Batson, C. D., & Shaw, L. (1991). Evidence for altruism: Toward a pluralism of prosocial motives. *Psychological Inquiry, 2,* 107–122.

Batson, C. D., & Ventis, W. L. (1982). *The religious experience: A social psychological perspective.* New York, NY: Oxford University Press.

Batson, C. D., Batson, J., Singlsby, J., Harrell, K., Peekna, H., & Todd, R. (1991). Empathic joy and the empathy-altruism hypothesis. *Journal of Personality and Social Psychology, 61,* 413–426.

Batson, C. D., Duncan, B. D., Ackerman, P., Buckley, T., & Birch, K. (1981). Is empathic emotion a source of altruistic motivation? *Journal of Personality and Social Psychology, 40,* 290–302.

Bauer, H. (1992). *Scientific literacy and the myth of the scientific method.* Urbana, IL: University of Illinois Press.

Bauer, P. J. (2006). Constructing a past in infancy: A neuro-developmental account. *Trends in Cognitive Sciences, 10,* 175–181.

Bauer, U. E., Briss, P. A., Goodman, R. A., & Bowman, B. A. (2014). Prevention of chronic disease in the 21st century: Elimination of the leading preventable causes of premature death and disability in the USA. *The Lancet, 384*(9937), 45–52.

Baugh, J. (2000). *Beyond Ebonics: Linguistic pride and racial prejudice.* New York, NY: Oxford University Press.

Baum, A., Cohen, L., & Hall, M. (1993). Control and intrusive memories as possible determinants of chronic stress. *Psychosomatic Medicine, 55,* 274–286.

Baum, H. S. (1987). *The invisible bureaucracy.* Oxford, England: Oxford University Press.

Baumeister R. F. (2008). Free will in scientific psychology. *Perspectives on Psychological Science, 3,* 14–19.

Baumeister, R. F. (Ed.). (2013). *Self-esteem: The puzzle of low self-regard.* New York, NY: Springer Science & Business Media.

Baumeister, R. F., & Leary, M. R. (1995). The need to belong: Desire for interpersonal attachments as a fundamental human motivation. *Psychological Bulletin, 117,* 497–529.

Baumeister, R. F., Campbell, J. D., Krueger, J. I., & Vohs, K. D. (2003). Does high self-esteem cause better performance, interpersonal success, happiness, or healthier lifestyles? *Psychological Science in the Public Interest, 4,* 1–44.

Baumeister, R. F., Catanese, K. R., & Vohs, K. D. (2001). Is there a gender difference in strength of sex drive? Theoretical views, conceptual distinctions, and a review of relevant evidence. *Personality and Social Psychology Review, 5,* 242–273.

Baumeister, R. F., Twenge, J. M., & Nuss, C. (2002). Effects of social exclusion on cognitive processes: Anticipated aloneness reduces intelligent thought. *Journal of Personality and Social Psychology, 83,* 817–827.

Baumrind, D. (1964). Some thoughts on ethics of research: After reading Milgram's "Behavioral study of obedience." *American Psychologist, 19,* 421–423.

Baumrind, D. (1971). Current patterns of parental authority. *Developmental Psychology Monographs, 4* (Pts. 1 & 2).

Baumrind, D. (1991). The influence of parenting style on adolescent competence and substance use. *Journal of Early Adolescence, 11,* 56–95.

Baumrind, D., Larzelere, R. E., & Cowan, P. A. (2002) Ordinary physical punishment: Is it harmful? Comment on Gershoff (2002). *Psychological Bulletin, 128,* 580–589.

Bausell, R. B. (2007). *The truth about complementary and alternative medicine.* Oxford, England: Oxford University Press.

Baxendale, S. (2004). Memories aren't made of this: Amnesia at the movies. *British Medical Journal, 18,* 1480–1483.

Bayard, M., Mcintyre, J., Hill, K. R., & Woodside, J. (2004). Alcohol withdrawal syndrome. *American Family Physician, 69,* 1442–1450.

Bayer, R. (1981). *Homosexuality and American psychiatry: The politics of diagnosis.* Princeton, NJ: Princeton University Press.

Bayer, R., & Spitzer, R. L. (1985). Neurosis, psychodynamics, and DSM-III: A history of the controversy. *Archives of General Psychiatry, 42,* 187–196.

Beall, A. T., & Tracy, J. L. (2013). Women are more likely to wear red or pink at peak fertility. *Psychological Science, 24*(9), 1837–1841.

Beaman, A., Barnes, P., Klentz, B., & McQuirk, B. (1978). Increasing helping rates through information dissemination: Teaching pays. *Personality and Social Psychology Bulletin, 4,* 406–411.

Beaman, C. P., Bridges, A. M., & Scott, S. K. (2007). From dichotic listening to the irrelevant sound effect: A behavioural and neuroimaging analysis of the processing of unattended speech. *Cortex, 43,* 124–134.

Beaton, A. A., Gruneberg, M. M., Hyde, C., Shufflebottom, A., & Sykes, R. N. (2005). Facilitation of receptive and productive foreign vocabulary learning using the keyword method: The role of image quality. *Memory, 13*(5), 458–471.

Beatty, J. (1982). Task-evoked pupillary responses, processing load, and the structure of processing resources. *Psychological Bulletin, 91,* 276–292.

Beauchaine, T. P., & Gatzke-Kopp, L. M. (2012). Instantiating the multiple levels of analysis perspective in a program of study on externalizing behavior. *Development and Psychopathology, 24,* 1003–1018. http://dx.doi.org/10.1017/S0954579412000508

Beauchamp, T. L., Ferdowsian, H. R., & Gluck, J. P. (2014). Rethinking the ethics of research involving nonhuman animals: introduction. *Theoretical Medicine and Bioethics, 35,* 91–96.

Beauregard, M., & Paquette, V. (2006). Neural correlates of a mystical experience in Carmelite nuns. *Neuroscience Letters, 405,* 186–190.

Bechtoldt, H., Norcross, J. C., Wyckoff, L. A., Pokrywa, M. L., & Campbell, L. F. (2001). Theoretical orientations and employment settings of clinical and counseling psychologists: A comparative study. *The Clinical Psychologist, 54,* 3–6.

Beck, A. T. (1967). *Depression: Clinical, experimental, and theoretical aspects* (Vol. 32). Philadelphia, PA: University of Pennsylvania Press.

Beck, A. T. (1976). *Cognitive therapy and the emotional disorders.* New York, NY: International Universities Press.

Beck, A. T. (1983). Treatment of depression. *New York Times Book Review, 88*(10), 35.

Beck, A. T. (1987) Cognitive models of depression. *Journal of Cognitive Psychotherapy, 1,* 5–37.

Beck, A. T. (2005). The current state of cognitive therapy: A 40-year retrospective. *Archives of General Psychiatry, 62,* 953–959.

Beck, A. T., (1964). Thinking and depression: 2. Theory and therapy. *Archives of General Psychiatry, 10,* 561–571.

Beck, A. T., & Dozois, D. J. (2011). Cognitive therapy: current status and future directions. *Annual Review of Medicine, 62,* 397–409.

Beck, A. T., Rush, A. J., Shaw, B. F., & Emery, G. (1979). *Cognitive therapy of depression.* New York, NY: Guilford Press.

Beck, H. P., Levinson, S., & Irons, G. (2009). A journey to John B. Watson's infant laboratory. *American Psychologist, 64,* 605–614.

Beck, J. G., Gudmundsdottir, B., Palyo, S. A., Miller, L. M., & Grant, D. M. (2006). Rebound effects following deliberate thought suppression: Does PTSD make a difference? *Behavior Therapy, 37,* 170–180.

Beck, J. S. (1995). *Cognitive therapy: Basics and beyond.* New York, NY: Guilford Press.

Beck, K., Javitt, D. C., & Howes, O. D. (2016). Targeting glutamate to treat schizophrenia: Lessons from recent clinical studies. *Psychopharmacology, 233,* 2425–2428.

Becker, A. E., Burwell, R. A., Gilman, S. E., Herzog, D. B., & Hamburg, P. (2002). Eating behaviors and attitudes following prolonged television exposure among ethnic Fijian adolescent girls. *British Journal of Psychiatry, 180,* 509–514.

Bedi, R. P., & Duff, C. T. (2014). Client as expert: A Delphi poll of clients' subjective experience of therapeutic alliance formation variables. *Counselling Psychology Quarterly, 27*(1), 1–18.

Bedny, M., Richardson, H., & Saxe, R. (2015). Visual cortex responds to spoken language in blind children. *Journal of Neuroscience, 35*(33), 11674–11681.

Beery, A. K. (2015). Antisocial oxytocin: Complex effects on social behavior. *Current Opinion in Behavioral Sciences, 6,* 174–182.

Begley, C. G., & Ioannidis, J. P. (2015). Reproducibility in science improving the standard for basic and preclinical research. *Circulation Research, 116,* 116–126.

Begley, S., & Kasindorf, M. (1979, December 3). Twins: Nazi and Jew. *Newsweek,* 139.

Bègue, L., & Subra, B. (2008). Alcohol and aggression: Perspectives on controlled and uncontrolled social information processing. *Social and Personality Psychology Compass, 2,* 511–538.

Bègue, L., Beauvois, J. L., Courbet, D., Oberlé, D., Lepage, J., & Duke, A. A. (2015). Personality predicts obedience in a Milgram paradigm. *Journal of Personality, 83,* 299–306.

Beier, M. E., & Ackerman, P. L. (2001). Current events knowledge in adults: An investigation of age, intelligence and non-ability determinants. *Psychology and Aging, 16,* 615–628.

Beilock, S. L. (2008). Math performance in stressful situations. *Current Directions in Psychological Science, 17,* 339–343.

Beilock, S. L., & Carr, T. H. (2005). When high-powered people fail: Working memory and "choking under pressure" in math. *Psychological Science, 16,* 101–105.

Beisteiner, R., Windischberger, C., Geißler, A., Gartus, A., Uhl, F., Moser, E., … Lanzenberger, R. (2015). FMRI correlates of different components of Braille reading by the blind. *Neurology, Psychiatry and Brain Research, 21*(4), 137–145.

Békésy, G. (1949). On the resonance curve and the decay period at different points along the cochlear partition. *Journal of the Acoustical Society of America, 21,* 245–254.

Bekinschtein, T. A., Shalom, D. E., Forcato, C., Herrera, M., Coleman, M. R., Manes, F. F., & Sigman, M. (2009). Classical conditioning in the vegetative and minimally conscious state. *Nature Neuroscience, 12,* 1343–1349.

Bell, A., P., & Weinberg, M. S. (1978). *Homosexualities: A study of diversity among men and women.* New York, NY: Simon & Schuster.

Bell, R. (1968). A reinterpretation of the direction of effects in studies of socialization. *Psychological Review, 75,* 81–95.

Bellamy, C. (1998). *The state of the world's children 1998.* New York, NY: Oxford University Press.

Bellezza, F. S. (1999). Mnemonic devices. In A. E. Kazdin (Ed.), *Encyclopedia of psychology.* Washington, DC: American Psychological Association.

Belli, R. F., Winkielman, P., Read, J. D., Schwarz, N., & Lynn, S. J. (1998). Recalling more childhood events leads to judgments of poorer memory: Implications for the recovered/false memory debate. *Psychonomic Bulletin & Review, 5,* 318–323.

Belliveau, F., & Richter, L. (1970). *Understanding human sexual inadequacy.* New York, NY: Bantam.

Bellon, A. (2006). Searching for new options for treating insomnia: Are melatonin and ramelteon beneficial? *Journal of Psychiatric Practice, 12,* 229–243.

Belonax Jr, J. J., & Bellizzi, J. A. (2015). Demand characteristics as determinants of behavior: An unconscious effect. In V. V. Beller, Th. R. Baird, P. T. Hertz, R. L. Jenkins, J. D. Linquist & S. W. Miller (Eds.), *The 1980's: A Decade of Marketing Challenges* (pp. 20–23). New York: Springer International Publishing.

Belsky, J. (1988). The "effects" of infant day care reconsidered. *Early Childhood Research Quarterly, 3,* 235–272.

Belsky, J., & Kelly, J. (1994). *The transition to parenthood.* New York, NY: Delacourte.

Bem, D. J. (1967). Self-perception: An alternative interpretation of cognitive dissonance phenomena. *Psychological Review, 74,* 183–200.

Bem, D. J. (1996). Exotic becomes erotic: A developmental theory of sexual orientation. *Psychological Review, 103,* 320–335.

Bem, D. J. (2011). Feeling the future: Experimental evidence for anomalous retroactive influences on cognition and affect. *Journal of Personality and Social Psychology, 100,* 407–425.

Bem, D. J., & Allen, A. (1974). On predicting some of the people some of the time: The search for cross-situational consistencies in behavior. *Psychological Review, 81,* 506–520.

Bem, D. J., & Funder, D. C. (1978). Predicting more of the people more of the time: Assessing the personality of situations. *Psychological Review, 85,* 485–500.

Bem, D. J., & Honorton, C. (1994). Does psi exist? Replicable evidence for an anomalous process of information transfer. *Psychological Bulletin, 115,* 4–18.

Bem, D. J., & McConnell, H. K. (1970). Testing the self-perception explanation of dissonance phenomena: On the salience of premanipulation attitudes. *Journal of Personality and Social Psychology, 14,* 23–31.

Bem, D., Tressoldi, P., Rabeyron, T., & Duggan, M. (2015). Feeling the future: A meta-analysis of 90 experiments on the anomalous anticipation of random future events. *F1000Research, 4,* 1188. doi: 10.12688/f1000research.7177.2

Ben-Porath, Y., & Tellegen, A. (2008). Empirical correlates of the MMPI-2 restructured clinical (RC) scales in mental health, forensic, and nonclinical settings: An introduction. *Journal of Personality Assessment, 90,* 119–121. http://dx.doi .org/10.1080/00223890701845120

Ben-Shakhar, G. (2011). Countermeasures. In B. Verschuere, G. Ben-Shakhar, E. Meijer (Eds.), *Memory detection: Theory and application of the concealed information test,* (pp. 200–214). Cambridge, England: Cambridge University Press.

Ben-Shakhar, G., & Elaad, E. (2003). The validity of psychophysiological detection of information with the Guilty Knowledge Test: A meta-analytic review. *Journal of Applied Psychology, 88,* 131–151.

Ben-Shakhar, G., Bar-Hillel, M., Bilu, Y., Ben-Abba, E., & Flug, A. (1986). Can graphology predict occupational success? Two empirical studies and some methodological ruminations. *Journal of Applied Psychology, 71,* 645–653.

Benasich, A. A., & Bejar, I. I. (1992). The Fagan Test of Infant Intelligence: A critical review. *Journal of Applied Developmental Psychology, 13,* 153–171.

Benassi, V. A., Sweeney, P. D., & Dufour, C. L. (1988). Is there a relation between locus of control orientation and depression? *Journal of Abnormal Psychology, 8,* 357–367.

Benavides-Varela, S., & Mehler, J. (2015). Verbal positional memory in 7-month-olds. *Child Development, 86*(1), 209–223.

Benbow, C. P., & Stanley, J. C. (1980). Sex differences in mathematical ability: Fact or artifact? *Science, 210,* 1262–1264.

Bender, D. A. (2008). What we don't know that we need to know. *Healthwatch. Newsletter, 71,* 4–5.

Benedetti, F. (2013). 2996–What is the placebo effect in psychiatry? *European Psychiatry, 28,* 1.

Benedetti, F., Lanotte, M., Lopiano, L., & Colloca, L. (2007). When words are painful: Unraveling the mechanisms of the nocebo effect. *Neuroscience, 147,* 260–271.

Benedetti, F., Lanotte, M., Lopiano, L., & Colloca, L. (2007). When words are painful: unraveling the mechanisms of the nocebo effect. *Neuroscience, 147,* 260–271.

Benish, S. G., Quintana, S., & Wampold, B. E. (2011). Culturally adapted psychotherapy and the legitimacy of myth: A direct-comparison meta-analysis. *Journal of Counseling Psychology, 58*(3), 279–289.

Benjamin, L. T., & Baker, D. B. (2004). *From séance to science: A history of the profession of psychology in America.* Belmont, CA: Wadsworth.

Bennett, C. M., Baird, A. A., Miller, M. B., & Wolford, G. L. (2009, June). *Neural correlates of interspecies perspective taking in the post-mortem Atlantic Salmon: An argument for multiple comparisons correction.* Poster presented at the 15th Annual Meeting of the Organization for Human Brain Mapping, San Francisco, CA.

Bennett, M. R. (1998). Monoaminergic synapses and schizophrenia: 45 years of neuroleptics. *Journal of Psychopharmacology, 12,* 289–304.

Benson, E. (2006, June). All that's gold doesn't glitter: How the Golden Fleece tarnished psychological science. *APS Observer.* Retrieved from http://www .psychologicalscience.org/index.php/publications/observer

Bent, S. (2008). Herbal medicine in the United States: Review of efficacy, safety, and regulation: Grand rounds at University of California, San Francisco Medical Center. *Journal of General Internal Medicine, 23,* 854–859.

Bentall, R. P. (2014). Hallucinatory experiences. In E. Cardeña, S. J. Lynn, & S. Krippner (Eds.), *Varieties of anomalous experiences* (2nd ed., 109–144). Washington, DC: American Psychological Association.

Bentley, K. J., & Walsh, J. (2006). *The social worker and psychotropic medication: Toward effective collaboration with mental health clients, families, and providers* (3rd ed.). Belmont, CA: Thompson.

Berenbaum, H. (2013). Classification and psychopathology research. *Journal of Abnormal Psychology, 122*(3), 894–901.

Berenbaum, S. A., & Hines, M. (1992). Early androgens are related to childhood sex-typed toy preference. *Psychological Science, 3,* 203–206.

Berg, J. H., & Archer, R. L. (1980). Disclosure or concern: A second look at liking for the norm breaker. *Journal of Personality, 48,* 245–257.

Berg, K. C., Crosby, R. D., Cao, L., Peterson, C. B., Engel, S. G., Mitchell, J. E., & Wonderlich, S. A. (2013). Facets of negative affect prior to and following binge-only, purge-only, and binge/purge events in women with bulimia nervosa. *Journal of Abnormal Psychology, 122*(1), 111.

Berger, H. (1929). Ueber das Elektroenkephalogramm des Menschen. *Archiv für Psychiatrie und Nervenkrankheiten, 87,* 527–570.

Berger, M., & Sarnyai, Z. (2015). "More than skin deep": Stress neurobiology and mental health consequences of racial discrimination. *Stress, 18*(1), 1–10.

Bergner, R. M. (1997). What is psychopathology? And so what? *Clinical Psychology: Science and Practice, 4,* 235–248.

Bergstrom, S. R. (1968). Acquisition of an avoidance reaction to the light in the protozoa tetrahymena. *Scandinavian Journal of Psychology, 9,* 220–224.

Berk, A. M., Vigorito, M., & Miller, R. R. (1979). Retroactive stimulus interference with conditioned emotional response retention in infant and adult rats: Implications for infantile amnesia. *Journal of Experimental Psychology: Animal Behavior Processes, 3,* 284–299.

Berk, M. S., & Andersen, S. M. (2000). The impact of past relationships on interpersonal behavior: Behavioral confirmation in the social-cognitive process of transference. *Journal of Personality and Social Psychology, 79,* 546–562.

Berkman, L. F., & Syme, S. L. (1979). Social networks, host resistance, and mortality: A nine year follow-up study of Alameda County residents. *American Journal of Epidemiology, 109,* 186–204.

Berkowitz, L. (1989). Frustration-aggression hypothesis: Examination and reformulation. *Psychological Bulletin, 106,* 59–73.

Berkowitz, L., & LePage, A. (1967). Weapons as aggression-eliciting stimuli. *Journal of Personality and Social Psychology, 7,* 202–207.

Berkun, M. M., Bialek, H. M., Kern, R. P., & Yagi, K. (1962). Experimental studies of psychological stress in man. *Psychological Monographs: General and Applied, 76,* 1–39.

Berlant, N. E., & Pruitt, S. D. (2003). Adherence to medical recommendations. In L. M. Cohen, D. E. McChargue, & F. L. Collins (Eds.), *The health psychology handbook* (pp. 208–224). Thousand Oaks, CA: Sage Publications.

Berlin, L. J., Ispa, J. M., Fine, M. A., Malone, P. S., Brooks-Gunn, J., Brady-Smith, C., … Bai, Y. (2009). Correlates and consequences of spanking and verbal punishment for low-income White, African American, and Mexican American toddlers. *Child Development, 80,* 1403–1420.

Berlyne, D. E. (1960). *Conflict, arousal, and curiosity.* New York, NY: McGraw-Hill.

Berman, J. D., & Straus, S. E. (2004). Implementing a research agenda for complementary and alternative medicine. *Annual Review of Medicine, 55,* 239–254.

Bernhardt, P. C., Dabbs, J. M., Fielden, J. A., & Lutter, C. D. (1998). Testosterone changes during vicarious experiences of winning and losing among fans at sporting events. *Physiology and Behavior, 65,* 59–62.

Berns, G. S., Chappelow, J., Zink, C. F., Pagnoni, G., Martin-Skurski, M. E., & Richards, J. (2005). Neurobiological correlates of social conformity and independence during mental rotation. *Biological Psychiatry, 58,* 245–253.

Bernstein, D. A., Borkovec, T. D., & Hazlett-Stevens, H. (2000). *New directions in progressive relaxation training: A guidebook for helping professionals.* Westport, CT: Praeger.

Bernstein, D. M., Laney, C., Morris, E. K., & Loftus, E. F. (2005). False memories about food can lead to food avoidance. *Social Cognition, 23,* 11–34.

Berntsen, D., Johannessen, K. B., Thomsen, Y. D., Bertelsen, M., Hoyle, R. H., & Rubin, D. C. (2012). Peace and war: Trajectories of posttraumatic stress disorder symptoms before, during, and after military deployment in Afghanistan. *Psychological Science, 23*(12), 1557–1565.

Berridge, C. W., & Arnsten, A. F. (2013). Psychostimulants and motivated behavior: arousal and cognition. *Neuroscience & Biobehavioral Reviews, 37*(9), 1976–1984.

Berry, C. M., Sackett, P. R., & Wiemann, S. A. (2007). A review of recent developments in integrity test research. *Personnel Psychology, 60,* 270–301.

Bersani, G., Clemente, R., Gherardelli, S., Bersani, F. S., & Manuali, G. (2012). Obstetric complications and neurological soft signs in male patients with schizophrenia. *Acta Neuropsychiatrica, 24*(6), 344–48.

Berscheid, E., & Reis, H. T. (1998). Attraction and close relationships. In D. Gilbert, S. Fiske, & G. Lindzey (Eds.), *The handbook of social psychology* (Vol. 2, 4th ed., pp. 193–281). New York, NY: McGraw-Hill.

Berzon, A. (2009, December 5). The gambler who blew $127 million. *Wall Street Journal.*

Besnard, P., Passilly-Degrace, P., & Khan, N. A. (2016). Taste of fat: a sixth taste modality? *Physiological Reviews, 96*(1), 151–176.

Beunen, G., & Malina, R. M. (1996). *The child and adolescent athlete.* Oxford, England: Blackwell.

Beutler, L. E. (2002). The dodo bird is extinct. *Clinical Psychology: Science and Practice, 9,* 30–34.

Beutler, L. E., & Harwood, T. M. (2002). What is and can be attributed to the therapeutic relationship. *Journal of Contemporary Psychotherapy, 32,* 25–33.

Beutler, L. E., Clarkin, J. F., & Bongar, B. (2000). *Guidelines for the systematic treatment of the depressed person.* Oxford, England: Oxford University Press.

Beutler, L. E., Machado, P. P., & Neufeldt, S. A. (1994). Therapist variables. In A. E. Bergin & S. L. Garfield (Eds.), *Handbook of psychotherapy and behavior change* (4th ed., pp. 259–260). New York, NY: Wiley.

Beyerstein, B. (1996). Graphology. In G. Stein (Ed.), *The encyclopedia of the paranormal* (pp. 309–324). Buffalo, NY: Prometheus.

Beyerstein, B. L. (1997, September/October). Why bogus therapies seem to work. *Skeptical Inquirer, 21,* 29–34.

Beyerstein, B. L. (1999). Whence cometh the myth that we only use ten percent of our brains? In S. Della Sala (Ed.), *Mind myths: Exploring everyday mysteries of the mind and brain* (pp. 1–24). Chichester, England: Wiley.

Beyerstein, B. L., & Beyerstein, D. F. (1992). *The write stuff: Evaluations of graphology—The study of handwriting analysis*. Buffalo, NY: Prometheus.

Beyerstein, B., & Hadaway, P. (1991). On avoiding folly. *Journal of Drug Issues, 20*, 689–700.

Bezdjian, S., Baker, L. A., & Tuvblad, C. (2011). Genetic and environmental influences on impulsivity: A meta-analysis of twin, family and adoption studies. *Clinical Psychology Review, 31*, 1209–1223. http://dx.doi.org/10.1016/j.cpr.2011.07.005

Bialystok, E. (1988). Levels of bilingualism and levels of linguistic awareness. *Developmental Psychology, 24*, 560–567.

Bialystok, E., Craik, F. I. M., & Luk, G. (2012). Bilingualism: Consequences for mind and brain. *Trends in Cognitive Sciences, 16*, 240–250.

Biasi, E., Silvotti, L., & Tirindelli, R. (2001). Pheromone detection in rodents. *Neuroreport, 12*, A81–A84.

Biederman, I., Cooper, E. E., Fox, P. W., & Mahadevan, R. S. (1992). Unexceptional spatial memory in an exceptional memorist. *Journal of Experimental Psychology: Learning, Memory, and Cognition, 18*, 654–657.

Biederman, J., Hirshfeld-Becker, D. R., Rosenbaum, J. F., Herot, C., Friedman, D., Snidman, N., … Faraone, S. V. (2001). Further evidence of association between behavioral inhibition and social anxiety in children. *American Journal of Psychiatry, 158*, 1673–1679.

Biegler, P., & Vargas, P. (2013). Ban the sunset? Nonpropositional content and regulation of pharmaceutical advertising. *American Journal of Bioethics, 13*, 3–13.

Bierbrauer, G. (1973). *Effect of set, perspective, and temporal factors in attribution*. Unpublished doctoral dissertation, Stanford University, Palo Alto, CA.

Biernbaum, M. A., & Ruscio, M. (2004). Differences between matched heterosexual and non-heterosexual college students on measures of defense mechanisms and psychopathological symptoms. *Journal of Homosexuality, 48*, 125–141.

Bigbee, J. (1990). Stressful life events and illness occurrence in rural versus urban women. *Journal of Community Health Nursing, 7*, 105–113.

Bikel, O. (Producer). (1995, April 11). *Frontline* [Television broadcast: "Divided Memories"]. New York, NY: Public Broadcasting Service.

Binet, A., & Simon, T. A. (1905). Méthode nouvelle pour le diagnostic du niveau intellectuel des anormaux. *L'Année Psychologique, 11*, 191–244.

Bink, M. L., & Marsh, R. L. (2000). Cognitive regularities in creative activity. *Review of General Psychology, 4*, 59–78.

Binkley, C. J., Beacham, A., Neace, W., Gregg, R. G., Liem, E. B., & Sessler, D. I. (2009). Genetic variations associated with red hair color and fear of dental pain, anxiety regarding dental care and avoidance of dental care. *Journal of the American Dental Association, 140*(7), 896–905.

Birch, S. A. J., & Bloom, P. (2003). Children are cursed: An asymmetric bias in mental state attribution. *Psychological Science, 14*, 283–286.

Birch, S. A. J., & Bloom, P. (2007). The curse of knowledge in reasoning about false beliefs. *Psychological Science, 18*, 382–386.

Birkley, E. L., Giancola, P. R., & Lance, C. E. (2012). Psychopathy and the prediction of alcohol-related physical aggression: The roles of impulsive antisociality and fearless dominance. *Drug and Alcohol Dependence, 128*, 58–63.

Birks, J. (2012). Cholinesterase inhibitors for Alzheimer's disease. *Cochrane Library*. Retrieved from http://onlinelibrary.wiley.com/doi/10.1002/14651858.CD005593/pdf/standard

Birmingham, C. L., Su, J., Hlynsky, J. A., Goldner, E. M., & Gao, M. (2005). The mortality rate from anorexia nervosa. *International Journal of Eating Disorders, 38*, 143–146.

Birnbaum, G., Glaubman, H., & Mikulincer, M. (2001). Women's experience of heterosexual intercourse—Scale construction, factor structure, and relations to orgasmic disorder. *Journal of Sex Research, 38*, 191–204.

Birren, J. E., & Renner, V. J. (1977). Research on the psychology of aging: Principles and experimentation. In J. E. Birren & K. W. Schaie (Eds.), *Handbook of the psychology of aging* (pp. 3–38). New York, NY: Van Nostrand Reinhold.

Bishop, G. F., Oldendick, R. W., & Tuchfarber, A. J. (1986). Opinions on fictitious issues: The pressure to answer survey questions. *Public Opinion Quarterly, 50*, 240–250.

Black, L. I., Clarke, T. C., Barnes, P. M., Stussman, B. J., & Nahin, R. L. (2015). Use of complementary health approaches among children aged 4–17 years in the United States: National Health Interview Survey, 2007–2012. *National Health Statistics Reports*, (78), 1–19.

Black, S. M., & Hill, C. E. (1984). The psychological well-being of women in their middle years. *Psychology of Women Quarterly, 8*, 282–292.

Blackmore, S. (1984). Accounting for out-of-body experiences. *Bulletin of the British Psychological Society, 37*, A53.

Blackmore, S. (1986). Out-of-body experiences in schizophrenia: A questionnaire surevey. *Journal of Nervous and Mental Disease, 174*, 615–619.

Blackmore, S. (1991). Lucid dreaming: Awake in your sleep? *Skeptical Inquirer, 15*, 362–370.

Blackmore, S. (1993). *Dying to live: Near-death experiences*. Buffalo, NY: Prometheus.

Blackmore, S. (2004). *Consciousness: An introduction*. New York, NY: Oxford University Press.

Blackmore, S. J. (1983). Divination with tarot cards: An empirical study. *Journal of the Society for Psychical Research, 52*, 97–101.

Blackwell, D. L., Lucas, J. W., & Clarke, T. C. (2014). Summary health statistics for US adults: national health interview survey, 2012. *Vital and health statistics. Series 10, Data from the National Health Survey*, (260), 1–161.

Blagys, M. D., & Hilsenroth, M. J. (2000). Distinctive features of short-term psychodynamic-interpersonal psychotherapy: A review of the comparative psychotherapy process literature. *Clinical Psychology-Science and Practice, 7*, 167–188.

Blair, C. (2006). How similar are fluid cognition and general intelligence? A developmental neuroscience perspective on fluid cognition as an aspect of human cognitive ability. *Behavioral and Brain Sciences, 29*, 109–160.

Blair, C., Gamson, D., Thorne, S., & Baker, D. (2005). Rising mean IQ: Cognitive demand of mathematics education for young children, population exposure to formal schooling, and the neurobiology of the prefrontal cortex. *Intelligence, 33*(1), 93–106. http://dx.doi.org/10.1016/j.intell.2004.07.008

Blair, L. (2013). *Birth order: What your position in the family really tells you about your character* (2nd ed.). London, England: Piatkus Books.

Blair, S. N., Kohl, H. W., Gordon, N. F., & Paffenberger, R. S. (1992). How much physical activity is good for health? *Annual Review of Public Health, 13*, 99–126.

Blanchard, R. (2008). Review and theory of handedness, birth order, and homosexuality in men. *Laterality: Asymmetries of Body, Brain, and Cognition, 13*, 51–70.

Blanchard, R., & Bogaert, A. F. (1996). Homosexuality in men and number of older brothers. *American Journal of Psychiatry, 153*, 27–31.

Blanchette, I., & Richards, A. (2003). Anxiety and the interpretation of ambiguous stimuli: Beyond the emotion-congruent effect. *Journal of Experimental Psychology: General, 13*, 294–309.

Blanchette, M. A., Stochkendahl, M. J., Da Silva, R. B., Boruff, J., Harrison, P., & Bussières, A. (2016). Effectiveness and economic evaluation of chiropractic care for the treatment of low back pain: A systematic review of pragmatic studies. *PloS One, 11*(8), e0160037.

Blaney, P. H. (1975). Implications of the medical model and its alternatives. *American Journal of Psychiatry, 132*, 911–914.

Blanke, O., & Dieguez, S. (2009). Leaving body and life behind: Out-of-body and near death experience. In S. Laureys (Ed.), *The neurology of consciousness* (pp. 303–325). Amsterdam, Netherlands: Elsevier.

Blanton, H., & Jaccard, J. (2008). Representing versus generalizing: Two approaches to external validity and their implications for the study of prejudice. *Psychological Inquiry, 19*, 99–105.

Blanton, H., & Jaccard, J. (2015). Not so fast: Ten challenges to importing implicit attitude measures to media psychology. *Media Psychology, 18*, 338–369.

Blanton, H., Klick, J., Mitchell, G., Jaccard, J., Mellers, B., & Tetlock, P. E. (2009). Strong claims and weak evidence: Reassessing the predictive validity of the IAT. *Journal of Applied Psychology, 94*(3), 567–582.

Blasco-Fontecilla, H., Delgado-Gomez, D., Legido-Gil, T., de Leon, J., Perez-Rodriguez, M. M., & Baca-Garcia, E. (2012). Can the Holmes-Rahe Social Readjustment Rating Scale (SRRS) be used as a suicide risk scale? An exploratory study. *Archives of Suicide Research, 16*(1), 13–28.

Blasi, A. (1980). Bridging moral cognition and moral action: A critical review of the literature. *Psychological Bulletin, 88*, 593–637.

Blass, T. (1999). The Milgram paradigm after 35 years. *Journal of Applied Social Psychology, 29*, 955–978.

Blass, T. (2004). *The man who shocked the world: The life and legacy of Stanley Milgram*. New York, NY: Perseus.

Blatt, S. J. (1974). Levels of object representation in anaclitic and introjective depression. *Psychoanalytic Studies of the Child, 29*, 107–157.

Blatt, S. J., Sanislow, C. A., Zuroff, D. C., & Pilkonis, P. A. (1996). Characteristics of effective therapists: Further analyses of data from the NIMH. *TDCRP, Journal of Consulting and Clinical Psychology, 64*, 1276–1284.

Blay, S. L., Andreoli, S. B., & Gastal, F. L. (2008). Prevalence of self-reported sleep disturbance among older adults and the association of sleep with service demand and medical conditions. *International Psychogeriatrics, 20*, 582–595.

Bleuler, E. (1911/1915). *Dementia praecox or the group of schizophrenias*. New York, NY: International Universities Press.

Bliss, T., Collingridge, G., & Morris, R. (2004). Long-term potentiation: Enhancing neuroscience for 30 years. Oxford, England: Oxford University Press.

Block, J. (1976). Issues, problems and pitfalls in assessing sex differences: A critical review of "The Psychology of Sex Differences." *Merrill Palmer Quarterly, 22*, 283–340.

Block, J. (1995). A contrarian view of the five-factor approach to personality description. *Psychological Bulletin, 117*, 187–215.

Block, J. (2006). In whom should Americans trust? Jeff Block's personal idea fountain. Retrieved from http://jeffblock.wordpress.com/?s=in+whom+should+americans+trust&searchbutton=go%21

Block, J. H., Block, J., & Gjerde, P. F. (1986). The personality of children prior to divorce: A prospective study. *Child Development, 57*, 827–840.

Block, J., & Block, J. H. (2006). Venturing a 30-year longitudinal study. *American Psychologist, 61*, 315–327.

Block, N. (1995). How heritability misleads about race. *Cognition, 56*, 99–128.

Blodgett, H. C. (1929). The effect of the introduction of reward upon the maze performance of rats. *University of California Publications in Psychology, 4*, 113–134.

Blom, R. M., Hennekam, R. C., & Denys, D. (2012). Body integrity identity disorder. *PloS one, 7*(4), e34702.

Blood, A. J., & Zatorre, R. J. (2001). Intensely pleasurable responses to music correlate with activity in brain regions implicated in reward and emotion. *Proceedings of the National Academy of Sciences, 98*, 11818–11823.

Frick, P. J., & Marsee, M. A. (2006). Psychopathy and developmental pathways to anti-social behavior in youth. In C. J. Patrick (Ed.), *Handbook of psychopathy* (pp. 353–374). New York, NY: Guilford Press.

Frick, P. J., & White, S. F. (2008). Research review: The importance of callous-unemotional traits for developmental models of aggressive and antisocial behavior. *Journal of Child Psychology and Psychiatry, 49*, 359–75.

Frick, P. J., Ray, J. V., Thornton, L. C., & Kahn, R. E. (2014). Can callous-unemotional traits enhance the understanding, diagnosis, and treatment of serious conduct problems in children and adolescents? A comprehensive review. *Psychological Bulletin, 140*, 1–57.

Friedkin, N. E. (2010). The attitude-behavior linkage in behavioral cascades. *Social Psychology Quarterly, 73*, 196–213.

Friedman, M., & Rosenman, R. H. (1959). Association of a specific overt behavior pattern with increases in blood cholesterol, blood clotting time, incidence of arcus senilis and clinical coronary artery disease. *Journal of the American Medical Association, 169*, 1286–1296.

Friedman, M., & Rosenman, R. H. (1974). *Type A behavior and your heart.* New York, NY: Alfred A. Knopf.

Friedman, R. A. (2006). Mental illness and violence: How strong is the link? *New England Journal of Medicine, 355*, 2064–2066.

Friedman, R. A. (2014). Antidepressants; black-box warning—10 years later. *New England Journal of Medicine, 371*(18), 1666–1668.

Friesen, W. V. (1972). *Cultural differences in facial expressions in a social situation: An experimental test of the concept of display rules.* Unpublished doctoral dissertation, University of California, San Francisco, CA.

Frieze, I. H., Peterson, J. E., Johnson, P. B., Ruble, D. N., & Zellman, G. (1978). *Women and sex roles: A social psychological perspective.* New York, NY: Norton.

Frijda, N. H. (1986). *The emotions.* Cambridge, England: Cambridge University.

Frisher M., Crome, I., Martino, O., & Croft, P. (2009). Assessing the impact of cannabis use on trends in diagnosed schizophrenia in the United Kingdom from 1996 to 2005. *Schizophrenia Research, 113*, 123–128.

Frisina, P. G., Borod, J. C., & Lepore, S. J. (2004). A meta-analysis of the effects of written disclosure on the health outcomes of clinical populations. *Journal of Nervous and Mental Disease, 192*, 629–634.

Fritch, J. W., & Cromwell, R. L. (2001). Evaluating Internet resources: Identity, affiliation, and cognitive authority in a networked world. *Journal of the American Society for Information science and Technology, 52*, 499–507.

Frith, C. D. (1992). *The cognitive neuropsychology of schizophrenia.* Hillsdale, NJ: Erlbaum.

Frontera, W. R., Meredith, C. N., O'Reilly, K. P., Knuttgen, H. H., & Evans, W. J. (1988). Strength conditioning in older men: Skeletal muscle hypertrophy and improved function. *Journal of Applied Physiology, 64*, 1038–1044.

Frontline (1995). *Divided memories* [Video]. Retrieved from http://www.youtube.com/watch?v=VWoxGEr0nmw

Frost, R. O., & Gross, R. C. (1993). The hoarding of possessions. *Behavioural Research and Therapy, 31*(4), 367–381.

Frost, R., Steketee, G., Tolin, D., & Brown, T. (2006). Diagnostic issues in compulsive hoarding. Paris: Paper presented at the European Association of Behavioural and Cognitive Therapies.

Fu, K. M., Johnston, T. A., Shah, A. S., Arnold, L., Smiley, J., Hackett, T. A., … Schroeder, C. E. (2003). Auditory cortical neurons respond to somatosensory stimulation. *Journal of Neuroscience, 23*, 7510–7515.

Fuhriman, A., & Burlingame, G. M. (1994). Group psychotherapy: Research and practice. In A. Fuhriman & G. M. Burlingame (Eds.), *Handbook of group psychotherapy: An empirical and clinical synthesis* (pp. 3–40). New York, NY: Wiley.

Fukuda, H., & Takahashi, J. (2005). Embryonic stem cells as a cell source for treating Parkinson's disease. *Expert Opinion on Biological Therapy, 5*, 1273–1280.

Fukuda, K., Ogilvie, R., Chilcott, L., Venditteli, A., & Takeuchi, T. (1998). High prevalence of sleep paralysis in Canadian and Japanese college students. *Dreaming, 8*, 59–66.

Fullana, M. A., Mataix-Cols, D., Caspi, A., Harrington, H., Grisham, J. R., Moffitt, T. E., & Poulton, R. (2009). Obsessions and compulsions in the community: Prevalence, interference, help seeking, developmental stability, and co-occurring psychiatric conditions. *The American Journal of Psychiatry, 166*, 329–336.

Fuller, R. L., Luck, S. J., Braun, E. L., Robinson, B. M., McMahon, R. P., & Gold, J. M. (2006). Impaired control of visual attention in schizophrenia. *Journal of Abnormal Psychology, 115*, 266–275.

Fulton, M. M., & Allen, E. R. (2005). Polypharmacy in the elderly: A literature review. *Journal of the American Academy of Nurse Practitioners, 17*, 123–132.

Funder, D. C. (1991). Global traits: A neo-Allportian approach to personality. *Psychological Science, 2*, 31–39.

Furnham, A. (2016). *All in the mind: Psychology for the curious.* New York, NY: John Wiley & Sons.

Furnham, A., & Cheng, H. (2000). Perceived parental behavior, self-esteem and happiness. *Social Psychiatry and Psychiatric Epidemiology, 35*, 463–470.

Furnham, A., & Fudge, C. (2008). The Five Factor model of personality and sales performance. *Journal of Individual Differences, 29*, 11–16.

Furnham, A., Batey, M., Anand, K., & Manfield, J. (2008). Personality, hypomania, intelligence and creativity. *Personality and Individual Differences, 44*, 1060–1069.

Furnham, A., Petrides, K. V., & Constantinides, A. (2005). The effects of body mass index and waist-to-hip ratio on ratings of female attractiveness, fecundity, and health. *Personality and Individual Differences, 38*, 1823–1834.

Furnham, A., Zhang, J., & Chamorro-Premuzic, T. (2006) The relationship between psychometric and self-estimated intelligence, creativity, personality and academic achievement. *Imagination, Cognition and Personality, 25*, 119–145.

Fuster, J. M. (2000). Executive frontal functions. *Experimental Brain Research, 133*, 66–70.

Gage, F. H. (2002). Neurogenesis in the adult brain. *Journal of Neuroscience, 22*, 612–613.

Gailliot, M. T., Peruche, B. M., Plant., E. A., & Baumeister, R. F. (2009). Stereotypes and prejudice in the blood: Sucrose drinks reduce prejudice and stereotyping. *Journal of Experimental Social Psychology, 45*, 288–290.

Galak, J., LeBoeuf, R. A., Nelson, L. D., & Simmons, J. P. (2012). Correcting the past: Failures to replicate psi. *Journal of Personality and Social Psychology, 103*, 933–948.

Galambos, S. J., & Hakuta, K. (1988). Subject-specific and task-specific characteristics of metalinguistic awareness in bilingual children. *Applied Psycholinguistics, 9*, 141–162.

Galanter, M. (1980). Psychological induction into the large group: Findings from a modern religious sect. *American Journal of Psychiatry, 137*, 1574–1579.

Galanter, M., Dermatis, H., & Santucci, C. (2012). Young people in Alcoholics Anonymous: The role of spiritual orientation and AA member affiliation. *Journal of Addictive Diseases, 31*(2), 173–182.

Galatzer-Levy, I. R., & Bonanno, G. A. (2014). Optimism and death predicting the course and consequences of depression trajectories in response to heart attack. *Psychological Science, 25*(12), 2177–2188.

Galatzer-Levy, I. R., & Bonanno, G. A. (2016). It's not so easy to make resilience go away: Commentary on Infurna and Luthar (2016). *Perspectives on Psychological Science, 11*, 195–198.

Galatzer-Levy, I. R., Bonanno, G. A., & Mancini, A. D. (2010). From marianthal to latent growth mixture modeling: A return to the exploration of individual differences in response to unemployment. *Journal of Neuroscience, Psychology, and Economics, 3*(2), 116–125.

Gallese, V., & Goldman, A. (1998) Mirror neurons and the simulation theory of mind-reading. *Trends in Cognitive Sciences, 2*, 493–501.

Gallo, E. (1994). Synchronicity and the archetypes: The imprecision of C. G. Jung's language and concepts. *Skeptical Inquirer, 18*, 376–403.

Gallo, L. C., & Matthews, K. A. (2003). Understanding the association between socioeconomic status and physical health: Do negative emotions play a role? *Psychological Bulletin, 129*, 10–51.

Gallup A. C. (2011). Why do we yawn? Primitive versus derived features. *Neuroscience and Biobehavioral Reviews, 35*, 765–769.

Gallup, G. G., Jr., & Suarez, S. D. (1985). Alternatives to the use of animals in psychological research. *American Psychologist, 40*, 1104–1111.

Galton, F. (1869). *Hereditary genius: An inquiry into its laws and consequences.* London, England: Macmillan.

Galton, F. (1876). The history of twin, as a criterion of the relative powers of nature and nurture. *Journal of the Anthropological Institute of Great Britain and Ireland, 5*, 391–406.

Galton, F. (1878). Composite portraits made by combining those of many different persons into a single resultant figure. *Journal of the Anthropological Institute of Great Britain and Ireland, 8*, 132.

Galton, F. (1880). Statistics of mental imagery. *Mind, 5*, 301–318.

Gamble, J. L., & Hess, J. J. (2012). Temperature and violent crime in Dallas, Texas: Relationships and implications of climate change. *Western Journal of Emergency Medicine, 13*, 239–246.

Gambrill, E. D. (1992). Self-help books: Pseudoscience in the guise of science? *Skeptical Inquirer, 16*(4), 389–399.

Gamer, M., Rill, H. G., Vossel, G., & Gädert, H. W. (2006). Psychophysiological and vocal measures in the detection of guilty knowledge. *International Journal of Psychophysiology, 60*, 76–87.

Gangestad, S. W., & Snyder, M. (2000). Self-monitoring: Appraisal and reappraisal. *Psychological Bulletin, 126*, 530–555.

Gangestad, S., & Scheyd, G. J. (2005). The evolution of human physical attractiveness. *Annual Review of Anthropology, 34*, 523–548.

Gangswisch, J. E., Babiss, L. A., Malaspina, D., Turner, J. B., Zammit, G. K., & Posner, K. (2010). Earlier parental set bedtimes as a protective factor against depression and suicidal ideation. *Sleep, 33*, 97–106.

Garatachea, N., Santos-Lozano, A., Sanchis-Gomar, F., Fiuza-Luces, C., Pereja-Galeano, H., Emanuele, E., & Lucía, A. (2014). Elite athletes live longer than the general population: A meta-analysis. *Mayo Clinic Proceedings, 89*(9), 1195–1200.

Garb, H. N. (1984). The incremental validity of information used in personality assessment. *Clinical Psychology Review, 4*, 641–655.

Garb, H. N. (1998). *Studying the clinician: Judgment, research, and psychological assessment.* Washington, DC: American Psychological Association.

Garb, H. N., Wood, J. M., Lilienfeld, S. O., & Nezworski, T. (2005). Roots of the Rorschach controversy. *Clinical Psychology Review, 25*, 97–118.

Garcia-Romeu, A., R Griffiths, R., & W Johnson, M. (2014). Psilocybin-occasioned mystical experiences in the treatment of tobacco addiction. *Current Drug Abuse Reviews, 7*(3), 157–164.

Garcia, J. R., MacKillop, J., Aller, E. L., Merriwether, A. M., Wilson, D. S., & Lum, J. K. (2010). Associations between dopamine D4 receptor gene variation with both infidelity and sexual promiscuity. *PLoS One, 5*(11), e14162.

Garcia, J., & Hankins, W. G. (1977). On the origin of food aversion paradigms. In L. M. Barker, M. R. Best, & M. Domjan (Eds.), *Learning mechanisms in food selection* (pp. 3–22). Houston, TX: Baylor University Press.

Garcia, J., & Koelling, R. A. (1966). The relation of cue to consequence in avoidance learning. *Psychonomic Science, 4*, 123–124.

Garcia, S. M., Weaver, K., Moskowitz, G. B., & Darley, J. M. (2002). Crowded minds: The implicit bystander effect. *Journal of Personality and Social Psychology, 83*, 843–853.

Gardini, S., Cloninger, C. R., & Venneri, A. (2009). Individual differences in personality traits reflect structural variance in specific brain regions. *Brain Research Bulletin, 79*, 265–270.

Gardner, H. (1983). *Frames of mind: The theory of multiple intelligences.* New York, NY: Basic Books.

Gardner, H. (1999). *Intelligence reframed: Multiple intelligences for the 21st century.* New York, NY: Basic Books.

Gardner, K. J., Dodsworth, J., & Selby, E. A. (2014). Borderline personality traits rumination, and self-injurious behavior: An empirical test of the emotional cascades model in adult male offenders. *Journal of Forensic Psychology Practice, 14*(5), 398–417.

Gardner, M. (1958). *Fads and fallacies in the name of science.* New York, NY: Dover.

Gardner, W. L., Gabriel, S., & Diekman, A. B. (2000). Interpersonal processes. In J. T. Cacioppo, L. G. Tassinary, & G. G. Berntson (Eds.), *Handbook of psychophysiology* (2nd ed., pp. 643–664). New York, NY: Cambridge University Press.

Garfield, S. L. (1978). Research on client variables. In S. Garfield & A. Bergin (Eds.), *Handbook of psychotherapy and behavior change* (pp. 191–232). New York, NY: Wiley.

Garmezy, N., Masten, A. S., & Tellegen, A. (1984). The study of stress and competence in children: A building block for developmental psychopathology. *Child Development, 55*, 97–111.

Garnier-Dykstra, L., Caldeira, K. M., Vincent, K. B., O'Grady, K. E., & Arria, A. (2012). Nonmedical use of prescription stimulants during college: Four-year trends in exposure opportunity, use, motives, and sources. *Journal of American College Health, 60*(3), 226–234. http://dx.doi.org/10.1080/07448481.2011.589876

Garrido, L., Furl, N., Draganski, B., Weiskopf, N., Stevens, J., Tan, G. C., … Duchaine, B. (2009). VBM reveals reduced gray matter volume in the temporal cortex of developmental prosopagnosics. *Brain, 132*, 3443–3455.

Garrido, L., Furl, N., Draganski, B., Weiskopf, N., Stevens, J., Tan, G. C. Y., … & Duchaine, B. (2009). Voxel-based morphometry reveals reduced grey matter volume in the temporal cortex of developmental prosopagnosics. *Brain, 132*(12), 3443–3455.

Garske, J. P., & Anderson, T. (2003). Toward a science of psychotherapy research: Present status and evaluation. In S. O. Lilienfeld, S. J. Lynn, & J. M. Lohr (Eds.), *Science and pseudoscience in clinical psychology* (pp. 145–175). New York, NY: Guilford Press.

Gartstein, M. A., Slobodskaya, H. R., Kirchhoff, C., & Putnam, S. P. (2013). Cross-cultural differences in the development of behavior problems: Contributions of infant temperament in Russia and US. *International Journal of Developmental Science, 7*(2), 95–104.

Gasperini, M., Scherillo, P., Manfredonia, M. G., Franchini, L., & Smeraldi, E. (1993). A study of relapse in subjects with mood disorder on lithium treatment. *European Neuropsychopharmacology, 3*, 103–110.

Gatchel, R. J. (2001). Biofeedback and self-regulation of physiological activity: A major adjunctive treatment modality in health psychology. In A. Baum, T. A. Revenson, & J. E. Singer (Eds.), *Handbook of health psychology* (pp. 95–103). Mahwah, NJ: Erlbaum.

Gatchel, R. J., & Baum, A. (1983). *An introduction to health psychology.* Reading, MA: Addison-Wesley.

Gatchel, R. J., & Oordt, M. S. (2003). *Clinical psychology and primary health care.* Washington, DC: American Psychological Association.

Gathercole, V. C. M. (2002a). Command of the mass/count distinction in bilingual and monolingual children: An English morphosyntactic distinction. In D. K. Oller & R. E. Eilers (Eds.), *Language and literacy in bilingual children* (pp. 175–206). Clevedon, England: Multilingual Matters.

Gathercole, V. C. M. (2002b). Grammatical gender in bilingual and monolingual children: A Spanish morphosyntactic distinction. In D. K. Oller & R. E. Eilers (Eds.), *Language and literacy in bilingual children* (pp. 207–219), Clevedon, England: Multilingual Matters.

Gaughan, E. T., Miller, J. D., & Lynam, D. R. (2012). Examining the utility of general models of personality in the study of psychopathy: A comparison of the HEXACO-PI-R and NEO PI-R. *Journal of Personality Disorders, 26*, 513–523. http://dx.doi.org/10.1521/pedi.2012.26.4.513

Gause, C., Morris, C., Vernekar, S., Pardo-Villamizar, C., Grados, M. A., & Singer, H. S. (2009). Antineuronal antibodies in OCD: Comparisons in children with OCD-only, OCD+chronic tics and OCD+PANDAS. *Journal of Neuroimmunology, 214*, 118–124.

Gautier, B. (2011, May 4). Top ten bizarre mental case studies. *Listverse.* http://listverse.com/2011/05/04/top-10-bizarre-mental-case-studies

Gawande, A. (2016, June 10). The mistrust of science. *New Yorker.* Retrieved from http://www.newyorker.com/news/news-desk/the-mistrust-of-science

Gawronski, B., LeBel, E. P., & Peters, K. R. (2007). What do implicit measures tell us? Scrutinizing the validity of three common assumptions. *Perspectives on Psychological Science, 2*, 181–193.

Gazzaniga, M. (2012). *Who's in charge? Free will and the science of the brain.* New York, NY: HarperCollins.

Gazzaniga, M. S. (2000). Cerebral specialization and interhemispheric communication: Does the corpus callosum enable the human condition? *Brain, 123*, 1293–1326.

Gazzaniga, M. S., Ivry, R., & Mangun, G. R. (2002). *Fundamentals of cognitive neuroscience* (2nd ed.). New York, NY: Norton.

Geake, J. (2008). Neuromythologies in education. *Educational Research, 80*, 123–133.

Geary, D. C. (1996). Sexual selection and sex differences in mathematical abilities. *Behavioral and Brain Sciences, 19*, 229–284.

Gebauer, J. E., Bleidorn, W., Gosling, S. D., Rentfrow, P. J., Lamb, M. E., & Potter, J. (2016). Big Five personality and religiosity: Agreeableness and conscientiousness constitute the basis of religiosity only in religious cultures. *Journal of Personality and Social Psychology*, awaiting volume and page numbers.

Gebremedhin, M., Ambaw, F., Admassu, E., & Berhane, H. (2015). Maternal associated factors of low birth weight: A hospital based cross-sectional mixed study in Tigray, Northern Ethiopia. *BMC Pregnancy and Childbirth, 15*(222), 1. doi: 10.1186/s12884-015-0658-1

Geddes, J. R., & Miklowitz, D. J. (2013). Treatment of bipolar disorder. *Lancet, 381*(9878), 1672–82.

Geen, R. G. (2001). *Human aggression* (2nd ed.). New York, NY: Taylor & Francis.

Geen, R. G., (1984). Preferred stimulation levels in introverts and extroverts: Effects on arousal and performance. *Journal of Personality and Social Psychology, 46*, 1303–1312.

Geier, A. B., Rozin, P., & Doros, G. (2006). Unit bias: A new heuristic that helps explain the effect of portion size on food intake. *Psychological Science, 17*, 521–525.

Geiser, S., & Studley, R. (2002). UC and the SAT: Predictive validity and differential impact of the SAT I and SAT II at the University of California. *Educational Assessment, 8*, 1–26.

Gellatly, A. R. (1987). Acquisition of a concept of logical necessity. *Human Development, 30*, 32–47.

Gelman, R., & Gallistel, C. (1978). *The child's understanding of number.* Cambridge, MA: Harvard University Press.

Genesee, F. (1985). Second language learning through immersion: A review of U.S. programs. *Review of Educational Research, 55*, 541–561.

Gentile, D. A. (2015). What is a good skeptic to do? The case for skepticism in the media violence discussion. *Perspectives on Psychological Science, 10*, 674–676.

Gentile, D. A., & Anderson, C. A. (2003). Violent video games: The newest media violence hazard. In D. A. Gentile (Ed.), *Media violence and children* (pp. 131–152). Westport, CT: Praeger.

Gentner, D., Loewenstein, J., Thompson, L., & Forbus, K. D. (2009). Reviving inert knowledge: Analogical abstraction supports relational retrieval of past events. *Cognitive Science, 33*, 1343–1382.

George, M. S., Sackeim, H., Rush, A. J., Marangell, L. B., Nahas, Z., Husain, M. M., … Ballenger, J. C. (2000). Vagus nerve stimulation: A new tool for treatment-resistant depression. *Biological Psychiatry, 47*, 287–295.

Geraerts, E., Bernstein, D. M., Merckelbach, H., Londers, C., Raymaekers, L., & Loftus, E. F. (2008). Lasting beliefs and their behavioral consequences. *Psychological Science, 19*, 749–753.

Geraerts, E., Smeets, E., Jelicic, M., van Heerden, J., & Merckelbach, H. (2005). Fantasy proneness, but not self-reported trauma is related to DRM performance of women reporting recovered memories of childhood sexual abuse. *Consciousness and Cognition, 14*, 602–612.

Gerard, S., Smith, B. H., & Simpson, J. A. (2003). A randomized controlled trial of spiritual healing in restricted neck movement. *Journal of Alternative and Complementary Medicine, 9*, 467–477.

Gergen, K. J. (1973). Social psychology as history. *Journal of Personality and Social Psychology, 26*, 309–320.

German, T. P., & Barrett, H. C. (2005). Functional fixedness in a technologically sparse culture. *Psychological Science, 16*, 1–5.

German, T. P., & Defeyter, M. A. (2000). Immunity to functional fixedness in young children. *Psychonomic Bulletin & Review, 7*, 707–712.

Gernsbacher, M. A., Dawson, M., & Goldsmith, H. H. (2005). Three reasons not to believe in an autism epidemic. *Current Directions in Psychological Science, 14*, 55–58.

Gershoff, E. T. (2002). Corporal punishment by parents and associated child behaviors and experiences: A meta-analytic and theoretical review. *Psychological Bulletin, 128*, 539–579.

Gershoff, E. T. (2013). Spanking and child development: We know enough now to stop hitting our children. *Child Development Perspectives, 7*, 133–137.

Gershoff, E. T., Lansford, J. E., Sexton, H. R., Davis-Kean, P., & Sameroff, A. J. (2012). Longitudinal links between spanking and children's externalizing behaviors in a national sample of White, Black, Hispanic, and Asian American families. *Child Development, 83*, 838–843.

Geschwind, N. (1983). Interictal behavior changes in epilepsy. *Epilepsia, 24*(Suppl. 1), S23–S30.

Gow, A. J., Johnson, W., Pattie, A., Brett, C. E., Roberts, B., Starr, J. M., & Deary, I. J. (2011). Stability and change in intelligence from age 11 to ages 70, 79, and 87: The lothian birth cohorts of 1921 and 1936. *Psychology and Aging, 26*(1), 232–240. http://dx.doi.org/10.1037/a0021072

Gowin, J. (2009, September 29). How "smart drugs" enhance us. *Psychology Today.* Retrieved from http://www.psychologytoday.com/blog/you-illuminated/200909/how-smart-drugs-enhance-us

Goyal, M., Singh, S., Sibinga, E. M., Gould, N. F., Rowland-Seymour, A., Sharma, R., ... & Ranasinghe, P. D. (2014). Meditation programs for psychological stress and well-being: A systematic review and meta-analysis. *JAMA Internal Medicine, 174*(3), 357–368.

Graber, J. A., Petersen, A. C., & Brooks-Gunn, J. (1996). Pubertal processes: Methods, measures, and models. In J. A. Graber, J. Brooks-Gunn, & A. C. Petersen (Eds.), *Transitions through adolescence: Interpersonal domains and context* (pp. 23–53). Hillsdale, NJ: Erlbaum.

Grace, A. A. (1991). The cortical regulation of dopamine system responsivity—A hypothesis regarding its role in the etiology of schizophrenia. *Schizophrenia Research, 4*, 345.

Graf, P. (1990). Life-span changes in implicit and explicit memory. *Bulletin of the Psychonomic Society, 28*, 353–358.

Graf, R. G. (1973). Speed reading: Remember the tortoise. *Psychology Today, 7*, 112–113.

Graham, J. R. (2011). *MMPI-2: Assessing personality and psychopathology.* New York, NY: Oxford University Press.

Graham, L. T., & Gosling, S. D. (2012). Impressions of World of Warcraft players' personalities based on their usernames: Interobserver consensus but no accuracy. *Journal of Research in Personality, 46*, 599–603.

Grana, R., Benowitz, N., & Glantz, S. A. (2014). E-cigarettes a scientific review. *Circulation, 129*(19), 1972–1986.

Grant, B. F., Goldstein, R. B., Saha, T. D., Chou, S. P., Jung, J., Zhang, H., ... & Hasin, D. S. (2015). Epidemiology of DSM-5 alcohol use disorder: results from the National Epidemiologic Survey on Alcohol and Related Conditions III. *JAMA psychiatry, 72*(8), 757–66.

Grant, B. F., Hansin, D. S., Stinson, F. S., Dawson D. A., June Ruan, W., Goldstein, R. B., ... Huang, B. (2005). Prevalence, correlates, co-morbidity, and comparative disability of DSM-IV generalized anxiety disorder in the USA: Results from the National Epidemiologic Survey on alcohol and related conditions. *Psychological Medicine, 35*, 1747–1759.

Grassian, S. (2006). Psychiatric effects of solitary confinement. *Washington University Journal of Law & Policy, 22*, 325.

Grawe, K., Donati, R., & Bernauer, F. (1998). *Psychotherapy in transition.* Seattle, WA: Hogrefe & Huber.

Gray, C. R., & Gummerman, K. (1975). The enigmatic eidetic image: A critical examination of methods, data, and theories. *Psychological Bulletin, 82*, 383–407.

Gray, J. (1981). A critique of Eysenck's theory of personality. In H. J. Eysenck (Ed.), *A model for personality* (pp. 246–276). New York, NY: Springer.

Gray, J. (1992). *Men are from Mars, women are from venus.* New York, NY: Harper-Collins.

Gray, J. A. (1982). *The neuropsychology of anxiety: An enquiry into the functions of the septo-hippocampal system.* Oxford, England: Oxford University Press.

Graybiel, A. M., Aosaki, T., Flaherty, A. W., & Kimura, M. (1994). The basal ganglia and adaptive motor control. *Science, 265*, 1826–1831.

Gredler, M. E. (2012). Understanding Vygotsky for the classroom: Is it too late? *Educational Psychology Review, 24*, 113–131.

Greeley, A. M. (1975). *The sociology of the paranormal: A reconnaissance* (Sage Research Papers in the Social Sciences, Vol. 3, Series No. 90-023). Beverly Hills, CA: Sage.

Greeley, A. M. (1987). Mysticism goes mainstream. *American Health, 6*, 47–49.

Greeley, J., & Oei, T. (1999). Alcohol and tension reduction: 1987–1997. In K. E Leonard & H. T. Blane (Eds.), *Psychological theories of drinking and alcoholism* (2nd ed., pp.14–53). New York, NY: Guilford Press.

Greely H. T., & Illes, J. (2007). Neuroscience-based lie detection: The urgent need for regulation. *American Journal of Law & Medicine, 33*, 377–431.

Greely H., Sahakian, B., Harris, J., Kessler, R. C., Gazzaniga, M., Campbell, P., & Farah, M. J. (2008). Towards responsible use of cognitive-enhancing drugs by the healthy. *Nature, 456*, 702–705.

Green, C. D. (1992). Is unified positivism the answer to psychology's disunity? *American Psychologist, 48*, 1057–1058.

Green, D. M., & Swets, J. A. (1966). *Signal detection theory and psychophysics.* New York, NY: Wiley.

Green, G. (1996). Early behavioral intervention for autism: What does research tell us? In C. Maurice, G. Green, & S. Luce (Eds.), *Behavioral intervention for young children with autism: A manual for parents and professionals* (pp. 29–44). Austin, TX: PRO-E.

Green, J. P. (2000). Treating women who smoke: The benefits of using hypnosis. In L. Hornyak & J. P. Green (Eds.), *Healing from within: The use of hypnosis in women's health care* (pp. 91–118). Washington, DC: American Psychological Association.

Green, J. P., & Lynn, S. J. (2005). Hypnosis vs. relaxation: Accuracy and confidence in dating international news events. *Applied Cognitive Psychology, 19*, 679–691.

Green, R. (1987). *The "sissy boy syndrome" and the development of homosexuality.* New Haven, CT: Yale University Press.

Greenberg, D. J., Hillman, D., & Grice, D. (1973). Infant and stranger variables related to stranger anxiety in the first year of life. *Development Psychology, 9*, 207–212.

Greenberg, D. L. (2004). President Bush's False 'Flashbulb' Memory of 9/11/01. *Applied Cognitive Psychology, 18*, 363–370.

Greenberg, G. (2013). *The book of woe: The DSM and the unmaking of psychiatry.* New York, NY: Blue Rider Press.

Greenberg, L. S., & Watson, J. C. (1998). Experiential therapy of depression: Differential effects of client-centered relationship conditions and process experiential interventions. *Psychotherapy Research, 8*, 210–224.

Greenberg, L. S., Elliot, R., & Lietaer, G. (1994). Research on humanistic and experiential psychotherapies. In A. E. Bergin & L. S. Garfield (Eds.), *Handbook of psychotherapy and behavior change* (4th ed., pp. 509–539). New York, NY: Wiley.

Greene, J. D., & Paxton, J. M. (2009). Patterns of neural activity associated with honest and dishonest moral decisions. *Proceedings of the National Academy of Sciences, 106*, 12506–12511.

Greene, R. L. (2000). *The MMPI-2: An interpretive manual* (2nd ed.). Boston, MA: Allyn & Bacon.

Greenfield, P. (1998). The cultural evolution of IQ. In U. Neisser (Ed.), *The rising curve: Long-term gains in IQ and related measures* (pp. 81–122). Washington, DC: American Psychological Association.

Greenglass, E. (2002). Proactive coping. In E. Frydenberg (Ed.), *Beyond coping: Meeting goals, vision, and challenges* (pp. 37–62). London, England: Oxford University Press.

Greenough, W. T. (1997). We can't just focus on the first three years. *American Psychological Association Monitor on Psychology, 28*, 19.

Greenspan, S., & Switzky, H. N. (Eds.). (2003). *What is mental retardation? Ideas for the new century.* Washington, DC: American Association on Mental Retardation.

Greenspan, S., & Woods, G. W. (2014). Intellectual disability as a disorder of reasoning and judgment: The gradual move away from intelligence quotient-ceilings. *Current Opinion in Psychiatry, 27*, 110–116.

Greenspan, S., Loughlin, G., & Black, R. S. (2001). Credulity and gullibility in people with developmental disabilities: A framework for future research. In L. M. Glidden (Ed.), *International Review of Research in Mental Retardation, Vol. 24* (pp. 101–135). New York, NY: Academic Press.

Greenwald, A. G. (2012). There is nothing so theoretical as a good method. *Perspectives on Psychological Science, 7*, 99–108.

Greenwald, A. G., & Gillmore, G. M. (1997). Grading leniency is a removable contaminant of student ratings. *American Psychologist, 52*, 1209–1217.

Greenwald, A. G., & Nosek, B. A. (2001). Health of the Implicit Association Test at age 3. *Zeitschrift für Experimentelle Psychologie, 48*, 85–93.

Greenwald, A. G., Banaji, M. R., & Nosek, B. A. (2015). Statistically small effects of the Implicit Association Test can have societally large effects. *Journal of Personality and Social Psychology, 108*, 553–561.

Greenwald, A. G., Leippe, M. R., Pratkanis, A. R., & Baumgardner, M. H. (1986). Under what conditions does theory obstruct research progress? *Psychological Review, 93*, 216–229.

Greenwald, A. G., McGhee, D. E., & Schwartz, J. L. K. (1998). Measuring individual differences in implicit cognition: The implicit association test. *Journal of Personality and Social Psychology, 74*, 1464–1480.

Greenwald, A. G., Spangenberg, E. R., Pratkanis, A. R., & Eskenazi, J. (1991). Double-blind tests of subliminal self-help audio tapes. *Psychological Science, 2*, 119–122.

Greenwood, C. R., Thiemann-Bourque, K., Walker, D., Buzhardt, J., & Gilkerson, J. (2011). Assessing children's home language environments using automatic speech recognition technology. *Communication Disorders Quarterly.* http://dx.doi.org/10.1177/1525740110367826

Gregory, R. J., Canning, S. S., Lee, T. W., & Wise, J. (2004). Cognitive bibliotherapy for depression: A meta-analysis. *Professional Psychology: Research and Practice, 35*, 275–280.

Gresham, L. G., & Shimp, T. A. (1985). Attitude toward the advertisement and brand attitudes: A classical conditioning perspective. *Journal of Advertising, 14*, 10–17, 49.

Griffiths S. (2014). *Hugs can make you feel younger: "Cuddle hormone" could improve bone health, and combat muscle wasting.* Available at: http://www.dailymail.co.uk/sciencetech/article-2654224/Hugs-make-feel-younger-Cuddle-hormone-improve-bone-health-combat-muscle-wasting.html#ixzz3UP2WNT2J

Griffiths, P. E. (1997). *What emotions really are: The problem of psychological categories.* Chicago, IL: Chicago University Press.

Griffiths, R. R., Johnson, M. W., Richards, W. A., Richards, B. D., McCann, U., & Jesse, R. (2011). Psilocybin occasioned mystical-type experiences: Immediate and persisting dose-related effects. *Psychopharmacology, 218*, 649–665.

Griffiths, R. R., Richards, W. A., Johnson, M. W., McCann, U. D., & Jesse, R. (2008). Mystical-type experiences occasioned by psilocybin mediate the attribution of personal meaning and spiritual significance 14 months later. *Journal of Psychopharmacology, 22*, 621–632.

Griffiths, R. R., Richards, W. A., McCann, U., & Jesse, R. (2006). Psilocybin can occasion mystical-type experiences having substantial and sustained personal meaning and spiritual significance. *Psychopharmacology, 187*(3), 268–283.

Griggs, R. (2015). Coverage of the Phineas Gage story in introductory psychology textbooks: Was Gage no longer Gage? *Teaching of Psychology, 42*, 195–202.

Griggs, R. A. (2015a). The disappearance of independence in textbook coverage of Asch's social pressure experiments. *Teaching of Psychology, 42*, 137–142.

Griggs, R. A. (2015b). The Kitty Genovese Story in Introductory Psychology Textbooks Fifty Years Later. *Teaching of Psychology, 42*(2), 149–152.

Griggs, R. A., & Whitehead, G. I. (2014). Coverage of the Stanford Prison Experiment in introductory social psychology textbooks. *Teaching of Psychology, 41*, 318–324.

Griggs, R. A., & Whitehead, G. I. (2015). Coverage of Milgram's Obedience Experiments in social psychology textbooks: Where have all the criticisms gone? *Teaching of Psychology, 42*, 315–322.

Grill, H. J., Schwartz, M. W., Kaplan, J. M., Foxhall, J. S., Breininger, J., & Baskin, D. G. (2002). Evidence that the caudal brainstem is a target for the inhibitory effect of leptin on food intake. *Endocrinology, 143*, 239–246.

Grings, W. W. (1973). Cognitive factors in electrodermal conditioning. *Psychological Bulletin, 79*, 200–210.

Grinker, R. R. (2007). *Unstrange minds: Remapping the world of autism.* New York, NY: Basic Books.

Grinker, R. R., & Werble, B. (1977). *The borderline patient.* New York, NY: Jason Aronson.

Grinnell, R. (2008). Word salad. In J. M. Grohol, *Encyclopedia of psychology.* Retrieved from http://psychcentral.com/encyclopedia

Grisso, T. (2003). *Evaluating competencies: Forensic assessments and instruments* (2nd ed). New York, NY: Kluwer.

Grob C. S., Danforth A. L., Chopra G. S., Hagerty, M., McKay, C. R., Halberstadt, A. L., & Greer, G. R. (2011) Pilot study of psilocybin treatment for anxiety in patients with advanced-stage cancer. *Archives of General Psychiatry, 68*, 71–78.

Grosjean, P. (2014). A history of violence: The culture of honor and homicide in the US south. *Journal of the European Economic Association, 12*(5), 1285–1316.

Groskreutz, M. (2013). Schedule of reinforcement. In F. R. Volkmar (Ed.), *Encyclopedia of Autism Spectrum Disorders* (pp. 2652–2657). New York, NY: Springer.

Gross, J. J., & Muñoz, R. F. (1995). Emotional regulation and mental health. *Clinical Psychology: Science & Practice, 2*, 151–164.

Gross, J., Byrne, J., & Fisher, C. (1965). Eye movements during emergent Stage 1 EEG in subjects with lifelong blindness. *Journal of Nervous and Mental Disease, 141*, 365–370.

Grossman, H. J. (Ed.). (1983). *Classification in mental retardation* (Rev. ed.). Washington, DC: American Association on Mental Deficiency.

Grossmann, T. (2015). The development of social brain functions in infancy. *Psychological Bulletin, 141*(6), 1266. doi:10.1037/bul0000002

Grove, W. M., & Tellegen, A. (1991). Problems in the classification of personality disorders. *Journal of Personality Disorders, 5*, 31–41.

Grubin, D. (2010). The polygraph and forensic psychiatry. *Journal of the American Academy of Psychiatry and the Law Online, 38*(4), 446–451.

Grunbaum, A. (1984). *The foundations of psychoanalysis: A philosophical critique.* Berkeley, CA: University of California Press.

Gruneberg, M. M., and Sykes, R. N. (1991). Individual differences and attitudes to the keyword method of foreign language learning. *Language Learning Journal, 4*, 60–62.

Grupe, D. W., & Nitschke, J. B. (2011). Uncertainty is associated with biased expectancies and heightened responses to aversion. *Emotion, 11*, 413–424.

Gu, Q. (2002). Neuromodulatory transmitter systems in the cortex and their role in cortical plasticity. *Neuroscience, 111*, 815–835.

Guan, J. H., & Wade, M. G. (2000). The effect of aging on adaptive eye–hand coordination. *Journals of Gerontology Series B—Psychological Sciences and Social Sciences, 55*, P151–P162.

Guéguen, N., & Pascual, A. (2000). Evocation of freedom and compliance: The "but you are free of" technique. *Current Research in Social Psychology, 5*, 264–270.

Guéguen, N., Pascual A., & Dagot L. (2002). The low-ball technique: An application in a field setting, *Psychological Reports, 91*, 81–84.

Guggisberg, A. G., Mathis, J., Schnider, A., & Hess, C. W. (2010). Why do we yawn? *Neuroscience and Biobehavioral Reviews, 34*, 1267–1276.

Guilford, J. P. (1954). *Psychometric methods* (2nd ed.). New York, NY: McGraw-Hill.

Guilford, J. P. (1967). *The nature of human intelligence.* New York, NY: McGraw-Hill.

Gulya, M., Galluccio, L., Wilk, A., & Rovee-Collier, C. (2001). Infants' long-term memory for a serial list: Recognition and reactivation. *Developmental Psychobiology, 38*, 174–185.

Gunnery, S. D., & Ruben, M. A. (2016). Perceptions of Duchenne and non-Duchenne smiles: A meta-analysis. *Cognition and Emotion, 30*, 501–515.

Gupta, S. (2007, May 24). Herbal remedies' potential dangers. *Time.* Retrieved from http://www.time.com/time/magazine/article/0,9171,1625175,00.html

Gupta, S., & Bonanno, G. A. (2010). Trait self-enhancement as a buffer against potentially traumatic events: A prospective study. *Psychological Trauma: Theory, Research, Practice, and Policy, 2*(2), 83.

Gurman, A. S., & Kniskern, D. P. (2014). *Handbook of family therapy.* London, UK: Routledge.

Gurven, M., von Rueden, C., Massenkoff, M., Kaplan, H., & Lero Vie, M. (2013). How universal is the Big Five? Testing the five-factor model of personality variation among forager–farmers in the Bolivian Amazon. *Journal of Personality and Social Psychology, 104*, 354–370.

Gustafsson, J. E. (1988). Hierarchical models of individual differences in cognitive abilities. In R. J. Sternberg (Ed.), *Advances in the psychology of human intelligence, Vol. 4* (pp. 35–71). Hillsdale, NJ: Erlbaum.

Gvion, Y., & Apter, A. (2011). Aggression, impulsivity, and suicide behavior: A review of the literature. *Archives of Suicide Research, 15*, 93–112.

Haack, L. J., Metalsky, G. I., Dykman, B. M., & Abramson, L. Y. (1996). Use of current situational information and causal inference: Do dysphoric individuals make "unwarranted" causal inferences? *Cognitive Therapy and Research, 20*, 309–331.

Haaga, D. A., Dyck, M. J., & Ernst, D. (1991). Empirical status of cognitive theory of depression. *Psychological Bulletin, 110*, 215–236.

Haber, R. N. (1979). Twenty years of haunting eidetic imagery: Where's the ghost? *Behavioral and Brain Sciences, 2*, 583–629.

Hackney, A. (2005). Teaching students about stereotypes, prejudice, and discrimination: An interview with Susan Fiske. *Teaching of Psychology, 32*, 196–199.

Haedt-Matt, A. A., & Keel, P. K. (2015). Affect regulation and purging: An ecological momentary assessment study in purging disorder. *Journal of Abnormal Psychology, 124*(2), 399–411.

Haeffel, G. (2010). When self-help is no help: Traditional cognitive skills training does not prevent depressive symptoms in people who ruminate. *Behaviour Research and Therapy, 48*, 152–157.

Haehner, A., Hummel, T., & Reichmann, H. (2014). A clinical approach towards smell loss in Parkinson's disease. *Journal of Parkinson's disease, 4*(2), 189–195.

Hafenbrädl, S., Waeger, D., Marewski, J. N., & Gigerenzer, G. (2016). Applied decision making with fast-and-frugal heuristics. *Journal of Applied Research in Memory and Cognition, 5*, 215–231.

Hafer, C. L., & Begue, L. (2005). Experimental research on just-world theory: Problems, developments, and future challenges. *Psychological Bulletin, 131*, 128–167.

Hagen, M. (2001). Damaged goods? What, if anything, does science tell us about the long-term effects of childhood sexual abuse? *Skeptical Inquirer, 24*(1), 54–59.

Hagiwara, N., Alderson, C. J., & McCauley, J. M. (2015). "We get what we deserve": the belief in a just world and its health consequences for Blacks. *Journal of Behavioral Medicine, 38*, 912–921.

Haidt, J. (2007) The new synthesis in moral psychology. *Science, 316*, 998–1002.

Haidt, J. (2012). *The righteous mind: Why good people are divided by politics and religion.* New York, NY: Vintage Books.

Haier, R. J. (2009, November/December). What does a smart brain look like? *Scientific American Mind*, 26–33.

Haier, R. J. (2009). Neuro-intelligence, neuro-metrics and the next phase of brain imaging studies. *Intelligence, 37*(2), 121–123. http://dx.doi.org/10.1016/j.intell.2008.12.006

Haier, R. J. (2009). Neuro-intelligence, neuro-metrics and the next phase of brain imaging studies. *Intelligence, 37*, 121–123.

Haier, R. J., Siegel, B. V., MacLachlan, A., Soderling, E., Lottenberg, S., & Buchsbaum, M. S. (1992). Regional glucose metabolic changes after learning a complex visuospatial/motor task: A positron emission tomographic study. *Brain Research, 570*, 134–143.

Haijma, S. V., Van Haren, N., Cahn, W., Koolschijn, P. C. M., Pol, H. E. H., & Kahn, R. S. (2013). Brain volumes in schizophrenia: a meta-analysis in over 18000 subjects. *Schizophrenia Bulletin, 39*(5), 1129–38.

Haimerl, C. J., & Valentine, E. (2001). The effect of contemplative practice on intrapersonal, interpersonal, and transpersonal dimensions of the self-concept. *Journal of Transpersonal Psychology, 33*, 37–52.

Haist, F., Shimamura, A. P., & Squire, L. R. (1992). On the relationship between recall and recognition memory. *Journal of Experimental Psychology: Learning, Memory, and Cognition, 18*, 691–702.

Hajjawi, O. S. (2014). Human brain biochemistry. *American Journal of BioScience, 2*, 122–134.

Haker, H., & Rössler, W. (2009). Empathy in schizophrenia: Impaired resonance. *European Archives of Psychiatry and Clinical Neuroscience, 259*, 352–361.

Halari, R., Hines, M., Kumari, V., Mehrotra, R., Wheeler, M., Ng, V., & Sharma, T. (2005) Sex differences and individual differences in cognitive performance and their relationship to endogenous gonadal hormones and gonadotropins. *Behavioral Neuroscience, 119*, 104–117.

Halberstadt, J., & Rhodes, G. (2003). It's not just the average face that's attractive: The attractiveness of averageness of computer-manipulated birds, fish, and automobiles. *Psychonomic Bulletin and Review, 10*, 149–156.

Haley, J. (1976). *Problem-solving therapy.* San Francisco, CA: Jossey-Bass.

Hall, C. S., & Nordby, V. J. (1972). *The individual and his dreams.* Winnipeg, Manitoba, Canada: New American Library.

Hall, C. S., & Van de Castle, R. (1966). *Content analysis of dreams.* New York, NY: Appleton-Century-Crofts.

Hall, D., & Buzwell, S. (2012). The problem of free-riding in group projects: Looking beyond social loafing as reason for non-contribution. *Active Learning in Higher Education*, 1469787412467123.

Hall, E. T. (1966). *The hidden dimension.* New York, NY: Anchor Books.

Hall, E. T. (1976). *Beyond culture.* New York, NY: Doubleday.

Hall, H. (2008). Puncturing the acupuncture myth. *Skeptic, 14*, 5.

Office of Technology Assessment. (1990). *The use of integrity tests for pre-employment screening.* Washington, DC: U.S. Congress Office of Technology Assessment.

Offit, P. A. (2008). Vaccines and autism revisited: The Hanna Poling case. *New England Journal of Medicine, 358,* 2089–2091.

Ofori, P. K., Biddle, S., & Lavallee, D. (2012). The role of superstition among professional footballers in Ghana. *Athletic Insight, 4,* 115–125.

Ogawa, S., Lee, T. M., Kay, A. R., & Tank, D. W. (1990). Brain magnetic resonance imaging with contrast dependent on blood oxygenation. *Proceedings of the National Academy of Sciences, 87,* 9868–9872.

Ogrodniczuk, J. S., & Piper, W. E. (1999). Use of transference interpretations in dynamically oriented individual psychotherapy for patients with personality disorders. *Journal of Personality Disorders, 13,* 297–311.

Oh, I.-S., Charlier, S. D., Mount, M. K., & Berry, C. M. (2014). The two faces of high self-monitors: Chameleonic moderating effects of self-monitoring on the relationships between personality traits and counterproductive work behaviors. *Journal of Organizational Behavior, 35,* 92–111.

Oh, S. H. (2013). Do collectivists conform more than individualists? Cross-cultural differences in compliance and internalization. *Social Behavior and Personality, 41,* 981–994.

Ohayon, M. M. (2000). Prevalence of hallucinations and their pathological associations in the general population. *Psychiatry Research, 97,* 153–164.

Ohayon, M. M. (2002). Epidemiology of insomnia: What we know and what we still need to learn. *Sleep Medicine Reviews, 6,* 97–111.

Ohayon, M. M. (2013). Narcolepsy is complicated by high medical and psychiatric comorbidities: a comparison with the general population. *Sleep Medicine, 14*(6), 488–492.

Ohlemiller, K. K., & Frisina, R. D. (2008). Age-related hearing loss and its cellular and molecular bases. In J. Schacht, A. N. Popper, & R. R. Fay (Eds.), *Springer handbook of auditory research: Auditory trauma, protection, and repair* (pp.145–162). Netherlands: Springer.

Ohlert, J., & Kleinert, J. (2012). Social loafing during preparation for performance situations. *Social Psychology, 11,* 1–7.

Ohman, A., & Mineka, S. (2001). Fears, phobias, and preparedness: Toward an evolved module of fear and fear learning. *Psychological Review, 108,* 483–522.

Ohman, A., & Mineka, S. (2003). The malicious serpent: Snakes as a prototypical stimulus for an evolved module of fear. *Current Directions in Psychological Science, 12,* 5–9.

Oishi, S., Diener, E., & Lucas, R. E. (2007). The optimal level of well-being: Can we be too happy? *Perspectives on Psychological Science, 2,* 346–360.

Oldfield, K. (1998). The GRE as fringe science. *Skeptic, 6*(1), 68–72.

Olds, J. (1959). Studies of neuropharmacologicals by electrical and chemical manipulation of the brain in animals with chronically implanted electrodes. In P. B. Bradley, P. Deniker, and C. Radouco-Thomas (Eds.), *Neuro-Psychopharmacology* (pp. 20–32). Amsterdam, the Netheralnds: Elsevier.

Olfson, M., & Marcus, S. C. (2010). National trends in outpatient psychotherapy. *American Journal of Psychiatry, 167,* 1456–1463.

Olguin, P., Fuentes, M., Gabler, G., Guerdjikova, A. I., Keck, P. E., & McElroy, S. L. (2016). Medical comorbidity of binge eating disorder. *Eating and Weight Disorders-Studies on Anorexia, Bulimia and Obesity,* 1–14. doi:10.1007/s40519-016-0313-5

Oliver, M. B., & Hyde, J. S. (1993). Gender differences in sexuality: A meta-analysis. *Psychological Bulletin, 114,* 29–51.

Olivier, J. D., Vinkers, C. H., & Olivier, B. (2013). The role of the serotonergic and GABA system in translational approaches in drug discovery for anxiety disorders. *Frontiers in Psychopharmacology, 4,* 74.

Olkin, R., & Taliaferro, G. (2005). Evidence-based practices have ignored people with disabilities. In J. C. Norcross, L. E. Beutler, & R. F. Levant (Eds.), *Evidence-based practices in mental health* (pp. 353–358). Washington, DC: American Psychological Association.

Olsen, S., Smith, S. S., Oei, T. P., & Douglas, J. (2012). Motivational interviewing (MINT) improves continuous positive airway pressure (CPAP) acceptance and adherence: A randomized controlled trial. *Journal of Consulting and Clinical Psychology, 80*(1), 151.

Olson, J. R., Marshall, J. P., Goddard, H. W., & Schramm, D. G. (2015). Shared religious beliefs, prayer, and forgiveness as predictors of marital satisfaction. *Family Relations, 64*(4), 519–533.

Olson, K.R., Durwood, L., DeMeules, M., & McLaughlin, K. A. (2016). Mental health of transgender children who are supported in their identities. *Pediatrics, 137*(3),1–8.

Olson, K.R., Key, A. C., & Eaton, N. R. (2015). Gender cognition in transgender children. *Psychological Science, 26,*467–474.

Olsson, A., Ebert, J. P., Banaji, M. R., & Phelps, E. A. (2005). The role of social groups in the persistence of learned fear. *Science, 309,* 785–787.

Oltmanns, T. F., & Turkheimer, E. (2009). Person perception and personality pathology. *Current Directions in Psychological Science, 18,* 32–36.

Olweus, D. (1993). *Bullying at school: What we know and what we can do.* Oxford, England: Blackwell.

Ondeck, D. M. (2003). Impact of culture on pain. *Home Health Care Management Practice, 15,* 255–257.

Ones, D. S., Viswesvaran, C., & Dilchert, S. (2005). Personality at work: Raising awareness and correcting misconceptions. *Human Performance, 18,* 389–404.

Ones, D. S., Viswesvaran, C., & Schmidt, F. L. (1993). Comprehensive meta-analysis of integrity test validities. *Journal of Applied Psychology, 78,* 679–703.

Onuma, T., & Sakai, N. (2016). Higher-order conditioning of taste-odor learning in rats: Evidence for the association between emotional aspects of gustatory information and olfactory information. *Physiology & Behavior, 164,* 407–416.

Oosterlaan, J., Geurts, H. M., Knol, D. L., & Sergeant, J. A. (2005). Low basal salivary cortisol is associated with teacher-reported symptoms of conduct disorder. *Psychiatry Research, 134*(1), 1–10. http://dx.doi.org/10.1016/j. psychres.2004.12.005

Open Science Collaboration. (2015). Estimating the reproducibility of psychological science. *Science, 349,* aac4716.

Open Science Collaboration. (2015). Estimating the reproducibility of psychological science. *Science, 349,* 943–950.

Opfer, J. E. and Gelman, S. A. (2011) Development of the animate-inanimate distinction. In *The Wiley-Blackwell handbook of childhood cognitive development (2nd ed.)* (U. Goswami, ed.), pp. 213–238, Wiley-Blackwell.

Oppenheim, R. W. (1991). Cell death during development of the nervous system. *Annual Review of Neuroscience, 14,* 453–501.

Opriş, D., Pintea, S., García-Palacios, A., Botella, C., Szamosközi, Ş., & David, D. (2012). Virtual reality exposure therapy in anxiety disorders: A quantitative meta-analysis. *Depression and Anxiety, 29*(2), 85–93.

Orathinkal, J., & Vansteenwegen, A. (2006). Religiosity and marital satisfaction. *Contemporary Family Therapy, 28,* 497–504.

Orlanksy, M. D., & Bonvillian, J. D. (1984). The role of iconicity in early sign language acquisition. *Journal of Speech and Hearing Disorders, 49,* 287–292.

Orlinsky, D. E., Grawe, K., & Parks, B. K. (1994). Process and outcome in psychotherapy—Noch einmal. In A. E. Bergin & S. L. Garfield (Eds.), *Handbook of psychotherapy and behavior change* (4th ed., pp. 270–376). New York, NY: Wiley.

Orne, M. T. (1962). On the social psychology of the psychological experiment: With particular reference to demand characteristics and their implications. *American Psychologist, 17,* 776–783.

Ornstein, P. A., Baker-Ward, L., Gordon, B. N., & Merritt, K. A. (1997). Children's memory for medical experiences: Implications for testimony. *Applied Cognitive Psychology, 11,* S87–S104.

Ortony, A., & Turner, T. J. (1990). What's basic about basic emotions? *Psychological Review, 97,* 315–331.

Osborn, A. F. (1957). Applied imagination: Principles and procedures of creative problem solving (Rev. ed.). New York, NY: Scribner.

Oshri, A., Rogosch, F. A., & Cicchetti, D. (2012). Child maltreatment and mediating influences of childhood personality types on the development of adolescent psychopathology. *Journal of Clinical Child & Adolescent Psychology, 42.* 187–201.

Ost, L. G. (2008). Efficacy of the third wave of behavioral therapies: A systematic review and meta-analysis. *Behaviour Research and Therapy, 46,* 296–321.

Ostwald, P. (1972). The sounds of infancy. *Developmental Medicine and Child Neurology, 14,* 350–361.

Oswald, F. L., Mitchell, G., Blanton, H., Jaccard, J., & Tetlock, P. E. (2015). Using the IAT to predict ethnic and racial discrimination: small effect sizes of unknown societal significance. *Journal of Personality and Social Psychology, 108,* 562–571.

Otero-Millan, J., Macknik, S. L., Robbins, A., McCamy, M., & Martinez-Conde, S. (2011). Stronger misdirection in curved than in straight motion. *Frontiers in Human Neuroscience, 5,* 375–378

Otgaar, H., Candel, I., Merckelbach, H., & Wade, K. (2009). Abducted by a UFO: Prevalence information affects young children's false memories for an implausible event. *Applied Cognitive Psychology, 23*(1), 115–125. http://dx.doi.org/10.1002/acp.1445

Otgarr, H., Scoboria, A., & Smeets, T. (2012). Experimentally evoking nonbelieved memories for childhood events. *Journal of Experimental Psychology: Learning, Memory, and Cognition.* Retrieved from http://www.ncbi.nlm.nih.gov/pubmed/22905934

Ott, R. (1995). The natural wrongs about animal rights and animal liberation. *Journal of the American Veterinary Medical Association, 207,* 1023–1030.

Otto, M. W., Smits, J. A. J., & Reese, H. E. (2005). Combined psychotherapy and pharmacotherapy for mood and anxiety disorders in adults: Review and analysis. *Clinical Psychology: Science & Practice, 12,* 72–86.

Overmier, J. B., & Murison, R. (2013). Restoring psychology's role in peptic ulcer. *Applied Psychology: Health and Well-Being, 5*(1), 5–27.

Overmier, J. B., & Seligman, M. E. P. (1967). Effects of inescapable shock upon subsequent escape and avoidance responding. *Journal of Comparative and Physiological Psychology, 63,* 28–33.

Overskeid, G. (2007). Looking for Skinner and finding Freud. *American Psychologist, 65,* 590–595.

Owen, P. R. (2012). Portrayals of schizophrenia by entertainment media: A content analysis of contemporary movies. *Psychiatric Services, 63*(7), 655–59.

Owens, R. E. (2011). *Language development: An introduction* (8th ed.). Upper Saddle River, NJ: Pearson.

Oxley, D. R., Smith, K. B., Alford, J. R., Hibbing, M. V., Miller, J. L., Scalora, M., … Hibbing, J. R. (2008). Political attitudes vary with physiological traits. *Science, 321,* 1667–1670.

Oyserman, D., Coon, H. M., & Kemmelmeier, M. (2002). Rethinking individualism and collectivism: Evaluation of theoretical assumptions and meta-analyses. *Psychological Bulletin, 128,* 3–72.

Ozer, E. J., Best, S. R., Lipsey, T. L., & Weiss, D. S. (2003). Predictors of post-traumatic stress disorder symptoms in adults: A meta-analysis. *Psychological Bulletin, 129*, 52–73.

Ozonoff S. (2011). Editorial: The first cut is the deepest: Why do the reported effects of treatments decline over trials? *Journal of Child Psychology and Psychiatry, 52*, 729–730.

Pace, T. W. W., Negi, L. T., Adame, D. D., Cole, S. P., Sivilli, T. I., Brown, T. D., … Raison, C. L. (2009). Effect of compassion meditation on neuroendocrine, innate immune and behavioral responses to psychosocial stress. *Psychoneuroendocrinology, 34*(1), 87–98. doi: http://dx.doi.org/10.1016/j.psyneuen.2008.08.011

Paffenbarger, R. S., Hyde, R. T., Wing, A. L., & Hsieh, C. C. (1986). Physical activity, all-cause mortality, and longevity of college alumni. *New England Journal of Medicine, 314*, 605–613.

Page, F. (2016). Tony Robbins hot coal walk injures dozens, authorities say. CNN. http://edition.cnn.com/2016/06/24/us/tony-robbins-hot-coal-walkers-burned/. Retrieved September 12, 2016.

Pagel, J. F. (2003). Non-dreamers. *Sleep Medicine, 4*, 235–241.

Pagoto, S., Schneider, K., Jojic, M., DeBiasse, M., & Mann, D. (2013). Evidence-based strategies in weight-loss mobile apps. *American Journal of Preventive Medicine, 45*(5), 576–582.

Pahnke, W. N., Kurland, A. A., Unger, S., Savage, C., & Grof, S. (1970). Experimental use of psychedelic (LSD) psychotherapy. *Journal of the American Medical Association, 212*, 1856.

Paivio, A. (1969). Mental imagery in associative learning and memory. *Psychological Review, 76*, 341–363.

Palsson, E., Klamer, D., Wass C., Archer, T., Engel, J. A., & Svensen, L. (2005). The effects of phencyclidine on latent inhibition in taste aversion conditioning: Differential effects of preexposure and conditioning. *Behavioural Brain Research, 157*, 139–146.

Pankow, A., Friedel, E., Sterzer, P., Seiferth, N., Walter, H., Heinz, A., & Schlagenhauf, F. (2013). Altered amygdala activation in schizophrenia patients during emotion processing. *Schizophrenia Research, 150*(1), 101–6.

Panksepp, J. (2004). Free will and the varieties of affective and conative selves. *Behavioral and Brain Sciences, 27*(5), 671–672. Retrieved from http://search.proquest.com/docview/620720288?accountid=14168

Panksepp, J. (2005). Beyond a joke: From animal laughter to human joy? *Science, 208*, 62–63.

Panksepp, J. (2007). Neurologizing the psychology of affects: How appraisal-based constructivism and basic emotion theory can coexist. *Perspectives in Psychological Science, 2*, 281–296.

Panksepp, J., & Panksepp, J. B. (2000). The seven sins of evolutionary psychology. *Evolution and Cognition, 6*, 108–131.

Pano, E. G., Hilscher, M. C., & Cupchik, G. C. (2008–2009). Responding to self-consciousness: An examination of everyday and dream episodes. *Imagination, Cognition, and Personality, 28*, 173–198.

Paolucci, E. O., & Violato, C. (2004). A meta-analysis of the published research on the affective, cognitive and behavioral effects of corporal punishment. *Journal of Psychology, 138*, 197–221.

Paris, J. (2000). *Myths of childhood*. New York, NY: Brunner/Mazel.

Paris, J. (2012). The rise and fall of dissociative identity disorder. *The Journal of Nervous and Mental Disease, 200*(12), 1076–79.

Park, B., & Rothbart, M. (1982). Perception of out-group homogeneity and levels of social categorization: Memory for the subordinate attributes of in-group and out-group members. *Journal of Personality and Social Psychology, 42*, 1051–1068.

Park, M. A. (1982). Palmistry: Science or hand jive? *Skeptical Inquirer, 5*, 198–208.

Park, N., Peterson, C., & Seligman, M. E. P. (2004). Strengths of character and well-being. *Journal of Social and Clinical Psychology, 23*, 603–619.

Park, R. (2002). *Voodoo science: The road from foolishness to fraud*. New York, NY: Oxford University Press.

Park, R. L. (2003, January 21). The seven warning signs of bogus science. *Chronicle Review*. Retrieved from http://chronicle.com/article/The-Seven-Warning-Signs-of/13674

Parke, R. (1996). *Fatherhood*. Cambridge, MA: Harvard University Press.

Parker, E. S., Cahill, L., & McGaugh, J. L. (2006). A case of unusual autobiographical remembering. *Neurocase, 12*, 35–49.

Parsons, C. E., Young, K. S., Bhandari, R., Ijzendoorn, M. H., Bakermans-Kranenburg, M. J., Stein, A., & Kringelbach, M. L. (2014). The bonnie baby: Experimentally manipulated temperament affects perceived cuteness and motivation to view infant faces. *Developmental Science, 17*(2), 257–269.doi:10.1111/desc.12112

Parsons, M. J., Moffitt, T. E., Gregory, A. M., Goldman-Mellor, S., Nolan, P. M., Poulton, R., & Caspi, A. (2015). Social jetlag, obesity and metabolic disorder: Investigation in a cohort study. *International Journal of Obesity, 39*(5), 842–848.

Pascalis, O., de Schonen, S., Morton, J., Deruelle, C., & Fabre-Grenet, M. (1995). Mother's face recognition by neonates: A replication and an extension. *Infant Behavior and Development, 18*, 79–85.

Pascolini, D., & Smith, A. (2009). Hearing impairment in 2008: A compilation of available epidemiological studies. *International Journal of Audiology, 48*(7), 473–485.

Pascual-Leone, J. (1989). An organismic process model of Witkin's field dependence-independence. In T. Globerson and T. Zelniker (Eds.), *Cognitive style and cognitive development* (pp. 36–70). Norwood, NJ: Ablex.

Pascual, A., Carpenter, C. J., Guéguen, N., & Girandola, F. (2016). A meta-analysis of the effectiveness of the low-ball compliance-gaining procedure. *European Review of Applied Psychology, 66*, 261–267.

Pasek, J., Stark, T. H., Krosnick, J. A., Tompson, T., & Keith Payne, B. (2014). Attitudes toward Blacks in the Obama era. *Public Opinion Quarterly, 78*, 276–302.

Pasework, R. A., & Pantle, M. L. (1979). Insanity plea: Legislator's view. *American Journal of Psychiatry, 136*, 222–223.

Pashler, H., & Wagenmakers, E. J. (2012). Editors' introduction to the special section on replicability in Psychological Science: A crisis of confidence? *Perspectives on Psychological Science, 7*, 528–530.

Pashler, H., McDaniel, M., Rohrer, D., & Bjork, R. (2009). Learning styles: Concepts and evidence. *Psychological Science in the Public Interest, 9*, 105–119.

Passini, F. T., & Norman, W. T. (1966). A universal conception of personality structure? *Journal of Personality and Social Psychology, 4*, 44–49.

Pate, R. R., Pratt, M., Blair, S. N., Haskell, W. L., Macera, C. A., Bouchard, C., … Wilmore, J. H. (1995). Physical activity and public health: A recommendation from the Centers for Disease Control and the American College of Sports Medicine. *Journal of the American Medical Association, 273*, 402–407.

Patel, G. A., & Sathian, K. (2000). Visual search: Bottom-up or top-down? *Frontiers in Bioscience, 5*, D169–D193.

Patihis, L., Frenda, S. J., LePort, A. K., Petersen, N., Nichols, R. M., Stark, C. E., … Loftus, E. F. (2013). False memories in highly superior autobiographical memory individuals. *Proceedings of the National Academy of Sciences, 110*(52), 20947–20952.

Patihis, L., Ho, L. Y., Tingen, I. W., Lilienfeld, S. O., & Loftus, E. F. (2014). Are the "memory wars" over? A scientist-practitioner gap in beliefs about repressed memory. *Psychological Science, 25*(2), 519–530.

Patihis, L., Lilienfeld, S. O., Ho, L. Y., & Loftus, E. F. (2014). Unconscious repressed memory is scientifically questionable. *Psychological Science, 25*(10), 1967–1968.

Patrick, C. J., & Iacono, W. G. (1989). Psychopathy, threat, and polygraph test accuracy. *Journal of Applied Psychology, 74*, 347–355.

Patterson, C. J. (1992). Children of lesbian and gay parents. *Child Development, 63*, 1025–1042.

Patton, C., Smith, S.F., & Lilienfeld, S.O. (2016). *Psychopathy and heroism in first-responders*. Manuscript in preparation.

Paul, A. M. (2004). *The cult of personality: How personality tests are leading us to miseducate our children, mismanage our companies, and misunderstand ourselves*. New York, NY: Free Press.

Paul, G., & Lentz, R. J. (1977). *Psychosocial treatment of chronic mental patients: Milieu versus social-learning programs*. Cambridge, MA: Harvard University Press.

Paulesu, E., Harrison, J., Baron-Cohen, S., Watson, J. D., Goldstein, L., Heather, J., … & Frith, C. D. (1995). The physiology of coloured hearing A PET activation study of colour-word synaesthesia. *Brain, 118*(3), 661–676.

Paulesu, E., Harrison, J., Baroncohen, S., Watson, J. D. G., Goldstein, L., Heather, J., … Frith C. D. (1995). The physiology of colored hearing—A PET activation study of color-word synesthesia. *Brain, 118*, 661–676.

Paulhus, D. L. (1991). Measurement and control of response bias. In J. P. Robinson & P. R. Shaver (Eds.), *Measures of personality and social psychological attitudes* (pp. 17–59). San Diego, CA: Academic Press.

Paulhus, D. L., Lysy, D. C., & Yik, M. S. M. (1998). Self-report measures of intelligence: Are they useful as proxy IQ tests? *Journal of Personality, 66*(4), 525–554. http://dx.doi.org/10.1111/1467-6494.00023

Paulus, P. B. (Ed.). (2015). *Psychology of group influence* (Vol. 22). New York: Psychology Press.

Paulus, P. B., Larey, T. S., & Ortega, A. H. (1995). Performance and perceptions of brainstormers in an organizational setting. *Basic and Applied Social Psychology, 17*, 249–265.

Paulus, T. M. (2004). Collaboration or cooperation? Small group interactions in a synchronous educational environment. In T. S. Roberts (Ed.), *Computer-supported collaborative learning in higher education* (pp. 100–124). Hershey, PA: Idea Group.

Paunonen, S. V., & LeBel, E. P. (2012). Socially desirable responding and its elusive effects on the validity of personality assessments. *Journal of Personality and Social Psychology, 103*(1), 158.

Pavlov, I. P. (1927). *Conditioned reflexes*. Oxford, England: Oxford University Press.

Pawliczek, C. M., Derntl, B., Kellermann, T., Gur, R. C., Schneider, F., & Habel, U. (2013). Anger under control: neural correlates of frustration as a function of trait aggression. *PloSone, 8*(10), e78503.

Paxton, A., & McCune, A. (2015). *Alcohol in the body. ABC of Alcohol* (5th ed., 12–14). West Sussex, UK: Wiley/Blackwell.

Paykel, E. S. (2003). Life events and affective disorders. *Acta Psychiatrica Scandinavia Supplement, 108*, 61–66.

Payne, J. D., & Kensinger, E. A. (2010). Sleep's role in the consolidation of emotional episodic memories. *Current Directions in Psychological Science, 19*(5), 290–295.

Pazhoohi, F., & Liddle, J. R. (2012). Identifying feminine and masculine ranges for waist-to-hip ratio. *Journal of Social, Evolutionary, and Cultural Psychology, 6*, 227–232.

Pearson, B. Z., & Fernández, S. C. (1994). Patterns of interaction in the lexical growth in two languages of bilingual infants and toddlers. *Language Learning, 44*, 617–653.

Pearson, B. Z., Fernández, S. C., & Oller, D. K. (1993). Lexical development in bilingual infants and toddlers: Comparison to monolingual norms. *Language Learning, 43*, 93–120.

Pearson, H. (2006). Mouse data hint at human pheromones. *Nature, 442*, 495.

Pearson, M. L., Selby, J. V., Katz, K. A., Cantrell, V., Braden, C. R., Parise, M. E., ... Eberhard, M. L. (2012). Clinical, epidemiologic, histopathologic and molecular features of an unexplained dermopathy. *PLoS One, 7*(1), e29908.

Pedersen, N. L., Plomin, R., McClearn, G. E., & Friberg, L. (1988). Neuroticism, extraversion, and related traits in adult twins reared apart and reared together. *Journal of Personality and Social Psychology, 55*, 950–957.

Pederson Mussell, M., Crosby, R. D., Crow, S. J., Knopke, A. J., Peterson, C. B., Wonderlich, S. A., & Mitchell, J. E. (2000). Utilization of empirically supported psychotherapy treatments for individuals with eating disorders: A survey of psychologists. *International Journal of Eating Disorders, 27*, 230–237.

Peever, J., Luppi, P. H., & Montplaisir, J. (2014). Breakdown in REM sleep circuitry underlies REM sleep behavior disorder. *Trends in Neurosciences, 37*(5), 279–288.

Pelkonnen, M., & Marttunen, M. (2003). Child and adolescent suicide: Epidemiology, risk factors, and approaches to prevention. *Psychiatric Drugs, 5*, 243–265.

Penfield, W. (1958). *The excitable cortex in conscious man*. Liverpool, England: Liverpool University Press.

Penn & Schoen and Berland Associates. (2008). *American Psychological Association benchmark study*. New York, NY: Author.

Pennebaker, J. W. (1997). Writing about emotional experiences as a therapeutic process. *Psychological Science, 8*, 162–166.

Pennebaker, J. W., & Graybeal, A. (2001). Patterns of natural language use: Disclosure, personality, and social integration. *Current Directions, 10*, 90–93.

Pennebaker, J. W., Kiecolt-Glaser, J., & Glaser, R. (1988). Disclosure of traumas and immune function: Health implications for psychotherapy. *Journal of Consulting and Clinical Psychology, 56*, 239–245.

Penner, L. A., Dovidio, J. F., Schroeder, D. A., & Piliavin, J. A. (2005). Prosocial behavior: Multilevel perspectives. *Annual Review of Psychology, 56*, 365–392.

Peppard, P. E., Young, T., Barnet, J. H., Palta, M., Hagen, E. W., & Hla, K. M. (2013). Increased prevalence of sleep-disordered breathing in adults. *American Journal of Epidemiology, 177*(9), 1006–1014.

Pepperberg, I. M. (2006). Cognitive and communicative abilities of grey parrots. *Applied Animal Behaviour Science, 100*, 77–86.

Perkins, D. N. (1981). *The mind's best work*. Cambridge, MA: Harvard University Press.

Perlin, M. L., (2016). The insanity defense: Nine myths that will not go away. In M. D. White (Ed.), *The insanity defense: Multidisciplinary views on its history, trends, and controversies*. New York, NY: Praeger.

Perlmutter, M. (1983). Learning and memory through adulthood. In M. W. Riley, B. B. Hess, & K. Bond (Eds.), *Aging in society: Selected reviews of recent research*. Hillsdale, NJ: Erlbaum.

Perrin, A. J., Cohen, P. N., & Caren, N. (2013). Are children of parents who had same-sex relationships disadvantaged? A scientific evaluation of the no-differences hypothesis. *Journal of Gay & Lesbian Mental Health, 17*(3), 327–336.

Perry, G. (2013). *Behind the shock machine: The untold story of the notorious Milgram psychology experiments*. New York: The New Press.

Perry, J. C. (1984). *The borderline personality disorder scale: Reliability and validity*. Unpublished manuscript, Department of Psychiatry, Harvard Medical School at the Cambridge Hospital, Cambridge, MA.

Perry, W. G., Jr. (1970). *Forms of intellectual and ethical development in the college years*. Oxford, England: Holt, Rinehart & Winston.

Persily, N. (Ed.). (2015). *Solutions to political polarization in America*. New York: Cambridge University Press.

Persinger, M. A. (1987). *Neuropsychological bases of God beliefs*. New York, NY: Praeger.

Persuh, M., Genzer, B., & Melara, R. D. (2012). Iconic memory requires attention. *Frontiers in Human Neuroscience, 6*, 1–8.

Pert, C. (1997). *Molecules of emotion*. New York, NY: Simon & Schuster.

Pert, C. B., Pasternak, G., & Snyder, S. H. (1973). Opiate agonists and antagonists discriminated by receptor binding in brain. *Science, 182*, 1359–1361.

Pertusa, A., Frost, R. O., Fullana, M. A., Samuels, J., Steketee, G., Tolin, D., ... Mataix-Cols, D. (2010). Refining the diagnostic boundaries of compulsive hoarding: A critical review. *Clinical Psychology Review, 30*(4), 371–386.

Pessah, M. A., & Roffwarg, H. P. (1972). Spontaneous middle ear muscle activity in man: A rapid eye movement sleep phenomenon. *Science, 178*, 773–776.

Peters, M. J. V., Horselenberg, R., Jelicic, M., & Merckelbach, H. (2007). The false fame illusion in people with memories about a previous life. *Consciousness and Cognition: An International Journal, 16*(1), 162–169. http://dx.doi.org/10.1016/j.concog.2006.02.002

Peterson, B. S., Thomas, P., Kane, M. J., Scahill, L., Zhang, H., Bronen, R., ... & Staib, L. (2003). Basal ganglia volumes in patients with Gilles de la Tourette syndrome. *Archives of General Psychiatry, 60*(4), 415–424.

Peterson, C. (2000). The future of optimism. *American Psychologist, 55*, 44–55.

Peterson, C., & Seligman, M. E. (2004). *Character strengths and virtues: A handbook and classification*. New York: Oxford University Press.

Peterson, C., & Seligman, M. E. P. (2003). *Character strengths and virtues: A handbook and classification*. New York, NY: Oxford University Press.

Peterson, C., Park, N., & Seligman, M. E. (2013). Orientations to happiness and life satisfaction: The full life versus the empty life. In A. D. Fave (Ed.), *The exploration of happiness* (pp. 161–173). Amsterdam, the Netherlands: Springer.

Peterson, C., Warren, K. L., & Short, M. M. (2011). Infantile amnesia across the years: A 2-year follow-up of children's earliest memories. *Child Development, 82*(4), 1092–1105. http://dx.doi.org/10.1111/j.1467-8624.2011.01597.x

Peterson, L. R., & Peterson, M. J. (1959). Short-term retention of individual verbal items. *Journal of Experimental Psychology, 58*, 193–198.

Petit, D., Pennestri, M. H., Paquet, J., Desautels, A., Zadra, A., Vitaro, F., ... & Montplaisir, J. (2015). Childhood sleepwalking and sleep terrors: A longitudinal study of prevalence and familial aggregation. *JAMA Pediatrics, 169*(7), 653–658.

Petitto, L. A., & Marentette, P. F. (1991). Babbling in the manual mode: Evidence for the ontogeny of language. *Science, 251*, 1493–1496.

Petri, G., Expert, P., Turkheimer, F., Carhart-Harris, R., Nutt, D., Hellyer, P. J., & Vaccarino, F. (2014). Homological scaffolds of brain functional networks. *Journal of the Royal Society Interface, 11*(101), 20140873.

Petrosino. A., Turpin-Petrosino, C., & Buehler, J. (2003, November). "'Scared Straight' and other juvenile awareness programs for preventing juvenile delinquency. Campbell Review Update I." In *The Campbell Collaboration Reviews of Intervention and Policy Evaluations (C2-RIPE)*. Philadelphia, PA: Campbell Collaboration. Retrieved from http://web.archive.org/web/20070927013116/http://www.campbellcollaboration.org/doc-pdf/ssrupdt.pdf

Petry, N. M., Tennen, H., & Affleck, G. (2000). Stalking the elusive client variable in psychotherapy research. In C. R. Snyder & R. Ingram (Eds.), *Handbook of psychological change: Psychotherapy processes and practices for the 21st century* (pp. 88–108). New York, NY: Wiley.

Pettigrew, T. F. (1958). Personality and sociocultural factors in intergroup attitudes: A cross-national comparison. *Journal of Conflict Resolution, 2*, 29–42.

Pettigrew, T. F. (1979). The ultimate attribution error: Extending Allport's cognitive analysis of prejudice. *Personality and Social Psychology Bulletin, 5*, 461–476.

Pettigrew, T. F. (1998). Intergroup contact theory. *Annual Review of Psychology, 49*, 65–85.

Pettigrew, T. F., & Tropp, L. R. (2008) How does intergroup contact reduce prejudice? Meta-analytic tests of three mediators. *European Journal of Social Psychology, 38*, 922–934.

Pettinati, H. M., Tamburello, T. A., Ruetsch, C. R., & Kaplan, F. N. (1994). Patient attitudes toward electroconvulsive therapy. *Psychopharmacological Bulletin, 30*, 471–475.

Petty, R. E., & Cacioppo, J. T. (1986). *Communication and persuasion: Central and peripheral routes to attitude change*. New York, NY: Springer Verlag.

Petty, R. E., & Wegener, D. T. (1999). The elaboration likelihood model: Current status and controversies. Dual-process theories in social psychology. In S. Chaiken & Y. Trope (Eds.), *Dual-process theories in social psychology* (pp. 37–72). New York, NY: Guilford Press.

Pew Research Center. (2006, February 13). Are we happy yet? Retrieved from http://pewresearch.org/pubs/301/are-we-happy-yet

Pew Research Center. (2009, December 9). Many Americans mix multiple faiths. Retrieved from http://www.pewforum.org/2009/12/09/many-americans-mix-multiple-faiths/#ghosts-fortunetellers-and-communicating-with-the-dead

Pezdek, K., Finger, K., & Hodge, D. (1997). Planting false childhood memories: The role of event plausibility. *Psychological Science, 8*, 437–441.

Pezdek, K., O'Brien, M., & Wasson, C. (2011). Cross-race (but not same-race) face identification is impaired by presenting faces in a group rather than individually. *Law and Human Behavior (0147-7307)* http://dx.doi.org/10.1037/h0093933

Pfaltz, M., Michael, T., Meyer, A., & Wilhelm, F. (2013). Reexperiencing symptoms, dissociation, and avoidance behaviors in daily life of patients with PTSD and patients with panic disorder with agoraphobia. *Journal of Traumatic Stress, 26*(4), 443–50.

Phillips, K. A., Menard, W., Fay, C., & Weisberg, R. (2005). Demographic characteristics, phenomenology, comorbidity, and family history in 200 individuals with body dysmorphic disorder. *Psychosomatics, 46*, 317–325.

Phillips, M. L., & Swartz, H. A. (2014). A critical appraisal of neuroimaging studies of bipolar disorder: toward a new conceptualization of underlying neural circuitry and a road map for future research. *American Journal of Psychiatry, 171*, 829–43.

Phillips, M. L., Chase, H. W., Sheline, Y. I., Etkin, A., Almeida, J. R., Deckersbach, T., & Trivedi, M. H. (2015). Identifying predictors, moderators, and mediators of antidepressant response in major depressive disorder: Neuroimaging approaches. *American Journal of Psychiatry, 172*(2), 124–138.

Phillips, M. L., Young, A. W., Senior, C., Brammer, M., Andrew, C., Calder, A. J., ... David, A. S. (1997). A specific neural substrate for perceiving facial expressions of disgust. *Nature, 389*, 495–498.

Phillips, M. R., Wolf, A. S., & Coons, D. J. (1988). Psychiatry and the criminal justice system: Testing the myths. *American Journal of Psychiatry, 145*, 605–610.

Phillips, W. T., Kiernan, M., & King, A. C. (2001). The effects of physical activity on physical and psychological health. In A. Baum, T. A. Revenson, & J. E. Singer (Eds.), *Handbook of health psychology* (pp. 627–660). Mahwah, NJ: Erlbaum.

Piaget, J. (1932). *The moral judgment of the child*. London, England: Kegan Paul.

Piasecki, T. M., Cooper, M. L., Wood, P. K., Sher, K. J., Shiffman, S., & Heath, A. C. (2014). Dispositional drinking motives: Associations with appraised alcohol effects and alcohol consumption in an ecological momentary assessment investigation. *Psychological Assessment, 26*(2), 363.

Piatelli-Palmarini, M. (1994). *Inevitable illusions: How mistakes of reason rule our minds*. New York, NY: Wiley.

Piccinelli, M., & Wilkinson, G. (2000). Gender differences in depression—Critical review. *British Journal of Psychiatry, 177*, 486–492.

Piccione, C., Hilgard, E. R., & Zimbardo, P. G. (1989). On the degree of stability of measured hypnotizability over a 25-year period. *Journal of Personality and Social Psychology, 56*, 289–295.

Pickel, K. L. (2007). Remembering and identifying menacing perpetrators: Exposure to violence and the weapon focus effect. In R. C. L. Lindsay, D. F. Ross, J. D. Read, & M. P. Toglia (Eds.), *The handbook of eyewitness psychology, volume II: Memory for people* (pp. 339–360). Mahwah, NJ: Erlbaum.

Pies, R. (2012). Bereavement, complicated grief, and the rationale for diagnosis in psychiatry. *Dialogues in Clinical Neuroscience, 14*(2), 111–113.

Piet, J., & Hougaard, E. (2011). The effect of mindfulness-based cognitive therapy for prevention of relapse in recurrent major depressive disorder: a systematic review and meta-analysis. *Clinical Psychology Review, 31*(6), 1032–1040.

Pietschnig, J., & Voracek, M. (2015). One century of global IQ Gains: A formal meta-analysis of the Flynn Effect (1909–2013). *Perspectives on Psychological Science, 10*, 282–306.

Pignotti, M., & Thyer, B. A. (2009). Some comments on *Energy Psychology: a review of the evidence:* Premature conclusions based on incomplete evidence? *Psychotherapy, Theory, Research, Practice, Training, 46*, 257–261.

Pignotti, M., & Thyer, B. A. (2015). New age and related novel unsupported therapies in mental health practice. In S.Lilienfeld, S.J. Lynn, & J. Lohr (Eds.), *Science and pseudoscience in clinical psychology*, 2nd Ed. (pp. 191–209). New York: Guilford Press.

Pihl, R. O. (1999). Substance abuse: Etiological considerations. In T. Millon, P. Blaney, & R. D. Davis (Eds.), *Oxford handbook of psychopathology* (pp. 249–276). New York, NY: Oxford University Press.

Pike, K. M., Hoek, H. W., & Dunne, P. E. (2014). Cultural trends and eating disorders. *Current Opinion in Psychiatry, 27*(6), 436–442.

Piliavin, I. M., Rodin, J., & Piliavin, J. A. (1969). Good samaritanism: An underground phenomenon? *Journal of Personality and Social Psychology, 13*, 289–299.

Pillemer, D. B. (1984). Flashbulb memories of the assassination attempt on President Reagan. *Cognition, 16*, 63–80.

Pinker, S. (1997). *How the mind works.* New York, NY: Norton.

Pinker, S. (2002). *The blank slate: The modern denial of human nature.* New York, NY: Penguin Press.

Pinker, S. (2005, February 14). The science of difference: Sex ed. *The New Republic, 232,*

Pinker, S. (2011). *The better angels of our nature: Why violence has declined.* New York, NY: Viking Press, 15–17.

Pinker, S. (2014, September 26). Why academics stink at writing. *Chronicle of Higher Education, 26.*

Pinsk, M. A., DeSimone, K., Moore, T., Gross, C. G., & Kastner, S. (2005). Representations of faces and body parts in macaque temporal cortex: A functional MRI study. *Proceedings of the National Academy of Sciences, 102*, 6996–7001.

Piper, A. (1993). "Truth serum" and "recovered memories" of sexual abuse: A review of the evidence. *Journal of Psychiatry & Law, 21*, 447–471.

Piper, A. (1997). *Hoax and reality: The bizarre world of multiple personality disorder.* Northvale, NJ: Jason Aronson.

Piske, T., MacKay, I. R. A., & Flege, J. E. (2001). Factors affecting degree of foreign accent in an L2: A review. *Journal of Phonetics, 29*, 191–215.

Pitman, R. K., Sanders, K. M., Zusman, R. M., Healy, A. R., Cheema, F., Lasko, N. B., … Orr, S. P. (2002). Pilot study of secondary prevention of posttraumatic stress disorder with propranolol. *Biological Psychiatry, 51*, 189–192.

Pittas, A. G., Hariharan, R., Stark, P. C., Hajduk, C. L., Greenberg, A. S., & Roberts, S. B. (2005). Interstitial glucose level is a significant predictor of energy intake in free-living women with healthy body weight. *Journal of Nutrition, 135*, 1070–1074.

Pittenger, D. J. (2005). Cautionary comments regarding the Myers-Briggs Type Indicator. *Consulting Psychology Journal: Practice and Research, 57*, 210–221.

Pittinger, C, & Duman, R. S. (2008). Stress, depression, and neuroplasticity: A convergence of mechanisms. *Neuropsychopharmacology Reviews, 33*, 88–109.

Pizzi, C., Cole, T. J., Richiardi, L., dos-Santos-Silva, I., Corvalan, C., & De Stavola, B. (2014). Prenatal influences on size, velocity and tempo of infant growth: Findings from three contemporary cohorts. *PloS One, 9*(2), e90291. doi:10.1371/journal.pone.0090291

Plait, P. C. (2002). *Bad astronomy: Misconceptions and misuses revealed from astrology to the moon landing "hoax."* New York, NY: Wiley.

Platek, S. M., Critton, S. R., Myers, T. E., & Gallup, G. G. (2003). Contagious yawning: The role of self-awareness and mental state attribution. *Cognitive Brain Research, 17*, 223–227.

Platek, S. M., Mohamed, F. B., & Gallup, G. G. (2005). Contagious yawning and the brain. *Cognitive Brain Research, 23*, 448–452.

Platt, J. R. (1964). Strong inference. *Science, 146*, 347–353.

Platt, S. A., & Sanislow, C. A. (1988). Norm-of-reaction: Definition and misinterpretation of animal research. *Journal of Comparative Psychology, 102*, 254–261.

Plomin, R. (2004). Genetics and developmental psychology. *Merrill-Palmer Quarterly Journal of Developmental Psychology, 50*, 341–352.

Plomin, R., & Crabbe, J. C. (2000). DNA. *Psychological Bulletin, 126*, 806–828.

Plomin, R., & Daniels, D. (1987). Why are children in the same family so different from one another? *Behavioral and Brain Sciences, 10*, 1–16.

Plomin, R., & Deary, I. J. (2015). Genetics and intelligence differences: Five special findings. *Molecular Psychiatry, 20*, 98–108.

Plomin, R., & Kovas, Y. (2005). Generalist genes and learning disabilities. *Psychological Bulletin, 131*, 592–617.

Plomin, R., & McClearn, G. E. (1993). *Nature, nurture, and psychology.* Washington, DC: American Psychological Association.

Plomin, R., & Petrill, S. A. (1997). Genetics and intelligence: What's new? *Intelligence, 24*(1), 53–77. http://dx.doi.org/10.1016/S0160-2896(97)90013-1

Plomin, R., Corley, R., DeFries, J. C., & Fulker, D. W. (1990). Individual differences in television viewing in early childhood: Nature as well as nurture. *Psychological Science, 1*, 371–377.

Plomin, R., DeFries, J. C., & Loehlin, J. C. (1977). Genotype-environment interaction and correlation in the analysis of human behavior. *Psychological Bulletin, 84*, 309–322.

Plomin, R., DeFries, J. C., Knopik, V. S., & Neiderhiser, J. M. (2016). Top 10 replicated findings from behavioral genetics. *Perspectives on Psychological Science, 11*(1), 3–23.

Plomin, R., DeFries, J. C., Knopik, V. S., & Neiderhiser, J. M. (2016). Top 10 replicated findings from behavioral genetics. *Perspectives on Psychological Science, 11*, 3–23.

Plomin, R., DeFries, J.C., McClearn, G.E., & Rutter, M. (1997). Behavioral genetics (3rd ed.). New york, NY: W.H. Freeman.

Plotkin, H. (2004). *Evolutionary thought in psychology: A brief history.* Oxford, England: Blackwell.

Plotnik, J. M., de Waal, F. B. M., & Reiss, D. (2006). Self-recognition in an Asian elephant. *Proceedings of the National Academy of Sciences, 103*, 17053–17057.

Plutchik, R. (2000). *Emotions in the practice of psychotherapy: Clinical implications of affect theories.* Washington, DC: American Psychological Association.

Plutchik, R. (2003). *Emotions and life: Perspectives from psychology, biology, and evolution.* Washington, DC: American Psychological Association.

Plutchik, R., & Kellerman, H. (Eds.). (1986). *Emotion: Theory, research, and experience: Biological foundations of emotion.* New York, NY: Academic Press.

Podczerwinski, E. S., Wickens, C. D., & Alexander, A. L. (2002) *Technical Report ARL-01-8/NASA-01-04.* Moffett Field, CA: NASA Ames Research Center.

Pohorecky, L. (1977). Biphasic action of ethanol. *Biobehavioral Review, 1*, 231–240.

Poizner, H., Klima, E. S., & Bellugi, U. (1987). *What the hands reveal about the brain.* Cambridge, MA: MIT Press.

Polderman, T. J., Benyamin, B., De Leeuw, C. A., Sullivan, P. F., Van Bochoven, A., Visscher, P. M., & Posthuma, D. (2015). Meta-analysis of the heritability of human traits based on fifty years of twin studies. *Nature Genetics, 47*, 702–709.

Poldrack, R. A. (2011). The iPhone and the brain. *New York Times,* 5.

Polivy, J., & Herman, C. P. (2002). If you first don't succeed. False hopes of self-change. *American Psychologist, 57*, 677–689.

Polivy, J., Schueneman, A. L., & Carlson, K. (1976). Alcohol and tension reduction: Cognitive and physiological effects. *Journal of Abnormal Psychology, 85*, 595–600.

Pollard, K. S., Salama, S. R., King, B., Kern, A. D., Dreszer, T., Katzman, S., … Hassler, D. (2006, October 13). Forces shaping the fastest evolving regions in the human genome. *PLoS Genetics, 2*(10), 168.

Pollini, R. A. Banta-Green, C. J., Cuevas-Mota, J., Metzner, M., Teshale, E., & Garfein, R. S. (2011). Problematic use of prescription-type opioids prior to heroin use among young heroin injectors. *Substance Abuse and Rehabilitation, 2*(1), 173–180.

Polusny, M. A., & Follette, V. M. (1996). Remembering childhood sexual abuse: A national survey of psychologists' clinical practices, beliefs, and personal experiences. *Professional Psychology: Research and Practice, 27*, 41–52.

Pontón, M. O., & Gorsuch, R. L. (1988). Prejudice and religion revisited: A cross-cultural investigation with a Venezuelan sample. *Journal for the Scientific Study of Religion, 27*, 260–271.

Poole, D. A., Lindsay, D. S., Memon, A., & Bull, R. (1995). Psychotherapists' opinions, practices, and experiences with recovery of memories of incestuous abuse. *Journal of Consulting and Clinical Psychology, 68*, 426–437.

Pope, H. G., Gruber, A. J., & Yergelun-Todd, D. (2001). Residual neuropsychologic effects of cannabis. *Current Psychiatry Report, 3*, 507–512.

Pope, H. G., Jr., & Hudson, J. I. (1992). Is childhood sexual abuse a risk factor for bulimia nervosa? *American Journal of Psychiatry, 149*, 455–463.

Pope, H. G., Jr., Poliakoff, M. B., Parker, M. P., Boynes, M., & Hudson, J. I. (2007). Is dissociative amnesia a culture-bound syndrome? Findings from a survey of historical literature. *Psychological Medicine, 37*, 225–233.

Popper, K. R. (1965). *The logic of scientific discovery.* New York, NY: Harper & Row.

Pornpitakpan, C. (2004). The persuasiveness of source credibility: A critical review of five decades' evidence. *Journal of Applied Social Psychology, 34*, 243–281.

Porsch, R. M., Middeldorp, C. M., Cherny, S. S., Krapohl, E., Van Beijsterveldt, C. E., Loukola, A., … Kaprio, J. (2016). Longitudinal heritability of childhood aggression. *American Journal of Medical Genetics Part B: Neuropsychiatric Genetics, 171*, 697–707.

Porter, S. B., & Baker, A. T. (2015). CSI (crime scene induction): Creating false memories of committing crime. *Trends in Cognitive Sciences, 19*(12), 716–718.

Porter, S., & Peace, K. A. (2007). The scars of memory: A prospective longitudinal investigation of the consistency of traumatic and positive emotional memories in adulthood. *Psychological Science, 18*, 435–441.

Porter, S., Yuille, J. C., & Lehman, D. R. (1999). The nature of real, implanted, and fabricated memories for emotional childhood events. *Law and Human Behavior, 23*, 517–537.

Posey, T. B., & Losch, M. E. (1983). Auditory hallucinations of hearing voices in 375 normal subjects. *Imagination, Cognition and Personality, 3,* 99–113.

Posner, G. P., & Sampson, W. (1999, Fall/Winter). Chinese acupuncture for heart surgery anesthesia. *The Scientific Review of Alternative Medicine, 3,* 15–19.

Posner, M. I., & Snyder, C. R. R. (1975). Facilitation and inhibition in the processing of signals. In P. M. A. Rabbitt & S. Dornic (Eds.), *Attention and performance* (pp. 669–682). New York, NY: Academic Press.

Post, J. M. (2010). The electronic revolution and the virtual communities of cooperation and hatred. Presentation at International Society of Political Psychology. Retrieved from http://www.ispp.org/meetings/abstract/the-electronic-revolution-and-the-virtual-communities-of-cooperation-and-ha

Posthuma, D., & de Geus, E. J. C. (2006). Progress in the molecular-genetic study of intelligence. *Current Directions in Psychological Science, 15,* 151–155.

Postle, B. R., & Kensinger, E. (2016). The unforgettable career of Suzanne Corkin. *Hippocampus, 26*(10), 1233–1237.

Postmes, T., & Spears, R. (1998). Deindividuation and antinormative behavior: A meta-analysis. *Psychological Bulletin, 123,* 238–259.

Potter, D. (2012). Same-sex parent families and children's academic achievement. *Journal of Marriage and Family, 74,* 556–571.

Potts, R. G. (2004). Spirituality, religion, and the experience of illness. In P. Camic & S. Knight (Eds.), *Clinical handbook of health psychology: A practical guide to effective interventions* (pp. 297–314). Cambridge, MA: Hogrefe & Huber.

Poulsen, S., Lunn, S., Daniel, S. I., Folke, S., Mathiesen, B. B., Katznelson, H., & Fairburn, C. G. (2014). A randomized controlled trial of psychoanalytic psychotherapy or cognitive-behavioral therapy for bulimia nervosa. *American Journal of Psychiatry, 171,* 109–116.

Powell, L. H., Shahabi, L., & Thoresen, C. E. (2003). Religion and spirituality: Linkages to physical health. *American Psychologist, 58,* 36–52.

Powell, R. A. (2010). Little Albert still missing. *American Psychologist, 65,* 299–300.

Powell, R. W., & Curley, M. (1984). Analysis of instinctive drift. 2. The development and control of species-specific responses in appetitive conditioning. *Psychological Record, 34,* 363–379.

Power, R. A., Steinberg, S., Bjornsdottir, G., Rietveld, C. A., Abdellaoui, A., Nivard, M. M., ... Cesarini, D. (2015). Polygenic risk scores for schizophrenia and bipolar disorder predict creativity. *Nature Neuroscience, 18,* 953–955.

Powers, D. E. (1993). Coaching for the SAT: A summary of the summaries and an update. *Educational Measurement: Issues and Practice, 12,* 24–39.

Powers, D. E., & Rock, D. A. (1999). Effects of coaching on SAT I: Reasoning test scores. *Journal of Educational Measurement, 36*(2), 93–118. http://dx.doi.org/10.1111/j.1745-3984.1999.tb00549.x

Poythress, N. G., Edens, J. F., Skeem, J. L., Lilienfeld, S. O., Douglas, K. S., Frick, P. J., ... Wang, T. (2010). Identifying subtypes among offenders with antisocial personality disorder: A cluster-analytic study. *Journal of Abnormal Psychology, 119*(2), 389–400.

Prasad, V. K., & Cifu, A. S. (2015). *Ending medical reversal: Improving outcomes, saving lives.* Baltimore, MD: Johns Hopkins University Press.

Prather, A. A., Janicki-Deverts, D., Hall, M. H., & Cohen, S. (2015). Behaviorally assessed sleep and susceptibility to the common cold. *Sleep, 38*(9), 1353–1359.

Prather, A. A., Janicki-Deverts, D., Hall, M. H., & Cohen, S. (2015). Behaviorally assessed sleep and susceptibility to the common cold. *Sleep, 38*(9), 1353–1359.

Pratkanis, A. R. (1995, July/August). How to sell a pseudoscience. *Skeptical Inquirer, 19,* 19–25.

Pratt, L. A., Brody, D. J., & Gu, Q. (2011).. NCHS Data Brief, No.76, October. U.S. Department of Health and Human Services, Atlanta: CDC.

Preckel, F., Holling, H., & Wiese, M. (2006). Relationship of intelligence and creativity in gifted and non-gifted students: An investigation of threshold theory. *Personality and Individual Differences, 40*(1), 159–170. http://dx.doi.org/10.1016/j.paid.2005.06.022

Premack, D. (1965). Reinforcement theory. In D. Levine (Ed.), *Nebraska Symposium on Motivation* (pp. 123–180). Lincoln, NE: University of Nebraska Press.

Premack, D., & Woodruff, G. (1978). Does the chimpanzee have a theory of mind? *Behavioral and Brain Sciences, 1,* 515–526.

Presley, S. (1997). *Why people believe in ESP for the wrong reasons.* Retrieved from http://www.rit.org/essays/esp.php

Price, J., & Davis, B. (2008). *The woman who can't forget: The extraordinary story of living with the most remarkable memory known to science.* New York, NY: Free Press.

Price, R. H., & Bouffard, D. L. (1974). Behavioral appropriateness and situational constraint as dimensions of social behavior. *Journal of Personality and Social Psychology, 30,* 579–586.

Priel, B., & de Schonen, S. (1986). Self-recognition: A study of a population without mirrors. *Journal of Experimental Child Psychology, 41,* 237–250.

Pringle, P. J., Geary, M. P. P., Rodeck, C. H., Kingdom, J. C. P., Kayamba-Kay's, S., & Hindmarsh, P. C. (2005). The influence of cigarette smoking on antenatal growth, birth size, and the insulin-like growth factor axis. *Journal of Clinical Endocrinology & Metabolism, 90,* 2556–2562.

Prinz, J. J. (2004). *Gut reactions: A perceptual theory of emotion.* New York, NY: Oxford University Press.

Proceedings of the National Academy of Sciences, 92(18), 8215–8218.

Prochaska, J. O., & DiClemente, C. C. (1982). Transtheoretical therapy: Toward a more integrative model of change. *Psychotherapy: Theory, Research, and Practice, 20,* 161–173.

Prochaska, J. O., & Norcross, J. C. (2007). *Systems of psychotherapy: A transtheoretical approach* (6th ed.). Pacific Grove, CA: Brooks/Cole.

Prochaska, J. O., & Norcross, J. C. (2013). Systems of psychotherapy: A transtheoretical analysis, 8th ed. Stamford, CT: Cengage Learning.

Proctor, R. W., & Capaldi, E. J. (2006). *Why science matters: Understanding the methods of psychological research.* Malden, MA: Blackwell.

Project MATCH Research Group. (1997). Matching alcoholism treatments to client heterogeneity: Project MATCH posttreatment drinking outcomes. *Journal of Studies on Alcohol, 58,* 7–29.

Pronin, E. (2008). How we see ourselves and how we see others. *Science, 320,* 1177–1180.

Pronin, E., Berger, J., & Molouki, S. (2007). Alone in a crowd of sheep: Asymmetric perceptions of conformity and their roots in an introspective illusion. *Journal of Personality and Social Psychology, 92,* 585–595.

Pronin, E., Gilovich, T., & Ross, L. (2004). Objectivity in the eye of the beholder: Divergent perceptions of bias in self versus others. *Psychological Review, 3,* 781–799.

Proske, U. (2006). Kinesthesia: The role of muscle receptors. *Muscle Nerve, 34,* 545–558.

Provine, R. R. (1996). Laughter. *American Scientist, 84,* 38–45.

Provine, R. R. (2000). *Laughter: A scientific investigation.* New York, NY: Viking Press.

Provine, R. R. (2005). Yawning. *American Scientist, 93,* 532–539.

Provine, R. R. (2012). *Curious behavior: Yawning, laughing, hiccupping, and beyond.* Cambridge, MA: Belknap Press.

Psychological Assessment Resources (2015, May 5). *Psychologists by the numbers.* http://blog.parinc.com/psychologists-by-the-numbers-2/

Punjabi, N. M., Caffo, B. S., Goodwin, J. L., Gottlieb, D. J., Newman, A. B., O'Connor, G. T., ... Samet, J. M. (2009) Sleep-disordered breathing and mortality: A prospective cohort study. *PLoS Medicine, 6*(8), e1000132. http://dx.doi.org/10.1371/journal.pmed.1000132

Purcell, K. (1963). Distinctions between subgroups of asthmatic children. *Pediatrics, 31*(3), 486–494.

Purcell, S. M., Wray, N. R., Stone, J. L., Visscher, P. M., O'Donovan, M. C., Sullivan, P. F., ... Fraser, G. (2009). Common polygenic variation contributes to risk of schizophrenia and bipolar disorder. *Nature, 460*(7256), 748–752.

Purves, D., Lotto, R. B., & Nundy, S. (2002). Why we see what we do. *American Scientist, 90,* 236.

Putman, V. L., & Paulus, P. B. (2009). Brainstorming, brainstorming rules, and decision making. *Journal of Creative Behavior, 42,* 23–29.

Quart, E. (2006, July/August). Extreme parenting. *The Atlantic.* Retrieved from http://www.theatlantic.com/doc/prem/200607/parenting

Quattrociocchi, Scalia, A., & Sunstein, C.R. (2016) Echo chambers on facebook. *SSRN.* http://www.law.harvard.edu/programs/olin_center/papers/pdf/Sunstein_877.pdf

Quenqua, D. (2012, February). They're, like, way ahead of the linguistic currrrve. *New York Times, 28.*

Quick, D. C. (1999, March/April). Joint pain and weather. *Skeptical Inquirer, 23,* 49–51.

Quick, J. C., Quick, J. D., Nelson, D. L., & Hurrell, J. J. (1997). *Preventive stress management in organizations.* Washington, DC: American Psychological Association.

Quick, V. M., McWilliams, R., & Byrd-Bredbenner, C. (2013). Fatty, fatty, two-by-four: Weight-teasing history and disturbed eating in young adult women. *American Journal of Public Health, 103*(3), 508–515.

Quidé, Y., Witteveen, A. B., El-Hage, W., Veltman, D. J., & Olff, M. (2012). Differences between effects of psychological versus pharmacological treatments on functional and morphological brain alterations in anxiety disorders and major depressive disorder: a systematic review. *Neuroscience & Biobehavioral Reviews, 36*(1), 626–644.

Quinn, P. C., & Eimas, P. D. (1996). Perceptual cues that permit categorical differentiation of animal species by infants. *Journal of Experimental Child Psychology, 63,* 189–211.

Quinn, P. C., & Liben, L. S. (2008). A sex difference in mental rotation in young infants. *Psychological Science, 19*(11), 1067–1070. http://dx.doi.org/10.1111/j.1467-9280.2008.02201.x

Quinn, P. C., & Liben, L. S. (2014). A sex difference in mental rotation in infants: Convergent evidence. *Infancy, 19,* 103–116.

Quiroga, R. Q., Reddy, L., Kreiman, G., Koch, C., & Fried, I. (2005). Invariant visual representation by single neurons in the human brain. *Nature, 435,* 1102–1107.

Quist, M. C., Watkins, C. D., Smith, F. G., DeBruine, L. M., & Jones, B. C. (2011). Facial masculinity is a cue to women's dominance. *Personality and Individual Differences, 50,* 1089–1093. http://dx.doi.org/10.1016/j.paid.2011.01.032

Rabinowitz, J., & Renert, N. (1997). Clinicians' predictions of length of psychotherapy. *Psychiatric Services, 48,* 97–99.

Rachlin, H. (1990). Why do people gamble and keep gambling despite heavy losses? *Psychological Science, 1,* 294–297.

Rachlin, H., & Logue, A. W. (1991). Learning. In M. Hersen, A. E. Kazdin, & A. S. Bellack (Eds.), *The clinical psychology handbook* (2nd ed., pp. 170–184). Elmsford, NY: Pergamon Press.

Rachman, S. (1977). The conditioning theory of fear-acquisition: A critical examination. *Behaviour Research and Therapy, 15,* 375–387.

Rachman, S. (1994). Psychological treatment of panic: Mechanisms. In B. E. Wolfe & J. D. Maser (Eds.), *Treatment of panic disorder: A consensus development conference* (pp. 133–148). Washington, DC: American Psychiatric Press.

Rachman, S., & Hodgson, R. J. (1968). Experimentally induced "sexual fetishism": Replication and development. *Psychological Record, 18*, 25–27.

Racine, E., Bar-Ilan, O., & Illes, J. (2006). Brain imaging: A decade of coverage in the print media. *Science Communication, 28*, 122–142.

Rader, C. M., & Tellegen, A. (1987). An investigation of synesthesia. *Journal of Personality and Social Psychology, 52*, 981–987.

Radvansky, G. A., Gibson, B. S., & McNerney, M. W. (2011). Synesthesia and memory: Color congruency, von restorff, and false memory effects. *Journal of Experimental Psychology: Learning, Memory, and Cognition, 37*(1), 219–229. http://dx.doi.org/10.1037/a0021329

Rafnsson, F. D., Jonsson, F. H., & Windle, M. (2006). Coping strategies, stressful life events, problem behaviors, and depressed affect. *Anxiety, Stress, & Coping, 19*, 241–257.

Rahim-Williams, B., Riley, J. L., Williams, A. K., & Fillingim, R. B. (2012). A quantitative review of ethnic group differences in experimental pain response: do biology, psychology, and culture matter? *Pain Medicine, 13*(4), 522–540.

Raimy, V. C. (Ed.). (1950). *Training in clinical psychology (Boulder Conference)*. New York, NY: Prentice Hall.

Rainey, D. W., & Larsen, J. D. (2002). The effect of familiar melodies on initial learning and long-term memory for unconnected text. *Music Perception, 20*, 173–186.

Rainville, P., Bechara, A., Naqvi, N., & Damasio, A. R. (2006). Basic emotions are associated with distinct patterns of cardiorespiratory activity. *International Journal of Psychophysiology, 61*, 5–18.

Rajaratnam, S. M., Polymeropoulos, M. H., Fisher, D. M., Roth, T., Scott, C., Birznieks, G., & Klerman, E. B. (2009). Melatonin agonist tasimelteon (VEC-162) for transient insomnia after sleep-time shift: Two randomised controlled multicentre trials. *Lancet, 373*, 482–491.

Raloff, J. (2009, September 12). Drugged money. *Science News, 176*(6), 9.

Ramachandran, V. S. (2000). Mirror neurons and imitation learning as the driving force behind "the great leap forward" in human evolution. Edge. Retrieved from http://www.edge.org/3rd_culture/ramachandran/ramachandran_p1.html

Ramachandran, V. S., & Rogers-Ramachandran, D. C. (1996). Synaesthesia in phantom limbs induced with mirrors. *Proceedings of the Royal Society of London, 263*, 377–386.

Ramaekers, J. G., Kauert, G., van Ruitenbeek, P., Theunissen, E. L., Schneider, E., & Moeller, M. R. (2006). High-potency marijuana impairs executive function and inhibitory motor control. *Neuropsychopharmacology, 31*, 2296–2303.

Ramer, D. G. (1980) The Premack Principle, self-monitoring, and the maintenance of preventive dental health behaviour. *Dissertation Abstracts International, 40*(11-B), 5415–5416.

Ramon, M., Busigny, T., & Rossion, B. (2010). Impaired holistic processing of unfamiliar individual faces in acquired prosopagnosia. *Neuropsychologia, 48*, 933–944.

Randi, J. (1982). *Flim-flam!* Amherst, NY: Prometheus.

Randoph-Seng, B., & Nielsen, M. E. (2007). Honesty: On effect of primed religious representations. *The International Journal for the Psychology of Religion, 17*, 303–315.

Ranehill, E., Dreber, A., Johannesson, M., Leiberg, S., Sul, S., & Weber, R. A. (2015). Assessing the Robustness of power posing No effect on hormones and risk tolerance in a large sample of men and women. *Psychological Science, 0956797614553946*.

Rankin, J. L. (2005). *Parenting experts: Their advice, the research, and getting it right.* Westport, CT: Praeger.

Rapaport M. H., Nierenberg, A. A., Howland, R., Dording, C., Schettler, P. J, & Mischoulon, D. (2011). The treatment of minor depression with St. John's Wort or citalopram: Failure to show benefit over placebo. *Journal of Psychiatric Research, 45*, 931–941.

Rapp, M. S. (1984). Differential diagnosis and treatment of the "housebound syndrome." *Canadian Medical Association Journal, 131*, 1041–44.

Rasmussen, K., Sampson, S. M., & Rummans, T. A. (2002). Electroconvulsive therapy and newer modalities for the treatment of medication-refractory mental illness. *Mayo Clinic Proceedings, 77*, 552–556.

Rasouli, R., & Razmizade, H. (2013). Effectiveness of stress inoculation training in reducing anxiety and stress in students. *International Journal of Behavioral Sciences, 7*(1), 43–48.

Rassin, E., Eerland, A., & Kuijpers, I. (2010). Let's find the evidence: An analogue study of confirmation bias in criminal investigations. *Journal of Investigative Psychology and Offender Profiling, 7*, 231–246.

Rathus, S.A., Nevid, J.S., & Fichner-Rathus, L. (2013). *Human sexuality in a world of diversity* (9th Ed.). Hoboken, NJ: Pearson.

Ratiu, P., Talos, I. F., Haker, S., Lieberman, D., & Everett, P. (2004). The tale of Phineas Gage, digitally remastered. *Journal of Neurotrauma, 21*, 637–643.

Rattenborg, N. C., Voirin, B., Cruz, S. M., Tisdale, R., Dell'Omo, G., Lipp, H-P.... . Vyssotski, A. (2016). Evidence that birds sleep in mid-flight. *Nature Communications*, doi:10.1038/ncomms12468

Raulin, M. L. (2003). *Abnormal psychology*. Boston, MA: Allyn & Bacon.

Raulin, M. L., & Lilienfeld, S. O. (2008). Research paradigms in the study of psychopathology. In P. H. Blaney & T. Milton (Eds.), *Oxford textbook of psychopathology*. (2nd ed., pp. 86–115). New York, NY: Oxford University Press.

Rauscher, F. H., Shaw, G. L., & Ky, K. N. (1993). Music and spatial task performance. *Nature, 365*, 611.

Raven, J., Raven, J. C., & Court, J. H. (1998). *Manual for Raven's Advanced Progressive Matrices*. Oxford, England: Oxford Psychologists Press.

Ray, J. V., Hall, J., Rivera-Hudson, N., Poythress, N. G., Lilienfeld, S. O., & Morano, M. (2012). The relation between self-reported psychopathic traits and distorted response styles: A meta-analytic review. *Personality Disorders: Theory, Research, and Treatment*. Retrieved from http://psycnet.apa.org/psycinfo/2012-01747-001

Rayner, K., Foorman, B. R., Perfetti, C. A., Pesetsky, D., & Seidenberg, M. S. (2002). How should reading be taught? *Scientific American, 286*, 84.

Rayner, K., Schotter, E. R., Masson, M. E., Potter, M. C., & Treiman, R. (2016). So much to read, so little time: How do we read, and can speed reading help? *Psychological Science in the Public Interest, 17*, 4–34.

Razoumnikova, O. (2000). Functional organization of different brain areas during convergent and divergent thinking: An EEG investigation. *Cognitive Brain Research, 10*, 11–18.

Reasoner, R. (2000). *Self-esteem and youth: What research has to say about it.* Port Ludlow, WA: International Council for Self-Esteem.

Rechtschaffen, A. (1998). Current perspectives on the function of sleep. *Perspectives in Biology and Medicine, 41*, 359–390.

Rechtschaffen, A., Verdone, P., & Wheaton, J. (1963). Reports of mental activity during sleep. *Canadian Psychiatry, 8*, 409–414.

Redding, R. E. (1998). How common-sense psychology can inform law and psycholegal research. *University of Chicago Law School Roundtable, 5*, 107–142.

Redding, R. E. (2004). Bias or prejudice? The politics of research on racial prejudice. *Psychological Inquiry, 15*, 289–293.

Redding, R. E. (2012). Likes attract the sociopolitical groupthink of (social) psychologists. *Perspectives on Psychological Science, 7*, 512–515.

Redick, T. S., Unsworth, N., Kelly, A. J., & Engle, R. W. (2012). Faster, smarter? Working memory capacity and perceptual speed in relation to fluid intelligence. *Journal of Cognitive Psychology, 24*(7), 844–854. http://dx.doi.org/10.1080/20445911.2012.704359

Reed, A. E., & Carstensen, L. L. (2012). The theory behind the age-related positivity effect. *Frontiers in Psychology, 3*, 339. http://dx.doi.org/10.3389/fpsyg.2012.00339

Reed, A. E., Chan, L., & Mikels, J. A. (2014). Meta-analysis of the age-related positivity effect: age differences in preferences for positive over negative information. *Psychology and Aging, 29*, 1–15.

Reed, E. W., & Reed, S. C. (1965). *Mental retardation: A family study*. Philadelphia, PA: W. B. Saunders.

Reese, H. W. (2010). Regarding Little Albert. *American Psychologist, 65*, 300–301.

Regan, D. T., & Totten, J. (1975). Empathy and attribution: Turning observers into actors. *Journal of Personality and Social Psychology, 32*, 850–856.

Regan, P. C., & Berscheid, E. (1999). *Lust: What we know about human sexual desire*. Thousand Oaks, CA: Sage.

Reger, G. M., Holloway, K. M., Candy, C., Rothbaum, B. O., Difede, J., Rizzo, A. A., & Gahm, G. A. (2011). Effectiveness of virtual reality exposure therapy for active duty soldiers in a military mental health clinic. *Journal of Traumatic Stress, 24*(1), 93–96.

Regnerus, M. (2012). How different are the adult children of parents who have same-sex relationships? Findings from the New Family Structures Study. *Social Science Research, 41*(4), 752–770.

Reich, K. H. (2010). Shortcomings of the human brain and remedial action by religion. *Cultural Studies of Science Education, 5*, 157–162.

Reichenbach, S., Sterchi, R., Scherer, M., Trelle, S., Bürgi, E., Bürgi, U., … Jüni, P. (2007). Meta-analysis: Chondroitin for osteoarthritis of the knee or hip. *Annals of Internal Medicine, 146*, 580–590.

Reicher, S. D., & Haslam, S. A. (2006). Rethinking the social psychology of tyranny: The BBC Prison Study. *British Journal of Social Psychology, 45*, 1–40.

Reicher, S. D., Haslam, A., & Smith, J. (2012). Working toward the experimenter: Reconceptualizing obedience within the Milgram paradigm as identification-based followership. *Perspectives on Psychological Science, 7*, 315–324.

Reichert, J., Richardson, J. T., & Thomas, R. (2015). "Brainwashing": Diffusion of a questionable concept in legal systems. *International Journal for the Study of New Religions, 6*, 3–26.

Reid, B. (2002, April 30). The nocebo effect: Placebo's evil twin. *Washington Post*, HE01.

Reimann, M., & Bechara, A. (2010). The somatic marker framework as a neurological theory of decision-making: Review, conceptual comparisons, and future neuroeconomics research. *Journal of Economic Psychology, 31*, 767–776.

Reis, F. L., Masson, S., deOliveira, A. R., & Brandao, M. L. (2004). Dopaminergic mechanisms in the conditioned and unconditioned fear as assessed by the two-way avoidance and light switch-off tests. *Pharmacology, Biochemistry and Behavior, 79*, 359–365.

Reisenzein, R. (1983). The Schachter theory of emotion: Two decades later. *Psychological Bulletin, 94*, 239–264.

Reiss, D., & Marino, L. (2001). Mirror self-recognition in the bottlenose dolphin: A case of cognitive convergence. *Proceedings of the National Academy of Sciences, 98*, 5937–5942.

Reiss, S. (2012). Intrinsic and extrinsic motivation. *Teaching of Psychology, 39* (2), 152–156.

Reiss, S., & McNally, R. J. (1985). The expectancy model of fear. In S. Reiss & R. R. Bootzin (Eds.), *Theoretical issues in behavior therapy* (pp. 107–121). New York, NY: Academic Press.

Renoult, L., Davidson, P. S., Palombo, D. J., Moscovitch, M., & Levine, B. (2012). Personal semantics: At the crossroads of semantic and episodic memory. *Trends in Cognitive Sciences, 16*, 550–558.

Rensink, R. A., O'Regan, J. K., & Clark, J. (1997). To see or not to see: The need for attention to perceive changes in scenes. *Psychological Science, 8*, 368–373.

Rentfrow, P. J., Gosling, S. D., & Potter, J. (2008). A theory of the emergence, persistence, and expression of geographic variation in psychological characteristics. *Perspectives on Psychological Science, 3*(5), 339–369.

Repetti, R., Taylor, S., & Seeman, T. (2002). Risky families: Family social environments and the mental and physical health of offspring. *Psychological Bulletin, 128*, 330–366.

Rescorla, R. A. (1990). The role of information about the response-outcome relation in instrumental discrimination learning. *Journal of Experimental Psychology: Animal Behavior Processes, 16*, 262–270.

Rescorla, R. A., & Wagner, A. R. (1972). A theory of Pavlovian conditioning: Variations in effectiveness of reinforcement and non-reinforcement. In A. H. Black & W. F. Prokasy (Eds.), *Classical conditioning II: Current research and theory*, (pp. 64–98). New York, NY: Appleton-Century-Crofts.

Resnick, A. G., & Ithman, M. H. (2009). The human sexual response cycle: Psychotropic side effects and treatment strategies. *Psychiatric Annals, 38*, 267–280.

Resnick, P. J., & Knoll, J. (2005). How to detect malingered psychosis. *Current Psychiatry, 4*, 13–25.

Resnick, S. M., Pham, D. L., Kraut, M. A., Zonderman, A. B., & Davatzikos, C. (2003). Longitudinal magnetic resonance imaging studies of older adults: A shrinking brain. *Journal of Neuroscience, 23*, 3295–3301.

Restak, R. (1984). *The brain.* New York, NY: Bantam.

Revelle, W. (2016). Hans Eysenck: Personality theorist. *Personality and Individual Differences, 103*, 32–39.

Revelle, W., Humphreys, M. S., Simon, L., & Gilliland, K. (1980). The interactive effect of personality, time of day, and caffeine: A test of the arousal model. *Journal of Experimental Psychology: General, 109*, 1–31.

Revonsuo, A. (2000). The reinterpretation of dreams: An evolutionary hypothesis of the function of dreaming. *Behavioral and Brain Sciences, 23*, 877–901.

Revonsuo, A., Tuominen, J., & Valli, K. (2015). The avatars in the machine: Dreaming as a simulation of social reality. In T. Metzinger, & J.M. Windt (Eds.), *Open MIND.* Frankfurt am Main: MIND Group.

Reyna, V. F., & Farley, F. (2006). Risk and rationality in adolescent decision making: Implications for theory, practice, and policy. *Psychological Science in the Public Interest, 7*, 1–44.

Reynolds, C. (Ed.). (2013). *Perspectives on bias in mental testing.* New York, NY: Springer Science & Business Media.

Reynolds, C. R. (1999). Cultural bias in testing of intelligence and personality. In C. Belar (Ed.), Sociocultural and individual differences, Vol. 10 of M. Hersen & A. Bellack (Eds.), *Comprehensive clinical psychology* (pp. 53–92). Oxford, England: Elsevier Science.

Reynolds, D. (2003, April 25). Panel recommends counseling for sterilization survivors. *Inclusion Daily Express.* Retrieved from http://www.inclusiondaily.com/news/institutions/nc/eugenics.htm#042503

Rhine, J. B. (1934). Extra-sensory perception of the clairvoyant type. *The Journal of Abnormal*

Rhodes, G., Halberstadt, J., & Brajkovich, G. (2001). Generalization of mere exposure effects to averaged composite faces. *Social Cognition, 19*, 57–70.

Ricciardelli, L. A. (1992). Bilingualism and cognitive development in relation to threshold theory. *Journal of Psycholinguistic Research, 21*, 301–316.

Richards, A. S., & Banas, J. A. (2015). Inoculating against reactance to persuasive health messages. *Health Communication, 30*, 451–460.

Richards, D. A., Ekers, D., McMillan, D., Taylor, R. S., Byford, S., Warren, F. C., … O'Mahen, H. (2016). Cost and outcome of behavioural activation versus cognitive behavioural therapy for depression (COBRA): A randomised, controlled, non-inferiority trial. *Lancet.* doi: http://dx.doi.org/10.1016/S0140-6736(16)31140-0

Richardson, R., Riccio, C., & Axiotis, R. (1986). Alleviation of infantile amnesia in rats by internal and external contextual cues. *Developmental Psychobiology, 19*, 453–462.

Richter, M. A., Summerfeldt, L. J., Antony, M. M., & Swinson, R. P. (2003). Obsessive-compulsive spectrum conditions in obsessive-compulsive disorder and other anxiety disorders. *Depression and Anxiety, 18*, 118–127.

Rickels, K., Hesbacher, P. T., Weise, C. C., Gray, B., & Feldman, H. S. (1970). Pills and improvement: A study of placebo response in psychoneurotic outpatients. *Psychopharmacologia, 16*(4), 318–328.

Rickford, J. R., & Rickford, R. J. (2000). *Spoken soul: The story of Black English.* New York, NY: Wiley.

Ridgway, S. H. (2002). Asymmetry and symmetry in brain waves from dolphin left and right hemispheres: Some observations after anesthesia, during quiescent hanging behavior, and during visual obstruction. *Brain, Behavior, and Evolution, 60*, 265–274.

Ridley, M. (2003). *Nature via nurture: Genes, experience, and what makes us human.* New York, NY: HarperCollins.

Ridley, M. (2003). *Nature via nurture: Genes, experience, and what makes us human.* New York, BY: HarperCollins Publishers.

Rieber, R. W. (1999). Hypnosis, false memory, and multiple personality: A trinity of affinity. *History of Psychiatry, 10*, 3–11.

Rieger, G., & Savin-Williams, R. C. (2012) The eyes have it: Sex and sexual orientation differences in pupil dilation patterns. *PLoS One, 7*(8), e40256. http://dx.doi.org/10.1371/journal.pone.0040256

Riesenhuber, M., & Poggio, T. (1999). Hierarchical models of object recognition in cortex. *Nature Neuroscience, 2*, 1019–1025.

Rietschel, M., & Treutlein, J. (2013). The genetics of alcohol dependence. *Annals of the New York Academy of Sciences, 1282*(1), 39–70.

Riley, J. R., Greggers, U., Smith, A. D., Reynolds, D. R., & Menzel, R. (2005) The flight paths of honeybees recruited by the waggle dance. *Nature, 435*, 205–207.

Rilling, J. K., King-Casas, B., & Sanfey, A. G. (2008). The neurobiology of social decision-making. *Current Opinion in Neurobiology, 18*, 159–165.

Rilling, M. (1996). The mystery of the vanished citations: James McConnell's forgotten 1960s quest for planarian learning, a biochemical engram, and celebrity. *American Psychologist, 51*, 1039.

Rimfeld, K., Kovas, Y., Dale, P. S., & Plomin, R. (2016). True grit and genetics: Predicting academic achievement from personality. *Journal of Personality and Social Psychology.*

Rimland, B. (2004). Association between thimerosol-containing vaccine and autism. *Journal of the American Medical Association, 291*, 180.

Rimmele, U., Davachi, L., & Phelps, E. A. (2012). Memory for time and place contributes to enhanced confidence in memories for emotional events. *Emotion, 12*(4), 834–846. http://dx.doi.org/10.1037/a0028003

Rind, B., Tromovitch, P., & Bauserman, R. (1998). A meta-analytic examination of assumed properties of child sexual abuse using college samples. *Psychological Bulletin, 124*, 22–53.

Ring, K. (1984). *Healing toward omega: In search of the meaning of the near-death experience.* New York, NY: Morrow.

Ringwalt, C. L., & Greene, J. M. (1993, March). *Results of school districts' drug prevention coordinators survey.* Paper presented at the Alcohol, Tobacco, and Other Drugs Conference on Evaluating School-Linked Prevention Strategies, San Diego, CA.

Risch, N., Herrell, R., Lehner, T., Liang, K. Y., Eaves, L., Hoh, J., … Merikangas, K. R. (2009). The interaction between the serotonin transporter gene (5-HTTLPR), stressful life events, and risk of depression: A meta-analysis. *Journal of the American Medical Association, 301*, 2462–2471.

Risen, J., & Gilovich, T. (2007). Informal logical fallacies. In R. J. Sternberg, H. L. Roediger, & D. F. Halpern (Eds.), *Critical thinking in psychology* (pp. 110–130). New York, NY: Cambridge University Press.

Ritchie, S. J., Wiseman, R., & French, C. C. (2012). Failing the future: Three unsuccessful attempts to replicate Bem's "Retroactive Facilitation of Recall" Effect. *PLoS One, 7*(3), e33423.

Ritschel, L. A., Ramirez, C. L., Jones, M., & Craighead, W. E. (2011). Behavioral activation for depressed teens: A pilot study. *Cognitive and Behavioral Practice, 18*(2), 281–299.

Ritzert, T. R., Forsyth, J. P., Sheppard, S. C., Boswell, J. F., Berghoff, C. R., & Eifert, G. H. (2016). Evaluating the effectiveness of ACT for anxiety disorders in a self-help context: Outcomes from a randomized wait-list controlled trial. *Behavior Therapy, 47*(4), 444–459.

Rizzolatti, G. (2005). The mirror neuron system and its function in humans. *Anatomy and Embryology, 210*(5), 419–421.

Rizzolatti, G., Fadiga, L., Gallese, V., & Fogassi, L. (1996) Premotor cortex and the recognition of motor actions. *Cognitive Brain Research, 3*, 131–141.

Robert, G., & Zadra, A. (2014). Thematic and content analysis of idiopathic nightmares and bad dreams. *Sleep, 37*(2), 409–417. doi: 10.5665/sleep.3426

Roberts, B. W. (2009). Back to the future: Personality and assessment and personality development. *Journal of Research in Personality, 43*, 137–145.

Roberts, B. W., & DelVecchio, W. F. (2000). The rank-order consistency of personality traits from childhood to old age: Review of longitudinal studies. *Psychological Bulletin, 126*, 3–25.

Roberts, C. J., & Lowe, C. R. (1975). Where have all the conceptions gone? *Lancet, i*, 498–501.

Roberts, N. A., Levenson, R. W., & Gross, J. J. (2008). Cardiovascular costs of emotion suppression cross ethnic lines. *International Journal of Psychophysiology, 70*, 82–87.

Roberts, R. E., Strawbridge, W. J., Deleger, S., & Kaplan, G. A. (2002). Are the fat more jolly? *Annals of Behavioral Medicine, 24*, 169–180.

Roberts, W. M., Howard, J., & Hudspeth, A. J. (1988). Hair cells: Transduction, tuning, and transmission in the inner ear. *Annual Review of Cell Biology, 4*, 63–92.

Robins, E., & Guze, S. B. (1970). Establishment of diagnostic validity in psychiatric illness: Its application to schizophrenia. *American Journal of Psychiatry, 126*, 983–987.

Robins, L. N., Helzer, J. E., & Davis, D. H. (1975). Narcotic use in Southeast Asia and afterward: An interview study of 898 Vietnam returnees. *Archives of General Psychiatry, 32*, 955–961.

Robinson, D. G., Woerner, M. G., McMeniman, M., Mendelowitz, A., & Bilder, R. M. (2004). Systematic and functional recovery from a first episode of schizophrenia or schizoaffective disorder. *American Journal of Psychiatry, 161*, 473–479.

Robinson, D. S. (2007). The role of dopamine and norepinephrine in depression. *Primary Psychiatry, 14*, 21–23.

Robinson, S. J., & Rollings, L. J. L. (2011). The effect of mood-context on visual recognition and recall memory. *Journal of General Psychology, 138*(1), 66–79. http://dx.doi.org/10.1080/00221309.2010.534405

Rochat, P. (2001). *The infant's world.* Cambridge, MA: Harvard University Press.

Rock, A. (2004). *The mind at night: The new science of how and why we dream.* New York, NY: Basic Books.

Rock, I., & Kaufman, L. (1962). The moon illusion, part 2. *Science, 136*, 1023–1031.

Roe, B. E., & Just, D. R. (2009). Internal and external validity in economics research: Tradeoffs between experiments, field experiments, natural experiments, and field data. *American Journal of Agricultural Economics, 91*, 1266–1271.

Roediger, H. L. (1990). Implicit memory: Retention without remembering. *American Psychologist, 45*(9), 1043.

Roediger, H. L., & Crowder, R. G. (1976). A serial position effect in recall of United States presidents. *Bulletin of the Psychonomic Society, 8*, 275–278.

Roediger, H. L., & DeSoto, K. A. (2014). Forgetting the presidents. *Science, 346*, 1106–1109.

Roediger, H. L., & Geraci, L. (2007). Aging and the misinformation effect: A neuropsychological analysis. *Journal of Experimental Psychology: Learning, Memory, and Cognition, 33*(2), 321–334. http://dx.doi.org/10.1037/0278-7393.33.2.321

Roediger, H. L., & McDermott, K. B. (1995). Creating false memories: Remembering words not presented in lists. *Journal of Experimental Psychology: Learning, Memory, and Cognition, 21*, 803–814.

Roediger, H. L., & McDermott, K. B. (1999). False alarms and false memories. *Psychological Review, 106*, 406–410.

Rogers, C. R. (1942). *Counseling and psychotherapy.* New York, NY: Houghton Mifflin.

Rogers, C. R. (1947). Some observations on the organization of personality. *American Psychologist, 2*, 358–368.

Rogers, C. R. (1957). The necessary and sufficient conditions of therapeutic personality change. *Journal of Consulting Psychology, 21*, 95–103.

Rogers, C. R. (1961). *On becoming a person.* Boston, MA: Houghton Mifflin.

Rogers, C. R., & Dymond, R. (1954). *Psychotherapy and personality change.* Chicago, IL: University of Chicago Press.

Rogers, M., & Smith, K. H. (1993). Public perceptions of subliminal advertising. *Journal of Advertising Research, 33*, 10–18.

Rogers, R. (2008). *Clinical assessment of malingering and deception.* New York, NY: Guilford Press.

Rogers, R. W., & Prentice-Dunn, S. (1981). Deindividuation and anger-mediated interracial aggression: Unmasking regressive racism. *Journal of Personality and Social Psychology, 41*, 63–73.

Rogoff, B. (1995). Observing sociocultural activities on three planes: Participatory appropriation, guided participation, and apprenticeship. In J. V. Wertsch, P. Pablo del R'o, & A. Alvarez (Eds.), *Sociocultural studies of mind* (pp. 139–163). Cambridge, England: Cambridge University Press.

Rogoff, B. (1998). Cognition as a collaborative process. In D. Kuhn & R. S. Seigler (Eds.), *Handbook of child psychology, Vol. 2: Cognition, perception, & language* (5th ed., pp. 679–744). New York, NY: Wiley.

Rogoff, B., & Chavajay, P. (1995). What's become of research on the cultural basis of cognitive development? *American Psychologist, 50*, 859–877.

Rohrer, D., & Pashler, H. (2012). Learning Styles: Where's the Evidence? *Medical Education, 46*, 634–635.

Rohrer, J. M., Egloff, B., & Schmukle, S. C. (2015). Examining the effects of birth order on personality. *Proceedings of the National Academy of Sciences, 112*, 14224–14229.

Rojas, R. (2013). *Neural networks: a systematic introduction.* Berlin, Germany: Springer-Verlag.

Rolls, E. T. (2004). The functions of the orbitofrontal cortex. *Brain & Cognition, 55*, 11–29.

Rolls, E. T. (2016). Motivation explained: Ultimate and proximate accounts of hunger and appetite. *Advances in Motivation Science, 3*, 289–238.

Romanczyk, R. G., Arnstein, L., Soorya, L. V., & Gillis, J. (2003). The myriad of controversial treatments for autism: A critical evaluation of efficacy. In S. O. Lilienfeld, S. J. Lynn, & J. M. Lohr (Eds.), *Science and pseudoscience in clinical psychology* (pp. 363–395). New York, NY: Guilford Press.

Romm, C. (2016, July 27). Toronto poop-themed restaurant defies human psychology. *Science of Us.* http://nymag.com/scienceofus/2016/07/torontos-poop-themed-restaurant-defies-human-psychology.html

Roney, J. R., Hanson, K. N., Durante, K. M., & Maestripieri, D. (2006). Reading men's faces: Women's mate attractiveness judgments track men's testosterone and interest in infants. *Proceedings of the Royal Society of London B, 273*, 2169–2175.

Rood, L., Roelofs, J., Bögels, S. M., Nolen-Noeksema, S., & Schouten, E. (2009). The influence of emotion-focused rumination and distraction on depressive symptoms in non-clinical youth: A meta-analytic review. *Clinical Psychology Review, 29*, 607–616.

Root, T. L., Thornton, L., Lindroos, A. K., Stunkard, A. J., Lichtenstein, P., Pedersen, N. L., … Bulik, C. M. (2010). Shared and unique genetic and environmental influences on binge eating and night eating: A Swedish twin study. *Eating Behaviors, 11*(2), 92.

Rosales-Lagarde, A., Armony, J. L., del Río-Portilla, Y., Trejo-Martínez, D., Conde, R., & Corsi-Cabrera, M. (2012). Enhanced emotional reactivity after selective REM sleep deprivation in humans: an fMRI study. *Frontiers in Behavioral Neuroscience*, Jun 18;6:25. doi: 10.3389/fnbeh.2012.00025. eCollection 2012.

Rosch, E. (1973). Natural categories. *Cognitive Psychology, 4*, 328–350.

Rose, H., & Rose, S. (2010). *Alas poor Darwin: Arguments against evolutionary psychology.*

Rose, R. J., & Ditto, W. B. (1983). A developmental-genetic analysis of common fears from early adolescence to early adulthood. *Child Development, 54*, 361–368.

Rose, S. (2009). Darwin 200: Should scientists study race and IQ? NO: Science and society do not benefit. *Nature, 457*, 786–788.

Rose, S. A., Feldman, J. F., Jankowski, J. J., & Van Rossem, R. (2012). Information processing from infancy to 11years: Continuities and prediction of IQ. *Intelligence.* http://dx.doi.org/10.1016/j.intell.2012.05.007

Rosebrock, L. E., Hoxha, D., Norris, C., Cacioppo, J. T., & Gollan, J. K. (2016). Skin conductance and subjective arousal in anxiety, depression, and comorbidity. *Journal of Psychophysiology.* DOI: 10.1027/0269-8803/a000176

Rosen, G. M. (1993). Self-help or hype? Comments on psychology's failure to advance self-care. *Professional Psychology: Research and Practice, 24*, 340–345.

Rosen, G. M. (2006). DSM's cautionary guideline to rule out malingering can protect the PTSD data base. *Journal of Anxiety Disorders, 20*, 530–535.

Rosen, G. M. (2015). Barnum Effect. In R. L. Cautin & S. O. Lilienfeld (Eds), *The Encyclopedia of Clinical Psychology.* New York, NY: Wiley.

Rosen, G. M., Glasgow, R. E., & Moore, T. E. (2003). Self-help therapy: The science and business of giving psychology away. In S. O. Lilienfeld, S. J. Lynn, & J. M. Lohr (Eds.), *Science and pseudoscience in clinical psychology* (pp. 399–424). New York, NY: Guilford Press.

Rosen, G. M., Glasgow, R. E., Moore, T., & Barrera, M. (2014). Self-Help therapy: Recent developments in the science and business of giving psychology away. In S.O. Lilienfeld, S.J. Lynn, & J. Lohr (Eds.), *Science and Pseudoscience in Clinical Psychology* 2nd Ed (pp. 245–274). New York: Guilford.

Rosenberg, H. (1993). Prediction of controlled drinking by alcoholics and problem drinkers. *Psychological Bulletin, 113*, 129–139.

Rosenberg, S. D., Rosenberg, H. J., & Farrell, M. P. (1999). The midlife crisis revisited. *Journal of Personality and Social Psychology, 77*, 415–427.

Rosenblum, D., & Lewis, M. (1999). The relations among body image, physical attractiveness, and body mass in adolescence. *Child Development, 70*, 50–64.

Rosenfarb, I. S., Bellack, A. S., & Aziz, N. (2006). Family interactions and the course of schizophrenia in African-American and white patients. *Journal of Abnormal Psychology, 115*, 112–120.

Rosenfeld, J. P. (2005). "Brain fingerprinting": A critical analysis. *Scientific Review of Mental Health Practice, 4*, 20–37.

Rosenhan, D. L. (1973). On being sane in insane places. *Science, 179*, 250–258.

Rosenhan, D. L., & Seligman, M. E. P. (1989). *Abnormal psychology.* New York, NY: Norton.

Rosenthal, G. T., Soper, B., Rachal, C., McKnight, R. R., & Price, A. W. (2004). The Profession of Psychology Scale: Sophisticated and naive students' responses. *Journal of Instructional Psychology, 31*, 202–205.

Rosenthal, R., & DiMatteo, M. R. (2001). Meta-analysis: Recent developments in quantitative methods for literature reviews. *Annual Review of Psychology, 52*, 59–82.

Rosenthal, R., & Fode, K. L. (1963). Psychology of the scientist: V. Three experiments in experimenter bias. *Psychological Reports, 12*, 491–511.

Rosenthal, R., & Rubie-Davies, C. M. (2015). Bob Rosenthal's lifetime of research into interpersonal expectancy effects. In C. M. Rubie-Davies, J. M. Stephens, & P. Watson (Eds.), *The Routledge international handbook of social psychology of the classroom*, 285. London, UK: Routledge, Taylor & Francis Group.

Rosenzweig, P. (2014). *The halo effect … and the eight other business delusions that deceive managers.* New York, NY: Simon and Schuster.

Rosenzweig, S. (1936). Some implicit common factors in diverse methods in psychotherapy. *American Journal of Orthopsychiatry, 6*, 412–415.

Roskies, A. L. (2007). Are neuroimages like photographs of the brain? *Philosophy of Science, 74*, 860–872.

Rosky, J. W. (2013). The (f) utility of post-conviction polygraph testing. *Sexual Abuse: A Journal of Research and Treatment, 25*, 259–281.

Rosnow, R. L. (1980). Psychology of rumor reconsidered. *Psychological Bulletin, 87*, 578–591.

Rosnow, R. L. (2002). The nature and role of demand characteristics in scientific inquiry. *Prevention and Treatment, 5*(1). Retrieved from http://psycnet.apa.org/index.cfm?fa=buy.optionToBuy&id=2003-04137-004

Ross, C. A. (1997). *Dissociative identity disorder: Diagnosis, clinical features, and treatment of multiple personality.* New York, NY: Wiley.

Ross, C. A., & Pam, A. (1995). *Pseudoscience in biological psychiatry: Blaming the body.* New York, NY: Wiley.

Ross, H., & Plug, C. (2002). *The mystery of the moon illusion.* Oxford, England: Oxford University Press.

Ross, L. (1977). The intuitive psychologist and his shortcomings: Distortions in the attribution process. In L. Berkowitz (Ed.), *Advances in experimental social psychology* (Vol. 10, pp. 173–220). New York: Academic Press.

Ross, L., & Nisbett, L. E. (1991). *The person and the situation: Essential contributions of social psychology.* New York, NY: McGraw-Hill.

Ross, L., & Ward, A. (1996). Naive realism: Implications for social conflict and misunderstanding. In T. Brown, E. Reed, & E. Turiel (Eds.), *Values and knowledge* (pp. 103–135). Hillsdale, NJ: Erlbaum.

Sekharan, P. C. (2013). Truth about Truth Detecting Techniques. *Journal of Forensic Research, Special Issue 11*, 2–11.

Selby, E. A, Anestis, M. D., Bender, T. W., & Joiner, T. E., Jr. (2009). An exploration of the emotional cascade model in borderline personality disorder. *Journal of Abnormal Psychology, 118* (2), 375–387.

Selby, E. A., & Joiner, T. E., Jr. (2009). Cascades of emotion: The emergence of borderline personality disorder from emotional and behavioral dysregulation. *Review of General Psychology, 12*(3), 219–229.

Selden, S. (1999). *Inheriting shame: The story of eugenics and racism in America.* New York, NY: Teachers College Press.

Seligman, D. (1994). *A question of intelligence.* New York, NY: Citadel Press.

Seligman, M. E. P. (1971). Phobias and preparedness. *Behavior Therapy, 2*, 307–320.

Seligman, M. E. P. (1975). *Helplessness: On depression, development, and death.* San Francisco, CA: W. H. Freeman.

Seligman, M. E. P. (1990). *Learned optimism.* New York, NY: Knopf.

Seligman, M. E. P., & Csikszentmihalyi, M. (2000). Positive psychology: An introduction. *American Psychologist, 55*, 5–14.

Seligman, M. E. P., & Hager, J. L. (1972). Sauce-bearnaise syndrome. *Psychology Today, 6*(3), 59.

Seligman, M. E. P., & Maier, S. F. (1967). Failure to escape traumatic shock. *Journal of Experimental Psychology, 74*, 1–9.

Seligman, M. E. P., & Pawelski, J. O. (2003). Positive psychology: FAQs. *Psychological Inquiry, 14*, 159–163.

Sellbom, M. (2016). Mapping the MMPI–2–RF specific problems scales onto extant psychopathology structures. *Journal of Personality Assessment*, Aug 2, 1–10. [Epub ahead of print.]

Sellbom, M., Lilienfeld, S.O., Fowler, K.A., & McCrary, K.L. (in press). The self-report assessment of psychopathy: Challenges, pitfalls, and promises. In C. J. Patrick (Ed.), *Handbook of psychopathy* (2nd edition). New York: Guilford.

Selye, H. (1956). *The stress of life.* New York, NY: McGraw-Hill.

Semple, R. J., & Lee, J. (2007). *Mindfulness-based cognitive therapy for anxious children: A manual for treating childhood anxiety.* Oakland, CA: New Harbinger Publications.

Serbin, L. A., & O'Leary, K. D. (1975). How nursery schools teach girls to shut up. *Psychology Today, 9*(7), 56–58.

Serpell, R. (1979). How specific are perceptual skills? *British Journal of Psychology, 70*, 365–380.

Sevdalis, N., & Harvey, N. (2007) Biased forecasting of postdecisional affect. *Psychological Science, 18*, 678–681.

Seyfarth, R. M., & Cheney, D. L. (1997). Behavioral mechanisms underlying vocal communication in nonhuman primates. *Animal Learning & Behavior, 25*, 249–267.

Shade, E. D., Ulrich, C. M., Wener, M. H., Wood, B., Yasui, Y., Lacroix, K., … McTiernan, A. (2004). Frequent intentional weight loss is associated with lower natural killer cell cytotoxicity in postmenopausal women: Possible long-term immune effects. *Journal of the American Dietetic Association, 104*, 903–912.

Shadish, W. R. (1995). The logic of generalization: Five principles common to experiments and ethnographies. *American Journal of Community Psychology, 23*, 419–428.

Shadish, W. R., Cook, T. D., & Campbell, D. T. (2002). *Experimental and quasi-experimental designs for generalized causal inference.* Boston, MA: Houghton Mifflin.

Shaffer, H. J. (2000). Addictive personality. In A. E. Kazdin (Ed.), *Encyclopedia of psychology* (Vol. 1, pp. 35–36). Washington, DC: American Psychological Association and Oxford University Press.

Shahly, V., Berglund, P. A., Coulouvrat, C., Fitzgerald, T., Hajak, G., Roth, T., … Kessler, R. C. (2012). The associations of insomnia with costly workplace accidents and errors: results from the America Insomnia Survey. *Archives of General Psychiatry, 69*(10), 1054–1063.

Shakeshaft, N. G., Trzaskowski, M., McMillan, A., Krapohl, E., Simpson, M. A., Reichenberg, A., … Plomin, R. (2015). Thinking positively: The genetics of high intelligence. *Intelligence, 48*, 123–132.

Shamsuzzaman, A. S., Gersh, B. J., & Somers, V. K. (2003). Obstructive sleep apnea: Implications for cardiac and vascular disease. *Journal of the American Medical Association, 290*, 1906–1914.

Shanab, M. E., & Yahya, K. A. (1977). A behavioral study of obedience in children. *Journal of Personality and Social Psychology, 35*, 530–536.

Shanahan, M. J., Hill, P. L., Roberts, B. W., Eccles, J., & Friedman, H. S. (2014). Conscientiousness, health, and aging: The life course of personality model. *Developmental Psychology, 50*, 1407–1425.

Shannon-Missal, L. (2013). *Americans' belief in God, miracles and heaven declines.* The Harris Poll #97, December 16, 2013.

Shapiro, A. K., Shapiro, E. S., Bruun, R. D., & Sweet, R. D. (1978). *Gilles de la Tourette Syndrome, G.* New York, NY: Raven Press.

Shapiro, D. A., & Shapiro, D. (1982). Meta-analysis of comparative therapy outcome studies: A replication and refinement. *Psychological Bulletin, 92*, 581–604.

Shapiro, F. (1995). *Eye movement desensitization and reprocessing: Basic principles, protocols, and procedures.* New York, NY: Guilford Press.

Shapiro, F., & Forrest, M. S. (1997). *EMDR: The breakthrough therapy for overcoming anxiety, stress, and trauma.* New York, NY: Basic Books.

Shapiro, S. L., & Walsh, R. (2003). An analysis of recent meditation research and suggestions for future directions. *The Humanistic Psychologist, 31*, 86–113.

Sharkin, B. (2013). *College students in distress: A resource guide for faculty, staff, and campus community.* New York, NY: Routledge.

Sharp, C., Monterosso, J., & Read Montague, P. (2012). Neuroeconomics: A bridge for translational research. *Biological Psychiatry, 72*, 87–92.

Sharpe, C., & Florek, A. (2016). Civil commitment: Examining mental illness, differential Diagnosis, attributes of risk, and application to case law. In T. R. Masson (Ed.), *Inside Forensic Psychology*, 144–72.

Shaw, P., Greenstein, D., Lerch, J., Clasen, L., Lenroot, R., Gogtay, N., … Giedd, J. (2006). Intellectual ability and cortical development in children and adolescents. *Nature, 440*, 676–679.

Shedler, J. (2010). The efficacy of psychodynamic psychotherapy. *American Psychologist, 65*, 98–109.

Shedler, J., & Block, J. (1990). Adolescent drug use and psychological health: A longitudinal inquiry. *American Psychologist, 45*, 612–630.

Sheehan, P. W. (1991). Hypnosis, context, and commitment. In S. J. Lynn & J. W. Rhue (Eds.), *Theories of hypnosis: Current models and perspectives* (pp. 520–541). New York, NY: Guilford Press.

Sheehan, P. W., & McConkey, K. M. (1982). *Hypnosis and experience: The exploration of phenomena and process.* Hillsdale, NJ: Erlbaum.

Sheehan, W., & Dobbins, T. (2003). The spokes of Venus: An illusion explained. *Journal for the History of Astronomy, 34*, 53–63.

Sheldon, K. M., & King, L. (2001). Why positive psychology is necessary. *American Psychologist, 56*, 216–217.

Sheldon, K. M., & Lyubomirsky, S. (2006). How to increase and sustain positive emotion: The effects of expressing gratitude and visualizing best possible selves. *The Journal of Positive Psychology, 1*, 73–82.

Sheldon, K. M., & Lyubomirsky, S. (2012). The challenge of staying happier testing the hedonic adaptation prevention model. *Personality and Social Psychology Bulletin, 38*, 670–680.

Sheldon, W. (1971). The New York study of physical constitution and psychotic pattern. *Journal of the History of the Behavioral Sciences, 7*, 115–126.

Shepard, R. N. (1990). *Mind sights: Original visual illusions, ambiguities, and other anomalies.* New York, NY: W. H. Freeman.

Shepperd, J. A., & Koch, E. J. (2005). Pitfalls in teaching judgment heuristics. *Teaching of Psychology, 32*, 43–46.

Sher, K. J. (1987). Stress response dampening. In H. T. Blane & K. E. Leonard (Eds.) *Psychological theories of drinking and alcoholism* (pp. 227–271). New York, NY: Guilford Press.

Sher, K. J., Grekin, E. R., & Williams, N. A. (2005). The development of alcohol use disorders. In S. Nolen-Hoeksema, T. D. Cannon, & T. Widiger (Eds.), *Annual Review of Clinical Psychology, 1*, 493–524.

Sher, K. J., Wood, M. D., Richardson, A. E., & Jackson, K. M. (2005). Subjective effects of alcohol 1: Effects of the drink and drinking context. In M. Earleywine (Ed.), *Mind-altering drugs: The science of subjective experience* (pp. 86–134). Washington, DC: American Psychological Association.

Sherif, M. (1936). *The psychology of social norms.* New York, NY: Harper.

Sherif, M., Harvey, O. J., White, B. J., Hood, W. R., & Sherif, C. W. (1961). *The Robbers Cave experiment: Intergroup conflict and cooperation.* Middletown, CT: Wesleyan University Press.

Shermer, M. (2002). *Why people believe weird things: Pseudoscience, superstition, and other confusions of our time* (2nd ed.). New York, NY: W. H. Freeman.

Shermer, M. (2008, October). Five ways brains scans mislead. *Scientific American*. http://www.scientificamerican.com/article.cfm?id=five-ways-brain-scans-mislead-us

Shermer, M. (2011). *The believing brain: From ghosts to Gods to politics and conspiracies— How we construct beliefs and reinforce them as truths.* New York, NY: Times Books.

Shih, H. I., Lin, C. C., Tu, Y. F., Chang, C. M., Hsu, H. C., Chi, C. H., & Kao, C. H. (2015). An increased risk of reversible dementia may occur after zolpidem derivative use in the elderly population: a population-based case-control study. *Medicine, 94*(17), e809.

Shimamura, A. P. (1992). Organic amnesia. In L. Squire (Ed.), *Encyclopedia of learning and memory* (pp. 30–35). New York, NY: Macmillan.

Shimamura, A. P., Berry, J. M., Mangels, J. A., Rusting, C. L., & Jurica, P. J. (1995). Memory and cognitive abilities in university professors: Evidence for successful aging. *Psychological Science, 6*, 271–277.

Shin, S. M., Chow, C., Camacho-Gonsalves, T., Levy, R. J., Allen, E., & Leff, S. H. (2005). A meta-analytic review of racial-ethnic matching for African American and Caucasian American clients and clinicians. *Journal of Counseling Psychology, 52*, 45–56.

Shiota, M. N., Keltner, D., & Mossman, A. (2007). The nature of awe: Elicitors, appraisals, and effects on self-concept. *Cognition and Emotion, 21*, 944–963.

Shipstead, Z., Redick, T. S., & Engle, R. W. (2012). Is working memory training effective? *Psychological Bulletin, 138*(4), 628–654. http://dx.doi.org/10.1037/a0027473

Shlien, J., & Levant, R. (1984). Introduction. In R. Levant & J. Shlien (Eds.), *Client-centered therapy and the person-centered approach: New directions in theory, research and practice* (pp. 1–16). New York, NY: Praeger.

Shoemaker, G. E., & Fagen, J. W. (1984). Stimulus preference and its effect on visual habituation and dishabituation in four-month-old infants. *Genetic Psychology Monographs, 109*, 3–18.

Shomstein, S., & Yantis, S. (2006). Parietal cortex mediates voluntary control of spatial and nonspatial auditory attention. *Journal of Neuroscience, 26*, 435–439.

Shors, T. J., & Matzel, L. D. (1999). Long-term potentiation: What's learning got to do with it? *Behavioral and Brain Sciences, 20*, 597–655.

Showalter, E. (1997). *Hystories: Hysterical epidemics and modern culture.* New York, NY: Columbia University Press.

Shrauger, J. S., & Schoeneman, T. J. (1979). Symbolic interactionist view of self-concept: Through the looking glass darkly. *Psychological Bulletin, 86*, 549–573.

Shumaker, S. A., & Czajkowski, S. M. (Eds.). (2013). *Social support and cardiovascular disease.* New York, NY: Springer Science & Business Media.

Sieff, E. M., Dawes, R. M., & Loewenstein, G. (1999). Anticipated versus actual reaction to HIV test results. *American Journal of Psychology, 112*, 297–311.

Siegel, J. (2005). Clues to the function of mammalian sleep. *Nature, 437*, 1264–1271.

Siegelbaum, S. A., Camardo, J. S., & Kandel, E. R. (1982, September 30). Serotonin and cyclic AMP close single K+ channels in Aplysia sensory neurons. *Nature, 299*, 413–417.

Siegler, R. S. (1992). The other Alfred Binet. *Developmental Psychology, 28*, 179–190.

Siegler, R. S. (1995). Children's thinking: How does change occur? In F. E. Weinert & W. Schneider (Eds.), *Memory performance and competencies: Issues in growth and development* (pp. 405–430). Hillsdale, NJ: Erlbaum.

Sigman, M., & Whaley, S. E. (1998). The role of nutrition in the development of intelligence. In U. Neisser (Ed.), *The rising curve: Long-term gains in IQ and related measures* (pp. 155–182). Washington, DC: American Psychological Association.

Sijtsma, K., & van der Ark, L. A. (2015). The many issues in reliability research: Choosing from a horn of plenty. *Nursing Research, 64*, 152–154.

Silventoinen, K., Sammalisto, S., Perola, M., Boomsma, D. I., Cornes, B. K., Davis, C., … Kaprio, J. (2003). Heritability of adult body height: A comparative study of twin cohorts in eight countries. *Twin Research, 6*, 399–408.

Silver, E., Cirincione, C., & Steadman, H. J. (1994). Demythologizing inaccurate perceptions of the insanity defense. *Law and Human Behavior, 18*, 63–70.

Silverman, S. (1987, July). Medical "miracles": Still mysterious despite claims of believers. *Newsletter of the Sacramento Skeptics Society*, Sacramento, CA, pp. 2–7.

Silvers, J. A., McRae, K., Gabrieli, J. D. E., Gross, J. J., Remy, K. A., & Ochsner, K. N. (2012). Age-related differences in emotional reactivity, regulation, and rejection sensitivity in adolescence. *Emotion.* http://dx.doi.org/10.1037/a0028297

Silvia, P. J. (2008). Interest—The curious emotion. *Current Directions in Psychological Science, 17*, 57–60.

Silvia, P. J. (2008). Interest—The curious emotion. *Current Directions in Psychological Science, 17*, 57–60.

Simeon, D., Gross, S., Guralnik, O., Stein, D. J., Schmeidler, J., & Hollander, E. (1997). Feeling unreal: 30 Cases of DSM-III-R depersonalization. *American Journal of Psychiatry, 154*, 1107–1113.

Simmons, D. A., & Neill. D. B. (2009) Functional interaction between the basolateral amygdala and the ventral striatum underlies incentive motivation for food reward. *Neuroscience, 159*, 1264–1273.

Simms, A., & Nichols, T. (2014). Social loafing: a review of the literature. *Journal of Management Policy and Practice, 15*, 58–67.

Simner, J., & Hubbard, E. M. (Eds.). (2013). *Oxford handbook of synesthesia.* Oxford, UK: Oxford University Press.

Simner, J., Mulvenna, C., Sagiv, N., Tsakanikos, E., Withery, S.A., Fraser, C., … Ward, J. (2006). Synaesthesia: The prevalence of atypical cross-modal experiences. *Perception, 35*, 1024–1033.

Simon-Moffat, A. (2002). New fossils and a glimpse of evolution. *Science, 25*, 613–615.

Simon, C. W., & Emmons, W. H. (1955). Learning during sleep? *Psychological Bulletin, 52*, 328–342.

Simon, G., von Korff, M., Saunders, K., Miglioretti, D. L., Crane, K., Van Belle, K., & Kessler, R. C. (2006). Association between obesity and psychiatric disorders in the U.S. population. *Archives of General Psychiatry, 63*, 824–830.

Simon, M. J., & Salzberg, H. C. (1985). The effect of manipulated expectancies on posthypnotic amnesia. *International Journal of Clinical and Experimental Hypnosis, 33*, 40–51.

Simon, R. I. (2006). Imminent suicide: The illusion of short-term prediction. *Suicide and Life-Threatening Behavior, 36*, 296–301.

Simons, D. J., & Chabris, C. F. (1999). Gorillas in our midst: Sustained inattentional blindness for dynamic events. *Perception, 28*, 1059–1074.

Simons, D. J., & Chabris, C. F. (2011). What people believe about how memory works: A representative survey of the U.S. population. *PLoS One, 6*(8), e22757. http://dx.doi.org/10.1371/journal.pone.0022757

Simons, D. J., Boot, W. R. Charness, N., Gatherole, S. E. Chabris, C. F., … Stine-Morrow, E. A. L (2016). Do brain training programs work. *Psychological Science in the Public Interest, 17*, 103–186.

Simons, R. C. (2001). Introduction to culture-bound syndromes. *Psychiatric Times, 18*(11), 283–292.

Simons, R. C., & Hughes, C. C. (1986). *The culture-bound syndromes: Folk illnesses of psychiatric and anthropological interest.* Boston, MA: D. Reidel.

Simonton, D. K. (1997). Creative productivity: A predictive and explanatory model of career trajectories and landmarks. *Psychological Review, 104*, 66–89.

Simonton, D. K. (1999). *Origins of genius.* New York, NY: Cambridge Press.

Simonton, D. K. (2006). Presidential IQ, openness, intellectual brilliance and leadership: Estimates and correlations for 42 U.S. chief executives. *Political Psychology, 27*, 511–526.

Simonton, D. K., & Song, A. V. (2009). Eminence, IQ, physical and mental health, and achievement domain: Cox's 282 geniuses revisited. *Psychological Science, 20*, 429–434.

Simpson, G. M., & Kline, N. S. (1976). Tardive dyskinesias: Manifestations, etiology, and treatment. In M. D. Yahr (Ed.), *The basal ganglia* (pp. 167–183). New York, NY: Raven Press.

Sinclair, R. R., & Tetrick, L. E. (2000). Implications of item wording for hardiness structure, relation with neuroticism, and stress buffering. *Journal of Research in Personality, 34*, 1–25.

Singer-Dudek, J., Choi, J., & Lyons, L. (2013). The effects of an observational intervention on the emergence of two types of observational learning. *European Journal of Behavior Analysis, 14*, 329–347.

Singer, M. (1979, January). Coming out of the cults. *Psychology Today*, 72–82.

Singer, M. T., & Nievod, A. (2003). New age therapies. In S. O. Lilienfeld, S. J. Lynn, & J. M. Lohr (Eds.), *Science and pseudoscience in clinical psychology* (pp. 176–204). New York, NY: Guilford Press.

Singh, D. (1993). Adaptive significance of female physical attractiveness: Role of waist-to-hip ratio. *Journal of Personality and Social Psychology, 65*, 293–307.

Singh, D. (1995). Female judgment of male attractiveness and desirability for relationships: Role of waist-to-hip ratio and financial status. *Journal of Personality and Social Psychology, 69*, 1089–1101.

Singh, S. P., Harley, K., & Suhail, K. (2013). Cultural specificity of emotional over involvement: a systematic review. *Schizophrenia Bulletin, 39*(2), 449–63.

Singh, S., & Ernst, E. (2008). *Trick or treatment: Alternative medicine on trial.* New York, NY: Bantam.

Sinkavich, F. J. (1995). Performance and metamemory: Do students know what they don't know? *Instructional Psychology, 22*, 77–87.

Skeem, J. L., Monahan, J., & Mulvey, E. P. (2002). Psychopathy, treatment involvement, and subsequent violence among civil psychiatric patients. *Law and Human Behavior, 26*, 577–603.

Skeem, J. L., Polaschek, D. L., Patrick, C. J., & Lilienfeld, S. O. (2011). Psychopathic personality bridging the gap between scientific evidence and public policy. *Psychological Science in the Public Interest, 12*(3), 95–162.

Skinner, B. F. (1938). *The behavior of organisms: An experimental analysis.* New York, NY: Appleton-Century-Crofts.

Skinner, B. F. (1948). Superstition in the pigeon. *Journal of Experimental Psychology, 38*, 168–172.

Skinner, B. F. (1953). *Science and human behavior.* New York, NY: Macmillan.

Skinner, B. F. (1969). *Contingencies of reinforcement.* East Norwalk, CT: Appleton-Century-Crofts.

Skinner, B. F. (1971). *Beyond freedom and dignity.* New York, NY: Knopf.

Skinner, B. F. (1974). *About behaviorism.* New York, NY: Vintage Books.

Skinner, B. F. (1990). Can psychology be a science of mind? *American Psychologist, 4*, 1206–1210.

Skinner, E., Edge, K., Altman, J., & Sherwood, H. (2003). Searching for the structure of coping: A review and critique of category systems for classifying ways of coping. *Psychological Bulletin, 129*, 216–219.

Slade, T., & Andrews, G. (2005). Latent structure of depression in a community sample: A taxometric analysis. *Psychological Medicine, 35*, 489–497.

Slater, A. (1997). Can measures of infant habituation predict later intellectual ability? *Archives of Diseases of the Child, 77*, 474–476.

Slater, L. (2004). *Opening Skinner's box: Great psychological experiments of the 20th century.* New York, NY: Norton.

Slavin, R. E., & Cooper, R. (1999). Improving intergroup relations: Lessons learned from cooperative learning programs. *Journal of Social Issues, 55*, 647–663.

Slegel, D. E., Benson, K. L., Zarcone, V. P., & Schubert, E. D. (1991). Middle-ear muscle activity and its association with motor activity in the extremities and head in sleep. *Lancet, 337*, 597–599.

Sloan, R. P., Bagiella, E., & Powell, T. (1999). Religion, spirituality, and medicine. *Lancet, 353*, 644–647.

Sloane, R. B., Staples, F., Cristol, A., Yorkston, N., & Whipple, K. (1975). *Psychotherapy versus behavior therapy.* Cambridge, MA: Harvard University Press.

Slopen, N., Kontos, E. Z., Ryff, C. D., Ayanian, J. Z., Albert, M. A., & Williams, D. R. (2013). Psychosocial stress and cigarette smoking persistence, cessation, and relapse over 9–10 years: A prospective study of middle-aged adults in the United States. *Cancer Causes & Control, 24*(10), 1849–1863.

Slovic, P., & Peters, E. (2006). Risk perception and affect. *Current Directions in Psychological Science, 15*, 322–325.

Slutske, W. S., Heath, A. C., Dinwiddie, S. H., Madden, P. A., & Bucholz, K. K. (1998). Common genetic risk factors for conduct disorder and alcohol dependence. *Journal of Abnormal Psychology, 107*, 363–374.

Smalheiser, N. R., Manev, H., & Costa, E. (2001) RNAi and memory: Was McConnell on the right track after all? *Trends in Neuroscience, 24*, 216–218.

Smalley, S., & Winston, D. (2010). *Fully present: The science, art, and practice of mindfulness.* Boston, MA: Da Capo Press.

Vaillancourt, T. (2012). Students aggress against professors in reaction to receiving poor grades: An effect moderated by student narcissism and self-esteem. *Aggressive Behavior*. http://dx.doi.org/10.1002/ab.21450

Vaillant, E., & Milofsky, E. (1980). Natural history of male psychological health: IX. Empirical evidence for Erikson's model of the life cycle. *American Journal of Psychiatry, 137*, 1348–1359.

Vaillant, G. E. (1977). *Adaptation to life*. Boston, MA: Little, Brown.

Vaillant, G. E., & Milofsky, E. S. (1982). Natural history of male alcoholism IV: Paths to recovery. *Archives of General Psychiatry, 39*, 127–133.

Vaitl, D., & Lipp, O. V. (1997). Latent inhibition and autonomic responses: A psychophysiological approach. *Behavioural Brain Research, 88*, 85–93.

Valdesolo, P., Park, J., & Gottlieb, S. (2016). Awe and scientific explanation. *Emotion, 16*, 937–940.

Valenstein, E. S. (1973). *Brain control*. New York, NY: Wiley.

Valenstein, E. S. (1986). *Great and desperate cures: The rise and decline of psychosurgery and other radical treatments for mental illness*. New York, NY: Basic Books.

Valentine, T., & Mesout, J. (2009). Eyewitness identification under stress in the London dungeon. *Applied Cognitive Psychology, 23*(2), 151–161. http://dx.doi.org/10.1002/acp.1463

Valentine, T., Darling, S., & Donnelly, M. (2004). Why are average faces attractive? The effect of view and averageness on the attractiveness of female faces. *Psychonomic Bulletin & Review, 11*, 482–487.

Vallée-Tourangeau, F., Euden, G., & Hearn, V. (2011). Eistellung defused: Interactivity and mental set. *Quarterly Journal of Experimental Psychology, 64*, 1889–1895.

Vallee, B. L. (1988, June). Alcohol in the Western world: A history. *Scientific American, 278*, 80–85.

Van Bavel, J. J., Packer, D. J., & Cunningham, W. A. (2008). The neural subtrates of in-group bias: A function magnetic resonance imaging investigation. *Psychological Science, 19*, 1131–1139.

van Bommel, M., van Prooijen, J. W., Elffers, H., & Van Lange, P. A. (2012). Be aware to care: Public self-awareness leads to a reversal of the bystander effect. *Journal of Experimental Social Psychology, 48*, 926–930.

Van Boven, L., & Gilovich, T. (2003). To do or to have? That is the question. *Journal of Personality and Social Psychology, 85*, 1193–1202.

Van de Castle, R. (1994). *Our dreaming mind*. New York, NY: Ballantine Books.

van de Mortel, T. F. (2008). Faking it: Social desirability response bias in self-report research. *Australian Journal of Advanced Nursing, 25*(4), 40.

van de Ven, N., Hoogland, C. E., Smith, R. H., van Dijk, W. W., Breugelmans, S. M., & Zeelenberg, M. (2015). When envy leads to schadenfreude. *Cognition and Emotion, 29*, 1007–1025.

van de Vijver, F., & Hambleton, R. K. (1996). Translating tests. *European Psychologist, 1*, 89–99.

Van den Heuvel, M. I., Johannes, M. A., Henrichs, J., & Van den Bergh, B. R. H. (2015). Maternal mindfulness during pregnancy and infant socio-emotional development and temperament: The mediating role of maternal anxiety. *Early Human Development, 91*(2), 103–108.

Van der Kloet, D., Giesbrecht, T., Lynn, S. J., Merckelbach, H., & de Zutter, A. (2012). Sleep normalization and decreases in dissociative experiences: Evaluation in an inpatient sample. *Journal of Abnormal Psychology, 121*, 140–150.

van der Kolk, B., Britz, R., Burr, W., Sherry, S., & Hartmann, E. (1984). Nightmares and trauma: A comparison of nightmares after combat with lifelong nightmares in veterans. *American Journal of Psychiatry, 141*, 187–190.

van der Maas, H. L., Dolan, C. V., Grasman, R. P., Wicherts, J. M., Huizenga, H. M., & Raijmakers, M. E. (2006). A dynamical model of general intelligence: the positive manifold of intelligence by mutualism. *Psychological Review, 113*, 842–961.

van der Worp, H. B., Howells, D. W., Sena, E. S., Porritt, M. J., Rewell, S., O'Collins, V., & Macleod, M. R. (2010). Can animal models of disease reliably inform human studies? *PLoS med, 7*(3), e1000245

Van Duijvenvoorde, A. C. K., Achterberg, M., Braams, B. R., Peters, S., & Crone, E. A. (2016). Testing a dual-systems model of adolescent brain development using resting-state connectivity analyses. *Neuroimage, 124*(Part A), 409–420.

Van Eeden, F. (1913). A study of dreams. *Proceedings of the Society for Psychical Research, 26*, 431–461.

Van Grootheest, D. S., Cath, D. C., Beekman, A. T., & Boomsma, D. I. (2007). *Psychological Medicine, 37*, 1635–1644.

Van Hal, G., Rosiers, J., Ponnet, K., & Wouters, E. (2013). Popping smart pills: prescription stimulant misuse by university and college students in Flanders. *The European Journal of Public Health, 23*(suppl 1), ckt126–300.

Van Hecke, M. L. (2007). *Blind spots: Why smart people do dumb things*. Amherst, NY: Prometheus.

Van Houtem, C. M. H. H., Laine, M. L., Boomsma, D. I., Ligthart, L., Van Wijk, A. J., & De Jongh, A. (2013). A review and meta-analysis of the heritability of specific phobia subtypes and corresponding fears. *Journal of Anxiety Disorders, 27*, 379–388.

Van Iddekinge, C. H., Roth, P. L., Raymark, P. H., & Odle-Dusseau, H. N. (2012). The criterion-related validity of integrity tests: An updated meta-analysis. *Journal of Applied Psychology, 97*, 499–530.

Van Ijzendoorn, M. H., & Bakermans-Kranenburg, M. J. (2012). Differential susceptibility experiments: Going beyond correlational evidence. *Developmental Psychology, 48*, 769–774.

Van Ijzendoorn, M. H., & De Wolff, M. S. (1997). In search of the absent father: Meta-analyses on infant–father attachment. *Child Development, 68*, 604–609.

Van Ijzendoorn, M. H., & Sagi, A. (1999). Cross-cultural patterns of attachment: Universal and cultural dimensions. In J. Cassidy & P. R. Shaver (Eds.), *Handbook of attachment: Theory, research, and clinical applications* (pp. 713–734). New York, NY: Guilford Press.

Van Kleef, E., Kavvouris, C., & van Trijp, H. C. (2014). The unit size effect of indulgent food: How eating smaller sized items signals impulsivity and makes consumers eat less. *Psychology & Health, 29*(9), 1081–1103.

Van Lange, P. A., Rinderu, M. I., & Bushman, B. J. (2016). Aggression and violence around the world: A model of CLimate, Aggression, and Self-control in Humans (CLASH). *Behavioral and Brain Sciences*. Awaiting volume and page numbers.

van Leeuwen, T. M., Singer, W., & Nikolić, D. (2015). The merit of synesthesia for consciousness research. *Frontiers in Psychology, 6*.

Van Litalie, T. B. (1990). The glucostatic theory 1953–1988: Roots and branches. *International Journal of Obesity, 14*, 1–10.

Van Lommel, P., van Wees, R., Meyers, V., & Elfferich, I. (2001). Near-death experiences in survivors of cardiac arrest: A prospective study in the Netherlands. *Lancet, 358*, 2039–2045.

Van Oudenhove, L., McKie, S., Lassman, D., Uddin, B., Paine, P., Coen, S., ... Aziz, Q. (2011). Fatty acid–induced gut-brain signaling attenuates neural and behavioral effects of sad emotion in humans. *The Journal of Clinical Investigation, 121*(8), 3094–3099.

Van Rooy, D. L., & Viswesvaran, C. (2004). Emotional intelligence: A meta-analytic investigation of predictive validity and nomological net. *Journal of Vocational Behavior, 65*, 71–95.

Van Wallendael, L. R., Cutler, B. L., Devenport, J., & Penrod, S. D. (2007). Mistaken identification = erroneous conviction? Assessing and improving legal safeguards. In M. P. Toglia, D. F. Ross, J. D. Read, & R. C. L. Lindsay (Eds.), *Handbook of eyewitness psychology, Vol II: Memory for people* (pp. 557–572). Mahwah, NJ: Erlbaum.

Vandello, J. A., Cohen, D., & Ransom, S. (2008). U.S. southern and northern differences in perceptions of norms about aggression: Mechanisms for the perpetuation of a culture of honor. *Journal of Cross-Cultural Psychology, 39*, 162–177.

VanderLaan D. P., & Vasey P. L. (2011). Male sexual orientation in Independent Samoa: Evidence for fraternal birth order and maternal fecundity effects. *Archives of Sexual Behavior, 40*, 495–503.

Vane, J. R. (1981). The Thematic Apperception Test: A review. *Clinical Psychology Review, 1*, 319–336.

Vanman, E. J., Paul, B. Y., Ito, T. A., & Miller, N. (1997). The modern face of prejudice and structural features that moderate the effect of cooperation on affect. *Journal of Personality and Social Psychology, 73*, 941–959.

Vanman, E. J., Saltz, J. L., Nathan, L. R., & Warren, J. A. (2004). Racial discrimination by low-prejudiced whites: Facial movements as implicit measures of attitudes related to behavior. *Psychological Science, 15*, 711–714.

Vartanian, L. R. (2000). Revisiting the imaginary audience and personal fable constructs of adolescent egocentrism: A conceptual review. *Adolescence, 35*, 639–661.

Vasquez, E. A., Pedersen, W. C., Bushman, B. J., Kelley, N. J., Demeestere, P., & Miller, N. (2013). Lashing out after stewing over public insults: The effects of public provocation, provocation intensity, and rumination on triggered displaced aggression. *Aggressive Behavior, 39*, 13–29.

Vaughan, E. B., Van Hulle, C. A., Beasley, W. H., Rodgers, J. L., & D'Onofrio, B. M. (2015). Clarifying the associations between age at menarche and adolescent emotional and behavioral problems. *Journal of Youth and Adolescence, 44*(4), 922–939. doi:10.1007/s10964-015-0255-7

Vazire, S. (2010). Who knows what about a person? The self–other knowledge asymmetry (SOKA) model. *Journal of Personality and Social Psychology, 98*, 281–300.

Veenstra, L., Schneider, I. K., & Koole, S. L. (2016). Embodied mood regulation: the impact of body posture on mood recovery, negative thoughts, and mood-congruent recall. *Cognition and Emotion*. DOI: 10.1080/02699931.2016.1225003

Veit, R., Flor, H., Erb, M., Hermann, C., Lotze, M., Grodd, W., & Birbaumer, N. (2002). Brain circuits involved in emotional learning in antisocial behavior and social phobia in humans. *Neuroscience Letters, 328*(3), 233–236.

Vellas, B., Coley, N., Ousset, P. J., Berrut, G., Dartigues, J. F., Dubois, B., ... Andrieu, S. (2012). Long-term use of standardised ginkgo biloba extract for the prevention of Alzheimer's disease (GuidAge): A randomised placebo-controlled trial. *The Lancet Neurology, 11*, 851–859.

Verdoux, H. (2004). Perinatal risk factors for schizophrenia: How specific are they? *Current Psychiatry Reports, 6*, 162–167.

Verhulst, B., Neale, M. C., & Kendler, K. S. (2015). The heritability of alcohol use disorders: a meta-analysis of twin and adoption studies. *Psychological Medicine, 45*(05), 1061–1072.

Vermetten, E., & Bremner, J. D. (2003). Olfaction as a traumatic reminder in posttraumatic stress disorder: Case reports and review. *Journal of Clinical Psychiatry, 64*, 202–207.

Vernon, P. A. (1987). *Speed of information processing and intelligence*. Norwood, NJ: Ablex.

Vernon, P. A., Villani, V. C., Vickers, L. C., & Harris, J. A. (2008). A behavioral genetic investigation of the Dark Triad and the Big 5. *Personality and Individual Differences, 44*, 445–452.

Vernon, P. E. (1971). *The structure of human abilities*. London, England: Methuen.

Verrier, D. B. (2012). Evidence for the influence of the mere-exposure effect on voting in the Eurovision Song Contest. *Judgment and Decision Making, 7*, 639–643.

Vervliet, B., Craske, M. G., & Hermans, D. (2013). Fear extinction and relapse: State of the art. *Annual Review of Clinical Psychology, 9*, 215–248.

Vetere, A. (2001). Structural family therapy. *Child Psychology and Psychiatry Review, 6*, 133–139.

Vickers, A. J., Cronin, A. M., Maschino, A. C., Lewith, G., MacPherson, H., Foster, N. E., … & Acupuncture Trialists' Collaboration. (2012). Acupuncture for chronic pain: individual patient data meta-analysis. *Archives of Internal Medicine, 172*(19), 1444–1453.

Victora, C. G., Horta, B. L., de Mola, C. L., Quevedo, L., Pinheiro, R. T., Gigante, D. P., … Barros, F. C. (2015). Association between breastfeeding and intelligence, educational attainment, and income at 30 years of age: A prospective birth cohort study from Brazil. *The Lancet Global Health, 3*, e199–e205.

Videbech, P., & Ravnkilde, B. (2004): Hippocampal volume and depression. A meta-analysis of MRI studies. *American Journal of Psychiatry, 161*, 1957–1966.

Vigen, T. (2015). *Spurious correlations: Correlation does not equal causation*. New York, NY: Hachette Books.

Vincent, P. (1971). Factors influencing patient noncompliance: A theoretical approach. *Nursing Research, 20*, 509–516.

Vinson, J. A., Demkosky, C. A., Navarre, D. A., & Smyda, M. A. (2012). High-antioxidant potatoes: Acute in vivo antioxidant source and hypotensive agent in humans after supplementation to hypertensive subjects. *Journal of Agricultural and Food Chemistry, 60*(27), 6749–6754.

Vitello, P. (2006, June 12). A ringtone meant to fall on deaf ears. *New York Times*. Retrieved from www.nytimes.com/2006/06/12/technology/12ring.html?_r=1&emc=eta1&oref=slogi

Vlach, H. A., & Sandhofer, C. M. (2011). Developmental differences in children's context-dependent word learning. *Journal of Experimental Child Psychology, 108*, 394–401.

Voevodsky, J. (1974). Evaluation of a deceleration warning light for reducing rear-end automobile collisions. *Journal of Applied Psychology, 59*, 270–273.

Vohs, K. D., Mead, N. L., & Goode, M. R. (2006). The psychological consequences of money. *Science, 314*, 1154–1156.

Volgmaier, M. M., Seidman, L. J., Niznikiewicz, M. A., Dickey, C. C., Shenton, M. E., & McCarley, R. W. (2000). Verbal and nonverbal neuropsychological test performance in subjects with schizotypal personality disorder. *American Journal of Psychiatry, 157*, 787–797.

Volkow, N. D., Wang, G. J., Fowler, J. S., & Ding, Y. (2005). Imaging the effects of methylphenidate on brain dopamine: New model on its therapeutic actions for attention-deficit/hyperactivity disorder. *Biological Psychiatry, 57*, 1410–1415.

von Dawans, B., Fischbacher, U., Kirschbaum, C., Fehr, E., & Heinrichs, M. (2012). The social dimension of stress reactivity acute stress increases prosocial behavior in humans. *Psychological Science, 23*(6), 651–660.

von Frisch, K. (1967). *The dance language and orientation of bees*. London, England: Oxford University Press.

von Känel, R., Dimsdale, J. E., Ziegler, M. G., Mills, P. J., Patterson, T. L., Lee, S. K., & Grant, I. (2001). Effect of acute psychological stress on the hypercoagulable state in subjects (spousal caregivers of patients with Alzheimer's disease) with coronary or cerebrovascular disease and/or systemic hypertension. *The American Journal of Cardiology, 87*(12), 1405–1408.

Von Stumm, S., Hell, B., & Chamorro-Premuzic, T. (2011). The hungry mind intellectual curiosity is the third pillar of academic performance. *Perspectives on Psychological Science, 6*, 574–588.

Voncken, M. J., Bogels, S. M., & deVries, K. (2003). Interpretation and judgmental biases in social phobias. *Behavior Research and Therapy, 41*, 1481–1488.

Vos, S. P. F., Huibers, M. J. H., Diels, L., & Arntz, A. (2012). A randomized clinical trial of cognitive behavioral therapy and interpersonal psychotherapy for panic disorder with agoraphobia. *Psychological Medicine, 1*(1), 1–12.

Voss, J. L., & Paller, K. A. (2008). Brain substrates of implicit and explicit memory: The importance of concurrently acquired neural signals of both memory types. *Neuropsychologia, 46*, 3021–3029.

Voss, J. L., Baym, C. L., & Paller, K. A. (2008). Accurate forced-choice recognition without awareness of memory retrieval. *Learning and Memory, 15*, 454–459.

Voss, U., Holzmann, R., Tuin, I., & Hobson, J. A. (2009a). Lucid dreaming: A state of consciousness with features of both waking and non-lucid dreaming. *Sleep, 32*(9), 1191–2000.

Voss, U., Tuin, I., Schermelleh-Engel, K., & Hobson, A. (2011). Waking and dreaming: related but structurally independent. Dream reports of congenitally paraplegic and deaf-mute persons. *Consciousness and Cognition, 20*(3), 673–687.

Voyer, D., Voyer, S., & Bryden, M. P. (1995). Magnitude of sex differences in spatial abilities: A meta-analysis and consideration of critical variables. *Psychological Bulletin, 117*, 250–270.

Voyles, E. C., Bailey, S. F., & Durik, A. M. (2015). New pieces of the jigsaw Classroom: Increasing accountability to reduce social loafing in student group projects. *The New School Psychology Bulletin, 13*, 11–20.

Vrba, J., & Robinson, S. E. (2001). Signal processing in magnetoencephalography. *Methods, 25*, 249–271.

Vriends, N., Pfaltz, M. C., Novianti, P., & Hadiyono, J. (2013). Taijin Kyofusho and social anxiety and their clinical relevance in Indonesia and Switzerland. *Frontiers in Psychology, 4*.

Vrieze, S., & Grove, W. G. (2009). Survey on the use of clinical and mechanical prediction methods in clinical psychology. *Professional Psychology: Research and Practice, 40*, 525–531.

Vrij, A. (2008). Nonverbal dominance versus verbal accuracy: A plea to change police practice. *Criminal Justice and Behavior, 35*, 1323–1335.

Vrij, A., Granhag, P. A., & Porter, S. B. (2010). Pitfalls and opportunities in nonverbal and verbal lie detection. *Psychological Science in the Public Interest, 11*, 89–121.

Vrught, A., & Kerkstra, A. (1984). Sex differences in nonverbal communication. *Semiotica, 50*, 141.

Vuksan, V., Rogovik, A. L., Jovanovski, E., & Jenkins, A. L. (2009). Fiber facts: Benefits and recommendations for individuals with type 2 diabetes. *Current Diabetes Reports, 9*, 405–411.

Vul, E., Harris, C., Winkielman, P., & Pashler, H. (2009). Puzzlingly high correlations in fMRI studies of emotion, personality, and social cognition. *Perspectives on Psychological Science, 4*, 274–290.

Vyse, S. A. (2000). *Believing in magic: The psychology of superstition*. New York, NY: Oxford University Press.

Vytal, K., & Hamann, S. (2010). Neuroimaging support for discrete neural correlates of basic emotions: A voxel-based meta-analysis, *Journal of Cognitive Neuroscience, 12*, 2864–2885.

Waalen, J. (2014). The genetics of human obesity. *Translational Research, 164*(4), 293–301.

Wachtel, P. L. (1973). Psychodynamics, behavior therapy, and the implacable experimenter: An inquiry into the consistency of personality. *Journal of Abnormal Psychology, 82*, 324–334.

Wachtel, P. L. (1977). *Psychoanalysis and behavior therapy: Toward an integration*. New York, NY: Basic Books.

Wachtel, P. L. (1997). *Psychoanalysis, behavior therapy, and the relational world*. Washington, DC: American Psychological Association.

Wade, K. A., Garry, M., Read, J. D., & Lindsay, D. S. (2002). A picture is worth a thousand lies: Using false photographs to create false childhood memories. *Psychonomic Bulletin & Review, 9*, 597–603.

Wagenmakers, E. J., Beek, T., Dijkhoff, L., Gronau, Q. F., Acosta, A., Adams, R. B., … & Bulnes, L. C. (2016). Registered Replication Report on Strack, Martin, and Stepper (1988). *Perspectives on Psychological Science*, 1745691616674458.

Wagenmakers, E.-J., Wetzels, R., Borsboom, D., & van der Maas, H. L. J. (2011). Why psychologists must change the way they analyze their data: The case of psi: Comment on Bem (2011). *Journal of Personality and Social Psychology, 100*, 426–432.

Wagenmakers, E.-J., Wetzels, R., Borsboom, D., van der Maas, H. L., & Kievit, R. A. (2012). An agenda for purely confirmatory research. *Perspectives on Psychological Science, 7*, 632–638.

Wager, T. D., Rilling, J. K., Smith, E. E., Sokolik, A., Casey, K. L., Davidson, R. J., … Cohen, J. D. (2004). Placebo-induced changes in fMRI in anticipation and experience of pain. *Science, 303*, 1162–1167.

Wagner, M. W., & Monnet, M. (1979). Attitudes of college professors toward extrasensory perception. *Zetetic Scholar, 5*, 7–16.

Wagner, R. K., & Torgesen, J. K. (1987). The nature of phonological processing and its causal role in the acquisition of reading skills. *Psychological Bulletin, 101*(2), 192–212.

Wagner, U., Gais, S., Haider, H., Verleger, R., & Born, J. (2004). Sleep inspires insight. *Nature, 427*, 352–355.

Wagstaff, G. (2008). Hypnosis and the law. *Criminal Justice and Behavior, 35*, 1277–1294.

Wahl, O. (1997). *Consumer experience with stigma: Results of a national survey*. Alexandria, VA: NAMI.

Wahl, O. F. (1976). Monozygotic twins discordant for schizophrenia: A review. *Psychological Bulletin, 83*, 91–106.

Wai, J., Cacchio, M., Putallaz, M., & Makel, M. C. (2010). Sex differences in the right tail of cognitive abilities: A 30-year examination. *Intelligence, 38*(4), 412–423.

Waid, W. M., & Orne, M. T. (1982). The physiological detection of deception. *American Scientist, 70*, 402–409.

Wainright, J. L., Russell, S. T., & Patterson, C. J. (2004). Psychosocial adjustment, school outcomes, and romantic relationships of adolescents with same-sex parents. *Child Development, 75*, 1886–1898.

Waite, L. J., Iveniuk, J., Laumann, E. O., & McClintock, M. K. (2015). Sexuality in older couples: Individual and dyadic characteristics. *Archives of Sexual Behavior*, 1–14. doi:10.1007/s10508-015-0651-9.

Wakefield, A. J., Murch, S., Anthony, A., Linnell, J., Casson, D. M., Malik, M., … Walker-Smith, J. A. (1998). Ileal lymphoid nodular hyperplasia, non-specific colitis, and regressive developmental disorder in children. *Lancet, 351*, 637–641.

Wakefield, J. C. (1992). The concept of mental disorder: On the boundary between biological facts and social values. *American Psychologist, 47*, 373–388.

Wakefield, J. C. (2006). Is behaviorism becoming a pseudo-science? Power versus scientific rationality in the eclipse of token economies by biological psychiatry in the treatment of schizophrenia. *Behavior and Social Issues, 15*, 202–221.

Wakefield, J. C., & First, M. B. (2012). Placing symptoms in context: The role of contextual criteria in reducing false positives in Diagnostic and Statistical Manual of Mental Disorders Diagnoses. *Comprehensive Psychiatry, 53*(2), 130–139.

Waldman, I. D. (2007a). Behavior genetic approaches are integral for understanding the etiology of psychopathology. In S. O. Lilienfeld & W. T. O'Donohue (Eds.), *The great ideas of clinical science: 17 principles that every mental professional should understand* (pp. 219–242). New York, NY: Routledge

Waldman, I. D., Lilienfeld, S. O., & Lahey, B. B. (1995). Toward construct validity in the childhood disruptive behavior disorders: Classification and diagnosis in DSM-IV and beyond. In T. H. Ollendick & R. J. Prinz (Eds.), *Advances in clinical child psychology* (Vol. 17, pp. 323–363). New York, NY: Plenum Press.

Walfish, S., McAlister, B., O'Donnell, P., & Lambert, M. J. (2012). An investigation of self-assessment bias in mental health providers. *Psychological Reports, 110*(2), 639.

Walker, E. F., & DiForio, D. (1997). Schizophrenia: A neural-diathesis stress model. *Psychological Review, 104*, 1–19.

Walker, E. F., & Lewine, R. J. (1990). Prediction of adult-onset schizophrenia from childhood home movies of the patients. *American Journal of Psychiatry, 147*, 1052–1056.

Walker, E. F., Kestler, L., Bollini, A., & Hochman, K. (2004). Schizophrenia: Etiology and course. *Annual Review of Psychology, 55*, 401–430.

Walker, G. H., Stanton, N. A., Baber, C., Wells, L., Gibson, H., Salmon, P., & Jenkins, D. (2010). From ethnography to the EAST method: A tractable approach for representing distributed cognition in air traffic control. *Ergonomics, 53*(2), 184–197. doi: 10.1080/00140130903171672

Walker, M. P., Brakefield, A., Morgan, J., Hobson, J. A., & Stickgold, R. (2002). Practice, with sleep, makes perfect. *Neuron, 35*, 205–211.

Wall, P. (2000). *Pain.* New York, NY: Columbia University Press.

Wallach, H., & Kirsch, I. (2003). Herbal treatments and antidepressant medication: Similar data, divergent conclusions. In S. O. Lilienfeld, S. J. Lynn, & J. M. Lohr (Eds.), *Science and pseudoscience in clinical psychology* (pp. 306–332). New York, NY: Guilford Press.

Wallechinsky, D., Wallace, D., & Wallace, H. (1977). *The book of lists.* New York, NY: Bantam.

Waller, N. G., Kojetin, B. A., Bouchard, T. J., Lykken, D. T., & Tellegen, A. (1990). Genetic and environmental influences on religious interests, attitudes, and values: A study of twins reared apart and together. *Psychological Science, 1*, 1–5.

Wallerstein, J. S. (1989, January 22). Children after divorce: Wounds that don't heal. *New York Times Magazine, 19*, 42.

Walonick, D. S. (1994). *Do researchers influence survey results with their question wording choices?* Retrieved from http://www.statpac.com/research-papers/researcher-bias.doc

Walsh, B. T. (1993). Binge eating in bulimia nervosa. In C. G. Fairburn & G. T. Wilson (Eds.), *Binge eating: Nature, assessment, and treatment* (pp. 37–49). New York, NY: Guilford Press.

Walsh, B. T., Hadigan, C. M., Kissileff, H. R., & LaChaussee, J. L. (1992). Bulimia nervosa: A syndrome of feast and famine. In G. H. Anderson & S. H. Kennedy (Eds.), *The biology of feast and famine.* New York, NY: Academic Press.

Walsh, F. (1999). Families in later life: Challenges and opportunities. In B. Carter & M. McGoldrick (Eds.), *The expanded family life cycle: Individual, family and social perspectives* (3rd ed., pp. 307–326). Boston, MA: Allyn & Bacon.

Walster, E., Berscheid, E., & Walster, G. W. (1973). New directions in equity theory and research. *Journal of Personality and Social Psychology, 25*, 151–176.

Walter, C. (2006). Why do we cry? *Scientific American Mind, 17*(6), 44.

Walters, G. D., & Greene, R. L. (1988). Differentiating between schizophrenia and manic inpatients by means of the MMPI. *Journal of Personality Assessment, 52*, 91–95.

Walton, D. E. (1978). An exploratory study: Personality factors and theoretical orientations of therapists. *Psychotherapy: Theory, Research, and Practice, 15*, 390–395.

Walton, G. M., & Spencer, S. J. (2009). Latent ability: Grades and test scores systematically underestimate the intellectual ability of negatively stereotyped students. *Psychological Science, 20*(9), 1132–1139. http://dx.doi.org/10.1111/j.1467-9280.2009.02417.x

Walum, H., Waldman, I. D., & Young, L. J. (2016). Statistical and methodological considerations for the interpretation of intranasal oxytocin studies. *Biological Psychiatry, 79*, 251–257.

Wampold, B. E. (2007). Psychotherapy: The humanistic (and effective) treatment. *American Psychologist, 62*(8), 857.

Wampold, B. E. (2010). The research evidence for the common factors models: A historically situated perspective. In B. M. Duncan, S. D. Miller, M. A. Hubble & B. E. Wampold, (Eds.) *The Heart and Soul of Therapy.* (2nd ed., 49–82). Washington, DC: American Psychological Association.

Wampold, B. E. (2015). How important are the common factors in psychotherapy? An update. *World Psychiatry, 14*(3), 270–277.

Wampold, B. E., & Imel, Z. E. (2015). *The great psychotherapy debate: The evidence for what makes psychotherapy work.* London, UK: Routledge.

Wampold, B. E., Minami, T., Baskin, T. W., & Tierney, S. C. (2002). A meta-(re)analysis of the effects of cognitive therapy versus "other therapies" for depression. *Journal of Affective Disorders, 68*, 159–165.

Wampold, B. E., Monding, W., Moody, M., Stich, I., Benson, K., & Ahn, H. (1997). A meta-analysis of outcome studies comparing bona fide psychotherapies: Empirically "all must have prizes." *Psychological Bulletin, 122*, 203–215.

Wang, C. S., Whitson, J. A., & Menon, T. (2012). Culture, control, and illusory pattern perception. *Social Psychological and Personality Science, 3*, 630–638.

Wang, D. D., & Kriegstein, A. R. (2009). Defining the role of GABA in cortical development. *The Journal of Physiology, 187*, 1873–1879.

Wang, D. J., Rao, H., Korczykowski, M., Wintering, N., Pluta, J., Khalsa, D. S., & Newberg, A. B. (2011). Cerebral blood flow changes associated with different meditation practices and perceived depth of meditation. *Psychiatry Research: Neuroimaging, 191*(1), 60–67.

Wang, J., Plöderl, M., Häusermann, M., & Weiss, M. G. (2015). Understanding suicide attempts among gay men from their self-perceived causes. *The Journal of Nervous and Mental Disease, 203*(7), 499–506.

Wang, P. S., Gruber, M. J., Powers, R. E., Schoenbaum, M., Speier, A., Wells, K. B., & Kessler, R. C. (2008). Disruption of existing mental health treatments and failure to initiate new treatment after hurricane Katrina. *American Journal of Psychiatry, 165*, 34–41.

Wang, Q. (2006). Culture and the development of self-knowledge. *Current Directions in Psychological Science, 15*, 182–187.

Wang, R., Li, J., Fang, H., M. Tian, & J. Liu. (2012). Individual differences in holistic processing predict face recognition ability. *Psychological Science, 23*, 169–177.

Wansink, B. (2009). *Mindless eating: Why we eat more than we think.* New York, NY: Bantam.

Wansink, B., Painter, J. E., & North, J. (2005). Bottomless bowls: Why visual cues of portion size may influence intake. *Obesity Research, 13*, 93–100.

Ward, B. W., Dahlhamer, J. M., Galinsky, A. M., & Joestl, S. S. (2014). Sexual orientation and health among US adults: National Health Interview Survey, 2013. *National Health Statistics Report, 77*(77), 1–10.

Ward, J. (2013). Synesthesia. *Annual Review of Psychology, 64*, 49–75. doi: 10.1146/annurev-psych-113011-143840

Ward, J. (2015) *The student's guide to cognitive neuroscience.* New York, NY: Psychology Press.

Ward, J., Huckstep B., & Tsakanikos E. (2006). Sound-colour synaesthesia: to what extent does it use cross-modal mechanisms common to us all? *Cortex, 42*, 264–280. doi: 10.1016/s0010-9452(08)70352-6

Wardell, D. (1999). Children in difficulty: A guide to understanding and helping. *Contemporary Psychology, 44*, 514–515.

Wardell, J. D., & Read, J. P. (2013). Alcohol expectancies, perceived norms, and drinking behavior among college students: Examining the reciprocal determinism hypothesis. *Psychology of Addictive Behaviors, 27*, 191–196.

Wark, D. M. (2006). Alert hypnosis: A review and case report. *American Jounral of Clinical Hypnosis, 48*, 291–300.

Warmelink, L., Vrij, A., Mann, S., Leal, S., Forrester, D., & Fisher, R. P. (2011). Thermal imaging as a lie detection tool at airports. *Law and Human Behavior, 35*, 40–48.

Warne, R. T., Yoon, M., & Price, C. J. (2014). Exploring the various interpretations of "test bias." *Cultural Diversity and Ethnic Minority Psychology, 20*, 570–582.

Warren-Gash, C., & Zeman, A. (2014). Is there anything distinctive about epileptic déjà vu? *Journal of Neurology, Neurosurgery & Psychiatry, 85*(2), 143–147.

Warren, G., Schertler, E., & Bull, P. (2009). Detecting deception from emotional and emotional cues. *Journal of Nonverbal Behavior, 33*, 59–69.

Waschbusch, D. A., & Hill, G. P. (2003). Empirically supported, promising, and unsupported treatments for children with attention-deficit/hyperactivity disorder. In S. O. Lilienfeld, S. J. Lynn, & J. M. Lohr (Eds.), *Science and pseudoscience in clinical psychology* (pp. 333–362). New York, NY: Guilford Press.

Wason, P. C. (1966). Reasoning. In B. M. Foss (Ed.), *New horizons in psychology* (pp. 135–151). Harmondsworth, England: Penguin.

Watanabe, S., Sakamoto, J., & Wakita, M. (1995). Pigeons' discrimination of paintings by Monet and Picasso. *Journal of the Experimental Analysis of Behavior, 63*, 65–174.

Waters, E., Matas, L., & Sroufe, L. A. (1975). Infants' reactions to an approaching stranger: Description, validation, and functional significance of wariness. *Child Development, 46*, 348–356.

Watkins, C. E., Campbell, V. L., Nieberding, R., & Hallmark, R. (1995). Contemporary practice of psychological assessment by clinical psychologists. *Professional Psychology: Science and Practice, 26*, 54–60.

Watkins, E. R., & Nolen-Hoeksema, S. (2014). A habit-goal framework of depressive rumination. *Journal of Abnormal Psychology, 123*(1), 24–34.

Watkins, L. R., & Maier, S. F. (2002). Beyond neurons: Evidence that immune and glial cells contribute to pathological pain states. *Physiological Reviews, 82*, 981–1011.

Watson, D., & Clark, L. A. (1984). Negative affectivity: The disposition to experience negative emotional states. *Psychological Bulletin, 96*, 465–490.

Watson, D., Clark, L. A., & Harkness, A. R. (1994). Structures of personality and their relevance to psychopathology. *Journal of Abnormal Psychology, 103*, 18–31.

Watson, J. B. (1913). Psychology as the behaviorist views it. *Psychological Review, 20*, 158–177.

Watson, J. B., & Rayner, R. (1920). Conditioned emotional reactions. *Journal of Experimental Psychology, 3*, 1–14.

Watson, R. I. (1973). Investigation into deindividuation using a cross-cultural survey technique. *Journal of Personality and Social Psychology, 25*, 342–345.

Watt-Smith, T. (2016). *Book of human emotions.* London, England: Profile Books Limited.

Watters, E. (2010). Crazy like us: The globalization of the American psyche. New York, NY: Free Press.

Watts, A. L., Lilienfeld, S. O., Smith, S. F., Miller, J. D., Campbell, W. K., Waldman, I. D., ... & Faschingbauer, T. J. (2013). The double-edged sword of grandiose narcissism implications for successful and unsuccessful leadership among US Presidents. Psychological Science, 24, 2379–2389.

Watts, A. L., Lilienfeld, S. O., Smith, S. F., Miller, J. D., Campbell, W. K., Waldman, I. D., ... & Faschingbauer, T. J. (2013). The double-edged sword of grandiose narcissism implications for successful and unsuccessful leadership among US Presidents. Psychological Science, 24, 2379–2389.

Watts, A. L., Salekin, R. T., Harrison, N., Clark, A., Waldman, I. D., Vitacco, M. J., & Lilienfeld, S. O. (2016). Psychopathy: Relations with three conceptions of intelligence. Personality Disorders: Theory, Research, and Treatment.

Watts, A.W., Smith, S.F., & Lilienfeld, S.O. (2014). Illusory correlation. In R.D. Cautin & S.O. Lilienfeld (Eds.). Encyclopedia of clinical psychology. New York: Wiley.

Watts, D. J. (2011). Everything is obvious*: Once you know the answer. New York, NY: Crown Business.

Watts, D. J. (2014). Common sense and sociological explanations. American Journal of Sociology, 120, 313–351.

Watzke, B., Rüddel, H., Jürgensen, R., Koch, U., Kriston, L., Grothgar, B., & Schulz, H. (2012). Longer term outcome of cognitive-behavioural and psychodynamic psychotherapy in routine mental health care: randomised controlled trial. Behaviour Research and Therapy, 50(9), 580–587.

Watzlawick, P., Beavin, J., & Jackson, D. D. (1967). Pragmatics of human communication: A study of interactional patterns, pathologies, and paradoxes. New York, NY: Norton.

Watzlawick, P., Weakland, J. H., & Fisch, R. (1974). Change: Principles of problem formation and problem resolution. New York, NY: Norton.

Waugh, N. C., & Norman, D. A. (1965). Primary memory. Psychological Review, 72, 89–104.

Waxman, S. R., & Booth, A. E. (2001). On the insufficiency of domain-general accounts of word-learning: A reply to Bloom and Markson. Cognition, 78, 277–279.

Wayment, H. A., & Peplau, L. A. (1995). Social support and well-being among lesbian and heterosexual women: A structural modeling approach. Personality and Social Psychology Bulletin, 21, 1189–1199.

Wearing, D. (2005). Forever today. New York, NY: Doubleday.

Weaver, I. C., Cervoni, N., Champagne, F. A., D'Alessio, A. C., Sharma, S., Seckl, J. R., ... Meaney, M. J. (2004). Epigenetic programming by maternal behavior. Nature Neuroscience, 8, 847–854.

Weaver, J. R., & Bosson, J. K. (2011). I feel like I know you: Sharing negative attitudes of others promotes feelings of familiarity. Personality and Social Psychology Bulletin, 37(4), 481–491.

Weaver, K., Garcia, S. M., Schwarz, N., & Miller, D. T. (2007). Inferring the popularity of an opinion from its familiarity: A repetitive voice can sound like a chorus. Journal of Personality and Social Psychology, 92, 821–833.

Wechsler, D. (1939). The measurement of adult intelligence. Baltimore, MD: Williams & Wilkins.

Wechsler, D. (1988). Wechsler Intelligence Scale for Children—Revised (WISC R). New York, NY: The Psychological Corporation.

Wechsler, D. (1997). The Wechsler Adult Intelligence Scale—Third edition (WAIS-III). San Antonio, TX: Harcourt Assessment.

Wechsler, D. (2008). Wechsler Adult Intelligence Scale, Fourth edition (WAIS-IV). Boston, MA: Pearson.

Weed, N. C., Ben-Porath, Y. S., & Butcher, J. N. (1990). Failure of Weiner and Harmon MMPI subtle scales as personality descriptors and as validity indicators. Psychological Assessment, 2, 281–285.

Weeks, G. R., & L'Abate, L. (2013). Paradoxical psychotherapy: Theory & practice with individuals, couples, & families. London, UK: Routledge.

Wegner, D. M. (2002). The illusion of conscious will. Cambridge, MA: MIT Press.

Wegner, D. M. (2004). Précis of the illusion of conscious will. Behavioral and Brain Sciences, 27, 649–692.

Wegner, D. M. (2005). The illusion of conscious will. Behavioral and Brain Sciences, 27, 649–692.

Wegner, D. M., Fuller, V. A., & Sparrow, B. (2003). Clever hands: Uncontrolled intelligence in facilitated communication. Journal of Personality and Social Psychology, 85, 5–19.

Wegner, D. M., Schneider, D. J., Carter, S. R., & White, T. L. (1987). Paradoxical effects of thought supression. Journal of Personality and Social Psychology, 53, 5–13.

Wei, M., Mallinckrodt, B., Larson, L. M., & Zakalik, R. A. (2005). Adult attachment, depressive symptoms, and validation from self versus others. Journal of Counseling Psychology, 52, 368–377.

Weidler, B. J., Multhaup, K. S., & Faust, M. E. (2012). Accountability reduces unconscious plagiarism. Applied Cognitive Psychology, 26(4), 626–634.

Weil, A. (2000). Spontaneous healing: How to discover and embrace your body's natural ability to maintain and heal itself. New York, NY: Ballantine Books.

Weil, R. S., & Rees, G. (2011). A new taxonomy for perceptual filling-in. Brain Research Reviews, 67(1–2), 40–55.

Weinberg, M. S., Williams, C. J., & Calhan, C. (1995). If the shoe fits ... Exploring male-homosexual foot fetishism. Journal of Sex Research, 31, 17–27.

Weinberg, R. A., Scarr, S., & Waldman, I. D. (1992). The Minnesota Transracial Adoption Study: A follow-up of IQ test performance at adolescence. Intelligence, 16, 117–135.

Weinberger, D. R. (1987). Implications of normal brain development for the pathogenesis of schizophrenia. Archives of General Psychiatry, 44, 660–669.

Weinberger, D. R., Elvevag, B., & Giedd, J. N., (2005). The adolescent brain: A work in progress, The National Campaign to Prevent Teen Pregnancy. Retrieved from http://www.teenpregnancy.org/resources/reading/pdf/BRAIN.pdf

Weinberger, N. M. (2006). Music and the brain. Scientific American, 291(5), 88–95.

Weiner, I. B. (1997). Current status of the Rorschach Inkblot Method. Journal of Personality Assessment, 68, 5–19.

Weinert, F. (1989). The impact of schooling on cognitive development: One hypothetical assumption, some empirical results, and many theoretical implications. EARLI News, 8, 3–7.

Weisberg, D. S., Keil, F. C., Goodstein, J., Rawson, E., & Gray, J. R. (2008). The seductive allure of neuroscience explanations. Journal of Cognitive Neuroscience, 20, 470–477.

Weisberg, L. A., Garcia, C., & Strub, R. L. (1996). Diseases of the peripheral nerves and motor neurons. In L. Weisberg, C. Garc'a, R. Strub, & E. Bouldin (Eds.), Essentials of clinical neurology (pp. 458–494). St. Louis, MO: Mosby.

Weisberg, R. W. (1994). Genius and madness? A quasi-experimental test of the hypothesis that manic-depression increases creativity. Psychological Science, 5, 361–367.

Weiskrantz, L. (1986). Blindsight: A case study and its implications. Oxford, England: Oxford University Press.

Weisner, W., & Cronshaw, S. (1988). A meta-analytic investigation of interview format and degree of structure on the validity of the employment interview. Journal of Occupational Psychology, 61, 275–290.

Weiss, B. L. (1988). Many lives, many masters. New York, NY: Simon & Schuster.

Weiss, L. H., & Schwarz, J. C. (1996). The relationship between parenting types and older adolescents' personality, academic achievement, adjustment, and substance use. Child Development, 67, 2101–2114.

Weisz, J. R., Weiss, B., Han, S. S., Granger, D. A., & Morton, T. (1995). Effects of psychotherapy with children and adolescents revisited: A meta-analysis of treatment outcome studies. Psychological Bulletin, 117, 450–468.

Welford, A. (1977). Mental workload as a function of demand, capacity, strategy and skill: Synthesis report. Travail Humain, 40, 283–304.

Weller, J. A., & Thulin, E. W. (2012). Do honest people take fewer risks? Personality correlates of risk-taking to achieve gains and avoid losses in HEXACO space. Personality and Individual Differences, 53, 923–926. http://dx.doi.org/10.1016/j.paid.2012.06.010

Welling, H. (1994). Prime number identification in idiots savants: Can they calculate them? Journal of Autism and Developmental Disorders, 24, 199–207.

Wellman, H. M., Cross, D., & Watson, J. (2001). Meta-analysis of theory-of-mind development: The truth about false belief. Child Development, 72, 655–684.

Wells, G. L., & Bradford, A. L. (1998). "Good, you identified the suspect": Feedback to eyewitnesses distorts their reports of the witnessing experience. Journal of Applied Psychology, 83, 360–376.

Wells, G. L., & Loftus, E. F. (Eds.). (1984). Eyewitness testimony: Psychological perspectives. New York, NY: Cambridge University Press.

Wells, G. L., Memon, A., & Penrod, S. D. (2006). Eyewitness evidence: Improving its probative value. Psychological Science in the Public Interest, 7, 45–75.

Wenger, W. (1983). Toward a taxonomy of methods for improving teaching and learning. Journal of the Society for Accelerative Learning and Teaching, 8, 75–90.

Wennberg, P. (2002). The development of alcohol habits in a Swedish male birth cohort. In S. P. Shohov (Ed.), Advances in psychology research, Vol. 15 (pp. 121–155). Hauppauge, NY: Nova Science.

Wenze, S. J., Gunthert, K. C., & German, R. E. (2012). Biases in affective forecasting and recall in individuals with depression and anxiety symptoms. Personality and Social Psychology Bulletin, 38, 895–906.

Werch, C. E., & Owen, D. (2002). Iatrogenic effects of alcohol and drug prevention programs. Journal of Studies on Alcohol, 63, 581–590.

Werker, J. F., & Tees, R. C. (2002). Cross-language speech perception: Evidence for perceptual reorganization during the first year of life. Infant Behavior & Development, 25, 121–133.

West, R. F., Meserve, R. J., & Stanovich, K. E. (2012). Cognitive sophistication does not attenuate the bias blind spot. Journal of Personality and Social Psychology, 103, 506–519.

West, T. A., & Bauer, P. J. (1999). Assumptions of infantile amnesia: Are there differences between early and later memories? Memory, 7, 257–278.

Westen, D. (1991). Clinical assessment of object relations using the TAT. Journal of Personality Assessment, 56, 56–74.

Westen, D. (1998). The scientific legacy of Sigmund Freud: Toward a psychodynamically informed psychological science. Psychological Bulletin, 124, 333–371.

Westen, D., Feit, A., & Zittel, C. (1999). Methodological issues in research using projective methods. In P. C. Kendall & J. N. Butcher (Eds.), Handbook of research methods in clinical psychology (2nd ed., pp. 224–240). New York, NY: Wiley.

Westen, D., Kilts, C., Blagov, P., Harenski, K., & Hamann, S. (2006). The neural basis of motivated reasoning: An fMRI study of emotional constraints on political judgment during the U.S. presidential election of 2004. *Journal of Cognitive Neuroscience, 18,* 1947–1958.

Westen, D., Novotny, C. M., & Thompson-Brenner, H. (2004). The empirical status of empirically supported psychotherapies: Assumptions, findings, and reporting in controlled clinical trials. *Psychological Bulletin, 130,* 631–663.

Westenberg, P. M., Blasi, A., & Cohn, L. D. (Eds.). (2013). *Personality development: Theoretical, empirical, and clinical investigations of Loevinger's conception of ego development.* Psychology Press.

Westphal, M., & Bonanno, G. A. (2004). Emotional self-regulation. In M. Beauregard (Ed.), *Consciousness, emotional self-regulation, and the brain* (pp. 1–34). Philadelphia, PA: Benjamins.

Wethington, E., Glanz, K., & Schwartz, M. D. (2015). Stress, coping, and health behavior. In K. Glanz, B. K. Rimer, & K. Viswanath (Eds.), *Health behavior: Theory, research, and practice* (pp. 226–242). San Francisco, CA: Jossey-Bass.

Wetzler, S. E., & Sweeney, J. A. (1986). Childhood amnesia: An empirical demonstration. In D. C. Rubin (Ed.), *Autobiographical memory* (pp. 191–201). New York, NY: Cambridge University Press.

Whaley, A. L., & Davis, K. E. (2007). Cultural competence and evidence-based practice in mental health services: A complementary perspective. *American Psychologist, 62,* 563–574.

Whalley, K. (2016). Psychiatric disorders: Linking genetic risk to pruning. *Nature Reviews Neuroscience, 17*(4), 199–99.

Whiting, B. B., & Edwards, C. P. (1988). *Children of different worlds: The formation of social behavior.* Cambridge, MA: Harvard University Press.

Whitley, B. E., & Lee, S. E. (2000). The relationship of authoritarianism and related constructs to attitudes towards homosexuality. *Journal of Applied Social Psychology, 30,* 144–170.

Whitson, J. A., & Galinsky, A. D. (2008). Lacking control increases illusory pattern perception. *Science, 322,* 115–117.

Whitson, J. A., Galinsky, A. D., & Kay, A. (2015). The emotional roots of conspiratorial perceptions, system justification, and belief in the paranormal. *Journal of Experimental Social Psychology, 56,* 89–95.

Whorf, B. L. (1956). *Language, thought, and reality: Selected writings of Benjamin Lee Whorf.* J. B. Carroll (Ed.). Cambridge, MA: MIT Press.

Wicherts, J. M., Dolan, C. V., & van der Maas, H. L. J. (2010). A systematic literature review of the average IQ of sub-Saharan Africans. *Intelligence, 38,* 1–20.

Wickelgren, W. A. (1965). Acoustic similarity and retroactive interference in short-term memory. *Journal of Verbal Learning and Verbal Behavior, 4,* 53–61.

Wicker, A. W. (1969). Attitudes versus actions: The relationship of verbal and overt behavioral responses to attitude objects. *Journal of Social Issues, 25,* 41–78.

Wicker, B., Keysers, C., Plailly, J., Royet, J. P., Gallese, V., & Rizzolatti, G. (2003). Both of us disgusted in my insula: The common neural basis of seeing and feeling disgust. *Neuron, 40,* 655–664.

Widiger, T. A. (2001). The best and the worst of us? *Clinical Psychology: Science and Practice, 8,* 374–377.

Widiger, T. A., & Clark, L. A. (2000). Toward DSM-V and the classification of psychopathology. *Psychological Bulletin, 126,* 946–963.

Widiger, T. A., & Costa P. T. (2012). Integrating normal and abnormal personality structure: The five-factor model. *Journal of Personality, 80,* 1471–1506.

Widom, C. S. (1977). A methodology for studying noninstitutionalized psychopaths. *Journal of Consulting and Clinical Psychology, 45,* 674–683.

Widom, C. S. (1989a). The cycle of violence. *Science, 244,* 160–166.

Widom, C. S. (1989b) Child abuse, neglect, and adult behavior: Research design and findings on criminality, violence, and child abuse. *American Journal of Orthopsychiatry, 59,* 355–367.

Wiemer, J., & Pauli, P. (2016). Fear-relevant illusory correlations in different fears and anxiety disorders: A review of the literature. *Journal of Anxiety Disorders, 42,* 113–128.

Wigal, T., Greenhill, L., Chuang, S., McGough, J., Vitiello, B., Skrobala, A., ... Stehli, A. (2006). Safety and tolerability of methylphenidate in preschool children with ADHD. *Journal of the American Academy of Adolescent Psychiatry, 45,* 1294.

Wilgus, J., & Wilgus, B. (2009). Face to face with Phineas Gage. *Journal of the History of the Neurosciences, 18,* 340–345.

Wilkins, L. K., Girard, T., & Cheyne, J. A. (2011). Ketamine as a primary predictor of out-of-body experiences associated with multiple substance use. *Conscoiusness and Cognition, 20*(3), 943–950.

Wilkowski, B., Hartung, C., Crowe, S., & Chai, C. (2012). Men don't just get mad; they get even: Revenge but not anger mediates gender differences in physical aggression. *Journal of Research in Personality, 46,* 546–555.

Willerman, L. (1979). *The psychology of individual and group differences.* San Francisco, CA: Freedman.

Willerman, R., Schultz, J. N., Rutledge, J. N., & Bigler, D. D. (1991). In vivo brain size and intelligence. *Intelligence, 15,* 223–228.

Williams, K. W., Scott, M. M., & Elmquist, J. K. (2009). From observation to experimentation: Leptin action in the mediobasal hypothalamus. *The American Journal of Clinical Nutrition, 89*(3), 985S–990S.

Williams, K., Harkins, S. G., & Latané, B. (1981). Identifiability as a deterrent to social loafing: Two cheering experiments. *Journal of Personality and Social Psychology, 40,* 303–311.

Williams, L., O'Connor, R. C., Grubb, N. R., & O'Carroll, R. E. (2011). Type D personality and illness perceptions in myocardial infarction patients. *Journal of Psychosomatic Research, 70*(2), 141–144.

Williams, S. L., Turner, S. M., & Peer, D. F. (1985). Guided mastery and performance desensitization treatments for severe acrophobia. *Journal of Consulting and Clinical Psychology, 53,* 234–247.

Williams, T. J., Pepitone, M. E., Christensen, S. E., Cooke, B. M., Huberman, A. D., Breedlove, N. J., ... Breedlove, S. M. (2000). Finger length patterns and human sexual orientation. *Nature, 404,* 455–456.

Williams, T. M. (Ed.). (1986). *The impact of television: A naturalistic study in three communities.* Orlando, FL: Academic Press.

Williams, T., & Davey, M. (2015, September 26). U.S. murders surged in 2015, FBI finds. *New York Times.* http://www.nytimes.com/2016/09/27/us/murder-crime-fbi.html?_r=0

Williams, W. M., & Ceci, S. J. (1997, September/October). "How'm I doing?" *Change, 29*(5), 13–23.

Williams, W. M., & Ceci, S. J. (1998). *Escaping the advice trap.* Kansas City, MO: Andrews McMeel.

Williamson, D. A., Womble, L. G., Smeets, M. A. M., Netemeyer, R. G., Thaw, J. M., Kutlesic, V., Gleaves, D. H. (2002). Latent structure of eating disorder symptoms: A factor analytic and taxometric investigation. *American Journal of Psychiatry, 159,* 412–418.

Williamson, K., & Cox, R. (2014). Distributed cognition in sports teams: Explaining successful and expert performance. *Educational Philosophy and Theory, 46*(6), 640–654.

Willingham, D. T. (2002). *Allocating student study time: "Massed" versus "distributed" practice.* Retrieved from http://www.aft.org/newspubs/periodicals/ae/summer2002/willingham.cfm

Willingham, D. T. (2004). Reframing the mind: Howard Gardner became a hero among educators simply by redefining talents as "intelligences." *Education Next, 4,* 18–24.

Willingham, D. T. (2007, Summer). Why is critical thinking so hard to teach? *American Educator, 31*(2), 8–19.

Willingham, D. T., Hughes, E. M., & Dobolyi, D. G. (2015). The scientific status of learning styles theories. *Teaching of Psychology, 42,* 266–271.

Wills, T. A., & Fegan, M. F. (2001). Social networks and social support. In A. S. Baum, T. A. Revenson, & J. E. Singer (Eds.), *Handbook of health psychology* (pp. 209–234). Mahwah, NJ: Erlbaum.

Wilson-Mendenhall, C. D., Barrett, L. F., & Barsalou, L. W. (2013). Neural evidence that human emotions share core affective properties. *Psychological Science, 24,* 947–956.

Wilson, C. (2005). What is autism? *New Scientist, 187,* 39.

Wilson, G. T., & O'Leary, K. D. (1980). *Principles of behavior therapy.* Englewood Cliffs, NJ: Prentice Hall.

Wilson, J. Q. (1993). *The moral sense.* New York, NY: Free Press.

Wilson, J. Q., & Herrnstein, R. J. (1985). *Crime and human nature: The definitive study of the causes of crime.* New York, NY: Simon & Schuster.

Wilson, N. (2003). Commercializing mental health issues: Entertainment, advertising, and psychological advice. In S. O. Lilienfeld, S. J. Lynn, & J. M. Lohr (Eds.), *Science and pseudoscience in clinical psychology* (pp. 425–459). New York, NY: Guilford Press.

Wilson, R. S., Schneider, J. A., Arnold, S. E., Tang, Y., Boyle, P.A., & Bennett, D. A. (2007). Olfactory identification and incidence of mild cognitive impairment in older age. *Archives of General Psychiatry, 64,* 802–808.

Wilson, S. C., & Barber, T. X. (1981). Vivid fantasy and hallucinatory abilities in the life histories of excellent hypnotic subjects ("somnambules"): Preliminary report with female subjects. In E. Klinger (Ed.), *Imagery: Concepts, results, and applications* (pp. 133–149). New York, NY: Plenum Press.

Wilson, T. D. (2002). *Strangers to ourselves: Discovering the adaptive unconscious.* Cambridge, MA: Harvard University Press.

Wilson, T. D. (2011). *Redirect: The surprising new science of psychological change.* Boston, MA: Little, Brown.

Wilson, T., Lisle, D., Schooler, J., Hodges, S. D., Klaaren, K. J., & LaFleur, S. J. (1993). Introspecting about reasons can reduce post-choice satisfaction. *Personality and Social Psychology Bulletin, 69,* 331–339.

Wimmer, H., & Perner, J. (1983). Beliefs about beliefs: Representation and constraining function of wrong beliefs in young children's understanding of deception. *Cognition, 13,* 103–128.

Windham, G. C., Hopkins, B., Fenster, L., & Swan, S. H. (2000). Prenatal active or passive tobacco smoke exposure and the risk of preterm delivery or low birth weight. *Epidemiology, 11,* 427–433.

Winer, G. A., Cottrell, J. E., Gregg, V., Fournier, J. S., & Bica, L. A. (2002). Fundamentally misunderstanding visual perception. Adults' belief in visual emissions. *American Psychologist, 57,* 417–424.

Winerman, L. (2005, October). The mind's mirror. *American Psychological Association Monitor, 36*(9). Retrieved from http://www.apa.org/monitor/oct05/mirror.html

Wing, L., & Potter, D. (2002). The epidemiology of autistic spectrum disorders: Is the prevalence rising? *Mental Retardation and Developmental Disabilities Research Reviews, 8,* 151–161.

Wing, R. R., & Hill, J. O. (2001). Successful weight loss maintenance. *Annual Review of Nutrition, 21,* 323–341.

Wing, R. R., & Jeffrey, R. W. (1999). Benefit of recruiting participants with friends and increasing social support for weight loss and maintenance. *Journal of Consulting and Clinical Psychology, 67*, 132–138.

Wing, R. R., & Polley, B. A. (2001). Obesity. In A. Baum, T. A. Revenson, & J. E. Singer (Eds.), *Handbook of health psychology* (pp. 263–279). Mahwah, NJ: Erlbaum.

Winiarski, A., Smith, S. F., & Lilienfeld, S. O. (2015). Pop psychology diagnoses. In A. Winiarski, S. F. Smith, & S. O. Lilieneld (Eds.), *The Encyclopedia of Clinical Psychology* (pp. 1–10). DOI: 10.1002/9781118625392.wbecp568

Wink, P. (1991). Two faces of narcissism. *Journal of Personality and Social Psychology, 61*, 590–597.

Winkelman, J. W., Buxton, O. M., Jensen, J. E., Benson, K. L., O'Connor, S. P., Wang, W., & Renshaw, P. F. (2008). Reduced brain GABA in primary insomnia: Preliminary data from 4T proton magnetic resonance spectroscopy (1HMRS). *Sleep, 31*, 1499–1506.

Winner, E. (1999). Uncommon talents: Gifted children, prodigies, and savants. *Scientific American Presents: Exploring Intelligence, 9*, 32–37.

Winnicott, D. (1958). *Collected papers—Through pediatrics to psychoanalysis.* New York, NY: Basic Books.

Winograd, E., & Killinger, W. A., Jr. (1983). Relating age at encoding in early childhood to adult recall: Development of flashbulb memories. *Journal of Experimental Psychology: General, 112*, 413–422.

Winograd, E., Peluso, J. P., & Glover, T. A. (1998). Individual differences in susceptibility to memory illusions. *Applied Cognitive Psychology, 12*, S5–S27.

Winter, A. (2005). The making of "truth serum." *Bulletin of the History of Medicine, 79*, 500–533.

Winton, W. M. (1987). Do introductory textbooks present the Yerkes-Dodson law correctly? *American Psychologist, 42*, 202–203.

Wisco, B. E., Marx, B. P., Wolf, E. J., Miller, M. W., Southwick, S. M., & Pietrzak, R. H. (2014). Posttraumatic stress disorder in the US veteran population: Results from the National Health and Resilience in Veterans Study. *Journal of Clinical Psychiatry, 75*(12), 1338–1346.

Wise, R. A., Safer, M. A., & Maro, C. M. (2011). What US law enforcement officers know and believe about eyewitness factors, eyewitness interviews and identification procedures. *Applied Cognitive Psychology, 25*(3), 488–500.

Wiseman, R. (2009). *Quirkology: The curious science of everyday lives.* New York: Pan Macmillan.

Witelson, S. F., Beresh, H., & Kiger, D. L. (2006). Intelligence and brain size in 100 postmortem brains, sex, lateralization and age factors. *Brain, 129*, 386–398.

Witelson, S. F., Kigar, D. L., & Harvey, T. (1999). The exceptional brain of Albert Einstein. *Lancet, 353*, 2149–2153.

Witelson, S. F., Kigar, D. L., Scamvougeras, A., Kideckel, D. M., Buck, B., Stanchev, P. L., … Black, S. (2008). Corpus callosum anatomy in right-handed homosexual and heterosexual men. *Archives of Sexual Behavior, 37*, 857–863.

Witt, M., & Wozniak, W. (2006). Structure and function of the vomeronasal organ. *Advances in Otorhinolaryngology, 63*, 70–83.

Witt, S. T., & Stevens, M. C. (2012). Overcoming residual interference in mental set switching: Neural correlates and developmental trajectory. *NeuroImage, 62*, 2055–2064.

Witty, P. A., & Jenkins, M. D. (1934). The educational achievements of a group of gifted Negro children. *Journal of Educational Psychology, 25*, 585–597.

Wixted, J. T., Mickes, L., Clark, S. E., Gronlund, S. D., & Roediger III, H. L. (2015). Initial eyewitness confidence reliably predicts eyewitness identification accuracy. *American Psychologist, 70*(6), 515.

Woehrer, C. E. (1982). The influence of ethnic families on intergenerational relationships and later life transitions. In F. M. Berardo (Ed.), *The Annals of the American Academy of Political and Social Science* (pp. 65–78). Beverly Hills, CA: Sage.

Wojcik, S. P., Hovasapian, A., Graham, J., Motyl, M., & Ditto, P. H. (2015). Conservatives report, but liberals display, greater happiness. *Science, 347*, 1243–1246.

Wojciszke, B. (2002). From the first sight to the last breath: A six-stage model of love. *Polish Psychological Bulletin, 33*, 15–25.

Wolfe, B. E. (2016). Existential-humanistic therapy and psychotherapy integration: A commentary. *Journal of Psychotherapy Integration, 26*(1), 56–60.

Wolfe, V. A., & Pruitt, S. D. (2003). Insomnia and sleep disorders. In L. M. Cohen, D. E. McChargue, & F. L. Collins (Eds.), *The health psychology handbook* (pp. 425–440). Thousand Oaks, CA: Sage.

Wolff PH (1969) The natural history of crying and other vocalizations in early infancy. In B.M. Foss (Ed.), Determinants of infant behaviour IV (pp 81–109. London, U.K.: Methuen & Co. Ltd.

Wolke, D., Rizzo, P., & Woods, S. (2002). Persistent infant crying and hyperactivity problems in middle childhood. *Pediatrics, 109*, 1054–1060.

Wolkowitz, O. M., Reus, V. I., & Mellon, S. H. (2011). Of sound mind and body: Depression, disease, and accelerated aging. *Dialogues in Clinical Neuroscience, 13*, 25–39.

Wollen, K. A., Weber, A., & Lowry, D. H. (1972). Bizarreness versus interaction of mental images as determinants of learning. *Cognitive Psychology, 3*, 518–523.

Woloshin, S., Schwartz, L. M., & Welch, H. G. (2002). Risk charts: Putting cancer in context. *Journal of the National Cancer Institute, 94*, 799–804.

Wolpe, J. (1990). *The practice of behavior therapy* (4th ed.). Elmsford, NY: Pergamon Press.

Wood, D., Bruner, J. A., & Ross, G. (1976). Role of tutoring in problem-solving. *Journal of Child Psychology and Psychiatry and Allied Disciplines, 17*, 89–100.

Wood, E., Desmarais, S., & Gugula, S. (2002). The impact of parenting experience on gender stereotyped toy play of children. *Sex Roles, 47*, 39–49.

Wood, J. M., & Lilienfeld, S. O. (1999). The Rorschach Inkblot Test: A case of overstatement? *Assessment, 6*, 341–351.

Wood, J. M., Garb, H. N., Nezworski, M. T., Lilienfeld, S. O., & Duke, M. C. (2015). A second look at the validity of widely used Rorschach indices: Comment on Mihura, Meyer, Dumitrascu, and Bombel (2013). *Psychological Bulletin, 131*, 236–249

Wood, J. M., Lilienfeld, S. O., Garb, H. N., & Nezworski, M. T. (2000). The Rorschach test in clinical diagnosis: A critical review, with a backward look at Garfield (1947). *Journal of Clinical Psychology, 56*, 395–430.

Wood, J. M., Lilienfeld, S. O., Garb, H. N., & Nezworski, M. T. (2010). The validity of the Rorschach Inkblot Test for discriminating psychopaths from non-psychopaths in forensic populations: A meta-analysis. *Psychological Assessment, 22*, 336–349.

Wood, J. M., Nezworski, M. T., & Stejskal, W. J. (1996). The comprehensive system for the Rorschach: A critical examination. *Psychological Science, 7*, 3–10.

Wood, M. J., Douglas, K. M., & Sutton, R. M. (2012). Dead and alive: Beliefs in contradictory conspiracy theories. *Social Psychological and Personality Science, 3*, 767–773.

Wood, W., Jones, M., & Benjamin, L. T. (1986). Surveying psychological public image. *American Psychologist, 41*, 947–953.

Wood, W., Wong, F. Y., & Chachere, J. G. (1991). Effects of media violence on viewers' aggression in unconstrained social interaction. *Psychological Bulletin, 109*, 371–383.

Woods, D. L., Wyma, J. M., Yund, E. W., Herron, T. J., & Reed, B. (2015). Factors influencing the latency of simple reaction time. *Frontiers in Human Neuroscience, 9*, 131.

Woods, S. C., Seeley, R. J., Porte, D., & Schwartz, N. W. (1998). Signals that regulate food intake and energy homeostasis. *Science, 280*, 1378–1383.

Woodworth, R. S. (1929). *Psychology* (Rev. ed.). Oxford, England: Holt.

Woody, E. Z., & Bowers, K. S. (1994). A frontal assault on dissociated control. In S. J. Lynn & J. W. Rhue (Eds.), *Dissociation: Clinical and theoretical perspectives* (pp. 52–79). New York, NY: Guilford Press.

Woody, E. Z., & Sadler, P (2008). Dissociation theories of hypnosis. In M. R. Nash & A. J. Barnier (Eds.), *The Oxford handbook of hypnosis* (pp. 81–110). New York, NY: Oxford University Press.

Wooldridge, T., & Lytle, P. P. (2012). An overview of anorexia nervosa in males. *Eating Disorders, 20*(5), 368–378.

Woolf, N. J. (1991). Cholinergic systems in mammalian brain and spinal cord. *Progress in Neurobiology, 37*, 475–524.

Woolf, N. J. (2006). Microtubules in the cerebral cortex: Role in memory and consciousness. In J. A. Tuszynski (Ed.), *The emerging physics of consciousness* (pp. 49–94). Berlin, Germany: Springer-Verlag.

Word, C. O., Zanna, M. P., & Cooper, J. (1974). Nonverbal mediation of self-fulfilling prophecies in interracial interaction. *Journal of Experimental Social Psychology, 10*, 109–120.

World Health Organization (WHO). (2004). *Global status report on alcohol 2004.* Geneva, Switzerland: WHO, Department of Mental Health and Substance Abuse.

World Health Organization (WHO). (2010). ICD-10 Version: 2010. *ICD-10 Version.* Retrieved from http://apps.who.int/classifications/icd10/browse/2010/en

World Health Organization (WHO). (2012). Visual impairments and blindness, Fact Sheet Number 282. Retrieved from http://www.who.int/mediacentre/factsheets/fs282/en

Wrangham, R. W., & Glowacki, L. (2012). Intergroup aggression in chimpanzees and war in nomadic hunter-gatherers. *Human Nature, 23*, 5–29. http://dx.doi.org/10.1007/s12110-012-9132-1

Wraw, C., Deary, I. J., Gale, C. R., & Der, G. (2015). Intelligence in youth and health at age 50. *Intelligence, 53*, 23–32

Wren, A. A., Wright, M. A., Carson, J. W., & Keefe, F. J. (2011). Yoga for persistent pain: New directions and directions for an ancient practice. *Pain, 152*(3), 477–480.

Wright Whelan, C., Wagstaff, G., & Wheatcroft, J. M. (2015). High stakes lies: Police and non-police accuracy in detecting deception. *Psychology, Crime & Law, 21*, 127–138.

Wu, C. H., Wang, C. C., Tsai, M. T., Huang, W. T., & Kennedy, J. (2014). Trend and pattern of herb and supplement use in the United States: Results from the 2002, 2007, and 2012 national health interview surveys. *Evidence-Based Complementary and Alternative Medicine, 2014*, (Article ID 872320), 1–7.

Wu, L. T., Woody, G. E., Yang, C., & Blazer, D. G. (2011). How do prescription opioid users differ from users of heroin or other drugs in psychopathology: Results from the National Epidemiologic Survey on Alcohol and Related Conditions. *Journal of Addiction Medicine, 5*(1), 28.

Wyatt, W. J. (2001) Some myths about behaviorism that are undone by B. F. Skinner's "The Design of Cultures." *Behavior and Social Issues, 11*, 28–30.

Wyatt, W., Posey, A., Welker, W., & Seamonds, C. (1984). Natural levels of similarities between identical twins and between unrelated people. *Skeptical Inquirer, 9*, 62–66.

Wysocki, C. J., & Preti, G. (2004). Facts, fallacies, fears, and frustrations with human pheromones. *Anatomical Record: Discoveries in Molecular, Cellular, & Evolutionary Biology, 281*, 1201–1211.

Yafeh, M., & Heath, C. (2003, September/October). Nostradamus' clever clairvoyance: The power of ambiguous specificity. *Skeptical Inquirer, 27*, 36–40.

Yaffe, K., Laffan, A. M., Harrison, S. L., Redline, S., Spira, A.P., Ensrud, K.E., ... Stone, K. L. (2011). Sleep-disordered breathing, hypoxia, and risk of mild cognitive impairment and dementia in older women. *Journal of the American Medical Association, 306*(6), 613–619.

Yagil, D. (2015). Display rules for kindness: Outcomes of suppressing benevolent emotions. *Motivation and Emotion, 39*, 156–166.

Yalom (1980). *Existential psychotherapy.* New York, NY: Basic Books.

Yalom, I. (1985). *The theory and practice of group psychotherapy.* New York, NY: Basic Books.

Yamaguchi, M., & Logan, G. D. (2016). Pushing typists back on the learning curve: Memory chunking in the hierarchical control of skilled typewriting. *Journal of Experimental Psychology: Learning, Memory, and Cognition.* http://dx.doi.org/10.1037/xlm0000288

Yamaguchi, S., & Ninomiya, K. (2000). Umami and food palatability. *Journal of Nutrition, 130*(4S Suppl.), 921S–926S.

Yamey, G., & Shaw, P. (2002). Is extreme racism a mental illness? No. *Western Journal of Medicine, 176*, 5.

Yan-Meier, L., Eberhart, N. K., Hammen, C. L., Gitlin, M., Sokolski, K., & Altshuler, L. (2011). Stressful life events predict delayed functional recovery following treatment for mania in bipolar disorder. *Psychiatry Research, 186*(2), 267–271.

Yang, S., & Sternberg, R. J. (1997). Taiwanese Chinese people's conceptions of intelligence. *Intelligence, 25*, 21–36.

Yang, Y., Kircher, T., & Straube, B. (2014). The neural correlates of cognitive behavioral therapy: Recent progress in the investigation of patients with panic disorder. *Behaviour Research and Therapy, 62*, 88–96.

Yapko, M. D. (1994). *Suggestions of abuse: True and false memories of childhood sexual trauma.* New York, NY: Simon & Schuster.

Yartz, A. R., & Hawk, L. W., Jr. (2001). Psychophysiological assessment of anxiety: Tales from the heart. In M. M. Antony, S. M. Orsillo, & L. Roemer (Eds.), *Practitioner's guide to empirically-based measures of anxiety* (pp. 25–30). New York, NY: Kluwer Academic/Plenum.

Yaseen, Z. S., Chartrand, H., Mojtabai, R., Bolton, J., & Galynker, I. I. (2013). Fear of dying in panic attacks predicts suicide attempt in comorbid depressive illness: Prospective evidence from the national epidemiological survey on alcohol and related conditions. *Depression and Anxiety, 30*(10), 930–39.

Yates, J. F., & Potworowski, G. A. (2012). Evidence-based decision management. In D. Rousseau (Ed.), *The Oxford handbook of evidence-based management* (pp. 198–222). Oxford, England: Oxford University Press.

Yeh, S.-L., He, S., & Cavanagh, P. (2012). Semantic priming from crowded words. *Psychological Science, 23*, 608–616.

Yerkes, R. M., & Dodson, J. D. (1908). The relation of strength of stimulus to rapidity of habit-formation. *Journal of Comparative Neurology and Psychology, 18*, 459–482.

Yogman, M., Garfield, C. F., & Committee on Psychosocial Aspects of Child and Family Health. (2016). Fathers' roles in the care and development of their children: The role of pediatricians. *Pediatrics, 138*(1), e20161128. doi: 10.1542/peds.2016–1128.

Young, J., & Cooper, L. M. (1972). Hypnotic recall amnesia as a function of manipulated expectancy. *Proceedings of the 80th Annual Convention of the American Psychological Association, 7*, 857–858.

Young, L. J., & Wang, Z. X., (2004) The neurobiology of pair bonding. *Nature Neuroscience, 7*, 1048–1054.

Young, L., & Nestle, M. (2002). The contribution of expanding portion sizes to the US obesity epidemic. *American Journal of Public Health, 92*, 246–249.

Young, M., Denny, G., Young, T., & Luquis, R. (2000). Sexual satisfaction among married women. *American Journal of Health Studies, 16*, 73–84.

Young, R. M., Oei, T. P. S., & Knight, R. G. (1990). The tension reduction hypothesis revisited: An alcohol expectancy perspective. *British Journal of Addiction, 85*, 31–40.

Young, S. G., Hugenberg, K., Bernstein, M. J., & Sacco, D. F. (2012). Perception and motivation in face recognition a critical review of theories of the cross-race effect. *Personality and Social Psychology Review, 16*(2), 116–142.

Young, S. M., & Pinsky, D. (2006). Narcissism and celebrity. *Journal of Research in Personality, 40*, 463–471.

Young, T. (1802). On the theory of light and colours. *Philosophical Transactions of the Royal Society of London, 92*, 12–48.

Young, W. C., Goy, R. W., & Phoenix C. H. (1964). Hormones and sexual behavior. *Science, 143*, 212–218.

Youngren, M. A., & Lewinsohn, P. M. (1980). The functional relationship between depressed and problematic interpersonal behavior. *Journal of Abnormal Psychology, 89*, 333–341.

Zabrucky, K., & Ratner, H. H. (1986). Children's comprehension monitoring and recall of inconsistent stories. *Child Development, 57*, 1401–1418.

Zadra, A. (1996). Recurrent dreams: Their relation to life events. In D. Barrett (Ed.), *Trauma and dreams* (pp. 231–247). Cambridge, MA: Harvard University Press.

Zaidel, D. W. (1994). A view of the world from a split brain perspective. In E. M. R. Critchley (Ed.), *The neurological boundaries of reality* (pp. 161–174). London, England: Farrand Press.

Zajonc, R. B. (1965). Social facilitation. *Science, 149*, 169–274.

Zajonc, R. B. (1968). Attitudinal effects of mere exposure. *Journal of Personality and Social Psychology Monographs, 9*, 1–27.

Zajonc, R. B. (1984). On the primacy of affect. *American Psychologist, 39*, 117–123.

Zajonc, R. B. (2000). Feeling and thinking: Closing the debate over the independence of affect. In J. P. Forgas (Ed.), *Feeling and thinking: The role of affect in social cognition* (pp. 31–58). New York, NY: Cambridge University Press.

Zajonc, R. B. (2001). Mere exposure: A gateway to the subliminal. *Current Directions in Psychological Science, 10*, 224–228.

Zajonc, R. B., Heingartner, A., & Herman, E. M. (1969). Social enhancement and impairment of performance in the cockroach. *Journal of Personality and Social Psychology, 13*, 83–92.

Zajonc, R. B., Murphy, S. T., & Inglehart, M. (1989). Feeling and facial efference: Implications for the vascular theory of emotion. *Psychological Review, 96*, 395–416.

Zak, P. J. (2012). *The moral molecule: The source of love and prosperity.* New York, NY: Dutton.

Zambianchi, M., & Bitti, P. E. R. (2014). The role of proactive coping strategies, time perspective, perceived efficacy on affect regulation, divergent thinking and family communication in promoting social well-being in emerging adulthood. *Social Indicators Research, 116*(2), 493–507.

Zanarini, M. C., Horwood, J., Wolke, D., Waylen, A., Fitzmaurice, G., & Grant, B. F. (2011). Prevalence of DSM-IV borderline personality disorder in two community samples: 6,330 English 11-year-olds and 34,653 American adults. *Journal of Personality Disorders, 25*(5), 607–619.

Zautra, A. J. (2003). *Emotions, stress, and health.* New York, NY: Oxford University Press.

Zavos, H., Gregory, A. M., & Eley, T. C. (2012). Longitudinal genetic analysis of anxiety sensitivity. *Developmental Psychology, 48*, awaiting page numbers.

Zborowski, M. J., & Garske, J. P. (1993). Interpersonal deviance and consequent social impact in hypothetically schizophrenia-prone men. *Journal of Abnormal Psychology, 102*, 482–489.

Zeidan, F., Adler-Neal, A. L., Wells, R. E., Stagnaro, E., May, L. M., Eisenach, J. C., ... Coghill, R. C. (2016). Mindfulness-meditation-based pain relief is not mediated by endogenous opioids. *Journal of Neuroscience, 36*(11), 3391–3397.

Zeier, J. D., Baskin-Sommers, A. R., Hiatt Racer, K. D., & Newman, J. P. (2012). Cognitive control deficits associated with antisocial personality disorder and psychopathy. *Personality Disorders: Theory, Research, and Treatment, 3*(3), 283–293.

Zeinah, M. M., Engel, S. A., Thompson, P. M., & Bookheimer, S. Y. (2003). Dynamics of the hippocampus during encoding and retrieval of face-name pairs. *Science, 299*, 577–580.

Zernike, K. (2000, May 31). Girls a distant 2nd in geography gap among U.S. pupils. *New York Times.* Retrieved from http://www.nytimes.com/2000/05/31/nyregion/girls-a-distant-2nd-in-geography-gap-among-us-pupils.html?pagewanted=1

Zhang, A. Y., & Snowden, L. R. (1999). Ethnic characteristics of mental disorders in five U.S. communities. *Cultural Diversity and Ethnic Minority Psychology, 5*, 134–136.

Zhang, L. (2006). Does student-teacher thinking style match/mismatch matter in students' achievement? *Educational Psychology, 26*, 395–409.

Zhong, C., Bohns, V. K., & Gino, F. (2010). A good lamp is the best police: Darkness increases self-interested behavior and dishonesty. *Psychological Science, 21*, 311–314.

Ziegler, M., Danay, E., Heene, M., Asendorpf, J., & Bühner, M. (2012). Openness, fluid intelligence, and crystallized intelligence: Toward an integrative model. *Journal of Research in Personality, 46*(2), 173–183. http://dx.doi.org/10.1016/j.jrp.2012.01.002

Zietsch, B. P., Verweij, K. J. H., Heath, A. C., Madden, P. A. F., Martin, N. G., Nelson, E. C., & Lynskey, M. T. (2012). Do shared etiological factors contribute to the relationship between sexual orientation and depression? *Psychological Medicine, 42*, 521–532.

Zillmann, D. (1988). Cognition-excitation interdependencies in aggressive behavior. *Aggressive Behavior, 14*, 51–64.

Zillmann, D., Katcher, A. H., & Milavsky, B. (1972). Excitation transfer from physical exercise to subsequent aggressive behavior. *Journal of Experimental Social Psychology, 8*, 247–259.

Zimbardo, P. G. (1997, May). What messages are behind today's cults? *American Psychological Association Monitor, 28*(5), 14.

Zimbardo, P. G. (2004a). Does psychology make a significant difference in our lives? *American Psychologist, 59*, 339–351.

Zimbardo, P. G. (2004b, May 9). Power turns good soldiers into "bad apples." *Boston Globe.* Retrieved from http://www.boston.com/news/globe/editorial_opinion/oped/articles/2004/05/09/power_turns_good_soldiers_into_bad_apples

Zimbardo, P. G. (2007). *The Lucifer effect: How good people turn evil.* New York, NY: Random House.

Zimbardo, P. G., Weisenberg, M., Firestone, I., & Levy, M. (1965). Communicator effectiveness in producing public conformity and private attitude change. *Journal of Personality, 33*, 233–255.

Zimmerman, F. J., Christakis, D. A., & Meltzoff, A. N. (2007) Associations between media viewing and language development in children under age 2 years. *The Journal of Pediatrics, 151*, 364–368.

Zimmerman, M. (1994). Diagnosing personality disorders: A review of issues and research methods. *Archives of General Psychiatry, 51*, 225–245.

Zimmermann, T. D., & Meier, B. (2006). The rise and decline of prospective memory performance across the lifespan. *The Quarterly Journal of Experimental Psychology, 59*(12), 2040–2046.

Zinbarg, R. E., & Barlow, D. H. (1996). The structure of anxiety and the anxiety disorders: A hierarchical model. *Journal of Abnormal Psychology, 105*, 81–193.

Zion, I. B., Tessler, R., Cohen, L., Lerer, E., Raz, Y., Bachner-Melman, R., … Ebstein, R. (2006). Polymorphisms in the dopamine D4 receptor gene (DRD4) contribute to individual differences in human sexual behavior: Desire, arousal and sexual function. *Journal for Molecular Psychiatry, 11*, 782–786.

Zivotofsky, A. Z., Edelman, S., Green, T., Fostick, L., & Strous, R. D. (2007). Hemisphere asymmetry in schizophrenia as revealed through line bisection, line trisection, and letter cancellation. *Brain Research, 1142*, 70–79.

Zlatevska, N., Dubelaar, C., & Holden, S. S. (2014). Sizing up the effect of portion size on consumption: a meta-analytic review. *Journal of Marketing, 78*(3), 140–154.

Zmyj, N., Prinz, W., & Daum, M. M. (2013). The relation between mirror self-image reactions and imitation in 14-and 18-month-old infants. *Infant Behavior and Development, 36*, 809–816.

Zohar, J., Greenberg, B., & Denys, D. (2012). Obsessive-compulsive disorder. *Neurobiology of Psychiatric Disorders E-Book: Handbook of Clinical Neurology (Series Editors: Aminoff, Boller and Swaab), 106*, 375–392.

Zola, S. (1997). The neurobiology of recovered memory, *Journal of Neuropsychiatry and Clinical Neurosciences, 9*, 449–459.

Zou, Y. M., Lu, D., Liu, L. P., Zhang, H. H., & Zhou, Y. Y. (2016). Olfactory dysfunction in Alzheimer's disease. *Neuropsychiatric Disease and Treatment, 12*, 869–875.

Zubin, J., & Spring, B. (1977). Vulnerability: A new view of schizophrenia. *Journal of Abnormal Psychology, 86*, 103–126.

Zuckerman, M. (1979). *Sensation seeking: Beyond the optimal level of arousal.* Hillsdale, NJ: Erlbaum.

Zuckerman, M. (1989). Personality in the third dimension: A psychobiological approach. *Personality and Individual Differences, 10*, 391–418.

Zuckerman, M. (1994). *Behavioral expressions and biosocial bases of sensation seeking.* New York, NY: Cambridge University Press.

Zuckerman, M., & Hopkins, J. (1966). Hallucinations or dreams: A study of arousal levels and reported visual sensations during sensory deprivation. *Perceptual and Motor Skills, 22*, 447–459.

Zuckerman, M., DePaulo, B. M., & Rosenthal, R. (1981). Verbal and non-verbal communication of deception. In L. Berkowitz (Ed.), *Advances in experimental and social psychology* (Vol. 14, pp. 1–59). New York, NY: Academic Press.

Zuger, B. (1988). Is early effeminate behavior in boys early homosexuality. *Comprehensive Psychiatry, 29*, 509–519.

Zullow, H. M., Oettingen, G., Peterson, C., & Seligman, M. E. P. (1988). Pessimistic explanatory style in the historical record. *American Psychologist, 43*, 673–682.

Zuroff, D. C., Mongrain, M., & Santor, D. A. (2004). Investing in the personality vulnerability research program: Current dividends and future growth: Rejoinder to Coyne, Thompson, and Whiffen. *Psychological Bulletin, 130*, 518–522.

Name Index

Subject Index

Credits

Text Credits

Chapter 1: p. 4: Based on a figure from Ilardi, Rand, & Karwoski, 2007; **p. 12:** Based on Gould, 1997; **p. 22:** ©Scott O Lilienfeld; **p. 34:** Based on data from the National Science Foundation, 2003; **p. 36:** Based on data from American Psychological Association [APA], 2007.

Chapter 2: p. 59: Source: Jon Mueller, Newspaper Headlines That Confuse Correlation With Causation; **p. 69:** © Scott O Lilienfeld.

Chapter 3: p. 87: Carlson, Neil R; Heth, Donald S; Miller, Harold L; Donahoe, John W; Buskist, William; Martin, G. Neil, Psychology: The Science of Behavior, 6th Ed., c.2007. Reprinted and Electronically reproduced by permission of Pearson Education Inc., Upper Saddle River, New Jersey; **p. 94:** Marieb, Elaine N; Hoehn, Katja, Human Anatomy and Physiology, 7th Ed., c.2007. Reprinted and Electronically reproduced by permission of Pearson Education, Inc., Upper Saddle River, New Jersey; **p. 110:** Based on Gazzaniga, M. S. (2000). Cerebral specialization and interhemispheric communication: Does the corpus callosum enable the human condition? Brain, 123, 1293–1326; M. Gazzaniga & J.E. LeDoux, (1978) The Integrated Mind. New York: Plenum Press.

Chapter 4: p. 125: Adapted from Ramachandran, V. S., & Hubbard, E. M. (2001). Synaesthesia: A window into perception, thought and language. Journal of Consciousness Studies, 8, 33–34. Published by kind permission of Jounal of Consciousness Studies, Imprint Academic, Exeter, UK; **p. 126:** Adapted from a demonstration by Clifford Pickover. © Scott O Lilienfeld; **p. 130:** Adapted from St. Luke's Cataract & Laser Institute. © Scott O Lilienfeld; **p. 131:** © Pearson Education; **p. 136:** Source: NIDCD, 1990; **p. 150:** Hill, 1915; **p. 151:** © 1995 Edward H. Adelson; **p. 151:** © Dale Purves and R. Beau Lotto, 2002; **p. 152:** Based on psychologists Max Wertheimer, Wolfgang Kohler, and Kurt Koffka; **p. 154:** "Christmas Lights Illusion" (c) 2002-2017 Gianni A. Sarcone, giannisarcone.com. All rights reserved; **p. 163:** Hines, 2003; Hyman, 1977; Rowland, 2001.

Chapter 5: p. 173: Source: Metzinger, T. (2009). The ego tunnel: The science of the mind and the myth of the self. New York, NY: Basic Books; **p. 182:** Source: Alvarado, C. S. (2000). Out-of-body experiences. In E. Cardeña, S. J. Lynn, & S. Krippner (Eds.), The variety of anomalous experiences (pp. 183–218). Washington, DC: American Psychological Association; **p. 183:** Source: Based on: Greyson, 2000; Moody, R. A. (1975). Life after life. Covington, GA: Mockingbird Books.Moody, R. A. (1977). Reflections on life after life. St. Simon's Island, GA: Mockingbird Books.

Chapter 6: p. 225: Based on Tolman & Honzik, 1930; **p. 228:** Based on Huesmann et al., 2003; **p. 234:** © Pearson Education.

Chapter 7: p. 242: Based on Atkinson, R. C., & Shiffrin, R. M. (1968). Human memory: A proposed system and its control processes. In K. W. Spence and J. T. Spence (Eds.), The psychology of learning and motivation: Advances in research and theory (Vol. 2, pp. 89–195). New York, NY: Academic Press. ©Scott O. Lilienfeld; **p. 243:** Based on Sperling, G. (1960). The information available in brief visual presentations. Psychological Monographs: General and Applied, 74 (11, Whole No. 498), 1–29. © Scott O. Lilienfeld; **p. 247:** Based on Paivio, A. (1969). Mental imagery in associative learning and memory. Psychological Review, 76, 341–363. © Scott O. Lilienfeld; **p. 248:** Adapted from Bahrick, H. P. (1984). Semantic memory content in permastore: Fifty years of memory for Spanish learning in school. Journal of Experimental Psychology: General, 113, 1–29; **p. 253:** Based on Nickerson, R. S., & Adams, J. J. (1979). Long-term memory for a common object. Cognitive Psychology, 11, 287–307. © Scott O. Lilienfeld; **p. 259:** Based on Ebbinghaus, H. (1885). Memory: A contribution to experimental psychology. New York, NY: Teachers College, Columbia University. © Scott O. Lilienfeld; **p. 261:** Based on Godden, D. R., & Baddeley, A. D. (1975). Context dependency in two natural environments: On land and underwater. British Journal of Psychology, 91, 99–104. © Scott O. Lilienfeld; **p. 263:** © Pearson Education; **p. 265:** © Pearson Education; **p. 267:** © Pearson Education; **p. 272:** Neisser, U., & Harsch, N. (1992). Phantom flashbulbs: False recollections of hearing the news about Challenger. In E. Winograd & U. Neisser (Eds.), Affect and accuracy in recall: Studies of flashbulb memories (pp. 9–31). Cambridge, England: Cambridge University.

Chapter 8: p. 284: The New York Review of Books; **p. 293:** © Pearson Education; **p. 293:** © Pearson Education; **p. 297:** © Pearson Education; **p. 305:** Based on Johnson & Newport, 1989; **p. 289:** © Scott O Lilienfeld; **p. 311:** © Pearson Education.

Chapter 9: p. 322: Based on Gardner, H. (1999). Intelligence reframed: Multiple intelligences for the 21st century. New York, NY: Basic Books. © Scott O Lilienfeld; **p. 323:** Based on Sternberg, R. J., & Wagner, R. K. (1993). Thinking styles inventory. Unpublished instrument.©Scott O Lilienfeld; **p. 328:** Retrieved from http://www.thinkbabynames.com/graph/1/0/Eugene/Eugene_Eugenio_Ewan_Gene_Geno. © Scott O Lilienfeld; **p. 329:** Based on data from http://www.uvm.edu/~lkaelber/eugenics/. © Scott O Lilienfeld; **p. 331:** Based on Raven, J., Raven, J. C., & Court, J. H. (1998). Manual for Raven's Advanced Progressive Matrices. Oxford, England: Oxford Psychologists Press. © Scott O Lilienfeld; **p. 337:** Based on Hauser, 2002. © Scott O Lilienfeld; **p. 338:** How to raise a genius: lessons from a 45-year study of super-smart children. 2016. © Nature Publishing Group. Reproduced with permission via CCC; **p. 344:** Flynn, J. R. (1999). Searching for justice: The discovery of IQ gains over time. American Psychologist, 54, 5–20; **p. 347:** Ivie, R., & Ray, K. N. (2005). Women in physics and astronomy,2005. College Park, MD: American Institute of Physics. Used with permission from the American Institute of Physics; **p. 350:** Based on Lewontin, R. C. (1970). Further remarks on race and the genetics of intelligence. Bulletin of the Atomic Scientists, 26, 23–25. © Scott O. Lilienfeld; **p. 355:** Based on Weisberg, R. W. (1994). Genius and madness? A quasi-experimental test of the hypothesis that manic-depression increases creativity. Psychological Science, 5, 361–367. © Scott O. Lilienfeld.

Chapter 10: p. 366: Marieb, Elaine N; Hoehn, Katja, Human Anatomy & Physiology, 7th Ed., ©2007. Reprinted and Electronically reproduced by permission of Pearson Education, Inc., Upper Saddle River, New Jersey; **p. 376:** Based on Jean Piaget, The Psychology Of The Child, 2008. © Scott O.Lilienfeld; **p. 380:** © Scott O Lilienfeld; **p. 383:** Based on Mix, (1999); **p. 385:** Based on Waters, Matas, & Sroufe, 1975; **p. 386:** Based on Kagan, Reznick, & Snidman, 1988; **p. 396:** Good, T. L., & Brophy, J. (1995). Contemporary educational psychology, 5th Ed., © 1995, **p.84.** Reprinted and Electronically reproduced by permission of Pearson Education, Inc., Upper Saddle River, New Jersey; **p. 398:** Kohlberg, L. (1981). The philosophy of moral development: Moral stages and the idea of justice. San Francisco, CA: Harper & Row.

Chapter 11: p. 409: Aronoff, J., Barclay, A. M., & Stevenson, L. A. (1988) The recognition of threatening facial stimuli. Journal of Personality and Social Psychology, 54, 647–655; **p. 414:** Science or Science Fiction?: Investigating the Possibility (and Plausibility) of Subliminal Persuasion, Laboratory Manual, Department of Psychology, Cornell University retrieved from http://www.csic.cornell.edu/201/subliminal/#appB; **p. 417:** © Microsoft Corporation; **p. 418:** Based on Duclos, S., Laird, J., Schneider, E., Sexter, M., Stern, L., & van Lighten, O. (1989). Emotion-specific effects of facial expressions and postures on emotional experience. Journal of Personality and Social Psychology, 57, 100–108. © Scott O. Lilienfeld; **p. 419:** Based on Ekman, P., O'Sullivan, M., & Frank, M. G. (1999). A few can catch a liar. Psychological Science, 10, 263–266. © Scott O. Lilienfeld; **p. 423:** Based on Duenwald, M. (2002, May 7). Religion and health: New research revives an old debate. New York Times, D5. © Scott O. Lilienfeld; **p. 424:** Based on Diener, E., & Seligman, M. E. P. (2004). Beyond money: Toward an economy of well-being. Psychological Science in the Public Interest, 5, 1–31. © Scott O. Lilienfeld; **p. 427:** Based on Pew Research Center. (2006, February 13). Are we happy yet? Retrieved from http://pewresearch.org/pubs/301/are-we-happy-yet. © Scott O. Lilienfeld; **p. 440:** Rathus, Spencer A; Nevid, Jeffrey S; Fichner-Rathus, Lois, Human Sexuality In A World Of Diversity, 7th Ed., ©2008, **p. 149.** Reprinted and Electronically reproduced by permission of Pearson Education, Inc., Upper Saddle River, New Jersey; **p. 443:** Hatfield, E., & Walster, G. W. (1978). A new look at love. Reading, MA: Addison-Wesley.

Chapter 12: p. 475: Centers for Disease Control and Prevention, 2007a, Division of Nutrition and Physical Activity National Center for Chronic Disease Prevention and Health Promotion; **p. 481:** Statistics taken from National Health Interview Statistics Report (Clarke et al., 2015).

Chapter 13: p. 492: Hartmann, W. K. (1992). Astronomy: The cosmic journey. Belmont, CA: Wadsworth. Reprinted with permission from William K. Hartmann; **p. 496:** Data from Jones, E. E., & Harris, V. A. (1967). The attribution of attitudes. Journal of Experimental Social Psychology, 3, 1–24. ©Scott O. Lilienfeld; **p. 497:** Adapted from Asch, S. E. (1955). Opinions and social pressure. Scientific American, 193, 31–35. © Scott O. Lilienfeld; **p. 497:** Adapted from Asch, S. E. (1955). Opinions and social pressure. Scientific American, 193, 31–35. © Scott O. Lilienfeld; **p. 508:** Interview conducted at the Columbus Zoo on September 29, 2005 by Sue Western, scriptwriter for "Bonobo: Missing in Action" (the BBC version of "The Last Great Ape"), and edited by Peter Tyson, editor in chief of NOVA Online (2548 words); **p. 515:** Fox, J. A. 2010. Heat wave has chilling effect on violent crime. Boston.com. Retrieved from http://boston.com/